Readings in

LATIN-AMERICAN CIVILIZATION

1492 to the present

Edited by **BENJAMIN KEEN**

ASSOCIATE PROFESSOR OF HISTORY

WEST VIRGINIA UNIVERSITY

Houghton Mifflin Company · BOSTON · NEW YORK · CHICAGO

DALLAS · ATLANTA · SAN FRANCISCO · *The Riverside Press Cambridge*

Preface

TEACHERS OF LATIN-AMERICAN HISTORY and civilization have long felt the need for a book of readings comparable in character and scope to the collections used in the fields of American and European history. This book represents an effort to fill that need. The great majority of the selections are source materials; that is, they were written by contemporaries of the events or things described. I have drawn on secondary works only when suitable contemporary material was lacking. Believing that personal narratives often convey the flavor and spirit of a period more vividly than official documents — and are generally better written — I have made relatively slight use of the latter. Many of the selections included here appear in English for the first time. When existing translations seemed inadequate I have translated the material anew. Brief introductions and headnotes provide the student with background information concerning the authors and subject matter of the readings.

Within the limits imposed by space considerations I have tried to make this anthology broadly representative of the major Latin-American creeds or ideals, political, social, and literary. Occasionally I have juxtaposed exponents of rival doctrines in direct debate. I do not expect that all teachers will agree with my relative emphasis on the various periods and topics, or with my choice of specific readings. Space limitations, the availability of material, and my own teaching experiences and historical points of view have influenced my judgment in these matters.

I have noted the sources of all readings. Omissions and interpolations in the text have been indicated in the usual manner. In order to save space, the footnotes which originally appeared with scholarly articles have often been omitted. My own notes carry the initials B.K. A glossary defines those foreign terms which seemed to require special definition.

Finally, I should like to express my appreciation to all who helped me to bring this project to its conclusion. In particular I wish to thank the following for assistance cheerfully rendered: Drs. Arthur J. O. Anderson and Charles E. Dibble of the School of American Research at the Museum of New Mexico; Professor Earl W. Thomas of Vanderbilt University; and Professors Francisco Herrera y Sánchez, Warren F. Manning, and J. C. Easton, all of West Virginia University.

B.K.

Morgantown, West Virginia

Contents

Part One – Ancient America – 1

Part Two – The Conquest of America – 39

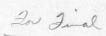

Part One

Ancient America

THE INDIAN PEOPLES of the Americas displayed wide cultural differences at the time of the coming of the white man. The variety of the physical environments of these groups partly explains this. The tropical rain forests of the Amazon Valley and the hard sod plains and hardwood forests of North America, for example, offered serious obstacles to cultivation by primitive peoples who lacked iron tools. As a result the inhabitants of these areas tended to rely for subsistence on the more precarious activities of hunting and food gathering, which in turn limited the growth of population and the general advance of culture. On the other hand, the semi-arid conditions of the Mexican and Andean highlands actually facilitated cultural development, as Professor Julian H. Steward suggests, because the land was easily tilled by digging-stick and irrigation farming. In such environments arose two of the advanced societies of ancient America: the Aztec and Inca civilizations. The brilliant civilization of the Maya Old Empire flowered in the tropical rain-forest area of Yucatan, but its agricultural system, on which the whole culture was based, probably originated in the Guatemalan highlands.

The distinctive economic feature of these civilizations was an intensive agriculture that made possible the development of a dense sedentary population and a considerable division of labor. The waging of predatory warfare by the Aztecs of Mexico and the Incas of Peru resulted in the growth of empires that on the part of the Aztecs represented little more than the systematic collection of tribute from their subjects, but in the case of the Incas reflected a remarkable and largely successful attempt at political and cultural integration of the vanquished peoples with their conquerors.

The religious life of the advanced societies of ancient America was characterized by belief in numerous deities and spirits identified with the forces of nature and by efforts to propitiate these divinities through prayer and sacrifice. Technical and artistic achievement found its highest expression in the sculpture and architecture of the Mayas, the ceramics and textiles of the ancient Peruvians, and the gold, silver, and feather work of the Aztecs. In the development of writing, astronomy, arithmetic, horology, and chronology, the Mayas were supreme.

1

I

The Mayas of Central America

IN THE TERRITORY formed by portions of southern Mexico and northern Central America, a notable Indian culture passed through two cycles of growth, flowering, and decay between the fourth and seventeenth centuries of the Christian Era. The economic basis of Maya civilization was an agricultural system that consisted essentially in felling the forest, burning the dried trees and brush, and planting corn in the cleared area. The political unit in Maya territory appears to have been the city-state, ruled by a hereditary monarch who probably combined religious with administrative and military functions. Tribute-paying commoners composed the great mass of the population, together with a considerable number of slaves. Maya religion, originally a simple nature worship, developed in time into an elaborate cult served by a numerous priesthood; in the New Empire period it was degraded by extensive human sacrifice, a borrowing from Mexican sources.

Maya civilization rose to great heights of architectural and artistic splendor in the lowlands of southern Yucatan in the eighth and ninth centuries of our era. The ensuing decline of the so-called Old Empire is not fully understood, but it has been convincingly ascribed to the gradual replacement of forest lands by man-made savannas that could not be tilled by Maya agricultural methods. Over a long period of time the great ceremonial centers in this region were abandoned by their inhabitants, who departed for northern Yucatan, to which Maya culture had been carried by earlier migrations. From the southwest came other migrants of Mexican (Toltec) origin, under a leader named Kukulcan, who gave a strong Mexican flavor to the architecture and religion of northern Yucatan.

Maya culture experienced a notable revival in its new homeland in the eleventh and twelfth centuries. The outbreak of strife between two leading city-states brought this period of economic and cultural renaissance to a close. By the time of the coming of the Spaniards all the larger ceremonial centers had been abandoned, and Yucatan was divided between numerous petty states that constantly warred with each other. These conditions paved the way for the Spanish conquest of the Mayas, and the fulfillment of an ancient native prophecy:

> On that day, a strong man seizes the land,
> On that day, things fall to ruin,
> On that day, the tender leaf is destroyed,
> On that day, the dying eyes are closed,
> On that day, three signs are on the tree,
> On that day, three generations hang there,
> On that day, the battle flag is raised,
> And they are scattered afar in the forests.

1. MAYA INDUSTRY, COMMERCE, AND AGRICULTURE

The Spanish Bishop Diego de Landa (1524–1579) is remembered by students of Maya culture for two achievements of very different types. One is his consignment to the flames of twenty-seven Maya hieroglyphic rolls as "works of the devil," the other his authorship of the famous Relation of the Things of Yucatan, *our principal source of information on the native way of life in northern Yucatan before and after the Conquest. In the extract from Landa given below, mention of the use of foreign trade, money, and credit points to the existence among the ancient Mayas of a fairly complex economy, in which exchange played a significant part. The references to cooperative effort in agriculture, hunting, and fishing*

2

suggest the importance of the communal element in Maya life.[1]

THE TRADES of the Indians were making pottery and carpentering. They earned a great deal by making idols out of clay and wood, with many fasts and observances. There were also surgeons, or, to be more accurate, sorcerers, who cured with herbs and many superstitious rites. And so it was with all the other professions. The occupation to which they had the greatest inclination was trade, carrying salt and cloth and slaves to the lands of Ulua and Tabasco, exchanging all they had for cacao and stone beads, which were their money; and with this they were accustomed to buy slaves, or other beads, because they were fine and good, which their chiefs wore as jewels in their feasts; and they had others made of certain red shells for money, and as jewels to adorn their persons; and they carried it in purses of net, which they had, and at their markets they traded in everything which there was in that country. They gave credit, lent and paid courteously and without usury. And the greatest number were the cultivators and men who apply themselves to harvesting the maize and other grains, which they keep in fine underground places and granaries, so as to be able to sell (their crops) at the proper time. Their mules and oxen are the people themselves. For each married man with his wife, they are accustomed to sow a space of four hundred feet, which they call a "hun uinic," measured with a rod of twenty feet, twenty feet wide and twenty feet long.

The Indians have the good habit of helping each other in all their labors. At the time of sowing those who do not have their own people to do their work, join together in groups of twenty, or more or less, and all together they do the work of all of them (each doing) his assigned share, and they do not leave it until everyone's is done. The lands today are common property, and so he who first occupies them becomes the possessor of them. They sow in a great number of places, so that if one part fails, another may supply its place. In cultivating the land they do nothing except collect together the refuse and burn it in order to sow it afterwards. They cultivate the land from the middle of January up to April, and they sow in the rainy season. They do this by carrying a little bag on their shoulders, and with a pointed stick they made a hole in the ground, and they drop there five or six grains, which they cover over with the same stick. It is a wonder how things grow, when it rains. They also joined together for hunting in companies of fifty more or less, and they roast the flesh of the deer on gridirons, so that it shall not be wasted, and when they reach the town, they make their presents to their lord and distribute the rest as among friends. And they do the same in their fishing.

2. THE SOCIAL ORDER

Ancient Maya society was highly stratified, with a fourfold division into classes: nobility, priesthood, commoners, and slaves, and over all a hereditary ruler with civil, religious, and military functions. The hierarchical order of society was reflected in the pattern of settlement in the Maya towns, where the homes of the nobles, priests, and the wealthy were clustered around the ceremonial center and the huts of the peasantry lay on the outskirts. For this, as for other aspects of Maya life, Bishop Landa's Relación *is our chief source.*[2]

AFTER THE DEPARTURE of Kukulcan, the nobles agreed, in order that the government should endure, that the house of the Cocoms should have the chief power; because it was the most ancient or the richest family, or because at this time he who was at the head of it was a man of the greatest worth. This being done, since within the enclosure there were only temples and houses for the lords and the high priest, they ordered that other houses should be constructed outside, where each one of them could keep some servants, and to which the people from their towns could repair, when they came to the city on business. Each one then established in these houses his mayordomo, who bore for his badge of office a short and thick stick, and they called him *caluac*. He kept account with the towns and with those who ruled them; and to them was sent notice of what was needed in the house of their lord, such as birds, maize, honey, salt, fish, game, cloth and other things, and the *caluac* always went to the house of his lord, in order to see what was wanted and provided it immediately, since his house was, as it were, the office of his lord.

1 Alfred M. Tozzer, "Landa's *Relación de las cosas de Yucatan,*" *Papers of the Peabody Museum of American Archeology and Ethnology,* Harvard University, Vol. 18, Cambridge, Mass., Harvard University Press, 1941, pp. 94–97. Reprinted by permission of the author and the Peabody Museum.

2 Tozzer, "Landa's *Relación,*" pp. 26, 62, 85–87. Reprinted by permission of the author and the Peabody Museum.

It was the custom to seek in the towns for the maimed and blind, and they supplied their needs.

The lords appointed the governors, and if they were acceptable confirmed their sons in the offices, and they charged them with the kind treatment of the poor people, the peace of the town and to occupy themselves in their work of supporting themselves and the lords.

All the lords were careful to respect, visit and to entertain the Cocom, accompanying him, making feasts in his honor and repairing to him with important business, and they lived in peace with each other amusing themselves with their accustomed pastimes of dancing, feasts and hunting. . . .

Before the Spaniards had conquered that country, the natives lived together in towns in a very civilized fashion. They kept the land well cleared and free from weeds, and planted very good trees. Their dwelling place was as follows: — in the middle of the town were their temples with beautiful plazas, and all around the temples stood the houses of the lords and the priests, and then (those of) the most important people. Then came the houses of the richest and of those who were held in the highest estimation nearest to these, and at the outskirts of the town were the houses of the lower class. And the Wells, if there were but few of them, were near the houses of the lords; and they had their improved lands planted with wine trees and they sowed cotton, pepper and maize, and they lived thus close together for fear of their enemies, who took them captive, and it was owing to the wars of the Spaniards that they scattered in the woods. . . .

Beyond the house, all the town did their sowing for the nobles; they also cultivated them (the fields) and harvested what was necessary for him and his household. And when there was hunting or fishing, or when it was time to get their salt, they always gave the lord his share, since these things they always did as a community. If the lord died, although it was the oldest son who succeeded him, the other children were very much respected and assisted and regarded as lords themselves. And they aided the other *principales* inferior to the lord in all these ways, according to whom he was and the favor which he enjoyed with his lord. The priests got their living from their offices and from offerings. The lords governed the town, settling disputes, ordering and settling the affairs of their republics, all of which they did by the hands of leading men, who were very well

obeyed and highly esteemed, especially the rich, whom they visited, and they held court in their houses, where they settled their affairs and business usually at night. And if the lords went out of their town, they took with them a great many people, and it was the same way when they went out of their homes.

3. THE RELIGIOUS LIFE

The great object of Maya religion and worship was, as Landa concisely puts it, "that they [the gods] should give them health, life, and sustenance." The principal divinities in the Maya pantheon represented those natural forces and objects that most directly affected the temporal welfare of the people. Such were the God of Rain; the God of the Heavens (who in one or another of his manifestations was the sun-god, the god of medicine, and the divine inventor of writing and books); the God of Corn; and the much-feared God of Death. The priesthood owed their influence to their assumed intimacy and power of intercession with the divine beings. Human sacrifice, vividly described below, was practiced from a very early period of the Old Empire, but it did not assume mass proportions among the Mayas until the tenth century, as a result of growing Mexican influence.[3]

THE NATIVES OF YUCATAN were as attentive to the matters of religion as to those of government, and they had a high priest whom they called *Ah Kin* Mai and by another name *Ahau Can* Mai, which means the Priest Mai, or the High-Priest Mai. He was very much respected by the lords and had no *repartimiento* of Indians, but besides the offerings, the lords made him presents and all the priests of the towns brought contributions to him, and his sons or his nearest relatives succeeded him in his office. In him was the key of their learning and it was to these matters that they dedicated themselves mostly; and they gave advice to the lords and replies to their questions. He seldom dealt with matters pertaining to the sacrifices except at the time of the principal feasts or in very important matters of business. They provided priests for the towns when they were needed, examining them in the sciences and ceremonies, and committed to them the duties of their office, and the good example to people and provided them with books and sent them forth. And they employed themselves in the duties of the temples and in teaching their sciences as well as in writing books about them.

3 Tozzer, "Landa's *Relación*," pp. 27–28, 108–113, 115–120. Reprinted by permission of the author and the Peabody Museum.

They taught the sons of the other priests and the second sons of the lords who brought them for this purpose from their infancy, if they saw that they had an inclination for this profession.

The sciences which they taught were the computation of the years, months and days, the festivals and ceremonies, the administration of the sacraments, the fateful days and seasons, their methods of divination and their prophecies, events and the cures for diseases, and their antiquities and how to read and write with the letters and characters, with which they wrote, and drawings which illustrate the meaning of the writings.

Their books were written on a large sheet doubled in folds, which was enclosed entirely between two boards which they decorated, and they wrote on both sides in columns following the order of the folds. And they made this paper of the roots of a tree and gave it a white gloss upon which it was easy to write. And some of the principal lords learned about these sciences from curiosity and were very highly thought of on this account although they never made use of them publicly. . . .

They had a very great number of idols and of temples, which were magnificent in their own fashion. And besides the community temples, the lords, priests and the leading men had also oratories and idols in their houses, where they made their prayers and offerings in private. And they held Cozumel and the well of Chichen Itza in the same veneration as we have for pilgrimages to Jerusalem and Rome, and so they used to go to visit these places and to offer presents there, especially to Cozumel, as we do to holy places; and if they did not go themselves, they always sent their offerings, and those who went there were in the habit of entering the abandoned temples also, as they passed by them, to offer prayers there and to burn copal. They had such a great quantity of idols that even those of their gods were not enough; for there was not an animal or insect of which they did not make a statue, and they made all these in the image of their gods and goddesses. They had some idols of stone, but very few, and others of wood, and carved but of small size but not as many as those of clay. The wooden idols were so much esteemed that they were considered as heirlooms and were (considered) as the most important part of the inherited property. They possessed no idols of metal, since there was no metal there. They knew well that the idols were the works of their hands, dead and without a divine nature; but they held them in reverence

on account of what they represented, and because they had made them with so many ceremonies, especially the wooden ones. The greatest idolaters were the priests, *Chilans,* the sorcerers and physicians, *Chacs,* and *Nacoms.* The office of the priest was to discuss and to teach their sciences, to make known their needs and the remedies for them, to preach and to publish the festival days, to offer sacrifices and to administer their sacraments. The duty of the *Chilans* was to give the replies of the gods to the people, and so much respect was shown to them that they carried them on their shoulders. The sorcerers and physicians performed their cures by bleedings of the parts which gave pain to the sick man; and they cast lots so as to know the future in their own duties and in other things. The *Chacs* were four old men who were always chosen anew for each occasion, to aid the priest in carrying on the festivals well and thoroughly. The *Nacoms* were two officers; the first was perpetual and did not bring much honor with it, since it was he that opened the breasts of the human victims whom they sacrificed. The second was a choice made of a captain for war and for other feasts. His duties lasted three years, and he was held in high honor. . . .

Besides the festivals in which they sacrificed persons in accordance with their solemnity, the priest or *Chilan,* on account of some misfortune or necessity, ordered them to sacrifice human beings, and everyone contributed to this, that slaves should be bought, or some in their devotion gave their little children, who were made much of, and feasted up to the day (of the festival), and they were well guarded, so that they should not run away or pollute themselves with any carnal sin. And in the meanwhile they led them from town to town with dancing, while the priests, Chilans and other officers fasted. And when the day arrived, they all came together in the court of the temple, and if the victim was to be sacrificed with arrows, they stripped him naked, and anointed his body with a blue color, and put a *coroza* on his head. When they had reached the victim, all, armed with bows and arrows, danced a solemn dance with him around the stake, and while dancing they put him up on it and bound him to it, all of them keeping on dancing and gazing at him. The foul priest in vestments went up and wounded the victim with an arrow in the parts of shame, whether it was a man or woman, and drew blood and came down and anointed the faces of the idols with it. And making a certain sign to the dancers, they began one after another to shoot, as they passed rapidly before him, still dancing, at his heart, which had been marked beforehand with a white mark. And in this way they made his whole chest one point like a hedgehog of arrows. If the heart of the victim was to be taken out, they led him with a great show and company of people of the temple, and having smeared him with blue and put on a *coroza,* they brought him up to the round altar, which was the place of sacrifice, and after the priest and his officials had anointed the stone with a blue color, and by purifying the temple drove out the evil spirit, the *Chacs* seized the poor victim, and placed him very quickly on his back upon that stone, and all four held him by the legs and arms, so that they divided him in the middle. At this came the executioner, the *Nacom,* with a knife of stone, and struck him with great skill and cruelty a blow between the ribs of his left side under the nipple, and he at once plunged his hand in there and seized the heart like a raging tiger and snatched it out alive and, having placed it upon a plate, he gave it to the priest, who went very quickly and anointed the faces of the idols with that fresh blood. Sometimes they made this sacrifice on the stone and high altar of the temple, and then they threw the body, now dead, rolling down the steps. The officials below took it and flayed it whole, taking off all the skin with the exception of the feet and hands, and the priest, all bare, covered himself, stripped naked as he was, with that skin, and the others danced with him. And this was considered as a thing of great solemnity amongst them. The custom was usually to bury in the court of the temple those whom they had sacrificed, or else they ate them, dividing him among those who had arrived (first) and the lords, and the hands, feet and head were reserved for the priest and his officials, and they considered those who were sacrificed as holy. If the victims were slaves captured in war, their master took their bones, to use them as a trophy in their dances as tokens of victory. Sometimes they threw living victims into the well of Chichen Itza, believing that they would come out on the third day, although they never appeared again.

4. A MAYA LEGEND OF THE CREATION OF THE FIRST MEN

The Quiché of Guatemala, a branch of the great Maya nation and the most powerful and cultured group inhabiting the Guatemalan highlands in pre-

Spanish times, had a Sacred Book or "Book of the People," that contained their mythology, religious beliefs, and traditional history. This book, the Popol Vuh, *was first written in the Quiché language, but in Latin script, by an unknown native who drew on the oral traditions of his people; it was translated into Spanish by Father Francisco Ximénez of the Dominican Order early in the eighteenth century, and was first published in Spanish in 1857. Authorities of the stature of Hubert H. Bancroft and Sylvanus G. Morley have praised it highly as "one of the rarest relics of aboriginal thought" and "the most distinguished example of native American literature that has survived the passing centuries." In contrast with the account in the* Popol Vuh *of the creation of the earth, which bears a suspicious resemblance to the Biblical story of Genesis, the following legend of the creation of the first men and their destruction has a strong and enjoyable indigenous flavor.*[4]

AND INSTANTLY the figures were made of wood. They looked like men, talked like men, and populated the surface of the earth.

They existed and multiplied; they had daughters, they had sons, these wooden figures; but they did not have souls, nor minds, they did not remember their Creator, their Maker; they walked on all fours, aimlessly.

They no longer remembered the Heart of Heaven and therefore they fell out of favor. It was merely a trial, an attempt at man. At first they spoke, but their face was without expression; their feet and hands had no strength; they had no blood, nor substance, nor moisture, nor flesh; their cheeks were dry, their feet and hands were dry, and their flesh was yellow.

Therefore, they no longer thought of their Creator nor their Maker, nor of those who made them and cared for them.

These were the first men who existed in great numbers on the face of the earth. . . .

Immediately the wooden figures were annihilated, destroyed, broken up, and killed.

A flood was brought about by the Heart of Heaven; a great flood was formed which fell on the heads of the wooden creatures.

Of tzite [wood], the flesh of man was made, but when woman was fashioned by the Creator and the Maker, her flesh was made of rushes. These were the materials the Creator and the Maker wanted to use in making them.

But those that they had made, that they had

[4] Reprinted from Adrian Recinos, *Popol Vuh, the Sacred Book of the Ancient Quiché Maya* (pp. 89–93), copyright 1952, by the University of Oklahoma Press. Reprinted by kind permission of the publisher.

created, did not think, did not speak with their Creator, their Maker. And for this reason they were killed, they were deluged. A heavy resin fell from the sky. The one called Xecotcovach came and gouged out their eyes; Camalotz came and cut off their heads; Cotzbalam came and devoured their flesh. Tucumbalam [5] came, too, and broke and mangled their homes and their nerves, and ground and crumbled their bones.

This was to punish them because they had not thought of their mother, nor their father, the Heart of Heaven, called Hurac'an. And for this reason the face of the earth was darkened and a black rain began to fall, by day and by night.

Then came the small animals and the large animals, and sticks and stones struck their faces. And all began to speak: their earthen jars, their griddles, their plates, their pots, their grinding stones, all rose up and struck their faces.

"You have done us much harm; you ate us, and now we shall kill you," said their dogs and birds of the barnyard.

And the grinding stones said: "We were tormented by you; every day, every day, at night, at dawn, all the time our faces went *holi, holi, huqui, huqui*, because of you. This was the tribute we paid you. But now that you are no longer men, you shall feel our strength. We shall grind and tear your flesh to pieces," said their grinding stones.

And then their dogs spoke and said: "Why did you give us nothing to eat? You scarcely looked at us, but you chased us and threw us out. You always had a stick ready to strike us while you were eating.

"Thus it was that you treated us. You did not speak to us. Perhaps we shall not kill you now; but why did you not look ahead, why did you not think about yourselves? Now we shall destroy you, now you shall feel the teeth of our mouths; we shall devour you," said the dogs, and then they destroyed their faces.

And at the same time, their griddles and pots spoke: "Pain and suffering you have caused us. Our mouths and our faces were blackened with soot; we were always put on the fire and you burned us as though we felt no pain. Now you shall feel it, we shall burn you," said their pots, and they all destroyed their [the wooden men's] faces. The stones of the hearth, which were heaped together, hurled themselves straight from the fire against their heads, causing them pain.

The desperate ones [the men of wood] ran as quickly as they could; they wanted to climb to the tops of the houses, and the houses fell down and threw them to the ground; they wanted to climb to the treetops, and the trees cast them far away; they wanted to enter the caverns, and the caverns repelled them.

So was the ruin of the men who had been created and formed, the men made to be destroyed and annihilated; the mouths and faces of all of them were mangled.

And it is said that their descendants are the monkeys which now live in the forests; these are all that remain of them because their flesh was made only of wood by the Creator and the Maker.

And therefore the monkey looks like man, and is an example of a generation of men which were created and made but were only wooden figures.

5. THE MAGICAL FEATS OF TWO MAYA HEROES

The Popol Vuh *concerns, among other matters, the adventures of the heroic twins Hunahpú and Xbalanqué, who set out for the gloomy land of Xibalba, a kind of Quiché underworld, to avenge the deaths of their father and uncle. Put to a series of grueling tests by the sardonic lords of Xibalba, including a trial of their skill at a strenuous kind of Mayan basketball, the brothers escape all the traps set for them by their enemies, and in a climactic scene overcome them by their magical prowess. The twins then ascend into heaven to become the sun and the moon. This Maya tale of high adventure is remarkable for its sustained dramatic interest, poetic fantasy, and touches of grim, barbaric humor. The following extract suggests the delight of the Maya in song, dance, and the art of juggling.*[6]

AND THE FOLLOWING DAY, two poor men presented themselves with old-looking faces and of miserable appearance, [and] ragged clothes, whose countenances did not commend them. So they were seen by all those of Xibalba.

[5] It is difficult to interpret the names of these enemies of man. Ximénez says that *Xecotcovach* was a bird, probably an eagle (*cot*) or sparrow hawk. The *Camalotz* which cut off men's heads was evidently the large vampire (*nima chicop*) Camazotz, bat of death. . . . *Cotzbalam* may be interpreted as the jaguar who lies in wait for his prey. *Tucumbalam* is another name for the danta or tapir.

[6] *Popol Vuh*, pp. 156–160, copyright 1952, by the University of Oklahoma Press. Reprinted by kind permission of the publisher.

And what they did was very little. They only performed the dance of the *puhuy* [owl or churn-owl], the dance of the *cux* [weasel], and the dance of the *iboy* [armadillo], and they also danced the *xtzul* [centipede] and the *chitic* [that walks on stilts].

Furthermore, they worked many miracles. They burned houses as though they really were burning and instantly they were as they had been before. Many of those of Xibalba watched them in wonder.

Presently they cut themselves into bits; they killed each other; the first one whom they had killed stretched out as though he were dead, and instantly the other brought him back to life. Those of Xibalba looked on in amazement at all they did, and they performed it, as the beginning of their triumph over those of Xibalba.

Presently word of their dances came to the ears of the lords Hun-Camé and Vucub-Camé. Upon hearing it they exclaimed: "Who are these two orphans? Do they really give you so much pleasure?"

"Surely their dances are very beautiful, and all that they do," answered he who had brought the news to the lords.

Happy to hear this, the [lords] then sent their messengers to call [the boys] with flattery. "Tell them to come here, tell them to come so that we may see what they do; that we may admire them and regard them with wonder," this the lords said. "So you shall say unto them," this was told to the messengers.

They arrived at once before the dancers and gave them the message of the lords.

"We do not wish to," the [boys] answered, "because, frankly, we are ashamed. How could we not but be ashamed to appear in the house of the lords with our ugly countenances, our eyes which are so big, and our poor appearance? Do you not see that we are nothing more than some [poor] dancers? What shall we tell our companions in poverty who have come with us and wish to see our dances and be entertained by them? How could we do our dances before the lords? For that reason, then, we do not want to go, oh, messengers," said Hunahpú and Xbalanqué.

Finally, with downcast faces and with reluctance and sorrow they went; but for a while they did not wish to walk, and the messengers had to beat them in the face many times, when they led them to the house of the lords.

They arrived, then, before the lords, timid and with head bowed; they came prostrating themselves, making reverences and humiliating themselves. They looked feeble, ragged, and their appearance was really that of vagabonds when they arrived.

They were questioned immediately about their country and their people; they also asked them about their mother and their father.

"Where do you come from?" [the lords] said.

"We do not know, Sir. We do not know the faces of our mother and father; we were small when they died," they answered, and did not say another word.

"All right. Now do [your dances] so that we may admire you. What do you want? We shall give you pay," they told them.

"We do not want anything; but really we are very much afraid," they said to the lord.

"Do not grieve, do not be afraid. Dance! And do first the part in which you kill yourselves; burn my house, do all that you know how to do. We shall marvel at you, for that is what our hearts desire. And afterwards, poor things, we shall give help for your journey," they told them.

Then they began to sing and dance. All the people of Xibalba arrived and gathered together in order to see them. Then they performed the dance of the *cux*, they danced the *puhuy*, and they danced the *iboy*.

And the lord said to them: "Cut my dog into pieces and let him be brought back to life by you," he said to them.

"Very well," they answered, and cut the dog into bits. Instantly they brought him back to life. The dog was truly full of joy when he was brought back to life, and wagged his tail when they revived him.

The lord said to them then: "Burn my house now!" Thus he said to them. Instantly they put fire to the lord's house, and although all the lords were assembled together within the house, they were not burned. Quickly it was whole again, and not for one instant was the house of Hun-Camé destroyed.

All of the lords were amazed, and in the same way the [boys'] dances gave them much pleasure.

Then they were told by the lord: "Now kill a man, sacrifice him, but do not let him die," he told them.

"Very well," they answered. And seizing a man, they quickly sacrificed him, and raising his heart on high, they held it so that all the lords could see it.

Again Hun-Camé and Vucub-Camé were

amazed. A moment afterward the man was brought back to life by them [the boys], and his heart was filled with joy when he was revived.

The lords were astounded. "Sacrifice yourselves now, let us see it! We really like your dances!" said the lords. "Very well, Sirs," they answered. And they proceeded to sacrifice each other. Hunahpú was sacrificed by Xbalanqué; one by one his arms and his legs were sliced off; his head was cut from his body and carried away; his heart was torn from his breast and thrown onto the grass. All the lords of Xibalba were fascinated. They looked on in wonder, but really it was only the dance of one man; it was Xbalanqué.

"Get up!" he said, and instantly [Hunahpú] returned to life. They [the boys] were very happy and the lords were also happy. In truth, what they did gladdened the hearts of Hun-Camé and Vucub-Camé, and the latter felt as though they themselves were dancing.

Then their hearts were filled with desire and longing by the dances of Hunahpú and Xbalanqué; and Hun-Camé and Vucub-Camé gave their commands.

"Do the same with us! Sacrifice us!" they said. "Cut us into pieces, one by one!" Hun-Camé and Vucub-Camé said to Hunahpú and Xbalanqué.

"Very well; afterward you will come back to life again. Perchance, did you not bring us here in order that we should entertain you, the lords, and your sons, and vassals?" they said to the lords.

And so it happened that they first sacrificed the one, who was the chief and [Lord of Xibalba], the one called Hun-Camé, king of Xibalba.

And when Hun-Camé was dead, they overpowered Vucub-Camé, and they did not bring either of them back to life.

The people of Xibalba fled as soon as they saw that their lords were dead and sacrificed. In an instant both were sacrificed. And this they [the boys] did in order to chastise them. Quickly the principal lord was killed. And they did not bring him back to life.

And another lord humbled himself then, and presented himself before the dancers. They had not discovered him, nor had they found him. "Have mercy on me!" he said when they found him.

All the sons and vassals of Xibalba fled to a great ravine, and all of them were crowded into this narrow, deep place. There they were crowded together and hordes of ants came and found them and dislodged them from the ravine. In this way [the ants] drove them to the road, and when they arrived [the people] prostrated themselves and gave themselves up; they humbled themselves and arrived, grieving.

In this way the Lords of Xibalba were overcome. Only by a miracle and by their [own] transformation could [the boys] have done it.

II

The Aztecs of Mexico

THE FIRST HIGH CIVILIZATION of ancient Mexico developed between about 400 and 300 B.C.; its seat was the great temple city of Teotihuacán, situated a short distance from the Mexico City of today. In the seventh century A.D. the Teotihuacán culture collapsed, for reasons that are obscure, and on its ruins arose the civilization of the Toltecs; these were Nahua-speaking Indians who invaded central Mexico in the eighth century and built a magnificent ceremonial center at Tollan, now Tula. In the tenth century the Toltec confederation broke up, and a time of strife and cultural decline ensued.

In the period that followed the passing of Toltec supremacy, a number of other Nahua-speaking tribes invaded the valley from the north and settled around the lakes that then covered much of its bottom. They borrowed freely from the rich civilization of their Toltec predecessors. One of the last groups to arrive was that of the Aztecs. Finding the most desirable sites occupied, they established themselves on a sandy islet in the Lake of Mexico. Here in the year 1325 they began to build the town of Tenochtitlán. The Aztecs gradually improved their economic position and perfected their military organization. In 1429, in alliance with the town of Tezcoco, they attacked and destroyed Azcapotzalco. This victory was a turning point in Aztec history.

The next step in the Aztec progress was the formation of a military alliance between Tenochtitlán and two other towns for the systematic conquest and plunder of other tribes. Some thirty towns, lying for the most part between Tenochtitlán and the Gulf coast, became tributaries of the Confederacy. Revolts of the tributary towns were frequent, and were growing in number and seriousness on the eve of the Spanish Conquest.

The economic basis of Aztec life was an intensive agriculture based on irrigation, the use of fertilizer, and the slash-and-burn method of cultivation. A numerous class of artisans produced a wide variety of manufactured products. By the time of the Conquest, Aztec society was definitely stratified. A "chief of men" chosen from a single family stood at the head of a ruling class of nobles and priests that was maintained in economic idleness by the labor of free commoners, serfs, and slaves.

The principal divinities worshipped in Tenochtitlán were the War and Rain Gods, and the most striking aspect of Aztec religion was the stupendous scale of human sacrifice. Artistic and technical progress was most marked in architecture, sculpture, gold and silver work, and the delicate craft of featherwork. The great Aztec cultural center was Tezcoco, where the remarkable Nezahualcoyotl (1379–1472), king, religious reformer, and philosopher, had his brilliant court, fostered literary and artistic activity, and established himself as a major poet in his own right.

1. AZTEC WARFARE

Warfare was the basis of Aztec existence, and warriors shared with priests the places of greatest honor and influence in Aztec society. Warriors who consistently distinguished themselves in battle were rewarded by admission into military orders, like the Knights of the Eagle or of the Tiger, which performed special dances and rituals. The successful warrior might also be rewarded by the grant of tribal land, worked by laborers attached to the soil; such grants often became hereditary estates. An important object of warfare was the procurement of captives to be sacrificed on the altars of the gods whose good will brought victory to the Aztec banners. Thus, in the words of the late Dr. George C. Vaillant, "war led to sacrifice and sacrifice led back to war, in ever-widening cycles." Our principal source of information concerning Aztec life and customs is the monumental work of the Spanish friar Bernardino de Sahagún (1499–1590), who carefully recorded a vast store of material obtained from native informants. His great General History of the Things of New Spain *contains the following native account of an Aztec military campaign.*[1]

THE RULER WAS KNOWN as the lord of men. His charge was war. Hence, he determined, disposed, and arranged how war would be made.

First he commanded masters of the youths and

[1] Drs. Arthur J. O. Anderson and Charles E. Dibble, translators and editors of the *Florentine Codex* (Fray Bernardino de Sahagún, *General History of the Things of New Spain*) (Santa Fe, School of American Research and University of Utah, 1950–   ), kindly permitted me to use this excerpt from the galley proofs of Book VIII of the *Florentine Codex*. B.K.

seasoned warriors to scan the [enemy] city and to study all the roads — where [they were] difficult, where entry could be made through them. This done, the ruler first determined, by means of a painted [plan], how was placed the city which they were to destroy. Then the chief noted all the roads — where [they were] difficult, and in what places entry could be made.

Then he summoned the general and the commanding general, and the brave warriors, and he commanded them how they were to take the road, what places the warriors were to enter, for how many days they would march, and how they would arrange the battle. And he commanded that these would announce war and send forth all the men dexterous in war to be arrayed, and to be supplied with provisions for war and insignia.

The ruler then consulted with all the majordomos — the men of the Petlacalco and of the Aztacalco, the majordomos of Quauhnauac and Uaxtepec, and [those] of Cuetlaxtlan, Tochpan, Tziuhcoac, Tepequacuilco, Uapan, Coatlixthauacan, Tlappan, Tlachco, Matlatzinco, Ocuillan, Xilotepec, Atotonilco, Axocopan, Itzcuincuitlapilco, Atocpan, and Ayotzintepec. He ordered them to take out all their [goods held in] storage, the tributes, costly articles — insignia of gold, and with quetzal feathers, and all the shields of great price.

And when the majordomos had delivered all the costly devices, the ruler then adorned and presented with insignia all the princes who were already able in war, and all the brave warriors, the men [at arms], the seasoned warriors, the fearless warriors, the Otomí, and the noblemen who dwelt in the young men's houses.

And when it had come to pass that the ruler adorned them, when he had done this to the brave warriors, then the ruler ordered all the majordomos to bear their goods, all the costly devices, and all the valuable capes there to battle, that the ruler might offer and endow with favors all the [other] rulers, and the noblemen, and the brave warriors, the men [at arms] who were about to go to war, who were to be extended as if made into a wall of men dexterous with arms. And the ruler forthwith called upon the rulers of Texcoco and Tlacopan and the rulers in all the swamp lands, and notified them to proclaim war in order to destroy a [certain] city. He presented them all with costly capes, and he gave them all insignia of great price. Then he also ordered the common folk to rise to go forth to war. Before them would go marching the brave warriors, the men [at arms], the lord general, and the commanding general.

The lords of the sun, it was said, took charge and directed in war. All the priests, the keepers of the gods, took the lead; they bore their gods upon their backs, and, by the space of one day, marched ahead of all the brave warriors and the seasoned warriors. These also marched one day ahead of all the men of Acolhuacan, who likewise marched one day ahead of all the Tepaneca, who similarly marched one day ahead of the men of Xilotepec; and these also marched one day ahead of all the so-called Quaquata. In like manner the [men of] other cities were disposed. They followed the road slowly and carefully.

And when the warlike lands were reached, the brave warrior generals and commanding generals then showed the others the way and arranged them in order. No one might break ranks or crowd in among the others; they would then and there slay or beat whoever would bring confusion or crowd in among the others. All the warriors were extended there, until the moment that Yacauitztli, [god of] the night, would descend — that darkness would fall. And when they already were to rise against the city to destroy it, first was awaited tensely the moment when fire flared up — when the priests brought [new] fire — and for the blowing of shell trumpets, when the priests blew them.

And when the fire flared up, then as one arose all the warriors. War cries were raised; there was fighting. They shot fiery arrows into the temples.

And when they first took a captive, one fated to die, forthwith they slew him there before the gods; they slashed his breast open with a flint knife.

And when the city had been overcome, thereupon were counted as many captives as there were, and as many Mexicans and Tlatilulcans as had died. Then they apprised the ruler that they had been orphaned for the sake of Uitzilopochtli; that men had been taken captive and been slain. And the ruler then commanded the high judges to go to tell and inform all in the homes of those who had gone to die in war, that there might be weeping in the homes of those who had gone to war to die. And they informed those in the homes of as many as had gone to take captives in war that they had received honors there because of their valor. And they were rewarded according to their merits; the ruler accorded favors to all — costly capes, breech clouts, chocolate, food, and devices, and lip rods and ear plugs. Even more did the ruler accord favors to the princes if they had taken captives. He gave them the offices of stewards, and all wealth without price — honor, fame, renown.

And if some had done wrong in battle, they then and there slew them on the battlefield; they beat them, they stoned them.

And if several claimed one captive, and one man said, "He is my captive," and another man also said, "He is my captive": if no man verified it, and also if no one saw how they had taken the captive, the lord of the sun decided between them. If neither had an advantage of the two who claimed the captive, then those who had taken four captives, the masters of the captives, decided that to neither one would the captive belong. He was dedicated to the Uitzcalco [or] they left him to the tribal temple, the house of the devil.

And when the city which they had destroyed was attained, at once was set the tribute, the impost. [To the ruler who had conquered them] they gave that which was there made. And likewise, forthwith a steward was placed in office, who would watch over and levy the tribute.

2. THE BATTLE OF AZCAPOTZALCO

A major turning point in the fortunes of the Aztec nation was the victory achieved in 1429, in alliance with the men of Tezcoco, over the dominant power in the lake region, the Tepanecs of Azcapotzalco. The Codex Ramirez, an important source of information on Aztec history, written by an unidentified native soon after the Spanish Conquest, contains a spirited

account of this affair. Written from an intensely parti-
san point of view, the narrative completely omits the
contribution of the Tezcocan allies to the outcome of
the struggle, and in other respects distorts the actual
course of events. Its chief interest consists in the in-
sight it gives into Aztec psychology and social rela-
tions.[2]

THEN THEY BEGAN TO MARCH against Azcapotzalco in perfect order and precision to the place
to which the king and the brave Atlacaellel, the
commander-in-chief, led them. When they approached the Azcapotzalcans the latter descried
them and immediately came down in good order
for the encounter. The latter were loaded down
with great riches, gold, silver, jewels, and feathers; they had rich devices on their shields and
weapons as became a powerful people who at
that time held sway over all that country. The
Mexicans, although poorly dressed, were full of
courage and confidence in the valor and subtlety
of their general.

The brave Atlacaellel, seeing that the enemy
was advancing with such vehemence, before they
actually came to blows, ordered that all the captains and the leaders and young men who
showed great intrepidity and desire for battle
be put in the wings of the army and that when
the signal was given these were to rush upon the
enemy, while the common people and soldiers
of lesser courage should remain where they were
(in the center), the king placing himself at the
head of them for the time being. If the enemy
were defeated these latter should not break rank
but together in one mass they were to enter the
city of Azcapotzalco.

The enemy was quite near as he said this, so
(those specially selected) placed themselves in
the wings as Atlacaellel had ordered and the
king Itzcohuatl struck a small drum suspended
from his shoulders and as he thus gave the signal
the Mexican army sprang forward with such
great shouts and shrieks that the enemy was
seized with fear. Then, attacking with impetuosity and with an invincible spirit, striking desperately to right and left, in no particular order,
they began to shout, "Mexico! Mexico!" and so
greatly did this disconcert the people of Azcapotzalco that they began to lose their order and
were defeated, many of the common people
being killed. The Mexicans, keeping up their

courage, captured great prizes and showed remarkable dexterity in wounding and killing the
enemy.

The people of Azcapotzalco began to retreat
to their city and the Mexicans, gaining upon
them, followed them. The Mexicans had exhibited no fear throughout the fighting and now
when they saw themselves victorious they rushed
with great boldness upon the enemy. Then the
Mexican king, seeing this, urged on his forces,
the king of Azcapotzalco doing the same. However, the Mexicans were so fired with enthusiasm that the people of Azcapotzalco could not
resist them, and fleeing from the field they retired to their city.

Then the spirited Atlacaellel, the general of
the Mexican army, let loose tremendous shouts
of "Victory! Victory!" and closing in upon the
enemy killed and wounded them most piteously.
The king, Itzcohuatl, then ordered that part of
the army under him to pillage the city, burn the
houses and sack whatever they found there, and
to spare neither man nor woman, young nor old.
This was done pitilessly and mercilessly and not
an object was left standing upright nor a person alive, except those who succeeded in escaping and who fled to the mountains. Even these
the Mexicans did not spare, for they followed
them like wild lions raging with fury and anger
and even pursued them to the most inaccessible
parts of the *sierras*. Then the people of Azcapotzalco prostrated themselves, surrendered their
weapons and promised to give (the Mexicans)
their lands, to work on their houses and plantations, to pay tribute to them forever and even
to supply them with stone, lime, and wood for
their houses. They also promised to give them
all necessary seeds and vegetables for their support. The general, Atlacaellel, taking pity upon
them, ordered the pursuit to cease and gathering
his people together he made the Azcapotzalcans
swear that they would fulfill what they had
promised. Then the Mexicans returned victorious and happy to their city, laden with great
riches and spoils which they had found in Azcapotzalco, for since it had been the court, all the
wealth of the Tepanecan nation had centered
there.

On the following day King Itzcohuatl of Mexico ordered all his chiefs to come together and
told them that they no doubt remembered that
the common people had obligated themselves to
perpetual service if the Mexicans were victorious, and that therefore it might be well to call
them and ask them to fulfill their promise. He
put this proposition before the common people

---

[2] The *Codex Ramirez*, in Paul Radin, "Sources and
Authenticity of the History of the Ancient Mexicans,"
University of California *Publications in American Archaeology and Ethnology*, Vol. 17, Berkeley, Cal., University of California Press, 1920, pp. 98–99. Reprinted by
permission of the University of California Press.

assembled there, and the latter admitted that they had promised all this; that the lords and leaders by their great bravery and valor had indeed merited victory and for that reason they were quite willing to accept their fate and keep their promise. So there they took the oath binding themselves to all the conditions mentioned before. And this was kept from that time on.

Then they went into the city of Azcapotzalco, where they divided the lands among themselves, giving the largest and the best portion to the royal crown; the next, to the captain-general Atlacaellel, and the remainder to the other leaders and nobles of Mexico, each one receiving land according to the manner in which he had distinguished himself in battle. To the common people they gave no land, except to those few who had shown spirit and courage. To the others they paid no attention at all and reviled them for their cowardice and their lack of courage, telling them that they were people who lacked the imagination to look ahead of them. Finally they gave land to the *barrios* so that they might use what they harvested from these lands for the service of their gods and the embellishment of their temples. This is the method to which they ever after adhered in apportioning lands gained by conquest.

3. THE UNVANQUISHED

To the east of the Valley of Mexico, but still within the central plateau, lived the warlike tribe of the Tlascalans. Although they claimed a common origin with the Aztecs, the Tlascalans stubbornly resisted Aztec aggression, and they were still enjoying full independence when Cortés and his men landed on the Mexican coast. Like the clash between Rome and Carthage, the prolonged strife between Aztecs and Tlascalans had an important element of commercial rivalry. The mestizo historian Muñoz Camargo (1528?–1599) describes the curiously modern technique of economic blockade used by the Aztecs against their enemies.[3]

WHEN THE LORDS of Tlascala learned of the growing might and prosperity of the Mexican realm . . . , they determined to arm and be on guard against any attack from such a great power as this; and so they watched over the frontiers of their lands and sought to keep the peace with all as they had always done. But all their precautions and prudence went for naught, for the men of Huexotzinco, Cholula, and other

provinces subject to the Mexicans, moved by mortal envy, sought by their wiles and craft to obstruct the trade of the Tlascalans wherever they could and to force them to withdraw into their own lands. And in order to incite the Mexicans all the more and move them to greater wrath, these subject peoples spoke mischievously against the Tlascalans, saying that by making friendships and by their trade they were gradually winning over provinces that the Mexicans had gained for themselves. . . .

The Tlascalans, seeing the great enmity of the Mexicans toward them, defended their interests as best they could, but since the power of the Mexicans was greater than their own, little by little they were forced to retreat to their own lands, losing the trade that they had once enjoyed. Engaged in this strife, they sent ambassadors to the Mexican princes, asking why they made war upon them, since they had given no cause for hostilities or for the maltreatment of their people, with whose commerce the Mexicans were interfering, seizing their wares and committing other outrages and injuries. To which the Mexicans replied that the great lord of Mexico was the lord of the whole world, to whom all men were vassals; that he would conquer them and force them to acknowledge him for their master; and whoever would not yield obedience unto him, them would he destroy and raze their towns to their foundations, settling them with new people. Let them therefore acknowledge him for their lord and yield themselves unto him, paying tribute as other provinces and realms were wont to do, for otherwise they would fall upon them. To which the ambassadors of Tlascala replied: "Most powerful lords, Tlascala is no vassal of yours; furthermore, not since they came out of the seven caves have the Tlascalans paid tribute or tax to any king or prince in the world, for they have always retained their freedom, and being unaccustomed to such service they will not obey you, for they would rather die than consent to such a thing. And know that what you demand of them they will require of you, and in this affair they will shed as much blood as the Chichimeca of Poyautlau shed in the war of Poyautlau that they fought with your ancestors.[4] And so we return with the reply that you have given us."

Learning of the arrogant reply of the Mexicans, the people of Tlascala thenceforth lived on their guard against whatever misfortune

[3] Diego Muñoz Camargo, *Historia de Tlaxcala*, México, 1947, pp. 119–123. (Excerpt translated by the editor.)

[4] A reference to a legendary affray between the Aztecs and the Tlascalans when the latter still inhabited the Valley of Mexico. B.K.

might befall them; and since the Mexicans had conquered the greater part of this New World and there remained nothing more for them to acquire from the one sea to the other, they thought that they could easily seize the province of Tlascala and subjugate it as they had done with the others. And so they fell upon the Tlascalans and engaged them in so many clashes and skirmishes that within a few years they had forced them back into their own lands and provinces. They kept the Tlascalans encircled for more than sixty years, depriving them of all their human wants, for they had no cotton with which to clothe themselves, nor gold and silver for their adornment, nor green plumes (which they favor most for their emblems and plumages), nor plumes of any other color for their festivals, nor cocoa to drink, nor salt for their food. All these and other things they lacked during the more than sixty years that they were encircled. They became so accustomed to eating no salt that to this day they have no taste for it and attach no worth to it, and even their children who have been reared among us use very little salt, although in view of its present abundance they have begun to form a liking for it.

4. THE HALLS OF MONTEZUMA

The political organization of the Aztec state on the eve of the Spanish Conquest represented a mixture of tribal democracy, theocracy, and royal absolutism, with the last two steadily gaining ascendancy over the first. The barbaric splendor and elaborate ceremonial that marked the household of the great war chief Montezuma are vividly described by an eyewitness, the conquistador and historian Bernal Díaz del Castillo (1492–1581?).[5]

THE GREAT MONTEZUMA was about forty years old, of good height and well proportioned, slender, and spare of flesh, not very swarthy, but of the natural colour and shade of an Indian. He did not wear his hair long, but so as just to cover his ears, his scanty black beard was well shaped and thin. His face was somewhat long, but cheerful, and he had good eyes and showed in his appearance and manner both tenderness and when necessary, gravity. He was very neat and clean and bathed once every day in the afternoon. He had many women as mistresses,

daughters of Chieftains, and he had two great Cacicas as his legitimate wives. He was free from unnatural offences. The clothes that he wore one day, he did not put on again until four days later. He had over two hundred chieftains in his guard, in other rooms close to his own, not that all were meant to converse with him, but only one or another, and when they went to speak to him they were obliged to take off their rich mantles and put on others of little worth, but they had to be clean, and they had to enter barefoot with their eyes lowered to the ground, and not to look up in his face. And they made him three obeisances, and said: "Lord, my Lord, my Great Lord," before they came up to him, and then they made their report and with a few words he dismissed them, and on taking leave they did not turn their backs, but kept their faces towards him with their eyes to the ground, and they did not turn their backs until they left the room. I noticed another thing, that when other great chiefs came from distant lands about disputes or business, when they reached the apartments of the Great Montezuma, they had to come barefoot and with poor mantles, and they might not enter directly into the Palace, but had to loiter about a little on one side of the Palace door, for to enter hurriedly was considered to be disrespectful.

For each meal, over thirty different dishes were prepared by his cooks according to their ways and usage, and they placed small pottery braziers beneath the dishes so that they should not get cold. They prepared more than three hundred plates of the food that Montezuma was going to eat, and more than a thousand for the guard. When he was going to eat, Montezuma would sometimes go out with his chiefs and stewards, and they would point out to him which dish was best, and of what birds and other things it was composed, and as they advised him, so he would eat, but it was not often that he would go out to see the food, and then merely as a pastime. . . .

Let us cease speaking of this and return to the way things were served to him at meal times. It was in this way: if it was cold they made up a large fire of live coals of a firewood made from the bark of trees which did not give off any smoke, and the scent of the bark from which the fire was made was very fragrant, and so that it should not give off more heat than he required, they placed in front of it a sort of screen adorned with figures of idols worked in gold. He was seated on a low stool, soft and richly worked, and the table, which was also low, was

---

5 Bernal Díaz del Castillo, *The True History of the Conquest of New Spain*, translated and edited by A. P. Maudsley, London, the Hakluyt Society, 1908–1916, 5 vols., II, 60–63.

made in the same style as the seats, and on it they placed the table cloths of white cloth and some rather long napkins of the same material. Four very beautiful cleanly women brought water for his hands in a sort of deep basin which they call *xicales*, and they held others like plates below to catch the water, and they brought him towels. And two other women brought him tortilla bread, and as soon as he began to eat they placed before him a sort of wooden screen painted over with gold, so that no one should watch him eating. Then the four women stood aside, and four great chieftains who were old men came and stood beside them, and with these Montezuma now and then conversed, and asked them questions, and as a great favour he would give to each of these elders a dish of what to him tasted best. They say that these elders were his near relations, and were his counsellors and judges of law suits, and the dishes and food which Montezuma gave them they ate standing up with much reverence and without looking at his face. He was served on Cholula earthenware either red or black. While he was at his meal the men of his guard who were in the rooms near to that of Montezuma, never dreamed of making any noise or speaking aloud. They brought him fruit of all the different kinds that the land produced, but he ate very little of it. From time to time they brought him, in cup-shaped vessels of pure gold, a certain drink made from cacao, and the women served this drink to him with great reverence.

Sometimes at meal-times there were present some very ugly humpbacks, very small of stature and their bodies almost broken in half, who are their jesters, and other Indians, who must have been buffoons, who told him witty sayings, and others who sang and danced, for Montezuma was fond of pleasure and song, and to these he ordered to be given what was left of the food and the jugs of cacao. Then the same four women removed the table cloths, and with much ceremony they brought water for his hands. And Montezuma talked with those four old chieftains about things that interested him, and they took leave of him with the great reverence in which they held him, and he remained to repose.

5. AZTEC INDUSTRY AND COMMERCE

Division of labor and perfection of craftsmanship among the Aztecs attained perhaps the highest point of development compatible with what was essentially an Upper Stone Age technology. The relatively vast scale on which the general exchange of goods and services was carried on is shown by the immense activity at the great market at Tenochtitlán, as described below[6] by Cortés in a letter to the Emperor Charles V. Trade was not confined to Aztec territory. The extension of inter-tribal contacts through war and diplomacy, and the rise of an aristocracy with luxurious tastes and the means to satisfy them, led to the development of a merchant class whose members traveled all over Mexico and beyond, exchanging the obsidian, cloth, and rope produced in the valley for shells, tropical feathers, jade, cacao, and many other articles. The second [7] of the two readings given below is a native account of the life of the Aztec trader.

THE CITY has many squares where markets are held, and trading is carried on. There is one square, twice as large as that of Salamanca, all surrounded by arcades, where there are daily more than sixty thousand souls, buying and selling, and where are found all the kinds of merchandise produced in these countries, including food products, jewels of gold and silver, lead, brass, copper, zinc, stone, bones, shells, and feathers. Stones are sold, hewn and unhewn, adobe bricks, wood, both in the rough and manufactured in various ways. There is a street for game, where they sell every sort of bird, such as chickens, partridges, quails, wild ducks, flycatchers, widgeons, turtle-doves, pigeons, reedbirds, parrots, owls, eaglets, owlets, falcons, sparrow-hawks and kestrels, and they sell the skin of some of these birds of prey with their feathers, heads, beaks, and claws. They sell rabbits, hares, and small dogs which they castrate, and raise for the purpose of eating.

There is a street set apart for the sale of herbs, where can be found every sort of root and medical herb which grows in the country. There are houses like apothecary shops, where prepared medicines are sold, as well as liquids, ointments, and plasters. There are places like our barber's shops, where they wash and shave their heads. There are houses where they supply food and drink for payment. There are men, such as in

6 *The Letters of Cortés to Charles V,* translated and edited by Francis A. McNutt, New York, 1908, 2 vols., I, 257–259. Reprinted by permission of the publishers, the Arthur H. Clark Company from Francis A. McNutt's *Fernando Cortés, His Five Letters of Relation to the Emperor Charles V.*

7 Arthur J. O. Anderson and Charles E. Dibble, *Florentine Codex* (Fray Bernardino de Sahagún, *General History of the Things of New Spain*), Book I, *The Gods* (Santa Fe, School of American Research and University of Utah, 1950), pp. 17–20. Reprinted by permission of the translators and the School of American Research.

Castile are called porters, who carry burdens. There is much wood, charcoal, brasiers, made of earthenware, and mats of divers kinds for beds, and others, very thin, used as cushions, and for carpeting halls, and bed-rooms. There are all sorts of vegetables, and especially onions, leeks, garlic, borage, nasturtion, water-cresses, sorrel, thistles, and artichokes. There are many kinds of fruits, amongst others cherries, and prunes, like the Spanish ones. They sell bees-honey and wax, and honey made of corn stalks, which is as sweet and syrup-like as that of sugar, also honey of a plant called maguey, which is better than most; from these same plants they make sugar and wine, which they also sell.

They also sell skeins of different kinds of spun cotton, in all colours, so that it seems quite like one of the silk markets of Granada, although it is on a greater scale; also as many different colours for painters as can be found in Spain and of as excellent hues. They sell deer skins with all the hair turned on them, and of different colours; much earthenware, exceedingly good, many sorts of pots, large and small, pitchers, large tiles, an infinite variety of vases, all of very singular clay, and most of them glazed and painted. They sell maize, both in the grain and made into bread, which is very superior in its quality to that of the other islands and mainland; pies of birds, and fish, also much fish, fresh, salted, cooked and raw, eggs of hens, and geese, and other birds in great quantity, and cakes made of eggs.

Finally, besides those things I have mentioned, they sell in the city markets everything else which is found in the whole country and which on acount of the profusion and number, do not occur to my memory, and which also I do not tell of, because I do not know their names.

Each kind of merchandise is sold in its respective street; and they do not mix their kinds of merchandise of any species; thus they preserve perfect order. Everything is sold by a kind of measure, and, until now, we have not seen anything sold by weight.

There is in this square a very large building, like a court of justice, where there are always ten or twelve persons, sitting as judges, and delivering their decisions upon all cases which arise in the markets. There are other persons in the same square who go about continually among the people, observing what is sold, and the measures used in selling, and they have been seen to break some which were false.

[YIACATECUTLI] was the god of the merchants. Greatly they esteemed him, arraying in paper the stout traveling staves with which they journeyed. Wheresoever they slept, there they set them up; before them they did penances, they drew [their] blood, they offered incense that they might be favored by their god, Yiacatecutli — thus they begged and implored his favor.

All manner of places they came to and entered. And hence they were named "the merchants who lead." They took their name from their god, Yiacatecutli.

These vanguard merchants went into the coast-lands, looking well for whatever goods there might be; they stretched over the southern coast-lands, they circled around the coast-lands.

They traveled exhausted by the heat and the winds; weakened, tired in the heat, they walked in great affliction. Their foreheads burned; they shaded the sun's heat with their hands [as] they plodded [under] its rays.

They betook themselves into the deserts; they climbed up and down canyons and mountains — all places. On elbow, on knee, they thus sped, they thus took much time.

Greatly were they wearied, much did they suffer, that they might find precious green stones, emeralds, turquoise, amber, gold; [and] feathers of all manner of birds — the [long tail feathers of the] quetzal and its black and green head and breast feathers; the red spoonbill; the blue cotinga; the parrot; the trupial; the eagle; and the skins of fierce animals, of ocelots.

And [they brought] vases, and incense-burners, and jars made of calabashes, spoons for stirring cacao, and stoppers for jars.

When they entered lands with which they were at war, and went among people who were far distant, they became like their enemies in their garments, their hair-dress, their speech, [that they might] mimic the natives.

And if they came to an evil pass, if they were discovered, then they were slain in ambush and served up with chili sauce. [But if] any — even one, even two — escaped alive, [such an one] informed Montezuma.

This one then gave him a gift, and decked him with his amber lip-plug. He did him honor, singling him out as a valiant warrior, thus making him a man of consequence.

And when those who returned arrived home, when they had come back, when they had reached and had contentment in their land, they feasted all, [especially] the merchants and the principal men, that they might make themselves celebrated.

It was called "the washing of the feet." They paid great honor to the cane, to the walking staff, of Yiacatecutli.

In the tribal temple they set it upright. They offered it an offering first, when they laid a feast. And when they summoned people to a banquet, they always offered it an offering when they ate.

And when they ceremoniously bathed and slew a man as a sacrifice, he whom they offered was the likeness of their god Yiacatecutli; or else one of [the following gods], or all of them, whom they worshipped — Chiconquiauitl, or Chalmecaciuatl, Axcomoquil, and Naxcitl, Cochimetl, Yacapitzauac. No one determined, [for] it was of their own free will, whether they should offer up one or two men.

They bought them there at the slave market at Atzcaputzalco; they sorted and arranged them, turning them around many times, examining them, buying the good ones — those of good bodies, without blemish, the best men, in good health, sick in no degree, who were marked by no marks on the body.

Such as these they slew on the feast-day, Panquetzaliztli, when the feast of Uitzilopochtli was celebrated.

Thereupon they garbed them in trappings like those of Yiacatecutli, which were assigned to them.

And before they slew them, first they let them be seen by the people. It was said: "They save them up [like gods]." Thus it was made known to the people that they would be offered up as sacrifices.

At this time they gave gifts and had a feast.

And their victims they set up in a good place, all in costly mantles which had been placed upon them. [And] they made them dance upon the roof-tops or in the market place. [And] they went singing, ending their song mocking death.

6. THE CONDITION OF THE AZTEC PEASANTRY

The unit of Aztec social organization was the clan, or calpulli; *this comprised a number of families that claimed descent from a common ancestor and was governed by a chief chosen by an elected council of elders. Twenty such clans, each occupying a distinct ward or quarter of the city, made up the population of* Tenochtitlán. *Each clan owned certain carefully bounded lands that were assigned in lots to individual families for their use but could not be transferred or sold. The rank and file of the clan membership, the* macehuales *or free peasantry, had to pay tribute in the form of labor on certain parts of the clan lands assigned for the support of the crown, the local chieftain, and the priesthood. The royal chronicler of the Indies, Gonzalo Fernández de Oviedo y Valdés (1478–1557), took a dim view of the condition of the Aztec common man before the Conquest. Oviedo was doubtless influenced by a desire to demonstrate the advantages of the new Spanish order, but his unvarnished picture of poverty and oppression is probably truer to life than the idealized conceptions of later writers.*[8]

THE INDIANS of New Spain, I have been told by reliable persons who gained their information from Spaniards who fought with Hernando Cortés in the conquest of that land, are the poorest of the many nations that live in the Indies at the present time. In their homes they have no furnishings or clothing other than the poor garments which they wear on their persons, one or two stones for grinding maize, some pots in which to cook the maize, and a sleeping mat. Their meals consist chiefly of vegetables cooked with chili, and bread. They eat little — not that they would not eat more if they could get it, for the soil is very fertile and yields bountiful harvests, but the common people and plebeians suffer under the tyranny of their Indian lords, who tax away the greater part of their produce in a manner that I shall describe. Only the lords and their relatives, and some principal men and merchants, have estates and lands of their own; they sell and gamble with their lands as they please, and they sow and harvest them but pay no tribute. Nor is any tribute paid by artisans, such as masons, carpenters, featherworkers, or silversmiths, or by singers and kettledrummers (for every Indian lord has musicians in his household, each according to his station). But such persons render personal service when it is required, and none of them is paid for his labor.

Each Indian lord assigns to the common folk who come from other parts of the country to settle on his land (and to those who are already settled there) specific fields, that each may know the land that he is to sow. And the majority of

8 Gonzalo Fernández de Oviedo y Valdés, *Historia general y natural de las Indias*, Asunción, Paraguay, 1944–45, 14 vols., X, 110–114. (Excerpt translated by the editor.)

them have their homes on their land; and between twenty and thirty, or forty and fifty
houses have over them an Indian head who is
called *tiquitlato,* which in the Castilian tongue
means "the finder (or seeker) of tribute." At
harvest time this *tiquitlato* inspects the corn-
field and observes what each one reaps, and
when the reaping is done they show him the
harvest, and he counts the ears of corn that each
has reaped, and the number of wives and children that each of the vassals in his charge possesses. And with the harvest before him he cal-
culates how many ears of corn each person in
that household will require till the next harvest,
and these he gives to the Indian head of that
house; and he does the same with the other
produce, namely kidney beans, which are a kind
of small beans, and chili, which is their pepper;
and *chia,* which is as fine as mustard seed, and
which in warm weather they drink, ground and
made into a solution in water and use for medicine, roasted and ground; and cocoa, which is a
kind of almond that they use as money, and
which they grind, make into a solution, and
drink; and cotton, in those places where it is
raised, which is in the hot lands and not the
cold; and pulque, which is their wine; and all
the various products obtained from the maguey
plant, from which they obtain food and drink
and footwear and clothing. This plant grows in
the cold regions, and the leaves resemble those
of the cinnamon tree, but are much larger. Of
all these and other products they leave the vassal only enough to sustain him for a year. And
in addition the vassal must earn enough to pay
the tribute of mantles, gold, silver, honey, wax,
lime, wood, or whatever products it is customary
to pay as tribute in that country. They pay this
tribute every forty, sixty, seventy, or ninety days,
according to the terms of the agreement. This
tribute also the *tiquitlato* receives and carries to
his Indian lord.

Ten days before the close of the sixty or hundred days, or whatever is the period appointed
for the payment of tribute, they take to the
house of the Indian lord the produce brought
by the *tiquitlatos;* and if some poor Indian
should prove unable to pay his share of tribute,
whether for reasons of health or poverty, or lack
of work, the *tiquitlato* tells the lord that such-
and-such will not pay the proportion of the
tribute that has been assigned to him; then the
lord tells the *tiquitlato* to take the recalcitrant
vassal to a *tianguez* or market, which they hold
every five days in all the towns of the land, and

there sell him into slavery, applying the proceeds of the sale to the payment of his tribute. . . .

All the towns have their own lands, long ago
assigned for the provision of the *orchilobos* or
ques or temples where they kept their idols; and
these lands were and are the best of all. And
they have this custom: At seeding time all would
go forth at the summons of the town council to
sow these fields, and to weed them at the proper
time, and to cultivate the grain and harvest it
and carry it to a house in which lived the pope
and the *teupisques, pioches, exputhles* and *pil-
toutles* (or, as we would say, the bishops, arch-
bishops, and canons and prebendaries, and even
choristers, for each major temple had these five
classes of officials). And they supported themselves from this harvest, and the Indians also
raised chickens for them to eat.

In all the towns Montezuma had his designated lands, which they sowed for him in the
same way as the temple lands; and if no garrison
was stationed in their towns, they would carry
the crops on their backs to the great city of
Temestitan [Tenochtitlán]; but in the garrison
towns the grain was eaten by Montezuma's soldiers, and if the town did not sow the land, it
had to supply the garrison with food, and also
give them chickens and all other needful provisions.

7. RELIGION AND RITUAL

*The Aztec inhabited a frightening universe peopled
by numerous gods and goddesses endowed with vast
powers and capricious tempers. The divinities held
in highest honor and most actively worshiped in
Tenochtitlán were the War God, Huitzilopochtli, and
the Rain God, Tlaloc, whose favor was considered essential to survival on the semi-arid Mexican plateau.
An imposing hierarchy of priests, said to have numbered five thousand in Tenochtitlán alone, acted as
intermediaries between gods and men. Human sacrifice on an immense scale played an important part in
Aztec religion and ritual. The following selection is
a native account of the awesome ceremonies that attended the spring festival held in the second month of
the Aztec year. The wearing of human skins symbolized the renewal of vegetation.[9]*

TLACAXIPEUALIZTLI. This feast came and was
thus celebrated; [it was] when all the captives

[9] Arthur J. O. Anderson and Charles E. Dibble, *Florentine Codex,* Book II, *The Ceremonies* (Santa Fe, School
of American Research and University of Utah, 1951), pp.
46–53. Reprinted by permission of the translators and
the School of American Research.

died, all those taken in war — the men, the women, the children.

Those who had taken captives, when, on the morrow, their prisoners were to die, then began the captives' dance, when the sun had passed noon. And they held an all-night vigil for their prisoners there in the tribal temple. And they placed [the captives] before the fire and took hair from the top of the captives' heads, when half the night had passed and when they made offerings of blood from the ear.

And when the dawn came, then they made them leave, that they might go to die, they who were to die appropriately to this feast day. For during the entire festival they were all flayed. Hence they called [the feast] Tlacaxipeualiztli.

And the captives were called *xipeme* and *tototecti*. Those who slew them were the priests. Those who had taken them captive did not kill them; they only brought them as tribute, only delivered them as offerings; [the priests] went laying hold of their heads, and seizing [the hair of] their heads. Thus they went leading them up to the top of the temple.

And when some captive faltered, fainted, or went throwing himself upon the ground, they dragged him.

And when one showed himself strong, not acting like a woman, he went with a man's fortitude; he bore himself like a man; he went speaking in manly fashion; he went exerting himself; he went strong of heart and shouting, not without courage nor stumbling, but honoring and praising his city.

He went with a firm heart, speaking as he went: "Already here I come! You will speak of me there in my home land!"

And so they were brought up [the pyramid temple steps] before [the sanctuary] of Uitzilopochtli.

Thereupon they stretched them, one at a time, down on the sacrificial stone; then they delivered them into the hands of six priests, who threw them upon their backs, and cut open their breasts with a wide-bladed flint knife.

And they named the hearts of the captives "precious eagle-cactus fruit." They lifted them up to the sun, the turquoise prince, the soaring eagle. They offered it to him; they nourished him with it.

And when it had been offered, they placed it in the eagle-vessel. And those captives who had died they called "eagle men."

Afterwards they rolled them over; they bounced them down; they came tumbling down head over heels, and end over end, rolling over and over; thus they reached the terrace at the base of the pyramid.

And here they took them up.

And the old men, the *quaquacuilti,* the old men of the tribal temples, carried them there to their tribal temples, where the captor had promised, undertaken, and vowed [to take a captive].

There they took [the slain captive] up, in order to carry him to the house [of the captor], so that they might eat him. There they portioned him out, cutting him to pieces and dividing him. First of all they reserved for Moctezuma a thigh and set forth to take it to him.

And [as for] the captor, they there applied the down of birds to his head and gave him gifts. And he summoned his blood relations, he assembled them, that they might go to eat at the house of him who had taken the captive.

And here they cooked each one a bowl of stew of dried maize, called *tlacatlaolli,* which they set before each, and in each was a piece of the flesh of the captive.

They named [the captor] the sun, white earth, the feather, because [he was] as one whitened with chalk and decked with feathers.

The pasting on of feathers was done to the captor because he had not died there in the war, but was yet to die, and would pay his debt [in war or by sacrifice]. Hence his blood relations greeted him with tears and encouraged him.

And on the morrow, the gladiatorial sacrifice was made. Until early morning, until dawn, they made them hold vigil, all night, until the dawn was ended. Thus did the captives, those to be sacrificed, pass the whole night until dawn. . . .

Thereupon began the gladiatorial sacrifice. The captives were spread out in order; the captors stood arranging and accompanying them. Then also the striped ones came forth; swiftly the ocelot [-costumed] warrior led and guided them; he came quickly to meet [the captives], displaying his shield and war club and lifting them up toward the sun [in dedication].

Then he turned back, retreated, turned to the rear; once again he went back.

In the same manner there then followed him, coming second, the eagle [-costumed warrior], who similarly lifted up [as an offering] to the sun his shield and his war club.

Once again emerged another ocelot [-costumed warrior], who came out as third, doing the same as he quickly came out.

Yet again an eagle [-costumed warrior] came out, doing just as had been done. All four [acted as if] fighting. They raised their shields and war clubs [as offerings] to the sun.

Now no longer did they delay, by turning back. When they came out, they came out dancing, they went in order. As if lying down on the ground, as if crawling along, flat on the ground, they went looking from side to side; they went up leaping and fighting.

And thereafter the Youallauan came forth, garbed like Totec; only he came last, after the others, behind the four great eagle and ocelot [warriors]; they lifted up their shields and war clubs, offering and dedicating them to the sun.

Then all the impersonators, the proxies, of all the gods emerged in order, ahead of all. They were called the lieutenants, the delegates, the images.

Similarly, they proceeded; they came in order; they came together. All came down. They came hence, from Iopico, from the very top of the [pyramid] Temple of Iopitli.

And when they had come down below, on the ground, on the earth, they gathered around the circular, flat, sacrificial stone; they seated themselves according to rank on large chairs called *quecholicpalli*.

And when they were seated, when they were arranged according to their importance, again the first in order was the chief priest, the Youallauan; because it was his right, his office, that he should slay, offer as sacrifice, [that] with his hands he should destroy — with his hands hack open each of the captives destined for sacrifice.

When this was done, then trumpets were sounded; conch shells, large sea shells, were blown; men put their fingers in their mouths and whistled, and there was singing. With singing of songs and blowing of trumpets they arrived. The Cozcateca placed themselves in order, their shoulders decked with feather banners, and they encircled the offering-stone.

One [of the captors] quickly seized a captive. The captor, he who owned the captive, seized him by the head to bring him to the offering-stone.

When he had brought him there, he offered him wine; and the captive raised the wine four times [as an offering], and afterwards drank it with a long hollow gourd.

Then still another man, [a priest] came out and cut the throat of a quail for the captive, him who was to be offered as a sacrifice; and when he had beheaded the quail, he raised [to the sun] the captive's shield, and cast the quail away, behind him.

Having done this, then they made [the cap-tive] climb upon the round sacrificial stone; and when they had lifted him on the offering-stone, the wolf [priest] came up to him, representing [a wolf], and known as "Old Wolf." [He came forth] as the uncle of the captive destined for the sacrifice.

Then he took the rope holding the captive, which reached and was attached to the center [of the stone]; then he tied it about the waist of the captive. And he gave him a war club, decked with feathers and not set with obsidian blades.

And he placed before him four pine cudgels, his missiles, with which to lay about him, with which to defend himself. And the captor when he had left his prisoner on the offering-stone, thereupon went away [to the place where] he had stood [before]. He stood dancing, looking upon, and studying, his captive.

Then [the fight] was begun; the contest [was started]. Carefully they studied where they would smite him in a dangerous place, and cut him — perchance the calf of the leg, or the thigh, or his head, or his middle.

And if some captive was valiant and courageous, with great difficulty he surpassed [his adversary]. He met and fought all four of the ocelot and eagle [warriors]. And if they could not weaken him, then came one who was left-handed. He then wounded his arm and threw him flat upon the surface. This one appeared as [the god] Opochtli. And although the captive might falter and faint, yet he acquitted himself as a man.

And when one went faltering, sinking down on all fours, reeling and overcome in the fray, uselessly and vainly holding the war club, which they snatched from him, thus his adversaries contended with him. And this useless one could now no longer do more; no more could he use his hands; no longer make himself do anything. No longer did he move; he did not speak. Then, faltering and fainting, he fell upon the surface, tumbling as if dead. He wished that he might stop breathing, that he might suffer [no longer], that he might perish, that he might cast off his burden of death.

And thereupon they quickly took and seized him, pushed him, and dragged him, and raised and stretched him out upon the edge of the round sacrificial stone.

And then, when the Youallauan went [forth], in the guise of Totec, he gashed [the captive's] breast, seized his heart, and raised it as an offering to the sun; and the priests placed it in the eagle vessel. And another man, a priest, carried the [hollow] eagle cane and set it in the breast of the captive, there where the heart had been; he stained it with blood; he submerged it well into the blood. Thereupon he offered [the blood] to the sun. It was said: "Thus he giveth [the sun] to drink."

And the captor thereupon took the blood of his captive into a green bowl with a feathered rim. The sacrificing priests came to pour it there. In it went the hollow cane, which also had feathers. And then the captor departed with it that he might nourish the demons. He went into and came out of all [shrines]; he omitted none; he forgot not the priests' dwellings in the tribal temples. On the lips of the stone images he placed the blood of his captive, giving them nourishment with the hollow cane. He went in festive attire.

And when he had gone to and reached all the places, then he took the insignia to the palace, and he caused his captive to be taken to the tribal quarters, where they had passed the night in vigil; here he flayed him. Afterwards he had [the flayed body] taken to his house, where they cut it up, that it might be eaten and shared, and, as was said, to bestow as a favor to others. . . .

And the captor might not eat the flesh of his captive. He said: "Shall I, then, eat my own flesh?" For when he took [the captive] he had said: "He is as my own beloved son." And the captive had said: "He is as my beloved father." And yet he might eat of someone else's captive.

And the captor kept the [captive's] skin for himself; he lent it to others. For twenty days the skin was carried by one person and another, worn for the entire feast. He who wore it gave everything given him, all that he had collected, to the captor. Afterwards [the captor] divided up [the gifts] among [all of] them. Thus he made use of his skin.

And when this was done, when they had finished with the gladiatorial sacrifice victims, then there was a dance and a procession about the round sacrificial stone, by all the impersonators [of the gods] and those who had fought the victims, all going ceremonially arrayed. In this way did they who did the slaying end [the ceremony]. All severally took with them the head of a captive, a sacrificial victim, and therewith danced. This was called "the dance with severed heads."

And the old wolf man grasped the rope [which had fastened the captives to the offering-stone] and raised it [as an offering] to the four directions. He went weeping and howling, like one bereaved; he wept for those who had suffered and died.

And also from the warring cities, from beyond [the mountains], those with whom there was war, were summoned, in secret, and came within, in secret, as Moctezuma's guests, the Nonoalca, the Cozcateca, the Cempoalteca, the Mecateca. [These ceremonies] were shown to them, and they were confounded. For thus they were undone and disunited.

8. THE AZTEC LITERARY HERITAGE

Although the Aztec system of hieroglyphics was not sufficiently developed to record formal compositions, there existed an extensive body of literature which Mexican youths were required to memorize in school and in their homes. This material was later written down in the Spanish alphabet by Indian students of the mission schools established in Mexico after the Conquest. Much of it deals with the exploits and misfortunes of the great Mexican culture hero Quétzalcóatl. The Song of Quétzalcóatl tells how the enchanter Titlacáhuan destroyed the wondrous city of Tula and forced the departure of Quétzalcóatl, its yellow-bearded god and prophet. After wandering over Mexico and performing many magical feats, Quétzalcóatl at last reached the Gulf of Mexico, where he fashioned a raft of serpents that bore him over the waters to the dominions of his master the Sun. Two selections from the Song of Quétzalcóatl, rendered into English by the late John H. Cornyn, follow.[10]

[THE SPLENDOR OF THE CITY OF TULA]

All the glory of the godhead
Had the prophet Quétzalcóatl;
All the honor of the people.
Sanctified his name and holy;
And their prayers they offered to him
In the days of ancient Tula.
There in grandeur rose his temple;
Reared aloft its mighty ramparts,
Reaching upward to the heavens.
Wondrous stout and strong the walls were,
High the skyward-climbing stairway
With its steps so long and narrow,
With its many steps so narrow
That there scarce was room for setting,
Room for placing of the footsteps.

. . . . .

And his people, they the Toltecs,
Wondrous skilled in all the trades were,
All the arts and artifices,

10 John H. Cornyn, *The Song of Quétzalcóatl*, Antioch, Ohio, Antioch College Press, 1930, pp. 78–82, 107–110. Reprinted by permission of Miss Eleanor Cornyn.

So that naught there was they knew not;
And as master workmen worked they,
Fashioned they the sacred emeralds;
Fashioned they the precious turquoise;
Smelted they both gold and silver.
Other arts and trades they mastered;
In all crafts and artifices
Skilled were they as wondrous workmen.
And in Quétzalcóatl all these
Arts and crafts had their beginning;
In him all were manifested.
He the master workman taught them
All their trades and artifices.

. . . . .

Very rich was Quétzalcóatl.
Nothing pleasing to the palate,
Nothing helpful to the body
Ever lacked they there in Tula.
Very large there grew the squashes;
Wondrous big and stout the squashes
So that one could scarcely span them
With the outstretched arms embracing.
Very long and thick the corn ears
So that in their arms they bore them.
Stoutly grew the amaranth stocks;
Wondrous tall the amaranth stocks;
And like trees they used to climb them.
Ready colored grew the cotton,
Red and yellow, rose and purple,
Green and bluish, verdigris,
Black and orange, gray and crimson,
Blushing like the ripening berry.
Ready colored grew the cotton
And no need was there to dye it.
Variegated, many-colored
Were the birds in ancient Tula.
There the bluish xiútótol;
There the quétzal and zácuan;
There the red-necked tláuhquéchol;
Birds of every hue and color;
Birds that sang with wondrous sweetness
Songs that gladdened all the listeners.

. . . . .

Wondrous rich were all the Toltecs;
Masters they of wealth uncounted;
Every need was satisfied them;
Nothing lacked they in their households;
Hunger never dwelt among them;
And the small corn never used they
Save to heat their thermal baths with.

[THE NECROMANCER TITLACÁHUAN LURES THE
PEOPLE OF TULA TO THEIR DEATH]

And you now shall hear of other
Magic of the necromancer,

The Enchanter, Titlacáhuan,
Who adorned himself with feathers,
With the precious Tócihuitli,
And waged war on Cóatépec;
And defeated Zácatépec.
Forth into the Place of Singing
Straightway goes the necromancer;
Goes the master priest enchanter,
To the Place of Inspiration
Where the songs come to the singer.
And he there begins composing,
Starts the weaving of his verses.
From the hill of Tzátzitépec
Loudly calls the public crier;
Shouts advising to the people;
Cries out to the Toltecs saying;
"You who hear my voice outreaching
Far o'er all the land of Tula,
Come ye here and come ye quickly!"
And full swiftly came the Toltecs,
At the call from Tzátzitépec.
Came they forth to Téxcalápan,
To the town upon the river,
Flowing past the cliffs uprising.
All the workers, all the masses
Hastened forth to Téxcalápan.
Came the young men and the maidens;
Came they forth in swarms unnumbered,
Mighty multitudes uncounted.
Then his song of deep enchantment
Straight began the necromancer;
Played his instrument of music,
Ever beating on his war drum;
And at once began the dancing.
Ever tramping go the people,
Marking time unto the music,
With their feet the measure stamping.
Swiftly move they in the dancing;
Move they to the ancient measure;
Joining hands they dance together.
Joyfully they sing the chorus;
Chant the song of vanished ages.
Grandly swells the choral music
Like the waves upon the ocean,
Breaking, ever breaking shoreward
Louder, louder grows the music;
Higher, higher swells the singing
Of the song the necromancer,
In the Place of Inspiration,
There and there alone composing,
Chanted in the Place of Singing.
As the song of the enchanter
Ever grandly swelling rises,
From his lips the people take it
And, repeating all together,

Sing they forth the magic chorus;
Chant they in the Place of Singing,
From the opening of the evening
Till the midnight wind is blowing.

As they dancing, ever dancing;
As they stamping, ever stamping,
Round and round about go swinging,
Crushed to earth they fall and falling
O'er the precipice are thrown
Sheer into the open canyon,
Downward unto death are driven;
Hurled to death are hosts unnumbered;
Straightway into cliffs converted.

And the others there remaining,
Forward moving, ever forward,
Press across the yawning canyon,
From whose depths the boulders rising
Cover all the gorge's pathway.
Straightway then the necromancer,
He the wondrous priest enchanter,
Breaks the bridge of stone asunder;

Hurls the struggling masses downward
Sheer into the moving water
Rushing underneath the roadway;
Into rocks forthwith converts them.

And so powerful was the magic
Of the wondrous priest enchanter
That the ever-dancing Toltecs
Nothing knew of all that happened;
Nothing knew of what befell them.
And thus to the place of singing,
Many times to Téxcalápan
Came they pressing ever forward;
Straight to death came rushing onward.
Forthwith then the grand enchanter
Hurled them from the cliffs uprising
Sheer into the yawning canyon.
And the Toltecs veiled their faces
That they might not view the corpses
Where they lay below extended;
See the many dead and dying.

III

The Incas of Peru

THE INCAS, the greatest empire-builders of ancient America, began their career of conquest as one of a number of tribes that inhabited the Cuzco region in the Andean Highlands. A strong strategic situation in the Valley of Cuzco and a marked cultural superiority to most of their neighbors favored the Incas in their schemes of conquest. True imperial expansion seems to have begun in the second quarter of the fifteenth century, in the reign of the Emperor Pachacuti. By 1525 the boundary markers of the "Children of the Sun" rested on the modern frontier between Ecuador and Colombia, to the north, and on the Maule River in Chile, on the south.

The principal economic activity of the Incas was an intensive agriculture that made wide use of irrigation, terracing, and fertilizer, supplemented by the raising of the llama for its wool and meat and of the alpaca solely for its fine wool. Special classes of craftsmen, such as silversmiths, jewelers, and tapestry weavers, manufactured only for the emperor, who distributed the surplus as gifts to the nobility. A large number of metals, including tin, copper, gold, and silver, were mined with tribute labor supplied by the neighboring villages. Copper and bronze were used extensively for tools and to a lesser extent for luxury articles.

The ayllu, a village community composed of individuals claiming descent from a common ancestor, was the unit of Inca social organization. As a result of the growth of Inca imperialism, the ayllu lost much of its original independence and democratic character. By the time of the Conquest a vast gulf separated the regimented and laborious life of the Inca commoner from the luxurious existence of the nobility.

The Incas worshiped a large number of divinities and an innumerable host of sacred places or objects. Most highly respected among their gods were a nameless Creator who had made all the other gods and all living creatures, and the sun, which was regarded as the divine ancestor of the Inca royal family. Their art work was marked by a high level of technical excellence. Their architecture, technically of a high order, was characteristically solid and functional, without the ornamental sculpture or relief carving found in Central American art. The Incas had no system of writing, but had developed an ingenious counting device and memory aid known as the *quipu*. Their literature consisted in the main of narrative poems dealing with mythology, history, and other subjects that were handed down from generation to generation. A melancholy and nostalgic spirit pervades many of the traditional Inca love songs, and the same plaintiveness characterizes the few examples of their music that have come down to us.

1. THE SOURCES OF INCA STRENGTH

Like the Romans and other great imperialist nations of antiquity, the Incas had a body of legends and myths that ascribed to their rulers a divine origin and afforded their soldiers a comforting assurance of supernatural favor and protection. This belief in divine favor, and in their "civilizing mission" among "the lesser breeds without the law," undoubtedly aided the Incas in their career of conquest. The Spanish lawyer and government official Polo de Ondegardo (1500?–1580?), did not believe the Inca claims of a lineage of great antiquity and miraculous origin. His report on this subject, based on exhaustive inquiry into Inca history and institutions, is remarkably sound in its chronology and shrewd in its analysis of the factors responsible for the successes of Inca imperialism. In this analysis special emphasis is placed on the cultural superiority of the Incas to all their neighbors, as shown in their agriculture, architecture, mode of warfare, and political organization.[1]

IT MUST BE UNDERSTOOD, in the first place, that the lineage of these Yncas was divided into two branches, the one called Hanan Cuzco, and the other Hurin Cuzco. From this it may be concluded (and there is no memory of anything to the contrary) that they were natives of the Valley of Cuzco, although some pretend that they came from other parts to settle there. But no credit should be given to them, for they also say that this happened before the flood. From what can be gathered and conjectured in considering the traditions of the present time, it is not more than three hundred and fifty to four hundred years since the Yncas only possessed and ruled over the valley of Cuzco as far as Urcos, a distance of six leagues, and to the Valley of Yucay, which is not more than five leagues.

Touching the Lords that the people can remember, their recollection does not carry them back beyond the time already stated. They preserve the memory of these Lords by their *Quipus*, but if we judge by the time that each is said to have lived, the historical period cannot be placed further back than four hundred years at the earliest.

It must have been at about that period that they began to dominate and conquer in the districts round Cuzco, and, as would appear from their records, they were sometimes defeated. For, although Andahuaylas, in the province of the Chancas, is only thirty leagues from Cuzco, they did not bring it under their sway until the time of Pachacutec Yupanqui Ynca, who defeated those Chancas. . . . On the other side of Cuzco is the road of Colla-suyu; and they also retain a recollection of the time when the Canas and Canches, whose country is even nearer, were paid to go with the Yncas to the wars, and not as vassals following their lords; and this was in the same battle in which Pacachutec Ynca fought against *Usco-vilca,* Lord of the Chancas. They also recollect the time when they extended their dominion along this road to the lake of Villcañota, the point where the Collao begins. Two powerful rivers flow out of this lake, one going to the north sea, and the other to the south. The lake was worshipped by the natives, before the Yncas advanced beyond this point. It was the successor of that lord who conquered the Chancas who began to advance beyond this point, and those provinces had no peace until the time of Tupac Ynca, of the Yncas, but each province also had its registers of wars, so that, if it were necessary, we might very easily fix the time when each province was subjugated by the Yncas.

But it is enough to understand that these Yncas at first extended their conquests by violence and war. There was no general opposition to their advance, for each province merely defended its land without aid from any other; so

[1] *Narratives of the Rites and Laws of the Yncas,* translated by Clements R. Markham, London, the Hakluyt Society, 1873, pp. 151–157.

that the only difficulty encountered by the Yncas was in the annexation of the districts around Cuzco. Afterwards all the conquered people joined them, so that they always had a vastly superior force as well as more cunning in the art of war. Thus it was seldom that they were completely defeated, although sometimes they were obliged to retreat, and desist from a war during a year.

No province ever attempted to disturb them in their own land, only seeking to be left in quiet possession of their own territories, and this seems to me to have been a great advantage to the Yncas. There is no memory of such an attempt in their registers; but after the districts were reduced to obedience, the great natural strength of this region conduced to its security. The four roads which diverge from Cuzco are all crossed by rivers that cannot be forded at any time in the years, while the land is very rugged and strong. There cannot, therefore, be a doubt that in this, and in possessing better discipline and more knowledge, lay the advantage they had over all the other nations of this region. This superiority is shown in their edifices, bridges, farms, systems of irrigation, and in their higher moral lives. If other nations have anything good, it has all been taught them by the Yncas. The Yncas also had a different system of warfare, and were better led, so that they could not fail to become lords over the rest. Thus they continued to extend their dominions and to subjugate their neighbours.

The second thing that may be taken for granted is that having resolved to conquer and subjugate other nations, the Yncas sought some colour and pretext for prosecuting their objects. The first story that these Yncas put forward, though it was not the idea which they finally asserted, was an idea that, after the deluge, seven men and women had come out of a cave which they call *Paccari-tampu*, five leagues from Cuzco, where a window was carved in masonry in most ancient times; that these persons multiplied and spread over the world. Hence every province had a like place of worship where people came forth after the universal destruction; and these places were pointed out by their old men and wizards, who taught them why and how the Yncas venerated the cave of *Paccari-tampu*. Thus in every province these places of worship are to be found, each one with a different tale attached to it.

With this title the Yncas were for a long time unable to conquer more than the provinces bor-

dering on Cuzco until the time of Pachacuti Ynca Yupanqui. His father had been defeated by the Chancas, and retreated to Cuzco, leaving his troops in a *Pucara* or fortress. Then the son formed an army out of the fugitives, and out of the garrison of Cuzco, and out of the men of Canes and Canches, and turned back to attack the Chancas. Before he set out his mother had a dream that the reason [for] the victory of the Chancas was that more veneration was shown for the Sun than *Pachayachachic*, who was the universal creator. Henceforward a promise was made that more sacrifices and prayers should be offered to that statue. Then the son was promised a victory over the Chancas, and that men should be sent from Heaven to reinforce him. With that title he went forth and conquered. . . . Sacrifices of many kinds were continually invented, and all who were subjugated were taught that Cuzco was the abode and home of the gods. Throughout that city there was not a fountain, nor a well, nor a wall, which they did not say contained some mystery, as appears in the report on the places of worship in that city, where more than four hundred such places are enumerated. All this continued until the arrival of the Spaniards; and even now all the people venerate the *huacas* given them by the *Yncas*.

The third thing to be understood is that as soon as the Yncas had made themselves lords of a province they caused the natives, who had previously been widely scattered, to live in communities, with an officer over every ten, another over every hundred, another over every thousand, another over every ten thousand, and an Ynca governor over all, who reported upon the administration every year, recording the births and the deaths that had occurred among men and flocks, the yield of the crops, and all other details with great minuteness. They left Cuzco every year, and returned in February to make their report, before the festival of Raymi began, bringing with them the tribute of the whole empire. This system was advantageous and good, and it was most important in maintaining the authority of the Yncas. Every governor, how great lord soever he might be, entered Cuzco with a burden on his back. This was a ceremony that was never dispensed with, and it gave great authority to the Yncas.

The fourth thing is that in every place where a settlement or village community was formed, the land was divided in the following manner: one portion was set apart for the support of religion, being divided between the Sun and the

Pachayachachic, and the thunder, which they called *Chuquilla*, and the *Pacha-mama* and their ministers, and other *huacas* and places of worship, both general and such as were peculiar to each village. It would take long to enumerate them, for they were so numerous that, if they had had nothing else to do, the sacrifices alone would have given them occupation. For each town was divided in the same way as Cuzco, and every notable thing was made an object of worship, such as springs, fountains, streams, stones, valleys and hill summits, which they called *apachetas*. Each of these things had its people, whose duty it was to perform the sacrifices, and who were taught when to sacrifice and what kind of things to offer up. Although in no part were there so many objects of worship as in Cuzco, yet the order and manner of worshipping was the same. . . .

Another share of the produce was reserved for the Ynca. This was stored in the granaries or sent to Cuzco, according to the necessities of the Government. For it was not always disposed of in the same way. The Ynca supplied with food all his garrisons, his servants, his relations, and the chiefs who attended upon him, out of this share of the tribute, which was brought to Cuzco from all parts of the country. In time of war the provisions from some parts were sent to others, in addition to the ordinary consumption, and there was such order in these arrangements that no mistake ever occurred. Sometimes the stores were sent from the magazines in the mountains to the coast, at others from the coast to the interior, according to the exigencies of each case, and this was done with never-failing speed and exactness. When there was no demand the stores remained in the magazines, and occasionally there was an accumulation sufficient for ten years.

2. PACHACUTI: CONQUEROR AND GIVER OF LAWS

The process of Inca territorial expansion effectively began in the reign of the Inca or Emperor Pachacuti, who assumed the imperial fringe about 1438 A.D. Together with his son, Topa Inca, an equally great conqueror, Pachacuti obtained the peaceful or forced submission of many provinces by the skillful use of claims of divine favor, fair promises, threats, and naked force. About 1471 the aged Pachacuti resigned the empire to Topa Inca, and soon thereafter, according to the rather imaginative account of the chronicler

Sarmiento de Gamboa, "he laid his head upon a pillow and expired, giving his soul to the devil, having lived a hundred and twenty-five years." A great organizer as well as a mighty warrior, Pachacuti is credited with many reforms and innovations, including the establishment of the territorial divisions and the elaborate administrative bureaucracy that made the wheels of the Inca Empire go round. He also appears to have established the official ascendancy of the cult of the Creator over the more traditional worship of the sun. His exploits are described by the Jesuit Father Bernabé Cobo (1582–1657) in a work that has been called "the best and most complete description of Inca culture in existence." [2]

PACHACUTIC married a lady named *Mama-Anahuarque*, a native of the town of Choco, near Cuzco, and founded the lineage called Ynnaca-Panaca. This king was the most valiant and warlike, the wisest and most solicitous of the public weal, of all the Incas; for he it was that gave to the land the order, laws, and statutes which were still in force at the time of the coming of the Spaniards. He established good order in all things; took away and added rites and ceremonies; enhanced the worship of his religion; decided with what sacrifices and solemnities the gods should be venerated; endowed the temples with magnificent edifices, rents, and a great number of priests and ministers; reformed the reckoning of time; divided the year into twelve months, attaching his name to each month, and designating the solemn festivals and sacrifices which should be held during the year. He composed many beautiful prayers with which to invoke the gods, and ordered the priests to recite these prayers when they offered their sacrifices. He was no less diligent and careful in matters touching the temporal welfare of the commonwealth, and so he showed his vassals how they should cultivate their fields and make use of the lands that were useless and barren because of their roughness and folds; he ordered the construction of terraces on the steep hillsides and the bringing of canals from the rivers to irrigate them; in fine, he overlooked nothing and established good order and harmony in everything; and that is why they gave him the name of Pachacutic, which means, "The Overturn of Time or of the World," for through his wise governance matters had so improved that the times appeared to have changed and the

2 Bernabé Cobo, *Historia del nuevo mundo*, Seville, 1890–93, 4 vols., III, 156–162. (Excerpt translated by the editor.)

world to have made a turn; and so his memory was much celebrated by the Indians, and they gave him more honor in their songs and poesy than to any other of the kings who preceded or succeeded him. . . .

After having shown himself most devoted to the sun and most diligent in ensuring that all adored him as their forefathers had done, one day he fell to considering how it could be that a thing so subject to movement as the sun — which never rests or pauses for a moment, since daily it revolves about the world — should be God; and from this train of thought he inferred that it must be nothing more than a messenger sent by the Creator to visit the Universe; besides which, if it were God, it would not permit the smallest cloud to impair its splendor and prevent its rays from shining down; and if it were the Universal Creator of all things, surely some day it would rest and from some place illuminate all the land and order what it wished to be done; and so it must be that there was another and more powerful Lord, who doubtless was the *Pachayachachic*. He communicated his thoughts to the members of his council, and with their assent determined that the *Pachayachachic* should be preferred above the sun, and in the city of Cuzco he raised a special temple called *Quishuar-Cancha;* and in it he placed a likeness of the Creator of the World, *Viracocha Pachayachachic,* made of gold, of the size of a ten-year-old boy, with the appearance of a man, very resplendent, standing with the right arm upraised, the hand almost closed, and the thumb and index fingers held up in the manner of one who gives commands. . . .

To his great wisdom Pachacutic united a great heart and enterprising spirit, with which he gained illustrious victories; so that he was equally fortunate in war and in peace. To his kingdom he added many extensive provinces which he and his captains conquered. He began his conquests in the provinces of Viticos and Vilcabamba, a land most difficult to subdue by reason of its roughness and numerous crags and dense forests. The Inca departed from Cuzco with his most valiant and select men; he entered the valley of Yucay and marched down stream as far as Tambo; he reached the valley of Amaybamba, and there was told that there was no bridge on the river by which he might proceed farther, for his foes had removed the bridge of Chuquichaca (meaning the Golden Bridge), and, confident that the Inca could not cross the river, had determined to resist him.

But such was the power of the Inca that he not only had a bridge made where that one had been, but many others in such places that the men of Vilcabamba were struck with fear and amazement, confessing that only the power of the Inca could achieve such great works.

When the Inca had completed the bridges, he ordered his army to march in good order, that the enemy might not take them by surprise, and at Cocospata, some twenty-five leagues from Cuzco, there came to him ambassadors from the *caciques* of Viticos and Vilcabamba, who told him that theirs was a rough land of cliffs and bush and forest, and very unhealthful; that his Highness might fall ill if he insisted on going forward, and hence that he should say what he wanted of the Lords of that land and they would do all that he required of them. The Inca would not accept this offer, and the reply with which he sent them away was: Let them say to their *caciques* that he swore by the sun, his father, that if they did not have the roads cleared and made smooth he would sacrifice them to the sun. The ambassadors, filled with sadness, returned bearing this threat and advised the warriors of their *caciques,* who were stationed along the roads in convenient places, that they should withdraw into the interior, for the power of the Inca was so great that he would destroy the whole province.

When the ambassadors returned the *caciques* of Vilcabamba were in the plains of Pampacona, at the foot of the mountains. And being informed of the great might of the Inca, and learning from their spies that he was on the march with his army while his engineers went before to clear and open the road, they lost heart, believing that if the Inca attacked them their destruction was certain. And in order to escape harm the chiefs of Vilcabamba resorted to a cruel ruse, for they summoned their captains on some pretext and had them beheaded in their presence. And the next day they carried the heads of their captains to the Inca and told him that they came in peace and that their only wish had been to obey him, but their captains against their will had taken up arms and advanced to obstruct the Inca's passage, for which disobedience and disrespect toward his Highness they had cut off their captains' heads, which they now offered to the Inca together with their own, to do with as he pleased. When the Inca had seen the heads of the dead captains and the good will and loyalty shown by the *caciques,* he received them affably, praised what they had done, and told them that he and the sun, his father, pardoned them and received them under their protection. The Inca did not advance beyond the plains of Pampacona; to this place came the other lords of the land to pay him homage, bringing great quantities of foodstuffs and presents for the army.

The *caciques*, for the greater pleasure of the Inca and to gain his favor, told him that they would give him an entire mountain of fine silver and some rich gold mines. The Inca was much pleased by this offering; he sent some of his people to see if it were so and to bring him some samples of gold and silver. They went with alacrity and found that the richness of the mines was much greater than had been described to the Inca, and they brought him many loads of gold and silver, whereat he rejoiced greatly. He remained there some time longer, causing a great quantity of gold and silver to be extracted. It was then that the mines of Vilcabamba began to be worked by order of Pachacutic, and his successors continued this work; and with the silver and gold that they obtained from them they assembled the riches found in Cuzco by the Spaniards. The Inca departed from Vilcabamba by the same road on which he had come, and on his arrival at Cuzco he ordered that this campaign and the discovery of the mines should be celebrated with public festivals, which lasted two months.

On their termination, word was brought to the Inca that a bastard brother of his, named Inca-Urco, was secretly conspiring to revolt and make himself tyrant over the kingdom. The Inca, without further inquiry into the matter, summoned his brother, and on the pretext of honoring him he entrusted him with the conduct of a certain war, and secretly ordered another of his captains to slay him in the heat of battle; and so it was done, and when the king received the news of the death of his brother he pretended great sorrow at it and ordered it to be observed with solemn obsequies and public lamentations.

He made another campaign in which he completed the pacification of the Charcas, who remained restless and endlessly hatched intrigues and revolts in order to throw off the Inca sway, for, believing that they were created to rule, they greatly resented being ruled by others. And having done all they could to regain their liberty, without success, they lost all hope of returning to be lords as before. And with a strange fury and desperation, taking for their leader a

valorous Indian by the name of Anco-Allo, many departed from their homeland, and embarking on rafts on an arm of the Marañón River, they plunged into the forests on the eastern slopes of the Andes, and nothing more was known of them. . . .

Having greatly enlarged his empire, this king devoted his remaining years to beautifying these provinces by erecting in their principal towns magnificent temples and palaces and some strong forts modeled on the buildings he had seen in Tiahuanaco. Among them were the edifices of Vilcas, Huarco, Lima-tambo, and the great fortress of Cuzco; in fine, the most sumptuous structures in the kingdom, whose ruins yet survive, were, according to Indian tradition, founded by King Pachacutic. This king also had a great idol, all of gold, named Inticllapa, which during his lifetime, and even down to the time of the coming of the Spaniards, was held in great veneration. They kept it in a very valuable golden litter and it is said that idol and litter, broken in pieces, were borne to Caxamarca as part of the ransom of the Inca Atahualpa, together with much more of the estate left by this Inca. The kindred of the Inca buried his body in Patallacta, whence they later moved it to Totocache, and there the licentiate Polo found it carefully guarded, and so well embalmed with a certain wax and preparation that it seemed to be alive.

3. THE WAY OF THE EMPEROR

At the time of the Conquest the Inca emperors were absolute rulers who claimed lineal descent from the sun. The elaborate formality and the atmosphere of religious awe that surrounded the emperor are well described by Cobo in his work on the Incas.[3]

THE INCAS presented a very majestic appearance by reason of their grooming and apparel and the pomp with which they went about and were served at home and abroad. They had a multitude of servants in their palaces; many of these were the sons of *caciques* and lords who were raised in the royal household so that they might acquire good manners. They considered it a sign of opulence to keep many servants and have many wives and concubines; they were served with all the rare, exquisite, and precious things that the land yielded, and had them brought for their pleasure from the outermost

[3] Cobo, *Historia*, III, 287–290. (Excerpt translated by the editor.)

limits of their Empire. The king ate seated on a small stool more than a *palmo* in height . . . ; it was of prettily painted wood, and was always covered with a thin mantle, even when the Inca was seated on it. The table was the floor, as with the other Indians, but there was a rich display of gold and silver plates, a multitude of dishes and delicate *chichas* or wines, and much bustling attendance of servants. The women brought him all the dishes at once in vessels of gold, silver, and clay; they were placed before him on very small thin rushes; he indicated whatever dish pleased him and it was brought to him by one of the serving women, who held it in her hand while he ate from it. When certain great festivals were held he would go out and dine in the plaza, accompanied by a noisy retinue. Everything that was salvaged from his table and everything that he had touched with his hands was kept by the Indians in chests; in one chest they would keep the rushes on which his food was placed, in another the chicken bones and meat scraps that were cleared from the table, and in another his cast-off garments. Finally, all that the Inca had ever touched was stored in a hut under the care of a principal Indian, and on a certain day of the year everything was burned; for they said that whatever had been touched by the Incas, the Children of the Sun, must be reduced to ashes and thrown to the winds, so that no one else might touch it. The king's bed was unremarkable; he slept on the floor on a large cotton mattress and covered himself with woolen blankets.

Whenever he journeyed, and frequently even in town, he was borne about on the shoulders of Indians in a litter lined with gold; it was considered a particular favor and honor to carry him. On the road he was accompanied by many *orejones,* his gentlemen and men-at-arms, for both protection and display. In advance of his litter went two or three hundred litter-bearers of the Lucana nation, dressed in livery, whose special office it was to carry him. They were changed when they grew tired, and went ahead sweeping the road. He also displayed his majesty by his leisurely rate of travel; when there was no urgent business he covered no more than four leagues a day, and wherever he made a stop they prepared him a repast as complete as if he were in his court.

The riches of these barbarian kings were so immense that they cannot easily be described. . . . The wealth that was collected in the city of Cuzco alone, as the capital and court of the empire, was incredible, for the principal houses of the dead kings were there, together with all the treasure that each had assembled in his lifetime. Since a new king never touched the estate or the fortune of his predecessor (which was applied solely to the service and worship of the deceased monarch) but instead built himself a new house and accumulated his own store of gold and silver and so forth, the treasure in this city was immense, for each king sought to outdo his predecessors in the luxury, brilliance, and pomp of his house. There, too, were the richest and most frequented temples of the kingdom, and the principal *guacas* and gods of the provinces, together with the famous and much revered sanctuary of the Sun, called *Coricancha* (meaning the House of Gold). This edifice was one of the world's richest shrines in gold and silver, and men came to it from all regions, bringing the most precious objects that they could offer for sacrifice. For all these reasons Cuzco was the richest city that has been found in the New World.

4. HOW THE INCAS FORMED A NATION

The Incas made a systematic attempt to unify the institutions and even the language of their extensive empire; that they had considerable success in the latter is shown by the fact that five sixths of the Indians of the Andean area still speak Quechua, the official language of the empire. The Incas obtained their results with the aid of an elaborate bureaucracy that brought every inhabitant of the empire under the direct and continuous control of an official appointed by the emperor. An important factor in the success of the Inca plan of unification was the famous policy of resettlement or colonization, described below by Father Cobo.[4]

THE ENTIRE EMPIRE of the Incas, though so extensive and composed of so many diverse nations, was a single commonwealth, ruled by the same laws, statutes, and customs and observing the same religion, rites, and ceremonies. . . .

The first thing that these kings did after conquering a province was to remove six or seven thousand families, more or less, as seemed best to them, taking into account the capacity and temper of the population, and to transfer these families to the quiet, peaceful provinces, assigning them to different towns. In their stead they introduced the same number of people, taken from the places to which the former families

4 Cobo, *Historia,* III, pp. 222–225. (Excerpt translated by the editor.)

had been sent or from such other places as seemed convenient; among these people were many nobles of royal blood. Those who were thus domiciled in new lands were called *mitimaes* — that is, newcomers or strangers, as distinct from the natives. This term applied to the new vassals as well as to the old ones who were sent in their places, since both went from their own to foreign lands; even today we use the word in this sense, calling *mitimaes* all those newcomers who have settled in the provinces of this kingdom. In these transfers of population they saw to it that the migrants, both the newly conquered persons and the others, were moved to lands whose climate and conditions were the same as, or similar to, those which they had left behind and in which they had been reared. . . .

The Incas introduced these changes of domicile in order to maintain their rule with greater ease, quiet, and security; for since the city of Cuzco, their capital, where they had their court and residence, was so distant from the provinces most lately acquired, in which there were many barbarous and warlike nations, they considered that there was no other way to keep them in peaceful submission. And since this was the principal purpose of the transfer, they ordered the majority of the *mitimaes* whom they sent to the recently conquered towns to make their homes in the provincial capitals, where they served as garrisons, not for wages or for a limited time but in perpetuity, both they and their descendants. As soldiers they received certain privileges to make them appear of nobler rank, and they were ordered always to obey the slightest commands of their captains and governors. Under this plan, if the natives revolted, the *mitimaes,* being devoted to the governors, soon reduced them to obedience to the Inca; and if the *mitimaes* rioted they were repressed and punished by the natives; thus, through this scheme of domiciling the majority of the people of some province in other parts, the king was made secure against revolts in his dominions, and the social and commercial intercourse among the different provinces was more frequent and the entire land was better supplied with all its needs. The Incas profited further by this transfer of their vassals from one part to another in that throughout the length and breadth of the Empire similarity and conformity prevailed in religion and government. All the nations learned and spoke the language of Cuzco, which thus came to be general throughout Peru; for through this change of domicile the newly conquered peoples, removed into the interior of the

kingdom, learned all this quickly and without difficulty or coercion, and the old vassals who were resettled in place of the new subjects who were being pacified taught it to the natives. The Incas required everyone to absorb their language, laws, and religion, with all the beliefs about these matters that were established at Cuzco; they either partly or wholly abolished their former usages and rites and made them receive their own. In order to introduce and establish these things more effectively, in addition to transferring people they would remove the principal idol from a conquered province and set it up in Cuzco with the same attendance and worship that it had formerly had; all this was seen to by persons who had come from that province, just as they had done when they had had the idol in their own country. For this reason Indians from every province of the kingdom were at all times in residence in the capital and court, occupied in guarding and ministering to their own idols. Thus they learned the usages and customs of the court; and when they were replaced by others according to their system of *mitas,* or turns, on their return to their own country they taught their people what they had seen and learned in the court.

5. THE VILLAGE BASIS OF INCA SOCIETY

The basic unit of Inca social organization was the ayllu, *a village community whose members claimed descent from a common ancestor and married exclusively within the group. Each* ayllu *owned certain lands, which were assigned to heads of families in accordance with their needs and redistributed every year to insure equal treatment and rotation of crops. In addition to cultivating their own lots, commoners were required to till certain community lands reserved for the imperial government and the Inca religion. The chronicler Garcilaso de la Vega (1539–1616), son of a Spanish noble and an Inca princess, drew an idyllic picture of Indian village life and of the relations between the Incas and their subjects. His account of a happy peasantry going forth with songs and rejoicing to labor in the service of their king is at serious variance with what is known of the chronic unrest and frequent revolts of conquered tribes against their Inca rulers.[5]*

IN THE MATTER of working and cultivating the fields they also established good order and harmony. First they worked the fields of the sun,

5 Garcilaso de la Vega, *Comentarios reales de los Incas,* Buenos Aires, 1943, 2 vols., I, 227–229. (Excerpt translated by the editor.)

then those of the widows and orphans and of those disabled by old age or illness: all such were regarded as poor people, and therefore the Inca ordered that their lands should be cultivated for them. In each town, or in each ward if the town was large, there were men assigned exclusively to look after the cultivation of the fields of the persons that we would call poor. These deputies were called *llactamayu,* or town councillors. It was their task, at the time of plowing, sowing, and harvesting the fields, to ascend at night towers that were made for this purpose, to blow on a trumpet or shell to attract attention, and loudly announce: "On such-and-such a day the fields of the disabled persons will be cultivated; let each betake himself to his assigned place." The people in each precinct already knew, by means of a list that had been made, to which fields they must go; these were the fields of their relatives or closest neighbors. Each one had to bring his own food, whatever he had in the house, so that the disabled persons would not have to provide for them. For they said that the aged, the sick, and the widows and orphans had trouble enough of their own, without being burdened with the troubles of others. If the disabled persons had no seeds they were provided from the storehouses, of which we shall have more to say hereafter. The fields of the soldiers who were away at war were also worked in common, for when their husbands were absent on army duty the wives were counted as widows. And so they performed this favor for them as for needy people. They took great care in the rearing of the children of those who were killed in the wars, until such time as they were married.

After the fields of the poor had been cultivated, each one tilled his own, and they helped each other in groups, cultivating their fields in turn. Then they tilled the fields of the *curaca,* the chief, and these were the last to be worked in each town or province. In the time of Huaina Capac, in a town of the Chacapuyas, one Indian town councillor gave precedence to the fields of the *curaca,* a relative of his, before those of a widow. He was hanged for breaking the rule that the Inca had established for the cultivation of the fields, and the gallows was set up on the land of the *curaca.* The Inca decreed that the fields of their vassals should have precedence before their own, for they said that the prosperity of his subjects was the source of good service to the king; that if they were poor and needy they could not serve well in war or in peace.

The last fields to be cultivated were those of the king. They worked them in common; all the Indians went to the fields of the king and the sun, generally with great good cheer and rejoicing, dressed in the vestments and finery that they kept for their principal festivals, adorned with gold and silver ornaments and wearing large feathered headdresses. When they plowed the land (and this was the labor that gave them the greatest pleasure), they sang many songs that they composed in praise of their Inca; thus they converted their work into merrymaking and rejoicing, because it was in the service of their God and of their kings.

6. INCA AGRICULTURE

The economic basis of Inca civilization was an intensive agriculture, which supported not only the laboring population but the large Inca armies, an enormous bureaucracy, and many other persons engaged in non-productive activities. Garcilaso de la Vega describes Inca agricultural technique.[6]

AFTER THE INCA had conquered some kingdom or province and had approved the government of the villages and the place of residence of the inhabitants according to his laws and the worship of his person, he ordered the cultivated land (land that would bear maize) to be enlarged, and for this purpose he sent for engineers to construct irrigation channels. From their works, both those that have fallen into ruin and those that remain in good order, it is clear that they were superb artisans. They dug as many channels as were required, according to how much useful land needed irrigation, for since this country is generally poor in grain-bearing land, they sought to increase it as much as possible. And because this land is underneath the torrid zone it must be irrigated, and they did this very carefully, never sowing a seed of grain without irrigation. They also built channels to water the pastures when the autumn rains were belated, for they wished to benefit the pasture lands as well as the sowed fields, since they had immense flocks. These channels for the pastures fell into ruin after the Spaniards entered the country, but their remains may still be seen.

After the channels had been made, they leveled the fields and arranged them in squares, to obtain the full benefit of the water. On the hills and slopes, where there was good land, they made terraces such as may be seen today in Cuzco and throughout Peru. To make these

6 Garcilaso de la Vega, *Comentarios,* I, 225–227, 230–231. (Excerpt translated by the editor.)

terraces they erected three strong walls of hewed stone, one in front and two at the sides, inclining slightly inward (as all their walls do) to sustain the weight of the earth, which they fill in until it is level with the top of the walls. Having constructed this terrace, they built another smaller one above it, and farther on one that was still smaller. In this manner they gradually covered the whole hill, grading it with their terraces like a stairway, and making use of all the land that was arable and could be irrigated. Where a hillside was rocky they removed the rocks and brought earth from elsewhere to construct terraces and make the place useful, rather than let it go to waste. The first terraces were large, of sufficient width and length for sowing one, two, and three hundred *fanegas* of seed, more or less, according to the situation of the site, and the next ones were smaller, and thus they continued to diminish as they ascended until the last terraces had room for two or three rows of maize. So much industry did the Incas display in the matter of increasing the land for the sowing of maize. In many places they would continue an irrigation canal for fifteen or twenty leagues in order to water a small quantity of grain land, lest it be wasted.

Having increased the arable area, they measured all the land in that province, each village separately, and divided the land into three parts: one for the sun, another for the king, and the remaining part for the natives. In the division they always took care that the natives had enough land to sow, preferring that they have too much rather than not enough. And when the population of the town or province increased, they took land from the portions of the sun and the Inca for the vassals; thus the king retained for himself and for the sun only those lands that would otherwise remain deserted, without an owner. The greater part of the terraces were allocated to the sun and to the Inca, since he had ordered their construction. Besides the cornfields that they irrigated, they divided dry, unirrigated land, where they planted other seeds and very important vegetables, such as the *papa* and *oca* and *añus*; these lands they also divided according to their system, a third part to the vassals and the same to the Sun and the Inca. And since these lands were sterile for lack of irrigation, they planted them for only one or two years, after which they distributed still other lands, letting the first ones lie fallow; in this manner they adjusted the use of their infertile lands so that they might always be productive.

The corn fields they planted every year, for they watered and fertilized them like a vegetable garden, and thus they always bore fruit. Along with corn they planted a seed that resembles rice, called *quinua,* which also grows in cold lands. . . .

They manured the land to make it fertile; in the valley of Cuzco, and nearly everywhere in the highlands, they used human manure in the cornfields, because they considered it the best. They collect it with much care and diligence, and dry and pulverize it to have it ready when the time for sowing comes. Throughout the Collao, a region more than one hundred and fifty leagues in length, where it is too cold to raise corn, they fertilize the fields sown to potatoes and other plants with the dung of llamas; they say it is more beneficial than any other manure.

On the sea coast, from below Arequipa to Tarapaca, a distance of more than two hundred leagues, they use no other manure than the droppings of sea birds, both large and small, which are to be found along the entire coast of Peru, and which fly in flocks so large as to be incredible to one who had not seen them. They breed on certain unpopulated islands along that coast, and the quantity of manure that they deposit on them is also incredible. From a distance the mounds of manure resemble snowy mountain peaks. In the time of the Inca kings they guarded these birds with such care that it was forbidden on pain of death to enter these islands during the breeding season, lest the birds should be disturbed and driven from their nests. It was similarly unlawful to kill them at any time either on the islands or elsewhere, also on pain of death.

Each island, by order of the Inca, was assigned for the use of a particular province; and if the island was large they gave it to two or three provinces. They set up markers so that the people of one province would not encroach on the district of another; and they made still more minute divisions, assigning to each village its share and to each of its inhabitants his portion, according to how much manure that he would require. The inhabitant of one village was punished with death if he took manure from the portion assigned to another, for this was regarded as theft; nor could he take more from the portion assigned to his village than had been allotted him in accordance with the requirements of his lands, and they punished the offender for his presumption in taking the excess. These bird droppings are a rich fertilizer.

7. INCA SUN WORSHIP

The chief of the Inca gods was a nameless creator, usually called Viracocha and Pachayachachic ("lord" and "instructor of the world"). First in importance after Viracocha was the Sun God, claimed by the Inca royal family as its divine ancestor. Father Cobo describes the elaborate cult of the Sun God among the Incas.[7]

THE GOD most respected by them after Viracocha was that most excellent of material creations, the sun; and the Incas, who boasted that they were the Children of the Sun, bent all their efforts toward exalting its authority and endowing it with a magnificent ritual, numerous priests, and frequent offerings and sacrifices. Not that much had to be done to inspire esteem for the sun among their people; they respected the objects of Nature in accord with the benefits that they obtained from them, and since the beneficial effects produced by this planet were so manifest and excellent, they held it in great regard. The authority and example of the Incas only served to make the external displays of worship more costly and elaborate. They believed that the Pachayachachic had given the sun power to create all the foods, together with the earth, whence came their regard for it as the greatest guaca of all after the Viracocha; and so they called it *Apu-Inti*, which means "My Lord Sun": they visualized it in the likeness of a man, and consequently they used to say that the moon was his wife and the stars their children.

They held the sun in such reverence throughout this kingdom of the Incas that I question whether in any other part of the world there ever prevailed a cult so respected and well served. This may be seen from the fact that to no other god did they dedicate so many and such magnificent temples; for there was not an important town where the sun did not have a temple with numerous priests and *mamaconas* and ample revenues for its maintenance. And the wealthiest and most sumptuous temple of all was that which the Inca kings had erected to the sun in their court, the temple called Coricancha, where they kept their principal and most venerated idol. It was an impressive image, called *Punchau*, which means "the day," all worked in finest gold with a wealth of precious stones, in the likeness of a human face, surrounded by rays, as we depict the sun; they placed it so that

it faced the east, and when the sun rose its rays fell on it; and since it was a sheet of finest metal the rays were reflected from it so brightly that it actually seemed to be the sun. The Indians were wont to say that the sun lent this image both its light and its power. From the spoils which the Spaniards obtained in the beautiful temple of Coricancha there fell to the lot of a soldier this splendid sheet of gold, and since at that time gambling was the popular pastime he lost it one night at play; from this came the saying used in Peru about heavy gamblers: "He gambles the sun away before it rises." This soldier was named Manso Serra; he later became a leading citizen of Cuzco, where I came to know a son of his, named Juan Serra. . . .

They regarded the eclipse of the sun as a grave matter, and when it occurred they consulted the diviners about its meaning; and having been told what it denoted, they made great and costly sacrifices, offering up various gold and silver figures, and killing a large number of sheep as well as many boys and girls. The sorcerers commonly asserted that the eclipse portended the death of some prince, and that the sun had gone into mourning for the loss that the world would suffer; when this happened all the women dedicated to the sun fasted for many days, wore mourning garments, and offered frequent sacrifices. The Inca retired to a secret spot, and there, having dealings with none, he fasted many days; during all this time no fire was lighted in the whole city.

8. THE SHEPHERD AND THE VIRGIN OF THE SUN

Only a few examples of Inca literature have come down to us in unmodified form. The lack of a system of writing, and the hostility of the Spanish priesthood to the Inca religious ideas that pervaded their literature, help to explain why so little material survives. The Inca hymns and prayers that have been preserved are described by one writer as notable for "their lofty thought and beauty of expression." The famous play Ollanta, cited by Markham as proof that the Incas composed dramatic pieces, is now generally thought to have been written after the Conquest. Of the long narrative poems that dealt with Inca mythology, legends, and history, and were memorized by each generation in turn, there remain only summaries in Spanish prose. Spanish chroniclers recorded a large number of Inca legends and fables, among them being many origin myths that explained the appearance of lakes, mountains, stones of unusual shape, and the

[7] Cobo, *Historia*, III, 324–327. (Excerpt translated by the editor.)

like. In this category belongs the following tale, which describes with unaffected simplicity the tragic romance of an Andean shepherd and a Virgin of the Sun.[8]

IN THE SNOW-CLAD Cordillera above the valley of Yucay, called Pitu-siray, a shepherd watched the flock of white llamas intended for the Inca to sacrifice to the Sun. He was a native of Laris, named Acoya-napa, a very well disposed and gentle youth. He strolled behind his flock, and presently began to play upon his flute very softly and sweetly, neither feeling anything of the amorous desires of youth, nor knowing anything of them.

He was carelessly playing his flute one day when two daughters of the Sun came to him. They could wander in all directions over the green meadows, and never failed to find one of their houses at night, where the guards and porters looked out that nothing came that could do them harm. Well! the two girls came to the place where the shepherd rested quite at his ease, and they asked him about his llamas.

The shepherd, who had not seen them until they spoke, was surprised, and fell on his knees, thinking that they were the embodiments of two out of the four crystalline fountains which were very famous in those parts. So he did not dare to answer them. They repeated their question about the flock, and told him not to be afraid, for they were children of the Sun, who was lord of all the land, and to give him confidence they took him by the arm. Then the shepherd stood up and kissed their hands. After talking together for some time the shepherd said that it was time for him to collect his flock, and asked their permission. The elder princess, named Chuqui-llantu, had been struck by the grace and good disposition of the shepherd. She asked him his name and of what place he was a native. He replied that his home was at Laris and that his name was Acoya-napa. While he was speaking Chuqui-llantu cast her eyes upon a plate of silver which the shepherd wore over his forehead, and which shone and glittered very prettily. Looking closer she saw on it two figures, very subtilely contrived, who were eating a heart. Chuqui-llantu asked the shepherd the name of that silver ornament, and he said it was called *utusi*. The princess returned it to the shepherd, and took leave of him, carrying well in her memory the name of the ornament and the figures, thinking with what delicacy they

were drawn, almost seeming to her to be alive. She talked about it with her sister until they came to their palace. On entering, the door-keeper looked to see if they brought with them anything that would do harm, because it was often found that women had brought with them, hidden in their clothes, such things as fillets and necklaces. After having looked well, the porters let them pass, and they found the women of the Sun cooking and preparing food. Chuqui-llantu said that she was very tired with her walk, and that she did not want any supper. All the rest supped with her sister, who thought that Acoya-napa was not one who could cause inquietude. But Chuqui-llantu was unable to rest owing to the great love she felt for the shepherd Acoya-napa, and she regretted that she had not shown him what was in her breast. But at last she went to sleep.

In the palace there were many richly furnished apartments in which the women of the Sun dwelt. These virgins were brought from all the four provinces which were subject to the Inca, namely Chincha-suyu, Cunti-suyu, Anti-suyu and Colla-suyu. Within, there were four fountains which flowed towards the four provinces, and in which the women bathed, each in the fountain of the province where she was born. They named the fountains in this way. That of Chincha-suyu was called *Chuclla-puquio*, that of Cuti-suyu was known as *Ocoruro-puquio, Sicilla-puquio* was the fountain of Anti-suyu, and *Llulucha-puquio* of Colla-suyu. The most beautiful child of the Sun, Chuqui-llantu, was wrapped in profound sleep. She had a dream. She thought she saw a bird flying from one tree to another, and singing very softly and sweetly. After having sung for some time, the bird came down and regarded the princess, saying that she should feel no sorrow, for all would be well. The princess said that she mourned for something for which there could be no remedy. The singing bird replied that it would find a remedy, and asked the princess to tell her the cause of her sorrow. At last Chuqui-llantu told the bird of the great love she felt for the shepherd boy named Acoya-napa, who guarded the white flock. Her death seemed inevitable. She could have no cure but to go to him whom she so dearly loved, and if she did her father the Sun would order her to be killed. The answer of the singing bird, by name *Checollo*, was that she should arise and sit between the four fountains. There she was to sing what she had most in her memory. If the fountains repeated her words,

8 C. R. Markham, *The Incas of Peru*, London, 1910, pp. 408–415.

she might then safely do what she wanted. Saying this the bird flew away, and the princess awoke. She was terrified. But she dressed very quickly and put herself between the four fountains. She began to repeat what she remembered to have seen of the two figures on the silver plate, singing:

"*Micuc isutu cuyuc utusi cucim.*"

Presently all the fountains began to sing the same verse.

Seeing that all the fountains were very favourable, the princess went to repose for a little while, for all night she had been conversing with the *checollo* in her dream.

When the shepherd boy went to his home he called to mind the great beauty of Chaqui-llantu. She had aroused his love, but he was saddened by the thought that it must be love without hope. He took up his flute and played such heart-breaking music that it made him shed many tears, and he lamented, saying: "Ay! ay! ay! for the unlucky and sorrowful shepherd, abandoned and without hope, now approaching the day of your death, for there can be no remedy and no hope." Saying this, he also went to sleep.

The shepherd's mother lived in Laris, and she knew, by her power of divination, the cause of the extreme grief into which her son was plunged, and that he must die unless she took order for providing a remedy. So she set out for the mountains, and arrived at the shepherd's hut at sunrise. She looked in and saw her son almost moribund, with his face covered with tears. She went in and awoke him. When he saw who it was he began to tell her the cause of his grief, and she did what she could to console him. She told him not to be downhearted, because she would find a remedy within a few days. Saying this she departed and, going among the rocks, she gathered certain herbs which are believed to be cures for grief. Having collected a great quantity she began to cook them, and the cooking was not finished before two princesses appeared at the entrance of the hut. For Chuqui-llantu, when she was rested, had set out with her sister for a walk on the green slopes of the mountains, taking the direction of the hut. Her tender heart prevented her from going in any other direction. When they arrived they were tired, and sat down by the entrance. Seeing an old dame inside they saluted her, and asked her if she could give them anything to eat.

The mother went down on her knees and said she had nothing but a dish of herbs. She brought it to them, and they began to eat with excellent appetites. Chuqui-llantu then walked round the hut without finding what she sought, for the shepherd's mother had made Acoya-napa lie down inside the hut, under a cloak. So the princess thought that he had gone after his flock. Then she saw the cloak and told the mother that it was a very pretty cloak, asking where it came from. The old woman told her that it was a cloak which, in ancient times, belonged to a woman beloved by Pachacamac, a deity very celebrated in the valleys on the coast. She said it had come to her by inheritance; but the princess, with many endearments, begged for it until at last the mother consented. When Chuqui-llantu took it into her hands she liked it better than before and, after staying a short time longer in the hut, she took leave of the old woman, and walked along the meadows looking about in hopes of seeing him whom she longed for.

We do not treat further of the sister, as she now drops out of the story, but only of Chuqui-llantu. She was very sad and pensive when she could see no signs of her beloved shepherd on her way back to the palace. She was in great sorrow at not having seen him, and when, as was usual, the guards looked at what she brought, they saw nothing but the cloak. A splendid supper was provided, and when every one went to bed the princess took the cloak and placed it at her bedside. As soon as she was alone she began to weep, thinking of the shepherd. She fell asleep at last, but it was not long before the cloak was changed into the being it had been before. It began to call Chuqui-llantu by her own name. She was terribly frightened, got out of bed, and beheld the shepherd on his knees before her, shedding many tears. She was satisfied on seeing him, and inquired how he had got inside the palace. He replied that the cloak which she carried had arranged about that. Then Chuqui-llantu embraced him, and put her finely worked *lipi* mantles on him, and they slept together. When they wanted to get up in the morning, the shepherd again became the cloak. As soon as the sun rose, the princess left the palace of her father with the cloak, and when she reached a ravine in the mountains, she found herself again with her beloved shepherd, who had been changed into himself. But one of the guards had followed them, and when he saw what had happened he gave the alarm with loud shouts. The lovers fled into the mountains which are near the town of Calca. Being tired after a long journey, they climbed to the top of a rock and went to sleep. They heard a great noise in their sleep, so they arose. The princess took one shoe in her hand and kept the other on her foot. Then looking towards the town of Calca both were turned into stone. To this day the two statues may be seen between Calca and Huayllapampa.

9. TWO VIEWS OF THE INCA EMPIRE

The debate on the nature of the Inca state that began soon after its downfall continues to be waged in our own times. Successive generations of historians, consciously or unconsciously influenced by political, social, or sentimental partialities, have found in the Inca Empire whatever type of governmental system or social order they perhaps wanted to find. Some of the pros and cons of this debate are presented in the selections given below, written by men who are not clearly identifiable with either of the two major schools and who are highly regarded for their honesty and objectivity. The first reading [9] *is from the* Chronicle of Peru, *written in 1551 by Cieza de León (1518–1560), a soldier who had traveled throughout the Andean region studying Indian customs and institutions. The second* [10] *is from the previously cited work of Father Cobo.*

SINCE THESE KINGS ruled over a land of such great length and vast provinces, and in part so rugged and full of snow-capped mountains and sandy, treeless, arid plains, they had to be very prudent in governing so many nations that differed so greatly in language, law, and religion, in order to maintain them in tranquillity and keep peace and friendship with them. Therefore, although the city of Cuzco was the head of their empire, . . . they stationed deputies and governors at various points; these men were the wisest, ablest, and most courageous that could be found, and none was so young but that he was in the last third of his age. And since the natives were loyal to such a governor and none dared to rebel, and he had the *mitimaes* on his side, no one, no matter how powerful, dared to rise against him; and if such a rebellion did take place, the village in which the uprising occurred was punished and the instigators were sent to

[9] Pedro de Cieza de León, *Del señorío de los Incas*, Buenos Aires, 1943, pp. 34–35. (Excerpt translated by the editor.)

[10] Cobo, *Historia*, III, 279–281. (Excerpt translated by the editor.)

Cuzco. Hence the kings were so greatly feared that if they traveled through the kingdom and merely permitted one of the hangings on their litters to be lifted so that their vassals might see them, the people raised such a great cry as to cause the birds flying on high to fall and be captured by hand; and so great was their fear that they dared not speak ill of even the shadow that the Inca cast. And this was not all; . . . if any of his captains or servants went out to visit some part of the kingdom, the people came out to receive him on the road with many presents, never failing, even if he were alone, to comply in detail with his every order.

So greatly did they fear their princes, in this extensive land, that every village was as well organized and governed as if their lord were present in it to punish those who disobeyed him. This fear arose from the power that these lords enjoyed, and from their justice, for all knew that if they did wrong they would certainly be punished and that neither pleas nor bribes would help them. And the Incas always did good works for their subjects, not permitting them to be wronged or burdened with excessive tribute or outraged in any way. They helped those who lived in barren provinces, where their forefathers had lived in great need, to make them fertile and abundant, providing them with the things they required; and to other provinces where they had insufficient clothing, for lack of sheep, they sent flocks of sheep with great liberality. In fine, it was understood that these lords knew not only how to be served by their subjects and to obtain tribute from them but also how to keep up their lands and how to raise them from their first rude condition to a civilized state and from destitution to comfort. And through these good works and through constantly presenting their principal men with wives and jewels, they gained the extreme good will of all, and were so greatly loved that I recall with my own eyes having seen aged Indians, visiting Cuzco, gaze upon the city with tearful lamentations, as they contemplated the present time and recalled the past, when that city so long housed their natural lords, who knew how to gain their service and friendship in other ways than those used by the Spaniards.

THE YOKE that weighed down the necks of these miserable Indians was so heavy that I doubt if all the men in the world, joining together to invent a species of subjection and tyranny as oppressive as that in which they lived, could improve on what the Incas achieved to keep these Indians in a state of submission.

And anyone who carefully considers the system they maintained in administering and conserving their empire will find that all was directed solely toward this end. I could easily prove this by describing in detail the actions they ordered for oppressing their subjects, but it will suffice to say that these poor people were not allowed to own anything privately without the permission of the Inca or his governors, not even to slaughter a sheep or to have two suits of clothes; nor could they eat what they chose, but they had to observe the wishes of the Inca or his governors; nor could they marry whomever they pleased, and still less could they marry off their daughters at their pleasure; nor (what is worse) were they masters of their own wives and children, for the lords took away the wives of some to give them to others, and they took their children to slay them in the sacrifices.

The *caciques* made the round of their districts several times a year, to make sure that the Indians had no more than was allowed them, for they were not permitted to possess gold or silver or to wear fine clothes. They could not own a flock of more than ten animals without special permission; this privilege the Inca would grant to the *caciques*, but in a specified number, which never exceeded fifty or a hundred heads; and the *caciques* themselves could not wear fine clothes unless they received them from the Inca as a reward for some distinguished service. Daughters ordinarily were in the power of their parents until the age of ten, and thereafter they were at the disposition of the Inca. All persons, no matter how noble their rank, when entering the presence of the king took off their sandals and placed light burdens on their shoulders as a sign of homage and reverence. In speaking to the Inca they kept their eyes lowered and did not look him in the face, while he maintained a visage of notable gravity and replied with few words, spoken in such a low voice that they could scarcely be heard. Only the great lords, by special privilege, seated themselves before him.

And since the Incas had no other aim in their method of government than to place their vassals daily in a state of greater subjection and servitude, to please them each of their governors and *caciques*, both high and low, applied himself to the attainment of their objective, which was to exhaust the strength of the Indians until they

were unable to raise their heads. And since the Incas were very capable men, they were not found wanting in the craft and skill required for the difficult task of taming nations so barbarous and indomitable. The principal method that they used for this purpose was to keep their subjects poor and continually occupied with excessive labors, so that being oppressed and abased they might lack the fire and spirit to aspire to revolt. To this end they built great fortresses, opened roads, constructed terraces on the hillsides, and compelled them to bring tribute to Cuzco from distances of three and four hundred leagues. With the same aim they introduced many cults and burdened them with many rites and sacrifices, so that when they were free from other labors and services this work alone sufficed to leave them without time to take breath or rest. . . .

Moreover, the Incas were much aided in their designs by the great esteem and respect that the Indians felt for them, through which these simple people came to believe that the Incas not only were different from other men in valor and strength but had close kinship, familiarity, and intercourse with the sun and with the *huacas,* basing this erroneous opinion on the testimony of the Incas themselves, who boasted of this relationship, and on the religious claims which the Incas always advanced in making their conquests. And by reason of these things, and because of the diligence with which the Incas propagated the worship of their religion, consuming in its honor so much wealth and so many people that it became the principal occupation of the whole land, the Indians concluded that the gods must be under a great sense of obligation and duty toward the Incas, never failing to favor their designs. They were daily confirmed in this view by the many victories that the Incas won over all kinds of nations, and by the fact that although at the outset they had been so few in number they had placed this whole great empire under their sway. And the esteem that the Indians felt for the Incas was not a little enhanced by the admirable order and harmony that they established in all matters, both in what concerned the good of the commonwealth and in the aggrandizement of the cult of their gods. To this also contributed the nonsense the Incas daily fed their subjects, as a result of which these simple people conceived the Incas to be very close to the gods and endowed with superhuman wisdom, particularly when they saw the beauty and majesty with which the Incas had adorned their court, for which the Indians felt great reverence. . . .

Nevertheless, I believe that these measures would not have sufficed to establish so firmly the power of the Incas and the subjection of these peoples if the Incas had not also resorted to severe measures, inflicting deaths and exemplary punishments upon those who attempted to overthrow the existing order. Actually, there were numerous revolts on the part of their subjects, who tried to regain their liberty by this means. . . . Many of these terrible chastisements are still fresh in the memories of living men, since their stories have been handed down from father to son. I will cite here two or three of these cases. In a place near Payta an Inca slew five thousand men at one time, and to strike greater fear into his subjects he ordered the

hearts of the slain men to be plucked out and placed around the fortress in a circle. In the towns of Otavalo and Caranque, Guaynacapac put to death all the males (except the boys), and for this reason the inhabitants of those towns were long called Guambracuna, which means "lads." . . . From which I conclude that it was through strictness and cruelty, more than by any other means, that the Incas succeeded in breaking the spirit of their subjects, in placing them in the strict servitude in which they kept them, and in developing in them the abject submissiveness with which they were obeyed and revered. For theirs was a slavery so rigorous that it is difficult to imagine a worse one, even if we reviewed all the governments of the world of which we have any knowledge.

Part Two

The Conquest of America

THE PECULIAR COURSE of Spain's development helps to explain her leadership in the exploration and conquest of America. Five centuries of struggle against the Moslems had made warfare almost a Spanish way of life, and had created a large class of titled fighting men who regarded manual labor and commerce with contempt. The crusading character of the Moorish Wars engendered a spirit of religious fanaticism that provided a convenient sanction for the conquest of New World pagans. Finally, Ferdinand and Isabella, the monarchs who brought the Moorish Wars to a successful conclusion, also created a unified Spain, free from internal strife, and thereby established favorable conditions for a mighty movement of overseas expansion.

The discovery of America by Columbus resulted from the search for an all-water route to the East that was promoted by the monarchs of Portugal and Spain in an effort to break the Italian monopoly of European commerce with the Orient.

From its primary base on Hispaniola the Spanish Conquest branched out to the other great Antilles (Puerto Rico, Cuba, Jamaica) and simultaneously sent out weak offshoots to the coasts of South and Central America. Slave-hunting and exploring expeditions gradually made the coasts of Central America and Mexico better known and revealed Indian societies far wealthier and more advanced than those found in the West Indies.

The discovery of these societies led to the invasion of Mexico by Hernando Cortés in 1519. The superstitious fears of the Aztec war chief Montezuma enabled Cortés to enter the Indian capital without opposition, but an unprovoked aggression by his lieutenant Alvarado precipitated a mortal struggle. Guatemoc, the last Aztec ruler, surrendered only when the city lay in ruins and its native defenders were dead or starving. From Mexico the stream of conquest flowed south into Guatemala and Honduras; in Nicaragua it joined another current formed by Spaniards coming north from Darien.

The town of Panama, founded in 1519 across the isthmus from Darien, became a base for expeditions seeking another golden kingdom that was rumored to lie southwards. After repeated failures, Francisco Pizarro and his companions achieved their aim of reaching and conquering the Inca Empire. However, before the Indian resistance was entirely overcome, the conquerors fell out among themselves, and by the time that peace was restored to Peru all the leading figures in the struggle had come to violent ends.

IV

The Hispanic Background

THE RUGGED IBERIAN PENINSULA had undergone successive invasions by foreign tribes or nations from very ancient times. The Iberians and Celts, who are believed to have come from North Africa and Central Europe respectively, were succeeded by Phoenicians, Greeks, and Carthaginians. These commercial nations established trading posts and cities on the coast but made no effort to establish control over the interior. Still later, Spain became a stake of empire in the great struggle for commercial supremacy between Rome and Carthage that ended with the decisive defeat of the latter in 201 B.C. For six centuries thereafter Rome was the dominant power in the peninsula.

Early in the fifth century the waning of Roman military power that accompanied the general crisis of the Empire made possible the invasion of Spain by a number of barbarian peoples of Germanic origin. By the last half of the century one of these groups of invaders, the Visigoths, had gained mastery over most of the peninsula. For most of its brief history the Visigothic Kingdom was plagued by internal strife; this generally arose out of disputes over the succession to the kingship, which was elective among the Germanic tribes. These divisions among the Goths played into the hands of their Moslem foes in North Africa. In A.D. 711 the latter crossed the straits and decisively defeated Roderic, the last Gothic king. Within a few years all Spain, aside from certain small districts in the mountainous north, had fallen into Moslem hands.

The Moslems, who had inherited the accumulated cultural wealth of the ancient Mediterranean and Eastern worlds, enriched this heritage with their own magnificent contributions to science, art, and literature. But for all its noble achievements, Moslem civilization rested on insecure foundations. The Moslem world was rent by fierce political and religious feuds over control of the empire. In Spain these internal differences were complicated by conflicts between the Arabs and the North African Berbers, recent converts to Mohammedanism and more fanatically devout than their teachers. These discords enabled the small Christian kingdoms that had arisen in the North to survive, to grow strong, and eventually to launch a general advance against the Moslem power. By the opening of the fifteenth century all of Spain except the small southeastern kingdom of Granada was in Christian hands.

A turning point in peninsular history was the marriage, in 1469, of the heirs apparent to the thrones of Aragon and Castile — Ferdinand and Isabella. The "Catholic Kings," as they are known in Spanish history, broke the power of the lawless grandees by force of arms, and by subtler means curbed the authority and independence of the proud Spanish towns. The crowning domestic achievement of their reign was the surrender of the city and kingdom of Granada in 1492, after a ten-year war. Unified politically and religiously, filled with martial and crusading zeal, and avid for the gold and silver that symbolized power and wealth in an age of dawning capitalism, Spain stood ready to launch the great enterprise of the Indies.

1. IN PRAISE OF SPAIN

The swift destruction of the Visigothic realm by Moslem invaders had a natural interest for early Spanish historians. According to legend, a certain Count Julian, seeking revenge for the seduction of his daugh-

ter by King Roderic, helped the Moors to enter Spain. In reality, the Moslems were invited to enter as allies of one of the parties contending for the Visigothic crown, but remained to conquer the land for themselves. The depth of feeling aroused by recollection of the disaster in a time of emergent Spanish nation-

alism is revealed in the following selection from the first general history of Spain, written at the behest of Alfonso the Sage of Castile (1252–1284).[1]

AND SO KING RODERICK and the Christians were vanquished and slain, and the noble Gothic nation, which had overthrown and humbled so many kingdoms, was itself defeated and abased, and its proud banners were trampled in the dust. The Goths, who had conquered Scythia, Pontus, Asia, Greece, Macedonia, and Illyria, and had robbed and ravaged these countries and even their womenfolk; who had subjugated all the eastern territory and imprisoned the great Cyrus, king of Babylonia, Syria, Media, and Hircania, and slain him in a wineskin full of blood; the people to whom the Romans, masters of the whole world, had bent the knee in surrender; they who had burned the Emperor Valentius in a fire and to whom the great Attila, king of the Huns, yielded in the battle of the Catalonian plains; that people before whom the Alani fled, leaving the Hungarian land, and to whom the Vandals abandoned Gaul in their flight; they whose victories had terrified the whole world as loud thunder terrifies men — that Gothic nation that had once been so fiery and proud, was destroyed in a single battle by the power of Mohammed the upstart, who had only recently come to notice. Let all learn from this that no one should boast of his estate — neither the rich man of his riches, nor the powerful man of his power, nor the strong man of his strength, nor the wise man of his wisdom, nor the noble of his high rank and good fortune. . . .

All the countries of the world, and their provinces, were honored by God in diverse ways, and to each He gave His gift, but of all the lands of the West Spain was most highly favored, for God gave her all the things that men desire. For when the Goths wandered through all the countries, harassing them with wars and battles and conquering many places in the provinces of Asia and Europe, inhabiting and studying every one in order to select the most favored spot in all the world, they found Spain to be the best, and they prized it above all others as the most richly endowed. Moreover, it is completely enclosed — on one side by the Pyrenees, which run to the sea, and on the others by the Ocean Sea and the Mediterranean. . . . Then this land of Spain is like God's Paradise, for it is watered by

five principal rivers, the Ebro, Duero, Tagus, Guadalquivir, and Guadiana. Each is separated from the others by great mountains and lands; the valleys and plains are broad and because of the goodness of the soil and the humor of the rivers they yield many fruits in abundance. . . .

Spain above all other lands is witty, daring, courageous in battle, light of heart, loyal to its lord, earnest in study, courtly in speech, endowed with all good things; no land in the world can match it for abundance or in number of strongholds, and few compare with it in size. Spain leads all other lands in greatness and loyalty. Ah, Spain! No tongue or intellect can recount thy good! . . . And this kingdom, so noble, so rich, so powerful, so honored, was separated and destroyed in a single attack because of discord among its people, who turned their swords against each other, as if they had no enemies to fight; and because of this everything was lost, for all the cities of Spain were captured and destroyed by the Moors.

2. THE CID CAMPEADOR: SYMBOL OF SPANISH NATIONALITY

The heroic figure of Ruy Dias de Vivar, the Cid Campeador or "Warrior Lord," as he was called by his Moslem soldiers, typifies in Spanish popular tradition the crusading era of Hispanic history. The real Cid, true to the ideals of his times, placed feudal above religious loyalties and ably served the Moslem kings of Saragossa and Valencia against not only Moorish foes but Christian princes. Furthermore, the Cid frequently displayed a chivalrous spirit in an age not remarkable for these virtues, and, in the words of the historian Altamira, "nobly personified the purest and loftiest type of the warrior nobility of his time." His greatest triumph was the seizure of the Moslem city of Valencia in the name of the king of Castile, in 1092. A thirteenth-century Spanish chronicler describes the aftermath of the victory.[2]

THAT NIGHT the Cid conferred with Alvar Fañez and Pero Bermudez and the other men of his council, and they decided what policy they would adopt with the Moors. On the next day all the Moors of Valencia assembled in the castle, as the Cid had ordered. The Cid seated himself on his dais, with all his nobles around him, and said:

"All you good men of the *aliama* of Valencia, you know how well I served and aided the king

[1] Ramón Menéndez Pidal, ed., *Primera crónica general de España*, Madrid, 1906, 2 vols., I, 310–312. (Excerpt translated by the editor.)

[2] Menéndez Pidal, *Primera crónica general*, I, 591–592. (Excerpt translated by the editor.)

of Valencia, and how many opportunities I let pass to take this city; now that God has seen fit to make me lord of Valencia, I want it for myself and for those who helped me to take it, subject only to the authority of my lord King Alfonso. You are all in my power, and I could easily take from you everything you have in the world — your persons, your wives, and your children. But I do not want to do this, and I therefore decree that the honorable men among you, who were always loyal to me, shall dwell in Valencia in their homes with their wives. However, each of you may keep only one animal — a mule —and one servant, and you may not own or use weapons unless by my order. All the others I order to leave Valencia and go to live outside the city in the Alcudia, where I once lived. You may keep your mosques in Valencia and outside in the Alcudia, and your *alfaquis* and your own laws; and you shall have your own judges and your sheriff besides those whom I have placed over you. You may keep all your estates, but you shall give me a tithe of all you grow, and I shall have supreme charge of justice and the coinage of money. Now, those who wish to remain with me on these terms may stay; as for the others, they may now leave, taking no possessions, and I shall order that no one harm them."

When the Moors of Valencia heard this they were sad, but the times were such that they had no choice. Within the hour all the Moors, except those that the Cid had ordered to remain, began to leave the town with their wives and children; and as they left the Christians who had dwelt in the Alcudia entered. History relates that so many people left Valencia that their departure required two days. . . . This business took a full two months to complete. And thereafter the Cid was called: "My Cid Campeador, Lord of Valencia."

3. THE CATHOLIC KINGS

The joint reign of Ferdinand of Aragon and Isabella of Castile was rich in dramatic and important events. Their reign has a dual aspect. Although they were constructive in their efforts to unify Spain, subdue feudal lawlessness, and activate Spanish industry, they nevertheless helped to initiate Spain's ultimate decay through their policies of religious intolerance and systematic weakening of the autonomy and democratic institutions of the Spanish towns. This negative aspect of their work was not apparent to the patriotic Jesuit Father Mariana (1535–1625), whose history of Spain contains a glowing tribute to the "Catholic Kings." [3]

TRULY IT WAS THEY who restored justice, previously corrupted and fallen into decay, to its proper place. They made very good laws for governing the towns and settling lawsuits. They defended religion and faith and established public peace, putting an end to discords and tumults, at home as well as abroad. They extended their dominions, not only in Spain but to the farthest parts of the earth. Most laudably, they distributed rich rewards and dignities not on the basis of noble birth or as private favors but according to individual merit, and thus encouraged their subjects to devote their intellects to good work and literature. There is no need to describe the benefits of all this; the results speak for themselves. Truly, where in the world are to be found more learned and saintly priests and bishops, or judges of greater wisdom and rectitude? Before their day one could list very few Spaniards distinguished in science; since their time who can count the Spaniards who have gained fame as scholars?

The king and queen were of average stature and well built; they carried themselves majestically, and their facial expressions were gravely pleasant. The king's naturally fair skin had been tanned in military campaigns; he wore his chestnut hair long and shaved his beard more often than necessary. He had wide eyebrows, a smooth face, a small crimson mouth, narrow teeth, wide shoulders, a straight neck, and a sharp voice; he spoke quickly and thought clearly; his manner was smooth, courteous, and kindly. He was skilled in the art of war, unexcelled in the business of government, and so conscientious that labor seemed to relax him. He was not self-indulgent; he ate simply and dressed soberly. He was a skilful horseman; as a youth he enjoyed playing cards and dice; as he grew older he practiced hawking, and took much pleasure in the flights of herons.

The queen had a pleasant face, blonde hair, and light blue eyes; she used no cosmetics and was exceedingly dignified and modest in appearance. She was devoted to religion and fond of literature; she loved her husband, but her love was mixed with jealousy and suspicion. She knew Latin, an accomplishment that King Fer-

[3] Juan de Mariana, *Historia de España*, Madrid, 1909, 2 vols., II, 239. (Excerpt translated by the editor.)

dinand lacked because he had not received a liberal education; he liked to read histories, however, and to talk with scholars. On the day of his birth, it is said, a certain saintly Carmelite friar of Naples said to King Alfonso, his uncle: "Today in the Kingdom of Aragon is born a child of thy lineage; heaven promises him new empires, great riches, and good fortune; he will be very devout, a lover of the good, and an excellent defender of Christianity." Considering human frailty, it was almost inevitable that among so many virtues there should be certain defects. The avarice that is charged against him can be excused by his lack of money and by the fact that the royal revenues were diverted from their proper use. The severe punishments that also are charged to him were occasioned by the disorder and depravity of the time. Foreign writers have implied that he was a crafty man and one who sometimes broke his word if it was to his advantage. I do not propose to discuss whether this be truth or fiction concocted out of hatred for our nation; I would only point out that malicious men often assign the name of vices to true virtues and, conversely, praise the deceitful vices that resemble virtues; for the rest, the king merely adapted himself to the times and to the language, methods, and strategies that were then in use.

4. THE SPANISH INQUISITION

All of Spain's troubles since the time of Ferdinand and Isabella should not be laid at the door of the Spanish Inquisition, but the operations of the Holy Office unquestionably contributed to the picture of economic decay that Spain presented by the close of the sixteenth century. The blows struck first at the Jews and later at the Conversos (Jewish converts and their descendants, who were frequently charged with heresy), fell on an important segment of Spain's merchant and banking class, the social group that in England and Holland was transforming economic life and preparing the way for the Industrial Revolution. As the great historian of the Spanish Inquisition, Charles Henry Lea, observed, "many causes contributed to [Spain's decline], but not the least among them was the bleeding to anemia, through centuries, of the productive classes and the insecurity which the enforcement of confiscation cast over all the operations of commerce and industry." The Santangel mentioned below was condemned by the civil court to burn at the stake, as the findings of the inquisitors required. Ironically, he was a kinsman of that Luis de Santangel,

Ferdinand's treasurer, who at the last moment persuaded Isabella to support Columbus's project, and who obtained at least half the money needed for the enterprise.[4]

IT APPEARS THAT the accused, the said Luis de Santangel, has openly and very clearly practiced heresy and apostasy from our holy Catholic Faith, performing and maintaining rites and ceremonies of the old law of Moses, as a true and consummate Jew, especially observing the Sabbath with entire faith and devotion, abstaining on that day from engaging in business, travel, or other lowly tasks, as much and as well as he could, keeping it a holiday with all zeal and devotion, as the Jews do, eating on that day meat and *amin* and many other Jewish foods, both those prepared in his house on Friday for use on Saturday and those brought and sent from the ghetto, getting and lighting clean candles on Friday evening in honor of the Sabbath, as the Jews do, donning a clean shirt and performing other ceremonies such as the Jews on that day are wont to perform. And likewise he zealously observed the holiday of the thin bread, eating ceremonially of the said thin bread, and of no other, this bread being sent to him by Jews, and on such days he would eat from new plates and bowls, keeping and observing the said holiday as best he could. Moreover, he observed the fasts that the Jews call the Great Kippur and Haman, abstaining from food until nightfall and then breaking fast with meat, as the Jews do. Moreover, he did not observe the Christian holidays, or attend mass, or observe the fasts of the Holy Mother Church, but on the contrary he ate meat at Lent; in particular, we find that he ate meat stewed in a pan on Good Friday. And that he continually prayed in the Judaic manner, his face turned to the wall, looking toward heaven through a window, bowing and reciting the psalms of David in Spanish, in the Judaic manner; and at the end of each psalm he said not *gloria patri* but instead *Adonai, Adonai,* and he had a psalter in the Spanish language that did not have *gloria patri* or the litany of the saints. And that he had faith and true hope in the said law of Moses, rather than in the evangelical law of our Lord Jesus Christ, defending the said law of Moses as superior to that of Jesus Christ; and that he gave oil for the

[4] Cited in: Manuel Serrano y Sanz, *Orígenes de la dominación española en América*, Madrid, 1918, pp. 114–116. (Excerpt translated by the editor.)

lamps of the synagogue, and other alms to Jews; and that he had no oratory or other Christian practice. Nor did he kneel at the sounding of the orisons or at the elevation of the Corpus Christi, or cross himself, or say "Jesus." And when riding horseback, if the beast should stumble, in place of saying "Jesus" he used to say *Sadday,* and *Adonai,* as the Jews do; and he abstained from eating the foods forbidden by the law of Moses as much as he could, eating instead the meat of animals slaughtered by Jewish hands, cleansing away the tallow, salting it to draw out the blood before cooking, and removing a certain small round body from the leg. Nor did he eat the flesh of game or birds that had been strangled, but instead he had his chickens and other fowls slaughtered by Jews; and the other game that he purchased he would kill or have killed with a well-sharpened knife, in the Judaic manner.

And as we already had information of the aforementioned matters, the said Luis de Santangel, suspecting this and suspecting that orders had been issued for his seizure, came before us with lying and deceitful words, saying that he, as a good Christian, wished to submit to our justice and confess completely certain errors that he had committed against the faith, and of his own will he bound himself to the punishment of a relapsed heretic if he should not tell the whole truth, and he gave in writing a certain confession in his handwriting, in which he confessed that he had observed certain Judaic ceremonies and fasts, by which it immediately became evident that he had committed perjury and relapsed into heresy, to which charge he had exposed himself of his own will; and after the above-cited confession, with the hope of being released from prison and even of having his goods returned, as we lawfully know, he made other confessions, more extensive than the first, although in none of these did he confess all the heresies that he had committed.

In fine, it appears that the said Luis de Santangel has been and is a negative, obdurate heretic, and that he came to seek reconciliation to the Holy Mother Church with a lying tale, and not in a sincere or contrite spirit, as the case required, and that he is unworthy of forgiveness or of admission to the Holy Mother Church; concerning all of which we have resolved and deliberated with learned men of good conscience, who have seen and examined the said process and the said confessions. And desiring to extirpate and eradicate completely, as by our office we are most strictly bound and held to do, in the name of the Church, all such vile, grave, and wicked errors, so that the name of Jesus Christ may be truly believed, exalted, adored, praised, and served, without any pretence, hypocrisy, or sham, and so that no one may bear the name of a Christian and the air of a lamb who is truly a Jew and has the heart of a wolf; and having before our eyes Our Lord, from whom proceed all just and righteous judgments, we find that we must pronounce and declare, as by these presents we do pronounce and declare, that the said Luis de Santangel has been and is a true heretic and apostate from the faith, negative and obdurate. . . . We moreover declare all his goods confiscated for the Treasury and exchequer of the King our lord. . . . And since the Holy Mother Church cannot and should not do anything more against the said heretic and apostate, except to withdraw from him its protection and remit him to the secular justice and arm that he may be punished and chastised according to his demerits, therefore, with the customary protestations established in canon law, we remit the said Luis de Santangel, heretic and apostate, to the excellent and virtuous Juan Garcez de Marcella, chief justice of the King our lord in this city, and to its judge and justices, that they may dispose of him as in law and justice they may decree.

5. THE FALL OF GRANADA

On January 2, 1492, the city and kingdom of Granada were surrendered to the Catholic Kings, bringing the ten-year Granadine war to a close. In the joyful procession that entered the last Moslem stronghold in Spain marched an obscure Genoese navigator named Cristoforo Colombo. The age of crusades had ended; the age of discovery and overseas conquest was about to begin. Father Mariana describes the last days and the fall of Moslem Granada.[5]

IT WAS BELIEVED that the siege of Granada would be of long duration; accordingly, the queen and her children came to the camp, for King Ferdinand had resolved not to make peace until Granada had fallen. With this intent he ordered the surrounding countryside laid waste, in order that the inhabitants of the city should be deprived of a source of foodstuffs; and on the site of the royal camp he built a strongly fortified town, which to this day bears the name of Santa

5 Mariana, *Obras,* II, 236, 238–240. (Excerpt translated by the editor.)

Fe. Within the walls were shops and lodgings, assigned according to the King's orders, and barracks, streets and squares, all laid out with admirable precision. Meanwhile various bands of people, sent out to plunder, clashed with the Moors who sallied from the city against them. In one skirmish the Christians advanced so far that they seized the Moorish artillery, captured many of the enemy, and compelled the rest to take refuge in the city. So great was the ardor of the Christians that they ventured to come closer than usual to the walls of the city and seized two towers that served the enemy as watchtowers and bastions and in which troops were stationed. . . . They gave the enemy no peace, although the Moors defended themselves with desperate bravery. Finally the Moors, wearying of so much harassment and seeing no prospect of relief, determined to negotiate a settlement.

Bulcacin Mulch, military governor of the city, went to the royal camp to discuss an agreement and capitulation. The King entrusted the negotiation to Gonzalo Fernández de Córdoba, later known as "The Great Captain," and to his own secretary, Hernando de Zafra. After conferring for several days they drew up an agreement, to which both parties pledged their faith on the 25th of November. The Moors were to surrender within sixty days the two castles, the towers, and the gates of the city. They were to render homage to King Ferdinand and to swear obedience and loyalty to him. All Christian captives were to be freed without ransom. As hostages for the fulfilment of these conditions, the Moors were to turn over within twelve days five hundred children of the principal citizens of Granada. They were to retain their estates, arms, and horses and surrender only their artillery. They would be permitted to keep their mosques and would have freedom to observe the ceremonies of their faith. They were to be governed according to their own laws, and to this end persons of their own nation would be designated to assist and advise the governors appointed by the king in ruling the Moors. Those who wished to depart for Africa could sell their goods, and ships were to be provided for their passage at such ports as they might designate. It was also agreed that the son of Boabdil, with the other hostages that he had previously given the king, should be returned to him, since with the surrender of the city and the fulfilment of the treaty no other security or hostage was necessary.

[A tumult among the Moslems of Granada, in protest against the capitulation agreement, is quelled by Boabdil, who fears new disorders. Ed.]

Boabdil, the "little king," immediately sent a letter to King Ferdinand, with a gift of two pure-blooded horses, a scimitar, and some harnesses. He told him of the rising in the city and said that speed was necessary to avoid trouble; he urged the king to come promptly, since small delays frequently brought about great changes. Since it was the will of God, he concluded, on the following day he would with good grace turn over the Alhambra and his kingdom to King Ferdinand as to a conqueror, but the king must not fail to come.

This letter reached the camp on New Year's Day, and King Ferdinand's satisfaction on reading it can easily be imagined. He ordered that everything should be made ready for the following day. . . . Changing from the mourning that he wore for the death of his son-in-law, Alonso, Prince of Portugal, to his royal vestments, the king set off for the castle with his retinue, all in formation and armed as if advancing to battle. A brilliant company and a splendid sight they were, indeed. Following them were the queen and her elder children, in sumptuous brocades and silks. When they had arrived with all this pomp and show near the fortress, Boabdil came out to meet them, accompanied by fifty men on horseback. He apparently intended to alight to kiss the hand of the conqueror, but the king would not permit it. Then, with downcast eyes and a melancholy expression, he said: "Invincible king, we are in your hands; we surrender to you this castle and kingdom; we trust that you will be fair and lenient in your dealings with us." He then placed in the king's hands the keys to the fortress. The king gave them to the queen, who gave them to the prince, her son; the latter placed them in the hands of Don Iñigo de Mendoza, Count of Tendilla, whom the king had appointed to hold the castle and be captain-general of the kingdom. . . . Surrounded by a large number of mounted men, the king then entered the city. He was followed by a group of lords and churchmen. Among the most distinguished were the prelates of Toledo and Seville, the master of the order of Santiago, the duke of Cadiz, and Fray Hernando de Talavera, lately made archbishop of Avila, of which city he had been bishop. Friar Hernando, having pronounced a prayer of thanksgiving, placed the standard of the cross that the cardinal of Toledo, as primate, carried before him, on the highest part of the principal tower, flanked on one side by the royal banner and on the other by that of Santiago. This was greeted by joyful shouts from the soldiers and the principal people. The king, kneeling with great humility, gave thanks to God that the empire and name of that evil people had been uprooted from Spain, and that the banner of the cross had been raised in the city where impiety had so long flourished. He implored Him to continue His favor and make it enduring and perpetual. When he had concluded this prayer, the grandees and lords approached the king to felicitate him on his acquisition of a new kingdom, and in order of rank each kissed the king's hand. They did the same with the queen and with the prince, his son.

I conclude by saying that with the entrance of the kings into Granada and their taking possession of that town, by the will of God the Moors were fortunately and forever subjected to Christian rule in that part of Spain. This was in the year 1492 of our salvation, on Friday the sixth of January — in the year 897 of the Hegira, on the eighth day of the month *rahib haraba,* according to Arabic count. This day, which for Christians is the joyful and solemn holiday of the Kings and of the Epiphany, became no less joyful for all Spain by virtue of this new victory, though a day of gloom to the Moors; for by the uprooting and destruction of impiety in our land its past disgrace and injuries were atoned for, and a sizable part of Spain was reunited with the Christian community and received its government and laws — a great joy in which the other nations of Christendom shared. . . . As a token of their satisfaction, and in acknowledgment of the divine source of this favor, the Pope, the cardinals, and the people of Rome made a solemn procession to the Spanish church of Santiago. There services were held, and in a sermon on the events of the day the preacher lauded the Spanish kings and the entire Spanish nation for their feats, their bravery, and their notable victories.

V

The Great Discoveries

ITALIAN MERCHANTS enjoyed a virtual monopoly of European trade with the Orient in the Middle Ages. The draining of their scanty store of gold and silver into the pockets of Italian and Levantine middlemen grew intolerable to the ambitious merchants and monarchs of Western Europe. Their answer to this problem was the search for an all-water route to the East, pursued with great energy in the fifteenth and sixteenth centuries. Little Portugal took a decisive lead in the race to find a waterway to the land of spices. The famous Prince Henry, known as the Navigator, initiated and organized explorations down the west coast of Africa that brought Portugal an unequaled prosperity based on trade in slaves and gold dust. Under Alfonso V and João II the effort to round Africa and reach India was vigorously pressed; success was finally achieved when Vasco da Gama made his way to Calicut in 1498.

The discovery of America was a by-product of the search for a sea road to the East. When Columbus, in about 1484, presented to the Portuguese ruler João II his plan for reaching the Orient by sailing west, the king's maritime committee rejected it, probably on sound technical grounds. Undismayed by the Portuguese rebuff, Columbus took his idea to the Spanish court. Eight years of discouraging delays elapsed before Queen Isabella agreed to support the "Enterprise of the Indies."

The voyages of Columbus laid a solid base for Spanish empire-building through the settlement of the island of Hispaniola, to which Castilian fortune-seekers flocked in large numbers. Columbus died in 1506, still believing that he had reached the mainland of Asia. It remained for Amerigo Vespucci, a Florentine merchant and navigator who made two important voyages of exploration along the north and east coasts of South America between 1499 and 1502, to announce the existence of a new continent that formed a "fourth part of the world."

The growing shortage of Indian labor, and the general lack of economic opportunities for new settlers on Hispaniola, stimulated Spanish adventurers to explore and conquer the remaining great Antilles between 1509 and 1511. In the same period, efforts to found colonies on the coasts of present-day Colombia and Central America failed disastrously, and the remnants of two expeditions were united under the able leadership of the conquistador Balboa to form the new settlement of Darien on the Isthmus of Panama. Indian accounts of a great sea and a land of gold to the south induced Balboa to make a laborious journey with a party of sixty-seven men across the isthmus to the shores of the Pacific. The discovery of the "South Sea" supported the belief that the so-called Indies formed no part of Asia, and posed the problem of finding a passage to the East across or around the American continents.

Ferdinand Magellan, a native of Portugal, was convinced that such a passage existed south of Brazil. Failing to interest the Portuguese crown in his project, Magellan turned to Spain, with greater success. The resulting voyage of circumnavigation of the globe represented an immense navigational feat and greatly increased Europe's fund of geographical knowledge. But from a practical point of view, aside from the acquisition of the Philippines for Spain, Magellan's exploit had little significance. His new route to the Orient was too long to have commercial importance. Disappointed in her dream of an easy access to the riches of the East, Spain turned with concentrated energy to the task of extending her American conquests, and to the exploitation of the human and natural resources of the New World.

1. PRINCE HENRY OF PORTUGAL: ADVANCE INTO THE UNKNOWN

At the threshold of the age of discovery and exploration stands the figure of Prince Henry of Portugal (1394–1460), somewhat misleadingly known as "the Navigator," since he apparently never sailed beyond sight of land. In Prince Henry were united a medieval crusading spirit with more modern traits: the desire to penetrate the secrets of unknown seas and lands and a lively appreciation of the importance of such discoveries for the expansion of Portuguese commerce. All these motives appear to have figured in his lifelong work of directing exploration down the west coast of Africa, but before his death the commercial motive had clearly become uppermost. The first of two selections from the chronicle of Gomes Eannes de Azurara (1410–1474), who enjoyed the friendship of the prince, affectionately portrays his appearance and character; the second describes the birth of the African slave trade with Portugal — the first bitter fruit of European overseas expansion.[1]

THE NOBLE PRINCE was of a good height and broad frame, big and strong of limb, the hair of

[1] Gomes Eannes de Azurara, *The Chronicle of the Discovery and Conquest of Guinea,* translated by C. R. Beazley and Edgar Prestage, London, the Hakluyt Society, 1896, 2 vols., I, 12–15, 81–83.

his head somewhat erect, his colour naturally fair, but by constant toil and exposure it had become dark. His expression at first sight inspired fear in those who did not know him, and when wroth, though such times were rare, his countenance was harsh. He possessed strength of heart and keenness of mind to a very excellent degree, and he was beyond comparison ambitious of achieving great and lofty deeds. Neither lewdness nor avarice ever found a home in his breast, for as to the former he was so restrained that he passed all his life in purest chastity, and as a virgin the earth received him again at his death to herself. . . .

His palace was a school of hospitality for the good and high born of the realm and still more for strangers, and the fame of it caused him a great increase of expense, for commonly there were to be found in his presence men from various nations, so different from our own that it was a marvel to well-nigh all our people; and none of that multitude could go away without some guerdon from the Prince.

All his days he spent in the greatest toil, for of a surety among the nations of mankind no one existed who was a sterner master to himself. It would be hard to tell how many nights he passed in which his eyes knew no sleep; and his body was so transformed by abstinence, that it seemed as if Henry had made its nature to be different from that of others. Such was the length of his toil and so rigorous was it, that as the poets have feigned that Atlas the giant held up the heavens upon his shoulders, for the great knowledge there was in him concerning the movements of the celestial bodies, so the people of our kingdom had a proverb that the great labours of this our prince conquered the heights of the mountains, that is to say, the things that seemed impossible to other men were made by his continual energy to appear light and easy.

The prince was a man of great wisdom and authority, very discreet and of good memory, but in some matters a little tardy, whether it was from the influence of the phlegm in his nature, or from the choice of his will, directed to some certain end not known to men. His bearing was calm and dignified, his speech and address gentle. He was constant in adversity, humble in prosperity. Never was hatred known to him, nor ill-will toward any man, however great the wrong done him; and such was his benignity in this respect, that wiseacres reproached him as wanting in distributive justice. And this they said, because he left unpunished some of his servants who deserted him at the siege of Tangier, which was the most perilous affair in which he ever stood before or after, not only becoming reconciled to them, but even granting them honourable advancement over others who had served him well, which in the judgment of men was far from their deserts, and this is the only shortcoming of his I have to record. The Infant drank wine only for a very small part of his life and that in his youth, but afterwards he abstained entirely from it.

He ever showed great devotion to the public affairs of this kingdom, toiling greatly for their good advancement and he much delighted in the trial of new undertakings for the profit of all, though with great expense of his own substance, and he keenly enjoyed the labour of arms, especially against the enemies of the holy Faith, while he desired peace with all Christians. Thus he was loved by all alike, for he made himself useful to all and hindered no one. His answers were always gentle and he showed great honour to the standing of every one who came to him, without any lessening of his own estate. A base or unchaste word was never heard to issue from his mouth. He was very obedient to the commands of Holy Church and heard all its offices with great devotion; aye and caused the same to be celebrated in his chapel, with no less splendour and ceremony than they could have been in the college of any Cathedral Church. . . . Well-nigh one-half of the year he spent in fasting and the hands of the poor never went away empty from his presence. . . . His heart knew not fear, save the fear of sin. . . .

ON THE NEXT DAY, which was the 8th of the month of August, very early in the morning, by reason of the heat, the seamen began to make ready their boats, and to take out their captives and carry them on shore, as they were commanded. And these, placed altogether in that field, were a marvellous sight, for amongst them were some white enough, fair to look upon and well proportioned, others were less white like mulattoes; others again were as black as Ethiops, and so ugly, both in features and in body, as almost to appear the images of a lower hemisphere. But what heart could be so hard as not to be pierced with piteous feeling to see that company? For some kept their heads low and their faces bathed in tears, looking one upon another; others stood groaning very grievously, looking up to the height of heaven, fixing their eyes upon it, crying out loudly, as if asking help of the Father of Nature; others struck their faces with the palms of their hands, throwing themselves at full length upon the ground; others made their lamentations in the manner of a dirge, after the custom of their country. And though we could not understand the words of their language, the sound of it right well accorded with the measure of their sadness. But to increase their sufferings still more, there now arrived those who had charge of the division of the captives and who began to separate one from another in order to make an equal partition of the fifths; and then it was needful to part fathers from sons, husbands from wives, brothers from brothers. No respect was shewn either to friends or relations, but each fell where his lot took him.

And who could finish that partition without very great toil, for as often as they had placed them in one part, the sons, seeing their fathers in another, rose with great energy and rushed over to them; the mothers clasped their other children in their arms, and threw themselves flat on the ground with them, receiving blows with little pity for their own flesh, if only they might not be torn from them.

The Infant was there, mounted upon a powerful steed, and accompanied by his retinue, making distribution of his favours, as a man who sought to gain but small treasure from his share;

for he made a very speedy partition of the forty-six souls that fell to him as his fifth. His chief riches lay in his purpose, and he reflected with great pleasure upon the salvation of those souls that before were lost. And certainly his expectation was not in vain, since, as we said before, as soon as they understood our language, they turned Christians with very little ado; and I who put together this history into the present volume, saw in the town of Lagos boys and girls (the children and grandchildren of those first captives) born in this land, as good and true Christians as if they had directly descended, from the beginning of the dispensation of Christ, from those who were first baptised.

2. THE MAN COLUMBUS

Christopher Columbus, like Prince Henry of Portugal, was a figure of transition whose thought and aspirations reflected both the waning Middle Ages and the rising new day of rationalism and capitalism. Medieval in his ardent and mystical faith, which led him to seek Scriptural authority for his enterprise of the Indies and to identify the Orinoco as one of the four rivers of Paradise, he was singularly modern in his questing, adventurous spirit and in his greed for gold and worldly honors. A major source of information about the Columbian epic is the monumental History of the Indies *of Bartolomé de las Casas (1474–1566), whose father and uncle accompanied Columbus on his second voyage, and who was with him on Hispaniola in 1500. Las Casas describes the appearance and character of the Discoverer.[2]*

As CONCERNS his appearance, he was fairly tall, his face long and giving an impression of authority, his nose aquiline, his eyes blue, his complexion light and tending to bright red; his beard and hair were fair in his youth but very soon turned gray from his labors. He was witty and gay in speech and, as the aforementioned Portuguese history relates, eloquent and boastful in his negotiations. His manner was serious, but not grave; he was affable with strangers and mild and pleasant with members of his household, whom he treated with dignity, and so he easily won the love of those who saw him. In short, he had the appearance of a man of great consequence. He was sober and moderate in eating and drinking, in dress and footwear; he would often say, whether jokingly or angrily: "God take you, don't you agree to that?" or "Why did you do that?" In the matter of Chris-

tian doctrine he was a devout Catholic; nearly everything he did or said he began with: "In the name of the Holy Trinity I shall do this" or "— this will come to pass," or "— may this come to pass." And at the head of everything he wrote he put: "Jesus and Mary, attend us on our way." I have many of these writings in my possession. Sometimes his oath was: "I swear by San Fernando"; when he wanted to affirm the truth of something very important, especially when writing to the King and Queen, he said: "I swear that this is true." He kept the fasts of the Church most faithfully, confessed and took communion very often, said the canonical offices like any churchman or monk, abhorred blasphemy and vain oaths, and was most devoted to Our Lady and the Seraphic Father Saint Francis. He appeared very grateful for benefits received at the divine hand; and it was almost a proverb with him, which he repeated frequently, that God had been especially good to him, as to David. When gold or precious objects were brought to him he would enter his chapel and kneel, asking the bystanders to do the same, saying: "Let us give thanks to the Lord, who made us worthy of discovering such great wealth." He was most zealous in the service of God; he was eager to convert the Indians and to spread the faith of Jesus Christ everywhere, and was especially devoted to the hope that God would make him worthy of helping to win back the Holy Sepulcher. . . . He was a man of great spirit and lofty thoughts, naturally inclined — as appears from his life, deeds, writings, and speech — to undertake great and memorable enterprises; patient and long-suffering . . . quick to forgive injuries, and wishing nothing more than that those who offended him should come to know their error and be reconciled with him. He was most constant and forbearing amid the endless incredible hardships and misfortunes that he had to endure, and always had great faith in the Divine Providence. And as I learned from him, from my own father, who was with him when he returned to settle the island of Hispaniola in 1493, and from other persons who accompanied and served him, he was always most loyal and devoted to the King and Queen.

3. "SAINT AUGUSTINE DOUBTS . . ."

Among the numerous legends that surround the Columbus story, perhaps the most popular of all is that which portrays Columbus as seeking to convince his bigoted and dull-witted opponents of the faculty of the University of Salamanca that the earth was

2 Bartolomé de las Casas, *Historia de las Indias*, México, 1951, 3 vols., I, 29–30. (Excerpt translated by the editor.)

round. In reality, the question of the sphericity of the earth never entered the discussions between Columbus and the committee appointed by Queen Isabella to consider his claims. The main issue, as Professor Morison points out, "was the width of the ocean; and therein the opposition was right." Of pedantry and excessive deference to the authority of the ancients, however, the committee was doubtless guilty, if we may trust Las Casas' lively account of the debate, in which he reveals a warm partisanship for Columbus.[3]

SOME SAID that it was impossible that after so many thousands of years these Indies should be unknown, if there were such places in the world, for surely Ptolemy and the many other astronomers, geographers, and sages that had lived would have known something of them, and would have left some reference to them in writing, since they had written of many other matters; hence, they said, to affirm what Columbus affirmed was to claim to know or divine more than anyone else. Others argued this way: The world is infinitely large, and therefore in many years of navigation it would be impossible to reach the end of Asia, as Christopher Columbus proposed to do by sailing westward. . . .

Still others, who vaunted their mathematical learning, talked about astronomy and geography, saying that only a very small part of this inferior sphere is land, all the rest being entirely covered with water, and therefore it could only be navigated by sailing along the shores or coasts, as the Portuguese did along the coasts of Guinea; the proponents of this view had read precious few books on navigation, and had done even less sailing themselves. They added that whoever sailed directly west, as Christopher Columbus proposed to do, could never return, for supposing that the world was round, and that going westward you went downhill, then once you had left the hemisphere described by Ptolemy, on your return you must go uphill, which ships could not do — truly a subtle and profound reason, and proof that the matter was well understood! Others cited Saint Augustine, who . . . denied the existence of antipodes . . . and their refrain was: "Saint Augustine doubts." Then someone had to bring up the business of the five zones, of which three, according to many, are totally uninhabitable; this was a commonly held opinion among the ancients, who, after all, did not know very much. Others adduced still other reasons, not worth mentioning

here since they came from the kind of people who disagree with everybody — who find any statement illogical, no matter how sound and clear it is, and never lack for reasons to contradict it. . . .

And so Christopher Columbus could give little satisfaction to those gentlemen whom the monarchs had convened, and therefore they pronounced his offers and promises impossible and vain and worthy of rejection. Having formed their opinion, they went to the monarchs and stated their views, persuading them that it did not become their royal authority to favor a project that was based on such weak foundations and that must appear vague and unfeasible to any sensible person, even an uneducated one, for if they sponsored it, they would lose the money that they spent on it and would weaken their own standing, with no benefit to anyone. Finally the monarchs sent a reply to Columbus, dismissing him for the time being, though not entirely depriving him of the hope of a return to the subject when their Highnesses should be less occupied with important business, as they were at that time by the War of Granada.

4. LANDFALL

Few records of navigation have the inherently dramatic quality of the straightforward log and journal kept by Columbus on his first voyage. Las Casas incorporated an abstract of this document, which has since vanished, in his History of the Indies. *The crisis of the voyage, to which Columbus' diary evidently made only meager reference, came on October 9–10, when the discoverer was apparently forced by a threat of mutiny to promise his fearful captains and crews that they would turn about if land were not sighted in three days. Landfall was made the following day. "Never again," justly writes Samuel Eliot Morison, "may mortal men hope to recapture the amazement, the wonder, the delight of those October days in 1492 when the New World gracefully yielded her virginity to the conquering Castilians."*[4]

MONDAY, Oct. 8th. Steered W.S.W. and sailed day and night eleven or twelve leagues; at times during the night, fifteen miles an hour, if the account can be depended upon. Found the sea like the river at Seville, *"thanks to God,"* says the Admiral. The air soft as that of Seville in April, and so fragrant that it was delicious to breathe it. The weeds appeared very fresh.

3 Bartolomé de las Casas, *Historia de las Indias*, I, 157–158. (Excerpt translated by the editor.)

4 *Journal of Christopher Columbus' First Voyage to America*, New York, A. & C. Boni, 1924, pp. 18–26. Reprinted by permission of the publisher.

Many land birds, one of which they took, flying towards the S.W.; also *grajaos,* ducks, and a pelican were seen.

Tuesday, Oct. 9th. Sailed S.W. five leagues, when the wind changed, and they stood W. by N. four leagues. Sailed in the whole day and night, twenty leagues and a half; reckoned to the crew seventeen. All night heard birds passing.

Wednesday, Oct. 10th. Steered W.S.W. and sailed at times ten miles an hour, at others twelve, and at others, seven; day and night made fifty-nine leagues' progress; reckoned to the crew but forty-four. Here the men lost all patience, and complained of the length of the voyage, but the Admiral encouraged them in the best manner he could, representing the profits they were about to acquire, and adding that it was to no purpose to complain, having come so far, they had nothing to do but continue on to the Indies, till with the help of our Lord, they should arrive there.

Thursday, Oct. 11th. Steered W.S.W.; and encountered a heavier sea than they had met with before in the whole voyage. Saw pardelas and a green rush near the vessel. The crew of the Pinta saw a cane and a log; they also picked up a stick which appeared to have been carved with an iron tool, a piece of cane, a plant which grows on land, and a board. The crew of the Niña saw other signs of land, and a stalk loaded with roseberries. These signs encouraged them, and they all grew cheerful. Sailed this day till sunset, twenty-seven leagues.

After sunset steered their original course W. and sailed twelve miles an hour till two hours after midnight, going ninety miles, which are twenty-two leagues and a half; and as the Pinta was the swiftest sailer, and kept ahead of the Admiral, she discovered land and made the signals which had been ordered. The land was first seen by a sailor called Rodrigo de Triana, although the Admiral at ten o'clock that evening standing on the quarterdeck saw a light, but so small a body that he could not affirm it to be land; calling to Pero Gutierrez, groom of the King's wardrobe, he told him he saw a light, and bid him look that way, which he did and saw it; he did the same to Rodrigo Sánchez of Segovia, whom the King and Queen had sent with the squadron as comptroller, but he was unable to see it from his situation. The Admiral again perceived it once or twice, appearing like the light of a wax candle moving up and down, which some thought an indication of land. But the Admiral held it for certain that land was near; for which reason, after they had said the *Salve* which the seamen are accustomed to repeat and chant after their fashion, the Admiral directed them to keep a strict watch upon the forecastle and look out diligently for land, and to him who should first discover it he promised a silken jacket, besides the reward which the King and Queen had offered, which was an annuity of ten thousand maravedis. At two o'clock in the morning the land was discovered, at two leagues' distance; they took in sail and remained under the squaresail lying to till day, which was Friday, when they found themselves near a small island, one of the Lucayos, called in the Indian language Guanahani. Presently they descried people, naked, and the Admiral landed in the boat, which was armed, along with Martín Alonzo Pinzon, and Vincent Yañez his brother, captain of the Niña. The Admiral bore the royal standard, and the two captains each a banner of the Green Cross, which all the ships had carried; this contained the initials of the names of the King and Queen each side of the cross, and a crown over each letter. Arrived on shore, they saw trees very green, many streams of water, and divers sorts of fruits. The Admiral called upon the two Captains, and the rest of the crew who landed, as also to Rodrigo de Escovedo, notary of the fleet, and Rodrigo Sánchez, of Segovia, to bear witness that he before all others took possession (as in fact he did) of that island for the King and Queen his sovereigns, making the requisite declarations, which are more at large set down here in writing. Numbers of the people of the island straightway collected together. Here follow the precise words of the Admiral: "As I saw that they were very friendly to us, and perceived that they could be much more easily converted to our holy faith by gentle means than by force, I presented them with some red caps, and strings of beads to wear upon the neck, and many other trifles of small value, wherewith they were much delighted, and became wonderfully attached to us. Afterwards they came swimming to the boats, bringing parrots, balls of cotton thread, javelins and many other things which they exchanged for articles we gave them, such as glass beads, and hawk's bells; which trade was carried on with the utmost good will. But they seemed on the whole to me, to be a very poor people. They all go completely naked, even the women, though I saw but one girl. All whom I saw were young, not above thirty years of age, well made, with fine shapes and faces; their hair short, and coarse like that of a horse's tail, combed toward the forehead, except a small portion which they suffer to hang down behind, and never cut. Some paint themselves with black, which makes them appear like those of the Canaries, neither black nor white; others with white, others with red, and others with such colours as they can find. Some paint the face, and some the whole body; others only the eyes, and others the nose. Weapons they have none, nor are acquainted with them, for I showed them swords which they grasped by the blades, and cut themselves through ignorance. They have no iron, their javelins being without it, and nothing more than sticks, though some have fish-bones or other things at the ends. They are all of a good size and stature, and handsomely formed. I saw some with scars of wounds upon their bodies, and demanded by signs the cause of them; they answered me in the same way, that there came people from the other islands in the neighbourhood who endeavored to make prisoners of them, and they defended themselves. I thought then, and still believe, that these were from the continent. It appears to me, that the people are ingenious, and would be good servants; and I am of opinion that they would very readily become Christians, as they appear to have no religion. They very quickly learn such words as are spoken to them. If it please our Lord, I intend at my return to carry home six of them to your Highnesses, that they may learn our language. I saw no beasts in the island, nor any sort of animals except parrots." These are the words of the Admiral.

5. AMERIGO VESPUCCI: MASTER MARINER AND HUMANIST

In one of his essays Ralph Waldo Emerson found it strange "that broad America must wear the name of a thief." For centuries the view prevailed that Amerigo Vespucci had foisted his name upon the continent by publishing accounts of a fictitious voyage in which he claimed to have reached the American mainland before Columbus. Modern research has largely untangled what Stefan Zweig called the "comedy of errors" surrounding the Vespucci problem, and has conclusively shown that the boastful documents attributed to him were forgeries. The authentic letters of Vespucci, describing two voyages that he made to South America in 1499 and 1501, reveal an urbane,

cultivated Renaissance figure who united to his impressive talent for astronomical and geographical observation an equal capacity for lively and realistic description of the fauna, flora, and inhabitants of the New World. These qualities appear in his Lisbon letter to Lorenzo de' Medici, reporting on his voyage to Brazil, in which he almost casually announces the existence of a new continent, thus refuting Columbus's theory that the lands he had discovered were a part of Asia.[5]

TO CONCLUDE, I was on the side of the antipodes; my navigation extended through one-quarter of the world; my zenith direction there made a right angle, at the center of the earth, with the zenith direction of the inhabitants of this Northern Hemisphere in the latitude of forty degrees. This must suffice.

Let us describe the country and the inhabitants and the animals and the plants and the other things I found in their habitations which are of general usefulness to human living.

This land is very pleasing, full of an infinite number of very tall trees which never lose their leaves and throughout the year are fragrant with the sweetest aromas and yield an endless supply of fruits, many of which are good to taste and conducive to bodily health. The fields produce many herbs and flowers and most delicious and wholesome roots. Sometimes I was so wonder-struck by the fragrant smells of the herbs and flowers and the savor of the fruits and the roots that I fancied myself near the Terrestrial Paradise. What shall we say of the multitude of birds and their plumes and colors and singing and their numbers and their beauty? I am unwilling to enlarge upon this description, because I doubt if I would be believed.

What should I tell of the multitude of wild animals, the abundance of pumas, of panthers, of wild cats, not like those of Spain, but of the antipodes; of so many wolves, red deer, monkeys, and felines, marmosets of many kinds, and many large snakes? We saw so many other animals that I believe so many species could not have entered Noah's ark. We saw many wild hogs, wild goats, stags and does, hares and rabbits, but of domestic animals, not one.

Let us come to rational animals. We found the whole land inhabited by people entirely

[5] Vespucci to Lorenzo di Pier Francesco de' Medici, Lisbon, 1502, quoted in Frederick J. Pohl, *Amerigo Vespucci, Pilot Major*, New York, Columbia University Press, 1945, pp. 131–135. Reprinted by permission of the Columbia University Press.

naked, the men like the women without any covering of their shame. Their bodies are very agile and well proportioned, of light color, with long hair, and little or no beard. I strove a great deal to understand their conduct and customs. For twenty-seven days I ate and slept among them, and what I learned about them is as follows:

Having no laws and no religious faith, they live according to nature. They understand nothing of the immortality of the soul. There is no possession of private property among them, for everything is in common. They have no boundaries of kingdom or province. They have no king, nor do they obey anyone. Each one is his own master. There is no administration of justice, which is unnecessary to them, because in their code no one rules. They live in communal dwellings, built in the fashion of very large cabins. For people who have no iron or indeed any metal, one can call their cabins truly miraculous houses. For I have seen habitations which are two hundred and twenty paces long and thirty wide, ingeniously fabricated; and in one of these houses dwelt five or six hundred persons. They sleep in nets woven out of cotton, going to bed in mid-air with no other coverture. They eat squatting upon the ground. Their food is very good: an endless quantity of fish; a great abundance of sour cherries, shrimps, oysters, lobsters, crabs, and many other products of the sea. The meat which they eat most usually is what one may call human flesh à la mode. When they can get it, they eat other meat, of animals or birds, but they do not lay hold of many, for they have no dogs, and the country is a very thick jungle full of ferocious wild beasts. For this reason they are not wont to penetrate the jungle except in large parties.

The men have a custom of piercing their lips and cheeks and setting in these perforations ornaments of bone or stone; and do not suppose them small ones. Most of them have at least three holes, and some seven, and some nine, in which they set ornaments of green and white alabaster, half a palm in length and as thick as a Catalonian plum. This pagan custom is beyond description. They say they do this to make themselves look more fierce. In short, it is a brutal business.

Their marriages are not with one woman only, but they mate with whom they desire and without much ceremony. I know a man who had ten women. He was jealous of them, and if it happened that one of them was guilty, he punished

her and sent her away. They are a very procreative people. They do not have heirs, because they do not have private property. When their children, that is, the females, are of age to procreate, the first who seduces one has to act as her father in place of the nearest relative. After they are thus violated, they marry.

Their women do not make any ceremony over childbirth, as do ours, but they eat all kinds of food, and wash themselves up to the very time of delivery, and scarcely feel any pain in parturition.

They are a people of great longevity, for according to their way of attributing issue, they had known many men who had four generations of descendants. They do not know how to compute time in days, months, and years, but reckon time by lunar months. When they wished to demonstrate something involving time, they did it by placing pebbles, one for each lunar month. I found a man of advanced age who indicated to me with pebbles that he had seen seventeen hundred lunar months, which I judged to be a hundred and thirty-two years, counting thirteen moons to the year.

They are also a warlike people and very cruel to their own kind. All their weapons and the blows they strike are, as Petrarch says, "committed to the wind," for they use bows and arrows, darts, and stones. They use no shields for the body, but go into battle naked. They have no discipline in the conduct of their wars, except that they do what their old men advise. When they fight, they slaughter mercilessly. Those who remain on the field bury all the dead of their own side, but cut up and eat the bodies of their enemies. Those whom they seize as prisoners, they take for slaves to their habitations. If women sleep with a male prisoner and he is virile, they marry him with their daughters. At certain times, when a diabolical frenzy comes over them, they invite their kindred and the whole tribe, and they set before them a mother with all the children she has, and with certain ceremonies they kill them with arrow shots and eat them. They do the same thing to the above-mentioned slaves and to the children born of them. This is assuredly so, for we found in their houses human flesh hung up to smoke, and much of it. We purchased from them ten creatures, male as well as female, which they were deliberating upon for the sacrifice, or better to say, the crime. Much as we reproved them, I do not know that they amended themselves. That which made me the more astonished at their wars and cruelty was that I could not understand from them why they made war upon each other, considering that they held no private property or sovereignty of empire and kingdoms and did not know any such thing as lust for possession, that is, pillaging or a desire to rule, which appear to me to be the causes of wars and of every disorderly act. When we requested them to state the cause, they did not know how to give any other cause than that this curse upon them began in ancient times and they sought to avenge the deaths of their forefathers. In short, it is a brutal business. Indeed, one man among them confessed to me that he had shared in the eating of the flesh of more than two hundred corpses, and this I assuredly believe. It was enough for me!

As to the nature of the land, I declare it to be the most agreeable, temperate, and healthful, for in all the time that we were in it, which was ten months, none of us died and only a few fell ill. As I have already said, the inhabitants live a long time and do not suffer from infirmity or pestilence or from any unhealthy atmosphere. Death is from natural causes or from the hand of man. In conclusion, physicians would have a wretched standing in such a place.

6. THE DISCOVERY OF THE PACIFIC

Vespucci's theory that the land mass said by Columbus to be part of Asia was really a new continent gained wide though not universal approval in the decade after 1502. If Vespucci was right, there was another ocean to cross between the New World and Asia. Confirmation of this view was forthcoming in 1513, when Balboa, standing "silent, upon a peak in Darien," looked out upon the waters of the Pacific. Although further exploration was required to dispel the lingering belief of some that the whole American land mass was a peninsula projecting from southeast Asia, after 1513 the work of discovery centered on the search for a waterway to the East through or around the American continents. The Spanish chronicler Oviedo, who came to Darien in 1514 in an official capacity, tells the story of Balboa's feat, with some mention of the exploits of his remarkable dog, Leoncico.[6]

FOR FOUR YEARS the Christians had been in Tierra-Firme; they fought under Captain Vasco Núñez de Balboa, and had made peace with certain *caciques,* in particular with the chief-

6 Oviedo y Valdés, *Historia general,* VII, 92–95. (Excerpt translated by the editor.)

tains of Careta, which lies on the west coast, twenty leagues west of Darien, and of Comogre, and both of them had been baptized. The *cacique* of Careta was called Chima, and they named him Don Fernando, and he had as many as two thousand Indian warriors; the *cacique* of Comogre was a greater lord, and his proper name was Ponquiaco, but they gave him the baptismal name of Don Carlos; he had more than three thousand warriors and ruled over more than ten thousand persons. These *caciques* had grown so peaceful that they sent messengers and canoes; they came and went to and from Darien to see the Christians and communicated with them as with friends. Vasco Núñez, filled with hope by the information that he had secretly obtained from these *caciques,* resolved to set out on Friday, the first day of September, 1513; and he departed from the town of Santa María de la Antigua with eight hundred men in a galleon and nine canoes to search out the secrets of the land, on the pretext of going to seek for mines. On the following Sunday, the fourth day of September, half of this company arrived at Careta in the canoes, and the galleon came later with the rest; there Vasco Núñez disembarked. The *cacique* Don Fernando received him and all his people very well, both those who came in the canoes and those in the galleon. After they had arrived and assembled, Captain Vasco Núñez selected those whom he wished to take with him and left there those who were to guard the galleon and the canoes, and set out for the interior on the sixth day of the month. After a two-day march over a rough, difficult, and mountainous route he approached the vicinity of the *cacique* of Ponca, only to find that he and his people had fled to the hills.

Before proceeding further, I should state that the town that the Christians now call Acla was founded in the abovementioned port of Careta. I also want to tell of a dog that belonged to Vasco Núñez, called Leoncico, a son of the dog Becerrico of the isle San Juan [Puerto Rico] and no less famous than his father. This dog gained for Vasco Núñez in this and other conquests more than a thousand gold pesos, for he received as large a share in the gold and slaves as a member of the company when the division was made. So, whenever Vasco Núñez went along, the dog was assigned wages and a share like the other captains; and he was so active that he earned his reward better than many sleepy comrades who like to gain at their ease what others reap by their toil and diligence. He was truly a marvelous dog, and could distinguish a peaceable from a wild Indian as well as I or any other who went to these wars. When Indians had been taken and rounded up, if any should escape by day or by night the dog had only to be told: "He's gone, go get him," and he would do it; and he was so keen a pointer that only by a miracle could a runaway Indian escape him. After overtaking him, if the Indian remained still the dog would seize him by the wrist or hand and would bring him back as carefully, without biting or molesting him, as a man could; but if the Indian offered resistance he would tear him to pieces. He was so much feared by the Indians that if ten Christians went with the dog they went in greater safety and accomplished more than twenty without him. I saw this dog, for when Pedrarias arrived in the following year, 1514, he was still alive, and Vasco Núñez lent him for some Indian wars that were made afterwards and gained his shares as was told above. He was a dog of middle size, reddish in color, with a black muzzle, and not elegant in appearance; but he was strong and robust, and had many wounds and scars of wounds that he had received fighting with the Indians. Later on, out of envy, someone gave the dog some poisoned food, and he died. . . .

On September 13 came the *cacique* of Ponca, reassured by Captain Vasco Núñez, who did him much honor, gave him shirts and hatchets, and made him as comfortable as he could. Since this *cacique* found himself so well treated, he told Vasco Núñez in secret a great deal about the secrets and treasures of the land, which gratified the captain; among other things, he said that a certain number of days' journey from there was another *pechry*, which in their language means "sea"; and he presented Vasco Núñez with some very finely worked pieces of gold. . . .

On the twentieth of that month, Vasco Núñez set out from the land of this *cacique* with certain guides that Ponca assigned to go with him till they reached the land of the *cacique* Torecha, with whom Ponca was at war; and on the twenty-fourth day of that month they came by night upon the *cacique* Torecha and his people. This was ten leagues beyond the land of Ponca, and was reached by a most difficult route and by crossing rivers in rafts, at great peril to themselves. And there they took some people and some gold and pearls, and Vasco Núñez obtained more extensive information concerning the interior and the other sea, to the South. In

Torecha he left some of his people, and set out with about seventy men; on the twenty-fifth of the month, the same day that he had left, he arrived at the village and seat of the *cacique* called Porque, who had absented himself; however, this did not matter to Vasco Núñez, and he went ahead, continuing his search for the other sea. And on Tuesday, the twenty-fifth of September of the year one thousand five hundred and thirteen, at ten o'clock in the morning, Captain Vasco Núñez, leading all the rest in the ascent of a certain bare mountain, saw from its peak the South Sea, before any other of his Christian companions. He joyfully turned to his men, raising his hands and eyes to the skies, praising Jesus Christ and his glorious mother the Virgin, Our Lady; then he sank on his knees and gave thanks to God for the favor that had been granted to him in allowing him to discover that sea and thereby to render such a great service to God and to the Catholic and Most Serene King of Castile, our lord. . . . And he ordered them all to kneel and give the same thanks to God for this grace, and to implore Him to let them discover and see the hoped-for great secrets and riches of that sea and coast, for the exaltation and increase of the Christian faith, for the conversion of the Indians of those southern regions, and for the greater glory and prosperity of the royal throne of Castile and its princes, both present and to come.

7. THE GREATEST VOYAGE IN HISTORY

Magellan's project for reaching the Spice Islands by way of a passage around South America was a logical sequel to the discoveries of Vespucci and Balboa, and had been anticipated by the former. Its principal defect was Magellan's understandable failure to conceive of the immensity of the ocean separating America from Asia. Though limited in its practical results, in point of duration, distance covered, and hardships suffered Magellan's accomplishment easily dwarfs the more celebrated first voyage of Columbus. Only one of the five ships that left Seville returned to port with its lucrative cargo of spices, and Magellan himself died in a skirmish with natives in the Philippines. His secretary, Antonio Pigafetta, describes the horrors of the crossing of the Pacific, and the circumstances of Magellan's death.[7]

[7] Antonio Pigafetta, *Magellan's Voyage around the World*, translated and edited by James A. Robertson, Cleveland, 1902, 2 vols., I, 91–93, 171–179. Reprinted by permission of the publishers, The Arthur H. Clark Company.

WEDNESDAY, Novmber 28, 1520, we debouched from that strait, engulfing ourselves in the Pacific Sea. We were three months and twenty days without getting any kind of fresh food. We ate biscuit, which was no longer biscuit, but powder of biscuits swarming with worms, for they had eaten the good. It stank strongly of the urine of rats. We drank yellow water that had been putrid for many days. We also ate some ox hides that covered the top of the main-yard to prevent the yard from chafing the shrouds, and which had become exceedingly hard because of the sun, rain, and wind. We left them in the sea for four or five days, and then placed them for a few moments on top of the embers, and so ate them; and often we ate sawdust from boards. Rats were sold for one-half ducado apiece, and even then we could not get them. But above all the other misfortunes the following was the worst. The gums of both the lower and upper teeth of some of our men swelled, so that they could not eat under any circumstances and therefore died. Nineteen men died from that sickness, and the giant together with an Indian from the country of Verzin. Twenty-five or thirty men fell sick [during that time], in the arms, legs, or in another place, so that but few remained well. However, I, by the grace of God, suffered no sickness. We sailed about four thousand leguas during those three months and twenty days through an open stretch in that Pacific Sea. In truth it is very pacific, for during that time we did not suffer any storm. We saw no land except two desert islets, where we found nothing but birds and trees, for which we called them the Ysolle Infortunate [i.e., the Unfortunate Isles]. They are two hundred leguas apart. We found no anchorage, [but] near them saw many sharks. The first islet lies fifteen degrees of south latitude, and the other nine. Daily we made runs of fifty, sixty, or seventy leguas at the catena or at the stern. Had not God and His blessed mother given us so good weather we would all have died of hunger in that exceeding vast sea. Of a verity I believe no such voyage will ever be made [again].

When we left that strait, if we had sailed continuously westward we would have circumnavigated the world without finding other land than the cape of the xi thousand Virgins. The latter is a cape of that strait at the Ocean Sea, straight east and west with Cape Deseado of the Pacific Sea. Both of these capes lie in a latitude of exactly fifty-two degrees toward the Antarctic Pole.

ON FRIDAY, April twenty-six, Zula, a chief of the island of Matan, sent one of his sons to present two goats to the captain-general, and to say that he would send him all that he had promised, but that he had not been able to send it to him because of the other chief Cilalulapu, who refused to obey the king of Spagnia. He requested the captain to send him only one boatload of men on the next night, so that they might help him and fight against the other chief. The captain-general decided to go thither with three boatloads. We begged him repeatedly not to go, but he, like a good shepherd, refused to abandon his flock. At midnight, sixty men of us set out armed with corselets and helmets, together with the Christian king, the prince, some of the chief men, and twenty or thirty balanguais. We reached Matan three hours before dawn. The captain did not wish to fight them, but sent a message to the natives by the Moro to the effect that if they would obey the king of Spagnia, recognize the Christian king as their sovereign, and pay us our tribute, he would be their friend; but that if they wished otherwise, they should wait to see how our lances sounded. They replied that if we had lances they had lances of bamboo and stakes hardened with fire. [They asked us] not to proceed to attack them at once, but to wait until morning, so that they might have more men. They said that in order to induce us to go in search of them; for they had dug certain pitholes between the houses in order that we might fall into them. When morning came forty-nine of us leaped into the water up to our thighs, and walked through water for more than two crossbow flights before we could reach the shore. The boats could not approach nearer because of certain rocks in the water. The other eleven men remained behind to guard the boats. When we reached land, those men had formed in three divisions to the number of more than one thousand five hundred persons. When they saw us, they charged down upon us with exceeding loud cries, two divisions on our flanks and the other on our front. When the captain saw that, he formed us into two divisions, and thus did we begin to fight. The musketeers and crossbowmen shot from a distance for about a half-hour, but uselessly; for the shots only passed through the shields which were made of thin wood and the arms [of the bearers]. The captain cried to them, "Cease firing! Cease firing!" but his order was not at all heeded. When the natives saw that we were shooting our muskets to no purpose, crying out they determined to stand firm, but they redoubled their shouts. When our muskets were discharged, the natives would never stand still, but leaped hither and thither, covering themselves with their shields. They shot so many arrows at us and hurled so many bamboo spears (some of them tipped with iron) at the captain-general, besides pointed stakes hardened with fire, stones, and mud, that we could scarcely defend ourselves. Seeing that, the captain-general sent some men to burn their houses in order to terrify them. When they saw their houses burning, they were roused to greater fury. Two of the men were killed near the houses, while we burned twenty or thirty houses. So many of them charged down upon us that they shot the captain through the right leg with a poisoned arrow. On that account, he ordered us to retire slowly, but the men took to flight, except six or eight of us who remained with the captain. The natives shot only at our legs, for the latter were bare; and so many were the spears and stones that they hurled at us, that we could offer no resistance. The mortars in the boats could not aid us as they were too far away. So we continued to retire for more than a good crossbow flight from the shore always fighting up to our knees in the water. The natives continued to pursue us, and picking up the same spear four or six times, hurled it at us again and again. Recognizing the captain, so many turned upon him that they knocked his helmet off his head twice, but he stood firmly like a good knight, together with some others. Thus did we fight for more than one hour, refusing to retire farther. An Indian hurled a bamboo spear into the captain's face, but the latter immediately killed him with his lance, which he left in the Indian's body. Then, trying to lay hand on sword, he could draw it out but halfway, because he had been wounded in the arm with a bamboo spear. When the natives saw that, they all hurled themselves upon him. One of them wounded him on the left leg with a large cutlass, which resembles a scimitar, only being larger. That caused the captain to fall face downward, when immediately they rushed upon him with

iron and bamboo spears and with their cutlasses, until they killed our mirror, our light, our comfort, and our true guide. When they wounded him, he turned back many times to see whether we were all in the boats. Thereupon, beholding him dead, we, wounded, retreated, as best we could, to the boats, which were already pulling off. The Christian king would have aided us, but the captain charged him before we landed, not to leave his balanghai, but to stay to see how we fought. When the king learned that the captain was dead, he wept. Had it not been for that unfortunate captain, not a single one of us would have been saved in the boats, for while he was fighting the others retired to the boats. I hope through [the efforts of] your most illustrious Lordship that the fame of so noble a captain will not become effaced in our times. Among the many virtues which he possessed, he was more constant than ever any one else in the greatest of adversity. He endured hunger better than all the others, and more accurately than any man in the world did he understand sea charts and navigation. And that this was the truth was seen openly, for no other had had so much natural talent nor the boldness to learn how to circumnavigate the world, as he had almost done. That battle was fought on Saturday, April twenty-seven, 1521. The captain desired to fight on Saturday, because it was the day especially holy to him. Eight of our men were killed with him in that battle, and four Indians, who had become Christians and who had come afterward to aid us were killed by the mortars of the boats. Of the enemy, only fifteen were killed, while many of us were wounded.

In the afternoon the Christian king sent a message with our consent to the people of Matan, to the effect that if they would give us the captain and the other men that had been killed, we would give them as much merchandise as they wished. They answered that they would not give up such a man, as we imagined [they would do], and that they would not give him up for all the riches in the world, but that they intended to keep him as a memorial.

VI

The Conquest of Mexico

IN 1517 AN EXPEDITION sent from Cuba under Hernández de Córdova discovered Yucatan and its Maya civilization, then in a decadent state. A second expedition, headed by Juan de Grijalva, followed the coasts of Yucatan and Mexico as far as the river Panuco, and obtained some idea of the wealth and splendor of the Aztec court. These discoveries resulted in a decision on the part of Governor Velásquez of Cuba to send still another expedition, under Hernando Cortés, to the Mexican mainland.

The thirty-four-year-old Cortés was a native of Estremadura in Spain who had come over to the Indies in 1504. In February, 1519, Cortés sailed from Cuba with a force of some six hundred men. He landed on the coast of the Mexican province of Tabasco in March of that year, defeated the local Indians in a sharp skirmish, and went on to drop anchor near the site of modern Veracruz. Becoming aware of the tributary towns' bitter discontent with Aztec rule, he decided to move upon the Mexican capital. Rich gifts of gold and other valuable objects sent by Montezuma, accompanied by warnings that the strangers should depart from Mexico, only confirmed Cortés in his determination to push into the interior.

In this crisis superstitious fears that identified the coming of Cortés with the prophesied return of the god Quetzalcoatl helped to paralyze the wills of Montezuma and his advisers. Visualizing both real and imaginary dangers, the Aztec leader was reduced to a hopelessly indecisive state of mind. As the Spanish invaders and their Indian allies approached the Aztec capital, Montezuma virtually capitulated, and he welcomed Cortés into Tenochtitlán as a representative of the rightful lord of Mexico.

The relations between the Aztecs and their white guests grew strained as Montezuma indignantly rejected Spanish proposals to substitute Christianity for the worship of his gods. Cortés now took decisive action; with a few followers he boldly entered Montezuma's rooms and forced him to come to the Spanish quarters as his prisoner. Montezuma was soon completely broken in spirit. However, an unprovoked massacre of many leading Aztec chiefs and warriors caused a popular uprising that forced the Spaniards to retreat into their quarters. The tribal council, having deposed the imprisoned Montezuma, elected a new chief who launched heavy attacks upon the Spanish forces. Cortés, fearing a long siege and famine, determined to evacuate the city. He accomplished this exploit at a terrible cost in lives. Performing a difficult retreat, the surviving Spaniards and their Indian auxiliaries at last reached the haven of friendly Tlascala.

In December, 1520, Cortés, his forces strengthened by the arrival of more Spaniards and by thousands of Indians who flocked to fight against their Aztec overlords, marched again on Tenochtitlán. Ferocious fighting began in late April of 1521, and it was not until the middle of August, 1521, that Guatemoc, the last Aztec war chief, surrendered to Cortés.

From the Valley of Mexico the process of conquest was gradually extended in all directions. Guatemala was reduced by Pedro de Alvarado; Honduras, by Cortés himself. In 1527 Francisco de Montejo began the conquest of Yucatan, but as late as 1542 the Mayas rose in a last desperate revolt that was crushed with great slaughter. Meanwhile, expeditions from Darien subjugated the Indians of Nicaragua, and thus the two streams of Spanish conquest, both originally starting from Hispaniola, came together again.

1. TWILIGHT OVER TENOCHTITLÁN

The last years of the Aztec domination were troubled by growing internal tensions and by presentiments of danger from outside the country. Revolts on the part of tributary tribes, restive under the mounting exactions of their Aztec masters, became more frequent, and were put down with increasing difficulty and ferocity. Then, one day in the year 1518, the agitated tribute-collector Pinotl arrived from the coast to inform Montezuma of the approach from the sea of winged towers containing men with white faces and heavy beards (Grijalva's expedition). Pinotl had spoken with the mysterious strangers, who later departed, promising to return. This event, presaging an early fulfilment of Quetzalcoatl's prophecy that he would return, caused the Aztec leaders grave misgivings. Their apprehensive frame of mind on the eve of the conquest is suggested by a native account of the "evil omens" that preceded the coming of the Spaniards.[1]

WHEN THE SPANIARDS had not yet arrived, by ten years, an omen first appeared in the heavens. It was like a tongue of fire, like a flame, as if showering the light of the dawn. It appeared as if it were piercing the heavens. [It was] wide at the base and pointed [at the head]. To the very midst of the sky, to the very heart of the heavens it extended; to the very midpoint of the skies stood stretched that which was thus seen off to the east. When it arose and thus came forth, when it appeared at midnight, it looked as if day had dawned. When day broke, later, the sun destroyed it when it arose. For a full year [the sign] came forth. (It was [in the year] Twelve House that it began.) And when it appeared, there was shouting; all cried out striking the palm of the hand against the mouth. All were frightened and waited with dread.

A second omen came to pass here in Mexico: of its own accord fire broke out in the house of the demon Uitzilopochtli, and flared greatly. No one had set fire to it; only of itself it burst into flames. It was called Itepeyoc, at the place named Tlacateccan. When [the fire] appeared, already the squared, wooden pillars were blazing; from within them emerged the flames, the tongues of fire, the blaze [which] speedily ate all the house beams. Thereupon there was an outcry; [the priests] said: "O Mexicans, hasten here

to put out [the fire! Bring] your earthen water jars!" And when they cast water upon it, when they sought to smother it, all the more did it flare. It could not be put out; it all burned.

A third omen: a temple was struck by a thunder bolt. It was only a straw hut, a place called Tzonmulco, Temple of Xiuhtecutli. It was raining not heavily; it only sprinkled, so that it was considered a bad omen. For, it was said, there was a mere summer flash; nor did thunder sound.

A fourth omen: there was yet sun when a comet fell. It became three parts. It departed from where the sun set and traveled toward where he came forth. As if sprinkling live coals, [so] its tail went extended a great distance. Far did its tail reach. And when it was seen, great was the uproar; like [the din of] shell rattles [the outcry] was overspread.

A fifth omen: the water [of the lake] foamed up. No wind stirred it. It was as if the water swirled, as if it boiled up with a cracking sound. Very far did it go, as it rose upward. And it reached the bases of the houses, and flooded them, and crumbled the houses. This was the great lake which stretcheth about us here in Mexico.

A sixth omen: often a woman was heard [as] she went weeping and crying out. Loudly did she call out at night. She walked about saying: "O my beloved sons, now we are about to go!" Sometimes she said: "O my beloved sons, whither shall I take you?"

A seventh omen: at one time the fisher folk who hunted or snared with nets took captive an ashen-hued bird like a cranc. Then they went to show it to Moctezuma, [who was] in the [room] Tlillan calmecatl. It was past noon, and still day time. On its head was as it were a mirror, round, circular, and as if pierced in the middle, where were to be seen the heavens, the stars — the Fire Drill [constellation]. And Moctezuma took it as an omen of great evil when he saw the stars and the Fire Drill. And when he looked at the bird's head a second time, a little beyond [the stars] he saw people who came as if massed, who came as conquerors, girt in war array. Deer bore them on their backs. And then he summoned the soothsayers and the sages. He said to them: "Do you not know what I have seen there, which was as if people came massed?" And when they would answer him, that which they looked at vanished. They could tell [him] nothing.

An eighth omen: often were discovered men

[1] Arthur J. O. Anderson and Charles E. Dibble, *Florentine Codex*, Book XII, The Conquest, Ch. 1 (Sahagún, *General History of the Things of New Spain*). MS. Used by kind permission of the authors.

of monstrous form, having two heads [but] only one body. They took them there to the Tlillan calmecatl, where Moctezuma beheld them; but when he looked at them, they then vanished.

2. PORTRAIT OF THE CONQUEROR

Historians and biographers do not agree in their estimate of the character and actions of Hernando Cortés. Some writers, recalling his treatment of Montezuma, the massacre of Cholula, and the torture and execution of the last Aztec war chief, Guatemoc, draw his portrait in unrelievedly sombre colors. Others see in him the creator of a Mexican nationality, and they extol his bravery, his intelligence, and his varied contributions to Mexican economic and educational life. The chronicler López de Gómara (1511?–1562?), who lived in Cortés' household as his private chaplain for some years, had no doubts concerning the righteousness of either Cortés' actions or the civilizing mission of the Spanish Conquest. His history of the conquest of Mexico, which is actually a biography of Cortés, contains an intimate and not altogether flattering description of his former patron.[2]

FERDINAND CORTES was of good size, broad in shoulders and chest, and of sallow complexion; his beard was light-colored, and he wore his hair long. He was very strong, high-spirited, and skilled in the use of arms. As a youth he was given to adventurous pranks, but in later years he acquired a mature dignity and thus became a leader in both war and peace. He was mayor of the town of Santiago de Barucoa [in Cuba], which fact the townspeople still regard as their chief title to fame. There he acquired a reputation for the qualities that he later displayed. He was passionately attracted to women, and indulged this proclivity without regard to time or place. It was the same with games of chance; he played dice exceedingly well and with great enjoyment. Although he drank moderately he was a very hearty eater and kept an abundant table. He bore hunger with great fortitude, as he showed on the march of Higueras and on the sea to which he gave his name. He was very contentious and so was involved in more lawsuits than became his condition. He spent freely on warfare, on women, on his friends, and to satisfy his whims, but showed himself niggardly in some things; hence some people called him a "wet-weather stream," one that ran high one

day and dry the next. He dressed neatly rather than richly, and kept himself scrupulously clean. He took pleasure in keeping a large house and family, with a great display of plate, both for use and for show. He bore himself like a lord, and with such gravity and discretion that it neither caused disgust nor appeared presumptuous. A story has it that as a boy he was told that he was fated to conquer many lands and become a very great lord. He was jealous of the honor of his own house but forward in the homes of others — a common trait of lustful men. He was devout and prayerful, and knew many prayers and psalms by heart; he was very charitable, and on his deathbed especially charged his son with the giving of alms. He usually gave the Church a thousand ducats a year, and sometimes he borrowed money for giving alms, saying that he redeemed his sins with the interest on the money. On his shields and coats of arms he put the motto: *Judicium Domini apprehendit eos, et fortitudo ejus corroboravit brachium meum*[3] — a text very appropriate to the conquest. Such was Ferdinand Cortés, Conqueror of New-Spain. . . .

3. CLASH AT TLASCALA

A major factor in the conquest of Mexico was the alliance formed between the invaders and the tough Tlascalan Indians, traditional foes of the Aztec Confederacy. To win that alliance, however, the Spaniards first had to prove in battle against the Tlascalans their fighting capacity and the superiority of their weapons. That doughty warrior and incomparable storyteller, Díaz del Castillo, describes the last major action in the war of Tlascala.[4]

THE NEXT MORNING, the 5th September, 1519, we mustered the horses. There was not one of the wounded men who did not come forward to join the ranks and give as much help as he could. The crossbowmen were warned to use the store of darts very cautiously, some of them loading while the others were shooting, and the musketeers were to act in the same way, and the men with sword and shield were instructed to aim their cuts and thrusts at the bowels [of their enemies] so that they would not dare to come as close to us as they did before. With our banner unfurled, and four of our comrades guarding

2 Francisco López de Gómara, *Conquista de Méjico*, in *Historiadores primitivos de las Indias*, edited by Enrique de Vedia, Madrid, 1852–1853, 2 vols., I, 454–455. (Excerpt translated by the editor.)

3 "The judgment of the Lord overtook them; and his strength supported my arm." B.K.

4 Bernal Díaz del Castillo, *The True History of the Conquest of New Spain*, tr. and ed. by A. P. Maudslay, London, the Hakluyt Society, 1908–1916, 5 vols., I, 237–240.

the standard-bearer, Corral, we set out from our camp. We had not marched half a quarter of a league before we began to see the fields crowded with warriors with great feather crests and distinguishing devices, and to hear the blare of horns and trumpets.

All the plain was swarming with warriors and we stood four hundred men in number, and of those many sick and wounded. And we knew for certain that this time our foe came with the determination to leave none of us alive excepting those who would be sacrificed to their idols.

How they began to charge on us! What a hail of stones sped from their slings! As for their bowmen, the javelins lay like corn on the threshing floor; all of them barbed and fire-hardened, which would pierce any armour and would reach the vitals where there is no protection; the men with swords and shields and other arms larger than swords, such as broadswords, and lances, how they pressed on us and with what mighty shouts and yells they charged upon us! The steady bearing of our artillery, musketeers, and crossbowmen, was indeed a help to us, and we did the enemy much damage, and those of them who came close to us with their swords and broadswords met with such sword play from us that they were forced back and they did not close in on us so often as in the last battle. The horsemen were so skillful and bore themselves so valiantly that, after God who protected us, they were our bulwark. However, I saw that our troops were in considerable confusion, so that neither the shouts of Cortés nor the other captains availed to make them close up their ranks, and so many Indians charged down on us that it was only by a miracle of sword play that we could make them give way so that our ranks could be reformed. One thing only saved our lives, and that was that the enemy were so numerous and so crowded one on another that the shots wrought havoc among them, and in addition to this they were not well commanded, for all the captains with their forces could not come into action and from what we knew, since the last battle had been fought, there had been disputes and quarrels between the Captain Xicotenga and another captain the son of Chichimecatecle, over what the one had said to the other, that he had not fought well in the previous battle; to this the son of Chichimecatecle replied that he had fought better than Xicotenga, and was ready to prove it by personal combat. So in this battle Chichimectecle and his men would not help Xicotenga, and we knew for a certainty that he had also called on

the company of Huexotzinco to abstain from fighting. Besides this, ever since the last battle they were afraid of the horses and the musketry, and the swords and crossbows, and our hard fighting; above all was the mercy of God which gave us strength to endure. So Xicotenga was not obeyed by two of the commanders, and we were doing great damage to his men, for we were killing many of them, and this they tried to conceal; for as they were so numerous, whenever one of their men was wounded, they immediately bound him up and carried him off on their shoulders, so that in this battle, as in the last, we never saw a dead man.

The enemy was already losing heart, and knowing that the followers of the other two captains whom I have already named, would not come to their assistance, they began to give way. It seems that in that battle we had killed one very important captain, and the enemy began to retreat in good order, our horsemen following them at a hard gallop for a short distance, for they could not sit their horses for fatigue, and when we found ourselves free from that multitude of warriors, we gave thanks to God.

In this engagement, one soldier was killed, and sixty were wounded, and all the horses were wounded as well. They gave me two wounds, one in the head with a stone, and one in the thigh with an arrow; but this did not prevent me from fighting, and keeping watch, and helping our soldiers, and all the soldiers who were wounded did the same; for if the wounds were not very dangerous, we had to fight and keep guard, wounded as we were, for few of us remained unwounded.

Then we returned to our camp, well contented, and giving thanks to God. We buried the dead in one of those houses which the Indians had built underground, so that the enemy should not see that we were mortals, but should believe that, as they said, we were Teules. We threw much earth over the top of the house, so that they should not smell the bodies, then we doctored all the wounded with the fat of an Indian. It was cold comfort to be even without salt or oil with which to cure the wounded. There was another want from which we suffered, and it was a severe one — and that was clothes with which to cover ourselves, for such a cold wind came from the snow mountains, that it made us shiver, for our lances and muskets and crossbows made a poor covering. That night we slept with more tranquillity than on the night before, when we had so much duty to do, with scouting, spies, watchmen and patrols.

4. THE SORCERERS' VISION

As the invaders, with their thousands of Indian auxiliaries, moved steadily up the sierra and across the Mexican plateau toward Tenochtitlán, the panicky Montezuma sent ambassadors who offered Cortés rich gifts, but simultaneously urged him to turn about and go home. This tactic failing, Montezuma sent a band of sorcerers and necromancers to conjure away the mysterious strangers. Their spells likewise failed to halt the irresistible advance of Cortés' army. A native history of the conquest elaborates the episode of the magicians into an impressive legend, in which the destruction of Tenochtitlán appears as the judgment of the gods upon the Aztecs for their crimes of imperialism and mass killings.[5]

AND MOCTEZUMA thereupon sent and charged the princes, when Tziuacpopocatzin led, and many others besides of his henchmen, to go to meet [Cortés] between Iztactepetl and Popocatepetl, there in Quauhtechcac. They laid before them golden streamers, quetzal feather streamers, and golden necklaces.

And when they had given them the gifts, they appeared to smile, rejoice exceedingly, and take great pleasure. Like monkeys they seized upon the gold. It was as if then they were satisfied, sated, and gladdened. For in truth they thirsted mightily for gold; they stuffed themselves with it, and hungered and lusted for it like pigs.

And they went about moving the golden streamer back and forth, and showed it to one another, all the while babbling; what they said was gibberish.

And when they saw Tziuacpopcatzin, they said: "Is this one perchance Moctezuma?" They spoke to those who came with them, their spies, those of Tlaxcala and Cempoalla. Thus in secret they questioned them. [These] said: "Not he, O our lords." This one was Tziuacpopcatzin, who was appearing in place of Moctezuma.

[The Spaniards] said to him: "Art thou perchance Moctezuma?" He replied: "I am your henchman; I am Moctezuma."

And these said to him: "Go thou hence. Why dost thou lie to us? Whom dost thou take us to be? Thou canst not fool us; thou canst not mock us. Thou canst not make us stupid, nor flatter us, nor become our eyes, nor trick us, nor misdirect our gaze, nor turn us back, nor destroy us, nor dazzle us, nor cast mud into our eyes, nor place a muddy hand over our faces. Thou art not [Moctezuma]. Now Moctezuma cannot hide from us. He cannot take refuge. Where can he go? [Is he] perchance a bird that he can fly? Or can he set out on his way under the earth? Is there somewhere a mountain pierced by a hole that he may enter? For we shall see him; for we shall listen to that [which cometh] from his lips."

Thus they only despised and belittled him. Thus came only to nothing still another of their welcomes and greetings.

Then they hurried straight and took the road direct [to Moctezuma].

And another company of messengers, who were soothsayers and sorcerers, and fire priests, also went and made their way to contend with them. But they could do nothing. They could not cast a spell on them; no more could they contend against and exert power over them. No longer could they succeed.

For a drunkard came along the way. They came up against him and stopped, stunned. They beheld him as one from Chalco, for so was he arrayed. He was dressed as a man from Chalco; he acted as a Chalcan. Like one besotted, he bore himself and acted like one who is drunk. With eight grass ropes was he bound about the chest. He accosted them, having come ahead of the outposts of the Spaniards.

And he rose up against them and said: "What do you come to do here again? What do you now wish? What would Moctezuma yet wish to do? Hath he perchance now come to his senses? Is he now filled with a great fear? For he hath committed a fault. He hath abandoned the common folk; he hath destroyed men. People have been struck upon the head; they have been bound [in wrappings for the dead]. He hath laughed at and deceived them!"

And when they had thus seen this, when they had heard his words, to no purpose did they give him attention, praying humbly to him and quickly setting up his earth pyramid, to keep him upon, and his straw bed. On no account would he look at it; vain was its erection. To no purpose had they made the earth pyramid. Just as if they had plunged him into his rage, he then chid and abused them, and spoke harshly. He said to them:

"Why do you vainly stand here? No longer

5 Arthur J. O. Anderson and Charles E. Dibble, Florentine Codex, Book XII, The Conquest, Chs. 12 and 13 (Sahagún, *General History of the Things of New Spain*). MS. Used by kind permission of the authors.

will there be a Mexico; [it is gone] forever. Go hence; it no more existeth. Turn about; look at what befalleth Mexico — what thus already cometh to pass!"

Then they look there; they quickly turned there to see. They beheld that already all the temples, the tribal temples, the priests' dwellings, and all the houses in Mexico burned; and [it looked] as if already there were fighting.

And when the soothsayers had seen this, it was as if they had lost heart; they could say nothing; it was as if they had been made to swallow something.

They said: "This is not for us to see; it must needs be that Moctezuma see what we have seen. For this is no common being; this is the youth Tezcatlipoca."

Then he vanished, and they saw him no more. And so the messengers went no further to encounter [the Spaniards]; they no longer pressed on toward them. From there the soothsayers and fire priests turned back and came to tell Moctezuma. There they and those who earlier [had gone with] Tziuacpopocatzin saw one another.

And when these messengers had come to arrive, just so they related to Moctezuma how this had come to pass and how they had beheld it. Moctezuma, when he heard it, only bowed his head; he stood with head downcast. He did not then speak, but only remained full of woe for a long time as if beside himself.

Finally he thus answered them, and said: "What can we do? What can be done? For we are finished; we have taken the [bitter] medicine. Shall we perhaps climb a mountain? Should we perhaps flee? For we are Mexicans. Shall we in truth perhaps enslave the Mexican domain? Unlucky are the poor old men and old women! And the children, who have no understanding — where may they be taken? What can be done? Where, in truth, can one go? For now we have taken the [bitter] medicine. Come what may, in whatsoever way it may befall, we shall marvel at it!"

5. THE MEETING OF CORTÉS AND MONTEZUMA

Few incidents in history have the romantic quality of the meeting between Cortés and Montezuma at the entrance to Tenochtitlán. Two worlds of culture met in the persons of the Indian chieftain and the Spanish conquistador. The remarkable speech of welcome made by Montezuma, as reported by Cortés, supports the view that Montezuma regarded the conqueror as an emissary of the departed Quetzalcoatl, about to return to his Mexican realm.[6]

I FOLLOWED the said causeway for about half a league before I came to the city proper of Temixtitan. I found at the junction of another causeway, which joins this one from the mainland, another strong fortification, with two towers, surrounded by walls, twelve feet high with castellated tops. This commands the two roads, and has only two gates, by one of which they enter, and from the other they come out. About one thousand of the principal citizens came out to meet me, and speak to me, all richly dressed alike according to their fashion; and when they had come, each one in approaching me, and before speaking, would use a ceremony which is very common amongst them, putting his hand on the ground, and afterward kissing it, so that I was kept waiting almost an hour, until each had performed his ceremony. There is a wooden bridge, ten paces broad, in the very outskirts of the city, across an opening in the causeway, where the water may flow in and out as it rises and falls. This bridge is also for defence, for they remove and replace the long broad wooden beams, of which the bridge is made, whenever they wish; and there are many of these bridges in the city, as Your Highness will see in the account which I shall make of its affairs.

Having passed this bridge, we were received by that lord, Montezuma, with about two hundred chiefs, all barefooted and dressed in a kind of livery, very rich, according to their custom, and some more so than others. They approached in two processions near the walls of the street, which is very broad, and straight, and beautiful, and very uniform from one end to the other, being about two thirds of a league long, and having, on both sides, very large houses, both dwelling places, and mosques. Montezuma came in the middle of the street, with two lords, one on the right side, and the other on the left, one of whom was the same great lord, who, as I said, came in that litter to speak with me, and the other was the brother of Montezuma, lord of that city Iztapalapan, whence I had come that day. All were dressed in the same manner, except that Montezuma was shod, and the other lords were barefooted. Each supported him below his arms, and as we

6 *The Letters of Cortés to Charles V*, translated and edited by F. A. McNutt, I, 232–236.

approached each other, I descended from my horse, and was about to embrace him, but the two lords in attendance prevented me, with their hands, that I might not touch him, and they, and he also, made the ceremony of kissing the ground. This done, he ordered his brother who came with him, to remain with me, and take me by the arm, and the other attendant walked a little ahead of us. After he had spoken to me, all the other lords, who formed the two processions, also saluted me, one after the other, and then returned to the procession. When I approached to speak to Montezuma, I took off a collar of pearls and glass diamonds, that I wore, and put it on his neck, and, after we had gone through some of the streets, one of his servants came with two collars, wrapped in a cloth, which were made of coloured shells. These they esteem very much; and from each of the collars hung eight golden shrimps executed with great perfection and a span long. When he received them, he turned towards me, and put them on my neck, and again went on through the streets, as I have already indicated, until we came to a large and handsome house, which he had prepared for our reception. There he took me by the hand, and led me into a spacious room, in front of the court where we had entered, where he made me sit on a very rich platform, which had been ordered to be made for him, and told me to wait there; and then he went away.

After a little while, when all the people of my company were distributed to their quarter, he returned with many valuables of gold and silver work, and five or six thousand pieces of rich cotton stuffs, woven, and embroidered in divers ways. After he had given them to me, he sat down on another platform, which they immediately prepared near the one where I was seated, and being seated he spoke in the following manner:

"We have known for a long time, from the chronicles of our forefathers, that neither I, nor those who inhabit this country, are descendants from the aborigines of it, but from strangers who came to it from very distant parts; and we also hold, that our race was brought to these parts by a lord, whose vassals they all were, and who returned to his native country, and had many descendants, and had built towns where they were living; when, therefore, he wished to take them away with him they would not go, nor still less receive him as their ruler, so he departed. And we have always held that those who descended from him would come to sub-

jugate this country and us, as his vassals; and according to the direction from which you say you come, which is where the sun rises, and from what you tell us of your great lord, or king, who has sent you here, we believe, and hold for certain, that he is our rightful sovereign, especially as you tell us that since many days he has had news of us. Hence you may be sure, that we shall obey you, and hold you as the representative of this great lord of whom you speak, and that in this there will be no lack or deception; and throughout the whole country you may command at your will (I speak of what I possess in my dominions), because you will be obeyed, and recognized, and all we possess is at your disposal.

"Since you are in your rightful place, and in your own homes, rejoice and rest, free from all the trouble of the journey, and wars which you have had, for I am well aware of all that has happened to you, between Puntunchan and here, and I know very well, that the people of Cempoal, and Tascaltecal, have told you many evil things respecting me. Do not believe more than you see with your own eyes, especially from those who are my enemies, and were my vassals, yet rebelled against me on your coming (as they say), in order to help you. I know they have told you also that I have houses, with walls of gold, and that the furniture of my halls, and other things of my service, were also of gold, and that I am, or make myself, a god, and many other things. The houses you have seen are of lime and stone and earth." And then he held up his robes, and showing me his body he said to me, "Look at me, and see that I am flesh and bones, the same as you, and everybody, and that I am mortal, and tangible." And touching his arms and body with his hands, "Look how they have lied to you! It is true indeed that I have some things of gold, which have been left to me by my forefathers. All that I possess, you may have whenever you wish.

"I shall now go to other houses where I live; but you will be provided here with everything necessary for you and your people, and you shall suffer no annoyance, for you are in your own house and country."

I answered to all he said, certifying that which seemed to be suitable, especially in confirming his belief that it was Your Majesty whom they were expecting. After this, he took his leave, and, when he had gone, we were well provided with chickens, and bread, and fruits, and other necessities, especially such as were required for the service of our quarters. Thus I passed six days well provided with everything necessary, and visited by many of the lords.

6. ALVARADO UNLEASHES THE STORM

Cortés' brilliantly conceived and executed plan for a bloodless seizure of power in Tenochtitlán-Mexico, with the captive Montezuma acting as his mouthpiece, appeared to have every prospect of success. The broken-spirited Montezuma, together with the principal Mexican chiefs, took a solemn oath of allegiance to the Spanish emperor and even connived at the seizure and imprisonment of his own rebellious brother and nephew. But Cortés had not taken into account the Aztec nation, increasingly resentful of the actions of the arrogant white strangers and increasingly doubtful of their divine attributes. Pedro de Alvarado's wanton attack on the celebrants of a great Aztec religious festival unleashed the storm that would probably have broken sooner or later.[7]

ALL HASTENED and ran, as they made their way toward the temple courtyard, in order there to dance the winding dance. And when all had assembled, then the start was made; then began the chanting and the winding dance. And those who had fasted twenty days, and those who had fasted a year, stood aside facing the others. Those who hemmed in [the dancers had] their pine cudgels; whomsoever tried to leave [the dance] they menaced with the pine cudgels. But one who would [leave to] urinate took off his net cape and his forked, heron feather head ornament. But one who did not at once obey, who would not be excluded, or who was mischievous, they soundly beat his back therefor, [or] his thighs, [or] his shoulders, and thrust him outside. They cast him out by force; they threw him on his face — he went falling on his face; he fell forth on his ear. No one in their hold took his leave.

The elder brothers of Uitzilcpochtli — those who had fasted for a year — were much feared, looked upon with terror and awe, and dreaded. And those at the head, the great leaders, the participants, might leave; they did not detain them. Yet all the small boys, those with the lock of hair at the back of the head, with back lock of hair, and those with the jar-shaped hair dress — they who had taken a captive with

others' help — the leaders, those called leaders of young men, who were unmarried, who had gone [to war] to take one or two [captives], they also held away. They said to them: "Go along there, knaves! You shall give a good example! Appear not before us!"

And after this, when already the feast was taking place, all were dancing and singing; there was song with dance, and the song resounded like the dashing of waves.

When now it was time, and the moment was opportune for the Spaniards to slay them, then they issued forth girt for battle; they came to block everywhere the ways leading out and in — the Eagle Gate, the Little Palace, the Point of Reeds, and the Mirror Serpent. And when they had closed them off and also various other places, [the people] were contained, so that nowhere could they get out.

And this having been done, they then entered the Temple Courtyard to slay them. They whose task it was to kill them went only afoot, each with [his] leather shield, some with their iron-studded shields, and each with iron sword. Then they surrounded those who danced, whereupon they went among the drums. Then they struck the arms of the one who beat the drums; they severed both his hands, and afterwards struck his neck, [so that] his neck [and head] flew off, falling far away. Then they pierced them all with iron lances, and they struck each with the iron swords. Of some they slashed open the back, and then their entrails gushed out. Of some, they split the head; they hacked the heads to pieces; their heads were completely cut up. And of some they hit the shoulder; they split open and cut their bodies to pieces. Some they struck on the shank; some on the thigh. Of some, they struck the belly, and then their entrails streamed forth. And when one in vain would run, he would only drag his entrails like something raw, as he tried to flee. Nowhere could he go. And one who tried to go out, there they struck and pierced him.

But some climbed the wall, and so succeeded in taking flight. Some entered the various tribal temples, and there escaped. And some eluded [the Spaniards] among [the dead]; they went in among those who had died, only feigning death, and were able to escape. But one who stirred, when they saw him, they pierced.

And the blood of the chieftains ran like water; it spread out slippery, and a foul odor rose from the blood. And the entrails lay as if dragged out. And the Spaniards walked everywhere,

[7] Arthur J. O. Anderson and Charles E. Dibble, Florentine Codex, Book XII, The Conquest, Chs. 19 and 20 (Sahagún, *General History of the Things of New Spain*). Used by kind permission of the authors.

searching in the tribal temples; they went making thrusts everywhere in case someone were hidden there. Everywhere they went, ransacking every tribal temple as they hunted.

And when [all this] became known, there then was a shout: "O chieftains! O Mexicans! Hasten here! Let all prepare the devices, shields, and arrows! Come! Hasten here! Already the chieftains have died; they have been put to death, destroyed, shattered, O Mexicans, O Chieftains!" Thereupon there was an outcry, a shouting, a shrieking with hands striking the lips. Quickly the chieftains marshalled themselves; as if working with a will they brought the arrows and shields. Then the fray was joined. They shot at them with barbed arrows, spears, and tridents, and they loosed darts with broad, obsidian points at them. It was as if a [mass of] deep yellow reeds spread over the Spaniards.

7. THE FALL OF TENOCHTITLÁN

For three months the Aztec nation fought for its independence with incredible valor and fortitude. Not until a great part of the city was in ruins, and the streets and canals were choked with corpses, did the gallant Guatemoc, the last Aztec war chief, surrender in the name of his people. An Aztec account of the fall of Tenochtitlán conveys with simple eloquence the pathos of the surrender and the terrible aftermath of the Conquest.[8]

AND WHEN NIGHT had fallen, then it rained and sprinkled at intervals. Late at night the flame become visible; just so was it seen, just so it emerged as if it came from the heavens. Like a whirlwind it went spinning around and revolving; it was as if embers burst out of it — some very large, some very small, some like sparks. Like a coppery wind it arose, crackling, snapping, and exploding loudly. Then it circled the dike and traveled toward Coyonacazco; then it went into the middle of the lake there to be lost.

None shouted; none spoke aloud.

And on the next day, nothing more happened. All remained quiet, and also our foes [so] remained.

But the Captain [Cortés] was watching from a roof-top at Amaxac — from the roof-top of [the house of] Aztauatzin — under a canopy. It was a many-colored canopy. He looked toward [us] common folk; the Spaniards crowded about him and took counsel among themselves.

8 Arthur J. O. Anderson and Charles E. Dibble, Florentine Codex, Book XII, The Conquest, Chs. 39 and 40 (Sahagún, *General History of the Things of New Spain*). MS. Used by kind permission of the authors.

And [on our side] were Quauhtemoc and the other noblemen — the vice ruler Tlacotzin, the lords' judge Petlauhtzin, the captain of the armies Motelchiuhtzin; the constable of Mexico; and the lord priest; and also the noblemen of Tlatilulco — the general Coyoueuetzin; the commanding general Temilotzin; the army commander Topantemoctzin; the chief justice Auelitoctzin; the captain of the armies Uitziliuitzin; and the courtier Uitzitzin. All of these noblemen were assembled at Tolmayecan; they appeared to consult among themselves how to do that which we were to undertake and how we should yield to [the Spaniards].

Thereafter only two [men] took Quauhtemoc in a boat. The two who took him and went with him were the seasoned warrior Teputzitoloc, and Yaztachimal, Quauhtemoc's page. And the one who poled [the boat] was named Cenyaotl.

And when they carried Quauhtemoc off, then there was weeping among all the common folk. They said: "Now goeth the young lord Quauhtemoc; now he goeth to deliver himself to the gods, the Spaniards!"

And when they had betaken themselves to bring and disembark him, thereupon all the Spaniards came to see. They drew him along; the Spaniards took him by the hand. After that they took him up to the roof-top, where they went to stand him before the Captain, the war leader. And when they had proceeded to stand him before [Cortés], they looked at Quauhtemoc, made much of him, and stroked his hair. Then they seated him with [Cortés] and fired the guns. They hit no one with them, but only made them go off above, [so that] they passed over the heads of the common folk. Then [some Mexicans] only fled. With this the war reached its end.

Then there was shouting; they said: "Enough! Let it end! Eat greens!" When they heard this, the common folk thereupon issued forth. On this, they went, even into the lagoon.

And as they departed, leaving by the great road, once more they there slew some, wherefore the Spaniards were wroth that still some again had taken up their obsidian-bladed swords and their shields. Those who dwelt in house clusters went straightway to Amaxac; they went direct to where the ways divide. There the common folk separated. So many went toward Tepeyacac, so many toward Xoxouiltitlan, so many toward Nonoalco. But toward Xolloco and toward Macatzintamal no one went.

And all who lived in boats and [in houses] on poles, and those at Tolmayecan, went into the water. On some, the water reached to the stomach; some, to the chest; and on some it reached to the neck. And some were all submerged, there in the deeps. Little children were carried on the backs [of their elders]; cries of weeping arose. Some went on happy and rejoicing as they traveled crowding on the road. And those who owned boats, all the boatmen, left by night, and even [continued to] leave all day. It was as if they pushed and crowded one another as they set out.

And everywhere the Spaniards were seizing and robbing the people. They sought gold; as nothing did they value the green stone, quetzal feathers, and turquoise [which] was everywhere in the bosoms or in the skirts of the women. And as for us men, it was everywhere in [our] breech clouts and in [our] mouths.

And [the Spaniards] seized and set apart the pretty women — those of light bodies, the fair [-skinned] ones. And some women, when they were robbed, covered their face with mud and put on old, mended shirts and rags for their shifts. They put all rags on themselves.

And also some of us men were singled out — those who were strong, grown to manhood, and next the young boys, of whom they would make messengers, who would be their runners, and who were known as their servers. And on some they burned [brand marks] on their cheeks; on some they put paint on their cheeks; on some they put paint on their lips.

And when the shield was laid down, when we gave way, it was the year count Three House and the day count was One Serpent.

8. THE SUN-GOD IN GUATEMALA

After his victory over the Aztecs, Cortés sent Pedro de Alvarado, called "Tunatiuh," the sun, by the Indians because of his yellow hair and ruddy complexion, to conquer the mountainous land of Guatemala, inhabited by powerful tribes of Maya stock. Alvarado's devastating progress through northern Central America is commemorated in the so-called Annals of the Cakchiquels, written in the Cakchiquel language by educated natives, probably during the early half of the seventeenth century.[9]

IT WAS ON THE DAY I Hunahpu when the Castilians arrived at Iximche with their chief, Tunatiuh. The people went forth to meet Tunatiuh with the chiefs Belehe Qat and Cahi Ymox.

[9] Pedro de Alvarado, *An Account of the Conquest of Guatemala*, edited by Sedley J. Mackie, New York, The Cortés Society, 1924, Appendix I, pp. 93–98.

Good was the heart of Tunatiuh when he entered the city with the chiefs. There was no fighting and Tunatiuh rejoiced when he entered Iximche. Thus did the Castilians enter of yore, O my children; but it was a fearful thing when they entered; their faces were strange, and the chiefs took them for gods. We, even we, your father, saw them when they first set foot in Iximche, at the palace of Tzupam where Tunatiuh slept. The chief came forth, and truly he frightened the warriors; he came from his chamber and called the rulers: "Why do you make war with me, when I also can make it?" said he. "Not at all. Why should so many warriors find their death? Do you see any pitfalls among them?" So replied the chiefs, and he went to the house of the chief Chicbal.

Then Tunatiuh agreed to join the chiefs in their wars, and the chiefs said to him: "O thou God, we have two wars, one with the Tzutuhils, one at Panatacat." Thus spake the chiefs. Only five days after, Tunatiuh went forth from the capital. Then the Tzutuhils were conquered by the Castilians. It was the day 7 Camey that the Tzutuhils were destroyed by the Castilians.

Twenty-five days afterwards Tunatiuh went forth from the capital to Cuzcatan, going there to destroy Atacat. On the day 2 Queh, Atacat was slain by the Castilians, with all his warriors. There went with Tunatiuh all his Mexicans to this battle.

On the day 10 Hunahpu he returned from Cuzcatan. He had been absent only forty days to make the conquest at Cuzcatan when he returned to the capital. Then Tunatiuh asked for a daughter of one of the chiefs, and she was given to Tunatiuh by the chiefs.

A DEMAND FOR MONEY IS MADE

Then Tunatiuh began to ask the chiefs for money. He wished that they should give him jars full of precious metals, and even their drinking cups and crowns. Not receiving anything, Tunatiuh became angry and said to the chiefs: "Why have you not given me the metal? If you do not bring me the precious metal in all your towns, choose then, for I shall burn you alive and hang you." Thus did he speak to the chiefs.

Then Tunatiuh cut from three of them the gold ornaments they wore in their ears. The chiefs suffered keenly from this violence, and wept before him. But Tunatiuh was not troubled, and said: "I tell you that I want the gold here within five days. Woe to you if you do not give it. I know my heart." So said he to the chiefs. The word was then given. The chiefs gathered together all their metals, those of the parents and children of the king, and all that the chiefs could get from the people.

While they were gathering the gold for Tunatiuh, a priest of the Demon showed himself. "I am the lightning; I will destroy the Castilians." So said he to the chiefs. "I will destroy them by fire. When I beat the drum let the chiefs come forth and go to the other bank of the river. This I shall do on the day 7 Ahmak." Thus did this priest of the Demon speak to the chiefs. Truly the chiefs thought that they should trust in the words of this man. It was when they were gathering the gold that we went forth.

HOW WE WENT FORTH FROM THE CITY

The day 7 Ahmak was that of the going forth. They deserted the city of Iximche on account of the priest of the Demon, and the chiefs left it. "Yes, truly, Tunatiuh shall die," said they. "There is no more war in the heart of Tunatiuh, as he now rejoices in the gold given him." Thus it was that our city was abandoned on the day 7 Ahmak on account of a priest of the Demon, O my children.

But what the chiefs did was soon known to Tunatiuh. Ten days after we had left the city, war was begun by Tunatiuh. On the day 4 Camey began our destruction. Then began our misery. We scattered in the forests; all our towns were taken, O my children; we were slaughtered by Tunatiuh. The Castilians entered the city and they arrived as to a deserted spot. From that time the Castilians were hated by the Cakchiquels. They made trenches, they dug pitfalls, that the horses might be killed, and war was waged by their men. Many men of the Castilians were slain, and many horses killed in the pitfalls. The Quichés and Tzutuhils were destroyed and all their villages ruined by the Cakchiquels. Only thus did the Castilians let them live, and only thus were they let live by all the villagers. One hundred and eighty days after the desertion of the city of Iximche was completed the ninth year (of the second cycle).

On the day 2 Ah was completed the 29th year after the Revolt.

During the tenth year the war continued with the Castilians. But the Castilians having received aid in this tenth year at Xepau, carried on the war with such vigor that they destroyed the forces of the nation.

Tunatiuh then went forth from Xepau, and so harassed us that the people would not come before him. There were lacking one hundred and twenty days to complete two years since we had abandoned the capital, now deserted, when Tunatiuh came there on his march in order to set fire to the city. On the day 4 Camey, two years less six months after the beginning of the war, he set fire to the capital and returned.

On the day 12 Ah was completed the 30th year after the Revolt.

VII

The Conquest of Peru

THE EPIC CONQUEST OF MEXICO challenged other Spaniards to match the exploits of Cortés and his companions. The work of discovering a golden kingdom reported to lie beyond the "South Sea" was undertaken by Francisco Pizarro, an illiterate Spanish soldier of fortune of whose early history little is known. Pizarro recruited two partners for his Peruvian venture: Diego Almagro, an adventurer of equally obscure antecedents, and Hernando de Luque, a priest who acted as financial agent for the trio. Two preliminary expeditions, fitted out from Panama in 1524 and 1526, yielded enough finds of gold and silver to confirm the existence of the elusive kingdom.

In December, 1531, Pizarro again sailed from Panama for the south with a force of some 200 men, and landed in the spring on the Peruvian coast. On their arrival the Spaniards learned that civil war was raging in the Inca Empire. Atahualpa, an illegitimate

*interval style
over assention*
the throne

son of the late emperor, had risen against the lawful heir to the throne, had defeated him
in a war marked by great slaughter, and had made him prisoner. Atahualpa was advancing toward the imperial capital of Cuzco when messengers brought him news of the
arrival of the white strangers. After an exchange of messages and gifts between the leaders,
the two armies advanced to a meeting at Cajamarca, high in the mountains.

There, in a famous scene, the priest Valverde stepped forward to harangue the bewildered Inca concerning his obligations to the Christian God and the Spanish king until
the angry monarch threw down a Bible which Valverde had handed him. At a signal
from Pizarro his ambushed soldiers, supported by cavalry and artillery, rushed forward to
slay hundreds of the terrified Indians and take the Inca prisoner. Later, after a farcical
trial, the Inca was found guilty of polygamy, idolatry, and the murder of his brother
Huascar, and was condemned to burn at the stake, a sentence commuted to strangling on
his acceptance of baptism.

Pizarro, posing as a defender of the legitimate Inca line, now proclaimed Huascar's
brother Manco the new Inca. But Manco was not content to play the part of a Quisling.
A formidable native insurrection, organized and led by Manco himself, broke out in
many sections of the empire. Defeated at last by a force under the command of Almagro,
just returned from an unprofitable expedition to Chile, the Inca retreated to a remote
part of the mountains, where he and his successors maintained a shadowy court for
many years.

Indian resistance had not yet ended when the Spaniards began fighting among themselves. Claiming that Cuzco was rightfully his, Almagro seized the city and made war
on the Pizarro brothers. Before the civil wars in Peru had run their course, four of the
Pizarro "brothers of doom" had met violent deaths; the Almagros, father and son, had
died on the block; a royal viceroy, Blasco Núñez de Vela, had been slain in battle, and
numberless others had lost their lives. Peace and order were not solidly established in the
country until the administration of the Viceroy Francisco de Toledo, who came out in
1569, a quarter-century after the beginning of the great civil wars.

1. RENDEZVOUS IN CAJAMARCA

*As the conquest of Peru unfolded, it repeated in a
number of important ways the sequence of events in
Mexico. Perhaps in direct imitation of Cortés, Pizarro
sought to win a quick and relatively bloodless victory
by seizing the person of the Inca Atahualpa, through
whom he may have hoped to rule the country, much
as Cortés had done with Montezuma. In one important respect, however, the Peruvian story differs from
that of Mexico. If Montezuma's undoing was his passive acceptance of the divinity of the invaders and
their inevitable triumph, Atahualpa erred disastrously
in his serious underestimation of the massed striking
power of the small Spanish forces. He had been led
to believe that the swords were no more dangerous
than women's weaving battens, that the firearms were
capable of firing only two shots, and that the horses
were powerless at night. This last illusion apparently
led to his delayed entry into Cajamarca at dusk, instead of at noon, as Pizarro had been told to expect.
Francisco de Jérez (1504–?), secretary to Pizarro and
an active participant in the conquest, describes the
fateful meeting at Cajamarca.[1]*

[1] *Reports on the Discovery of Peru,* translated by C. R.
Markham, London, the Hakluyt Society, 1872, pp. 52–56.

WHEN THE GOVERNOR saw that it was near sunset, and that Atabaliba did not move from the
place to which he had repaired, although troops
still kept issuing out of his camp, he sent a Spaniard to ask him to come into the square to see
him before it was dark. As soon as the messenger came before Atabaliba, he made an obei-
sance to him, and made signs that he should
come to where the Governor waited. Presently
he and his troops began to move, and the Spaniard returned and reported that they were coming, and that the men in front carried arms concealed under their clothes, which were strong
tunics of cotton, beneath which were stones and
bags and slings; all of which made it appear that
they had a treacherous design. Soon the van of
the enemy began to enter the open space. First
came a squadron of Indians dressed in a livery
of different colours, like a chess board. They
advanced, removing the straws from the ground,
and sweeping the road. Next came three squadrons in different dresses, dancing and singing.
Then came a number of men with armour, large
metal plates, and crowns of gold and silver.
Among them was Atabaliba in a litter lined with
plumes of macaws' feathers, of many colours,

and adorned with plates of gold and silver. Many Indians carried it on their shoulders on high. Next came two other litters and two hammocks, in which were some principal chiefs; and lastly, several squadrons of Indians with crowns of gold and silver.

As soon as the first entered the open space they moved aside and gave space to the others. On reaching the centre of the open space, Atabaliba remained in his litter on high, and the others with him, while his troops did not cease to enter. A captain then came to the front and, ascending the fortress near the open space, where the artillery was posted, raised his lance twice, as for a signal. Seeing this, the Governor asked the Father Friar Vicente if he wished to go and speak to Atabaliba, with an interpreter? He replied that he did wish it, and he advanced, with a cross in one hand and the Bible in the other, and going amongst them: "I am a Priest of God, and I teach Christians the things of God, and in like manner I come to teach you. What I teach is that which God says to us in this Book. Therefore, on the part of God and of the Christians, I beseech you to be their friend, for such is God's will, and it will be for your good. Go and speak to the Governor, who waits for you."

Atabaliba asked for the Book, that he might look at it, and the Priest gave it to him closed. Atabaliba did not know how to open it, and the Priest was extending his arm to do so, when Atabaliba, in great anger, gave him a blow on the arm, not wishing that it should be opened. Then he opened it himself, and, without any astonishment at the letters and paper, as had been shown by other Indians, he threw it away from him five or six paces, and, to the words which the monk had spoken to him through the interpreter, he answered with much scorn, saying: "I know well how you have behaved on the road, how you have treated my Chiefs, and taken the cloth from my storehouses." The monk replied: "The Christians have not done this, but some Indians took the cloth without the knowledge of the Governor, and he ordered it to be restored." Atabaliba said: "I will not leave this place until they bring it all to me." The monk returned with this reply to the Governor. Atabaliba stood up on the top of the litter, addressing his troops and ordering them to be prepared. The monk told the Governor what had passed between him and Atabaliba, and that he had thrown the Scriptures to the ground. Then the Governor put on a jacket of cotton, took his sword and dagger, and, with the Spaniards who

were with him, entered amongst the Indians most valiantly; and, with only four men who were able to follow him, he came to the litter where Atabaliba was, and fearlessly seized him by the arm, crying out *Santiago*. Then the guns were fired off, the trumpets were sounded, and the troops, both horse and foot, sallied forth.

On seeing the horses charge, many of the Indians who were in the open space fled, and such was the force with which they ran that they broke down part of the wall surrounding it, and many fell over each other. The horsemen rode them down, killing and wounding, and following in pursuit. The infantry made so good an assault upon those that remained that in a short time most of them were put to the sword. The Governor still held Atabaliba by the arm, not being able to pull him out of the litter because he was raised so high. Then the Spaniards made such a slaughter amongst those who carried the litter that they fell to the ground, and, if the Governor had not protected Atabaliba, that proud man would there have paid for all the cruelties he had committed.

The Governor, in protecting Atabaliba, received a slight wound in the hand. During the whole time no Indian raised his arms against a Spaniard. So great was the terror of the Indians at seeing the Governor force his way through them, at hearing the fire of the artillery, and beholding the charging of the horses, a thing never before heard of, that they thought more of flying to save their lives than of fighting. All those who bore the litter of Atabaliba appeared to be principal chiefs. They were all killed, as well as those who were carried in the other litters and hammocks. One of them was the page of Atabaliba, and a great lord, and the others were lords of many vassals, and his Councillors. The chief of Caxamalca was also killed, and others; but, the number being very great, no account was taken of them, for all who came in attendance on Atabaliba were great lords. The Governor went to his lodging, with his prisoner Atabaliba, despoiled of his robes, which the Spaniards had torn off in pulling him out of the litter. It was a very wonderful thing to see so great a lord, who came in such power, taken prisoner in so short a time.

2. DEATH OF A HERO

Pizarro, suspecting that Atahualpa planned to lead a revolt against Spanish rule, presided over a grotesque trial which ended in the execution of the Inca for his alleged crimes. The Spaniards proclaimed a new puppet Inca in the person of the youthful Manco, brother of the murdered Huascar. Three years after his inaugural, taking advantage of growing discontent with Spanish rule, Manco led and directed a nation-wide uprising against the invaders. A large Indian army laid siege to Cuzco for ten months, but failed by a narrow margin to take the city. Defeated at last by superior Spanish weapons and tactics, and by food shortages in his army, Manco retreated to a fastness in the Andean mountains, where he and his successors maintained a kind of Inca government-in-exile until 1572, when a Spanish military expedition entered the mountains, broke up the imperial court, and captured the last Inca, Tupac Amaru, who was beheaded in a solemn ceremony at Cuzco. Pedro Pizarro (1514–1571?), a first cousin of the conqueror of Peru and a participant in the defense of Cuzco, relates an incident of the siege, the Spanish capture of the key Inca fortress of Sacsahuaman.[2]

WHEN HERNANDO PIZARRO arrived [at the fortress] it had already dawned, and we were all of this day and the next fighting with the Indians who had collected together on the two topmost levels, which could only be gained by means of thirst, awaiting the time when their water should give out, and so it happened that we were here two or three days until their water came to an end, and when it had given out, they hurled themselves from the highest walls, some in order to flee, and others in order to kill themselves, and others surrendered, and in this way they began to lose courage, and so was gained one level.

And we arrived at the last level [which] had as its captain an *orejon* so valiant that the same might be written of him as has been written of some Romans. This *orejon* bore a shield upon his arms and a sword in his hand and a cudgel in the shield-hand and a morion upon his head. These arms this man had taken from Spaniards who had perished upon the roads, as well as many others which the Indians had in their possession. This *orejon*, then, marched like a lion from one end to another of the highest level of all, preventing the Spaniards who wished to mount with ladders from doing so, and killing the Indians who surrendered, for I understand that he killed more than thirty Indians because they [tried] to surrender and to glide down from

2 Pedro Pizarro, *Relation of the Discovery and Conquest of the Kingdoms of Peru*, translated and edited by Philip A. Means, New York, The Cortés Society, 1921, 2 vols., II, 313–317.

the level, and he attacked them with blows upon the head from the cudgel which he carried in his hand. Whenever one of his men warned him that some Spaniard was climbing up in some place, he rushed at him like a lion, with his sword and grasping his shield.

Seeing this, Hernando Pizarro commanded that three or four ladders be set up, so that while he was rushing to one point, they might climb up at another, for the Indians which this *orejon* had with him were all now either surrendered or lacking in courage, and it was he alone who was fighting. And Hernando Pizarro ordered those Spaniards who climbed up not to kill this Indian but to take him alive, swearing that he would not kill him if he had him alive. Then, climbing up at two or three places, the Spaniards won the level. This *orejon*, perceiving that they had conquered him and had taken his stronghold at two or three points, threw down his arms, covered his head and face with his mantle and threw himself down from the level to a spot more than one hundred *estados* below, where he was shattered. Hernando Pizarro was much grieved that they had not taken him alive.

Having won this fortress, Hernando Pizarro stationed here fifty infantrymen with a captain named Juan Ortiz, a native of Toledo, providing them with many vessels in which they had water and food, and fortifying the part where they were to be. And he left them some cross-bows and arquebuses, and we went down to Cuzco. And the taking of the fortress was the reason why the Indians withdrew a little, giving up the part of the city which they had gained. In this manner we were on the alert during more than two months, tearing down some *andenes* by night so that the horsemen might go up by that route, because the Indians always withdrew at night to the strongest and most secure place, and this withdrawal was always to some strong *andenes*.

3. THE KNIGHTS OF THE CLOAK

A heavy atmosphere of intrigue, broken by recurrent cycles of murderous violence, hung over Peru in the time of the great civil wars. The last Indian resistance had not yet ended when fighting began between one group of the conquerors, headed by the Pizarro brothers, and another led by Diego de Almagro, over possession of the city of Cuzco. Defeated in battle, Almagro suffered death on the block, but left behind him a large group of supporters who brooded over their poverty and supposed wrongs. Twelve of them, contemptuously dubbed by Pizarro's secretary "the knights of the cape" because they allegedly had only one cloak among them, planned and carried out the assassination of the conqueror of Peru. The Spanish chronicler and official Agustín de Zárate (1520?–?), who came to Peru in 1543 with the Viceroy Blasco Núñez Vela, gives a detailed account of the episode.[3]

IT WAS so widely known in Lima that a plot was afoot to slay the Marquis that many told him of it. He replied that the heads of the others were surety for his own; and to those who advised him to go about attended by guards, he said that he would not have it appear that he was on guard against the judge that his majesty was sending to Peru.

One day Juan de Herrada complained to the Marquis, saying that it was bruited about that he (Pizarro) meant to slay the men of Chile. The Marquis swore that he never had such a design. Juan de Herrada said that this was hard to believe, when they saw him buying many lances and other arms. When the Marquis heard this he reassured them affectionately, saying that the lances were not brought for use against them. And he took some oranges, which were highly prized, being the first grown in that country, and gave them to Juan de Herrada, and whispered that if he had need of anything, he (Pizarro) would provide it. Juan de Herrada kissed his hands for this favor, and, leaving the Marquis secure and confident, he departed for his house, where he, together with the most important men of his faction, agreed to kill the Marquis the following Sunday, since they had not done so on Saint John's Day, as they had planned. . . .

On Saturday of that week, one of them revealed the plot in confession to the priest of the great church, and that night the priest went to tell the story to Antonio Picado, secretary to the Marquis, and asked him to take him to his master. The secretary took him to the house of Francisco Martín, brother of the Marquis, where he was dining with his children. When the priest told him what he had learned, Pizarro changed countenance somewhat, but later on he told his secretary that he believed nothing of the sort, because a few days previously Juan de Herrada had come to speak to him very humbly, and the man who had told that story

to the priest must want to ask some favor of him, and had invented that tale to place him (Pizarro) under obligation.

Nevertheless, Pizarro sent for Doctor Juan Velásquez, his lieutenant, and because an indisposition kept the doctor from coming, the Marquis went to his house that night, accompanied only by his secretary and two or three others, by the light of a torch. Finding his lieutenant in bed, he related all that had happened. The lieutenant reassured him, saying that his lordship should not fear; that as long as he had his judge's wand in his hand no one would dare revolt. In which it seems that he kept his word, for when he later fled (as will presently be told) when they came to kill the Marquis, he let himself down from a window into the garden, holding the wand between his teeth.

For all these assurances, the Marquis was so uneasy that on Sunday he did not go to hear Mass at church, but ordered Mass said in his house, for greater security. And when Doctor Juan Velásquez and Captain Francisco de Chaves (who was at that time the leading man in the country, after the Marquis) came out of Mass, they went with many others to the house of the Marquis. When his closest neighbors had paid their respects they returned to their houses, and the doctor and Francisco de Chaves remained to dine with the Marquis. After they had eaten, which must have been between eleven and one o'clock in the afternoon, knowing that all the townspeople were quiet and that the servants of the Marquis had gone to eat, Juan de Herrada and some eleven or twelve others sallied from his house, which must have been more than 300 steps from that of the Marquis, because between them lay the whole length of the square and a good part of the street. And as soon as they came out they unsheathed their swords and shouted as they went along: "Death to the tyrant and traitor who has caused the death of the judge sent by the king!" . . .

Arrived at the house of the Marquis, they left one of their number at the door with a naked sword (which he had blooded in a sheep that was in the yard), crying out: "The tyrant is dead! The tyrant is dead!" Some citizens wanted to offer aid, but when they heard this they returned to their homes, believing it to be the truth. So Juan de Herrada and his men stormed upstairs. Meanwhile the Marquis, who had been warned of their coming by some Indians at the door, had ordered Francisco de

[3] Agustín de Zárate, *Historia del descubrimiento y conquista del Perú*, in *Historiadores primitivos de las Indias*, II, 496–498. (Excerpt translated by the editor.)

Chaves to close the doors of his room and the large hall, while he went in to arm himself. But Chaves became so excited that without closing any doors he ran out to the stairs, asking "What was that noise?" One of them gave Chaves a sword thrust; and he, seeing himself wounded, put his hand to his sword saying: "What! Do you slay your friends too?" Whereupon all the others gave him many wounds.

So, leaving him dead, they ran toward the hall of the Marquis, at which more than twelve Spaniards who were there fled, jumping from some windows into the garden, and among them Doctor Juan Velásquez, with his judge's wand between his teeth, as was told above, in order to let himself down from the window. And the Marquis, who was arming in his chamber, with his brother Francisco Martín and two other gentlemen, and two grown pages, one named Juan de Vargas, son of Gómez de Tordoya, and the other named Escandón, seeing their enemies so close, without waiting to tie the straps of their cuirasses, ran with sword and shield to the door, where Pizarro and his men defended themselves so valiantly that for a long time they prevented their entry, the Marquis crying: "At them, brother, death to the traitors!"

The men of Chile fought until they slew Francisco Martín, and one of the pages took his place. After a while they realized that Pizarro's group were defending themselves so well that there might be time for help to arrive, and they might be thus surrounded and easily killed. So they determined to end the business quickly by putting forward one of their best-armed men, who gave the Marquis such trouble in killing him that the rest were able to get through the door. Then they all fell upon him with such fury that he was exhausted and could no longer brandish his sword. Then they slew him with a thrust in the throat. As he fell to the floor he called for confession; and as his life ebbed away he made the sign of a cross on the floor and kissed it, and so yielded up his soul to God. His two pages also died; of the men of Chile four died, and others were wounded.

4. How the New Laws Were Received in Peru

The assassins of Pizarro proclaimed Almagro's half-breed son, commonly known as "Almagro the lad," governor of Peru. But their triumph was of short duration. From Spain came a judge, Vaca de Castro, sent by Charles V to advise Pizarro concerning the government of his province. Assuring himself of the loyalty of Pizarro's principal captains, Castro made war on Almagro the lad, defeated his army on the "bloody plains of Chupas," and promptly had him tried and beheaded as a traitor to the king. Presently fresh troubles arose. Early in 1544 a new viceroy, Blasco Núñez Vela, arrived in Lima to proclaim the edicts known as the "New Laws of the Indies." These laws, the fruit of years of devoted labor on the part of Father Bartolomé de las Casas to save the Indians from destruction, evoked outraged cries and appeals for their suspension from the Spanish landowners in Peru. When these pleas failed, the desperate conquistadores rose in revolt and found a leader in Gonzalo Pizarro, brother of the murdered Marquis. The chronicler Gómara describes the reception accorded the New Laws in Peru.[4]

Blasco Núñez entered Trujillo amid great gloom on the part of the Spaniards; he publicly proclaimed the New Laws, regulating the Indian tributes, freeing the Indians, and forbidding their use as carriers against their will and without pay. He took away as many vassals as these laws permitted, and vested them in the crown. The people and the town council petitioned for repeal of these ordinances, except for those which regulated Indian tribute and prohibited the use of Indians as carriers; of these provisions they approved. He did not grant their appeal, but instead set very heavy penalties for those judges who should fail to execute the laws, saying that he brought an express order of the emperor for their enforcement, without hearing or granting any appeal. He told them, however, that they had reason to complain of the ordinances; that they should take their case to the emperor; and that he would write to the king that he had been badly informed to order those laws.

When the citizens perceived the severity behind his soft words, they began to curse. Some said that they would leave their wives. Actually, some were ready to leave them for any reason, good or bad, since many had married their ladyloves or camp-followers only on account of an order that stripped them of their estates if they did not do so. Others said that it would be much better not to have a wife and children to maintain, if they were to lose the slaves who

[4] Gómara, *Historia de las Indias*, in *Historiadores primitivos de las Indias*, I, 251. (Excerpt translated by the editor.)

supported them by their labors in mines, fields, and other pursuits; others demanded payment for the slaves that were being taken from them, since they had bought them from the crown fifth [5] and they bore the royal brand and mark. Still others said that they were ill-requited for their labors and services, if in their declining years they were to have no one to serve them; these showed their teeth, decayed from eating toasted corn in the conquest of Peru; others displayed many wounds, bruises, and great lizard bites; the conquerors complained that after wasting their estates and shedding their blood in gaining Peru for the emperor, he was depriving them of the few vassals that he had given them. The soldiers said that they would not go to conquer other lands, since they were denied the hope of holding vassals, but instead would rob right and left all they could; the royal lieutenants and officials complained bitterly of the loss of their allotments of Indians, though they had not maltreated them, and held them not by virtue of their officers but in return for their labors and services.

The priests and friars also declared that they could not support themselves nor serve their churches if they were deprived of their Indian towns; the one who spoke most shamelessly against the viceroy and even against the king was Fray Pedro Múñoz, of the Mercedarian Order, saying how badly the king rewarded those who had served him so well, and that the New Laws smelled of calculation rather than of saintliness, for the king was taking away the slaves that he had sold without returning the money received for them, and that he was taking away Indian towns from monasteries, churches, hospitals, and the conquistadores who had gained them; and, what was worse, they were laying a double tribute and tax on the Indians whom they took away in this fashion and vested in the crown, and that the Indians themselves were weeping over this. There was bad blood between this friar and the viceroy because the latter had stabbed the friar one evening in Málaga, when the viceroy was *corregidor* there.

5. THE PLEASANTRIES OF CARBAJAL

The first phase of the great revolt in Peru ended auspiciously for Gonzalo Pizarro with the defeat and death of the Viceroy Núñez Vela in a battle near Quito. Pizarro now became the uncrowned king of the country. The rebel leader owed much of his initial

[5] The *quinto*, or royal share of the spoils of war. B.K.

military success to the resourcefulness and demoniac energy of his eighty-year-old field commander and principal adviser, Francisco de Carbajal. To these qualities Carbajal united an inhuman cruelty that became legendary in Peru. Garcilaso de la Vega, who as a youth witnessed the terrors of Carbajal's regime in Cuzco, gives some examples of the curious wit and humor of Francisco de Carbajal.[6]

THE MASTER of the camp, Francisco de Carbajal, priding himself on his soldierly appearance, almost invariably wore, in place of a cape, a Moorish cloak of purple color, with a border and a hood; I saw him in this dress many times. On his head he wore a hat lined with black taffeta and a very plain silk braid; he trimmed the hat with numerous black and white hen feathers, crossed to form the figure X. He wore this finery to set an example to his soldiers; one of the things he most earnestly urged upon them was to wear plumes, no matter of what kind; for he said that plumes were the proper adornment and device of soldiers, and not of civilians, for in the latter it indicated frivolity, whereas in the former it was a mark of gallantry. . . .

Francisco de Carbajal had a fund of diverting stories that he would tell on all occasions. I wish I remembered them all and could write them down here, for they were amusing. I shall tell those that I remember of the more decent kind, lest the freedom of his language (which was very great) give offense.

In pursuing Diego Centeno, one day Carbajal captured three soldiers of the kind that he called "weavers," who changed sides as their advantage required. Since he never pardoned such men when he caught them, he ordered these to be hanged. After two had been hanged, the third, seeking some pretext for a pardon, called out: "Pardon me, your worship, for I have eaten your bread!" And actually, as his soldier, he had often eaten at his table. To which Carbajal replied: "A curse on bread that had such evil use!" And turning to the hangman, he said: "Since this gentleman has eaten of my bread, hang him over there, on the highest branch of all. . . ."

Earlier, I mentioned that Francisco de Carbajal strangled Doña María Calderón and hung her from a window of her house. . . . I shall now relate what I omitted before. Doña María Calderón, though in the power of her enemies,

[6] Garcilaso de la Vega, *Historia general del Perú*, Buenos Aires, 1944, 3 vols., II, 269–274. (Excerpt translated by the editor.)

spoke quite openly against Gonzalo Pizarro and his tyranny, and in ordinary conversation could say nothing but evil of him. Carbajal, who learned of it, sent her one, two, and more warnings to desist from such remarks, on the basis that they were neither discreet nor good for her health. She received the same warning from other persons who feared that harm would come to her. Doña María Calderón, instead of curbing her speech and mending her ways, henceforth spoke with even greater freedom and disrespect, which obliged Carbajal to come to her house in order to correct the situation. There he said to her: "Fellow godparent" (which she was, in reality), "do you know that I have come to strangle you?" She, in her usual debonair way, thinking that Carbajal was joking, replied: "Go to the Devil, you crazy drunk, I don't care to listen to your jokes." Carbajal said: "I am not joking, really, for I have come to twist your neck so that your ladyship may not speak so much evil; and to prove it to your ladyship, I order these African soldiers to strangle you," signaling to three or four Negroes that he always took with him for such exploits. They immediately strangled her and hung her from a window that looked out upon the street. Carbajal, passing below her, raised his eyes and said, "For the life of me, fellow godparent, I don't know what I shall do if you don't learn a lesson from this."

6. THE MAN WHO WOULD BE KING

After his victory over the viceroy Vela, Carbajal and other advisers urged Pizarro to proclaim himself King of Peru. But Pizarro, a weaker man than his iron-willed lieutenant, hesitated to avow the revolutionary meaning of his actions. The arrival of a smooth-tongued envoy of the crown, La Gasca, who announced suspension of the New Laws and offered pardons and rewards to all repentant rebels, caused a trickle of desertions from Pizarro's ranks that in time became a flood. As his army melted away, Carbajal is said to have hummed the words of an old Spanish song: "These my hairs, mother, two by two the breeze carries them away." In the sequel the rebellion collapsed almost without a struggle, and its leaders ended on the gallows or the block. Garcilaso de la Vega describes the execution of Gonzalo Pizarro.[7]

IT REMAINS ONLY for me to tell of the pitiful

[7] Garcilaso de la Vega, *Historia general del Perú*, II, 276–277. (Excerpt translated by the editor.)

death of Gonzalo Pizarro. He spent all of his last day in confession. . . . The ministers of justice, coming and going, sought to hasten the execution of his sentence. One of the gravest of them, angered by the delay, said loudly: "Well! Are they not done with the fellow yet?" All the soldiers who heard him took offense at his disrespect and hurled a thousand oaths and insults at him, but though I remember many of them and knew the man, I will not set them down here nor give his name. He went without saying a word, before it came to blows, something he had reason to fear in view of the indignation and annoyance that the soldiers displayed at his rudeness. A little later Gonzalo Pizarro came out and mounted a saddled mule that was held ready for him. He was covered with a cape; although one author says that his hands were tied, it was not so. They threw one end of a halter over the neck of the mule, in compliance with the law. In his hands he bore an image of Our Lady, to whom he was most devoted. He continually implored her to intercede for his soul. Halfway along he asked for a crucifix. A priest, one of the twelve that accompanied him, gave him one. Gonzalo Pizarro took it and gave the priest the image of Our Lady, kissing with great affection the hem of the dress of the image. With the crucifix in his hands, never taking his eyes from it, he came up to the platform that had been made for his execution. This he ascended, and, standing at one side, he spoke to the people who were watching him. Among them were all the men of Peru, soldiers and citizens, excepting only the grandees who had turned against him — and even some of them were there, disguised and muffled up. He said in a loud voice:

"Gentlemen, your worships know well that my brothers and I gained this empire. Many of your worships hold *repartimientos* of Indians that the Marquis, my brother, gave you; many others hold them from me. Moreover, many of your worships owe me money that you borrowed from me; many others have received money from me as free gift. I die so poor that even the clothes I wear belong to the executioner who will cut off my head. I have nothing with which to ensure the good of my soul. Therefore I appeal to those of your worships who owe me money, as well as those who do not, to grant me the alms and charity of having as many masses as possible said for my soul, for I place hopes in God that by the blood and passion of Our Lord Jesus Christ, His Son, and through the alms that your worships grant me, He will have pity of me and will pardon my sins. And may your worships remain with God."

Before he had finished his plea for alms, there arose a general lament, with great moans and sobs and tears, from those who heard his pitiful words. Gonzalo Pizarro kneeled before the crucifix that he bore, and which was placed on a table on the platform. The executioner, who was named Juan Enríquez, came up to place a bandage over his eyes. Gonzalo Pizarro said to him: "I do not need it." And when he saw that Enríquez was raising the sword to cut off his head, he said: "Do your task well, brother Juan." He meant that he should do the job cleanly, and not prolong the agony, as frequently happens. The executioner replied: "I promise it to your Lordship." Saying this, with his left hand he raised his beard, which was long, about eight inches, and round, for it was not the fashion in those days to clip beards. And with one back stroke he cut off his head as easily as if it were a lettuce leaf and held it in his hand, and the body fell slowly to the ground. Such was the end of this good gentleman. The executioner, true to his trade, wanted to despoil him of his clothing, but Diego Centeno, who had come to inter the body safely,

forbade him to approach it and promised him a good sum of money for the clothing. And so they bore the body to Cuzco; they buried Pizarro in his clothes, for there was no one to offer him a burial shroud. They buried him in the Convent of Nuestra Señora de las Mercedes, in the same chapel where were buried the two Don Diegos de Almagro, father and son, in order that they might be equal and comrades in all things — in their common conquest of the land, in the common death of all three on the executioner's block, and in the pauper's burial of all three in a common grave, as if they even lacked earth enough to cover each one separately. Fortune made them equal in all things, as if to prevent any one of them from lording it over the others and as if to prevent all three from setting themselves above the Marquis Francisco Pizarro, who was brother of the one and comrade of the other and who was likewise slain and buried in a pauper's grave, as was told above. Thus all four were brothers and comrades in all and for all. Such is the way of the world (as those remarked who viewed these matters dispassionately) with those who serve it most and best, for such was the end of those who won that empire called Peru.

VIII

The Quest for El Dorado

FROM ITS ORIGINAL base in the West Indies, and from the two new centers of Mexico and Peru, the great movement of Spanish expansion radiated in all directions.

The North American mainland early attracted the attention of Spanish gold-seekers and slave-hunters based in the West Indies. In 1513 Ponce de León, governor of Puerto Rico, sailed west and discovered a subtropical land to which he gave the name La Florida. In the 1520's another expedition, ineptly led by Pánfilo de Narváez, met with disaster in the vast, indefinite expanse then called La Florida. Only four survivors of the venture, among them its future chronicler, Cabeza de Vaca, reached safety in Mexico after a lengthy, circuitous trek over the plains of Texas. Cabeza de Vaca's tales of adventure, with their hints of populous cities just beyond the horizon, inspired the conquistador Hernando de Soto to try his fortune in La Florida. After three years of unprofitable wanderings and struggles with Indians in the great area between South Carolina and Arkansas, the discoverer of the Mississippi died in the wilderness of a fever.

The glowing account of a certain Fray Marcos, who claimed to have seen in the distant northern lands one of the legendary Seven Cities of Cibola, induced Viceroy Antonio de Mendoza to send an expedition there under the command of Francisco Vásquez de Coronado. Coronado, disillusioned by the humble reality of the Zuñi pueblos of Arizona, the original of the Cibola myth, went on to discover the Grand Canyon of the Colorado, and then pushed east in search of still another El Dorado, this time called Quivira. In the spring of 1542 Coronado, much chagrined at his failure to find any treasure, returned to Mexico.

The golden will-o'-the-wisp that lured Spanish knights into the deserts of the Southwest also beckoned to them from South American jungles and mountains. From the town of Santa Marta, on the coast of present-day Colombia, an expedition led by Jiménez de Quesada departed in 1539 on a difficult pilgrimage through jungles and mountains in search of a legendary Gilded Chieftain; they suffered incredible hardships before they finally emerged on the cool plateau of Bogotá. There they met and conquered the Chibchas — the last advanced Indian culture discovered by the Spaniards.

In the southern reaches of the continent, which contained little gold or silver, new agricultural and pastoral settlements arose. Pedro de Valdivia, a captain under Pizarro, laid the foundations of the colony of Chile in struggle with the tough Araucanian Indians, losing his life in battle in 1553. In the same period Buenos Aires was founded on the Plate estuary by Pedro de Mendoza, but was soon abandoned by its famished inhabitants, who moved upstream to the newly risen town of Asunción in Paraguay. Not until 1580 was Buenos Aires permanently refounded by colonists coming downstream from Asunción.

1. ADVICE TO A WOULD-BE CONQUEROR

The conquest of America, like similar enterprises before and after, or like our own gold rushes, attracted a wide variety of types. A common figure in the conquest was the adventurer, who frequently had a military background and not infrequently a past that he preferred to forget; such, assuredly, were the "fine-feathered birds and great talkers" that Oviedo warns against below. But there were other thousands of young and high-spirited hidalgos, "men of good family who were not reared behind the plow," who sailed in the ships bound for the Indies. In the matter of motives, it is probably safe to assume that of the trinity of motives usually assigned to the Spanish conquistador ("God, Gold, and Glory"), the second was uppermost in the minds of most.[1]

SIR CAPTAIN: Understand me and understand yourself. When you make up a company to go to the Indies, and especially in Seville (for it is there, on the steps of the cathedral, that the soldiers are wont to gather), you should first examine the face of each; having scrutinized the face, you will see part of the evil beneath. But because the outward aspect may deceive you in the choice of a soldier, you should make secret inquiry concerning his habits, his mode of life, his skills, and his nationality; for even in that sacred place[2] there are some who will lie about

their countries and even their own names for the sake of going to the Indies. And do not attach much importance to his height and his well-combed beard, but rather try to find out whether he is of good character and family, and a frank and modest man. And if he tells you that he was in the battle of Ravenna, dismiss him, if he is a Spaniard, since he remained alive or was not taken prisoner; and do the same if he speaks of the battle of Pavia; and dismiss him if he tells you that he was in the sack of Genoa or Rome, since he did not get rich; and if he was there, and gambled his wealth away or lost it, do not trust him. Those slashed hose and shoes will not do at all for such lands as the Indies, full of ambushes and thick with trees and hawthorns, where there are so many rivers to swim and so many swamps and bogs to cross.

The dress and the person should conform to your needs; above all do not take a man whose faith is suspect, or one less than twenty-five or more than fifty years old. And do not take such fine-feathered birds and great talkers as those I mentioned above, for in the many years that I have seen them in the Indies, and before that in Europe, I have found that few turn out well. As long as there is gold, or they suspect that they will get it through your hands, they will serve you diligently; but be careful, for the min-

1 Gonzalo Fernández de Oviedo y Valdés, *Historia general*, V, 213–218. (Excerpt translated by the editor.)

2 The first chronicler of the Indies alludes here to the immemorial custom of meeting at the cathedral of Seville to arrange all manner of contracts, which gave rise likewise to the practice of hiring and negotiating with soldiers

bound for the Indies, who usually were found on the steps, in the yard, lined with orange trees, and at the gates of the cathedral. . . . The soldiers awaited outside the church the results of the conferences that the merchants and captains held within; from these conferences commonly developed the great American enterprises and expeditions. [José Amador de los Ríos.]

ute that things do not go their way they will either slay you or sell you or forsake you, when they find that you promised them more in Spain than you can produce. . . .

And before you begin this examination, examine yourself, and make sure that your aim is to serve God and your king by converting the Indians and treating them well, and by finding a way to lead them to the Republic of Christ. Do not enslave them without cause, or stain your hands with blood without cause or justice, or rob them or remove them from the lands where God created them; he gave them life and humanity not to help you carry out any evil design but in order to save them. . . . And do not say that you are going to the Indies to serve the king and to employ your time as a brave man and an *hidalgo* should; for you know that the truth is just the opposite; you are going solely because you want to have a larger fortune than your father and your neighbors. However, you can do everything you want to do without hurting others or jeopardizing your soul. And do not seek any estate or treasure that might cost you such a price, if in so doing you lose that invaluable treasure by which you were redeemed and God freed you from Hell. . . .

COMRADE AND FRIEND: If you decide to go to the Indies, when you are in Seville ascertain first of all whether the captain with whom you are going is a man who will fulfill what he promises, and learn on the basis of what word or guaranty you are entrusting your life and person to his will — because many of these captains promise what they do not have, know, or understand; and they pay for your person with words that are worth less than feathers; because feathers, though the wind bear them away, at least have some substance and you know their purpose, which is to float in the air aimlessly; but the words of a liar are without substance and, having been said, are invisible and vanish like air. . . . Do you not see that he speaks of what is yet to come, and promises what he neither has nor understands? And once you are free of the perils of the sea and the land, which are innumerable, and come to the Indies, if he should succeed, he neither knows nor rewards you; and if you fall ill, he does not heal you; and if you should die, he will not bury you. . . . And if he gives you an allotment of Indians, he does not care to ascertain whether you are competent to teach them or whether you yourself have more need of a teacher than of governing others, in order that both your consciences may be at rest. And since these estates are acquired unjustly, God permits them to be lost, and you with them. . . .

I observe that for every man who has made his fortune in these parts and has returned to Castile with or without it, an incomparably larger number have lost both their fortunes and their lives. You will say: What should I do? Shall I hold back from going to the Indies, where so many go and return rich — men who were formerly poor and do not measure up to me in ability, merit, or capacity for work? Is it fitting that for lack of courage I should fail to do what so many have done who are older than I and not of such good health and presence? I do not counsel you not to go to the Indies, nor to go there; but I do counsel you, whether you come or not, first to justify yourself with God and to commend yourself to Him. I am aware that it is proper and necessary to seek one's fortune, especially for men of good family who were not reared behind the plow; but let the undertaking be well thought out, and once you have determined upon it, never let greed turn you aside from the loyalty that you owe, and never let necessity give occasion for you to be considered an ingrate or to tarnish your good name; for if you only set your mind to it, in the Indies as elsewhere you can live without offense to your fellow-men.

2. THE ADVENTURES OF CABEZA DE VACA

Few chronicles of exploration have the charm and interest of the narrative of Cabeza de Vaca (?–1557), one of the four survivors of Narváez's disastrous expedition to the land of Florida. In refreshing contrast to other Spanish accounts of the Conquest, Cabeza de Vaca's has few scenes of bloodshed and destruction, for, like Robinson Crusoe, it is essentially an absorbing tale of how one individual managed to survive and even prosper modestly in a strange and difficult environment. Honest and humane, Cabeza de Vaca fared reasonably well at the hands of the Indians, who often fed him from their own pitifully meager stocks; in time he achieved an exalted reputation among them as a medicine-man of great powers. In the last stages of his great trek over the Texan plains, Cabeza de Vaca was followed by thousands of adoring Indians, "clouds of witnesses" to his healing arts.[3]

[3] "The Narrative of Álvar Núñez Cabeza de Vaca," edited by Frederick W. Hodge, in *Spanish Explorers in the Southern United States*, New York, 1907, pp. 96–99, 109–110. Reprinted by permission of the publishers, Charles Scribner's Sons.

THOSE WHO THERE received us, after they had touched us went running to their houses and directly returned, and did not stop running, going and coming, to bring us in this manner many things for support on the way. They fetched a man to me and stated that a long time since he had been wounded by an arrow in the right shoulder, and that the point of the shaft was lodged above his heart, which, he said, gave him much pain, and in consequence, he was always sick. Probing the wound I felt the arrow-head, and found it had passed through the cartilage. With a knife I carried, I opened the breast to the place, and saw the point was aslant and troublesome to take out. I continued to cut, and, putting in the point of the knife, at last with great difficulty I drew the head forth. It was very large. With the bone of a deer, and by virtue of my calling, I made two stitches that threw the blood over me, and with hair from a skin I stanched the flow. They asked me for the arrow-head after I had taken it out, which I gave, when the whole town came to look at it. They sent it into the back country that the people there might view it. In consequence of this operation they had many of their customary dances and festivities. The next day I cut the two stitches and the Indian was well. The wound I made appeared only like a seam in the palm of the hand. He said he felt no pain or sensitiveness in it whatsoever. This cure gave us control throughout the country in all that the inhabitants had power, or deemed of any value, or cherished. . . .

We left there, and travelled through so many sorts of people, of such diverse languages, the memory fails to recall them. . . . We drew so many followers that we had not use for their services. While on our way through these vales, every Indian carried a club three palms in length, and kept on the alert. On raising a hare, which animals are abundant, they surround it directly and throw numerous clubs at it with astonishing precision. Thus they cause it to run from one to another; so that, according to my thinking, it is the most pleasing sport which can be imagined, as oftentimes the animal runs into the hand. So many did they give us that at night when we stopped we had eight or ten back-loads apiece. Those having bows were not with us; they dispersed about the ridge in pursuit of deer; and at dark came bringing five or six for each of us, besides quail, and other game. Indeed, whatever they either killed or found, was put before us, without themselves daring to take anything until we had blessed it, though they should be expiring of hunger, they having so established the rule, since marching with us.

The women carried many mats, of which the men made us houses, each of us having a separate one, with all his attendants. After these were put up, we ordered the deer and hares to be roasted, with the rest that had been taken. This was done by means of certain ovens made for the purpose. Of each we took a little and the remainder we gave to the principal personage of the people coming with us, directing him to divide it among the rest. Every one brought his portion to us, that we might breathe upon and give it our benediction; for not until then did they dare eat any of it. Frequently we were accompanied by three or four thousand persons, and as we had to breathe upon and sanctify the food and drink for each, and grant permission to do the many things they would come to ask, it may be seen how great was the annoyance. The women first brought us prickly pears, spiders, worms, and whatever else they could gather; for even were they famishing, they would eat nothing unless we gave it to them.

In company with these, we crossed a great river coming from the north, and passing over some plains thirty leagues in extent, we found many persons coming a long distance to receive us, who met us on the road over which we were to travel, and welcomed us in the manner of those we had left. . . .

We passed through many territories and found them all vacant: their inhabitants wandered fleeing among the mountains, without daring to have houses or till the earth for fear of Christians. The sight was one of infinite pain to us, a land very fertile and beautiful, abounding in springs and streams, the hamlets deserted and burned, the people thin and weak, all fleeing or in concealment. As they did not plant, they appeased their keen hunger by eating roots and the bark of trees. We bore a share in the famine along the whole way; for poorly could these unfortunates provide for us, themselves being so reduced they looked as though they would willingly die. They brought shawls of those they had concealed because of the Christians, presenting them to us; and they related how the Christians at other times had come through the lands, destroying and burning the towns, carrying away half the men, and all the women and the boys, while those who had been able to escape were wandering about fugitives. We found them so alarmed they dared not remain anywhere. They would not nor could they till the earth, but preferred to die rather than live in dread of such cruel usage as they received. Although these showed themselves greatly delighted with us, we feared that on our arrival among those who held the frontier, and fought against the Christians, they would treat us badly and revenge upon us the conduct of their enemies; but, when God our Lord was pleased to bring us there, they began to dread and respect us as the others had done, and even somewhat more, at which we no little wondered. Thence it may at once be seen that, to bring all these people to be Christians and to the obedience of the Imperial Majesty, they must be won by kindness, which is a way certain, and no other is.

3. THE PRAIRIE AND THE BUFFALO

The strange tales told by Cabeza de Vaca and his three companions on their arrival in Mexico in 1536, and the even stranger story told by a certain Fray Marcos, who claimed to have seen in the far north one of the Seven Golden Cities of Cibola (from a great distance, it was true), persuaded Viceroy Antonio de Mendoza to send there an expedition commanded by Francisco Vásquez de Coronado. For two years Spanish knights in armor pursued the elusive realm of gold through the future states of Arizona, New Mexico, Colorado, Oklahoma, Kansas, and possibly Nebraska. Intruders in the great plains that left no trace of their passage, the Spaniards were only repelled by their immensity, and returned home bitterly disappointed with their failure to find treasure. Pedro de Castañeda, a soldier in Coronado's army of whose life very little is known, describes the prairie and its curious denizen — the American buffalo.[4]

WHO COULD BELIEVE that 1,000 horses and 500 of our cows and more than 5,000 rams and ewes and more than 1,500 friendly Indians and servants, in travelling over those plains, would leave no more trace where they had passed than if nothing had been there — nothing — so that it was necessary to make piles of bones and cowdung now and then, so that the rear guard could follow the army. The grass never failed to become erect after it had been trodden down, and, although it was short, it was as fresh and straight as before.

Another thing was a heap of cow bones, a crossbow shot long, or a very little less, almost twice a man's height in places, and some eighteen feet or more wide, which was found on the edge of a salt lake in the southern part, and this in a region where there are no people who could have made it. The only explanation of this which could be suggested was that the waves which the north winds must make in the lake had piled up the bones of the cattle which had died in the lake, when the old and weak ones who went into the water were unable to get out. The noticeable thing is the number of cattle that would be necessary to make such a pile of bones.

Now that I wish to describe the appearance of the bulls, it is to be noticed first that there was not one of the horses that did not take flight when he saw them first, for they have a narrow, short face, the brow two palms across from eye to eye, the eyes sticking out at the side, so that, when they are running, they can see who is following them. They have very long beards, like goats, and when they are running they throw their heads back with the beard dragging on the ground. There is a sort of girdle round the middle of the body. The hair is very wooly, like a sheep's, very fine, and in front of the girdle the hair is very long and rough like a lion's. They have a great hump, larger than a camel's. The horns are short and thick, so that they are not seen much above the hair. In May they change the hair in the middle of the body for a down, which makes perfect lions of them. They rub against the small trees in the little ravines to shed their hair, and they continue this until only the down is left, as a snake changes his skin. They have a short tail, with a bunch of hair at the end. When they run, they carry it erect like a scorpion. It is worth noticing that the little calves are red and just like ours, but they change their color and appearance with time and age.

Another strange thing was that all the bulls that were killed had their left ears slit, although these were whole when young. The reason for this was a puzzle that could not be guessed. The wool ought to make good cloth on account of its fineness, although the color is not good, because it is the color of buriel.[5]

Another thing worth noticing is that the bulls travelled without cows in such large numbers

[4] "The Narrative of the Expedition of Coronado, by Pedro de Castañeda," edited by F. W. Hodge, in *Spanish Explorers in the Southern United States*, pp. 382–384. Reprinted by permission of the publishers, Charles Scribner's Sons.

[5] The kersey, or coarse woollen cloth out of which the habits of the Franciscan friars were made. Hence the name Grey Friars.

that nobody could have counted them, and so far away from the cows that it was more than forty leagues from where we began to see the bulls to the place where we began to see the cows. The country they travelled over was level and smooth that if one looked at them the sky could be seen between their legs, so that if some of them were at a distance they looked like smooth-trunked pines whose tops joined, and if there was only one bull it looked as if there were four pines. When one was near them, it was impossible to see the ground on the other side of them. The reason for all this was that the country seemed as round as if a man should imagine himself in a three-pint measure, and could see the sky at the edge of it, about a crossbow shot from him, and even if a man only lay down on his back he lost sight of the ground.

I have not written about other things which were seen nor made any mention of them, because they were not of so much importance, although it does not seem right for me to remain silent concerning the fact that they venerate the sign of the cross in the region where the settlements have high houses. For at a spring which was in the plain near Acuco they had a cross two palms high and as thick as a finger, made of wood with a big square twig for its crosspiece, and many little sticks decorated with feathers around it, and numerous withered flowers, which were the offerings. In a graveyard outside the village at Tutahaco there appeared to have been a recent burial. Near the head there was another cross made of two little sticks tied with cotton thread, and dry withered flowers. It certainly seems to me that in some way they must have received some light from the cross of Our Redeemer, Christ, and it may have come by way of India, from whence they proceeded.

4. IN THE LAND OF AMAZONS

The dream of spices played its part in inspiring the saga of Spanish exploration and conquest. Attracted by accounts of an eastern land where cinnamon trees grew in profusion, in 1539 Gonzalo Pizarro led an expedition from Quito across the Andes and down the forested eastern slopes of the mountains. Cinnamon was found, but in disappointingly small quantity. Lured on by the customary Indian tall tales of rich kingdoms somewhere beyond the horizon, the treasure-hunters plunged deep into the Amazonian wilderness. Gonzalo's lieutenant Orellana, sent with a party down a certain stream in search of food, found the current too strong to return, and went on to enter a great river whose course he followed in two makeshift boats for a distance of eighteen hundred leagues, eventually emerging from its mouth to reach Spanish settlements in Venezuela in safety. On the banks of the great stream Orellana battled hostile Indians whose womenfolk joined in the fray, on which account he gave the river its Spanish name of Amazonas. Father Gaspar de Carvajal (1504?–1584), whose narrative is the principal source of information on the expedition, describes its encounter with the "Amazons" — an excellent illustration of the myth-making process among the Spaniards of the Conquest.[6]

ON THE FOLLOWING THURSDAY we passed by other villages of medium size, and we made no attempt to stop there. All these villages are the dwellings of fishermen from the interior of the country. In this manner we were proceeding on our way searching for a peaceful spot to celebrate and to gladden the feast of the blessed Saint John the Baptist, herald of Christ, when God willed that, on rounding a bend which the river made, we should see on the shore ahead many villages, and very large ones, which shone white. Here we came suddenly upon the excellent land and dominion of the Amazons. These said villages had been forewarned and knew of our coming, in consequence whereof they [i.e., the inhabitants] came out on the water to meet us, in no friendly mood, and, when they had come close to the Captain, he would have liked to induce them to accept peace, and so he began to speak to them and call them, but they laughed, and mocked us and came up close to us and told us to keep on going and [added] that down below they were waiting for us, and that there they were to seize us all and take us to the Amazons.

The Captain, angered at the arrogance of the Indians, gave orders to shoot at them with the crossbows and arquebuses, so that they might reflect and become aware that we had wherewith to assail them; and in this way damage was inflicted on them and they turned about towards the village to give the news of what they had seen; as for us, we did not fail to proceed and to draw close to the village, and before we were within half a league of putting in, there were along the edge of the water, at intervals, many squadrons of Indians, and, in proportion as we kept on going ahead, they gradually came to-

[6] *The Discovery of the Amazon,* translated by Bertram T. Lee and edited by H. C. Heaton, New York, American Geographical Society, 1934, pp. 212–214. Reprinted by permission of the American Geographical Society.

gether and drew close to their living quarters.

There was in the center of this village a very great horde of fighters, formed in a good squadron, and the Captain gave the order to have the brigantines beached right there where these men were, in order to go look for food, and so it came about that, as we began to come in close to land, the Indians started to defend their village and to shoot arrows at us, and as the fighters were in great numbers it seemed as if it rained arrows; but our arquebusiers and crossbowmen were not idle, because they did nothing but shoot, and although they killed many, they [i.e. the Indians] did not become aware of this, for in spite of the damage that was being done to them they kept it up, some fighting and others dancing: and here we all came very close to perishing, because as there were so many arrows our companions had all they could do to protect themselves from them, without being able to row, in consequence whereof they did [so much] damage to us that before we could jump out on land they had wounded five of us, of whom I was one, for they hit me in one side with an arrow, which went in as far as the hollow region, and, if it had not been for [the thickness of] my clothes, that would have been the end of me.

In view of the danger that we were in, the Captain began to cheer up the men at the oars and urge them to make haste to beach the brigantines, and so, although with hard work, we succeeded in beaching the boats and our companions jumped into the water, which came up to their chests: here there was fought a very serious and hazardous battle, because the Indians were there mixed in among our Spaniards, who defended themselves so courageously that it was a marvelous thing to behold. More than an hour was taken up by this fight, for the Indians did not lose spirit, rather it seemed as if it was being doubled in them, although they saw many of their own number killed, and they passed over them [i.e. their bodies], and they merely kept retreating and coming back again.

I want it to be known what the reason was why these Indians defended themselves in this manner. It must be explained that they are the subjects of, and tributaries to, the Amazons, and, our coming having been made known to them, they went to them to ask help, and there came as many as ten or twelve of them, for we ourselves saw these women, who were there fighting in front of all the Indian men as women captains, and these latter fought so courageously that the Indian men did not dare to turn their

backs, and anyone who did turn his back they killed with clubs right there before us, and this is the reason why the Indians kept up their defense for so long. These women are very white and tall, and have hair very long and braided and wound about the head, and they are very robust and go about naked, [but] with their privy parts covered, with their bows and arrows in their hands, doing as much fighting as ten Indian men, and indeed there was one woman among these who shot an arrow a span deep into one of the brigantines, and others less deep, so that our brigantines looked like porcupines.

5. THE EL DORADO OF SIR WALTER RALEIGH

The life and death of Sir Walter Raleigh, courtier, poet, historian, and promoter of colonial enterprise, are curiously linked to the quest for El Dorado. In 1594 Raleigh came into possession of captured Spanish papers containing a fantastic story of a golden kingdom supposed to be located near the headwaters of the Caroni River, a tributary of the Orinoco. So vast was the capital city of the kingdom that one had to walk through its golden streets for two days in order to reach the center. In 1595 Raleigh, as credulous as any Spanish conquistador, outfitted an expedition to search for the golden city of Manoa. He traveled up the Orinoco to its junction with the Caroni, but decided that his force was too small to attempt further exploration and returned to England to publish a glowing account of the mythical kingdom. In the reign of the pro-Spanish James I Raleigh fell out of favor with the crown and was sentenced to death on charges of conspiracy, but was reprieved without annulment of the sentence. After spending twelve years in the Tower he was released in 1616 on the basis of his assurances that he would bring the king a great store of El Dorado treasure. His second expedition to Guiana was a dismal failure, and on his return to England, Raleigh, aged sixty-six, was beheaded by orders of the king. Raleigh's description of the "Rich and Beautiful Empire of Guiana" incorporates just about all the elements that ever entered into the legend of El Dorado, including the themes of lost Inca treasure, the Gilded Chieftain, and a warlike tribe of women.[7]

THE EMPIRE OF GUIANA is directly east from Peru towards the sea, and lieth under the equinoctial line, and it hath more abundance of gold than any part of Peru, and as many or

7 Sir Walter Raleigh, *The Discovery of Guiana*, London, 1887, pp. 24, 32–33, 41–45, 142–143.

more great cities than ever Peru had when it flourished most. It is governed by the same laws, and the emperor and people observe the same religion and the same form and policies in government as was used in Peru, not differing in any part; and as I have been assured by such of the Spaniards as have seen Manoa, the imperial city of Guiana, which the Spaniards call El Dorado, that for the greatness, for the riches, and for the excellent seat, it far exceedeth any of the world, at least of so much of the world as is known to the Spanish nation; it is founded upon a lake of salt water of two hundred leagues long, like unto *mare caspiu*.[8] . . .

[The] Guianians, and also the borderers, and all others in that tract which I have seen, are marvellous great drunkards, in which vice I think no nation can compare with them; and at the times of their solemn feasts, when the Emperor carouseth with his captains, tributaries, and governors, the manner is thus: All those that pledge him are first stripped naked, and their bodies anointed all over with a kind of white balsam (by them called Curai), of which there is great plenty, and yet very dear, amongst them, and it is of all others the most precious, whereof we have had good experience: when they are anointed all over, certain servants of the Emperor having prepared gold made into fine powder, blow it through hollow canes upon their naked bodies, until they be all shining from the foot to the head, and in this sort they sit drinking by twenties and hundreds, and continue in drunkenness sometimes six or seven days together; the same is also confirmed by a letter written into Spain which was intercepted, which Master Robert Dudley told me he had seen. . . .

Undoubtedly those that trade with the Amazons return much gold, which (as is aforesaid) cometh by trade from Guiana, by some branch of a river that falleth from the country into the Amazons, and either it is by the river which passeth by the nations called Tisnados, or by Carepuna. I made inquiries amongst the most ancient and best travelled of the Orinocoponi, and I had knowledge of all the rivers between Orinoco and Amazons, and was very desirous to understand the truth of those warlike women, because of some it is believed, of others not: and though I digress from my purpose, yet I will set down what hath been delivered me for truth of those women; and I spoke with a cazique, or lord of people, that told me he had been in the river, and beyond it also.

The nations of these women are on the south side of the river, in the provinces of Topago, and their chiefest strengths and retreats are in the islands situated on the south side of the entrance, some sixty leagues within the mouth of the said river. The memories of the like women are very ancient as well in Africa as in Asia; in Africa those that had Medusa for queen, others in Scythia, near the rivers of Tanais and Thermadon; we find also that Lampedo and Marthesia were queens of the Amazons; in many histories they are verified to have been, and in divers ages and provinces; but they which are not far from Guiana do accompany with men but once in a year, and for the time of one month, which I gather by their relation to be in April.

At that time all the kings of the borders assemble, and the queens of the Amazons, and after the queens have chosen, the rest cast lots for their valentines. This one month they feast, dance, and drink of their wines in abundance, and the moon being done, they all depart to their own provinces. If they conceive and be delivered of a son, they return him to the father, if of a daughter, they nourish it and retain it; and as many as have daughters send unto the begetters a present, all being desirous to increase their own sex and kind; but that they cut off the right dug of the breast I do not find to be true.

It was further told me that if in the wars they took any prisoners that they used to accompany with those also at what time soever, but in the end for certain they put them to death; for they are said to be very cruel and bloodthirsty, especially to such as offer to invade their territories. These Amazons have likewise great store of these plates of gold, which they recover by exchange chiefly for a kind of green stone, which the Spaniards call Piedras Hijadas, and we use for spleen stones, and for the disease of the stone we also esteem them: of these I saw divers in Guiana, and commonly every king or cazique hath one, which their wives for the most part wear, and they esteem them as great jewels. . . .

To conclude, Guiana is a country that hath yet her maidenhead, never sacked, turned, nor wrought, the face of the earth hath not been torn, nor the virtue and salt of the soil spent by manuring, the graves have not been opened for gold, the mines not broken with sledges, nor their images pulled down out of their temples. It hath never been entered by any army of strength, and never conquered or possessed by any Christian prince. It is besides so defensible, that if two forts be built in one of the provinces

8 The Caspian Sea. B.K.

which I have seen the flood setteth in so near the bank, where the channel also lieth, that no ship can pass up but within a pike's length of the artillery, first of the one, and afterwards of the other; which two forts will be sufficient guard both to the Empire of Inga, and to a hundred other several kingdoms lying within the said river, even to the city of Quito in Peru.

6. JOURNEY'S END

Of the many bold captains who rode under the banner of Castile to the conquest of America, few lived to enjoy in peace and security the fruits of their valor, their sufferings, and their cruelties. "He that killeth with the sword must be killed with the sword," recalled the old conquistador Oviedo. Certainly there was a kind of poetic justice about the ends met by such notorious and hardened Indian slave-catchers and tormentors as Balboa, Ponce de León, and Pedro de Alvarado. But fortune was little kinder to the humane and thoughtful Cabeza de Vaca, who spent his last years in the shadow of poverty and imprisonment; or to Hernando de Soto, who protested against the farcical trial and execution of Atahualpa and later died broken-hearted on the shores of the Mississippi. Oviedo presents a partial roll-call of the great adelantados, or leaders of conquering expeditions, and relates the ends to which they came.[9]

I DO NOT LIKE the title of *adelantado,* for actually that honor and title is an evil omen in the Indies, and many who bore it have come to a pitiable end. So it was with Don Bartholomew Columbus, the first adelantado in the Indies, brother of the first admiral, who left behind him neither heirs nor any other enduring thing. Look at Ponce de León, adelantado of Florida, slain by the Indians; the adelantado Rodrigo de Bastidas, treacherously slain by the dagger blows of his own soldiers; the adelantado Diego Velásquez, who spent infinite sums on the discovery of New Spain, only to see another enjoy it and himself disappointed. Consider Vasco Núñez de Balboa, adelantado of the South Sea, and its first discoverer, who was beheaded as a traitor, and others with him, although they were all innocent of treason; the adelantado Lucas Vásquez de Ayllón, his Majesty's judge on the Royal Audience that sits here in Santo Domingo, who spent his estate and died in the discovery of a certain province that was given him in the northern regions, and whose body was flung in the

sea; Francisco de Garay, adelantado of Panuco, who wasted his substance in arming and going to settle a land he knew nothing of, and who lost everything and finally died, although some say he was poisoned.

Antonio Sedeño spent much money on the conquest of Trinidad and Meta, and in the end was ruined and died disastrously; Diego de Ordaz, somewhat madder than the others, left and lost all he had and sought to settle the River Marañón, and in the end, departing for Spain, died and was cast in the sea; the adelantado Hernando de Soto, governor of the isle of Cuba, after returning to Spain loaded with gold, went to settle the mainland [of North America] and died there, leaving no trace or memory of himself. The adelantado Simón de Alcazaba was treacherously slain by his soldiers; the adelantado Diego de Almagro died a good and Catholic death; and, finally, his comrade Francisco Pizarro and his brothers, especially Hernando Pizarro, were slain against all reason and justice by those who were not their judges — but there is another world after this.

The adelantado Francisco Pizarro, later a marquis, was wickedly slain by his enemies and soldiers; the adelantado Pedro de Heredia, governor of Cartagena, is still alive, and no one can tell how he will end; a worse fate than others befell the adelantado Francisco de Orellana, who went to the River Marañón in search of the tribe of the Amazons — or, to put it better, in search of death, although he did not know it — and so met his end at the mouth of the river.... The adelantado Pedro de Mendoza went to the River Plate and wasted and lost all he had, and sailing for Spain, died and was cast into the sea; the adelantado Pánfilo de Narváez and his followers suffered an even worse fate, for some were eaten by their fellows, and of six hundred men only three escaped, while Narváez drowned in the sea; the adelantado Pedro de Alvarado lived and died violently, for his horse rolled down a steep hill, with him helplessly entangled underneath, and dragged him from cliff to cliff, ..aving him in such a state that he died soon after, but not before receiving the Sacraments like a good Catholic....

And thus, prudent reader, you may see what sort of title is that of adelantado, that leaves in such conditions those who have held it in the Indies; and it seems to me that after what I have said of the adelantados named above, no man of sound sense will seek to obtain this title in that part of the world.

---

[9] Gonzalo Fernández de Oviedo y Valdés, *Historia general,* V, 150–152. (Excerpt translated by the editor.)

Part Three

The Foundations of Colonial Life

THE SPANISH MONARCHS early had to contend with the problem of devising a workable Indian labor policy for the colonies. Left to themselves, the conquistadores would obviously bring about the speedy extinction of the natives or become great feudal barons independent of royal authority. Royal intervention resulted in the abolition of Indian slavery and helped to stabilize the chaotic labor situation in the colonies. Nevertheless, the economic life of the Indies continued to be based on Indian forced labor, whether this took the form of the *encomienda,* the *repartimiento,* or peonage.

Agriculture, the principal economic activity of the Spanish colonies, was aided by the introduction of new European plants and animals. Although the silver and gold mines employed only a tiny proportion of the total colonial labor force, they yielded enormous revenues to the crown and to the fortunate Spaniards who "struck it rich." The most widely-developed manufacturing industry was that of textiles; this was carried on in the home or in workshops everywhere in the colonies.

The Spanish commercial system was restrictive and exclusive to an extreme degree. Colonial discontent with the resulting régime of scarcity and intolerably high prices stimulated the growth of a contraband trade that eventually surpassed the legal traffic in volume and importance.

Social status in the colonies was nominally based on the criteria of race, family, and occupation. The Indians (save for the favored descendants of native ruling houses and nobility) and the Negroes constituted hereditary servile castes, subject to numerous restrictions and burdens. In practice, racial lines were not so strictly drawn. Wealth, rather than gentle birth or racial purity, was the distinguishing characteristic of the colonial aristocracy.

The supreme governing authority for the Indies was the Council of the Indies. In consultation with the king, this body framed laws for the colonies, nominated all high colonial officials, and acted as a court of last resort in cases appealed from colonial tribunals. In particular, it named the viceroys, powerful officials who ruled over vast jurisdictions from their capitals at Mexico City, Lima, Bogotá, and Buenos Aires.

Next to the crown, with which it was indissolubly united, the Church was the most powerful institution in the Indies. The friars or regular clergy were the first priests to come to the Indies; later an ecclesiastical organization patterned on that of Spain, complete with bishoprics and archbishoprics, was erected. In addition to their religious duties, the clergy established and maintained schools, hospitals, and asylums of various kinds. Other clerics worked to convert and domesticate the wild Indians of the desert and jungle; the most celebrated of these mission establishments was that of the Jesuits in Paraguay. As in Spain, the colonial Inquisition was active in ferreting out and punishing heresy, as well as many minor offenses.

IX

The Evolution of Spain's Indian Policy

THE CENTRAL PROBLEM of Spain's Indian policy was that of devising a workable labor system for the American colonies. The first decade of colonial experience demonstrated that the Indians, left to the tender mercies of the conquistadores, would either become an extinct race, as actually happened on the once densely-populated island of Hispaniola, or would rise in revolts that might threaten the very existence of the Spanish Empire in America. The crown naturally regarded these alternatives with distaste.

The situation created on the island of Hispaniola by the arrival of Columbus's second expedition has been aptly summed up in the phrase "Hell on Hispaniola." Columbus, anxious to prove to the crown the value of his discoveries, resorted to the expedient of compelling the natives to bring in a daily tribute of gold dust. When the Indians revolted they were hunted down, and hundreds were sent to Spain as slaves. Later, yielding to the pressure of rebellious settlers, Columbus divided the lands of the island among them in *repartimientos,* or shares, with the grantee enjoying the right to use the forced labor of the Indians living on his land. This system, formalized under the administration of Governor Ovando and sanctioned by the crown, became the *encomienda.*

In operation, the *encomienda* in the West Indies became a hideous slavery. The first voices raised against this state of affairs were those of a company of Dominican friars who arrived in Hispaniola in 1510. Their spokesman was Father Antonio Montesino, who on Advent Sunday, 1511, ascended the church pulpit to threaten the Spaniards of the island with damnation for their offenses against the Indians.

The agitation begun by the Dominicans raised the larger question of the legality of Spain's claim to the Indies. To satisfy the royal conscience, a distinguished jurist, Doctor Palacios Rubios, drew up a document, the *requerimiento,* which was supposed to be read by all conquistadores to the Indians before making war upon them. This document called upon the natives to acknowledge the supremacy of the Church and the Pope and the sovereignty of the Spanish monarchs over their lands by virtue of the papal donation of 1493, on pain of suffering the disasters of war and enslavement.

The famous Father Bartolomé de las Casas now entered the lists against Indian slavery and the doctrines of Palacios Rubios. He argued that the papal grant of America to the Spanish crown had been made solely for the purpose of conversion, and carried with it no temporal power or possession. Love, reason, and persuasion, he insisted, were the only ways to lead the Indians to the true faith.

Las Casas appeared to have won a brilliant but largely illusive victory in the promulgation of the New Laws of 1542. Faced with revolt in Peru and the threat of revolt elsewhere, the Spanish crown offered the colonists a compromise. The laws forbidding enslavement and forced personal service by *encomienda* Indians were reaffirmed, but the right of *encomenderos* to continue collecting fixed amounts of tribute from the natives was confirmed. In Yucatan and Chile the *encomienda* survived till the last quarter of the eighteenth century.

Indian forced labor, legally separated from the *encomienda,* soon appeared in another guise. The demand of the colonists for cheap labor on their estates, in mines, and in domestic service was satisfied by legal conscription of Indians, working in shifts or relays. There also emerged a pattern of Indian debt servitude or peonage. A class of free paid laborers also existed at an early date and came into fairly wide use in mining areas.

1. WANTED: A LABOR POLICY

From the first days of the conquest the Spanish crown faced a problem of harmonizing the demand of the conquistadores for cheap Indian labor, frequently employed in a wasteful and destructive manner, with the interest of the crown in the preservation of a large, contented, and productive native population and with the requirements of the Christian ethic. The pious Isabella, first to face the problem, resolved its contradictions in a way that became typical of Spanish legislation on the subject. The Indians were to be forced *to labor, but as* free *men. This verbal reconciliation of opposites is well illustrated by the important order of December 20, 1503, which laid the basis for the* encomienda *system.*[1]

MEDINA DEL CAMPO, Dec. 20, 1503. Isabella, by the Grace of God, Queen of Castile, etc. In as much as the King, my Lord, and I, in the instruction we commanded given to Don Fray Nicholas de Ovando, Comendador mayor of Alcantara, at the time when he went to the islands and mainland of the Ocean Sea, decreed that the Indian inhabitants and residents of the island of Española, are free and not subject . . . and as now we are informed that because of the excessive liberty enjoyed by the said Indians they avoid contact and community with the Spaniards to such an extent that they will not even work for wages, but wander about idle, and cannot be had by the Christians to convert to the Holy Catholic Faith; and in order that the Christians of the said island . . . may not lack people to work their holdings for their maintenance, and may be able to take out what gold there is on the island . . . and because we desire that the said Indians be converted to our Holy Catholic Faith and taught in its doctrines; and because this can better be done by having the Indians living in community with the Christians of the island, and by having them go among them and

associate with them, by which means they will help each other to cultivate and settle and increase the fruits of the island and take the gold which may be there and bring profit to my kingdom and subjects:

I have commanded this my letter to be issued on the matter, in which I command you, our said Governor, that beginning from the day you receive my letter you will compel and force the said Indians to associate with the Christians of the island and to work on their buildings, and to gather and mine the gold and other metals, and to till the fields and produce food for the Christian inhabitants and dwellers of the said island; and you are to have each one paid on the day he works the wage and maintenance which you think he should have . . . and you are to order each cacique to take charge of a certain number of the said Indians so that you may make them work wherever necessary, and so that on feast days and such days as you think proper they may be gathered together to hear and be taught in matters of the Faith. . . . This the Indians shall perform as free people, which they are, and not as slaves. And see to it that the said Indians are well treated, those who become Christians better than the others, and do not consent or allow that any person do them any harm or oppress them.

I, THE QUEEN

2. THE STRANGE SERMON OF FATHER MONTESINO

The struggle for justice for the Indians was begun by a small group of Dominican friars, who were horrified by the sights that they daily saw on the island of Hispaniola. They delegated one of their number, Father Antonio Montesino, to preach a sermon that would drive home to the Spanish settlers the wickedness of their deeds. Father Antonio's tremendous denunciation produced much dismay and anger among his listeners, but apparently not a single conversion. In the sequel, the infuriated townspeople called upon the Dominicans to retract their sentiments in next

[1] Quoted in Lesley B. Simpson, *The Encomienda in New Spain,* Berkeley, Calif., University of California Press, 1929, pp. 30–31. Reprinted by permission of the University of California Press.

Sunday's sermon; otherwise the friars should pack up and get ready to sail for home. (This would not have been at all difficult, observes Las Casas, with quiet humor, for all they had on earth would have gone into two small trunks.) In reply, Father Montesino mounted the pulpit the following Sunday and let loose a second and even more terrible blast against Spanish mistreatment of the Indians. Las Casas describes the opening round in the great controversy over Spain's Indian policy.[2]

SUNDAY having arrived, and the time for preaching, Father Antonio Montesino rose in the pulpit, and took for the text of his sermon, which was written down and signed by the other friars, "I am the voice of one crying in the wilderness." Having made his introduction and said something about the Advent season, he began to speak of the sterile desert of the consciences of the Spaniards on this isle, and of the blindness in which they lived, going about in great danger of damnation and utterly heedless of the grave sins in which they lived and died.

Then he returned to his theme, saying: "In order to make your sins known to you I have mounted this pulpit, I who am the voice of Christ crying in the wilderness of this island; and therefore it behooves you to listen to me, not with indifference but with all your heart and senses; for this voice will be the strangest, the harshest and hardest, the most terrifying that you ever heard or expected to hear."

He went on in this vein for a good while, using cutting words that made his hearers' flesh creep and made them feel that they were already experiencing the divine judgment. . . . He went on to state the contents of his message.

"This voice," said he, "declares that you are in mortal sin, and live and die therein by reason of the cruelty and tyranny that you practice on these innocent people. Tell me, by what right or justice do you hold these Indians in such cruel and horrible slavery? By what right do you wage such detestable wars on these people who lived mildly and peacefully in their own lands, where you have consumed infinite numbers of them with unheard-of murders and desolations? Why do you so greatly oppress and fatigue them, not giving them enough to eat or caring for them when they fall ill from excessive labors, so that they die or rather are slain by you, so that you may extract and acquire gold every day? And what care do you take that they receive religious

instruction and come to know their God and creator, or that they be baptized, hear mass, or observe holidays and Sundays?

"Are they not men? Do they not have rational souls? Are you not bound to love them as you love yourselves? How can you lie in such profound and lethargic slumber? Be sure that in your present state you can no more be saved than the Moors or Turks who do not have and do not want the faith of Jesus Christ."

Thus he delivered the message he had promised, leaving his hearers astounded. Many were stunned, others appeared more callous than before, and a few were somewhat moved; but not one, from what I could later learn, was converted.

When he had concluded his sermon he descended from the pulpit, his head held high, for he was not a man to show fear, of which indeed he was totally free; nor did he care about the displeasure of his listeners, and instead did and said what seemed best according to God. With his companion he went to their straw-thatched house, where, very likely, their entire dinner was cabbage soup, unflavored with olive oil. . . . After he had left, the church was so full of murmurs that . . . they could hardly complete the celebration of the mass.

3. THE LAUGHTER OF DOCTOR PALACIOS RUBIOS

The dispute over Indian policy that had begun on the island of Hispaniola and was carried to Spain by the contending parties stimulated discussion of a fundamental question: By what right did Spain claim to rule over America and wage war on its native peoples? The strong tradition of legalism in Spanish life and history, as well as the pious professions of the Catholic Kings, required that a satisfactory reply be devised to this query. King Ferdinand, who is not particularly remembered by historians for scrupulosity in dealing with his fellow European monarchs, summoned a committee of theologians to deliberate on the matter. The fruit of their discussions was the famous requerimiento, *drawn up by Doctor Palacios Rubios. This document called upon the Indians to acknowledge the supremacy of the Church, the Pope, and the Spanish kings and to permit the faith to be preached to them. Not until they had rejected these demands, which would be made known to them by interpreters, could war be legally waged on them. The chronicler Oviedo, who accompanied the expedition of Pedrarias Dávila to the South American mainland in 1514, records in*

2 Las Casas, *Historia de las Indias,* II, 441–442. (Excerpt translated by the editor.)

his great history the first use made of the Require-
ment, and the ironic laughter of Doctor Palacios
Rubios as he listened to Oviedo's account of his ex-
perience with this curious manifesto.[3]

AFTER CROSSING this river we entered a village of
some twenty huts; we found it deserted, and the
general entered one of the houses, accompanied
by all the captains who were there, by the licentiate Espinosa, who was the royal comptroller,
factor, and governor, and by his lieutenant Juan
de Ayora, and in the presence of all I said to
him:

"Sir, it seems to me that these Indians do not
care to hear the theology of this requirement,
nor do you have anyone who can make them
understand it. Your worship had better put this
paper away until we have caught an Indian and
put him in a cage, where he can gradually master its meaning, and the bishop can help to
make it clear to him."

And I gave the general the requirement, and
he took it, amid the hearty laughter of all who
were there. While we were all resting in those
huts, waiting for the sun to go down, our senti-
nels gave the alarm at about two o'clock in the
afternoon. And down a very wide and handsome road, bordered with many trees that had
been planted for adornment, came more than a
thousand Indian bowmen, with much noise and
blowing on certain large shells which are called
cobos and are heard at a great distance. . . .

The general quickly left the village to meet
the Indians on the road and arrayed his men in
battle formation, each line separated from the
other by a distance of two hundred paces. He
also ordered a bronze cannon of about two hundred pounds to be loaded. Two greyhounds,
highly praised by their masters, were to be placed
on our wings; we were to fire when he gave the
signal; and at that instant the dogs should be
loosed and we were all to fall upon the enemy
and conduct ourselves like valiant men.

I should have preferred to have that requirement explained to the Indians first, but no effort
was made to do so, apparently because it was
considered superfluous or inappropriate. And
just as our general on this expedition failed to
carry out this pious proceeding with the Indians,
as he was supposed to do before attacking them,
the captains of many later expeditions also neglected the procedure and did even worse things,
as will be seen. Later, in 1516, I asked Doctor

Palacios Rubios (who had written that proclamation) if the consciences of the Christians were
satisfied with that requirement, and he said yes,
if it were done as the proclamation required.
But I recall that he often laughed when I told
him of that campaign and of others that various
captains later made. I could laugh much harder
at him and his learning (for he was reputed to
be a great man, and as such had a seat on the
Royal Council of Castile), if he thought that the
Indians were going to understand the meaning
of that requirement until many years had
passed.

4. BARTOLOMÉ DE LAS CASAS: GOD'S ANGRY MAN

Among the many personalities who intervened in
the great controversy over Spain's Indian policy, the
figure of Bartolomé de Las Casas (1474–1566) has per-
haps grown most in stature with the passing of the
centuries. By scholars he is most highly regarded for
his monumental History of the Indies, *which is indis-*
pensable to every student of the first phase of the
Spanish conquest. The world generally knows him
best for his flaming tract against Spanish cruelty to
the Indians, the Brief Account of the Destruction of
the Indies *(1552), a work soon translated into most of*
the languages of Europe and joyously used by Spain's
imperialist rivals to discredit her colonial enterprise.
Opponents of Las Casas have severely criticized his
palpable misstatements concerning the size of Indian
populations and the numbers slain by the Spaniards,
overlooking, perhaps, what John Fiske pointed out
long ago: that "the arithmetic of Las Casas is . . . no
worse than that of all the Spanish historians of that
age. With every one of them the nine digits seem to
have gone on a glorious spree." Typical of the tone
and contents of the Brief Account *is its description of*
the Spanish conquest of Cuba.[4]

IN THE YEAR 1511 the Spaniards passed over to
the island of Cuba, which as I said, is as long as
from Valladolid to Rome, and where there were
great and populous provinces. They began and
ended in the above manner, only with incomparably greater cruelty. Here many notable
things occurred.

A very high prince and lord, named Hatuey,
who had fled with many of his people from Hispaniola to Cuba, to escape the calamity and inhuman operations of the Christians, having re-

---

[3] Gonzalo Fernández de Oviedo y Valdés, *Historia gen-*
eral, VII, 131–132. (Excerpt translated by the editor.)

[4] "The Brevíssima Relación," in: Francis A. McNutt,
Bartholomew de las Casas, New York, 1909, Appendix I,
pp. 328–332.

ceived news from some Indians that the Christians were crossing over, assembled many or all of his people, and addressed them thus.

"You already know that it is said the Christians are coming here; and you have experience of how they have treated the lords so and so and those people of Hayti (which is Hispaniola); they come to do the same here. Do you know perhaps why they do it?" The people answered no; except that they were by nature cruel and wicked. "They do it," said he, "not alone for this, but because they have a God whom they greatly adore and love; and to make us adore Him they strive to subjugate us and take our lives." He had near him a basket full of gold and jewels and he said. "Behold here is the God of the Christians, let us perform *Areytos* before Him, if you will (these are dances in concert and singly); and perhaps we shall please Him, and He will command that they do us no harm."

All exclaimed: it is well! it is well! They danced before it, till they were all tired, after which the lord Hatuey said: "Note well that in any event if we preserve the gold, they will finally have to kill us to take it from us: let us throw it into this river." They all agreed to this proposal, and they threw the gold into a great river in that place.

This prince and lord continued retreating before the Christians when they arrived at the island of Cuba, because he knew them, but when he encountered them he defended himself; and at last they took him. And merely because he fled from such iniquitous and cruel people, and defended himself against those who wished to kill and oppress him, with all his people and offspring until death, they burnt him alive.

When he was tied to the stake, a Franciscan monk, a holy man, who was there, spoke as much as he could to him, in the little time that the executioner granted them, about God and some of the teachings of our faith, of which he had never before heard; he told him that if he would believe what was told him, he would go to heaven where there was glory and eternal rest; and if not, that he would go to hell, to suffer perpetal torments and punishment. After thinking a little, Hatuey asked the monk whether the Christians went to heaven; the monk answered that those who were good went there. The prince at once said, without any more thought, that he did not wish to go there, but rather to hell so as not to be where Spaniards were, nor to see such cruel people. This is the renown and honour, that God and our faith

have acquired by means of the Christians who have gone to the Indies.

On one occasion they came out ten leagues from a great settlement to meet us, bringing provisions and gifts, and when we met them, they gave us a great quantity of fish and bread and other victuals, with everything they could supply. All of a sudden the devil entered into the bodies of the Christians, and in my presence they put to the sword, without any motive or cause whatsoever, more than three thousand persons, men, women, and children, who were seated before us. Here I beheld such great cruelty as living man has never seen nor thought to see.

Once I sent messengers to all the lords of the province of Havana, assuring them that if they would not absent themselves but come to receive us, no harm should be done them; all the country was terrorized because of the past slaughter, and I did this by the captain's advice. When we arrived in the province, twenty-one princes and lords came to receive us; and at once the captain violated the safe conduct I had given them and took them prisoners. The following day he wished to burn them alive, saying it was better so because those lords would some time or other do us harm. I had the greatest difficulty to deliver them from the flames but finally I saved them.

After all the Indians of this island were reduced to servitude and misfortune like those of Hispaniola, and when they saw they were perishing inevitably, some began to flee to the mountains; others to hang themselves, together with their children, and through the cruelty of one very tyrannical Spaniard whom I knew, more than two hundred Indians hanged themselves. In this way numberless people perished.

There was an officer of the King in this island, to whose share three hundred Indians fell; and by the end of three months he had, through labour in the mines, caused the death of two hundred and seventy; so that he had only thirty left, which was the tenth part. The authorities afterwards gave him as many again, and again he killed them: and they continued to give, and he to kill, until he came to die, and the devil carried away his soul.

In three or four months, I being present, more than seven thousand children died of hunger, their fathers and mothers having been taken to the mines. Other dreadful things did I see.

Afterwards the Spaniards resolved to go and

hunt the Indians who were in the mountains, where they perpetrated marvellous massacres. Thus they ruined and depopulated all this island which we beheld not long ago; and it excites pity, and great anguish to see it deserted, and reduced to a solitude.

5. ALL MANKIND IS ONE

What was perhaps Las Casas' finest hour came in 1550, when he rose to answer the eminent humanist Juan Ginés de Sepúlveda (1490?–1572?), author of a treatise which sought to prove that wars against the Indians were just. The background of the great debate, held before a junta of theologians summoned by Charles V to decide the matter, was a general reaction in the Spanish court against Las Casas' liberal views, signalized by the partial repeal of the New Laws of 1542. All further conquests in the New World were ordered suspended while the great battle of words raged in Valladolid. Sepúlveda, a disciple of Aristotle, invoked his theory that some men are slaves by nature and thus made to serve others in order to show that the Indians must be made to serve the Spaniards for their own good as well as for that of their masters. Furthermore, the spread of the faith would be served by their subjugation. The highest point of Las Casas' argument was his eloquent affirmation of the equality of all races, the essential oneness of mankind. The outcome of the debate was inconclusive, with the judges finding themselves unable to reach agreement. The first [5] of the following extracts is from Sepúlveda's treatise on the subject of Indian wars; the second [6] is taken from Las Casas' Apologetical History of the Indies.

Now COMPARE these [Spanish] traits of prudence, intelligence, magnanimity, moderation, humanity, and religion with the qualities of these little men in whom you will scarcely find even vestiges of humanity; who not only are devoid of learning but do not even have a written language; who preserve no monuments of their history, aside from some vague and obscure reminiscense of past events, represented by means of certain paintings; and who have no written laws but only barbaric customs and institutions. And if we are to speak of virtues, what moderation or mildness can you expect of men who are given to all kinds of intemper-

ance and wicked lusts, and who eat human flesh?

And do not believe that before the coming of the Christians they lived in that peaceful reign of Saturn that the poets describe; on the contrary, they waged continuous and ferocious war against each other, with such fury that they considered a victory hardly worth while if they did not glut their monstrous hunger with the flesh of their enemies, a ferocity all the more repellent since it was not joined to the invincible valor of the Scythians, who also ate human flesh. For the rest, these Indians are so cowardly that they almost run at the sight of our soldiers, and frequently thousands of them have fled like women before a very few Spaniards, numbering less than a hundred. . . .

Could one give more convincing proof of the superiority of some men to others in intelligence, spirit, and valor, and of the fact that such people are slaves by nature? For although some of them display a certain talent for craftsmanship this is not proof of human intelligence, for we know that animals, birds, and spiders do certain work that no human industry can completely imitate. And as regards the mode of life of the inhabitants of New Spain and the province of Mexico, I have already said that they are considered the most civilized of all. They themselves boast of their public institutions, for they have cities constructed in an orderly fashion, and kings, not hereditary but elected by popular vote; and they carry on commerce among themselves in the manner of civilized people.

But see how they deceive themselves, and how much I disagree with their opinion, for in these same institutions I see proof on the contrary of the rudeness, the barbarism, and the inherently slavish nature of these people. For the possession of habitations, of a fairly rational mode of life, and of a kind of commerce is something that natural necessity itself induces, and only serves to prove that they are not bears or monkeys and are not completely devoid of reason. But on the other hand, they have no private property in their state, and they cannot dispose of or bequeath to their heirs their houses or fields, since they are all in the power of their lords, whom they improperly call kings, at whose pleasure, rather than at their own, they live, attentive to their will and caprice rather than to their own freedom. And the fact that they do all this in a voluntary and spontaneous manner and are not constrained by force of

[5] Juan Ginés de Sepúlveda, *Tratado sobre las justas causas de la guerra contra los indios,* México, 1941, pp. 105–113. (Excerpt translated by the editor.)

[6] Las Casas, *Apologética historia de las Indias,* Madrid, 1909, pp. 128–129. (Excerpt translated by the editor.)

arms is certain proof of the servile and abased spirit of these barbarians. . . .

Such, in sum, are the disposition and customs of these little men — barbarous, uncivilized, and inhumane; and we know that they were like this before the coming of the Spaniards. We have not yet spoken of their impious religion and of the wicked sacrifices in which they worshiped the devil as their God, believing that they could offer no better tribute than human hearts. . . . How can we doubt that these peoples, so uncivilized, so barbarous, contaminated with so many infidelities and vices, have been justly conquered by such an excellent, pious, and just king as the late Ferdinand the Catholic, and the present Emperor Charles, and by a nation that is most humane and excels in every kind of virtue?

FROM THESE EXAMPLES, both ancient and modern, it is clear that no nation exists, no matter how rude and uncivilized, barbarous, gross, savage or almost brutal it may be, that cannot be persuaded into a good way of life and made domestic, mild, and tractable — provided that diligence and skill are employed, and provided that the method that is proper and natural to men is used: namely, love and gentleness and kindness. . . .

For all the peoples of the world are men, and the definition of all men, collectively and severally, is one: that they are rational beings. All possess understanding and volition, being formed in the image and likeness of God; all have the five exterior senses and the four interior senses, and are moved by the objects of these; all have the natural capacity or faculties to understand and master the knowledge that they do not have; and this is true not only of those that are inclined toward good but of those that by reason of their depraved customs are bad; all take pleasure in goodness and in happy and pleasant things; and all abhor evil and reject what offends or grieves them. . . .

Thus all mankind is one, and all men are alike in what concerns their creation and all natural things, and no one is born enlightened. From this it follows that all of us must be guided and aided at first by those who were born before us. And the savage peoples of the earth may be compared to uncultivated soil that readily brings forth weeds and useless thorns, but has within itself such natural virtue that by labor and cultivation it may be made to yield sound and beneficial fruits.

6. INDIAN FORCED LABOR IN GUATEMALA

Las Casas died in 1566, at the great age of ninety-two, in a convent outside Madrid. Three Spanish kings had listened respectfully to his advice on Indian affairs, had sometimes acted upon that advice, and in their Indian legislation gave pious lip-service to the principles he advocated. But the realities of colonial existence overruled the voice of morality and religion. Legal slavery and personal service under the enco-mienda system had largely disappeared by 1700, but their place had been effectively taken by a system of labor conscription under which all adult male Indians were required to give a certain amount of their time to work in mines and factories and on farms, ranches, and public works, receiving a small wage for their labor. In New Spain this institution was known as the repartimiento. *Its operation in this area is described by Thomas Gage (1600?–1656), an observant though highly biased Englishman who spent twelve years as a priest in Guatemala before turning apostate and coming home to write an anti-Spanish book about his experiences. Frequent references in Gage's book to Indians who had grown rich by farming and trading testify that not all natives shared in the general misery of their race; in one town he found an Indian "who alone had bestowed upon the church five thousand ducats."* [7]

THE MISERABLE CONDITION of the Indians of that country is such that though the Kings of Spain have never yielded to what some would have, that they should be slaves, yet their lives are as full of bitterness as is the life of a slave. For which I have known myself some of them that have come home from toiling and moiling with Spaniards, after many blows, some wounds, and little or no wages, who have sullenly and stubbornly lain down upon their beds, resolving to die rather than to live any longer a life so slavish, and have refused to take either meat or drink or anything else comfortable and nourishing, which their wives have offered unto them, that so by pining and starving they might consume themselves. Some I have by good persuasions encouraged to life rather than to a voluntary and wilful death; others there have been that would not be persuaded, but in that wilful way have died.

The Spaniards that live about that country (especially the farmers of the Valley of Mixco,

7 Thomas Gage, *The English-American: A New Survey of the West Indies,* edited by A. P. Newton, London, 1946, pp. 230–233.

Pinola, Petapa, Amatitlan, and those of the Sacatepequez) allege that all their trading and farming is for the good of the commonwealth, and therefore whereas there are not Spaniards enough for so ample and large a country to do all their work, and all are not able to buy slaves and blackamoors, they stand in need of the Indians' help to serve them for their pay and hire; whereupon it hath been considered that a partition of Indian labourers be made every Monday, or Sunday in the afternoon to the Spaniards, according to the farms they occupy, or according to their several employments, calling, and trading with mules, or any other way. So that for such and such a district there is named an officer, who is called *juez repartidor,* who according to a list made of every farm, house, and person, is to give so many Indians by the week. And here is a door opened to the President of Guatemala, and to the judges, to provide well for their menial servants, whom they commonly appoint for this office, which is thus performed by them. They name the town and place of their meeting upon Sunday or Monday, to the which themselves and the Spaniards of that district do resort. The Indians of the several towns are to have in a readiness so many labourers as the Court of Guatemala hath appointed to be weekly taken out of such a town, who are conducted by an Indian officer to the town of general meeting; and when they come thither with their tools, their spades, shovels, bills, or axes, with their provision of victuals for a week (which are commonly some dry cakes of maize, puddings of *frijoles,* or French beans, and a little chilli or biting long pepper, or a bit of cold meat for the first day or two) and with beds on their backs (which is only a coarse woolen mantle to wrap about them when they lie on the bare ground) then are they shut up in the townhouse, some with blows, some with spurnings, some with boxes on the ear, if presently they go not in.

Now all being gathered together, and the house filled with them, the *juez repartidor,* or officer, calls by the order of the list such and such a Spaniard, and also calls out of the house so many Indians as by the Court are commanded to be given him (some are allowed three, some four, some ten, some fifteen, some twenty, according to their employments) and delivereth unto the Spaniard his Indians, and so to all the rest, till they be all served; who when they receive their Indians, take from them a tool, or their mantles, to secure them that they

run not away; and for every Indian delivered unto them, they give unto the *juez repartidor,* or officer, half a real, which is three-pence an Indian for his fees, which mounteth yearly to him to a great deal of money; for some officers make a partition or distribution of four hundred, some of two hundred, some of three hundred Indians every week, and carrieth home with him so many half hundred reals for one, or half a day's work. If complaint be made by any Spaniard that such and such an Indian did run away from him, and served him not the week part, the Indian must be brought, and surely tied to a post by his hands in the market-place, and there be whipped upon his bare back. But if the poor Indian complain that the Spaniards cozened and cheated him of his shovel, axe, bill, mantle, or wages, no justice shall be executed against the cheating Spaniard, neither shall the Indian be righted, though it is true the order runs equally in favour of both Indian and Spaniard. Thus are the poor Indians sold for threepence apiece for a whole week's slavery, not permitted to go home at nights unto their wives, though their work lie not above a mile from the town where they live; nay some are carried ten or twelve miles from their home, who must not return till Saturday night late, and must that week do whatsoever their master pleaseth to command them. The wages appointed them will scarce find them meat and drink, for they are not allowed a real a day, which is but sixpence, and with that they are to find themselves, but for six days' work and diet they are to have five reals, which is half a crown. This same order is observed in the city of Guatemala, and towns of Spaniards, where to every family that wants the service of an Indian or Indians, though it be but to fetch water and wood on their backs, or to go of errands, is allowed the like from the nearest Indian towns.

7. INDIAN FORCED LABOR IN PERU

Indian forced labor in Peru, commonly known as the mita, *produced even greater evils there than in New Spain. The situation was most disastrous in the highland areas, with the silver mines of Potosí and the Huancavelica mercury mine enjoying particular notoriety as death-traps for Indian laborers. To the operations of the* mita, *Spanish observers frequently attributed the depopulation of Indian villages that is frequently mentioned in seventeenth- and eighteenth-century accounts. Vásquez de Espinosa (?–1630), a*

Carmelite friar who traveled widely in the Indies between 1612 and 1620, gives a restrained description of labor conditions in the Potosí mines at that period.[8]

ACCORDING TO His Majesty's warrant, the mine owners on this massive range have a right to the *mita* of 13,300 Indians in the working and exploitation of the mines, both those which have been discovered, those now discovered, and those which shall be discovered. It is the duty of the Corregidor of Potosí to have them rounded up and to see that they come in from all the provinces between Cuzco over the whole of El Collao and as far as the frontiers of Jarija and Tomina; this Potosí Corregidor has power and authority over all the Corregidors in those provinces mentioned; for if they do not fill the Indian *mita* allotment assigned each one of them in accordance with the capacity of their provinces as indicated to them, he can send them, and does, salaried inspectors to report upon it, and when the remissness is great or remarkable, he can suspend them, notifying the Viceroy of the fact.

These Indians are sent out every year under a captain whom they choose in each village or tribe, for him to take them and oversee them for the year each has to serve; every year they have a new election, for as some go out, others come in. This works out very badly, with great losses and gaps in the quotas of Indians, the villages being depopulated; and this gives rise to great extortions and abuses on the part of the inspectors toward the poor Indians, ruining them and thus depriving the caciques and chief Indians of their property and carrying them off in chains because they do not fill out the *mita* assignment, which they cannot do, for the reasons given and for others which I do not bring forward.

These 13,300 are divided up every 4 months into 3 *mitas,* each consisting of 4,433 Indians, to work in the mines on the range and in the 120 smelters in the Potosí and Tarapaya areas;

8 Antonio Vásquez de Espinosa, *Compendium and Description of the West Indies,* translated by C. U. Clark, Washington, the Smithsonian Institution, 1942, pp. 623–625.

it is a good league between the two. These *mita* Indians earn each day, or there is paid each one for his labor, 4 reals. Besides these there are others not under obligation, who are *mingados* or hire themselves out voluntarily: these each get from 12 to 16 reals, and some up to 24, according to their reputation of wielding the pick and knowing how to get the ore out. These *mingados* will be over 4,000 in number. They and the *mita* Indians go up every Monday morning to the locality of Guayna Potosí which is at the foot of the range; the Corregidor arrives with all the provincial captains or chiefs who have charge of the Indians assigned them, and he there checks off and reports to each mine and smelter owner the number of Indians assigned him for his mine or smelter; that keeps him busy till 1 P.M., by which time the Indians are already turned over to these mine and smelter owners.

After each has eaten his ration, they climb up the hill, each to his mine, and go in, staying there from that hour until Saturday evening without coming out of the mines; their wives bring them food, but they stay constantly underground, excavating and carrying out the ore from which they get the silver. They all have tallow candles, lighted day and night; that is the light they work with, for as they are underground, they have need of it all the time. The mere cost of these candles used in the mines on this range will amount every year to more than 3,000,000 pesos, even though tallow is cheap in that country, being abundant; but this is a very great expense, and it is almost incredible, how much is spent for candles in the operation of breaking down and getting out the ore.

These Indians have different functions in the handling of the silver ore; some break it up with bar or pick, and dig down in, following the vein in the mine; others bring it up; others up above keep separating the good and the poor in piles; others are occupied in taking it down from the range to the mills on herds of llamas; every day they bring up more than 8,000 of these native beasts of burden for this task. These teamsters who carry the metal do not belong to the *mita,* but are *mingados* — hired.

X

The Economic Foundations of Colonial Life

THE ECONOMIC LIFE of the Spanish-American colonies reflected both New and Old World influences. Side by side with the subsistence-and-tribute economy of the Indians, there arose a Spanish commercial agriculture producing food stuffs or raw materials for sale in local or distant markets. To some extent this agriculture served internal markets, as in the mining areas of Mexico and Peru, or intercolonial trade, as in the case of the wine industry of Peru, but its dominant trait, which became more pronounced with the passage of time, was that of production for export to European markets. Spain imposed certain restrictions on colonial agriculture, in the mercantilist spirit of the age, but this legislation was largely ineffective.

Stock-raising was another important economic activity in the colonies. The introduction of domestic animals represented a major Spanish contribution to American economic life, since ancient America, aside from a limited region of the Andes, had no domestic animals for use as food or in transportation. By 1600 the export of hides from Hispaniola to Spain had assumed large proportions, and meat had become so abundant on the island that the flesh of slain wild cattle was generally left to rot. The export of hides also became important during the seventeenth century in the Plate area.

Mining, as the principal source of royal revenue, received the special attention and protection of the crown. Silver, rather than gold, was the principal product of the American mines. The great mine of Potosí in Upper Peru was discovered in 1545; the rich mines of Zacatecas and Guanajuato in New Spain were opened up in 1548 and 1558 respectively. Silver mining was greatly stimulated in 1556 by the introduction of the *patio* process for separating silver from the ore with quicksilver. As in other times and places, the mining industry brought prosperity to a few and either failure or small success to the great majority.

The Spaniards found a flourishing handicrafts industry in the advanced culture areas of Mexico, Central America, and Peru. Throughout the colonial period the majority of the natives continued to supply their own needs for pottery, clothing, and other household requirements. With the coming of the Spaniards new manufacturing industries arose in the towns, stimulated by the high prices of imported Spanish goods. The artisans were organized in guilds (from which Indians were excluded as masters), which included silversmiths, goldbeaters, weavers, and the like.

The period up to 1700 also witnessed a remarkable growth of factory-type establishments (*obrajes*) that produced cheap cotton and woolen goods for popular consumption. A number of towns in New Spain (Puebla, Guadalajara, Cholula, and others) were centers of the textile industry. Other factory-type establishments produced soap, chinaware, leather, and other products. Internal and intercolonial trade, based on regional specialization and particularly on the rise of mining centers that consumed large quantities of agricultural produce and manufactures, steadily increased in the sixteenth and seventeenth centuries.

1. THE INDIAN AGRICULTURAL HERITAGE

The Indian contributions to colonial and world agriculture were extremely rich and varied. A partial list includes such important products as maize, the potato and sweet potato, pineapple, peanut, cultivated strawberry, lima and kidney beans, squash and pump- *kin, cacao, rubber, and tobacco. To Europeans of the era of colonization, some of the new American plants appeared to have strange and possibly supernatural qualities. The learned Jesuit José Acosta (1539?–1600) sought to satisfy Spanish curiosity about the natural productions of the New World in his scientific and historical work, the* Natural and Moral History of the Indies *(1590). Among the plants described by Father*

Acosta are maize, the Indian staff of life; cacao, source of the refreshing chocolate drink first used by the Mayas; coca, the magic plant that imparted endurance to the weary frame of the Peruvian Indian; and maguey, the Mexican tree of wonders.[1]

TURNING TO PLANTS, I shall speak first of those which are more peculiar to the Indies and afterwards of those which are common both to those lands and to Europe. And because plants were created principally for the maintenance of man, and man sustains himself above all by bread, I should speak first of their bread. . . . The Indians have their own words to signify bread, which in Peru is called *tanta* and in other parts is given other names. But the quality and substance of the bread the Indians use is very different from ours, for they have no kind of wheat, barley, millet, panic grass, or any grain such as is used in Europe to make bread. Instead they have other kinds of grains and roots, among which maize, called Indian wheat in Castile and Turkey grain in Italy, holds the first place.

And just as wheat is the grain most commonly used by man in the regions of the Old World, which are Europe, Asia, and Africa, so in the New World the most widely used grain is maize, which is found in almost all the kingdoms of the West Indies: in Peru, New Spain, the New Kingdom of Granada, Guatemala, Chile, and in all the Tierra Firme.[2] In the Windward Isles, which are Cuba, Hispaniola, Jamaica, Puerto Rico, it does not seem to have been used in earlier times; to this day they prefer to use yucca and cassava, of which more later. I do not think that maize is at all inferior to our wheat in strength and nourishment; but it is stouter and hotter and engenders more blood, so that if people who are not accustomed to it eat it in excess they swell up and get the itch.

Maize grows on canes or reeds; each one bears one or two ears, to which the grains are fastened, and though the grains are big they hold a large number of them, and some contain seven hundred grains. The seeds are planted one by one. Maize likes a hot and humid soil. It grows in many parts of the Indies in great abundance; a yield of three hundred *fanegas* from a sowing is not uncommon. There are various kinds

of maize, as of wheat; one is large and nourishing; another, called *moroche,* is small and dry. The leaves of the maize and the green cane are a choice fodder for their beasts of burden, and when dry are also used as straw. The grain gives more nourishment to horses than barley, and therefore it is customary in those countries to water their horses before giving them maize to eat, for if they drank after feeding they would swell up and have gripes, as they do when they eat wheat.

Maize is the Indian bread, and they commonly eat it boiled in the grain, hot, when it is called *mote* . . . ; sometimes they eat it toasted. There is a large and round maize, like that of the Lucanas, which the Spaniards eat as a delicacy; it has better flavor than toasted chickpeas. There is another and more pleasing way of preparing it, which consists in grinding the maize and making the flour into pancakes, which are put on the fire and are later placed on the table and eaten piping hot; in some places they call them *arepas.* . . .

Maize is used by the Indians to make not only their bread but also their wine; from it they make beverages which produce drunkenness more quickly than wine made of grapes. They make this maize wine in various ways, calling it *azua* in Peru and more generally throughout the Indies *chicha.* The strongest sort is made like beer, steeping the grains of maize until they begin to break, after which they boil the juice in a certain way, which makes it so strong that a few drinks will produce intoxication. In Peru, where it is called *sora,* its use is forbidden by law because of the terrific drinking it occasions. But the law is little observed, for they use it anyway, and stay up whole days and nights, dancing and drinking. . . .

The cacao tree is most esteemed in Mexico and coca is favored in Peru; both trees are surrounded with considerable superstition. Cacao is a bean smaller and fattier than the almond, and when roasted has not a bad flavor. It is so much esteemed by the Indians, and even by the Spaniards, that it is the object of one of the richest and largest lines of trade of New Spain; since it is a dry fruit, and one that keeps a long time without spoiling, they send whole ships loaded with it from the province of Guatemala. Last year an English corsair burned in the port of Guatulco, in New Spain, more than one hundred thousand *cargas* of cacao. They also use it as money, for five cacao beans will

---

[1] José de Acosta, *Historia natural y moral de las Indias,* México, 1940, pp. 265–266, 285–289. (Excerpt translated by the editor.)

[2] The northern coast of South America. B.K.

buy one thing, thirty another, and one hundred still another, and no objections are made to its use. They also use it as alms to give to the poor.

The chief use of this cacao is to make a drink that they call chocolate, which they greatly cherish in that country. But those who have not formed a taste for it dislike it, for it has a froth at the top and an effervescence like that formed in wine by dregs, so that one must really have great faith in it to tolerate it. In fine, it is the favorite drink of Indians and Spaniards alike, and they regale visitors to their country with it; the Spanish women of that land are particularly fond of the dark chocolate. They prepare it in various ways: hot, cold, and lukewarm. They usually put spices and much chili in it; they also make a paste of it, and they say that it is good for the chest and the stomach, and also for colds. Be that as it may, those who have not formed a taste for it do not like it.

The tree on which this fruit grows is of middling size and well-made, with a beautiful top; it is so delicate that to protect it from the burning rays of the sun they plant near it another large tree, which serves only to shade it; this is called the mother of the cacao. There are cacao plantations where it is raised as are the vine and the olive in Spain. The province of Guatemala is where they carry on the greatest commerce in this fruit.

The cacao does not grow in Peru; instead they have the coca, which is surrounded with even greater superstition and really seems fabulous. In Potosí alone the commerce in coca amounts to more than 5,000,000 pesos, with a consumption of from 90 to 100,000 hampers, and in the year 1583 it was 100,000. . . . This coca that they so greatly cherish is a little green leaf which grows upon shrubs about one *estado* high; it grows in very warm and humid lands and produces this leaf, which they call *trasmitas*, every four months. Being a very delicate plant, it requires a great deal of attention during cultivation and even more after it has been picked. They pack it with great care in long, narrow hampers and load it on the sheep of that country, which carry this merchandise in droves, bearing one, two, and three thousand hampers. It is commonly brought from the Andes, from valleys of insufferable heat, where it rains the greater part of the year, and it costs the Indians much labor and takes many lives, for they must leave their highlands and cold climates in order to cultivate it and carry it away. Hence there

have been great disputes among lawyers and wise men about whether the coca plantations should be done away with or no — but there they still are.

The Indians prize it beyond measure, and in the time of the Inca kings plebeians were forbidden to use coca without the permission of the Inca or his governor. Their custom is to hold it in their mouths, chewing and sucking it; they do not swallow it; they say that it gives them great strength and is a great comfort to them. Many serious men say that this is pure superstition and imagination. To tell the truth, I do not think so; I believe that it really does lend strength and endurance to the Indians, for one sees effects that cannot be attributed to imagination, such as their ability to journey two whole days on a handful of coca, eating nothing else, and similar feats. . . . All would be well, except that its cultivation and commerce endanger and occupy so many people. . . .

The maguey is the tree of wonders, to which the newly-come Spaniards, or *chapetones* (as they call them in the Indies), attribute miracles, saying that it yields water and wine, oil and vinegar, honey, syrup, thread, needles, and a thousand other things. The Indians of New Spain value it greatly, and they commonly have one or several of these trees near their homes to supply their needs. It grows in the fields, and there they cultivate it. Its leaves are wide and thick, with strong, sharp points which they use as fastening pins or sewing needles; they also draw a certain fibre or thread from the leaves.

They cut through the thick trunk when it is tender; there is a large cavity inside, where the sap rises from the roots; it is a liquor which they drink like water, since it is fresh and sweet. When this liquor is boiled it turns into a kind of wine, and if it is left to sour it becomes vinegar. But when boiled for a longer time it becomes like honey, and cooked half as long it turns into a healthful syrup of good flavor, superior in my judgment to syrup made of grapes. Thus they boil different substances from this sap, which they obtain in great quantity, for at a certain season they extract several *azumbres* a day.

2. SPAIN'S CONTRIBUTIONS TO NEW WORLD AGRICULTURE

The colonial era saw a notable exchange of agricultural gifts between the Old and the New Worlds. The

Spanish crown displayed much solicitude for the agricultural development of the Indies, and paid particular attention to the shipping of trees, plants, seeds, and agricultural implements of all kinds. Father Acosta gives an account of the transit of Spanish plants to America and of the rapid rise there of a commercial agriculture producing wine, wheat, sugar, and other products.[3]

THE INDIES have been better repaid in the matter of plants than in any other kind of merchandise; for those few that have been carried from the Indies into Spain do badly there, whereas the many that have come over from Spain prosper in their new homes. I do not know whether to attribute this to the excellence of the plants that go from here or to the bounty of the soil over there. Nearly every good thing grown in Spain is found there; in some regions they do better than in others. They include wheat, barley, garden produce and greens and vegetables of all kinds, such as lettuce, cabbage, radishes, onions, garlic, parsley, turnips, carrots, eggplants, endive, salt-wort, spinach, chickpeas, beans, and lentils — in short, whatever grows well here, for those who have gone to the Indies have been careful to take with them seeds of every description. . . .

The trees that have fared best there are the orange, lemon, citron, and others of that sort. In some parts there are already whole forests and groves of orange trees. Marvelling at this, I asked on a certain island who had planted so many orange trees in the fields. To which they replied that it might have happened that some oranges fell to the ground and rotted, whereupon the seeds germinated, and, some being borne by the waters to different parts, gave rise to these dense groves. This seemed a likely reason. I said before that orange trees have generally done well in the Indies, for nowhere have I found a place where oranges were not to be found; this is because everywhere in the Indies the soil is hot and humid, which is what this tree most needs. It does not grow in the highlands; oranges are transported there from the valleys or the coast. The orange preserve which is made in the islands is the best I have ever seen, here or there.

Peaches and apricots also have done well, although the latter have fared better in New Spain. . . . Apples and pears are grown, but in moderate yields; plums give sparingly; figs are abundant, chiefly in Peru. Quinces are found everywhere, and in New Spain they are so plentiful that we received fifty choice ones for half a *real*. Pomegranates are found in abundance, but they are all sweet, for the people do not like the sharp variety. The melons are very good in some regions, as in Tierra Firme and Peru. Cherries, both wild and cultivated, have not so far prospered in the Indies. . . . In conclusion, I find that hardly any of the finer fruits is lacking in those parts. As for nuts, they have no acorns or chestnuts, nor, as far as I know, have any been grown over there until now. Almonds grow there, but sparingly. Almonds, walnuts, and filberts are shipped there from Spain for the tables of epicures. I have not seen any medlars or services, but those do not matter. . . .

By profitable plants I mean those plants which not only yield fruit but bring money to their owners. The most important of these is the vine, which gives wine, vinegar, grapes, raisins, verjuice, and syrup — but the wine is the chief concern. Wine and grapes are not products of the islands or of Tierra Firme; in New Spain there are vines which bear grapes but do not yield wine. The reason must be that the grapes do not ripen completely because of the rains which come in July and August and hinder their ripening; they are good only for eating. Wine is shipped from Spain and the Canary Islands to all parts of the Indies, except Peru and Chile, where they have vineyards and make very good wine. This industry is expanding continually, not only because of the goodness of the soil, but because they have a better knowledge of winemaking.

The vineyards of Peru are commonly found in warm valleys where they have water channels; they are watered by hand, because rain never falls in the coastal plains, and the rains in the mountains do not come at the proper time. . . . The vineyards have increased so far that because of them the tithes of the churches are now five and six times what they were twenty years ago. The valleys most fertile in vines are Victor, near Arequipa; Yca, hard by Lima; and Caracaro, close to Chuquiavo. The wine that is made there is shipped to Potosí and Cuzco and various other parts, and it is sold in great quantities, because since it is produced so abundantly it sells at five or six ducats the jug, or *arroba*, whereas Spanish wine (which always arrives with the fleets) sells for ten and twelve. . . . The wine trade is no small affair, but does not exceed the limits of the province.

[3] Acosta, *Historia natural de las Indias*, pp. 311–315. (Excerpt translated by the editor.)

The silk which is made in New Spain goes to other provinces — to Peru, for example. There was no silk industry before the Spaniards came; the mulberry trees were brought from Spain, and they grow well, especially in the province called Misteca, where they raise silkworms and make good taffetas; they do not yet make damasks, satins, or velvets, however.

The sugar industry is even wider in scope, for the sugar not only is consumed in the Indies but is shipped in quantity to Spain. Sugar cane grows remarkably well in various parts of the Indies. In the islands, in Mexico, in Peru, and elsewhere they have built sugar mills that do a large business. I was told that the Nasca [Peru] sugar mill earned more than thirty thousand pesos a year. The mill at Chicama, near Trujillo [Peru], was also a big enterprise, and those of New Spain are no smaller, for the consumption of sugar and preserves in the Indies is simply fantastic. From the island of Santo Domingo, in the fleet in which I came, they brought eight hundred and ninety-eight chests and boxes of sugar. I happened to see the sugar loaded at the port of Puerto Rico, and it seemed to me that each box must contain eight *arrobas*. The sugar industry is the principal business of those islands — such a taste have men developed for sweets!

Olives and olive trees are also found in the Indies, in Mexico, and in Peru, but up to now they have not set up any mills to make olive oil. Actually, it is not made at all, for they prefer to eat the olives, seasoning them well. They find it unprofitable to make olive oil, and so all their oil comes from Spain.

3. THE RISE OF THE CATTLE INDUSTRY

The Spanish introduction of all kinds of domestic animals made possible a large increase in the food supply of the Americas and in the productivity of American agriculture. Their increase in this land of almost infinite pasturage soon outstripped potential demand and utilization, and herds of wild cattle became a common phenomenon in some parts of the Spanish colonies. Although the salting process and the preparation of jerked beef (meat cut into strips and dried in the sun) were used on a limited scale before 1700, exports of cattle products before that time were largely limited to hides and tallow.[4]

I FIND THREE KINDS of animals in the Indies: some were brought there by the Spaniards;

[4] Acosta, *Historia natural de las Indias*, pp. 317–318. (Excerpt translated by the editor.)

others are of the same kind we have in Europe but were not brought over by Spaniards; and still others are indigenous to the Indies and are not found in Spain. In the first category are sheep, cows, goats, pigs, horses, donkeys, dogs, cats, and the like, for all these species are found in the Indies. The sheep have greatly multiplied, and if their wool could profitably be exported to Europe it would be one of the greatest sources of wealth in the Indies, for the flocks have immense pastures, and in some places the grass never gets parched. So great is the extent of pasture land in Peru that there are no private pastures; everyone pastures his flocks where he pleases. For this reason there is usually an abundance of cheap meat there, as well as of the other products of sheep, such as cheese, milk, and the like. For a time the wool went entirely to waste, until they set up workshops in which they make cloth and blankets. This industry has greatly helped the poor people of that land, since the cloth of Castile is very expensive.

There are a variety of workshops in Peru, but a much greater number in New Spain. Nevertheless, either because the wool is inferior or because the workmen are less expert, the cloth that comes from Spain is much finer than what is made here. There used to be men who owned seventy and even a hundred thousand head of sheep, and even today some men have herds nearly as large. In Europe this would be a great fortune, but there it is only modest wealth. In most parts of the Indies, sheep do not do very well, because the grass is so high and the soil so overgrown that only the cattle can graze there.

There are two kinds of cattle. Some are domesticated and wander in herds, as in Charcas and other provinces of Peru, and in all New Spain. They use these tame cattle as do the Spaniards — for their meat, butter, and calves, and as oxen for tilling the ground. The other kind runs wild in the woods and hills, and because of the wildness and density of the forests, and also because of the great number of these cattle, they have no brands or masters; as with any other wild game, whoever kills an animal is its owner. The cattle have multiplied so greatly in Santo Domingo, and in other islands of that region, that they wander by the thousands through the forests and fields, all masterless. They hunt these beasts only for their hides; whites and Negroes go out on horseback, equipped with a kind of hooked knife, to chase the cattle, and any animal that falls to their knives is theirs. They kill it and carry the hide home, leaving the flesh to rot — no one wants it, since meat is so plentiful. They told me in Santo Domingo that in some parts an infection has been caused by the rotting of so much flesh.

The export of hides to Spain forms one of the principal industries of the islands and New Spain. The fleet that came in 1587 brought 35,444 hides from Santo Domingo. From New Spain came 74,350 hides, valued at 96,532 pesos. When one of these fleets discharges, it is a wonderful thing to see the river at Seville, and the sandbar where they unload so many hides and so much merchandise.

There are also large numbers of goats, which in addition to the usual products — kids, milk, and so forth — yield the lucrative tallow, which rich and poor alike commonly use for lighting, because its abundance makes it cheaper than oil. . . . Tanned goat hides are also used to make footwear, but I do not believe them to be as good as those which are brought from Castile.

4. THE PROMISE OF THE PAMPA

Buenos Aires, situated on the edge of a large plain of marvelous fertility, and the natural outlet for the trade of the vast region drained by the Paraná River and its affluents, remained a provincial village or town of little importance for the greater part of the colonial period. Spanish prohibition of any seaborne commerce with the outside world, only occasionally relieved by grudging permission to send licensed vessels to Spain or Brazil, hampered the development of the teeming livestock resources of the region. In the seventeenth century the aggressive drive of Dutch, English, and other foreign merchants to break into the Spanish-American markets brought a marked growth of clandestine trade in the Plate area, and some economic relief to its inhabitants. A Frenchman by the name of Acarette, of whom very little is known, left an interesting and on the whole reliable account of his visit to Buenos Aires in 1657. However, an Argentine editor of Acarette's book questions his enthusiastic estimates of the number of cattle on the pampa at that date. The same editor doubts the truth of Acarette's story that herds of wild cattle were used to prevent hostile landings, and suggests that the traveler was the victim of a joke of fun-loving porteños *(citizens of Buenos Aires).*[5]

ALL THE WEALTH of these inhabitants consists in livestock, which multiply so prodigiously in this

[5] Acarette, *Relación de un viaje al Rio de la Plata . . . ,* edited by Julio Cesar González, Buenos Aires, 1943, pp. 45–46. (Excerpt translated by the editor.)

province that the plains are almost completely covered with them — particularly bulls, cows, sheep, horses, mares, donkeys, pigs, deer, and others — to such an extent that if it were not for the vast number of dogs that devour the calves and other young animals they would devastate the country. The people make such great profits from the skins and hides of these animals that a single example will suffice to show how it could be increased in good hands. Each of the twenty-two Dutch ships that we found in Buenos Aires was loaded with 13 to 14,000 bull hides, whose value was at least 300,–000 *livres* or 33,500 pounds sterling. These hides were bought by the Dutch at seven or eight *reales* apiece — that is, less than an English crown — and were sold in Europe for at least twenty-five English shillings.

When I expressed my surprise at the sight of such an infinite number of heads of cattle, they told me of a stratagem that they use when they fear the landing of some enemy: They drive such a multitude of bulls, cows, horses, and other animals toward the beach that it becomes impossible for any number of men, though they have no fear of the fury of the animals, to open a way for themselves through such an immense assemblage of beasts.

The first inhabitants of this place put their personal brands on the animals that they could trap and put in enclosures, but they multiplied so rapidly that they had to let them go, and now they merely kill as many as they need when they have occasion to sell a considerable number of hides. At present they only brand those horses and mules that they catch to break in and train for their own use. Some individuals carry on a large business sending these draft animals to Peru, where a pair brings fifty *patacones,* or eleven pounds, thirteen shillings, and four pence. The majority of the cattle-dealers are very rich, but of all the merchants, those who trade in European goods are most important, and many of them are reputed to be worth from 200 to 300,000 crowns, or 67,000 pounds sterling. By these standards a merchant who is not worth more than 15 or 20,000 crowns is considered a mere retailer.

5. THE POTOSÍ MINE

Spain's proudest possession in the New World was the great silver mine of Potosí in Upper Peru (present-day Bolivia), whose flow of treasure attained gigantic proportions between 1579 and 1635. More than any other colonial resource, the fantastic wealth of Potosí captivated the Spanish imagination. The following selection gives some account of this wealth and of mining practices in the late sixteenth century.[6]

IT APPEARS from the royal accounts of the House of Trade of Potosí, and it is affirmed by venerable and trustworthy men, that during the time of the government of the licentiate Polo, which was many years after the discovery of the hill, silver was registered every Saturday to the value of 150 to 200,000 pesos, of which the King's fifth (*quintos*) came to 30 to 40,000 pesos, making a yearly total of about 1,500,000 pesos. According to this calculation, the value of the daily output of the mine was 30,000 pesos, of which the King's share amounted to 6,000 pesos. One more thing should be noted in estimating the wealth of Potosí; namely, that accounts have been kept of only the silver that was marked and taxed. But it is well known in Peru that for a long time the people of that country used the silver called "current," which was neither marked nor taxed. And those who know the mines well conclude that at that time the bulk of the silver mined at Potosí paid no tax, and that this included all the silver in circulation among the Indians, and much of that in use among the Spaniards, as I could observe during my stay in that country. This leads me to believe that a third — if not one half — of the silver production of Potosí was neither registered nor taxed. . . . [It should also be noted that] although the mines of Potosí have been dug to a depth of two hundred *estados*, the miners have never encountered water, which is the greatest possible obstacle to profitable operations, whereas the mines of Porco, so rich in silver ore, have been abandoned because of the great quantity of water. For there are two intolerable burdens connected with the search for silver: the labor of digging and breaking the rock, and that of getting out the water — and the first of these is more than enough. In fine, at the present time His Catholic Majesty receives on the average a million pesos a year from his fifth of the silver of Potosí, not counting the considerable revenue he derives from quicksilver and other royal perquisites. . . .

The hill of Potosí contains four principal veins: the Rich vein, that of Centeno, the vein called "of Tin," and that of Mendieta. All these veins are in the eastern part of the hill, as if

6 Acosta, *Historia natural de las Indias*, pp. 238–243. (Excerpt translated by the editor.)

facing the sunrise; there is no vein to the west. These veins run from north to south, or from pole to pole. They measure six feet at their greatest width, and a *palmo* at the narrowest point. From these veins issue others, as smaller branches grow out of the arms of trees. Each vein has different mines that have been claimed and divided among different owners, whose names they usually bear. The largest mine is eighty yards in size, the legal maximum; the smallest is four yards. By now all these mines are very deep. In the Rich vein there are seventy-eight mines; they are as deep as one hundred and eighty and even two hundred *estados* in some places. In the Centeno vein there are twenty-four mines. Such are as much as sixty and even eighty *estados* deep, and the same is true of the other veins and mines of that hill. In order to work the mines at such great depths, tunnels (*socavones*) were devised; these are caves, made at the foot of the mountain, that cross it until they meet the veins. Although the veins run north to south, they descend from the top to the foot of the mountain — a distance calculated at more than 1200 *estados*. And by this calculation, although the mines run so deep it is six times as far again to their root and bottom, which some believe must be extremely rich, being the trunk and source of all the veins. But so far experience has proven the contrary, for the higher the vein the richer it is, and the deeper it runs the poorer the yield. Be that as it may, in order to work the mines with less cost, labor, and risk, they invented the tunnels, by means of which they can easily enter and leave the mines. They are eight feet wide and one *estado* high, and are closed off with doors. With the aid of these tunnels they get out the silver ore without difficulty, paying the owner of the tunnel a fifth of all the metal that is obtained. Nine tunnels have already been made, and others are being dug. A tunnel called "of the Poison" (*del Veneno*), which enters the Rich vein, was twenty-nine years in the making, for it was begun in 1556 (eleven years after the discovery of those mines) and was completed on April 11, 1585. This tunnel crossed the vein at a point thirty-five *estados* from its root or source, and from there to the mouth of the mine was 135 *estados*; such was the depth that they had to descend to work those mines. This tunnel (called the *Crucero*) is 250 yards in length, and its construction took twenty-nine years; this shows how much effort men will make to get silver from the bowels of the earth. They labor there in perpetual darkness, not knowing day from night; and since the sun never penetrates these places, they are not only always dark but very cold, and the air is very thick and alien to the nature of men. And that is why those who enter there for the first time get seasick, as it were, being seized with nausea and stomach cramps, as I was. The miners always carry candles, and they divide their labor so that some work by day and rest by night and others work at night and rest during the day. The silver ore is generally of a flinty hardness, and they break it up with bars. Then they carry the ore on their backs up ladders made of three cords of twisted cowhide, joined by pieces of wood that serve as rungs, so that one man can climb up and another come down at the same time. These ladders are ten *estados* long, and at the top and bottom of each there is a wooden platform where the men may rest, because there are so many ladders to climb. Each man usually carries on his back a load of two *arrobas* of silver ore tied in a cloth, knapsack fashion; thus they ascend, three at a time. The one who goes first carries a candle tied to his thumb, because, as I mentioned, they receive no light from above; thus, holding with both hands, they climb that great distance, often more than 150 *estados* — a fearful thing, the mere thought of which inspires dread. So great is the love of silver, which men suffer such great pains to obtain.

6. THE COLONIAL FACTORY

The Mexican city of Puebla was a leading industrial center in the colonial period, with numerous workshops (obrajes) *producing cotton, woolen, and silk cloth, hats, chinaware, and glass. The Englishman Gage, who visited Puebla not many years after the visit described below, observed that "the cloth which is made in it . . . is sent far and near, and [is] judged now to be as good as the cloth of Segovia, which is the best that is made in Spain." It is noteworthy that many of the factory owners, who treated their native employees so mercilessly, were themselves Indians or mestizos.*[7]

THERE ARE in this city large woolen mills in which they weave quantities of fine cloth, serge, and grogram, from which they make handsome

[7] Vásquez de Espinosa. *Description of the West Indies,* translated by C. U. Clark, pp. 133–134.

profits, this being an important business in this country. . . . To keep their mills supplied with labor for the production of cloth and grogram, they maintain individuals who are engaged and hired to ensnare poor innocents; seeing some Indian who is a stranger to the town, with some trickery or pretext, such as hiring him to carry something, like a porter, and paying him cash, they get him into the mill; once inside, they drop the deception, and the poor fellow never again gets outside that prison until he dies and they carry him out for burial. In this way they have gathered in and duped many married Indians with families, who have passed into oblivion here for 20 years, or longer, or their whole lives, without their wives or children knowing anything about them; for even if they want to get out, they cannot, thanks to the great watchfulness with which the doormen guard the exits. These Indians are occupied in carding, spinning, weaving, and the other operations of making cloth and grogram; and thus the owners make their profits by these unjust and unlawful means.

And although the Royal Council of the Indies, with the holy zeal which animates it for the service of God our Lord, of His Majesty, and of the Indians' welfare, has tried to remedy this evil with warrants and ordinances, which it constantly has sent and keeps sending, for the proper administration and the amelioration of this great hardship and enslavement of the Indians, and the Viceroy of New Spain appoints mill inspectors to visit them and remedy such matters, nevertheless, since most of those who set out on such commissions, aim rather at their own enrichment, however much it may weigh upon their consciences, than at the relief of the Indians, and since the mill owners pay them well, they leave the wretched Indians in the same slavery; and even if some of them are fired with holy zeal to remedy such abuses when they visit the mills, the mill owners keep places provided in the mills in which they hide the wretched Indians against their will, so that they do not see or find them, and the poor fellows cannot complain about their wrongs. This is the usual state of affairs in all the mills of this city and jurisdiction, and that of Mexico City; the mill owners and those who have the mills under their supervision, do this without scruple, as if it were not a most serious mortal sin.

XI

Commerce, Smuggling, and Piracy

SPAIN'S COLONIAL COMMERCIAL SYSTEM was unusually restrictive, exclusive, and regimented in character, even by the mercantilist standards of that day. Control over all colonial trade, under the Royal Council of the Indies, was vested in the *Casa de Contratación*, or House of Trade, established in 1503. Trade with the colonies was restricted until the eighteenth century to the wealthier merchants of Seville and Cadiz, who were organized in a guild that exercised great influence in all matters relating to colonial trade. With the aim of safeguarding the Seville monopoly and preventing contraband trade, only three American ports, Veracruz in New Spain, Cartagena in New Granada, and Nombre de Dios (later Portobello) on the Isthmus of Panama, were licensed to receive the Spanish merchant fleets. Inevitably the system generated colonial discontent and stimulated the growth of contraband trade.

The Spanish kings, on the basis of the papal donation of 1493 and the treaty of Tordesillas with Portugal of the following year, laid claim to all America except that portion which belonged to Portugal. By virtue of this title, all foreigners were forbidden to navigate American waters or trade on American coasts, on pain of destruction of ships and crews. The rising merchant classes and ambitious monarchs of northern Europe were unwilling to accept these pretensions. French, Dutch, and English mariners participated in the mounting offensive against Spain's monopoly in the New World, but England soon emerged as the principal threat to Spain's empire in America. Slave-trading, smuggling, and outright banditry were the various forms of the British offensive against the Spanish empire in America. "No peace beyond the line" was the formula that described the chronic warfare that raged in American waters east of the meridian of the Azores and south of the Tropic of Cancer, even while peace prevailed in Europe.

In the seventeenth century piracy and contraband were supplemented by efforts to found foreign colonies in the forbidden waters of the Spanish Main. The net result of a century of colony-building and attempts to wrest territory from Spain measured in square miles was meager: England held the large island of Jamaica, and divided with Holland and France possession of a number of small islands in the Lesser Antilles. In this period piracy became a highly-organized and large-scale activity. Piracy entered on a decline after the signing of the treaty of Madrid (1670) between England and Spain, by which the English government agreed to aid in suppressing the corsairs in return for Spanish recognition of its sovereignty over the British West Indian islands.

Contraband trade attained ever larger proportions in the course of the sixteenth and seventeenth centuries. Buenos Aires became a funnel through which foreign traders poured immense quantities of merchandise that penetrated as far as Peru. The European establishments in Jamaica and the Lesser Antilles formed another focus of forbidden trade with the Spanish colonies. This traffic, to which the colonists were driven by their unsatisfied needs, and to which the venality of local officials materially contributed, did untold damage to Spanish royal and private interests.

---

1. ON THE SEA-ROAD TO THE INDIES

Throughout the sixteenth century men and goods were carried to the colonies in much the same tiny vessels as those with which Columbus had made his memorable discovery. Danger and hardship attended

the long voyage to the Indies from the time a ship left the port of Seville at San Lucar to thread its careful way down the shoal-ridden Guadalquivir to the Mediterranean. Father Tomás de la Torre, one of a number of Dominican friars who accompanied Bishop Bartolomé de las Casas when the Protector of the In-

*dians came to Mexico in 1544, describes the trials of
an Atlantic crossing in the days of the Galleons.*[1]

AFTER BOARDING OUR SHIP we passed the day
there, exposed to a burning sun. On the following day (July 10) we hoisted sails with a very
feeble wind, because the sailors said that once
on the high seas we could navigate with any
kind of wind. That day all the other ships got
off that difficult and dangerous sandbar at San
Lucar. Only ours remained in the middle of
the bar and its dangers. They put the blame on
the land pilot; but it was really the fault of our
sailors, who had ballasted the ship badly, loading all the cargo above deck. That day the fleet
moved three leagues out, while we remained on
the bar in front of the town, enduring miseries
that made a good beginning to our labors and
perils.

When the townspeople saw that the ship remained there they thought that something had
happened, and the Duke [of Alba] sent a boat
to express the regrets of himself and his lady,
and to say that if boats were needed to get the
ship off the bar he would send them. But the
crazy sailors, very haughty about all that concerned their business, wanted no help.   The
captain of the fleet sent a small vessel to let us
know that he would wait for us only a day or
two. . . . The pilot and master of the ship,
named Pedro de Ibarra, went to give an account
of himself and to complain of the land pilot,
who, in accordance with prevailing custom, is
supposed to take the ships off the bar. . . .

The following day, which was Friday, July 11,
we raised sails and with perfectly dry eyes lost
sight of our Spain. The wind was good but
weak. The sea quickly gave us to understand
that it was not meant to be the habitation of
men, and we all became so deathly sick that
nothing in the world could move us from where
we lay. Only the Father Vicar and three others
managed to keep their feet, but these three were
so ill that they could do nothing for us; the
Father Vicar alone served us all, placing basins
and bowls before us so that we could bring up
our scanty meals, which did us no good at all.
There were four or five neophytes in our company, on their way to serve God in the Indies,
who usually took care of us, but they also became sick and had to be nursed themselves. We

could not swallow a mouthful of food, although
we were quite faint, but our thirst was intense.

One could not imagine a dirtier hospital, or
one that resounded with more lamentations,
than ours. Some men went below deck, where
they were cooked alive; others roasted in the
sun on deck, where they lay about, trampled
upon, humiliated, and indescribably filthy; and
although after several days some of them had
recovered, they were not well enough to serve
those who were still sick. His Lordship the
Bishop donated his own hens to the sick, for we
had not brought any, and a priest who was going as a schoolteacher to Chiapa helped the
Father Vicar. . . . We were a pitiful sight indeed, and there was no one to console us, since
nearly everyone was in the same condition.

When we left Spain the war with France was
at its height, so we departed in great fear of the
enemy. On the afternoon of that day those
who could raise their heads saw sixteen sails.
They feared that they were Frenchmen, and all
that night the fleet was much alarmed, although
the enemy had greater reason to fear us, because of our superior numbers. But in the
morning nothing could be seen, so we decided it
was a fleet coming from the Indies. . . . In the
evening our stomachs quieted down and we did
not vomit, but the heat, especially below deck,
was intolerable.

Saturday morning we saw a large boat, and,
thinking that it was a French spy, a ship went
after it. The bark began to escape, when the
ship fired a shot, whereupon the bark lowered
its sails, was recognized as Spanish, and was permitted to go in peace. The crews of the vessels
that heard the shot thought that we had run into
Frenchmen and that the ships were firing at each
other. When we below deck heard the noise of
arms being got ready, we were alarmed and suddenly recovered enough to say a litany; some
even confessed themselves. Others made a joke
of the whole affair. When we learned it was
nothing at all, we returned to our former supine
misery. After this there was no more disturbance.

So that those who do not know the sea may
understand the suffering one endures there,
especially at the beginning of a voyage, I shall
describe some things that are well known to anyone who has sailed on it. First, a ship is a
secure prison, from which no one may escape,
even though he wears neither shackles nor irons;
so cruel is this prison that it makes no distinctions among its inmates but makes them all suf-

---

[1] Fray Tomás de la Torre, *Desde Salamanca, España,
hasta Ciudad Real, Chiapas, Diario del viaje, 1544–1545,*
edited by Frans Blom, México, 1945, pp. 70–73. (Excerpt
translated by the editor.)

fer alike. The heat, the stuffiness, and the sense
of confinement are sometimes overpowering.
The bed is ordinarily the floor. Some bring a
few small mattresses; ours were very poor, small,
and hard, stuffed with dog hairs; to cover us we
had some extremely poor blankets of goat's wool.
Add to this the general nausea and poor health;
most passengers go about as if out of their minds
and in great torment — some longer than others,
and a few for the entire voyage. There is very
little desire to eat, and sweet things do not go
down well; there is an incredible thirst, sharp-
ened by a diet of hardtack and salt beef. The
water ration is half an *azumbre* daily; if you
want wine you must bring your own. There are
infinite numbers of lice, which eat men alive,
and you cannot wash clothing because the sea
water shrinks it. There is an evil stink, especially below deck, that becomes intolerable
throughout the ship when the pump is working
— and it is going more or less constantly, depending on how the ship sails. On a good day
the pump runs four or five times, to drain the
foul-smelling bilge water.

These and other hardships are common on
board ship, but we felt them more because they
were so foreign to our usual way of living. Furthermore, even when you are enjoying good
health there is no place where you can study or
withdraw for a little while, and you have to sit
all the time, because there is no room to walk
about. . . . The most disturbing thing of all is
to have death constantly staring you in the face;
you are separated from it by only the thickness
of one board joined to another with pitch.

2. THE PATTERN OF COLONIAL TRADE

*The Spanish colonial trade system was restrictive
and exclusive to a degree unusual even in that age of
mercantilist policies. But Spanish industry, handicapped by its guild organization and technical backwardness, was unable to supply cheap and abundant
manufactures in return for colonial foodstuffs and raw
materials, as required by the implied terms of the
mercantilist bargain. Nor was it in the interest of the
merchant monopolists of Seville, who throve on a
régime of scarcity and high prices, to permit an abundant flow of manufactures to the colonies. Inevitably
the more advanced industrial nations of northern
Europe sought to enter by force or guile into the large
and unsatisfied Spanish-American markets. Foreign
interest in the commercial possibilities of Spanish
America gave rise to a considerable body of pamphlets
and books dealing with that part of the world. John*

*Campbell (1708–1775), a popular writer on politics
and history, composed one of the best-informed works
of this type. His book went through numerous edi-
tions in the eighteenth century, suggesting the strong
interest that Englishmen took in its subject. Here
Campbell discusses the operation of the Spanish fleet
system.[2]*

IT HAS BEEN ALWAYS the ruling maxim in the
Spanish councils to preserve by all means possible the commerce with the West Indies, not
only to the Spanish nation, but to the crown of
Spain. On this principle they restrained, with
great punctuality, all strangers from passing into
their American dominions; and though there
have been formerly some instances of foreigners
passing through the Spanish settlements, and
even residing in them, yet they are so rare, and
attended with such extraordinary circumstances,
that instead of admiring that such things have
happened, we ought rather to wonder that they
have not happened more frequently, considering the strong passion that strangers have always had for penetrating unknown countries,
especially such countries as Mexico and Peru,
rich in themselves, and represented much richer
than they were. . . . Thus we see that the lawful
commerce between Europe and Spanish America is entirely in the hands of the Spaniards, and
absolutely subject to the direction of the crown.

The method in which this trade is carried on
is well enough known in general, but few enter
far enough into its particulars. In order to give
as distinct an account of this matter as possible,
we shall speak of the Galleons, the Flota, the
Flotilla, Register-Ships, and Guardas Costas; and
when we have done this, the reader will perfectly comprehend the mystery of the Spanish
policy in this point.

A Galleon is, properly speaking, a very large
man-of-war, of three or four decks, built in a
manner now altogether out of fashion, except in
Spain; and the reason why it is still used there,
is, that it affords a great deal of room for merchandise, with which the king's ships are generally so much crowded, as to be in no condition of defending themselves. That fleet which
we call the Galleons, consists of eight such men-
of-war. Of these there are three very large ones,
styled *la Capitana*, *la Almiranta*, and *el Gobierno*; two others which are less, *la Patacha*, and
la Margarita, each of fifty guns; and an advice
frigate of forty. The merchant-men which sail

2 John Campbell, *The Spanish Empire in America*, London, 1747, pp. 279–286.

with this fleet, and purchase their licences at a very high rate, are in number from twelve to sixteen, and burthen at least a third part bigger than is expressed in their respective schedules. These ships are intended to carry all that is necessary, either of warlike stores, or merchandise for Peru: and this is the specific difference between this fleet and the Flota, which is intended for Mexico. In time of peace, the Galleons sail regularly once a year from Cadiz, at no set time, but according to the king's pleasure, and the convenience of the merchants. From Cadiz the Galleons steer directly for the Canaries, where, if the Flota sailed with them, as it sometimes does, they anchor together in the haven of Gomera. Thence they bear away for the Antilles, and when they arrive at that height, the Flota separates, and the Galleons bear away for Cartagena. As soon as they double Cape de la Vela, and appear before the mouth of Rio de la Hacha, advice is sent to all parts, that every thing may be got ready for their reception. In the harbour of Cartagena they remain a month, and land there all the goods designed for the Audience of the Terra Firma. Then they sail to Porto Bello, where they continue during the fair, which lasts five or six weeks; and having landed the merchandise intended for Peru, and received the treasure and rich commodities sent from thence on board, they sail again to Cartagena, where they remain till they return to Spain, which is usually within the space of two years. When they have orders to return, they sail first to the Havana, and having there joined the Flota, and what other ships are returning to Europe, they steer through the gulf of Florida, and so to the height of Carolina, where meeting with the western winds, they shape their course then for the Azores. They take in fresh water and provisions at Tercera, and thence continue their voyage to Cadiz.

The Flota consists, as well as the Galleons, of a certain number of men-of-war, and of a certain number of merchant ships. The former are seldom more than three, *la Capitana, la Almiranta,* and *la Patacha.* The latter are usually about sixteen, in burthen between five hundred and a thousand tons. This fleet sails about the month of August, that by the favour of the winds which reign about November, they may the more easily pursue their voyage to Vera Cruz. In their passage they call at Puerto Rico, to take in fresh water and provisions, then pass in sight of Hispaniola, Jamaica, and Cuba; and, according to the season of the year, and the nature of the

winds, pass either by the coast of Yucatan, or higher thro' the gulf of Vera Cruz, two hundred and sixty leagues in twelve days, or thereabouts; in all eighteen hundred and ten leagues in about sixty-two days. As the Flota is designed to furnish not only Mexico, but the Philippine Islands also, as we have before remarked in speaking of the trade of Acapulco, with European goods, they are obliged to remain there for a considerable space; and, when it is necessary, they winter in that port. The cargo with which they return, is not so rich as that of the Galleons; but some writers say, that it increases annually in its value, which must be owing to the progress made in settling what the Spaniards call the Kingdom of New Mexico.

It is usually in the month of May that the Flota leaves Vera Cruz, though sometimes it is detained in that harbour till August. Then the ships that compose it, sail for the Havana; for though the Galleons and the Flota seldom leave Spain, yet they generally return, together. As soon as they are safely arrived in the Havana, they detach a few of the lightest and cleanest ships to Europe, who, besides money and merchandise, carry also an exact account of the contents both of the Galleons and Flota. These ships are called by the Spaniards, with propriety enough, the Flotilla, i.e. the little fleet. The principal reason for sending them in this manner into Spain, is to give the court of Madrid an opportunity of judging what convoy may be necessary, in case of any alteration of affairs, to be sent to escort the grand fleet, as also to regulate the *Indulto* which may be levied on the merchants in proportion to their interest in the Galleons and Flota. But the reader may possibly incline to enquire what obliges this great fleet to remain so long at the Havana? To which two causes may be assigned, viz. waiting for a wind, or for the register-ships which they are to convoy home.

A register-ship is so called, from its being registered with all the effects embarked in Spain, in the books kept for that purpose in the Chamber of Seville. As this general account will not probably appear satisfactory, I shall endeavour to state the matter more fully. A company of merchants having, as they conceive, just grounds to imagine that European goods are greatly wanted at some particular ports in the West Indies, they draw up a memorial or petition, containing these reasons in the clearest and concisest terms, and lay it before the Council of the Indies. The prayer of this petition is, that they may have leave to send a ship of three hundred ton burthen, or under, to the port they mention. When leave is obtained, they pay a certain sum to the crown, which is generally between thirty and fifty thousand pieces of eight, besides presents, and those no small ones, to the king's officers, from the greatest to the last. That this however may not induce any suspicion of fraud, they register their ship and cargo, that it may appear consistent with their petition and licence, and yet (such a fatality there attends on all custom-house actions) this ship of under three hundred tons generally carries upwards of six hundred tons of goods, and affords accommodation for passengers besides. Copies from the register are transmitted to the governor and royal officers at the port, to which the register-ship is bound; and such is their diligence, such their integrity, that when the ship comes to an anchor in the port, they make a very narrow enquiry, and yet there is seldom or never any fraud discovered, but, on the contrary, this ship of six or seven hundred tons returns into Europe with an authentic certificate from all the King of Spain's officers, that she does not carry quite three hundred, together with a bill of lading in the same strain of computation. By these register-ships there is sometimes a gain of two, or three hundred per cent, which enables the owners to pay so bountifully for cheating the King, having first got the money by robbing his subjects.

3. THE GREAT FAIR AT PORTOBELLO

After 1584 the chief port of entry for the legal commerce with South America was the little town of Portobello on the Isthmus of Panama. For a few weeks during the year a brisk trade, strictly supervised by royal officials, was plied in the town square. In the 1730's, when the Portobello fair was visited by two youthful Spanish scientists and naval officers, Jorge Juan (1713–1773), and Antonio Ulloa (1716–1795), it had long passed its heyday, principally because of the growing influx of foreign interlopers into colonial trade, but it still presented a scene of considerable business activity.[3]

THE TOWN OF PORTO BELLO, so thinly inhabited, by reason of its noxious air, the scarcity of provisions, and the soil, becomes, at the time of the galleons, one of the most populous places in all South America. Its situation on the isthmus betwixt the south and north sea, the goodness of

its harbour, and its small distance from Panama, have given it the preference for the rendezvous of the joint commerce of Spain and Peru, at its fair.

On advice being received at Carthagena, that the Peru fleet had unloaded at Panama, the galleons make the best of their way to Porto Bello, in order to avoid the distempers which have their source from idleness. The concourse of people, on this occasion, is such, as to raise the rent of lodging to an excessive degree; a middling chamber, with a closet, lets, during the fair, for a thousand crowns, and some large houses for four, five, or six thousand.

The ships are no sooner moored in the harbour, than the first work is, to erect, in the square, a tent made of the ship's sails, for receiving its cargo; at which the proprietors of the goods are present, in order to find their bales, by the marks which distinguish them. These bales are drawn on sledges, to their respective places by the crew of every ship, and the money given them is proportionally divided.

Whilst the seamen and European traders are thus employed, the land is covered with droves of mules from Panama, each drove consisting of above an hundred, loaded with chests of gold and silver, on account of the merchants of Peru. Some unload them at the exchange, others in the middle of the square; yet, amidst the hurry and confusion of such crowds, no theft, loss, or disturbance, is ever known. He who has seen this place during the *tiempo muerto,* or dead time, solitary, poor, and a perpetual silence reigning everywhere; the harbour quite empty, and every place wearing a melancholy aspect; must be filled with astonishment at the sudden change, to see the bustling multitudes, every house crowded, the square and streets encumbered with bales and chests of gold and silver of all kinds; the harbour full of ships and vessels, some bringing by the way of Rio de Chape the goods of Peru, as cacao, quinquina, or Jesuit's bark, Vicuña wool, and bezoar stones; others coming from Carthagena, loaded with provisions; and thus a spot, at all other times detested for its deleterious qualities, becomes the staple of the riches of the old and new world, and the scene of one of the most considerable branches of commerce in the whole earth.

The ships being unloaded, and the merchants of Peru, together with the president of Panama, arrived, the fair comes under deliberation. And for this purpose the deputies of the several parties repair on board the commodore of the gal-

3 George Juan and Antonio de Ulloa, *A Voyage to South America,* London, 1772, 2 vols., I, pp. 103–105.

leons, where, in presence of the commodore, and the president of Panama; the former, as patron of the Europeans, and the latter, of the Peruvians; the prices of the several kinds of merchandizes are settled; and all preliminaries being adjusted in three or four meetings, the contracts are signed, and made public, that every one may conform himself to them in the sale of his effects. Thus all fraud is precluded. The purchases and sales, as likewise the exchanges of money, are transacted by brokers, both from Spain and Peru. After this, every one begins to dispose of his goods; the Spanish brokers embarking their chests of money, and those of Peru sending away the goods they have purchased, in vessels called chatas and bongos, up the river Chagre. And thus the fair of Porto Bello ends.

Formerly this fair was limited to no particular time; but as a long stay, in such a sickly place, extremely affected the health of the traders, his Catholic majesty transmitted an order, that the fair should not last above forty days, reckoning from that in which the ships came to an anchor in the harbour; and that, if in this space of time the merchants could not agree in their rates, those of Spain should be allowed to carry their goods up the country to Peru; and accordingly the commodore of the galleons has orders to reimbark them, and return to Carthagena; but otherwise, by virtue of a compact between the merchants of both kingdoms, and ratified by the king, no Spanish trader is to send his goods, on his own account, beyond Porto Bello: and, on the contrary, those of Peru cannot send remittances to Spain, for purchasing goods there.

4. JOHN HAWKINS: MERCHANT ADVENTURER

The famous trading voyage of John Hawkins to Hispaniola in 1563 opened the great struggle between England and Spain for world supremacy. Half honest trader, half corsair, Hawkins came to the Indies heavily armed and ready to compel the colonists to deal with him at cannon point, but he showed himself scrupulously correct in his business dealings with the Spaniards, even to the point of paying the royal license and customs dues. Hawkins owed the success of his first two American voyages to the needs of the Spanish settlers, who were ready to trade with a Lutheran heretic or the Devil himself to satisfy their desperate need for slave labor and European goods.

To cover up these violations of Spanish law, the venal local officials made a thin pretense of enforcement. But by 1567 the pretense had worn too thin, the Spanish government had taken alarm, and angry orders went out to drive the English contrabandists away. An official report describes the reception accorded to Hawkins on his third voyage, at the town of Rio de la Hacha on the Venezuelan coast.[4]

ON JUNE 10 of the current year John Hawkins, English corsair, arrived off the port of this city. He came in command of ten very handsome ships, which he said belonged to the queen of England, his mistress. As soon as he had arrived off this port he sent me a letter in which he offered me great gifts, if I would permit him to trade; and if I would not, he made great threats. I answered him what your majesty has ordered and provided in your majesty's royal orders and provisions, and that I would by no means yield a single point from the tenor of those commands.

In view of my determination, after much argument, he landed his forces three-quarters of a league down the coast, beyond all my defences and bulwarks, and out of range of the artillery which in your majesty's service I have placed here. Seeing this, I went out with all the men there were in this town to see if I could manage to prevent him from landing; although inasmuch as the enemy's number was so overwhelming and we were so few, it seemed to me to be madness to attempt to oppose the attack of such superior forces.

The Englishman having landed his party, with what few persons were available in the place I manned a fort which is built on the road by which he must advance, and there disputed his passage as fully as I was able. From that work I inflicted serious damage on him, but because of his superior numbers we were unable to prevent him from taking the fort, for from his pinnaces and shallops he played so many guns on the fort, not a man dared to remain in any part of it. When he had taken the fort, he also took the town.

I assembled the people of the place in as good order as possible and retired to a point from which I could prevent his advance, although my force was badly cut up. My hope was to keep a fighting body together that the enemy might not

4 *Spanish Documents Concerning English Voyages to the Caribbean, 1527–1568*, translated and edited by Irene A. Wright, London, the Hakluyt Society, 1929, pp. 120–123.

forget himself and begin to capture the women, children, aged and ill, who were scattered over the adjacent countryside.

When he had taken the town the Englishman again sent word to permit trade, saying that unless I did so he would burn and destroy the town and invade the interior and capture and steal whatever he might find. I answered him to do as he pleased, since I preferred to lose my worldly goods rather than to yield a jot of your majesty's commands. Immediately upon the messenger's arrival there he began to fire the town and that day he burned about half of it.

The next day in the morning he set out with as many as four hundred men and his field artillery, to invade the land. I opposed him with the few men I had. Wherever he turned I preceded him, doing what damage I could to his men, and burning and destroying the fields and food crops and farmhouses belonging to the people of the town. Seeing that their very owners were destroying their own houses and estates, the Englishman returned to the town in very desperate humour and burned the government house and another large portion of the town. Excepting only certain houses he needed to shelter his men, he left no others standing. He spared about one-third of the town and burned two-thirds of it.

That night a negro and mulatto, slaves of mine, deserted to the enemy and told him they would lead him to the place, seven leagues from this city, where I had buried your majesty's royal treasure-chest, and that night they fell on a tent where I had all my goods, and where some poor and sick people and some women were in hiding. They seized these and robbed their poverty and stole everything I had, and threatened them that unless they were ransomed they would be killed. They released a prisoner that he might come to tell me the pitiable lamentations of the rest. In order that such grievous cruelty might not be carried out, for 4000 *pesos* gold I redeemed them and what remained to be burned of the town, including its holy church, on condition that they deliver to me the mulatto and the negro aforesaid.

I paid over the 4000 *pesos* and the enemy released the prisoners. Although they promised to restore the property that had been taken from them, they did not fulfil this promise. On the contrary, they stole it and carried it off. They reembarked and delivered to me the mulatto and the negro and I handed them over to your majesty's royal law that they might be punished and made an example to all the rest on this coast, and so the mulatto was hung and the negro quartered.

Before they cleared, after this ransom had been arranged, because they were unable to feed them, the English set a certain number of negroes ashore rather than throw them overboard. Some were children not over six years of age, and some were old males and old females (over a hundred years). Although the Englishman left them in recompense for the damage he did the town, acting with the royal officials I took possession of them all for your majesty and delivered them to a certain person to feed them through two or three months and so put them into condition that they might be worth something. We are now selling them off little by little despite the fact that the burghers demand them, alleging that the Englishman left them to pay for the damage done the town. I assure your majesty that had he left as many again it would not cover the damage he did here.

5. "No Peace Beyond the Line"

Returning from his third voyage to the Indies, Hawkins encountered storms in the Florida channel that forced him to seek refuge in the port of Veracruz in September, 1568. There he was attacked by a large Spanish fleet bringing the new viceroy of Mexico, Don Martin Enriquez. Only two of the English ships managed to get away; one was commanded by Hawkins, the other by his cousin, Francis Drake. Four years later Drake left England with four small ships, bound for the Isthmus of Panama. In actions marked by audacity and careful planning he stormed and plundered the town of Nombre de Dios, escaping at dawn; later he made the most lucrative haul in the history of piracy by capturing the pack-train carrying Peruvian silver from the Pacific side of the isthmus to Nombre de Dios. In 1577 Drake set sail again on an expedition that had the secret sponsorship and support of Queen Elizabeth. Its objects were to "singe the King of Spain's beard" by seizing his treasure-ships and ravaging his colonial towns; to explore the whole Pacific coast of America, taking possession of the regions beyond the limits of Spanish occupation; and to display English maritime prowess through a second circumnavigation of the globe. Drake achieved these ends without shedding the blood of a single Spaniard. The involuntary respect and liking that he inspired even in a Spanish enemy appear in the following letter from Don Francisco de Zárate to Viceroy En-

ríquez of New Spain, describing his captivity on board the Golden Hind.[5]

ON THE FOLLOWING DAY, which was Sunday, in the morning, he dressed and decked himself very finely and had his galleon decorated with all its flags and banners. He also ordered that all the men on our ship be passed to another one of his, which he had taken on this same coast, and which had served for this purpose since he reached the coast of Chile, where he had on his hands a ship laden with a large quantity of gold and many others laden with silver. He had entered the port of Callao de Lima and cut the cables of all the ships that were in port. As the wind was from the land, they all went out to sea, where he had time to sack them at his will. Before he proceeded to do the same to ours he said to me: "Let one of your pages come with me to show me your apparel." He went from his galleon at about nine in the morning and remained until towards dusk, examining everything contained in the bales and chests. Of that which belonged to me he took but little. Indeed he was quite courteous about it. Certain trifles of mine having taken his fancy, he had them brought to his ship and gave me, in exchange for them, a falchion and a small brazier of silver, and I can assure Your Excellency that he lost nothing by the bargain. On his return to his vessel he asked me to pardon him for taking the trifles, but that they were for his wife. He said that I could depart the next morning, when the breeze would rise, for which I gave him thanks. . . .

This general of the Englishmen is a nephew * of John Hawkins, and is the same who, about five years ago, took the port of Nombre de Dios. He is called Francisco Drac, and is a man about 35 years of age, low of stature, with a fair beard, and is one of the greatest mariners that sails the seas, both as a navigator and as a commander. His vessel is a galleon of nearly four hundred tons, and is a perfect sailor. She is manned with a hundred men, all of service, and of an age for warfare, and all are as practised therein as old soldiers from Italy could be. Each one takes particular pains to keep his arquebuse clean. He treats them with affection, and they treat him with respect. He carries with him nine or ten cavaliers, cadets of English noblemen.

These form a part of his council which he calls together for even the most trivial matter, although he takes advice from no one. But he enjoys hearing what they say and afterwards issues his orders. He has no favourite.

The aforesaid gentlemen sit at his table, as well as a Portuguese pilot, whom he brought from England, who spoke not a word during all the time I was on board. He is served on silver dishes with gold borders and gilded garlands, on which are his arms. He carries all possible dainties and perfumed waters. He said that many of these had been given him by the Queen.

None of these gentlemen took a seat or covered his head before him until he repeatedly urged him to do so. This galleon of his carries about thirty heavy pieces of artillery and a great quantity of firearms with the requisite ammunition and lead. He dines and sups to the music of viols. He carries trained carpenters and artisans, so as to be able to careen the ship at any time. Besides being new, the ship has double lining. I understood that all the men he carries with him receive wages, because, when our ship was sacked, no man dared take anything without his orders. He shows them great favour, but punishes the least fault. He also carries painters who paint for him pictures of the coast in its exact colours. This I was most grieved to see, for each thing is so naturally depicted that no one who guides himself according to these paintings can possibly go astray. I understood from him that he had sailed from his country with five vessels, four sloops (of the long kind) and that half of the armada belonged to the Queen.

6. THE BROTHERHOOD OF THE COAST

The seventeenth century saw a marked increase in privateering and piratical activity in Spanish-American waters. Chronic warfare between Spain and her European rivals, and Spain's stubborn refusal to concede the right of other powers to trade or navigate in the waters "beyond the line," provided these powers with a convenient pretext for tolerating and even fomenting piratical enterprise against Spanish colonial shipping and coastal towns. Jamaica, captured by the British in 1655; the western end of the island of Hispaniola; and the neighboring island of Tortuga became the principal lairs of the buccaneers. The typical pirate captain of the latter half of the seventeenth century was quite free of patriotic or religious zeal, and plied his trade in the calculating spirit of a businessman engaged in a likely speculation. John Esquemeling, a Dutch ex-corsair who wrote a valuable

---

[5] *New Light on Drake*, translated and edited by Zella Nuttall, London, the Hakluyt Society, 1914, pp. 204–208.

* Zárate was mistaken: Drake was Hawkins' cousin. B.K.

account of the exploits of the leading pirates of his time, describes the mode of operation of the "Brethren of the Coast," the name the buccaneers commonly gave to themselves.[6]

Before the Pirates go out to sea, they give notice to every one that goes upon the voyage, of the day on which they ought precisely to embark, intimating also to them their obligation of bringing each man in particular so many pounds of powder and bullets as they think necessary for that expedition. Being all come on board, they join together in council, concerning what place they ought first to go to wherein to get provisions — especially of flesh, seeing that they scarce eat anything else. And of this the most common sort among them is pork. The next food is tortoises, which they are accustomed to salt a little. Sometimes they resolve to rob such or such hog-yards, wherein the Spaniards often have a thousand heads of swine together. They come to these places in the dark of the night, and having beset the keeper's lodge, they force him to rise, and give them as many heads as they desire, threatening withal to kill him in case he disobeys their commands or makes any noise. Yea, these menaces are oftentimes put in execution, without giving any quarter to the miserable swine-keepers, or any other person that endeavours to hinder their robberies.

Having got provisions of flesh sufficient for their voyage, they return to their ship. Here their allowance, twice a day to every one, is as much as he can eat, without either weight or measure. Neither does the steward of the vessel give any greater proportion of flesh, or anything else to the captain than to the meanest mariner. The ship being well victualled, they call another council, to deliberate towards what place they shall go, to seek their desperate fortunes. In this council, likewise, they agree upon certain Articles, which are put in writing, by way of bond or obligation, which every one is bound to observe, and all of them, or the chief, set their hands to it. Herein they specify, and set down very distinctly, what sums of money each particular person ought to have for that voyage, the fund of all the payments being the common stock of what is gotten by the whole expedition; for otherwise it is the same law, among these people, as with other Pirates, *No prey, no pay.* In the first place, therefore, they mention how much the Captain ought to have for his ship.

Next the salary of the carpenter, or shipwright, who careened, mended and rigged the vessel. This commonly amounts to one hundred or an hundred and fifty pieces of eight, being, according to the agreement, more or less. Afterwards for provisions and victualling they draw out of the same common stock about two hundred pieces of eight. Also a competent salary for the surgeon and his chest of medicaments, which usually is rated at two hundred or two hundred and fifty pieces of eight. Lastly they stipulate in writing what recompense or reward each one ought to have, that is either wounded or maimed in his body, suffering the loss of any limb, by that voyage. Thus they order for the loss of a right arm six hundred pieces of eight, or six slaves; for the loss of a left arm five hundred pieces of eight, or five slaves; for a right leg five hundred pieces of eight, or five slaves; for the left leg four hundred pieces of eight, or four slaves; for an eye one hundred pieces of eight, or one slave; for a finger of the hand the same reward as for the eye. All which sums of money, as I have said before, are taken out of the capital sum or common stock of what is got by their piracy. For a very exact and equal dividend is made of the remainder among them all. Yet herein they have also regard to qualities and places. Thus the Captain, or chief Commander, is allotted five or six portions to what the ordinary seamen have; the Master's Mate only two; and other Officers proportionate to their employment. After whom they draw equal parts from the highest even to the lowest mariner, the boys not being omitted. For even these draw half a share, by reason that, when they happen to take a better vessel than their own, it is the duty of the boys to set fire to the ship or boat wherein they are, and then retire to the prize which they have taken.

They observe among themselves very good orders. For in the prizes they take, it is severely prohibited to every one to usurp anything in particular to themselves. Hence all they take is equally divided, accordingly to what has been said before. Yea, they make a solemn oath to each other not to abscond, or conceal the least thing they find amongst the prey. If afterwards any one is found unfaithful, who has contravened the said oath, immediately he is separated and turned out of the society. Among themselves they are very civil and charitable to each other. Insomuch that if any wants what another has, with great liberality they give it one to another. As soon as these Pirates have taken any

---

[6] John Esquemeling, *The Buccaneers of America*, London, 1893, pp. 58–60.

prize of ship or boat, the first thing they endeavour is to set on shore the prisoners, detaining only some few for their own help and service, to whom also they give their liberty after the space of two or three years. They put in very frequently for refreshment at one island or another; but more especially into those which lie on the Southern side of the Isle of Cuba. Here they careen their vessels, and in the meantime some of them go to hunt, others to cruize upon the seas in canoes, seeking their fortune. Many times they take the poor fishermen of tortoises, and, carrying them to their habitations, they make them work so long as the Pirates are pleased.

7. DOING BUSINESS IN THE SMUGGLING WAY

Smuggling was the principal weapon employed by the rising industrial powers of Europe to batter down the wall of commercial monopoly that surrounded Spain's American possessions. Colonial merchants and consumers alike were glad of the opportunity to buy cheap foreign wares and dispose of their own surplus products. The royal officials in the colonies, corrupt almost to a man, most often connived with local merchants at the introduction of contraband goods. A useful survey of the subject appears in Campbell's work on the Spanish empire in America.[7]

THE METHODS taken by his most Catholic Majesty for effectually securing the commerce of his American dominions to the inhabitants of Old Spain, is the grand source of the little respect paid him in the Indies, and of the great weakness of his government at home. The inhabitants of the Spanish America consider gold and silver as commodities, which they have, and would willingly barter for some other commodities, which they have not, and which would be more useful to them than large heaps of either of those metals. It seems therefore to these people a great hardship, that either proper care is not taken to furnish them with what they want from Spain, or that they should not be allowed to supply themselves some other way. The native Spaniards, who have the government of the Indies entirely in their hands, treat such complaints with haughtiness natural to that nation, which renders them universally odious and insupportable. . . .

When folks are in such a situation, there need

7 John Campbell, *The Spanish Empire in America*, pp. 306–310, 315–319.

be no wonder at their endeavouring to carry on a clandestine trade, as, on the other hand, one cannot think it strange that their neighbours, who live under better governments, who have at cheap rates all that these Spaniards want, and yet stand in need of the silver and gold with which they abound, should be very willing to commence such an intercourse as might take away all their wants. Sometimes governors have winked at this, not from a principle of avarice only, that they might share in the profits resulting from such a trade, but also from a sense of the necessity of dispensing with laws so ill executed as to deserve no respect. For, to be sure, that rule of justice, which connects the Spanish plantations to Spain, requires that the government of Spain should have a reciprocal regard for those plantations; and a neglect on one part infers licence on the other. Upon this principle it was, that before the treaty of Utrecht the English at Jamaica furnished the Spaniards at Porto Bello with Negroes, with the knowledge at least, if not by the permission of the governors. The inhabitants of Peru never could be without slaves. The government of Old Spain never could, indeed never attempted to supply them, but permitted sometimes the Genoese, sometimes the French to carry on this trade; and when they did not do it effectually, the deficiency was made good by such a commerce as I before mentioned with the English, though without any formal licence, but by a connivance, the less criminal for its being absolutely necessary.

The situation of the island of Jamaica, together with the conveniences of building and freighting sloops from thence, engaged the inhabitants in this, and in other branches of traffic. Such as settle themselves in these distant parts of the world, do it generally from a spirit of getting, and therefore the grand point with them is always how to get most. They therefore for a long tract of time, and by various methods, not necessary to be insisted on here, supplied the Spaniards at Carthagena, Porto Bello, Rio de la Hacha, and other places with European commodities of all sorts, notwithstanding the mighty hazard they ran in the management of so dangerous a business, their own lives, and those of their customers, being alike exposed, and frequently forfeited to what the Spaniards call justice. They likewise carried on a trade with the Indians of Darien, to their great profit, but with equal risk, for the Spaniards were wont to shew no mercy either to English or Indians that fell into their hands; which is so much the harder, since the latter never were their subjects, nor ever will have any intercourse with them. By degrees the gains by this commerce tempted so many persons to be concerned in it, and the ships made use of were so well manned, and of such force, that the Spaniards grew less timorous than formerly; so that at last the commerce by the Galleons was greatly affected; for, knowing where to buy goods cheaper, the merchants would not give the prices usually demanded at the fairs of Carthagena and Porto Bello. . . .

The little island of St. Thomas, which lies in the North Seas, about fourteen leagues off Porto Rico, is the sole colony possessed by the Danes in the West Indies; nor would it be worth the keeping, but as it serves to maintain an illicit trade with the Spanish islands in its neighbourhood. We may form some idea of the vast advantages flowing from this contraband commerce, from this very particular, especially if we consider that the Hamburgers have likewise a factory in this little isle purely on the same score. In order to maintain this correspondence, they transport from the Danish colonies in Africa a considerable number of slaves for the supply of Porto Rico, and sometimes of the Spanish part of the island of St. Domingo. Under color of this trade, a commerce in European goods is carried on; and we may easily discern how hard the Spaniards are to it for the necessaries, or at least the conveniences of life, when we find them trading to a place which is a free port to privateers and pirates of all nations, who there vend openly, and in the very sight of the Spaniards, what they have taken from them in the basest and most barbarous manner possible, and yet so tame are they, that they not only bear this with patience, but will even purchase commodities from these very buccaneers. Of late years other nations have made an advantage of this free port, and keep warehouses there of all sorts of commodities, for the service of such customers, as will run the hazard of coming at them; and in time of war the privateers never want a market in this place.

The Portuguese at Rio Janeiro entertain also a very beneficial correspondence with their Spanish neighbours. The goods with which they supply them, are sugars, indigo, tobacco, wines, brandies, and rums, with some European goods, and sometimes slaves. The inhabitants of this colony are far more industrious than the rest of the Brazil planters; and this gives them an opportunity of gaining considerably by the inhabitants of Buenos Ayres, and other places on the River of Plate. . . .

Besides these methods of trading, which we have hitherto spoken of, there is another common to all nations, with the mention of which we shall conclude. Ships frequently approach the Spanish coasts under pretence of wanting water, wood, provisions, or more commonly, in order to stop a leak. The first thing that is done in such a case, is to give notice to the governor of their great distress, and, as a full proof thereof, to send a very considerable present. By this means leave is obtained to come on shore, to erect a warehouse, and to unlade the ship, but then all this is performed under the eye of the king's officers, and the goods are regularly entered in a register as they are brought into the warehouse, which when full is shut up, and the doors sealed. All these precautions taken, the business is effectually carried on in the night by a back-door, and the European goods being taken out, indigo, cochineal, vinellos, tobacco, and above all bars of silver and pieces of eight are very exactly packed in the same cases, and placed as they stood before. But then, that such as have bought may be able to sell publicly, a new scheme takes place. A petition is presented to the governor, setting forth the stranger's want of money to pay for provisions, building the warehouse, timber for repairing the ship, and a proportionable number of such like items; in consideration of all which, leave is desired to dispose of some small part of their cargo, in order to discharge these debts. This being obtained in the usual manner, something of each sort of goods which had been privately sold, is now publicly brought to market, and purchased by those persons respectively who had larger quantities in their warehouses before. Thus the whole of this scene of iniquity is transacted with all the formal solemnity which could attend an act of justice and compassion.

8. A FOREIGN VIEW OF THE SPANISH COMMERCIAL SYSTEM

By the opening of the eighteenth century it was apparent to thoughtful Spaniards and foreign observers alike that the Spanish commercial policy in the colonies was a dismal failure from the point of view of the general interests of the mother country. The English publicist Campbell offered a shrewd analysis of the reasons for this failure. Historians generally concur in his argument that it sprang not from any want of intelligence or industry in such able rulers as Charles V and Phillip II, but from an incorrect policy that neglected the development of domestic commerce and industry and squandered the vast revenues obtained from the colonies in ruinous European wars aiming at the achievement of "universal empire." [8]

THERE IS NOTHING more common than to hear Spain compared to a sieve, which, whatever it receives, is never the fuller. How common soever the comparison may be, most certainly it is a very true one; but the means by which all this immense wealth, or at least the far greatest part of it is drawn from the Spaniards, and conveyed to other nations, and in what proportions, is neither so well, nor so generally understood. To account for this shall be our present task. . . .

If after the discovery of the New World, as the Spaniards justly enough called it, the government had encouraged trade or manufactures, there is great probability that the supreme direction of the affairs of Europe would have fallen into the hands of the Catholic Kings. For, if all the subjects of Spain, without restraint, had traded to these far distant regions, this must have created such a maritime force, as no other nation could have withstood. Or, supposing the trade had been restrained as it is at present, yet, if manufactures had been encouraged, so as that the greatest part of the trade of the West Indies had been driven without having recourse to foreigners, such prodigious sums of money must have rested in Spain, as would have enabled its monarchs to have given law to all their neighbours. But, by neglecting these obvious, and yet certain rules for establishing solid and extensive at least, if not universal dominion, her kings had recourse to those refinements in policy, which, however excellent they may seem in theory, have never yet been found to answer in practice. They were for fixing their commerce by constraint, and for establishing power by the sword; the first, experience has shewn to be impracticable, and the latter, perhaps was the only method whereby they could have missed that end they used it to obtain. In short, by repeated endeavours to secure the wealth of the Indies to Spain absolutely, they scattered it throughout Europe, and, by openly grasping at universal monarchy, they alarmed those they might

have subdued; so that in process of time, some of those they intended for slaves became their equals and allies, and some their masters.

Yet the princes that took these steps were not either rash and hasty, or voluptuous and profuse, but, on the contrary, were esteemed by all the world the wisest monarchs of their respective times, and, in many things deserved to be so esteemed. They erred, not through want of capacity, or want of application, as their successors did, but for want of considering things in a right light, occasioned purely by their fixing their eyes on that dazzling meteor, universal empire. . . .

From what has been said it is evident, that however wise, however penetrating these princes might be, they certainly overshot themselves in their schemes concerning the Western Indies. Instead of looking upon it as an estate, they seemed to think it only a farm, of which they were to make presently the most they could. In doing this, it must be owned, they acted with skill and vigour, for they drew immense sums from thence, which they wasted in Europe to disturb others, and in the end to destroy their own state. Mr. Lewis Roberts, author of the *Map of Commerce,* an excellent book for the time in which it was written, tells us, that it appeared by the records in the custom-house of Seville, that in the space of seventy-four years, computing backwards from the time in which he wrote, the kings of Spain had drawn into that country from America, two hundred and fifty millions of gold, which make about ninety-one millions sterling. He also observes that . . . Philip II . . . spent more in his reign than all his predecessors in the whole of their respective reigns; though no less than 62 kings had reigned before him. Yet this cunning, this ambitious monarch left his subjects in a manner quite exhausted, and, by establishing a most pernicious system of politics, left the total ruining of his dominions by way of legacy to his successors, a point which with wonderful obstinacy they have pursued ever since.

All who are in any degree acquainted with the history of Europe know, that for a long course of years Spain maintained wars in Flanders, Germany, Italy, and sometimes in Ireland, which created a prodigious expense of treasure and of troops; neither of which from the death of Charles V they were in any condition to spare. As families were reduced by the expense of serving in the army, they were inclined to seek new fortunes in the West Indies: and thus

---

[8] Campbell, *The Spanish Empire in America,* pp. 291–299.

numbers went over thither, not to cultivate the country, or to improve trade, but to strip and plunder those who were there before them. Other great families again concurred with the measures of the crown, in hopes of vice-royalties, and other valuable offices in its conquests: but if ever their schemes were beneficial to their families, which may admit of doubt, certain it is that they contributed more and more to the ruin of the Spanish nation. For, though his Catholic Majesty once possessed Naples, Sicily, Sardinia, Milan, with other territories in Italy, besides all the Low Countries, and some other provinces which are now lost; yet, for want of attending to commerce, and by having no sort of economy, all this turned to his prejudice; and it plainly appeared towards the close of the last century, that with all their boasted sagacity and firmness, the Spaniards had ruined themselves by acquiring too great power, and rendered themselves beggars by misusing their immense riches. With swelling titles and wide dominions, they were despicably weak, and scarce any but copper money was to be seen in a country, which received above twenty millions annually from its plantations.

Before I quit this topic, I must take notice of another thing, which is certainly very extraordinary. This wrong turn in the Spanish policy had a wonderful effect; it made all the enemies of that nation rich, and all its friends poor. Everybody knows that the United Provinces not only made themselves free and independent, but rich and powerful also, by their long war with Spain. Our maritime power was owing to the same cause. If Philip II had not disturbed Queen Elizabeth, our fleet might have been as inconsiderable at the close of her reign as it was at the beginning, when we were pestered with pirates even in the narrow seas. Our plantations abroad were in a great measure owing to expeditions against the Spaniard. Our manufactures at home were the consequence of affording refuge to the king of Spain's protestant subjects. When Queen Elizabeth's successor closed with Spain, he suffered by it, while France, the only country then at war with Spain, was a gainer. I say nothing of Cromwell's breach with Spain, and the advantages he drew from it, because the world seems well enough apprized of all I could say on that subject already. . . .

By so long a series of mismanagement the Spaniards have brought their affairs into so wretched a situation, that they neither have, nor can have any very great benefit from their vast dominions in America. They are said to be stewards for the rest of Europe; their Galleons bring the silver into Spain, but neither wisdom nor power can keep it there; it runs out as fast as it comes in, nay, and faster; insomuch that the little Canton of Bern is really richer, and has more credit, than the king of Spain, notwithstanding his Indies. At first sight this seems to be strange and incredible; but when we come to examine it, the mystery is by no means impenetrable. The silver and rich commodities which come from the Indies come not for nothing (the king's duties excepted) and very little of the goods or manufactures for which they come, belong to the subjects of the crown of Spain. It is evident, therefore, that the Spanish merchants are but factors, and that the greatest part of the returns from the West Indies belong to those foreigners for whom they negotiate.

XII

Class and Caste in the Spanish Colonies

THE SOCIAL ORDER THAT AROSE in the Spanish colonies on the ruins of the old Indian societies was based, like that of Spain, on feudal principles. All agricultural and mechanical labor was regarded as degrading. The various races and racial mixtures were carefully distinguished, and a trace of Negro or Indian blood legally sufficed to deprive an individual of the right to hold public office or enter the professions and of the other rights and privileges of white men. In practice, racial lines were not so strictly drawn. For a stipulated sum a wealthy *mestizo* or mulatto could often purchase from the Spanish crown a certificate placing him in the category of whites.

Wealth, not gentle birth or racial purity, was the true distinguishing characteristic of the colonial aristocracy. Legally, the creoles and peninsular Spaniards were equal. In practice, the former suffered from a system of discrimination that denied them employment in high church and government posts and in large-scale commerce. The resulting cleavage in the colonial upper class grew wider with the passage of time, and must be considered a major cause of the creole Wars of Independence.

The mestizo caste had its main origin in a multitude of irregular unions between Spaniards and native women, although mixed marriages were not uncommon, especially in the early colonial period. The mass of mixed-bloods were consigned to an inferior social status by their poverty and illegitimate birth. The mestizo caste tended to become a lower middle class of artisans, overseers, shopkeepers, and the like.

By contrast with the mestizo, no ambiguity marked the position of the Indian in the social scale. Aside from a small and privileged group of hereditary chiefs and their families, the Indians formed a distinct servile class, burdened with many tribute and labor obligations. They lived apart from the whites, in their own communities of pre-Conquest origin, or in towns established by the Spaniards. In many regions they preserved quite intact their ancestral social organization, language, and other culture traits. On numerous occasions they rose against their oppressors in revolts that were generally crushed with great severity.

The virtual disappearance of the native population of the Antilles, and the rapid growth of sugar-cane cultivation in the islands, created an insistent demand on the part of the colonists for Negro slave labor. A numerous Negro and mixed population came into being in the regions of plantation culture, notably in the West Indies and on the coasts of Mexico and Venezuela; smaller numbers were found in all the large colonial towns, where they were chiefly used as household servants.

Negro slavery in the Spanish colonies has been described as patriarchal and humane by comparison with the operations of the system in the English and French colonies. Emancipation was legally possible, and occurred with some frequency during the colonial period. Whether slaves or freedmen, Negroes occupied the lowest position in the social scale. Unless redeemed by wealth or singular talents, mulattoes and other racial mixtures containing Negro blood shared this disfavor. Many found employment in the mines, in the mechanical trades, as confidential servants, and in the colonial militia, where they formed separate units under the command of white officers.

1. THE STRUCTURE OF CLASS AND CASTE

The population of the Spanish colonies formed a melting pot of races, white, red, and black. Their progressive amalgamation was retarded but not halted by a caste system that assigned different social values to the respective races and mixtures. A white skin was a symbol of social superiority, but not all whites belonged to the privileged economic group. The Spaniard compelled by poverty to choose his mate from the colored races generally doomed his descendants to an inferior economic and social status. On the other hand, the mestizo or mulatto son of a wealthy Spanish landowner, if acknowledged and made his father's legal heir, as occasionally happened, could often purchase from the crown a certificate of white blood or even a title of nobility. The Spanish travelers Juan and Ulloa describe the complicated structure of class and caste of a colonial town — the Caribbean port of Cartagena.[1]

THE INHABITANTS may be divided into different casts or tribes, who derive their origin from a coalition of Whites, Negroes, and Indians. Of each of these we shall treat particularly.

The Whites may be divided into two classes, the Europeans, and Creoles, or Whites born in the country. The former are commonly called *Chapetones*, but are not numerous; most of them either return into Spain after acquiring a competent fortune, or remove up into inland provinces in order to increase it. Those who are settled at Carthagena, carry on the whole trade of that place, and live in opulence; whilst

[1] George Juan and Antonio de Ulloa, *Voyage to South America*, I, pp. 29–32.

the other inhabitants are indigent, and reduced to have recourse to mean and hard labour for subsistence. The families of the White Creoles compose the landed interest; some of them have large estates, and are highly respected, because their ancestors came into the country invested with honourable posts, bringing their families with them when they settled here. Some of these families, in order to keep up their original dignity, have either married their children to their equals in the country, or sent them as officers on board the galleons; but others have greatly declined. Besides these, there are other Whites, in mean circumstances, who either owe their origin to Indian families, or at least to an intermarriage with them, so that there is some mixture in their blood; but when this is not discoverable by their colour, the conceit of being Whites alleviates the pressure of every other calamity.

Among the other tribes which are derived from an intermarriage of the Whites with the Negroes, the first are the Mulattoes. Next to these the *Tercerones,* produced from a White and a Mulatto, with some approximation to the former, but not so near as to obliterate their origin. After these follow the *Quarterones,* proceeding from a White and a *Terceron.* The last are the *Quinterones,* who owe their origin to a White and *Quarteron.* This is the last gradation, there being no visible difference between them and the Whites, either in colour or features; nay they are often fairer than the Spaniards. The children of a White and *Quinteron* are also called Spaniards, and consider themselves as free from all taint of the Negro race. Every person is so jealous of the order of their tribe or cast, that if, through inadvertence, you call them by a degree lower than what they actually are, they are highly offended, never suffering themselves to be deprived of so valuable a gift of fortune.

Before they attain the class of the *Quinterones,* there are several intervening circumstances which throw them back; for between the Mulatto and the Negro, there is an intermediate race, which they call *Sambos,* owing their origin to a mixture between one of these with an Indian, or among themselves. They are also distinguished according to the class their fathers were of. Betwixt the *Tercerones* and the Mulattoes, the *Quarterones* and the *Tercerones,* etc. are those called *Tente en el Ayre,* suspended in the air, because they neither advance nor recede. Children, whose parents are a *Quarteron* or

Quinteron, and a Mulatto or *Terceron,* are *Salto atras* retrogrades; because, instead of advancing towards being Whites, they have gone backwards towards the Negro race. The children between a Negro and *Quinteron* are called *Sambos de Negro, de Mulatto, de Terceron,* etc.

These are the most known and common tribes or Castas; there are indeed several others proceeding from their intermarriages; but, being so various, even they themselves cannot easily distinguish them; and these are the only people one sees in the city, the *estancias,* and the villages; for if any White, especially women, are met with, it is only accidental, these generally residing in their houses; at least, if they are of any rank or character.

These casts, from the Mulattoes, all affect the Spanish dress, but wear very slight stuffs on account of the heat of the climate. These are the mechanics of the city; the Whites, whether Creoles or *Chapetones,* disdaining such a mean occupation follow nothing below merchandise. But it being impossible for all to succeed, great numbers not being able to procure sufficient credit, they become poor and miserable from their aversion to those trades they follow in Europe, and, instead of the riches which they flattered themselves with possessing in the Indies, they experience the most complicated wretchedness.

The class of Negroes is not the least numerous, and is divided into two parts; the free and the slaves. These [last] are again subdivided into Creoles and *Bozales,* part of which are employed in the cultivation of the *haciendas* or *estancias.* Those in the city are obliged to perform the most laborious services, and pay out of their wages a certain quota to their masters, subsisting themselves on the small remainder. The violence of the heat not permitting them to wear any cloaths, their only covering is a small piece of cotton stuff about their waist; the female slaves go in the same manner. Some of these live at the *estancias,* being married to the slaves who work there; while those in the city sell in the markets all kind of eatables, and cry fruits, sweet-meats, cakes made of the maize, and cassava, and several other things about the streets. Those who have children sucking at their breast, which is the case of the generality, carry them on their shoulders, in order to have their arms at liberty; and when the infants are hungry, they give them the breast either under the arm or over the shoulder, without taking them from their backs. This will perhaps appear incredible; but their breasts, being left to grow without any pressure on them often hang down to their very waist, and are not therefore difficult to turn over their shoulders for the convenience of the infant.

2. THE COLONIAL CITY: MEXICO

Mexico City and Lima were the two great centers of urban civilization in colonial Spanish America. In each an uncrossable chasm separated the world of the white upper class, flaunting its wealth in gay apparel, richly ornamented dwellings, and colorful pageants, from that of the sullen Indian, Negro, and mixed-blood proletariat, living in wretched huts amid incredible squalor. In the sixteenth and seventeenth centuries a spirit of violence pervaded the life of the colonial city. Brawls, duels, and murders were commonplace among the gentry as well as the lower classes; and occasionally the latter erupted in blindly destructive tumults against el mal gobierno (the rotten government). The renegade English priest Thomas Gage paints a vivid picture of Mexico City in 1625.[2]

AT THE REBUILDING of this city there was a great difference betwixt an inhabitant of Mexico, and a Conqueror; for a Conqueror was a name of honour, and had lands and rents given him and to his posterity by the King of Spain, and the inhabitant or only dweller paid rent for his house. And this hath filled all those parts of America with proud Dons and gentlemen to this day; for every one will call himself a descendant from a Conqueror, though he be as poor as Job; and ask him what is become of his estate and fortune; he will answer that fortune hath taken it away, which shall never take away a Don from him. Nay, a poor cobbler, or carrier that runs about the country far and near getting his living with half-a-dozen mules, if he be called Mendoza, or Guzman, will swear that he descended from those dukes' houses in Spain, and that his grandfather came from thence to conquer, and subdued whole countries to the Crown of Spain, though now fortune have frowned upon him, and covered his rags with a threadbare cloak.

When Mexico was rebuilt, and judges, aldermen, attorneys, town-clerks, notaries, scavengers, and serjeants with all other officers necessary for the commonwealth of a city were appointed, the fame of Cortez and majesty of the city was blown abroad into far provinces, by means whereof it was soon replenished with Indians again, and with Spaniards from Spain, who soon

conquered above four hundred leagues of land, being all governed by the princely seat of Mexico. But since that first rebuilding, I may say it is now rebuilt the second time by Spaniards, who have consumed most of the Indians; so that now I will not dare to say there are a hundred thousand houses which soon after the Conquest were built up, for most of them were of Indians.

Now the Indians that live there, live in the suburbs of the city, and their situation is called Guadalupe. In the year 1625, when I went to those parts, this suburb was judged to contain five thousand inhabitants; but since most of them have been consumed by the Spaniards' hard usage and the work of the lake. So that now there may not be above two thousand inhabitants of mere Indians, and a thousand of such as they call there mestizoes, who are of a mixed nature of Spaniards and Indians, for many poor Spaniards marry with Indian women, and others that marry them not but hate their husbands, find many tricks to convey away an innocent Uriah to enjoy his Bathsheba. The Spaniards daily cozen them of the small plot of ground where their houses stand, and of three or four houses of Indians built up one good and fair house after the Spanish fashion with gardens and orchards. And so is almost all Mexico new built with very fair and spacious houses with gardens of recreation.

Their buildings are with stone, and brick very strong, but not high, by reason of the many earthquakes, which would endanger their houses if they were above three storeys high. The streets are very broad, in the narrowest of them three coaches may go, and in the broader six may go in the breadth of them, which makes the city seem a great deal bigger than it is. In my time it was thought to be of between thirty and forty thousand inhabitants — Spaniards, who are so proud and rich that half the city was judged to keep coaches, for it was a most credible report that in Mexico in my time there were above fifteen thousand coaches. It is a byword that at Mexico there are four things fair, that is to say, the women, the apparel, the horses, and the streets. But to this I may add the beauty of some of the coaches of the gentry, which do exceed in cost the best of the Court of Madrid and other parts of Christendom; for there they spare no silver, nor gold, nor precious stones, nor cloth of gold, nor the best silks from China to enrich them. And to the gallantry of their horses the pride of some doth add the cost of bridles and shoes of silver.

The streets of Christendom must not compare

2 Thomas Gage, *The English-American*, pp. 89–92.

with those in breadth and cleanness, but especially in the riches of the shops which do adorn them. Above all, the goldsmiths' shops and works are to be admired. The Indians, and the people of China that have been made Christians and every year come thither, have perfected the Spaniards in that trade. The Viceroy that went thither the year 1625 caused a popinjay to be made of silver, gold, and precious stones with the perfect colours of the popinjay's feathers (a bird bigger than a pheasant), with such exquisite art and perfection, to present unto the King of Spain, that it was prized to be worth in riches and workmanship half a million of ducats. There is in the cloister of the Dominicans a lamp hanging in the church with three hundred branches wrought in silver to hold so many candles, besides a hundred little lamps for oil set in it, every one being made with several workmanship so exquisitely that it is valued to be worth four hundred thousand ducats; and with such-like curious works are many streets made more rich and beautiful from the shops of goldsmiths.

To the by-word touching the beauty of the women I must add the liberty they enjoy for gaming, which is such that the day and night is too short for them to end a primera when once it is begun; nay gaming is so common to them that they invite gentlemen to their houses for no other end. To myself it happened that passing along the streets in company with a friar that came with me that year from Spain, a gentlewoman of great birth knowing us to be *chapetons* (so they call the first year those that come from Spain), from her window called unto us, and after two or three slight questions concerning Spain asked us if we would come in and play with her a game at primera.

Both men and women are excessive in their apparel, using more silks than stuffs and cloth. Precious stones and pearls further much their vain ostentation; a hat-band and rose made of diamonds in a gentleman's hat is common, and a hat-band of pearls is ordinary in a tradesman; nay a blackamoor or tawny young maid and slave will make hard shift but she will be in fashion with her neck-chain and bracelets of pearls, and her ear-bobs of some considerable jewels. The attire of this baser sort of people of blackamoors and mulattoes (which are of a mixed nature, of Spaniards and blackamoors) is so light, and their carriage so enticing, that many Spaniards even of the better sort (who are too too prone to venery) disdain their wives for them.

Their clothing is a petticoat of silk or cloth, with many silver or golden laces, with a very broad double ribbon of some light colour with long silver or golden tags hanging down before, the whole length of their petticoat to the ground, and the like behind; their waistcoats made like bodices, with skirts, laced likewise with gold or silver, without sleeves, and a girdle about their body of great price stuck with pearls and knots of gold (if they be any ways well esteemed of), their sleeves are broad and open at the end, of holland or fine China linen, wrought some with coloured silks, some with silk and gold, some with silk and silver, hanging down almost unto the ground; the locks of their heads are covered with some wrought coif, and over it another of network of silk bound with a fair silk, or silver, or golden ribbon which crosseth the upper part of their forehead, and hath commonly worked out in letters some light and foolish love posy; their bare, black, and tawny breasts are covered with bobs hanging from their chains of pearls.

And when they go abroad, they use a white mantle of lawn or cambric rounded with a broad lace, which some put over their heads, the breadth reaching only to their middle behind, that their girdle and ribbons may be seen, and two ends before reaching to the ground almost; others cast their mantles only upon their shoulders, and swaggers-like, cast the one end over the left shoulder that they may the better jog the right arm, and shew their broad sleeve as they walk along; others instead of this mantle use some rich silk petticoat to hang upon their left shoulder, while with their right arm they support the lower part of it, more like roaring boys than honest civil maids. Their shoes are high and of many soles, the outside whereof of the profaner sort are plated with a list of silver, which is fastened with small nails of broad silver heads.

Most of these are or have been slaves, though love have set them loose at liberty to enslave souls to sin and Satan. And there are so many of this kind both men and women grown to a height of pride and vanity, that many times the Spaniards have feared they would rise up and mutiny against them. And for the looseness of their lives, and public scandals committed by them and the better sort of the Spaniards, I have heard them say often who have professed more religion and fear of God, they verily thought God would destroy that city, and give up the country into the power of some other nation. . . .

Great alms and liberality towards religious houses in that city commonly are coupled with great and scandalous wickedness. They wallow in the bed of riches and wealth, and make their alms the coverlet to cover their loose and lascivious lives. From hence are the churches so fairly built and adorned. There are not above fifty churches and chapels, cloisters and nunneries, and parish churches in that city; but those that are there are the fairest that ever my eyes beheld, the roofs and beams being in many of them all daubed with gold, and many altars with sundry marble pillars, and others with brazil-wood stays standing one above another with tabernacles for several saints richly wrought with golden colours, so that twenty thousand ducats is a common price of many of them. These cause admiration in the common sort of people, and admiration brings on daily adoration in them to those glorious spectacles and images of saints.

Besides these beautiful buildings, the inward riches belonging to the altars are infinite in price and value, such as copes, canopies, hangings, altar cloths, candlesticks, jewels belonging to the saints, and crowns of gold and silver, and tabernacles of gold and crystal to carry about their sacrament in procession, all which would mount to the worth of a reasonable mine of silver, and would be a rich prey for any nation that could make better use of wealth and riches. I will not speak much of the lives of the friars and nuns of that city, but only that there they enjoy more liberty than in the parts of Europe (where yet they have too much) and that surely the scandals committed by them do cry up to Heaven for vengeance, judgment, and destruction.

In my time in the cloister of the Mercenarian friars which is entitled for the Redemption of Captives, there chanced to be an election of a Provincial to rule over them, to the which all the priors and heads of the cloisters about the country had resorted, and such was their various and factious difference that upon the sudden all the convent was in an uproar, their canonical election was turned to mutiny and strife, knives were drawn, many wounded, the scandal and danger of murder so great, that the Viceroy was fain to interpose his authority and to sit amongst them and guard the cloister until their Provincial was elected.

It is ordinary for the friars to visit their devoted nuns, and to spend whole days with them, hearing their music, feeding on their sweetmeats, and for this purpose they have many chambers which they call *locutorios,* to talk in, with wooden bars between the nuns and them, and in these chambers are tables for the friars to dine at; and while they dine the nuns recreate them with their voices. Gentlemen and citizens give their daughters to be brought up in these nunneries, where they are taught to make all sorts of conserves and preserves, all sorts of needlework, all sorts of music, which is so exquisite in that city that I dare be bold to say that the people are drawn to their churches more for the delight of the music than for any delight in the service of God. More, they teach these young children to act like players, and to entice the people to their churches make these children to act short dialogues in their choirs, richly attiring them with men's and women's apparel, especially upon Midsummer Day, and the eight days before their Christmas, which is so gallantly performed that many factious strifes and single combats have been, and some were in my time, for defending which of these nunneries most excelled in music and in the training up of children. No delights are wanting in that city abroad in the world, nor in their churches, which should be the house of God, and the soul's, not the sense's delight.

The chief place in the city is the market-place, which though it be not as spacious as in Montezuma his time, yet is at this day very fair and wide, built all with arches on the one side where people may walk dry in time of rain, and there are shops of merchants furnished with all sorts of stuffs and silks, and before them sit women selling all manner of fruits and herbs; over against these shops and arches is the Viceroy his palace, which taketh up almost the whole length of the market with the walls of the house and of the gardens belonging to it. At the end of the Viceroy his palace is the chief prison, which is strong of stone work. Next to this is the beautiful street called *La Plateria,* or Goldsmiths Street, where a man's eyes may behold in less than an hour many millions' worth of gold, silver, pearls, and jewels. The street of St. Austin is rich and comely, where live all that trade in silks; but one of the longest and broadest streets is the street called Tacuba, where almost all the shops are of ironmongers, and of such as deal in brass and steel, which is joining to those arches whereon the water is conveyed into the city, and is so called for that it is the way out of the city to a town called Tacuba; and this street is mentioned far and near, not so much for the length and breadth of it, as for a small commodity of needles which are made there, and for proof are the best of all those parts. For stately buildings the street called *del Aquila*, the Street of the Eagle, exceeds the rest, where live gentlemen, and courtiers, and judges belonging to the Chancery, and is the palace of the Marques del Valle from the line of Ferdinando Cortez; this street is so called from an old idol an eagle of stone which from the Conquest lieth in a corner of that street, and is twice as big as London stone.

The gallants of this city shew themselves daily, some on horseback, and most in coaches, about four of the clock in the afternoon in a pleasant shady field called *la Alameda*, full of trees and walks, somewhat like unto our Moorfields, where do meet as constantly as the merchants upon our exchange about two thousand coaches, full of gallants, ladies, and citizens, to see and to be seen, to court and to be courted, the gentlemen having their train of blackamoor slaves some a dozen, some half a dozen waiting on them, in brave and gallant liveries, heavy with gold and silver lace, with silk stockings on their black legs, and roses on their feet, and swords by their sides; the ladies also carry their train by their coach's side of such jetlike damsels as before have been mentioned for their light apparel, who with their bravery and white mantles over them seem to be, as the Spaniard saith, *mosca en leche,* a fly in milk. But the train of the Viceroy who often goeth to this place is wonderful stately, which some say is as great as the train of his master the King of Spain. At this meeting are carried about many sorts of sweetmeats and papers of comfits to be sold, for to relish a cup of cool water, which is cried about in curious glasses, to cool the blood of those love-hot gallants. But many times these their meetings sweetened with conserves and comfits have sour sauce at the end, for jealousy will not suffer a lady to be courted, no nor sometimes to be spoken to, but puts fury into the violent hand to draw a sword or dagger and to stab or murder whom he was jealous of, and when one sword is drawn thousands are presently drawn, some to right the party wounded or murdered; others to defend the party murdering, whose friends will not permit him to be apprehended, but will guard him with drawn swords until they have conveyed him to the sanctuary of some church, from whence the Viceroy his power is not able to take him for a legal trial.

3. THE COLONIAL CITY: LIMA

A little more than a hundred years after the Englishman Gage visited Mexico City, the young Spanish scientists Juan and Ulloa came to Lima, proud capital of the viceroyalty of Peru, and the seat of the most corrupt, sophisticated, and extravagant society in the Americas. The upper class, following the lead of Spain, where French manners were winning ascendancy, had acquired an urbanity and polish foreign to the early conquistadores. Pleasure and dissipation were the order of the day, with cockfighting, bullfights, gambling, balls, and the theater among the principal amusements. The women of the city enjoyed a reputation for beauty, gala dress, captivating manners, and a passion for intrigue. Juan and Ulloa offer their impressions of life and manners in eighteenth-century Lima.[3]

THE INHABITANTS of Lima are composed of whites, or Spaniards, Negroes, Indians, Mestizos, and other casts, proceeding from the mixture of all three.

The Spanish families are very numerous; Lima according to the lowest computation, containing sixteen or eighteen thousand whites. Among these are reckoned a third or fourth part of the most distinguished nobility of Peru; and many of these dignified with the stile of ancient or modern Castilians, among which are no less than 45 counts and marquises. The number of knights belonging to the several military orders is also very considerable. Besides these are many families no less respectable and living in equal splendor; particularly 24 gentlemen of large estates, but without titles, tho' most of them have ancient seats, a proof of the antiquity of their families. One of these traces, with undeniable certainty, his descent from the Incas. The name of this family is Ampuero, so called from one of the Spanish commanders at the conquest of this country, who married a Coya, or daughter of the Inca. To this family the kings of Spain have been pleased to grant several distinguishing honours and privileges, as marks of its great quality: and many of the most eminent families in the city have desired intermarriages with it.

All those families live in a manner becoming their rank, having estates equal to their gener-

3 Juan and Ulloa, *A Voyage to South America,* II, pp. 53–60.

ous dispositions, keeping a great number of slaves and other domestics, and those who affect making the greatest figure, have coaches, while others content themselves with calashes or chaises, which are here so common, that no family of any substance is without one. It must be owned that these carriages are more necessary here than in other cities, on account of the numberless droves of mules which continually pass thro' Lima, and cover the streets with their dung, which being soon dried by the sun and the wind, turns to a nauseous dust, scarce supportable to those who walk on foot. These chaises, which are drawn by a mule, and guided by a driver, have only two wheels, with two seats opposite to each other, so that on occasion they will hold four persons. They are very slight and airy; but on account of the gildings and other decorations, sometimes cost eight hundred or a thousand crowns. The number of them is said to amount to 5 or 6000; and that of coaches is also very considerable, tho' not equal to the former.

The funds to support these expenses, which in other parts would ruin families, are their large estates and plantations, civil and military employments or commerce, which is here accounted no derogation to families of the greatest distinction; but by this commerce is not to be understood the buying and selling by retail or in shops, every one trading proportional to his character and substance. Hence families are preserved from those disasters too common in Spain, where titles are frequently found without a fortune capable of supporting their dignity. Commerce is so far from being considered as a disgrace at Lima, that the greatest fortunes have been raised by it; those on the contrary, being rather despised, who not being blessed with a sufficient estate, through indolence, neglect to have recourse to it for improving their fortunes. This custom, or resource, which was established there without any determinate end, being introduced by a vain desire of the first Spaniards to acquire wealth, is now the real support of that splendor in which those families live; and whatever repugnance these military gentlemen might originally have to commerce, it was immediately removed by a royal proclamation, by which it was declared that commerce in the Indies should not exclude from nobility or the military orders; a very wise measure, and of which Spain would be still more sensible, were it extended to all its dependencies.

At Lima, as at Quito, and all Spanish Amer-

ica, some of the eminent families have been long since settled there, whilst the prosperity of others is of a later date; for being the center of the whole commerce of Peru, a greater number of Europeans resort to it, than to any other city; some for trade, and others, from being invested in Spain with considerable employments: among both are persons of the greatest merit; and tho' many after they have finished their respective affairs, return home, yet the major part induced by the fertility of the soil, and goodness of the climate, remain at Lima, and marry young ladies remarkable equally for the gifts of fortune as those of nature; and thus new families are continually settled.

The Negroes, Mulattoes, and their descendants, form the greater number of the inhabitants; and of these are the greatest part of the mechanics; tho' here the Europeans also follow the same occupations, which are not at Lima reckoned disgraceful to them, as they are at Quito; for gain being here the universal passion, the inhabitants pursue it by means of any trade, without regard to its being followed by Mulattoes, interest here preponderating against any other consideration.

The third, and last class of inhabitants are the Indians and Mestizos, but these are very small in proportion to the largeness of the city, and the multitudes of the second class. They are employed in agriculture, in making earthen ware, and bringing all kinds of provisions to market, domestic services being performed by Negroes and Mulattoes, either slaves or free, though generally by the former.

The usual dress of the men differs very little from that worn in Spain, nor is the distinction between the several classes very great; for the use of all sorts of cloth being allowed, every one wears what he can purchase. So that it is not uncommon to see a Mulatto, or any other mechanic dressed in a tissue, equal to any thing that can be worn by a more opulent person. They all greatly affect fine cloaths, and it may be said without exaggeration, that the finest stuffs made in countries, where industry is always inventing something new, are more generally seen at Lima than in any other place; vanity and ostentation not being restrained by custom or law. Thus the great quantities brought in the galleons and register ships notwithstanding they sell here prodigiously above their prime cost in Europe, the richest of them are used as cloaths, and worn with a carelessness little suitable to their extravagant price; but in this article the men are greatly exceeded by the women, whose passion for dress is such as to deserve a more particular account.

In the choice of laces, the women carry their taste to a prodigious excess; nor is this an emulation confined to persons of quality, but has spread thro' all ranks, except the lowest class of negroes. The laces are sewed to their linen, which is of the finest sort, though very little of it is seen, the greatest part of it, especially in some dresses, being always covered with lace; so that the little which appears seems rather for ornament than use. These laces too must be all of Flanders manufacture, no woman of rank condescending to look on any other.

Their dress is very different from the European, which the custom of the country alone can render excusable; indeed to Spaniards at their first coming over it appears extremely indecent. Their dress consists of a pair of shoes, a shift, a petticoat of dimity, an open petticoat, and a jacket, which in summer, is of linen, in winter of stuff. To this some add a mantellette, that the former may hang loose. The difference between this dress and that worn at Quito, though consisting of the same pieces is, that at Lima it is much shorter, the petticoat which is usually tied below the waist, not reaching lower than the calf of the leg, from whence, nearly to the ankle, hangs a border of very fine lace, sewed to the bottom of the under petticoat; through which the ends of their garters are discovered, embroidered with gold or silver, and sometimes set with pearls; but the latter is not common. The upper petticoat, which is of velvet, or some rich stuff, is fringed all round, and not less crowded with ornaments, than those described in the first volume of this work. But be the ornaments what they will, whether of fringe, lace, or ribbands, they are always exquisitely fine. The shift's sleeves, which are a yard and a half in length, and two yards in width, when worn for ornament, are covered with rolls of laces, variegated in such a manner as to render the whole truly elegant. Over the shift is worn the jacket, the sleeves of which are excessively large, of a circular figure, and consist of rows of lace, or slips of cambrick or lawn, with lace disposed betwixt each, as are also the shift sleeves, even of those who do not affect extraordinary ornament. The body of the jacket is tied on the shoulders with ribbands fastened to the back of their stays; and the round sleeves of it being tucked up to the shoulders, are so disposed together with those of the shift, as to form what

may be term'd four wings. If the jacket be not buttoned or clasped before, it is agreeably fastened on the shoulders; and indeed the whole dress makes a most elegant figure. They who use a close vest, fasten it with clasps, but wear over it the loose jacket, already described. In the summer they have a kind of veil, the stuff and fashion of which is like that of the shift and body of the vest, of the finest cambrick or lawn, richly laced: But in winter the veil worn in their houses is of baize; when they go abroad full dressed, it is adorned like the sleeves. They also use brown baize, finely laced and fringed, and bordered with slips of black velvet. Over the petticoat is an apron of the same stuff as the sleeves of the jacket, hanging down to the bottom of it. From hence some idea may be formed of the expense of a dress, where the much greater part of the stuff is merely for ornament; nor will it appear strange, that the marriage shift should cost a thousand crowns, and sometimes more.

One particular on which the women here extremely value themselves, is the size of their feet, a small foot being esteemed one of the chief beauties; and this is the principal fault they find with the Spanish ladies, who have much larger feet than those of Lima. From their infancy they are accustomed to wear straight shoes, that their feet may not grow beyond the size of which they esteem beautiful; some of them do not exceed five inches and a half, or six inches in length, and in women of a small stature they are still less. Their shoes have little or no sole, one piece of Cordovan serving both for that and the upper leather, and of an equal breadth and roundness at the toe and heel, so as to form a sort of long figure of eight; but the foot not complying with this figure, brings it to a greater regularity. These shoes are always fastened with diamond buckles, or something very brilliant in proportion to the ability of the wearer, being worn less for use than ornament; for the shoes are made in such a manner, that they never loosen of themselves, nor do the buckles hinder their being taken off. It is unusual to set these buckles with pearls, a particular to be accounted for, only from their being so lavish of them in the other ornaments of dress, as to consider them as of too little value. The shoemakers, who are no strangers to the foible of the sex, take great care to make them in a manner very little calculated for service. The usual price is three half crowns a pair, those embroidered with gold or silver cost from eight to ten crowns. The latter, however, are but little worn, the encumbrance of embroidery being suited rather to enlarge than diminish the appearance of a small foot.

They are fond of white silk stockings, made extremely thin, that the leg may appear the more shapely; the greatest part of which is exposed to view. These trifles often afford very sprightly sallies of wit in their animadversions on the dress of others.

Hitherto we have considered only the more common dress of these ladies; the reader will conceive a still higher idea of their magnificence, when he is informed of the ornaments with which they are decorated in their visits, and upon public occasions. We shall begin with their manner of dressing the hair, which being naturally black, and capable of reaching below their waists, they dispose in such a manner as to appear perfectly graceful. They tie it up behind in six braided locks, through which a golden bodkin a little bent is inserted, and having a cluster of diamonds at each end. On this the locks are suspended so as to touch the shoulder. On the front and upper part of the head they wear diamond egrets, and the hair is formed into little curls, hanging from the forehead to the middle of the ear, with a large black patch of velvet on each temple. Their earrings are of brilliants, intermixed with tuffs of black silk, covered with pearls, resembling those already described in the first volume. These are so common an ornament, that besides their necklaces, they also wear about their necks rosaries, the beads of which are of pearls, either separate or set in clusters to the size of a large filbert; and those which form the cross are still larger.

Besides diamond rings, necklaces, girdles, and bracelets, all very curious both with regard to water and size, many ladies wear other jewels set in gold, or for singularity sake, in tombago. Lastly, from their girdle before is suspended a large round jewel enriched with diamonds; much more superb than their bracelets, or other ornaments. A lady covered with the most expensive lace instead of linen, and glittering from head to foot with jewels, is supposed to be dressed at the expense of not less than thirty or forty thousand crowns. A splendor still the more astonishing, as it is so very common.

A fondness for expense in these people, does not confine itself to rich apparel; it appears no less in the strange neglect, and the small value they seem to set upon them, by wearing them

in a manner the most careless, and by that means bringing upon themselves fresh expenses in repairing the old or purchasing new jewels; especially pearls on account of their fragility.

The most common of the two kinds of dresses worn when they go abroad, is the veil and long petticoat; the other is a round petticoat and mantelet. The former for church, the latter for taking the air, and diversions; but both in the prevailing taste for expense, being richly embroidered with silver or gold.

The long petticoat is particularly worn on holy Thursday; as on that day they visit the churches, attended by two or three female Negro or mulatto slaves, dressed in an uniform like pages.

4. THE MESTIZO: SEED OF TOMORROW

The mestizo arose from a process of racial fusion that began in the first days of the Spanish Conquest and has continued down to the present. The Spanish jurist Juan de Solórzano Pereira (1575–1655) discusses the status of the mestizo in colonial law and opinion.[4]

TURNING NOW to the persons called mestizos and mulattoes, of whom there are great numbers in the Indies, first let me say that the name mestizo was assigned to the former because they represent a mixture of blood and nationality. . . .

As for the mulattoes, although for the same reason they belong in the class of mestizos, yet as the offspring of Negro women and white men, or the reverse, which is the most strange and repulsive mixture of all, they bear this specific name which compares them to the species of the mule. . . .

If these men were born of legitimate wedlock and had no other vices or defects, they could be regarded as citizens of those provinces and could be admitted to honor and office in them, as is argued by Victoria and Zapata. I am of the opinion that such an intention was the basis of certain royal decrees that permit mestizos to take holy orders and mestizas to become nuns, and admit mestizos to municipal offices and notaryships.

But because they are most often born out of adultery or other illicit unions, since few Spaniards of honorable position will marry Indian or Negro women . . . , they bear the taint of illegitimacy and other vices which they take in, as it were, with their milk. And these men, I

4 Juan de Solórzano Pereira, *Política indiana*, Madrid, 1930, 5 vols., I, 445–448. (Excerpt translated by the editor.)

find by many other decrees, are forbidden to hold any responsible public office, whether it is that of Protector of the Indians, councilman, or notary public, unless they acknowledge this defect at the time of application and receive special dispensation from it; and those who have gained office in any other way are not allowed to keep it.

There are other decrees that forbid them to take holy orders, unless by special dispensation.

I shall content myself for the present with saying that if these mestizos (especially those in the Indies) possess recognized and assured virtue, and sufficient ability and learning, they could be extremely useful in matters relating to the Indians, being, as it were, their countrymen, and knowing their languages and customs. . . .

But returning to the question of curacies, although for the reason given above it would be convenient to entrust them to mestizos, great care must be taken with this, for we see that the majority of them come from a vicious and depraved environment, and it is they who do the most harm to the Indians. . . . And for this reason many decrees forbid them to visit or live in the Indian towns, and compel them to live in the Spanish towns, or in such towns as may be formed and populated by mestizos and mulattoes. These same decrees order that mestizas married to Spaniards, if charged with adultery, shall be tried and punished like Spanish women.

There are other decrees, of later date, issued in 1600 and 1608, directed to the viceroys of Peru Don Luis de Velasco and the marquis of Montes Claros, saying that the king had learned that the number of mestizos, mulattoes, and *zambahigos* (the children of Negro men and Indian women, or the reverse) was increasing sharply, and ordering them to take appropriate measures that men of such mixtures, vicious in their majority, should not cause injury and disturbances in that kingdom — a thing always to be feared from such people, especially if to the sins that arise from their evil birth are added those that spring from idleness and poor upbringing.

For this reason, although by the ordinances of the viceroy of Peru, Don Francisco de Toledo, they are exempt from paying tribute, by later decrees of the years 1600, 1612, 1619, by the celebrated decrees concerning personal service of 1601 and 1609, and by many others that have been successively promulgated, it is ordered that they pay tribute. And the same decrees command the viceroys to see that the mestizos and mulattoes, like the Indians, are made to labor in the mines and fields. . . .

For it does not appear just that this labor [of the mines], which requires such physical strength . . ., should be assigned entirely to the wretched Indians, while the mestizos and mulattoes, who are of such evil caste, race, and character, are left to idleness; this contravenes the rule that lewdness should not be more favored than chastity, and that the offspring of legitimate marriage should be more privileged than the illegitimate, as is taught by Saint Thomas and other authorities. . . .

From this abuse results the fact that many Indian women desert their Indian husbands and neglect the children that they have by them, seeing them subject to tribute-payments and personal services, and desire, love, and spoil the children that they have out of wedlock by Spaniards or even by Negroes, because they are free and exempt from all burdens — a condition that plainly should not be permitted in any well-governed state.

5. THE INDIAN TOWN

Among the various races and mixtures that composed the population of the Spanish empire in America, the Indians formed a nation apart. Most of them lived in their own self-governing communities, in which Spaniards other than the village priest were forbidden to reside. In many regions they maintained intact their ancient clan or tribal organization, language, dress, and customs. Thomas Gage, who spent twelve years as a priest in Guatemala, and amassed a tidy fortune from the piety and credulity of his native parishioners, describes the life of the Indian town.[5]

THEIR ORDINARY CLOTHING is a pair of linen or woollen drawers broad and open at the knees, without shoes (though in their journeys some will put on leathern sandals to keep the soles of their feet) or stockings, without any doublet, a short coarse shirt, which reacheth a little below their waist, and serves more for a doublet than for a shirt, and for a cloak a woollen or linen mantle (called *aiate*) tied with a knot over one shoulder, hanging down on the other side almost to the ground, with a twelvepenny or two shilling hat, which after one good shower of rain like paper falls about their necks and eyes; their bed they carry sometime about them, which is that woollen mantle wherewith they wrap themselves about at night, taking off their shirt and drawers, which they lay under their

[5] Thomas Gage, *The English-American*, pp. 234–247.

head for a pillow; some will carry with them a short, slight, and light mat to lie, but those that carry it not with them, if they cannot borrow one of a neighbour, lie as willingly in their mantle upon the bare ground as a gentleman in England upon a soft down-bed, and thus do they soundly sleep, and loudly snort after a day's work, or after a day's journey with a hundred-weight upon their backs.

Those that are of the better sort, and richer, and who are not employed as *tamemez* to carry burdens, or as labourers to work for Spaniards, but keep at home following their own farms, or following their own mules about the country, or following their trades and callings in their shops, or governing the towns, as *alcaldes,* or *alguaziles,* officers of justice, may go a little better apparelled, but after the same manner. For some will have their drawers with a lace at the bottom, or wrought with some coloured silk or crewel, so likewise the mantle about them shall have either a lace, or some work of birds on it; some will wear a cut linen doublet, others shoes, but very few stockings or bands about their necks; and for their beds, the best Indian Governor or the richest, who may be worth four or five thousand ducats, will have little more than the poor *tamemez;* for they lie upon boards, or canes bound together, and raised from the ground, whereon they lay a board and handsome mat, and at their heads for man and wife two little stumps of wood for bolsters, whereon they lay their shirts and mantles and other clothes for pillows, covering themselves with a broader blanket than is their mantle, and thus hardly would Don Bernabé de Guzman the Governor of Petapa lie, and so do all the best of them.

The women's attire is cheap and soon put on; for most of them also go barefoot, the richer and better sort wear shoes, with broad ribbons for shoe-strings, and for a petticoat, they tie about their waist a woollen mantle, which in the better sort is wrought with divers colors, but not sewed at all, pleated, or gathered in, but as they tie it with a list about them; they wear no shift next their body, but cover their nakedness with a kind of surplice (which they call *guaipil*) which hangs loose from their shoulders down a little below their waist, with open short sleeves, which cover half their arms; this *guaipil* is curiously wrought, especially in the bosom, with cotton, or feathers. The richer sort of them wear bracelets and bobs about their waists and necks; their hair is gathered up with

fillets, without any coif or covering, except it be the better sort. When they go to church or abroad, they put upon their heads a veil of linen, which hangeth almost to the ground, and this is that which costs them most of all their attire, for that commonly it is of Holland or some good linen brought from Spain, or fine linen brought from China, which the better sort wear with a lace about. When they are at home at work they commonly take off their *guaipil,* or surplice, discovering the nakedness of their breasts and body. They lie also in their beds as do their husbands, wrapped up only with a mantle, or with a blanket.

Their houses are but poor thatched cottages, without any upper rooms, but commonly one or two only rooms below, in the one they dress their meat in the middle of it, making a compass for fire, with two or three stones, without any other chimney to convey the smoke away, which spreading itself about the room filleth the thatch and the rafters so with soot that all the room seemeth to be a chimney. The next unto it is not free from smoke and blackness, where sometimes are four or five beds according to the family. The poorer sort have but one room, where they eat, dress their meat, and sleep. Few there are that set any locks upon their doors, for they fear no robbing nor stealing, neither have they in their houses much to lose, earthen pots, and pans, and dishes, and cups to drink their chocolate being the chief commodities in their house. There is scarce any house which hath not also in the yard a stew, wherein they bathe themselves with hot water, which is their chief physic when they feel themselves distempered.

Among themselves they are in every town divided into tribes, which have one chief head, to whom all that belong unto that tribe do resort in any difficult matters, who is bound to aid, protect, defend, counsel, and appear for the rest of his tribe before the officers of justice in any wrong that is like to be done unto them. When any is to be married, the father of the son that is to take a wife out of another tribe goeth unto the head of his tribe to give him warning of his son's marriage with such a maid. Then that head meets with the head of the maid's tribe, and they confer about it. The business commonly is in debate a quarter of a year; all which time the parents of the youth or man are with gifts to buy the maid; they are to be at the charges of all that is spent in eating and drinking when the heads of the two tribes do meet with the rest of the kindred of each side, who sometimes sit in conference a whole day, or most part of a night. After many days and nights thus spent, and a full trial being made of the one and other side's affection, if they chance to disagree about the marriage, then is the tribe and parents of the maid to restore back all that the other side hath spent and given. They give no portions with their daughters, but when they die their goods and lands are equally divided among their sons. If anyone want a house to live in or will repair and thatch his house anew, notice is given to the heads of the tribes, who warn all the town to come to help in the work, and everyone is to bring a bundle of straw, and other materials, so that in one day with the help of many they finish a house, without any charges more than of chocolate, which they minister in great cups as big as will hold above a pint, not putting in any costly materials, as do the Spaniards, but only a little aniseed, and chilli, or Indian pepper; or else they half fill the cup with *atole,* and pour upon it as much chocolate as will fill the cup and colour it.

In their diet the poorer sort are limited many times to a dish of *frijoles,* or Turkey beans, either black or white (which are there in very great abundance, and are kept dry for all the year) boiled with chilli; and if they can have this, they hold themselves well satisfied; with these beans, they make also dumplings, first boiling the bean a little, and then mingling it with a mass of maize, as we do mingle currents in our cakes, and so boil again the *frijoles* with the dumpling of maize mass, and so eat it hot, or keep it cold; but this and all whatsoever else they eat, they either eat it with green biting chilli, or else they dip it in water and salt, wherein is bruised some of that chilli. But if their means will not reach to *frijoles,* their ordinary fare and diet is their *tortillas* (so they call thin round cakes made of the dough and mass of maize) which they eat hot from an earthen pan, whereon they are soon baked with one turning over the fire; and these they eat alone either with chilli and salt, and dipping them in water and salt with a little bruised chilli. When their maize is green and tender, they boil some of those whole stalks or clusters, whereon the maize groweth with the leaf about, and so casting a little salt about it, they eat it. I have often eat of this, and found it as dainty as our young green peas, and very nourishing, but it much increaseth the blood. Also of this green

and tender maize they make a furmety, boiling the maize in some of the milk which they have first taken out of it by bruising it. The poorest Indian never wants this diet, and is well satisfied as long as his belly is thoroughly filled.

But the poorest that live in such towns where flesh meat is sold will make a hard shift but that when they come from work on Saturday night they will buy one half real, or a real worth of fresh meat to eat on the Lord's day. Some will buy a good deal at once, and keep it long by dressing it into *tasajos,* which are bundles of flesh, rolled up and tied fast, which they do when, for example's sake, they have from a leg of beef sliced off from the bone all the flesh with the knife, after the length, form, and thinness of a line, or rope. Then they take the flesh and salt it, (which being sliced and thinly cut, soon takes salt) and hang it up in their yards like a line from post to post, or from tree to tree, to the wind for a whole week, and then they hang it in the smoke another week, and after roll it up in small bundles, which become as hard as a stone, and so as they need it they wash it, boil it and eat it. This is America's powdered beef, which they call *tasajo.* . . .

As for drinking, the Indians generally are much given unto it; and drink if they have nothing else of their poor and simple chocolate, without sugar or many compounds, or of *atole,* until their bellies be ready to burst. But if they can get any drink that will make them mad drunk, they will not give it over as long as a drop is left, or a penny remains in their purse to purchase it. Among themselves they use to make such drinks as are in operation far stronger than wine; and these they confection in such great jars as come from Spain, wherein they put some little quantity of water, and fill up the jar with some molasses or juice of the sugar-cane, or some honey for to sweeten it; then for the strengthening of it, they put roots and leaves of tobacco, with other kind of roots which grow there, and they know to be strong in operation, and in some places I have known where they have put in a live toad, and so closed up the jar for a fortnight, or month's space, till all that they have put in him be thoroughly steeped and the toad consumed, and the drink well strengthened, then they open it, and call their friends to the drinking of it (which commonly they do in the night time, lest their priest in the town should have notice of them in the day), which they never leave off until they be mad and raging drunk. This drink they call *chicha,* which stinketh most filthily, and certainly is the cause of many Indians' death, especially where they use the toad's poison with it. . . .

And thus having spoken of apparel, houses, eating and drinking, it remains that I say somewhat of their civility, and religion of those who lived under the government of the Spaniards. From the Spaniards they have borrowed their civil government, and in all towns they have one, or two, *alcaldes,* with more or less *regidores* (who are as aldermen or jurats amongst us) and some *alguaziles,* more or less, who are as constables, to execute the orders of the *alcalde* (who is a mayor) with his brethren. In towns of three or four hundred families, or upwards, there are commonly two *alcaldes,* six *regidores,* two *alguaziles mayores,* and six under, or petty, *alguaziles.* And some towns are privileged with an Indian Governor, who is above the *alcaldes* and all the rest of the officers. These are changed every year by new election, and are chosen by the Indians themselves, who take their turns by the tribes or kindreds, whereby they are divided. Their offices begin on New Year's Day, and after that day their election is carried to the city of Guatemala (if in that district it be made) or else to the heads of justice, or Spanish governors of the several provinces, who confirm the new election, and take account of the last year's expenses made by the other officers, who carry with them their town-book of accounts; and therefore for this purpose every town hath a clerk, or scrivener, called *escribano* who commonly continueth many years in his office, by reason of the paucity and unfitness of Indian scriveners who are able to bear such a charge. This clerk hath many fees for his writings and informations, and accounts, as have the Spaniards, though not so much money or bribes, but a small matter, according to the poverty of the Indians. The Governor is also commonly continued many years, being some chief man among the Indians, except for his misdemeanours he be complained of, or the Indians in general do all stomach him.

Thus they being settled in a civil way of government they may execute justice upon all such Indians of their town as do notoriously and scandalously offend. They may imprison, fine, whip, and banish, but hang and quarter they may not; but must remit such cases to the Spanish governor. So likewise if a Spaniard passing by the town, or living in it, do trouble the peace, and misdemean himself, they may lay hold on him, and send him to the next Spanish justice, with a full information of his offence, but fine him, or keep him about one night in prison they may not. This order they have against Spaniards, but they dare not execute it, for a whole town standeth in awe of one Spaniard, and though he never so heinously offend, and be unruly, with oaths, threatenings, and drawing of his sword, he maketh them quake and tremble, and not presume to touch him; for they know if they do they shall have the worst, either by blows, or by some misinformation which he will give against them. . . .

Amongst themselves, if any complaint be made against any Indian, they dare not meddle with him until they call all his kindred, and especially the head of that tribe to which he belongeth; who if he and the rest together find him to deserve imprisonment, or whipping, or any other punishment, then the officers of justices, the *alcaldes* or mayors, and their brethren the jurats inflict upon him that punishment which all shall agree upon. But yet after judgment and sentence given, they have another, which is their last appeal, if they please, and that is to their priest and friar, who liveth in their town, by whom they will sometimes be judged, and undergo what punishment he shall think fittest.

XIII

The Political Institutions of the Indies

To COLUMBUS, CORTÉS, PIZARRO, and other conquistadores, the Spanish kings granted sweeping political powers that made these men practically sovereign in the territories that they had won or proposed to subdue. But royal jealousy of the great expeditionary leaders was quick to show itself. Their authority was soon revoked or strictly limited, and the institutions that had been employed in Spain to achieve centralized political control were transferred to America for the same end.

The Council of the Indies, chartered in 1524, stood at the head of the Spanish imperial administration almost to the close of the colonial period. Under the king (active royal participation in its work varied from monarch to monarch) it was the supreme legislative, judicial, and executive institution of colonial government. One of its most important functions was the nomination of all high colonial officials to the king. It also framed a vast body of legislation for the colonies — the famous Laws of the Indies.

The principal royal agents in the colonies were the viceroys, the captains-general, and the *audiencias*. The viceroys and captains-general had essentially the same functions, differing only in the greater importance and extent of the territory assigned to the jurisdiction of the former. At the end of the Hapsburg era in 1700 there were two great American viceroyalties. The viceroyalty of New Spain, with its capital at Mexico City, included all the Spanish possessions north of the isthmus of Panama; that of Peru, with its capital at Lima, embraced all of Spanish South America, except for the coast of Venezuela. Captains-general, theoretically subordinate to the viceroys but in practice virtually independent of them, governed subdivisions of these vast political jurisdictions.

Each viceroy or captain-general was assisted in the performance of his duties by an audiencia which was the highest court of appeal in its district and also served as the viceroy's council of state. Although the viceroy had supreme executive and administrative powers and was not legally obligated to heed the advice of the audiencia, its immense prestige and its right to correspond directly with the Council of the Indies made it a potential check on the viceregal authority.

Provincial administration in the Indies was entrusted to royal officials who governed districts of varying size and importance from their chief towns and who were most commonly styled *corregidores*. One of their principal duties was to protect the Indians from fraudulent or extortionate practices on the part of the whites, but there is ample testimony that the corregidor was himself the worst offender in this respect.

All royal officials in the Indies, from the viceroy down, faced a *residencia* or judicial review of their conduct at the end of their terms of office. As a general rule, however, the judicious use of bribery and influence could get an erring governor over this last hurdle.

The only political institution in the Indies that at all satisfied local aspirations to self-government was the town council, generally known in the colonies as the *cabildo*. Despite its undemocratic character, inefficiency, and waning prestige and autonomy, the cabildo was not devoid of potential significance. As the only political institution in which the creoles were largely represented, and upon which popular pressure could be in some measure exerted, it was destined to play an important part in the creole seizure of power in the coming age of revolution.

1. THE STRUCTURE OF COLONIAL GOVERNMENT

The shifting pattern of Spain's administration of the Indies in the sixteenth century reflected the steady growth of centralized rule in Spain itself and the application of a trial-and-error method to the problems of colonial government. By the middle of the century the political organization of the Indies had assumed the definitive form that it was to retain, with slight variations, until late in the eighteenth century. The Mexican historian and statesman Lucas Alamán (1792–1853) included an informative sketch of colonial governmental institutions in his classic History of Mexico. *His account, somewhat abstract and idealized, suggests Alamán's sympathy with the old Spanish regime, but gains much value from his familiarity with the colonial climate of opinion in which he passed his youth and early manhood.*[1]

AMONG THE MANY KINGDOMS and lordships that were united in the kings of Spain by inheritance, marriage, and conquest were included the *East and West Indies, islands, and Tierra firme of the Ocean Sea,* the name given to the immense possessions that these kings held on the continent of America and adjacent islands, the Philippine Islands, and others in the eastern seas. These vast dominions were ruled by special laws promulgated in various times and circumstances and later brought together in a code called the *Compilation of Laws of the Kingdoms of the Indies,* authorized by King Charles II on May 18, 1680.

[1] Lucas Alamán, *Historia de Méjico*, México, 1849–52, 5 vols., I, 31–34, 40–43. (Excerpt translated by the editor.)

At the same time the monarch ordered that all the decrees and orders given to the audiencias that did not contravene the compiled laws should continue in force, and that where these laws did not suffice those of Castile, known as the Laws of Toro, should apply.

The discovery and conquest of America coincided with the changes that Charles V made in the fundamental laws of Castile and that his son Philip completed by destroying the *fueros* [privileges] of Aragón. The *cortes* of Castile, Aragón, Valencia, and Catalonia, which formerly had met separately, were transformed and gradually declined in importance until they were reduced to a meeting in Madrid of some representatives or deputies of a few cities of Castile and Aragón, solely for the ceremony of acknowledging and taking the oath of allegiance to the heirs to the throne. All the high functions of government, both legislative and administrative, were vested in the councils, of which there were established in Madrid as many as the monarchy had parts. These councils were in no way dependent upon each other, and had no other relation to each other than that of being under a single monarch. Thus there was the Council of Castile, which was called "royal and supreme" and which the kings had always maintained, though in different forms, to aid them with its advice, and with whose concurrence the dispositions of the monarch had the force of laws, *as if they were proclaimed in the cortes,* a phrase that filled the gap caused by the disappearance of these bodies.

There were also Councils of Aragón, Flanders, and Italy, in addition to those which had jurisdiction over particular departments, such as the Council of the Inquisition, over matters of faith; the Council of the Orders, for the towns that belonged to the military orders of knighthood; and that of the *Mesta,* for the problems arising from the migratory herds of sheep. When, at the beginning of the eighteenth century, the monarchy was reduced in Europe by the War of the Spanish Succession to the Spanish peninsula and adjacent islands, the first three councils were suppressed. Although these councils were endowed with great powers, they derived their authority entirely from that of the monarch, in whose name they performed all their acts and who was the fountainhead and first principle of all power.

Although the Indies were incorporated in the crown of Castile, "from which they could not be alienated totally or in part, under any condition, or in favor of any person," its government was not on that account made at all dependent on the council established for that kingdom; on the contrary, particular care was taken to establish for the colonies a government entirely independent and separate from the Council of Castile. In 1542 was created "the Council of the Indies," to which were assigned the same exemptions and privileges enjoyed by that of Castile; the same power of making laws in consultation with the king; and the same supreme jurisdiction in the East and West Indies and over their natives, even though resident in Castile, subjecting to it the audiencia of the commerce of Seville and expressly forbidding all the councils and tribunals of Spain, except that of the Inquisition, to take cognizance of any question relating to the Indies.

The Council of the Indies, then, was the legislative body in which were framed the laws that governed those vast dominions, it being declared that no law or provision should be obeyed in the colonies that had not passed through the council and had not been communicated by it; it was the supreme court, to which were brought all suits that by reason of the large sums involved could be appealed to this last resort; and, finally, it was the consultative branch of the government in all the weighty matters in which it was judged fitting to hear the Council's opinion. It was also charged with the duty of submitting to the king, through its chamber composed of five councilors, lists of . . . candidates from which were filled the vacant bishoprics, canonates, and judgeships of the audiencias. In order to enable it to perform this task more adequately, the viceroys were required to inform the council privately, at stated intervals, concerning residents of the territory under their command who might be worthy of filling these posts. . . .

The first governors [in the colonies] were the conquistadores themselves, either under the terms of their capitulations or agreements with the king, as in the case of Pizarro in Peru, or by choice of their soldiers, later confirmed by the crown, as happened with Cortés in New Spain. Later the governmental authority was transferred to the same bodies that were appointed to administer justice, called audiencias. Finally the Emperor Charles V created in Barcelona on November 20, 1542, the two viceroyalties of Mexico and Peru, to which were added in the eighteenth century those of Santa Fe and Buenos Aires, the other provinces remaining under captains-general and presidents, who exercised the same functions as the viceroys and differed from them only in title.

The authority of these high functionaries varied greatly according to the times. In the epoch of the creation of the first viceroyalties it was almost without limits, for the king declared: "In all the cases and affairs that may arise, they may do whatever appears fitting to them, and they can do and dispose just as we would do and dispose . . . in the provinces in their charge . . . saving only what is expressly forbidden them to do. . . ."

In the period we are discussing the power of the viceroys was moderated by prudent compromises, reflected in the participation of other bodies in the different branches of government, although the viceroys retained all the glitter and pomp of their supreme authority. In the arduous and important tasks of public administration . . . they were obliged to consult with the *real acuerdo,* the name given to a sitting of the audiencia when it acted as the viceroy's council, although he was not bound to accept the advice of the *oidores* or judges. . . . The viceroy was also subject to the *residencia,* which was a judicial review held immediately at the end of his term of office, and to which the judge who was appointed for this purpose summoned all who desired to complain of some offense or injustice.

From the decisions of this judge there was no appeal except to the Council of the Indies. But although all these restrictions had a very laudable object — to limit and bring within the scope of the laws an authority that bordered on the royal — distance and the very extent of that authority frequently made these precautions illusory. A viceroy of Mexico . . . said in this connection: "If he who comes to govern (this kingdom) does not repeatedly remind himself that the most rigorous *residencia* is that which the viceroy must face when he is judged by the divine majesty, he can be more sovereign than the Grand Turk, for there is no evil action that he may contrive for which he will not find encouragement, nor any tyranny that he may practice which will not be tolerated. . . ."

The period of time that a viceroy could remain in office was at first indefinite, and the first two viceroys of New Spain retained their positions for many years. It was later fixed at a period of three years, which was commonly renewed for those who distinguished themselves by their services, or for those who were the objects of the king's favor; finally it was increased to five years. . . . The salary also varied, and in Mexico, from the time of the Marquis de Croix in 1766, it was 60,000 pesos a year. . . .

The authority exercised by the audiencias in their respective districts may be likened to that enjoyed by the council over all the Indies. These bodies were held in much respect, not only because they possessed great powers, acted as councils to the viceroys with the name of *acuerdo,* and were supreme tribunals from which there was no appeal (save in particular cases, to the Council of the Indies) but also because of their members' reputation for honesty, their discreet conduct and bearing, and even their distinctive attire on public occasions. . . .

This combination of circumstances made these posts very desirable and their holders objects of envy. Appointments were made according to an established scale, with the judges progressing from less important audiencias to those of higher rank.

In order that these magistrates might be entirely independent and devote themselves to the administration of justice without relations of interest, friendship, or kinship in the place where they exercised their functions, they were strictly forbidden to engage in any kind of commerce or business; to borrow or lend money; to own lands, whether vegetable gardens or estates; to pay visits or attend betrothals and baptisms; to associate with merchants; to receive gifts of any kind; or to attend pleasure or gambling parties. These prohibitions also extended to their wives and children. In order to marry they had to obtain a license from the king, on pain of loss of their positions; and if such a license was granted they were generally transferred to another audiencia. The number of *oidores* varied according to the rank of the audiencia. These tribunals were found not only in the viceregal capitals but wherever else they were necessary.

Such was the general system of government of the kingdoms or large divisions of the Indies.

2. A VICEROY ENTERS LIMA

A colonial viceroy was regarded as the very image of his royal master. He enjoyed an immense delegated authority, which was augmented by the distance that separated him from Spain and by the frequently spineless or venal nature of lesser officials. A court modeled on that of Spain, a numerous retinue, and the constant display of pomp and circumstance bore witness to his exalted status. The Spanish travellers Juan and Ulloa describe the elaborate and colorful ceremonies that attended the entrance of such an official into Lima, capital of the viceroyalty of Peru.[2]

[2] Juan and Ulloa, *Voyage to South America,* II, 46–52.

ON THE LANDING of the viceroy at Paita, two hundred and four leagues from Lima, he sends a person of great distinction, generally some officer of his retinue, to Lima, with the character of an ambassador; and, by a memoir, informs his predecessor of his arrival, in conformity to his majesty's orders, who had been pleased to confer on him the government of that kingdom. On this ambassador's arrival at Lima, the late viceroy sends a messenger to compliment him on his safe arrival; and on dismissing the ambassador, presents him with some jewel of great value, and a jurisdiction or two which happen at that time to be vacant, together with an indulgence of officiating by deputy, if most agreeable to him. The corregidor of Piura receives the new viceroy at Paita, and provides litters, mules, and every other necessary for the viceroy and his retinue, as far as the next jurisdiction. He also orders booths to be built at the halting-places in the deserts; attends him in person, and defrays all the expences, till relieved by the next corregidor. Being at length arrived at Lima, he proceeds, as it were incognito, through the city to Callao, about two leagues and a half distant. In this place he is received and acknowledged by one of the ordinary alcaldes of Lima, appointed for that purpose, and also by the military officers. He is lodged in the viceroy's palace, which on this occasion is adorned with astonishing magnificence. The next day, all the courts, secular and ecclesiastical, wait on him from Lima, and he receives them under a canopy in the following order: The audiencia, the chamber of accounts, the cathedral chapter, the magistracy, the consulado, the inquisition, the tribunal de Cruzada, the superiors of the religious orders, the colleges, and other persons of eminence. On this day the judges attend the viceroy to an entertainment given by the alcalde; and all persons of note take a pride in doing the like to his attendants. At night there is a play, to which the ladies are admitted veiled, and in their usual dress, to see the new viceroy.

The second day after his arrival at Callao, he goes in a coach provided for him by the city, to the chapel de la Legua, so called from its being about-half-way between Callao and Lima, where he is met by the late viceroy, and both alighting from their coaches, the latter delivers to him a truncheon as the ensign of the government of the kingdom. After this, and the usual compliments, they separate.

If the new viceroy intends to make his public entry into Lima in a few days, he returns to Callao, where he stays till the day appointed; but as a longer space is generally allowed for the many preparatives necessary to such a ceremony, he continues his journey to Lima, and takes up his residence in his palace, the fitting up of which on this occasion is committed to the junior auditor, and the ordinary alcalde.

On the day of public entry, the streets are cleaned, and hung with tapestry, and magnificent triumphal arches erected at proper distances. At two in the afternoon the viceroy goes privately to the church belonging to the monastery of Montserrat, which is separated by an arch and a gate from the street, where the cavalcade is to begin. As soon as all who are to assist in the procession are assembled, the viceroy and his retinue mount on horses, provided by the city for this ceremony, and the gates being thrown open, the procession begins in the following order:

The militia; the colleges; the university with the professors in their proper habits; the chamber of accounts; the audiencia on horses with trappings; the magistracy, in crimson velvet robes, lined with brocade of the same colour, and a particular kind of caps on their heads, a dress only used on this occasion. Some members of the corporation who walk on foot, support the canopy over the viceroy; and the two ordinary alcaldes, which are in the same dress, and walk in the procession, act as equerries, holding the bridle of his horse. This part of the ceremony, though prohibited by the laws of the Indies, is still performed in the manner I have described; for the custom being of great antiquity, the magistrates have not thought proper to alter it, that the respect to the viceroy might not suffer any diminution, and no person has yet ventured to be the first in refusing to comply with it.

This procession is of considerable length, the viceroy passing through several streets till he comes to the great square, in which the whole company draw up facing the cathedral, where he alights, and is received by the archbishop and chapter. Te Deum is then sung before the viceroy, and the officers placed in their respective seats; after which he again mounts his horse and proceeds to the palace-gate, where he is received by the audiencia, and conducted to an apartment in which a splendid collation is provided, as are also others for the nobility in the antichambers.

On the morning of the following day, he returns to the cathedral in his coach, with the retinue and pomp usual in solemn festivals, and public ceremonies. He is preceded by the whole troop of horse-guards, the members of the several tribunals in their coaches, and after them the viceroy himself with his family, the company of halberdiers bringing up the rear. On this occasion all the riches and ornaments of the church are displayed; the archbishop celebrates in his pontifical robes the mass of thanksgiving; and the sermon is preached by one of the best orators of the chapter. From hence the viceroy returns to the palace attended by all the nobility, who omit nothing to make a splendid figure on these occasions. In the evening of this, and the two following days, the collations are repeated, with all the plenty and delicacy imaginable. To increase the festivity, all women of credit have free access to the halls, galleries, and gardens of the palace, when they are fond of shewing the dispositions of their genius, either by the vivacity of repartees, or spirited conversations, in which they often silence strangers of very ready wit.

This shew and ceremony is succeeded by bull-feasts at the city's expense, which continue five days; the three first for the viceroy, and the two latter in compliment of the ambassador who brought advice of his arrival, and the great honour conferred on him by the sovereign in the government of this kingdom.

This ambassador, who, as I before observed, is always a person of eminent quality, makes also a public entrance into Lima on horseback on the day of his arrival, and the nobility being informed of his approach, go out to receive and conduct him to the palace, from whence they carry him to the lodgings prepared for him. This ceremony used to be immediately followed by feasts and public diversions; but in order to avoid that inconvenience, just when the city is everywhere busied in preparing for the reception of the viceroy, they are deferred, and given at one and the same time as above recited.

The bull-feasts are succeeded by that ceremony, in which the university, the colleges, the convents and nunneries acknowledge him as their vice-royal protector. This is also accompanied with great splendour; and valuable prizes are bestowed on those who make the most ingenious compositions in his praise. These ceremonies, which greatly heighten the magnificence of this city, are so little known in Europe, that I shall be excused for enlarging on them.

They are begun by the university, and the rector prepares a poetical contest, adapted to display either the wit or learning of the competitors. After publishing the themes, and the prizes to be given to those who best handle the subjects they have chosen, he waits on the viceroy to know when he will be pleased to honour the university with his presence; and, the time being fixed, every part of the principal court is adorned with the utmost magnificence. The prizes which are placed in order distinguish themselves by their richness, while the pillars and columns are hung with emblematical devices, or pertinent apothegms on polished shields, surrounded by the most beautiful mouldings.

The reception is in the following order. On the viceroy's entering the court he is conducted to the rectorial chair, which, on this occasion, glitters with the magnificence of an Eastern throne. Opposite to it sits the rector, or, in his absence, one of the most eminent members of that learned body, who makes a speech, in which he expresses the satisfaction the whole university feels in such a patron. After this the viceroy returns to his palace, where, the day following, the rector presents him with a book, containing the poetical contest, bound in velvet, and plated at the corners with gold, accompanied with some elegant piece of furniture, whose value is never less than eight hundred or a thousand crowns.

The principal end of the university in this ceremony being to ingratiate itself with the viceroy and his family, the rector contrives that the poetical pieces which gain the prizes, be made in the name of the principal persons of his family, and accordingly the most distinguished prizes are presented to them; and there being 12 subjects in the contest, there are three prizes for each, of which the two inferior fall to those members, whose compositions are most approved of. These prizes are pieces of plate, valuable both for their weight and workmanship.

The university is followed by the colleges of St. Philip and St. Martin, with the same ceremonies, except the poetical contest.

Next follow the religious orders, according to the antiquity of their foundation in the Indies. These present to the viceroy the best theses maintained by students at the public acts.

The viceroy is present at them all, and each disputant pays him some elegant compliment, before he enters on his subject.

The superiors of the nunneries send him their congratulatory compliments, and when he is pleased in return to visit them, they entertain him with a very fine concert of musick, of which the vocal parts are truly charming: and at his retiring they present him with some of the chief curiosities which their respective institutes allow to be made by them.

Besides these festivities and ceremonies, which are indeed the most remarkable; there are also others, some of which are annual, in which the riches and liberality of the inhabitants are no less conspicuous. Particularly on new-year's day, at the election of alcaldes, who being afterwards confirmed by the viceroy, appear publickly on horseback the same evening, and ride on each side of him, in very magnificent habits ornamented with jewels, and the furniture of their horses perfectly answerable. This cavalcade is very pompous, being preceded by the two companies of horse-guards, the halberdiers, followed by the members of the tribunals in their coaches, the viceroy's retinue, and the nobility of both sexes.

On twelfth-day in the morning, and the preceding evening, the viceroy rides on horseback through the town, with the royal standard carried in great pomp before him. This is performed in commemoration of the building of the city, which, as we have already observed, was begun on this day; solemn vespers are sung in the cathedral, and a mass celebrated; and the ceremony is concluded with a cavalcade, like that on new-year's day.

The alcaldes chosen for the current year, give public entertainments in their houses, each three nights successively; but that the feasts of one might not interfere with those of another, and occasion resentments, they agree for one to hold his feasts the three days immediately succeeding the election, and the other on twelfth-day and the two following. Thus each has a great number of guests, and the entertainments are more splendid and sumptuous. The other feasts in the course of the year, are not inferior to these either with regard to numbers or expense; at least the number of them must excite a high idea of the wealth and magnificence of Lima.

3. "I HAVE SEEN CORRUPTION BOIL AND BUBBLE . . . " [3]

Corruption became structural in the government of the Indies in the seventeenth century. Colonial officials, high and low, prostituted their trusts in innumerable and ingenious ways. An audacious adventurer who had an intimate knowledge of conditions in the colonies, Gabriel Fernández de Villalobos, Marquis of Varinas (1642?–?), showered Charles II with memorials in which he sought to guide the mon-

[3] Shakespeare, *Measure for Measure*, Act V, Scene I.

arch through the bewildering thicket of official misdeeds and warned him that failure to remedy the situation must lead to the loss of the Indies. He was rewarded for his pains by imprisonment in a North African fortress. The following extract from one of his memorials illuminates the technique of a grafting viceroy.[4]

I SHALL ASSUME that your Majesty has everywhere excellent ministers, conscientious and learned, and that the Indies are today and have often before been governed by viceroys and *oidores* of notable piety and integrity. . . . And certainly some were distinguished by all the virtues; there was one, in particular, of such zeal and integrity that on departing from Mexico City after completing his term of office he received with kindness an Indian who offered him a bouquet of flowers, saying: "This is the first gift I have received in this kingdom." A great viceroy was this, my lord, who died so poor that King Philip II (may he be with God) paid his debts out of the royal treasury. And it may be that these virtues (in addition to the merits of his family) later won for his sons the favor of Philip IV, your Majesty's father.

There were viceroys before and after him who worked in the same righteous spirit. For that reason, in this discourse I shall neither name names nor accuse anyone in particular; I shall speak instead of the evils that I have seen and of the remedies that are necessary. . . .

Your Majesty may assume that a high official driven by an immoderate desire to make his fortune will operate in the following manner:

First, he will utilize or sell (to put it more precisely), for his own profit and at high prices, every kind of judicial office, *alcaldías mayores, corregimientos,* commissions, and *residencias.*

Second, he will also sell the rights to *encomiendas,* licenses, and concessions — authorizations to do various things that are forbidden by the laws and ordinances but that the viceroy may allow.

Third, he will dispose in the same way of all kinds of military positions, such as the titles and commissions of lieutenants, captains, generals, recruiting officers, garrison commanders, constables, and many non-existent posts.

Fourth, he will do the same with all that relates to the public finances, selling drafts on the royal treasury (which is the ruin of your Majesty's estate) and disposing of the offices of revenue

[4] *Colección de documentos inéditos . . . de las antiguas posesiones españolas de Ultramar,* Madrid, 1885–1932, 25 vols. XII, 226–231. (Excerpt translated by the editor.)

collectors, of judges appointed to make various investigations, of officials charged with collecting the royal fifth and making financial settlements, of inspectors of the mines and lands, of *alcaldes* with jurisdiction over water rights, and so forth. . . .

Such, my lord, are the articles of faith that your ministers of the Indies observe most diligently.

The minister who does these things, my lord, clearly will be guided not by reason but by his own convenience, and therefore he will surround himself with individuals who will advance his interests; and will encourage these men to commit excesses, while he will always persecute and humiliate the just and virtuous, for these are the only ones he fears.

Such a minister must also seek the good will of superiors as well as inferiors, and share his spoils with them, so that they will write favorably of him to Spain and so that his trickery will be concealed. He must also try to persuade the tribunals to close their eyes to his actions, sometimes through terrorizing them, sometimes by bribing them. . . .

Such viceroys and presidents must also go about in fear and distrust of the people, who see what goes on and murmur, complain, denounce it publicly, and compose satires and squibs. . . .

All these things together, and each one separately, contribute to the total destruction of the Indies, for every item is a source of political offenses and scandalous crimes that cause infinite miseries.

4. THE CORREGIDOR: ENEMY OF THE PEOPLE

The provincial governor — or corregidor, the title he most commonly bore — occupied a key position in the political hierarchy of the Indies. His supreme authority on the local level, under the viceroy, from whom he usually bought his position, gave him immense power for good or evil. By common consent, he generally employed that power for bad ends. The worst abuse of his authority arose in connection with the practice of repartimiento, *the mandatory purchase of goods from the corregidor by the Indians of his district. The Marquis of Varinas describes in vivid detail the operations of the repartimiento.*[5]

THIS CORREGIDOR or governor, president or *alcalde mayor*, whose office cost him 10 or 12,000 pesos, must acquire a stock of goods worth 20,000

pesos to sell in his province, in order to make a profit on the money he has expended. . . . He sells this merchandise to his poor subjects at six or eight times its true value, and buys up the products of the Indians and Spaniards at four or five times below the current price of the country, using force and threats . . . to enrich himself and slake his unnatural thirst for money, as soon as he takes up the tasks of government. . . .

The goods that this official receives from the merchants who outfit him, he purchases at steep prices; and he must increase their cost to the Indians accordingly. So the unhappy judge, dragging the chains of his many debts, arrives in his district, which he finds filled with naked Indians and impoverished Spaniards burdened with children and obligations, whose total possessions, if put up at public auction, would not yield 6,000 pesos. Withal, this judge must squeeze out of them more than 30,000 pesos in two years in order to pay his debts, and half as much again if he wishes to make a profit from his office. And if he cannot do this he is beyond salvation (as they say in the Indies), since he is considering only his temporal welfare and forgetting that such a policy may consign him to eternal perdition, as will inevitably ensue if he does not make restitution.

When this judge enters upon his office, his sole concern is to find means of paying off his large debts and to make a profit from his employment; and since time is short, his needs immense, the land exhausted, and his vassals poor, he must use violence and cruelty to attain what equity, moderation, and kindness will not secure.

To this end he must monopolize the products of the land, compelling his miserable vassals to sell all their fruits to him, who, rod in hand, is judge and inspector, merchant, corregidor, and interpreter of his own contract. . . .

Let your Majesty's ministers of the Council of the Indies, and your Majesty's confessor, take note that the distribution of goods by the corregidor, made to enable him to buy the products of the district, is never carried out by arrangement with the Indians who have to buy this merchandise. The customary practice is for the Spanish governor to turn the goods over to the Indian *alcaldes* and bosses and to fix prices in collusion with them. . . . The Indian bosses never object to the high prices, for they do not have to buy anything; their principal con̶ is to avoid having to shoulder any ̶ burden and to ingratiate themselve̶ corregidores, so that they may keep t̶

[5] *Colección de documentos inéditos*, XII, 237–239, 245–246, 249–256. (Excerpt translated by the editor.)

Having agreed on prices and received the goods, the Indian bosses, who are stupid and heartless, count the people living in each town; they make no exception of the widows or of the poor, sick, and aged, but treat all alike, and assign to them by heads the payment they must make for these goods. They take the merchandise, according to the assessment made by the corregidor, to each one's house, place it before him, and tell him the reckoning; he must pay this in the allotted time or else go to rot in prison. As a clear example of the injustice of this distribution, the Indians are often seen wearing scapularies of various colors . . . which fell to their lot in the distribution and of which they can make no other use. . . .

Your Majesty may imagine from these and similar facts how these Indians fear prison, the threat of which compels the Indian bosses and commoners to submit to their governors; and no wonder, for the Indian prison is a fearful thing. It is a small dark room, without windows or other vent than a very small door. There they must perform their bodily functions, chained by the feet; there are no beds; and as the Indians are brought from other towns, they generally forget to give them any food. They suffer from hunger and thirst and a terrible stench; and since these unhappy beings have been raised in the open country they consider imprisonment worse than death, and therefore many prefer to take their own lives. . . .

At the conclusion of one year, the period for which his office is granted (with a second year possible by way of extension), the judge makes another deal with the superior officer who appointed him, and adds another 1 or 2,000 pesos to the original price, unless this sum was included in the original agreement. If he did not do this he would be completely ruined, for in the first year he was occupied with the distribution of his goods . . . and he must have the second year to collect payment for his merchandise. . . . In any case the judge almost always ends "over-extended" (as they say), with the district owing him for the goods that he distributed — and these debts represent not only the profit that he hoped to make but the sums that he must pay out. On this account the judge resorts to the following expedients, which are all new and greater injustices and injuries to the service of God and of your Majesty:

First, seeing that the end of his term of office and the arrival of a successor are near, the corregidor tries to collect payment from Your Majesty's vassals in four days . . . for goods that he had sold on credit for a much longer period.

Second, after his successor has been named he makes a deal with him (if he is the judge of residence), paying him a certain sum; if he is not the judge, he uses this money to have a judge appointed who will absolve him of all guilt.

Third, in any case he will try to obtain a pledge from his successor that he will not permit any inhabitant to lodge any complaints or charges against him in the *residencia,* making it clear to him that whatever befalls the old judge will happen to the new one, since he must of necessity manage his affairs in the same way as his predecessor.

Fourth, since the debt with which he began his term of office — of 10, 12, and 200,000 pesos, with interest added — is so large that his subjects, though exploited with such great severity, simply cannot furnish this sum of money . . . , he must choose one of two courses of action. He may remain in the vicinity until he has collected all that is owed him — which is his profit — all the rest having gone to pay his outfitters, his creditors, the official who appointed him, and the judge of residence. In this case Your Majesty's vassals, and the judge who succeeds him, are saddled with a very burdensome and offensive guest who not only obstructs their industry but impoverishes them with his collections. Or he may sell his debts to his successor, taking a partial loss; and since these obligations grow with the passage of time, they come to form an unbearable burden on the Spanish and Indian settlements, so that the people become impoverished and leave their homes, and the district is soon depopulated through these intolerable injuries.

Fifth, the evil ministers often resort to the following expedient: Sometimes, in order to leave no debts outstanding when they quit office, they sell or hire the Indians to owners of workshops to satisfy their debts, using trivial offenses as pretexts. . . . At other times they use for pretexts the arrears in the tribute they owe Your Majesty. In other places they commit still greater offenses and violence for the same cause, compelling the Indians to cultivate fields for them, which gives rise to a mass of injuries more numerous than the seeds of grain gathered from the land, for with this pretext fifty Indians are forced to pay the tributes of five hundred. So these Indians must pass their lives in endless labor, lacking food, clothing, or time in which to plant for themselves and their families. They go about continually harassed — men, women, the aged, boys, widows, young girls, and married women, sowing and plowing with their own hands, unaided by oxen or other animals, and threshing the grain with their feet, all without recompense. . . .

Sixth, since the first question put in the *residencia* asks the witnesses under oath whether the judge engaged in any business dealings on his own account, it becomes necessary to keep from the judge of residence what everybody else knows. Hence, by one means or another — threats or pleas for mercy, or bad conscience — all are made to swear that the corregidor engaged in no business dealings, either personally or through intermediaries; and this is sworn to by the same persons to whom the judge forcibly sold and distributed the steers, mules, and other merchandise in which he traded during his term of office, and whose grain and other supplies he monopolized. . . .

Thus, through such perjury and sins of sacrilege on the part of the persons he suborned, the corregidor obtains an acquittal and quits his office — one which he secured through bribery and fraud, which he entered with usury and oppression, whose duties he performed with violence and injury, and which he left committing sacrilege, bearing false witness before God concerning his actions.

5. City Government in the Indies

The birth of the colonial city coincided with the passing of the freedom and authority of the communes or towns of Spain. Under the circumstances it was inconceivable that Spain's rulers should permit any development of municipal democracy or autonomy in the colonies. From the outset the right of the king to appoint municipal officials was accepted without question. Philip II began the practice — which later became general — of selling posts in the town councils to the highest bidders, with the right of resale or bequest, on condition that a certain part of their value be paid to the crown at each transfer. Inevitably, this system caused such an office to be regarded as a source of social prestige or profit, rather than as a public trust for which the holder was answerable to the citizenry. Gonzalo Gómez de Cervantes, a leading citizen of Mexico, of whose life little is known, criticized the practice and suggested its reform in a memorial addressed to a member of the Council of the Indies, dated 1599.[6]

[6] Gonzalo Gómez de Cervantes, *La vida económica y social de Nueva España al finalizar el siglo XVI*, edited by

It is well known and understood that Mexico is the head of all this kingdom and that all the other cities, towns, and places of this New Spain acknowledge it as such. All the more reason, then, that its *regidores* (councilmen) should be outstanding men, of quality, experience, and mature judgment. And the lack of such men has been a cause of many different things, that show a serious weakness. The proof of this is that the majority of the regidores are youths who even twenty years from now will not have enough experience to govern a city; and it is a sorry thing to see those who have not yet left off being children, already made city fathers.

This evil arises from the permission granted by His Majesty for the sale of these offices — whereby they go to those who can pay the most for them, and not to those who would render the best honor and service to the commonweal. It is shameful that such youths should be preferred for the posts of regidores and other important positions over mature and eminent men who should occupy those offices. Truly, it would redound much more to the service of His Majesty and to the increase of his kingdom, if he gave these council seats to qualified persons, descendants of conquistadores, and others who have served him; they would regard their king and country with greater love, if His Majesty rewarded them for their merits and services, and would be inspired to serve him still more.

It is not seemly that those who yesterday were shopkeepers or tavern-keepers, or engaged in other base pursuits, should today hold the best offices in the country while gentlemen and descendants of those who conquered and won the land go about poor, dejected, degraded, and neglected. And it is the city that suffers most from this injustice, because the fixing of market prices, the supervision of weights and measures in the markets, and other very important matters are in a state of great disorder. It would be a very efficacious remedy, if his Majesty were to add a dozen council seats and give them to men of quality, maturity, wisdom, and merit — not by way of sale, but as gifts — and if he were to do the same with the seats that fall vacant. If such a policy were adopted, everything pertaining to his royal estate and the preservation of this realm would be greatly served and advanced.

Alberto María Carreño, México, 1944, pp. 93–94. (Excerpt translated by the editor.)

XIV

The Church in the Indies

THE CONTROLLING INFLUENCE of the Catholic Church in the social and spiritual life of the colonies was deeply rooted in the Spanish past. During the long centuries of struggle against the Moslems, the Church, in whose name the Wars of Reconquest were waged, acquired immense wealth and an authority second only to that of the crown. The Catholic Kings, Ferdinand and Isabella, particularly favored the clergy and the spread of its influence as a means of achieving their ideals of national unity and royal absolutism. The Spanish Inquisition, founded by them in 1480, had political as well as religious uses, and under their great-grandson Philip II it became "the strongest bulwark of the omnipotence of the crown."

Royal control over ecclesiastical affairs, in both Spain and the Indies, was solidly founded on the institution of the *patronato real* (royal patronage). As applied to the colonies, this consisted in the absolute right of the Spanish kings to nominate all church officials, collect ecclesiastical tithes, and found churches and monasteries in America. The Spanish monarchs regarded the patronage of the Church as their most cherished prerogative, and reacted sharply to all encroachments upon it.

Beginning with Columbus's second voyage, one or more clergymen accompanied every expedition that sailed for the Indies, and they came in swelling numbers to the subjugated territories. They converted prodigious numbers of natives, who as a rule willingly accepted the new and more powerful divinities of the invaders; frequently they championed the rights of the Indians against their Spanish oppressors. Unfortunately, some lost their apostolic fervor as the high religious excitement of the first strenuous years dissolved; many of the later arrivals preferred ease and profit to a life of austerity and service. From first to last, the colonies were a scene of unedifying strife between regular and secular clergy over their fields of jurisdiction.

The missionary impulse of the first friars survived longest on the frontier, "the Rim of Christendom." The most notable instance of successful missionary effort, at least from an economic point of view, was that of the Jesuit establishments in Paraguay.

The Inquisition was established in the Indies by Philip II in 1569. Its great privileges, its independence of other courts, the secrecy of its proceedings, and the dread with which the charge of heresy was generally regarded by Spaniards made the Inquisition an effective check on "dangerous thoughts," whether religious, political, or philosophical. The great mass of cases tried by its tribunals, however, had to do with offenses against morality or minor deviations from orthodox religious conduct.

By the first decades of the eighteenth century the morals of the clergy had declined to a condition that the Mexican historian Lucas Alamán, himself a leader of the clerical party in the period of independence, could only characterize as "scandalous." Yet the power of the Church, founded upon its immense wealth, its many bonds with the state, and the fanaticism of the masses, was not significantly diminished by the moral decline of many of the clergy. It was destined to survive the wreck of the Spanish colonial system and to play an important role in the life of the new Spanish-American republics.

1. THE ROYAL PATRONAGE

The privilege of the patronato real *was to some extent implied in the papal grant of the newly-discovered western lands to the king of Castile in 1493, "with free, full, and absolute power, authority, and*

jurisdiction." By later bulls, issued in 1501 and 1508, the Papacy conceded to King Ferdinand and his successors the exclusive right of patronage over the Church in the New World. The following decree of Philip II, dated July 10, 1574, fully defines that right, and claims it not only on the basis of the papal con-

138

cessions but on the ground that the Indies had been discovered and acquired at the expense of the crown of Castile.[1]

THE KING, to our viceroy of the provinces of Peru, or to any other person or persons who for the time may be in charge of the government of that country. As you know, the right of ecclesiastical patronage, throughout the whole dominion of the Indies, belongs to us, not only because it was at our expense and that of the Catholic sovereigns, our predecessors, that that part of the world was discovered and acquired, and that churches and monasteries were built and endowed therein, but also because that right was granted to us by bulls issued by the supreme pontiffs, of their own accord; and in order to preserve it, and maintain our just title thereto, we order and command that said right of patronage, one and undivided throughout the whole dominion of the Indies, may always remain preserved to us and to our royal Crown, without any possibility of our losing it, either wholly or in part, and that we may never be understood as conceding the right of patronage by favour or disfavour, by statute or by any other action that we ourselves, or the sovereigns our successors, may take.

And, moreover, that neither by custom, nor by prescription, nor by any other title, shall any person or persons, or ecclesiastical or secular communities, churches, or monasteries, be able to use the right of patronage, except the person who in our name and with our authority and power shall exercise it; and that no person, be he a layman or an ecclesiastic, no order, convent, religion, community, of whatever state, condition, quality and rank it may be, may dare to intermeddle on any occasion or by any reason whatever, either judicially or extrajudicially, in any affair that may concern our royal patronage, neither to prejudice us respecting it, nor to appoint to any church or benefice, or ecclesiastical office, nor to accept such appointment when made in any part of the dominion of the Indies, without our nomination or the nomination of the person whom we by law or by patent shall have authorized; and whoever shall act contrary to this, shall, in case of being a layman, incur a loss of the privileges which he shall hold from us in the whole dominion of the Indies, and he shall be incompetent to hold others, and shall be for ever banished from all our kingdoms and dominions, and in case of being an ecclesiastic, he shall be regarded as a stranger and an alien in all our kingdoms and dominions, and shall not be able to hold any benefice or ecclesiastical office therein, and shall, moreover, incur the other penalties established against such acts by the laws of these kingdoms; and our viceroys, audiencias, and royal justices shall proceed with all rigour against those who shall so stand or act in opposition to our right of patronage, proceeding on the charge or demand of our fiscals, or of any party whatsoever who may ask for such prosecution; and great diligence shall be observed in the conduct of the case. We wish and command that there shall not be erected, instituted, founded, or constituted any cathedral or parochial church, monastery, hospital, votive church, or any other pious or religious place without our express consent, or that of the person who shall have our authority and commission for this purpose. And again, that there shall not be instituted or established any archbishopric, dignity, canonry, prebend, benefice, either simple or parochial, or any other benefice, or ecclesiastical or religious office, without our express permission, or that of the person on whom we shall have conferred full power and authority for the purpose.

2. THE COMING OF THE FRIARS

Hard on the heels of the conquistador came the priest. Even before all fighting in Mexico had ceased, Cortés wrote to the Emperor Charles V urgently asking that missionaries be sent from Spain. In June, 1524, twelve Franciscan friars, led by Father Martín de Valencia, landed on the shores of Mexico and began their barefooted pilgrimage toward the capital. There Cortés received them with a humility that confounded the Indian chiefs summoned for the occasion. Father Gerónimo de Mendieta (1525–1604), a Franciscan friar who passed many years of his life in New Spain, where he wrote an important ecclesiastical history of the colony, records the arrival of the first friars in Mexico.[2]

WHEN THE GOVERNOR, Don Fernando Cortés, learned of the arrival of these friars, whose coming he had so greatly desired and worked for, he was very joyful and gave thanks to God for this mercy. Then he ordered some of his servants to go out on the road to meet them, to receive them

[1] Quoted in Bernard Moses, *The Spanish Dependencies in South America*, New York, 1914, 2 vols., II, 219–221.

[2] Gerónimo de Mendieta, *Historia eclesiástica indiana*, México, 1945, 4 vols., II, 51–55. (Excerpt translated by the editor.)

in his name, and to look after them. He did this so that they might not lack anything, and so that they might suffer no mishap, for the affairs of the country were not entirely settled, since it had been conquered only recently, and the few Spaniards in it were collected in Mexico City, and feared new disturbances. One of these servants was Juan de Villagomez, who told me the story that I write down here.

While these friars journeyed toward Mexico City (which lies sixty leagues from their port of debarkation) on foot and unshod, and wanting no special care for themselves, the governor summoned all the Indian caciques and principal men of the largest towns around Mexico City, so that they might all join him in receiving the ministers of God who came to teach them His law, show them His will, and guide them along the road of salvation.

These servants of God, passing through Tlascala, stopped there for a few days to rest from their journey and to view the city, which was famed for its size. They remained there till market day, when most of the people of that province are wont to gather to obtain provisions for their families. And they marveled to see such a multitude of souls, a greater throng than they had ever seen before. They praised God with great joy to see such a plentiful harvest placed before them. And though they could not speak to them in their language, they made signs (like mutes), pointing to heaven, to convey that they came to teach them the treasures and wonders that were to be found on high.

The Indians trailed behind them (like boys following someone who is performing a novel trick), and wondered to see their threadbare garments, so different from the gallant attire of the Spanish soldiers. And they said to each other: "Who are these men that look so poor? What kind of clothing are they wearing? They are not like the other Christians of Castile." And they frequently uttered a word in their language, saying: *"motolinea, motolinea."* One of the fathers, named Fray Toribio de Benavente, asked a Spaniard the meaning of this word that they used so frequently. The Spaniard replied, "Father, *motolinea* means poor." Then Fray Toribio said: "That shall be my name as long as I live"; thereafter he always signed himself Fray Toribio Motolinea.

When they had arrived at Mexico, the governor, accompanied by all the Spanish gentlemen and the leading Indians who were assembled for that purpose, came out to receive them; he went from one to another, kneeling before each and kissing his hands. The same was done by Don Pedro de Alvarado and the other Spanish captains and gentlemen. The Indians, seeing this, imitated the Spaniards and also kissed the hands of the fathers. Such is the power of example when given by superiors. . . .

When the governor had shown the new guests to their lodgings and had seen to their needs, he returned to the Indian caciques and principal men (who stood as if stunned by this unusual event) and said to them:

"Do not marvel that I, who am captain-general, governor, and lieutenant of the Emperor of the World, should render obedience and submission to these shabbily dressed men who have come to us from Spain. For the power that governors enjoy . . . extends only to the bodies and estates of men, which are the outward and visible part that is perishable and corruptible on this earth. But the dominion that these men wield is over men's immortal souls, each of which has greater worth and price than all the gold or silver or precious stones in the world, or than the heavens themselves. For God has endowed them with power to guide men's souls to heaven to enjoy eternal glory, if they will accept their aid. But if they reject it, they are damned and must go to Hell to suffer eternal torments, as happened to all your forebears for lack of ministers to teach them knowledge of the God who created us. . . .

"And so that the same may not happen to you, and lest through ignorance you go where your fathers and grandfathers went before you, these priests of God, whom you call *teopixques,* have come to show you the way of salvation. Regard them, therefore, with much esteem and reverence as the guides of your souls, messengers of the most high God, and your spiritual fathers. Listen to their teachings and heed their advice and commands, and see to it that all the rest obey them, for such is my will and that of the Emperor our Lord, and of God himself . . . , who sent them to this land."

3. DIALOGUE IN YUCATAN

Some of the early friars in the Indies were saintly and courageous men who preached not only the gospel of Christ but the message of justice to the Indians. Their zeal in this cause won them the hatred of Spanish encomenderos *and mine owners and the gratitude of the natives. Objectively their altruism served the long-range interests of Spanish imperialism, for it helped to overcome the spiritual resistance of the Indians to their conquerors and aided in stabilizing the social and economic life of the colonies. But their sincerity and good will cannot be questioned. Their point of view is well expressed in a dialogue overheard in a Yucatan village by Father La Torre, one of the Dominican friars who accompanied Las Casas when the great fighter for Indian rights came to southern Mexico as Bishop of Chiapas in 1544.[3]*

THE SUN had already set when we came to a clean-looking little church, decorated with branches. We were much pleased and greatly heartened, believing that where these signs appeared we were certain to find charity. After saying a prayer we continued on our way as if spellbound, for we knew nothing of these people and did not know how to talk to them. This was our first encounter with the Indians, who certainly could do as they pleased with us without fear of resistance; it was we who were afraid of them.

So we came to a village where many Indians were sitting about. When they saw us they rose and gave us seats, which were small stools, no larger than the distance between the extended thumb and forefinger of one hand. . . . The father vicar said, "Let us stay here this night, for God has prepared this lodging for us." The Indians, seeing how miserable we were, owing to the cold of the lagoon, made a great bonfire, the first that we had needed since leaving Spain. Then the chief came with half a pumpkin shell filled with water; he washed our feet, and they gave us each two tortillas and a piece of fresh fish and another of sweet potato. We ate and felt much better, and were filled with devotion and wonder to see the charity of these Indians, who the Spaniards claimed were so bestial.

At night came Ximénes, who knew their language, and through him we asked them why they had treated us so kindly. They replied that on the road an Indian had seen us and realized that we were thirsty and had told them so, and for that reason they had sent that pumpkin shell of water and accorded us that hospitality, because they knew that we came from Castile for their good. We took great pleasure in the reply of these barbarians.

That night there arrived a peasant who came with the bishop [Las Casas], Zamora by name, and after we had all lain down to sleep, some on boards and others on small mats that the In-

dians make of rushes . . . , Zamora, the recently-arrived peasant from Castile, and Ximénes, an oldtimer in the country and a conqueror of Yucatan, began to talk, and because their conversation was very diverting I shall set down here what I remember of it.

Said Ximénes to Zamora:

"You chose a poor place to stable that beast of yours for the night; the Indians will surely take it and eat it."

Said Zamora:

"Let them eat it, by God; we Christians owe them a good deal more than that."

Ximénes:

"What the devil do you mean by that?"

Zamora:

"I mean that you've robbed them of their property and taken their sons from them and made them slaves in their own land."

Ximénes:

"They owe us more than that, for we are Christians."

Zamora:

"Christians? A Christian is known by his works."

Ximénes:

"We are Christians, and we came to this land to make Christians of them."

Zamora:

"I'll bet you came over here because your deviltries made Spain too hot a place for you, or else you would not have left your own country. I swear to God that no one comes to the Indies for any other reason, and myself first of all."

Ximénes:

"God alone knows why each man came over; but the main thing is that we conquered this country."

Zamora:

"And that is why you expect the Indians to give you their food and property — because you murdered them in their own houses! Good friends you proved to be, indeed!"

Ximénes:

"You would not say that if you had shed your blood in the war."

Zamora:

"I dare say that even if they had killed you they would not go to Hell, because you made war on them."

Ximénes:

"They are dogs, and will not believe in God."

Zamora:

"And very good preachers they had in you, for certain."

---

[3] F. Tomás de la Torre, *Desde Salamanca . . . hasta . . . Chiapas*, pp. 150–152. (Excerpt translated by the editor.)

Ximénes:

"Surely, Zamora, you will not go back to Castile."

Zamora:

"The devil take me if I carry away a cent that I did not earn with my spade; the Indians owe me nothing."

While this dialogue went on the rest of us kept quiet, lying in the dark, but we could hardly keep from laughing at the humor of Zamora's remarks. On the other hand, we were confounded by the clarity and simplicity of the judgments of this illiterate peasant, who said only what his reason dictated. . . .

4. THE JESUIT MISSION EMPIRE

In the wilderness of eastern Paraguay, a region favored by a genial climate and fertile soil, two Jesuit priests, Joseph Cataldino and Simon Mazetta, began missionary work among the Guarani Indians in 1609. Eventually more than thirty missions or reductions had arisen in the area; they formed the principal field of Jesuit activity in America until their expulsion in 1767. Their strict discipline, centralized organization, and absolute control over the labor of thousands of docile Indians enabled the Jesuits to turn their missions into a highly profitable business enterprise. The self-imposed isolation of the Jesuit mission empire aroused the curiosity of European philosophers and literati; Voltaire gave an ironic and fanciful description of it in his witty satire on the follies and vices of the age, Candide. *Félix de Azara (1742–1804), a distinguished Spanish soldier and scientist who came to Paraguay on an official assignment in 1781, fourteen years after the expulsion of the Jesuits, describes the life and government of the missions.*[4]

HAVING SPOKEN of the towns founded by the Jesuit fathers, and of the manner in which they were founded, I shall discuss the government which they established in them. . . .

In the town of Candelaria there was a father, a kind of provincial, named *Superior of the Missions,* who had authority from the Pope to confirm the Indians and was the chief of all the curacies or towns. In each one resided two priests, a curate and a sub-curate, who had certain assigned functions. The sub-curate was charged with all the spiritual tasks, and the curate with every kind of temporal responsibility. Since the latter required much knowledge

4 Félix de Azara, *Descripción y historia del Paraguay y del Rio de la Plata,* Asunción, Paraguay, 1896, 2 vols., I, 338–352. (Excerpt translated by the editor.)

and experience, the curates were always priests of notable gravity, who had earlier been provincials or rectors of their colleges; whether or not they knew the language of the Indians was not considered important. Their predecessors in office left them copious diaries, with directions for the management of labor, workshops, and so forth. The curates, in sum, were masters of all. Although each town had its Indian *corregidor, alcaldes,* and *regidores,* who comprised a municipal council like that of a Spanish town, they had no jurisdiction, and were in effect nothing more than the executors of the orders of the curate, who invariably handed down mild judgments in all cases, civil and criminal, but did not permit an appeal to other Spanish judges or *audiencias.*

The curate allowed no one to work for personal gain; he compelled everyone, without distinction of age or sex, to work for the community, and he himself saw to it that all were equally fed and dressed. For this purpose the curates placed in storehouses all the fruits of agriculture and the products of industry, selling in the Spanish towns their surplus of cotton, cloth, tobacco, vegetables, skins, yerba maté, and wood, transporting them in their own boats down the nearest rivers, and returning with implements and whatever else was required.

From the foregoing one may infer that the curates disposed of the surplus funds of the Indian towns, and that no Indian could aspire to own private property. This deprived them of any incentive to use reason or talent, since the most industrious, able, and worthy person had the same food, clothing, and pleasures as the most wicked, dull, and indolent. It also follows that although this form of government was well designed to enrich the communities it also caused the Indian to work at a languid pace, since the wealth of his community was of no concern to him. . . .

It must be said that although the fathers were supreme in all respects, they employed their authority with a mildness and restraint that command admiration. They supplied everyone with abundant food and clothing. They compelled the men to work only half a day, and did not drive them to produce more. Even their labor was given a festive air, for they went in procession to the fields, to the sound of music and carrying a little image in a litter, for which they always constructed a bower; and the music did not cease until they had returned in the same way they had set out. They gave them many holidays, dances, and tournaments, dressing the actors and the members of the municipal councils in gold or silver tissue and the most costly European garments, but they permitted the women to act only as spectators.

They likewise forbade the women to sew; this occupation was restricted to the musicians, sacristans, and acolytes. But they made them spin cotton; and the cloth that the Indians wove, after satisfying their own needs, they sold together with the surplus cotton in the Spanish towns, as they did with the tobacco, vegetables, yerba maté, wood, and skins. The curate and his companion, or sub-curate, had their own plain dwellings, and they never left them except to take the air in the great enclosed yard of their college. They never walked through the streets of the town or entered the house of any Indian or let themselves be seen by any woman — or, indeed, by any man, except for those indispensable few through whom they issued their orders. If some ailing person required spiritual aid, they brought him from his miserable dwelling to a clean room near the college that was set apart for that purpose, and the sub-curate, carried in a sedan with great pomp, administered the holy sacraments to him there.

When they appeared in the church, although it was only to say mass, it was with the greatest ceremony, wearing costly garments, surrounded and assisted by about a hundred sacristans, acolytes, and musicians. All their churches were the largest and most magnificent in that part of the world, filled with great altars, pictures, and gilding; the ornaments could not be better or more costly in Madrid or Toledo. All this is convincing evidence that the Jesuits spent on churches and their accessories, and in attiring the actors and municipal officers on festival days, the vast sums that they could have appropriated for themselves if they had been ambitious.

The streets of their towns were five paces wide. The buildings were one-story structures, each consisting of a long hall that originally housed all the subjects of a chieftain; they were later divided into little rooms, each seven *varas* long, one to each family. These rooms had no window, chimney, or kitchen, and their entire furnishings consisted of a cotton hammock, for the master of the house; the others slept on skins on the floor, without any partitions between them. The food of the Indians cost the priests little or nothing, since they had a surplus of meat from the increase of the herds on their estates. For clothing they gave each man a cap,

a shirt, stockings, and a poncho, all made of cotton cloth, a thick, coarse, light-colored material. They made them shave their hair, and did not permit them to wear anything on their feet. The women also went barefooted, and their only garment was a *tipos* or sleeveless shirt of the same material as was described above, girdled at the waist. . . .

From what I could learn, in visiting all the towns, none of the Indians understood Spanish, nor could they read or write, except for a few who were taught to read and write in Guarani in order to keep accounts of what was taken into and out of the storehouses and so forth. They had no scientific knowledge and only a few crafts, since they only wove cloth for their own garments and for slaves or very poor people; but some were taught the trades of ironsmith and silversmith and painting, sculpture, music, dancing, and so forth, in which they were instructed by Jesuits brought especially for this purpose.

All were baptized and knew how to say their prayers, which all the boys and unmarried girls had to recite in a chorus under the portico of the church at dawn. Yet those who have replaced the Jesuits assert that there was little true religion among the Indians. This is not strange, in view of the fact that the Indians themselves say that there were few Jesuit curates capable of preaching the gospel in Guarani. . . . As a partial remedy for this deficiency, the Jesuits had certain clever Indians learn a few sermons, which they preached in the town square after some festival or tournament; I have heard some of these, and they contained a good deal of nonsense, which the orator drew out of his head. . . .

In the year 1768, the Jesuits turned their towns over to an equal number of friars; but theirs was only the spiritual power, while the temporal power formerly enjoyed by the Jesuit curate was entrusted to a secular administrator. There was also established a military governor of all the missions of the Parana and Uruguay rivers. It could be said that these towns only changed hands, but the Jesuits were more able, moderate, and frugal, and regarded their towns as their own handiwork and private possession, and so loved them and worked for their good. The secular governors, on the other hand, and the administrators whom they appointed, not only lacked the intelligence of the Jesuits but regarded the wealth of the communities as a mine which was theirs to exploit for a short time. It is not strange, therefore, that the towns have grown poor, and that the Indians are compelled to work harder and are more poorly fed and clothed.

5. IN THE HANDS OF THE INQUISITION

Among the first victims of the Inquisition in Spanish America were a number of English mariners who were set on the Mexican shore by Sir John Hawkins, at their own request, after Hawkins had escaped with two battered ships from a severe naval defeat at Spanish hands in the harbor of Veracruz. After a residence of some six years in the country, during which time they were fairly well treated by the colonists, the Englishmen were rounded up and brought to Mexico City to be tried for heresy by the Inquisition. Miles Philips, one who lived to return to England and tell the tale, recorded his ordeal in a narrative first published by Richard Hakluyt (1552?–1616?) in his great documentary collection dealing with English voyages. Modern archival research has confirmed the essential reliability of this and other accounts in Hakluyt of the experiences of Englishmen in Mexico during the sixteenth century.[5]

NOW AFTER THAT SIX YEARS were fully expired after our first coming into the Indies, in which time we had been imprisoned and served in the said countries as is before truly declared, in the year of our Lord one thousand five hundred seventy four, the Inquisition began to be established in the Indies, very much against the minds of the Spaniards themselves. For never until this time since their first conquering and planting in the Indies, were they subject to that bloody and cruel Inquisition.

The chief Inquisitor was named Don Pedro Moya de Contreras, and John de Bovilla his companion, and John Sanchez the fiscal, and Pedro de los Rios, the secretary. They being come and settled, and placed in a very fair house near unto the white friars, considering with themselves that they must make an entrance and beginning of that their most detestable Inquisition here in Mexico, to the terror of the whole country, thought it best to call us that were Englishmen first in question, and so much the rather, for that they had perfect knowledge and intelligence that many of us were become very rich, as has been already declared, and therefore we were a very good booty and prey to the Inquisitors.

5 "The Voyage of Miles Philips . . . ," in Richard Hakluyt, *The Principal Navigations, Voyages, Traffiques and Discoveries of the English Nation*, London, n.d., 8 vols., VI, 318–323.

So that now again began our sorrows afresh, for we were sent for, and sought out in all places of the country, and proclamation made upon pain of losing of goods and excommunication, that no man should hide or keep secret any Englishman or any part of their goods. By means whereof we were all soon apprehended in all places, and all our goods seized and taken for the Inquisitor's use, and so from all parts of the country we were conveyed and sent as prisoners to the city of Mexico, and there committed to prison in sundry dark dungeons, where we could not see but by candle light, and were never past two together in one place, so that we saw not one another, neither could one of us tell what was become of another.

Thus we remained close imprisoned for the space of a year and a half, and others for some less time, for they came to prison ever as they were apprehended. During which time of our imprisonment, at the first beginning we were often called before the Inquisitors alone, and there severely examined of our faith, and commanded to say the Pater Noster, the Ave Maria, and the Creed in Latin, which God knows a great number of us could not say, otherwise than in the English tongue. And having the said Robert Sweeting who was our friend at Tescuco always present with them for an interpreter, he made report for us, that in our own country speech we could say them perfectly, although not word for word as they were in Latin.

Then did they proceed to demand of us upon our oaths what we did believe of the Sacrament, and whether there did remain any bread or wine after the words of consecration, yea or no, and whether we did not believe that the host of bread which the priest did hold up over his head, and the wine that was in his chalice, was the very true and perfect body and blood of our Savior Christ, yea or no. To which if we answered not yea, then was there no way but death. Then they would demand of us what we did remember of ourselves, what opinions we had held, or had been taught to hold contrary to the same while we were in England. To which we for the safety of our lives were constrained to say, that never we did believe, nor had been taught otherwise than . . . before we had said.

Then would they charge us that we did not tell them the truth, that they knew the contrary, and therefore we should call ourselves to remembrance, and make them a better answer at the next time, or else we should be racked, and made to confess the truth whether we would or no. And so coming again before them the next time, we were still demanded of our belief while we were in England, and how we had been taught, and also what we thought or did know of such our own company as they did name unto us, so that we could never be free from such demands, and at other times they would promise us, that if we would tell them truth, then we should have favor and be set at liberty, although we very well knew their fair speeches were but means to entrap us to the hazard and loss of our lives.

Howbeit God so mercifully wrought for us by a secret means that we had, that we kept us still to our first answer, and would still say that we had told the truth unto them, and knew no more by ourselves nor any other of our fellows than as we had declared, and that for our sins and offenses in England against God and our Lady, or any of his blessed Saints, we were heartily sorry for the same, and did cry God mercy, and besought the Inquisitors for God's sake, considering that we came into those countries by force of weather, and against our wills, and that never in our lives we had either spoken or done anything contrary to their laws, and therefore they would have mercy upon us.

Yet all this would not serve; for still from time to time we were called upon to confess, and about the space of three months before they proceeded to their severe judgment, we were all racked, and some enforced to utter that against themselves, which afterwards cost them their lives. And thus having gotten from our own mouths matter sufficient for them to proceed in judgment against us, they caused a large scaffold to be made in the middle of the market place in Mexico right over against the head church, and fourteen or fifteen days before the day of their judgment, with the sound of a trumpet, and the noise of their *atabales*, which are a kind of drums, they did assemble the people in all parts of the city. Before whom it was then solemnly proclaimed, that whosoever would upon such a day repair to the market place, they should hear the sentence of the holy Inquisition against the English heretics, Lutherans, and also see the same put in execution.

Which being done, and the time approaching of this cruel judgment, the night before they came to the prison where we were, with certain officers of that holy hellish house, bringing with them certain fool's coats which they had prepared for us, being called in their language San Benitos, which coats were made of yellow cotton and red crosses upon them, both before and behind. They were so busied in putting on their coats about us, and bringing us out into a large yard, and placing and pointing us in what order we should go to the scaffold or place of judgment upon the morrow, that they did not once suffer us to sleep all that night long.

The next morning being come, there was given to every one of us for our breakfast a cup of wine, and a slice of bread fried in honey and so about eight of the clock in the morning, we set forth of the prison, every man alone in his yellow coat, and a rope about his neck, and a great green wax candle in his hand unlighted, having a Spaniard appointed to go upon either side of every one of us. And so marching in this order and manner toward the scaffold in the market place, which was a bow shoot distant or thereabouts, we found a great assembly of people all the way, and such a throng, that certain of the Inquisitors officers on horseback were constrained to make way, and so coming to the scaffold, we went up by a pair of stairs, and found seats ready made and prepared for us to sit down on, every man in order as he should be called to receive his judgment.

We being thus set down as we were appointed, presently the Inquisitors came up another pair of stairs, and the viceroy and all the chief justices with them. When they were set down and placed under the cloth of estate agreeing to their degrees and calling, then came up also a great number of friars, white, black, and gray, about the number of 300 persons, they being set in the places for them appointed. Then was there a solemn Oyes made, and silence commanded, and then presently began their severe and cruel judgment.

The first man that was called was one Roger the chief armorer of the *Jesus,* and he had judgment to have three hundred stripes on horseback, and after condemned to the galleys as a slave for ten years.

After him were called John Gray, John Brown, John Rider, John Moon, James Collier, and one Thomas Brown. These were adjudged to have 200 stripes on horseback, and after to be committed to the galleys for the space of eight years.

Then was called John Keyes, and was adjudged to have 100 stripes on horseback, and condemned to serve in the galleys for the space of six years.

Then were severally called the number of fifty-three one after another, and every man had his several judgment, some to have 200 stripes on horseback, and some 100, and condemned for slaves to the galleys, some for six years, some for eight and some for ten.

And then was I Miles Philips called, and was adjudged to serve in a monastery for five years, without any stripes, and to wear a fool's coat, or San Benito, during all that time.

Then were called John Storie, Richard Williams, Robert Cook, Paul Horsewell and Thomas Hull. The six were condemned to serve in monasteries without stripes, some for three years and some for four, and to wear the San Benito during all the said time. Which being done, and it now drawing toward night, George Rively, Peter Momfrie, and Cornelius the Irishman were called and had their judgment to be burned to ashes, and so were presently sent away to the place of execution in the market place but a little from the scaffold, where they were quickly burned and consumed. And as for us that had received our judgment, being sixty-eight in number; we were carried back that night to prison again.

And the next day in the morning being Good Friday, the year of our Lord 1575, we were all brought into a court of the inquisitors' palace, where we found a horse in a readiness for every-one of our men which were condemned to have stripes, and to be committed to the galleys, which were in number sixty and so they being enforced to mount up on horseback naked from the middle upward, were carried to be showed as a spectacle for all the people to behold throughout the chief and principal streets of the city, and had the number of stripes to everyone of them appointed, most cruelly laid upon their naked bodies with long whips by sundry men appointed to be the executioners thereof. And before our men there went a couple of criers which cried as they went: "Behold these English dogs, Lutherans, enemies to God," and all the way as they went there were some of the Inquisitors themselves, and of the familiars of that rakehell order, that cried to the executioners, "Strike, lay on those English heretics, Lutherans, God's enemies."

And so this horrible spectacle being showed round about the city, they returned to the Inquisitors' house, with their backs all gore blood, and swollen with great bumps, and were then taken from their horses, and carried again to prison, where they remained until they were sent into Spain to the galleys, there to receive the rest of their martyrdom. And I and the six other with me which had judgment, and were condemned amongst the rest to serve an appren-ticeship in the monastery, were taken presently and sent to certain religious houses appointed for the purpose.

6. THE SOURCES OF CATHOLIC POWER

By the last decades of the colonial era the discipline of the clergy had become seriously relaxed, and the unity of the Church was rent by unseemly squabbles between regular and secular clergy and between creole and peninsular priests. Yet the influence of the Church in colonial society, except among a tiny hand-ful of converts to the new materialistic doctrines of the encyclopedists, remained undiminished. In the following excerpt the Mexican historian Alamán ex-plains the sources of Catholic power.[6]

THE IMMENSE INFLUENCE of the Church rested on three foundation-stones: respect for religion, remembrance of its great benefactions, and its immense wealth. The people, poorly instructed in the essentials of religion, tended to identify it in large part with ceremonial pomp; they found relief from the tedium of their lives in the religious functions, which, especially during Holy Week, represented in numerous proces-sions the most venerated mysteries of the re-demption. The festivals of the Church, which should have been entirely spiritual, were thus transformed into so many profane performances, marked by displays of fireworks, dances, plays, bullfights and cockfights, and even such forbid-den diversions as cards and the like, in order to celebrate at great cost the festivals of the patron saints of the towns, into which the Indians poured the greater part of the fruits of their labor. It was this vain pomp, attended by little true piety, that led the viceroy whom I have frequently cited [the Duke of Linares] to remark that "in this realm all is outward show, and though their lives are steeped in vices, the ma-jority think that by wearing a rosary about their necks and kissing the hand of the priest they are made Catholics, and that the Ten Command-ments can be replaced by ceremonies."

The Indians continued to regard the regular clergy with the respect that the first mission-aries had justly gained by protecting them against the oppression and violence of the con-quistadores and by instructing them not only in religion but in the arts necessary for subsistence. This respect, which grew to be a fanatical ven-eration, presented no dangers as long as it was

6 Alamán, *Historia de Méjico*, I, 64–70. (Extract trans-lated by the editor.)

accorded to men of admirable virtue, and the government, to which they were very devoted and obedient, found in these exemplary ecclesiastics its firmest support; but it could become highly dangerous if a clergy of debased morals wished to abuse this influence for its own ends. This danger to the government was made still greater by the very precaution that Archbishop Haro had advised to avoid it, for since the high Church positions were intrusted to Europeans, the Americans, who generally enjoyed only the less important posts and benefices, exerted greater influence over the people with whom they were placed in more immediate contact.

The wealth of the clergy consisted not so much in the estates that it possessed, numerous though they were (especially the urban properties in the principal cities like Mexico City, Puebla, and others), as in capital invested in quitrent mortgages on the property of individuals; the traffic in mortgages and the collection of interest made of every chaplaincy and religious brotherhood a sort of bank. The total property of the clergy, both secular and regular, in estates and loans of this kind, certainly was not less than half of the total value of the real estate of the country.

The town council of Mexico City, seeing the multitude of monasteries and nunneries that were being founded, and the large number of persons destined for the ecclesiastical profession, together with the great sums devised to pious foundations, petitioned King Philip IV in 1644 "that no more convents of nuns or monks be established, since the number of the former was excessive, and the number of their woman servants even greater; that limits be placed upon the estates of the convents and that they be forbidden to acquire new holdings, complaining that the greater part of the landed property of the land had come into the hands of the religious by way of donations or purchases, and that if steps were not taken to remedy the situation they would soon be masters of all; that no more religious be sent from Spain, and that the bishops be charged not to ordain any more clerics, since there were already more than six thousand in all the bishoprics without any occupation, ordained on the basis of tenuous chaplaincies; and, finally, that there should be a reform in the excessive number of festivals, which increased idleness and gave rise to other evils." The *cortes* assembled in Madrid at that period petitioned the king to the same effect, and similar reforms were earlier proposed by the Coun-

cil of Castile, but nothing was done, and things continued in the same state. . . .

In addition to the revenues derived from these estates and loans, the secular clergy had the tithes, which in all the bishoprics of New Spain amounted to some 1,800,000 pesos annually, although the government received a part of this sum. . . . In the bishopric of Michoacán the tithes were farmed out; this made their collection more rigorous and oppressive, since private interest devised a thousand expedients to burden even the least important products of agriculture with this assessment.

The clergy had a privileged jurisdiction, with special tribunals, and a personal *fuero* which in former times had been very extensive but had greatly diminished with the intervention of the royal judges in criminal cases and with the declaration that the secular courts had jurisdiction in cases involving both principal and interest of the funds of the chaplaincies and pious foundations. The viceroy decided conflicts between ecclesiastical and civil courts, and this prerogative was one of those that gave the greatest luster to his authority.

From the instructions of the Duke of Linares to his successor and from the secret report made by Don Jorge Juan and Don Antonio Ulloa to King Ferdinand VI, it appears that the customs of the clergy had declined at the beginning of the eighteenth century to a point of scandalous corruption, especially among the friars charged with the administration of the curacies or doctrines. In the epoch of which I speak this corruption was particularly notable in the capitals of some bishoprics and in smaller places, but in the capital of the realm the presence of the superior authorities enforced more decorum. Everywhere, it should also be said, there were truly exemplary ecclesiastics, and in this respect certain religious orders stood out. The Jesuits, above all others, were remarkable for the purity of their customs and for their religious zeal, a notable contrast appearing in the above-cited work by Juan and Ulloa between their comments on the Jesuits and their references to other orders. Their expulsion left a great void, not only in the missions among the barbarians whom they had in charge but in the matter of the instruction and moral training of the people. . . . No less commendable were the friars of the order of Saint James, those of the order of Saint Philip, whose oratories had largely replaced those of the Jesuits, and among the hospitaller orders the Bethlehemites, who devoted themselves to primary education and the care of hospitals.

Into these religious orders the rivalry of birth had also penetrated, excepting always the Jesuits, who had no chapters or tumultuous elections and whose prelates were named in Rome by the general of the order, with regard only to the merit and virtue of individuals. Not only did there prevail in some of them the strife between "*gachupines* and creoles," but there were entire communities composed almost exclusively of one or the other element.

Part Four

The Spanish Colonies
in the Eighteenth Century

IN THE EIGHTEENTH CENTURY Spanish America felt the influence of the vast changes that were ushering in the modern world. The Industrial Revolution, greatly increasing the demand for Latin-American raw materials, helped to create a wealthy class of creole landlords, mineowners, and merchants. The Enlightenment, teaching creole youth to reason and to question, prepared them intellectually for the coming struggle for independence. And Spain herself, in which the new Bourbon dynasty was engaged in a supreme effort to modernize Spanish economic and political life, stimulated progressive change in the colonies through her reform policies.

The colonial policy of the Bourbon kings had two principal aims: to regain for Spain a major share of the trade of her colonies, wrested from her by English and other foreign contrabandists, and to increase the royal revenues from the colonies. To achieve the first of these aims the Bourbons gradually abolished the system of fleets and fairs, while preserving the principle of peninsular monopoly. Between the stimulus given by this and other commercial reforms and that offered by the increasing European market for Spanish-American staples, the colonial economy experienced a marked expansion in the eighteenth century.

The second Bourbon ambition, that of increasing the royal revenues from the colonies, was to be achieved by making their administration more efficient. Accordingly the intendant system of government, borrowed from France, was introduced in the colonies. Many of the viceroys and intendants of the reform era were men of great diligence and enlightened views, but the intendants' subordinates, the subdelegates, generally continued the evil practices of the *corregidor*.

Spanish-American colonial culture was basically on extension of the richer culture of the mother country. The Church enjoyed a virtual monopoly of education, which was restricted with few exceptions to the Indian aristocracy and the children of well-to-do Spaniards. Colonial writing, born in the twilight of the Golden Age of Spanish literature, produced only one truly great figure, the Mexican poetess Sor Juana Inés de la Cruz. Largely isolated from foreign influences and vigilantly watched over by the Inquisition, most colonial political and religious thought was expressed within the limits approved by Church and State.

In the eighteenth century the Enlightenment made a cautious entrance into the colonies. Under official auspices, efforts were made to establish schools of a more modern and useful type. The first true colonial newspapers and reviews appeared, promoting the rise of a secular and critical spirit through their articles on economic and scientific subjects. The forbidden writings of the French Encyclopedists and other European writers circulated among the educated classes in increasing quantity.

The creole upper class enjoyed greater opportunities for material and cultural enrichment in the Bourbon era, but the same was not true of Indians, mestizos, and other laboring groups. The intolerable conditions of the common people led to major revolutionary outbreaks in Peru, Bolivia, and Colombia (1780–1783) that were sternly suppressed by Spanish arms.

XV

The Bourbon Reforms and Spanish America

SPAIN MADE A REMARKABLE RECOVERY in the eighteenth century from the state of abject weakness into which she had fallen under the last Hapsburg kings. This revival is associated with the reigns of three princes of the Houses of Bourbon: Philip V (1700–1746), grandson of Louis XIV of France, and his two sons, Ferdinand VI (1746–1759) and Charles III (1759–1788).

The work of national reconstruction reached its maximum under Charles III. During his reign Spanish industry, agriculture, and trade made marked gains. Clerical influence suffered a setback as a result of the expulsion of the Jesuits in 1767 and of decrees restricting the authority of the Inquisition. Under the cleansing influence of able and honest ministers, a new spirit of austerity and service began to appear among public officials.

In the field of colonial reform the Bourbons moved slowly and cautiously, as was natural in view of the fact that powerful vested interests were identified with the old order of things. The *Casa de Contratación,* or House of Trade, was gradually reduced in importance until it finally disappeared in 1790. A similar fate overtook the venerable Council of the Indies, although it was not abolished until 1854. Most of its duties were entrusted to a colonial minister appointed by the king. The Bourbons alternately suspended and tried to rehabilitate the fleet system of sailing, but in the end it was abandoned, the Portobello fleet disappearing in 1740, the Veracruz fleet in 1789. The Portobello and Veracruz fairs vanished contemporaneously. In the same period the trading monopoly of Cadiz was gradually eliminated. The success of the "free trade" policy was reflected in a spectacular increase in the value of Spain's commerce with Spanish America.

The eighteenth century witnessed a steady growth of agricultural, pastoral, and mining production in Spanish America. By contrast with these signs of progress, the once-flourishing colonial handicrafts industry declined, owing to the influx of cheap European wares with which the native products could not compete. Contraband trade, never completely eliminated under the Bourbons, reached vast proportions during the frequent intervals of warfare in which British naval power swept Spanish shipping from the seas.

The most important Bourbon political reform was the transfer to the colonies, between 1782 and 1790, of the intendant system, already introduced in Spain from France. The intendants were expected to relieve the over-burdened viceroys of many of their duties, especially in financial matters, and to develop agriculture, industry, and commerce and generally to promote the welfare of their respective districts. Many of the viceroys and intendants of the reform period were able and progressive men, devoted to the interests of the crown and their subjects. But the same cannot be said of the majority of their subordinates, who, like their predecessors, the *corregidores,* soon became notorious for their oppressive practices. Following the triumph of reaction in Spain after 1788, the familiar evils of administrative corruption, mismanagement, and indifference to the public interest reappeared on a large scale in the colonies as in the mother country.

1. CHARLES III: REFORMER-KING

Gaspar Melchor de Jovellanos (1744–1811) was a leading collaborator of Charles III in the work of reform. Of noble birth, broadly cultured, abreast of the most advanced thought of his time, Jovellanos devoted himself principally to the improvement of Spanish agriculture. His report on this subject, vigorously attacking the evils of entailed estates and mortmain, is a classic of Spanish economic literature. His eulogy of Charles III, presented before the Economic Society of Madrid on November 8, 1788, not only depicts the many-sided battle of the great king against peninsular backwardness but reveals the basic premises of the intellectual vanguard of the reform movement.[1]

THE ENUMERATION of the measures and establishments with which this beneficent monarch won our love and gratitude has already been the object of more eloquent discourses. My design barely permits me to mention them. The founding of new agricultural colonies, the division of the communal lands, the reduction of the privileges of the stock raisers, the abolition of price-fixing and the free circulation of grain, by which he improved the state of agriculture; the encouragement of technical training, the reform of the guild system, the increase of industrial establishments, and the generous provision of privileges and exemptions in favor of industry; the breaking of the ancient chains that bound our internal commerce, the opening of new ports to foreign trade, the establishment of peace in the Mediterranean and of periodic communication and free trade with our overseas colonies in the interest of commerce . . . , and above all, the founding of those patriotic and model groups [the Economic Societies], to whose consideration he submitted all that concerned the common weal: What ample and glorious cause is this for eulogizing Charles III, and for calling him the Father of His Country!

But let us not deceive ourselves: The path of

[1] Gaspar Melchor de Jovellanos, *Obras escogidas,* Madrid, 1940, 5 vols., III, 64–82. (Excerpt translated by the editor.)

reform would have brought Charles III a highly transient glory if his vigilance had not sought to perpetuate in his dominions the good to which he aspired. His wisdom enabled him to perceive that the best-meditated laws do not as a rule suffice to bring prosperity to a nation, much less to maintain it. . . . Charles understood that he could do nothing for his people if he did not first prepare it to receive these reforms — if he did not infuse into it that spirit upon which their perfection and stability completely depend.

You, gentlemen, you who are cooperating with such zeal for the achievement of his paternal designs, are aware of the spirit that the nation lacked. Useful sciences, economic principles, a general spirit of enlightenment — that is what Spain owes to the reign of Charles III. . . .

At the opening of the eighteenth century the first Bourbon prince passed over the Pyrenees, and amid the horrors of a war as just as it was sanguinary he from time to time turned his eyes to the people, which fought generously for its rights. Philip, knowing that he could not make his people happy if he did not instruct it, founded academies, erected seminaries, established libraries, and subsidized literature and literary men; in a reign of almost half a century he taught Spain the value of enlightenment.

Ferdinand, in a shorter but more prosperous and peaceful reign, followed in the footsteps of his father; he developed the merchant marine, stimulated industry, promoted internal trade, housed and rewarded the fine arts, and protected talent; and in order to augment more rapidly the sum total of useful knowledge, at the same time that he sent many promising youths through Europe to acquire this precious commodity he received with favor foreign savants and artisans and rewarded their brilliance with prizes and pensions. Thus he prepared the road that Charles III later trod so gloriously.

This pious sovereign, determined to admit light into his dominions, began by removing the obstacles that could hinder its progress. This was his first care. Ignorance yet held out in its trenches, but Charles would completely smash them. Truth battled on his side, and at its sight all the shadows would vanish.

For long centuries the philosophy of Aristotle had tyrannized over the republic of letters, and though scorned and expelled from almost all Europe it was still revered in our schools. Of little utility in itself, since it was based entirely on speculation and not at all on experience and had been garbled in the versions of the Arabs, to whom Spain owed this unfortunate gift, it was completely corrupted by the ignorance of its commentators.

Its sectaries, divided into bands, had obscured it among us with new subtleties, invented to support the empire of each sect . . . Charles dissipated, destroyed, annihilated at one blow those parties, and by admitting freedom of philosophy into our academic halls he attracted to them a treasure-trove of philosophic knowledge, which already circulates in the minds of our youth and begins to restore the sway of reason. Nowadays one rarely hears among us those barbarous words, those obscure judgments, those vain and subtle reasonings that were once the glory of the peripatetic philosopher [Aristotle] and the delight of his believers; and, finally, even the very names of Thomists, Scotists, Suarists, have fled from our schools, together with the names of Froilan, González, and Losada, their leaders, once so celebrated and now neglected and forgotten. . . .

Charles began by promoting the study of the exact sciences, without whose aid little or no progress can be made in the investigation of the truths of nature. Madrid, Seville, Salamanca, and Alcalá saw the rebirth of their ancient schools of mathematics, Barcelona, Valencia, Zaragoza, Santiago, and nearly all the universities established mathematical studies anew. The force of demonstration replaced the subtlety of syllogisms. The study of physics, based on experiment and calculation, was perfected; together with it arose the other sciences within its jurisdiction: chemistry, mineralogy, metallurgy, natural history, botany. . . .

But still another science was necessary to make profitable use of all the others. . . . Hardly had Charles ascended the throne when the spirit of examination and reform surveyed all aspects of the public economy. The activity of the government aroused the curiosity of the citizens. Then was born the study of this science, which at that time attracted the major attention of European thinkers. Spain read the most celebrated writers in the field, examined their ideas, analyzed their works. There was discussion, controversy, writing; and Spain began to have economists.

2. THE BOURBON COMMERCIAL REFORMS

The Bourbon reforms in the field of colonial trade represented a supreme effort to recover for Spain a dominant position in the markets of Spanish America. The reform program provided for a stricter enforcement of the laws against contraband; more importantly, it included a series of measures designed to liberalize the commerce between Spain and her colonies while retaining the principle of peninsular trade monopoly. The fundamental reasons for the ultimate failure of this well-conceived program were, first, Spain's industrial weakness, which the best efforts of the Bourbons were unable to overcome, and, second, her closely related inability to keep her sea-lanes to America open in time of war with England, when foreign traders again swarmed in Spanish-American ports. Yet the Bourbon reforms, combined with a rising European demand for Spanish-American products, helped to produce a remarkable expansion of colonial trade and prosperity in the last half of the eighteenth century. The Mexican historian Alamán surveys the beneficial effects of these reforms on the commerce of New Spain.[2]

COMMERCE WITH SPAIN, the only one that was permitted, was restricted until 1778 to the port of Cadiz, where were assembled, under the inspection of the *audiencia* and the House of Trade of Seville, all the goods bound for America. They were carried there in the fleets, which departed each year and whose routes were minutely prescribd by the laws, and in the interval there was no other communication than that of the dispatch boats and the storeships coming with quicksilver. On the arrival of the fleets a great fair was held at Panama, for all South America, and another in Jalapa for New Spain, whence this town acquired the name of Jalapa of the Fair.

This order of things gave rise to a double monopoly: that enjoyed by the houses of Cadiz and Seville which made up the cargoes and that which was secured at the fairs by the American merchants, who made agreements among themselves whereby particular merchants acquired complete control over certain lines of goods. Since the supply of these goods was not renewed for a long time, it was in their power to raise prices at will, whence arose the high prices of

2 Alamán, *Historia de Méjico*, I, 110–113, 109–110. (Excerpt translated by the editor.)

some commodities, especially when maritime war prevented the arrival of the fleets for several years. This condition gave occasion for the arbitrary measures of certain viceroys in fixing retail prices in favor of the consumer, as was done by the second Duke of Albuquerque in 1703.

Commerce with Asia was reduced to a single vessel, known as the "China-ship," which was sent once a year from Manila and, passing in sight of San Blas, arrived at Acapulco, to which came the buyers for the fair that was held there; after the fair it sailed again, carrying the cash proceeds of the sale of the goods that it had brought, the subvention with which the royal treasury of Mexico aided that of Manila, the criminals condemned to serve time in those islands, and those dissipated youths whom their families had consigned to this kind of exile as a disciplinary measure, called "being sent to China." Commerce between New Spain and Peru, Guatemala, and New Granada by way of the Pacific was prohibited for a variety of reasons.

By the ordinance of October 12, 1778, all this system of commerce with Europe was changed. The fleets ceased to come, the last being the one that arrived at Vera Cruz in January of that year, under the command of Don Antonio de Ulloa, so celebrated for his voyage to Peru and his secret report to the king on the state of that kingdom. Commerce thus became free for all Spanish ships sailing from habilitated ports in the peninsula, but it could only be carried on in New Spain through the port of Vera Cruz, and European goods could not be introduced from Havana or any other American place but must be brought directly from Spain.

The results of this change were very important, not only because of the abundance of goods and price reductions that it yielded but also because it ended the monopoly and the vast profits acquired with little labor by the *flotistas,* the name given to the monopolists. These men, finding it impossible to continue their former practices, retired from commerce and invested their capital in agriculture and mining, which they greatly stimulated, especially the latter. Their places were taken by a larger number of individuals, who in order to prosper had to display much activity, and thus instead of a few large capitals there arose many small ones, which, distributed among all the towns, contributed largely to their betterment.

In this same period were lifted the odious restrictions on commerce among the provinces or kingdoms of America; and a royal decree of January 17, 1774, promulgated in the Prado, conceded freedom of trade in the Pacific, though only in the goods and productions of the respective provinces. Later declarations broadened this freedom, removing the restrictions imposed by the aforementioned order in regard to European and Asiatic goods. . . .

The exclusive colonial system of Spain provided great and valuable compensations for the prohibitions that it imposed. If one glances at the balance of trade of Vera Cruz, the only port habilitated in that period for trade with Europe and the West Indies, for the year 1803, one of the last years of peace with England, it will be seen that of the total exports to Spain, worth 12,000,000 pesos, more than a third, or 4,500,000, were in the form of produce, including not only 27,000 *arrobas* of cochineal of a value of 2,200,-000 pesos but also 150,000 pounds of indigo, worth 260,000 pesos, and 500,000 *arrobas* of sugar of the value of 1,500,000 pesos, besides 26,600 *quintales* of logwood and 17,000 *quintales* of cotton. Among the exports to various points in America one notes 20,000 *tercios* of flour, 14,700 *varas* of coarse frieze, 1,300 *varas* of baize, 1,760 boxes of soap, and 700 boxes of ordinary Puebla chinaware; all this, with other minor articles, comes to a value of more than 600,000 pesos a year.

The effect of these exports was to give a great value to the sugarcane plantations, while the flour of Puebla, flowing down to Vera Cruz to satisfy not only the needs of that place but also those of Havana, the other islands, and Yucatan, left the provisioning of the markets of Mexico City to the wheatfields of Querétaro and Guanajuato, adding to their value and bringing prosperity to the wheat farmers of those provinces. All this active traffic infused animation and life into our internal commerce. Mexican agriculture today would gladly exchange the sterile freedom to cultivate vines and olives for an exportation of 500,000 *arrobas* of sugar and 20,000 *tercios* of flour.

3. THE EXPANSION OF AGRICULTURE

Stimulated by the Bourbon commercial reforms, and perhaps even more by the growing European demand for sugar, tobacco, coffee, hides, and other American staples, colonial agricultural and pastoral production rose sharply in the last half of the eighteenth century. Contrary to a common belief, by the end of the colonial period the value of this production considerably exceeded that of the precious metals.

This increase, however, was made possible by more extensive use of land and labor rather than by employment of improved implements or techniques. Agricultural progress was also held back by the growing concentration of land in a few hands, with much arable land being kept idle. The great Prussian scientist Alexander von Humboldt (1769–1859), who spent the years 1799–1804 in travel through Mexico and northern South America, describes the condition of Mexican agriculture.[3]

The produce of the earth is the sole basis of permanent opulence. It is consolatory to see that the labour of man for half a century, has been more directed towards this fertile and inexhaustible source, than towards the working of mines, of which the wealth has not so direct an influence on the public prosperity, and merely changes the nominal value of the annual produce of the earth. The territorial impost levied by the clergy, under the name of tenth, or tithe, measures the quantity of that produce, and indicates with precision the progress of agricultural industry, if we compare the periods, in the intervals of which the price of commodities has undergone no sensible variation. The following is a view of the value of these tithes; taking for example two series of years, from 1771 to 1780, and 1780 to 1789:

Names of Dioceses	Periods	Value of Tithes in Piastres	Periods	Value of Tithes in Piastres
Mexico	1771–1780	4,132,630	1781–1790	7,082,879
Puebla de los Angeles	1770–1779	2,965,601	1780–1789	3,508,884
Valladolid de Mechoacan	1770–1779	2,710,200	1780–1789	3,239,400
Oaxaca	1771–1780	715,974	1781–1790	863,237
Guadalaxara	1771–1780	1,889,724	1781–1790	2,579,108
Durango	1770–1779	913,028	1780–1789	1,080,313

The result of this view is, that the tithes of New Spain have amounted in these six dioceses:

From 1771 to 1779 —
to 13,357,157
From 1779 to 1789 —
to 18,353,821
} Double Piastres, or pezzos fuertes.

Consequently the total augmentation has been, in the last ten years, five millions of piastres, or two-fifths of the total produce. The same data also indicate the rapidity of the progress of agriculture, in the intendancies of Mexico, Guadalaxara, Puebla, and Valladolid, compared with the provinces of Oaxaca and New Biscay. The tithes have been nearly doubled in the archbishopric of Mexico; for those which were levied during the ten years anterior to 1780, were to those levied ten years afterwards, in the proportion of 10 to 17. In the intendancy of Durango or New Biscay, this augmentation has been only in the proportion of 10 to 11.

The celebrated author of the *Wealth of Nations,* estimates the territorial produce of Great Britain, from the produce of the landtax. In the political view of New Spain, which I presented to the court of Madrid in 1803, I had hazarded a similar valuation, from the value of the tithes payable to the clergy. The result of this operation was, that the annual produce of the land amounted at least, to 24 millions of piastres. The results, which I came to in drawing up my first view, have been discussed with much sagacity, in a memoir presented by the municipal body of the town of Valladolid de Mechoacan, to the king, in the month of October 1805, on the occasion of passing an edict, relative to the property of the clergy. According to this memoir, a copy of which I have before me, we must add to these 24 millions of piastres, three millions for the produce of cochineal, vanilla, jalap, pimento of Tabasco, sarsaparilla which pay no tithes; and 2 millions for sugar and indigo, which yield only to the clergy a duty of 4 per cent. If we adopt these data, we shall find that the total agricultural produce amounts annually to 29 millions of piastres, or to more than 145 millions of francs, which, reducing them to a natural measure, and taking for basis the actual price of wheat in Mexico, 15 francs for 10 myriagrammes of wheat, are equal to 96 mil-

3 Alexander von Humboldt, *Political Essay on the Kingdom of New Spain*, London, 1822–1823, 4 vols., III, 95–101.

lions of myriagrammes of wheat. The mass of precious metals annually extracted from the mines of the kingdom of New Spain, scarcely represent 74 millions of myriagrammes of wheat, which proves the interesting fact, that the value of the gold and silver of the Mexican mines is less, by almost a fourth, than the value of the territorial produce.

The cultivation of the soil, notwithstanding the fetters with which it is everywhere shackled, has lately made a more considerable progress, on account of the immense capitals laid out in land, by families enriched either by the commerce of Vera Cruz and Acapulco, or by the working of the mines. The Mexican clergy scarcely possess land (*bienes raíces*) to the value of two or three millions of piastres; but the capitals which convents, chapters, religious societies, and hospitals have laid out in lands, amount to the sum of 441/2 millions of piastres, or more than 222 millions of livres tournois. The following is a view of these capitals, called *capitales de capellanías y obras de la juridicción ordinaria,* extracted from an official paper:

	Piastres
Archbishopric of Mexico	9,000,000
Bishopric of Puebla	6,500,000
Bishopric of Valladolid (very accurate valuation)	4,500,000
Bishopric of Guadalaxara	3,000,000
Bishoprics of Durango, Monterey, and Sonora	1,000,000
Bishoprics of Oaxaca and Merida	2,000,000
Obras Pias of the regular Clergy	2,500,000
Endowments of Churches and Communities of Monks and Nuns	16,000,000

. . . When we read the excellent work on agrarian laws, presented to the council of Castille in 1795, we perceive that notwithstanding the difference of climate and other local circumstances, Mexican agriculture is fettered by the same political causes which have impeded the progress of industry in the Peninsula. All the vices of the feudal government have passed from the one hemisphere to the other; and in Mexico these abuses have been so much the more difficult to the supreme authority to remedy the evil, and display its energy at an immense distance. The property of New Spain, like that of Old Spain, is in a great measure in the hands of a few powerful families, who have gradually absorbed the smaller estates. In America, as well as Europe, large commons are condemned to the pasturage of cattle, and to perpetual sterility.

4. THE REVIVAL OF MINING

The eighteenth century saw a marked revival of the silver-mining industry in the Spanish colonies. Peru and Mexico both shared in this advance, but the Mexican mines, whose production had been rising quite consistently since the sixteenth century, forged far ahead of their Peruvian rivals in the Bourbon era. As in the case of agriculture, the increase in production was primarily due not to improved technique but rather to the opening of many new as well as old mines and the growth of the labor force. Although the Bourbon kings and their colonial agents exerted themselves to overcome the backwardness of the mining industry, their efforts were largely frustrated by the traditionalism of the mineowners and by lack of capital to finance necessary changes.[4]

WHEN WE TAKE A GENERAL view of the mining operations of New Spain, and compare them with those of the mines of Freiberg, the Hartz, and Schemnitz, we are surprised at still finding in its infancy, an art which has been practised in America for these three centuries, and on which, according to the vulgar prejudice, the prosperity of these ultramarine establishments depends. The causes of this phenomenon cannot escape those who, after visiting Spain, France, and the western parts of Germany, have seen that mountainous countries still exist in the centre of civilized Europe, in which the mining operations partake of all the barbarity of the middle ages. The art of mining cannot make great progress, where the mines are dispersed over a great extent of ground, where the government allows to the proprietors the full liberty of directing the operations without control, and of tearing the minerals from the bowels of the earth, without any consideration of the future. Since the brilliant period of the reign of Charles the 5th, Spanish America has been separated from Europe, with respect to the communication of discoveries useful to society. The

[4] Humboldt, *Political Essay on the Kingdom of New Spain,* III, 231–246.

imperfect knowledge which was posesssed in the 16th century relative to mining and smelting, in Germany, Biscay, and the Belgic provinces, rapidly passed into Mexico and Peru, on the first colonization of these countries; but since that period, to the reign of Charles the third, the American miners have learned hardly anything from the Europeans, but the blowing up with powder those rocks which resist the *pointrole*. This King and his successor have shown a praiseworthy desire of imparting to the colonies all the advantages derived by Europe from the improvement in machinery, the progress of chemical science, and their application to metallurgy. German miners have been sent at the expense of the court to Mexico, Peru, and the kingdom of new Granada; but their knowledge has been of no utility, because the mines of Mexico are considered as the property of the individuals, who direct the operations, without the government being allowed to exercise the smallest influence. . . .

After the picture which we have just drawn of the actual state of the mining operations, and of the bad economy which prevails in the administration of the mines of New Spain, we ought not to be astonished at seeing works, which for a long time have been most productive, abandoned whenever they have reached a considerable depth, or whenever the veins have appeared less abundant in metals. We have already observed, that in the famous mine of Valenciana, the annual expenses rose in the space of fifteen years from two millions of francs to four millions and a half. Indeed, if there be much water in this mine, and if it require a number of horse baritels to draw it off, the profit must, to the proprietors, be little or nothing. The greatest part of the defects in the management which I have been pointing out, have been long known to a respectable and enlightened body, the *Tribunal de Minería* of Mexico, to the professors of the school of mines, and even to several of the native miners, who without having ever quitted their country, know the imperfection of the old methods; but we must repeat here, that changes can only take place very slowly among a people who are not fond of innovations, and in a country where the government possesses so little influence on the works which are generally the property of individuals, and not of shareholders. It is a prejudice to imagine, that the mines of New Spain on account of their wealth, do not require in their management the same intelligence and the same economy which are necessary to the preservation of the mines of Saxony and the Hartz. We must not confound the abundance of ores with their intrinsic value. The most part of the minerals of Mexico being very poor, as we have already proved, and as all those who do not allow themselves to be dazzled by false calculations very well know, an enormous quantity of gangue impregnated with metals must be extracted, in order to produce two millions and a half of marcs of silver. Now it is easy to conceive that in mines of which the different works are badly disposed, and without any communication with one another, the expense of extraction must be increased in an alarming manner, in proportion as the shafts (*pozos*) increase in depth, and the galleries (*cañones*) become more extended.

The labour of a miner is entirely free throughout the whole kingdom of New Spain; and no Indian or Mestizo can be forced to dedicate themselves to the working of mines. It is absolutely false, though the assertion has been repeated in works of the greatest estimation, that the court of Madrid sends out galley slaves to America, to work in the gold and silver mines. The mines of Siberia have been peopled by Russian malefactors; but in the Spanish colonies this species of punishment has been fortunately unknown for centuries. The Mexican miner is the best paid of all miners; he gains at the least from 25 to 30 francs per week of six days, while the wages of labourers who work in the open air, husbandmen for example, are seven livres sixteen sous, on the central table land, and nine livres twelve sous near the coast. The miners, *tenateros* and *faeneros* occupied in transporting the minerals to the place of assemblage (*despachos*) frequently gain more than six francs per day, of six hours. Honesty is by no means so common among the Mexican as among the German or Swedish miners; and they make use of a thousand tricks to steal very rich specimens of ores. As they are almost naked, and are searched on leaving the mine in the most indecent manner, they conceal small morsels of native silver, or red sulphuret and muriate of silver in their hair, under their arm-pits, and in their mouths; and they even lodge in their anus, cylinders of clay which contain the metal. These cylinders are called *longanas,* and they are sometimes found of the length of thirteen centimetres, (five inches). It is a most shocking spectacle to see in the large mines of Mexico, hundreds of workmen, among whom there are a great number of very respectable men, all compelled to allow themselves to be searched on leaving the pit or the gallery. A register is kept of the minerals found in the hair, in the mouth, or other parts of the miners' bodies. In the mine of Valenciana at Guanaxuato, the value of these stolen minerals, of which a great part was composed of the *longanas,* amounted between 1774 and 1787, to the sum of 900,000 francs.

5. COLONIAL INDUSTRY IN DECLINE

In the last half of the eighteenth century, colonial manufacturing, after experiencing a long and steady growth, began to decline because of the influx of cheap European wares with which the domestic products could not compete. The textile and wine industries of western Argentina fell into decay as they lost their markets in Buenos Aires and Montevideo to lower-priced foreign wines and cloth. The textile producers of the province of Quito in Ecuador complained of injury from the same cause. In the Mexican manufacturing center of Puebla, production of chinaware, of which the city had long been a leading center, slumped catastrophically between 1793 and 1802. Industrial decadence was accompanied by a falling-off of internal trade in some areas as Spanish-American economic life became increasingly geared to the export of agricultural and pastoral products and the import of European finished goods. Humboldt's account of his visits to Mexican manufacturing centers clearly reveals the weakness and backwardness of colonial industry.[5]

THE OLDEST CLOTH MANUFACTORIES of Mexico are those of Tezcuco. They were in great part established in 1592 by the viceroy Don Louis de Velasco II, the son of the celebrated constable of Castille, who was second viceroy of New Spain. By degrees, this branch of national industry passed entirely into the hands of the Indians and Mestizos of Querétaro and Puebla. I visited the manufactories of Querétaro in the month of August 1803. They distinguish there the great manufactories, which they call *obrajes,* from the small, which go by the name of *trapiches.* There were 20 *obrajes,* and more than 300 *trapiches* at that time, who altogether wrought up 63,900 *arrobas* of Mexican sheep-wool. According to accurate lists, drawn up in 1793, there were at that period at Querétaro, in the *obrajes* alone, 215 looms, and 1500 workmen who manufactured 6,042 pieces, or 226,522 *varas* of cloth (*paños*); 287 pieces, or 39,718

5 Humboldt, *Political Essay on the Kingdom of New Spain,* III, 462–469.

varas of ordinary woollens (*xerguatillas*); 207 pieces, or 15,369 *varas* of baize (*bayetas*); and 161 pieces, or 17,960 *varas* of serge (*xergas*). In this manufacture they consumed 46,270 *arrobas* of wool, the price of which only amounted to 161,-945 piastres. They reckon in general seven *arrobas* to one piece of *xerguatilla,* and five *arrobas* to one piece of *xerga.* The value of the cloths and woollen stuffs of the *obrajes* and *trapiches* of Querétaro at present amounts to more than 600,000 piastres, or three millions of francs per annum.

On visiting these workshops, a traveller is disagreeably struck, not only with the great imperfection of the technical process in the preparation for dyeing, but in a particular manner also with the unhealthiness of the situation, and the bad treatment to which the workmen are exposed. Free men, Indians, and people of colour, are confounded with the criminals distributed by justice among the manufactories, in order to be compelled to work. All appear half naked, covered with rags, meagre, and deformed. Every workshop resembles a dark prison. The doors, which are double, remain constantly shut, and the workmen are not permitted to quit the house. Those who are married are only allowed to see their families on Sunday. All are unmercifully flogged, if they commit the smallest trespass on the order established in the manufactory.

We have difficulty in conceiving how the proprietors of the *obrajes* can act in this manner with free men, as well as how the Indian workman can submit to the same treatment with the galley slaves. These pretended rights are in reality acquired by stratagem. The manufacturers of Querétaro employ the same trick, which is made use of in several of the cloth manufactories of Quito, and in the plantations, where from a want of slaves, labourers are extremely rare. They choose from among the Indians the most miserable, but such as show an aptitude for the work, and they advance them a small sum of money. The Indian, who loves to get intoxicated, spends it in a few days, and having become the debtor of the master, he is shut up in the workshop, under the pretence of paying off the debt by the work of his hands. They allow him only a real and a half, or 20 sous tournois per day of wages; but in place of paying it in ready money, they take care to supply him with meat, brandy, and clothes, on which the manufacturer gains from fifty to sixty per cent; and in this way the most industrious workman is forever in debt, and the same rights are exercised over him which are believed to be acquired over a purchased slave. I knew many persons in Querétaro, who lamented with me the existence of these enormous abuses. Let us hope that a government friendly to the people, will turn their attention to a species of oppression so contrary to humanity, the laws of the country, and the progress of Mexican industry.

With the exception of a few stuffs of cotton mixed with silk, the manufacture of silks is at present next to nothing in Mexico. In the time of Acosta, towards the conclusion of the sixteenth century, silk worms brought from Europe were cultivated near Panuco, and in la Misteca, and excellent taffeta was there manufactured with Mexican silk.

On my passage through Querétaro, I visited the great manufactory of cegars (*fábrica de puros y cigarros*), in which 3000 people, including 1900 women, are employed. The halls are very neat, but badly aired, very small, and consequently excessively warm. They consume daily in this manufacture 130 reams (*resmas*) of paper, and 2770 pounds of tobacco leaf. In the course of the month of July, 1803, there was manufactured to the amount of 185,288 piastres; viz. 2,654,820 small chests (*caxillas*) of cegars, which sell for 165,926 piastres, and 289,-799 chests of *puros* or cegars, which are not enveloped in paper. The expense of manufacture of the month of July alone, amounted to 31,789 piastres. It appears that the royal manufactory of Querétaro annually produces more than 2,200,000 piastres, in *puros* and *cigarros*.

The manufacture of hard soap is a considerable object of commerce at Puebla, Mexico, and Guadalaxara. The first of these towns produces nearly 200,000 *arrobas* per annum; and in the intendancy of Guadalaxara, the quantity manufactured is computed at 1,300,000 *livres tournois*. The abundance of soda which we find almost everywhere at elevations of 2000 or 2500 metres, in the interior table land of Mexico, is highly favourable to this manufacture. . . .

The town of Puebla was formerly celebrated for its fine manufactories of delf ware (*loza*) and hats. We have already observed that, till the commencement of the eighteenth century, these two branches of industry enlivened the commerce between Acapulco and Peru. At present there is little or no communication between Puebla and Lima, and the delf manufactories have fallen so much off, on account of the low price of the stone ware and porcelain of Europe imported at Vera Cruz, that of 46 man-ufactories which were still existing in 1793, there were in 1802 only sixteen remaining of delf ware, and two of glass.

6. POLITICAL REFORM: THE INTENDANT SYSTEM

The intendant reform was made by Charles III in the interests of greater administrative efficiency and increased royal revenues from the colonies. Among their many duties, the intendants were expected to further the economic development of their districts by promoting the cultivation of new crops, the improvement of mining, the building of roads and bridges, and the establishment of consulados *(chambers of commerce) and Economic Societies. At the height of the reform era many of these officials were capable and cultivated men who earnestly sought to foster the material and cultural welfare of the regions in their charge. The historian Alamán gives a glowing account of the favorable consequences of the establishment of the intendant system in New Spain and of the accomplishments of two model intendants.[6]*

THE PRINCIPAL SOURCE of profit of the *alcaldes mayores* consisted in the traffic they carried on under the pretext of getting the Indians to work, as was recommended by the laws. They assigned them certain tasks and purchased the product at low prices, paying for it in necessary articles of dress and food that were overpriced. Having all authority in their hands, they compelled the Indians to fulfill these contracts with great punctuality, and reaped large profits thereby. This was particularly true in those districts where there was some valuable product, such as cochineal in Oaxaca, which constituted a monopoly for those officers and for the merchants who equipped them with capital and goods. Meanwhile the Indians were cruelly oppressed. A miserable system of administration was this, in which the pecuniary advantage of the governors was rooted in the oppression and misery of the governed! The Duke of Linares, in his vigorous and concise style, characterized it in a few words: "Although the jurisdiction of the *alcaldes mayores* is most extensive, I can define it very briefly, for it amounts to this: They are faithless to God from the time they enter upon their employment, by breaking the oath they have taken; they are faithless to their king, because of the *repartimientos* they engage in; and they sin against the common Indians, by tyrannizing over them as they do."

6 Alamán, *Historia de Méjico*, I, 73–76. (Excerpt translated by the editor.)

The whole order of things, so unjust and oppressive, ceased with the promulgation of the Ordinance of Intendants, published by Minister [José de] Gálvez on December 4, 1786, and limited at that time to New Spain alone, but later extended, with appropriate modifications, to all Spanish America. In it, under the titles of "the four departments of justice, police, finance, and war," were set forth the most comprehensive rules for the administration of the country in these spheres and for the encouragement of agriculture, industry, and mining. The whole territory of the vice-royalty, including Yucatán and the *provincias internas,* was divided into twelve intendancies, which took the names of their capitals. The corregimiento of Querétaro was retained for civil and judicial matters, but it was made financially dependent on the intendancy of Mexico. To the posts of intendants were appointed men of integrity and intelligence in the performance of their functions. Among those who distinguished themselves by their special merit were the intendants of Guanajuato and Puebla.

Minister Gálvez, at the time when he was in power, sought to place all his relatives in high posts, and their actions justified this preference. Don Matías, his brother, and Don Bernardo, his nephew, succeeded each other as viceroys of Mexico; the latter married in New Orleans, while in command of the expedition that reconquered the Floridas, Doña Felicitas Saint-Maxent, whose two sisters, Doña Victoria and Doña Mariana, married Don Juan Antonio de Riaño and Don Manuel de Flon, respectively. At the time of the creation of the intendancies, the former was assigned that of Valladolid, where he remained only a short time, being transferred immediately to the more important one of Guanajuato; and Flon was placed over that of Puebla.

The strict and honorable Flon reformed great abuses, encouraged all the branches of industry in his province, and notably beautified its capital. Riaño, of equal integrity but of a mild and affable disposition, had served in the royal navy, and to a knowledge of mathematics and astronomy, natural in that profession, united a taste for literature and the fine arts. These interests, and in particular his delight in architecture, he introduced to Guanajuato; through his influence there were erected, not only in the capital but in all the province, magnificent structures, whose building he himself supervised, even instructing the stonecutters in the art of hewing stone. He promoted the study of the Latin classics and of the best Spanish writers; it was owing to his influence that the young men of Guanajuato devoted themselves to the study of the Castilian tongue and to its correct pronunciation.

French, the native tongue of his wife, was spoken in their home, and he introduced among the youth of the provincial capital a taste for that language and its literature, together with an elegance of manners unknown in other cities of the province. He was also responsible for the development of interest in drawing and music and for the cultivation of mathematics, physics, and chemistry in the school that had formerly been maintained by the Jesuits. To that end he zealously patronized Don José Antonio Rojas, professor of mathematics in that school and a graduate of the School of Mines. He also established a theater, promoted the cultivation of olives and vines, and diligently fostered the mining industry, the chief wealth of that province, by encouraging the rich citizens of Guanajuato to form companies for the exploitation of old and abandoned mines as well as new ones.

7. "THE MORE IT CHANGES . . ."

Plus ça change, plus c'est la même chose could be fairly applied to Spain's Indian policy. The Ordinance of Intendants, by abolishing the offices of corregidor and alcalde mayor and forbidding their successors, the subdelegates, to engage in the infamous repartimiento, promised to inaugurate a new and better day for the Indian. Despite the complacent observation of Alamán (see the previous selection) that the old order of things, "so unjust and oppressive, ceased with the promulgation of the Ordinance of Intendants," other observers came to different conclusions. In Peru, the intendant Demetrio O'Higgins asserted in an official report that the subdelegates continued to force the Indians to trade with them, in violation of the laws; that the curates oppressed the natives in the many ways described by Juan and Ulloa half a century before; and that the wretched Indians were being despoiled of their lands by the Spaniards. And in Mexico an enlightened prelate, Bishop Manuel Abad Queipo of Michoacán, denounced the entire system of subjection and segregation of the Indians and mixed castes and flatly stated that the natives were worse off than they had been before the intendant reform.[7]

THE POPULATION OF NEW SPAIN is composed of some four and a half million inhabitants, who can be divided into three classes: Spaniards, In-

[7] José María Luis Mora, *Obras sueltas,* Paris, 1837, 2 vols., I, 55–57. (Excerpt translated by the editor.)

dians, and castes. The Spaniards number one tenth of the total population but possess almost the entire property or wealth of the kingdom. The other two classes, forming the other nine tenths, can be divided into two parts castes, the other part pure Indians. The Indians and castes are employed in domestic service, agricultural labors, and the ordinary tasks of commerce and industry — that is to say, they are servants and day-laborers for the Spaniards. Consequently there arises between them and the Spaniards that opposition of interests and views that is typical of those who have nothing and those who have everything — between superiors and inferiors. Envy, theft, and unwilling service are the traits of the latter; arrogance, exploitation, and harsh treatment, the qualities of the former. These evils are to a certain extent common to all the world. But in America they are immeasurably greater because there are no gradations or intermediate states: all are either rich or wretched, noble or infamous.

In effect, the two classes of Indians and castes are sunk in the greatest abasement and degradation. The color, ignorance, and misery of the Indians places them at an infinite distance from a Spaniard. The ostensible privileges which the laws accord them do them little good and in most respects injure them greatly. Shut up in a narrow space of six hundred *varas,* assigned by law to the Indian towns, they possess no individual property and are obliged to work the communal lands. This cultivation is made all the more hateful by the fact that in recent years it has become increasingly difficult for them to enjoy any of the fruits of their labor. Under the new intendant system they cannot draw on the communal funds [*caja de comunidad*] without special permission from the office of the royal exchequer [*junta superior de la real hacienda*] in Mexico City.

Forbidden by law to commingle with the other castes, they are deprived of the instruction and assistance that they should receive from contact with these and other people. They are isolated by their language, and by a useless, tyrannical form of government. In each town there are found eight or ten old Indians who live in idleness at the expense of their fellows and artfully try to perpetuate their ancient customs, usages, and gross superstitions, ruling them like despots. Incapable, by law, of making a binding contract or of running into debt to the extent of more than five pesos — in a word, of any dealings at all — they cannot learn anything or

better their fortune or in any way raise themselves above their wretched condition. Solorzano, Fraso, and other Spanish authors have wondered why the privileges granted them have redounded to their injury; but it is greater cause for wonder that such men as these should have failed to understand that the source of the evil lies in these very privileges. They are an offensive weapon employed by the white class against the Indians, and never serve to defend the latter. This combination of causes makes the Indians indifferent to their future and to all that does not excite the passions of the moment.

The castes are declared infamous by law, as descendants of Negro slaves. They are subject to the payment of tribute, which is punctiliously recorded; as a result, this obligation has become a brand of slavery which neither the passage of time nor the mixture of successive generations can ever obliterate. There are many of these who in their color, physiognomy, and conduct could pass for Spaniards if it were not for this impediment, which reduces them all to the same state. . . .

The Indians as well as the castes are governed directly by magistrates of districts [*justicias territoriales*] whose conduct has measurably contributed to the situation in which they find themselves. The *alcaldes mayores* considered themselves not so much justices as merchants, endowed with the exclusive privilege . . . of trading in their province and of extracting from it in a five-year term of office from thirty to two hundred thousand pesos. Their usurious and arbitrary *repartimientos* caused great injuries. But despite this state of affairs two favorable circumstances commonly resulted, one being that they administered justice with impartiality and rectitude in cases in which they were not parties, the other being that they fostered agriculture and industry, in their own interests.

The Spanish government undertook to put an end to these abuses by replacing the *alcaldes mayores* with the subdelegates. But since the latter were not assigned any fixed salary, the remedy proved much worse than the evil. If they adhere to the schedule of fees, among a wretched folk who litigate only against each other, they will inevitably perish of hunger. They must of necessity prostitute their posts, swindle the poor, and traffic in justice. For the same reason it is extremely difficult for the intendants to find suitable individuals to fill these posts. They are sought, therefore, only by bankrupts or by those whose conduct and talents unfit them for success in the other walks of life. Under these conditions, what benefits, what protection, can these ministers of law dispense to the abovementioned two classes? How can they attract their good-will and respect, when extortion and injustice are virtually their livelihood?

XVI

Colonial Culture and the Enlightenment

COLONIAL CULTURE IN ALL ITS ASPECTS was a projection of contemporaneous Spanish culture and only faintly reflected native American influences. Colonial culture thus suffered from all the infirmities of its parent but inevitably lacked the breadth and vitality of Spanish literature and art, the product of a much older and more mature civilization.

The Church enjoyed a virtual monopoly of colonial education on all levels. Poverty condemned the great majority of the natives and mixed castes to illiteracy. The Universities of Lima and Mexico City, both chartered in 1551, were the first permanent institutions of higher learning. Since they were modeled on the Spanish University of Salamanca, their organization, curricula, and methods of instruction were alike medieval.

Within the limits imposed by official censorship and their own backgrounds, colonial scholars, especially those of the sixteenth and early seventeenth centuries, were able to make impressive contributions in the fields of history, anthropology, linguistics, geography, and natural history. The second half of the seventeenth century saw a decline in the quantity and quality of scholarly production. Nevertheless, in this period two remarkable men, Carlos Sigüenza y Góngora, in Mexico, and Pedro de Peralta Barnuevo, in Peru, foreshadowed the eighteenth-century enlightenment by the universality of their interests and by their concern with the practical uses of science.

Colonial literature, with some notable exceptions, was a pallid reflection of prevailing literary trends in the mother country. Among a multitude of poetasters towered a strange and rare genius, one of the greatest poets of the New World, Sor Juana Inés de la Cruz. Sor Juana could not escape the pressures of her environment. Rebuked by the Bishop of Puebla for her worldly interests, she ultimately gave up her books and scientific instruments and devoted the remainder of her brief life to religious devotions and charitable works.

Colonial art drew its principal inspiration from Spanish sources, but Indian influence was visible, particularly in sculpture and architecture. As might be expected, religious motifs dominated the sculpture and painting. In architecture the colonies followed Spanish examples, with the severely classical style of the sixteenth century giving way in the seventeenth to the highly ornamented baroque, and in the eighteenth to the even more ornate churrigueresque.

In the eighteenth century Spanish America began to awake from its medieval sleep. A lively contraband in unorthodox ideas accompanied the growing trade between the colonies and non-Spanish lands. Spain, now under the sway of the enlightened Bourbon kings, herself contributed to the intellectual renovation of the colonies. Spanish or foreign scientific expeditions to Spanish America, authorized and sometimes financed by the crown, stimulated the growth of scientific interests. The expulsion of the Jesuits (1767) removed from the scene the ablest exponents of scholasticism and cleared the way for modest projects of educational reform. But the most significant cultural activity took place outside academic halls — in the Economic Societies, organized for the promotion of useful knowledge; in private gatherings and coffee houses, where young men ardently discussed the advantages of free trade and the rights of men; and in the colonial press, in which the new secular and critical spirit found articulate expression.

1. THE COLONIAL UNIVERSITY

The colonial university was patterned on similar institutions in Spain and faithfully reproduced their medieval organization, curricula, and methods of instruction. Indifference to practical or scientific studies, slavish respect for the authority of the Bible, Aristotle, the Church Fathers, and certain medieval schoolmen, and a passion for hair-splitting debate of fine points of theological or metaphysical doctrine were among the features of colonial academic life. "In ordinary circumstances," writes Professor Lanning, "the regimen produced men of stupendous rote memory, along with imposing but inappropriate and artificial allusions to the ancients and the myths." In the following selection a Spanish friar describes the University of Lima in the first quarter of the seventeenth century.[1]

THE UNIVERSITY and Royal Schools are so distinguished that they need envy no other in the world, since they were established by the Emperor Charles V, and later by Philip II, both of glorious memory; they enlarged, ennobled and enriched them, with the same privileges as the University of Salamanca; they endowed the professorial chairs of Prime with 1,000 assay pesos, and those of Vespers with 600, per annum. The Prime chairs are in Theology, Scholastics, Scripture, Law, and Canons; the Vespers, in the Institutes, the Code, the Decretals, three in Philosophy, one in the Indian language for the training of the priests who are to be parish priests or doctrineros; before they are commissioned, they have to be examined and certificated by the Professor of the language.

The Professors are in major part natives of the Indies and especially of this city, where it would appear that the skies, as usually in the Indies, train outstanding and unusual intellects in subtlety and facility, so that in general they are very able and keen witted; this is obvious from the professorial positions which they occupy and the pulpits, where remarkable men distinguish themselves in their mastery of science and oratory; but they are unfortunate in living far from the eyes of His Majesty. For after all their labors, since there are so few professorial chairs and so many candidates, and there cannot be many lawyers, after having drudged and done brilliantly, and having spent in attaining the degrees of Licentiate and Doctor, 3,500 pesos, they lose heart, unless they have private means, at seeing themselves unrewarded; so the clerics

take benefices and Indian curacies in order to live, and many abandon their books and studies, and never take their degrees.

This University's faculty is important, for it comprises more than 80 Doctors and Masters; the members of the Circuit Court join them, for at the end of the year the fees amount to many ducats. The lecture halls in the schools are excellent, and the chapel very fine, but the most remarkable feature is the amphitheater, where [are held] the public functions and commencements; it is very large and imposing; the display at the granting of whatever degrees are given, is also imposing. They [the faculty] invite the city's nobility as an escort, and meet at the house of the Doctor-to-be in a blare of trumpets, flageolets, and bugles, with a banner which hangs from a window of the house over a canopy on crimson velvet cushions and has the arms of the University and of the graduating Doctor; these are likewise set up in the theater erected in the Cathedral under the royal arms; they remind and notify the invited guests and doctors, who form an escort the evening before; the nobility follow the banner, then the Beadles with their silver maces, then the Masters and Doctors with their insignia, in order of age, closing with the Dean of the faculty and the graduating Doctor; and in this order they repair to the Rector's house, where the members of the Circuit Court await them; with the Rector in their center, they continue in the procession, in order of age. And in this same order the following day they parade till they arrive at the Cathedral, where the theater and the stage have been decorated and provided with seats; Mass is said for them, and at its close after leaving the Cathedral, the newest Doctor of the faculty delivers his burlesque invective, and the Chancellor gives him his degree, just as is done at Salamanca.

2. THE TENTH MUSE

The conditions of colonial life did not favor the development of a rich literature. Isolation from foreign influences, the strict censorship of all reading matter, and the limited audience for writing of every kind made literary creation difficult. "A narrow and dwarfed world," the discouraged Mexican poet Bernardo Balbuena (1568–1627) called the province of New Spain. To make matters worse, in the seventeenth century colonial literature succumbed to the Spanish literary fad of Gongorismo (so called after the poet Luis de Góngora) — the cult of an obscure, involved, and artificial style. Amid "a flock of jangling

---

[1] Vásquez de Espinosa, *Description of the West Indies*, translated by C. V. Clark, pp. 444–446.

magpies," as one literary historian describes the Gongorist versifiers of the seventeenth century, appeared an incomparable songbird, known to her admiring contemporaries as "the tenth muse" — Sor Juana Inés de la Cruz (1651–1695). English and American translators have tried, without great success, to capture the "curious light music" of her poems, "the most gentle and delicate that have ever come from the pen of a woman." Rebuked by the Bishop of Puebla, who wrote under the pseudonym of "Sor Filotea," for her interest in secular learning, Sor Juana replied in a letter that is both an important autobiographical document and an eloquent defense of the rights of women to education and intellectual activity.[2]

I WAS LESS THAN THREE YEARS OLD when my mother sent an older sister to be taught reading at a school for small children, of the kind called *Amigas*. Moved by sisterly affection and by a mischievous spirit, I followed her; and seeing her receive instruction, I formed such a strong desire to learn to read that I tried to deceive the schoolmistress, telling her that *my mother wanted her to give me lessons*. She did not believe me, since it was incredible; but to humor me she acquiesced. I continued to come and she to teach me, no longer in jest but in earnest; and I learned so quickly that I already knew how to read by the time my mother heard about the lessons from the teacher, who had kept them secret in order to break the pleasant news to her and receive her reward all at once. I had concealed it from my mother for fear that I would be whipped for acting without permission. The lady who taught me still lives — God keep her — and can testify to this.

I remember that at that time, although I had the healthy appetite of most children of that age, I would not eat cheese because I heard that it made one dull-witted, and the desire to learn prevailed more with me than hunger, so powerful in children. Later, at the age of six or seven, when I already knew how to read and write, as well as to sew and do other women's tasks, I heard that in Mexico City there was a university, and schools where the sciences were taught. No sooner had I heard this than I began to badger my mother with pleas that she let me put on men's clothing and go to Mexico City, where I could live with some relatives and attend the university. She would not do it, and quite rightly, too, but I satisfied my desire by

2 Sor Juana, *Carta atenagórica, Respuesta a Sor Filotea*, edited by E. Abreu Gómez, México, 1934, pp. 54–58, 66–70. (Excerpt translated by the editor.)

reading in a large number of books that belonged to my grandfather, and neither punishments nor rebukes could stop me. Hence when I came to Mexico City men wondered not so much at my intelligence as at my memory and knowledge, at an age when it seemed I would do well to know how to talk.

I began to study Latin, in which I had barely twenty lessons; and so intense was my application that although women (especially in the flower of their youth) naturally cherish the adornment of their hair, I would cut it off four or six fingers' length, making it a rule that if I had not mastered a certain subject by the time it grew back, I would cut it off again . . . , for it did not seem right to me that a head so empty of knowledge, which is the most desirable adornment of all, should be crowned with hair. I became a nun, for although I knew that the religious state imposed obligations (I speak of incidentals and not of the fundamentals) most repugnant to my temperament, nevertheless, in view of my total disinclination to marriage, it was the most becoming and proper condition that I could choose to ensure my salvation. To achieve this I had to repress my wayward spirit, which wished to live alone, without any obligatory occupation that might interfere with the freedom of my studies or any conventual bustle that might disturb the restful quiet of my books. These desires made me waver in my decision, until, having been told by learned persons that it was temptation, with divine favor I conquered and entered the state which I so unworthily occupy. I thought that I had fled from myself, but — wretched me! — I brought myself with me and so brought my greatest enemy, that thirst for learning which Heaven gave me — I know not whether as a favor or chastisement, for repress it as I might with all the exercise that the conventual state offers, it would burst forth like gunpowder; and it was verified in me that *privatio est causa appetitus* [deprivation is the cause of appetite].

I renewed or rather continued (for I never truly ceased) my labors (which were my rest in all the leisure time that my duties left me) of reading and more reading, of studying and more studying, with no other teacher than the books themselves. You will readily comprehend how difficult it is to study from these lifeless letters, denied the living voice and explanation of a teacher, but I joyfully endured all this labor for love of learning. Ah, if it had been for love of God, as was fitting, how worthy it would have been! True, I sought to direct it as much as possible to His service, for my aspiration was to study theology, since it seemed a notable defect to me, as a Catholic, not to know all that can be learned in this life about the Divine Mysteries; and since I was a nun, and not a lay person, it seemed to me an obligation of my state to study literature. . . . So I reasoned, and convinced myself — though it could well be that I was only justifying what I already wanted to do. And so, as I have said, I directed the steps of my studying toward the heights of Sacred Theology; it seemed to me that in order to arrive there I should climb the stairway of the human sciences and arts; for how should I understand the language of the Queen of Sciences if I did not know that of her handmaidens?

How, without Logic, could I know the general and particular rules by which the Sacred Scripture was written? Without Rhetoric, how should I understand its figures, tropes, and turns of speech? Without Physics, how might I penetrate so many questions of the nature of animals, of sacrifices, that have so many symbolic meanings, some declared and others hidden? And how might I know whether the healing of Saul by the sound of David's harp proceeded from the natural force and virtue of music or from a supernatural power that God placed in David? Without Arithmetic, how should I comprehend the great Temple of Solomon, where God himself was the master architect who drew up the specifications and the plan and the Wise King was but the foreman who executed it — where there was not a base without its mystery, not a column without its symbol, not a cornice without an allusion or architrave without significance — and so on in all its parts, so that even the smallest fillet not only served to embellish but symbolized greater things? Without extensive knowledge of the rules and facts of History, how should one comprehend the Historical Books? How, without ample knowledge of both branches of the Law, could I understand the Legal Books? Without vast erudition, how should I comprehend the many points of profane history mentioned in the Sacred Scripture, so many pagan rites, customs, modes of speech? Without much reading of the Church Fathers, how could one understand the obscure teaching of the Prophets? . . .

At one time my enemies persuaded a very saintly and guileless prelate, who believed that study was a matter for the Inquisition, to forbid me to study. I obeyed her (for the three months or so that she had power over me) in what concerned my reading, but as for the absolute ban on study, this was not in my power to obey, for although I did not study in books, I studied everything that God created, and all this universal machine served me as a textbook. I saw nothing without reflecting upon it; everything I heard moved me to thought. This was true of the smallest and most material things, for since there is no creature, however lowly, in which one does not recognize the *me fecit Deus* [God made me], so there is no object that will not arouse thought, if one considers it as one should. Thus I looked at and wondered about everything, so that even the people I spoke to, and what they said to me, aroused a thousand speculations in me. How did such a variety of temperaments and intellects come about, since we are all of the same species? What could be the hidden qualities and traits that caused these differences? If I saw a figure I would consider the proportion of its lines and measure it in my mind and reduce it to other figures. Sometimes I would walk about in the front part of a dormitory of ours (a very spacious room); I noticed that although the lines of its two sides were parallel and the ceiling was level, the lines seemed to run toward each other and the ceiling seemed to be lower at a distance than it was close by — from which I inferred that visual lines run straight but not parallel, forming a pyramidal figure. And I speculated whether this could be the reason that caused the ancients to wonder whether the world was a sphere or not. Because although it appeared spherical, this might be an optical illusion, presenting concavities where they perhaps did not exist. . . .

This habit is so strong in me that I see nothing without reflecting upon it. I noticed two little girls playing with a top, and I had hardly seen the movement and the object when I began, with my usual madness, to consider the easy motion of the spherical form — and how the impulse, once given, continued independently of its cause, for there was the top dancing at a distance from the girl's hand — the motive cause. Not content with this, I had some flour brought and strewn on the floor, in order to learn whether the top's motion described perfect circles or not; and I discovered that they were only spiral lines that gradually lost their circular character as the impulse diminished. Other children were playing at pins (which is the most infantile game known to children). I began to study the figures they formed, and seeing, by chance, that three pins formed a triangle, I set about joining one to the other, remembering that this is said to have been the figure of the mysterious ring of Solomon, in which were depicted some shadowy hints and representations of the most Sacred Trinity, by virtue of which it worked many miracles; it is said that David's harp had the same figure and that for this reason Saul was healed by its sound; the harps we use today have almost the same shape.

But what shall I say, my lady, of the secrets of nature that I have discovered while cooking? I observe that an egg coheres and fries in butter or oil but breaks up in sugar syrup; that to keep sugar fluid it is sufficient to pour on it a little water containing a quince or some other sour fruit; that the yolk and white of an egg are so opposed that each one separately will mix with sugar, but not both together. I shall not weary you with such trifles, which I mention only to give you an adequate notion of my character and which, I am sure, will make you laugh; but, my lady, what can we women know except kitchen philosophy? Lupercio Leonardo aptly said: "It is possible to philosophize while preparing dinner." And I often say, observing these trifles: "If Aristotle had been a cook, he would have written much more." . . .

Although I had no need of examples, I have nevertheless been aided by the many that I have read about, in both divine and profane writings. For I have seen a Deborah giving laws, both military and political, and governing a people in which there were so many learned men. I read of that sage Queen of Sheba, so learned that she dared to test with enigmas the wisdom of the wisest of men, and suffered no reproof for it but instead was made the judge of unbelievers. I observe so many illustrious women — some adorned with the gift of prophecy, like Abigail; others, with that of persuasion, like Esther; others with piety, like Rahab; others with perseverance, like Anna, mother of Samuel; and an infinite number of others, endowed with still other kinds of graces and virtues.

If I turn my gaze to the pagans, I first encounter the Sibyls, chosen by God to prophesy the principal mysteries of our faith, in verses so learned and elegant that they arouse our wonder. I see the Greeks adore as goddess of learning a woman like Minerva, daughter of the first Jupiter and teacher of all the wisdom of Athens. I see a Bola Argentaria, who aided her husband Lucan to write the great "Battle of Pharsalia."

I see a Zenobia, Queen of Palmyra, as wise as she was brave. An Aretea, the most learned daughter of Aristippus. A Nicostrata, inventor of Latin letters and most learned in Greek. An Aspasia of Miletus, who taught philosophy and rhetoric and was teacher of the philosopher Pericles. A Hypatia, who taught astronomy and studied for a long time in Alexandria. A Leontia, of Greek birth, who wrote against the philosopher Theophrastus and convinced him. A Jucia, a Corinna, a Cornelia, and finally all that multitude of women who won renown under the names of Greeks, Muses, Pythonesses and in the end were nothing more than learned women, regarded and venerated as such by the ancients. Not to mention an infinite number of others of whom the books tell, such as the Egyptian Catherine, who not only read but overcame in debate the wisest sages of Egypt. I see a Gertrude study, write, and teach. And there is no need to wander far afield, for I see a holy mother of my own order, Paula, learned in Hebrew, Greek, and Latin, and most skillful in interpreting the Scriptures — so much so, in fact, that her biographer, the great and saintly Jerome, declared himself unequal to his task. He said, in his usual serious, forceful way: "If all the members of my body were tongues, they would not be enough to proclaim the wisdom and virtue of Paula." He bestowed the same praise on the widow Blesilla and the illustrious virgin Eustoquio, both daughters of the same Paula; for her learning the latter won the name "Prodigy of the World." Fabiola, a Roman lady, was also most learned in the Sacred Scripture. Proba Falconia, a Roman matron, wrote an elegant work in Virgilian measures about the mysteries of our sacred faith. It is well known that our Queen Isabel, wife of Alfonso XII, wrote on astronomy. And . . . in our own time there flourishes the great Christina Alexandra, Queen of Sweden, as learned as she is brave and magnanimous, and there are also the excellent Duchess of Abeyro and the Countess of Vallambrosa.

3. THE MOVEMENT FOR EDUCATIONAL REFORM

In the eighteenth century the Enlightenment came to Spanish America. Foreign travelers and merchants helped to spread the new gospel of rationalism and progress, but much of the liberal impulse stemmed from Spain, where the Bourbon kings were engaged in a major effort at national reconstruction. From Spain came viceroys and intendants with "French" ideas, determined to change the face of their provinces and the thinking of their backward subjects. To achieve this last aim they founded, or tried to found, printing presses, theaters, public libraries, and schools of a more useful and modern kind than the existing Church-controlled institutions. Typical of these men was Viceroy Manuel de Guirior of New Granada (1773–1776), whose recommendations for educational reform, it is worth noting, were rejected by the king's ministers, presumably because of clerical opposition.[3]

THE INSTRUCTION OF YOUTH and the encouragement of the sciences and arts are among the fundamental principles of good government and are the source of the happiness and prosperity of a state. . . . Conscious of this fact, and of the zeal with which our prudent king and his government have worked to establish sound methods of instruction, I determined to make my contribution to the worthy project begun by his Excellency, my predecessor, of founding a public university. . . . By this means, at a small cost, the kingdom could make happy its young men, who at present are denied instruction in the useful sciences and the sound methods and good taste introduced by Europe in the study of belles-lettres, and are occupied in futile debate of the abstract questions posed by Aristotle.

Knowing that His Majesty had been informed of this project, and that a decision had been delayed by the opposition of the Dominican convent in this city, which at present enjoys the sole right of granting degrees, and wishing to put an end to this unhappy state of affairs before its evil effects become incurable, I determined in consultation with the illustrious prelate and the ministers who composed the *junta superior de aplicaciones* to commission the attorney of the *audiencia*, Don Francisco Antonio Moreno y Escandón, a man of sound training and one who had all the necessary qualifications for the task, to prepare a plan of study, adapted to local conditions, that might serve as a model for other educational establishments and help to eliminate existing abuses. After he had drawn up this plan, very intelligently and in entire conformity to the royal intentions, it was examined by the same *junta superior* and approved with universal acclaim and expressions of gratitude to Don Francisco for his zeal. It was also ordered that the plan should be carried out without delay, with the said Moreno acting

as royal director of education, until such time as His Majesty . . . should make known his sovereign will.

Despite the opposition of some persons educated in the ancient fashion — notably that of the regular clergy (who were aggrieved because they had formerly monopolized education in their cloisters and were conscious of their inability to teach certain subjects which they would have to learn anew), a beginning was made with the new method in the two *colegios* of this city. . . . This has had such happy results that one year sufficed to demonstrate the progress made by the students in arithmetic, algebra, geometry, and trigonometry, and in jurisprudence and theology, whose true principles they found in the Church Councils, the ancient canons, Sacred Scripture, and the Church Fathers. . . . I am confident that your Excellency, moved by zeal in this cause, will not heed the appeals and clamors of the abovementioned convent, supported by the regular clergy, but will firmly insist that this reform be carried forward, demonstrating to His Majesty and the Royal Council of the Indies the advantages to the kingdom and monarchy of continuing this method and the urgent need for a university, a workshop in which could be formed heroes capable of making this nation happy. . . .

To this end, I have proposed to His Majesty that a beginning, at least, should be made of the university establishment, with the well-founded hope that time and circumstances will bring it to a state of greater perfection, meantime endowing it with many of the revenues of the Jesuit temporalities. . . . I have also informed His Majesty that all the books found in the *colegios* of the defunct Jesuit Society have been taken to form a public library in this capital, to which persons of literary tastes may come to obtain instruction in all subjects. A spacious room has been set apart for this worthy purpose. . . . In times to come this library can be enriched with new books, and with machines or instruments of which men of science will make profitable use.

4. THE RISE OF THE SCIENTIFIC SPIRIT

The intellectual atmosphere of the Spanish colonies was not conducive to scientific inquiry or achievement. As late as 1773 the Colombian botanist Mutis was charged with heresy for giving lectures on the Copernican system in Bogotá, and the prosecutor of the Inquisition asserted that Mutis was "perhaps the only man in Latin America to uphold Copernicus." In

[3] "Relación del Excmo. Sr. de Guirior," in *Relaciones de los virreyes del Nuevo Reino de Granada*, edited by José Antonio García y García, New York, 1867, pp. 144–147. (Excerpt translated by the editor.)

the closing decades of the eighteenth century, however, the growing volume of economic and intellectual contacts with Europe, as well as the patronage and protection of enlightened governors, created more favorable conditions for scientific activity. Science made its greatest strides in the wealthy province of New Spain, where the expansion of the mining industry stimulated interest in such fields as geology, chemistry, mathematics, and metallurgy. In Mexico City arose a School of Mines, the first in the New World, a Botanical Garden, and an Academy of Fine Arts. The learned Humboldt had high praise for the state of scientific studies in New Spain at the opening of the nineteenth century.[4]

NO CITY OF THE NEW CONTINENT, without even excepting those of the United States, can display such great and solid scientific establishments as the capital of Mexico. I shall content myself here with naming the School of Mines, directed by the learned Elhuyar, to which we shall return when we come to speak of the mines; the Botanic Garden; and the Academy of Painting and Sculpture. This academy bears the title of *Academia de los Nobles Artes de México*. It owes its existence to the patriotism of several Mexican individuals, and to the protection of the minister Gálvez. The government assigned it a spacious building, in which there is a much finer and more complete collection of casts than is to be found in any part of Germany. We are astonished on seeing that the Apollo of Belvidere, the group of Laocoon, and still more colossal statues, have been conveyed through mountainous roads at least as narrow as those of St. Gothard; and we are surprised at finding these masterpieces of antiquity collected together under the torrid zone, in a table land higher than the convent of the great St. Bernard. The collection of casts brought to Mexico cost the king 200,000 francs. The remains of the Mexican sculpture, those colossal statues of basaltes and porphyry, which are covered with Aztec hieroglyphics, and bear some relation to the Egyptian and Hindoo style, ought to be collected together in the edifice of the academy, or rather in one of the courts which belong to it. It would be curious to see these monuments of the first cultivation of our species, the works of a semibarbarous people inhabiting the Mexican Andes, placed beside the beautiful forms produced under the sky of Greece and Italy.

The revenues of the Academy of Fine Arts at Mexico amount to 125,000 francs, of which the government gives 60,000, the body of Mexican miners nearly 25,000, the *consulado*, or association of merchants of the capital, more than 1500. It is impossible not to perceive the influence of this establishment on the taste of the nation. This influence is particularly visible in the symmetry of the buildings, in the perfection with which the hewing of stone is conducted, and in the ornaments of the capitals and stucco relievos. What a number of beautiful edifices are to be seen at Mexico! nay, even in provincial towns like Guanaxuato and Querétaro! These monuments, which frequently cost a million and million and a half of francs, would appear to advantage in the finest streets of Paris, Berlin, and Petersburg. M. Tolsa, professor of sculpture at Mexico, was even able to cast an equestrian statue of King Charles the Fourth; a work which, with the exception of the Marcus Aurelius at Rome, surpasses in beauty and purity of style everything which remains in this way in Europe. Instruction is communicated gratis at the Academy of Fine Arts. It is not confined alone to the drawing of landscapes and figures; they have had the good sense to employ other means for exciting the national industry. The academy labours successfully to introduce among the artisans a taste for elegance and beautiful forms. Large rooms, well lighted by Argand's lamps, contain every evening some hundreds of young people, of whom some draw from relievo or living models, while others copy drawings of furniture, chandeliers, or other ornaments in bronze. In this assemblage (and this is very remarkable in the midst of a country where the prejudices of the nobility against the castes are so inveterate) rank, colour, and race is confounded: we see the Indian and the Mestizo sitting beside the white, and the son of a poor artisan in emulation with the children of the great lords of the country. It is a consolation to observe, that under every zone the cultivation of science and art establishes a certain equality among men, and obliterates for a time, at least, all those petty passions of which the effects are so prejudicial to social happiness.

Since the close of the reign of Charles the Third, and under that of Charles the Fourth, the study of the physical sciences has made great progress, not only in Mexico, but in general in all the Spanish colonies. No European government has sacrificed greater sums to advance the knowledge of the vegetable kingdom than the Spanish government. Three botanical expeditions, in Peru, New Granada, and New Spain, under the direction of MM. Ruíz and

[4] Humboldt, *Political Essay on the Kingdom of New Spain*, I, 212–223.

Pavón, Don José Celestino Mutis, and MM. Sesse and Mocino, have cost the state nearly two millions of francs. Moreover, botanical gardens have been established at Manilla and the Canary Islands. The commission destined to draw plans of the canal of los Guines was also appointed to examine the vegetable productions of the island of Cuba. All these researches, conducted during twenty years in the most fertile regions of the new continent, have not only enriched science with more than four thousand new species of plants, but have also contributed much to diffuse a taste for natural history among the inhabitants of the country. The city of Mexico exhibits a very interesting botanical garden within the very precincts of the viceroy's palace. Professor Cervantes gives annual courses there, which are very well attended. This savant possesses, besides his herbals, a rich collection of Mexican minerals. M. Mocino, whom we just now mentioned as one of the coadjutors of M. Sesse, and who has pushed his laborious excursions from the kingdom of Guatemala to the north-west coast or island of Vancouver and Quadra; and M. Echeverría, a painter of plants and animals, whose works will bear a comparison with the most perfect productions of the kind in Europe, are both of them natives of New Spain. They had both attained a distinguished rank among savants and artists before quitting their country.

The principles of the new chemistry, which is known in the Spanish colonies by the equivocal appellation of new philosophy (*nueva filosofía*), are more diffused in Mexico than in many parts of the peninsula. A European traveller cannot undoubtedly but be surprised to meet in the interior of the country, on the very borders of California, with young Mexicans who reason on the decomposition of water in the process of amalgamation with free air. The School of Mines possesses a chemical laboratory; a geological collection, arranged according to the system of Werner; a physical cabinet, in which we not only find the valuable instruments of Ramsden, Adams, Le Noir, and Louis Berthoud, but also models executed in the capital even, with the greatest precision, and from the finest wood in the country. The best mineralogical work in the Spanish language was printed at Mexico, I mean the *Manual of Oryctognosy,* composed by M. Del Rio, according to the principles of the school of Freyberg, in which the author was formed. The first Spanish translation of Lavater's *Elements of Chemistry* was also published

at Mexico. I cite these isolated facts because they give us the measure of the ardour with which the exact sciences are begun to be studied in the capital of New Spain. This ardour is much greater than that with which they addict themselves to the study of languages and ancient literature.

Instruction in mathematics is less carefully attended to in the University of Mexico than in the School of Mines. The pupils of this last establishment go farther into analysis; they are instructed in the integral and differential calculi. On the return of peace and free intercourse with Europe, when astronomical instruments (chronometers, sextants, and the repeating circles of Borda) shall become more common, young men will be found in the most remote parts of the kingdom capable of making observations, and calculating them after the most recent methods. I have already indicated in the analysis of my maps the advantage which might be drawn by the government from this extraordinary aptitude in constructing a map of the country. The taste for astronomy is very old in Mexico. Three distinguished men, Velásquez, Gama, and Alzate, did honour to their country towards the end of the last century. All the three made a great number of astronomical observations, especially of eclipses of the satellites of Jupiter. Alzate, the worst informed of them, was the correspondent of the Academy of Sciences at Paris. Inaccurate as an observer, and of an activity frequently impetuous, he gave himself up to too many objects at a time. We have already discussed in the geographical introduction the merits of his astronomical labours. He is entitled to the real merit, however, of having excited his countrymen to the study of the physical sciences. The *Gazetta de Litteratura,* which he published for a long time at Mexico, contributed singularly to give encouragement and impulsion to the Mexican youth.

The most remarkable geometrician produced by New Spain since the time of Siguenza was Don Joaquín Velásquez Cárdenas y León. All the astronomical and geodesical labours of this indefatigable savant bear the stamp of the greatest precision. He was born on the 21st July, 1732, in the interior of the country, at the farm of Santiago Acebedocla, near the Indian village of Tizicapan; and he had the merit, we may say, of forming himself. At the age of four he communicated the small pox to his father, who died of them. An uncle, parish-priest of

Xaltocan, took care of his education, and placed him under the instruction of an Indian of the name of Manuel Asentizio; a man of great natural strength of mind, and well versed in the knowledge of the Mexican history and mythology. Velásquez learned at Xaltocan several Indian languages, and the use of the hieroglyphical writings of the Aztecs. It is to be regretted that he published nothing on this very interesting branch of antiquity. Placed at Mexico in the Tridentine college, he found neither professor, nor books, nor instruments. With the small assistance which he could obtain, he fortified himself in the study of the mathematics and the ancient languages. A lucky accident threw into his hands the works of Newton and Bacon. He drew from the one a taste for astronomy, and from the other an acquaintance with the true methods of philosophising. While poor and unable to find any instrument even in Mexico, he set himself, with his friend M. Guadalaxara (now professor of mathematics in the Academy of Painting), to construct telescopes and quadrants. He followed at the same time the profession of advocate, an occupation which in Mexico, as well as elsewhere, is much more lucrative than that of looking at the stars. What he gained by his professional labours was laid out in purchasing instruments in England. After being named professor in the university, he accompanied the *visitador* Don José de Gálvez in his journey to Sonora. Sent on a commission to California, he profited by the serenity of the sky in that peninsula to make a great number of astronomical observations. He first observed there that in all the maps, for centuries, through an enormous error of longitude, this part of the new continent had always been marked several degrees farther west than it really was. When the Abbé Chappe, more celebrated for his courage and his zeal for the sciences than for the accuracy of his labours, arrived in California, he found the Mexican astronomer already established there. Velásquez had constructed for himself, in Mimosa planks, an observatory at St. Anne. Having already determined the position of this Indian village, he informed the Abbé Chappe that the moon's eclipse on the 18th June, 1769, would be visible in California. The French astronomer doubted the truth of this assertion, till the eclipse actually took place. Velásquez by himself made a very good observation of the transit of Venus over the disk of the sun on the 3d June, 1769. He communicated the result, the very morning of the transit, to the Abbé Chappe, and to the Spanish astronomers, Don Vicente Doz and Don Salvador de Medina. The French traveller was surprised at the harmony between the observation of Velásquez and his own. He was no doubt astonished to meet in California with a Mexican, who, without belonging to any academy, and without having ever left New Spain, was able to observe as well as the academicians. In 1773 Velásquez executed the great geodesical undertaking, of which we have given some of the results in the geographical introduction, and to which we shall again return in speaking of the drain of the lakes of the valley of Mexico. The most essential service which this indefatigable man rendered to his country was the establishment of the Tribunal and the School of Mines, the plans for which he presented to the court. He finished his laborious career on the 6th of March, 1786, while first director-general of the *Tribunal de Minería,* and enjoying the title of *Alcalde del Corte honorario.*

After mentioning the labours of Alzate and Velásquez, it would be unjust to pass over the name of Gama, the friend and fellow-labourer of the latter. Without fortune, and compelled to support a numerous family by a troublesome and almost mechanical labour, unknown and neglected during his life by his fellow-citizens, who loaded him with eulogies after his death, Gama became by his own unassisted efforts an able and well-informed astronomer. He published several memoirs on eclipses of the moon, on the satellites of Jupiter, on the almanac and chronology of the ancient Mexicans, and on the climate of New Spain; all of which announce a great precision of ideas and accuracy of observation. If I have allowed myself to enter into these details on the literary merit of three Mexican savants, it is merely for the sake of proving from their example, that the ignorance which European pride has thought proper to attach to the Creoles is neither the effect of the climate nor of a want of moral energy; but that this ignorance, where it is still observable, is solely the effect of the isolation and the defects in the social institutions of the colonies.

5. COLONIAL JOURNALISM IN ACTION

Colonial newspapers and reviews played a significant part in the development of a critical and reformist spirit and a nascent sense of nationality among the educated creoles of Spanish America. They appeared in increasing number in the period after 1780. Subjected to an oppressive censorship by Church and

State, and beset by chronic financial difficulties, they generally had short and precarious lives. More important than the routine news items they carried were the articles they housed on scientific, economic, and social questions. The Semanario del Nuevo Reino de Granada, *edited between 1808 and 1811 by the distinguished Colombian scientist Francisco José de Caldas (1771–1816), was notable for the high quality of its contents. Caldas himself contributed many of the articles in the* Semanario, *including a brilliant essay on the geography of New Granada, from which the following excerpt is taken.*[5]

WHETHER WE LOOK north or south, whether we examine the most populous or the most deserted places in this colony, everywhere we find the stamp of indolence and ignorance. Our rivers and mountains are unknown to us; we do not know the extent of the country in which we were born; and the study of our geography is still in the cradle. This capital and humiliating truth should shake us out of our lethargy; it should make us more attentive to our interests; it should draw us to every corner of New Granada to measure, examine, and describe it. This truth, engraved in the hearts of all good citizens, will bring them together in order to collect information, donate funds, and recruit men of learning, sparing neither labor nor expense to obtain a detailed reconnaissance map of our provinces. I am not speaking now of an ordinary map; reduced scales and economy must disappear from the minds of our countrymen. Two square inches, at least, should represent a league of terrain. Here should appear the hills, mountains, pastures, forests, lakes, marshes, valleys, rivers, their turns and velocities, straits, cataracts, fisheries, all settlements, all agricultural activities, mines, and quarries — in fine, everything above the surface of our land. These features, brought together, will produce a superb map, worthy of New Granada. The statesman, the magistrate, the philosopher, the businessman, will come to look at it to obtain information needed in the performance of their duties; the traveler, the botanist, the mineralogist, the biologist, the soldier, and the agriculturist will see their concerns depicted in majestic strokes. . . . Each province will copy its own section and will guard it religiously. Our youth will be trained in the study of these sections, and in a few years we shall have men capable of conceiving and carrying out great plans. Everywhere we shall hear only of projects: projects of roads, navigation canals, new branches of industry, naturalization of foreign plants; the flame of patriotism will be lighted in every heart; and the ultimate result will be the glory of our monarch and the prosperity of this colony.

If a geographical-economic expedition were formed to survey the whole viceroyalty, composed of an astronomer, a botanist, a mineralogist, a zoologist, and an economist, with two or more draftsmen; if all the provinces contributed toward a fund set up by the wealthy, and especially by the landowners; if the merchants did the same in view of their financial interest in the project; if the Chamber of Commerce [*Consulado*] of Cartagena supported the enterprise as actively as it promotes other projects of the same nature; if the governmental leaders supported it with all their authority — there is no doubt that in a few years we would have the glory of possessing a masterpiece of geographical and political knowledge, and would have laid the foundations of our prosperity.

If this project presents difficulties, there remains no other recourse than to improve our educational system. If instead of teaching our youths trifles . . . , we gave them some acquaintance with the elements of astronomy and geography, and taught them the use of some easily-mastered instruments; if practical geometry and geodesy were substituted for certain metaphysical and useless subjects; if on finishing their courses they knew how to measure the earth, make a survey, determine a latitude, use a compass — then we would have reason to hope that these youths, dispersed throughout the provinces, would put into practice the principles they had learned in school, and would make a map of their country. Six months devoted to these interesting studies would qualify a young man to work on the great enterprise of the geography of this colony. I ask the persons responsible for our public education to consider and weigh whether it is more profitable to the State and Church to spend many weeks in sustaining airy systems and all that heap of futile or merely speculative questions than to devote this time to the study of the globe and the land that we inhabit. What do we care about the dwellers on the moon? Would it not be better to learn about the dwellers on the fertile banks of the Magdalena?

The religious orders who have in their charge the missions of the Orinoco, Caqueta, Andaquies, Mocoa, and Maynas should educate the

[5] Francisco José de Caldas, *Semanario del Nuevo Reino de Granada,* Bogotá, 1942, 3 vols., I, 51–54. (Excerpt translated by the editor.)

young missionaries in these important subjects. These apostolic men would bring to the barbarians both the light of salvation and that of the useful sciences. Zealous imitators of Fathers Fritz, Coleti, Magnio, and Gumilla, they would leave us precious monuments of their activity and learning. Exact maps, geographical determination, descriptions of plants and animals, and important information about the customs of the savages whom they are going to civilize would be the fruits of these studies. They would serve them as a relief from the tedium and weariness that are inseparable from their lofty ministry.

The rudiments of arithmetic, plane geometry, and trigonometry, of which we possess good compendiums; the use of the graphometer, the gnomon, the quadrant (with some knowledge of how to draw a meridian), and the use of the barometer and the thermometer qualify a young man to assist in the advance of our geographical knowledge.

We have two chairs of mathematics, and that of philosophy offers some instruction in these sciences; thanks to the wise and generous Mutis, we already have an astronomical observatory, where practical experience can be obtained in the use of certain instruments; we have books, and we lack nothing necessary to working for the good of our country. My love for the fatherland dictated these reflections. If they are useful to my countrymen, I am already rewarded for the labor they cost me; if not, they will pardon me, taking into account the purity of my intentions.

6. A COLONIAL FREETHINKER

The circulation and influence of forbidden books among educated colonials steadily increased in the closing decades of the eighteenth century and the first years of the nineteenth. In Mexico, writes Professor Jiménez Rueda, "Voltaire and the encyclopedists, Jean Jacques Rousseau and Montesquieu, were read by village curates, by canons of provincial cathedrals, and by lawyers in the capital. Pictures of Voltaire were even sold in the bookstalls by the Gate of the Augustine friars, and the books of all of them passed from hand to hand, although surreptitiously, because the Holy Office still kept watch." Encyclopedist influence is strongly evident in the work of the Mexican writer Fernández de Lizardi (1776–1827), whose stormy life spanned the declining years of the colony and the first years of its independence. His masterpiece, El periquillo sarniento (The Itching Parrot), the first true Spanish-American novel, depicted with harsh realism and biting satire the conditions of Mexican life in the late colonial period. First published in Mexico City in 1816, incomplete because of official censorship, it was later reprinted in its entirety. The following episode from The Itching Parrot, *laid in Manila, illustrates Lizardi's emphatic dissent from social folly and prejudice of every kind.[6]*

I SAID BEFORE that a virtuous man has few misfortunes to relate. Nevertheless, I witnessed some strange affairs. One of them was as follows:

One year, when a number of foreigners had come from the port to the city for reasons of trade, a rich merchant who happened to be a Negro went down a street. He must have been bound on very important business, because he strode along very rapidly and distractedly, and in his headlong progress he inadvertently ran into an English officer who was paying court to a rich young creole lady. Such was the shock of the collision that if the girl had not supported him the officer would have fallen to the ground. As it was, his hat fell off and his hair was disheveled.

The officer's pride was greatly wounded, and he immediately ran toward the Negro, drawing his sword. The poor fellow was taken by surprise, and since he carried no arms he probably believed that it was all up with him. The young lady and the officer's companions restrained him, but he raged at the Negro for some time, protesting a thousand times that he would vindicate his injured honor.

So much abuse did he heap on the innocent black that the latter finally said to him in English: "Sir, be quiet; tomorrow I shall be waiting in the park to give you satisfaction with a pistol." The officer accepted, and there the matter rested.

I, who witnessed this incident and knew some English, having learned the hour and place assigned for the duel, took care to be there punctually to see how the affair would end.

At the appointed time both men arrived, each accompanied by a friend who acted as his second. As soon as they met the Negro drew two pistols, presented them to the officer, and said to him: "Sir, I did not intend yesterday to offend you; my running into you was an accident. You heaped abuse on me and even wished to wound

6 José Joaquín Fernández de Lizardi, *El periquillo sarniento*, México, 1897, 2 vols., II (D), 3–7. (Excerpt translated by the editor.)

or kill me. I had no arms with which to defend myself against you. I knew that a challenge to a duel was the quickest means of quieting you, and now I have come to give you satisfaction with a pistol, as I said I would."

"Very well," said the Englishman, "let's get on. It gives me no satisfaction to fight with a Negro, but at least I shall have the pleasure of killing an insolent rascal. Let's choose our pistols."

"All right," said the Negro, "but you should know that I no more intend to offend you today than I did yesterday. It seems to me that for a man of your position to decide to kill a man for such a trifle is not a matter of honor but a mere caprice. But if the explanation I gave you means nothing, and only killing will do, I don't propose to be guilty of murder or to die without cause, as must happen if your shot or my shot finds its target. So let luck decide who has justice on his side. Here are the pistols; one of them is loaded with two balls and the other is empty. Look them over, give me the one you don't want, and let us take our chances."

The officer was surprised by this proposal. The others said that it was highly irregular — that both must fight with the same weapons; and they offered other arguments that did not convince the Negro, who insisted that the duel must take place on his terms, so that he might have the consolation of knowing that if he killed his opponent it was because Heaven had ordered it or especially favored him — and if he were killed, it would be no fault of his but pure chance, as when a ship is wrecked at sea. He added that since the arrangement favored neither party, since no one knew who would get the loaded pistol, refusal to accept his proposal could only be attributed to cowardice.

No sooner had the ardent young man heard this than he took up the pistols, selected one, and gave the other to the Negro.

The two men turned their backs to each other, walked a short distance, and then turned to face each other. At that moment the officer fired at the Negro — but in vain, for he had chosen the empty pistol.

He stood there as if stunned, believing with the others that he would be the defenceless victim of the Negro's wrath. But the latter, with the greatest generosity, said to the officer: "Sir, we have both come out with whole skins; the duel is over; you had to accept it with the conditions I imposed, and I could wage it on no other terms. I could fire at you if I wished, but if I never sought to offend you before, how could I do it now, seeing you disarmed? Let us be friends, if you consider yourself satisfied; but if only my death can appease you, take the loaded pistol and aim it at my breast."

Saying this, he presented the horrible weapon to the officer. The latter, moved by this extraordinary generosity, took the pistol and fired it in the air. Approaching the Negro with outstretched arms, he embraced him, saying with the greatest tenderness:

"Yes, friends we are and friends we shall be eternally; forgive my vanity and madness. I never believed that Negroes were capable of such greatness of soul." "That prejudice still has many followers," said the Negro, warmly embracing the officer.

We who witnessed this incident were eager to strengthen the bonds of this new friendship, and I, who knew them least of all, hastened to introduce myself to them as their friend, and to beg them to take a glass of punch or wine with me at the nearest coffeehouse.

XVII

The Revolt of the Masses

INNUMERABLE SERVILE REVOLTS, large and small, punctuated the colonial period of Spanish-American history. Before Spanish rule had been firmly established the Indians rose against their new masters in many regions. The revolutionary wave subsided in the seventeenth century but rose again to great heights in the eighteenth, as a result of new burdens imposed on the common people.

The expansion of colonial economic life under the Bourbon dynasty failed to better the lot of the Indian and mestizo peasantry and artisans. On the contrary, Bourbon efforts to increase the royal revenues, by creating governmental monopolies and privileged companies, and by imposing new taxes, actually intensified the sufferings of the lower classes. This circumstance helps to explain the popular character of the revolts of 1780–1781, as distinct from the creole wars of independence of the next generation.

In November, 1779, José Gabriel Tupac-Amaru, a direct descendant of the last Inca, raised the standard of revolt in Peru by ambushing the hated *corregidor* Arriaga near the town of Tinta and putting him to death after a summary trial. By the first months of 1780 the southern highlands of the viceroyalty were aflame with rebellion. Although the various revolutionary movements lacked a unified direction, the rebel leaders generally recognized Tupac-Amaru as their chief, and they continued to invoke his name even after his death.

Tactical errors — such as the failure of Tupac-Amaru to attack Cuzco before the arrival of Spanish reinforcements, poor communications between the rebel forces, the superior arms and organization of the royalist armies, and divisions among the native nobility — doomed the rebellion to defeat. Despite some initial successes, the rebel chieftain was soon completely routed. Tupac-Amaru, members of his family, and his leading captains were captured and put to death, in some cases with ferocious cruelty.

The revolt of the *Comuneros* in New Granada, like that in Peru, had its origin in intolerable economic conditions. The disturbances began in Socorro, an important manufacturing town in the north, and rapidly spread to other communities. Under the command of hesitant or unwilling creole leaders, a multitude of Indian and mestizo peasants and artisans marched upon Bogotá, capturing or putting to flight the small forces sent from the capital. An agreement reached on June 4, 1781, satisfied virtually all the demands of the rebels, and was sanctified by the archbishop by a special religious service. Secretly, however, the Spanish commissioners signed another document declaring the agreement void as obtained by force. The jubilant insurgents scattered and returned to their homes. Only José Antonio Galán, a young mestizo peasant leader, kept his small force intact and sought to keep the revolt alive.

Having achieved their objective of disbanding the rebel host, the Spanish officials prepared to crush the insurrection completely. The Viceroy Flores openly repudiated the agreement with the *Comuneros*. Spanish troops moved into the disaffected area and seized large numbers of prisoners. Galán, who vainly urged a new march on Bogotá, was seized by a renegade leader and handed over to the Spaniards, who put him to death by hanging on January 30, 1782. The revolt of the *Comuneros* had ended.

1. THE PLAN OF TUPAC-AMARU

The general causes of the great revolt in Peru are sufficiently clear. More obscure are the precise aims that the rebel leader, Tupac-Amaru, set for himself. It is difficult to believe that the well-educated José Gabriel, who had had years of experience in dealing with Spanish officialdom, seriously believed that he could obtain sweeping reforms from the crown by negotiation, even from positions of strength, especially after his execution of the corregidor *Arriaga. More plausible is the view that his professions of loyalty to Spain represented a mask by means of which he hoped to utilize the still strong faith of the Indians in the mythical benevolence of the Spanish king and perhaps to soften his punishment in case of defeat. If this view is correct, it follows that his true object*

was the establishment of an independent Peruvian state, with himself as king or Inca. Such a state would have been essentially Spanish in religion and in political and social organization. The fiscal, or prosecuting attorney, of the viceroyalty of Buenos Aires offers a shrewd and convincing argument in favor of the thesis that the rebel leader aimed at independence.[1]

WHAT IS WORTHY OF ATTENTION in this affair is not so much the pitiful death of the corregidor Don Antonio de Arriaga, the theft of his fortune, the seizure of the arms that he had in his

[1] "Vista del fiscal del virreinato de Buenos Aires, enero 15 de 1781," in: Manuel de Odriozola (ed.), *Documentos históricos del Perú*, Lima, 1863, pp. 132–133. (Excerpt translated by the editor.)

house, or the outrages committed by the perfidious Tupac-Amaru, as the astuteness, the painstaking care, and the deceptions with which he managed to perform them and to subvert that and other provinces, preparing them to carry out his reprehensible secret designs.

It appears that in order to seize the corregidor Arriaga, in his own house, he arranged a banquet for his victim. In order to summon the military chiefs, caciques, and Indians of the province, he compelled the unhappy corregidor to issue or sign orders to that effect. In order to drag him to the gallows in the presence of the multitude with no disturbance, he published a decree, pretending that he acted on His Majesty's orders. On the same pretext, after this horrible deed, he departed for the neighboring province of Quispicanchi, in order to perpetrate similar atrocities on the corregidor and as many Spaniards as he could find, and as soon as he had returned to his town of Tungasuca issued orders to the caciques of neighboring provinces to imitate his example.

And although in the provinces of Azangaro and Carabaya, which belonged to this viceroyalty of Buenos Aires, his wicked designs failed to bear fruit, thanks to the loyalty with which his commissioner Don Diego Chuquiguanca (the cacique and governor of the town of Azangaro) and his sons turned over the dispatches, of which copies are found in the file on this case, the fact is that the province of Quispicanchi, since the flight of Don Fernando Cabrera, its present corregidor, is under the sway of the rebel Tupac-Amaru; and he himself asserts in one of the papers written at Chuquiguanca that four more provinces obey his orders. And, knowing as he did the natives' great respect for the orders of the king and their hatred of the corregidores and their European associates, he probably did not find it difficult to incite them to execute the supposed orders of the king.

But the essence of the careful planning and perfidy of the traitor Tupac-Amaru consists in this, that after speaking so often of the royal orders which authorized him to proceed against the corregidores and other Europeans, in his orders, letters, and messages, and in the edicts which he dispatched to Don Diego Chuquiguanca, in order to revolutionize that province and Carabaya, he now says nothing about the orders of the king, and proceeds as the most distinguished Indian of the royal blood and principal line of the Incas to liberate his countrymen from the injuries, injustices, and slavery which the European corregidores had inflicted on them, while the superior courts turned a deaf ear to their complaints. From which it follows that he repeatedly used the name of the king — in a vague way, not specifying our present ruler, Charles III — only to secure the acquiescence of the natives of those provinces in the violence done to Arriaga and to induce them to do the same to other corregidores. And considering these aims partially achieved, he transforms himself from a royal commissioner into a redeemer from injustices and burdens, moved only by pity for his compatriots, preparing the way for them to acclaim him as king, or at least to support their benefactor with arms, until they have raised him to the defunct throne of the tyrannical pagan kings of Peru, which is doubtless the goal of his contrivings.

Actually, he has already succeeded in assembling a large number of Indians, as noted by Colonel Don Pedro la Vallina (who was his prisoner) in a letter contained in the file on this case — and with their aid, it is stated, he defeated and slew some 300 men who came out to halt his advance on Cuzco, and took their weapons to arm the rebels who follow him. He took these first successful steps in his titanic enterprise after certain other things had occurred: the rising that took place in Arequipa as a result of the establishment of a customshouse; the rioting that with less cause broke out in the city of La Paz; the disturbances that occurred in the provinces of Chayanta for the same reason; and the rumors that the natives in other provinces were somewhat restless. When one considers that the rebel Tupac-Amaru, informed of these events, offers the natives freedom, not only from customshouse duties but from sales taxes, tributes, and forced labor in the mines, it must be admitted that he offers them a powerful inducement to follow him, and that there is imminent danger that the party of rebellion will progressively increase unless the most energetic effort is made to slay this insolent rebel, the prime mover of this conspiracy, so that others may be deterred from joining the rebellion and abandoning their loyalty to their legitimate monarch and natural lord, to the detriment of themselves and the commonwealth.

2. A HEROINE OF THE REVOLT

Micaela, the wife of Tupac-Amaru, played a leading role in the great revolt. From the first she was the rebel leader's principal adviser, and in his absence assumed full direction of the movement. After the initial victory over the small Spanish force sent from Cuzco, she strongly advised an immediate march on the city, to take advantage of the chaos and panic that reigned there. The capture of Cuzco, ancient capital of the Inca Empire and center of Spanish power in the highlands, would have been a stroke of the greatest moral and military significance. Tupac-Amaru decided instead to invade the provinces to the south, promising to return immediately and advance on Cuzco — a promise he failed to keep. By the time he returned, reinforcements had reached Cuzco from Lima, and the golden opportunity had vanished. The bitterness of Micaela's letter to José Gabriel reflects her appreciation of the immensity of his blunder. Despite these harsh reproaches, her letters to Tupac-Amaru contain "notes of profound and laconic tenderness." ("Chepe" was an affectionate nickname for her husband.) [2]

DEAR CHEPE:

You are causing me mortal concern. While you saunter through the villages, wasting two days in Yauri, showing no sense of urgency, our soldiers are rightly becoming bored, and are leaving for their homes.

I simply cannot endure all this any longer, and I am ready to give myself up to the Spaniards and let them take my life when I see how lightly you regard this serious matter that threatens the lives of all of us. We are surrounded by enemies and constantly insecure; and on your account the lives of all my sons, and of all our people, are in danger.

I have warned you again and again not to dally in those villages, where there is nothing to do — but you continue to saunter, ignoring the fact that the soldiers are running short of food. They are receiving their pay, but the money will not last forever. Then they will all depart, leaving us to pay with our lives, because you must have learned by this time that they came only for reasons of self-interest, and to get all they could out of us. They are already beginning to desert; they are frightened by the rumor spread by Vargas and Oré that the Spaniards of Lampa, united with those of other provinces and Arequipa, are going to surround you, and so they want to get away, fearing the punishment that might befall them. Thus we will lose all the people that I have gotten together

2 Micaela Bastidas to José Gabriel Tupac Amaru, Dec. 6, 1780, in: Francisco A. Loáyza (ed.), *Mártires y heroínas*, Lima, 1945, pp. 48–51. (Excerpt translated by the editor.)

for the descent on Cuzco, and the forces at Cuzco will unite with the soldiers from Lima, who have been on the march for many days.

I must tell you all this, though it pains me. If you want to ruin us, continue to sleep and commit such follies as that of passing alone through the streets of Yauri, and even climbing to the church tower — actions certainly out of place at this time, and that only dishonor you and gain you disrespect.

I believed that you were occupied day and night with arranging these affairs, instead of showing an unconcern that robs me of my life. I am already a shadow of myself and beside myself with anxiety, and so I beg you to get on with this business.

You made me a promise, but henceforth I shall not heed your promises, for you did not keep your word.

I do not care for my life, but for the lives of my poor children, who need all my help. If the enemy comes from Paruro, as I suggested in my last letter, I am prepared to march to meet them, leaving Fernando in a secure place, for the Indians are not capable of acting by themselves in these perilous times.

I gave you plenty of warnings to march immediately on Cuzco, but you took them all lightly, giving the Spaniards time to prepare as they have done, placing cannon on Picchu Mountain, and devising other measures so dangerous that you are no longer in a position to attack them. God keep you many years. Tungasuca, December 6, 1780.

I must also tell you that the Indians of Quispicanchi are tired of serving as guards so long a time. In fine, God must want me to suffer for my sins. Your wife.

After I had finished this letter, a messenger arrived with the definite news that the enemy from Paruro is in Acos; I am going forward to attack them, even if it costs me my life.

3. THE DEATH OF TUPAC-AMARU

The rebel attack on Cuzco came too late. The strong resistance of the reinforced Spanish defenders and their Indian auxiliaries (the majority of combatants on both sides were natives), the superiority of the Spanish armaments, the constant desertions from Tupac-Amaru's undisciplined host, and the treason of the captured Spaniard who commanded the rebel artillery and systematically misdirected the fire of his pieces were among the reasons for its failure. In January, 1781, Tupac-Amaru suddenly abandoned the siege and began a rapid withdrawal toward his base in the province of Tinta. The Spaniards soon launched a powerful offensive. The insurgent forces were defeated in fierce battles, and Tupac-Amaru evacuated Tinta, fleeing southward with the apparent intention of organizing a new resistance in the highlands around Lake Titicaca. During the disorderly retreat he, his wife, his sons, and a number of his captains were seized by treachery and handed over to the Spaniards. After a summary trial, on May 15, 1781, the visitador *Areche handed down sentences whose ferocity revealed how thin was the veneer of Enlightenment over the medieval mentality of Bourbon Spain. A contemporary account describes the death of Tupac-Amaru and other leaders of the rebellion.*[3]

ON FRIDAY, May 18, 1781, the militia of Cuzco, armed with spears and some firearms, surrounded the public square, and the corps of mulattoes and Indians from Huamanga district, with fixed bayonets, surrounded the four-sided gallows. Then the following persons were brought forth: José Berdejo, Andres Castelu, the *zambo* Antonio Oblitas (the executioner of the corregidor Arriaga), Antonio Bastidas, Francisco Tupac-Amaru, Tomasa Condemaita, the woman cacique of Acos, Hipólito Tupac-Amaru, son of the traitor, his wife Micaela Bastidas, and the rebel leader himself. They were all brought out together in chains, in baskets of the kind they use to bring yerba maté leaves from Paraguay, and dragged along behind a harnessed horse. Accompanied by their guards and by priests who offered them spiritual consolation, they were brought to the foot of the scaffold, and there the executioners meted out the following deaths to them:

Berdejo, Castelu, the zambo, and Bastidas were simply hanged. Francisco Tupac-Amaru, the rebel's uncle, and his son Hipólito, had their tongues cut out before they were thrown down the steps of the gallows. The Indian woman Condemaita was strangled on a little scaffold provided with an iron screw made for this purpose, the first ever seen here. The Indian and his wife witnessed all these punishments, even that of their son Hipólito, who was the last to go to the gallows. Then Micaela went up to the scaffold, where, in the presence of her husband, her tongue was cut out and she was garroted, suffering infinite agony all the while, because since her neck was very slender the screw could not strangle her, and the executioners had to dispatch her by tying ropes

around her neck, each pulling in a different direction, and kicking her in the stomach and breast. Last to die was the rebel leader, José Gabriel. He was brought into the middle of the square, and there the executioner cut out his tongue. Then they took off his chains and laid him on the ground. They tied four ropes to his hands and feet and attached the ropes to the girths of four horses, which four mestizos drove in four different directions. Cuzco had never before seen a spectacle of this kind. Either because the horses were not very strong or because the Indian was really made of iron, they simply could not tear him apart, although they tugged at him for a long time, while he dangled in the air like a spider. Finally the visitador Areche, moved by compassion, decided to end his sufferings and sent an order from the Jesuit College, from whose windows he was watching these punishments, that the executioner should cut off his head, and so it was done. Then they laid his body under the gallows and cut off his arms and legs. They did the same to the women, and the heads of the others were cut off and sent to be displayed in various towns. The bodies of the Indian and his wife were borne to Picchu, where a great bonfire was made, into which they were thrown and reduced to ashes, which were thrown into the air and into the little river that runs through there. Such was the end of José Gabriel Tupac-Amaru and Micaela Bastidas, whose pride and arrogance reached such a pitch that they called themselves Kings of Peru, Chile, Quito, Tucuman, and other parts, even including the Grand Paititi, with other follies of the same kind.

A considerable number of people gathered on this day, but no one gave a cry or even spoke; many, and I among them, noted that there were no Indians in that multitude, at least not in their customary dress; if there were any there, they must have been disguised in cloaks or ponchos. Sometimes things happen as if the Devil had planned them to confirm these Indians in their abuses and superstitions. I say this because, although the weather had been very fine and dry, that day dawned with the sky heavily overcast, and at twelve o'clock, when the horses were tugging at the Indian, there arose a gust of wind followed by a downpour that forced all the people and even the guards to run for shelter. This has caused the Indians to say that the heavens and the elements were mourning the death of their Inca, whom the inhuman or impious Spaniards were putting to death with such cruelty.

[3] Odriozola, *Documentos históricos del Perú*, pp. 161–162. (Excerpt translated by the editor.)

4. A CHARTER OF LIBERTY

Although produced by the same causes, the rising of the Comuneros *in New Granada was a relatively peaceful affair by contrast with the vast upheaval in Peru. Its reformist spirit was reflected in the insurgent slogan:* Viva el rey y muera el mal gobierno (*Long live the king, and down with the rotten government!*) *But in view of its organization and its effort to form a common front of all colonial groups with grievances against Spanish authority (excepting only the Negro slaves), the revolt of the* Comuneros *marked an advance over the chaotic course of events to the south. A central committee, or* común, *elected in the town of Socorro by thousands of peasants and artisans from adjacent towns, directed the insurrection. Each of the towns in revolt also had a* común *and a captain chosen by popular election. The popular basis of the* Comunero *movement is evident from the terms which the rebel delegates presented to the Spanish commissioners, and which the latter signed and later repudiated. A number of important or typical articles follow.*[4]

1. The tax entitled Armada de Barlovento [5] must be abolished so completely that its name shall never again be heard in this kingdom. . . .

4. In view of the poverty of this kingdom, stamped paper shall circulate only in sheets of half *real,* for the use of ecclesiastics, religious, Indians, and poor people, and in sheets of two *reales* for the legal titles and lawsuits of persons of some wealth; and no other stamped paper shall circulate. . . .

5. The new tax on tobacco shall be completely abolished. . . .

7. Considering the miserable state of all the Indians, who go about more poorly clothed and fed than hermits, and whose small knowledge, limited faculties, and meager harvests prevent them from paying the high tribute which the *corregidores* exact with such severity, not to mention the stipends assigned to their curates: The total annual tribute of the Indians shall be only four pesos, and that of mulattoes subject to tribute shall be two pesos. The curates shall not collect from the Indians any fee for the administration of holy oils, burials, and weddings, nor shall they compel them to serve as mayordomos at their saints' festivals. The cost of these festivals shall (except when some pious person

offers to bear them) be borne by the brotherhood. . . . Furthermore, those Indians who have been removed from their towns but whose lands have not been sold or transferred shall be returned to their lands of immemorial possession; and all the lands which they at present possess shall be theirs, not only for their use but as their property, which they may use as the owners thereof. . . .

9. The *alcabala,* henceforth and forever, shall be two per cent of all fruits, goods, cattle, and articles of every kind when sold or exchanged. . . .

10. Since the cause of the widespread commotions in this kingdom and in that of Lima has been the imprudent conduct of the *visitadores,* who tried to squeeze blood out of stones and destroy us with their despotic rule, until the people of this kingdom, ordinarily so docile and submissive, were made desperate by their growing extortions and could no longer tolerate their tyrannical rule . . . , we demand that Don Juan Gutiérrez de Piñeres, *visitador* of the royal audiencia, be expelled from this kingdom to Spain, where our Catholic Monarch, reflecting on the results of his arbitrary conduct, shall do with him as he thinks best. And never again must officials be sent us who would treat us so severely and unwisely, for in such a case we shall again join together to repel any oppression that may be directed against us on any pretext whatever. . . .

18. All the officers on the present expedition, with the ranks of commander-general, captains-general, territorial captains, lieutenants, ensigns, sergeants, and corporals, shall retain their respective appointments, and shall be obliged to assemble their companies on Sunday afternoon of each week to train them in the use of arms, both offensive and defensive, against the event that an effort be made to break the agreements that we are now making in good faith, and also to aid His Majesty in resisting his enemies. . . .

21. In filling offices of the first, second, and third classes, natives of America shall be privileged and preferred over Europeans, who daily manifest their antipathy toward us . . . , for in their ignorance they believe that they are the masters and that all Americans of any kind are their inferiors and servants. And so that this irrational view may disappear, Europeans shall be employed only in case of necessity and according to their ability, good will, and attachment to the Americans, for since we are all subjects of the same king and lord we should live like brothers, and whoever strives to lord it over others and advance himself against the rule of

---

[4] Manuel Briceño, *Los comuneros,* Bogotá, 1880, Appendix, pp. 122–132. (Excerpt translated by the editor.)

[5] This was a tax designed to strengthen the *armada de barlovento,* the Spanish squadron guarding the Windward Islands. B.K.

equality must be removed from among us. . . .

32. The order greatly reducing the number of grocery stores has had the result that the stores licensed in each town are owned by the wealthiest or most favored individuals. We therefore ask, as a matter of public benefit, that the right to establish stores be granted to all inhabitants of the kingdom, as was formerly the case, without limitation as to their number.

5. TUPAC-AMARU AND THE COMUNEROS

The revolt of Tupac-Amaru had repercussions among the Indians of New Granada. In the eastern lowlands, where the powerful missions and their priests replaced the corregidores *as symbols of Spanish oppression, the news that a great king of their race had arisen was carried from town to town and caused wild rejoicing and revolts against Spanish authority among the Indians. In this region the popularly-chosen* comúnes *pledged loyalty to the Inca. At Silos, in the district of Pamplona, where a great throng of Indians took an oath of allegiance to their distant king, the following decree of Tupac-Amaru was published.[6]*

DON JOSÉ I, by the grace of God Inca, King of

[6] Briceño, *Los comuneros,* pp. 139–140. (Excerpt translated by the editor.)

Peru, Santafe, Quito, Chile, Buenos Aires, and the continents of the South Sea, Duke of the Superlativa, Lord of the River of the Amazons, with dominion over the Grand Paititi, commissioner and distributor of the divine mercy. . . .

Whereas it has been determined by my council in prolonged sessions, on repeated occasions, both secret and public, that the Kings of Castile have usurped the crown and dominions of Peru, imposing an intolerable number of taxes, tributes, duties, excises, monopolies, tithes, fifths, viceroys, audiencias, corregidores, and other ministers, all equally tyrannical, who sold justice at auction. . . . ,

For these causes, and by reason of the cries which have risen up to heaven, in the name of Almighty God I order that henceforth no man shall pay money to any Spanish officer, excepting the tithe to priests and a moderate tribute and fifth to his natural King and Lord; and for the speedier observance of the abovesaid, I order that an oath of allegiance to my royal crown be taken in all the cities, towns, and villages of my dominions, and that I be informed without delay which vassals are faithful and loyal, so that I may reward them, and which ones are disloyal, so that I may mete out condign punishment to them.

Part Five

Colonial Brazil

PEDRO ALVARES CABRAL, a Portuguese sea captain bound for India in the wake of Vasco da Gama's voyage, discovered Brazil in 1500. For several decades thereafter, Portugal's rulers neglected Brazil in favor of the Far East and its trade. However, as the profits of the Oriental spice trade declined, the Portuguese turned with increasing interest to the "Isle of Santa Cruz," as Brazil was then called. The export of brazilwood and the raising of sugar cane formed the principal economic activities of the early colonists. After 1550 large numbers of Negro slaves were imported to meet the needs of an expanding plantation economy.

French and Dutch invaders challenged Portuguese possession of Brazil in the sixteenth and seventeenth centuries but were beaten off by the colonists, practically unaided by the mother country. Meanwhile adventurous gold-seekers and slave-hunters from São Paulo pushed deep into the interior, far beyond the Line of Demarcation of 1494. In 1695 the Paulistas discovered gold in the region later called Minas Gerais — a timely find, for the first sugar cycle of the Northeast had about run its course as a result of competition from more efficient West-Indian producers. But the mineral cycle, marked by rapid and wasteful exploitation of the more accessible deposits of gold and diamonds, was of short duration. At the close of the colonial period the Northeast, revived by a growing European demand for cotton, sugar, and other of Brazil's staples, again enjoyed economic primacy.

Like Spain, Portugal governed her empire with the aid of a royal council at home and an apparatus of viceroys, governors, judges, and inspectors overseas, but her administrative machinery for Brazil was less elaborate than that of the Spanish Indies. As in the Spanish colonies, the Church was under royal control but lacked the vast wealth and influence of its Spanish counterpart. The Jesuits led all other clergy in the work of converting the Indians, and in educational and humanitarian activities.

The nucleus of the social organization of the colony was the great estate, or fazenda, a self-sufficient patriarchal community centered about the Big House and its owner. Slavery cast a heavy shadow over every aspect of colonial life. One of its greatest evils was the resulting prejudice against labor — a prejudice that condemned to idleness or vagabondage many whites and free mixed-bloods who could neither aspire to be masters nor lower themselves by performing tasks ordinarily carried out by slaves.

XVIII

The Formation of Colonial Brazil

PEDRO ALVARES CABRAL, a Portuguese captain sent to follow up Gama's great voyage to India, accidentally discovered Brazil in 1500 and claimed it for his country. Projects of trade and conquest in the Far East claimed Portugal's chief attention at this time, but she did not completely neglect her new possession. Brazilwood, source of a valued red dye, was the first staple of the colony, but sugar soon established its economic leadership. Raids on Indian voyages and, after 1550, the importation of Negro slaves provided labor for the plantations and sugar mills.

The second half of the seventeenth century saw a crisis in the Brazilian sugar industry, which was faced with severe competition from newly-risen Dutch, English, and French sugar colonies in the West Indies. As the first economic cycle of colonial Brazil drew to a close, a second opened with the discovery of gold and diamonds in the regions of Minas Gerais, Goiaz, and Mato Grosso, lying west and south of Baía and Pernambuco. But the gold and diamonds were found in limited quantities, and production declined sharply after 1760.

As the interior provinces of Minas Gerais and Goiaz sank into decay, the Northeast enjoyed a revival based on the increasing European demand for sugar, cotton, and other semi-tropical products. Between 1750 and 1800 Brazilian cotton production made large strides, but as rapidly declined in the face of competition from the more efficient cotton growers of the United States. The beginnings of the coffee industry, future giant of the Brazilian economy, also date from the late colonial period.

Until the decree of January 28, 1808, which opened the ports of Brazil to the trade of all nations, the commerce of the colony was restricted to Portuguese nationals and ships. A significant exception was made in the case of Great Britain, Portugal's protector and ally. By the Treaty of 1654, British merchants were permitted to trade between Portuguese and Brazilian ports. English ships frequently neglected the formality of touching at Lisbon, and plied a direct contraband commerce with the colony. The decree of free trade of 1808 only confirmed Great Britain's actual domination of Brazilian commerce.

1. THE BRAZILIAN INDIAN

At the time of the coming of the Portuguese, the Brazilian coast from the Amazon River to the Rio de la Plata was inhabited by a large number of Indian tribes closely related in language and culture. These tribes made their living by farming, hunting, and fishing, waged constant war against one another, and practiced ritual cannibalism. They generally accorded a friendly welcome to Europeans, until efforts to enslave them aroused their hostility. Pero de Magalhães, author of an important early chronicle of Brazil, describes the life and customs of the Brazilian Indian.[1]

IT IS IMPOSSIBLE to enumerate or to know the multitude of barbarous people which Nature has sown throughout this land of Brazil, because no one can safely travel through the *sertão*, nor travel overland without finding villages of Indians armed against all peoples; and as they are so numerous God granted that they are enemies one against the other, and that there is amongst them great hatred and discord, because otherwise the Portuguese would not be able to live in the land, nor overcome the great power of the inhabitants. There were many of these Indians on the coast near the Captaincies; the whole coast was inhabited by them when the Portuguese began to settle the country; but, because these Indians revolted against them and practised much treachery upon them, the Governors and Captains of the land overthrew them little by little, and killed many of

[1] Pero de Magalhães, *The Histories of Brazil*, translated and edited by John B. Stetson, Jr., New York. The Cortés Society, 1922, 2 vols., II, 165–174.

them; the others fled to the *sertão*; thus the coast remained unpopulated by the natives, near the Captaincies; however, some Indian villages, peaceful and friendly toward the Portuguese, were left.

All the people of the coast have the same language; it lacks three letters, namely, *f*, *l* and *r*, a fact worthy of wonder because they also have neither *F*aith, *L*aw, nor *R*uler; hence they live without justice and in complete disorder. The Indians go naked without any covering whatever, the males as well as the females; they do not cover any portion of their body, but all that Nature gave them goes uncovered. They all live in villages; there may be seven or eight houses in each. These houses are built long like ropewalks; and each one of them is filled with people, each of whom has his stand on one side or the other, and the net in which he sleeps hung up there; thus they are all together, ranged in order, one after the other, and in the middle of the house there is an open aisle for passage. As I have said, there is among them no king nor justice, but in each village there is a head-man who is like a Captain, to whom they give voluntary obedience, but not through force; if this head-man dies, his son takes his place; he serves no other purpose than to go with them to war to take council with them as to the method they should employ in fighting, but he does not punish their wrong-doing, nor does he command them in any respect against their wills. This head-man has three or four wives; he has the greatest consideration for the first one and has more respect for her than for the others; they do this as a matter of position and dignity. They do not worship anything, nor do they believe that there is in another life glory for the good nor suffering for the wicked; they all believe that after this life ends their souls die with their bodies. Thus they live like beasts without thought, without regard and without restraint. These Indians are warlike and wage great wars, one tribe against the other; they are never at peace with one another, nor can they live on friendly terms, because one tribe fights against another, many are killed and so their hatred goes on increasing more and more [with each encounter], and they remain real enemies perpetually. The arms with which they fight are bows and arrows; whatever they aim at they hit; they are very accurate with this arm and much feared in war; they are expert in its use, and are much inclined to fight; they are very valiant and impetuous against their adversaries; and

therefore it is a strange sight to witness two or three thousand naked men on opposite sides, shooting arrows at one another with shrieks and cries; all during this contest they are not still a moment, but leap from one place to another with much agility, so that the enemy can not aim at them nor shoot at any particular person: some of the old women are accustomed to gather up the arrows on the ground and serve them while they fight. This is a very bold people which fears death but little; when they go to war, it always seems to them that victory is certain and that none of their company is to die; and when they leave they say, "We are going out to kill," without any other thought, nor do they believe that they themselves can be conquered.

They spare the life of none of their captives, but kill all and eat them, so that their wars are very perilous and should be considered seriously, because one of the reasons which have been the undoing of many Portuguese has been the great indifference with which they regarded fighting with the Indians, and the small concern which they felt for it; and so many of them have died miserably for not having prepared themselves as they should have; among them there have been disastrous deaths, and this is happening at each step in those regions. If at the time of their impetuous rush these Indians do not kill, but capture some of their enemies, they bring them alive to their villages, whether they be Portuguese or of some enemy Indian tribe. As soon as they arrive at their houses, they place a very thick rope about the neck of the captive in order that he may not flee; they hang up for him a net in which to sleep, and give him an Indian girl, the most beautiful and honoured in the village, to sleep with him; she is also charged with guarding him, and he goes nowhere unaccompanied by her. The Indian girl is charged with providing him well with food and drink; and after they have kept him in this way five or six months, or as long as they please, they decide to kill him. They celebrate great ceremonies and feasts in those days, and prepare much wine on which to get drunk; this is made of the root of a plant called *aypim* which is first boiled; after it is cooked, some Indian virgins chew it and spit the juice into large jars, and in three or four days they drink it. On the morning of the day on which they kill the captive, they take him to bathe in a stream, if there is one near the village, with much singing and dancing; when they arrive with him in the village they tie about his waist four cords, one stretching in each direction, with three or four Indians attached to each end; in this way they lead him to the middle of the plaza, and pull so much on each of these cords that it is impossible for him to move in any direction; they leave his hands free because they enjoy seeing him defend himself with them. The man who is designated to kill him first decks his whole body with parrot feathers of many colours; this executioner must be the most valiant and most honoured of the country. He carries in his hand a sword of very hard, heavy wood, with which they are accustomed to kill; and he comes up to the victim saying many things to him, threatening his entire posterity and his relatives: having insulted him with many injurious words, he gives him a heavy blow on the head which breaks his head in pieces and kills him on the spot. There is an old Indian woman by with a gourd in her hand who, as soon as the victim falls, approaches very quickly and puts this to his head, in order to catch the brains and blood. Finally, they cook or roast and eat every part of him, so that none of him remains. This they do more for the sake of vengeance than on account of hatred or to satisfy their appetites. After they have eaten the flesh of these enemies, they remain more confirmed in their hatred; because this injury is felt keenly, they are always desirous of taking vengeance. If the girl with whom the captive slept is pregnant, they kill the child she bears, after it is weaned; they cook it and say that that child, boy or girl, is verily their enemy, and therefore they are very desirous of eating its flesh and taking vengeance upon it. And because the mother knows the end destined for the child, often when she is pregnant she kills the child in the womb and produces abortion. It sometimes happens that she falls so deeply in love with the captive and becomes so enamoured of him that she flees with him to his country, in order to save his life; hence there are living today some Portuguese who have thus escaped. Many Indians have saved themselves in the same manner, although some of them are so brutish that they do not wish to flee after they have been taken. Once there was an Indian already tied in the plaza to be killed, and they gave him his life; he did not desire it, but wished them to kill him, for, said he, his relatives would not consider him brave, and all of them would avoid him; hence it comes about that they do not fear death; and when that hour arrives they are imperturbable, and show no sadness in that

pass. Finally, those Indians are very inhuman and cruel; no piety moves them; they live like brute beasts without the order or concord of men; they are very dissolute and given to sensuality, yielding to vice as though they lacked human reason; although they always have certain reserve, the males and females in their congress, thereby manifesting a certain sense of modesty. They all eat human flesh and consider it the best of their dishes, not that of their friends with whom they are at peace, but that of their enemies. These Indians have this quality, that whatever they eat, however small the quantity, they must invite all present to share with them; this is the only charitable conception found among them. They eat whatever insects grow in the country, rejecting none, no matter how poisonous, except spiders. The male Indians have the custom of pulling out all their beard, and do not allow hair to grow on any part of the body except the head, and they pull it out even from the lower part of this. The females pride themselves much on their hair, and wear it braided with ribbons. The males are accustomed to wear the lips pierced and a stone placed in the hole for decoration; there are others who have the entire face full of holes, thereby appearing very ugly and disfigured; this is done to them when they are children. Some of these Indians also have the entire body painted with a certain dye, in lines of many patterns; they always paint themselves with the same designs; they do not wear these designs unless they have performed some deed of valour. Moreover, the males as well as the females are accustomed to dye themselves with the juice of a fruit which is called *genipapo*; this is green when squeezed out, and after they have placed it on their bodies and it has dried, it turns very black; however much one bathes, it can not be removed for nine days; they do all this for adornment. The Indian women are faithful to their husbands and are very friendly with them, because adultery is not tolerated. Most of the men marry their nieces, the daughters of their brothers or sisters; these are their true wives, and the fathers of the women can not refuse their request. In these regions there are some Indian women who take an oath of chastity, and hence do not marry, or have commerce with men in any respect; nor would they consent to it, even if their refusal meant death. These give up all functions of women and imitate the men, pursuing the functions of the latter as though they were not women; they cut their hair, wearing it in the same way as the males, they go to war with their bows and arrows, and hunt; in a word, they always go in company with the men, and each one has a woman to serve her, who provides food for her as if they two were married. The Indian men live very much at ease; they think about nothing except eating, drinking, and killing people; for this reason, they grow very fat, and when anything worries them they become very thin; if any one is vexed at anything, he eats earth; and in this way many of them die like beasts. All are prone to follow the advice of the old women; their every suggestion is acted upon, and is believed to be true; hence it occurs that many inhabitants will not buy the old women [for slaves], so that these will not have an opportunity to cause their slaves to flee. When these Indian women give birth, their first act after birth is to wash themselves in a river, after which they are just as lusty as if they had not given birth. Instead of the woman, her husband remains in his hammock, and is visited and treated as though he were the one who had given birth. When one of these Indians dies, they are accustomed to bury him in a hole seated upon his feet, with the net in which he slept at his back, and then for the first few days they place something to eat over the grave.

2. THE PORTUGUESE COLONIZER

Unlike the Spanish conquistadores, who roamed through jungles and mountains in search of golden kingdoms, their Portuguese counterparts were content to remain on the fertile coast of Northeast Brazil, where they established a plantation economy producing sugar for the world market. Yet the Portuguese colonizer could deal hard blows when necessity required, as shown by the story of Duarte Coelho, who undertook to settle the captaincy of Pernambuco. Gabriel Soares de Souza, a planter of Baía who wrote one of the earliest and most valuable accounts of colonial Brazil, tells of Duarte's exploits.[2]

THE TOWN OF OLINDA is the capital of the captaincy of Pernambuco, which was settled by Duarte Coelho, a gentleman of whose courage and chivalry I shall not speak here in detail, for the books that deal with India are full of his deeds. After Duarte Coelho returned from India to Portugal to seek a reward for his services,

he sought and obtained from His Highness the grant of a captaincy on this coast; this grant began at the mouth of the São Francisco River in the northwest and ran fifty leagues up the coast toward the captaincy of Tamaracá, ending at the Igaruçu River. . . . Since this brave captain was always disposed to perform great feats, he determined to come in person to settle and conquer this his captaincy. He arrived there with a fleet of ships that he had armed at his own cost, in which he brought his wife and children and many of their kinsmen, and other settlers. With this fleet he made port at the place called Pernambuco, which in the native language means "hidden sea," because of a rock nearby that is hidden in the sea. Arriving at this port, Duarte Coelho disembarked and fortified himself as well as he could on a high point free of any dominating peaks, where the town is today. There he built a strong tower, which still stands in the town square, and for many years he waged war against the natives and the French who fought at their side. Frequently he was besieged and badly wounded, with the loss of many of his people, but he courageously persisted in his aim, and not only defended himself bravely but attacked his enemies so effectively that they abandoned the neighboring lands. Later his son, of the same name, continued to wage war on them, harassing and capturing these people, called Cayté, until they had abandoned the whole coast and more than fifty leagues in the interior. In these labors Duarte spent many thousands of *cruzados* that he had acquired in India, and this money was really well spent, for today his son Jorge de Albuquerque Coelho enjoys an income of ten thousand *cruzados,* which he obtains from the retithe,[3] from his tithe of the fishing catch, and from the quit rent paid him by the sugar-mills (fifty of these have been established in Pernambuco, and they produce so much sugar that the tithes on it yield nineteen thousand *cruzados* a year).

This town of Olinda must have about seven hundred householders, but there are many more within the limits of the town, since from twenty to thirty people live on each of these plantations, aside from the many who live on farms. Hence if it were necessary to assemble these people with arms, they could place in the field more than three thousand fighting men, together

---

2 Gabriel Soares de Souza, *Tratado descriptivo do Brasil em 1587,* São Paulo, 1938, pp. 27–29. (Excerpt translated by the editor.)

3 The retithe was a tenth of all tithes collected by the king in his capacity of Master of the Order of Christ; it was paid to the donatory. B.K.

with the inhabitants of the town of Cosmos, which must have four hundred mounted men. These people could bring from their estates four or five thousand Negro slaves and many Indians. This captaincy is so prosperous that there are more than a hundred men in it who have an income of from one to five thousand *cruzados,* and some have incomes of eight to ten thousand *cruzados.* From this land many men have returned rich to Portugal who came here poor, and every year this captaincy sends forty to fifty ships loaded with sugar and brazilwood; this wood is so profitable to His Majesty that he has lately farmed out the concession for a period of ten years at twenty thousand *cruzados* a year. It seems to me that such a powerful captaincy, which yields this kingdom such a great store of provisions, should be better fortified, and should not be exposed for a corsair to sack and destroy — which could be prevented with little expense and less labor.

3. THE SLAVE-HUNTERS

The expanding plantation economy of the Brazilian Northeast required a steady supply of cheap labor. The Portuguese met the problem with raids on Indian villages, returning with trains of captives who were sold to plantation owners. These aggressions were the primary cause of the chronic warfare between the natives and the whites. Indian labor was quite unsatisfactory from an economic point of view, and after 1550 it began to be replaced by that of Negro slaves imported from Africa. But the supply of African slaves was often cut off or sharply reduced by the activities of Dutch privateers and other foreign foes, and Brazilian slave-hunters continued to find a market for their human prey throughout the seventeenth century. The men of São Paulo, lacking the sugar and brazilwood on which the prosperity of the Northeast was based, turned to slave-hunting as a lucrative occupation. The prospect of finding gold in the interior made their expeditions doubly attractive. As the coastal Indians were exterminated or fled before the invaders, the bandeirantes, *the "men of the banner," pushed ever deeper south and west, expanding the frontiers of Brazil in the process. Almost the only voices raised against their predatory activities were those of the Jesuit missionaries. One of them, believed to be the famous Father Anchieta (1534–1597), describes the devastation wrought by the slave-hunters.[4]*

4 *Cartas, Informações, Fragmentos Históricos e Sermões do Padre Joseph de Anchieta, S. J. (1554–1594),* Rio de Janeiro, 1933, pp. 377–378. (Excerpt translated by the editor.)

THE NUMBER OF INDIANS that have been destroyed in this captaincy of Baía in the past twenty years passes belief; who would think that so many people could be destroyed in so short a time? In the fourteen churches maintained by the Fathers they had brought together 40,000 souls, by count, and even more, counting those who came after — yet today it is doubtful whether the three churches that remain have 3,500 souls together. Six years ago an honored citizen of this city, a man of good conscience and a city official at the time, said that in the two preceding years 20,000 souls, by count, had been brought from the back country of Arabó and that all of them went to the Portuguese plantations. These 20,000, added to the 40,000 of the churches, come to 60,000. Now for the past six years the Portuguese have been bringing Indians for their plantations, one bringing 2,000, another 3,000, some more, others less; in six years this must come to 80,000 souls or more. Now look at the sugar-mills and plantations of Baía, and you will find them full of Guinea Negroes but very few natives; if you ask what happened to all those people, they will tell you that they died.

In this way God has severely punished the Portuguese for the many offenses that they committed and still commit against these Indians, for they go into the interior and deceive these people, inviting them to go to the coast, where, they say, they would live in their villages as they did in their lands, and the Portuguese would be their neighbors. The Indians, believing this, go with them, and for fear they will change their minds the Portuguese destroy their gardens. On arrival at the coast they divide the Indians among themselves, some taking the women, others their husbands, and still others the children, and they sell them. Other Portuguese go into the interior and entice the Indians by saying that they will take them to the churches of the Fathers; and by this means they seduce them from their lands, for it is common knowledge in the backlands that only the Indians in the churches where the Fathers reside enjoy liberty and all the rest are captives. Matters reached such a point that a certain Portuguese, going into the back country in search of Indians, shaved his head like a priest, saying that he was a Father seeking Indians for the churches. This happened at a time when Father Gaspar Lourenço was bound for the interior, and he found these people on the road. When they heard that the Father was going into the backlands they said: "How can that be, when he who brings us says that he is a Father, and that is why we go with him?" And the Portuguese with the shaven head hid himself, not wanting the priest to see him.

The Portuguese travel 250 and 300 leagues to find the Indians, for the nearest ones are by now a great distance away, and since the land is now depopulated most of them die on the road from hunger. There have been Portuguese who seized on the road certain Indians who were enemies of the ones they were bringing, killed them, and gave their flesh to their captives to eat. And when all these people arrive at the coast, seeing that the Portuguese do not keep the promises they made in the interior but separate them from each other, some flee into the forests, never to emerge again, and others die from grief and chagrin that they, who had been free men, should be made slaves.

4. AIMORÉ: WORD OF TERROR

The Brazilian Indian did not accept the loss of his land and liberty without a struggle. Indian resistance to white aggression was handicapped by the fatal propensity of the tribes to war against each other, a situation that the Portuguese utilized for their own advantage. Forced to retreat into the interior by the superior arms and organization of the whites, the natives often returned to make destructive forays on isolated Portuguese communities. As late as the first part of the nineteenth century stretches of the Brazilian shore were made uninhabitable by the raids of Indians who lurked in the forests and mountains back of the coast. "The coast from Espiritu Santo to Buhia was practically abandoned," says the historian Calogeras, "and even today reveals large gaps in its population as a consequence of these attacks." One tribe that never sought or granted a truce to the whites was that of the ferocious Aimorés. The chronicler Soares de Souza describes their mode of life and warfare.[5]

IT SEEMS PROPER at this point to state what kind of people are those called Aimorés, who have done so much damage to this captaincy of Ilheos, as I have said. The coast of this captaincy used to be inhabited by the Tupiniquins, who abandoned it from fear of these brutes and went to live in the back country; at the present time there are only two very small Tupiniquin villages, situated near the sugar mills of Henrique Luiz.

These Aimorés are descended from other people that they call Tapuias, from whom departed

[5] Soares de Souza, *Tratado Descriptivo do Brazil*, pp. 58–60. (Excerpt translated by the editor.)

in olden times certain families that went to live in very rugged mountains, fleeing from a defeat inflicted on them by their enemies; and there they lived many years without seeing any other people; and their descendants gradually lost their language, and developed a new one that is not understood by any other nation in the whole country of Brazil. These Aimorés are so savage that the other barbarians consider them worse than barbarians. Some of these were taken alive in Porto Seguro and in Ilheos, and they would not eat, preferring to die like savages.

This people first came to the sea at the River Caravellas, hard by Porto Seguro, and roamed this countryside and the beaches as far as the River Camamú; from there they began to launch attacks near Tinharé, descending to the shore only when they came to make an attack. This people is of the same color as the others, but they are larger and of more robust build. They have no beards or any other hair except on their heads, because they pluck out the hairs on the other parts of their bodies. They fight with very large bows and arrows, and are such excellent bowmen that they never miss a shot; they are marvelously light on their feet, and great runners.

These barbarians do not live in villages or houses like other people, and so far no one has come across their dwellings in the woods; they go from one place to another through the woods and fields; they sleep on the ground on leaves; and if it rains they go up to the foot of a tree and squat there, covering themselves with leaves; no other furnishings have ever been found among them. These savages do not have gardens or raise any food; they live on wild fruit and the game they kill, which they eat raw or poorly roasted, when they have a fire. Both men and women cut their hair short, shearing it with certain canes of which they gather a great number; their speech is rough, projected from their throats with much force; like Basque, it is impossible to write down.

These barbarians live by robbing everyone they encounter, and one never sees more than twenty or thirty bowmen at one time. They never fight anyone face to face, but always employ treachery, for they attack in the fields and roads which they travel, waiting in ambush for other Indians and all other sorts of persons, each hidden behind a tree and never missing a shot. They use up all their arrows, and if the people turn on them they all flee in different directions, but if they see that their pursuers have dropped their guard they stop and find a place to hide until their pursuers have passed, when they shoot them in the back with their arrows at will. They do not know how to swim, and any river that cannot be forded presents an adequate defense against them; but in order to find a crossing they will go many miles along the river in search of one.

These savages eat human flesh for sustenance — unlike the other Indians, who only eat it for the sake of revenge and in memory of their ancient hatreds. The captaincies of Porto Seguro and Ilheos have been destroyed and almost depopulated by fear of these barbarians, and the sugar mills have stopped working because all the slaves and the other people have been killed by them. The people on most of the plantations and those who have escaped from them have become so afraid of them that if they merely hear the word "Aimorés" they leave their plantations in search of refuge, the white men among them. In the twenty-five years that this plague has afflicted these two captaincies, they have killed more than 300 Portuguese and 3,000 slaves.

The inhabitants of Baía used to send letters to the people of Ilheos, and men traveled this road along the shore without danger. But when the Aimorés realized this they decided to come to these beaches to wait for the people who passed there, and there they killed many Portuguese and many more slaves. These bandits are such fleet runners that no one could escape them on foot, except those who take refuge in the sea; they dare not enter the ocean, but wait for them to come on shore until nightfall, when they retire. For this reason the road is forbidden, and no one travels it except at great risk of his life. If some means is not found to destroy these savages they will destroy the plantations of Baía, through which they roam at will. Since they are such intractable enemies of all mankind, it was not possible to learn more about their mode of life and customs.

5. THE DUTCH IN BRAZIL

The dyewood, the sugar, and the tobacco of Portuguese Brazil early excited the cupidity of foreign powers. For almost a century (1520–1615) the French, aided by friendly Indians, made sporadic efforts to establish themselves in the country. A greater threat to Portuguese sovereignty over Brazil came from the Dutch, who seized and occupied for a quarter of a century (1630–1654) the richest sugar-growing portions of

the Brazilian coast. Under the administration of Prince Maurice of Nassau (1637–1644) Dutch Brazil, with its capital at Recife, was the scene of a brilliant scientific and artistic activity. But in 1654 the Dutch, weakened by revolt and war with England, were forced to evacuate the province, and before long almost all trace of their presence had disappeared. Robert Southey (1774–1843), author of a classic history of colonial Brazil, sums up the achievements of the Dutch in Brazil.[6]

FROM THE POTENGI to the S. Francisco, the Dutch were in possession when the restoration of the Portuguese monarchy made them apparently secure in their conquests. This portion of Brazil was then called New Holland, in the maps; that appellation, however, was destined to designate a more extensive country in a different part of the world; and the New Holland of the West India Company, like the Antarctic France of Villegagnon, soon became an empty name, exemplifying the shortsightedness of presumptuous ambition. The Dutch deserved to lose these possessions for the treachery with which they attempted to extend their conquests during the truce, the baseness with which they sought to take advantage of the helpless state of Portugal, their blind unfeeling avarice, and that brutal cruelty which in all their foreign territories has characterized them: but they were not without some redeeming qualities. Under Prince Mauritz of Nassau great efforts were made for exploring the country, civilizing the Tapuyas, and improving the general condition of the people. His bridges, his palace, and his city, remain monuments of his wise and splendid administration; but they are not the only, nor the most durable materials. He took out with him scholars, naturalists, and draughtsmen. His actions were celebrated in Latin verse by Franciscus Plante, and by Barlaeus in a Latin history worthy of the reputation of its author. The work of Marcgraff and Piso is the first which appeared upon the natural history of Brazil; and the views in Barlaeus were the first graphic representations of Brazilian scenery and manners.

Elias Herckmann was sent by Nassau into the interior of Pernambuco in search of mines. The attempt was unsuccessful; but he discovered vestiges of some forgotten people who possessed the country before the present race of savages, and of whom not even the most vague tradition

6 Robert Southey, *History of Brazil*, London, 3 vols., 1810–1819, II, 651–659.

had been preserved. He found two huge perfectly round stones, manifestly rounded by art, and placed by art one upon another, the largest being uppermost; they were sixteen feet in diameter, and the thickness such that a man standing on the ground could scarcely reach to the middle: and on the following day he came to some other stones, of such magnitude that it seemed impossible for any human strength to have moved them; they were piled up like altars, and Herckmann compares them to some monuments at Drent in Belgium. . . .

Great and commendable zeal was shown, not only under Nassau's administration, but as long as the Dutch continued in the country, for promulgating the reformed religion. There were Protestant ministers at Olinda, Itamaraca, Paraiba, Cape St. Augustines, and Serinhaem, and three at Recife. Some of them acquired the Tupi, and with what success they had labored among the Indians may be apprehended by the jealousy with which Vieyra regarded those who had been under their pastoral care. They laboured in civilizing as well as converting them. It has been seen, that in the Serra de Ibiapaba paper and sealing wax were in use, and that there were Indians there as well able to read and understand the laws as the Portuguese themselves. But although the government meant well toward the aboriginal inhabitants, and some of the clergy did their duty with eminent zeal and success, the conduct of the Dutch in general, both to the Indians and Negroes, was marked with that deep depravity which has characterized them in all their colonies. During the war their privateers seized all the Indians whom they found fishing, and kidnapped as many as they could catch on shore, and sold them to the Sugar Islands. Of six thousand four hundred imported Negroes, more than fifteen hundred died within a year and a half, and Nassau himself imputed this frightful mortality to their unwholesome or insufficient food on the voyage, and to their sufferings. It appears also that these wretched slaves frequently attempted to murder their inhuman masters, and when they failed in the attempt, delivered themselves by poison from a life of insupportable misery.

The conquerors introduced some improvements while they held the country. A people who were accustomed to such cleanliness at home could not tolerate the filth of a Portuguese city, and the streets of Recife under their government were regularly cleaned. They cultivated culinary herbs, which were soon propagated in every garden, and found their way into every kitchen; but the war put an end to horticulture, and this benefit seems to have been only transient. They reared vines with some success, procured a succession of grapes, and made a wine the excellence of which is expressed by saying that it was not inferior to the Cretan. The soldiers preferred mandioc to wheat, thinking it a stronger food. In other points the Dutch were more tenacious of old habits. Though the Brazilians, as it was said, dreamt of disease and death if they dwelt upon the lowlands, the Hollanders, with that obstinate attachment to swamps and standing water which has cost the lives of so many thousands at Batavia, built everywhere upon the plains and morasses. Such situations were suited to their mode of fortification, and they had need to fortify themselves. They experienced less injury than had been predicted, probably less than any other people would have done: their diet, which was more generous than that of the Portuguese, and their habit of smoking, serving to counteract the pernicious effects of marsh exhalation, and their constitutions also being habituated to such an atmosphere. Their women, however, suffered greatly from the change of climate; for they neither drank nor smoked; and, as was the case at first with the Portuguese women, they reared very few children. They found it necessary to have Indian or Negress nurses, whose custom it was never to wean the infant until the end of the second year, and rarely so soon.

The whole country which they possessed, from the Potengi to the Lagoas, was cultivated only in patches. The cultivation usually extended from twelve to fifteen miles inland, seldom farther, and never more than one or two and twenty; but none of the Dutch settled more than eight miles from the coast, as much for fear of the savages and the Portuguese, as for the convenience of trade. Between one *freguezia* or parish, and another, there was usually a solitary track of ten or twelve miles, perhaps of greater extent. Salt works and fishermen's huts were sometimes found in these uncultivated parts, but all the rest was a wilderness, which the settled part of the inhabitants had never explored. The admirable industry of the Dutch had not time to display itself; and what branches of industry they found there suffered considerably during the war. A lucrative fishery upon the coast was entirely neglected after their conquest; they attempted to restore it during the truce, but the renewal of hostilities put an end to it. The Portuguese government permitted only ten thousand *quintaes* of Brazil to be felled yearly, that valuable wood being the property of the crown. The Dutch felled it without restriction, and cut down young trees as well as old: Nassau recommended that the Portuguese system should be observed, and that severe penalties should be inflicted upon those who destroyed the young trees. They were not acquainted with the process of making sugar when they arrived. When Vieyra argued for the cession of these provinces he urged their unskilfulness as a reason why the sugar trade would not be injured by it, that of the Portuguese captaincies bearing a better price and being in greater demand. But it is not possible that any nation can keep arts of this kind to itself, so as always to prevent other people, under circumstances equally favorable, from rivalling them. Under the expulsion of the Dutch they carried with them some Negroes who were perfectly acquainted with the management of an *Engenho;* these men instructed the French at Guadaloupe, and thus enabled them first to compete with the Portuguese sugar, and soon to supersede it in many of its markets.

Before the invasion Olinda was the most flourishing of all the colonial possessions of the Portuguese, and perhaps, it is said, the richest. Ships of all sizes were continually arriving and departing, yet there was scarcely tonnage to carry away the sugar, more of which was raised at that time in Pernambuco than in Bahia. The ships from Peru which put back on their voyage, or which had evaded the duties in the port from whence they sailed, discharged the best part of their treasures here. Those who were not served in plate were regarded as poor. The women were not satisfied with wearing silks and satins, unless they were of the richest embroidery, and they were so profusely decked with jewels that it seemed, says F. Manoel do Salvador, as if pearls, rubies, emeralds, and diamonds had been showered upon them. Every new fashion in apparel, or in the furniture of swords and daggers, was instantly followed by the men, and the choicest delicacies of Portugal and the Western Islands were regularly imported for their tables. "The place," says the Friar, "hardly appeared like earth; it seemed rather an image of Paradise, as far as opulence and dissipation could make it so." The war proved fatal to this prosperity. "When first I beheld Olinda," says Vieyra, "the nobleness of her edifices, her temples and her towers, her valleys everywhere adorned, and her hills covered with green and loftiest palms, she seemed like a beautiful and most delicious garden, worthy of her name, and of being pictured that all the world might behold her. Now what is there but a desert, a solitude, a shapeless carcass, a dismal sepulchre without a name!" A flourishing city had risen at the port, but Recife had not succeeded to the splendor of its former capital. When Rennefort visited it in 1666 it contained, according to his computation, about three hundred indifferent houses, besides some others so wretchedly constructed that he seems to have considered them as hovels unworthy of being included in the account. They were all of only one floor. There were about an hundred more in S. Antonio, as Mauritias was now called, the founder having given place to the favorite saint of the Portuguese. But the works of that founder outlasted his name; the Governor resided in his palace; and the French traveler speaks with delight of the fragrance and beauty of the groves which Prince Mauritz had planted with such magnificence.

Though the Dutch were twenty-five years in the country, there had been very little intermixture of the two nations; the difference of religion was too great an obstacle, both parties being sincere, and regarding each other's religion with mutual contempt, mingled however, on the part of the Papists, with the fiercest and most intolerant abhorrence. The few intermarriages which occurred were with Portuguese women. Most of these would naturally follow their husbands upon their expulsion; but if the husbands chose to remain in the country among their new connections, if they did not conform themselves to the dominant superstition, their children fell into it of course, and in another generation no trace remained either of the religion, language, or manners of Holland. The ambitious struggle which the Dutch carried on so long, with such inhumanity, and such an expense of treasure and blood, produced no other benefit than that of proving, as a warning for other powers, how impossible it is to effect a permanent conquest of Brazil. A people of such determined nationality as the Portuguese, in such a country, are invincible by any human force.

6. THE RISE AND FALL OF VILLA RICA

When the Dutch withdrew from Brazil they transferred their skills in sugar growing to their West Indian colonies. English and French planters in the

Caribbean area also began to compete with Brazilian sugar producers. Thanks to their superior techniques and closer proximity to European ports, the West Indian growers were able to take over many of Brazil's best foreign markets. By the last decade of the seventeenth century the sugar cycle of the Northeast had about run its course. It was at this time of acute depression that the discovery of gold in Minas Gerais (1690) gave a new stimulus to Brazil's economic life, led to the first effective settlement of the interior, and began a major shift in the center of economic and political gravity from north to south. Like its predecessor, the mineral cycle was marked by rapid and superficial exploitation of the new sources of wealth, followed by an even swifter decline. The story of the rise and fall of the gold-mining center of Villa Rica is told by John Mawe (1764–1829), who visited it at the opening of the nineteenth century.[7]

THE HISTORY OF AN ESTABLISHMENT which, twenty years after its foundation, was reputed the richest place on the globe, was an object of considerable interest to me, and I made many inquiries respecting it from some of the best informed men on the spot. It appears that the first discovery of this once rich mountain was effected by the enterprising spirit of the Paulistas, who, of all the colonists in Brazil, retained the largest share of that ardent and indefatigable zeal for discovery which characterized the Lusitanians of former days. They penetrated from their capital into these regions, braving every hardship, and encountering every difficulty which a savage country, infested by still more savage inhabitants, opposed to them. They cut their way through impervious woods, carrying their provisions with them, and occasionally cultivating small patches of land to afford them food to retreat to, in case of necessity, as well as to keep up a communication with their city, St. Paul's. Every inch of ground was disputed by the barbarous Indians, here called Bootocoodies, who were constantly either attacking them openly or lying in ambush, and but too frequently succeeded in surprising some of them, or their negroes, whom they immediately sacrificed to their horrible appetite for human flesh. They believed the negroes to be the great monkeys of the wood. The bones of the unfortunate sufferers were frequently found exposed, shocking testimonies of the barbarity of their murderers, whom the Paulistas, roused to revenge, invariably shot, wherever they met them. These examples of vengeance answered their desired

end; the Indians, terrified as well by the noise as by the fatal effect of the fire-arms, fled with precipitation, believing that the white men commanded lightning and thunder.

It does not appear that in exploring this territory they received any assistance whatever from the Aborigines; they followed the course of rivers, occasionally finding gold, of which they skimmed the surface, and continued to proceed until they arrived at the mountain which is our present subject. Its riches arrested their course; they immediately erected temporary houses and began their operations. The principal men of the party that first settled here, were Antonio Dias, Bartholomew Rocinho, Antonio de Ferrera (filho), and Garcia Ruis. It appears that they took the most direct way to the place, for the roads they then opened are the same which are still used. The fame of their success soon reached the city of St. Paul's; fresh adventurers arrived in great numbers, bringing with them all the negroes they had means to purchase. Other adventurers went from St. Paul's to Rio de Janeiro to procure more negroes, their own city being drained; and thus the news of the lately discovered gold-mountain being made known in the Brazilian capital, men of all descriptions went in crowds to this land of promise by the way of St. Paul's, which was the only route then known. The first settlers might have prevented the exposure of their good fortune, had they been able to moderate their joy, and consented to act in concert; but as gold was in such great abundance, every individual appropriated a lot of ground, and thus became a capitalist. Each strove which should make the most of his treasure in the shortest time, and thus there was a continual demand for more negroes, more iron, etc. and, in the general eagerness to obtain them, the secret which all were interested in keeping was disclosed. The Paulistas, independent in spirit, and proud of their wealth, were desirous of giving laws to the new-comers; but the latter determining to oppose this measure, formed themselves into a party under the guidance of Manuel Nuñez Viana, an adventurer of some consequence, who strenuously asserted their claim to equal rights and advantages. Disputes arose on both sides, and were at length aggravated into hostilities, which proved unfavourable to the Paulistas, the great part of whom fled to a considerable station of their own, and there awaited reinforcements. Viana and his followers, without loss of time, went in pursuit of their foes, whom they found on a plain near the site of St. João del Rey. The two

7 John Mawe, *Travels in the Interior of Brazil,* London, 1815, pp. 171–177.

parties met on the borders of a river, and a sanguinary battle took place, which ended in the
defeat of the Paulistas, who afterwards made the
best terms they could. The slain were buried on
the margin of the river, which, from that circumstance took the name of Rio dos Mortos.

The Paulistas, bent on revenge, but weakened
by defeat, appealed to the sovereign, King
Pedro, denouncing Viana and his followers as
rebels who were attempting to take the district
to themselves, and set up an independent government. The King's ministers, apprized of the
state of affairs, and learning by report the immense riches of the country, immediately sent
a chief, with a competent body of troops, to take
advantage of the strife between the two parties;
which, in a country tenable by a few men on
account of its numerous strong-holds, was a
most fortunate circumstance. The name of this
chief was Albuquerque; a man of enterprize and
perseverance, in all respects qualified for the
service on which he was sent. His appearance at
first occasioned much confusion and discontent
among both parties; and though he was not
openly opposed, yet he was in continual alarm.
The Paulistas now saw that the riches which
they in conjunction with their rivals might have
retained, were about to be seized by a third
party which would reduce them both to subordination. Disturbances prevailed for some time,
but reinforcements continually arriving from
Government, tranquillity was at length perfectly
established; and in the year 1711 a regular town
began to be formed; a government-house, a
mint, and a depot for arms were built. A code
of laws was enacted for the regulation of the
mines; all gold-dust found was ordered to be
delivered to officers appointed for that purpose;
a fifth in weight was taken for the King, and the
remaining four parts were purified, melted into
ingots at the expence of Government, then as-
sayed, marked according to their value, and delivered to the owners, with a certificate to render
them current. For the greater convenience of
trade, gold-dust was likewise permitted to circulate for small payments. Notwithstanding
these strict regulations, a considerable quantity
of the precious metal in its original state found
its way to Rio de Janeiro, Bahia, and other
ports, clandestinely, without paying the royal
fifth, until Government, apprized of this illicit
traffic, established registers in various parts for
the examination of all passengers, and stationed
soldiers to patrol the roads. By these means,
gold in immense quantities was seized and con-

fiscated; the persons on whom any was found
forfeited all their property, and, unless they had
friends of great influence, were sent as convicts
to Africa for life. The greatest disgrace was attached to the name of smuggler; and such was
the rigour of the law against offenders of this
description, that every person quitting the district was obliged to take a certificate stating
whither he was going, and what he carried with
him. This regulation is still in force, and is
rigorously observed.

Villa Rica soon enjoyed a considerable trade
with Rio de Janeiro; the returns were negroes,
iron, woollens, salt, provisions of various kinds,
and wine, all which at that time bore amazingly
high profits.

About the year 1713, when Dr. Bras de Silvia
was appointed governor, the quantity of gold
produced was so considerable that the royal fifth
amounted to half a million sterling annually.
The mountain became pierced like a honey-
comb, as the miners worked every soft part they
could find, and penetrated as far as they could,
conveying the *cascalhão* which they dug out to
a convenient place for washing. In rainy weather
the torrents of water running down the sides
of the mountain, carried away much earthy matter containing delicate particles of gold, which
settled in the ground near its base. When the
waters abated, this rich deposit gave employment to numbers of the poorer sort of people,
who took it away and washed it at their convenience.

Antonio Dias, the person already mentioned
as one of the leaders of the Paulistas, who discovered the place, having become extremely rich,
built a fine church, and dying soon after, bequeathed to it considerable funds. It still bears
his name. Five or six others were begun and
soon finished, as neither wood nor stone was
wanting, and the inhabitants were all ready to
contribute a share of their property, and to
employ their negroes in furtherance of these
pious works. A law highly creditable to the
wisdom of the Portuguese government was now
enacted, to prohibit friars from entering the territory of the mines. What treasures were thus
saved to the state, and what a number of persons were thus continued in useful labour, who
would else have become burthensome to the
community!

The town now underwent many improvements; its streets were more regularly built, and
some parts of the side of the mountain were
levelled to afford more convenient room for the

construction of houses, and the laying out of gardens. Reservoirs were formed, from which water was distributed by means of conduits to all parts, and public fountains were erected in the most convenient and central situations. The mint and smelting-houses were enlarged, and rendered more commodious for the transaction of business. About this period the inhabitants amounted to twelve thousand or upwards; those who possessed mines were either the first settlers or their descendants, and as the best part of the district was occupied, the new adventurers who continued to arrive from time to time were obliged to enter into the service of the existing owners until they had learned their methods of working, after which they generally went in search of fresh mines, proceeding along the water-courses and ravines, where they sometimes discovered new sources of wealth. Between the years 1730 and 1750 the mines were in the height of their prosperity; the King's fifth during some years of that period is said to have amounted to at least a million sterling annually.

The mines which produced this immense wealth at length became gradually less abundant; and, as the precious metal disappeared, numbers of the miners retired, some to the mother-country, loaded with riches, which tempted fresh adventurers, and many to Rio de Janeiro and other sea-ports, where they employed their large capitals in commerce.

Villa Rica at the present day scarcely retains a shadow of its former splendour. Its inhabitants, with the exception of the shop-keepers, are void of employment; they totally neglect the fine country around them, which, by proper cultivation, would amply compensate for the loss of the wealth which their ancestors drew from its bosom. Their education, their habits, their hereditary prejudices, alike unfit them for active life; perpetually indulging in visionary prospects of sudden wealth, they fancy themselves exempted from that universal law of nature which ordains that man shall live by the sweat of his brow. In contemplating the fortunes accumulated by their predecessors, they overlook the industry and perseverance which obtained them, and entirely lose sight of the change of circumstances which renders those qualities now doubly necessary. The successors of men who rise to opulence from small beginnings seldom follow the example set before them, even when trained to it; how then should a Creolian, reared in idleness and ignorance, feel any thing of the benefits of industry! His negroes constitute his principal property, and them he manages so ill, that the profits of their labour hardly defray the expences of their maintenance: in the regular course of nature they become old and unable to work, yet he continues in the same listless and slothful way, or sinks into a state of absolute inactivity, not knowing what to do from morning to night. This deplorable degeneracy is almost the universal characteristic of the descendants of the original settlers; every trade is occupied either by mulattoes or negroes, both of which classes seem superior in intellect to their masters, because they make a better use of it.

XIX

Government and Church

THE PORTUGUESE CROWN first governed Brazil through donatories or lords proprietors who were given almost complete authority in their territories in return for assuming the responsibilities of colonization. In 1549, convinced that the system had failed to achieve its ends, the king issued a decree limiting the powers of the donatories and creating a central government for all of Brazil. The first captain-general of the colony was Thomé de Souza, and Baía was selected as his capital. Governors appointed by the king, and subordinate to the captain-general, gradually replaced the donatories as the political and military leaders of the captaincies.

During the period of the Spanish Captivity (1580–1640), Spain established a *Conselho da India* for the administration of the Portuguese colonies. After Portugal regained her independence, this body continued to have charge of Brazilian affairs. As the colony expanded, new captaincies or provinces were created. In 1763 the captain-general of Rio de Janeiro replaced his colleague at Baía as head of the colonial administration in Brazil, with the title of viceroy. In practice, however, his authority over the other governors was negligible.

Official inefficiency and corruption seem to have been as common in colonial Brazil as in the Spanish Indies. During the reform administration of the Marquis de Pombal (1756–1777) the situation improved, but apparently without lasting effects.

The Brazilian Church lacked the immense wealth and influence of its counterpart in the Spanish Indies. By comparison with the Spanish monarchs, the Portuguese kings seemed almost niggardly in their dealings with the Church. But their control over its affairs was equally absolute.

In Brazil, as in the Spanish colonies, the Jesuits carried on intensive missionary work among the Indians. The priests aimed at the settlement of their Indian converts in villages completely isolated from the whites. Their efforts in this direction led to many conflicts with the Portuguese landowners, who wanted to enslave the Indians for work on their plantations. The clash of interests was most severe in São Paulo, whose halfbreed slave-hunters bitterly resented Jesuit interference with their operations.

Like their colleagues in the Spanish colonies, the Brazilian clergy — always excepting the Jesuits and some other orders — were often criticized for their worldly lives and indifference to their charges. Yet such educational and humanitarian establishments as existed were almost exclusively provided by the clergy, and from its ranks came most of the few distinguished names in Brazilian colonial science, learning, and literature.

1. THE ADMINISTRATION OF COLONIAL BRAZIL

The government of Portuguese Brazil broadly resembled that of the Spanish Indies in its spirit, its structure, and its vices. Henry Koster, an astute observer of Brazilian life in the early nineteenth century, describes the political and financial administration of the important province of Pernambuco.[1]

THE CAPTAINCIES-GENERAL, or provinces of the first rank, in Brazil, of which Pernambuco is one, are governed by captains-general, or governors, who are appointed for three years. At the end of this period, the same person is continued or not, at the option of the supreme government. They are, in fact, absolute in power: but before the person who has been nominated to one of these places can exercise any of its functions, he is under the necessity of presenting his credentials to the *Senado da Câmara,* the chamber or municipality of the principal town. This is formed of persons of respectability in the place. The governor has the supreme and sole command of the military force. The civil and criminal causes are discussed before, and determined by, the *Ouvidor* and *Juiz de Fora,* the two chief judicial officers, whose duties are

somewhat similar: but the former is the superior in rank. They are appointed for three years, and the term may be renewed. It is in these departments of the government that the opportunities of amassing large fortunes are most numerous; and certain it is, that some individuals take advantage of them in a manner which renders justice but a name. The governor can determine in a criminal cause without appeal; but if he pleases, he refers it to the competent judge. The *Procurador da Coroa,* attorney-general, is an officer of considerable weight. The *Intendente da Marinha,* port admiral, is likewise consulted on matters of first importance; as are also the *Escrivão da Fazenda Real,* chief of the treasury, and the *Juiz da Alfândega,* comptroller of the customs. These seven officers form the *Junta,* or council, which occasionally meets to arrange and decide upon the affairs of the captaincy to which they belong.

The ecclesiastical government is scarcely connected with that above mentioned; and is administered by a bishop and a dean and chapter with his vicar-general etc. The governor cannot even appoint a chaplain to the island of Fernando de Noronha, one of the dependencies of Pernambuco; but acquaints the bishop that a priest is wanted, who then nominates one for the place.

The number of civil and military officers is

[1] Henry Koster, *Travels in Brazil,* London, 2 vols., 1816, I, 46–50.

enormous; inspectors innumerable — colonels without end, devoid of any objects to inspect — without any regiments to command; judges to manage each trifling department of which the duties might all be done by two or three persons. Thus salaries are augmented; the people are oppressed; but the state is not benefitted.

Taxes are laid where they fall heavy upon the lower classes: and none are levied where they could well be borne. A tenth is raised in kind upon cattle, poultry, and agriculture, and even upon salt; this in former times appertained, as in other Christian countries, to the clergy.[2] All the taxes are farmed to the highest bidders, and this among the rest. They are parcelled out in extensive districts, and are contracted for at a reasonable rate; but the contractors again dispose of their shares in small portions: these are again retailed to other persons: and as a profit is obtained by each transfer the people must be oppressed, that these men may satisfy those above them and enrich themselves. The system is in itself bad, but is rendered still heavier by this division of the spoil. The tenth of cattle, as I have already said, is levied in kind upon the estates in the interior of the country: and, besides this, a duty of 320 *reis per arroba* of 32 lbs. is paid upon the meat at the shambles, which amounts to about twenty-five *per cent.* Fish pays the tenth, to a duty of ten *per cent.* and moveables to five *per cent.* Besides these, there are many other taxes of minor importance. Rum, both for exportation and home consumption, pays a duty of 80 *reis per canada,*[3] which is sometimes a fourth of its value; but may be reckoned as from fifteen to twenty *per cent.* Cotton pays the tenth, and is again taxed at the moment of exportation 600 *reis per arroba*, of 32 lbs, or about 1¼ *d. per* lb. Nothing can be more injudicious, than this double duty upon the chief article of exportation from that country to Europe. The duties at the custom house are fifteen *per cent.* upon imports, of which the valuation is left in some measure to the merchant to whom the property belongs. Here, I think, ten *per cent.* more might be raised without being felt. A tax is paid at Pernambuco for lighting the streets of the Rio de Janeiro, whilst those of Recife remain in total darkness.

Now, although the expenses of the provincial governments are great, and absorb a very considerable proportion of the receipts, owing to the number of officers employed in every department, still the salaries of each are, in most instances, much too small to afford a comfortable subsistence. Consequently peculation, bribery, and other crimes of the same description, are to be looked for: and they become so frequent as to escape all punishment or even notice; though there are some men whose character is without reproach. The governor of Pernambuco receives a salary of 4,000,000 *reis,* or about 1000 £ *per annum.* Can this be supposed to be sufficient for a man in his responsible situation, even in a country in which articles of food are cheap? His honour, however, is unimpeached; not one instance did I ever hear mentioned of improper conduct in him. But the temptation and the opportunities of amassing money are very great, and few are the persons who can resist them.

2. LOCAL GOVERNMENT: THE CAPITÃO-MÔR

Away from the few large towns, local government in colonial Brazil in effect meant government by the great landowners or fazendeiros. *In the* câmaras, *or municipal councils, the power of these rural magnates was sometimes checked by representatives of the crown or of urban interests, but on their vast estates they were absolute lords. To their personal influence the great planters often joined the authority of office, for the royal governors invariably appointed the* capitães-môres, *or district militia officers, from among them. Armed with unlimited power to command, arrest, and punish, the* capitão-môr *(captain-major) became a popular symbol of despotism and oppression. The following selection from Koster's book illustrates his comment that "the whole aspect of the government of Brazil is military."* [4]

I BECAME ACQUAINTED and somewhat intimate with the *Capitão-môr* of a neighbouring district, from frequently meeting him, in my evening

[2] When Brazil was in its infancy, the clergy could not subsist on their tithes, and therefore petitioned the government of Portugal to pay them a certain stipend, and receive the tenths for its own account: this was accepted: but now the tenths have increased in value twenty-fold, the government still pays to the vicars the same stipends. The clergy of the present day, bitterly complain of the agreement made by those to whom they have succeeded.

[3] A great confusion exists in Brazil respecting measures. Every captaincy has its own, agreeing neither with those of its neighbours, nor with the measures of Portugal, though the same names are used invariably: thus a *canada* and an *alqueire* in Pernambuco represent a much greater quantity than the same denominations in Portugal, and less than in some of the other provinces of Brazil.

[4] Henry Koster, *Travels in Brazil*, I, 252–255.

visits to a Brazilian family. He was about to make the circuit of his district, in the course of a few weeks, and invited one of my friends and myself to accompany him in this review or visit to his officers, to which we readily agreed. It was arranged that he should make us acquainted in due time with the day which he might appoint for setting out, that we might meet him at his sugar-plantation, from whence we were to proceed with him and his suite further into the country.

The *Capitães-môres*, captains-major, are officers of considerable power. They have civil as well as military duties to perform, and ought to be appointed from among the planters of most wealth and individual weight in the several *Termos*, boundaries or districts. But the interest of family or of relations about the Court, have occasioned deviations from this rule: and persons very unfit for these situations, have been sometimes nominated to them. The whole aspect of the government in Brazil is military. All men between the ages of sixteen and sixty, must be enrolled either as soldiers of the line, as militiamen, or as belonging to the body of *Ordenanças*. Of the regular soldiers, I have already spoken in another place. Of the second class, each township has a regiment, of which the individuals, with the exception of the major and adjutant, and in some cases the colonel, do not receive any pay. But they are considered as embodied men; and as such are called out upon some few occasions, in the course of the year, to assemble in uniform, and otherwise accoutred. The expense which must be incurred in this respect, of necessity, precludes the possibility of many persons becoming members of this class, even if the government were desirous of increasing the number of militia regiments. The soldiers of these are subject to their captains, to the colonel, and to the governor of the province. The colonels are either rich planters, or the major or lieutenant-colonel of a regiment of the line is thus promoted to the command of one of these; in this case, and in this case only, he receives pay. I am inclined to think, that he ought to possess some property in the district, and that any deviation from this rule is an abuse; but I am not certain that the law so ordains. The majors and the adjutants are likewise occasionally promoted from the line; but whether they are regularly military men or planters, they receive pay; as their trouble, in distributing orders, and in other arrangements connected with the regiment, is considerable.

The third class, that of the *Ordenanças*, consisting of by far the largest portion of the white persons, and of free mulatto men of all shades, have for their immediate chiefs, the *Capitães-môres*, who serve without pay: and all the persons who are connected with the *Ordenanças*, are obliged likewise to afford their services gratuitously. Each district contains one *Capitão-mór*, who is invariably a person possessing property in the part of the country to which he is appointed. He is assisted by a major, captains, and *alferes*, who are lieutenants or ensigns, and by sergeants and corporals. The duties of the *Capitão-mór* are to see that every individual under his command has in his possession some species of arms; either a firelock, a sword, or a pike. He distributes the governor's orders through his district; and can oblige any of his men to take these orders to the nearest captain, who sends another peasant forwards to the next captain, who sends another peasant forwards to the next captain, and so forth; all which is done without any pay. A *Capitão-mór* can also imprison for twenty-four hours, and send under arrest for trial a person who is accused of having committed any crime, to the civil magistrate of the town to which his district is immediately attached. Now, the abuses of this office of *Capitão-mór* are very many: and the lower orders of free persons are much oppressed by these great men, and by their subalterns, down to the corporals. The peasants are often sent upon errands which have no relation to public business; for leagues and leagues these poor fellows are made to travel, for the purpose of carrying some private letter of the chief, of his captains, or of his lieutenants, without any remuneration. Indeed, many of these men in place, seldom think of employing their slaves on these occasions, or of paying the free persons so employed. This I have witnessed times out of number; and have heard the peasants in all parts of the country complain: it is a most heavy grievance. Nothing so much vexes a peasant as the consciousness of losing his time and trouble in a service which is not required by his sovereign. Persons are sometimes confined in the stocks for days together, on some trifling plea; and are at last released without being sent to the civil magistrate, or even admitted to a hearing. However, I am happy to say, that I am acquainted with some men, whose conduct is widely different from what I have above stated; but the power given to an individual is too great, and the probability of being called to an account for its abuse too remote, to insure the exercise of it in a proper manner.

The free mulattos and free negroes, whose names are upon the rolls, either of the militia regiments which are commanded by white officers, or by those of their own class and colour, are not, properly speaking, subject to the *Capitães-môres*. These officers, and the colonels of militia, are appointed by the supreme government: and the subaltern officers are nominated by the governor of each province.

3. CRUSADERS OF THE JUNGLE

The Jesuits, who enjoyed great influence in the Portuguese court until the middle of the eighteenth century, early established their leadership in the religious and educational life of Brazil. The first Fathers, led by Manoel de Nobrega, came in 1549 with the captain-general Thomé de Souza. Four years later the famous Father Anchieta arrived in Brazil. Far to the south, on the plains of Piratininga, Nobrega and Anchieta established a colegio or school for Portuguese, mixed-blood, and Indian children that became a model institution of its kind. Around this settlement gradually arose the town of São Paulo, an important point of departure into the interior for "adventurers in search of gold and missionaries in search of souls." The English historian Southey, whose bitter anti-Catholic bias did not blind him to the heroism and devotion of Anchieta and his colleagues, describes their apostolic labor.[5]

WHEN THOMÉ DE SOUSA had been Governor four years, he petitioned to be recalled, and D. Duarte da Costa was sent out to succeed him. Seven Jesuits accompanied the new Governor; among them were Luis da Gram, who had been Rector of the College at Coimbra, and Joseph de Anchieta, then only a Temporal Coadjutor, but destined to be celebrated in Jesuitical history as the Thaumatourgos of the New World. Loyola, the Patriarch, as he is called, of the Company, or more probably Laynez, by whose master-hand the whole machine was set in motion, had already perceived the importance of this mission, and delegated new powers to Nobrega, erecting Brazil into an independent Province, and appointing him and Luis de Gram joint Provincials. As neither of these Fathers had yet taken the fourth vow, which is the last and highest degree in the order, they were instructed now to take it before the Ordinary; and they were directed to choose out Con-

[5] Southey, *History of Brazil,* I, 261–266.

sultores, or Advisers, from their companions, one of whom was to go with them upon all their journeys.

Nobrega's first act, after this accession of power, was to establish a College in the plains of Piratininga. Such an establishment was necessary because the Society was now numerous; they had very many children of both colours to support, and the alms upon which they subsisted were not sufficient to maintain them all in one place. The spot chosen was ten leagues from the sea, and about thirteen from St. Vicente, upon the great Cordillera which stretches along the coast of Brazil. The way was by a steep and difficult ascent, broken with shelves of level ground, and continuing about eight leagues, when a track of delightful country appeared in that temperate region of the air. Here were lakes, rivers, and springs, with rocks and mountains still rising above, and the earth as fertile as a rich soil and the happiest of all climates could render it. The best fruits of Europe thrive there, the grape, the apple, the peach, fig, cherry, mulberry, melon, and water-melon, and the woods abound with game.

Thirteen of the Company, under Manoel de Paiva, were sent to colonize here, where Nobrega had previously stationed some of his converts. Anchieta went with them as schoolmaster. Their first mass was celebrated on the feast of the Conversion of St. Paul, and from this, as from a good omen, they named their College after the Saint, a name which extended to the town that arose there, and has become famous in the history of South America. The plains of Piratininga had not yet been improved by European culture: nature indeed had fitted them for an earthly Paradise, but they were as nature left them, unassisted by human art. "Here we are," says Anchieta, in a letter written to Loyola, "sometimes more than twenty of us in a little hut of wicker work and mud, roofed with straw, fourteen paces long and ten wide. This is the school, this is the infirmary, dormitory, refectory, kitchen, and store-room. Yet we covet not the more spacious dwellings which our brethren inhabit in other parts, for our Lord Jesus Christ was in a straiter place when it was his pleasure to be born among beasts in a manger; and in a far straiter when he deigned to die for us upon the Cross." It was not however for want of room that Anchieta and his brethren and his pupils were thus crowded. They herded together in this way to keep themselves warm, for against the cold they were miserably provided. Fire indeed they had, but they had smoke with it, not having contrived a chimney; and sometimes cold was thought the more endurable evil of the two, and they studied in the open air. They slept in hammocks, and had no bed-clothes: for door there was a mat hung up at the entrance; their dress was calculated for a lower region; what little clothing it consisted of was cotton; they were bare-footed, and without breeches. Banana-leaves served them for a table, and napkins, says Anchieta, may well be excused when there is nothing to eat, for they had no other food than what the Indians gave them, sometimes alms of mandioc flour, and less frequently fish from the brooks, and game from the forest.

Many scholars, both Creoles and Mamalucos, came here from the nearest settlements. Anchieta taught them Latin, and learnt from them the Tupinamban, of which he composed a grammar and vocabulary, the first which were made. Day and night did this indefatigable man, whose life without the machinery of miracles, is sufficiently honorable to himself and to his order, labour in discharging the duties of his office. There were no books for the pupils; he wrote for every one his lesson on a separate leaf, after the business of the day was done, and it was sometimes day-light before this task was completed. The profane songs which were in use he parodied into hymns in Portuguese, Castilian, Latin, and Tupinamban; the ballads of the natives underwent the same travesty in their own tongue; how greatly should we have been indebted to Anchieta had he preserved them! In this language also he drew up forms of interrogations for the use of Confessors, suitable to all occasions, and wrote dialogues for the Catechumens, expounding the whole Christian, or rather Catholic faith. "I serve," says he, "as physician and barber, physicking and bleeding the Indians, and some of them have recovered under my hands when their lives were not expected, because others had died of the same diseases. Besides these employments, I have learnt another trade which necessity taught me, that is, to make *alpargatas*; I am now a good workman at this, and have made many for the brethren, for it is not possible to travel with leathern shoes among these wilds." The *alpargata* is a sort of shoe, of which the upper part is made of hemp, or any such substance — here they were of cordage from a species of wild thistle, which it was necessary to prepare for the purpose. . . . For bleeding he had no other instrument than a penknife; there was a scruple about this branch of his pro-

fession, because the clergy are forbidden to shed blood; they sent to ask Loyola's opinion, and his answer was, that charity extended to all things.

About three leagues from Piratininga, was a settlement called St. André, inhabited chiefly by Mamalucos. This breed, so far from being a link which should bind together the two races in friendly intercourse, was more desperately inimical to the natives than even the Portuguese themselves were. They hated the Jesuits for opposing the custom, as they termed it, of the land, and for interfering with what they called the liberty of making slaves. The conversion and civilization of the Indians was regarded by these wretches as measures necessarily destructive to their interests, and they devised an ingenious mode of prejudicing them against Christianity. Cowardice, they said, was the motive which induced them to be baptized; they were afraid to meet their enemies in battle, and so took shelter under the protection of the Church. Of all reproaches, this was the most cutting which could be made to a savage; they added, that the Jesuits were a set of fellows turned out of their own country as idle vagabonds, and that it was disgraceful for men who could use the bow to be under their control. Some of the adjoining tribes, instigated by these ruffians, advanced to attack Piratininga, but were met and defeated by the converts. During the night they returned to the field to carry off the dead bodies of their enemies, and feast upon them. They found fresh heaps of earth, and concluding that the bodies which they sought were buried there, dug them up and carried them away in the darkness. At daylight, when they reached their settlements, they recognized the features of their own dead, and their expected feast was changed into lamentation.

4. THE JESUIT INDIAN POLICY

The Jesuits aimed at the settlement of their Indian converts in aldeas, *or villages, where they would live completely segregated from the white colonists, under the tutelage of the priests. The Jesuit Indian program led to many clashes with the Portuguese planters, who wanted to enslave the natives for work on their estates. In an angry protest to the* Mesa de Conciencia, *a royal council entrusted with responsibility for the religious affairs of the colony, the planters charged that the Indians in the Jesuit villages "were true slaves, who labored as such not only in the* colegios *but on the so-called Indian lands, which in the end became the estates and sugar mills of the*

Jesuit Fathers." Replying to these and other accusations, Father Anchieta explained the Jesuit Indian policy.[6]

EVERY DAY, in the morning, the Fathers teach the Indians doctrine and say mass for those who want to hear it before going to their fields; after that the children stay in school, where they learn reading and writing, counting, and other good customs pertaining to the Christian life; in the afternoon they conduct another class especially for those who are receiving the sacred sacraments. Daily the Fathers visit the sick with certain Indians assigned for this purpose, and if they have some special needs they attend to them, and always administer to them the necessary sacraments. All this they do purely for love of God and for no other interest or profit, for the Fathers get their food from the *colegio,* and they live with the Indians solely because of love of their souls, which have such great need of them. The Fathers make no use of them on plantations, for if the *colegio* needs them for certain tasks, and they come to help, they work for wages, . . . and not through force but of their own free will, because they need clothing or implements. For although it is their natural tendency to go about naked, all those who have been raised in the Jesuit schools now wear clothes and are ashamed to go about naked. It is not true, as some say, that the Fathers are the lords of the villages.

When the Portuguese come to the villages in search of Indian labor, the Fathers help them all they can, summoning one of the Indian headmen to take the Portuguese to the houses of the natives to show them the goods they have brought, and those who wish to go they permit to leave without impediment. If the Fathers object at times, it is because the Indians have not finished their farm work, and they have to do this for the sake of their wives and children. In other cases, the Indians are not getting along with their wives, and once they leave for the homes of the Portuguese they never return; such Indians the Father also restrains from going, so that they may continue living with their wives. . . .

The Indians are punished for their offenses by their own magistrates, appointed by the Portuguese governors; the only chastisement consists in being put in the stocks for a day or two, as the magistrate considers best; they use no chains or other imprisonment. If some Indian who went to work for the Portuguese returns before completing his time, the Father compels him to return to work out his time, and if the Indian cannot go for some good reason the Father arranges matters to the satisfaction of his employer.

The Fathers always encourage the Indians to cultivate their fields and to raise more provisions than they need, so that in case of necessity they might aid the Poruguese by way of barter; in fact, many Portuguese obtain their food from the villages. Thus one could say that the Fathers are truly the fathers of the Indians, both of their souls and of their bodies.

5. "YOU ARE ALL IN MORTAL SIN . . . !"

The clash of interests between Brazilian planters and slave-hunters, on the one hand, and the Jesuit missionaries, on the other, reached a climax about the middle of the seventeenth century, an era of great activity on the part of the bandeirantes *of São Paulo. In various parts of Brazil the landowners rose in revolt, expelled the Jesuits, and defied royal edicts proclaiming the freedom of the Indians. In 1653 the Jesuit Antonio Vieyra (1608–1697), a priest of extraordinary oratorical and literary powers, arrived in Brazil with full authority from the king to settle the Indian question as he saw fit. During Lent Vieyra preached a famous sermon to the people of Maranhão, in which he denounced Indian slavery in terms comparable to those used by Father Montesino on Santo Domingo in 1511. The force of Vieyra's tremendous blast was somewhat weakened by his suggestion that Indian slavery should be continued under certain conditions, and by the well-known fact that the Company itself had both Indian and Negro slaves. The following excerpt from Vieyra's sermon gives some notion of his burning eloquence.*[7]

ALEXANDER AND CAESAR were lords of the world, but their souls are now burning in Hell, and will burn there for all eternity. Who will tell me now how to ask Caesar and Alexander what it profits them to have been masters of the world, and if they find that it has proved a good bargain to give their souls in exchange for it? Alexander! Julius! Was it good for you to have been masters of the world, and to be now where you are? They cannot answer me, . . . but answer me ye who can! Would any of you choose at this time to be Julius Caesar? God forbid that we should! How? Were they not masters of the

---

[6] *Cartas . . . do Joseph de Anchieta,* pp. 381–382. (Excerpt translated by the editor.)

[7] Southey, *History of Brazil,* II, 475–479.

world? They were so, but they lost their own souls. . . . Oh blindness! And it seems ill to you, for Alexander and for Caesar to have given their souls for the whole world, . . . and it seems well to you to give your own souls for what is not the world, nor hath the name of it! . . . At how different a price now . . . does the Devil purchase souls from that which he formerly offered for them — I mean in this country. The Devil has not a fair in the world where they go cheaper! In the Gospel he offers all the kingdoms of the earth for a single soul: he does not require so large a purse to purchase all that are in Maranhão. It is not necessary to offer worlds, it is not necessary to offer cities, nor towns, nor villages; it is enough for the Devil to point at a plantation and a couple of Tapuyas, and down goes the man upon his knees to worship him. Oh what a market! A Negro for a soul, and the soul the blacker of the two! This Negro shall be your slave for the few days that you may have to live, and your soul shall be my slave through all eternity, as long as God is God; this is the bargain which the Devil makes with you! . . .

Do ye know, Christians, do ye know, nobles and people of Maranhão, what is the fast which God requires of you this Lent? It is that ye loosen the bands of injustice, and that you set those free whom you hold captives, and whom you oppress. These are the sins of Maranhão; these are what God commands me to announce: "Shew my people their transgression!" Christians, God commands me to undeceive you, and I undeceive you on the part of God! You are all in mortal sin! you are all living and dying in a state of condemnation, and you are all going straight to Hell! Many are already there, and you also will soon be there with them, except you change your lives! Now mark the reasoning. Every man who holds another unjustly in servitude, being able to release him, is certainly in a state of condemnation. . . . My brethren, if there be any who doubt upon this matter, here are the Laws, here are the Lawyers, let the question be asked. You have three Orders of Religioners in the State, and among them so many subjects of such virtue and such learning: ask them . . . examine the matter . . . inform yourselves. But Religioners are not necessary: go to Turkey, go to Hell, for there can neither be Turk so beturked in Turkey, nor Devil so bedeviled in Hell, as to affirm that a free man may be a slave. But you will say to me, this people, this republic, this state cannot be supported without Indians. Who is to bring us a pitcher of water or a bundle of wood? Who is to plant our mandioc? Must our wives do it? Must our children do it? In the first place, as you will presently see, these are not the straits in which I would place you: but if necessity and conscience require it, then I reply, yes! And I repeat it, yes! You and your wives and your children ought to do it! We ought to support ourselves with our own hands; for better is it to be supported by the sweat of one's own brow than by another's blood. O ye riches of Maranhão! What if these mantles and cloaks were to be wrung? They would drip blood!

XX

Masters and Slaves

RACE MIXTURE PLAYED A DECISIVE ROLE in the formation of the Brazilian people. The scarcity of white women in the colony, the freedom of the Portuguese from Puritanical attitudes, and the despotic power of the great planters over their Indian and Negro slave women, all gave impetus to miscegenation. Color lines were drawn, but less sharply than in the Spanish Indies, and in colonial Brazil the possession of wealth more easily expunged the taint of Negro blood.

Slavery played as important a role in the social organization of colonial Brazil as did race mixture in its ethnic make-up. The social consequences of the system were almost entirely negative. Slavery corrupted both master and slave, fostered harmful attitudes with respect to the dignity of labor, and retarded the economic development of Brazil. The virtual monopolization of labor by slaves sharply limited the number of socially acceptable occupations in which whites or free mixed-bloods could engage. This gave rise to a numerous class of vagrants, beggars, "poor whites," and other degraded or disorderly elements who would not or could not compete with slaves in agriculture and industry.

The nucleus of Brazilian social as well as economic organization was the large estate; this centered about the Big House and constituted a patriarchal community that included the owner and his family, his chaplain and overseers, his slaves, and his *agregados,* or retainers — freemen of low social status who received the landowner's protection and assistance in return for a variety of services. In the sugar-growing Northeast the great planters became a distinct aristocratic class, possessed of family traditions and pride in their name and blood.

By contrast with the decisive importance of the *fazenda,* or large estate, most of the colonial towns were mere appendages of the countryside, dominated politically and socially by the rural magnates. But in a few large cities, such as Baía and Rio de Janeiro, were found other social groups that disputed or shared power with the great landowners: high officials of the colonial administration; dignitaries of the Church; wealthy professional men, especially lawyers; and the large merchants, almost exclusively peninsulars, who monopolized the export-import trade and financed the industry of the planters.

1. THE WORLD OF THE SUGAR PLANTATION

The Jesuit priest João Antonio Andreoni (1650–1715), who came to Brazil in 1667 and spent the rest of his life there, wrote a valuable account of the agricultural and mineral resources of the colony. His book, published in Lisbon in 1711, was promptly suppressed by the Portuguese government on the grounds that the information it contained might prove helpful to Portugal's European rivals. The following excerpts from Andreoni's book illustrate Gilberto Freyre's point that "the Big House completed by the slave shed represents an entire economic, social, and political system." [1]

IF THE PLANTATION OWNER must display his capacity in one thing more than another, it is in the proper choice of persons to administer his estate. . . .

The first choice that he must make with care, on the basis of secret information concerning the conduct and knowledge of the person in question, is that of a chaplain to whom he must entrust the teaching of all that pertains to the Christian way of life. For the principal obligation of the planter is to teach, or have taught, his family and slaves. This should be done not by some slave born in Brazil, or by some overseer who at best can only teach them their prayers and the laws of God and the Church by word of mouth, but by one who can explain to them what they should believe and what they must

do, and how they must do it, and how they are to ask God for what they need. And for this reason, if he must pay the chaplain a little more than is customary, the planter should understand that he could not put the money to better use. . . .

The chaplain should live outside the planter's house; this is best for both, because he is a priest and not a servant, a familiar of God and not of men. He should not have any woman slave in his house, unless she be of advanced years, nor should he trade in anything, either human or divine, for all this is opposed to his clerical state and is prohibited by various Papal orders.

It is customary to pay a chaplain, when he is free to say masses during weekdays, forty or fifty thousand *reis* a year, and with what he gains from the saying of masses during the week he can earn a respectable salary — and well earned too, if he does all the things described above. If he is expected to teach the children of the plantation owner, he should receive a just additional compensation. . . .

On the day that the cane is brought to be ground, if the plantation owner does not invite the Vicar, the chaplain blesses the mill and asks God to grant a good yield and to guard those who work in it from all misfortune. When the mill stops grinding at the end of the harvest, he sees to it that all give thanks to God in the chapel. . . .

The arms of the plantation owner, on which he relies for the good governance of his people and estate, are his overseers. But if each should aspire to be the head, it would be a monstrous government and would truly resemble the dog

[1] André João Antonil (João Antonio Andreoni), *Cultura e Opulencia do Brazil por Suas Drogas e Minas,* edited by Affonso de E. Tauny, São Paulo, 1923, pp. 77–83, 91–102. (Excerpts translated by the editor.)

Cerberus, to whom the poets fancifully ascribe three heads. I do not say that the overseers should not possess authority, but I say that this authority must be well ordered and subordinate, not absolute, so that the lesser are inferior to the greater, and all to the master whom they serve.

It is fitting that the slaves should understand that the chief overseer has power to command and reprove them, and to punish them when necessary, but they should also know that they have recourse to the master and that they will be heard as justice requires. Nor must the other overseers suppose that their powers are unlimited, especially in what concerns punishment and seizure. The plantation owner, therefore, must make very clear the authority given to each, and especially to the chief overseer; and if they exceed their authority he should check them with the punishment that their excesses deserve — but not before the slaves, lest another time they rise against the overseer, and so that he may not bear the shame of being reproved before them and hence not dare to govern them. It will suffice if the master let a third party make known to the injured slave, and to some of the oldest slaves on the estate, that the master was much displeased with the overseer for the wrong that he had committed, and that if he did not amend his ways he would be immediately dismissed.

The overseers must on no account be permitted to kick slaves — in particular to kick pregnant slave women in the belly — or to strike slaves with a stick, because blows struck in anger are not calculated, and they may inflict a mortal head wound on some valuable slave that cost a great deal of money. What they may do is to scold them and strike them a few times on the back with a liana whip, to teach them a lesson. To seize fugitive slaves and any who fight and slash each other and get drunk, so that the master may have them punished as they deserve, is to show a diligence worthy of praise. But to tie up a slave girl and lash her with a liana whip until the blood runs, or to place her in the stocks or in chains for months at a time (while the master is in the city) simply because she will not go to bed with him, or to do the same to a slave who gave the master a faithful account of the overseer's disloyalty, violence, and cruelty, and to invent pretended offenses to justify the punishment — this may not be tolerated on any account, for it would be to have a ravening wolf rather than a well-disposed and Christian overseer.

It is the obligation of the chief overseer of the plantation to govern the people, and to assign them to their tasks at the proper time. It is his duty to learn from the master who should be notified to cut their cane, and to send them word promptly. He should have the boats and carts ready to go for the cane and should prepare the forms and fuel. He should apprise the master of everything that is needed to equip the sugar-mill before the start of grinding, and when the season is over he should put everything away in its place. He must see that each performs his task, and if some disaster occurs he should hasten to the scene to give what help he can. . . .

The slaves are the hands and feet of the plantation owner, for without them you cannot make, preserve, and increase a fortune, or operate a plantation in Brazil. And the kind of service they give depends on how they are treated. It is necessary, therefore, to buy a certain number of slaves each year and assign them to the canefields, the manioc fields, the sawmills, and the boats. And because they are usually of different nations, and some more primitive than others, and differ greatly in physical qualities, the assignments should be made with great care. Those who come to Brazil are the Ardas, Minas, Congos, others from S. Thomé, Angola, Cape Verde, and some from Mozambique, who come in the India ships. The Ardas and Minas are robust. Those who come from Cape Verde and S. Thomé are weaker. The slaves from Angola, raised in Loanda, are more capable of acquiring mechanical skills than those who come from the other regions that I have named. Among the Congos there are also some who are quite industrious, and good not only for work in the canefields but for mechanical tasks and housework.

Some arrive in Brazil very barbarous and dull-witted, and continue so throughout their lives. Others in a few years become clever and skillful, not only in learning Christian doctrine but in mastering trades, and they can be used to handle a boat, carry messages, and perform any other routine task. . . . It is not well to remove a slave against his will from the plantation where he has been raised since childhood, for he may pine away and die. Those slaves who were born in Brazil, or were raised from infancy in the homes of whites, form an affection for their masters and give a good account of themselves; one of these who bears his captivity well is worth four slaves brought from Africa.

The mulattoes are even more apt for every task; but many of them, taking advantage of the favor of their masters, are haughty and vicious and swagger about, always ready for a brawl. Yet they and the mulatto women commonly have it best of all in Brazil, because the white blood in their veins (sometimes that of their own masters) works such sorcery that some owners will tolerate and pardon anything they do; not only do they not reprove them, but it seems that all the caresses fall to their share. It is hard to say whether the masters or the mistresses are more at fault in this respect, for there are some of both sexes who permit themselves to be ruled by mulattoes, and not those of the best sort, either, thus verifying the proverb that says that Brazil is the Hell of the Negroes, the Purgatory of the Whites, and the Paradise of the mulattoes — but let some distrust or feeling of jealousy change love into hatred, and it comes forth armed with every kind of cruelty and severity. It is well to make use of their capabilities, if they will make good use of them (as some do, to be sure), but they should not be treated with such intimacy that they lose respect, and from slaves turn into masters. To free mulatto women of loose habits is surely an iniquitous thing, because the money with which they purchase their freedom rarely comes out of any other mines than their own bodies, and is gained with repeated sins; and after they are freed they continue to be the ruination of many.

Some masters are opposed to the marriage of male and female slaves, and they not only are indifferent to their living in concubinage but consent and actually encourage them to live in that state, saying: "You, so-and-so, will in due time marry so-and-so"; and after that they permit them to live together as if they were already man and wife. It is said that the reason why masters do not marry such couples off is because they fear that if they tire of the match they may kill each other with poison or witchcraft, for among them there are notable masters of this craft. Others, after marrying off their slaves, keep them apart for years as if they were unwed, and this they cannot do in good conscience. Others are so negligent in what concerns the salvation of the slaves that they keep them for a long time in the canefields or at the sugar-mill without baptism. Furthermore, of those who have been baptized, many do not know who is their Creator, what they should believe, what law they should observe, how to commend themselves to God, why Christians go to Church, why they adore the Church, what to say to the Father when they kneel before him

and when they speak into his ear, whether they have souls and if these souls die, and where they go when they leave the body. . . .

In what concerns food, clothing, and rest from labor, clearly these things should not be denied them, for in all fairness the master should give a servitor sufficient food, medicine for his sicknesses, and clothing so that he may be decently covered and not go about half-naked in the streets; he should also regulate their labor so that it is not beyond their strength and endurance. In Brazil they say that the slaves must have the three P's, namely, a stick, bread, and a piece of cloth (*páo, pão, e panno*). And though they make a bad beginning, commencing with the stick, which stands for punishment, yet would to God that the bread and clothing were as abundant as the punishment! For it is frequently inflicted for some offense not wholly proved, or else invented, and with instruments of great severity (even if the crimes were proved), such instruments as are not used on brute beasts. To be sure, some masters take more account of a horse than of a half-dozen slaves, for the horse is cared for, and has a groom to find him hay, and wipe his sweat away, and a saddle, and a gilded bridle. . . .

Some masters have the custom of giving their slaves one day a week to plant for themselves, sometimes sending the overseer along to see that they do not neglect their work; this helps to keep them from suffering hunger or from daily milling about the house of the master to beg him for a ration of flour. But to deny them both flour and a day for planting, and to expect them to work in the fields by day, from sunrise to sundown, and in the sugar-mill by night, with little rest from labor — how shall such a master escape punishment before the Tribunal of God? If to deny alms to one who needs it is to deny it to Christ our Lord, as the Good Book says, what must it be to deny food and clothing to one's slaves? And how shall that master justify his conduct, who gives woolens and silks and other fineries to her who works his perdition and then denies four or five yards of cotton, and a few more of woolen cloth, to the slave who dissolves in sweat to serve him, and barely has time to hunt for a root and a crab-fish for his meal? And if on top of this the punishment is frequent and excessive, the slaves will either run away into the woods or commit suicide, as is their custom, by holding their breath or hanging themselves — or they will try to take the lives of those who do them such great evil, resorting, if necessary, to diabolical arts, or they will clamor so loudly to the Lord that he will hear them and do to their masters what he did to the Egyptians when they vexed the Jews with extraordinary labor, sending terrible plagues against their estates and sons, as we read in the Sacred Scripture. . . .

Not to punish their excesses would be a serious fault, but these offenses should first be verified, so that innocent people may not suffer. The accused should be given a hearing, and if the charges are proved the culprits should be chastised with a moderate lashing, or by placing them in chains or in the stocks for a short period. But to punish them overhastily, with a vengeful spirit, with one's own hand, with terrible instruments, and perhaps to burn them with fire or heated sealing wax, or to brand the poor fellows in the face — why, this is intolerable in barbarians, to say nothing of Christian Catholics. . . . And if, having erred by reason of their frailty, they themselves come to beg the master's pardon, or find sponsors (*padrinhos*) to accompany them, in such cases it is customary in Brazil to pardon them. And it is well for them to know that this will obtain them forgiveness, for otherwise they may one day flee to some fugitive-slave settlement (*mucambo*) in the forest, and if they are captured they may kill themselves before the master can lash them, or some kinsman will take it upon himself to avenge them by the use of witchcraft or poison. Completely to deny them their festivities, which are their only consolation in their captivity, is to condemn them to sadness and melancholy, to apathy and sickliness. Therefore masters should not object if they crown their kings and sing and dance decently for a few hours on certain days of the year, or if they amuse themselves in proper ways of an afternoon, after having celebrated in the morning the holiday of Our Lady of the Rosary, of Saint Benedict, and of the patron-saint of the plantation chapel. . . .

Since the management of a sugar plantation requires so many large outlays, as described above, it is plain that the owner must carefully watch the expenses of his household. . . .

It is a poor thing to have the reputation of being a miser, but it is no credit to bear the name of a prodigal. He who decides to assume the burdens of a plantation must either retire from the city, shunning its diversions, or maintain two houses — which is notably deleterious to the one from which he is absent and also doubly expensive. To keep one's sons on the plantation is to create country bumpkins who can only talk of dogs, horses, and cattle. To leave them in the city is to permit them to fall into vicious habits and contract shameful diseases that are not easily cured. To avoid both extremes, the best course is to place them in the household of some responsible and honorable relative or friend, where they will have no opportunity to make a false step — a friend who will faithfully keep the parent informed of their good or bad conduct and of their improvement or neglect of their studies. The lad's mother should not be permitted to send him money or to send secret orders for that purpose to the father's correspondent or cashier; nor must it be forgotten that money requested for the purchase of books can also be used for gambling. The father should therefore instruct his attorney or agent not to give the boy anything without his order. For these young fellows can be very ingenious in their pleas for money, and can devise all manner of plausible reasons and pretexts, especially when they are supposed to be engaged in some course of studies. They are perfectly willing to spend three years of pleasant life at the expense of their father or uncle, who is in his sugar-cane fields and has no idea of what goes on in town. So when a father boasts that he has an Aristotle in the Academy, it may be that he really has an Asinius or an Apricius in the city. But if the father decides to keep his children at home, content to let them learn to read, write, and count, together with some knowledge of events or history, to enable them to converse in company, he should not fail to watch over them, especially when they reach a certain age. For the broad countryside is also a place of much freedom, and can breed thistles and thorns. And if one constructs a fence for cattle and horses to keep them from leaving the pasture, why should one not keep children within bounds, both inside and outside the house, if experience proves that it is necessary? . . . The good example of the father, however, is the best lesson in conduct; and the surest means of achieving peace of mind is to marry off the girls, and the boys as well, at the proper time. If they are content to marry within their station, they will find houses where they can make good matches and receive their rewards.

2. The Free Population

Freemen and slaves formed the two great legal categories into which the Brazilian colonial population was divided. However, not all freemen belonged to the master class. Unable or unwilling to compete with slave labor in agriculture and industry, the majority maintained a precarious existence on the margins of a society dominated by the great landholding class. Perhaps the most hopeful feature of Brazilian colonial life was the gradual blurring of the color line through race mixture — a circumstance that gave free mulattoes and other mixed-bloods a greater social mobility than was possible in any other slave society of modern times.[2]

IN THE PORTUGUESE South American dominions, circumstances have directed that there should be no division of casts, and very few of those degrading and most galling distinctions which have been made by all other nations in the management of their colonies. That this was not intended by the mother country, but was rather submitted to from necessity, is to be discovered in some few regulations, which plainly show that if Portugal could have preserved the superiority of the whites, she would, as well as her neighbors, have established laws for that purpose. The rulers of Portugal wished to colonize to an unlimited extent: but their country did not contain a population sufficiently numerous for their magnificent plans. Emigrants left their own country to settle in the New World, who were literally adventurers; for they had not any settled plans of life, and they were without families. Persons of established habits, who had the wish to follow any of the ordinary means of gaining a livelihood, found employment at home; neither could Portugal spare them, nor did they wish to leave their native soil. There was no superabundance of population: and therefore every man might find occupation at home, if he had steadiness to look for it. There was no division in political or religious opinion. There was no necessity of emigration, save that which was urged by crimes. Thus the generality of the men who embarked in the expeditions which were fitted out for Brazil, were unaccompanied by females: and therefore, naturally, on their arrival in that country, they married, or irregularly connected themselves with Indian women, and subsequently with those of Africa. It is true that orphan girls were sent out by the government of Portugal: but these were necessarily few in number. In the course of another generation, the colonists married the women of mixed casts, owing to the impossibility of obtaining those of their own colour: and the fre-

quency of the custom, and the silence of the laws upon the subject, removed all idea of degradation, in thus connecting themselves. Still the European notions of superiority were not entirely laid aside: and these caused the passing of some regulations, by which white persons were to enjoy certain privileges. Thus, although the form of trial for all casts is the same, in certain places only, can capital punishment be inflicted upon the favoured race. The people of colour are not eligible to some of the chief offices of government: nor can they become members of the priesthood.

From the mildness of the laws, however, the mixed casts have gained ground considerably. The regulations which exist against them are evaded, or rather they have become obsolete. Perhaps the heroic conduct of Camarão and Henrique Dias, the Indian and negro chieftains, in the famous and most interesting contest, between the Pernambucans and the Dutch, and the honours subsequently granted by the crown of Portugal to both of them, may have led to the exaltation of the general character of the much-injured varieties of the human species of which they were members. Familiarity between the chieftains of the several corps must be the consequence of their embarkation in the same cause, when the war is one of skirmishes, of ambuscades, of continual alarm, of assistance constantly afforded to each other; a patriotic war, against a foreign invader, in which difference of religion exists, and each party mortally hates the other. On these occasions all men are equal; or he only is superior whose strength and whose activity surpasses that of others. The amalgamation of casts which is caused by this consciousness of equality could not have had a fairer field for its full accomplishment, than the war to which I have alluded: and the friendships which were formed under these circumstances would not easily be broken off. Although the parties who had been so united might have been in their situations in life very far removed from each other, still the participation of equal danger must render dear the companions in peril, and make the feelings, which had been roused on these occasions, of long duration; they would continue to act, long after the cessation of the series of occurrences which had called them forth.

The free population of Brazil at the present time consists of Europeans; Brazilians, that is, white persons born in Brazil; mulattos, that is, the mixed cast between the whites and blacks,

[2] Koster, *Travels in Brazil,* II, 167–187.

and all the varieties into which it can branch; mamalucos, that is, the mixed casts between the whites and Indians, and all its varieties; Indians in a domesticated state, who are called generally Tapuyas; negroes born in Brazil, and manumitted Africans; lastly, mestizos, that is, the mixed cast between the Indians and negroes. Of slaves, I shall speak by and by more at large; these are Africans, creole negroes, mulattos, and mestizos. The maxim of the Civil law, *partus sequitur ventrem*, is in force here as well as in the colonies of other nations.

These several mixtures of the human race have their shades of difference of character as well as of colour. First we must treat of the whites. The Europeans who are not in office, or who are not military men, are, generally speaking, adventurers who have arrived in that country with little or no capital. These men commence their career in low situations of life, but by parsimony and continual exertion directed to one end, that of amassing money, they often attain their object, and pass the evening of their lives in opulence. These habits fail not, oftentimes, to give a bias to their dispositions, which is unallied to generosity and liberality. They look down upon the Brazilians, or rather they wish to consider themselves superior to them; and until lately the government took no pains to remove the jealousy which existed between the two descriptions of white persons; and even now, not so much attention is paid to the subject as its great importance seems to require.[3]

The Brazilian white man of large property, who draws his descent from the first Donatory of a province, or whose family has for some generations enjoyed distinction, entertains a high opinion of his own importance, which may sometimes appear ridiculous; but which much oftener leads him to acts of generosity, — to the adoption of liberal ideas, — to honourable conduct. If he has been well educated and has had the good fortune to have been instructed by a priest whose ideas are enlightened, who gives a proper latitude for difference of opinion, who tolerates as he is tolerated, then the character of a young Brazilian exhibits much to admire. Surrounded by numerous relatives, and by his immediate dependents living in a vast and half-civilized country, he is endued with much independence of language and behaviour, which are softened by the subordination which has been imbibed during his course of education. That this is general, I pretend not to say. Few persons are instructed in a proper manner; and again, few are those who profit by the education which they have received; but more numerous are the individuals who now undergo necessary tuition, for powerful motives have arisen to urge the attainment of knowledge.

I have heard it often observed, and I cannot help saying, that I think some truth is to be attached to the remark, in the country of which I am now treating, that women are usually less lenient to their slaves than men: but this doubtless proceeds from the ignorant state in which they are brought up. They scarcely receive any education; and have not the advantages of obtaining instruction from communication with persons who are unconnected with their own way of life; of imbibing new ideas from general conversation. They are born, bred, and continue surrounded by slaves without receiving any check, with high notions of superiority, without any thought that what they do is wrong. Bring these women forward, educate them, treat them as rational, as equal beings, and they will be in no respect inferior to their countrymen. The fault is not with the sex, but in the state of the human being. As soon as a child begins to crawl, a slave of about its own age, and of the same sex, is given to it as a playfellow, or rather as a plaything. They grow up together: and the slave is made the stock upon which the young owner gives vent to passion. The slave is sent upon all errands, and receives the blame of all unfortunate accidents; — in fact, the white child is thus encouraged to be overbearing, owing to the false fondness of its parents. Upon the boys the effect is less visible in after-life, because the world curbs and checks them: but the girls do not stir from home, and therefore have no opportunities of wearing off these pernicious habits. It is only surprising that so many excellent women should be found among them, and by no means strange that the disposition of some of them should be injured by this unfortunate direction of their infant years.

As vegetation rapidly advances in such climates, so the animal sooner arrives at maturity than in those of less genial warmth; and here again education is rendered doubly necessary to lead the mind to new ideas, to curb the passions, to give a sense of honour, and to instil feelings of that species of pride which is so neces-

---

[3] The majority of the clergy of Pernambuco, both regular and secular, are of Brazilian parentage. The governor is an European, and so are the major part of the chief officers, civil, military, and ecclesiastical but the bishop is a Brazilian, and so is the *ouvidor*.

sary to a becoming line of conduct. The state of society, the climate, and the celibacy of the numerous priesthood, cause the number of illegitimate children to be very great. But here the *roda dos engeitados,* and a custom which shews the natural goodness of the people, prevent the frequent occurrence of infanticide, or rather render it almost unknown. An infant is frequently during the night laid at the door of a rich person; and on being discovered in the morning is taken in, and is almost invariably allowed to remain: it is brought up with the children of the house (if its colour is not too dark to admit of this), certainly as a dependent, but not as a servant. However, a considerable tinge of colour will not prevent it from being reared with the white children. These *engeitados,* or rejected ones, as individuals who are so circumstanced are called, are frequently to be met with: and I heard of few exceptions to the general kindness with which they are treated. Public feeling is much against the refusing to accept and rear an *engeitado.* The owner of a house, who is in easy circumstances, and yet sends the infant from his own door to the public institution which is provided for its reception, is generally spoken of in terms of indignation. Sometimes a poor man will find one of these presents at his door: and he will generally place it at the landholder's threshold on the following night. This is accounted excusable and even meritorious; for at the Great House the child has nearly a certainty of being well taken care of.

I have observed that, generally speaking, Europeans are less indulgent to their slaves than Brazilians. The former feed them well: but they require from the poor wretches more labour than they can perform, whilst the latter allow the affairs of their estates to continue in the way in which they have been accustomed to be directed. This difference between the two descriptions of the owners is easily accounted for. The European has probably purchased part of his slaves on credit; and has, during the whole course of his life, made the accumulation of riches his chief object. The Brazilian inherits his estate: and as nothing urges him to the necessity of obtaining large profits, he continues the course that has been pointed out to him by the former possessors. His habits of quietude and indolence have led him to be easy and indifferent: and although he may not provide for the maintenance of his slaves with so much care as the European, still they find more time to seek

for food themselves. That avaricious spirit which deliberately works a man or a brute animal until it is unfit for farther service, without any regard to the well-being of the creature, which is thus treated as a mere machine, as if it was formed of wood or iron, is, however, seldom to be met with in those parts of the country which I visited. Instances of cruelty occur (as has been, and will yet be seen), but these proceed from individual depravity, and not from systematic, coldblooded, calculating indifference to the means by which a desired end is to be compassed.

Notwithstanding the relationship of the mulattos on one side to the black race, they consider themselves superior to the mamalucos. They lean to the whites; and from the light in which the Indians are held, pride themselves upon being totally unconnected with them. Still the mulattos are conscious of their connection with men who are in a state of slavery, and that many persons, even of their own colour, are under these degraded circumstances. They have therefore always a feeling of inferiority in the company of white men, if these white men are wealthy and powerful. This inferiority of rank is not so much felt by white persons in the lower walks of life: and these are more easily led to become familiar with individuals of their own colour who are in wealthy circumstances. Still the inferiority which the mulatto feels, is more that which is produced by poverty than that which his colour has caused; for he will be equally respectful to a person of his own cast, who may happen to be rich.[4] The degraded state of the people of colour in the British colonies is most lamentable. In Brazil, even the trifling regulations which exist against them, remain unattended to. A mulatto enters into holy orders, or is appointed a magistrate, his papers stating him to be a white man, but his appearance plainly denoting the contrary. In conversing on one occasion with a man of colour who was in my service, I asked if a certain *Capitão-môr* was not a mulatto man: he answered, "he was, but is not now." I begged him to explain, when he added, "Can a *Capitão-môr* be a mulatto man?" I was intimately acquainted with a priest, whose complexion and hair plainly denoted from whence he drew his origin. I liked him much. He was a well-educated and

[4] The term of *Senhor* or *Senhora* is made use of to all free persons, whites, mulattos, and blacks: and in speaking to a freeman of whatever class or colour the manner of address is the same.

intelligent man. Besides this individual instance, I met with several others of the same description.

The regiments of militia, which are called mulatto regiments, are so named from all the officers and men being of mixed casts; nor can white persons be admitted into them. The principal officers are men of property: and the colonel, like the commander of any other regiment, is only amenable to the governor of the province. In the white militia regiments, the officers ought to be by law white men. But in practice they are rather reputed white men, for very little pains are taken to prove that there is no mixture of blood. Great numbers of the soldiers belonging to the regiments which are officered by white men, are mulattos, and other persons of colour. The regiments of the line, likewise, (as I have elsewhere said) admit into the ranks all persons excepting negroes and Indians. But the officers of these must prove nobility of birth. However, as certain degrees of nobility have been conferred upon persons in whose families there is much mixture of blood, this proof cannot be regarded as being required against the mulatto or mamaluco part of the population. Thus an European adventurer could not obtain a commission in these regiments, whilst a Brazilian, whose family has distinguished itself in the province in former times, will prove his eligibility without regard to the blood which runs in his veins. He is noble, let that flow from whence it may.[5]

The late colonel of the mulatto regiment of Recife, by name Nogueira, went to Lisbon, and returned to Pernambuco with the Order of Christ, which the Queen had conferred upon him. A chief person of one of the provinces is the son of a white man and a woman of colour. He has received an excellent education; is of generous disposition; and entertains most liberal views upon all subjects. He has been made a colonel, and a degree of nobility has been conferred upon him; likewise the Regent is sponsor to one of his children. Many other instances might be mentioned. Thus has Portugal, of late

years from policy, continued that system into which she was led by her peculiar circumstances in former times. Some of the wealthy planters of Pernambuco, and of the rich inhabitants of Recife, are men of colour. The major part of the best mechanics are also of mixed blood.

It is said that mulattos make bad masters: and this holds good oftentimes with persons of this description, who have been in a state of slavery, and become possessed of slaves of their own, or are employed as managers upon estates. The change of situation would lead to the same consequences in any race of human beings; and cannot be accounted peculiar to the mixed casts. I have seen mulattos of free birth, as kind, as lenient, and as forbearing to their slaves and other dependents, as any white man.

Marriages between white men and women of colour are by no means rare; though they are sufficiently so to cause the circumstance to be mentioned when speaking of an individual who has connected himself in this manner. But this is not said with the intent of lowering him in the estimation of others. Indeed the remark is only made if the person is a planter of any importance, and the woman is decidedly of dark colour; for even a considerable tinge will pass for white. If the white man belongs to the lower orders, the woman is not accounted as being unequal to him in rank, unless she is nearly black. The European adventurers often marry in this manner, which generally occurs when the woman has a dower. The rich mulatto families are often glad to dispose of their daughters to these men, although the person who has been fixed upon may be in indifferent circumstances; for the colour of the children of their daughters is bettered; and from the well-known prudence and regularity of this set of men, a large fortune may be hoped for even from very small beginnings. Whilst I was at Jaguaribe, I was in the frequent habit of seeing a handsome young man, who was a native of the island of St. Michael's. This person happened to be with me on one occasion when the commandant from the Sertão was staying at my house. The commandant asked him if he could read and write: and being answered in the negative, said, "then you will not do:" and turning to me added, "I have a commission from a friend of mine to take with me back to the Sertão a good-looking young Portuguese of regular habits, who can read and write, for the purpose of marrying him to his daughter." Such commissions (*encommendas*) are not unusual.

---

5 To this statement some explanation is necessary, owing to the regulations of the Portuguese military service. Privates are sometimes raised to commissions by the intermediate steps of corporals, quartermasters, and sergeants. These men gain their ensigncies without any relation to their birth: and though a decidedly dark-coloured mulatto might not be so raised, a European of low birth would. It is to enable a man to become a cadet, and then an officer without serving in the ranks, that requires nobility of birth.

Still the Brazilians of high birth and large property do not like to intermarry with persons whose mixture of blood is *very* apparent: and hence arise peculiar circumstances. A man of this description becomes attached to a woman of colour; connects himself with her; and takes her to his home, where she is in a short time visited even by married women. She governs his household affairs: acts and considers herself as his wife; and frequently after the birth of several children, when they are neither of them young, he marries her. In connections of this nature, the parties are more truly attached than in marriage between persons who belong to two families of the first rank; for the latter are entered into from convenience rather than from affection. Indeed the parties, on some occasions, do not see each other until a few days before the ceremony takes place. It often occurs, that inclination, necessity, or convenience induces or obliges a man to separate from the person with whom he is connected. In this case, he gives her a portion; and she marries a man of her own rank, who regards her rather as a widow than as one whose conduct has been incorrect. Instances of infidelity in these women are rare. They become attached to the men with whom they cohabit: and they direct the affairs of the houses over which they are placed with the same zeal that they would display if they had the right of command over them. It is greatly to the credit of the people of that country, that so much fidelity should be shewn on one side; and that this should so frequently as it is, be rewarded by the other party, in the advancement of those who have behaved thus faithfully, to a respectable and acknowledged situation in society. It should be recollected too that the merit of moral feelings must be judged of by the standard of the country, and not by our own institutions. I have only spoken above of what occurs among the planters; for in large towns, man is pretty much the same everywhere.

The Mamalucos are more frequently to be seen in the Sertão than upon the coast. They are handsomer than the mulattos: and the women of this cast particularly surpass in beauty all others of the country. They have the brown tint of mulattos: but their features are less blunt, and their hair is not curled. I do not think that the men can be said to possess more courage than the mulattos. But whether from the knowledge which they have of being of free birth on both sides, or from residing in the interior of the country where the government is more loose, they appear to have more independence of character, and to pay less deference to a white man than the mulattos. When women relate any deed of danger that has been surmounted or undertaken, they generally state that the chief actor in it was a large mamaluco, *mamalucão;* as if they thought this description of men to be superior to all others. Mamalucos may enter into the mulatto regiments; and are pressed into the regiments of the line as being men of colour, without any regard to the sources from which their blood proceeds.

Of the domesticated Indians I have already elsewhere given what accounts I could collect, and what I had opportunities of observing. The wild Indians are only now to be met with at a great distance from the coast of Pernambuco: and although they are very near to Maranhão, and are dreaded neighbors, I had no means of seeing any of them.

I now proceed to mention that numerous and valuable race of men, the creole negroes; a tree of African growth, which has thus been transplanted, cultivated, and much improved by its removal to the New World. The creole negroes stand alone and unconnected with every other race of men: and this circumstance alone would be sufficient, and indeed contributes much to the effect of uniting them to each other. The mulattos, and all other persons of mixed blood, wish to lean towards the whites, if they can possibly lay any claim to relationship. Even the mestizo tries to pass for a mulatto, and to persuade himself and others, that his veins contain some portion of white blood, although that with which they are filled proceeds from Indian and negro sources. Those only who have no pretensions to a mixture of blood, call themselves negroes, which renders the individuals who do pass under this denomination, much attached to each other, from the impossibility of being mistaken for members of any other cast. They are of handsome persons, brave and hardy, obedient to the whites, and willing to please. But they are easily affronted: and the least allusion to their colour being made by a person of lighter tint, enrages them to a great degree; though they will sometimes say, "a negro I am, but always upright." They are again distinct from their brethren in slavery, owing to their superior situation as free men.

The free creole negroes have their exclusive regiments, as well as the mulattos, of which every officer and soldier must be perfectly black. There are two of these regiments for the province of

Pernambuco, which consists of indefinite numbers of men, who are dispersed all over the country. These regiments are distinguished from each other by the names of Old Henriques and New Henriques. The name of Henriques is derived from the famous chieftain, Henrique Díaz, in the time of the Dutch war. I have heard some of the most intelligent of those with whom I have conversed, speak in enthusiastic terms of the aid which he gave to the whites in that struggle. I have seen some portion of one of these regiments, in Recife, accompanying the procession of our Lady of the Rosary, the patroness of negroes. They were dressed in white cloth uniforms, turned up with scarlet: and they looked very soldier-like. They were in tolerable discipline; and seemed to wish to go through the duty of the day in the best manner that they were able. They acted with an appearance of zeal and the desire of excelling. Those of which I speak, formed a finer body of men than any other soldiers which I had an opportunity of seeing in that country. On gala days, the superior black officers in their white uniforms, pay their respects to the governor, exactly in the same manner that the persons of any other cast, holding commissions of equal rank, are expected to go through this form. These men receive no pay, so that their neat appearance on such occasions bespeaks a certain degree of wealth among them; neither are the privates nor any other persons belonging to these regiments paid for their services. Some of the whites rather ridicule the black officers, but not in their presence; and the laugh which is raised against them is caused perhaps by a lurking wish to prevent this insulted race from the display of those distinctions which the government has wisely conceded to them, but which hurt the European ideas of superiority. The old regiment of Henriques was, at the time that I resided in Pernambuco, without a colonel: and I heard much discussion on several occasions among the creole negroes, about the fittest person to be appointed to the vacant situation.

The creole negroes of Recife are, generally speaking, mechanics of all descriptions: but they have not yet reached the higher ranks of life, as gentlemen, as planters, and as merchants. Some of them have accumulated considerable sums of money; and possess many slaves, to whom they teach their own trade: or these slaves are taught other mechanical employments by which they may become useful. They work for their owners, and render them great profits; for every description of labour is high, and that which requires any degree of skill bears a higher comparative value than the department of which a knowledge is more easily attained. The best church and image painter of Pernambuco is a black man, who has good manners, and quite the air of a man of some importance, though he does not by any means assume too much. The negroes are excluded from the priesthood; and from the offices which the mulattos may obtain through their evasion of the law, but which the decided and unequivocal colour of the negro entirely precludes him aspiring to. In law all persons who are not white, and are born free, class equally. Manumitted slaves are placed upon the same footing as persons born free. However, although the few exclusions which exist against the negroes, are degrading; still in some instances they are befriended by them. They are unable, owing to their colour, to serve in the regiments of the line, or in any regiments excepting those which are exclusively their own. But by means of this regulation they escape the persecutions under which the other casts suffer during the time of recruiting. The officers and men of the Henrique regiments are so united to each other, that the privates and subalterns are less liable to be oppressed by any white men in office even than the soldiers of the mulatto regiments. Of these latter, officers, having a considerable tinge of white, sometimes lean towards the wishes of the *capitão-môr,* or some other rich white officer, instead of protecting his soldiers.

The men whose occupation it is to apprehend runaway negroes, are, almost without exception, creole blacks. They are called *capitães-do-campo,* captains of the field; are subject to a *capitão-môr do campo* who resides in Recife; and receive their commissions either from the governor or from this officer. By these they are authorized to apprehend and take to their owners any slaves who may be found absent from their homes without their master's consent. Several of these men are to be found in every district, employing themselves in such pursuits as they think fit, when their services are not required in that calling which forms their particular duty. They are men of undaunted courage; and are usually followed by two or three dogs, which are trained to seek out, and, if necessary, to attack and bring to the ground those persons whose apprehension their masters are desirous of effecting. The men who bear these commissions can oblige any unauthorized person to give up to them an apprehended negro, for the purpose of being by them returned to his owner.

It is scarcely necessary to name the mestizos; for they usually class with the mulattos; nor are they to be easily distinguished from some of the darker varieties of this cast. A dark coloured man, of a disagreeable countenance, and badly formed person, is commonly called a mestizo, without any reference to his origin.

3. NEGRO SLAVERY IN BRAZIL

At the close of the colonial period, according to the best available data, Negro slaves constituted one third of the total population of Brazil. On a base of Negro slave labor rested all the important large-scale economic activities of the colony: the cultivation of sugar cane, cotton, and tobacco. How the system functioned at the opening of the nineteenth century is told by Henry Koster with a wealth of factual detail.[6]

THE INDIAN SLAVERY has been for many years abolished in Brazil: and the individuals who are now in bondage in that country are Africans, and their descendants on both sides, or individuals whose mothers are of African origin: and no line is drawn at which the near approach to the colour and blood of the whites entitles the child, whose mother is a slave, to freedom. I have seen several persons who were to all appearance of white origin, still doomed to slavery.

Slaves, however, in Brazil, have many advantages over their brethren in the British colonies. The numerous holidays of which the Catholic religion enjoins the observance, give to the slave many days of rest or time to work for his own profit: thirty-five of these, and the Sundays besides, allow him to employ much of his time as he pleases. Few masters are inclined to restrain the right of their slaves to dispose of these days as they think fit: or, at any rate, few dare, whatever their inclinations may be, to brave public opinion in depriving them of the intervals from work which the law has set apart as their own, that their lives may be rendered less irksome. The time which is thus afforded, enables the slave, who is so inclined, to accumulate a sum of money: however this is by law his master's property, from the incapability under which a slave labours of possessing any thing which he can by right call his own. But I believe there is no instance on record in which a master attempted to deprive his slave of these hard-earned gains. The slave can oblige his master to manu-

6 Koster, *Travels in Brazil*, II, 189–215, 238–243.

mit him, on tendering to him the sum for which he was first purchased, or the price for which he might be sold, if that price is higher than what the slave was worth at the time he was first bought. This regulation, like every one that is framed in favour of slaves, is liable to be evaded, and the master sometimes does refuse to manumit a valuable slave: and no appeal is made by the sufferer, owing to the state of law in that country, which renders it almost impossible for the slave to gain a hearing; and likewise this acquiescence in the injustice of the master proceeds from the dread, that if he was not to succeed, he would be punished, and that his life might be rendered more miserable than it was before. Consequently a great deal depends upon the inclinations of the master, who will, however, be very careful in refusing to manumit, owing to the well-known opinion of every priest in favour of this regulation, to the feelings of the individuals of his own class in society, and to those of the lower orders of people: and likewise he will be afraid of losing his slave. He may escape with his money: and the master will then run much risk of never seeing him again, particularly if the individual is a creole slave. In general, therefore, no doubts are urged, when application is made for manumission by a slave to his master; who is indeed oftentimes prepared for it by the habits of industry and regularity of his slave, and by common report among the other slaves and free persons upon the estate, that the individual in question is scraping together a sum of money for this purpose. The master might indeed deprive the slave of the fruits of his labours: but this is never thought of; because the slave preserves his money in a secret place, or has entrusted it to some person upon whom he can depend, and would suffer any punishment rather than disclose the spot in which his wealth lies concealed. A still more forcible reason than any other, for the forbearance of the master, is to be found in the dread of acting against public opinion: in the shame which would follow the commission of such an act; and perhaps the natural goodness which exists in almost every human being, would make him shun such gross injustice, would make him avoid such a deed of baseness.

A slave is often permitted by his owner to seek a master more to his liking; for this purpose a note is given, declaring that the bearer has leave to enter into the service of any one, upon the price which the master demands being paid by the purchaser. With this the slave applies to any individual of property whom he may wish to serve; owing to having heard a good report of his character towards his slaves, or from any other cause. This is a frequent practice; and at least admits the possibility of escape from a severe state of bondage to one that is less irksome.

A considerable number of slaves are manumitted at the death of their masters: and indeed some persons of large property fail not to set at liberty a few of them during their own lifetime. A deed of manumission, however simply it may be drawn out, cannot be set aside. A register of these papers is preserved at the office of every notary-public by which any distress that might be occasioned by the loss of the originals is provided against; for the copy, of course, holds good in law. A slave who has brought into the world, and has reared ten children, ought to be free, for so the law ordains. But this regulation is generally evaded: and besides, the number of children is too great for many women to be benefited by it. The price of a new-born child is 5£ (20,000 *mil-reis*) and the master is obliged to manumit the infant at the baptismal font, on the sum being presented. In this manner, a considerable number of persons are set at liberty; for the smallness of the price enables many freemen who have had connections with female slaves to manumit their offspring; and instances occur of the sponsors performing this most laudable act. Not infrequently female slaves apply to persons of consideration to become sponsors to their children, in the hopes that the pride of these will be too great to allow of their godchildren remaining in slavery. Thus by their own exertions, by the favour of their masters, and by other means, the individuals who gain their freedom annually, are very numerous.

The comforts of slaves in different situations are widely disproportionate. Whilst some are doomed to an existence of excessive toil and misery, from the nature of their occupations and the characters of their masters, others lead a comparatively easy life. It is true, that in countries of which the workmen are free, the daily labour is unequally divided: but their wages are proportioned accordingly: and as each man is a free agent, he seeks that employment to which his bodily and mental powers are befitted. The slave is purchased for a certain purpose; and is to follow the line of life which his master has chalked out for him.

He is not to be occupied in that which he would himself prefer, or at any rate his wishes are not consulted upon the subject. The price for which a slave is to be obtained, and the convenience of the purchaser are oftener consulted, than the fitness of his bodily strength to the labour which it is his lot to be ordered to perform. Besides the obligation of following an unsuitable trade, or at any rate of following one which he has not chosen, he has to endure the still incomparably greater grievance of bearing with a tyrannical, an inconsiderate, or a peevish master, whose commands are not to be called in question, whose will is absolute, and from whom the possibility of appeal is far removed, and that of redress placed at a still greater distance. Masters are punished by the payment of fines, for cruelty to their slaves, if any account of such behaviour should reach the ear of the Ouvidor of the province. But I never heard of punishment having been carried farther than this trifling manner of correction. The emoluments which proceed from this mode of chastising the offenders, weigh heavily in its favour. The injury which the slave has received is not, I am afraid, the only cause which urges the exaction of the stipulated penalty; of this the slave does not receive any part.

All slaves in Brazil follow the religion of their masters; and notwithstanding the impure state in which the Christian church exists in that country, still such are the beneficent effects of the Christian religion, that these, its adopted children, are improved by it to an infinite degree; and the slave who attends to the strict observance of religious ceremonies, invariably proves to be a good servant. The Africans, who are imported from Angola, are baptized in lots before they leave their own shores: and on their arrival in Brazil they are to learn the doctrines of the church, and the duties of the religion into which they have entered. These bear the mark of the royal crown upon their breasts, which denotes that they have undergone the ceremony of baptism, and likewise that the king's duty has been paid upon them. The slaves which are imported from other parts of the coast of Africa, arrive in Brazil unbaptized, and before the ceremony of making them Christians can be performed upon them, they must be taught certain prayers, for the acquirement of which one year is allowed to the master, before he is obliged to present the slave at the parish church. The law is not always strictly adhered to as to the time, but it is never evaded altogether. The religion of the master teaches him that it would be extremely sinful to allow his slave to remain a

heathen: and indeed the Portuguese and Brazilians have too much religious feeling to let
them neglect any of the ordinances of their
church. The slave himself likewise wishes to be
made a Christian; for his fellow-bondmen will,
otherwise, in every squabble or trifling disagreement with him, close their string of opprobrious
epithets with the name of *pagão* (pagan). The
unbaptized negro feels that he is considered as
an inferior being: and although he may not be
aware of the value which the whites place upon
baptism, still he knows that the stigma for
which he is upbraided, will be removed by it;
and therefore he is desirous of being made equal
to his companions. The Africans who have
been long imported, imbibe a Catholic feeling;
and appear to forget that they were once in the
same situation themselves. The slaves are not
asked whether they will be baptized or not.
Their entrance into the Catholic church is
treated as a thing of course: and indeed they
are not considered as members of society, but
rather as brute animals, until they can lawfully
go to mass, confess their sins, and receive the
sacrament.

The slaves have their religious brotherhoods
as well as the free persons: and the ambition of
the slave very generally aims at being admitted
into one of these, and at being made one of the
officers and directors of the concerns of the
brotherhood. Even some of the money which
the industrious slave is collecting for the purpose of purchasing his freedom, will oftentimes
be brought out of its concealment for the decoration of a saint, that the donor may become of
importance in the society to which he belongs.
The negroes have one invocation of the Virgin
(or I might almost say one virgin) which is peculiarly their own. Our Lady of the Rosary is
even sometimes painted with a black face and
hands. It is in this manner that the slaves are
led to place their attention upon an object in
which they soon take an interest, but from which
no injury can proceed towards themselves, nor
can any through its means be by them inflicted
upon their masters. Their ideas are removed
from any thought of the customs of their own
country; and are guided into a channel of a
totally different nature, and completely unconnected with what is practised there. The election of a King of Congo by the individuals who
come from that part of Africa, seems indeed as
if it would give them a bias towards the customs
of their native soil. But the Brazilian Kings of
Congo worship Our Lady of the Rosary; and are

dressed in the dress of white men. They and
their subjects dance, it is true, after the manner
of their creole blacks, and mulattos, all of whom
dance after the same manner: and these dances
are now as much the national dances of Brazil,
as they are of Africa. The Portuguese language
is spoken by the slaves: and their own dialects
are allowed to lie dormant until they are by
many of them quite forgotten. No compulsion
is resorted to, to make them embrace the habits
of their masters: but their ideas are insensibly
led to imitate and adopt them. The masters at
the same time imbibe some of the customs of
their slaves; and thus the superior and his dependent are brought nearer to each other. I
doubt not that the system of baptizing the newly
imported negroes, proceeded rather from the
bigotry of the Portuguese in former times than
from any political plan: but it has had the most
beneficial effects. The slaves are rendered more
tractable. Besides being better men and women,
they become more obedient servants. They are
brought under the control of the priesthood:
and even if this was the only additional hold
which was gained by their entrance into the
church, it is a great engine of power which is
thus brought into action.

But in no circumstance has the introduction
of the Christian religion among the slaves been
of more service than in the change which it has
wrought in the men regarding the treatment of
their women, and in the conduct of the females
themselves. . . .

The slaves of Brazil are regularly married according to the forms of the Catholic church.
The banns are published in the same manner as
those of free persons: and I have seen many
happy couples (as happy at least as slaves can
be) with large families of children rising around
them. The masters encourage marriages among
their slaves; for it is from these lawful connections that they can expect to increase the number of their creoles. A slave cannot marry without the consent of his master; for the vicar will
not publish the banns of marriage without this
sanction. It is likewise permitted that slaves
should marry free persons. If the woman is in
bondage, the children remain in the same state:
but if the man is a slave, and she is free, their
offspring is also free. A slave cannot be married until the requisite prayers have been learnt,
the nature of confession be understood, and the
Sacrament can be received. Upon the estates
the master or manager is soon made acquainted
with the predilections of the slaves for each

other; and these being discovered, marriage is forthwith determined upon, and the irregular proceedings are made lawful. In towns there is more licentiousness among the negroes, as there is among all other classes of men. The passion of love is supposed only to exist in a certain state of civilization, and this may be granted without at the same time declaring that negroes are incapable of lasting attachment, without supposing that the regard of each sex is mere animal desire, unconnected with predilection. That species of affection which is heightened until personal possession is almost forgotten, doubtless is not felt by human beings who are in a state of barbarism; but still a negro may be attached: he may fix upon one object in preference to all others. That this is the case, I can vouch. I have known and have heard of many instances in which punishments and other dangers have been braved to visit a chosen one; in which journeys by night have been made after a day of fatigue; in which great constancy has been shewn, and a determination that the feelings of the heart shall not be controlled.

The great proportion of men upon many of the estates, produce, of necessity, most mischievous consequences. A supply is requisite to keep up the number of labourers. The women are more liable to misconduct, and the men imbibe unsettled habits. But if an adequate number of females are placed upon the estate, and the slaves are trained and taught in the manner which is practised upon well-regulated plantations, the negroes will be as correct in their behaviour, as any other body of men: and perhaps their conduct may be less faulty than that of other descriptions of persons, who have less to occupy their time, though their education may be infinitely superior. That many men and many women will be licentious, has been and is still the lot of human nature, and not the peculiar fault of the much injured race of which I speak. . . .

As the voyage from the coast of Africa to the opposite shores of South America is usually short, for the winds are subject to little variation, and the weather is usually fine, the vessels which are employed in this traffic are generally speaking small, and are not of the best construction. The situation of captain or master of a slave ship is considered of secondary rank in the Portuguese merchant-service: and the persons who are usually so occupied, are vastly inferior to the generality of the individuals who command the large and regular trading vessels be-

tween Europe and Brazil. The slave ships were formerly crowded to a most shocking degree; nor was there any means of preventing this. But a law has been passed for the purpose of restricting the number of persons for each vessel. However, I more than suspect, that no attention is paid to this regulation. . . . The rules of the port direct that they shall be disembarked, and taken to St. Amaro, which is an airy spot, and sufficiently distant from the town to prevent the admittance of any infectious disorder, if such should exist among the newly-imported negroes; and yet the place is at a convenient distance for the purchasers, St. Amaro being situated immediately opposite to Recife, upon the island bank of the expanse of waters which is formed by the tide, on the land site of the town. However, like many others, this excellent arrangement is not attended to: and even if the slaves are removed for a few days to St. Amaro, they are soon conveyed back to the town. Here they are placed in the streets before the doors of the owners, regardless of decency, of humanity, and of due attention to the general health of the town. The small pox, the yaws, and other complaints have thus frequent opportunities of spreading. It is probable, that if the climate was not so very excellent as it is, this practice would be discontinued; but if it was not put a stop to, and the country was subject to pestilential complaints, the town would not be habitable.

In the day-time, some of the streets of Recife are in part lined with miserable beings, who are lying or sitting promiscuously upon the footpath, sometimes to the number of two or three hundred. The males wear a small piece of blue cloth round their waists, which is drawn between the legs and fastened behind. The females are allowed a larger piece of cloth, which is worn as a petticoat: and sometimes a second portion is given to them, for the purpose of covering the upper parts of the body. The stench which is created by these assemblages is almost intolerable to one who is unaccustomed to their vicinity. . . . These people do not, however, seem to feel their situation, any farther than that it is uncomfortable. Their food consists of salt meat, the flour of the mandioc, beans, and plantains occasionally. The victuals for each day are cooked in the middle of the street in an enormous caldron. At night they are driven into one or more warehouses: and a driver stands to count them as they pass. They are locked in: and the door is again opened at daybreak on the following morning. The wish of these wretched creatures to escape from this state of inaction and discomfort is manifested upon the appearance of a purchaser. They start up willingly, to be placed in the row for the purpose of being viewed and handled like cattle: and on being chosen they give signs of much pleasure. I have had many opportunities of seeing slaves bought; for my particular friends at Recife lived opposite to slave-dealers. I never saw any demonstrations of grief at parting from each other: but I attribute this to the dread of punishment, if there had been any flow of feeling, and to a resigned or rather despairing sensation, which checks any shew of grief, and which has prepared them for the worst, by making them indifferent to whatever may occur: besides, it is not often that a family is brought over together; the separation of relatives and friends has taken place in Africa. It is among the younger part of the assemblage of persons who are exposed for sale, that pleasure is particularly visible at the change of situation, in being removed from the streets of the town; the negroes of more advanced age do whatever the driver desires, usually with an unchanged countenance. I am afraid that very little care is taken to prevent the separation of relatives who may chance to come over in the same ship: and any consideration on this point lies entirely with the owner of the cargo. A species of relationship exists between the individuals who have been imported in the same ship. They call each other *malungos:* and this term is much regarded among them. The purchaser gives to each of his newly bought slaves a large piece of baize and a straw hat; and as soon as possible marches them off to his estate. I have often in travelling met with many parties going up to their new homes, and have observed that they were usually cheerful; — any thing is better than to sit at the door of the slave merchant in Recife. The new master, too, does every thing in his power to keep them in good humour at first, whatever his conduct may afterwards be towards them.

The slaves which are usually brought to Pernambuco, are known under the names of Angola, Congo, Rebolo, Anjico, Gabam, and Mosambique. These last have only been imported of late years, owing, I rather imagine, to the difficulty with which slaves have been obtained on the western coast of Africa, caused by the vigilance of the British cruisers in that quarter, and the vexations to which some of the slave ships have been liable from detention, although they were ultimately suffered to proceed on their voyages.

The Angola negroes make the best slaves. Many of them have been in bondage in their own country: and therefore to these the change is for the better. Some of them have even served the whites in the city of Loanda, which is the principal Portuguese settlement upon the coast of Africa. But others were free in Angola, and consequently to these is allotted a life of disappointment and vexation, whenever they remember their own country. The negroes from Angola are however usually tractable; and may be taught to perform the menial services of a house or stable without much pains being taken with them; and they often shew great attachment, fidelity, and honesty. The Angola negroes are those who most commonly exert themselves to purchase their own freedom. The Congo negroes partake much of the character of the Angolans, being equally tractable: but they are steadier, and are particularly adapted to the regular routine of field labour. They are less quick in their movements than the Angolans; and do not seem to be so spirited and courageous; they obtain in a short period a knowledge of the Portuguese language. The Rebolos can scarcely in persons be distinguished from the two former, being stoutly made, and not tall. They have a black skin; but it is not shining; and the features are flat. They seem to be a branch of the Angolans and Congos: but they are more obstinate, and more subject to despond than the others. These three tribes appear to have belonged originally to the same nation; for many parts of their character are similar; their persons are of the same mould; and the dialects of each sufficiently resemble each other to be understood by all the three.

The Anjico negroes shew many marks of being of another nation. They make good slaves, if they are well treated, and are yet preserved under due control. They are difficult to train; and bear a heavy yoke impatiently. There is in them much independence of character, if they dared to shew it. There is also much cunning, and the desire and capability of over-reaching. Their persons are tall, and well formed. Their skins are of a glossy black; their eyes are expressive: and their countenances plainly denote, that it is not by their own will that they continue in slavery. They are not, however, numerous. Great neatness is shown by them in their household arrangements, and they often exert themselves to obtain money; but they are less careful and prudent than the nations of which I have already treated. All the Anjico negroes have three gashes on each cheek, which are cut in a circular form from the ear to the mouth.

The *Gabam,* or Gaboon negroes, have not been very long introduced: and from the well known general character of the nation, they are sold at a reduced price. I have heard many persons state that they are cannibals. They appear to be in a still more savage state than any of the former-mentioned nations; and are much given to despondency and consequent suicide. Indeed ten and even twenty that have been purchased together have, in some instances, in the course of a short period, all died from despair, or have put an end to their lives in a more summary manner. It is with difficulty that the Gaboons can be taught to perform any labour above that of the simplest description; and sometimes they remain for years unbaptized, from the great trouble which is required in making them articulate any sounds to which they have not been accustomed. Yet it is rather that they *will* not be taught, than they *cannot* learn; for I have heard many planters say, that if a Gabam negro can be made cheerful, and be induced to take an interest in those persons who are around him and his occupations, he becomes a most useful and intelligent slave. The *Gabam* negroes are tall and handsome: and their skins are very black and shining. The features of many of them are good, being much less flat and blunt than those of their countrymen in general.

The Mosambique negroes are a poor and ugly race of beings, languid and inactive, and subject to despondency. Their colour inclines to brown: but still they have completely the negro features. As the price of these slaves is much below that of any other description of negroes, some of the planters have taken them on trial: but they are said to have many of the bad qualities of the Gaboons, without their hardiness.

A negro will sometimes tell his master, that he is determined to die, and too often the effects of his resolve begin shortly afterwards to be perceived. He becomes thin, loses his appetite, and dies almost a skeleton. One of the means which it is very generally said that these miserable beings employ for the purpose of destroying themselves, is that of eating considerable quantities of lime and earth, which either produces emaciation or dropsy. But it is strange that a habit of eating lime and earth should be contracted in some instances by African and likewise by creole children, and as frequently by free children as by those who are in slavery. This practice is treated as if it were a disorder: but it is accounted a habit, which, by attention from those who have the charge of the children — in watching and punishing them, may be conquered without the aid of medicine. I know of some instances in which no medical treatment was deemed necessary: but the individuals recovered by means of chastisement and constant vigilance. It is a subject upon which I was often led to converse: and I discovered that most of the free-born families were acquainted with the practice from experience among their own children, or those of their neighbours; and that they always considered it as a habit and not as a disease. Among adults, however, slaves are infinitely more subject to it than free persons.

Pernambuco has never experienced any serious revolt among the slaves; but at Bahia there have been several commotions. I believe that Bahia contains fewer free people than Pernambuco in proportion to the number of slaves. But I cannot avoid attributing the quietude of the latter in some measure to the circumstance of a few of the Gold Coast negroes being imported into it, whilst at Bahia the principal stock of slaves is from that part of Africa. It is by the *Mina* negroes, in Bahia, that the revolts have been made, and by the *Koromanties,* in Jamaica, in 1760. These are, I believe, the same people under different names; and they are represented as possessing great firmness of mind and body, and ferociousness of disposition.

The Obeah-men, of the Columbian islands [the West Indies], and the *Mandingueiros* of Brazil, are evidently, from their practices, the same description of persons. The religion which the Brazilian slaves are taught, has likewise a salutary effect upon this point; for it tends to lessen or entirely removes the faith which was previously entertained by the Africans respecting the incantations of their countrymen. The superstitions of their native land are replaced by others of a more harmless nature. The dreadful effects of faith in the *Obeah*-men, which sometimes occur in the British colonies, are not experienced in Brazil from the *Mandingueiros.* Belief in their powers is certainly not extinguished: and indeed even some or the creoles imbibe a notion of the efficacy of their spells: but the effects of these are not generally felt. . . .

From the vastness of the country, it might be supposed that if a slave escapes from his master, the chances would be against his return: but this is not the case. The Africans particularly are generally brought back. They are soon distinguished by their manner of speaking the Portuguese language; and if any one of them cannot give a good account of himself, he will not be allowed to remain long unmolested; for the profit arising from the apprehension of a runaway slave is considerable. Besides, the manumitted African generally continues to reside in the neighbourhood of the estate upon which he has served as a slave; so that when a man of this description, that is, an African, comes without being known, to settle in a district, suspicion immediately arises that he is not free. The manumitted creoles remove to where they are not known; because they do not wish that the state in which they were born should reach their new place of residence. An African must have been brought to Brazil as a slave: and therefore his situation of a freeman proves that his character is good, or he could not have obtained his liberty. But a creole may have been born free, and consequently his former state as a slave wishes to conceal. Creole slaves, and more especially mulattos, often do escape, and are never afterwards heard of by their masters: but even these are sometimes brought back. . . .

Some of the negroes who escape, determine to shun the haunts of man. They conceal themselves in the woods, instead of attempting to be received into some distant village as free persons. They form huts, which are called *mocambos,* in the most unfrequented spots; and live upon the game and fruit which their places of retreat afford. These persons sometimes assemble to the number of ten or twelve, and then their dislodgement is difficult; for their acquaintance with the woods around give them the advantage over any party which may be sent to attack them. Sometimes a whole neighbourhood is disturbed by one of these communities, who rob the provision grounds, steal calves, lambs and poultry; and stories are told of the Gabam negroes stealing children.

The slaves of Maranhão are in a less favourable state than those of Pernambuco, on the whole. But the system which is followed repecting them is radically the same. Their food is usually rice, which is said to disagree with the most of the nations which come from Africa; and the treatment which they receive upon the estates in that part of the country, is said to be more rigorous; but of this I cannot myself speak, for I had no opportunities of judging.

Negroes who are decidedly of incorrigible character, are shipped from Pernambuco to Maranhão: and though the cause for which these transportations are made, is well known, they are often sold to great advantage. Nothing tends so much to keep a slave in awe, as the threat of sending him to Maranhão, or to Pará.

That the general character of persons who are in a state of slavery should be amiable, and that goodness should predominate, is not to be expected. But we ought rather to be surprised at the existence of that degree of virtue which is to be found among those who are reduced to a situation of so much misery. Slaves are much inclined to pilfer, and particularly towards their masters this is very frequent. Indeed many of them scarcely think that they are acting improperly in so doing. Drunkenness is common among them. A direct answer is not easily obtained from a slave: but the information which is required is learnt by means of four or five questions put in various ways. The necessity for this is frequently caused by stupidity, or from ignorance of the language in which the slave is addressed, rather than from any wish to deceive. It is in their behaviour to their families and companions, that the good part of the human being is displayed: and natural enough it is that it should be so. The negroes shew much attachment to their wives and children, to their other relations if they should chance to have any, and to their *malungos* or fellow passengers from Africa. The respect which is paid to old age, it is extremely pleasing to witness. Superannuated Africans, upon the estates, are never suffered to want any comforts with which it is in the power of their fellow slaves to supply them. The old negroes are addressed by the term of pai and mai, father and mother. The masters likewise add this term to the name of their older slaves, when speaking to them. That the generality of the slaves should shew great attachment to their masters, is not to be expected: why should they? The connection between the two descriptions of persons, is not one of love and harmony, of good producing gratitude, of esteem and respect; it is one of hatred and discord, of distrust, and of continual suspicion; one of which the evil is so enormous, that if any proper feelings exist in those who are supposed to benefit from it, and in those who suffer under it, they proceed from our nature, and not from the system.

It will be seen from the above statement, that the slaves of those parts of Brazil which I have had opportunities of seeing, are more favourably situated than those of the Columbian islands [the West Indies]. But still they are slaves: and in this word is included, great misery, great degradation, great misfortune.

4. THE SOCIAL CONSEQUENCES OF SLAVERY

A forerunner of the Brazilian abolitionists of a later day, Luiz dos Santos Vilhena, regius professor of Greek in Baía from 1787 to 1798, boldly assailed the system of slave labor on which the sugar culture of his province was based. Slavery, and not an enervating tropical climate, he affirmed, was responsible for the dissolute manners and idleness of the Portuguese living in Brazil. The following excerpt from his book on Brazil, written in the form of letters to a Portuguese friend, illustrates the vigor and forthrightness of his attack.[7]

THE NEGRO WOMEN and a majority of the mulatto women as well, for whom honor is a delusion, a word signifying nothing, are commonly the first to corrupt their master's sons, giving them their first lessons in sexual license, in which from childhood on they are engulfed; and from this presently arises a veritable troop of little mulattoes whose influence on family life is most pernicious. But it often happens that those who are called the old masters, to distinguish them from their sons, are the very ones who set a bad example for their families through their conduct with their female slaves, giving pain to their wives and perhaps causing their death. Frequently their black favorites contrive to put the legitimate children out of the way, to avoid any difficulties in the event of the master's death.

There are other men who never marry, simply because they cannot get out of the clutches of the harpies in whose power they have been since childhood. There are ecclesiastics, and not a few, who from old and evil habit, forgetting their character and station, live a disorderly life with mulatto and Negro women, by whom they have sons who inherit their property; in this and other ways many of the most valuable properties of Brazil pass into the hands of haughty, arrogant vagabond mulattoes, to the great detriment of the State. This is a matter well deserving of His Majesty's attention, for if these sugar mills and great plantations are not prevented

[7] Luiz dos Santos Vilhena, *Recopilação de Noticias Soteropolitanas e Brasilicas*, Baía, 2 vols., 1921–1922, edited by Braz do Amaral, I, 138–142. (Excerpt translated by the editor.)

from falling into the hands of these mulattoes, who ordinarily are profligate and set little store by these splendid properties, having come by them so easily, in due time they will all fall into their hands and be ruined, as has happened to the greater part of those that came into the possession of such owners.

You must also know that the passion for having Negroes and mulattoes in the house is so strong here that only death removes them from the household in which they were born; there are many families that have sixty, seventy, and more superfluous persons within their doors. I speak of the city, for in the country this would not be remarkable. All this black brood, whether mulattoes or Negroes, are treated with the greatest indulgence, and that is why they are all vagabonds, insolent, bold, and ungrateful. . . .

The Negroes are harmful in still another way to the State of Brazil. For since all the servile labors and mechanical arts are in their charge, few are the mulattoes, and fewer still the white men, who will deign to perform such tasks. . . .

It has been observed that he who comes here as servant to some public official continues to be a good servant until he realizes that the work he does for his master is performed in other households by Negroes and mulattoes, whereupon he begins to plead with his master to find him some public employment not open to Negroes. Some masters yield to their entreaties, finding themselves so badgered and badly served that they are driven to distraction. But if they delay in finding them jobs, their servants leave them, preferring to be vagabonds and go about dying from hunger, or to become soldiers and sometimes bandits, to working for an honored master who pays them well and supports and cherishes them — and this only to avoid having to do what Negroes do in other households.

The same occurs with the serving women who accompany the ladies that come to Brazil. The same prejudice induces them to take to the streets; they prefer suffering all the resulting miseries to living in a home where they are honored and sheltered.

The girls of this country are of such disposition that the daughter of the poorest, most abject individual, the most neglected little mulatto wench, would rather go to the scaffold than serve a Duchess, if one were to be found in this country; that is the reason for the great number of ruined and disgraced women in this city.

The whites born in this land must either be soldiers, merchants, notaries, clerks, court officials, judges, or Treasury officials or else hold some other public occupation that is barred to Negroes, such as surgeon, apothecary, pilot, shipmaster or sea-captain, warehouse clerk (*caxeiro do trapiche*), and so forth. A few others are employed as sculptors, goldsmiths, and the like.

Many used to attend the school established by His Majesty in this city, a school that once boasted of excellent students who prepared for the Church and other learned professions. But when their fathers saw that the school was the fixed target at which the recruiting officers and soldiers aimed their shots, and that their sons were being snatched away for garrison duty, against which their immunities, privileges, and exemptions availed them nothing, they became convinced that the State had no further need of ecclesiastics or members of other learned professions . . . , and decided that they would not sacrifice their sons by exposing them to the enmity of autocratic and thoughtless soldiers. . . .

Is it not obvious that the inactivity of the whites is the reason for the laziness of the blacks?

Why should a man not dig the ground in Brazil who in Portugal lived solely by his hoe? Why should one not labor here who in Portugal knew nothing more than to put one hand to the plough-handle and another to the goad?

Why should a man go about here with his body upright who came here bent with labor?

Why should he who knows only obedience want only to command? Why should he who was always a plebeian strut about with the air of a noble?

How plentifully would these blessed lands produce, dear friend, if they were cultivated by other hands than those of savage Negroes, who do no more than scratch their surface!

What great profits they would yield if cultivated by sensible and intelligent men, and if sound views of political economy changed the prevailing system!

No land could boast of greater opulence and plenty than Baía if it were ruled wisely, and if henceforth admittance were denied to slaves, the causes of its backwardness and poverty.

Part Six

The Independence of Latin America

MANY FACTORS COMBINED TO CAUSE the Latin-American Wars of Independence. The discontent of the creole class with Spanish restrictions on its economic and political activity, the influence of French and English liberal doctrines, the powerful example of the American and French Revolutions, and foreign interest in the liquidation of the Spanish Empire in America — all played a part in producing the great upheaval.

The immediate cause of the Spanish-American revolutions was the occupation of Spain by French troops in 1808. Napoleon's intervention provoked an uprising of the Spanish people, headed by *juntas,* or local governing committees. Creole leaders in the colonies soon took advantage of Spain's distresses. Professing loyalty to "the beloved Ferdinand VII," a prisoner in France, they forced the removal of allegedly unreliable Spanish officials and formed governing juntas to rule in the name of the captive king. Their claims of loyalty did not convince the Spanish authorities, and fighting soon broke out between patriots and loyalists.

Simón Bolívar led the struggle for independence in northern South America, and José de San Martín directed the military efforts of the patriots to the south. In 1822 the enigmatic San Martín resigned command of his army, leaving to Bolívar the task of completing the conquest of Peru, the last Spanish stronghold in the New World. The battle of Ayacucho, won by Sucre, virtually ended the war. Brazil achieved a relatively peaceful separation from Portugal in 1822, under the leadership of Prince Pedro and his adviser José Bonifacio de Andrada.

The Mexican revolution, initiated in 1810 by the creole priest Manuel Hidalgo, was continued after his death by another liberal curate, José María Morelos. These men attempted to combine the creole ideal of independence with a program of social reform in behalf of the Indian and mixed-blood masses. The radicalism of Hidalgo and Morelos alienated many creole conservatives, who joined the royalist forces to suppress the revolt. Later, fearing the loss of their privileges as a result of the liberal revolution of 1820 in Spain, the same conservative coalition schemed to bring about a separation from the mother country. They found an agent in the ambitious creole officer Agustín de Iturbide. His Plan of Iguala offered a compromise solution temporarily acceptable to liberals and conservatives, to creoles and many Spaniards. Slight loyalist opposition was swiftly overcome, and in September, 1822, a national congress proclaimed the independence of the Mexican Empire.

XXI

The Background of the Wars of Independence

IN THE CLOSING YEARS of the eighteenth century a small number of Spanish-Americans began to dream of independence and even to work for the overthrow of Spanish rule. Most of them came from the wealthy and cultivated creole class, which had become increasingly resentful of Spanish restrictions on its economic and political activity.

From the writings of French and English philosophers enlightened creoles learned to regard the colonial system as unjust and irrational and to believe that all rightful authority derived from the people. The success of the North American and French Revolutions encouraged a few daring spirits to organize conspiracies, which were, however, easily discovered and crushed by the Spanish Government. Creole timidity and political inexperience and the indifference of the masses would probably have long delayed the achievement of Spanish-American independence if external factors had not hastened its coming.

British efforts to conquer new markets for England's expanding industry and commerce weakened Spain's hold on her American possessions. The British invasions of La Plata (1806–1807), defeated by the people of Buenos Aires without Spanish aid, placed arms in creole hands and inspired the *porteños* with confidence in their own powers. French attempts to dominate Spain influenced still more decisively the fate of the Spanish colonies. In 1808 Napoleon forced the abdication of Charles IV and his son Ferdinand VII, and placed his brother Joseph on the Spanish throne. To these insults the Spanish people responded with a great insurrection against French occupation troops. Local juntas arose in the regions under patriot control. Later a central junta assumed leadership of the movement in the name of the captive King Ferdinand VII.

In the colonies the creole radicals watched the course of events in Spain with secret satisfaction. Confident that the French armies would crush all Spanish opposition, they prepared to take power into their own hands under the pretence of loyalty to Ferdinand. Early in 1810 news reached the colonies that French armies had overrun Andalusia and were threatening Cadiz, last stronghold of the Spanish cause. Swiftly the creole leaders moved into action. In Caracas, Buenos Aires, Bogotá, and Santiago they organized popular demonstrations that compelled the royal authorities to yield control to local juntas dominated by the creole element. But their hopes of a relatively peaceful transition to independence were doomed to failure.

1. THE CLEAVAGE WITHIN

By the close of the colonial period the creoles and peninsular Spaniards had become two mutually hostile castes, differing in their occupations and ideas. The Spaniards justified their privileged status by reference to the alleged indolence and incapacity of the natives. The creoles vented their spleen by describing the Europeans as mean and grasping parvenus. The pro-Spanish historian Alamán offers many revealing details of the cleavage within the colonial upper class in his classic History of Mexico.[1]

[1] Alamán, *Historia de Méjico*, I, 8–14. (Excerpt translated by the editor.)

THE NUMBER of peninsular Spaniards who resided in New Spain in 1808 was in the neighborhood of 70,000. They occupied nearly all the principal posts in the administration, the Church, the judiciary, and the army; commerce was almost exclusively in their hands; and they possessed large fortunes, consisting of cash, which they employed in various lines of business and in all kinds of farms and properties. Those who were not officeholders had generally left their country at a very early age, belonged to poor but honest families, especially those who came from the Basque provinces and the mountains of Santander, and were for the most part of good character. Since they aimed to make their fortune, they were ready to gain it by every kind of productive labor; neither great distances, perils, nor unhealthy climates frightened them. Some came to serve in the house of some relative or friend of the family; others were befriended by their countrymen. All began as clerks, subject to a severe discipline, and from the first learned to regard work and thrift as the only road to wealth. There was some relaxation of manners in Mexico City and Vera Cruz, but in all the cities of the interior, no matter how rich or populous, the clerks in each house were bound to a very narrow and almost monastic system of order and regularity. This Spartan type of education made of the Spaniards living in America a species of men not to be found in Spain herself, and one which America will never see again.

As their fortunes improved or their merits won recognition, they were often given a daughter of the house in marriage, particularly if they were relatives — or they might set up their own establishments; but all married creole girls, for very few of the women there had come from Spain, and these were generally the wives of officeholders. With financial success and kinship to the respectable families of the town came respect, municipal office, and influence, which sometimes degenerated into absolute dominance. Once established in this manner, the Spaniards never thought of returning to their country, and they considered that their only proper concerns were the furthering of their business affairs, the advancement of their communities, and the comfort and dignity of their families. Thus every wealthy Spaniard came to represent a fortune formed for the benefit of the country, a prosperous family rooted in Mexican soil, or, if he left no family, a source of pious and beneficial foundations designed to shelter orphans and succor the needy and disabled — foundations of which Mexico City presents so many examples. These fortunes were formed through the arduous labors of the field, the long practice of commerce, or the more risky enterprise of the mines. Although these occupations did not usually permit rapid enrichment, the economy practiced by these families, who lived frugally, without luxurious furniture or clothing, helped them to attain this goal. Thus all the towns, even the less important ones, included a number of families of modest fortunes, whose parsimony did not prevent the display of liberality on occasions of public calamity or when the needs of the state required it. . . .

The creoles rarely preserved these economical habits or pursued the professions that had enriched their fathers. The latter, amid the comforts that their wealth afforded, likewise failed to subject their sons to the severe discipline in which they themselves had been formed. Wishing to give their sons a more brilliant education, suitable to their place in society, they gave them a training that led to the Church or to the practice of law, or left them in a state of idleness and liberty that was deleterious to their character. Some sent their sons to the seminary of Vergara, in the province of Guipuzcoa in Spain, after that institution had won renown as a school providing general instruction, and if this practice had become general it not only would have contributed greatly to the diffusion of useful knowledge in America but would have aided in formation of more durable bonds between Spanish America and the mother country. From the other and pernicious kind of rearing resulted this state of affairs: The European clerks, married to the master's daughters, carried on his business and became the principal support of the family, increasing their wives' inheritances, whereas the creole sons wasted their substance and in a few years were ruined — at which time they looked about for some trifling desk job that would barely keep them alive in preference to an active and laborious life that would assure them an independent existence.[2] The classical education that some of them had received, and the aristocratic manner that they affected in their days of idleness and plenty, made them scornful of the Europeans, who seemed to them mean and covetous because they were economical and active; they regarded these men as inferiors because they engaged in trades and occupations which they considered unworthy of the station to which their own fathers had raised them. Whether it was the effect of

[2] Hence the well-known proverb: "The father a merchant, the son a gentleman, the grandson a beggar," which characterized in a few words this transition from wealth gained by labor to idleness and prodigality, and from that to misery.

This prodigality had a long history. Balbuena, in his *Grandeza mejicana*, a poem written in 1603, includes among the circumstances that made life in Mexico City pleasanter than anywhere else in the world,

"That prodigal giving of every ilk,
    Without a care how great the cost,
    Of pearls, of gold, of silver, and of silk. . . ."

this vicious training or the influence of a climate that conduced to laxity and effeminacy, the creoles were generally indolent and negligent; of sharp wits, rarely tempered by judgment and reflection; quick to undertake an enterprise but heedless of the means necessary to carry it out; giving themselves with ardor to the present, but giving no thought to the future; prodigal in times of good fortune and resigned and long-suffering in adversity. The effect of these unfortunate propensities was the brief duration of their wealth; the assiduous efforts of the Europeans to form fortunes and pass them on to their children may be compared to the bottomless barrel of the Danaïdes, which no amount of water could fill. It resulted from this that the Spanish race in America, in order to remain prosperous and opulent, required a continuous accretion of European Spaniards who came to form new families, while those established by their predecessors fell into oblivion and indigence.

Although the laws did not establish any difference between these two classes of Spaniards, or indeed with respect to the mestizos born to either class by Indian mothers, a distinction came to exist between them in fact. With it arose a declared rivalry that, although subdued for a long time, might be feared to break out with the most serious consequences when the occasion should offer. As has been said, the Europeans held nearly all the high offices,[3] as much because Spanish policy required it as because they had greater opportunity to request and obtain them, being near the fountainhead of all favors. The rare occasions on which creoles secured such high posts occurred through fortunate coincidences or when they went to the Spanish capital to solicit them. Although they held all the inferior posts, which were much more numerous, this only stimulated their ambition to occupy the higher posts as well. Although in the first two centuries after the Conquest the Church offered Americans greater opportunities for advancement, and during that period many obtained[4] bishoprics, canonships, pulpits, and lucrative benefices, their opportunities in this sphere had gradually been curtailed. . . .The Europeans also dominated the cloisters, and in order to avoid the frequent disturbances caused by the rivalry of birth some religious orders had provided for an alternation of offices, electing European prelates in one election and Americans in the next; but as a result of a distinction introduced between the Europeans who had come from Spain with the garb and those who assumed it in America, the former were favored with another term, resulting in two elections of Europeans to one of creoles. If to this preference in administrative and ecclesiastical offices, which was the principal cause of the rivalry between the two classes, are added the fact that . . . the Europeans possessed great riches (which, though the just reward of labor and industry, excited the envy of the Americans . . .); the fact that the wealth and power of the peninsulars sometimes gained them more favor with the fair sex, enabling them to form more advantageous unions; and the fact that all these conditions combined had given them a decided predominance over the creoles — it is not difficult to explain the jealousy and rivalry that steadily grew between them, resulting in a mortal enmity and hatred.

2. THE CRIME OF ANTONIO NARIÑO

Antonio Nariño (1765–1823), a cultivated and wealthy creole of Bogotá, incurred Spanish wrath when he translated and printed on his own press the French Declaration of the Rights of Man (1789). For this subversive activity he was sentenced to imprisonment in Africa for ten years. He lived to become a leader and patriarch of the independence movement in New Granada, and to witness its triumph. The following excerpt is from an official report to the Spanish king on Nariño's trial.[5]

IN THE COURSE of the search that was made among the papers of Nariño, one of the follow-

[3] Of the one hundred and seventy viceroys who governed in America until 1813, only four had been born there — and that by chance, as the sons of officeholders. Three of them were viceroys of Mexico: Don Luis de Velasco, son of the Luis de Velasco who also held that office and died in Mexico in 1564; Don Juan de Acuna, Marquis of Casafuerte, born in Lima, who governed the viceroyalty between 1722 and 1734 and died there, being buried in the church of San Cosme de Mexico; and the Count of Revilla Gigedo, who was born in Havana while his father was captain-general of the island of Cuba, whence he was transferred to the viceroyalty of Mexico. The three were models of probity, capacity, and zeal. Of the six hundred and two captains general and presidents, fourteen had been creoles. . . .

[4] Of the seven hundred and six bishops who held office in Spanish America until 1812, one hundred and five were creoles, although few held miters of the first class. . . .

[5] Eduardo Posada, ed., *El Precursor*, Bogotá, 1903, Appendix, pp. 607–609, 612–614. (Excerpt translated by the editor.)

ing tenor was found: "I have the idea of founding in this city a reading club along the lines of those to be found in some casinos of Venice; the members would meet in a spacious room, and after the expenses of lighting, etc., had been met, the rest would be spent for the purchase of the best newspapers, foreign journals, and other similar periodicals, according to the amount of the subscription. We would meet at certain hours, read the newspapers, criticize them, and converse about various matters, in this way passing some entertaining though useful hours. Members of the society might include Don José María Lozano, Don José Antonio Ricaurte, Don Francisco Zea, Don Francisco Tobar, Don Joaquín Camacho, Dr. Iriarte. . . ."

There was also found among his papers a plan for a study, with various inscriptions to Liberty, Reason, Philosophy, and others, among which the most notable is the following: "He snatched the lightning from the heavens, and the scepter from the hands of tyrants"; and above: "God, not Plato and Franklin," and a chain on a pedestal. Asked about this plan and the inscriptions, he said that it was all in his own handwriting; that the design was a rough sketch that he had made as a plan for his study, some seven or eight months previously; that the inscriptions to Philosophy, Reason, and Minerva were his work, and the others by the authors that he cited. . . .

Asked how he could think of placing in his study at the foot of the picture of Franklin the inscription which said: "He snatched the lightning from the heavens, and the scepter from the hands of tyrants," the second part of which was so scandalous and offensive to all legitimate monarchs, and consequently to Your Majesty, he replied that his attention had been caught by the first part of the inscription, which alluded to the electricity of the skies, in which his interest was well known; that he could see no reason for omitting the second part, knowing that it had been published in France without objection from the royal government; and that he had never imagined that it might be censured as offensive to Your Majesty, whom he regarded as a most humane and just king.

He was asked how he could say this, when in his declaration Don Gabriel José Manzano . . . told how one day, when the accused was in Manzano's store for the purpose of buying a certain article, Manzano had said of its quality "that it was fit for a king," and Nariño had scornfully replied, "Drop that business of kings,"

which sounded very bad to Manzano, and made him believe . . . that the accused sustained sentiments and principles opposed to the legitimate authority of kings, and consequently to that of Your Majesty. He replied that the deposition on which the charge was based was false and calumnious, and that he had not the slightest recollection of the incident. . . .

On July 2, 1795, the prosecutors Berrio and Blaya, on the basis of the facts that emerged from the summary and his confession, charged Nariño and his accomplice Don Diego Espinosa with guilt in having published that seditious book, making most criminal use of the printing press, and demanded that both suffer the appropriate serious penalties which they had incurred under the laws and the royal dispositions. They pointed out that as far as the principal offense of publication was concerned, both had confessed and were convicted, offering no defense that might extenuate or lessen their offense or the malice with which they had committed it, for the sole aim of making five or six hundred pesos could not have moved Nariño to make this clandestine publication, since as treasurer of tithes he had many thousands at his disposal. The prosecutors also pointed out that the body of the offense, the cited book, was not attached to the proceedings, but a sufficient idea of its contents was given in the declaration of Don Francisco Carrasco, who had read it and had it in his possession, and who said that it contained a chapter that said or taught *that it was permissible for a man to do anything that did not injure his fellowmen; that it was permissible, in point of religion, for a man to think freely and express his thoughts, and that this was liberty;* that with respect to the power of kings, it stated *that since their power emanated from the people, the latter could set them up and remove them, and that their power was tyrannical,* and that this was the substance of this book. They said that even brief reflection on such expressions or phrases would show the extent of the crime committed here — they were contrary to the liberty of which they prated; they were subversive of all political order; they destroyed the union of men and aspired toward anarchy; they detached vassals from just obedience to their sovereign and denied his legitimate authority and rights; they tended directly against the very sovereignty of monarchs, and were anti-Catholic. . . . They further said that it was notable that this book was published at just the right time to assault the minds of the unwary, when all Europe was threatened with seductions, calamities, and scenes of blood and slaughter, when perils besieged us on all sides, and when Your Majesty was engaged in saving his vassals from the most unheard-of barbarism, and from all the horrors of infidelity.

3. AN ABORTIVE CONSPIRACY

In 1797, three years after Nariño published the Declaration of the Rights of Man *in Bogotá, a conspiracy against Spanish rule was discovered in the town of La Guaira in Venezuela. The ringleaders fled to Trinidad, but one of them, José María España, having ventured to return to Venezuela, was seized and hanged. Among the papers of the conspirators was discovered a document of forty-four articles that embodied their program. French revolutionary influence is clearly evident in this document, which is considerably to the left of the constitution actually adopted by the Venezuelan revolutionists in 1811. Among its main provisions were the following.*[6]

IN THE NAME of the Sacred Trinity and of Jesus, Mary, and Joseph, Amen:

The commanders of the provinces of Tierra Firme of South America, gathered in the place of N. to deal with and confer about the measures that should be adopted to restore to the American people their freedom, after a mature examination and long reflection, agreed, among other matters, that for the time being all the towns should observe the following articles:

1. All the inhabitants shall preserve union, constancy, and faith among themselves, and all shall form the firm resolution to die before abandoning this just cause.

2. Since this enterprise is of common interest, no one shall be permitted to regard it with indifference: the individual who holds back from this affair shall be immediately arrested, and such proceedings shall be taken against him as justice demands; whoever opposes it in any way shall be immediately punished as a declared enemy of the good of the Fatherland.

3. Whoever under cover of this revolution (daughter of reason, justice, and virtue) for private purposes sets fire to any buildings, commits any murder, strikes any person, perpetrates any robbery, treats any woman improperly, or steals any papers, shall be immediately and severely punished, without regard to his class.

[6] Pedro Grases, *La conspiración de Gual y España y el ideario de la independencia,* Caracas, 1949, pp. 170–178. (Excerpt translated by the editor.)

4. The soldier or patriot who during the revolution distinguishes himself in any action shall be substantially rewarded, as will anyone who is disabled, and finally whoever has the misfortune to perish shall have his name immortalized and his family rewarded in proportion to his merit.

5. As soon as any town receives notice of this essential resolution, the townspeople will arm themselves as well as they can, and divided into various bands, each under the command of an elected head, shall proclaim in all the streets and squares: Long live the American people! They shall seize all offices and places where there are public moneys, papers, military stores, and foodstuffs, sealing their doors and leaving at each a sufficient number of soldiers and patriots for their custody, not permitting these doors to be opened or any papers, moneys, or any other effects to be moved without the express order of the Governing Junta or the military commander and Chief of the Revolution.

6. All officials presently employed in the Treasury or the army and in the administration of justice shall be immediately deposed by edicts, and the people shall be summoned to meet at a designated time and place for the election of an interim Governing Junta, the number of its members to be proportionate to the population and circumstances of each town. Only those landowners can be elected members of this Junta who have previously given unequivocal proof of their continued patriotism. . . .

11. All ecclesiastics, churches, and convents shall continue to receive their revenues as before the Revolution, but if any of them, against the divine doctrines of the gospel and the Sacred Books, should preach, exhort, disseminate papers, or commit any other action against the general welfare, stripping himself of his character of spiritual minister to become a defender of tyranny, he shall be treated as a traitor to the Fatherland and punished with the rigor of the laws. . . .

14. The cultivation and sale of tobacco shall be free, from the very beginning of the Revolution in each town; such foodstuffs as bread, rice, vegetables, roots, garden stuff, fruits, etc., shall also be free from all duty, but all other kinds of contributions and tributes shall remain on their present footing, reduced by one fourth, until the Junta General makes a decision. . . .

16. It shall be the care of the Governing Juntas to establish good order in their respective towns, to encourage by all possible means agri-

culture, industry, arts, and commerce, and more particularly the planting of all articles that are basic necessities, so that the towns and the army may not lack the essentials of daily living at any time. . . .

18. All our towns and harbors shall be open to all the nations of the world, preserving the greatest harmony with them and the most exact neutrality toward the belligerent powers. . . .

19. By these presents we proclaim the natural equality of all the inhabitants of the provinces and districts. The whites, Indians, mixed-bloods (*pardos*) and Negroes are advised to live in the greatest harmony, regarding each other as brothers in Jesus Christ and as made equal by God; they should seek to surpass each other only in merits and virtue, which are the only two true and real distinctions among men, and the only ones to exist in the future among the inhabitants of our republic.

33. By virtue of this equality the payment of Indian tribute — with which the tyrannical government insultingly stamped and oppressed the Indians, and which was imposed upon the lands that were forcibly usurped from them — is abolished; it shall be one of the cares of our government to insure their ownership of the lands that they possess, or of others that may be more useful to them, affording them the means to be as happy as other citizens.

34. Slavery is abolished as repugnant to humanity. By virtue of this provision, all masters shall present to the Governing Junta of their respective towns the number of their slaves with a sworn list of their names, country of origin, age, sex, employment, original cost, and number of years of service, together with a note of their conduct and indispositions, if any, in order that the Junta General may determine the amounts that should justly be paid to the respective owners out of the public funds. . . .

36. All these new citizens shall take an oath of loyalty to the Fatherland, and the able-bodied males shall serve in the militia until the liberty of the people is secured, or as long as the circumstances require. In the interim, so that agriculture may not suffer the least injury, the slaves employed in agriculture shall remain with their former masters, but on condition of receiving a just wage and proper treatment, and in order to avoid any excesses on either part, no slave or new citizen of this kind may leave his master without just cause, approved by one of the members of the Governing Junta, who shall be named by the judge in these cases.

37. When the liberty of the Fatherland is secured, these new citizens will be discharged and will receive all the aid that may be judged necessary for their regular establishment. . . .

43. In all the towns, from this very instant, the rights of men will be published for the intelligence and government of all. . . .

44. In token of the unity, harmony, and equality which should reign constantly among all the inhabitants of the Tierra Firme, the national device shall be a cockade of four colors, namely: white, blue, yellow, and red.

The significance of the four colors:

The four colors of the united patriots, who are mixed-bloods (*pardos*), Negroes, whites, and Indians.

The union of the four provinces that compose the State: Caracas, Maracaibo, Cumaná, and Guayana.

The four foundations of the rights of men are equality, liberty, property, and security.

4. THE GREAT FORERUNNER

Of all the precursores or forerunners of Spanish-American independence, none had a more remarkable history than Francisco de Miranda (1750–1816). A high point of Miranda's career was his effort to revolutionize Venezuela with the aid of North American volunteers — the ill-fated Leander *expedition of 1806. On board the* Leander *as it headed toward the coast of Venezuela and disaster was one James Biggs, who later wrote the following sketch of Miranda.[7]*

FROM THIS NARRATIVE, in connection with the prior history of General Miranda, you will receive an impression of his character not so favourable, as that entertained by many persons. I have related facts. They must be allowed to speak for themselves. His imagination and feelings were an overmatch for his judgment. He is more rash and presumptuous in projects, than dexterous in extricating himself from difficulties. In religion he is reputed skeptical; but in our hearing he never derided subjects of this nature. He used formerly to talk infidelity, to the offence of the serious; experience has taught him caution, or he has changed his sentiments. It is said upon good authority, that he partook the sacrament at Coro. He is too much of an enthusiast in his favourite objects to allow his

[7] James Biggs, *The History of Don Francisco de Miranda's Attempt to Effect a Revolution in South America,* Boston, 1808, pp. 288–291.

means to be enfeebled by moral scruples. I am willing to believe he has as much conscience as the impetuous passions of such men generally admit.

I make a few remarks on his person, manners, and petty habits.

He is about five feet ten inches high. His limbs are well proportioned; his whole frame is stout and active. His complexion is dark, florid, and healthy. His eyes are hazel-coloured, but not of the darkest hue. They are piercing, quick, and intelligent, expressing more of the severe than the mild feelings. He has good teeth, which he takes much care to keep clean. His nose is large and handsome, rather of the English than Roman cast. His chest is broad and flat. His hair is grey, and he wears it tied long behind, with powder. He has strong grey whiskers, growing on the outer edges of his ears, as large as most Spaniards have on their cheeks. In the contour of his visage, you plainly perceive an expression of pertinaciousness and suspicion. Upon the whole, without saying he is an elegant, we may pronounce him a handsome man. He has a constant habit of picking his teeth. When sitting, he is never perfectly still; his foot or hand must be moving to keep time with his mind, which is always in exercise. He always sleeps a few moments after dinner, and then walks till bedtime, which with him is about midnight. He is an eminent example of temperance. A scanty or bad meal is never regarded by him as a subject of complaint. He uses no ardent spirits; seldom any wine. Sweetened water is his common beverage. Sweetness and warmth, says he, are the two greatest physical goods; and acid and cold are the greatest physical evils in the universe.

He is a courtier and gentleman in his manners. Dignity and grace preside in his movements. Unless when angry, he has a great command of his feelings; and can assume what looks and tones he pleases. His demeanour is often marked by hauteur and distance. When he is angry he loses discretion. He is impatient of contradiction. In discourse, he is logical in the arrangement of his thoughts. He appears conversant on all subjects. His iron memory prevents his ever being at a loss for names, dates, and authorities.

He used his mental resources and colloquial powers with great address to recommend himself to his followers. He assumed the manners of a father and instructor to the young men. He spoke of the prospect of success, and of the preparations made for him, with great confidence. The glory and advantages of the enterprize were described in glowing colours. At another time, he detailed his travels, his sufferings and escapes, in a manner to interest both their admiration and sympathy. He appeared the master of languages, of science and literature. In his conversations, he carried his hearers to the scenes of great actions, and introduced them to the distinguished characters of every age. He took excursions to Troy, Babylon, Jerusalem, Rome, Athens and Syracuse. Men famed as statesmen, heroes, patriots, conquerors, and tyrants, priests and scholars, he produced, and weighed their merits and defects. Modern history and biography afforded him abundant topics. He impressed an opinion of his comprehensive views, his inexhaustible fund of learning; his probity, his generosity, and patriotism. After all, this man of blazoned fame, must, I fear, be considered as having more learning than wisdom; more theoretical knowledge than practical talent; too sanguine and too opinionated to distinguish between the vigour of enterprize and the hardiness of infatuation.

5. THE FORGING OF A REBEL

In his valuable brief autobiography, Manuel Belgrano (1770–1821), one of the Fathers of Argentine Independence, describes the influences and events that transformed a young creole of wealth and high social position into an ardent revolutionary. The French Revolution, disillusionment with Bourbon liberalism, the English invasions, and finally the events of 1808 in Spain all played their part in this process.[8]

THE PLACE OF MY BIRTH was Buenos Aires; my parents were Don Domingo Belgrano y Peri, known as Pérez, a native of Onella in Spain, and Doña María Josefa González Casero, a native of Buenos Aires. My father was a merchant, and since he lived in the days of monopoly he acquired sufficient wealth to live comfortably and to give his children the best education to be had in those days.

I studied my first letters, Latin grammar, philosophy, and a smattering of theology in Buenos Aires. My father then sent me to Spain to study law, and I began my preparation at Salamanca; I was graduated at Valladolid, continued my

8 Ricardo Levene, ed., *Los sucesos de mayo contados por sus actores*, Buenos Aires, 1928, 60–71. (Excerpt translated by the editor.)

training at Madrid, and was admitted to the bar at Valladolid. . . .

Since I was in Spain in 1789, and the French Revolution was then causing a change in ideas, especially among the men of letters with whom I associated, the ideals of liberty, equality, security, and property took a firm hold on me, and I saw only tyrants in those who would restrain a man, wherever he might be, from enjoying the rights with which God and Nature had endowed him. . . .

When I completed my studies in 1793 political economy enjoyed great popularity in Spain; I believe this was why I was appointed secretary of the *consulado* of Buenos Aires, established when Gardoqui was minister. The official of the department in charge of these matters even asked me to suggest some other well-informed persons who could be appointed to similar bodies to be established in the principal American ports.

When I learned that these consulados were to be so many Economic Societies that would discuss the state of agriculture, industry, and commerce in their sessions, my imagination pictured a vast field of activity, for I was ignorant of Spanish colonial policy. I had heard some muffled murmuring among the Americans, but I attributed this to their failure to gain their ends, never to evil designs of the Spaniards that had been systematically pursued since the Conquest.

On receiving my appointment I was infatuated with the brilliant prospects for America. I had visions of myself writing memorials concerning the provinces so that the authorities might be informed and provide for their well-being. It may be that an enlightened minister like Gardoqui, who had resided in the United States, had the best of intentions in all this. . . .

I finally departed from Spain for Buenos Aires; I cannot sufficiently express the surprise I felt when I met the men named by the king to the council which was to deal with agriculture, industry, and commerce and work for the happiness of the provinces composing the viceroyalty of Buenos Aires. All were Spanish merchants. With the exception of one or two they knew nothing but their monopolistic business, namely, to buy at four dollars and sell for eight. . . .

My spirits fell, and I began to understand that the colonies could expect nothing from me who placed their private interests above those of the community. But since my position gave me

an opportunity to write and speak about some useful topics, I decided at least to plant a few seeds that some day might bear fruit. . . .

I wrote various memorials about the establishment of schools. The scarcity of pilots and the direct interest of the merchants in the project presented favorable circumstances for the establishment of a school of mathematics, which I obtained on condition of getting the approval of the Court. This, however, was never secured; in fact, the government was not satisfied until the school had been abolished, because although the peninsulars recognized the justice and utility of such establishments, they were opposed to them because of a mistaken view of how the colonies might best be retained.

The same happened to a drawing school which I managed to establish without spending even half a real for the teacher. The fact is that neither these nor other proposals to the government for the development of agriculture, industry, and commerce, the three important concerns of the consulado, won its official approval; the sole concern of the Court was with the revenue that it derived from each of these branches. They said that all the proposed establishments were luxuries, and that Buenos Aires was not yet in a condition to support them.

I promoted various other useful and necessary projects, which had more or less the same fate, but it will be the business of the future historian of the consulado to give an account of them; I shall simply say that from the beginning of 1794 to July, 1806, I passed my time in futile efforts to serve my country. They all foundered on the rock of the opposition of the government of Buenos Aires, or that of Madrid, or that of the merchants who composed the consulado, for whom there was no other reason, justice, utility, or necessity than their commercial interest. Anything that came into conflict with that interest encountered a veto, and there was nothing to be done about it.

It is well known how General Beresford entered Buenos Aires with about four hundred men in 1806. At that time I had been a captain in the militia for ten years, more from whim than from any attachment to the military art. My first experience of war came at that time. The Marqués de Sobremonte, then viceroy of the provinces of La Plata, sent for me several days before Beresford's disastrous entrance and requested me to form a company of cavalry from among the young men engaged in commerce. He said that he would give me veteran officers to train them; I sought them but could not find any, because of the great hostility felt for the militia in Buenos Aires. . . .

The general alarm was sounded. Moved by honor, I flew to the fortress, the point of assembly; I found there neither order nor harmony in anything, as must happen with groups of men who know nothing of discipline and are completely insubordinate. The companies were formed there, and I was attached to one of them. I was ashamed that I had not the slightest notion of military science and had to rely entirely on the orders of a veteran officer — who also joined voluntarily, for he was given no assignment.

This was the first company, which marched to occupy the *Casa de las Filipinas*. Meanwhile the others argued with the viceroy himself that they were obliged only to defend the city and not to go out into the country; consequently they would agree only to defend the heights. The result was that the enemy, meeting with no opposition from veteran troops or disciplined militia, forced all the passes with the greatest ease. There was some stupid firing on the part of my company and some others in an effort to stop the invaders, but all in vain, and when the order came to retreat and we were falling back I heard someone say: "They did well to order us to retreat, for we were not made for this sort of thing."

I must confess that I grew angry, and that I never regretted more deeply my ignorance of even the rudiments of military science. My distress grew when I saw the entrance of the enemy troops, and realized how few of them there were for a town of the size of Buenos Aires. I could not get the idea out of my head, and I almost went out of my mind, it was so painful to me to see my country under an alien yoke, and above all in such a degraded state that it could be conquered by the daring enterprise of the brave and honorable Beresford, whose valor I shall always admire.

[A resistance movement under the leadership of Santiago Liniers drives the British out of Buenos Aires. A second English invasion, commanded by General John Whitelocke, is defeated, and the entire British force is compelled to surrender. B.K.]

General Liniers ordered the quartermaster-general to receive the paroles of the officer prisoners; for this reason Brigadier-General Crawford, together with his aides and other high officers, came to his house. My slight knowledge of French, and perhaps certain civilities that I showed him, caused General Crawford to prefer to converse with me, and we entered upon a discussion that helped to pass the time — although he never lost sight of his aim of gaining knowledge of the country and, in particular, of its opinion of the Spanish Government.

So, having convinced himself that I had no French sympathies or connections, he divulged to me his ideas about our independence, perhaps in the hope of forming new links with this country, since the hope of conquest had failed. I described our condition to him, and made it plain that we wanted our old master or none at all; that we were far from possessing the means required for the achievement of independence; that even if it were won under the protection of England, she would abandon us in return for some advantage in Europe, and then we would fall under the Spanish sword; that every nation sought its own interest and did not care about the misfortunes of others. He agreed with me, and when I had shown how we lacked the means for winning independence, he put off its attainment for a century.

How fallible are the calculations of men! One year passed, and behold, without any effort on our part to become independent, God Himself gave us our opportunity as a result of the events of 1808 in Spain and Bayonne. Then it was that the ideals of liberty and independence came to life in America, and the Americans began to speak frankly of their rights.

6. THE ECONOMIC FACTOR IN THE REVOLUTION

In the twilight years of the Spanish Empire in America, contraband trade with the Indies assumed vast proportions. Spain, locked in a desperate struggle with Napoleonic France, could not provide her colonies with the goods and shipping services that they must have. In August, 1809, two English merchants petitioned Viceroy Cisneros for permission to sell their cargoes in Buenos Aires. Cisneros called on representatives of various interests to give their opinions in the matter. Speaking for the cattle-raisers, the creole lawyer Mariano Moreno (1778–1811) came forward with a vigorous brief in favor of free trade. Faced with an empty treasury and creole military supremacy, the viceroy reluctantly sanctioned a limited free trade with allied and neutral nations. Moreno's slashing attack on Spanish mercantilism foreshadowed the revolution that was less than one year away.[9]

THE RESOURCES of the Royal Treasury being exhausted by the enormous expenditure which has lately been required, your Excellency, on assuming the reins of Government, was deprived of the means of providing for the safety of the provinces committed to your charge. The only mode of relieving the necessities of the country, appears to be to grant permission to the English merchants to introduce their manufactures into the town, and to re-export the produce of the Interior, by which the revenue will be at once increased, and an impulse given to industry and trade.

Your Excellency possesses powers sufficient for the adoption of any measures that the safety of the country may require, but a natural desire to ensure the result of these measures, by adapting them to the peculiar situation of the viceroyalty, induced your Excellency to consult the Cabildo of this city, and the Tribunal of the Real Consulado, before any definitive resolution was taken.

The intentions of your Excellency had barely transpired, when several of the merchants manifested their discontent and dissatisfaction. Groups of European shopkeepers were formed in all the public places, who, disguising their jealousy and personal apprehensions under the most specious pretences, affected to deplore, as a public calamity, the diminution of the profits, which they have hitherto derived from the contraband trade. At one time, with hypocritical warmth, they lamented the fatal blow which the interests of the Mother-country were about to receive, and at another, they predicted the ruin of the colony, and the total destruction of its commerce: others again announced the universal distress that the free exportation of the precious metals would bring upon us, and pretended to feel a lively interest in the fate of our native artisans (whom they have always hitherto despised), endeavouring to enlist in their cause the sacred name of religion, and the interests of morality.

Never, certainly, has America known a more critical state of affairs, and never was any European governor so well entitled as your Excellency to dispense at once with the maxims of past ages; for if, in less dangerous times, the laws

have often been allowed to sleep, when their observance might have checked the free action of the Government, surely your Excellency cannot now be condemned for the adoption of a measure, by which alone the preservation of this part of the monarchy can be effected.

Those should be doomed to eternal infamy, who maintain that, under present circumstances, it would be injurious either to Spain, or to this country, to open a free intercourse with Great Britain. But even supposing the measure to be injurious, still it is a necessary evil, and one which, since it cannot be avoided, ought at least to be made use of for the general good, by endeavouring to derive every possible advantage from it, and thus to convert it into a means of ensuring the safety of the state.

Since the English first appeared on our coasts, in 1806, the merchants of that nation have not lost sight of the Rio de la Plata in their speculations. A series of commercial adventures has followed, which has provided almost entirely for the consumption of the country; and this great importation, carried on in defiance of laws and reiterated prohibitions, has met with no other obstacles than those necessary to deprive the Custom-house of its dues, and the country of those advantages which it might have derived from a free exportation of its own produce in return.

The result of this system has been to put the English in the exclusive possession of the right of providing the country with all the foreign merchandize that it requires; while the Government has lost the immense revenues which the introduction of so large a proportion of foreign manufacturers ought to have produced, from too scrupulous an observance of laws, which have never been more scandalously violated than at the moment when their observance was insisted upon by the merchants of the capital. For what, Sir, can be more glaringly absurd than to hear a merchant clamouring for the enforcement of the prohibitive laws, and the exclusion of foreign trade, at the very door of a shop filled with English goods, clandestinely imported?

To the advantages which the Government will derive from the open introduction of foreign goods, may be added those which must accrue to the country from the free exportation of its own produce.

Our vast plains produce annually a million of hides, without reckoning other skins, corn, or tallow, all of which are valuable, as articles of foreign trade. But the magazines of our resident merchants are full; there is no exportation; the

---

[9] "Extracts from a representation, addressed to the viceroy of Buenos Aires. . . ," in Henry G. Ward, *Mexico in 1827,* London, 2 vols., 1828, II, Appendix, 479–483.

capital usually invested in these speculations is already employed, and the immense residue of the produce, thrown back upon the hands of the landed-proprietors, or purchased at a price infinitely below its real value, has reduced them to the most deplorable state of wretchedness, and compelled them to abandon a labour which no longer repays them for the toil and expense with which it is attended.

The freedom of trade in America was not proscribed as a real evil, but because it was a sacrifice required of the colonies by the Mother-country. The events which led to the gradual increase of this exclusive commerce, till it became a monopoly of the Cadiz merchants, are well known.

Well informed men exclaimed in vain against a system so weak, so ruinous, and so ill judged; but inveterate evils are not to be cured at once. Minor reforms had paved the way for a system founded upon sounder principles, when the late extraordinary events, changing entirely the political state of Spain, destroyed by one unforeseen blow all the pretexts by which the prohibitory laws had been previously supported. — The new order of things which the Mother-country has proclaimed as the happy commencement of national prosperity, has completely changed the motives for the prohibitory system, and demonstrated, in their fullest extent, the advantages that must result to the country from a free trade. Good policy, therefore, and the natural wish to apply a remedy to pressing evils, are converted into a positive duty, which the first magistrate of the state cannot, in reason, or justice, neglect.

Is it just that the fruits of our agricultural labours should be lost, because the unfortunate provinces of Spain can no longer consume them? Is it just that the abundant productions of the country should rot in our magazines, because the navy of Spain is too weak to export them? Is it just that we should increase the distress of the Mother-country, by the tidings of our own critical and vacillating state, when the means are offered to us of consolidating our safety upon the firmest basis? Is it just, that, when the subjects of a friendly and generous nation present themselves in our ports, and offer us, at a cheap rate, the merchandize of which we are in want, and with which Spain cannot supply us, we should reject the proposal, and convert, by so doing, their good intentions to the exclusive advantage of a few European merchants, who, by means of a contraband trade, render themselves masters of the whole imports of the country? Is

it just, that when we are entreated to sell our accumulated agricultural produce, we should, by refusing to do so, decree at the same time the ruin of our landed-proprietors, of the country, and of society together?

If your Excellency wishes to diminish the extraction of specie, which has taken place latterly to so great an extent, there is no other mode of effecting it than to open the ports to the English, and thus to enable them to extend their speculations to other objects. It is one of the fatal consequences of the contraband trade, that the importer is absolutely compelled to receive the value of his imports in the precious metals alone. His true interest, indeed, consists in exchanging them at once for articles that may become the objects of a new speculation; but the risks with which the extraction of bulky commodities must be attended, under a system of strict prohibition, induce him to sacrifice this advantage to the greater security which exports in specie afford, and to deprive himself of the hope of new profits, and the country of the sale of its most valuable produce.

Yet the *apoderado* of the Cadiz monopolists maintains, "that a free trade will be the ruin of our agriculture." This luminous discovery is worthy of his penetration. The free exportation of the produce is declared to be detrimental to the interests of the producer! What, then, is to be the mode of encouraging him in his labours? According to the principles laid down by our merchants, the agricultural produce should be allowed to accumulate, — purchasers are to be deterred from entering the market, by the difficulties of exporting the articles bought up, to countries where they might be consumed; and this system is to be persevered in until, after ruining the landholders by preventing them from disposing of the fruits of their labours, the superfluous produce itself is to be disposed of, in order to fill up the ditches and marshes in the vicinity of the town.

Yes, Sir, this is the deplorable state to which our agriculture has been reduced during the last few years. The marshes around the town have been actually filled up with wheat; and this miserable condition, which forms a subject of lamentation with all true friends to their country, and scandalizes the inhabitants of the whole district, is the natural fate of a province, in which, as soon as an inclination is shown to apply a remedy to these evils, men are found daring enough to assert, "That by giving value, or in other words, a ready market, to the agricultural produce, agriculture will be ruined."

XXII

The Liberation of South America

CREOLE PROFESSIONS OF LOYALTY to the "beloved Ferdinand," a prisoner in France, did not impress the Spanish authorities. Learning of the upheaval in Caracas, they declared the colony in revolt and proclaimed a blockade of its ports. Accordingly, in July, 1811, Venezuela declared its independence from Spain. Other provinces soon followed its example, although Argentina delayed the act of separation until 1816.

Simón Bolívar led the movement for independence in northern South America. A turning point in the northern war came when Bolívar routed a Spanish army at Boyacá, high in the mountains of New Granada (1819). The liberation of Venezuela and Ecuador soon followed. From the union of New Granada, Venezuela, and Ecuador arose a gigantic new state, Colombia, with Bolívar as its first president.

The austere figure of José de San Martín dominated the war for independence in southern South America. From its base in Buenos Aires the revolution flowed into the Banda Oriental (Uruguay) and other provinces of the old viceroyalty of La Plata, but was thrown back at the rugged borders of Upper Peru (Bolivia). San Martín's bold design for total victory proposed a march across the Andes to liberate Chile, followed by an attack on Lima from the sea.

San Martín planned and executed the campaign of the Andes with consummate skill. The battle of Maipú (1818) ended Spanish rule in Chile. However, final victory in Peru escaped San Martín's grasp. In September, 1822, after a meeting with Bolívar that revealed serious political differences between the two men, he resigned his command; he soon afterwards departed for Europe. It remained for Bolívar to complete the work of continental liberation. In December, 1824, his lieutenant Sucre accepted the surrender of La Serna, the last Spanish viceroy in the New World.

Brazil made a fairly peaceful transition to independence. The flight of the Portuguese royal family to Brazil in 1808 as a result of the French invasion of the kingdom gave new importance and privileges to the colony. In 1820, after the fall of Napoleon, a jealous Portuguese *cortes* demanded the return of King João, and he reluctantly complied. But his son Pedro, supported by the Brazilian landed aristocracy, rejected a similar demand, issued the famous cry of "independence or death," and in December, 1822, was formally proclaimed constitutional Emperor of Brazil.

1. MAN OF DESTINY

There is no more controversial figure in Latin-American history than that of Simón Bolívar (1783–1830). To his admirers or worshippers he is the Liberator of a continent; Waldo Frank calls him "the culture hero of our hemisphere." To his critics he is the proverbial "man on horseback," an ambitious schemer who sacrificed San Martín to his passion for power and glory. Louis Peru de Lacroix, a French member of Bolívar's staff, wrote the following description of the Liberator in a diary that he kept during their stay at Bucaramanga in 1828.[1]

[1] Monseñor Nicolás E. Navarro, ed., *Diaria de Bucaramanga, estudia crítico*, Caracas, 1935, pp. 327, 329–331. (Excerpt translated by the editor.)

THE GENERAL-IN-CHIEF, Simón José Antonio Bolívar, will be forty-five years old on July 24 of this year, but he appears older, and many judge him to be fifty. He is slim and of medium height; his arms, thighs, and legs are lean. He has a long head, wide between the temples, and a sharply pointed chin. A large, round, prominent forehead is furrowed with wrinkles that are very noticeable when his face is in repose, or in moments of bad humor and anger. His hair is crisp, bristly, quite abundant, and partly gray. His eyes have lost the brightness of youth but preserve the luster of genius. They are deep-set, neither small nor large; the eyebrows are thick, separated, slightly arched, and are grayer than the hair on his head. The nose is aquiline and well formed. He has prominent cheekbones, with hollows beneath. His mouth is rather large, and the lower lip protrudes; he has white teeth and an agreeable smile.... His tanned complexion darkens when he is in a bad humor, and his whole appearance changes; the wrinkles on his forehead and temples stand out much more prominently; the eyes become smaller and narrower; the lower lip protrudes considerably, and the mouth turns ugly. In fine, one sees a completely different countenance: a frowning face that reveals sorrows, sad reflections, and sombre ideas. But when he is happy all this disappears; his face lights up, his mouth smiles, and the spirit of the Liberator shines over his countenance. His Excellency is clean-shaven at present. . . .

The Liberator has energy; he is capable of making a firm decision and sticking to it. His ideas are never commonplace — always large, lofty, and original. His manners are affable, having the tone of Europeans of high society. He displays a republican simplicity and modesty, but he has the pride of a noble and elevated soul, the dignity of his rank, and the *amour-propre* that comes from consciousness of worth and leads men to great actions. Glory is his ambition, and his glory consists in having liberated ten million persons and founded three republics. He has an enterprising spirit, combined with great activity, quickness of speech, an infinite fertility in ideas, and the constancy necessary for the realization of his projects. He is superior to misfortunes and reverses; his philosophy consoles him and his intelligence finds ways of righting what has gone wrong. . . .

He loves a discussion, and dominates it through his superior intelligence; but he sometimes appears too dogmatic, and is not always tolerant enough with those who contradict him. He scorns servile flattery and base adulators. He is sensitive to criticism of his actions; calumny against him cuts him to the quick, for none is more touchy about his reputation than the Liberator. . . .

His heart is better than his head. His bad temper never lasts; when it appears, it takes possession of his head, never of his heart, and as soon as the latter recovers its dominance it immediately makes amends for the harm that the former may have done. . . .

The great mental and bodily activity of the Liberator keeps him in a state of constant moral and physical agitation. One who observes him at certain moments might think he is seeing a madman. During the walks that we take with him he sometimes likes to walk very rapidly, trying to tire his companions out; at other times he begins to run and leap, to leave the others behind; then he waits for them to catch up and tells them they do not know how to run. He does the same when horseback riding. But he acts this way only when among his own people, and he would not run or leap if he thought that some stranger was looking on. When bad weather prevents walking or riding, the Liberator rocks himself swiftly back and forth in his hammock or strides through the corridors of his house, sometimes singing, at other times reciting verses or talking with those who walk beside him. When conversing with one of his own people, he changes the subject as often as he does his position; at such times one would say that he has not a bit of system or stability in him. How different the Liberator seems at a private party, at some formal gathering, and among his confidential friends and aides-de-camp! With the latter he seems their equal, the gayest and sometimes the maddest of them all. At a private party, among strangers and people less well known to him, he shows his superiority to all others by his easy and agreeable ways and good taste, his lively and ingenious conversation, and his amiability. At a more formal gathering, his unaffected dignity and polished manners cause him to be regarded as the most gentlemanly, learned, and amiable man present. . . .

In all the actions of the Liberator, and in his conversation, as I have already noted, one observes an extreme quickness. His questions are short and concise; he likes to be answered in the same way, and when someone wanders away from the question he impatiently says that that is not what he asked; he has no liking for a diffuse answer. He sustains his opinions with force and logic, and generally with tenacity. When he has occasion to contradict some assertion, he says: "No, sir, it is not so, but thus. . . ." Speaking of persons whom he dislikes or scorns, he often uses this expression: "That (or those) c***." He is very observant, noting even the least trifles; he dislikes the poorly educated, the bold, the windbag, the indiscreet, and the discourteous. Since nothing escapes him, he takes pleasure in criticizing such people, always making a little commentary on their defects. . . .

I have already said that the Liberator can assume an air of dignity when among persons who do not enjoy his full confidence or with whom he is not on terms of familiarity; but he throws it off among his own people. In church he carries himself with much propriety and respect, and does not permit his companions to deviate from this rule. One day, noticing that his physician, Dr. Moore, sat with his legs crossed, he had an aide-de-camp tell him that it was improper to cross one's legs in church, and that he should observe how *he* sat. One thing that His Excellency does not know, when at Mass, is when to kneel, stand up, and sit down. He never crosses himself. Sometimes he talks to the person beside him, but only a little, and very softly.

The ideas of the Liberator are like his imagination: full of fire, original, and new. They lend considerable sparkle to his conversation, and make it extremely varied. When His Excellency praises, defends, or approves something, it is always with a little exaggeration. The same is true when he criticizes, condemns, or disapproves of something. In his conversation he frequently quotes, but his citations are always well chosen and pertinent. Voltaire is his favorite author, and he has memorized many passages from his works, both prose and poetry. He knows all the good French writers and evaluates them competently. He has some general knowledge of Italian and English literature and is very well versed in that of Spain.

The Liberator takes great pleasure in telling of his first years, his voyages, and his campaigns, and of his relations and old friends. His character and spirit dispose him more to criticize than to eulogize, but his criticisms or eulogies are never baseless; he could be charged only with an occasional slight exaggeration. I have never heard his Excellency utter a calumny. He is a lover of truth, heroism, and honor and of the public interest and morality. He detests and scorns all that is opposed to these lofty and noble sentiments.

2. THE POLITICAL IDEAS OF BOLÍVAR ✓

The political organization of the new Spanish-American states claimed much of Bolívar's attention. Rejecting a monarchical solution as unsuited to the conditions of the New World, he advocated a highly centralized republican government headed by a strong executive. Distrustful of the masses, he proposed to limit the suffrage and office-holding to the propertied and educated elite. The following excerpts from his celebrated message to the Congress of Angostura (1819), concerning a proposed new constitution for the Republic of Venezuela, illustrate his political views at that stage of his career.[2]

LET US REVIEW the past to discover the base upon which the Republic of Venezuela is founded.

America, in separating from the Spanish monarchy, found herself in a situation similar to that of the Roman Empire when its enormous framework fell to pieces in the midst of the ancient world. Each Roman division then formed an independent nation in keeping with its location or interests; but this situation differed from America's in that those members proceeded to reëstablish their former associations. We, on the contrary, do not even retain the vestiges of our original being. We are not Europeans; we are not Indians; we are but a mixed species of aborigines and Spaniards. Americans by birth and Europeans by law, we find ourselves engaged in a dual conflict: we are disputing with the natives for titles of ownership, and at the same time we are struggling to maintain ourselves in the country that gave us birth against the opposition of the invaders. Thus our position is most extraordinary and complicated. But there is more. As our role has always been strictly passive and political existence nil, we find that our quest for liberty is now even more difficult of accomplishment; for we, having been placed in a state lower than slavery, had been robbed not only of our freedom but also of the right to exercise an active domestic tyranny. Permit me to explain this paradox.

In absolute systems, the central power is unlimited. The will of the despot is the supreme law, arbitrarily enforced by subordinates who take part in the organized oppression in proportion to the authority that they wield. They are charged with civil, political, military, and religious functions; but, in the final analysis, the satraps of Persia are Persian, the pashas of the Grand Turk are Turks, and the sultans of Tartary are Tartars. China does not seek her mandarins in the homeland of Genghis Khan, her conqueror. America, on the contrary, received everything from Spain, who, in effect, deprived her of the experience that she would have gained from the exercise of an active tyranny by not allowing her to take part in her own domestic affairs and administration. This exclu-

2 Vicente Lecuna, comp., and Harold A. Bierck, Jr., ed., *Selected Writings of Bolívar*, New York, Colonial Press, 1951, 2 vols., I, 175–191. Reprinted by kind permission of the Banco de Venezuela.

sion made it impossible for us to acquaint ourselves with the management of public affairs;
nor did we enjoy that personal consideration,
of such great value in major revolutions, that
the brilliance of power inspires in the eyes of
the multitude. In brief, Gentlemen, we were
deliberately kept in ignorance and cut off from
the world in all matters relating to the science
of government.

Subject to the three-fold yoke of ignorance,
tyranny, and vice, the American people have
been unable to acquire knowledge, power, or
[civic] virtue. The lessons we received and the
models we studied, as pupils of such pernicious
teachers, were most destructive. We have been
ruled more by deceit than by force, and we have
been degraded more by vice than by superstition. Slavery is the daughter of darkness: an
ignorant people is a blind instrument of its own
destruction. Ambition and intrigue abuse the
credulity and experience of men lacking all
political, economic, and civic knowledge; they
adopt pure illusion as reality; they take license
for liberty, treachery for patriotism, and vengeance for justice. This situation is similar to
that of the robust blind man who, beguiled by
his strength, strides forward with all the assurance of one who can see, but, upon hitting every
variety of obstacle, finds himself unable to re-
trace his steps.

If a people, perverted by their training, succeed in achieving their liberty, they will soon
lose it, for it would be of no avail to endeavor to
explain to them that happiness consists in the
practice of virtue; that the rule of law is more
powerful than the rule of tyrants, because, as the
laws are more inflexible, every one should submit to their beneficent austerity; that proper
morals, and not force, are the bases of law; and
that to practice justice is to practice liberty.
Therefore, Legislators, your work is so much the
more arduous, inasmuch as you have to reëdu-
cate men who have been corrupted by erroneous
illusions and false incentives. Liberty, says
Rousseau, is a succulent morsel, but one difficult
to digest. Our weak fellow-citizens will have to
strengthen their spirit greatly before they can
digest the wholesome nutriment of freedom.
Their limbs benumbed by chains, their sight
dimmed by the darkness of dungeons, and their
strength sapped by the pestilence of servitude,
are they capable of marching toward the august
temple of Liberty without faltering? Can they
come near enough to bask in its brilliant rays

and to breathe freely the pure air which reigns
therein? . . .

The more I admire the excellence of the federal Constitution of Venezuela, the more I am
convinced of the impossibility of its application
to our state. And to my way of thinking, it is a
marvel that its prototype in North America endures so successfully and has not been overthrown at the first sign of adversity or danger.
Although the people of North America are a
singular model of political virtue and moral
rectitude; although that nation was cradled in
liberty, reared on freedom, and maintained by
liberty alone; and — I must reveal everything —
although those people, so lacking in many respects, are unique in the history of mankind, it
is a marvel, I repeat, that so weak and complicated a government as the federal system has
managed to govern them in the difficult and
trying circumstances of their past. But, regardless of the effectiveness of this form of government with respect to North America, I must say
that it has never for a moment entered my mind
to compare the position and character of two
states as dissimilar as the English-American and
the Spanish-American. Would it not be most
difficult to apply to Spain the English system of
political, civil, and religious liberty: Hence, it
would be even more difficult to adapt to Venezuela the laws of North America. Does not
L'Esprit des Lois state that laws should be suited
to the people for whom they are made; that it
would be a major coincidence if those of one
nation could be adapted to another; that laws
must take into account the physical conditions
of the country, climate, character of the land,
location, size, and mode of living of the people;
that they should be in keeping with the degree
of liberty that the Constitution can sanction respecting the religion of the inhabitants, their
inclinations, resources, number, commerce, habits, and customs? This is the code we must consult, not the code of Washington! . . .

Venezuela had, has, and should have a republican government. Its principles should be the
sovereignty of the people, division of powers,
civil liberty, proscription of slavery, and the abolition of monarchy and privileges. We need
equality to recast, so to speak, into a unified
nation, the classes of men, political opinions,
and public customs.

Among the ancient and modern nations, Rome
and Great Britain are the most outstanding.
Both were born to govern and to be free and

both were built not on ostentatious forms of freedom, but upon solid institutions. Thus I recommend to you, Representatives, the study of the British Constitution, for that body of laws appears destined to bring about the greatest possible good for the peoples that adopt it; but, however perfect it may be, I am by no means proposing that you imitate it slavishly. When I speak of the British government, I only refer to its republican features; and, indeed, can a political system be labelled a monarchy when it recognizes popular sovereignty, division and balance of powers, civil liberty, freedom of conscience and of press, and all that is politically sublime? Can there be more liberty in any other type of republic? Can more be asked of any society? I commend this Constitution to you as that most worthy of serving as model for those who aspire to the enjoyment of the rights of man and who seek all the political happiness which is compatible with the frailty of human nature.

Nothing in our fundamental laws would have to be altered were we to adopt a legislative power similar to that held by the British Parliament. Like the North Americans, we have divided national representation into two chambers; that of Representatives and the Senate. The first is very wisely constituted. It enjoys all its proper functions, and it requires no essential revision, because the Constitution, in creating it, gave it the form and powers which the people deemed necessary in order that they might be legally and properly represented. If the Senate were hereditary rather than elective, it would, in my opinion, be the basis, the tie, the very soul of our republic. In political storms this body would arrest the thunderbolts of the government and would repel any violent popular reaction. Devoted to the government because of a natural interest in its own preservation, a hereditary senate would always oppose any attempt on the part of the people to infringe upon the jurisdiction and authority of their magistrates. It must be confessed that most men are unaware of their best interests, and that they constantly endeavor to assail them in the hands of their custodians — the individual clashes with the mass, and the mass with authority. It is necessary, therefore, that in all governments there be a neutral body to protect the injured and disarm the offender. To be neutral, this body must not owe its origin to appointment by the government or to election by the people, if it is to enjoy a full measure of independence which neither fears nor expects anything from these two sources of authority. The hereditary senate, as a part of the people, shares its interests, its sentiments, and its spirit. For this reason it should not be presumed that a hereditary senate would ignore the interests of the people or forget its legislative duties. The senators in Rome and in the House of Lords in London have been the strongest pillars upon which the edifice of political and civil liberty has rested.

At the outset, these senators should be elected by Congress. The successors to this Senate must command the initial attention of the government, which should educate them in a *colegio* designed especially to train these guardians and future legislators of the nation. They ought to learn the arts, sciences, and letters that enrich the mind of a public figure. From childhood they should understand the career for which they have been destined by Providence, and from earliest youth they should prepare their minds for the dignity that awaits them.

The creation of a hereditary senate would in no way be a violation of political equality. I do not solicit the establishment of a nobility, for as a celebrated republican has said, that would simultaneously destroy equality and liberty. What I propose is an office for which the candidates must prepare themselves, an office that demands great knowledge and the ability to acquire such knowledge. All should not be left to chance and the outcome of elections. The people are more easily deceived than is Nature perfected by art; and, although these senators, it is true, would not be bred in an environment that is all virtue, it is equally true that they would be raised in an atmosphere of enlightened education. Furthermore, the liberators of Venezuela are entitled to occupy forever a high rank in the Republic that they have brought into existence. I believe that posterity would view with regret the effacement of the illustrious names of its first benefactors. I say, moreover, that it is a matter of public interest and national honor, of gratitude on Venezuela's part, to honor gloriously, until the end of time, a race of virtuous, prudent, and persevering men who, overcoming every obstacle, have founded the Republic at the price of the most heroic sacrifices. And if the people of Venezuela do not applaud the elevation of their benefactors, then they are unworthy to be free, and they will never be free.

A hereditary senate, I repeat, will be the fundamental basis of the legislative power, and therefore the foundation of the entire government. It will also serve as a counterweight to both government and people; and as a neutral power it will weaken the mutual attacks of these two eternally rival powers. In all conflicts the calm reasoning of a third party will serve as the means of reconciliation. Thus the Venezuelan senate will give strength to this delicate political structure, so sensitive to violent repercussions; it will be the mediator that will lull the storms and it will maintain harmony between the head and the other parts of the political body.

No inducement could corrupt a legislative body invested with the highest honors, dependent only upon itself, having no fear of the people, independent of the government, and dedicated solely to the repression of all evil principles and to the advancement of every good principle —a legislative body that would be deeply concerned with the maintenance of a society, for it would share the consequences, be they honorable or disastrous. It has rightly been said that the upper house in England is invaluable to that nation because it provides a bulwark of liberty; and I would add that the Senate of Venezuela would be not only a bulwark of liberty but a bastion of defense, rendering the Republic eternal.

The British executive power possesses all the authority properly appertaining to a sovereign, but he is surrounded by a triple line of dams, barriers, and stockades. He is the head of the government, but his ministers and subordinates rely more upon law than upon his authority, as they are personally responsible; and not even decrees of royal authority can exempt them from this responsibility. The executive is commander in chief of the army and navy; he makes peace and declares war; but Parliament annually determines what sums are to be paid to these military forces. While the courts and judges are dependent on the executive power, the laws originate in and are made by Parliament. To neutralize the power of the King, his person is declared inviolable and sacred; but, while his head is left untouched, his hands are tied. The sovereign of England has three formidable rivals: his Cabinet, which is responsible to the people and to Parliament; the Senate [sic], which, representing the nobility of which it is composed, defends the interests of the people; and the House of Commons, which serves as the representative body of the British people and provides them with a place in which to express their opinions. Moreover, as the judges are responsible for the enforcement of the laws, they do not depart from them; and the administrators of the exchequer, being subject to prosecution not only for personal infractions but also for those of the government, take care to prevent any misuse of public funds. No matter how closely we study the composition of the English executive power, we can find nothing to prevent its being judged as the most perfect model for a kingdom, for an aristocracy, or for a democracy. Give Venezuela such an executive power in the person of a president chosen by the people or their representatives, and you will have taken a great step toward national happiness.

No matter what citizen occupies this office, he will be aided by the Constitution, and therein being authorized to do good, he can do no harm, because his ministers will cooperate with him only insofar as he abides by the law. If he attempts to infringe upon the law, his own ministers will desert him, thereby isolating him from the Republic, and they will even bring charges against him in the Senate. The ministers, being responsible for any transgressions committed, will actually govern, since they must account for their actions. The obligation which this system places upon the officials closest to the executive power, that is to take a most interested and active part in governmental deliberations and to regard this department as their own, is not the smallest advantage of the system. Should the president be a man of no great talent or virtue, yet, notwithstanding his lack of these essential qualities, he will be able to discharge his duties satisfactorily, for in such a case the ministry, managing everything by itself, will carry the burdens of the state.

Although the authority of the executive power in England may appear to be extreme, it would, perhaps, not be excessive in the Republic of Venezuela. Here the Congress has tied the hands and even the heads of its men of state. This deliberative assembly has assumed a part of the executive functions, contrary to the maxim of Montesquieu, to wit: A representative assembly should exercise no active function. It should only make laws and determine whether or not those laws are enforced. Nothing is as disturbing to harmony among the powers of government as their intermixture. Nothing is more dangerous with respect to the people than a weak executive; and if a kingdom has deemed it necessary to grant the executive so many powers, then in a republic these powers are infinitely more indispensable.

If we examine this difference, we will find that

the balance of power between the branches of government must be distributed in two ways. In republics the executive should be the stronger, for everything conspires against it; while in monarchies the legislative power should be superior, as everything works in the monarch's favor. The people's veneration of royal power results in a self-fascination that tends greatly to increase the superstitious respect paid to such authority. The splendor inherent in the throne, the crown, and the purple; the formidable support that it receives from the nobility; the immense wealth that a dynasty accumulates from generation to generation; and the fraternal protection that kings grant to one another are the significant advantages that work in favor of royal authority, thereby rendering it almost unlimited. Consequently, the significance of these same advantages should serve to justify the necessity of investing the chief magistrate of a republic with a greater measure of authority than that possessed by a constitutional prince.

A republican magistrate is an individual set apart from society, charged with checking the impulse of the people toward license and the propensity of judges and administrators toward abuse of the laws. He is directly subject to the legislative body, the senate, and the people: he is the one man who resists the combined pressure of the opinions, interests, and passions of the social state and who, as Carnot states, does little more than struggle constantly with the urge to dominate and the desire to escape domination. He is, in brief, an athlete pitted against a multitude of athletes.

This weakness can only be corrected by a strongly rooted force. It should be strongly proportioned to meet the resistance which the executive must expect from the legislature, from the judiciary, and from the people of a republic. Unless the executive has easy access to all the [administrative] resources, fixed by a just distribution of powers, he inevitably becomes a nonentity or abuses his authority. By this I mean that the result will be the death of the government, whose heirs are anarchy, usurpation, and tyranny. Some seek to check the executive authority by curbs and restrictions, and nothing is more just; but it must be remembered that the bonds we seek to preserve should, of course, be strengthened, but not tightened.

Therefore, let the entire system of government be strengthened, and let the balance of power be drawn up in such a manner that it will

be permanent and incapable of decay because of its own tenuity. Precisely because no form of government is so weak as the democratic, its framework must be firmer, and its institutions must be studied to determine their degree of stability. Unless this is done, we must plan on the establishment of an experimental rather than a permanent system of government; and we will have to reckon with an ungovernable, tumultuous, and anarchic society, not with a social order where happiness, peace, and justice prevail.

Legislators, we should not be presumptuous. We should be moderate in our pretensions. It is not likely that we will secure what mankind has never attained or that which the greatest and wisest nations have not acquired. Complete liberty and absolute democracy are but reefs upon which all republican hopes have foundered. Observe the ancient republics, the modern republics, and those of most recent origin: Virtually all have attempted to establish themselves as absolute democracies, and almost all have seen their just aspirations thwarted. The men who covet legitimate institutions and social perfection are indeed worthy of commendation. But who has told these men that they now possess the wisdom or practice the virtue that is so forcefully demanded by the union of power with justice? Only angels, not men, can exist free, peaceful, and happy while exercising every sovereign power.

The people of Venezuela already enjoy the rights that they may legitimately and easily exercise. Let us now, therefore, restrain the growth of immoderate pretensions which, perhaps, a form of government unsuited to our people might excite. Let us abandon the federal forms of government unsuited to us; let us put aside the triumvirate which holds the executive power and center it in a president. We must grant him sufficient authority to enable him to continue the struggle against the obstacles inherent in our recent situation, our present state of war, and every variety of foe, foreign and domestic, whom we must battle for some time to come. Let the legislature relinquish the powers that rightly belong to the executive; let it acquire, however, a new consistency, a new influence in the balance of authority. Let the courts be strengthened by increasing the stability and independence of the judges and by the establishment of juries and civil and criminal codes dictated, not by antiquity nor by conquering kings, but by the voice of Nature, the cry of Justice, and the genius of Wisdom.

My desire is for every branch of government and administration to attain that degree of vigor which alone can insure equilibrium, not only among the members of the government, but also among the different factions of which our society is composed. It would matter little if the springs of a political system were to relax because of its weakness, so long as this relaxation itself did not contribute to the dissolution of the body social and the ruination of its membership. The shouts of humanity, on the battlefields or in tumultuous crowds, denounce to the world the blind, unthinking legislators who imagined that experiments with chimerical institutions could be made with impunity. All the peoples of the world have sought freedom, some by force of arms, others by force of law, passing alternately from anarchy to despotism, or from despotism to anarchy. Few peoples have been content with moderate aims, establishing their institutions according to their means, their character, and their circumstances. We must not aspire to the impossible, lest, in trying to rise above the realm of liberty, we again descend into the realm of tyranny. Absolute liberty invariably lapses into absolute power, and the mean between these two extremes is supreme social liberty. Abstract theories create the pernicious idea of unlimited freedom. Let us see to it that the strength of the public is kept within the limits prescribed by reason and interest; that the national will is confined within the bonds set by a just power; that the judiciary is rigorously controlled by civil and criminal laws, analogous to those in our present Constitution — then an equilibrium between the powers of government will exist, the conflicts that hamper the progress of the state will disappear, and those complications which tend to hinder rather than unite society will be eliminated.

3. THE GREAT CAMPAIGN

A turning point in the struggle for independence in northern South America came in 1819, when Bolívar crossed the Colombian Andes with his army and attacked the Spanish forces in New Granada from a completely unexpected direction. Victory on the field of Boyacá crowned one of the most daring and brilliantly executed campaigns in history. In the following selection Daniel F. O'Leary (1800–1854),

Bolívar's English aide-de-camp and biographer, describes the epic campaign of 1819.[3]

WHILE BOLÍVAR assembled his army in Tame, the royalist forces in New Granada, perfectly equipped and under the command of the ablest officers of the expeditionary army, were quartered in the following manner: Four thousand men garrisoned the northern frontier, separating the provinces of Cundinamarca and Tunja from the plains of Casanare; three thousand well disciplined and well paid men, Spaniards and Americans, guarded the city of Santa Fe and other towns of the interior and the littoral. The cavalry mounted excellent horses; the artillery was well operated and lacked nothing. Add to these resources, which alone were probably enough to defend the country, the natural obstacles presented by the terrain, and Bolívar's project must seem a fantasy. But he counted less on the material force of his army than on the resources of his own genius and on the iron will that made his name so dreaded by the enemies of his country.

From Tame to Pore, the capital of Casanare, the road was inundated. "The territory through which the army had to make its first marches was a small sea, rather than solid land," says Santander in his account of this campaign. On July 27 they encountered obstacles of another kind.

The gigantic Andes, which are considered uncrossable at this season, imposed a seemingly insuperable barrier to the march of the army. For four days the troops battled against the difficulties of these rugged roads — if precipices can be called roads.

The plainsmen regarded these stupendous heights with astonishment and terror, and marveled at the existence of a land so different from their own. As they ascended, each new elevation increased their surprise, for what they had taken for the last peak was only the beginning of other and still loftier mountains, from whose crests they could discern ranges whose summits appeared to lose themselves in the eternal clouds of the firmament. Men who on their plains were accustomed to cross torrential rivers, tame savage horses, and conquer in bodily combat the wild bull, the tiger, and the crocodile were frightened by the forbidding aspect of these

[3] Daniel F. O'Leary, *Bolívar y la emancipación de Sur-América,* Madrid, 1915, 2 vols., I, 664–682. (Excerpt translated by the editor.)

strange surroundings. Losing hope of overcoming such stupendous difficulties, their horses already dead from fatigue, they decided that only madmen could persevere in the enterprise, in a climate whose temperature numbed their senses and froze their bodies. As a result, many of them deserted.

The mules carrying the munitions and arms fell under the weight of their burdens; few horses survived the five days of marching; and the fallen animals of the forward division obstructed the road and increased the difficulties of the rear guard. It rained incessantly day and night, and the cold grew worse as they ascended. The cold water, to which the troops were not accustomed, caused diarrhea among them. It seemed as if sorcery had conjured up this accumulation of mishaps in order to destroy the hopes of Bolívar. He alone remained firm among reverses the least of which would have discouraged a weaker spirit. He inspired the troops with his presence and example, speaking to them of the glory that awaited them, and of the abundance that reigned in the country that they were going to liberate. The soldiers listened to him with pleasure and redoubled their efforts.

On the 27th the vanguard dispersed a royalist force of 300 men, advantageously posted in front of Paya, a town in the cordillera. This strong position could bar the passage of an army; the royalist detachment was more than sufficient to defend it against 6,000 men; but the timidity of the Spanish commander saved the army and opened to Bolívar the road to New Granada. . . .

After some days of rest, the army resumed its march on July 2. The royalist detachment which had been beaten at Paya retired to Labranza Grande, which was reached by a road that was considered the only passable one at that season of the year. There was another, across the páramo of Pisba, but it was so rough that it was hardly used even in the summer. The Spaniards considered it unusable and therefore neglected its defense; Bolívar selected it for precisely that reason. The passage of Casanare through plains covered with water, and that of the portion of the Andes which lay behind us, though rugged and steep was in every way preferable to the road which the army was to take.

At many points immense fallen rocks and trees, and slides caused by the constant rains that made walking dangerous and uncertain, completely obstructed its advance. The soldiers, who had received rations of meat and arracacha

for four days, threw them away and kept only their rifles, for the climb presented enough difficulties without any burdens. The few surviving horses perished during this day.

As darkness fell the army reached the foot of the páramo of Pisba, where it passed a frightful night. It was impossible to have a fire, because there were no dwellings in the vicinity and a steady drizzle, accompanied by hail and a freezing wind, quenched the bonfires made in the open as quickly as they were lighted.

Since the troops were nearly naked, and the majority were natives of the burning plains of Venezuela, it is easier to conceive than to describe their cruel sufferings. The following day they reached the páramo itself, a dismal and inhospitable desert, devoid of all vegetation because of its height. On that day the effect of the piercingly cold air was fatal to many soldiers; many fell suddenly ill while on the march and expired in a few minutes. Flogging was used, with success in some cases, to revive frozen soldiers; a colonel of cavalry was saved in this way.

During this day's march my attention was called to a group of soldiers who had stopped near where I had seated myself, overcome with fatigue. Seeing anxiety written on their faces, I asked one of them what was wrong; he replied that the wife of a soldier of the Rifles Battalion was in labor. The next morning I saw the same woman, her babe in her arms, and apparently in the best of health, marching in the rear guard of the battalion. After the birth she had walked for two leagues along one of the worst roads in that rough terrain.

One hundred men would have sufficed to destroy the patriot army while crossing the páramo. On the march it was impossible to keep the soldiers together because even the officers could barely stand the hardships of the road, much less attend to the troops. That night was more terrible than the preceding ones, and although the encampment was more sheltered and the rain less frequent, many soldiers died from the effects of their sufferings and privations. As the parties of ten or twenty men descended together from the páramo, the President [Bolívar] congratulated them on the approaching conclusion of the campaign, telling them that they had already conquered the greatest obstacles of the march.

On the 6th the division of Anzoátegui reached Socha, the first town in the province of Tunja; the vanguard had arrived there on the preceding day. The soldiers, seeing behind them the crests of the mountains, covered with clouds and mists, spontaneously vowed to conquer or die rather than retreat through those mountains, for they feared them more than the most formidable enemy. In Socha the army received a cordial welcome from the inhabitants of that place and its vicinity. Bread, tobacco, and *chicha,* a beverage made from corn and cane-juice syrup, rewarded the troops for their sufferings and inspired greater hopes for the future. But as the hardships of the soldier diminished, the cares of the general increased. . . .

Great was the royalist surprise to learn that they had unwelcome guests in the shape of an enemy army; it seemed incredible that Bolívar should have begun operations and overcome such great obstacles at a time of the year when few dared to undertake even the shortest journeys. . . .

Meanwhile the enemy remained in his positions, giving no sign that he wished to accept combat on the plain. After vain efforts to commit him to an action, Bolívar ordered a flank movement in an effort to encircle his right wing. At dawn on the 25th of July, anniversary of the patron saint of Spain and the birthday of Bolívar, the army began to cross the Sogamoso river, which runs through the plains of Bonza.

At midday, as the army defiled through the swamp of Vargas, the enemy appeared on the heights in front.

Since nine in the morning Barreiro had observed the movement of the patriots and had speedily acted to counter it. Both armies immediately got ready for battle. The republicans were forced to occupy an unfavorable position, which Bolívar sought to improve by sending Santander with his division to the heights that dominated the left wing of the Army of Liberation, whose right wing was protected by a swamp.

Barreiro began the action by sending the first battalion *del Rey* against the left wing of the patriot army, to be followed by an attack on its shoulder. Seeing that this corps had seized the heights, where Santander offered very feeble resistance, Barreiro struck at the center of the line with such force that the Rifles and Barcelona battalions broke and gave way.

At that moment all seemed lost, but Bolívar flew to reunite the shattered corps, ordering Colonel Rook and his British Legion to dislodge the enemy from the heights that he had occupied. The fearless Englishman carried out his assignment with brilliant success.

Now the royalist general, fiery and tireless, made a second furious attack on the front of the patriot army. But he gained only a temporary advantage, for Bolívar, making judicious use of his small reserve, decided the fate of the battle with a magnificent cavalry charge.

One word or the efforts of a single individual have sometimes succeeded in calming an insurrection or gaining a triumph. At that critical moment, when everything seemed to favor the Spaniards, who already counted on the complete destruction of the patriot army, and when all — except Bolívar — despaired of victory, Rondón appeared with his squadron of *llaneros.* Bolívar shouted words of encouragement and cried to their leader: "Colonel, save the fatherland!" Rondón, followed by his brave soldiers, immediately hurled himself upon the advancing enemy squadrons and threw them back, with a heavy loss of life. The infantry imitated Rondón's feat, and the royalists could not withstand the impetus of the combined attack.

The night put an end to the bloody battle, whose outcome seemed doubtful at certain moments. Twice that day the Army of Liberation believed that all was lost.

Barreiro's communiqué pays tribute to the valor of our troops. "Desperation," he says, "inspired them with an unheard-of valor. Their infantry and cavalry left the gullies into which they had been hurled, and rushed with fury up the heights which they had lost. Our infantry could not resist them. . . ."

The bravery of Rondón and the calm bravery of the few British troops contributed substantially to victory, or rather to saving the liberating army of New Granada from destruction. In the general order published the next day, Bolívar acknowledged the merits of these brave foreigners by conferring on them the "Cross of Liberators," a distinction which they well deserved. . . .

Bolívar's activity and energy appeared to redouble even as his difficulties increased. He never showed himself more worthy of his reputation than after the battle of Vargas. General Páez had not lived up to his agreement to invade New Granada by way of Cúcuta, because he either could not or would not leave the plains of the Apure, so there was no longer any reason to hope for aid from that quarter. The army could rely only on the talents of Bolívar and the expedients that his genius might suggest. Actually, these were enough, as the course of events was to show. . . .

After the expected munitions and the convalescents from the hospital had arrived, and after the army had been augmented by numbers of patriotic volunteers, on August 3 the army began its advance on the enemy. Barreiro was forced to evacuate the town of Paipa, and as the patriots approached he withdrew his advance guards to the heights dominating the road to Tunja.

At nightfall the patriots crossed the Sogamoso River and encamped within half a league from the royalists. [The following day Bolívar recrossed the river, apparently returning to his former position at Bonza; but at nightfall he gave a counterorder, crossed the river once more, and, leaving the enemy behind, began a rapid march on Tunja by way of Toca. Ed.] At eleven in the morning he occupied the city and took as prisoners the few soldiers of the garrison, for the governor of Tunja had left that same morning for Barreiro's headquarters with the third *Numancia* battalion and an artillery brigade. The patriot army was received in Tunja with the same joyful demonstrations that had greeted it everywhere.

Bolívar's daring movement terrified the Spaniards and decided the fate of the campaign. The enemy learned of the movement only the next morning, when Barreiro set out for Tunja by the principal road. During the night he turned slightly to the right, and the next morning he entered Motavita, a village a short distance from the city.

A cavalry detachment which had followed his movements, stabbing at his rear guard, caused him a good deal of trouble during the night, and took all his stragglers as prisoners.

On the 7th, Barreiro continued his march, and as soon as Bolívar, by a personal reconnaissance, had assured himself of its direction, he ordered the army to march toward the same point, with the intention of cutting the enemy off from Santa Fe.

At two in the afternoon the first royalists reached the bridge of Boyacá. They were passing over it when the patriot vanguard attacked their rear; simultaneously Santander's division appeared on the heights which dominated the position where Barreiro had drawn up his army.

The battle began with skirmishes between scouts. Meanwhile a column of royalist chasseurs crossed the bridge under the command of Colonel Jiménez and drew up in battle formation. But Barreiro, finding himself unable to do the same with the bulk of his army, ordered it to withdraw about three quarters of a mile from the bridge, and thereby gave the patriots time to cut him off from Santa Fe.

Bolívar immediately ordered Santander to force the bridge, and Anzoátegui simultaneously to attack the right wing and the center of the royalist position. The combat now became general; the Spanish infantry fought very bravely for some time, until Anzoátegui and his lancers enveloped their right wing and took the artillery on which the Rifles battalion had made a frontal attack; the fleeing cavalry was cut down, and when the infantry saw this they surrendered. A bayonet charge decided the day. Jiménez, who defended the bridge and was holding Santander's division in check, fell back when he saw Barreiro's plight, and the rout became general.

Sixteen hundred men laid down their arms. Barreiro, his second-in-command, Jiménez, and the majority of the chiefs and officers were taken prisoner. Artillery, munitions, arms, banners, money, and baggage fell into the hands of the victor. Bolívar personally pursued the fugitives as far as Venta Quemada, where he spent that night.

On the following morning an act of just retribution took place. Vinoni, the traitor, who had played a leading part in the uprising at and surrender of the castle of Puerto Cabello to the Spaniards, was recognized by Bolívar among the prisoners taken during the pursuit; he was immediately hanged.

4. THE ARMY OF THE ANDES

For Argentines the figure of José de San Martín has the same heroic and legendary quality that Bolívar possesses for the peoples of northern South America. Modest and reserved, San Martín was something of an enigma to his contemporaries, and we lack a description as revealing of the man as Perú de Lacroix's sketch of Bolívar. From the military point of view, San Martín's chief claim to greatness is his masterful campaign of the Andes, prelude to the decisive attack on Peru. To this day the standard biography of San Martín is the classic life by Bartolomé Mitre (1821–1906), distinguished Argentine soldier, historian, and statesman. Mitre describes San Martín's painstaking preparations for the passage of the Andes.[4]

SAN MARTÍN tried to convince the enemy that he planned to invade Chile in the south, whereas

[4] Bartolomé Mitre, *Historia de San Martín y de la emancipación sudaméricana*, Buenos Aires, 1944, 2 vols., I, 319–334. (Excerpt translated by the editor.)

he actually intended to strike in the center. This was a fixed major objective of his "war of nerves," and that is why he deceived friend and enemy alike with misleading communications and incomplete confidences, guarding his secret until the last moment. In order to confirm Marcó, the Spanish governor of Chile, in his mistaken views, he devised a new stratagem, which, like all his ruses, bore the stamp of novelty and of a brain fertile in expedients.

Since 1814, San Martín, as governor of Cuyo, had cultivated friendly relations with the Pehuenche Indians, then masters of the eastern slopes of the cordillera south of Mendoza, in order to ensure the safe transit of his secret Chilean agents through the passes they dominated, and to have them on his side in case of an enemy invasion. At the time he assembled his army in the encampment of Plumerillo he decided to renew these relations, with the double object of deceiving the enemy with respect to his true plans, and of giving greater security and importance to the secondary operations which he planned to carry out by way of the southern passes. For this purpose he invited them to a general parley in the Fort of San Carlos, above the boundary line of the Diamond River, with the ostensible object of seeking permission to pass through their lands. He sent ahead trains of mules loaded with hundreds of barrels of wine and skins filled with aguardiente; with sweets, bright-colored cloths, and glass beads for the women; and, for the men, horse gear, foodstuffs of all kinds, and all the old clothes that the province could supply, in order to dazzle the allies. On the appointed day the Pehuenches approached the fort with barbaric pomp, blowing their horns, flourishing their long plumed lances, and followed by their women. The warriors were naked from the waist up and wore their long hair untied; all were in fighting trim. Each tribe was preceded by a guard of mounted grenadiers, whose correctly martial appearance contrasted with the savage appearance of the Indians. On approaching the esplanade of the fort, the women went to one side, and the men whirled their lances about by way of greeting. There followed a picturesque sham fight in Pehuenche style, with the warriors riding at full speed around the walls of the redoubt, from whose walls a gun fired a salvo every five minutes, to which the braves responded by striking themselves on the mouth and whooping with joy.

The solemn meeting that followed was held on the parade ground of the fort. San Martín asked permission to pass through the lands of the Pehuenches in order to attack the Spaniards through the Planchón and Portillo passes. The Spaniards, he told them, were foreigners, enemies of the American Indian, whose fields and herds, women and children, they sought to steal. The Colo-colo of the tribes was a white-haired ancient called Necuñan. After consulting the assembly and obtaining their opinions with suitable gravity, he told the general that with the exception of three caciques, with whom they could deal later, all accepted his proposals, and they sealed the treaty of alliance by embracing San Martín, one after another. In proof of their friendship they immediately placed their arms in the keeping of the Christians and gave themselves up to an orgy that lasted for eight consecutive days. On the sixth day the general returned to his headquarters to await the result of these negotiations, whose object he kept secret from even his most intimate confidants.

The creole diplomat had foreseen that the Indians, with their natural perfidy — or the dissident caciques, at any rate — would report his pretended project to Marcó, as actually happened. But just in case they should not do so, he hastened to communicate it to the Spanish leader directly by means of one of his characteristic ruses, in which he was aided by a coincidence that he had also foreseen. During the reorganization of his army he had cut the supposed communications of the Spaniards of Cuyo with Marcó, and the latter, ignorant of everything that was taking place east of the Andes, sent emissaries to obtain information from the individuals whom he believed to be his official correspondents. Such was San Martín's vigilance that for two years not a single royalist spy had been able to penetrate into Cuyo without being captured in the cordillera by patriot guards who had been warned by secret agents in Chile. The last letters of the Spanish governor met the same fate. With these letters in his possession, San Martín summoned the supposed correspondents to his presence, — among them was Castillo de Albo, — showed them the incriminating letters, and with pretended anger (it is said that he even threatened them with a pistol that he had on his desk) forced them to write and sign replies that he dictated. In these replies he announced that "about the 15th of October" a squadron was preparing to leave Buenos Aires for an unknown destination. It was "composed of a frigate, three corvettes, two brigantines, and two transports, all under the command of the Englishman Teler [Taylor]." "San Martín," they added, "has held a general parley with the Pehuenche Indians. The Indians have agreed to everything; we shall see how they carry out their pledges; caution and more caution; for lack of it our people have suffered imprisonment and spoliations. Everything is known here." In another he said that a French engineer had left Mendoza in order to construct a bridge over the Diamond River. San Martín's letters, sent by an emissary who played the role of a double spy, were delivered to Marcó, who believed everything in them, lost his head entirely, and turned the whole province upside down to guard against a double invasion. At the same time San Martín informed the government of Buenos Aires that the purpose of the parley was to get the Indians "to assist the passage of the army with live stock and horses at the stipulated prices," while to his confidant, Guido, he wrote: "I concluded with all success my great parley with the Indians of the south; they not only will aid the army with livestock but are committed to take an active part against the enemy." As can be seen, San Martín was a well of large and small mysteries, with the naked truth hidden at the bottom.

Marcó, disheartened by the alarming news from his supposed correspondents in Cuyo, and by the simultaneous rising of the guerrillas of Manuel Rodríguez, who extended their excursions between the Maule and the Maipo and made armed assaults on villages in the very vicinity of the capital, dictated a series of senseless and contradictory measures that revealed the confusion in his mind and the fear in his heart. He ordered the ports to be fortified and attempted to convert some of them into islands with the object of preventing a disembarkation; at the same time he equipped a squadron to act against the imaginary fleet of Buenos Aires. He commanded that entrenchments should be thrown up in the pass of Uspallata, that the southern provinces of the kingdom should be mapped and that the entrances to the Maule and Planchón passes should be surveyed; but before these tasks had been completed he ordered strengthening of the guards at all the passes of the cordillera, from north to south. First he concentrated his troops and then he dispersed most of them again, moving them about in empty space. Finding no inspiration in himself, after jerking about like a puppet manipulated by San Martín, he finished by reproducing the man's very gestures, like a monkey; in imitation of the patriot general he held a parley with the Araucanian Indians, but failed to devise a rational plan of defense.

The objective of the astute Argentine leader was fulfilled: the captain-general of Chile sought to defend all its land and sea frontiers simultaneously; consequently he dispersed his army and thus became weak everywhere, never suspecting the point of the true attack. To crown his confusion, the spies he sent to obtain accurate information either did not return or served San Martín by bringing back false reports that led him to commit new errors. Some of his advisers urged him to take the offensive; others, that he persevere in his absurd waiting plan; and only one of them, his secretary, Dr. Judas Tadeo Reyes, the least knowledgeable in warfare, suggested the plan he should have followed: concentrate the 50,000 veteran troops in the capital, disperse the militia troops about the country, and await the invasion in that posture. However, by this time Marcó was so distraught that good and bad counsels were equally useless. He himself graphically depicted his deplorable morale at this time (February 4, 1817): "My plans are reduced to continual movements and variations according to developments and news of the enemy, whose astute chief at Mendoza, kept informed of my situation by his innumerable lines of communication and the disloyal spies who surround me, seeks to surprise me."

But it was not only the threat of impending invasion that made Marcó uneasy. His resources were scanty, and as a result of the stupid system of taxation established by Osorio and continued and intensified by himself, the very sources of further contributions were exhausted. In order to defray the public expenses he levied a tax on exports of grain and flour and imports of wine and sugar; simultaneously he decreed a forced loan of 400,000 pesos to be collected from individuals with an annual income of 1,000 pesos, not excluding civil and military officers, and payable in cash. The sole result of these measures was the spread of demoralization and discontent, which fanned the sparks of insurrection lighted by the agents of San Martín, who announced his immediate arrival at the head of a powerful liberating army. . . .

The situation was quite different in the encampment at Mendoza: here there was a methodical activity, an automatic obedience coupled with an enthusiasm born of understanding. A superior will, that knew what it wanted and what it was doing, directed all, inspiring the soldiers with the feeling that victory was certain. In Mendoza it was known what Marcó did, thought, or was going to do, whereas Marcó did not even know what he wanted to do. Everyone worked, each performing the task assigned to him, and they all trusted in their general. Pack mules and war horses were assembled; thousands of horseshoes were forged for the animals; pack-saddles were made for the beasts of burden; fodder and provisions were stored; and herds of cattle were rounded up for the passage of the cordillera. Leaders, officers, and soldiers devoted themselves to their respective duties and positions. The arsenal turned out hundreds of thousands of cartridges. The forges blazed day and night, repairing arms and casting projectiles. The indefatigable Father Luis Beltran supervised the construction of new machines by means of which, as he put it, the cannon would fly over the tops of the mountains like condors. The ingenious friar had invented, or rather adapted, a kind of narrow carriage (called *zorra*) of rude but solid construction which, mounted on four low wheels and drawn by oxen or mules, replaced the mounts of the cannon; the guns themselves would be carried on the backs of mules along the narrow, tortuous paths of the cordillera until they reached the plain on the other side. As a precaution, long slings were made in which the carriages and cannon would be hoisted over rough places between mules, as if in litters, one after the other; sleds of hide were also prepared in which heavy objects might be hauled up by hand or by a portable winch when the gradients were too steep for the mules.

Meantime the general-in-chief, silent and reserved, planned for everyone, inspected everything, and provided for all contingencies in the most minute detail, from food and equipment for men and beasts to the complicated machines of war, even seeing the cutting edge of his soldiers' sabres.

The army needed a healthful and nourishing food that would restore the soldiers' strength and would be suited to the frigid temperatures through which they must pass. San Martín found this in a popular dish called *charquican,* composed of beef dried in the sun, roasted, ground to powder, mixed with fat and chili pepper, and well pounded. A soldier could carry enough of this in his knapsack to last him eight days. Mixed with hot water and roasted maize meal it made a nutritious and appetizing porridge. . . . After providing for his soldiers' stomachs, San Martín took thought for their feet — the vehicles of victory. In order to obtain footwear without burdening the treasury, he asked the *cabildo* of Mendoza to collect and send to the camp the scraps of cowhide discarded every day by the slaughterhouses of the city. From these pieces he had the soldiers make *tamangos,* a kind of closed sandal often used by the Negroes. . . . He carried economy to extreme lengths in order to show, in his own words, that great enterprises can be accomplished with small means. An order of the day, made public to the sound of drums, asked the people to bring to special depots old woolen rags that could be used to line the *tamangos,* because, San Martín declared, "the health of the soldiers is a powerful machine that if well directed can bring victory; and our first concern is to protect their feet." The horns of slaughtered cattle were used to make canteens, necessary in crossing the waterless stretches of the cordillera. Another decree ordered all the cloth remnants in the stores and tailor shops of the city to be collected, and San Martín distributed them to the soldiers to make into straps for their knapsacks.

The sabres of the mounted grenadiers had lost their sharpness; San Martín had them given a razor-like edge and placed them in the hands of his soldiers, saying they were for cutting off Spanish heads. It was not enough to sharpen swords; arms had to be trained to use them; and martial instruments were needed to nerve the soldiers and to take the place of the officer's voice in battle. San Martín chose the trumpet, an instrument rarely used by American cavalry at that time. The army had only three trumpets. San Martín had some made out of tin, but they were mute. In his application to the government San Martín wrote: "The trumpet is as necessary for the cavalry as is the drum for the infantry. . . . "

The general gave the matter of horseshoes his closest attention. Before making a decision he held conferences with veterinarians, blacksmiths, and muleteers; after carefully listening to them, he adopted a model of a horseshoe which he sent to the government, telling the officer who carried it to guard it as if it were made of gold and to present it to the Minister of War. . . . The army needed thirty thousand horseshoes with a double set of nails. In two months they were forged by artisans who toiled day and night in the shops of the arms factory in Buenos Aires and in the forges of Mendoza.

How was the army to cross the deep ravines

and torrents that lay before it? How were the heavy materials of war to ascend and descend the steep slopes of the mountains? And finally, how were the carriages and their loads to be rescued from the depths into which they might fall? These were problems that had to be solved. For river passages a rope bridge of a given weight and length (60 *varas*) was devised, and the piece of cable which was to be shown to the government as a model was entrusted to an officer with the same solemnity as the horseshoe. "It is impossible to transport the artillery and other heavy objects over the narrow defiles and slopes of the cordillera, or to rescue material fallen from the path," wrote San Martín, "without the aid of two anchors and four cables, of a weight that can be transported on muleback." With this apparatus, moved by a winch, the difficulties of the passage were overcome. . . .

Amid this official correspondence concerning the movement of men, materials, and money, an exchange of letters of mixed character took place between the two protagonists of our story: General San Martín and Pueyrredón, Director of the United Provinces of La Plata. Passionately devoted to the same cause, they aided and comforted each other, until they and their mission became one. . . .

"You don't ask for much," the Director would write San Martín, "and I feel bad because I don't have the money to get these things for you; but I shall do my best, and by the beginning of October I shall have gotten together thirty thousand pesos for the use of the army." But hardly had Pueyrredón assumed direction of the government and begun to make good his promises when there broke out in Córdoba a confused anarchical revolt that threatened to throw the entire Republic into chaos. . . .

When the brief uprising of Córdoba had been crushed, the general of the Andes renewed his insistent urging, as has been shown from the official correspondence. The Director provided everything, and when he had satisfied all demands he took up his pen and wrote with humorous desperation and comradely forthrightness: "I am sending official letters of thanks to Mendoza and the other cities of Cuyo. I am sending the officers' commissions. I am sending the uniforms you asked for and many more shirts. I am sending 400 saddles. I am sending off today by post two trumpets — all I could find. In January I shall send 1387 *arrobas* of dried beef. I am sending the 200 spare sabres that you asked for. I am sending 200 tents or pavilions; that's

all there are. I am sending the world, the flesh, and the devil! I don't know how I shall get out of the scrape I'm in to pay for all this, unless I declare bankruptcy, cancel my accounts with everyone, and clear out to join you, so that you can give me some of the dried beef I'm sending you. Damn it, don't ask me for anything else, unless you want to hear that they found me in the morning dangling from a beam in the Fort!" . . .

When everything was ready the general of the expedition asked for instructions concerning his military and political courses of action. The government, inspired by the same lofty aims as the general, drew up instructions infused with a broad, generous, and resolute spirit, in harmony with San Martín's continental plan; and formulated, in words which deeds were to make good, the liberation policy of the Argentine Revolution in respect to the other peoples of South America, on the basis of independence and liberty for each one of them. "The consolidation of American independence" (said Article 1) "and the glory of the United Provinces of South America are the only motives of this campaign. The general will make this clear in his proclamations; he will spread it through his agents in every town, and will propagate it by every possible means. The army must be impressed with these principles. Care must be taken that not a word is said of pillage, oppression, conquest, or retaining possession of the liberated country." . . .

With these instructions in his portfolio, all decisions made, and the army poised at the eastern entrances to the Andes, San Martín, one foot already in the stirrup, wrote (January 24, 1817) his last letter to his most intimate confidant: "This afternoon I set out to join the army. God grant me success in this great enterprise."

5. THE INTERVIEW OF GUAYAQUIL

Historical controversy still rages in Latin America about the famous meeting between Bolívar and San Martín at Guayaquil, in July, 1822. One view is that San Martín came to Guayaquil in search of military aid from Bolívar, was rebuffed by the Liberator, and magnanimously determined to quit Peru, leaving the way open for Bolívar to complete the work he had begun. Other students deny that San Martín asked Bolívar for more troops at the conference; they say that San Martín's departure from Peru was motivated by personal reasons and had nothing to do with the generals' discussion. The following account of this private conference was given by Bolívar to his secretary, J. G. Pérez.[5]

General Headquarters, Guayaquil, July 29, 1822. The 12th [year].

MY DEAR GENERAL SUCRE:

I have the honor of informing you that on the 26th, at nine o'clock in the morning, His Excellency the Protector of Perú entered this city.

No sooner did the Protector see His Excellency the Liberator aboard the ship that had brought him than he expressed in the most cordial terms the sentiments that had heightened his desire to meet the Liberator, to embrace him, and to assure him of his true and lasting friendship. He congratulated His Excellency on his remarkable perseverance amidst the adversities that he had met with in defense of the cause of freedom and on the victory which had crowned his heroic achievements. Altogether, the Protector protested his friendship for His Excellency in terms of high eulogy and lavish praise.

His Excellency replied in the noble and gracious terms that propriety and gratitude demand in such circumstances.

The Protector opened the conferences in a most frank manner. The principal topics were as follows:

The situation recently experienced in this province, because of the ferment of political opinions, was discussed. Of his own accord the Protector told His Excellency that he had not interfered in the tangled affairs of Guayaquil, that he had not the slightest part in them, and that the fault was theirs, meaning the opposition. His Excellency replied that his desire to consult that city had been realized, for on the 28th the electors would meet, and that he was counting upon the will of the people and a plurality of votes in the assembly. The Protector thereupon changed the subject and went on to talk of military matters and of the expedition which is about to depart [for Perú].

The Protector complained a great deal about his command and, above all, about his comrades-in-arms who had recently abandoned him in Lima. He asserted that he was going to retire to Mendoza, that he had left a sealed note to be presented to the Congress, renouncing the Pro-

tectorate, that he would also refuse the election which he expected to win; and that, as soon as he had won the first victory, he would give up his military command and not await the war's end. But, he added, before retiring he would give thought to laying the foundations of the [Peruvian] government. He stated that this government should not be democratic, as democracy did not suit Perú; and lastly he said that an independent, unattached prince should be brought from Europe to rule Perú. His Excellency replied that to invite European princes would please neither America nor Colombia, as they were extraneous to our people, and that for his part His Excellency would oppose them if he were able, yet without interfering in whatever form of government any country might desire. His Excellency set forth all his ideas on the nature of governments, repeating all that he had said in his speech to the Congress of Angostura. The Protector replied that the securing of a prince was a matter for the future.

It can be assumed that his plan is to erect a monarchy by offering the crown to several European princes, and finally to grant the throne to the one receiving the most popular support or having the strongest force to offer. If the Protector is sincere in what he says, no one is further than he from occupying such a throne. He appears to be convinced of the difficulties inherent in leadership.

The Protector applauded highly the federation of the American states as being the very foundation of our political existence. He regards Guayaquil as the most suitable place for the headquarters of such a federation. He believes Chile will have no objections to joining it, but that Buenos Aires, because of the lack of unity and method in that country, will refuse. He said that nothing was closer to his heart than to have the federation between Colombia and Perú continue, even in the absence of other states.

The Protector believes the enemy is weaker than he, and that the enemy's leaders, though daring and able, are not to be greatly feared. He will immediately open his campaign with a maritime expedition to Intermedios and from Lima, defending that capital by a frontal march on the enemy.

In their very first talks, the Protector, of his own accord, told his Excellency that the matter of boundaries between Colombia and Perú would be settled satisfactorily and without the slightest difficulty. He would undertake to spon-

[5] José Gabriel Pérez to General Antonio José Sucre, Guayaquil, July 29, 1822, in Lecuna and Bierck, *Selected Writings of Bolívar*, I, 340–343. Reprinted by kind permission of the Banco de Venezuela.

sor it in the Congress, where he did not lack friends.

The Protector told His Excellency that he might ask anything he wished of Perú, as his answer would never be anything but yes, yes, yes; and that he hoped that Colombia would reciprocate. This offer of services and friendship is without qualification, and it displays a frankness and a sense of satisfaction that appear to be sincere. The Protector's visit to Colombia was not official in character; it was merely a visit to His Excellency the Liberator for no ulterior purpose, political or military. He did not so much as refer to the troops that Colombia is about to send to Perú.

Early yesterday morning the Protector departed. On taking leave, he displayed the same cordiality, affection, and sincerity toward His Excellency as at their first meeting.

6. AYACUCHO

The departure of San Martin from Peru left the country in the hands of weak and incompetent politicians. Threatened by a strong Spanish counter-offensive, the Peruvian leaders called on Bolivar to save the new state from destruction. Bolivar responded to their summons. The battle of Ayacucho, fought on December 9, 1824, was the last major action in the Spanish-American Wars of Independence.[6]

QUINUA, AN INDIAN VILLAGE, is on the western extremity of the plain of Ayacucho, the shape of which is nearly square, about a league in circumference, and flanked right and left by deep, rugged, ravines. In the rear of the plain, or towards the west, is a gradual descent of two leagues to the main road from Guamanga to Guanta, which runs along the base of a mountain range, that rises like a wall with no apparent outlet. The eastern boundary of the plain is formed by the abrupt and rugged ridge of Condorkanki; which gigantic bulwark, running north and south, overlooks the field of Ayacucho. A little below the summit of this ridge was perched the royalist army.

The liberating army was drawn up on the plain, in front of the Spaniards, at an interval of about a mile, having Quinua in the rear, each corps being formed in close column, to await the attack of the royalists. . . .

During the night of the 8th, a brisk fire was maintained between the royalist and patriot

[6] John Miller, *Memoirs of General Miller, in the Service of the Republic of Peru*, London, 1828, 2 vols., II, 194–202.

outposts. It was the object of Sucre to prevent the royalists descending in the night. For this purpose the bands of two battalions were sent with a company near to the foot of the ridge, and continued playing for some time whilst a sharp fire was kept up. This feint had the desired effect, for the royalists did not stir from their lines.

The viceroy's position in the night of the 8th was very much exposed: his infantry, occupying the front of the ridge of Condorkanki, was within musket-range of the foot of the hill. The fire from two or three battalions, deployed into line, might have obliged the royalists to abandon their position. As it was, a lieutenant-colonel and two or three men, within the Spanish encampment, were killed, as they sat round their fires, by chance balls from the patriot company at the foot of the hill.

The night of the 8th was one of deep and anxious interest. A battle was inevitable on the following day, and that battle was to decide the destinies of South America. The patriots were aware that they had to contend with twice their own numbers; and that nothing but a decisive victory could save them and their country from ignominious servitude. The patriot *soldier* might indeed expect to escape with *life*, reduced to the condition of a slave; but with the patriot generals and officers, it was only a choice between death and victory. They knew full well what would be the cruel policy of the Spaniards if they proved victorious. The viceroy was, it is true, a man of humane disposition, but the individual who counselled Monet to shoot two patriot officers in the pass of San Mateo, and the other man (if such he may be called) who ran his sword through the wounded and defenceless Major Gumer, on the field at Lea, were, with others, of a character equally sanguinary, amongst the advisers of La Serna; and it is extremely probable that unsparing executions would have been resorted to in the hope of destroying the very germ of future insurrection. Every one felt that the approaching battle was to have no common result.

The morning of the 9th dawned particularly fine. At first there was a chilliness in the air which seemed to influence the minds of the men, but when the sun rose above the mountain, the effects of its genial warmth became manifest in the renovated spirits of the soldiers. The men on both sides were observed rubbing their hands, and exhibiting every token of content and satisfaction. At nine A.M. the division of Villalobos began to descend. The viceroy, on foot, placed himself at its head; and the files wound down the craggy side of Condorkanki, obliquing a little to their left. The division Monet, forming the royalist right, commenced at the same time to defile directly into the plain. The cavalry, leading their horses, made the same movement, though with greater difficulty, between the infantry of each division. As the files arrived on the plain, they formed into column. This was a moment of extraordinary interest. It appeared as though respiration were suspended by feelings of anxiety, mingled with doubts and hope.

It was during this operation, which had an imposing effect, that Sucre rode along his own line, and, addressing a few emphatic words to each corps, recalled to memory its former achievements. He then placed himself in a central point, and, in an inspiring tone of voice, said, "that upon the efforts of that day depended the fate of South America;" then pointing to the descending columns, he assured his men, "that another day of glory was about to crown their admirable constancy." This animating address of the general produced an electric effect, and was answered by enthusiastic "vivas."

By the time that rather more than half the royalist divisions, Monet and Villalobos, had reached and formed upon the arena, Sucre ordered the division Córdova and two regiments of cavalry to advance to the charge. The gallant Córdova placed himself about fifteen yards in front of his division, formed into four parallel columns with the cavalry in the intervals. Having dismounted, he plunged his sword into the heart of his charger, and turning to the troops, exclaimed, "there lies my last horse; I have now no means of escape, and we must fight it out together!" Then waving his hat above his head, he continued, *Adelante, con paso de vencedores* (Onward with the step of conquerors). These words were heard distinctly throughout the columns, which, inspired by the gallant bearing of their leader, moved to the attack in the finest possible order. The Spaniards stood firmly and full of apparent confidence. The viceroy was seen, as were also Monet and Villalobos, at the head of their divisions, superintending the formation of their columns as they reached the plain. The hostile bayonets crossed, and for three or four minutes the two parties struggled together, so as to leave it doubtful which would give way. At this moment the Colombian cavalry, headed by Colonel Silva, charged. This brave officer fell covered with wounds, but the intrepidity of the onset was irresistible. The royalists lost ground, and were driven back with great slaughter. The vice-king was wounded and taken prisoner. As the fugitives climbed the sides of Condorkanki, the patriots, who had deployed, kept up a well-directed fire, and numbers of the enemy were seen to drop and roll down, till their progress was arrested by the brush-wood, or some jutting crag.

Miller, who had followed up Córdova's division, perceiving its complete success, returned to the regiment of Úsares de Junín, which fortunately had been left in reserve.

At dawn of day, the royalist division Valdés commenced a detour of nearly a league. Descending the sides of Condokanki on the north, Valdés had placed himself on the left of the patriots at musket-shot distance, separated by a ravine. At the important moment of the battle, just described, he opened a heavy fire from four field-pieces and a battalion in extended files. By this, he obliged two battalions of the Peruvian division La Mar to fall back. The Colombian battalion Bargas, sent to support the Peruvian division, also began to give way. Two royalist battalions crossed the deep ravine, already spoken of, on the left, and advanced in double quick time in pursuit of the retiring patriots. At this critical juncture, Miller took upon himself to lead the hussars of Junín against the victorious Spaniards, and by a timely charge drove them back, and followed them across the ravine, by which time he was supported by the *granaderos a caballo* and by the division La Mar, which had rallied. The brave Colonel Plaza crossed the ravine at the head of the legion on the left. Lieutenant-Colonel Morán, at the head of the battalion Bargas, made a similar movement on the right of the cavalry. These two battalions and the cavalry, mutually supporting and rivalling each other in valour, repeated their charges with such resolution, that the division Valdés was broken; its artillery taken; its cavalry obliged to fly in disorder; and its infantry dispersed.

The royalists had now lost the battle, and fled to the ridge from which they had descended, in the morning, with so much confidence.

The action lasted an hour. Fourteen hundred royalists were killed, and seven hundred wounded, and they lost fifteen pieces of artillery.

The loss on the part of the patriots was three hundred and seventy killed, and six hundred and nine wounded.

Bolivar's ideas of government

The single piece of artillery belonging to the patriots did considerable execution on the royalist columns, and was of service also in attracting a heavy fire from their artillery, which if it had been directed upon the patriot columns, would have occasioned the loss to be more considerable.

The plan of the royalists was to wait until Valdés had outflanked the left of Sucre's position, from which having driven him, the whole army was to advance and complete the victory. The mistake of the viceroy in attacking at all, originated in suffering himself to be impelled to it by the eagerness of his troops. Their patience had been worn out, by the terrible marches, which appeared to them to be endless. At Guamanguilla, a system of pasquinading had been adopted. The tents of La Serna, Canterac, and others, had various lampoons pasted on them, and it may be fairly said that they were goaded by their own soldiers into a general action contrary to their own judgment.

The royalists, upon regaining the heights of Condorkanki, rallied as many of their defeated troops as they possibly could. The patriot divisions La Mar and Lara gained the summit of the heights at about 1 P.M. Before sunset Canterac sued for terms, and an hour afterward rode down to the tent of Sucre, where a capitulation was agreed upon. The Viceroy La Serna, Generals Canterac, Valdés, Carratala, Monet, Villalobos, Ferras, Bedoya, Somocursio, Cacho, Atero, Landazuri, García-Camba, Pardo, Vigil, and Tur; 16 colonels, 68 lieutenant-colonels, 484 officers, 3200 rank and file, became prisoners of war. The rest had dispersed.

The battle of Ayacucho was the most brilliant ever fought in South America. The troops on both sides were in a state of discipline which would have been creditable to the best European armies. The ablest generals and chiefs of either party were present, and it is difficult to say which army most panted for an appeal to the sword, as every man fought with undaunted bravery. What the patriots wanted in numbers was made up by enthusiasm, and by a perfect knowledge that, if beaten, retreat was utterly impracticable. It was not a victory of mere chance, but the result of the most determined valour, and of an irresistible onset, conceived and executed at the proper moment.

7. THE VISION OF BOLÍVAR

The most grandiose of Bolívar's political conceptions was that of a league of friendship and mutual assistance uniting all the Latin-American states, under the leadership and protection of Great Britain. To achieve this project, Bolívar invited these and other nations to a Congress, which was held at Panama in 1826. In the end this assembly proved an almost total failure. On the eve of the meeting Bolívar wrote down a statement of the advantages to be gained from the proposed confederacy. This document suggests that fear of the Holy Alliance, on the one hand, and of Negro and Indian insurrections, on the other, partly influenced Bolívar's decision to summon the Congress of Panama.[7]

THE CONGRESS OF PANAMA will bring together all the representatives of America and a diplomat-agent of His Britannic Majesty's government. This Congress seems destined to form a league more extensive, more remarkable, and more powerful than any that has ever existed on the face of the earth. Should Great Britain agree to join it as a constituent member, the Holy Alliance will be less powerful than this confederation. Mankind will a thousand times bless this league for promoting its general welfare, and America, as well as Great Britain, will reap from it untold benefits. A code of public law to regulate the international conduct of political bodies will be one of its products.

1. The New World would consist of independent nations, bound together by a common set of laws which would govern their foreign relations and afford them a right to survival through a general and permanent congress.

2. The existence of these new states would receive fresh guarantees.

3. In deference to England, Spain would make peace, and the Holy Alliance would grant recognition to these infant nations.

4. Domestic control would be preserved untouched among the states and within each of them.

5. No one of them would be weaker than another, nor would any be stronger.

6. A perfect balance would be established by this truly new order of things.

7. The power of all would come to the aid of any one state which might suffer at the hands of a foreign enemy or from internal anarchic factions.

8. Differences of origin and color would lose their influence and power.

9. America would have nothing more to fear from that tremendous monster who has de-

[7] Lecuna and Bierck, *The Selected Writings of Bolívar,* II, 561–562. Reprinted by kind permission of the Banco de Venezuela.

voured the island of Santo Domingo, nor would she have cause to fear the numerical preponderance of the aborigines.

10. In short, a social reform would be achieved under the blessed auspices of freedom and peace, but the fulcrum controlling the beam of the scales must necessarily rest in the hands of England.

Great Britain would, of course, derive considerable advantage from this arrangement.

1. Her influence in Europe would progressively increase, and her decisions would be like those of destiny itself.

2. America would serve her as an opulent domain of commerce.

3. America would become the center of England's relations wtih Asia and Europe.

4. British subjects in America would be considered the equals of American citizens.

5. The relations between England and America would in time become those between equals.

6. British characteristics and customs would be adopted by the Americans as standards for their future way of life.

7. In the course of the centuries, there might, perhaps, come to exist one single nation throughout the world — a federal nation.

These ideas are in the minds of many Americans in positions of importance who impatiently await the inauguration of this project at the Congress of Panama, which may afford the occasion to consumate the union of the new states and the British Empire.

8. A LETTER TO DOM PEDRO

Brazil made a swift and relatively bloodless transition to independence. The immediate causes of separation were the efforts of a jealous Portuguese cortes to revoke the liberties and concessions won by Brazil since 1808 and to force the departure of the prince regent, Dom Pedro, from Brazil. Messages of support from juntas throughout the country, such as the following from the junta of São Paulo, encouraged the prince to defy the Lisbon government and to issue his famous "fico" (I remain).[8]

SIR,

We had already written to your Royal Highness, before we received the extraordinary gazette of the 11th instant, by the last courier: and we had hardly fixed our eyes on the first decree of the Cortes concerning the organization of the

[8] Maria Graham, *Journal of a Voyage to Brazil, and Residence There, During Part of the Years 1821, 1822, and 1823,* London, 1824, pp. 174–177.

governments of the provinces of Brazil, when a noble indignation fired our hearts: because we saw impressed on it a system of anarchy and slavery. But the second, in conformity to which Your Royal Highness is to go back to Portugal, in order to travel *incognito* only through Spain, France, and England, inspired us with horror.

They aim at no less than disuniting us, weakening us, and in short, leaving us like miserable orphans, tearing from the bosom of the great family of Brazil the only common father who remained to us, after they had deprived Brazil of the beneficent founder of the kingdom, Your Royal Highness's august sire. They deceive themselves; we trust in God, who is the avenger of injustice; He will give us courage, and wisdom.

If, by the 21st article of the basis of the constitution, which we approve and swear to because it is founded on universal and public right, the deputies of Portugal were bound to agree that the constitution made at Lisbon could then be obligatory on the Portuguese resident in that kingdom; and, that, as for those in the other three parts of the world, it should only be binding when their legitimate representatives should have declared such to be their will: How dare those deputies of Portugal, without waiting for those of Brazil, legislate concerning the most sacred interest of each province, and of the entire kingdom? How dare they split it into detached portions, each isolated, and without leaving a common centre of strength and union? How dare they rob Your Royal Highness of the lieutenancy, granted by Your Royal Highness's august father, the King? How dare they deprive Brazil of the privy council, the board of conscience, the court of exchequer, the board of commerce, the court of requests, and so many other recent establishments, which promised such future advantage? Where now shall the wretched people resort in behalf of their civil and judicial interests? Must they now again, after being for twelve years accustomed to judgment at hand, go and suffer, like petty colonists, the delays and chicanery of the tribunals of Lisbon, across two thousand leagues of ocean, where the sighs of the oppressed lose all life and all hope? Who would credit it, after so many bland, but deceitful expressions of reciprocal equality and future happiness!

In the session of the 6th of August last, the deputy of the Cortes, Pereira do Carmo, said (and he spoke the truth) that the constitution was the social compact, in which were expressed and declared the conditions on which a nation might wish to constitute itself a body politic: and that the end of that constitution is the general good of each individual who is to enter into that social compact. How then dares a mere fraction of the great Portuguese nation, without waiting for the conclusion of this solemn national compact, attack the general good of the principal part of the same, and such is the vast and rich kingdom of Brazil; dividing it into miserable fragments, and, in a word, attempting to tear from its bosom the representative of the executive power, and to annihilate by a stroke of the pen, all the tribunals and establishments necessary to its existence and future prosperity? This unheard-of despotism, this horrible political perjury, was certainly not merited by the good and generous Brazil. But the enemies of order in the Cortes of Lisbon deceive themselves if they imagine that they can thus, by vain words and hollow professions, delude the good sense of the worthy Portuguese of both worlds.

Your Royal Highness will observe that, if the kingdom of Ireland, which makes part of the United Kingdom of Great Britain, besides that it is infinitely small compared to the vast kingdom of Brazil, and is separated from England but by a narrow arm of the sea, which is passed in a few hours, yet possesses a governor-general or viceroy, who represents the executive power of the King of the United Kingdom, how can it enter the head of any one who is not either pro-

foundly ignorant, or rashly inconsiderate, to pretend, that the vast kingdom of Brazil, should remain without a centre of activity, and without a representative of the executive power; and equally without a power to direct our troops, so as that they may operate with celerity and effect, to defend the state against any unforeseen attack of external enemies, or against internal disorders and factions, which might threaten public safety, or the reciprocal union of the province!

We therefore entreat Your Royal Highness with the greatest fervour, tenderness, and respect to delay your return to Europe, where they wish to make you travel as a pupil surrounded by tutors and spies: We entreat you to confide boldly in the love and fidelity of your Brazilians, and especially of your Paulistas, who are all ready to shed the last drop of their blood, and to sacrifice their fortunes, rather than lose the adored Prince in whom they have placed their well-founded hopes of national happiness and honour. Let Your Royal Highness wait at least for the deputies named by this province, and for the magistracy of this capital, who will as soon as possible present to Your Highness our ardent desires and firm resolutions; and deign to receive them, and to listen to them, with the affection and attention, which your Paulistas deserve from you.

May God preserve your Royal Highness's august person many years.

XXIII

The War for Mexican Independence

IN MEXICO, AS IN OTHER SPANISH-AMERICAN COLONIES, news of the impending fall of Spain to French armies caused widespread agitation and inspired creole projects for separation from the mother country. In September, 1810, the patriot priest Manuel Hidalgo launched a revolt by calling on the Indians of his parish to rise against their Spanish rulers. After his first victories Hidalgo issued decrees abolishing slavery and personal tribute and ordering the restoration of their lands to the Indian communities. These measures gave the Mexican revolution a popular character that was largely absent from the movement for independence in South America. But they alienated many wealthy creoles who also desired independence — but without social revolution.

Hidalgo proved unable to weld his Indian hordes into a disciplined army, or to capitalize on his early victories. Less than one year after the revolt had begun, he was captured and executed by the royalists. Another capable priest, José María Morelos, assumed leadership of the revolutionary struggle. Morelos liberated a large part of Mexico, maintained order in the regions under his control, and summoned a congress that proclaimed Mexican independence and framed a republican constitution for the country. Morelos shared Hidalgo's vision of the war as a social revolution, going beyond his master in his advocacy of agrarian reform. Like Hidalgo, Morelos had differences over policy with creole associates that seriously hampered him in his conduct of the war. In 1815 he was captured by the Spaniards, and after a speedy trial suffered the fate of Hidalgo.

After the death of Morelos, the revolution declined into a guerrilla war waged by many rival chiefs, some of whom were mere brigands. Royalist armies gradually extinguished the remaining centers of resistance. By 1820 only two patriot leaders — Vicente Guerrero and Guadalupe Victoria — were carrying on the struggle for independence.

At the opening of that year a revolution in Spain compelled Ferdinand VII to swear loyalty to the liberal Constitution of 1812. News of this development raised liberal hopes in Mexico and threw conservative churchmen and army officers into a panic. Fearing the loss of their privileges, they schemed to separate Mexico from the mother country. Their instrument was the creole officer Agustín de Iturbide, hitherto a merciless foe of the insurgents. His Plan of Iguala won the support of all creole monarchists and the temporary adherence of republican insurgents. Iturbide's "Army of the Three Guarantees" swiftly overcame scattered loyalist resistance. On September 28, 1821, the independence of the Mexican Empire was officially proclaimed, and eight months later a national congress elected Iturbide emperor of the new realm.

1. HIDALGO: TORCHBEARER OF THE REVOLUTION

Miguel Hidalgo (1753–1811), the scholarly white-haired priest of the town of Dolores and onetime rector of the college of San Nicolás at Valladolid, hardly seemed fitted by background and disposition to head a revolution. It was Hidalgo, nevertheless, who overcame the waverings of his associates when their conspiracy was discovered, and who transformed what had been planned as an upper-class creole revolt into a rising of the masses. Alamán, historian and bitter enemy of the revolution — who knew Hidalgo in the peaceful years before the great upheaval — describes the curate of Dolores.[1]

DON MIGUEL HIDALGO, being neither austere in his morals nor very orthodox in his opinions, did not concern himself with the spiritual administration of his parish, which he had turned over, together with half the income of his curacy, to a priest named Don Francisco Iglesias. Knowing French — a rather rare accomplishment at that period, especially among churchmen — he formed a taste for technical and scientific books and zealously promoted various agricultural and industrial projects in his parish. He considerably furthered viticulture, and today that whole region produces abundant harvests of grapes; he also encouraged the planting of mulberry trees for the raising of silkworms.

In Dolores eighty-four trees planted by him are still standing, in the spot called "the mulberry trees of Hidalgo," as well as the channels that he had dug for irrigating the entire plantation. He established a brickyard and a factory for the manufacture of porcelain, constructed troughs for tanning hides, and promoted a variety of other enterprises.

All this, plus the fact that he was not only generous but lavish in money matters, had won him the high regard of his parishioners — especially the Indians, whose languages he had mastered. It also gained him the esteem of all who took a sincere interest in the advancement of the country, men like Abad y Queipo, the bishop-elect of Michoacán, and Riaño, the intendant of Guanajuato. It seems, however, that he had little basic knowledge of the industries which he fostered, and even less of that systematic spirit which one must have to make substantial progress with them. Once, being asked by Bishop Abad y Queipo what method he used for picking and distributing the leaves to the silkworms according to their age, and for separating the dry leaves and keeping the silkworms clean — concerning which the books on the subject give such elaborate instructions — he replied that he followed no particular order, that he threw down the leaves as they came from the tree and let the silkworms eat as they wished. "The revolution," exclaimed the bishop, who told me this anecdote, "was like his raising of silkworms, and the results were what might be

[1] Alamán, *Historia de Méjico*, I, 352–354. (Excerpt translated by the editor.)

expected!" Nevertheless, he had made much progress, and obtained enough silk to have some garments made for himself and for his stepmother. He also promoted the raising of bees, and brought many swarms of bees to the hacienda of Jaripeo when he bought that estate.

He was very fond of music, and not only had it taught to the Indians of his parish, where he formed an orchestra, but borrowed the orchestra of the provincial battalion of Guanajuato for the frequent parties that he gave in his home. Since his residence was a short distance from Guanajuato, he often visited the capital and stayed there for long periods of time. This gave me an opportunity to see him and to know him. He was fairly tall and stoop-shouldered, of dark complexion and quick green eyes; his head bent a little over his chest and was covered by sparse gray hair, for he was more than sixty years old.[2] He was vigorous, though neither swift nor active in his movements; short of speech in ordinary conversation but animated in academic style when the argument grew warm. He was careless in dress, wearing only such garb as small-town curates commonly wore in those days.

2. THE STORMING OF THE GRANARY

Hidalgo unleashed a storm of Indian revolt with his Grito de Dolores. *Under the banner of the Virgin of Guadalupe he led his peasant army to the liberation of Mexico. Some creoles joined him, but the majority recoiled before the elemental violence and radicalism of the movement. The spirit of the insurrection found expression in the first large-scale action of the war, in which Hidalgo's Indians and the miners of Guanajuato joined to storm the Alhóndiga de Granaditas, a large stone building used by the government for the storage of grain.[3]*

A LITTLE BEFORE TWELVE a numerous rabble of Indians — a few armed with rifles, the majority with lances, clubs, slings, and bows and arrows — appeared in sight on the causeway of Our Lady of Guadalupe, which leads into the city from the Marfil road. The vanguard of this group passed over the bridge of the same name as the causeway and arrived in front of the barricade at the foot of Mendizábal hill. Don Gilberto de Riaño, to whom his father had entrusted command of that spot as the most dangerous one, ordered them to stop in the name of

the king; as the multitude continued to advance, he gave the order to fire. A number of Indians were killed, and the rest retreated precipitately. On the causeway, a native of Guanajuato told them they should go to Cuarto hill, and he himself led them there.

Meanwhile Hidalgo's other foot soldiers, amounting to some 20,000 Indians, joined by the miners and the common people of Guanajuto, occupied the heights and all the houses fronting on the granary. The soldiers from Celaya, armed with rifles, took up positions there, while a cavalry corps of some 2,000 men, composed of dragoons of the regiment *de la reina,* and country people armed with lances, with Hidalgo at their head, ascended the road called *de la yerbabuena* as far as the place known as "the racetracks" and from there descended to the city. Hidalgo stopped at the barracks of the cavalry regiment *del príncipe,* where he remained during the action. The column continued its march across the whole city, finally halting at the street *de Belén.* In their march the soldiery looted a candy store and released from jail all prisoners of both sexes, numbering between 300 and 400 persons, among them criminals guilty of grave offenses. The male prisoners were impressed into the insurgent ranks for the attack on the granary.

The intendant, noticing that the majority of the enemy were grouping in front of the barricade at the entrance to the street *de los Pozitos,* commanded by Captain Pedro Telmo Primo, decided it was necessary to reinforce that point with twenty infantrymen from the company of civilians attached to the battalion. With more daring than prudence, he himself led them to the position where they were needed; he was accompanied by his aide, Don José María Bustamante. He was returning, and was already on the stairs leading to the door of the granary, when he received a rifle bullet above his left eye and died immediately. The shot came from the window of one of the houses in the square of the granary, facing east; it was said that it had been fired by a corporal of the infantry regiment of Celaya. . . .

The mob gathered on Cuarto hill began to hurl stones, by hand and with slings, so thickly that they exceeded the heaviest fall of hail. The attackers were aided by swarms of Indians and their allies from Guanajuato, who continually brought up from the Cata River the round stones which cover the bed of that stream; so great was the discharge of stones during the

---

2 Hidalgo was actually fifty-seven years old in 1810. B.K

3 Alamán, *Historia de Méjico,* I, 425–433. (Excerpt translated by the editor.)

short time that the attack lasted, that the roof of the granary was raised about eight inches above its ordinary level. It proved impossible to hold the barricades, and after withdrawing the troops that were defending them, Captain Escalera, who was guarding the entrance, closed the door. As a result the Europeans who occupied the hacienda of Dolores were cut off and had no recourse but to sell their lives dearly; the cavalry on the back of the River Cata were in the same or a worse plight. Nor could the roof be long defended, dominated as it was by the hills of Cuarto and San Miguel. . . . Notwithstanding the heavy casualties caused by the continuous fire of the troops stationed on the roof, the number of assailants was so great that the fallen were quickly replaced by others, and their loss was not felt.

As a result of the abandonment of the barricades and the withdrawal of the troops defending the roof, the mob poured in a confused mass down all the avenues to the foot of the granary; those in front were pushed forward by those behind them and thus could not retreat, like waves of the sea that force each other onward until they dash against the rocks. Courage could not display itself; cowardice could not impel to flight. The cavalry was completely swept away, having no opportunity to use its arms and horses. Captain Castilla was killed; a number of soldiers died; the majority went over to the victors. Only the brave Don José Francisco Valenzuela, turning his horse about, rode three times up the slope, opening a way for himself with his sword. Torn from his saddle and suspended on the points of the lances of the mob about him, he managed to kill some of the men nearest to him before he received a mortal wound. He shouted "Long live Spain!" until he breathed his last. He was a native of Irapuato and a lieutenant of the company from that town.

On the corner of the streets of *los Pozitos* and *los Mandamientos* was a store which sold splits of torch pine to miners, who used them to light their way to their place of work. The mob broke in the doors and carried all this combustible material away, heaping it up at the door of the granary, after which they set fire to it; meanwhile skilled miners, protected by huge earthen jars, like Roman soldiers with the *testudo,* approached the rear of the structure and attempted to make a breach in order to dynamite it. The defenders hurled quicksilver flasks filled with powder through the windows on the mob; when they exploded they caused great havoc, but gaps

in the crowd were immediately filled up, and the fallen were trampled underfoot and suffocated. This explains why so few attackers were wounded and so many killed. . . .

While Don Gilberto Riaño, thirsting to avenge his father, aided by Don Miguel Bustamante and others, was hurling quicksilver flasks or grenades on the assailants, the *asesor* of the intendency thrust out a white cloth as a flag of truce; but the populace, attributing to perfidy an act that was merely the result of the confusion prevailing among the defenders, renewed the combat with greater fury. Then the *asesor* had a soldier let down from a window to negotiate with the insurgents; the unhappy man was dead before he reached the ground. Father Martín Septiem, trusting in his priestly character and in an image of Christ that he carried, attempted to leave the building. A rain of stones shattered the image, but the father, using the cross which he held in one hand as an offensive weapon, managed, though badly wounded, to push his way through the multitude. Meanwhile some of the Spaniards, beside themselves with terror, threw money out the window in the hope of placating the mob; others clamored for surrender; and still others, persuaded that their last hour had come, threw themselves at the feet of the priests who were there, to receive absolution.

Berzábal, seeing the door in flames, assembled as many as posisble of his soldiers and grouped them in front of the entrance. As the burning door collapsed, he ordered them to fire pointblank at the attackers. Many perished, but the momentum of those in the rear carried those in front over the bodies of the fallen and into the building, sweeping everything before them with irresistible force, and the courtyard, stairs, and corridors of the granary were soon crowded with the Indians and the populace. Berzábal, retreating with a handful of surviving soldiers to a corner of the courtyard, defended the banners of the battalion with the standard-bearers Marmolejo and González. When both of them had fallen, he seized the banner; clutching them with his left hand, he defended himself first with his sword, and when that was broken, with a pistol, until, pierced by many lances, he fell still holding the banners he had sworn to defend. . . .

All resistance now ceased, and only an occasional shot was heard from some isolated defender, such as the Spaniard Ruymayor, who kept the Indians at bay until he had used up all his cartridges. The Europeans in the hacienda of Dolores tried to escape by a back door which opened on the wooden bridge spanning the Cata River. But they found that it had already been taken by the attackers, and so had to retreat to the draw-well, a high vantage point, where they defended themselves until their munitions gave out, causing heavy losses to the insurgents. It was said that Don Francisco Iriarte alone, the man who had warned the intendant from San Juan de los Llanos of the start of the revolution, and who was an excellent shot, killed eighteen. The few who remained alive fell or threw themselves into the well and drowned.

The taking of the granary of Granaditas was entirely the work of the populace of Guanajuato, joined by the numerous gangs of Indians led by Hidalgo. Hidalgo and his lieutenants could do no more than lead their people to the hills and begin the attack. Once it was begun, it was impossible to give any orders, since there was no one to receive orders and carry them out; there was no order in that confused mob, and no subordinate officers to direct it. The Indians, throwing themselves with extraordinary bravery into the first military action they had ever seen, could not turn back, for the mob, pressing upon those who went in front, compelled them to advance and instantly took the space left by the fallen. The resistance of the defenders, though courageous, lacked all order and plan, owing to the early death of the intendant, and the early end of the action must be attributed to this, for by four in the afternoon everything was over.

3. THE REFORMS OF HIDALGO

Hidalgo and Morelos attempted to combine the creole ideal of independence with a program of social justice for the oppressed classes of the Mexican population. The following decrees of Hidalgo, issued after his capture of Guadalajara, help to explain why many conservative creoles fought on the Spanish side against the patriots.[4]

DON MIGUEL HIDALGO Y COSTILLA, generalissimo of America, etc. By these presents I order the judges and justices of the district of this capital to proceed immediately to the collection of the rents due to this day by the lessees of the lands belonging to the Indian communities, the said rents to be entered in the national treasury. The lands shall be turned over to the Indians for

their cultivation, and they may not be rented out in the future, for it is my wish that only the Indians in their respective towns shall have the use of them. Given in my headquarters of Guadalajara, December 5, 1810. . . .

Don Miguel Hidalgo y Costilla, generalissimo of America, etc. From the moment that the courageous American nation took up arms to throw off the heavy yoke that oppressed it for three centuries, one of its principal aims has been to extinguish the multitude of taxes that kept it in poverty. Since the critical state of our affairs does not permit the framing of adequate provisions in this respect, because of the need of the kingdom for money to defray the costs of the war, for the present I propose to remedy the most urgent abuses by means of the following declarations. First: All slaveowners shall set their slaves free within ten days, on pain of death for violation of this article. Second: The payment of tribute by all the castes that used to pay it shall henceforth cease, and no other taxes shall be collected from the Indians. Third: In all judicial business, documents, deeds, and actions, only ordinary paper shall be used, and the use of sealed paper is abolished.

4. THE PLAN OF IGUALA

By a notable irony, the work begun by Hidalgo and Morelos was consummated by a creole officer, Agustín de Iturbide (1783–1824), who for nine years had fought the insurgents with great effectiveness. Behind Iturbide were conservative churchmen, army officers, and officials, who preferred separation from Spain to submission to the liberal Constitution of 1812, imposed on Ferdinand VII by his revolted army. Lorenzo de Zavala (1788–1836), a brilliant Mexican statesman, publicist, and historian, describes the origin and triumph of the Plan of Iguala.[5]

THE YEAR 1820 was born among stormy portents. The gathering of troops on the island of León for dispatch to South America aroused no special interest, for experience had shown the futility of such expeditions. But the news of the first moves made by the army in the palm grove of the port of Santa María, under the orders of the Count of La Bisbal, to reëstablish the constitution of 1812, caused excitement in Mexico and inspired consternation in Viceroy Apodaca. He perceived that the seeming tranquillity of

4 Alamán, *Historia de Méjico*, II, 25–26. (Excerpt translated by the editor.)

5 Lorenzo de Zavala, *Ensayo histórico de los revoluciones de México*, México, 1918, 2 vols., I, 69–79. (Excerpt translated by the editor.)

Mexico was an illusion, for the times were out of joint; he feared to lose in a moment the fruit of his labors and, above all, the glory he had acquired by bringing peace to Mexico — the result of a combination of circumstances that could produce only a momentary effect. The viceroy issued circulars announcing that the rumors being spread about the temper of the troops in Spain were false: *Never was the royal government more solidly established, or military discipline better; never did the king have greater proof of the love of his people and of his armies.* This was said in the government press, the only newspaper permitted to appear; the bishops and priests preached the same thing; but the only result of these measures was to increase alarm and to awaken hopes that were never extinguished. The very concern of the government, and its effort to discredit the news of this movement, only gave them greater currency. Commerce, that reliable index of developments and infallible barometer of political conditions, revealed more through its precautionary measures than any statements the government agents could make to conceal the situation from the public. The efforts of the unfortunate Lacy, in Cataluña, and of the martyred Porlier, in Galicia, were so many proofs that Spain had but temporarily accepted the yoke of an arbitrary power. . . . I shall now try to describe briefly and as exactly as possible the state of Mexican public opinion in these circumstances.

The upper clergy and the privileged classes, who saw the revolutionary principles of 1812 rising again to threaten their revenues and their benefices, united as if by instinct to oppose an insuperable barrier, as they thought, to the reestablishment of the Spanish constitution, which had so greatly weakened their influence. The first news of the cry of Riego in the town of Las Cabezas, on January 1, 1820, were received with terror by all those who lived on the credulity and ignorance of the people. Apodaca, a fanatical supporter of the royal power and of the abuses of superstition, formed the project of offering Ferdinand VII an asylum in Mexico against the enterprises of the constitutionalists, assuring him of a throne in a land to which the new doctrines would have no access. What a flattering prospect for the canons and aristocratic classes this was — to make Mexico the center of their power and to form a court that would dispense jobs and honors! The Mexican counts and marquises already saw themselves made grandees of the *first class,* raised to eminent titles and vying with the ancient Spanish nobility in pride, in wealth, and in ignorance! The project tended inevitably toward independence; to be sure, the Mexicans would have been glad to be independent, but it is very doubtful that they would have acquiesced to absolute power. Constitutional monarchy had become fashionable; the Mexicans would have wanted to keep in step with their peninsular fathers; the desire for a republic was not the plan of Apodaca and his advisers. In seeking to revive Napoleon's ancient project to transfer the royal family to Mexico, they only envisioned raising a throne for despotism and placing the immense barrier of the Atlantic between liberal ideas and the new monarchy. As if the example of the United States were not enough to excite new strivings on the part of the people! As if the progress made by the doctrines of anti-legitimacy and the sovereignty of the people among the Mexicans could be destroyed by this step! Futile efforts of a dying power, that only deceived itself with these illusions!

The rapidity with which the new revolution, headed by Riego, Quiroga, and other celebrated leaders, spread throughout Spain burst in a moment the bubble of Viceroy Apodaca. But from his plan there emerged another, in which the viceroy certainly had no part, no matter what may be said by some people who only judge by appearances and do not examine the background and causes of events. Frustrated in their first project, the clergy and the self-styled nobles decided that the moment had arrived to form a plan of independence which would assure a monarchy for Mexico and would summon a prince of the ruling house of Spain to occupy the throne. The idea was not new; the Count of Aranda had proposed it to Charles III fifty years before. It seemed to reconcile the interests of the different parties, it established independence, it made the monarchy secure, it gave guarantees to the Spaniards, and the people received a form of government best suited to their new needs and to their customs and habits. Amid these circumstances the elections of deputies for the Spanish *cortes* took place, and all those named for this mission agreed to present proposals to the assembly that harmonized with this solution. Amid this chaos of opinion and of parties, the viceroy was much perplexed. In April, 1820, arrived a royal order that required everyone to swear loyalty to the constitution. It was obeyed without resistance; the press began to speak freely once again; the dungeons opened to release prisoners held for political opinions; the Inquisition and the tribunal of public security disappeared; liberal ideas had triumphed in both worlds. New enterprises were set on foot — great projects that began under good auspices — and a man was needed, a man who would be valiant, active, energetic, enterprising. Where could he be found?

Popular revolutions present anomalies whose origin or causes are unknowable. Men who have followed one party, who have fought for certain principles, who have suffered for their loyalty to certain views or persons, suddenly change and adopt a completely different line of conduct. Who would ever have thought that the Mexican officer who had shed the blood of so many of his compatriots to maintain his country in slavery was destined to place himself at the head of a great movement that would destroy forever the Spanish power? What would have been thought of a man's sanity if in 1817 he had said that Iturbide would occupy the place of Morelos or would replace Mina? Yet the astonished Mexicans and Spaniards saw this happen.

Don Agustín de Iturbide, colonel of a battalion of provincial troops and a native of Valladolid de Michoacán, was endowed with brilliant qualities, and among his leading traits were uncommon bravery and vigor. To a handsome figure he united the strength and energy necessary to endure the great exertions of campaigning, and ten continuous years of this activity had fortified his natural qualities. He was haughty and domineering, and it was observed that to stay in favor with the authorities he had to remain at a distance from those who were in a position to give him orders. Every time that he came to Mexico City or other places where there were superiors, he gave indications of his impatience. . . . It is said that he was involved in a plan hatched at Valladolid in 1809 for the achievement of independence but withdrew because he was not placed in command, though his rank at the time did not qualify him for leadership. Be that as it may, there is no doubt that Iturbide had a superior spirit, and that his ambition was supported by that noble resolution that scorns dangers and does not retreat before obstacles of every kind. He had faced danger and difficulty in combat; he had learned the power of Spanish weapons; he had taken the measure of the chiefs of both parties — and one must confess that he did not err in his calculations when he set himself above all of them.

He was conscious of his superiority, and so did not hesitate to place himself at the head of the national party, if he could only inspire the same confidence in his compatriots. He discussed his project with men whose talents would be useful to him in the political direction of affairs, and henceforth he threw himself heart and soul into forming a *plan* that would offer guarantees to citizens and monarchists and at the same time would remove all cause for fear on the part of the Spaniards.

Anyone who examines the famous Plan of Iguala (so called because it was made public in that town for the first time), bearing in mind the circumstances of the Mexican nation at the time, will agree that it was a masterpiece of politics and wisdom. All the Mexicans desired *independence,* and this was the first basis of that document. The killings of Spaniards that had taken place, in reprisal for those that the Spaniards had committed during the past nine years, required a preventive, so to speak, to put an end to such atrocious acts, which could not fail to arouse hostility among the 50,000 Spaniards who still resided in the country. It was necessary to make plain the intentions of the new chief in this respect. Accordingly, he seized upon the word *union* as expressing the solidarity that should exist between creoles and Spaniards, regarded as citizens with the same rights. Finally, since the Catholic religion is the faith professed by all Mexicans, and since the clergy has a considerable influence in the country, the preservation of this church was also stated to be a fundamental basis, under the word *religion.* These three principles, *independence, union,* and *religion,* gave Iturbide's army its name of "the Army of the Three Guarantees." The representative monarchical system was established, and various articles stated the elementary principles of this form of government and the individual rights guaranteed to the people. Finally, the Spaniards were given freedom to leave the country with all their property. The expeditionary forces were offered the privilege of returning to Spain at the expense of the public treasury; those who chose to stay would be treated like Mexican soldiers. As can be seen, the plan reconciled all interests, and, raising New Spain to the rank of an independent nation, as was generally desired, with its immense benefits it silenced for the time being the particular aspirations of those who wanted the *republic* on the one hand and the *absolute monarchy* on the other. All the sons of the country united around the principle of *nationality*, putting aside for the moment their different ideals. We shall soon see the sprouting of these germs of ideas, as yet enveloped in mists or suppressed by the great matter of the common cause.

Don Agustín Iturbide made all these preparations in the greatest secrecy, and to conceal his projects more effectively he entered or pretended to enter the church of San Felipe Neri to take part in religious exercises. There, it is said, was framed the document I mentioned. This display of piety, and the prudence and reserve with which he managed the affair, inspired the viceroy, who also was devout, to entrust him with the command of a small division assigned to pursue Don Vicente Guerrero, whose forces had increased considerably after the arrival of the news of the Spanish revolution. At the end of the year 1820 Colonel Iturbide set out from Mexico City, charged with the destruction of Guerrero but actually intending to join him at the first opportunity to work with him for the achievement of national independence. A few days after his departure from the capital, Iturbide drew near to Guerrero's camp. The latter had routed Colonel Berdejo, also sent out in his pursuit, in a minor clash, and this provided Iturbide with an opportunity to send Guerrero a letter inviting the patriot leader to abandon the enterprise that had cost the country so much futile bloodshed: "Now that the King of Spain has offered liberal institutions and confirmed the social guarantees of the people, taking an oath to support the Constitution of 1812, the Mexicans will enjoy a just equality, and we shall be treated like free men." He added: "The victories that you have recently gained over the government forces should not inspire you with confidence in future triumphs, for you know that the fortunes of war are mutable, and that the government possesses great resources."

This letter was written very artfully, for at the same time that it suggested a desire to enter into agreements and relations with the insurgents it aroused no suspicion in the viceroy, who interpreted it as reflecting the same policy that had been so useful to him in pacifying the country. Presumably the persons employed by Iturbide to deliver these letters carried private instructions explaining his intentions. General Guerrero replied, with the energy that he always showed in defending the cause of independence and liberty, that he was resolved "to continue defending the national honor, until victory or death"; that he was "not to be deceived by the flattering promise of liberty given by the Spanish constitutionalists, who in the matter of independence [hold] the same views as the most die-hard royalists; that the Spanish constitution [offers] no guarantees to the Americans." He reminded Iturbide of the exclusion of the castes in the Cadiz constitution; of the diminution of the American representatives; and, finally, of the indifference of the viceroys to these liberal laws. He concluded by exhorting Iturbide to join the national party, and invited him to take command of the national armies, of which Guerrero himself was then the leader. The vigorous tone of this letter, the sound observations that it contained, the convincing logic of its judgments, produced an astounding effect upon the Mexicans. Iturbide needed no persuasion; we have seen him depart from Mexico City with the intent of proclaiming the independence of the country, and the only matter left unsettled was the precise method of beginning the work, with himself as the leader of the daring enterprise.

He received this letter in January, 1821, and replied to General Guerrero, in a few lines, that he wished to "confer with [him] about the means of working together for the welfare of the kingdom" and hoped that he (Guerrero) "would be fully satisfied concerning his intentions." An agreement was reached for an interview between the two men.[6] General Guerrero himself supplied me with details of what took place at this meeting. The conference was held in a town in the State of Mexico. . . . The two chiefs approached each other with some mutual distrust, although that of Guerrero was plainly the more justified. Iturbide had waged a cruel and bloody war on the independents since 1810. The Spanish leaders themselves hardly equaled this unnatural American in cruelty; and to see him transformed as if by magic into a defender of the cause that he had combated, would naturally arouse suspicions in men like the Mexican insurgents, who had often been the victims of their own credulity and of repeated betrayals. Nevertheless, Iturbide, though sanguinary, inspired confidence by the conscientiousness with which he proceeded in all matters. He was not believed capable of an act of treachery that would stain his reputation for valor and noble conduct. For himself, he had very little to fear from General

6 Historians are not in agreement concerning the time of the first meeting between Iturbide and Guerrero. For a discussion of the controversy, see William S. Robertson, *Iturbide of Mexico*, Durham, N.C., Duke University Press, 1952, pp. 64–65. B.K.

Guerrero, a man distinguished from the beginning for his humanity and for his loyalty to the cause he was defending. The troops of both leaders were within cannon-shot of each other; Iturbide and Guerrero met and embraced. Iturbide was the first to speak: "I cannot express the satisfaction I feel at meeting a patriot who has supported the noble cause of independence and who alone has survived so many disasters, keeping alive the sacred flame of liberty. Receive this just homage to your valor and to your virtues." Guerrero, who also was deeply moved, replied: "Sir, I congratulate my country, which on this day recovers a son whose valor and ability have caused her such grievous injury." Both leaders seemed to feel the strain of this memorable event; both shed tears of strong emotion. After Iturbide had revealed his plans and ideas to Señor Guerrero, that leader summoned his troops and officers, and Iturbide did the same. When both armies had been joined, Guerrero addressed himself to his soldiers, saying: "Soldiers: The Mexican who appears before you is Don Agustín de Iturbide, whose sword wrought such grave injury for nine years to the cause we are defending. Today he swears to defend the national interests; and I, who have led you in combat, and whose loyalty to the cause of independence you cannot doubt, am the first to acknowledge Señor Iturbide as the chief of the national armies. Long live independence! Long live liberty!" From that moment everyone acknowledged the new leader as general-in-chief, and he now dispatched to the viceroy a declaration of his views and of the step he had taken. Iturbide sent General Guerrero to seize a convoy of Manila merchants bound for the port of Acapulco with 750,000 pesos; he himself set out for the town of Iguala, forty leagues to the south of Mexico City, where he published the plan which I have outlined. The Spanish troops began to leave Iturbide's division, but the old patriot detachments began to reassemble everywhere to come to his aid.

All Mexico was set in motion by the declaration of Iguala. Apodaca immediately ordered General Liñán to march with a large division against the new leader, to strangle in its cradle this movement of threatening aspect. But this was not the tumultuous cry of Dolores of 1810; the viceroy was not dealing with a disorderly mob of Indians armed with sickles, stones, and slings and sending up the confused cry "Death to the *gachupines,* long live Our Lady of Guadalupe!" He faced a chief of proven bravery, who, supported by the national will and followed by trained leaders, spoke in the name of the people and demanded rights with which they were well acquainted. . . . While this chief was making extraordinary progress in the provinces, the capital was in the greatest confusion. The Spaniards residing in Mexico City attributed the successes of Iturbide to the ineptitude of Apodaca, who a short time before, according to them, had been the peacemaker, the tutelar angel, of New Spain; now this same man suddenly turned into an imbecile incapable of governing. They stripped him of his command, replacing him with the Brigadier Francisco Novella. This fact alone suffices to give an idea of the state of confusion in which the last defenders of the Spanish government found themselves. Reduced to the support of the expeditionary forces, the dying colonial regime immediately revealed the poverty of its resources. . . . Of the 14,000 soldiers sent to defend the imaginary rights of the Spanish government, only 6,000, at the most, remained — and what could they do against the Mexican army, which numbered at least 50,000 men? Arms, discipline — everything was equal except morale, which naturally was very poor among troops suddenly transported to a strange land, two thousand leagues away from their country. . . . Was it surprising that they surrendered, in view of the situation? Thus, between the end of February, when Iturbide proclaimed his plan of Iguala, and September 27, when he made his triumphant entry into Mexico City, only six months and some days elapsed, with no other memorable actions than the sieges of Durango, Querétaro, Córdoba, and the capital. It was at this time that General Antonio López de Santa-Anna, then lieutenant-colonel, began to distinguish himself.

Part Seven

Latin America in the Nineteenth Century

THE MANY REVOLUTIONS AND CIVIL WARS that occurred in Latin America in the nineteenth century were not all mere struggles for offices and spoils. Social, regional and ideological cleavages contributed to some of these conflicts, and to the bitterness with which they were fought. The economic advance of the second half of the century, uniting the governing classes in the pursuit of prosperity, helped to stabilize political life. Government by oligarchy continued, but revolutions became less frequent and peaceful transfers of power more common.

For many years after independence the economy of the new states remained much as it had been in colonial times. After 1850 a mounting European demand for Latin-American raw materials stimulated rapid economic development. This expansion, beneficial in some respects, was harmful in others; it led to excessive dependence on a few staples and accentuated the colonial character of the Latin-American economy.

Independence left the colonial way of life basically intact. The creole aristocracy, augmented by a number of mestizos who had distinguished themselves in war and politics, continued its leisurely and luxurious existence, generally based on income from absentee landownership. The condition of the Indian and mestizo laboring classes had changed little, and generally for the worse. Only in a few countries, such as Argentina and Uruguay, to which European immigrants came in considerable numbers after 1860, did significant middle-class groups arise.

Latin-American literature took its first faltering steps toward independence by breaking with Spanish classical models and turning for inspiration to the French and English romantics. Creole romanticism produced some of its finest achievements in the writings of exiles from Rosas' Argentina — notably Sarmiento's *Facundo*. Toward the end of the century arose a group of brilliant poets — the Modernists — who turned their backs on an uncongenial reality and embraced the creed of "Art for Art's Sake."

The long, constructive reign of Dom Pedro II (1840–1889) dominates Brazilian history in the nineteenth century. Despite his many virtues and accomplishments, the processes of economic change gradually undermined the social foundations on which the Empire rested. In 1888 the Brazilian Assembly abolished slavery — a serious blow at the rural aristocracy that had been the monarchy's chief support. One year later a group of military conspirators staged a coup, sent Dom Pedro into exile, and proclaimed a republic.

XXIV

Dictators and Revolutions

AFTER THE WINNING OF INDEPENDENCE Spanish America began a long uphill struggle to achieve stable, democratic government. The new states lacked a strong middle class, experience in self-government, and the other advantages with which the United States began their independent career. The result was an age of violence, of alternate dictatorship and revolution. Its symbol was the *caudillo,* or "strong man," whose power was always based on force, no matter what the constitutional form.

Whatever their methods, the caudillos generally displayed some regard for republican ideology and institutions. Political parties, usually called Conservative and Liberal, were active in most of the new states. Conservatism drew its main support from the landed aristocracy, the Church, and the military; liberalism attracted the merchants and professional men of the towns. Regional conflicts often cut across the lines of social cleavage, complicating the political picture.

As a rule the conservatives regarded with sympathy the social arrangements of the colonial era and favored a highly centralized government; the liberals, inspired by the success of the United States, advocated a federal form of government, guarantees of individual rights, lay control of education, and an end to special privileges for the clergy and the military. Neither party displayed much interest in the problems of the landless, debt-ridden peasantry that formed the majority of every nation.

After the middle of the nineteenth century a growing trade with Europe helped to stabilize political conditions in Latin America. The new economic order demanded peace and continuity in government. Old party lines dissolved as conservatives adopted the "positivist" dogma of science and progress, while liberals abandoned their concern with constitutional methods and civil liberties in favor of an interest in material prosperity. A new type of "progressive" caudillo — Díaz in Mexico, Núñez in Colombia, Guzmán Blanco in Venezuela — symbolized the politics of acquisition. The cycle of dictatorship and revolution continued in many lands, but the revolutions became less frequent and devastating.

As the century drew to a close, in a number of countries dissatisfied middle-class and laboring groups combined to form parties, called Radical or Democratic, that challenged the traditional domination of political affairs by the landed aristocracy. But the significance of this movement, like that of the small socialist groups that arose in Argentina and Chile in the 90's, still lay in the future.

1. THE AGE OF VIOLENCE

"There is no good faith in America," wrote Bolivar in 1829, "nor among the nations of America. Treaties are scraps of paper; constitutions, printed matter; elections, battles; freedom, anarchy; and life, a torment." Many Spanish-American observers echoed Bolivar's cry of despair during the chaotic half-century that followed the winning of independence. A fiery Chilean liberal, Francisco Bilbao (1823–1865), *subjected republican government in Latin America to a penetrating critique in his essay* America in Danger, *written in 1862.[1]*

THE CONQUEST OF POWER is the supreme goal.

This leads to the immoral doctrine that "the end justifies the means. . . ."

But since there are constitutional provisions that guarantee everyone his rights, and I can-

[1] Francisco Bilbao, *La América en peligro,* Santiago de Chile, 1941, pp. 34–40. (Excerpt translated by the editor.)

not violate them, I invoke the system of "preserving the form."

If the constitution declares: "Thought is free," I add: "within the limits established by law" — and since the law referred to is not the constitutional provision but one that was issued afterwards, I inscribe in it the exceptions of Figaro. "Thought is free," but there can be no discussion of dogma or exposition of systems that attack morality. And who is to judge? A commission or jury named in the last analysis by the authorities. And we have the colonial "censorship" reëstablished under the guise of the freest institution of all, the jury. Sublime victory of duplicity! "But the form has been preserved."

The electoral power is the only power exercised by the "sovereign people," and it exercises this power not to make the laws but to select the persons who will make them. Very well. The majority vote, then is the expression . . . of the popular will.

That is the basis of republican power, and that is why free and legitimate elections establish the legitimacy of power.

The election is free, it is said; but what if I control the election returns? What if I, the established power, name the inspector of the election returns, if the law permits one to vote twenty times a day in the same election? What if I dominate the elections and frighten my opponents away with impunity?

What happens then? Why, the government party is perpetuated in office, and the popular will is flouted and swindled.

But "the form has been preserved," and long live free elections!

"The domicile is inviolable," but I violate it, adding: "save in the cases determined by law." And the "cases" are determined in the last analysis by the party in power.

"The death penalty in political cases is abolished," but I shoot prisoners because I consider that these are not "political cases"; and since I am the infallible authority I declare that these political prisoners are bandits, and "the form has been preserved."

The Executive can be accused before the Chamber of Deputies and is subject to impeachment for one year after leaving office.

But that Chamber has been selected by me, and functions for one year after my departure. The persons who must judge me are my employees, my *protégés*, my creatures, my accomplices. Will they condemn me? No. Nor will they dare to accuse me. I am vindicated, and the "form" has saved me. Montt smiles over the bodies of his eight thousand victims.[2]

"The press is free." But I name the jury, and, backed by the authority of that free institution, I can accuse, harass, persecute; I can silence free speech. Then there reigns, absolute and sovereign, the opinion of one party. I spread the shroud of infamy over the corpse of the vanquished and cry: "The press is free!"

All liberal publicists, it can be said, accept the doctrine of "the separation of powers," as indispensable for the safety of the Republic.

But if the Executive has the power to name the judges; if the Executive participates in the framing of the laws; if the Executive can use the electoral law to name the members of Congress, what remains, in the last analysis, of the famous separation of powers?

"The guarantees established by this constitution cannot be suspended." But if I have the power to declare a province or the Republic in a state of siege, authorized to do so, as in Chile, by a "Council of State" appointed by the President, what security can a citizen have?

This miserable Machiavellianism has "preserved the forms" at the cost of plunging Chile into bloodshed and reaction for a space of thirty years.

There is discussion, the press is free; citizens come together, for they have the right of assembly; an enlightened public opinion almost unanimously clamors for reforms; preparations are made for elections that will bring to power representatives of the reform movement; and then the Executive Power declares the province or the Republic in a state of siege, and the suspended guarantees soar over the abyss of "legal" dictatorship and constitutional despotism!

And then? Either resignation or despair, or civil war, etc., etc. Then revolution raises its terrible banner, and blood flows in battles and on scaffolds. Respect for law and authority is lost, and only force holds sway, proclaiming its triumph to be that of liberty and justice. . . .

We have seen that our republican constitutions bear in themselves the germ of "legal despotism," a monstrous association of words that well describes the prostitution of the law. And since despotism, being "legal," is vindicated, the result is that the sentiment of justice is erased from the consciences of men.

Its place is taken by sophistry, duplicity, and

2 The reference is to the Chilean Liberal revolt of 1851, crushed by the Administration of President Montt with a heavy loss of life. B.K.

intrigue, used to win power at all cost, for power legitimizes everything. . . .

Experience proves that in the legal combat of the parties the party in power always gains the victory. Experience shows that the party that conducts itself loyally is swindled and routed. What can be the result of this state of affairs? That justice is forgotten, and success becomes justice. To win, then, is the supreme desideratum.

Then the debased conscience alters even the countenances of men, and their words, in the expression of Talleyrand, serve only "to mask their thought."

Then chaos emerges. Words change their meaning, the tongues of men become as twisted as serpents, their speech grows pompous and hollow, the language of the press is like the tinsel thrown on a grave to adorn "a feast of worms," and the prostitution of the word crowns the evolution of the lie.

The conservative calls himself a progressive.

The liberal protests that he is a loyal Catholic.

The Catholic swears by liberty.

The democrat invokes dictatorship, like the rebels in the United States, and defends slavery.

The reactionary asserts that he wants reform.

The educated man proclaims the doctrine that "all is for the best in the best of all possible worlds."

The "civilized man" demands the extermination of the Indians or of the gauchos.[3]

The "man of principles" demands that principles yield to the principle of the public good. There is proclaimed, not the sovereignty of justice, presiding over the sovereignty of the people, but the sovereignty of "the end" — which legitimizes every "means."

The absolutist proclaims himself the savior of society.

And if it governs with *coups d' état,* states of siege, or permanent or transitory dictatorships, while the constitutional guarantees are flouted, mocked, or suppressed, the party in power will tell you: civilization has triumphed over barbarism, authority over anarchy, virtue over crime, truth over the lie. . . .

We have behind us a half-century of independence from Spain. How many years of true liberty have any of the new nations enjoyed?

That is difficult to say; it is easier to reckon the years of anarchy and despotism that they have endured.

Shall Paraguay be the "model," with its forty years of dictatorship?

Or shall it be the Argentine Republic, with its provincial and national dictatorships, culminating in the twenty-year tyranny of Rosas?

And who knows what is to come?

Shall it be Chile, beginning with the dictatorship of O'Higgins and continuing with an intermittent dictatorship of thirty consecutive years?

Shall it be Bolivia, with its terrifying succession of sanguinary dictatorships?

Shall it be Peru, which has had more dictators than legal presidents?

Shall it be Ecuador, with its twenty years of the dictatorship of Flores?

Shall it be New Granada? And there one almost finds the exception, but Obando, the liberal legal president, was "overthrown for being a dictator."

Shall it be Venezuela, with its twenty years of Monagas?

Shall it be the little republics of Central America, and even Mexico? But this will suffice.

And these dictatorships have proclaimed all the principles.

The *pelucones,*[4] the conservatives, the reds, the liberals, the democrats, the Unitarians, the Federalists, all have embraced dictatorship. With the best of intentions the parties genially proclaim: "dictatorship in order to do good."

That is to say: despotism in order to secure liberty.

Terrible and logical contradiction!

2. FACUNDO: BARBARIAN CAUDILLO

The caudillo appeared in many guises. A common type in the first period after independence was the barbarian chieftain, whose rule represented dictatorship in its crudest, most lawless form. A specimen of this breed was Juan Facundo Quiroga, master under Rosas of the Argentine province of San Juan, and the terrible hero of a memorable book by Domingo Faustine Sarmiento (1811–1888).[5]

FACUNDO, as he was long called in the interior, or General Don Facundo Quiroga, as he afterwards became, when society had received him into its bosom and victory had crowned him with laurels, was a stoutly built man of low stat-

[3] An ironic reference to D. F. Sarmiento's book, *Civilization and Barbarism, The Life of Juan Facundo Quiroga.* B.K.

[4] Literally, "bigwigs," nickname given to Chilean conservatives by their liberal opponents in the period after the winning of independence. B.K.

[5] D. F. Sarmiento, *Life in the Argentine Republic in the Days of the Tyrants: or Civilization and Barbarism,* translated by Mrs. Horace Mann, New York, 1868, pp. 76–90.

ure, whose short neck and broad shoulders supported a well-shaped head, covered with a profusion of black and closely curling hair. His somewhat oval face was half buried in this mass of hair and an equally thick black, curly beard, rising to his cheek-bones, which by their prominence evinced a firm and tenacious will. His black and fiery eyes, shadowed by thick eyebrows, occasioned an involuntary sense of terror in those on whom they chanced to fall, for Facundo's glance was never direct, whether from habit or intention. With the design of making himself always formidable, he always kept his head bent down, to look at one from under his eyebrows, like the Ali Pacha of Monovoisin. The image of Quiroga is recalled to me by the Cain represented by the famous Ravel troupe, setting aside the artistic and statuesque attitudes, which do not correspond to his. To conclude, his features were regular, and the pale olive of his complexion harmonized well with the dense shadows which surrounded it.

The formation of his head showed, notwithstanding this shaggy covering, the peculiar organization of a man born to rule. Quiroga possessed those natural qualities which converted the student of Brienne into the genius of France, and the obscure Mameluke who fought with the French at the Pyramids, into the Viceroy of Egypt. Such natures develop according to the society in which they originate, and are either noble leaders who hold the highest place in history, ever forwarding the progress of civilization, or the cruel and vicious tyrants who become the scourges of their race and time.

Facundo Quiroga was the son of an inhabitant of San Juan, who had settled in the Llanos of Lo Rioja, and there had acquired a fortune in pastoral pursuits. In 1779, Facundo was sent to his father's native province to receive the limited education, consisting only of the arts of reading and writing, which he could acquire in its schools. After a man has come to employ the hundred trumpets of fame with the noise of his deeds, curiosity or the spirit of investigation is carried to such an extent as to scent out the insignificant history of the child, in order to connect it with the biography of the hero: and it is not seldom that the rudiments of the traits characteristic of the historical personage are met amid fables invented by flattery. The young Alcibiades is said to have lain down at full length upon the pavement of the street where he was playing, in order to insist that the driver of an approaching vehicle should yield the way to avoid running over him. Napoleon is reported to have ruled over his fellow-students, and to have entrenched himself in his study to resist an apprehended insult. Many anecdotes are now in circulation relating to Facundo, many of which reveal his true nature. In the house where he lodged, he could never be induced to take his seat at the family table; in school he was haughty, reserved, and unsocial; he never joined the other boys except to head their rebellious proceedings or to beat them. The master, tired of contending with so untamable a disposition, on one occasion provided himself with a new and stiff strap, and said to the frightened boys, as he showed it to them, "This is to be made supple upon Facundo." Facundo, then eleven years old, heard this threat, and the next day he tested its value. Without having learned his lesson, he asked the headmaster to hear it himself, because, as he said, the assistant was unfriendly to him. The master complied with the request. Facundo made one mistake, then two, three, and four; upon which the master used his strap upon him. Facundo, who had calculated everything, down to the weakness of the chair in which the master was seated, gave him a buffet, upset him on his back, and, taking to the street in the confusion created by this scene, hid himself among some wild vines where they could not get him out for three days. Was not such a boy the embryo chieftain who would afterwards defy society at large?

In early manhood his character took a more decided cast, constantly becoming more gloomy, imperious, and wild. From the age of fifteen years he was irresistibly controlled by the passion for gambling, as is often the case with such natures, which need strong excitement to awaken their dormant energies. This made him notorious in the city, and intolerable in the house which afforded him its hospitality; and finally under this influence, by a shot fired at one Jorge Peña, he shed the first rill of blood which went to make up the wide torrent that marked his way through life.

On his becoming an adult, the thread of his life disappears in an intricate labyrinth of bouts and broils among the people of the surrounding region. Sometimes lying hid, always pursued, he passed his time in gambling, working as a common laborer, domineering over everybody around him, and distributing his stabs among them. . . .

The most connected account of this obscure and roaming part of his life that I can procure is as follows:

Towards 1806, he went to Chili with a consignment of grain on his parent's account. This he gambled away, as well as the animals, which had brought it, and the family slaves who had accompanied him.

He often took to San Juan and Mendoza droves of the stock on his father's estate, and these always shared the same fate; for with Facundo, gambling was a fierce and burning passion which aroused the deepest instincts of his nature. These successive gains and losses of his must have worn out his father's generosity, for at last he broke off all amicable relations with his family.

When he had become the terror of the Republic, he was once asked by one of his parasites, "What was the largest bet you ever made in your life, General?" "Seventy dollars," replied Quiroga, carelessly, and yet he had just won two hundred dollars at one stake. He afterwards explained that once when a young man, having only seventy dollars, he had lost them all at one throw. But this fact has its characteristic history. Facundo had been at work for a year as a laborer upon the farm of a lady, situated in the Plumerillo, and had made himself conspicuous by his punctuality in going to work, and by the influence and authority which he exercised over the other laborers. When they wanted a holiday to get drunk in, they used to apply to Facundo, who informed the lady, and gave her his word, which he always fulfilled, to have all the men at work the next day. On this account the laborers called him "the father." At the end of a year of steady work, Facundo asked for his wages, which amounted to seventy dollars, and mounted his horse without knowing where he was bound, but seeing a collection of people at a grocery store, he alighted, and reaching over the group around the card-dealer, bet his seventy dollars on one card. He lost them and remounting, went on his way, careless in what direction, until after a little time a justice, Toledo by name, who happened to be passing, stopped him to ask for his passport. Facundo rode up as if about to give it to him, pretended to be feeling for something in his pocket, and stretched the justice on the ground with a stab. Was he taking his revenge upon the judge for his recent loss at play? or was it this purpose to satisfy the irritation against civil authority natural to a gaucho outlaw, and increase, by this new deed, the splendor of his rising fame? Both are true explanations. This mode of revenging himself for misfortunes upon whatever first offered itself, had many examples in his life. When he was addressed as General, and had colonels at his or-

ders, he had two hundred lashes given one of them in his house at San Juan, for having, as he said, cheated at play. He ordered two hundred lashes to be given to a young man for having allowed himself a jest at a time when jests were not to his taste; and two hundred lashes was the penalty inflicted on a woman in Mendoza for having said to him as he passed, "Farewell, General," when he was going off in a rage at not having succeeded in intimidating a neighbor of his, who was as peaceable and judicious as Facundo was rash and gaucho-like.

Facundo reappears later in Buenos Aires, where he was enrolled in 1810 as a recruit in the regiment of Arribeños, which was commanded by General Ocampo, a native of his own province, and afterwards president of Charcas. The glorious career of arms opened before him with the first rays of the sun of May; and doubtless, endowed with such capacity as his, and with his destructive and sanguinary instincts, Facundo, could he have been disciplined to submit to civil authority and ennobled in the sublimity of the object of the strife, might some day have returned from Peru, Chili, or Bolivia, as a General of the Argentine Republic, like so many other brave gauchos who began their careers in the humble position of a private soldier. But Quiroga's rebellious spirit could not endure the yoke of discipline, the order of the barrack, or the delay of promotion. He felt his destiny to be to rule, to rise at a single leap, to create for himself, without assistance, and in spite of a hostile and civilized society, a career of his own, combining bravery and crime, government and disorganization. He was subsequently recruited into the army of the Andes, and enrolled in the Mounted Grenadiers. A lieutenant named García took him for an assistant, and very soon desertion left a vacant place in those glorious files. Quiroga, like Rosas, like all the vipers that have thriven under the shade of their country's laurels, made himself notorious in after-life by his hatred for the soldiers of Independence, among whom both the men above named made horrible slaughter.

Facundo, after deserting from Buenos Aires, set out for the interior with three comrades. A squad of soldiery overtook him; he faced the pursuers and engaged in a real battle with them, which remained undecided for awhile, until, after having killed four or five men, he was at liberty to continue his journey, constantly cutting his way through detachments of troops which here and there opposed his progress, until he arrived at San Luis. He was, at a later day, to traverse the same route with a handful of men to disperse armies instead of detachments, and proceed to the famous citadel of Tucumán to blot out the last remains of Republicanism and civil order.

Facundo now reappears in the Llanos, at his father's house. At this period occurred an event which is well attested. Yet one of the writers whose manuscripts I am using, replies to an inquiry about the matter, "that to the extent of his knowledge Quiroga never attempted forcibly to deprive his parents of money," and I could wish to adopt this statement, irreconcilable as it is with unvarying tradition and general consent. The contrary is shocking to relate. It is said that on his father's refusal to give him a sum of money which he had demanded, he watched for the time when both parents were taking an afternoon nap to fasten the door of the room they occupied, and to set fire to the straw roof, which was the usual covering of the building of the Llanos! [6]

But what is certain in the matter is that his father once requested the governor of La Rioja to arrest him in order to check his excesses, and that Facundo, before taking flight from the Llanos, went to the city of La Rioja, where that official was to be found at the time, and coming upon him by surprise, gave him a blow, saying as he did so, "You have sent, sir, to have me arrested. There, have me arrested now!" On which he mounted his horse and set off for the open country at a gallop. At the end of a year he again showed himself at his father's house, threw himself at the feet of the old man whom he had used so ill, and succeeded amid the sobs of both, and the son's assurances of his reform in reply to the father's recriminations, in reestablishing peace, although on a very uncertain basis.

But no change occurred in his character and disorderly habits; races, gambling parties, and expeditions into the country were the occasions of new acts of violence, stabbings, and assaults on his part, until he at length made himself intolerable to all, and rendered his own position very unsafe. Then a great thought which he announced without shame got hold of his mind. The deserter from the Arribeños regiment, the mounted grenadier who refused to make himself immortal at Chacabuco or Maipú, determined

to join the montonera of Ramírez, the off-shoot from that led by Artigas, whose renown for crime and hatred for the cities on which it was making war, had reached the Llanos, and held the provincial government in dread. Facundo set forth to join those buccaneers of the pampa. But perhaps the knowledge of his character, and of the importance of the aid which he would give to the destroyers, alarmed his fellow provincials, for they informed the authorities of San Luis, through which he was to pass, of his infernal design. Dupuis, then (1818) governor, arrested him, and for some time he remained unnoticed among the criminals confined in the prison. This prison of San Luis, however, was to be the first step in his ascent to the elevation which he subsequently attained. San Martín had sent to San Luis a great number of Spanish officers of all ranks from among the prisoners taken in Chili. Irritated by their humiliations and sufferings, or thinking it possible that the Spanish forces might be assembled again this party of prisoners rose one day and opened the doors of the cells of the common criminals, to obtain their aid in a general escape. Facundo was one of these criminals, and as soon as he found himself free from prison, he seized an iron bar of his fetters, split the skull of the very Spaniard who had released him, and passing through the group of insurgents, left a wide path strewn with the dead. Some say that the weapon he employed was a bayonet, and that only three men were killed by it. Quiroga, however, always talked of the iron bar of the fetters, and of fourteen dead men. This may be one of the fictions with which the poetic imagination of the people adorns the types of brute force they so much admire; perhaps the tale of the iron bar is an Argentine version of the jaw-bone of Samson, the Hebrew Hercules. But Facundo looked upon it as a crown of glory, in accordance with his idea of excellence, and whether by bar or bayonet, he succeeded, aided by other soldiers and prisoners whom his example encouraged, in suppressing the insurrection and reconciling society to himself by this act of bravery, and placing himself under his country's protection. Thus his name spread everywhere, ennobled and cleansed, though with blood, from the stains which had tarnished it.

Facundo returned to La Rioja covered with glory, his country's creditor: and with testimonials of his conduct, to show in the Llanos, among gauchos, the new titles which justified the terror his name began to inspire; for there is some-

---

[6] The author afterwards learned that Facundo related this story to a company of ladies, and one of his own early acquaintances testified to his having given his father a blow on one occasion.

thing imposing, something which subjugates and controls others in the man who is rewarded for the assassination of fourteen men at one time.

Something still remains to be noticed of the previous character and temper of this pillar of the Confederation. An illiterate man, one of Quiroga's companions in childhood and youth, who has supplied me with many of the above facts, sends me the following curious statements in a manuscript describing Quiroga's early years: "His public career was not preceded by the practice of theft; he never committed robbery even in his most pressing necessities. He was not only fond of fighting, but would pay for an opportunity, or for a chance to insult the most renowned champion in any company. He had a great aversion to respectable men. He never drank. He was very reserved from his youth, and desired to inspire others with awe as well as with fear, for which purpose he gave his confidants to understand that he had the gift of prophecy, in short a soothsayer. He treated all connected with him as slaves. He never went to confession, prayed, or heard mass; I saw him once at mass after he became a general. He said of himself that he believed in nothing." The frankness with which these words are written prove their truth.

And here ends the private life of Quiroga, in which I have omitted a long series of deeds which only show his evil nature, his bad education, and his fierce and bloody instincts. The facts stated appear to me to sum up the whole public life of Quiroga. I see in them the great man, the man of genius, in spite of himself and unknown to himself; a Caesar, Tamerlane, or Mohammed. The fault is not his that thus he was born. In order to contend with, rule, and control the power of the city, and the judicial authority, he is willing to descend to anything. If he is offered a place in the army, he disdains it, because his impatience cannot wait for promotion. Such a position demands submission, and places fetters upon individual independence; the soldier's coat oppresses his body, and military tactics control his steps, all of which are insufferable! His equestrian life, a life of danger and of strong excitements, has steeled his spirit and hardened his heart. He feels an unconquerable and instinctive hatred for the laws which have pursued him, for the judges who have condemned him, and for the whole society and organism from which he has felt himself withdrawn from his childhood, and which regards him with suspicion and contempt. With these remarks is connected by imperceptible links the

motto of this chapter, "He is the natural man, as yet unused either to repress or disguise his passions; he does not restrain their energy, but gives free rein to their impetuosity. This is the character of the human race." And thus it appears in the rural districts of the Argentine Republic. Facundo is a type of primitive barbarism. He recognized no form of subjection. His rage was that of a wild beast. The locks of his crisp black hair, which fell in meshes over his brow and eyes, resembled the snakes of Medusa's head. Anger made his voice hoarse, and turned his glances into dragons. In a fit of passion he kicked out the brains of a man with whom he had quarreled at play. He tore off both the ears of a woman he had lived with, and had promised to marry, upon her asking him for thirty dollars for the celebration of the wedding; and laid open his son Juan's head with an axe, because he could not make him hold his tongue. He violently beat a beautiful young lady at Tucumán, whom he failed either to seduce or to subdue, and exhibited in all his actions a low and brutal yet not a stupid nature, or one wholly without lofty aims. Incapable of commanding noble admiration, he delighted in exciting fear; and this pleasure was exclusive and dominant with him to the arranging all his actions so as to produce terror in those around him, whether it was society in general, the victim on his way to execution, or his own wife and children. Wanting ability to manage the machinery of civil government, he substituted terror for patriotism and self-sacrifice. Destitute of learning, he surrounded himself with mysteries, and pretended to a foreknowledge of events which gave him prestige and reputation among the commonalty, supporting his claims by an air of impenetrability, by natural sagacity, an uncommon power of observation, and the advantage he derived from vulgar credulity.

The repertory of anecdotes relating to Quiroga, and with which the popular memory is replete, is inexhaustible; his sayings, his expedients, bear the stamp of an originality which gives them a certain Eastern aspect, a certain tint of Solomonic wisdom in the conception of the vulgar. Indeed, how does Solomon's advice for discovering the true mother of the disputed child differ from Facundo's method of detecting a thief in the following instances: —

An article had been stolen from a band, and all endeavors to discover the thief had proved fruitless. Quiroga drew up the troop and gave orders for the cutting of as many small wands of equal length as there were soldiers; then, having had these wands distributed one to each man, he said in a confident voice, "The man whose wand will be longer than the others tomorrow morning is the thief." Next day the troop was again paraded, and Quiroga proceeded to inspect the wands. There was one whose wand was, not longer but shorter than the others. "Wretch!" cried Facundo, in a voice which overpowered the man with dismay, "it is thou!" And so it was; the culprit's confusion was proof of the fact. The expedient was a simple one; the credulous gaucho, fearing that his wand would really grow, had cut off a piece of it. But to avail one's self of such means, a man must be superior in intellect to those about him, and must at least have some knowledge of human nature.

Some portions of a soldier's accoutrements having been stolen and all inquiries having failed to detect the thief, Quiroga had the troops paraded and marched past him as he stood with crossed arms and a fixed, piercing, and terrible gaze. He had previously said, "I know the man," with an air of assurance not to be questioned. The review began, many men had passed, and Quiroga still remained motionless, like the statue of Jupiter Tonans or the God of the Last Judgment. All at once he descended upon one man, and said in a curt and dry voice. "Where is the saddle?" "Yonder, sir," replied the other, pointing to a thicket. "Ho! four fusileers!" cried Quiroga. What revelation was this? that of terror and guilt made to a man of sagacity.

On another occasion, when a gaucho was answering to charges of theft which had been brought against him, Facundo interrupted him with the words, "This rogue has begun to lie. Ho, there! a hundred lashes!" When the criminal had been taken away, Quiroga said to some one present, "Look you, my master, when a gaucho moves his foot while talking, it is a sign he is telling lies." The lashes extorted from the gaucho the confession that he had stolen a yoke of oxen.

At another time he was in need of a man of resolution and boldness to whom he could intrust a dangerous mission. When a man was brought to him for this purpose, Quiroga was writing; he raised his head after the man's presence had been repeatedly announced, looked at him and returned to his writing with the remark, "Pooh! that is a wretched creature. I want a brave man and a venturesome one!" It turned out to be true that the fellow was actually good for nothing.

Hundreds of such stories of Facundo's life, which show the man of superior ability, served

effectually to give him a mysterious fame among the vulgar, who even attribute superior powers to him.

3. IN DEFENSE OF CONSERVATISM

At the opposite pole from barbarian caudillos like Facundo were those chieftains, more common in the period after 1860, who stimulated economic development and often ruled with outward regard for constitutional forms. Rafael Núñez (1825–1894), president-dictator of Colombia from 1885 to 1894, was also a distinguished poet and publicist. In the following essay, written in 1882, Núñez expounds his conservative political philosophy.[7]

IN THE TIME OF PRAXITELES a sculpture competition was held in Cos, and the celebrated Greek artist presented two admirable statues, one nude, the other clothed. The morality of that remote period was much inferior to our own; nevertheless, the judges of the contest decided in favor of the draped statue, which was awarded the prize.

Now, after the passage of so many centuries, there has arisen in France a literary school called naturalism or realism (or nudity), whose founder, Èmile Zola, is the author of several works that I have rapidly examined. I had already been repelled by their naked portrayal of human vices when there fell into my hands a recent book that alludes to this literary fashion, and which cites the entirely adverse judgment pronounced upon it by the most powerful literary genius of the age: Victor Hugo.

He energetically condemns the new school. "Why must one descend into the gutter," he asks, "in order to tell the truth? Why, lofty ideas are no less truthful than the others; and as for myself, I prefer the former. . . ."

In contemporary politics there is the same fatal tendency toward realism, which is particularly evident in some sections of the parties called Liberal. To this school of thought must be attributed the frightful failure of the first French Republic and the errors which led to it. Voltaire, perhaps unconsciously, despite his prodigious talent, prepared the way for that dizzy flight of French popular thought by teaching men to use the scalpel of free investigation beyond the limits marked out by a prudent and fruitful wisdom.

Human reason has certain inalienable rights,

7 *Los mejores artículos políticos de Rafael Núñez,* Bogotá, 1936, pp. 95–103. (Excerpt translated by the editor.)

but in its investigation of truth it is often led astray under the influence of superficial stimuli. Believing the number of premises to be complete, in many cases it draws conclusions that are naturally erroneous, as if an accountant were to compute a sum and left one or more figures out of his calculation.

In the domain of politics, to which I must limit myself at present, an analysis merits little faith if it does not provide the elements for the solution of simple problems. These problems can later be converted into axioms; but the formulation of political axioms is not so easy to achieve as is generally believed.

In its first impulse the French Revolution of '89 sought only a limited reform. It is certain that Mirabeau, for one, and Lafayette, for another, sought only this. That reform was necessary, because the traditional abuses of the feudal monarchy were of such magnitude that they would have inevitably dragged France to her ruin.

The king did not understand the situation, because he was absolutely lacking in political capacity; but the revolutionaries, in their turn, proposed in a short time to dismantle the ancient and time-honored structure of monarchy, placing on public view, in the manner of an anatomical dissection, the whole skeleton of political power.

Sieyès affirmed that the Third Estate was everything. His demonstration was equivalent to saying that all the rest was nothing. That demonstration was not without an element of truth, but it fell short, by little or by much, of being the whole truth.

To suppress the king, the clergy, and the nobility, with the stroke of a pen, was the same as making the clock strike in a second the hours of several centuries.

The lowest social group rushed in to fill the void, as happens with columns of air when some atmospheric space becomes vacant; and a social storm broke over France.

The privileges of the aristocracy were not defensible in the light of abstract reason, but it was a grave error to suppose that their total and immediate abolition was desirable.

The quality that we call prestige, in relation to a given political order of things, certainly cannot withstand the cold scrutiny of a philosopher; but that prestige must have some reason for existence, when its disappearance can cause so many misfortunes. I believe that truths are always relative, because they depend upon the time and the measure in which they are applied.

The French Revolution waged a determined campaign against all the prevailing prejudices (and prejudices they were, from an elevated point of view); but all that series of measures aimed at the extirpation of abuses and errors became a vortex that swallowed up the principal actors in the projected social and political renovation. Instead of a glorious ascent, France suffered a disastrous collapse; and there was a moment when the elegant *Marseillaise* was considered aristocratic and royalist and was replaced by the vulgar *Carmagnole*.

The ninth of Thermidor marks the beginning of the reaction, but the true reaction did not openly appear until the eighteenth of Brumaire, which cleared the way for the establishment of the Napoleonic dynasty. The very novelty of the terms I have just used demonstrates to what an absurd point the revolutionary dreamers carried their spirit of reform.

There you have in a few words the story of a great experiment in political realism, made by one of the most courageous and intelligent peoples in the world.

A similar experiment, on a much smaller scale, was made among us. It yielded some excellent fruits, as was also true of the great French Revolution. But here, as in republican France, it was proposed to turn society upside down, and this daring effort produced other fruit whose intense and poisonous bitterness soon made itself felt.

It would be unjust to deny that in the first period of that daring revolution the leaders of our political life proceeded in good faith. This was also true of the Girondist leaders of the French Revolution at its beginning; nor can one question the sincerity of Robespierre when he framed the Declaration of the Rights of Man, and when he took a determined stand against war and capital punishment from the tribune of the parliament.

In the first period, to which I have referred, the dominant tendency could be described as idealistic or chimerical, but since extremes always meet, this exaggerated idealism gradually led to an exaggerated realism.

Indirect and public elections were replaced by direct and secret elections, because it was believed that this last system was more sound. Popular voting was applied to all important offices, including those of a judicial order. The ignorance of the masses, meantime, was all but complete. Simultaneously there began the senseless effort to weaken the influence and power of religious feeling, which among us invariably and exclusively takes the form of Catholic faith. Under the pretext, in fine, of combating prejudices and errors, our politicians unclothed, bared, and dissected nearly everything, completely oblivious of what might be called a political sense of shame and of the limitations of human reason.

At the beginning of this article I showed the depths to which literary realism may descend. A like degradation must occur with respect to experiments in political realism. From the hoped-for "true Republic" one goes on to anarchy or despotism, just as from the abolition of religious worship one descends to a sterile and melancholy disbelief, and from the suppression of the aesthetic in art one falls into the sewer of the novels called naturalistic. . . .

Fortunately, we already stand in the dawn of reaction. . . . The shadows flee, and a beautiful twilight emerges. That it may grow and assume an aspect of complete and definitive light, it is only necessary for us to have confidence in our powers and conviction in our hearts.

4. REFORM BY REVOLUTION

Mexico and Argentina were the main battlefields of the struggle between liberalism and conservatism in nineteenth-century Latin America. The movement to which Mexican historians give the name La Reforma, *led by men of such intellectual and moral stature as Benito Juárez and Melchor Ocampo, represented an ambitious effort to transform backward Mexico into a progressive middle-class state. Its climactic moment was the adoption of the Constitution of 1857, which ushered in the War of the Reform, which was swiftly followed by the French Intervention. Justo Sierra (1848–1912), brilliant Mexican historian and educator, records the movement of events between the establishment of Santa Anna's last dictatorship and the outbreak of the War of the Reform.[8]*

JUÁREZ, retired to private life by the triumph of the ill-omened Plan of Jalisco, expected from the moment of Santa Anna's coup a policy of persecution and repression of all liberals. He was not surprised, therefore, by his arrest in May, 1853, in Etla, nor by his confinement to Jalapa, nor by his violent abduction from a friend's house in Puebla by the wrathful hand

[8] Justo Sierra, *Obras completas*, I, *Juárez, su obra y su tiempo*, México, 1948, pp. 87–113. (Excerpt translated by the editor.)

of the famous Pepe Santa Anna (who considered it an honor to play the part of a bravo in the service of his father, and who lived the life of a sultan in the sacred city of clericalism), nor by his imprisonment for some days in the horrible dungeons of San Juan de Ulúa, nor by his exile. . . .

In the middle of 1853 Juárez was in New Orleans. There he found a group of outstanding men who awaited with unshakable faith the end of Santa Anna's tyranny, and who thought constantly about the means of securing the triumph of reform ideas in Mexico. All respected Juárez; his reputation as a governor of unwavering integrity had preceded him in that beehive of ideas and noble ambitions. But the salient personality was that of Ocampo, man of thought and action, agriculturist, naturalist, economist, a public man from love for the public good, with no other ambition than that of doing something for his country. To comprehend the moral grandeur of this disciple of Rousseau and student of Proudhon it is necessary to take into account his absolute disinterest. There is no longer any mystery about the irregular but exalted origin of Señor Ocampo; the mistress of the Hacienda of Pateo bequeathed to him her property . . . and the fortune thus acquired he employed for the good of others, improving labor conditions in the regions over which his influence extended and converting his estates into experimental stations for the acclimation of useful plants, for trials of new cultures, and for the production of exquisite botanical specimens. Into this as in all else Ocampo put all the warmth of his passionate soul. A friend of his told me that on one occasion, in the garden of the little station of La Tejería on the railroad from Veracruz to Mexico City, then just begun (this was in 1859), he found the illustrious reformer kneeling with tearful emotion before some splendid Yucatecan lilies in bloom. . . .

The influence, the ascendancy of Ocampo over the New Orleans group was immense; it was evident in the case of Juárez — nor could it be otherwise. Both men had firm liberal convictions; both had been governors, one in Oaxaca and the other in Michoacán; both had advocated peace and condemned revolutions, joining in support of an honest Federalism and the honorable and moderate administrations of Herrera and Arista; both had bitterly denounced the unprincipled and equivocal revolt of Jalisco. But while Juárez as governor had made concessions to the Church in an obvious effort to placate it,

Ocampo had thrown down the gauntlet to the clergy in the matter of parochial obventions. In New Orleans the aspect of things changed; there, assisted by Mata and Ponciano Arriaga, they hammered out the party program on the basis of which the Constitution of '57 would soon be formed. Complete emancipation of the civil power — and not only complete but definitive; to wit: radical destruction of the power of the Church in all that did not concern its strictly spiritual influence, by suppressing the *fueros* and religious communities, and nationalizing church property. The North American scene fortified and confirmed the libertarian ideas of the exiles; they saw clearly the close relation between liberty and prosperity. On one occasion Juárez and Mata walked together along the levee of New Orleans. The future president was astounded by the immense commercial activity he saw taking place in the course of a single hour at that point on the banks of the Mississippi. "The explanation of all this," said Mata, "is a single freedom — that of internal trade; abolish our *alcabalas,* and our prosperity would be as great as theirs." These were the lessons that the Anglo-Saxon world taught the exiles. They helped to keep their convictions firm; all their hatred for the tutelage of the clergy had as its complement a devotion to freedom of conscience, incompatible with the authority of the Church. Hence their lively desire, not only to renew in a future constitution the great charter of individual liberties which the ecclesiastical domination nullified, but to find a way of making them effective by making all administrative action subject to judicial review (*Juicio de Amparo*). . . .

The tyranny of Santa Anna had succeeded in unifying the once formless Liberal Party, which worked as a solid phalanx to overthrow the despot; and one could say that the time arrived when all conspired against him — even the bureaucrats, even the soldiers. Sensible conservatives, convinced that Santa Anna's dictatorship was not a government nor an institution, but a vice, viewed without grief, though not without misgivings, the fall of the despot. Their hope was Comonfort — and the man who was the chief, the soul of the revolution of Ayutla was truly capable of inspiring hope. . . .

The Revolution of Ayutla, converted into the War of the Reform and then into a struggle with an exotic monarchy based on foreign aid, constitutes the Great Mexican Revolution of our period of independence. It was the work of our national Jacobins, a great and good work. But it began slowly, thanks to the tenacious hopes of Comonfort, who believed that he could avoid war. To aid him in this effort, while keeping alive the promises of the revolution, was the work of Juárez, named by President Álvarez Secretary of Justice and Ecclesiastical Affairs in his coalition cabinet. . . .

Juárez rendered a great service to the ideals of the *puros* [9] by acceding to the request of General Álvarez and remaining in the ministry when Ocampo left. Without him the reform measures would have been indefinitely postponed, until the time — for which Comonfort yearned — when all would agree to them. Comonfort's apprehensions were well founded, to be sure; he feared that the clergy would convert a political conflict into a religious question, and that the civil strife would be transformed into a religious war. Truly a calamity that would completely ruin the country! Juárez, no writer of books replete with projects of vengeance and social catastrophe, but a responsible lawgiver, well understood that to convince Comonfort of the convenience of a great reform measure, albeit attenuated, was better and more feasible than to draft a complete code of transcendent reforms that would have died stillborn without the aid of Comonfort's victorious sword. Juárez thus rendered a major service to the liberal cause.

This happened after General Álvarez, named provisional president by the junta assembled in Cuernavaca, lost hope that the Congress would assemble in Dolores and decided to come to Mexico City, establishing himself with his ministry in the capital of the Republic. Juárez and Comonfort were the two representative figures of that government.

The Juárez Law organized the administration of justice and set in it the foundation stone of the Reform. Excitement ran high; the conservative newspapers raised the cry of alarm against every effort at innovation; the liberal newspapers with equal insistence demanded a program of struggle, not of peace (no one thought of peace except Comonfort, the Minister of War). General Álvarez thought only of retirement; he urged that Comonfort, his inevitable and necessary successor as provisional president of the Republic, should not be embarrassed by a reform law proclaimed even before the meeting of the Constituent Assembly. In November, 1855, appeared the Juárez Law; Article 42 suppressed

[9] The radical (as opposed to the moderate) wing of the Liberal Party. B.K.

the special tribunals (there still were many —
of commerce, the treasury, etc.) and exempted
from this suppression the ecclesiastical and military tribunals. But they were only to continue
temporarily. The first (until the passage of a
law that should definitively regulate the ecclesiastical privileges) would have jurisdiction only
over common offenses of members of the clergy.
Civil affairs were to be under the exclusive control of the common courts. Moreover, ecclesiastics were given the right to reject trial by ecclesiastical courts of a penal character. With respect to the military, something very similar was
provided; jurisdiction over civil affairs was also
taken away from the military courts, and it was
retained only for purely military or mixed
offenses, and only if the responsible parties were
soldiers.

A true daughter of the Revolution of Ayutla,
the Juárez Law was a revolutionary law; given
by an authority which had the revolution for
its sole source of power, it declared that as a
general (federal) law the states could neither
modify nor change it. The uproar was great but
had been anticipated; Comonfort made common
cause with his cabinet; and the protests of the
bishop who sought to have the point referred to
the judgment of the Pope and the Supreme
Court (which objected to an organic court law
framed without consulting its opinion) did not
deter Juárez from putting the law into immediate effect. In a short time it had assumed the
character of a *res adjudicata*, as the jurists say,
and so it has been down to our time, because
the conquests of the Reform had this peculiarity: once established in law they have been converted into enduring facts; they have been enlarged, but never altered or revoked. . . .

The clergy and the army felt the blow of the
formidable adversary that rose before them and
prepared for combat. Their protests and complaints were the agitated whirlpool that shows
on the surface; below was the danger, the permanent conspiracy, the conspiracy that united
in intimate contact soldiers and churchmen, that
now expanded until it became international,
now convulsively contracted to center about the
curacies of the mountains, the larger towns,
from which sparks constantly flew up, presaging
the imminent conflagration. Could the immense
popularity of Comonfort quench the fire? Many
believed it — but not the bishops, not the heads
of Santa Anna's favorite corps, not honest but
hopelessly deluded conservatives like Haro and
Tamáriz, not the young officers swollen with

ambition and bravado like Osollo and Mira-
món, not Father Miranda.

In December, 1855, General Álvarez resigned
and named Comonfort as his substitute; that is
why he was called the substitute president. The
great doctrine of conciliation was to be put fully
into practice. Ocampo had insisted that it would
fail; but if it succeeded, revolution would be
replaced by a normal evolution, and peace,
blessed peace, would be a fact. . . . Yet war
raised its threatening visage everywhere: a rising
in Guanajuato, where Doblado, an individual of
many expedients and few scruples, had raised
the banner of Comonfort with no plausible motive, was crushed by a piece of paper — a very
sensible, worthy, and biting letter from Juan
Álvarez — and Doblado bowed his head; the
mountains of Querétaro burned with religion
and *fueros*; the indefatigable Mejía was on the
war path; Uraga sought to take advantage of
the discontent of the "old army" with the Juárez
Law; Jalisco and the whole North were restless,
and bands of outlaws roamed the country in
search of spoil. In the Bajío the situation was
returning to normal. In Puebla, on the other
hand, there broke out a blaze which had to be
isolated and smothered before it could spread to
the entire country.

The Bishop of Puebla (Don Pelagio Antonio
de Labastida y Dávalos, future Archbishop of
Mexico) had acquired by his merits, fine intelligence, and social graces, an immense prestige
in Puebla society. From the highest to the lowest, that society lived in the Church and by the
Church; the aristocratic families were all petri-
fied, embalmed in devotion and mysticism about
this canon, that curate, such-and-such a friar,
and at the foot of one or another image of Christ
or of Our Lady. Life there consisted of pious
exercises, of saints' festivals, of processions, of
novenas. As for mortal sin, a microbe which
pullulated at the bottom of the most angelic
beatitudes, it did not show on the transparent
surface of that life, as clear as water; high-pow-
ered miscroscopes had not yet come into use.
And the populace, vicious and dirty, but much
less so than the rabble of the capital, only lived
by what it obtained from the convents, by the
crumbs of the Church, by the protection and
charity of the priests.

And that is why all that concerned the Church
touched them to the quick, reached the inner-
most recesses of their beings, of their interests,
of their loves and hates. And with slight shades
of difference it was the same everywhere in the

Republic, with the exception of some coastal towns, where the salty sea air diluted somewhat the influence of the clergy. The bishops, like Señor Labastida, publicly affirmed that they did not mix in political affairs, that they reproved armed revolts, and that they counseled obedience to the government as long as its dispositions were not in conflict with the Catholic conscience; and what they affirmed they doubtless believed and practiced. This was least of all true, however, of the Bishop of Puebla, who shortly after the events that unfolded in his diocese in the year 1856 showed very plainly what an ardent politician he was. . . .

Given the national character, however, even if the bishops had not prompted or desired the revolt it inevitably followed from their protests. These protests affirmed that the Church was suffering grave offenses, unjust attacks that were causing irreparable injury to national Catholicism; the Juárez Law . . . they proclaimed to be a rude assault on the most obvious rights of the Church. But how could the clergy resist the attack except by defending themselves, and what better defense than to overthrow the government? All this was clear, and the Catholic populace proceeded with more logic than its prelates, though with less understanding of the situation.

Taking advantage of the feverish atmosphere of Puebla, large groups of the permanent army — on whose support Comonfort, clinging tenaciously to his illusions, still counted — false to their commitments, to their honor, to their oaths, seized the city, which all the spokesmen for military and clerical reaction had made their headquarters. The president determined to atone for his naiveté by striking a hard blow, during the very days when the Constituent Assembly was gathering. The campaign, very prudently and energetically directed, once again placed in bold relief the distinguished soldierly traits of the leader of the Revolution of Ayutla: a desire to spare his soldiers' blood, respect for the advice of experts in the technical aspects of war, and a serene bravery that gave him a kind of heroic aura. The soldiers of the national guard adored him.

Once master of Puebla, where the populace, ever ready to cheer the victor, gave him a friendly reception, the President returned to Mexico City in a better position to sustain two great struggles — one against the clergy, ordering the confiscation of the property of the bishopric of Puebla, and the second against the permanent army, humiliating, degrading, and irritating the officer class. Bishop Labastida, who resisted the orders of the government, was exiled; it was a sound political measure. Clearly, in a city like Puebla the funds of the Church, with or without the wishes of its head, only served to foment conspiracies; it was necessary to deprive the fire of oil, and to give the proof of energy for which the Liberal Party loudly clamored by putting a hand on the most rebellious of the prelates. Away to Europe to conspire went the bishop; he conspired furiously, incessantly, from that moment. Thereby he revealed what lay at the bottom of his heart; Comonfort had not been mistaken.

The degradation of the officers, on the other hand, produced contrary effects. These men thought of nothing but revenge, of settling scores, and they thought about it with pleasure. The future General Sostenes Rocha, who at the time was a petty officer in the Sappers and who was one of the officers stripped of their ranks and confined to towns south of Puebla, relates in his colorful memoirs (as yet unpublished) the ruses to which all these culprits, who naturally regarded themselves as heroes, resorted in order to keep alive. . . . One by one they succeeded in escaping from their confinements, drawn to the counter-revolutionary center in Mexico City or called to military posts in certain states (as happened with Rocha), and it is clear that the stages of their flight were from convent to convent, and from curacy to curacy. It would have been better for the country and for Comonfort to have shot three or four of the principal officers and to have imprisoned the rest for two or three years; such energy would have spared the country a great deal of suffering. The writer of these lines cannot forget that as a student, representing the School of Law, he went to plead with President Juárez to spare the life of a great impenitent revolutionary, captured almost *in flagrante delicto* while assaulting a treasure-train under government convoy. The prisoner had a name intimately linked to a glorious date. "It is well," replied Señor Juárez to my petition, "I had already decided to pardon him. But do not forget, and let your friends know, that by pardoning a man of this kind, who thinks that politics signifies disorders and barrackroom revolts, I am sentencing to death many hundreds of innocent people." Perhaps these words could be applied to the perennial clemency of Comonfort. . . .

The Juárez Law was the lighted fuse, and its first result the explosion of Puebla, a tremendous rising with its train of sanguinary combats, a costly and difficult campaign, the military degradation of the old army, the confiscation of Church property in that priestly city, and the exile of Bishop Labastida. Comonfort gave constant proofs of his private religiosity, as if to match the professions of obedience made by the clergy each time it questioned the right of the government to subject all social classes to its jurisdiction. . . . The attitude taken by the Church, its decision to struggle for its privileges by appealing to religious sentiments (exciting them not against the government but in favor of the Church) gave the sessions of Congress a certain solemn and religious tone. When one heard Zarco, Mata, and Arriaga speak of the fundamental conformity between the Constitution and the Gospel, when they discussed religious tolerance, the Constituent Assembly resembled an assembly of Puritans on the eve of the great English religious wars. All this raised to the highest pitch the political fever of the country. And the press with its immense clamor echoed the tribune and the pulpit; the time of Religious Wars appeared to be drawing near for Mexico. Comonfort meditated — that is to say, he vacillated. Later he sent an agent to Rome in search of reconciliation and an agreement; as might be expected, the Pope would not receive him. Pius IX, a great heart filled with all the fire of apostolic zeal, a warrior and martyr by nature but of small intelligence when compared with his successor, dismissed the Mexican minister from the pontifical throne with the same wrathful and tremulous hand that hurled anathema against the Reform. Very logical, perhaps, but infinitely imprudent and improvident. Heads grew heated in Mexico on receipt of this news, and when an undecided person had made up his mind, he was no longer a simple friend of the civil power but a resolute enemy of the Church. To this attitude of the Pontiff must be ascribed the anti-Catholic tone of the reform press and the iconoclastic and "War-to-the-friar" character of the Three Years' War. . . .

Comonfort, no Mirabeau, Napoleon, or Cromwell, yielded here and yielded there, and believed that he was advancing in zigzag fashion; in reality he was zigzagging into the abyss. With the sword of Damocles over the head of the press (the Lafragua Law), he was stern toward the conservative journals and excessively timid with the revolutionary ones. . . . He attached the property of the bishopric of Puebla and exiled the bishop; this show of energy frightened the high clergy, but some months later its effect was nullified by the suspension of the process of seizure. . . . The suppression of the Company of Jesus caused a profound uproar, intensified by the feverish excitement with which the people followed the discussions of the Constituent Congress. . . . When the Bishop of Puebla, awaiting in Havana the possible revocation of his exile, learned of the suppression of the Company, he understood that the fight had just begun, and departed for Rome.

Arriving in Spain, he found even greater cause for despair: The Lerdo Law had been promulgated in June (1856). With a severe preamble that summarized the economic reasons justifying the law, and which could be reduced to the necessity of putting in circulation an almost unproductive mass of wealth, the minister of the treasury set forth in articles as clear as his character and intellect the conditions under which disentail should take place. The law left in the hands of the actual possessors the estates or urban properties belonging to civil (philanthropic, public educational) or ecclesiastical corporations. Calculating the value of the property by the rent or lease at six per cent, the resulting sum should constitute a mortgage on the disentailed estate, which was to pay six per cent interest to the corporation. This species of mortgage could on no condition result in a return of the estate to the corporation, but under certain conditions enumerated in the law it could be put up at auction. . . .

During the days that Congress discussed the article of the draft constitution that related not to freedom of worship but to religious toleration, the capital, and before long the whole Republic, lived in an atmosphere saturated with the electric tension that presages combat. All upper-class Mexico, the governing classes *en masse*, arose as one man and presented to the Congress eloquent memorials pleading that it vote down the Satanic article. This work of the devil, claimed to be a source of evils compared with which the Deluge was child's play, declared: "There shall not be promulgated any law or order that prohibits or impedes the exercise of any religious cult; but since the Roman, Catholic, Apostolic Faith has been the exclusive religion of the Mexican people, the Congress of the Union shall seek to protect it by means of just and prudent laws, providing they do not injure the interests of the people or the rights of national sovereignty." The authors of the project could be criticized for not having dared to carry their thinking to its logical conclusion by proclaiming complete freedom of worship, without any privileged religion, as a consequence of the separation of Church and State. However, the tremendously excited state of public opinion probably intimidated them — not personally, to be sure, for Arriaga, Mata, Zarco had the courage of their convictions, but as a commission of the fundamental code they believed that only their project had any chance of success. They were mistaken; it was badly beaten in the breach, and under the formidable pressure of the government and popular opinion (the bourgeoisie and the illiterate class), the article disappeared from the draft. . . .

The constitution was voted; the great promise of Ayutla, in the words of the members, was fulfilled. Trembling with horror, the society that lived in the shadow of the belfry saw the ancient Gómez Farías, the founder of the reform government, take an oath of loyalty to the new law on bended knees, his hand on the Bible; then the whole country was summoned to take the same oath. The Church, with some hesitation (some bishops and ecclesiastical dignitaries swore loyalty), because it understood that upon its attitude depended peace or war, loosened the folds of its long mantle and chose war, like the Roman senator in Carthage. The nation, placed under a kind of interdict, displayed nervousness, almost epilepsy. Some refused to swear; others retracted their oaths; all who swore fell under the ban of excommunication. The crisis was at the very base of society; in the family, in the home; in the terrible anguish of the public official wavering between his religious duty and the prospect of misery; in the sobs, the appeals, the reproaches of mothers and wives; in the homes of the liberals themselves. . . .

Comonfort, terribly moved by this social crisis, daily confronted by the mute and tearful pleading of his mother, was content at the time he took the oath to ask for immediate reform of the constitution: a really senseless action. His indecision was immense. One idea had taken hold of his brain: *it was impossible to govern with the constitution*. The Executive, he believed, was made so impotent in the face of the action of a unitary Congress and the right of intervention — which could be incessant — of the judicial power, that only an uninterrupted succession of extraordinary powers could enable the President to govern; and these powers, painful experience told him, were usually denied, so that authority might remain in revolutionary hands.

Yet special powers were indispensable. The whole interior of the country was up in arms. Puebla witnessed a new revolt, a new siege, a new victory of the government, a new waste of blood and money that exhausted the resources of the treasury at a time when the foreign horizons darkened. The question of the Spanish claims became increasingly urgent and alarming. . . . In fine, the foreign intervention that Paredes had asked for, that Santa Anna had demanded, was in the air of the Mexican Gulf. Money and more money was needed to conjure away the storm. Where was it to come from? The proceeds of the tax on disentails were negligible or nil; the clergy had stopped with its interdict a movement that might have saved both it and the government of Comonfort.

[Under these conditions elections are held for the first congress and president under the Constitution of 1857, and for the members of the Supreme Court, whose president was also to be Vice President. Comonfort is elected President; Juárez becomes his Vice President. Comonfort's requests for special powers and a revision of the Constitution are rejected by the Liberal majority in the Congress. In November, 1857, General Félix Zuloaga, an instrument of conservative military and clerical groups, "pronounces" for a Comonfort dictatorship, dismisses Congress, and arrests Juárez. B.K.]

The Plan of Tacubaya repealed the Constitution of 1857 as unsuited to the usages and manners of the country, placed dictatorial powers in the hands of Comonfort, and referred to a future constituent assembly whose decisions were to be reviewed by the people *(ad referendum)*. Comonfort adhered to the Plan two days later. Never did a more modest Caesar, or one with less confidence in himself and his future, pronounce "the die is cast"; he pronounced it almost inaudibly. This man, who was no longer at peace with himself, was to bring peace to the Republic!

Zuloaga was a conservative four-square; if he had joined the liberal ranks it was from personal loyalty to Comonfort and nothing more. Now, brought to the fore, he was surrounded by counter-revolutionaries who hemmed him in, brought pressure upon him. What did they want? The Constitution no longer existed. There was talk of a grouping or coalition of certain states of the interior, of forces that came and went, of Parodi, of Degollado, of Arteago, of Doblado. True, the Archbishop had declared for the Plan of Tacubaya, and the priest Valdovinos had blessed it. The Church had joyfully "pronounced" in its favor! But this was not enough; the Council of Conservatives, *moderados*, and *puros* formed by Comonfort no longer gave satisfaction. He must go on to destroy the coalition, and above all and before all else he must repeal the Juárez Law; and above all and right away he must repeal the Lerdo Law, the law of disentail; he must return everything to the Church — but quickly, quickly!

The unhappy Comonfort said: "But this law has created new interests, new rights, new positions, and all under my pledge, my signature, my protection!" "What would you do if you were in my position?" the President asked the conservative leader José M. Cuevas. "Repeal the Lerdo Law and put myself in the hands of the conservatives," replied the lawyer. "And if you were in my place, with my background, my ideas, would you do it?" the anxious Comonfort asked. "Not I," replied the reactionary gentleman. "Thanks," Comonfort concluded, "I shall never do it." The next day Zuloaga's brigade "Re-pronounced," disavowing Comonfort as President. And Comonfort, gathering the few forces left to him, declared the Constitution of 1857 re-established. It was a tragic retraction. Twenty days later, standing on the stern of an American ship as it steamed out of Veracruz, he watched the Mexican coasts recede in the distance, and his political dreams merged with the clouds, with the shadows. . . .

On the day of Zuloaga's second "pronouncement" (January 11, 1858), Juárez was released by order of Comonfort. The two old friends probably did not speak to each other. Juárez could not recognize Comonfort as President, despite his repentance. Comonfort had accused, judged, and sentenced himself. Juárez, president of the Supreme Court, replaced him, according to the Constitution. It was Comonfort's last service to the liberal cause, though not to his country, for which he died obscurely six years later. The effort to achieve reform by way of persuasion and clemency had failed. The tremendous Three Years' War had begun.

5. ROADS TO THE FUTURE

Another important struggle between Spanish-American liberalism and conservatism took place in Argentina between 1830 and 1852. Against the tyranny of Juan Manuel Rosas, representing the narrow interests and views of the great cattlemen of the province of Buenos Aires, the cultured youth of the Capital rose in romantic but ineffective revolt. In 1852 Rosas fell, buried under the weight of the many enmities, domestic and foreign, that his policies had aroused. On the eve of the convention of 1853, summoned to draft a new constitution for Argentina, appeared a book by Juan Bautista Alberdi (1810–1884), entitled Bases and Points of Departure for the Political Organization of the Argentine Republic, *which strongly influenced the work of the delegates. The following selections from this book illustrate the optimistic, "civilizing," and pragmatic temper of Argentine liberalism in the age of Alberdi, Mitre, and Sarmiento.*[10]

OUR YOUTH should be trained for industrial life, and therefore should be educated in the arts and sciences that would prepare them for industry. The South-American type of man should be one formed for the conquest of the great and oppressive enemies of our progress: the desert; material backwardness; the brutal and primitive nature of this continent.

We should therefore endeavor to draw our youth away from the cities of the interior, where the old order with its habits of idleness, conceit, and dissipation prevails, and to attract them to the coastal towns so that they may obtain inspiration from Europe, which extends to our shores, and from the spirit of modern life.

The coastal towns, by their very nature, are better schools than our pretentious universities. . . .

Industry is the grand means of promoting morality. By furnishing men with the means of getting a living you keep them from crime, which is generally the fruit of misery and idleness. You will find it useless to fill the minds of youths with abstract notions about religion if you leave them idle and poor. Unless they take monastic vows they will be corrupt and fanatical at the same time. England and the United States have arrived at religious morality by way of industry; Spain has failed to acquire industry and liberty by means of religion alone. Spain has never been guilty of irreligion, but that did not save her from poverty, corruption, and despotism. . . .

The railroad offers the means of righting the topsy-turvy order that Spain established on this continent. She placed the heads of our states where the feet should be. For her ends of isolation and monopoly this was a wise system; for our aims of commercial expansion and freedom it is disastrous. We must bring our capitals to the coast, or rather bring the coast into the in-

10 Juan Bautista Alberdi, *Bases y puntos de partida para la organización política de la República Argentina*, Buenos Aires, 1943, pp. 62–63, 85–88, 90–92, 240–242. (Excerpts translated by the editor.)

terior of the continent. The railroad and the electric telegraph, the conquerors of space, work this wonder better than all the potentates on earth. The railroad changes, reforms, and solves the most difficult problems without decrees or mob violence.

It will forge the unity of the Argentine Republic better than all our congresses. The congresses may declare it "one and indivisible," but without the railroad to connect its most remote regions it will always remain divided and divisible, despite all the legislative decrees.

Without the railroad you will not have political unity in lands where distance nullifies the action of the central government. Do you want the government, the legislators, the courts of the coastal capital to legislate and judge concerning the affairs of the provinces of San Juan and Mendoza, for example? Bring the coast to those regions with the railroad, or vice versa; place those widely separated points within three days' travel of each other, at least. But to have the metropolis or capital a twenty days' journey away is little better than having it in Spain, as it was under the old system, which we overthrew for presenting precisely this absurdity. Political unity, then, should begin with territorial unity, and only the railroad can make a single region of two regions separated by five hundred leagues.

Nor can you bring the interior of our lands within reach of Europe's immigrants, who today are regenerating our coasts, except with the powerful aid of the railroads. They are or will be to the life of our interior territories what the great arteries are to the inferior extremities of the human body: sources of life. . . .

The means for securing railroads abound in these lands. Negotiate loans abroad, pledge your national revenues and properties for enterprises that will make them prosper and multiply. It would be childish to hope that ordinary revenues may suffice for such large expenditures; invert that order, begin with expenditures, and you will have revenues. If we had waited until we had sufficient revenues to bear the cost of the War of Independence against Spain, we would still be colonists. With loans we obtained cannons, guns, ships, and soldiers, and we won our independence. What we did to emerge from slavery, we should do to emerge from backwardness, which is the same as slavery; there is no greater title to glory than civilization.

But you will not obtain loans if you do not have national credit — that is, a credit based on the united securities and obligations of all the towns of the state. With the credits of town councils and provinces you will not secure railroads or anything notable. Form a national body, consolidate the securities of your present and future revenues and wealth, and you will find lenders who will make available millions for your local and general needs; for if you lack money today, you will have the means of becoming opulent tomorrow. Dispersed and divided, expect nothing but poverty and scorn. . . .

The great rivers, those "moving roads," as Pascal called them, are yet another means of introducing the civilizing action of Europe into the interior of our continent by means of her immigrants. But rivers that are not navigated do not, for practical purposes, exist. To place them under the exclusive domination of our poor banners is to close them to navigation. If they are to achieve the destiny assigned to them by God of populating the interior of the continent, we must place them under the law of the seas — that is, open them to an absolute freedom of navigation. . . .

Let the light of the world penetrate every corner of our republics. By what right do we maintain our most beautiful regions in perpetual brutality? Let us grant to European civilization what our ancient masters denied. In order to exercise their monopoly, the essence of their system, they gave only one port to the Argentine Republic; and we have preserved the exclusivism of the colonial system in the name of patriotism. No more exclusion or closure, whatever be the pretext that is invoked. No more exclusivism in the name of the Fatherland. . . .

What name will you give a land with 200,000 leagues of territory and a population of 800,000? A desert. What name will you give the constitution of that country? The constitution is a desert. Very well, the Argentine Republic is that country — and whatever its constitution, for many years it will be nothing more than the constitution of a desert.

But what constitution best fits a desert? One that will help to make it disappear: one that will enable it in the shortest possible time to cease being a desert and become a populated country. This, then, should and must be the political aim of the Argentine constitution and in general of all South American constitutions. The constitutions of unpopulated countries can have no other serious and rational end, at present and for many years to come, than to give the solitary and abandoned countryside the population it requires, as a fundamental condition for its development and progress.

Independent America is called upon to complete the work begun and left unfinished by the Spain of 1450. The colonization, the settlement of this world, new to this day despite the three hundred years that have passed since its discovery, must be completed by the sovereign and independent American states. The work is the same; only its authors are different. At that time Spain settled our lands; today we settle them ourselves. All our constitutions must be aimed at this great end. We need constitutions, we need a policy of creation, of settlement, of conquest of the solitude and the desert. . . .

The end of constitutional policy and government in America, then, is essentially economic. In America, to govern is to populate.

XXV

The Pattern of Economic Activity

FOR MANY YEARS AFTER INDEPENDENCE the Latin-American economy remained substantially the same as in colonial times. The large estate or *hacienda,* generally operated with primitive methods, continued to dominate economic life. The mining industry only slowly recovered from the paralysis to which the great wars had reduced it. Free trade brought increased commercial activity to the coasts, but this was offset by the deepening stagnation of the interior. Widespread banditry and political disorders seriously hampered economic revival.

After 1850 the quickening tempo of the Industrial Revolution in Europe and North America stimulated considerable change in the Latin-American economy. In response to a mounting foreign demand for raw materials and foodstuffs, Latin-American producers increased their output of these commodities. Encouraged by a growing political stability, European capital flowed into the area, creating railroads, docks, processing plants, and other facilities needed to expand and modernize production and trade. The pace and degree of economic progress of the various countries was very uneven, depending largely on their geographical position and natural resources.

A marked feature of the new economic order was its extreme one-sidedness. One or two products became the basis of each country's prosperity, making it highly vulnerable to fluctuations in the world demand and price of these commodities. Meanwhile, other sectors of the economy remained stagnant or actually declined through diversion of labor and land to the export industries. Two other characteristics of the late nineteenth-century economic expansion were: (1) It took place mostly within the framework of the semi-feudal hacienda system of land tenure and labor relations, and (2) it was accompanied by a steady growth of foreign corporate control over the natural and man-made resources of the continent. As a result, the profits of the system, instead of being widely diffused, tended to flow into the hands of a small number of native and foreign landlords, merchants, and concessionaires.

1. THE JUNGLE ROUTE

The Railway Age came to Latin America between 1850 and 1870. The building of new means of transport took a heavy toll of life; every sleeper on a tropical line, it was said, represented a man. An extraordinary project was the Madeira-Mamoré Railway in the depths of the Amazonian jungle, twice begun and abandoned, resumed in 1907 and completed in 1913. Designed to provide an outlet for Bolivian rubber to the Atlantic, it proved a complete financial failure when the rubber boom collapsed. The English writer H. M. Tomlinson (1873–   ), who inspected the road in 1910, tells its tragic early history.[1]

AND NOW IT SEEMS time to explain why we are bound for the centre of the American continent, where the unexplored jungle still persists, and

---

[1] H. M. Tomlinson, *The Sea and the Jungle,* New York, 1928, pp. 160–165. Reprinted by permission of Mr. H. M. Tomlinson and the British Society of Authors.

disease or death, so the legends tell us, comes to all white men who stay there for but a few months. If you will get your map of the Brazils, begin from Para, and cruise along the Amazon to the Madeira River — you turn south just before Manaos — when you have reached Santo Antonio on the tributary stream you have traversed the ultimate wilderness of a continent, and stand on the threshold of Bolivia, almost under the shadows of the Andes. If you find any pleasure in maps, flying in shoes of that kind when affairs pursue you too urgently (and I suppose you do, or you would not be so far into this narrative), you will hardly thank me when I tell you it is possible for an ocean steamer exceeding 23 feet in draught to make such a journey, and so break the romance of the obscure place at the end of it. But it must be said. Even one who travels for fun should keep to the truth in the matter of a ship's draught. As a reasonable being you would prefer to believe the map; and that clearly shows the only way there (when the chance comes for you to take it) must be by canoe, a long and arduous journey to a seclusion remote, and so the more deeply desired. It certainly hurts our faith in a favourite chart to find that its well-defined seaboard is no barrier to modern traffic, but that, journeying over those pink and yellow inland areas, which should have no traffic with great ships, a large cargo steamer, full of Welsh coal, can come to an anchorage, still with many fathoms under her, at a point where the cartographer, for lack of place-names and other humane symbols, has set the word Forest, with the letters spread widely to the full extent of his ignorance, and so promised us sanctuary in plenty. I suppose that in a few years those remote wilds, somehow cleared of Indians, jungle, and malaria — though I do not see how all this can be done — will have no further interest for us, because it will possess many of the common disadvantages of civilization's benefits: it will be a point on a regular route of commerce. I am really sorry for you; but in the sad and cruel code of the sailor I can only reply as Jack did when he got the sole rag of beef in the hash, "Blow you, Bill. I'm all right." I had the fortune to go when the route was still much as it was in the first chapter of Genesis. "But after all," you question me, hopeful yet, "nothing can be done with 5000 tons of Welsh cargo in a jungle."

People with the nose for dollars can do wonders. It would be unwise to back such a doughty opponent as the pristine jungle with its malaria against people who smell money there. In the early seventies there was a man with one idea, Colonel George Church. His idea was to give to Bolivia, which the Andes shuts out from the Pacific, and two thousand miles of virgin forest from the Atlantic, a door communicating with the outside world. He said, for he was an enthusiast, that Bolivia is the richest country in the world. The mines of Potosí are in Bolivia. Its mountains rise from fertile tropical plains to Arctic altitudes. The rubber tree grows below, and a climate for barley is found in a few days' journey towards the sky. But the riches of Bolivia are locked up. Small parcels of precious goods may be got out over the Andean barrier, on mule back; or they may dribble in a thin stream down the Beni, Mamoré, and Madre de Dios rivers — rivers which unite not far from the Brazilian boundary to form the Rio Madeira. The Beni is a very great and deep river which has a course of 1500 miles before it contributes its volume to the Madeira. The Rio Madeira, a broad and deep stream in the rainy season, reaches the Amazon in another 1100 miles. But between Guajara-Merim and San Antonio the Madeira comes down to a terrace 250 miles in length of nineteen dangerous cataracts. The Bolivian rubber collectors shoot those rapids in their batelaoes, large vessels carrying sometimes ten tons of produce and a crew of a dozen men, when the river is full. Many are overturned, and the produce and the men are lost. The Madeira traverses a country notorious even on the Amazon for its fever, and quite unexplored a mile inland anywhere on its banks; the rubber hunters, too, have to reckon with wandering tribes of hostile Indians.

The country is like that to-day. Then judge its value for a railway route in the early 'seventies. But Colonel Church was a New Englander, and again he was a visionary, so therefore most energetic and compelling; he soon persuaded the practical business folk, who seldom know much, and are at the mercy of every eloquent dreamer, to part with a lot of money to buy his Bolivian dream. We do really find the Colonel, on 1st November 1871, solemnly cutting the first sod of a railway in the presence of a party of Indians, with the wild about him which had persisted from the beginning of things. What the Indians thought of it is not recorded. Anyhow, they seem to have humoured the infatuated man who stopped to cut a square of grass in the land of the Parentintins, the men who go stark naked, and make musical instruments out of the shin bones of their victims.

An English company of engineering contractors was given the job of building the line, and a small schooner, the *Silver Spray,* went up to San Antonio with materials in 1872. Her captain, and some of her officers, died on the way. A year later the contractors confessed utter defeat. The jungle had won. They declared that "the country was a charnel-house, their men dying like flies, that the road ran through an inhospitable wilderness of alternating swamp and porphyry ridges, and that, with the command of all the capital in the world, and half its population, it would be impossible to build the road." (There is a quality of bitterness in their vehement hate which I recognise. I heard the same emotional chord expressed concerning that land, though not because of failure there, only two years ago.)

But the Bank of England held a large sum in trust for the pursuance of this enterprise, and after the lawyers had attended to the trust money in long debate in Chancery, there was yet enough of it left to justify the indefatigable colonel in beginning the railway again. That was in 1876. Messrs. Collins, of Philadelphia, obtained the contract. The road, of metre gauge, was to be built in three years. The matter excited the United States into a wonderful attention. The press there went slightly delirious, and the excited *Eagle* was advised that "two Philadelphians are to overcome the Madeira rapids, and to open up to the world a land as fair as the Garden of the Lord." The little steamer *Mercedita,* of 856 tons, with 54 engineers and material, was despatched to San Antonio on 2nd January 1878. Her departure was made an important national occasion, and it is an historic fact, which may be confirmed by a reference to the files of Philadelphian papers of that date, that strong men, as well as women and children, sobbed aloud on the departure of the steamer. The vessel arrived at San Antonio on the 16th February. They had barely started operations when, so they said, a Brazilian official told them, betraying some feeling, "when the English came here they did nothing but smoke and drink for two days, but Americans work like the devil." Yet, by all accounts, the English method was right. I prefer it, on the Amazon. The preface to work there should be extended to three or even more days of drinking and smoking.

Yet it must be said that if ever men should have honour for holding to a duty when it was far more easy, and even more reasonable, to leave it, then I submit the claim of those American engineers. Having lived in the place where many of them died, and knowing their story, I feel a certain kinship. There is no monument to them. No epic has been written of their tragedy. But their story is, I should think, one of the saddest in the annals of commerce. Of the 941 who left for San Antonio at different times, 221 lost their lives, mostly of disease, though 80 perished in the wreck of the transport ship. That is far higher a mortality rate than that of, say, the South African or the American Civil War.

Few of those men appeared to know the tropics. They thought "the tropics" meant only prodigal largess of fruits and sun and a wide latitude of life — a common mistake. The enterprise became a lingering disaster. Their state was already bad when a supply ship was lost; and they hopefully waited, ill and starving, but with a gallant mockery of their lot, as their letters and diaries attest, for food and medicine which were not to reach them. The doctors continued the daily round of the host of the fever-stricken, given them quinine, which was a deceit made of flour. The wages of all ceased for legal reasons, and they were in a place where little is cultivated, and so most food has to be imported in spite of a tariff which usually doubles the price of every necessary of life. Some of the survivors, despairing and heroic souls, attempted to escape on rafts down the river; they might as well have tried to cut their way through the thousand miles of forest between them and Manaos. The railway undertaking collapsed again, and the clearing, the huts, and the workshops, and the short line that was actually laid, were left for the vines and weeds to bury. But now again the conquering forest is being attacked. The Madeira-Mamoré Railway has been recommenced, and our steamer, the *Capella,* is taking up supplies for the establishment at Porto Velho, from which the new railway begins, three miles this side of San Antonio.

2. MEXICO IN TRANSITION

In no other Latin-American country was the connection between economic progress and the coming of the railroads so strikingly evident as in Mexico. The importance of the subject inspired a North American historian, Bernard Moses (1846–1930), to write a book describing the changes that had taken place and speculating concerning those yet to come.[2]

ONE OF THE MOST STRIKING THINGS in the economic history of Mexico is the completeness and

2 Bernard Moses, *The Railway Revolution in Mexico,* San Francisco, 1895, pp. 7–12, 30–37, 56–63.

persistence of her isolation. By destroying this isolation, she has suddenly been brought under the influences that make for social changes, and we discover here an excellent example of the transition from a stagnant to a progressive society. In order to determine to what extent the building of railways has been influential in effecting these changes, we have to take account of the fact that the Spaniards acquired from the Moors, during their long association with them in the Peninsula, an indifference to roads suited to vehicles with wheels, and that the colonists who went out from Spain in the sixteenth century carried this indifference to the New World. Settlements were made and cities grew to importance, with no other means of communicating with the world at large than that offered by the Indian trail or the mule path. . . .

By referring to Spain's restrictions on trade and in America, the accomplishment of ends with rude means, and the employment of human and animal power directly with little use of mechanical appliances, we indicate the early character of Mexico's economic system, a system which became so thoroughly rooted in custom that its main characteristics were preserved well into this century; and some of its features are conspicuous in the Mexican life of the present. Fruit is still carried into the City of Mexico on the backs of men, over distances requiring journeys of several days; and when you buy it there in the market, you think it still cheap, from which may be inferred how little must be the daily compensation of these men, and, in relation to the result, how great the expenditure of force.

The revival in Mexico is a result of the attempt now making to set aside an antiquated economic system and introduce that which the most progressive nations have adopted. Probably the most conspicuous force thus far observable as helping to effect this change, has come through the introduction of railways.

When the railway was introduced into England and France, it came as a rival to all sorts of wheeled vehicles drawn by properly fed and trained animals over roads that were excellent specimens of well-executed public works. When the railway was introduced into Mexico, it came as a rival of the half-starved donkey and the not overfed Indian. The transition from the freight wagons and passenger coaches on the great roads of France was less striking than the transition from the beasts of burden on the rough trails of Mexico. The time of the revolution in the two cases was also important. In the one case it happened before the habit of much travel and the practice of extensive shipments had become fully developed; in the other case it came when the leading nations had become filled with the turmoil of travel and the transportation of goods, when these, in fact, had become the characteristic features of modern civilized life.

A conspicuous means by which the introduction of railways has contributed to the economic revival in question is the influence which they have exerted on political affairs. As long as the history of Mexico was one of successive revolutions, one party after another laying lawless hands on private property, economic improvement was impossible; for security, the essential condition of such improvement was wanting. Manufacturers would not flourish when the factories might be plundered without redress. Goods would not be transported when they might be seized by one party or the other, under the pretext of military necessity.

And the means for escaping from this state of things were not at hand. Over the territory of the republic, extending from northwest to southeast a distance of 1,900 miles, and covering an area of 768,500 square miles, it was impossible to move soldiers and the munitions of war with sufficient rapidity to prevent uprisings, at points remote from the capital, from gaining numbers and prestige. Before the Federal forces could intervene, a local government might be overthrown, and the excluded authorities themselves be placed in the attitude of revolutionists. Rapid transportation, therefore, became necessary for the preservation of peace and the maintenance of legitimate authority; and this has been furnished by the railways.

The revolutionist has now not adequate time to gather and effectively organize his forces before he is overwhelmed by a superior force acting under orders from the capital. Thus the first important service which the railways have rendered to Mexico is to make possible the maintenance of civil order and the security of property — by this means furnishing a direct incentive to industry and commerce.

And the demand for peace and security is bred by peace itself, and grows stronger and becomes more universal the larger becomes the number of persons who have accumulations at stake. Already the desire for peace constitutes a phase of a new national sentiment. In the words of one of the most thoughtful writers on economic affairs in Mexico, "the Mexican people do not want to return to the habits of revolutionary days. They are becoming accumulators of wealth, and a new generation has grown up, composed of young lawyers, planters, and men of affairs, who lead laborious lives and are well fitted to guide the destinies of the republic in the early years of the coming century." . . .

In contrast with this isolation of the colonial days, mark the present relation of Mexico to the rest of the world. The port of Vera Cruz is open to the vessels of all nations, and two railways connect it with the capital and the other interior towns. By a system of jetties, constructed by the Mexican Central Railway, the bar that closed the harbor of Tampico has been scoured away, and ocean vessels now ascend the river Panuco seven miles, to the ancient town of Tampico. Here they may anchor in perfect safety and discharge their cargoes and passengers without lighterage or transfer. Thus there has been opened to Mexican shipping an inland harbor on the eastern coast, free from the storms which make the roadstead of Vera Cruz sometimes inconvenient and dangerous. And the new port of Tampico has already regular lines of steamers connecting it with New York, Mobile, Havana, and European ports. While this is the first inland port that has been opened on the eastern coast of Mexico the western shore has, it is true, good harbors; but they are of comparatively little advantage, for two reasons: They are not readily accessible to the markets of Europe and the eastern part of the United States; and they have as yet no means of communication with the important cities of Central Mexico, except the pack mule and the burden-bearing Indian. But by the Mexican Gulf Railway, running northwestward to Monterey, and by the branch of the Mexican Central, which runs through San Luis Potosí, the port of Tampico is brought into immediate communication with the great internal system of Mexican railways. . . .

The railways have not only opened ways into the country, but are in themselves the moving forces of an industrial revolution. For it is a mistake to suppose that the only function of a railway corporation, having once set its road in operation, is the somewhat passive one of receiving the business brought to it without its initiative. Capital in large masses must itself, through its agents, make the conditions of its own existence. It goes with its products to places where they have not been previously desired, and creates a demand for them. When a large amount of capital has been gathered and organized for doing a specific work, the principle of the life of that capital is having that work to do. Suppose that in the time of active railway construction in a given country a large plant for making rails has come into existence. When the roads which it was built to supply are completed, the original occupation of this capital appears to be gone. It must now be transformed at a loss, or lie idle at a loss, or those who act for it must become instrumental in creating a demand for its products elsewhere. Thus the existence of such plants in England, called into being by a strong domestic demand for rails, becomes a force in extending the railway systems of other countries. The managers may, rather than allow the capital to lie idle or be transformed, agree to terms which make the building of railways profitable in Russia or the Argentine Republic. Thus the capital organized for the construction of rails and the equipment of railways becomes a permanent missionary of railway civilization. The same thing is true of the enormous amounts of capital organized for the construction of sewing machines. If certain nations are supplied so that there might be naturally a falling off in the demand, this must not be; otherwise the value of the plant is diminished; hence other people must be made to demand sewing machines. Thus the missionary force of the capital involved in the making of the machines has carried them to the four quarters of the earth. They may be found in huts in Mexico, where the dwelling itself and all else that it contains is not of half the value of the machine. These are only instances of the aggressive force of large masses of organized capital, prompted by the instinct of self-preservation in the organization.

The capital that has gone into Mexican railways is subject to the same law. It cannot be passive; it must be a reforming agency. The people among whom the roads have been constructed, whether they have hitherto felt the need of them or not, must feel the need of them. It is not a question of greater or less happiness — the railway has come and commanded other forms of life, and millions of capital depend on this command being obeyed, and it will be obeyed. Men may not, hitherto, have wished to go to Mexico; they will be made to wish this thing especially. The ordinary man or the poor peon who has never left his native valley, will be indifferent at first. His mind is not easily inflamed. There will gradually be awakened in him a desire to see the great city, and the great city will inspire in him the wish for things he has never possessed. His wants will be increased; he will feel the necessity of work; continuous work will make him a man; and the railway will bring to him for his earnings things of which he never dreamed. What nobody wanted at first will at last be demanded by everybody; and organized capital in the form of railways will have succeeded in creating demands for its services by the compensation for which it may be maintained and increased.

3. PERU IN THE GUANO AGE

Two gross and lowly substances, guano and nitrates, played in the economy of independent Peru the role assigned to gold and silver in colonial days. More than 70,000 Chinese coolies were brought to the country in the nineteenth century to work on the guano islands. An Englishman who visited Peru in the seventies, and who formed no very complimentary opinion of its governing class, describes the uncertain and odoriferous basis of the Peruvian economy in that period.[3]

WHETHER IT BE TRUE, or only a poetical way of putting it, that Yarmouth was built on red herrings, Manchester on cotton, Birmingham on brass, Middlesborough on pigs of iron, and the holy Roman Catholic Church in China on Peruvian bark, it is true that the Government of Peru has for more than a generation subsisted on guano, and the foundations of its greatness have been foundations of the same; the ordure of birds — pelicans, penguins, boobies, and gulls of many kinds, and many kinds of ducks, all of marine habits, and deriving their living solely from the sea and the sky which is stretched above it.

This precious Guano, or Huano, according to the orthography of the sixteenth century, had long been in use in Peru before Peru was discovered by the Spaniards. It was well enough known to those famous agriculturists, the Incas, who five centuries ago used it as a servant. With the change which changed the Incas from off the face of the earth, came the strangest change of all — guano ceased to be the servant or helper of the native soil; it became the master of the people who occupy it, the Peruvian people, the Spanish Peruvians who call themselves Republicans.

No disgrace or ignominy need have come upon

Peru for selling its guano and getting drunk on the proceeds, if it had not trampled its own soil into sand, and killed not only the corn, the trees, and flowers which grow upon it, but also the men who cultivate those beautiful and necessary things.

During the time that Peru has been a vendor of guano, it has sold twenty million tons of it, and as the price has ranged from £12 to £12 10s and £13 the ton, Peru may be said to have turned a pretty penny by the transaction. What she has done with the money is a very pertinent question, which will be answered in its right place.

The amount of guano still remaining in the country amounts to between seven and eight million tons. There are men of intelligence even in Peru who affirm that the quantity does not reach five million tons. One of my informants, a man intimately connected with the export and sale of this guano, assured me that there are not at this hour more than two million tons in the whole of the Republic, and he had the best possible means at his disposal for ascertaining its truth. I have since discovered, however, that men who deal in guano do not always speak with a strict regard for the truth.

As this is one of the vexed questions of the hour to some of my countrymen, the violent lenders of money, Jews, Greeks, infidels and others; although I have no sympathy with them, yet on condition that they buy this book I will give them a fair account of the guano which I have actually seen, and where it exists.

I was sent to Peru for the express purpose of making this examination. I may therefore expect that my statements will be received with some consideration. They have certainly been prepared with much care, and, I may add, under very favourable circumstances.

My visits to the existing guano deposits were made after they had been uncovered of the stones which had been rolled upon them by the turbulent action of a century of earthquakes, the sand which the unresisted winds of heaven for the same period had heaped upon them from the mainland, and the slower but no less degrading influence of a tropical sun, attended with the ever humid air, dense mists, fogs and exhalations, and now and then copious showers of rain. Moreover, my visits were made after a certain ascertained quantity of guano had been removed, and my measurements of the quantity remaining were therefore easily checked.

Last year the Pabellon de Pica was reported

3 Alexander J. Duffield, *Peru in the Guano Age*, London. 1877, pp. 70–79.

to contain eight million tons of guano. At that time it was covered from head to foot with more than fifty feet of sand and stones. The principal slopes are now uncovered. Before this painful and expensive process had been completed, various other courageous guesses had been made, and the Government engineers were divided among themselves in their estimates. One enthusiastic group of these loyal measurers contended for five million tons, another for three million five hundred and twenty thousand six hundred and forty, and another, unofficial and disinterested, placed it at less than a million tons.

My own measurements corroborate this latter calculation. There may be one million tons of guano on the Pabellon de Pica. The exact quantity will only be known after all the guano has been entirely removed and weighed.

The Pabellon de Pica is in form like a pavilion, or tent, or better still, a sugar-loaf rising a little more than 1000 feet above the sea which washes its base. It is connected by a short saddle with the mountain range, which runs north and south along the whole Peruvian coast, attaining a height here of more than 5000 feet in isolated cones, but maintaining an average altitude of 3000 feet.

When a strong north wind rages on these sandy pampas, the dust, finer than Irish blackguard, obscures the sky, disfigures the earth, and makes mad the unhappy traveller who happens to be caught in its fury. A mind not troubled by the low price of Peruvian bonds, or whether even the next coupon will be paid, might imagine that the gods, in mercy to the idleness of man, were determined to cover up those dunghills from human sight; and hence the floods, and cataracts of sand and dust which have been poured upon them from above.

If it could be conceived that an almighty hand, consisting of nineteen fingers, each finger six hundred feet long, with a generous palm fifteen hundred feet wide had thrust itself up from below, through this loaf of sugar, or dry dung, to where the dung reaches on the Pabellon, some idea might be formed of the frame in which, and on which the guano rests.

The man who reckoned the Pabellon to contain eight million tons of guano, took no notice of the Cyclopean fingers which hold it together, or the winstone palm in which it rests. There are eighteen large and small gorges formed by the nineteen stone fingers. Each gorge was filled with a motionless torrent of stones and sand,

and these had to be removed before the guano could be touched.

So hard and compact had the guano become, that neither the stones nor the sand had mixed with it; when these were put in motion and conducted down into the sea below, the guano was found hard and intact, and it had to be blasted with gunpowder to convey it by the wooden shoots to the ships' launches that were dancing to receive it underneath. The process was as dangerous as mining, and quite as expensive, to the Peruvian Government; for, although the loading of the guano is let out by contract, the contractors — a limited company of native capitalists — will, as a matter of course, claim a considerable sum for removing stones and sand, and equally as a matter of course, they will be paid: and they deserve to be paid. No hell has ever been conceived by the Hebrew, the Irish, the Italian, or even the Scotch mind for appeasing the anger and satisfying the vengeance of their awful gods, that can be equalled in the fierceness of its heat, the horror of its stink, and the damnation of those compelled to labour there, to a deposit of Peruvian guano when being shovelled into ships. The Chinese who have gone through it, and had the delightful opportunity of helping themselves to a sufficiency of opium to carry them back to their homes, as some believed, or to heaven, as fondly hoped others, must have had a superior idea of the Almighty, than have any of the money-making nations mentioned above, who still cling to an immortality of fire and brimstone.

4. A CHILEAN NITRATE PLANT

From the War of the Pacific (1879–1883) Chile emerged with rich prizes in the form of the nitrate and copper deposits of the provinces of Atacama and Taracapá, annexed from Bolivia and Peru, respectively. English capital flowed in large quantities into the nitrate and copper industries; between 1880 and 1910 the production of nitrogen increased tenfold. A famous London Times *correspondent, William H. Russell (1820–1907), recorded his impressions of a Chilean nitrate mine and mill in a readable travel book.*[4]

IN THE DAYTIME PRIMITIVA, for all the electric lighting, shows to more advantage than at night. You see that every portion of the machinery and all the accessories are beautifully kept, that the

4 William H. Russell, *A Visit to Chile and the Nitrate Fields of Tarapacá*, London, 1890, pp. 176–194.

three great chimneys are bright red, that the boilers are fronted with white tiles, that the *bateas* or vats — drawn up like a battalion of soldiers in company columns — are painted scarlet. At the same time the more you see, the more the dimensions of the factory grow upon you. The main buildings, some sixty or seventy yards distant from the house of the administrator, run along at the foot of a high bank and abut upon it, and above them are the engine-house to work the crushers, the cabins of the attendants, and the pillar and look-out steps of the electric lighthouse. This is the centre of the *estaciamento*, the heart and head of the great nitrate-producing establishment of Primitiva.

As I was standing in front of the door of the house before we set out on our day's work, surveying the curious sights and listening to the strange sounds near at hand, I asked one of the staff, "What extent does Primitiva cover?" The answer was, "Twelve square miles." "How much of that has been worked?" "I should say about three square miles, but some of that ground has been only partially worked. We begin at the outer parts of the estate and work gradually back towards the *máquina*." "Well, how long do you suppose the *caliche* grounds you have to work will last?" "That is a question to which no answer can be given, because we do not know what the output is to be. If the present *máquina* were worked at the present rate — that is, if the general number of quintals per day which has been turned out on the average were not exceeded — I believe there is *caliche* enough here to last for the next thirty years. Even then, if nitrate of soda became very dear and commanded high prices, there is plenty of stuff, which it is not worth our while to deal with at present, that might be worked at a profit." "But supposing that the manufacture of nitrate of soda were pushed to the utmost, and that all the force of the *máquina* were exerted to turn it out in quantities, without reference to price or cost, how long would the *caliche* last?" "The answer must be conjectural. I could go into the figures, but even then there would be no certainty, for there can be no average of the quality of the *caliche* over nine square miles. However, I would say that with the very largest possible production of nitrate the beds would last for fifteen or eighteen years to come." "And what would happen then?" "That is beyond my ken. So far as this ground is concerned we can continue, I firmly believe, yielding nitrate

of soda sufficient to pay most handsome dividends for more than twenty — ay, or twenty-five — years to come. Can the same be said of any other mining work? — coal? — diamonds? — gold? — silver? — copper? Certainly not! Here comes your carriage."

And so my wife and I set out in a two-wheeled cabriolet provided with a hood and drawn by a pair of mules, ridden by a Chilean Postillon de Longjumeau, to explore the nitrate fields and processes, under the guidance of Mr. Teare, who heedless of the fine dust, which rose like smoke from the ground on the slightest provocation, rode alongside us. The ladies, escorted by Colonel North, Mr. Humberstone, and all the riding men, took to the saddle on horses from the stables, which were well stocked with them, and with very fine mules. The moment the cavalcade was in motion the equestrians were lost, in clouds not altogether celestial, as completely as Homeric heroes; but presently there arose a brisk breeze, as there generally does in the morning on the pampas, and the annoyance was blown away to leeward as fast as it was made.

The limits of the various estates on the pampas are marked by slabs, like milestones, or by mounds of earth at regular intervals. In less than half an hour driving across country to the westward, we came to the scene of operations, or rather to one of them. The vicinity of this *tiro* was marked by pits, around the edges of which were masses of earth in wall-like mounds. This accumulation was formed by the broken *costra*, and all that remained of the *caliche* bed were excavations resembling upon a small scale the craters of volcanoes; these pits were worked-out mines.

The technical words used in describing the section of a nitrate mine are — *chuca*, the outer covering, the surface of the ground, generally friable, varying in thickness, sometimes scarcely existent; the *costra*, or bed of harder earth beneath the *chuca*, resting on the *caliche;* then the *caliche* itself, which varies from a few inches to 10 or 12 ft. in thickness; then, under the rock-like mass of the nitrate bed, the soft stratum of earth or sand called *cova*.

We approached a group of men engaged in breaking up the *caliche* and separating it from the *costra*. The hole into which we peered was about 7 ft. deep, and for about 15 ft. on either side of it the earth was heaved up and cracked in deep fissures by an explosion of the mine fired the night before. Around us were also the great blocks of *costra* and *caliche* not yet separated, which had been blown up. Two little forests of iron bars or "jumpers" were stuck into the ground near at hand to be used by-and-by. The material from which nitrate of soda is evolved resembles rock salt, sometimes seeming so white and so pure that it should need very little manufacturing to fit it for the market. . . . The appearance of *caliche* is no safe guide; the actual quality of it can only be tested in the chemist's office. As in all strata formed as *caliche* is supposed to be, there is great difference in the thickness of the seams, so in the nitrate grounds the strata of the *caliche,* of the covering of it, and of the matter on which it rests, differ materially in depth; the *costra* may be an inch or several feet thick, the *cova* or earth underlying the *caliche* may be reached by the *barreteros* very readily, or they may spend weary hours in the *tiro* in driving the "jumper" through *costra* and *caliche* before they arrive at the *cova* where the powder is to be placed for the mine. When the hole has been made to the *cova* it is enlarged by means of a gigantic spoon till it is sufficiently wide to let down a little boy, the powder-monkey, or as he is called, the *destazador,* whose business it is to scrape away the soft earth under the *caliche* till he has hollowed out the *taza* or cup for the charge of powder for the breaking up of the bed. The *barretero* has sunk the shaft, the *destazador* has scraped out the *taza,* the *particular* then charges the *tiro* with a bag of powder, to which is attached a fuse long enough to allow the men of the working party to retire to a safe distance, and fires it. In adjusting the strength of the charge considerable knowledge, to be gained only by experience, is required; the object being — not to produce a volcanic eruption — but to disintegrate the ground thoroughly, so as to split it in every direction, and enable the *particular,* or man in charge of the working party, to judge whether it is worth while to clean the *caliche* and load it on the carts for the factory. When the smoke has cleared away the *particular* and his workmen come to examine the ground. As he is paid by the number of cartloads that he sends away from the *tiro,* he has to decide whether he will load the carts from the bed or try another, because he must put good *caliche* into the carts for the crusher or he will be docked of his pay. The *corrector,* or overseer, argues with him over the price per cartload — 35 to 42 quintals are a cartload — before the rate is fixed. It is said that sharp eyes are needed to prevent very inferior stuff being mixed up with good *caliche* in the loads put on

the carts, but of this I have only report. The *particular,* having had the price fixed per cart, proceeds with the help of his gang and the carters, to place the loads in fixed weights on the carts or in the small trucks on the portable railway.

With the early morning, just at daybreak, begins the labour of loading the carts. The *caliche,* broken up into suitable blocks, is piled, when it is separated from the *costra,* in stacks by the side of the tiro. All the arrangements for the working of an *oficina* are minute in the division of labour responsibility. The *capataz,* who has under him mounted men, controls the carters and directs their labour. The carts are kept going between the mine and the *máquina* all day with very little interruption. Mules when exhausted are allowed to find their own way to the stables, their places being taken by others always kept for the purpose. When the animals have to struggle through very bad ground, the horsemen of the *capataz* hitch on and help them. As each cart arrives at the factory, the contents of it are inspected by the man *(bolelero)* who is in charge of the crushers, and who determines whether the material shall be tipped over to be crushed up or rejected. The crushers are placed a few feet below the ridge, or incline, up which the carts are drawn. The *caliche* is thrown into them by the *acendradores,* by whom it is delivered over to the *carreros* to be placed in the boiling tanks by hand or by mechanical appliances. The crushers are insatiable. Worked by steam they munch their *caliche* all day and night, and disgorge it in coarse-grained powder into the cars on the tramway, which discharge their contents into the *cachuros* or boiling tanks. In some *máquinas* the iron cars or tanks travel upon a railway raised over the *cachuro* with the ground *caliche.* The bottom of the cart or tank opens on hinges and the contents fall into the boiling tanks. In these tanks commences the chemical change undergone by the *caliche,* of which some account will be found further on.

When we reached the *tiro* we found some of our equestrian friends and Mr. Humberstone already there, examining the *caliche* of the recently exploded mine. There were masses of the stuff lying about which might easily be mistaken for fragments of marble. The workmen, muscular fellows lightly clad, were chiselling away the *costra* from the *caliche,* splitting up the blocks which sometimes offered such resistance to the sledge that it is necessary to break them up with gunpowder. How they stood the smother and heat, in air filled with saline particles, and with a fine dust which settled down like a second skin in a few minutes on clothes, face and hands, was a marvel. But habit has made these men capable of enduring such and greater discomforts — "though" said one of the staff, "they do take good long drinks when they get a chance and when the day's work is over" —that is by sundown or earlier. It is then that the *tiros* are generally completed and that the mines are fired.

5. ON AN ARGENTINE ESTANCIA

In the late sixties the changes that were to transform the Argentine livestock industry — the fencing of the ranges, the building of the railroads, the establishment of alfalfa ranges, the coming of refrigerator ships — still lay in the future or had barely begun. An English settler describes operations on the typical estancia *or cattle-ranch of that day.*[5]

THE GREAT CATTLE ESTABLISHMENTS, estancias, as before said, occupy lands for the most part more distant than those devoted to sheep farming in the province of Buenos Aires; but there are many estancias within the sheep farming districts still occupied by cattle, or on which both sheep and cattle are bred.

There are many tracts of land on a large estancia, say of ten to twenty-five square leagues, as well as certain districts or lines of country, which are unsuitable for sheep; for instance, low strong land, with rank reedy grasses, often flooded, and on some of which the "leech" is generated. On such land horses and cattle hold their own.

In the Uruguay and Entre-Ríos cattle prevail almost everywhere, and there are comparatively few estancias whereon sheep alone are reared; but here, as in Buenos Aires, the sheep are gradually encroaching on to the previously pure cattle lands.

The distribution of a cattle estancia is similar to that of a sheep farm: — the estancia house, with horse corrales and cattle corrales, and *puestos* in different parts of the ground for the herdsmen. Each *puestero* has his herd *(rodeo)* of cattle and tract of land appointed to him.

There is a *capataz* (overlooker) to a certain number of *puestos,* and a *mayordomo,* or manager, over all: there are also immense troops of wild mares and horses. A *rodeo,* or herd, is var-

5 Wilfrid Latham, *The States of the River Plate,* London, 1868, pp. 34–46.

ious in size, consisting of a few hundreds or a few thousands semi-wild cattle. The *puestero* tends the cattle and keeps them within certain limits, and prevents their mixing with other herds. On some establishments they are brought up to what is called *el rodeo,* a bare piece of ground near the station or *puesto,* at sundown, or they are only thus gathered up occasionally. They are settled to rest on the rodeo by *peones* riding round them; it is from this practice of herding them —*rodeando,* surrounding or riding round — that both the ground and the herd take the name of *rodeo.*

In these estancias we see the true type of the gaucho of the Pampas — a type now-a-days rarely found in the sheep districts — men familiar only with the plain on which they were born and have lived, without ever having known or seen anything beyond it.

Their faces are blackened by exposure, their long black and matted hair reaching the shoulders and mingling with the beard. They are rarely off horseback. They are dressed in long wide cotton drawers, and a garment called *chiripá,* in lieu of trowsers, girdled round the waist with a long woven belt *(faja),* a leather punch-belt, into which is thrust, across the loins, a long knife, a shirt and poncho, a coloured handkerchief over the head, and felt hat. The skin of a colt's hind legs, freed from the hair, and dried and softened by rubbing, serves for boots, the point of the "hock" forming the heel, and the big and second toes protruding. They wear huge iron spurs, with rowels three inches in diameter, and have rarely known any other bed than their *recado* (saddle) stretched on the ground, their *ponchos,* or cloaks, with the saddle-cloths, forming their covering. Their horse-gear is their sole furniture. The lasso, when not in use, is coiled and fastened behind the *recado,* and lies over the rump of the horse. With balls *(bolas)* for balling wild horses slung in the belts, a powerful bit in the horse's mouth, and hide reins, the man and his outfit are complete. He rarely knows any other food than beef, *asado,* with or without salt; his luxuries are *maté,* Paraguay tea, sucked through a tube from a gourd, and cigarettes. Born to the horse, as it were, the gaucho is a splendid horseman, dexterous with the lasso. In full career after a wild bull or cow, he swings the lasso and throws it unerringly over the animal's horns; then on his checking the horse, the lasso, which is fastened to a ring in the broad hide girth of the saddle, is drawn taut, and the animal swung round or thrown.

A single man will thus catch and kill his meat in the plain; the animal being thrown, the trained horse will stand or move onwards in such a way as to keep the lasso tight, and prevent the animal from rising, while the gaucho dismounts, hamstrings, and kills it with his long knife. Swinging the "balls," the gaucho will pursue the wild horse's stride; the balls wind round the fleeing animal's hind legs, and cause it to fall. If his horse falls with him, even at full gallop, the gaucho rarely comes to grief, for loosing his knee hold, he is impelled forward on his legs, and catches his horse before he is up.

As an instance of the extraordinary sagacity and cleverness of a horse perfectly trained to work among cattle, I will relate an encounter which took place on the town killing-grounds, at the southern extremity of the city of Buenos Aires, and witnessed by my son. An unusually large and powerful bull was loosed from one of the corrales; he was approached in the usual way by the lasso-men, whom he charged, freeing himself from the lassos; he became infuriated, and charged and charged again with such velocity that none of them could succeed in throwing him; he unhorsed two of the men, disembowelling one of the horses, and injuring the rider; he gored another horse in the leg, and finally beat his antagonists out of the ground. There was a moment of suspense, for none seemed willing to try their chances against him, when from the far side of the killing-ground an old man was seen to approach cautiously on a somewhat lean and ancient-looking roan horse. A cry was raised by the beaten lasso-men to warn the old man, and induce him to return and avoid what appeared to be certain death; but the old man heeded not, and availing himself of the diversion of the bull's attention to the cries in the front, ran his horse, breast on, against the infuriated animal's flanks, which staggered and then instantly charged. The old man dexterously avoided the onslaught, cast his lasso over the horns, and, at the same moment, drew a rug (pellón) from off his saddle, shook it in front of the bull, and threw it forward. At the same instant he slipped from his saddle unperceived by the beast, whose attention was drawn off by the rug, and away went the horse, the bull charging him. The horse having no weight on his back, headed and turned with great rapidity, got a strain on the lasso, and continued to "work" the bull until he finally threw him, and then keeping the lasso taut, moving with every struggle of the bellowing animal, prevented him

from rising, till the old man approached on foot and gave him the coup de grâce.

The events in cattle estancia life are those of branding the young cattle with the owner's mark, cutting the young bulls, and parting out cattle sold for the markets or saladeros.

The marking or branding is a great time. The mayordomos and capatazes of the neighbouring estancias have notice to attend, if they wish, so as to part out the cattle of their employers' brands if any should have strayed or become mixed. The peones of the estancia are mounted on their cleverest horses; the cattle are driven into the estancia corrales, and a large fire, wherein to heat the brands, is made of cattle bones outside the corral. Girths and saddles are looked to, and rearranged, if not quite in order, this being a matter of the greatest importance, as on the girth (cincha and recado) the whole strain of the work falls. Lassos are buckled on and held in coils in the hand. The group is picturesque, with the cattle in the corrales, the large fires outside, the dense smoke curling and rolling along the plain, the groups of boys and men at the fires, the "stokers" and the brands men half enveloped in the smoke, and on the alert to climb the posts of the corrales in case of danger. In addition to these may be seen twenty-five or thirty horsemen, freed from all superfluous garments, with coloured handkerchiefs tied round the head, many and bright-coloured shirts, chiripás, of all colours, scarlet, drab and scarlet, blue, green, and white, while mayordomos and capatazes look on, distinguished by their gay horse trappings and their huge silver spurs.

When the work is begun, the animals are drawn out of the corral as required, the lassos are cast over the horns and round the hind legs, and the young bull is thrown to the ground and kept stretched, so as to be unable to rise. One of the brandsmen darts from the fires, steadies himself by placing one foot on the prostrate animal, and plants the brand. The castrators perform their operation. The lassos are slackened and cast off, the animal rises; some trot quietly off, downcast and surly; others glare round and charge the nearest man, horse, or group, furiously. Away gallop the horsemen, with loud wild shouts and laughter — the pursued to escape, others to draw off the maddened animal from those that are hard pressed, edging him away farther into the open, where he is left. The day winds up with the asado (roast) in the usual way, and the men "yarn" over the feats of the day, as hunting men are wont to do, of the "run" and its incidents. The guitar and the ditty are, as usual, in requisition, and the younger men frolic and spar with their knives.

The parting out of cattle sold for the *saladeros* is another busy time. A certain number, hundreds or thousands, are sold, of a specified age and condition. The purchaser picks from the herds such as correspond with the definition in the contract; these are parted out from the herd, and for this purpose trained oxen, termed *sinualeros* or decoys, are placed at a certain distance. The selected animals are parted out and chased by the *peones* until they join the group of *sinualeros;* when the number is complete they are driven off for their destination. The *tropas* (droves) are accompanied by a chief drover and *peones,* corresponding to the number of head of cattle, usually one man to every hundred head. They travel with their change horses *(tropilla),* headed by a mare with a bell, which go in front of the cattle. Behind these, driving them, and keeping the cattle from rushing forward, rides one or more *peones;* others are on the flanks of and behind the *tropa.* At night time the cattle are stopped, and the *peones* ride round them until they settle and lie down. Horses are picketed, fires lit of thistles, bones, or what can be picked up, and the *asado* put down to roast, an animal having been killed to furnish it.

There are other events than those of routine in the cattle estanciero's life — events rather of the past than the present, or only occurring now-a-days in particular districts, viz. the gathering of wild cattle to be gradually reduced to the semi-wild, and confined *(aquerenciado)* to particular or determined tracts of grazing ground.

In the province of Buenos Aires this work is now very rare, or, at most, it is of a modified form. In the interior of the Banda Oriental, in Entre-Ríos, and in Corrientes there is still something to be done in this way on the vast estancias of a dozen or twenty leagues in extent, which in a certain sense have still to be reclaimed from the wilds. It is not very long since a friend of mine, who has a magnificent estancia on the Rio Negro, in the Banda Oriental — over which, as the crow flies, one can ride thirty miles, the camps "broken," that is, diversified with wood, water, hill and dale — a charming wilderness, where cattle perfectly wild roamed at will — had a gathering of this kind, from which I take my data.

The business is undertaken by a sort of gaucho chief, or captain, who gets a price per head brought in and located. He engages his band, over whom he rules with an iron hand — I might say a "hand of steel," for the "cold steel" would not be wanting on occasion. He knows every foot of ground in the Republic, and rarely knows other canopy than that of the heaven.

In the present instance he has undertaken a large gathering, and his band is over eighty to a hundred men. To his lieutenants he gives his orders, stationing them at different points, from which, at an appointed time, like "army corps," they manoeuver driving the cattle through wood, over hill, and across streams, towards the rendezvous. More than one thousand head, gathering now from different points, draw near to the rendezvous, thence to be directed to a *rincón* — a tongue of land, narrow at the entrance, and surrounded, except at this entrance, by a deep and wood-fringed river.

The critical moment has arrived. The captain of the band has taken his station on elevated ground, flag in hand, with which he makes his signals; the men move silently, obeying the signals — "Close in on the right" — "Stand in the centre" — "Retire on the left": bellowing, lowing herds — the deep low tones of venerable and stately bulls rolling through the still air — like skirmishers, issue from the woods or pour over the hills; slowly they come at first, then break into a trot. "Stand to the right." A point (of cattle) too quickly comes. "Stand" — "Stand all" — they slack their pace and break up into knots; strange bulls bellow at other strange bulls, trot forward, or with nose to ground tear up with their hoofs the firm earth. Ten days the band has worked. From all points the cattle come; and now one instant, one false manoeuvre, and the work is lost; for the cattle will charge away, a stampede of more than a thousand head of mighty horned brutes crashing through every obstacle — Ha! the flag is waved from right and left to centre, lashing the air in quick successive flouts — reinforcements for the centre; the cattle break; yes! no! the practiced eye of the captain detects every indication of movement in the "mob" — "Steady!" — the flag but flouts the breeze as held aloft — the manoeuvering towards the centre has checked the threatened break — and now "Push on" — "Close in" — "Close in all." They (the cattle) head for the *rincón* — "Hurrah!" My friend Don Juan sits on his horse apart from the workers, eagerly watching them. There has been an animal or two left in the wood — a faithful and practised *peón* is close at hand — suddenly he cries *"Cuidado, patrón!"*

"Look out, master!" in a quick ringing tone; an infuriated animal is close upon Don Juan, who instantly spurs his horse, which has scarcely sprung into the gallop before the bull is upon him; and man and horse go down. Fortunately the well-trained horse has dodged the horns, and the shoulder of the brute has struck his quarters; the *peón* is upon the beast, and pressing close, with loud shouts, lasso whirling, and horse at speed, so that the brute cannot turn to gore the fallen, runs him far, and forcing him into a wood, leaves him beyond the power of mischief. Don Juan is up and in the saddle again, shaken but uninjured. "Look! look!" the wary captain gesticulates, beating the air with his bright-coloured flag. "Hold hard!" — "Check!" to the left; "Stand!" to the right and centre. Now, now! they enter the neck of the the *rincón*. "On, on!" silence is no longer kept — wild whoops — whirling lassos, a tearing gallop! charge, charge on the rear — charge the close phalanx now — more than one thousand head, a forest of horned crested brutes, heading all for the goal — a hundred voices ring through wood and vale, and over plain and hill, and the wild, sharp cries of the gaucho band are heard above the rolling thunder of many thousand hoofs trampling the trembling earth: "Hurrah! dismount — slack the girths of the panting steeds — light fires along the line — guard the neck of the *rincón!*" The cattle break up and spread themselves, restless or furious but without cohesion — they are safe — a couple or three of the brutes are lassoed, killed, and soon are seething masses — supper for the hungry gaucho band.

The cattle are long-horned, ranging generally from small to medium size, and of varied quality, according to the locality and nature of the pasturage on which they are reared and bred. In some *partidos* (districts), owing to the nature of the pasture, the cattle vary, yielding larger carcase and heavier hide, lighter hide and more grease, and being of smaller or larger size. On some of the Banda Oriental *campos,* and in parts of Entre Ríos, they are fully as large as those of Buenos Ayres, and the hides exported are heavier, partly, it is true, because the bullocks, or neats, are as a rule killed when somewhat older, but in part from the stronger nature of the pasture, the greater shelter of trees — or from other causes. The oxen, when fully matured (five or six years of age), are powerful and weighty, carrying enormous horns, and make very good draught animals. Except on the lines of railways, nearly all the transport of goods, and produce from and to the country is effected in large, ungainly carts, with huge, hard wood, and untired wheels, to which six oxen are yoked by the horns. The cows are but scanty milkers as a rule; there are, however, some marked exceptions.

The dairies for supplying the town with milk are of the most primitive fashion, consisting of a hut and a corral, a greater or less number of cows, and a tract of *campo* to graze them on. The cows are milked once in twenty-four hours — at dawn of day — and the milk at once transferred to a number of small, round tin cans, which fit into hide-lashings on each side of the saddle, or pad, of the milkman's horse, on which he mounts half-sitting half-kneeling, and trots off to the city to supply his customers. The calves are allowed to run with the cows during the day, but parted from them and shut up in the pen or corral in the evening, the cows being left at liberty to graze. In a few better regulated establishments good cross-bred (shorthorn cross) cows are kept, a little lucerne soiling and hay being supplied to them when grass is scanty; and in some of these are milk-rooms, or dairies. Excellent butter is made in such establishments, which commands a high price, especially in the winter time. In the spring, when milk is abundant, some of the milkmen make an inferior kind of cheese, and also butter.

During the past dozen years, many English-bred cattle have been imported for the purpose of crossing with and improving the native breed. The majority of those imported, both bulls and cows, have been of the shorthorn variety.

The value and the importance of this movement can hardly be over-estimated. Nevertheless it has not found general favour, as few have hitherto derived that direct pecuniary benefit which is needful to give it wide-spread acceptation.

To understand this, we must take into consideration the use to which most of the cattle of the country are put, and from which they take their value, together with the position and management of the cattle establishments.

The chief value of our cattle at present is in the hide; and secondly, in the tallow and grease. The cross of the shorthorn does not, to any very great extent, raise the weight of the hide, and in this particular, apparently, does not augment the value of the cattle in a degree commensurate with the cost of introducing high blood into the herds. The introduction of these higher class animals, whose good qualities have been perfected under domestication, high breeding, selection, and feeding among the semi-wild herds of the plain, where, subjected to similar treatment and obliged to seek their food as best they can, they are exposed to all the vicissitudes to which the common herds are, as it were, born, is not likely to lead to immediate appreciable advantage in any other respect. Acquiring thus the habits of the half-wild cattle of the country, the cross-breeds, after a few generations, where cross-bred bulls only are used, make little more fat and not much more beef than the common stock. The often precarious and unequal feeding or pasture, the long driving of the animals to the slaughter, unfit the cattle for any purpose beyond the common one of hide-salting and steaming for grease. Ninety-nine out of a hundred of the estancieros know no other use for their cattle, and have no conception of any other principle of breeding than that of a state of nature and immediate and palpable benefit alone would induce them to step out of the accustomed course, and in many cases not even this would induce them to take the trouble. It is not likely, therefore, that cattle-refining will, for some time to come, attain any wide-spread development. The spirited pioneers of the attempt find themselves without the support which they anticipated; they find no sufficient sale for the bulls which they breed, so that the improvement is limited to their own herds. On these estab-lishments the ultimate result cannot be doubtful, as the principle of greater domestication is applied, and the best pasture lands are dedicated to the cross-bred herds. The tolerably even growth of the young animals is thus secured, and the breeding stock not allowed to fall into absolute low condition. A decidedly improved stock will, therefore, be created on these estancias, and at no very distant day their superior qualities as beef-makers and fat-producers will be recognised, and a profitable use will be found for them. The cities and large towns cannot long continue indifferent to the existence in their vicinity of animals that will yield a superior meat, in much larger proportion per head, under a system of at least "half-fatting," and the call from Europe for meat supplies must sooner or later induce the possessors of well-bred herds to take steps to put their neats (steers) into a condition that will give beef a quality more or less "up to the mark" of European requirements. The problem of ways and means of putting cattle into at least fair condition has yet to be solved. As it is totally new ground, men hesitate to take the initiative. The growing necessity, however, must compel it, and a company of breeders and others might very well make the venture; they could do so with small individual risk, and with every prospect of a highly satisfactory result.

XXVI

The Way of Life

INDEPENDENCE MODIFIED THE SOCIAL STRUCTURE of the former Spanish colonies in some respects. The revolution, throwing "careers open to talents," enabled some mestizos of humble origin to rise high in the military, political, and social scale. Verbally, at least, the new republican constitutions established the equality of all men before the law. All of the new states (except Brazil) had abolished slavery by 1855. Indian tribute had also legally disappeared by that date.

Independence, however, left intact the basis of social life: the system of great estates. In fact, concentration of land continued at a more rapid pace under the republic as creole *hacendados* took advantage of the lapse of Spanish protective legislation to acquire by various means the lands of neighboring Indian communities. Lavish grants of land from the public domain aided the process of engrossment. Concentration of land was accompanied by a rise in the number of landless peons, economically and socially dependent on the feudal *patrón*.

A patriarchal family organization, highly ceremonial conduct, and economic idleness were characteristic traits of the creole landed aristocracy. European dress, manners, and ideas first conquered in the capitals and coastal cities, more receptive to innovation than sleepy provincial towns. After 1860 large contingents of European immigrants arrived in Argentina, Uruguay, Brazil, and Chile, helping to strengthen the middle class and its ideals in those countries.

1. THE WORLD OF THE HACIENDA

A significant social development of the nineteenth century was the definitive triumph of the hacienda over the Indian landholding village. The lapse of Spanish protective legislation, and new republican codes that forced the partition of village lands materially contributed to this outcome. The decisive role of the hacienda in the life of nineteenth-century Mexico emerges from the following account of the institution by a noted North American scholar.[1]

THE HACIENDAS OF MEXICO are the most conspicuous feature of the land system of the country. They give to agricultural Mexico its distinctive cast, and, by their great size, create the impression that the entire land is divided into vast rural estates. These properties, indeed, are the only type of agricultural holding immediately visible to the traveler in many parts of Mexico, just as the *hacendado* is the only type of agriculturist whose interests reach beyond the immediate neighborhood of his home. As will appear later, there are other kinds of holdings, particularly in the more remote districts, but it is the hacienda that first attracts attention, and its prominence justifies its consideration in the first place.

Many of the haciendas are of very great extent; it is estimated that 300 of them contain at least 25,000 acres each; 116 have not less than 62,500; 21 have approximately 75,000 acres; while 11 are believed to have 250,000 acres apiece. The Mexican hacienda seldom contains less than 2,500 acres — whether situated in the arid plains of the north, where land is worth little or nothing, or in the densely settled areas of the Mesa Central, where the price of land is high even in comparison with that of agricultural lands in other countries. In places one may see the low stone boundary walls of a single farm running as far as the eye can reach, over hills, valleys, and plains, and a traveler on horse-back may journey for several days in crossing one of these vast estates.

The great size of these holdings is due, in part, to the fact that the typical hacienda aspires to be self-sustaining, and the variety of a countryside is taxed to render it independent. Hence, for the many different products required, different kinds of land must be included within its limits. In the first place, a large acreage of valley land is needed for the production of grain. These hundreds or thousands of acres of arable land form the nucleus of the estate. An hacendado would not, however, be satisfied to hold valley lands alone; for, in his economy, the products of the hills are only less important than those of the lowlands. Thus, the farm requires a supply of water, for irrigation as well as for the live stock; the hacienda must, therefore, include some stream, which should be controlled up to its headwaters in order to assure the undisputed use of the supply. Again, grazing land is needed for the herds of cattle, horses, sheep, and goats; this is found upon the park-like mountain sides and the alpine meadows. . . . Timber, also, is a prime necessity and is derived either from the deciduous trees that grow along the lower mountain slopes or from the pine forests that clothe the tops of the higher ridges. The products even of the waste land are likewise essential, since from this are obtained stone and lime for building purposes, clay for adobe huts, coarse grass for thatched roofs, salt, and the wild fruits and herbs which are gathered for household use. The administration of such extensive properties necessarily presents great difficulties. To facilitate management many of the larger ones are divided into several units styled *estancias* or *ranchos*, each under its own *mayordomo*. Even with such subdivision most of the haciendas are too vast to be developed intensively, and large areas lie completely unused. This is particularly the case where hilly country impedes communication, as upon the dissected slopes of the plateau and on the Mesa del Sur.

The haciendas are settlements complete in themselves. Indeed, few of these estates have less than a hundred, while many of them have

[1] George M. McBride, *The Land Systems of Mexico,* New York, American Geographical Society, 1923, pp. 25–34, 38–42. Reprinted by permission of the American Geographical Society.

as many as a thousand inhabitants. In Michoacán there are two haciendas, Huaracha and
Buenavista, each of which maintains over two
thousand persons; while in Morelos, México,
Puebla, Durango, Veracruz, Querétaro, and Chihuahua there are others in which the number is
not much smaller. Furthermore, the haciendas
are all named; they appear on the maps; and
they are important units of public administration, often being incorporated as *municipios*.
They include all the customary accessories of an
independent community, such as a church, a
store, a post office, a burying ground, and sometimes a school or a hospital. Workshops are
maintained, not only for the repair but even for
the manufacture of machinery and of the numerous implements required upon the estate. The
permanent population consists of an *administrador,* one or more mayordomos, a group of
foremen, and the regular peons, together with
the families of these individuals. Besides these,
there are several classes of hangers-on, less permanently attached to the farm. Among the latter
are usually a priest or two, clerks, accountants,
storekeepers, hired shepherds and cattlemen,
and often a number of families who rent small
pieces of land from the hacienda. Over this
aggregation the owner presides in a more or less
patriarchal manner, the degree of paternal care
or of tyranny varying with the character of the
individual and with that of his superior employees.

In colonial times nearly all the owners of these
large estates were Spaniards — *conquistadores,*
explorers, and government officials. During the
War of Independence (1810–1821) most of these
Spaniards were compelled to leave the country,
and, in many cases, their properties passed, by
means more or less irregular, into the hands of
creoles or mestizos. The hacendados have, however, always been predominantly of European
descent. Since this group of landed proprietors
has, at all times, composed the highest social
class in Mexico, its members have tended to
intermarry or to become affiliated with the foreigners who have settled in the country. In recent times many foreigners have acquired landholdings in Mexico, most conspicuous among
the number being Spaniards, who, enriched by
successful ventures in trade or in the mines have
invested their fortunes in the old Mexican estates which from time to time have come upon
the market. During the prosperous days of the
Díaz regime, Americans from north of the Rio

Grande not infrequently acquired possession of
some large hacienda.

The life of a Mexican hacendado is a curious
mixture of primitive rusticity and modern luxury, of self-indulgence and fatherly solicitude
for his dependents, of stern administration of
paternal discipline and an intermittent supervision of his mayordomo and numerous foremen.
The hacendado lives in a spacious *casa de hacienda,* built of stone or adobe and roofed with
red tiles. Flower gardens adorn the large open
patios, while fruits and vegetables of several
climates are grown in nearby plots. Some one or
several patios are devoted to the needs of the
farm, the rooms opening into them serving as
granaries, tool sheds, workshops, and sometimes
even as stables. The doors and windows of the
house are usually heavily barred, and in most
cases the entire establishment is surrounded by
a high, thick wall. In fact the casa of an hacendado must serve not only as a dwelling but as
a place of defense, either against the bandits
who have always infested the hills of Mexico or,
in case of an uprising, against the owner's own
tenants. But the typical Mexican landowner
spends relatively little of his time within this
citadel. He usually maintains a residence in
the capital or some other large city, where he
spends the greater part of the year. If the income of his property makes it possible, he may
go to Europe or to the United States. Only during the most active seasons, while planting or
harvesting is in progress or on some special occasion, does he remain long upon his estate. In
his absence the management devolves upon the
mayordomo or administrador. The hacendado
is, therefore, less an agriculturist than a landowner, less a farmer than an absentee landlord,
and his interest in the property is due less to
its economic possibilities than to its character
as an ancestral estate.

The laborers on the haciendas, in most parts
of Mexico, are of Indian blood or are mestizos
in whom the Indian element predominates, although many of these have abandoned their
aboriginal costume and have forgotten their
native tongue. The purity of race of the peon is
most strongly marked in the regions where, as
in the Mesa Central and Yucatan, the Spaniards
found the country already settled with an agricultural population which could be reduced to
serfdom. In other parts of the country, notably
upon the semi-arid plains of the north, where
the aboriginal element alone has never been

able to thrive and where, as a consequence, no such supply of native labor was found, the white element predominates among the *brazos,* or hands, employed upon the estates.

The peons upon a Mexican hacienda are theoretically free. They have been so ever since the War for Independence and, to a large extent, since the early colonial period. As a matter of fact, however, many of them are held upon the estate in a bondage no less real because it is sanctioned only by custom and enforced only by economic conditions. In the first place, many of these peons have proprietary claims on the land which they and their ancestors have occupied and cultivated for generations. While, it is true, their tenure has no legal status, it has generally been recognized by the owners of the haciendas and has survived in custom because it has proved advantageous to the landlord no less than to the native. Furthermore, the peons feel an attachment to the land that a stranger unacquainted with their psychology can hardly appreciate. Upon it their ancestors have lived for many generations, have followed the one occupation of tilling these fields, and have looked to the owner as their patron. As a result, the peons not only feel that the land belongs to them but that they belong to it, and a deep-rooted sentiment binds them to the estate. In the second place, the peons have, until recently, been bound to the haciendas by a system of economic bondage which was tacitly concurred in by the officers of the law. This system was designed by the Spaniards, in colonial times, to replace the explicit slavery which the crown prohibited. By a system of advance payments, which the peons were totally unable to refund, the hacendados were able to keep them permanently under financial obligations and hence to oblige them to remain upon the estates to which they belonged. Occasionally, indeed, a neighboring hacendado might agree to take over the debt that was owing, but, in such a case, the peon merely experienced a change of masters and a removal from the surroundings to which he was attached. The system of payments in advance is prohibited in the new Constitution of 1917, but, until agrarian conditions undergo a complete change, it will probably survive in spite of the law, as it has for sixty years in defiance of the Constitution of 1857. Furthermore, the peons are bound to the haciendas by mere necessity. Were they to leave, there is no unoccupied land upon which they might settle; and, if

this were to be found, they have neither tools, seeds, stock, nor savings with which to equip farms of their own. During the recent revolution, when land was offered free to peons of Nuevo León, few of them were able to take advantage of the opportunity (so residents of the district say) because of this complete lack of capital.

The daily wages paid to the peons who work on the haciendas have always been very low. The law of 1656 fixed at three reales the amount to be paid to an Indian who was bound by debt. Humboldt reported that, in 1804, the country laborers in Mexico received about 28 centavos. Poinsett, in 1822, stated that wages in central Mexico varied from 25 to 50 centavos. Romero, in 1891, gave 36 centavos as the average, for the whole country, of the daily wages paid to field hands. The wages of the peons remained at that level until near the close of the Díaz administration, although, in the meantime, the peso had sunk to about half its earlier value. At the beginning of the twentieth century the increasing demand for labor was making itself felt, with varying results in different parts of the country, so that the scale of wages showed a considerable range. In Aguascalientes, Nuevo León, and San Luis Potosí a minimum of 19 to 20 centavos per day was being paid, while in regions where labor was scarce, as in Morelos, Sonora, Chiapas, and Baja California, the daily wage ranged from 65 centavos to 1.50 pesos. The Constitution of 1917 has provided for the fixing of a minimum wage, but as yet the conditions in the rural districts have prevented the application of this regulation.

The wages of the peon are seldom paid in money. Ordinarily for his labor he is given a due bill or time check to be negotiated at the store maintained by the hacienda — with obvious results. On the other hand, the actual wage earned is not the only compensation that the peon receives. Certain perquisites, if one might so describe them, have been established by custom, which alleviate the lot of the Indian laborer. Thus he occupies a hut upon the estate without being called upon to pay rent. He is usually allowed a *milpa,* a piece of land for his own use, and this may provide at least a part of his living. Moreover, while he is forced to resort to the hacienda store, he enjoys a credit there sufficient to tide him over in the event of a general crop failure. Actually, however, so meager is the compensation received by the peon that he is kept in the most abject poverty, and few opportunities of escape from the bondage imposed by the established system ever present themselves. Obviously, this situation has greatly encouraged the emigration of rural laborers from Mexico to the southwestern part of the United States. Official figures given by the U. S. Bureau of Immigration show that between 1899 and 1919 there was an average yearly movement of 10,320 immigrants from Mexico into this country, in addition to the seasonal migration. These figures are thought to represent only a part of the actual movement, since conditions on the border make it easy for the immigrant to avoid registration. The full tide of emigration of Mexican laborers is thought by some to reach as high as 100,000 a year. The problem has repeatedly demanded the attention of Mexican officials, both state and federal, but no means has been found for limiting the exodus. In an interview accorded the writer, Señor Pastor Rouaix, ex-Minister of Agriculture, declared that the movement was directly traceable to the land system existing in Mexico; that the largest migration was from the states of Querétaro and Michoacán, where the hacienda system is particularly well developed; and that, in his opinion, emigration would continue until the Mexican peon was enabled to possess a house and land of his own.

The Mexican peon usually lives in a village. This is either a settlement of laborers established upon the hacienda itself or an Indian pueblo that lies surrounded by, or at the edge of, the estate. Of recent years some hacendados have adopted the plan of building new settlements for their peons, and occasionally these groups of huts erected on a common plan and constructed of brick and corrugated iron, may be seen in orderly array in some open space about a casa de hacienda, in striking contrast with the cluster of little adobe houses scattered among ancient groves of scraggly, gnarled trees and remains of stone walls that characterize the typical Mexican pueblo. The home of the peon and his family generally consists of a single-roomed hut, which contains, by way of furnishings, little more than the pile of mats and blankets upon which the family sleeps, with possibly a home-made table, some rough chairs, a wooden chest or two for the trinkets and clothes worn on fiestas, and the inevitable candles burning before the picture of some saint or of the Virgin. The peon has neither corrals nor outhouses attached to his dwelling; he needs no such additional buildings, since he possesses neither implements nor stock of his own save the ubiquitous pig and a few fowls. The only thing that gives the place the aspect of a home is the presence of plants that are grown around it, for, next to his children and music, the Mexican loves flowers. Indeed, in traveling through the country, the presence of yards, outhouses, and gardens about the dwellings is evidence that one has passed from an hacienda into a region of small independent holdings.

The foregoing description of labor conditions applies chiefly to the haciendas on the Mesa Central, parts of the plateau of Oaxaca, the highland of Chiapas, and in the agricultural section of the peninsula of Yucatan, regions where the system of large agricultural holdings has reached its highest development. In other parts of the country conditions are different. In the Mesa del Norte, including the states of Chihuahua, Coahuila, Nuevo León, Durango, Zacatecas, and parts of San Luis Potosí, where the native population has always been limited in numbers, the system just described has not become general. As stated earlier, this part of the country was occupied only after the arrival of the Europeans, and the men who actually cultivate the land have never been attached as serfs to the soil. The same may be said of the other regions that were settled chiefly after the arrival of the Spaniards, such as the grasslands on the Gulfward slope in Tamaulipas, San Luis Potosí, and northern Veracruz, and the arid or semi-arid escarpment along the western coast. In the humid *tierra caliente* of Veracruz, Tabasco, Campeche, and the isthmus of Tehuantepec plantations have also been developed within recent times. Here, again, there was no established agricultural population upon which the newcomers might rely and, in this case, labor was forcibly recruited from uncivilized Indian tribes, which were often reduced to virtual slavery, from the *enganchados,* or laborers kidnapped on the plateau, and from the Yaquis who were expelled from their lands in southern Sonora. . . .

In the eyes of the Mexicans the value of an hacienda does not lie in the money return yielded by the annual crops. The actual return in money is often very small. With intensive cultivation the broad acres might be made to yield a large income; but, with an absentee owner, a hired administrator, and poorly paid peons, the typical Mexican hacienda yields little more than enough to feed its numerous population. The economic value to the owner lies rather in the supplies which it furnishes, the cheap service which it provides for his household, and the amount of money which he can obtain on a mortgage. As Molina Enríquez says, *"La hacienda no es negocio."*

At the present time two important factors are operating to affect the economic value of the Mexican hacienda. On the one hand there is the "unearned increment." This increase is likely to be rapid in a country such as Mexico, where most of the habitable areas are already densely settled and where the amount of arable land is so reduced that the agricultural products in an average year barely suffice for the domestic consumption. On the other hand under the present system of cultivation the productivity of the land seems to be decreasing at a rather alarming rate. Humboldt estimated that the average yield of corn lands on the Bajío of Guanajuato, in his time, was 150 grains for each grain planted, which has been reckoned as a yield of 75 hectoliters per hectare, or about 86.1 bushels per acre. This is probably an exaggeration, but, even so, it suggests an actual return far above the present yield, which may be taken for the same region to be between 8 and 10 hectoliters per hectare, or from 9 to 12 bushels per acre. For typical agricultural lands near Monterrey an estimate of 7 to 25 bushels per acre has been given, varying with the amount of water supplied. This would represent a decline in productivity of at least 50 per cent within about a century and a quarter. It is not at all surprising that under the present system, "the most wasteful of extensive cultivation," the soil should become exhausted. With no careful administration, with the poorest of poor labor, with no attempt at rotation of crops — except that intended to get two or three crops from the same area each year with little attention to the use of artificial fertilizers, the lands of the haciendas cannot but deteriorate. Furthermore, the ruthless cutting of timbered areas leaves the slopes of the hills denuded, exposes them to gullying during the tropical showers of the summer time and to abrasion by the strong mountain winds. Except in the districts where small holdings prevail, and where care of the land is necessarily more imperative, one sees little effort made to conserve the resources of the farm lands or to introduce improvements in the methods of agriculture. The deterioration involved cannot but tend to offset in some degree the natural increase in the economic value of the properties.

The hacienda has, however, a social value which far outweighs its economic worth in the eyes of the average Mexican. Every Mexican aspires to be a landowner; and the life of the hacendado holds a charm unrivaled by the attractions of any other occupation. The elements which make this appeal are sufficiently obvious; pride of proprietorship, a minimum of toil, the leisurely oversight of an estate, and unlimited opportunity for the exercise of authority over humble servitors. Furthermore, the life of the hacendado offers ample occasion for the display of fine horses, expensive trappings, and picturesque accouterments; while the rounds of supervision call for periods of life in the open and provide the subtle attraction of occasional personal hardships and dangers. Herein lies the real value of a Mexican hacienda to its owner. The hacendado, the "man on horseback" of whom Blasco Ibáñez often speaks in his characterization of Mexico, is the real hero of the nation. A large rural estate is the goal of ambition of every true Mexican, and the sentimental value that attaches to these holdings is an influence in the life of the nation that far eclipses the economic value of the properties.

The haciendas and their owners have, in most respects, dominated the life of Mexico. This domination is less economic than social or political. Opinions differ as to the proportion of the nations's food supply that is derived from the haciendas and from the smaller properties. Statistics that would settle the question have, apparently, never been compiled; but, even if the smaller farms supply the greater part of the food for public consumption, it is the haciendas, with their greater ability to hold their produce for a favorable price, that control the markets. In matters of wages and conditions of work the haciendas also exert a determining influence.

The social and political influence of the haciendas is more direct and powerful. Throughout the history of Mexico the landholding class has generally dominated social conditions. It has set the standards of morals, education, and amusement for the middle class and has determined the conditions under which the manual laborer must live. Moreover, the great landholders have ruled the country. This small class, numbering 8,000 to 10,000 proprietors, has at all times exercised a preponderant influence in national affairs and has usually been in control in individual states. In truth, while the Indian element has through its politico-agrarian pueblo and its *caciques* maintained a fair degree of local self-government, the great landholders have been the only group in the country whose training and experience have fitted them to deal with the larger aspects of national government. In the colonial period their influence constantly thwarted the benevolent measures of the home government; and since the birth of the republic legislation has been dictated by them, and largely in their interest. If, as has sometimes happened in revolutionary periods, landholders were unable to prevent the enactment of laws opposed to their interests, they have usually succeeded in controlling the enforcement of the objectionable laws. In the War for Independence they blocked the democratic tendencies of Morelos and Hidalgo and substituted for these leaders the aristocratic regime of Iturbide. In the middle of the nineteenth century the great proprietors supported Maximilian in his struggle against the Juárez reform movement. Though ultimately defeated in that contest, they succeeded later in nullifying the agrarian program by their influence in the land legislation of the Díaz administration. Working hand in hand with the clerical party, they have uniformly constituted the conservative element, opposing, as contrary to their interests, most of the liberal measures put forward.

2. FIESTA AT SAN AGUSTÍN

As in colonial days, the creole aristocracy of the republican era generally resided in the cities, leaving their great estates in the charge of Administrators. Frances Calderón de la Barca (1804–1882), the Scottish-born wife of a Spanish minister to Mexico, described upper-class society in the age of Santa Anna in a series of sprightly letters. A high point in the life of the capital's fashionable world was the annual three-day festival of dancing, cockfighting, and gambling at the village of San Agustín, near Mexico City.[2]

SINCE MY LAST LETTER we have been at San Agustín de las Cuevas, which, when I last saw it, was a deserted village, but which during three days in the year presents the appearance of a vast bee-hive or ant-hill. San Agustín! At the name how many hearts throb with emotion! How many hands are mechanically thrust into empty pockets! How many visions of long-vanished golden ounces flit before aching eyes! What faint crowing of wounded cocks! What

2 Frances Calderón de la Barca, *Life in Mexico during a Residence of Two Years in that Country*, London, 1843, pp. 163–168.

tinkling of guitars and blowing of horns come upon the ear! Some, indeed, there be, who can look round upon their well-stored hacienda and easy-rolling carriages, and remember the day, when with threadbare coat, and stake of three modest ounces, they first courted Fortune's favours, and who, being then indigent, and enjoying an indifferent reputation, found themselves, at the conclusion of a few successive San Agustíns, the fortunate proprietors of gold, and land, and houses; and, moreover, with an unimpeachable fame; for he who can fling gold-dust in his neighbour's eyes, prevents him from seeing too clearly. But these favourites of the blind goddess are few and far between; and they have for the most part, with a view to greater security, become holders or sharers of banks at San Agustín, thus investing their fortune in a secure fund; more so decidedly, if we may believe the newspaper reports, than in the bank of the United States at this present writing.

Time, in its revolutions whirling all things out of their places, has made no change in the annual fete of San Agustín. Fashions alter. The graceful mantilla gradually gives place to the ungraceful bonnet. The old painted coach, moving slowly like a caravan, with Guido's Aurora painted on its gaudy panels, is dismissed for the London-built carriage. Old customs have passed away. The ladies no longer sit on the door-sills, eating roast duck with their fingers, or with the aid of tortillas. Even the *Chinampas* have become stationary, and have occasionally joined the continent. But the annual fete of San Agustín is built on a more solid foundation than taste or custom, or floating soil. It is founded upon that love of gambling, which is said to be a passion inherent in our nature, and which is certainly impregnated with the Mexican constitution, in man, woman, and child. The beggars gamble at the corners of the streets or under the arches; the little boys gamble in groups in the villages; the coachmen and footmen gamble at the doors of the theatre while waiting for their masters.

But while their hand is thus kept in all the year round, there are three days sacredly set apart annually, in which every accommodation is given to those who are bent upon ruining themselves or their neighbours; whilst every zest that society can afford, is held out to render the temptation more alluring. As religion is called in to sanctify everything, right or wrong; as the robber will plant a cross at the mouth of his cave, and the pulque-shops do occasionally call themselves "Pulquerías of the Most Holy Virgin," so this season of gambling is fixed for the fete of *Pascua* (Whitsunday), and the churches and the gambling-houses are thrown open simultaneously.

The village is in itself pretty and picturesque; and, as a stone at its entry informs us, was built by the active Viceroy Revillagigedo, with the product, as —— assured us, of two lotteries. It is charmingly situated, in the midst of handsome villas and orchards, whose high walls, overtopped by fruit-trees, border the narrow lanes. At this season the trees are loaded with the yellow chabacano and the purple plum, already ripe; while the pear-trees are bending under the weight of their fruit. The gardens are full of flowers; the roses in their last bloom, covering the crowd with their pink leaves, and jasmine and sweet-peas in profusion, making the air fragrant. The rainy season has scarce set in, though frequent showers have laid the dust, and refreshed the air. The country villas are filled with all that is gayest and most distinguished in Mexico, and every house and every room in the village has been hired for months in advance. The ladies are in their most elegant toilets, and looking forward to a delightful whirl of dancing, cock-fighting, gambling, dining, dressing, and driving about.

The high-road leading from Mexico to San Agustín is covered with vehicles of every description; carriages, diligences, hackney-coaches, carts, and carratelas. Those who are not fortunate enough to possess any wheeled conveyance, come out on horse, ass, or mule; single, double, or treble, if necessary; and many hundreds, with visions of silver before their eyes, and a few *clacos* (pence), hid under their rags, trudge out on foot. The President himself, in carriage-and-six, and attended by his aides-de-camp, sanctions by his presence the amusements of the fete. The Mexican generals and other officers follow in his wake, and the gratifying spectacle may not unfrequently be seen, of the president leaning from his box in the *plaza de gallos*, and betting upon a cock, with a coatless, bootless, hatless, and probably worthless ragamuffin in the pit. Every one, therefore, however humble his degree, has the pleasure, while following his speculative inclinations, of reflecting that he treads in the steps of the magnates of the land; and, as Sam Weller would say, "Vot a consolation that must be to his feelings!"

At all events, nothing can be gayer than the appearance of the village, as your carriage makes its way through the narrow lane into the principal plaza, amidst the assembled crowd of coaches and foot-passengers; though the faces of the people bear evidence that pleasure alone has not brought them to San Agustín. All round the square are the gambling-houses, where for three nights and three days every table is occupied. At the principal *montes* nothing is played but gold, but as there is accommodation for all classes, so there are silver tables in the inferior houses, while outside are rows of tables on which are heaps of copper, covered with a rugged awning, and surrounded by *léperos* and blanketed Indians, playing *monte* in imitation of their betters, though on a scale more suited to their finances.

Having left Mexico early in the morning, we stopped to breakfast at San Antonio, a noble hacienda, about four leagues from Mexico, belonging to the Dowager Marquesa de Vivanco, where we breakfasted with a large party. It is a fine solid mass of building, and as you enter the courtyard, through a deep archway, the great outhouses, stables, and especially the granary, look like remains of feudalism, they are on so large and magnificent a scale. It is an immense and valuable property, producing both maize and maguey, and the hospitality of the family, who are amongst our earliest friends here, is upon as large a scale as everything that belongs to them. We had a splendid breakfast, in a fine old hall, and stayed but a short time to visit the gardens and the chapel, as we were anxious to arrive at San Agustín in time for the cock-fight.

It is singular, that while San Agustín is situated in the midst of the most fertile and productive country, there should lie opposite to it, and bounded as it were by the graceful Peruvian trees and silver poplars which surround a small church on the other side of the high-road, a great tract of black lava, sterile, bleak, and entirely destitute of vegetation, called the *Pedregal*. This covers the country all along to San Agustín and to the base of the mountain of Ajusco, which lies behind it, contrasting strangely with the beautiful groves and gardens in its neighbourhood, and looking as if it had been cursed for some crime committed there. The high-road, which runs nearly in a direct line from the hacienda to San Agustín, is broad and in tolerable repair; but before arriving there, it is so little attended to, that during the rainy season it might be passed in canoes; yet this immense formation of ferruginous lava and porphyritic rock lies conveniently in its vicinity. A large sum, supposed to be employed in mending the road, is collected annually at the toll, close to San Antonio. For each carriage two dollars are asked, and for carts and animals in proportion. The proprietor of this toll or *postazgo* is also the owner of the *plaza de gallos,* where a dollar is paid for entry, the sums produced by which go exclusively to enrich the same individual. The government has no advantage from it. . . .

The last day of the fete is considered the best, and it is most crowded on that day both by families from Mexico and by foreigners who go solely for pleasure, though not unfrequently tempted to do a little business on their own account. In fact, the temptations are great; and it must be difficult for a young man to withstand them.

We went to the *gallos* about three o'clock. The plaza was crowded, and the ladies in their boxes looked like a parterre of different-coloured flowers. But whilst the Señoras in their boxes did honour to the fete by their brilliant toilet, the gentlemen promenaded round the circle in jackets, high and low being on the same *curtailed* footing, and certainly in a style of dress more befitting the exhibition. The president and his suite were already there, also several of the foreign ministers.

Meanwhile, the cocks crowed valiantly, bets were adjusted, and even the women entered into the spirit of the scene, taking bets with the gentlemen *sotto voce* in their boxes, upon such and such favourite animal. As a small knife is fastened to the leg of each cock, the battle seldom lasted long, one or other falling every few minutes in a pool of blood. Then there was a clapping of hands, mingled with the loud crowing of some unfortunate cock, who was giving himself airs previous to a combat where he was probably destined to crow his last. It has a curious effect to European eyes, to see young ladies of good family, looking peculiarly feminine and gentle, sanctioning, by their presence, this savage diversion. It is no doubt the effect of early habit, and you will say that at least it is no worse than a bull-fight; which is certain — yet cruel as the latter is, I find something more *en grande,* more noble, in the

"Ungentle sport, that oft invites
The Spanish maid, and cheers the Spanish swain;"

in the roaring of the "lord of lowing herds," the galloping of the fine horses, the skill of the riders, the gay dresses, the music, and agile matador; in short, in the whole pomp and circumstances of the combat, than when one looks

quietly on to see two birds peck each other's eyes out, and cut each other to pieces. Unlike cock-pits in other countries, attended by blacklegs and pickpockets and gentlemanly *roués,* by far the largest portion of the assembly in the pit was composed of the first young men in Mexico, and for that matter, of the first old ones also. There was neither confusion, nor noise, nor even loud talking, far less swearing, amongst the lowest of those assembled in the ring; and it is this quiet and orderly behaviour which throws over all these incongruities a cloak of decency and decorum, that hides their impropriety so completely, that even foreigners who have lived here a few years, and who were at first struck with astonishment by these things, are now quite reconciled to them.

As far as the company went, it might have been the House of Representatives in Washington; the ladies in the gallery listening to the debates, and the members in the body of the house surrounding Messrs. —— and ——, or any other two vehement orators; applauding their biting remarks and cutting sarcasms, and encouraging them to crow over each other. The president might have been the speaker, and the corps diplomatique represented itself.

We had an agreeable dinner at the E——s, and afterwards accompanied them to the Calvario, a hill where there was a ball *al fresco,* which was rather amusing, and then paid a visit to the family of General Morán, who has a beautiful house and gardens in the neighbourhood. We found a large party assembled, and amongst them the president. Afterwards, accompanied by the —— minister, and the ladies of our party, we went to take a view of the gambling-tables, and opened our eyes at the heaps of gold, which changed owners every minute. I saw C——a, a millionaire, win and lose a thousand ounces apparently with equal indifference. A little advocate having won two thousand five hundred ounces, wisely ordered his carriage and set off for Mexico, with the best fee he had ever received in his life. Ladies do not generally look on at the tables, but may if they please, and especially if they be strangers. Each gambling-room was well fitted up, and looked like a private apartment.

We then returned home and dressed for the ball, which was given in the evening in the *plaza de gallos.* We first went upstairs to a box, but I afterwards took the advice of M. de —— and came down to see the dancers. There were ladies in full dress, and gentlemen in white jackets — rather inconsistent. The company, though perfectly quiet and well-behaved, were not very select, and were, on that account, particularly amusing. Madame de —— and I walked about, and certainly laughed much more than we should have done in a more distinguished society.

About two in the morning we returned to Mexico, and as I this moment receive a note from the American minister, informing me that the packet from Vera Cruz is about to sail, I shall send off my letters now; and should we still be here next year, I shall then give you a more detailed description of the fete, of the ball, both at Calvario and in the cock-pit, and also of the "high life below stairs" gambling, at which the scenes are *impayable*. In one respect the fashions of San Agustín are altered from what they were a few years ago, when the Señoras used to perform five elaborate and distinct toilets daily; the first in the morning, the second for the cock-fight, the third for the dinner, the fourth for the ball on the hill of Calvary, and the fifth for the ball in the evening. I am told that as they danced in the open air, on the hill, with all their diamonds and pearls on, in the midst of an immense concourse of people, a great many jewels were constantly lost, which the *léperos* used afterwards to search for, and pick up from the grass; a rich harvest. Though they still dress a great deal, they are contented with changing their toilet twice, or at the most, three times in the course of the day.

Upon the whole, these three days are excessively amusing, and as all ranks and conditions are mingled, one sees much more variety than at a ball in the city.

3. The Disinherited

Social inequalities in republican Mexico were as great as under Spanish rule. The capital and other cities swarmed with beggars, thieves, and vagabonds of all descriptions. These outcasts were commonly called léperos. *Guillermo Prieto (1818–1897), a brilliant portrayer of Mexican society in the nineteenth century, describes life in the capital's lower depths.[3]*

THE LOWER CLASSES, who inhabited the suburbs and some central points of the city, lived in a misery that today, fortunately, must appear completely incredible.

There were Indian huts in Tarasquillo and the suburbs of Santiago Tlalteloco, Tepito and Santa Clarita, La Viga, San Antonio Abad, etc.

[3] Guillermo Prieto, *Memorias de mis tiempos*, México, 1948, 2 vols. I, pp. 205–207. (Excerpt translated by the editor.)

The walls made of cane and adobe; the roof of thatch or shingle; inside, the *tlecuitl* — a pot filled with water. In the more luxurious huts, a sleeping-mat (*petate*) . . . .

Naked walls, scabby dogs, sores, walking mummies, and every kind of deformity; hunchbacks, contorted faces, knock-kneed and epileptic beings. . . .

The men like domino pieces of six, and blank, bare skin above and cotton trousers below; the women with a short woolen shawl floating over the breast and shoulder, and wrapped about in a long cloth. Pull it back, and you make the wearer spin like a top.

The true *lépero*, generally speaking, is a mestizo, illegitimate, born out of adultery, sacrilegious, and full of mischief. To his rascality he joins a sprightly wit, capacity for generous actions, courage, and really remarkable traits of gratitude, all on a base of idleness, fanaticism, and a powerful inclination toward robbery, drunkenness and love. . . .

The *lépero* is shrewd, and knows how to adopt an abject manner; he appears most submissive when he is most vindictive and harbors the worst intentions; he tends to be an unbeliever and a mocker of religion; he delights in tormenting lay priests, sacristans, and church people in general; he hates cops and soldiers, domestic servants or "cats"; he is a skillful but unsteady worker, a swindler, a vagrant, and a gambler.

Love, pulque, and fighting are the stuff of his life; for the first he needs a legal wife and a sweetheart; for the second, friends; for the third — any occasion will do. Jail doesn't scare him, although he distrusts and keeps out of the way of informers, scribes, and clerks of the courts of justice.

The lépero will have no part of assault, of midnight assassination, of dark and planned conspiracy.

My teacher rightly used to say to me: "The lépero is not to be defined or explained; you can only surprise him in some act that typifies him: a robber, knife in hand, will despoil you of your watch; the lépero will step on your corn, as if by accident, and while you howl with pain he will disappear with your watch."

A robber will pawn a stolen piece of jewelry or will lose it at play; a lépero will call you aside and mysteriously offer you a ring, convincing you that it had been stolen; it turns out the ring is counterfeit. There is a good deal of baseness in the lépero, but he appreciates intelligence; he is fond of men of wit and discernment.

"How could you steal those spoons from the café?" a judge asked a lépero.

"Well, they said I could have anything I liked — so I took the spoons without botherin' nobody."

To add to the contradictions of his character, which I have tried to sketch in these confused lines, the lépero is courageous; he hates ingratitude and perfidy toward a comrade; he prides himself on his disinterest; very rarely will he betray an accomplice or abandon a friend in misfortune.

His mind is a chaos. Bestial superstitions, perverted moral maxims, confused notions of liberty and rights, collusion with the saints to commit robbery . . . a very sea!

4. CITY IN THE ANDES

In drowsy provincial towns, untouched by the wave of change that swept over more favored regions, the colonial way of life maintained its supremacy to the end of the century. Professor James Orton (1830–1877) of Vassar College, sent by the Smithsonian Institution to study the Equatorial Andes and the Amazon, offers his unflattering impressions of Quito, capital of Ecuador, as seen in 1867.[4]

QUITONIANS CLAIM for their capital eighty thousand inhabitants; but when we consider that one fourth of the city is covered with ecclesiastical buildings, and that the dwelling-houses are but two stories high, we see that there is not room for more that half that number. From thirty thousand to forty thousand is the estimate of the venerable Dr. Jameson, who has resided here for a generation. Census taking is as difficult as in Constantinople; the people hide themselves to escape taxation. The women far outnumber the men. The white population — a stiff aristocracy of eight thousand souls — is of Spanish descent, but not more than half a dozen can boast of pure blood. The coarse black hair, prominent cheek-bones, and low foreheads, reveal an Indian alliance. This is the governing class; from its ranks come those uneasy politicians who make laws for other people to obey, and hatch revolutions when a rival party is in power. They are blessed with fair mental capacity, quick perception, and uncommon civility; but they lack education and industry, energy and perseverance. Their wealth, which is not great, consists mainly

in *haciendas*, yielding grain, cotton, and cattle. The Aguirre family is one of the noblest and wealthiest in the city; their mansion is on the Grand Plaza, facing the Capitol. The pure Indians of Quito number perhaps 10,000; not all those seen in the city are citizens, as many *serranos,* or mountaineers, come in to sell produce. They are the serfs that do the drudgery of the republic; they are the tillers of the soil, and beasts of burden. Many sell themselves for money in advance, and then are ever kept in debt. Excepting a few Zambos (the children of Indians and Negroes), and a very few foreigners and Negroes, the remainder, constituting the bulk of the population, are Cholos — the offspring of whites and Indians. They are not strictly half-breeds, for the Indian element stands out most prominent. Though a mixed race, they are far superior to their progenitors in enterprise and intelligence. They are the soldiers, artisans, and tradesmen who keep up the only signs of life in Quito. "I know not the reason," says Darwin, "but men of such origin seldom have a good expression of countenance." This may be true on the pampas, but Quito, where there is every imaginable mixture of Indian and Spaniard, is wonderfully free from ugly features. It may be owing to the more peaceful and civilized history of this mountain city.

As to dress, black is the color of etiquette, but is not so national as in Madrid. The upper class follow *la mode de Paris,* gentlemen adding the classic cloak of Old Spain. This modern toga fits an Ecuadorian admirably; it favors habits of inactivity, preventing the arms from doing anything, and covers a multitude of sins, especially pride and poverty. The *poncho,* so peculiar to the West Coast and to the Gauchos of Buenos Ayres, is a piece of cloth of divers colors, with a slit in the centre, through which the head is passed. It is the only variable article of the wardrobe. It is an excellent riding habit, and is made of heavy woolen for mountain travel, and of silk or cotton for warmer altitudes. No gentleman will be seen walking in the streets of Quito under a poncho. Hence citizens are divided into men with ponchos, and gentlemen with cloaks. Pañuelon is the most essential article of female gear. It answers to the mantilla of the mother country, though it is not worn so gracefully as on the banks of the Tagus. Andean ladies are not troubled with the distressing fluctuations in the style of hats; a bonnet in Quito is as much out of place as a turban in New York.

4 James Orton, *The Andes and the Amazon,* New York, 1870, pp. 68–84.

When the daughter of our late minister resident appeared in the cathedral with one, the innovation was the subject of severe remark. The Spanish hair is the glory of the sex. It is thick and black (red, being a rarity, is considered a beauty), and is braided in two long tresses. A silk dress, satin shoes, and fancy jewelry complete the visible attire of the belles of Quito.

The ordinary costume of the Indians and Cholos consists of a coarse cotton shirt and drawers, and silk, cotton, or woolen poncho of native manufacture, the females adding a short petticoat, generally of a light blue or "butternut" color, belted around the waist with a figured woolen belt woven by themselves. The head, arms, legs, and feet are often bare, but, by those who can afford it, the head is covered with a straw or white felt broad-brim, and the feet protected by sandals, called *alpargatas*, made of the fibres of the aloe. They are very fond of bracelets and necklaces. Infants are usually swathed from neck to feet with a broad strip of cloth, so that they look like live mummies.

Quitonians put us to shame by their unequaled courtesy, cordiality, and good nature, and are not far below the grave and decorous Castilian in dignified politeness. Rudeness, which some Northerners fancy is a proof of equality and independence, we never met with, and duels and street quarrels are almost unknown. We detected none of the touchy sensitiveness of the punctilious Spanish *hidalgos*. Their compliments and promises are without end; and, made in the magnificent and ceremonious language of Spain, are overwhelming to a stranger. Thus a fair Quitonian sends by her servant the following message to another lady: "Go to the Señorita Fulana de Tal, and tell her that she is my heart and the dear little friend of my soul; tell her that I am dying for not having seen her, and ask her why she does not come to see me; tell her that I have been waiting for her more than a week, and that I send her my best respects and considerations; and ask her how she is, and how her husband is, and how her children are, and whether they are all well in the family; and tell her she is my little love, and ask her whether she will be kind enough to send me that pattern which she promised me the other day." This highly important message the servant delivers like a parrot, not omitting a single compliment but rather adding thereto.

A newly-arrived foreigner is covered with promises: houses, horses, servants, yea, every-thing is at his disposal. But, alas! the traveler soon finds that this ceremony of words does not extend to deeds. He is never expected to call for the services so pompously proffered. So long as he stays in Quito he will not lose sight of the contrast between big promise and beggarly performance. This outward civility, however, is not hypocritical; it is mere mechanical prattle; the speaker does not expect to be taken at his word. The love of superlatives and the want of good faith may be considered as prominent characteristics. "The readiness with which they break a promise or an agreement (wrote Colonel Hall forty years ago) can only be equaled by the sophistical ingenuity with which they defend themselves for having done so." The Quitonians, who are sensible of their shortcomings, have this standing apology: "Our vices we owe to Spain; our virtues to ourselves." . . .

Ecuador boasts of one University and eleven colleges; yet the people are not educated. Literature, science, philosophy, law, medicine, are only names. Nearly all young gentlemen are doctors of something; but their education is strangely dwarfed, defective, and distorted; and their knowledge, such as they have, is without power, as it is without practice. The University of Quito has two hundred and eighty-five students, of whom thirty-five are pursuing law, and eighteen medicine. There are eleven professors. They receive no fees from the students, but an annual salary of $300. The library contains eleven thousand volumes, nearly all old Latin, Spanish, and French works. The cabinet is a bushel of stones cast into one corner of a lumber-room, covered with dust, and crying out in vain for a man in the University to name them. The College of Tacunga has forty-five students; a fine chemical and philosophical apparatus, but no one to handle it; and a set of rocks from Europe, but only a handful from Ecuador. The College of Riobamba has four professors, and one hundred and twenty students. In the common schools, the pupils study in concert aloud, Arab fashion. There are four papers in the republic; two in Guayaquil, one in Cuenca, and one in Quito. *El Nacional,* of the capital, is an official organ, not a newspaper; it contains fourteen duodecimo pages, and is published occasionally by the Minister of the Interior. Like the *Gazeta* of Madrid, it is one of the greatest satires ever deliberately published by any people on itself. There is likewise but one paper in Cuzco, *El Triunfo del Pueblo.*

The amusements of Quito are few, and not

very amusing. Indo-Castilian blood runs too slowly for merry-making. There are no operas or concerts, no theatres or lectures, no museums or menageries. For dramas they have revolutions; for menageries, bull-baitings. A bull-bait is not a bull-fight. There is no coliseum or amphitheatre; no *matador* gives the scientific death-wound. Unlike their fraternity in the ring of Seville, where they are doomed to die, the animals are only doomed to be pothered; they are "scotched, not killed." They are teased and tormented by yelling crowds, barking dogs, brass bands, red ponchos, tail-pulling, fire-crackers, wooden lances, and such like. The Plaza de Toros is the Plaza de San Francisco. This sport is reserved for the most notable days in the calendar: Christmas, New Year's, Inauguration Day, and Independence Day — the 10th of August.

Cock-fights come next in popularity, and are *bona fide* fights. Often the roosters are so heroic that both leave their blood in the arena, and never crow again. Little knives are fastened to the natural spurs, with which the fowls cut each other up frightfully. The interesting scene takes place on Sundays and Thursdays, near the Church of Santa Catalina, and is regulated by a municipal tribunal. The admission fee of five cents, and the tax of two per cent on bets yield the city a monthly revenue of $100.

Other pastimes are carnivals and masquerades. Carnival is observed by pelting one another with eggs and sprinkling with water. Whoever invented this prelude to Lent should be canonized. Masquerades occur during the holidays, when all classes, in disguise or fancy dress, get up a little fun at each other's expense. The monotony of social life is more frequently disturbed by fashionable funerals than by these amusements; and, as the principal families are inter-related, the rules of condolence keep the best part of society in mourning, and the best pianos and guitars silent for at least six months in the year.

A word about the ladies of Quito. We concur in the remark of our minister, Mr. Hassaurek, that "their natural dignity, gracefulness, and politeness, their entire self-possession, their elegant but unaffected bearing, and the choiceness of their language, would enable them to make a creditable appearance in any foreign drawing-room." Their natural talents are of a high order; but we must add that the señoras are uneducated, and are incapable of either great vices or great virtues. Their minds, like the soil of their native country, are fertile, but uncultivated; and their hearts, like the climate, are of a mean temperature. Prayer-books and French novels (imported, as wanted, for there is not a book-store in the city) are the alpha and the omega of their literature; Paris is considered the centre of civilization. They are comely, but not beautiful; Venus has given her girdle of fascination to few. Sensible of this, they paint. . . .

The ladies of Quito give few entertainments for lack of ready money. They spend much of their time in needle work and gossip, sitting like Turkish sultanas on divans or the floor. They do not rise at your entrance or departure. They converse in a very loud, unmusical voice. We never detected bashfulness in the street or parlor. They go to mass every morning, and make visits of etiquette on Sundays. They take more interest in political than in domestic affairs. Dust and cobwebs are unmistakable signs of indifference. Brooms are rarities; such as exist are besoms made of split stick. Since our return, we have sent to a Quitonian gentleman, by request, a package of broom-corn seed, which, we trust, will be the forerunner of a harvest of brooms and cleaner floors in the high city. Not only the lords, but also the ladies, are inveterate smokers. Little mats are used for spittoons.

Perhaps Quitonian ladies have too many Indian servants about them to keep tidy; seven or eight is the average number for a family. These are married, and occupy the ground floor, which swarms with nude children. They are cheap, thievish, lazy, and filthy. No class, pure-blood or half-breed, is given to ablution, though there are two public baths in the city. Washerwomen repair to the Machangara, where they beat the dirty linen of Quito over the smooth rocks. We remember but two or three tablecloths which entirely covered the table, and only one which was clean. There are but two daily meals; one does not feel the need of more; they are partaken at nine and three, or an hour earlier than in Guayaquil. When two unwashed, uncombed cooks bend over a charcoal fire, which is fanned by a third unkempt individual, and all three blinded by smoke (for there is no chimney), so that it is not their fault if capillaries and something worse are mingled with the stew, with onions to right of them, onions to left of them, onions in front of them, and *achote* already in the pot in spite of your repeated anathemas and expostulations — *achote*, the same red coloring matter which the wild Indians use for painting their bodies and dyeing their cloth — and with several aboriginal wee ones romping about the kitchen, keen must be the appetite that will take hold with alacrity as the dishes are brought on by the most slovenly waiter imagination can body forth.[5] The aim of Ecuadorian cookery is to eradicate all natural flavor; you wouldn't know you were eating chicken except by the bones. Even coffee and chocolate somehow lose their fine Guayaquilian aroma in this high altitude, and the very pies are stuffed with onions. But the beef, minus the garlic, is most excellent, and the *dulce* unapproachable.

5. THE WAY OF THE GAUCHO

Before the coming of the railroad and the other changes that created modern Argentina, the pampa was the home of a primitive, patriarchal society whose central figure was the colorful gaucho. In his masterpiece Facundo (1845), *the Argentine writer Domingo F. Sarmiento (1811–1888) portrayed with a magnificent blend of romanticism and realism the gaucho way of life.*[6]

COUNTRY LIFE . . . has developed all the physical but none of the intellectual powers of the gaucho. His moral character is of the quality to be expected from his habit of triumphing over the obstacles and the forces of nature; it is strong, haughty, and energetic. Without instruction, and indeed without need of any, without means of support as without wants, he is happy in the midst of his poverty and privations, which are not such to one who never knew nor wished for greater pleasures than are his already. Thus if the disorganization of society among the gauchos deeply implants barbarism in their natures, through the impossibility and uselessness of moral and intellectual education, it has, too, its attractive side to him. The gaucho does not labor; he finds his food and raiment ready to his hand. If he is a proprietor, his own flocks yield him both; if he possesses nothing himself, he finds them in the house of a patron or a relation. The necessary care of the herds is reduced to excursions and pleasure parties; the branding, which is like the harvesting of farmers, is a festival, the arrival of which is received with transports of joy, being the occasion of the as-

sembling of all the men for sixty miles around and the opportunity for displaying incredible skill with the lasso. The gaucho arrives at the spot on his best steed, riding at a slow and measured pace; he halts at a little distance and puts his leg over his horse's neck to enjoy the sight leisurely. If enthusiasm seizes him, he slowly dismounts, uncoils his lasso, and flings it at some bull, passing like a flash of lightning forty paces from him; he catches him by one hoof, as he intended, and quietly coils his leather cord again. . . .

THE RASTREADOR

The most conspicuous and extraordinary of the occupations to be described is that of the *rastreador,* or track-finder. All the gauchos of the interior are rastreadores. In such extensive plains, where paths and lines of travel cross one another in all directions, and where the pastures in which the herds feed are unfenced, it is necessary often to follow the tracks of an animal, to distinguish them among a thousand others, and to know whether it was going at an easy or a rapid pace, at liberty or led, laden or carrying no weight.

This is a generally understood branch of household knowledge. I once happened to turn out of a by-way into the Buenos Aires road, and my guide, following the usual practice, cast a look at the ground. "There was a very nice little Moorish mule in that train," said he, directly. "D. N. Zapata's it was — she is good for the saddle, and it is very plain she was saddled this time; they went by yesterday." The man was traveling from the Sierra de San Luis, while the train had passed on its way from Buenos Aires, and it was a year since he had seen the Moorish mule, whose track was mixed up with those of a whole train in a path two feet wide. And this seemingly incredible tale only illustrates the common degree of skill — the guide was a mere herdsman, and no professional rastreador.

The rastreador proper is a grave, circumspect personage, whose declarations are considered conclusive evidence in the inferior courts. Consciousness of the knowledge he possesses gives him a certain reserved and mysterious dignity. Everyone treats him with respect; the poor man because he fears to offend one who might injure him by a slander or an accusation; and the proprietor because of the possible value of his testimony. A theft has been committed during the

[5] We noticed at Riobamba a custom which formerly prevailed also at Quito. As soon as the guests have finished, and before they have risen, the Indian waiter kneels devoutly down beside the table, and offers thanks in a very solemn, touching tone.

[6] Mrs. Horace Mann, tr., *Life in the Argentine Republic in the Days of the Tyrants*, New York, 1866, pp. 32–41.

night; no one knows anything of it; the victims of it hasten to look for one of the robber's footprints, and on finding it, they cover it with something to keep the wind from disturbing it. They then send for the rastreador, who detects the track and follows it, only occasionally looking at the ground as if his eyes saw in full relief the footsteps invisible to others. He follows the course of the streets, crosses gardens, enters a house, and, pointing to a man whom he finds there, says coldly: "That is he!" The crime is proved, and the criminal seldom denies the charge. In his estimation, even more than in that of the judge, the rastreador's deposition is a positive demonstration; it would be ridiculous and absurd to dispute it. The culprit accordingly yields to a witness whom he regards as the finger of God pointing him out. I have had some acquaintance myself with Calibar, who has practiced his profession for forty consecutive years in one province. He is now about eighty years old, and of venerable and dignified appearance, though bowed down by age. When his fabulous reputation is mentioned to him, he replies: "I am good for nothing now; there are the boys." The "boys" who have studied under so famous a master are his sons. The story is that his best horse-trappings were once stolen while he was absent on a journey to Buenos Aires. His wife covered one of the thief's footprints with a tray. Two months afterwards Calibar returned, looked at the footprint, which by that time had become blurred and could not have been made out by other eyes, after which he spoke no more of the circumstances. A year and a half later Calibar might have been seen walking through a street in the outskirts of the town with his eyes on the ground. He turned into a house, where he found his trappings, by that time blackened by use and nearly worn out. He had come upon the trail of the thief nearly two years after the robbery.

In 1830, a criminal under sentence of death having escaped from prison, Calibar was employed to search for him. The unhappy man, aware that he would be tracked, had taken all the precautions suggested to him by the image of the scaffold, but they were taken in vain. Perhaps they only assured his destruction; for as Calibar's reputation was hazarded, his jealous self-esteem made him ardent in accomplishing a task which would demonstrate the wonderful sharpness of his sight though it insured the destruction of another man. The fugitive had left as few traces as the nature of the ground would permit; he had crossed whole squares on tiptoe; afterwards he had leaped upon low walls; he had turned back after crossing one place; but Calibar followed him without losing the trail. If he missed the way for a moment, he found it again, exclaiming: "Where are you?" Finally the trail entered a water-course in the suburbs in which the fugitive had sought to elude the rastreador. In vain! Calibar went along the bank without uneasiness or hesitation. At last he stops, examines some plants, and says: "He came out here; there are no footprints, but these drops of water on the herbage are the sign!" On coming to a vineyard, Calibar reconnoitered the mud walls around it and said: "He is in there." The party of soldiers looked till they were tired, and came back to report the failure of the search. "He has not come out," was the only answer of the rastreador, who would not even take the trouble to make a second investigation. In fact, he had not come out, but he was taken and executed the next day.

In 1831 some political prisoners were planning an escape; all was ready, and outside help had been secured. On the point of making the attempt, "What shall be done about Calibar?" said one. "To be sure, Calibar!" said the others in dismay. Their relations prevailed upon Calibar to be ill for four full days after the escape, which was thus without difficulty effected.

What a mystery is this of the rastreador! What microscopic power is developed in the visual organs of these men! How sublime a creature is that which God made in His image and likeness!

THE BAQUEANO, OR PATHFINDER

Next to the rastreador comes the *baqueano*, a personage of distinction, and one who controls the fate of individuals and of provinces. The baqueano is a grave and reserved gaucho, who knows every span of a hundred and fifty thousand square miles of plain, wood, and mountain! He is the most thorough topographer, the only man whom a general consults in directing the movements of his campaign. The baqueano is always at his side. Modest and mute as a garden wall, he is in possession of every secret of the campaign; the fate of the army, the issue of a battle, the conquest of a province, all depend upon him. The baqueano almost always discharges his duty with fidelity, but the general does not place full confidence in him.

Conceive the situation of a commander condemned to be attended by a traitor, from whom he has to obtain the information without which he cannot succeed. A baqueano finds a little path crossing the road which he is following; he knows to what distant watering-place it leads. If he finds a thousand such paths, some of them even three hundred miles apart, he is acquainted with each and knows whence it comes and whither it goes. He knows the hidden fords of a hundred rivers and streams above or below the ordinary place of crossing. He can point out a convenient path through a hundred distinct and extensive swamps.

In the deepest darkness of the night, surrounded by boundless plains or by forests, while his companions are astray and at a loss, he rides around them inspecting the trees; if there are none, he dismounts and stoops to examine the shrubs and satisfies himself of his points of the compass. He then mounts and reassures his party by saying: "We are in a straight line from such a place, so many miles from the houses; we must travel southwards." And he sets off in the direction he has indicated, without uneasiness, without hurrying to confirm his judgment by arriving at the town, and without answering the objections suggested to the others by fear or bewilderment.

If even this is insufficient, or if he finds himself upon the pampas in the impenetrable darkness, he pulls up herbs from different places, smells their roots and the earth about them, chews their foliage, and, by often repeating this proceeding, assures himself of the neighborhood of some lake or stream, either of salt or of fresh water, of which he avails himself upon finding it to set himself exactly right. It is said that General Rosas knows the pasturage of every estate in the south of Buenos Aires by its taste.

If the baqueano belongs to the pampas, where no road exists, and a traveler asks him to show the way straight to a place a hundred and fifty miles off, he pauses a moment, reconnoiters the horizon, examines the ground, fixes his eyes upon some point, and gallops off straight as an arrow until he changes his course for reasons known only to himself, and keeps up his gallop day and night till he arrives at the place named.

The baqueano also announces the approach of the enemy; that is, that they are within thirty miles; and he also detects the direction in which they are approaching by means of the movements of the ostriches, deer, and guanacos which fly in certain directions. At shorter distances he notices the clouds of dust and estimates the number of the hostile force by their density. "They have two thousand men," he says, "five hundred," "two hundred"; and the commander acts upon this assumption, which is almost always infallible. If the condors and crows are wheeling in circles through the air, he can tell whether there are troops hidden thereabouts, or whether a recently abandoned camp, or simply a dead animal is the attractive object. The baqueano knows how far one place is from another, the number of days and hours which the journey requires, and, besides, some unknown byway through which the passage may be made in half the time, so as to end in a surprise; and expeditions for the surprise of towns a hundred and fifty miles away are thus undertaken, and generally with success, by parties of peasants. This may be thought an exaggeration. No! General Rivera, of the Banda Oriental, is a simple baqueano, who knows every tree that grows anywhere in the Republic of Uruguay. The Brazilians would not have occupied that country if he had not aided them; nor, but for him, would the Argentines have set it free.

This man, at once general and baqueano, overpowered Oribe, who was supported by Rosas, after a contest of three years; and at the present day were he in the field against it, the whole power of Buenos Aires, with its numerous armies, which are spread all over Uruguay, might gradually fade away by means of a surprise today, by a post cut off tomorrow, by some victory which he could turn to his own advantage by his knowledge of some route to the enemy's rear or by some other unnoticed or trifling circumstance.

General Rivera began his study of the ground in 1804, when making war upon the government as an outlaw; afterwards he waged war upon the outlaws as a government officer; next upon the King as a patriot; and later upon the patriots as a peasant; upon the Argentines as a Brazilian chieftain; and upon the Brazilians as an Argentine general; upon Lavalleja as President; upon President Oribe as a proscribed chieftain; and finally upon Rosas, the ally of Oribe, as a general of Uruguay; in all which positions he has had abundance of time to learn something of the art of the baqueano.

THE GAUCHO OUTLAW

The example of this type of character, to be found in certain places, is an outlaw, a squatter, a kind of misanthrope. He is Cooper's Hawkeye or Trapper, with all the knowledge of the wilderness possessed by the latter, and with all his aversion to the settlements of the whites, but without his natural morality or his friendly relations with the savages. The name of gaucho outlaw is not applied to him wholly as an uncomplimentary epithet. The law has been for many years in pursuit of him. His name is dreaded — spoken under the breath, but not in hate, and almost respectfully. He is a mysterious personage; his abode is the pampas; his lodgings are the thistle-fields; he lives on partridges and hedgehogs, and whenever he is disposed to regale himself upon a tongue, he lassos a cow, throws her without assistance, kills her, takes his favorite morsel, and leaves the rest for the carrion birds. The gaucho outlaw will make his appearance in a place just left by soldiers, will talk in a friendly way with the admiring group of good gauchos around him, provide himself with tobacco and yerba mate, which makes a refreshing beverage, and if he discovers the soldiers, he mounts his horse quietly and directs his steps leisurely to the wilderness, not even deigning to look back. He is seldom pursued; that would be killing horses to no purpose, for the beast of the gaucho outlaw is a bay courser, as noted in his own way as his master. If the gaucho outlaw ever happens to fall unawares into the hands of the soldiers, he sets upon the densest masses of his assailants and breaks through them with the help of a few slashes left by his knife upon the faces or bodies of his opponents; and lying along the ridge of his horse's back to avoid the bullets sent after him, he hastens toward the wilderness, until, having left his pursuers at a convenient distance, he pulls up and travels at his ease. The poets of the vicinity add this new exploit to the biography of the desert hero, and his renown flies through all the vast region around. Sometimes he appears before the scene of a rustic festival with a young woman whom he has carried off and takes a place in the dance with his partner, goes through the figures of the *cielito,* and disappears, unnoticed. Another day he brings the girl he has seduced to the house of her offended family, sets her down from his horse's croup, and, heedless of the parents' curses by which he is followed, quietly betakes himself to his boundless abode.

This white-skinned savage, at war with society and proscribed by the laws, is no more depraved at heart than the inhabitants of the settlements. The reckless outlaw who attacks a whole troop does no harm to the traveler. The gaucho outlaw is no bandit or highwayman; murderous assaults do not suit his temper, as robbery would not suit the character of the *churriador* (sheep-stealer). To be sure, he steals; but this is his profession, his trade, his science. He steals horses. He arrives, for instance, at the camp of a train from the interior; its master offers to buy of him a horse of some unusual color, of a particular shape and quality, with a white star on the shoulder. The gaucho collects his thoughts, considers a moment, and replies, after a short silence: "There is no such horse alive." What thoughts have been passing through the gaucho's mind? In that moment his memory has traversed a thousand estates upon the pampa; he has seen and examined every horse in the province, with its marks, color, and special traits, and he has convinced himself that not one of them has a star on its shoulder; some have one on their foreheads, others have white spots on their haunches. Is this power of memory amazing? No! Napoleon knew two hundred thousand soldiers by name and remembered, when he saw any one of them, all the facts relating to him. Therefore, if nothing impossible is required of him, the gaucho will deliver upon a designated day and spot just such a horse as has been asked for, and with no less punctuality if he has been paid in advance. His honor is as sensitive upon this point as that of a gambler about his debts.

Sometimes he travels to the country about Córdoba or Santa Fe. Then he may be seen crossing the pampa behind a small body of horses; if anyone meets him, he follows his course without approaching the newcomer unless he is requested to do so.

6. THE COMING OF THE IMMIGRANT

Between 1860 and 1880 the trickle of European immigration into Argentina changed into a flood. The newcomers — mostly Italians, Spaniards, French, Belgians, and English-Irish — made important contributions to the expansion and improvement of the cattle industry, sheep raising, and agriculture. Most of them, however, remained in Buenos Aires and other cities, where they speedily established their leadership in industry, commerce, and the professions. Wilfrid Latham, a pioneer English sheep raiser in La Plata, describes some of the economic and social changes wrought by the new immigration.[7]

7 Wilfrid Latham, *The States of the River Plate*, London, 1868, pp. 312–331.

AFTER THE STORMING of Monte Video by General Beresford (1806) and the capitulation of General Whitelock in Buenos Ayres (1807), and more especially after the War of Independence, many foreigners, chiefly British, found their way to these countries. After the notification of the treaty with Great Britain conceding to her subjects unrestricted trading rights, with protection for their lives, properties, stock, and merchandise, and exemption from military service, forced loans and all other exactions whatsoever, many British subjects settling in Buenos Ayres and the Banda Oriental purchased properties and live stock, entered into local trades and industries, or initiated new or improved systems of industry, mechanical trades, pastoral and agricultural pursuits, effecting great improvements in produce, and expanding the commerce between the two nations.

A considerable impulse was given to the commerce and industry of these infant republics by the early rulers, and especially in Buenos Ayres by Rivadavia, an earnest advocate of education, free institutions, commerce, and immigration.

During the long dictatorship of General Rosas, however, the Argentine States fell under the moral depression which corresponded to their political circumstances and the policy of the Dictator. Far from affording facilities for commerce (which worked its way by the force of necessity and of the innate capacity of the countries for it) and for the development of trade with the interior, vexatious restrictions and exactions were imposed. The great artery of water communication, the Paraná, was kept closed to the world; Paraguay was hermetically sealed, under the barbaric despot Francia, neither ingress nor egress being permitted. The raw or rudely prepared produce of the provinces on the banks of the Paraná was dropped down the river to Buenos Ayres in small craft and *chalapas* (rude flat-bottomed boats), and the unwieldy ox-carts or mules with their packs toiled their sluggish course to or from the interior provinces, bringing their scant produce or taking up manufactured goods, which paid full duties to Buenos Ayres, and again to the several provinces.

The population, utterly prostrate as they were, had little heart, though they felt an eager desire, for industrial undertakings. Scarcely any buildings were erected in town or country, while many fell into dilapidation; and those who were really wealthy in their large estates and number of live stock lived retired in the plainest, if not the coarsest manner. Of education there was next to none.

In the chief city of the Republic (Buenos Ayres) there was scarcely a conveyance to be had (I write of twenty or twenty-five years ago) other than some dozen rumbling old *galeras,* oblong square boxes swung on four wheels (much like a hammock) by rawhide "springs" — i.e. ropes — and drawn by horses yoked to a pole by rawhide thongs attached to a large ring fixed to the broad belt or girth which secures the *bastos,* a sort of saddle, on which rode grotesque-looking gauchos. These conveyances pitched amid the deep ruts and mud-holes as a cock-boat pitches in a heavy breaking sea. Only a few streets were paved wretchedly for a short distance round about the principal square . . . , and the approaches to the city were, in the winter, mere water-courses, alternating at every few yards with cesspools, through which it was scarcely possible (often for weeks together utterly impossible) to pass with horse-*galera* or ox-cart.

Land and stock stood at its lowest. Men feared to purchase and many were eager to sell: they were afraid of owning property lest it should be confiscated or robbed from them.

Some of the best lands in the province of Buenos Ayres were bought and sold at mere nominal figures; 40,000$ or 60,000$ m/c — about 350£ or 342£ — were the current prices for a square league of land, and even shortly after the fall of Rosas the very best of lands were purchased for 80,000$ = 700£. Cattle as they ran, 25$ or 30$ = 3s. 6d. or 4s. 2d., and for slaughter 40$ or 50$. Sheep, 4$, 6$, and 8$, according to class = 7d. or 14d. each.

By continual issues of irredeemable paper — a measure to which the Dictator, to the infinite prejudice of the country, resorted whenever he needed funds, the country under his government being absolutely without credit — the paper currency was depreciated to 1/30 and 1/35 part of its original nominal value. There was scarcely any gold or silver coin in circulation, where before there had been abundance. The massive services of silver which were at one time common in almost every house, were beaten up, sold, and exported.

Few natives, out of the immediate circle of Rosas, ventured to make any improvement on their estates, and they were as slow to introduce the sheep industry on them as they were to improve their sheep stock when they had it. A universal feeling of mistrust pervaded all. They knew not when every peon on their establishments might be carried off for military service, or what contributions, exactions, or confiscations might be looked for. The protection which their treaties secured to foreigners placed them under these circumstances at an advantage over the natives, inasmuch as the former were absolutely exempt from military service and from forced contributions, horses excepted, which were considered articles of war; and any injury to their properties, or the taking of their cattle in intestinal warfare, constituted claims for compensation under the existing treaties.

Induced by the low price of land and the greater security which they enjoyed, foreigners, more especially the British, purchased largely of the lands offered for sale, and devoted themselves to the sheep industry and the improvement of the almost valueless native or Creole sheep. Several large establishments were formed expressly for their improvement by crossing with Merino rams. The most important of these was the establishment of Messrs. Sheridan, Harratt, Hannah, Thwaites, &c. Very many others followed in their wake, including several native estancieros, who gradually drifted into the current, taking from those more advanced establishments the cross-bred stock. Owing to the depressing influence of the Dictatorship and the backward state of the country generally, the sheep stock remained at a lower level, both as to quality and value, than would have been the case under brighter circumstances. The natural increase was, however, not checked: there was superabundance of room with excellent pasture, and this class of stock ran comparatively little or no risk from predatory inroads in troubled times, as they were not easy to drive and were of little value as booty to the chiefs or as provision for the men of the cavalry levies which constituted the military force of the country. A few hundred ox or cow hides were at all times a tempting bait, whereas sheepskins were troublesome, and in those days of little, or indeed no value, except at that period of the year when they were in wool.

When Rosas fell, large numbers of foreigners, principally Irish immigrants, were already engaged in this pastoral industry on the estancias both of foreigners and natives. They were especially desirable as shepherds, inasmuch as they could not be taken for military service, besides taking more kindly to the occupation than the more roving habits of the gaucho admitted of. They were, moreover, particularly sought after by the native estancieros as *medianeros* (on halves), as the sheep, in which they, as British

subjects, thus became interested as partners, came more or less under the protective action of the treaty with Great Britain.

The fall of Rosas readmitted into Buenos Ayres the political exiles, men of intellect and education, who had been obliged to fly from their country during the Dictatorship. During their exile they had come in contact with a more advanced civilization, and learned in adversity to appreciate constitutional order and industrial development. Henceforth they exercised a marked influence in forming and modifying public opinion.

It would be too much to say that the majority even of these men understood clearly the application of the principles of political progress and economic science; but there were some who did, and most of these had experienced the benefits of their working, and speaking thus of the wonderful things they had seen, they left on the minds of others the impressions which they had received themselves when dwelling among men who had been born to the knowledge and habit of material progress and constitutional freedom. In this way they predisposed large numbers of their countrymen to defer to, and to a certain extent take tone from, the intelligent portion of the foreign residents whose interests had been engrafted into those of the country; and they also aided to make more widely known the value of the practical lessons which the merely industrial settlers were working out.

It might perhaps be too much to say that all classes were disposed to acknowledge the value of the influences to which they were subjected. Human nature is substantially the same everywhere, though guided more or less by circumstances and opportunities; but generally it is enough if the knowledge acquired is brought to bear with effect. At the same time, it is only just to say that probably in no country have foreigners been more esteemed; nay, under the advantages of security and exemption which they enjoyed over the natives in the periods of trouble, it is remarkable that there was not a very much stronger feeling of jealousy. Causes creditable to both natives and foreigners tended to prevent the growth of such prejudices — on the one side, the good sense of the people of the country, who saw that foreigners were fostering and improving their industries and were almost exclusively the parties who would or could purchase those things or properties which they wished to sell; on the other, the sympathy of foreigners with the people in their troubles and under their oppressions, and even their readiness to protect and shelter them to the best of their ability, as well as to preserve their properties. These interweavings of mutual interests, conveniences, and sympathies never fail to bring about a social modification. But foreigners have exercised a direct material influence on the conditions and destinies of these countries in addition to the powerful though less direct influence of industry.

During the great struggle in the Banda Oriental, when the director Rosas proposed to crush the party of progress in its last refuge, the foreign element came into play with marked effect. A very large foreign population existed in Monte Video at the time of the siege, and it was mainly through its instrumentality that the city held her own. The pecuniary means were largely supplied by and through the resident foreign capitalists, and as a consequence the bulk of the state properties passed into their hands, together with private estate lands and other properties of immense extent and value. Nine years of military occupation, and the siege of the city, had driven numbers of its people to sell their possessions: nay more, the force with which the city of Monte Video directly maintained her position was foreign. The defenders of the city were chiefly volunteer corps of Italians under Garibaldi, French, Spaniards, Basques, and others, who followed their avocations when not on duty — which fell in turns to the different corps — and received their rations for the service rendered. The frugal and industrial habits of these men enabled them to live when the native city and suburban population, untrained to persistent industry and devoid of the resources incidental to habits of frugality, could not subsist. The native population of the city and its neighbourhood was, as it were, worn out, and the result is now seen in the industries, as well as in the large extent of land or other properties, which remain in the hands of foreigners, and gives to that state (Banda Oriental) a surprising elasticity of recuperative energy under conditions of singular political disadvantage. It has been, as we have stated, the centre of intrigues for neighbouring states and the scene of continual intestinal broil, into which the native population is on all occasions pressed. Foreigners not being personally interfered with, nor sensibly impeded in their avocations, are enabled to do more than maintain the industrial status of the country; hence its products and its trade and substantial wealth continually increase. Moreover, so relatively small is the pro-

portion of those men who at the present time are available for intestinal struggles, that the effects of irregular warfare are to a certain extent neutralized; and the time is not distant when, from the same fact, such warfare will be impossible. Indeed, it has been already much modified in character by the large foreign interests and other influences brought to bear upon it. Supplies taken from the estates of foreigners must be paid for, and the victorious party has to pay for all.

In Buenos Ayres the direct material intervention of foreigners in the politics of the country has been merely nominal; but these economic and industrial interests and influences are of longer standing, and are more deeply rooted than in any other part of the Confederation. These interests are of greater value than any in the Banda Oriental. The former have been developed by fusion; the latter are rather the result of absorption. . . .

Liberated from the incubus of the Dictatorship, and confiding in the perpetuity of the new order, men awoke as from a cataleptic swoon, and entered with enthusiasm into all questions of material progress — the progress achieved strengthening in its turn the principle to which it owed its origin. The system of municipalities was adopted in both town and country, the members being duly elected by popular vote from among the district residents, foreign and native; municipal schools were established, with a free press alike for foreigners as for natives. Moles and wharfs shot up, and a large extent of street surface was paved in the city of Buenos Ayres; the streets were lighted with gas; carriages, cabs, and omnibuses crowded them; houses — almost palaces — sprang up in every block; and the city increased rapidly in extent and population — the latter doubling itself in a single decade. Railways, canals, and telegraphs were projected, and are now in operation; steamers, in quick succession, coursed the rivers and connected every town of any importance with the commercial centres of Buenos Ayres and Montevideo; rural industries were prosecuted with eagerness, if with little skill, and men of all nationalities began to root themselves to the soil.

Foremost among the actors in industrial undertakings were, as a matter of course, the foreign residents, and foreign capitalists cooperating from without.

The purchases of lands by foreigners were very large indeed, and the multiplication of sheep was as rapid as the increase of commerce:

value so rose as to overshoot equilibrium. Near the cities, the enclosure of lands for agricultural and horticultural purposes, scarcely before known, went on year by year to such an extent that to-day, around the city of Buenos Ayres, all the lands over a radius of 15 to 20 miles are subdivided and enclosed as farms or market-gardens, cultivated by Italians, Basques, French, British, and Germans. Mechanical trades kept pace with, and contributed to, the general progress, these being, as a matter of course, almost monopolized by foreigners, as it was only from the immigrant ranks that the demand for skilled or other labour could be even partially supplied.

The comparatively useless native population of the suburbs, who lived by growing pumpkins and watermelons and exchanging them for the few pence that sufficed to purchase beef at a farthing to a halfpenny a pound, or doing odd jobs, to obtain the luxuries of maté and sugar (the work of one or two days sufficing to procure enough for a week's feasting), gradually gave place to immigrants of industrial habits, to vegetable and fruit gardeners, fodder growers, artisans, tillers of the soil, flayers, salters, porters, boatmen, and launchmen. The poorer immigrants from other countries bettered their condition and, in many instances, speedily rose to opulence, while they conferred incalculable benefits on the country of their adoption. . . .

In the earlier period of immigration, when the foreign element was at the minimum as compared with the native, the influence of the former was slight; indeed, foreign settlers and their children, subjected to the strongest modifying influence, caught, in sensible degree, the prevailing infection, and frequently acquired the most undesirable habits with the greatest facility; and it is only in comparatively recent years, and in the presence of a rapidly increasing immigrant population, that European influence has asserted itself as an irresistible modifying force now extending itself with giant strides.

In the higher and middle classes of the natives, this modification is perhaps more marked than in the lower. There have been more opportunities and more influences operating materially and intellectually. Naturally polished, elegant, intelligent, and fluent to eloquence, many have travelled under compulsion as exiles, and, since the development of steam communication with Europe, for pleasure and improvement, they have mingled much with foreign residents, polished, intellectual, and (more especially) practical, and there have been many intermarriages.

In commerce, industrial undertakings, and all business transactions there has been continuous and close contact. On political and politico-economic questions there has been a free interchange of views. Very many of the natives speak and read both English and French, and the standard literature of Europe and America — as well as light literature — fills their libraries, is extensively read and by many eagerly and profitably studied.

There is unquestionably a great charm in the polished circles of the native society. The courteous welcome accorded to the intelligent foreigner, and the refined deference with which they meet the expression of practical views, redound to the credit of their good sense and kindly feeling; while their appreciation of the benefits accruing to their country from immigrant settlers, and more especially from the educated and intellectual portion of them, testifies to their discernment. They are particularly anxious that practical men among the resident foreigners should accept seats on their municipal boards, or assist at consultations and discussions on questions of political and social economy. The wish to work out an adequate reformation is widely felt among the more intelligent of the upper class, who see clearly that the position of a nation in which a very large portion of the population and possessors of property takes comparatively little direct part in the working of its social and economic system is abnormal, and that a new country, mainly dependent on colonists for the development of its resources, needs the direct cooperation of all educated and thinking men. There are resisting elements still strong, both among natives and foreigners, and certain stumbling-blocks, which a little time and another step or two in political development and social modification will surmount — at least in the great centres of material progress.

Two periods in the life of these countries are distinguished by the assertion of the principle of political and industrial progress — viz. the present and that of Rivadavia — but differing both in the character of the influences in operation and in their results. Rivadavia had lived in France when the French Socialist school was still at its zenith, and when the ideas born of the French Revolution, modified by the Empire and the Restoration, held feverish sway in Europe. The scheme of development which he propounded to his country was naturally somewhat tainted with these influences, and at best speculative and exaggerated. It broke down, and its failure contributed perhaps in no slight degree to rouse the spirit of contention which led to struggles, arrested at length only by the reassertion of the principles of progress under riper circumstances. The present political and social systems have not sprung, meteor-like, from the luminous brain of an individual, but are the result of influences emanating from new conditions and the circumstances and relations which follow the course of accomplished facts — the substitution of the influences of an essentially practical age for the French ideal of the Rivadavia period.

The progress already made and the modifications already effected in the Province of Buenos Ayres since the fall of Rosas are so great as to place it in an exceptional position in the Argentine Confederation, and mark it out as the central power from which all civilizing influences radiate. The population of its chief city has increased from 70,000 or 80,000 to 200,000; its commerce has been quadrupled; an immense foreign capital is invested in industrial undertakings, lands, stock, and buildings, and employed in commercial, banking, and industrial pursuits, and an exceedingly large foreign population is rooted to the soil. The native population, or certain classes of it, have fairly entered the lists of commercial and industrial development, and have immense stakes in it; and the interests of foreigners and natives are amalgamated to such an extent as to create a paramount mutual interest in the maintenance of order and constitutional government. Railways connect the interior of the province with the capital. A diligence service is established between the outlying districts with the termini and stations along the lines of rail, and a fleet of steam-vessels puts the various river ports in daily communication with the great emporium of trade. Ocean steamers, arriving and departing every two or three days, maintain a close and continuous intercourse with the older world, making its well-tried systems familiar to all classes of the people, and conveying to them a continuous stream of capital, and practical men to work with it. The combination of influences and mutually dependent interests thus created constitute the strongest guarantees for order and stability, while they furnish the means of maintaining them. It is scarcely possible now that the confusion and disorder which have characterised South American republics can recur in Buenos Ayres. Here therefore we have a centre from which all the influences concentrated in it must inevitably radiate. We may add with truth that they are being so extended already.

XXVII

Toward A Latin-American Culture

POLITICAL INDEPENDENCE did not at once free Latin America from cultural subjection to Spain and Portugal. Young writers took the first step toward literary emancipation by breaking with Hispanic classic traditions and adopting as their models the great French and English poets of the romantic school. The romantic revolt found a spokesman of prodigious talent in the Argentine Domingo Faustino Sarmiento, who illustrated his artistic ideas in the formless masterpiece *Facundo* (1845). Romantic freedom of expression soon triumphed everywhere. In 1867 the movement, already in decline, produced its finest prose flower, the delicate love story *María* by the Colombian Jorge Isaacs.

Romanticism, uncovering the picturesque qualities of hitherto neglected scenes and groups, awoke interest in the Indian (generally idealized beyond recognition by his interpreters) and in other national or regional types. In Argentina this trend yielded a rich literature of the gaucho, crowned by the epic poem of José Hernández, *The Gaucho Martín Fierro* (1872). In the same year Ricardo Palma began to publish his ironic and sparkling evocations of life in colonial Lima, *The Peruvian Traditions* (1872–1906).

As the century drew to a close, a galaxy of poetic talents drew on a variety of foreign sources (the French post-romantics, Whitman, Poe, etc.) to create a new literary movement known as Modernism. Artificial and exotic in its origins, Modernism nevertheless succeeded in forging a new, ornate poetry and prose, "entirely new, new in form and vocabulary and subject matter and feeling." The greatest of these escapist poets was the Nicaraguan Rubén Darío, whose first book of verse and prose, *Azure,* appeared in 1888.

Brazilian literature, like that of Spanish America, broke with classicism to fall under the spell of romanticism and then went on to assimilate such European late-nineteenth-century styles as Parnassianism, realism, and naturalism. In the urban novels of Machado de Assis (1839–1908), a master of ironic realism, Brazilian letters displayed a precocious maturity. At the turn of the century (1902) appeared an impressive study of rural Brazil, *Rebellion in the Backlands (Os Sertões),* by Euclydes da Cunha, generally regarded as marking the birth of modern Brazilian literature.

1. THE GREAT TEACHER

The Venezuelan Andrés Bello (1781–1865), distinguished poet, scholar, and educator, made important contributions to the development of Hispanic culture. His Spanish grammar, published in 1857, ended the domination of Latin grammatical rules and forms over the language, and won acceptance by the Spanish Academy. His poem on The Agriculture of the Torrid Zone *(1826), despite its classic form, stimulated the rise of literary "Americanism." In Chile, where he lived from 1829 till his death, he founded the National University, served as its first rector, and helped to train a whole generation of Chilean writers. Conservative in politics and letters, he nevertheless encouraged and protected younger men of more liberal tendencies. The following excerpt from the literary memoirs of* José Victorino Lastarria (1817–1888) *illustrates the attitude of mingled respect and dissent with which some of his disciples came to regard the great teacher.*[1]

IN 1834 PROFESSOR BELLO taught two courses in his own home: one in Grammar and Literature, the other in Roman and Spanish Law. . . .

His teaching of these subjects revealed his immense knowledge and grasp of the material, but his method suffered from a certain narrowness of approach, reflecting the influence of the epoch in which he himself had been trained. The language study was a complete course in philology, covering general and historical grammar, and included the most minute points of grammatical analysis. In these classes Bello continued his practice of writing his textbooks as he taught. His treatise on the inflection of the verb and the most interesting chapters of his *Grammar* were minutely discussed in these long and pleasant conferences with his students.

In his teaching Professor Bello was extremely

serious and formal, disliking all interruption. He never troubled to explain in detail, but simply talked. He always began with the exposition of the question, in order to stimulate his students to think. But he did all the thinking and discussing, generally smoking an enormous Havana cigar, speaking calmly, choosing his words carefully, and never moving one muscle of his face, except when some pleasantry of Domingo Tagle's made him forget himself. Then he would unbend and laugh freely.

His choice library served as our classroom, and the students consulted the authorities right there, under the teacher's direction. We debated every question of law in exhaustive detail.

This method of instruction could have been most useful if given a philosophical direction, but since it aimed solely at mastery of details, it only served to form sophistical lawyers and pedants. Professor Bello was a philosopher, but in his teaching he clung to certain traditional practices that he later abandoned. For example, although he delivered his lectures on Roman law (today so well known) in Spanish, he insisted, over our objections, that we memorize the Institutes of Justinian and study the commentaries of Vinnius in Latin. . . .

The influence of his teaching at that period was immense — it almost amounted to a dictatorship. Professor Bello's students went out from the classroom to spread their teacher's ideas and methods. He personally urged the instructors in the *colegios* of Santiago to foster the study of language and literature. He lamented the corruption of the Castilian speech in Chile, and converted young teachers into fanatical purists who infected their students with the same finicky spirit. From 1835 to 1842 all the educated youth of Santiago were sophists in law and rhetoricians in literature. The spirit of philosophical inquiry penetrated their minds like a flash

[1] J. V. Lastarria, *Recuerdos literarios*, Santiago de Chile, 1885, pp. 65–70. (Excerpt translated by the editor.)

of light while they were studying political science and philosophy at the National Institute; but once they had enrolled in the advanced courses and become part of the circle of elegant sophists and rhetoricians, that light went out, never to shine again. A backward social milieu and an atmosphere of political reaction were largely responsible for this state of affairs.

2. THE ROMANTIC REVOLT

A famous debate arose in Chile in 1842 between Andrés Bello, conservative arbiter of literary taste, and the young exile from Rosas's Argentina, D. F. Sarmiento, who upheld a democratic freedom of expression and the superiority of contemporary French literature over all others. Before the controversy had ended, Sarmiento had silenced his opponent and converted Bello's chief disciple, Lastarria, to his own beliefs. One of Sarmiento's most impassioned outbursts was provoked by a disparaging review of Victor Hugo's romantic play, Ruy Blas, *in the conservative* Literary Weekly.[2]

WHEN THE EXCITEMENT CAUSED by its appearance had passed, a distinguished figure who had never been one of its partisans defined Romanticism with this simple phrase: freedom of thought. Others called it a renovation — that is, a solemn and energetic protest against the categories in which the old social order had encased all of creation; the admission of things formerly scorned, hated, and viewed with loathing, not excluding ugliness in the physical sphere, evil in the moral sphere, and the unusual and strange in the intellectual sphere. Romanticism, then, was a true literary insurrection, like the political uprisings that preceded it. It demolished all the ancient barriers that were thought immovable; it overturned and destroyed all that stood in its path. But it failed to construct anything and disappeared the day it had concluded its task.

What has arisen to take its place? What, at least, aspires to fill its place? Socialism, if you will excuse the word — that is, the ideal of enlisting science, art, and politics in the service of the people, with the sole aim of improving their condition, of fostering liberal tendencies, of combating reactionary prejudices, and of redeeming the people, the mulatto, and all the disinherited. Béranger, gallantly fighting for the people, founded this literary school in France; in Spain,

Bretón de los Herreros has used the theater as a weapon against the Carlists, not disdaining to use the new language of modern Spain, and admitting into his plays the verbal lapses, slang, and vulgarities of popular speech. . . .

The powerful genius of Victor Hugo, having shattered and pulverized all literary chains, felt the necessity of a work of reconstruction, of using the new art to correct the ills of society. He wished to depict a decaying society, a crumbling social structure, a decrepit nobility devoid of virtues, a monarchy about to fall — and to set amid this mire and rottenness a man of the people, whose plebeian rags conceal his genius, but who understands and feels the evils that afflict the nation, who shakes his head and mutters between his teeth: If I were king! If I were the chief minister! If I were the royal favorite! Hugo finds this man in the livery of a lackey; he contrives an opportunity for him to become the chief minister, the royal favorite, and presently the former lackey assumes the dignity proper to genius, kicks out of the royal palace the crowd of venal and corrupt nobles, like Cromwell dismissing the members of the Long Parliament, and sets about establishing order and remedying the ills of the people that he himself had witnessed, felt, and suffered, as do all the oppressed. Hugo develops the idea admirably; the minister-lackey displays in all his actions the stamp of genius and audacity. But in order to resolve the plot, he introduces a trival theatrical effect. He ends by making the lackey, fully conscious of his power, his genius, and his love for the queen, submit to his former master and don his livery again. Thus Hugo destroys like a toy the grand work that he had so brilliantly begun.

Now let's come to the point. Along comes the *Weekly* and proclaims that it can't help "protesting against Victor Hugo, when in *Ruy Blas* he depicts a lackey, who had never been anything but a lackey, as madly in love with a queen, and filled with thoughts and aspirations that would hardly befit one of the haughtiest grandees of Spain. . . . " "Such monstrosities," says the *Weekly*, "are not to be found in nature. . . . "

What does the *Weekly* mean by "a lackey who had never been anything but a lackey"? Does it want him to have been a lawyer, or a noble, or rich — or just *what* does it think he should have been? This is the most stupid statement ever written. Does the *Weekly* believe that the livery of a lackey can cancel out the genius and audac-

[2] *El Mercurio*, July 28, 1842, in *Sarmiento en el destierro*, edited by Armando Donoso, Buenos Aires, 1927, pp. 128–132. (Excerpt translated by the editor.)

ity with which a man is naturally endowed? Does it perhaps suppose that one must have gone to the University and studied the classics in order to possess common sense, perspicacity, and lofty views? . . .

How many popes have been lackeys? How many great leaders began as shepherds? How many great kings knew how to read? During the revolutions, how many thousands of Ruy Blases forged their way to the front by their talents, their virtues, their genius, their valor? The *Weekly* doubtless attributes the extraordinary talents of Napoleon to his college career — and Napoleon, to be sure, never wore the livery of a lackey. But what about Junot the drummer-boy, and Lannes the sergeant, and Kléber, who was the first to understand Napoleon, and King Murat, son of an innkeeper, and all the guerrilla generals of Spain; and what of Godoy, Prince of the Peace, Ruy Blas, and Mehemet Ali, who civilized his country by overcoming its national prejudices and resistance, and understood all that the most colossal genius could comprehend, and O'Connell, and . . . ? Ah, it's a tiresome business, replying to such stupidities. The Spanish-American War of Independence threw up many a Ruy Blas who took advantage of that great social upheaval to emerge from the mass, shoulder a rifle, and end the campaign as a general, a governor, a representative of the people. To this day every republic in America has its share of generals and diplomats who began their careers as genuine lackeys.

It takes a real "classic" to do such violence to human nature, to take the dress for the man, to distort contemporary history and the history of all periods. And then, to find it absurd that a lackey of genius should have loftier ideas than a stupid Spanish grandee! A grandee of Spain! What Spanish grandee of our times has had even middling capacity and talents? The majority of distinguished Spaniards have been plebeians. The *Weekly* is astonished that a lackey should dare to fall in love with a queen! Ask us for a list of queens who have granted their favors to lackeys and cooks, and we shall send it to you. . . .

But the author of all this rubbish sees in the livery of a lackey nothing but the livery; a lackey cannot have more talent than his master, or greater capacity than the author of the article on Romanticism.

This scribbler takes a lackey for nothing more than a lackey. He does not see that the lackey is the peon, the worker, the sailor, the tavern-keeper, the *roto,* the man, in fine, who occupies a lowly place in society but nevertheless may be an exceptional individual. He does not know that a lad raised in the street once saw a man painting and said, inspired, "I also can paint," and that boy's name was Correggio; he does not know that the child Pascal solved problems that his father, a mathematician of repute, could not solve in ten years of labor. He does not know that the majority of men of genius were born lackeys.

3. THE ACADEMY OF LETRÁN

"In the Academy of Letrán," says the Mexican literary historian González Peña, "was incubated the generation which later filled half a century of the history of Mexican literature." The history of this remarkable institution, in which classicists and romanticists sat peacefully side by side, is told by one of its founders, the distinguished poet and statesman Guillermo Prieto.[3]

NOW LET ME TELL how this wonderful Academy came to be.

At a fixed hour four of us were accustomed to meet in the room of José María Lacunza, who enjoyed our meetings so much that he let no business, large or small, interfere with them.

There he would sit at his ease, wearing his coffee-colored work coat, laughing insolently at some joke or other; he wore neither bonnet nor slipper, nor any other part of the "lawyer's uniform," as we call it today.

There sat Juan Lacunza in his gray sackcoat, Manuel Toniat Ferrer and I in our plain overcoats, all with rolls of verses in our pockets. Now J. M. Lacunza, assuming a solemn air, gravely and deliberately recited some composition, say, his *To the Stars.* . . .

After the author had read his composition we would criticize its defects, and sometimes there would be a tremendous row.

The composition was approved or corrected by strict majority vote. These literary exercises had the ostensible aspect of a game, but thanks to Lacunza's encyclopedic knowledge they became real courses of study, usually directed by him. Taking for his cue an imitation of Herrera or Fray Luis de León, he would discuss Spanish literature; at another time, in connection with a translation of Ossian or Byron, he

3 Guillermo Prieto, *Memorias de mis tiempos*, México. 1948, 2 vols., I, 120–126, 153–155. (Excerpt translated by the editor.)

would lecture on English literature. And we, not to be outdone, would pay our respects to Goethe and Schiller, or drag Horace and Virgil in by the beard.

We carried on in this fashion for more than two years, shut up within the four walls of Lacunza's little room. But the news of our meetings leaked out, and we, for our part, wished to bring in friends infected with the same malady of scribbling.

One afternoon in June, 1836, this desire became inordinately strong, I cannot say why. Then and there we valiantly decided to set ourselves up as an Academy that would bear the name of our *colegio;* and to invite our friends to join if they had our unanimous approval.

We organized ourselves that very moment, and Lacunza made the inaugural address.

I cannot explain it, but somehow, although all was as before, the audience appeared more attentive, and the orator grew so inspired that he delivered a grandiloquent, moving, magnificent speech.

When he had finished, amid embraces and applause, the pitcher of water on the adjacent table seemed to be casting glances of cold disillusionment at us.

"We must have a banquet," said Juan; "let's dig into our pockets."

The collection turned up a *real* and a half.

We had to do without the liquor and biscuits.

We agreed to buy a pineapple and use some lumps of sugar, wrapped up in a piece of paper, that were waiting for the coffee to be brought in.

We sliced the pineapple, spread the sugar over it and . . . the banquet was a splendid affair, made still more agreeable by noisy improvisations.

We agreed to have no rules; our fundamental unwritten law provided that a candidate for membership must present a composition in verse or prose, and approval of the candidacy was all that was required for membership.

Having read the composition, the author named a defender, and himself plunged into the debate.

The president was to be the individual whose compositions for the past month had shown the greatest merit; he was to hold office for a month, designating as secretary the first person whose name occurred to him. . . .

One afternoon, gloomy and rainy for certain, someone knocked at the door of the Academy. He proved to be a little old man in a red checkered overcoat; a black suit, new and correct; a white tie, badly made; and a shabby hat with an uptilted brim behind.

The ancient walked with a painful stoop. He had a brown skin, brilliant, expressive black eyes, and a truly Olympian brow, full of majesty.

The little old fellow knocked, entered the room without further ado, and quietly sat down among us, saying:

"I've come to see what my boys are doing."

The Academy rose to its feet and broke into stormy applause that visibly moved the venerable one. The name of Quintana Roo — for that was the name of the visitor — was uttered by every tongue, and by overwhelming acclamation he was elected our permanent president.

The joy over this nomination was as ardent as it was sincere; we felt as if *la patria* herself had paid us an affectionate visit.

Quintana at nineteen had been the adviser and inspiration of the great Morelos. Rich in the purest and most benevolent sentiments; a star in the brilliant pleiade that contained the names of Zavala, Cos, Justo Sierra, and other famous statesmen; an eloquent writer who made known abroad the ideals of our War of Independence, causing Blanco White to say that there could be no slavery where there existed thinkers like Quintana; surrounded by a romantic aura thanks to his love affair with Leona Vicario, the enchanting heroine of the insurrection; honorable, wise, modest, and displaying a simplicity through which shone his goodness and delicacy — such was our president, who accepted his well-deserved post with a voice trembling with emotion.

Quintana was a distinguished latinist, and his conversation was sprinkled with citations from Cicero, Horace, and Virgil.

He himself had struck the lyre with archaic passion, celebrating the glories of *la patria;* at the end of the war for independence he had broken out in epic style:

> Refresh, O Muse! the poetic fire
> Of one who striking on his wingéd lyre,
> Foretold in accents of inspired song
> The glorious ending of his country's wrong.

In his writings on mining, in his polemic on the forms of government, in his correspondence with Benjamin Constant concerning freedom of the press, Quintana was a monument to his country's glory and a star of the first magnitude in our nascent literature.

Quintana's accounts of the War of Independence were fascinating; he brought out with great naturalness the causes of our independence, describing the guiding spirits, the obstacles presented by the opinions of the half-educated, the magic power of instincts that overcame all theories, the store of goodness, love, and redemption among patriots of different positions, of different levels of education, and of social classes that ranged from the most civilized to the most barbarous groups, all confounded in the disorder of the times.

Quintana enthralled us when he told tales of the revolution.

One night, in his house, he related an incident that took place on the eve of the Congress of Chilpancingo.

"Morelos," he told me, "was a robust, broad-faced, brown-skinned priest, of great energy in his walk and movements, of sweet and sonorous voice.

"We were in a small one-room farmhouse; on a small white table burned a tallow candle that cast a pale, flickering light.

"Morelos said to me:

"'Sit down and listen to me, Mr. Lawyer. I must speak tomorrow and I'm afraid of talking nonsense; I am ignorant and want to say what is in my heart. Listen carefully to me, and when I finish, correct me to make sure that I speak sense.'

"I sat down," continued Quintana. "Morelos walked up and down. He had on a white jacket, and a handkerchief tied around his head. Suddenly he stopped before me and began his speech.

"Then, speaking in his own plain way, filled with colloquialisms and even grammatical errors, he developed for me his views concerning the rights of man, the division of powers, the separation of Church and State, freedom of trade, and all those admirable concepts that are embodied in the Constitution of Chilpancingo. . . .

"I listened to him with astonishment, overwhelmed by that simple eloquence, as grandiose as the sight of a volcano; he continued, and I stood up, entranced. He ended magnificently and said to me: 'Now, what do you say?'

"'I say, God bless you' (throwing myself into his arms); 'pay no attention to me, and don't leave out a single word; it was wonderful.'

"'Out on you for a foolish lawyer,' said Morelos, while I remained astounded at the flight that his talent and great heart (for he really had very little education) had given that immortal leader of our independence." . . .

Here let me make some brief reflections on the Academy of Letrán, in order to show that I do not at all exaggerate its importance in regarding it as one of the sources — perhaps the most important source — of Mexican literature.

To be sure, I cannot cite any geniuses like Shakespeare, Calderón, Cervantes, Byron, Goethe, and other stars of the first magnitude of other nations. But it was important that for the first time, in a scientific and conscientious manner, we should have initiated discussions, expressed doctrines, and established principles that were either completely unknown or buried in the libraries of a few learned men.

The extremely gloomy picture that Sr. Pimentel draws in his valuable book, entitled *Critical History of the Sciences and Letters in Mexico*, is most exact; sermons of incomprehensible obscurity; mystical verses that sometimes contained true blasphemies; salutations to successive Spanish kings; cold imitations of Latin and Spanish poets; such was the vassalage of our literature until the beginning of the present century, when Navarrete and Tagle appeared like happy omens for the future of Mexican letters. . . .

The neglect of primary education was great, the study of Latin much preferred and esteemed. The result was that public figures of the highest stature and men with all kinds of doctors' degrees wrote *abrazo* with an *h,* like the character in the *Blind Hen.*

The discussions of the Academy obliged us to study Sicilia, Salva, and other grammarians, and our poetic and literary productions gained in correctness. . . .

The Academy had even greater significance in that it democratized literary studies, recognizing merit without regard to age, social position, wealth, or any other consideration.

And nothing could be more natural. The Academy, born of four penniless students, became a place where men of exalted station rubbed shoulders with and gave the palm to office apprentices, book clerks, and vagabonds like Ignacio Ramírez. It was the scene of a spontaneous evolution in which knowledge, light, inspiration, and genius achieved a noble and generous supremacy.

Never before had meetings of this kind been held in Mexico.

But for me the great and transcendent significance of the Academy was its decided tendency to "Mexicanize" our literature, emancipating it from all other literatures and giving it a specific character. . . .

Pesado in his novel entitled *The Inquisitor of Mexico;* Pacheco in his *Creole;* Ortego in *Netzula;* Rodríguez Galván in *Girl,* in *Manolito the Dude,* in *The Viceroy's Favorite;* Calderón in his *Adela;* and I in my *Insurgent,* dealt with the following themes: Pesado, with the horrors of the Inquisition; Pacheco, with the degraded condition of the Mexican creoles; Ortega with the Aztecs; Rodríguez, Calderón, and I, with our national customs. . . .

The Academy, or more properly speaking, Rodríguez Galván, published three little volumes with the title of *New Year,* in 1837, 1838, and 1839. These volumes remain as mementos of the literary labor that I have described, and whose importance shall be recognized the day that a fundamental study of our literature is undertaken.

4. A GAUCHO EPIC

The appearance of poems, stories, and novels that depicted with naturalness, sympathy, and skillful use of popular idiom the life and customs of national groups hitherto neglected by literature, marked a new and higher stage of Latin-American cultural emancipation. In Argentina the new genre found its supreme expression in the epic The Gaucho Martín Fierro *(1872) by José Hernández (1834–1886). No mere romance,* Martín Fierro *embodied a noble appeal in behalf of the gaucho against the forces of "civilization" that were destroying the old free life of the plains. Walter Owen has written an English adaptation that admirably conveys the spirit of the original. The following lines are from the opening of the poem.*[4]

I sit me here to sing my song
  To the beat of my old guitar;
For the man whose life is a bitter cup,
With a song may yet his heart lift up,
As the lonely bird on the leafless tree,
  That sings 'neath the gloaming star.

May the shining Saints of the heavenly band,
  That sing in the heavenly choir,
    Come down and help me now to tell
    The good and ill that me befell,
And to sing it true to the thrumming strings;
  For such is my desire.

4 José Hernández, *The Gaucho Martín Fierro,* adapted from the Spanish and rendered into English verse by Walter Owen, New York, 1936, pp. 1–5. Copyright, 1936, by Rinehart & Co., Inc., and reprinted by permission of Rinehart & Co., Inc., Publishers.

Come down ye Saints that have helped me
  In many a perilous pass;
    For my tongue is tied and my eyes grow dim,
    And the man that calls, God answers him,
And brings him home to his own roof-tree,
  Out of many a deep morass.

O many singers have I seen,
  That have won a singer's wreath,
    That have talked a lot as they passed the pot,
    Of the songs they sang and the songs they wrought,
Till their voices rusted in their throats,
  As a knife rusts in its sheath.

Now all that a son of the plains may do,
  To none shall I give best;
    And none may daunt with a windy vaunt,
    Or bristle my scalp with a phantom gaunt,
And as song is free to all that will, —
  I will sing among the rest.

I will sing my song till my breath gives out,
  I will sing when they bury me;
    And singing I'll come where the angels roam
    The rolling plains of their starry home, —
Into this world I came to sing,
  As I sang on my mother's knee.

And let my tongue be glib and sweet,
  My words be not halt nor few,
    And the men to come that I shall not see,
    In days to be will remember me,
By the song I sang in the days gone by,
  That now I sing to you.

In a grassy hollow I'll sit me down,
  And sing of the days long done,
    Like the ancient wind that sighing goes,
    Through the prairie grass, I will sing my woes,
The hands I held and the cards I played,
  And the stakes I lost and won.

'Tis little I have of bookman's craft,
  Yet once let me warm to the swing
    And the lilt and beat of the plainsman's song, —
    I will sing you strong, I will sing you long,
And the words will out like the tumbling rout
  Of waters from a spring.

With my mellow guitar across my knee,
  The flies even give me room,
    And the talk is stilled, and the laugh and jest,
    As I draw the notes from its sounding breast;
The high string sighs, and the middles weep,
  And the low strings mourn and boom.

I am the best of my own at home,
  And better than best afar;
    I have won in song my right of place,
    If any gainsay me; — face to face,
Let him come and better me, song for song,
  Guitar against guitar.

I step not aside from the furrowed track,
  Though they loosen their hilts as they come;
    Let them speak me soft, I will answer soft,
    But the hard may find me a harder oft;
In a fight they have found me quick as they,
  And quicker far than some.

When trouble's afoot — now Christ me save,
  And Christ me save from sin, —
    I feel my heart grow big and strong,
    And my blood rise up like a rolling song,
For life is a battle, it seems to me,
  That a man must fight to win.

A son am I of the rolling plain,
  A gaucho born and bred;
    For me the whole great world is small,
    Believe me, my heart can hold it all;
The snake strikes not at my passing foot,
  The sun burns not my head.

I was born on the mighty Pampas' breast,
  As the fish is born in the sea;
    Here was I born and here I live,
    And what seemed good to God to give,
When I came to the world; it will please him too,
  That I take away with me.

And this is my pride: to live as free
  As the bird that cleaves the sky;
    I build no nest on this careworn earth,
    Where sorrow is long, and short is mirth,
And when I am gone none will grieve for me,
  And none care where I lie.

I have kept my feet from trap or trick
  In the risky trails of love;
    I have roamed as free as the winging bird,
    And many a heart my song has stirred,
But my couch is the clover of the plain,
  With the shining stars above.

And every one that hears my song,
  With this he will agree:
    I sought no quarrel, nor drew a knife,
    Save in open fight and to guard my life,
And that all the harm I have done to men
  Was the harm men wished to me.

Then gather around and hearken well
  To a gaucho's doleful story,
    In whose veins the blood of the Pampas runs,
    Who married a wife and begat him sons,
Yet who nevertheless is held by some
  As a bandit grim and gory.

5. THE POET OF THE SWANS

Spanish-American Modernism in its first phase (ca. 1890–1910) represented more than a reaction against the outworn ideals and forms of romanticism; it was an effort to escape from "a world they never made" on the part of the gifted, sensitive young poets who created the movement. Most escapist of them all was the prodigiously talented Nicaraguan Rubén Darío (1867–1916), who peopled his verses with "satyrs, nymphs, centaurs, peacocks, and swans." His poem entitled Yo soy aquel *("I am the Man"), is particularly valuable for its autobiographical details and its literary confession of faith.[5]*

I am the singer who of late put by
  The verse azulean and the chant profane,
Across whose nights a rossignol would cry
  And prove himself a lark at morn again.

Lord was I of my garden-place of dreams,
  The heaping roses and swan-haunted brakes;
Lord of the doves; lord of the silver streams,
  Of gondolas and lyres upon the lakes.

And very eighteenth century; both old
  And very modern; bold, cosmopolite;
Like Hugo daring, like Verlaine half-told,
  And thirsting for illusions infinite.

From infancy, 'twas sorrow that I knew;
  My youth — was ever youth my own indeed? —
Its roses still their perfume round me strew,
  Their perfume of a melancholy seed —

A reinless colt, my instinct galloped free,
  My youth bestrode a colt without a rein;
Drunken I went, a belted blade with me;
  If I fell not — 'twas God who did sustain —

Within my garden stood a statue fair,
  Of marble seeming yet of flesh and bone,
A gentle spirit was incarnate there
  Of sensitive and sentimental tone.

[5] *Hispanic Anthology*, collected and arranged by Thomas Walsh, New York, 1920, pp. 606–613. Reprinted by courtesy of the Hispanic Society of America.

So timid of the world, it fain would hide
　　And from its walls of silence issue not,
Save when the spring released upon its tide
　　The hour of melody it had begot —

The hour of sunset and the hidden kiss;
　　The hour of gloaming twilight and retreat;
The hour of madrigal, the hour of bliss,
　　Of "I adore thee" and "Alas" too sweet.

And 'mid the gamut of the flute, perchance,
　　Would come a ripple of crystal mysteries
Recalling Pan and his old Grecian dance
　　With the intoning of old Latin keys.

With such a sweep and ardor so intense
　　That on the statue suddenly were born
The muscled goat-thighs shaggy and immense
　　And on the brows the satyr's pair of horn.

As Góngora's Galatea, so in fine
　　The fair marquise of Verlaine captured me;
And so unto the passion half divine
　　Was joined a human sensuality;

All longing, and all ardor, the mere sense
　　And natural vigor; and without a sign
Of stage effect or literature's pretence —
　　If there was ever soul sincere — 'twas mine.

The ivory tower awakened my desire;
　　I longed to enclose myself in selfish bliss,
Yet hungered after space, my thirst on fire
　　For heaven, from out the shades of my abyss.

As with the sponge the salt sea saturates
　　Below the oozing wave, so was my heart
Tender and soft, bedrenched with bitter fates
　　That world and flesh and devil here impart.

But, through the grace of God, my conscience
　　Elected unto good its better part;
If there were hardness left in any sense,
　　It melted soft beneath the touch of Art.

My intellect was freed from baser thought,
　　My soul was bathed in the Castalian flood,
My heart a pilgrim went, and so I caught
　　The harmony from out the sacred wood.

O sacred wood! O rumor, that profound
　　Stirs from the sacred woodland's heart divine!
O plenteous fountain in whose power is wound
　　And overcome our destiny malign!

Grove of ideals, where the real halts,
　　Where flesh is flame alive, and Psyche floats;
The while the satyr makes his old assaults,
　　Let Philomel loose her azure-drunken throats.

Fantastic pearl and music amorous
　　A-down the green and flowering laurel tops;
Hypsipyle stealthily the rose doth buss
　　And the faun's mouth the tender stalklings crops.

There, where the god pursues the flying maid,
　　Where springs the reed of Pan from out the mire,
The Life Eternal hath its furrows laid
　　And wakens the All-Father's mystic choir.

The soul that enters there, disrobed should go
　　A-tremble with desire and longing pure,
Over the wounding spine and thorn below, —
　　So should it dream, be stirred, and sing secure.

Life, Light, and Truth, as in a triple flame
　　Produce the inner radiance infinite;
Art, pure as Christ, is heartened to exclaim:
　　"I am indeed the Life, the Truth, the Light!"

The Life is mystery; the Light is blind;
　　The Truth beyond our reach both daunts and fades;
The sheer perfection nowhere do we find;
　　The ideal sleeps a secret in the shades.

Therefore to be sincere is to be strong.
　　Bare as it is what glitter hath the star;
The water tells the fountain's soul in song
　　And voice of crystal flowing out afar.

Such my intent was, — of my spirit pure
　　To make a star, a fountain music-drawn,
With horror of the thing called literature —
　　And mad with madness of the gloam and dawn.

From the blue twilight such as gives the word
　　Which the celestial ecstasies inspire.
The haze and minor chord, — let flutes be heard!
　　Aurora, daughter of the Sun, — sound, lyres!

Let pass the stone if any use the sling;
　　Let pass, should hands of violence point the dart.
The stone from out the sling is for the waves a thing,
　　Hate's arrow of the idle wind is part.

Virtue is with the tranquil and the brave;
　　The fire interior burneth well and high;
The triumph is o'er rancor and the grave;
　　Toward Bethlehem — the caravan goes by!

6. THE LAST DAYS OF CANUDOS

Native and foreign critics agree in regarding Os Sertões, *by Euclydes da Cunha (1856–1909), as Brazil's greatest book. The work deals, among other things, with the siege of Canudos in 1896–97, when a handful of wretched backwoodsmen, led by the mystic Antonio Conselheiro, heroically resisted a federal army of some six thousand men. In his style — now lush and sensuous, now rugged; in his unsparing realism; and in his outspoken but unsentimental sympathy with the semibarbarous folk of the backlands, Cunha blazed a trail for the regional and social novelists who dominate the Brazilian literary scene today. The following excerpt from* Os Sertões *records some incidents from the last stand of Canudos.*[6]

FLOUNDERINGS OF THE VANQUISHED

Something then happened that was truly extraordinary and wholly unexpected. The battered enemy now appeared of a sudden to have obtained a new lease on life and began displaying an incredible degree of vigor. Even yet the troops that had faced him from the start of the conflict had not really come to know him; or, rather, they knew him only from the glimpses they had had of him, as an astute foe, slipping away among the maze of dugouts and luring them on, indomitably repelling the most valiant of charges, and without an equal when it came to eluding the most unforeseen of attacks. He was beginning to loom as a hero in their eyes.

Hemmed in on all sides by thousands of bayonets, the jagunço was merely stimulated and his resistance stiffened; it was as if all this were not more than a fresh incentive to battle. And battles there were, from the twenty-third on, persistent as never before, at all points along the line, involving the entire circumference of the siege as the enemy fought furiously, blindly, trench by trench. It was like a huge and stormy wave that had broken in a tumultuous whirlpool of battle. Halted, dammed, by the advance trenches to the east, it came flowing back with a gleaming wake of rifle fire in the direction of Cambaio, dashing against the steep slopes which there descend to the river; under the direct fire of our trenches above, it then took a northerly course and burst, foaming, down the bed of the Vasa-Barris until it was shattered on the stock-

[6] *Rebellion in the Backlands,* tr. by Samuel Putnam from *Os Sertões* by Euclydes da Cunha, Chicago, University of Chicago Press, 1944, pp. 435–444. Copyright, 1944, by the University of Chicago Press, and reprinted by permission.

ades which formed a dike on that side; whereupon it roared southward, and our men could see it rising and falling, swift and turbulent, within the settlement itself. Having crossed the village, it rose along the bottom of the outlying spurs of Mount Favella — our troops raining fire all the while — and then gave another bound to the east, twisting and writhing noisily, to fall upon the left flank of the Baian Fifth. Repelled here, it once more subsided before the barrier formed by the Twenty-sixth and then drew back from this point to the center of the square, in a serpentine course of many turns and bends. A moment later it was breaking against the "black line." Barely to be made out now in the fitful light of battle, it again surged northward, against the same points as before; ever repulsed, ever attacking, the eddying wave of jagunços came on and on, with the irrespressible rhythm of a cyclone. And then it stopped. The furious tornado was followed by a sudden and complete stillness; and absolute silence fell upon both camps. The besieging forces maintained their battle formation, but they were given at least a moment's respite.

Then there came the thunder of cannon fire, directed at the new church; and above the ruined cornices of that rubbish heap, parlously clinging to swaying blocks of stone, figures could be seen darting about madly here and there in all directions. In addition to the case shots which burst in a spray of bullets, whole sections of the wall, pounded by the artillery, now fell upon them. This was more than they could endure and they were forced to come down, falling and sliding like monkeys, to seek refuge in the near-by ruins of the "Sanctuary." But they would spring up again, unexpectedly, at some point along the line, would launch an attack and be repelled; they would then attack the neighboring trenches and again be driven back, and so on, until they had completed once again the enormous circle of rotating assaults.

Those who, only the day before, had looked with disdain upon this adversary burrowing in his mud huts, were now filled with astonishment, and, as in the evil days of old, but still more intensely new, they felt the sudden strangling grip of fear. No more displays of foolhardy courage. An order was issued that the bugles should no longer be sounded, the only feasible call to arms being that which the foe himself so eloquently gave. The hillocks were now depopulated, and there was no more swaggering and

strutting about in defiance of the enemy's bullets. Men renowned for their courage now
crept cautiously along, scrambling through covered passageways, stooping low and bounding
across the points which were exposed to the
jagunços' fire. Once more, the matter of communications became extremely difficult. The
supply trains, the moment they appeared over
the brow of the hills along the Calumby Road,
were now subjected to a violent attack, and a
number of the men in this service fell wounded
on the last stage of the haul, at the entrance to
the camp.

In brief, the situation had suddenly become
quite unnatural. For one thing, it was hard to
understand how the jagunços, after all these
months of fighting, came to be so well supplied
with ammunition. For they were not in the least
sparing of it. On certain occasions, when the
firing was heaviest, it was as if a prolonged gust
of wind were howling over the camp. At such
times one could hear the smooth hiss of Mann-
licher and Mauser bullets, the deep, sonorous
hum of Comblains, the harsh crack of trabucos,
sharp as machine-gun fire — projectiles of every
species, hurtling over every point of our far-
flung lines: over the headquarters tents; over the
hilltops, all the way to the sheltered neck of
Mount Favella, where the supply-train drivers
and the wounded were resting; over all our
trenches; over the long, winding bed of the river
and the most deeply hidden of the depressions;
bursting through the leather awning of the field-
hospital shed, causing the patients to start up
in a spasm of fear; shattering glass vials in the
military pharmacy annexed to the hospital;
swooping inexplicably low to graze the leafy
bowers and falling within a palm's breadth of
the hammocks to startle the exhausted combatants who were snatching a moment's respose;
beating like a shower of rocks against the thick
walls of the huts that housed the engineering
commission and the First Column headquarters; flaying with the whine of a lash the folds
of the tents large and small, the huts and awn-
ings everywhere; spraying the hillsides, cracking,
ricocheting, bounding off, falling on the schist
folds, rending and shattering them to bits, with
an incomparable profusion of grapeshot.

The battle was feverishly approaching a decisive climax, one that was to put an end to the
conflict. Yet this stupendous show of resistance
on the part of the enemy made cowards of the
victors.

THE PRISONERS

On the twenty-fourth the first prisoners were
brought in. At first, our troops had picked up
no more than half-a-dozen terrified children,
from four to eight years of age, whom they had
found straggling along the road; but a more
thorough search of the captured huts resulted
in their taking a number of women and
wounded men. These latter were few in number
and were in a deplorable state indeed. One of
them, in a half-fainting condition, supported
under the armpits by a soldier on either side,
had a scar on his naked bosom which stood out
sharply, the mark left by the saber which had
laid him low. Another of the prisoners was the
aged and dying curiboca who had not been able
to discharge his rifle at the soldiers. He had the
appearance of an exhumed corpse limping
along. Months ago he had been wounded in the
abdomen by the splinters from a grenade, and
in his belly were two red-bordered cicatrized
holes through which his intestines had pro-
truded. His voice, a stifled cry, died in his
throat. They did not question him but left him
in the shade of a tent to continue enduring the
agony which he had been suffering for three
whole months perhaps.

Some of the women gave information of a revealing character. Villa Nova the day before
had slipped away from the settlement, by the
Varzea da Ema trail. For some time now they
had felt the pangs of hunger, since practically
all their provisions were reserved for the fighting men. A still more important revelation concerned the failure of the Counselor to make his
appearance for quite a long while. In addition
to this, now that all their means of egress had
been cut off, the inhabitants of the settlement
were beginning to suffer the growing tortures of
thirst.

That was as far as their information went.
Those who revealed these facts were in so weakened a condition that they were barely able to
reply to questions. There was one man alone
who did not, like the others, show the effects of
the privations they had endured. Sturdily built,
of medium height and broad shouldered — a
perfect specimen of backland Hercules of the
kind to be seen at fairs, with a bony framework
that was like iron, and gnarled and prominent
joints — he was, everything went to show, a
frontline fighter, possibly one of those acrobatic
warriors who had clung so agilely to the ruined

cornices of the new church. Originally white, he was sunburned all over and his face was spotted with freckles. From his girdle there dangled, to a point below his knee, the empty sheath of a scraping knife. They had captured him in the thick of the fight. Having valiantly attacked and brought down three or four soldiers, he would have made good his escape had he not been knocked silly by a slanting bullet which struck him in the left eye socket. They now brought him, throttled like a wild beast, into the tent of the First Column commander. There they loosened their hold on him, and, as he stood there panting from the struggle, he raised his head, one eye gleaming brightly, the other filled with blood, in a glance that was terrifying. Awkwardly, he stammered a few words which they could not make out; then, taking off his broadbrimmed leather hat, he said something about sitting down. This was a supreme act of insolence on the bandit's part! Powerful hands laid hold of him and brutally tumbled him through the other door. Outside, with no protest on his part, they ran a rope around his neck, then dragged him over to the right side of the camp, where the poor fellow and his sinister guards were swallowed up in the bosom of the caatinga.

The Execution

As soon as they reached the first sheltered spot, a horrible but commonplace incident occurred. In such cases the soldiers would invariably demand that the victim shout a viva to the Republic, a demand that was seldom complied with. This was but the customary prologue to the cruel scene that was to follow. Seizing the prisoner by the hair, they would bend his head backward to expose his throat and then would decapitate him. Not infrequently, however, the greedy assassins were too impatient to wait for these lugubrious preparations, and matters would then be expedited with a quick thrust of the knife, a single thrust in the lower belly, ripping out the guts.

We had brave men among us who looked forward eagerly to such repugnant acts of cowardice as this — acts which were given the tacit and explicit sanction of the military leaders. Despite their three centuries of backward development, the sertanejos by no means carried off the palm from our troops when it came to deeds of barbarism.

Deposition by the Author

It is our purpose rudely to unveil these barbarities by making a deposition in the matter.

The incident which we have narrated was a common enough one, a mere insignificant detail in the whole of things. It all began under the spur of an irritation occasioned by the first reverses which our troops met with and had ended by becoming the coolly accepted practice, a mere trifle from the point of view of the larger exigencies of the war. The moment an able-bodied jagunço, capable of supporting the weight of a musket, had been taken prisoner, there was not a second to be wasted in futile deliberation. Off with his head, out with his guts. One or another commanding officer might put himself to the trouble of making an expressive gesture; but, if he did so, it was so useless as to provoke surprises; it was something the soldier, accustomed to and eager for his task, could well dispense with.

That task, as we have seen, was a simple one. Fasten a leather thong around the victim's neck in the form of a halter or slipknot, then drag him along between the rows of tents; no need to worry about anyone's being shocked by the procedure and no need to fear that the prey might escape, for, at the least sign of resistance or attempted flight, all one had to do was to give a tug on the rope and the lasso would anticipate the work of the knife, and strangulation would take the place of beheading. They would go on until they came to the first deep concavity in the hills, a precaution which in itself was a superfluous formality, and then would stab the fellow to death. At this point, depending upon the humor of the executioner, certain slight variations might be introduced. As is well known, the one thing the sertanejo fears above everything else is dying by cold steel; not from fear of death but from fear of the consequences of this particular kind of death; for they believe that, so dying, their souls will not be saved.

Our men exploited this naive superstition. They would frequently promise the jagunço the reward of a bullet if he would give them desired information. The information was rarely forthcoming. In the majority of cases the prisoners would remain stoically mute and unshakable — facing eternal perdition. The soldiers would then demand that they shout viva's to the Republic; or for this sorry jest they would substitute mocking insults and cruel allusions, as the brutal and hilarious chorus drove home their barbed jibes. After that they would lose no time in beheading their prisoner or hacking his abdomen with knife thrusts. This obscure, unchronicled tragedy would take place against the somber and impoverished background of the hilly slopes, bristling with stones and cacti; and, with bursts of ghoulish laughter, the killers would then return to camp. There, no one asked them any questions about what had happened; for, as has been said, the episode was utterly and lamentably commonplace. The jagunços themselves, when taken prisoner, knew very well the fate that awaited them. The inhabitants of the settlement knew all about this summary brand of justice, and this it was, in good part, which led to their putting up so frenzied a resistance. In view of all the odious tortures they had suffered in the course of this campaign, they would assuredly have given themselves up to any other adversary, but, in the case of the one who confronted them, they chose to fight until the death.

And when at last, captured and throttled, they were led into the presence of our military leaders, they were by that time already resigned to the deplorable fate that was in store for them. Their bearing was uniformly marked by a strange serenity, a serenity that was hard to explain in view of the many and discordant types of character to be found among them — mestizos of every sort, with temperaments as varied as were the shadings of their skin. Some of these beings on the lowest rung of our racial ladder displayed an incredible haughtiness in the presence of their captors. Let us note an example or two.

There was one Negro, one of the few pure blacks that were there, who, having been captured during the latter part of September, was brought before the commander of the First Column, General João da Silva Barbosa. He was still panting and exhausted from the engagement in which he had been taken and from having been dragged and shoved along by the soldiers. Tall and lean in appearance, his gaunt and slightly stooping frame showed all the rigors of hunger and of battle, his emaciation causing him to seem even taller than he was. His inordinately long hair afforded but a glimpse of his narrow brow, and his markedly prognathous face, all but lost in his cottony beard, was a bruised and filthy mask. He reeled as he walked; and his tottering, infirm step, his woolly head, the scant bit of his countenance that was to be seen, his flattened nose, thick lips, his crookedly protruding teeth, his tiny eyes sparkling brightly in their deep sockets, his long, bare, dangling arms — all this gave him the wizened appearance of a sickly orangutan.

They did not waste any time on him; for he was an animal, not worth questioning. The general of the brigade, João da Silva Barbosa, from the hammock where he lay convalescing from his recent wound, made a gesture, and a corporal attached to the engineering commission, who was famous for such exploits, at once grasped the meaning of it and brought out the rope. Of diminutive stature himself, he had difficulty in adjusting the halter about the condemned man's throat; whereupon the prisoner calmly gave him a hand, fastening about his own neck the noose that was to throttle him.

Near by, looking on at this scene, were a headquarters lieutenant of the first class and a fifth-year medical student. They now beheld a change come over the poor fellow the moment he took his first few steps toward his execution. That begrimed and filthy body, barely supported by the long, withered limbs beneath, now of a sudden took on admirably — and terribly — sculpturesque lines, exhibiting a plasticity that was nothing less than stupendous. It was a statuesque masterpiece, modeled out of the mire. The Negro's stooping frame was now rigid and erect, striking a pose that was exceedingly beautiful in the pride of bearing it expressed; head up, shoulders thrown back, chest out, with all the defiant hauteur of a nobleman of old, as a pair of flashing eyes lighted up the manly face. Resolutely, impassively, he followed where his captor led — silently, his face immovable, his flabby muscles standing out against the bones of his skeleton-like figure, and with an impeccable demeanor. Truly, he was a statue, an ancient statue of a Titan, buried four centuries ago and now exhumed, blackened and mutilated, in that enormous ruin heap of Canudos. It was an inversion of roles, a shameful antinomy.

Yet these things created no impression.

One concession at least they made to that respect which was due the human race: they did not slaughter the women and children. There was, however, a proviso attached to this: the prisoners must not give signs of being dangerous. There was the case of the forty-year-old mameluca who on one occasion was captured and brought to the tent of the commander-in-chief. The general was not feeling well and interrogated her from his campaign cot, surrounded by a large number of officers. The usual questions were put to her, as to how many fighting men there were in the settlement, what conditions were like there, what resources they possessed, and so forth, questions which ordinarily met with an "I don't know!" or a wavering and ambiguous "How should I know?" But this woman was impudent, aggressive, and irascible and very imprudently gave vent to her feelings.

"It's no use asking me all those questions. You know very well that you are done for. You are not besieging us; you are our prisoners. You won't be able to go back as the other expeditions did. The fact is, you are going to be worse off than they were — You're going to remain here, every man of you, blindly groping your way over these hills." These words were accompanied by gestures that were rude and unrestrained and quite unsuited to the occasion.

All this was irritating. She was a dangerous old shrew and deserved no consideration at the hands of the conquerors. As they left the tent a sub-lieutenant and a few privates seized her; and this woman, this demon in petticoats, this witch who was prophesying defeat when victory was near at hand — she was beheaded.

The timid ones were generally spared but were looked upon as inconvenient encumbrances, useless pieces of baggage. This was the case with one old woman who, with her two grandchildren around ten years of age, had been billeted next the slope where the cavalry detachment was encamped. The stunted little ones were so weak that they could no longer stand and had gone back to creeping. They cried terribly from hunger; and the grandmother, driven to despair by their plight, would go from tent to tent begging for leftovers of food; then she would hasten back and wrapping their bodies in the remnants of old shirts, would lull them to sleep. Busily, tirelessly, she watched over them like this, going here, there, and everywhere in search of an old blouse, a crust from a soldier's knapsack, or a bit of water. Bent over with age and suffering, staggering, reeling from side to side, shaken by a consumptive's hacking cough, she was a sight to move even the hardest of hearts. She was something in the nature of a chastisement, as she came and went like the impertinent and persevering ghost of an old remorse.

Decapitation, our men flatly averred, was infinitely preferable. For this was not a campaign; it was a slaughter-house. It was a matter not of law but of vengeance. A tooth for a tooth. There were the ashes of Moreira Cesar; others must burn. There was the decapitated trunk of Colonel Tamerindo; other heads must fall. Revenge thus knew two poles — fire and the knife. For all this they found justification. There was Colonel Carlos Telles, who once had spared a captive sertanejo. The assassin's ferocity beat a retreat in the presence of this generous-souled hero. But he had paid for it; he had paid for this unpardonable lapse, for the luxury of being kindhearted. The jagunço whose life he had saved had succeeded in escaping afterward, and he it was who had fired the shot which removed the colonel from the scene of action. They believed such stories as these; they made them up, seeking in advance an absolution for their misdeeds. At other times they deliberately exaggerated their feelings. There were their martyred friends who, having fallen into the enemy's treacherous snares, had been ruthlessly slain. Not only that; the jagunços had made sport of their corpses, hanging them up like scarecrows along the road. Their own merciless acts of savagery were thus transformed into acts of compassion for their dead comrades, acts of mourning. Bathed in tears, they washed their hands in blood.

A CRY OF PROTEST

What was more, they had not to fear the formidable judgment of posterity: for History would not go as far as that. Concerned with the fearful physiognomy of peoples amid the majestic ruins of vast cities, against the supremely imposing background of cyclopic coliseums, with the glorious butchery of classic battles and the epic savagery of great invasions, History would have no time for this crude slaughter pen.

The backlands are a refuge for the criminal. Whoever goes along these trails and, by the side of the road, sees a cross standing above the grave of the assassin's victim does not pause to investigate the crime but lifts his hat and passes on. The punitive powers of the constituted authorities assuredly do not extend to these regions. In this case the crime was a public one. The government's chief representative in Monte Santo knew all about it, and he kept silent, thereby covering it with the mantle of a culpable indifference. The offenders knew that they would go unpunished, and they were further protected by anonymity and by the tacit complicity of the only ones who were in a position to repress the crimes in question. The result was, all the accumulated rancors burst forth, as a criminal multitude, armed to the teeth and paid to kill, fell upon the wretched backlands populace.

Canudos was appropriately enough surrounded by a girdle of mountains. It was a parenthesis, a hiatus. It was a vacuum. It did not exist. Once having crossed that cordon of mountains, no one sinned any more. An astounding miracle was accomplished and time was turned backward for a number of centuries. As one came down the slopes and caught sight of the enormous bandits' den that was huddled there, he well might imagine that some obscure and bloody drama of the Stone Age was here taking place. The setting was sufficiently suggestive. The actors, on one side and the other, Negroes, caboclos, white and yellow skinned,

bore on their countenances the indelible imprint of many races — races which could be united only upon the common plane of their lower and evil instincts. A primitive animality, slowly expunged by civilization, was here being resurrected intact. The knot was being undone at last. In place of the stone hatchet and the harpoon made of bone were the sword and the rifle; but the knife was still there to recall the cutting edge of the ancient flint, and man might flourish it with nothing to fear — not even the judgment of the remote future.

But, nevertheless, for the light of a future day, let this passage stand, even though it be one marked by no brilliance, uncompromising, angry, unedifying by reason of the subject matter, brutal, violent, because it is a cry of protest, somber as the bloodstain that it reflects.

XXVIII

Brazil: From Empire to Republic

MORE FORTUNATE THAN HER SPANISH-AMERICAN NEIGHBORS, independent Brazil made a relatively easy and rapid transition to a stable political order. To the troubled reign of Dom Pedro I (1822–1831) and the stormy years of the Regency (1831–1840) succeeded the long and serene reign of Dom Pedro II (1840–1889). Brazil's ruling class of great landowners deliberately sacrificed "liberty with anarchy for order and security," in the words of Professor Manchester, and vested the young Emperor, called to rule at the age of fifteen, with virtually absolute power. The generally upward movement of Brazilian economic life and the tact, wisdom, and firmness of the Emperor contributed to the success with which the system functioned for half a century.

Only one serious foreign crisis — the exhausting Paraguayan War (1874–1879) — marred Dom Pedro's reign. Economic and social change dominated the period. As the sugar-growing Northeast and its patriarchal slave society declined because of competition from foreign sugars, coffee-raising São Paulo, which was gradually shifting to the use of free immigrant labor, gained in prosperity and importance. The rise (after 1850) of banks, corporations, stock exchanges, and other institutions of capitalism further weakened the position of the old-style plantation aristocracy.

The new business and land-owning groups, employing free labor, grew increasingly impatient with the highly centralized imperial régime and the dominant influence of slave-owning fazendeiros within it. Rising anti-slavery agitation was accompanied by a slower growth of republican propaganda. Popular pressure for emancipation became irresistible. In 1888 the Brazilian parliament, with the approval of the Emperor's daughter, passed a law abolishing slavery. One year later, weakened by the defection of a large portion of the rural aristocracy, by quarrels with the Church, and by discontent on the part of the Army, the Empire was overthrown, Dom Pedro departed into exile, and the victorious rebels proclaimed Brazil a federative republic.

1. DOM PEDRO II: A POLITICAL PORTRAIT

Historians and biographers of Dom Pedro II (1825–1891) have written sufficiently concerning his amiable, democratic traits, his patronage of arts and letters, and his scholarly tastes and accomplishments. But Dom Pedro's best claim to fame is the consummate skill with which he guided the Brazilian ship of state for almost half a century. Joaquim Nabuco (1849–1910), famous Brazilian abolitionist, diplomat, and historian, paid tribute to the Emperor's political wisdom in his monumental biography of his own statesman-father, first published in 1897.[1]

THE COMMANDING FIGURE of the Second Empire was that of the Emperor himself. To be sure, he did not govern directly and by himself; he respected the Constitution and the forms of the parliamentary system. But since he determined the fate of every party and every statesman, making or unmaking ministries at will, the sum of power was effectively his. Cabinets had short and precarious lives, holding office only as long as it pleased the Emperor. Under these conditions there was but one way to govern, and that was in agreement with him. To oppose his plans, his policies, was to invite dismissal. One or another minister might be ready to quit the government and the office on whose duties he had just entered, but cabinets clung to life, and the party imposed obedience to the royal will from love of offices, of patronage. So the ministers passively assented to the role that the Emperor assigned to them. The senate, the council of state, lived by his favor and grace. No leader wished to be "incompatible." He alone represented tradition and continuity in government. Since cabinets were short-lived and he was permanent, only he could formulate policies that required time to mature. He alone could wait, temporize, continue, postpone, sowing in order to reap in due season. Whenever he needed to display his own unquestioned authority he shunted the most important statesmen away from the throne. Olinda, perhaps because he had been a kind of rival to the Crown in 1840, only returned to the government in 1848 — to be quickly dismissed — when the Emperor already governed alone, and after Olinda had skillfully served his apprenticeship and no longer put his old political pupil in the shade.

1 Joaquim Nabuco, *Um Estadista do Imperio: Nabuco de Araujo, Sua Vida, Suas Opiniões, Sua Epoca*, São Paulo, 1936, 2 vols., II, 374–385. (Excerpt translated by the editor.)

Bernardo Pereira de Vasconcellos, who had opposed the proclamation of the Emperor's majority, died in 1850 without ever having been made minister. Honorio Hermeto Carneiro Leão, also . . . an opponent of the declaration of Dom Pedro's majority — another independent, a great vassal who bent the knee to no man — was called in 1843 and dismissed in February, 1844. Having these examples before them, younger men learned that without the Emperor's confidence and approval they were nothing. . . .

On one point he had strong feelings and was very sensitive: He must not be suspected of having favorites. After completing his political apprenticeship he dispensed with the counsels of Aureliano Coutinho and reduced him to the position of a statesman just as dependent, just as ignorant of the high mysteries of state, as the others. He did not want towering personalities at his side and in his counsels, men who might employ his prestige to govern as if they had power of their own over the nation. He never conceded to any statesman that position of unquestioned leadership that Queen Victoria had to recognize — after parliamentary self-government had been perfected in her reign — in Gladstone and Disraeli, for example, as independent leaders of the respective parties, possessing a mutual right to return to head the government. No one but he knew what the next day would bring. He set the course of administration, now steering in one direction, now in another; and only he knew the true course of the ship of state. So it was with the slave question; in 1865 or 1866, when Olinda headed the cabinet, the Emperor made his decision. Olinda opposed him, but Dom Pedro won Nabuco, Saraiva, Paula Souza to his side; in the Conservative camp he had the support of Pimenta Bueno. The Paraguayan War crossed his path, and he yielded, putting off the project. Later, with a more amenable president of the council, Zacharias, he pushed the work in the council of state, entrusting to both parties the framing of the future law. Zacharias, however, fell out with Caxias. The war was a primary interest, Caxias was necessary to its success; Zacharias was sacrificed, and with him the Liberal Party. The Conservative Party came to power with a government headed by Itaborahy. The Emperor now put the slave question aside as secondary, in his opinion, to the war; but as soon as the war had ended, the infallible clock of the Palace of São Christovão struck the hour of emancipation. . . .

The work of government was carried on in

this fashion; what are the Emperor's wishes, what does the Emperor not wish? The statesman who would not adjust to these conditions condemned himself to complete failure. For this reason the advocates of a new idea accomplished nothing until they had awakened the interest of the Emperor and gained his sympathy. Once that was attained, all parties and governments followed the Emperor's lead like an avalanche. So it was with everything, especially in the great question of his reign, slavery; the pronouncements of Rio-Branco in 1871, of Dantas in 1884, of Cotegipe in 1885, only came after Dom Pedro had been won over to their point of view. In 1888 Cotegipe took advantage of the absence of the Emperor to carry out immediate abolition, but if the Emperor had been in the country he also would have been summoned to solve the problem, though in another way.

His power, however, was a spontaneous, natural phenomenon, the result of our social and political condition. If that power had no check it was not because of the Emperor, but because it was impossible to have free elections with a people like the Brazilian, and because free elections would only have made the electorate more attached to the government, whatever it might be — that is, to the power that had the right to make appointments. That is why his power was indestructible. In effect, there was only one means — short of a republican revolution — of compelling him to surrender his personal power: to confront the omnipotent Crown with independent chambers. But that was just the impossibility; that was the great illusion of the propagandists for direct elections, and afterward of the statesmen who expected direct elections to bring about a regeneration of the representative system. That was the dream of the Liberals of 1868, of Paulino de Souza's Conservatives, and of the Baron of Cotegipe. When, after long resisting the project, the Emperor, who in the end always let himself be conquered — but professing to be only conquered and not convinced — yielded, and Saraiva obtained his direct elections, what were the consequences? That as a result of the first experiment in honest elections anarchy and corruption prevailed everywhere; that the parliament came to reflect the general sickness of the localities — the thirst for jobs and influence, the dependence on the government. . . .

The Emperor always exercised his power: (1) within the limits of the Constitution; (2) in accord with the fictions and usages of the English parliamentary system as adapted by our own parties; and (3) yielding always to public sentiment and opinion. "The honor of my reign can only consist in complying with the Constitution which I swore to obey." The distinguishing feature of his government was the sacrament of form; from the day on which his majority was proclaimed to that of his abdication he never abandoned his role of constitutional monarch. Then, too, the progress of affairs in his reign was not his work; he was only the clock, the regulator, that marked the time or gave the rhythm. In matters of politics, to be sure, the minister never proposed and the chambers never approved any measure that he had not sanctioned; it was he who sounded both sides of the channel that was being navigated. But the origin of his inspirations was to be found elsewhere. If everything that was deliberate and personal in his reign reflected the Emperor's directing will and consciousness, the march of events always proceeded ahead of the wishes of the imperial mover or moderator. Every day, everywhere, his individual action was annulled by the action of social forces over whose agents, reactions, and collisions he had no control. . . .

The Emperor inspired and directed, but he did not govern. He might check on every nomination, every decree, every word of his ministers, but the responsibility for their actions was theirs. He rarely intervened in the political and administrative machinery — the parties with their adherents and official hierarchies, their personnel and transactions. He did not even wish to know about the internal life of the parties, nor did he establish direct and personal relations with them, but only with the leaders who one day would be presidents of the council. We have seen how he proceeded with the latter: he always reserved the right to dismiss them when he chose; that right he always possessed. All ministries had their elements of disintegration. He could impede or facilitate the process of dissolution, as he pleased; there was always an anxious opposition party at his orders, awaiting a summons; within the ministerial camp itself there were rivalries to be used; and he always had at hand the instrument of dissolution. Throughout his reign, from 1840 to 1889, all the statesmen who served under him were conscious that their mandates were not final, their positions uncertain and dependent. . . . But even if their mandates were precarious, even if they entered upon their duties knowing that the first serious disagreement with the monarch must lead to their dismissal, nevertheless the Emperor scrupulously respected the sphere of ministerial action. Nor could the ministers complain of the observations made by the Emperor in the council, for in his role of devil's advocate he elucidated questions, clarified his nominations, deduced precedents, compared the reports brought to him from all quarters . . . , lending to each administration the prestige of his high position and the assistance of his vast experience. At the same time he left to the ministers the political patronage, the distribution of jobs among their partisans, and the administration of affairs, including the realization of the ideas they had advocated while in the opposition. In many branches he hardly intervened at all — in the fields of justice and finance, for example.

That is why the most eminent men of the period were proud to hold those positions and competed for them, despite their uncertain tenure and the qualified nature of their mandates. It was from their number, from a small circle in parliament, that the Emperor always made his choices. He was, in fact, free only to alternate the parties, to pass from one group to the group in opposition, on the same conditions, choosing from what was always a league of chieftains the name that best pleased him at that juncture. Thus they were not royal ministers, creatures of the Palace; they were parliamentary ministers, like those of France in the reign of Louis Philippe, not like those of England in the reign of Queen Victoria. The Emperor could dismiss them, as the electorate dismisses them in the United Kingdom, but aside from this difference — that there was no electoral power capable of sustaining its representatives in the case of an appeal to the country — the ministerial mandate was the same. Yet to aspire to hold office, under existing conditions, was both honorable and legitimate. The Emperor was not to blame for the absence of free elections; the parties were infinitely more responsible for this condition than he, who had almost nothing to do with the abuses that corrupted the elections. The monarch did not degrade his ministers; he respected them, treated them with dignity. As a governor he sought only one glory for himself: to make Brazil a model of liberty among the nations. The truth about his reign is summed up in the epigram attributed to Ferreira Vianna: "The Emperor passed fifty years in maintaining the pretense that he ruled over a free people" — that is, in upholding Brazil's reputation before the world, concealing the general indifference of its citizenry toward public affairs, toward their rights and liberties; in practicing and cherishing the cult of the Constitution as the political divinity of the Empire.

If the Constitution was Brazil's Palladium, Parliament was its Forum; it was for seventy years the center of the political life of the country, the scene of struggles for power and liberty. It was not a great historical theater, to be sure, but Brazilians of the old colonial stocks — whatever the feelings of the new nationalities that may in time replace them — will always regard its ruins with veneration. Nothing would have been impossible there for a true political genius, endowed with real ambition and capable of making his ideals come true; unhappily, we never had a statesman who united to genius the qualities of ambition, independence, and will power. Had one existed, he would have found no obstacle in Dom Pedro II. *He* was not responsible for the degeneration of the political spirit of the chambers, in which once had risen men like Villela Barbosa, Vasconcellos, Alves Branco, and Paula Souza. It is absurd, when one observes that the majority of these men evolved from Conservatives into Liberals, in some cases, and from Liberals into Conservatives, in others, to suppose that it was the Emperor who determined these regular movements of opinion from one to another social pole. He was not the source of that skepticism, or indifference, or political lukewarmness, that replaced the ancient fervor, seriousness, and persistence of the epoch of solid and austere character. . . .

As with parliament, so with the council of state. A grand political conception was this council of state, one that even England might envy us, heard in all the great questions, guardian of the political traditions of the Empire, in which the opposition was called to collaborate in the wise government of the country, where the opposition had to reveal its plans, its alternatives, its mode of attacking the great problems whose solution fell to the lot of the ministry. This admirable product of the Brazilian genius, which complemented the other and equally admirable device of the Moderative Power, taken from Benjamin Constant, united about the Emperor the finest political talents of both sides, with all their accumulated experience, whenever it was necessary to confer about some serious public issue. It made the opposition, up to a certain point, a participant in the government of the country, the superintendent of its interests, the depository of the secrets of state.

That was the system of the Empire from 1840 to 1889. Political life went on in the chambers,

in the press, in the provinces, as in England —
but the parties did not display moderation,
would not resign themselves to free elections;
and as a result the last word belonged, willy-
nilly, to the power that named the ministers,
and not to the chambers from which they came.
But the difference was hardly apparent, because
the Emperor did not upset situations abruptly
or capriciously, being always guided by public
opinion or necessity. The fact is that this dual
mechanism, monarchical-parliamentary, in which
the monarch, as well as parliament, was a director, instead of being a kind of automaton
moved by the chambers, ensured the tranquillity and security of the country for four generations. Had the Emperor not had the supreme
direction, had he not been the independent arbiter of the parties, had he been limited to signing the decrees presented to him, had he been
helpless to change the situation except through
the effect of elections, his reign would very
likely have been nothing more than a continuation of the regency or an anticipation of the
Republic, and the imperial power, slave and instrument of the oligarchy, would have disappeared in a few years in the whirlpool of factions. Men intellectually superior to the Emperor, governing in his name, statesmen of
greater capacity than his own, dispensing with
his intervention and accustoming the country to
regard the throne as vacant, would only have
unleashed the forces of anarchy against themselves — while he, by the sagacious and moderate exercise of his role of constitutional emperor, kept his authority intact for half a century, whereas his father, the founder of the Empire, had only managed to stay in power for nine
years, and the three regencies for four, two, and
three years. . . . In all likelihood the author of
this nineteenth-century miracle of South American politics would have died in the palace of
São Christovão and today would be resting in
the burial ground of the Ajuda, were it not for
the illness that began to weaken his mind in
1887, making him — who wished to appear a
sort of philosopher-king, such as José Bonifacio
de Andrada dreamed that Dom Pedro I might
be, a crowned Benjamin Franklin — timid, almost vexed, to be ruling in America in European fashion.

There was much that was noble about this
imperial policy, a policy of always pushing
down the road that seemed straight to him,
scorning the resistance that must be overcome,
heedless of the resentments that might one day
cut off his retreat. It was a decided and resolute

policy that sought to prevent the formation of
maires du palais, of personalities that might put
him in the shade; that sought to extinguish the
old revolutionary foci of the First Empire and
of the Regency, military and political; that
worked to extirpate feudalism, defiant of justice, superior to the law, an asylum for outlaws;
that struck down with one blow the powerful
slave traffic; that later carried the Five Years'
War to the last stronghold of López in the
Aquidaban; that attempted to achieve the gradual extinction of slavery in his realm; that
sought to subject the Church to the temporal
power. But the inner and profound characteristic of the royal policy was its indifference to
the interests of the throne. . . .

At bottom, Dom Pedro II had the same attitude toward the throne as Dom Pedro I. Neither
would maintain himself in power by bloodshed;
they would be emperors only as long as the
country wanted them, only as long as *everyone*
wanted them; they would not haggle with the
people. The one willingly made the sacrifice of
May 13, 1822, when he implicitly renounced for
love of Brazil the crown of Portugal and its
Empire; the other did not regret years of self-
abnegation and sacrifice for his country. Deposed, he went into exile, burdened with debts
which were nothing compared with the chari-
ties that he had provided out of his civil list.
And he paid these debts, in what was perhaps
the only case of its kind in the history of monarchy, by selling the furniture and jewels of his
palace at public auction, leaving to the State
his library, his only wealth (except his property
in Petropolis), without even disputing ownership of the properties of São Christovão.

The Emperor's persistent policy of indifference toward consequences was thus a policy of
tacit renunciation. It was not the policy of a
sovereign convinced that the monarchy was necessary to the country and determined to regard
it as his primary political interest. If they dismissed him, the fault would not be his; an
honorable settlement of this kind would do for
him. In one of his notes the Emperor wrote:

"If the mistaken conduct of the monarchical
parties should give victory to the republicans,
what will that prove? The monarch will not on
that account cease to be an honest and disinterested man — disinterested in all that does not
touch the welfare of his country, which for him
cannot exist outside the Constitution."

This voluntary dependence of his on the good
will of the country was so strong that, deposed
from the throne, he did not once affirm his right

to rule by virtue of any of the old pacts — that of the Independence, of the Constitution, of April 7, of his majority, and much less by virtue of his traditional Portuguese right.

His was a policy entirely independent of circumstances, indifferent to the personal consequences of his actions. It did not lean on any class, corporation, or party; it presumed the general good will; it rested on the spirit of progress, on trust in his rectitude, on the movement imparted to society by new reforms, on confidence in the general good sense, on disinterested support that would frustrate the intrigues of private interests and assure the unimpeded progress of the nation. . . . If the result should prove the contrary, the royal stoic would resign his throne without a murmur, regretting only for love of Brazil — perhaps his only passion — that he must die in a foreign land, and leaving for posterity to say: *Victrix causa diis placuit, sed victa Catoni.*[2]

2. Life and Manners at Mid-Century

In the 1850's the condition of Rio de Janeiro's streets still offered some justification for the outraged comment of an earlier English traveler who called it "the most squalid and filthy abode of humans under the sun." The life and manners of Rio's inhabitants impressed some uncharitable foreign visitors as being almost as archaic and backward as the city's sanitary regulations. Less severe in their strictures than most visitors were two North American clergymen who wrote the following account of daily life in the capital.[3]

THE CITY-HOME is not an attractive place; for the carriage-house and stable are upon the first floor, while the parlor, the alcoves, and the kitchen are in the second story. Not unfrequently a small area or court-yard occupies the space between the coachhouse and the stable, and this space separates, on the second floor, the kitchen from the dining-room. . . .

The access to the staircase is through the great door whence the carriage thunders out on *festas* and holidays. At night it is shut by iron bars of prison-like dimensions. Every lock, bolt, or mechanical contrivance seem as if they might have come from the Pompeiian department of the

Museo Borbonico at Naples. The walls, composed of broken bits of stone cemented by common mortar, are as thick as those of a fortress.

In the daytime you enter the great door and stand at the bottom of the staircase; but neither knocker nor bell announce your presence. You clap your hands rapidly together; and, unless the family is of the highest class, you are sure to be saluted by a slave from the top of the stairs with "Quem é?" (Who is there?) If you should behold your friends in the balcony, you not only, if intimate, salute by removing the hat, but move quickly the fingers of your hand, as if you were beckoning to some one.

The furniture of the parlor varies in costliness according to the degree of style maintained; but what you may always expect to find is a cane-bottomed sofa at one extremity and three or four chairs arranged in precise parallel rows, extending from each end of it toward the middle of the room. In company the ladies are expected to occupy the sofas and the gentlemen the chairs.

The town-residences in the old city always seemed to me gloomy beyond description. But the same cannot be said of the new houses, and of the lovely suburban villas, with their surroundings of embowering foliage, profusion of flowers, and overhanging fruits. Some portions of the Santa Theresa, Larangeiras, Botafogo, Catumby, Engenho Velho, Praia Grande, São Domingo, cannot be surpassed for their beautiful and picturesque houses in the Brazilian style.

There are various classes of society in Brazil as well as elsewhere, and the description of one would not hold good for another; but, having sketched the house, I shall next endeavor to trace the inmates from infancy to adult life.

The Brazilian mother almost invariably gives her infant to a black to be nursed. As soon as the children become too troublesome for the comfort of the senhora, they are despatched to school; and woe betide the poor teachers who have to break in those vivacious specimens of humanity! Accustomed to control their black nurses, and to unlimited indulgence from their parents, they set their minds to work to contrive every method of foiling the efforts made to reduce them to order. This does not arise from malice, but from want of parental discipline. They are affectionate and placable, though impatient and passionate, — full of intelligence, though extremely idle and incapable of prolonged attention. They readily catch a smattering of knowledge: French and Italian are easy to them, as cognate tongues with their own.

---

[2] "For if the victor had the gods on his side, the vanquished had Cato." Lucan, *Pharsalia*, Book I, verse 128. B. K.

[3] D. P. Kidder and J. C. Fletcher, *Brazil and the Brazilians*, Philadelphia, 1857, pp. 162–178.

Music, singing, and dancing suit their volatile temperaments; and I have rarely heard better amateur Italian singing than in Rio de Janeiro and Bahia. Pianos abound in every street, and both sexes become adept performers. The opera is maintained by the Government, as it is in Europe, and the first musicians go to Brazil. Thalberg triumphed at Rio de Janeiro before he came to New York. The manners and address of Brazilian ladies are good, and their carriage is graceful. It is true that they have no fund of varied knowledge to make a conversation agreeable and instructive: but they chatter nothings in a pleasant way, always excepting a rather high tone of voice, which I suppose comes from frequent commands given to Congo or Mozambique. Their literary stores consist mostly of the novels of Balzac, Eugène Sue, Dumas *père et fils,* George Sand, the gossiping *pacotilhas* and the *folhetim* of the newspapers. Thus they fit themselves to become wives and mothers.

Dr. P. da S——, a gentleman who takes a deep interest in all matters of education, and whose ideas are practically and successfully applied to his own children, who possesses solid acquirements as well as graceful accomplishments, once said to me, "I desire with all my heart to see the day when our schools for girls will be of such a character that a Brazilian daughter can be prepared, by her moral and intellectual training, to become a worthy mother, capable of teaching her own children the elements of education and the duties which they owe to God and man: to this end, sir, I am toiling." Such schools are increasing, and some are very excellent: but, in eight cases out of ten, the Brazilian father thinks that he has done his duty when he has sent his daughter for a few years to a fashionable school kept by some foreigner: at thirteen or fourteen he withdraws her, believing that her education is finished. If wealthy, she is already arranged for life, and in a little time the father presents to his daughter some friend of his own, with the soothing remark, *"Minha Filha,* this is your future husband." A view of diamonds, laces, and carriages dazzles her mental vision, she stifles the small portion of heart that may be left her, and quietly acquiesces in her father's arrangement, probably consoling herself with the reflection that it will not be requisite to give her undivided affections to the affianced companion, — that near resemblance of her grandfather. Now the parents are at ease. The care of watching that ambitious young lady devolves on her husband, and thenceforth he alone is

responsible. He, poor man, having a just sense of his own unfitness for such a task, places some antique relative as a duenna to the young bride, and goes to his counting-house in happy security. At night he returns and takes her to the opera, there to exhibit the prize that his *contos* have gained, and to receive the congratulations of his friends on the lovely young wife that he has bought. "'Tis an old tale"; and Brazil has not a monopoly of such marriages.

Then the round of errors recommences: her children feel the effects of the very system that has rendered the mother a frivolous and outward being. She sallies forth on Sundays and *festas,* arm-in-arm with her husband or brother, the children preceding, according to their age, all dressed in black silk, with neck and arms generally bare, or at most a light scarf or cape thrown over them, their luxuriant hair beautifully arranged and ornamented, and sometimes covered with a black lace veil: prayer-book in hand, they thus proceed to church. Mass being duly gone through and a contribution dropped into the poor-box, they return home in the same order as before.

It is often a matter of surprise to Northerners how the Brazilian ladies can support the rays of that unclouded sun. Europeans glide along under the shade of bonnets and umbrellas; but these church-going groups pass on without appearing to suffer, seldom using even a small parasol.

You remark, in these black-robed, small-waisted young ladies, a contrast to the ample dame who follows them. A Brazilian matron generally waxes wondrously broad in a few years, — probably owing to the absence of outdoor exercise, of which the national habits deprive her. It cannot be attributed to any want of temperance; for we must always remember that Brazilian ladies rarely take wine or any stimulant. On "state occasions," when healths are drunk they only touch it for form's sake. During many years of residence, I cannot recall a single instance of a lady being even suspected of such vice, which, in their eyes is the most horrible reproach that can be cast upon the character. *Está bebido* (he is drunk,) — pronounced in the high and almost scolding pitch of a Brazilian woman, — is one of the severest and most withering reproaches. In some parts of the country the expression for a dram is *um baieta Inglez* (an English overcoat;) and the term for an intoxicated fellow, in the northern provinces is *Elle está bem Inglez* (he is very

English). The contrast between the general so-briety of all classes of Brazilians and the steady drinking of some foreigners and the regular "blow-out" of others is painful in the extreme.

Wives in Brazil do not suffer from drunken husbands; but many of the old Moorish preju-dices make them the objects of much jealousy. There is, however, an advance in this respect; and, far more frequently than formerly, women are seen out of the church, the ballroom, and the theatre.

Nevertheless, — owing to the prevailing opin-ion that ladies ought not to appear in the streets unless under the protection of a male relative, — the lives of the Brazilian women are dull and monotonous to a degree that would render mel-ancholy a European or an American lady.

At early dawn all the household is astir, and the principal work is performed before nine o'clock. Then the ladies betake themselves to the balconies for a few hours, to "loll about generally," to gossip with their neighbors, and to look out for the milkman and for the *quitan-deiras*. The former brings the milk in a cart of novel construction to the foreigner, — or at least he has never seen such a vehicle used for this purpose before going to Brazil. The cow is the milk-cart! Before the sun has looked over the mountains, the *vacca,* accompanied by her calf, is led from door to door by a Portuguese peas-ant. A little tinkling bell announces her pres-ence. A slave descends with a bottle and re-ceives an allotted portion of the refreshing fluid, for which he pays about sixpence English. One would suppose that all adulteration is thus avoided. The inimitable Punch says, if in the human world the "child is father to the man," in the London world the pump is father to the cow, — judging from the results, (i.e. the milk sold in that vast metropolis). Alas! mankind is the same in Brazil that it is in London. Milk may be obtained pure from the cow if you stand in the balcony and watch the operation; other-wise your bottle is filled from the tin can carried by the Oportoense, and which can has often times a due proportion of the water that started from the top of Corcovado and has gurgled down the aqueduct and through the fountain at the corner of the street.

The *quitandeiras* are the vendors of vege-tables, oranges, guavas, maracujas, (fruits of the "passion-flower,") mangoes, *doces,* sugarcane, toys, etc. They shout out their stock in a lusty voice, and the different cries that attract atten-tion remind one of those of Dublin or Edin-burgh. The same nasal tone and high key may be noticed in all. Children are charmed when their favorite old black tramps down the street with toys or *doces.* Here she comes, with her little African tied to her back and her tray on her head. She sings, —

> "Cry meninas, cry meninos,
> Papa has money in plenty,
> Come buy, ninha, ninha, come buy!" —

and, complying with the invitation, down run the little meninos and meninas to buy *doces* doubly sugared, to the evident destruction of their gastric juices and teeth. Be it remarked, *en passant,* that no profession has more patron-age in Rio than that of dentistry.

At length there appears at the head of the street that charm of a Brazilian lady's day, — the pedlar of silks and muslins. He announces his approach by the click of his *covado* (measur-ing stick), and is followed by one or more blacks bearing tin cases on their heads. He walks up-stairs sure of welcome; for, if they need nothing of his wares, the ladies have need of the amuse-ment of looking them over. The negroes de-posit the boxes on the floor and retire. Then the skilful Italian or Portuguese displays one thing after another; and he manages very badly if he cannot prevail on the economical lady to become the possessor of at least one cheap bar-gain. As to payment, there is no need of haste: he will call again next week, or take it by instal-ments, — just as the senhora finds best; only he should like senhora to have that dress, — it suits her complexion so well; he thought of the sen-hora as soon as he saw it; and the price, — a mere *nada.* Then, too, he has a box of lace, some just made, — a new pattern for the ends of tow-els, — insertion for pillow-cases, and trimmings for undergarments.

Some families have negresses who are taught to manufacture this lace, — the thread for which is brought from Portugal, — and their fair own-ers make considerable profit by exchanging the products of their lace-cushions for articles of clothing. One kind of needlework in which they excel is called *crivo.* It is made by drawing out the threads of fine linen and darning in a pat-tern. The towels that are presented to guests after dinner are of the most elaborate workman-ship, consisting of a broad band of *crivo* fin-ished by a trimming of wide Brazilian thread-lace.

These Italian and Portuguese pedlars sell the

most expensive and beautiful articles. A Brazilian lady's wardrobe is almost wholly purchased at home. Even if she does not buy from the *moscato,* she despatches a black to the Rua do Ouvidor or Rua da Quitanda, and orders an assortment to be sent up, from which she selects what is needed. The more modern ladies begin to wear bonnets, but these are always removed in church. Almost every lady makes her own dresses, or, at least, cuts them out and arranges them for the slaves to sew, with the last patterns from Paris near her. She sits in the midst of a circle of negresses, for she well knows that "as the eye of the master maketh the horse fat," so the eye of the mistress maketh the needle to move. She answers to the description of the good woman in the last chapter of Proverbs: — "She riseth up while it is yet night, and giveth a portion to her maidens; she maketh fine linen (*crivo* and lace) and selleth it;" and, though her hands do not exactly lay hold on the spindle and distaff, yet "she looketh well to the ways of her household, and eateth not the bread of idleness," always excepting that taken on the balcony.

We may infer that the habits of servants were the same in Solomon's time as in Brazil at the present day, judging by the amount of trouble they have always given their mistresses. A lady of high rank in Brazil declared that she had entirely lost her health in the interesting occupation of scolding negresses, of whom she possessed some scores, and knew not what occupation to give them in order to keep them out of mischief. A lady of noble family one day asked a friend of mine if she knew any one who desired to give out washing, as she (the senhora) had nine lazy servants at home for whom there was no employment. She piteously told her story, saying, "We make it a principle not to sell our slaves, and they are the torment of my life, for I cannot find enough work to keep them out of idleness and mischief." Another, a marchioness, said that her blacks "would be the death of her."

Slavery in Brazil, setting aside any moral consideration of the question, is the same which we find the "world over," — viz.: It is an expensive institution, and is, in every way, very poor economy. When I have looked upon the careless, listless work of the bondman, and have watched the weariness of flesh to the owner, I have sometimes thought the latter was most to be pitied. Any cruelty that may be inflicted upon the blacks by the whites is amply avenged by the vices introduced in families, and the troublesome anxiety given to masters. . . .

In many families a cup of strong coffee is taken at sunrise, and then a substantial meal later in the morning. Dinner is usually served about one or two o'clock, — at least where the hours of foreigners have not been adopted. Soup is generally presented, and afterward meat, fish, and pastry at the same time. Except at dinners of ceremony, an excellent dish, much relished by foreigners, always finds a place on a Brazilian table. It is compounded of the *feijão,* or black beans of the country, mingled with some *carne secca* (jerked beef) and fat pork. Farinha, or mandioca-flour, is sprinkled over it, and it is worked into a stiff paste. This farinha is the bread for the million, and is the principal food of the blacks throughout the country, who would consider it much deteriorated by being eaten in any other manner than with the fingers. It is an excellent and nutritious diet, and with it they can endure the hardest labor. Coffee or maté are often taken after dinner, and the use of tea is becoming more common. The "cha nacional" bids fair to rival that of China; but the maté, though not generally used in the Middle and Northern provinces, is considered more wholesome than tea, being less exciting to the nerves. Some families have supper frequently of fish; but in others nothing substantial is taken after dinner, and they retire very early to rest. Rio is as quiet at ten o'clock P.M. as European cities at two in the morning. Even the theatre-goers make but little noise, as they are generally on foot, — at least if they reside in the city. So much do the places of public amusement depend on the pedestrians, that if the evening is decidedly rainy it is usual to postpone the performance until another night. It must be remembered that half an hour's rain transforms the streets of Rio into rushing canals, all the drainage being on the surface. On a drenching day, the *pretos de ganho,* or porters, who lounge at the corner of every street, make a good harvest by carrying people on their backs across these impromptu streams. Sales are often announced with this condition: — "The weather permitting." . . .

The Fluminensian lady has occasionally some respite from slave-watching and household cares, when the senhor takes her to Petropolis or Tijuca, or perhaps gives her a few weeks of fresh air at Constancia or Nova Fribourgo. Such visits are not, however, so frequent as one would wish, and the senhora must content herself with *festas*, the opera, and a ball, as a relief from her usual round of duties. An evening-party in Rio generally means a ball. Familiar intercourse with the higher families is difficult of attainment by foreigners; but when the stranger is admitted he is received *en famille*, and all ceremony is laid aside. In such home-circles the evenings are often spent in music, dancing, and games of romps. Here men of highest position are sometimes seen unbending their stiff exteriors, and joining heartily in innocent mirth. A game called *"pilha tres"* is a favorite, and is quite as wild and noisy as "pussy wants a corner." An American gentleman informed me that on one occasion he joined in this play with a Minister of the Empire, the Viscountess (his wife,) two Senators, an ex-Minister-plenipotentiary, three foreign Chargés d'Affaires, and the ladies and children of the family. No one feared any loss of dignity by thus laying aside, for the moment, his ordinary gravity, and all seemed to enjoy themselves in the highest degree.

The Brazilians have large families, and it is not an uncommon thing to find ten, twelve, or fifteen children to a single mother. I saw a gentleman — a planter — in the province of Minas-Geraes, who was one of twenty-four children by the same mother. I afterward was presented to this worthy matron at Rio de Janeiro. . . .

The education of the Brazilian boy is better than that of his sister. There is, however, a great deal of superficiality: he is made a "little old man" before he is twelve years of age, — having his stiff black silk hat, standing collar, and cane; and in the city he walks along as if everybody were looking at him, and as if he were encased in corsets. He does not run, or jump, or trundle hoop, or throw stones, as boys in Europe and North America. At an early age he is sent to a *collegio,* where he soon acquires the French language and the ordinary rudiments of education in the Portuguese. Though his parents reside in the city, he boards in the *collegio,* and only on certain occasions does he see his father or mother. He learns to write a "good hand," which is a universal accomplishment among the Brazilians; and most of the boys of the higher classes are good musicians, become adept in the Latin, and many of them are taught to speak English with creditable fluency. The examination was formerly a great anniversary, when the little fellows were starched up in their stiffest clothes and their minds were "crammed" for the occasion. The boys acted their parts, and the various *professores,* in exaltation of their office, read or

delivered *memoriter* speeches to the admiring parents; and the whole was wound up by some patron of the school crowning with immense wreaths the "good boys" who stood highest during the session. The *collegio* then took a vacation of a few weeks, and commenced again with its boarders, the "very young gentlemen" students. But these things have greatly changed for the better, and many *collegios* are ably conducted.

The principals of these establishments, when gifted with good administrative capacities, reap large sums. One with whom I was acquainted had, after a few years' teaching 20,000$000 (ten thousand dollars) placed out at interest. The *professores* do not always reside in the *collegio,* but teach by the hour for a stipulated sum, and are thus enabled to instruct in a number of schools during the day. The English language has become such a *desideratum* at Rio, that every *collegio* has its *professor Inglez.*

There has recently been a great improvement in the *collegio* as well as in the public schools. The *professores* were summoned, by a commission under the Superintendent of Public Instruction, to appear at the Military Academy, and there to be examined as to their qualifications for giving instruction. If they passed their examination, which was most rigid, they received a license to teach, for which they had to pay a certain fee. The principals also were required to undergo an examination, if the commission should think it proper; and they were not permitted to carry on their *collegios* without a certificate. The educational authorities also asserted their right to visit these private academies at any hour of the day or night, to examine the proficiency of the scholars at any time during the term, to investigate their sleeping-apartments, their food, and whatever appertained to their mental or physical well-being. This was not a mere threat, but schools were actually visited, and some were reformed more rapidly than agreeably. The system of "cramming" was in a measure broken up, and the Empire thus took under its control the instruction given in the private as well as in the public *aulas.* This educational innovation at the capital is owing to energetic measures taken by the Visconde de Itaborahy, and Dr. Manuel Pacheco da Silva, who is at present the President of the first classical institution of Rio de Janeiro, the Imperial College of D. Pedro II. The note of reform was sounded; every duty connected with teachers or scholars was fully investigated, and the revolution was made, notwithstanding the complaints of *professores* who were degraded as incompetent, and parents who found their children rigidly examined and only promoted in the public schools after convincing proofs of real progress.

There is a common-school system throughout the Empire, more or less modified by provincial legislation. The General Government during the years 1854–55 educated 65,413 children: there were probably as many more of whom we have no Government report who were educated by private tuition and under provincial authority. When, therefore, we consider the number of slaves and Indians in Brazil, and also when we reflect that the common-school system is in its infancy, it is an encouraging proportion. There seems to be an inquiry among the educated men and the statesmen as to the plan best adapted to the country. Once in the interior I was aroused from my slumbers by a loud knocking at the door. I hastily opened it, and saw a respectably-dressed Brazilian, who informed me that he was a school-teacher, and, learning that an American was in the village and would leave that morning, he had made bold to come at this early hour (the sun was just peeping over the palm-trees) to ask me if I could either give him an account of the American system of teaching, or could send him documents on that subject. In the same place another teacher spoke to me of Horace Mann's reports on the common schools of Massachusetts!

3. Negro Slavery Under the Empire

Under the Empire, as in colonial times, Negro slavery formed the massive base of virtually all of Brazil's significant economic activity. The condition and prospects of the Negro race in Brazil aroused the lively interest of foreign visitors. Two North American travelers present a summary view of the situation.[4]

THE SUBJECT OF SLAVERY in Brazil is one of great interest and hopefulness. The Brazilian Constitution recognizes, neither directly nor indirectly, color as a basis of civil rights; hence, once free, the black man or the mulatto, if he possess energy and talent, can rise to a social position from which his race in North America is debarred. Until 1850, when the slave-trade was effectually put down, it was considered cheaper, on the country-plantations, to use up a slave in five or seven years and purchase another, than

[4] D. P. Kidder and J. C. Fletcher, *Brazil and the Brazilians*, pp. 132–138.

to take care of him. This I had, in the interior, from intelligent native Brazilians, and my own observation has confirmed it. But, since the inhuman traffic with Africa has ceased, the price of slaves has been enhanced, and the selfish motives for taking greater care of them have been increased. Those in the city are treated better than those on the plantations: they seem more cheerful, more full of fun, and have greater opportunities for freeing themselves. But still there must be great cruelty in some cases, for suicides among slaves — which are almost unknown in our Southern States — are of very frequent occurrence in the cities of Brazil. Can this, however, be attributed to cruelty? The negro of the United States is the descendant of those who have, in various ways, acquired a knowledge of the hopes and fears, the rewards and punishments, which the Scriptures hold out to the good and threaten to the evil: to avoid the crime of suicide is as strongly inculcated as to avoid that of murder. The North American negro has, by this very circumstance, a higher moral intelligence than his brother fresh from the wild freedom and heathenism of Africa; hence the latter, goaded by cruelty, or his high spirit refusing to bow to the white man, takes that fearful leap which lands him in the invisible world.

In Brazil everything is in favor of freedom; and such are the facilities for the slave to emancipate himself, and, when emancipated, if he possess the proper qualifications, to ascend to higher eminences than those of a mere free black, that *fuit* will be written against slavery in this Empire before another half-century rolls around. Some of the most intelligent men that I met with in Brazil — men educated at Paris and Coimbra — were of African descent, whose ancestors were slaves. Thus, if a man have freedom, money, and merit, no matter how black may be his skin, no place in society is refused him. It is surprising also to observe the ambition and the advancement of some of these men with negro blood in their veins. The National Library furnishes not only quiet rooms, large tables, and plenty of books to the seekers after knowledge, but pens and paper are supplied to such as desire these aids to their studies. Some of the closest students thus occupied are mulattoes. The largest and most successful printing-establishment in Rio — that of Sr. F. Paulo Brito — is owned and directed by a mulatto. In the colleges, the medical, law, and theological schools, there is no distinction of color. It must, however, be admitted that there is a certain — though by no means strong — prejudice existing all over the land in favor of men of pure white descent.

By the Brazilian law, a slave can go before a magistrate, have his price fixed, and can purchase himself; and I was informed that a man of mental endowments, even if he had been a slave, would be debarred from no official station, however high, unless it might be that of Imperial Senator.

The appearance of Brazilian slaves is very different from that of their class in our own country. Of course, the house-servants in the large cities are decently clad, as a general rule; but even these are almost always barefooted. This is a sort of badge of slavery. On the tables of fares for ferry-boats, you find one price for persons wearing shoes (calçadas), and a lower one for those descalças, or without shoes. In the houses of many of the wealthy Fluminenses you make your way through a crowd of little woolly-heads, mostly guiltless of clothing, who are allowed the run of the house and the amusement of seeing visitors. In families that have some tincture of European manners, these unsightly little bipeds are kept in the background. A friend of mine used frequently to dine in the house of a good old general of high rank, around whose table gambolled two little jetty blacks, who hung about their "pai" (as they called him) until they received their portions from his hands, and that, too, before he commenced his own dinner. Whenever the lady of the house drove out, these pets were put into the carriage, and were as much offended at being neglected as any spoiled only son. They were the children of the lady's nurse, to whom she had given freedom. Indeed, a faithful nurse is generally rewarded by manumission.

The appearance of the black male population who live in the open air is anything but appetizing. Their apology for dress is of the coarsest and dirtiest description. Hundreds of them loiter about the streets with large round wicker-baskets ready to carry any parcel that you desire conveyed. So cheaply and readily is this help obtained, that a white servant seldom thinks of carrying home a package, however small, and would feel quite insulted if you refused him a preto de ganho to relieve him of a roll of calico or a watermelon. These blacks are sent out by their masters, and are required to bring home a certain sum daily. They are allowed a portion of their gains to buy their food, and at night sleep on a mat or board in the lower purlieus of the house. You frequently see horrible cases of elephantiasis and other diseases, which are doubtless engendered or increased by the little care bestowed upon them.

The coffee-carriers are the finest race of blacks in Brazil. They are almost all of the Mina tribe, from the coast of Benin, and are athletic and intelligent. They work half clad, and their sinewy forms and jetty skins show to advantage as they hasten at a quick trot, seemingly unmindful of their heavy loads. This work pays well, but soon breaks them down. They have a system among themselves of buying the freedom of any one of their number who is the most respected. After having paid their master the sum required by him daily, they club together their surplus to liberate the chosen favorite. There is now a Mina black in Rio remarkable for his height, who is called "The Prince," being, in fact, of the blood-royal of his native country. He was a prisoner of war, and sold to Brazil. It is said that his subjects in Rio once freed him by their toil: he returned, engaged in war, and was a second time made prisoner and brought back. Whether he will again regain his throne I know not; but the loss of it does not seem to weigh heavily on his mind. He is an excellent carrier; and, when a friend of mine embarked, the "Prince" and his troop were engaged to transport the baggage to the ship. He carried the largest case on his head the distance of two miles and a half. This same case was pronounced unmanageable in Philadelphia by the united efforts of four American negroes, and it had to be relieved of half its contents before they would venture to lift it up-stairs.

From time to time the traveller will meet with negroes from those portions of Africa of which we know very little except by the reports of explorers like the intrepid Livingstone and Barth. I have often thought that the slaves of the United States are descended not from the noblest African stock, or that more than a century of bondage has had upon them a most degenerating effect. We find in Brazil very inferior spiritless Africans, and others of an almost untamable disposition. The Mina negro seldom makes a good house-servant, for he is not contented except in breathing the fresh air. The men become coffee-carriers, and the women quitandeiras, or street pedlars.

These Minas abound at Bahia, and in 1838 plunged that city into a bloody revolt, — the last which that flourishing municipality has experienced. It was rendered the more dreadful on account of the secret combinations of these

Minas, who are Mohammedans, and use a language not understood by other Africans or by the Portuguese.

When the delegation from the English Society of Friends visited Rio de Janeiro in 1852, they were waited upon by a deputation of eight or ten Mina negroes. They had earned money by hard labor and had purchased their freedom, and were now desirous of returning to their native land. They had funds for paying their passage back again to Africa, but wished to know if the coast were really free from the slavers. Sixty of their companions had left Rio de Janeiro for Badagry (coast of Benin) the year before, and had landed in safety. The good Quakers could scarcely credit this last information, thinking it almost impossible that any who had once been in servitude "should have been able and bold enough to make so perilous an experiment:" but the statement of the Minas was confirmed by a Rio ship-broker, who put into the hands of the Friends a copy of the charter under which the sixty Minas sailed, and which showed that they had paid four thousand dollars passage money. A few days after this interview, Messrs. Candler & Burgess received from these fine-looking specimens of humanity "a paper beautifully written in Arabic by one of their chiefs, who is a Mohammedan."

In Rio the blacks belong to many tribes, some being hostile to each other, having different usages and languages. The Mina negroes still remain Mohammedans, but the others are nominal Roman Catholics.

Many of them, however, continue their heathen practices. In 1839, Dr. Kidder witnessed in Engenho Velho a funeral, which was of the same kind as those curious burial-customs which the African traveller beholds on the Gaboon River. You can scarcely look into a basket in which the *quitandeiras* carry fruit without seeing a *fetisch*. The most common is a piece of charcoal, with which, the abashed darkey will inform you, the "evil eye" is driven away. There is a singular secret society among the negroes, in which the highest rank is assigned to the man who has taken the most lives. They are not so numerous as formerly, but from time to time harm the unoffending. These blacks style themselves *capoeiros,* and during a *festa* they will rush out at night and rip up any other black they chance to meet. They rarely attack the whites, knowing, perhaps, that it would cost them too dearly.

The Brazilians are not the only proprietors of slaves in the Empire. There are many Englishmen who have long held Africans in bondage, some for a series of years, and others have purchased slaves since 1843, when what is called the Lord Brougham Act was passed. By this act it is made unlawful for Englishmen to buy or sell a slave in any land, and by holding property in man they are made liable, were they in England, to prosecution in criminal courts. The English mining-company, whose stockholders are in Great Britain, but whose field of operations is S. João del Rey in Brazil, own about eight hundred slaves, and hire one thousand more.

Frenchmen and Germans also purchase slaves, although they have not given up allegiance to their respective countries.

If it be asked, "Who will be the laborers in Brazil when slavery is no more?" the reply is that the supply will come from Germany, Portugal, the Azores and Madeira, and other countries.

It is a striking fact that emigrants did not begin to arrive from Europe by thousands until 1852. In 1850 and '51 the African slave-trade was annihilated, and in the succeeding year commenced the present comparatively vigorous colonization. Each year the number of colonists is increasing, and the statesmen of the Empire are now devoting much attention to discover the best means for thus promoting the advancement of the country.

Almost every step in Brazilian progress has been prepared by a previous gradual advance: she did not leap at once into self-government. She was raised from a colonial state by the residence of the Court from Lisbon, and enjoyed for years the position of a constituent portion of the Kingdom of Portugal. The present peaceful state of the Empire under D. Pedro II was preceded by the decade in which the capabilities of the people for self-government were developed under the Regency. The effectual breaking up of the African slave-trade is but the precursor of a more important step.

4. THE ANTI-SLAVERY IMPULSE

Negro slavery was the great domestic issue of Dom Pedro's reign. The agricultural interest that regarded slavery as necessary for its survival fought a delaying rear-guard action against the irresistible advance of anti-slavery sentiment. After 1880 the abolitionist movement assumed the character of a popular crusade. In Joaquim Nabuco, son of a distinguished liberal statesman of the Empire, Brazilian abolitionism found a leader of towering intellectual and moral stature.

His eloquent indictment of slavery, O Abolicionismo (1883), made a profound impression in Brazilian intellectual circles. In one chapter of this book, Nabuco examines the social and political consequences of slavery in Brazil.[5]

HISTORY KNOWS NO EXAMPLE of a free government founded on slavery. The governments of antiquity were not based on the same principles of individual liberty as modern states; they represented a very different social order. Since the French Revolution there has been only one notable case of democracy combined with slavery — the United States; but the southern states of the Union never were free governments. American liberty, taking the Union as a whole, actually only dates from Lincoln's Proclamation freeing the millions of slaves in the South. Far from being free, the states south of the Potomac were societies organized on the basis of the violation of all human rights. American statesmen like Henry Clay or Calhoun, who compromised or identified themselves with slavery, did not properly calculate the force of the antagonism that was later to prove so formidable. The ensuing course of events — the rebellion in which the North saved the South from committing suicide through the formation of a separate slave power, and the manner in which the rebellion was crushed — proves that in the United States slavery did not affect the social constitution as a whole, as is the case with us. The superior part of the organism remained intact, and even strong enough to bend the hitherto dominant section of the country to its will, despite all its complicity with that section.

Among us there is no dividing line. There is no section of the country that differs from another. Contact is synonymous with contagion. The whole circulatory system, from the great arteries to the capillaries, serves as a channel for the same impurities. The whole body — blood, constituent elements, respiration, force and activity, muscles and nerves, intelligence and will, not only the character but the temperament, and above all the energy — is affected by the same cause. . . .

In the southern states of the American Union a social color line was drawn. The slaves and their descendants did not form part of society. Race mixture took place on a very small scale. Slavery devastated the soil, obstructed industrial growth, prepared the way for economic bank-

ruptcy, impeded immigration — produced, in fine, all the results of that kind that we know in Brazil; but American society was not formed from units created in that process. . . .

In Brazil just the opposite occurred. Brazilian slavery, though based on the difference between the two races, never developed a prejudice against dark skin, and was infinitely more sagacious in that respect. The contacts between the races, from the first colonization by the donatories until today, have produced a mixed population; and the slave who receives his certificate of freedom simultaneously acquires the rights of citizenship. Thus there are no perpetual social castes among us; there is not even a fixed division into classes. The slave, as such, practically does not exist for society, for he may not even have been registered by his master, who in any case can alter the registration at will. For the rest, registration in itself means nothing, since the government does not send inspectors to the fazendas, nor are the masters obliged to account for their slaves to the authorities. This being, who enjoys no more right of protection by society than any other piece of personal property, on the day after he has gained his freedom becomes a citizen like any other, with full political rights. Furthermore, in the very shadow of his own captivity he can buy slaves, perhaps — who knows? — some child of his old master. This proves the confusion of classes and individuals, and the unlimited extent of social crossings between slaves and free men, which make the majority of Brazilian citizens political mixedbloods, so to speak, in whom two opposed natures struggle: that of the master by birth and that of the domesticated slave.

Our slavery extended its privileges to all without distinction: white men and black, *ingenuos* and freedmen, slaves, foreigners and natives, rich and poor; and in this way it acquired a redoubled capacity for absorption and an elasticity incomparably greater than it would have had if there were a racial monopoly of the institution, as in the South of the United States. In 1845, the year of the Aberdeen Bill,[6] Macaulay said in the House of Commons: "I think it not improbable that the black population of Brazil will be free and happy within eighty or a hundred years. I do not see a reasonable prospect of a like change in the United States." He appears to have been as correct in his insight into the rela-

---

[5] Joaquim Nabuco, *O Abolicionismo*, São Paulo, 1938, pp. 167–195. (Excerpt translated by the editor.)

[6] A bill that empowered the British government to take unilateral measures to suppress the Brazilian slave trade. The act aroused great resentment in Brazil. B.K.

tive happiness of the Negro race in the two countries as he was wrong in his belief that the United States would lag behind us in the emancipation of its slaves. What deceived the great English orator in this case was his assumption that the color line was a social and political force in favor of slavery. On the contrary, its chief strength consists in banishing race prejudice and opening the institution to all classes. But for this very reason the greatest possible ethnic chaos prevailed among us, and the confusion that reigns in the regions where the process of national unity is working itself out with all those heterogenous elements reminds one of the proud disorder of the incandescent stars.

Athens, Rome, and Virginia were, to draw an analogy from chemistry, simple mixtures in which the different elements retained their individual properties; Brazil, on the other hand, is a compound in which slavery represents the causal affinity. The problem that awaits solution is how to make a citizen of this compound of master and slave. The problem of the American South was very different, because there the two species did not mix. Among us slavery did not exert its influence exclusively below the Roman line of *libertas;* it also exerted it within and above the sphere of *civitas;* it leveled all the classes, except the slaves, who always live in the social depths; but it leveled them by degrading them. Hence the difficulty, in analyzing its influence, of discovering some feature in the temperament of the people, or in the aspect of the country, or even in the social heights most distant from the slave huts, which should not be included in the national synthesis of slavery. Consider our different social classes. They all present symptoms of retarded or impeded development, or what is worse, of artificial, premature growth. . . .

An important class whose development is impeded by slavery comprises the cultivators who are not landowners and the dwellers in the countryside and the hinterlands in general. We have already seen the unhappy state of this class, which constitutes nearly our entire population. Since they lack all independence and are dependent on another man's whims, the words of the Lord's Prayer, "Give us this day our daily bread," have for the members of this class a concrete and real significance. Their plight is not that of workers, who, dismissed from one factory, can find work in another establishment, or of day laborers who can go to the labor market to offer their services, or of families which can

emigrate; they constitute a class without means or resource — taught to consider work a servile occupation, having no market for its products, and far removed from a region of wage labor (if there is such an *El Dorado* in our country) — a class that consequently must resign itself to living and raising its children in dependency and misery.

This is the picture which a compassionate sugarmill owner presented of a section — the most fortunate section — of this class at the Agricultural Congress held in Recife in 1878:

"The cultivator who is not a sugarmill owner leads a precarious life; his labor is not remunerated; his personal dignity is not respected; he is at the mercy of the sugarmill owner on whose land he lives. There is not even a written contract to bind the interested parties; everything is based on the absolute will of the sugarmill owner. In exchange for a dwelling, often of the most wretched kind, and for permission to cultivate a patch of manioc, invariably situated in the most unproductive land — in return for this the sharecropper divides equally with the sugarmill owner the sugar obtained from his crop. The owner also gets all the syrup and rum derived from the sugarcane; all the refuse — an excellent fuel for the manufacture of sugar; and all the sugarcane leaves, which provide a succulent food for his cattle. Thus the landowner receives the lion's share — all the more unjustly when it is remembered that the sharecropper bears all the expense of planting, cultivation, cutting, and preparation of the cane, and of its transport to the sugarmill." . . .

And this is a favored class, that of the sharecroppers, below which there are others who have nothing of their own, tenants who have nothing to sell the landowner and who lead a nomadic existence, having no obligations to society and denied all protection by the State.

Consider now the other classes whose development is retarded by slavery — the working and industrial classes, and the commercial classes in general.

Slavery does not permit the existence of a true working class, nor is it compatible with the wage system and the personal dignity of the artisan. The artisan himself, in order to escape the stigma with which slavery brands its workers, attempts to widen the gulf that separates him from the slave, and becomes imbued with a sense of superiority that is base in one who himself emerged from the servile class or whose parents were slaves. For the rest, there can be no strong, respected, and intelligent working class where the employers of labor are accustomed to order slaves about. As a result, the workers do not have the slightest political influence in Brazil.

Slavery and industry are mutually exclusive terms, like slavery and colonization. The spirit of the former, spreading through a country, kills every one of the human faculties from which industry springs — initiative, inventiveness, individual energy, and every one of the elements that industry requires — the formation of capital, an abundance of labor, technical education of the workers, confidence in the future. Agriculture is the only Brazilian industry that has flourished in native hands. Commerce has prospered only in the hands of foreigners. . . . The advent of industry has been singularly retarded in our country, and it is barely making its entrance now.

Brazilian large-scale commerce does not possess the capital available to foreign commerce, in either the export or the import trade; and retail trade, at least as concerns its prosperous sector, with its own life, is practically a foreign monopoly. At various times in our history this has provoked popular demonstrations, proclaiming that retail commerce must become Brazilian, but this cry was characteristic of the spirit of exclusivism and hatred of competition, no matter how legitimate, in which slavery reared our people. More than once it was accompanied by uprisings similar in character but actuated by religious fanaticism. Those who supported the program of closure of Brazilian ports, and of annulling all the progress made since 1808, were unaware that if we took retail commerce away from foreigners it would not pass into native hands but would simply create a permanent shortage of goods — because it is slavery, not nationality, that prevents any significant development of Brazilian retail trade.

In relation to commerce, slavery proceeds in this fashion: It shuts off to trade, whether from distrust or from a spirit of routine, all of the interior except the provincial capitals. Aside from the towns of Santos and Campinas in São Paulo, Petropolis and Campos in Rio de Janeiro, Pelotas in Rio Grande do Sul, and a few other cities, outside the capitals you will not find a business establishment that is more than a little shop selling articles necessary for life, and these are generally crudely made or adulterated. Just as you will find nothing that betokens intellectual progress — neither bookstores nor newspapers — so will you find no

trace of commerce except in the ancient rudimentary form of the store-bazaar. Consequently, aside from the articles that are ordered directly from the capital, all commercial transactions take the form of barter, whose history is the history of our whole interior. Barter, in fact, is the "pioneer" of our commerce, and represents the limits within which slavery is compatible with local exchange.

Yet commerce is the fountainhead of slavery, and its banker. A generation ago it supplied plantation agriculture with African slaves; many rural properties fell into the hands of slave traders; and the fortunes made in the traffic (for which counterfeit money sometimes had a great affinity), when not converted into town and country houses, were employed in assisting agriculture by way of loans at usurious rates. At present the bond between commerce and slavery is not so dishonorable for the former, but their mutual dependence continues to be the same. The princes of commerce are slave owners; coffee always reigns on the exchanges of Rio and Santos; and commerce, in the absence of industry and free labor, can function only as an agent of slavery, buying whatever it offers and selling whatever it needs. That is why in Brazil commerce does not develop or open new perspectives for the country; it is an inactive force, without stimuli, and conscious that it is merely an extension of slavery, or rather the mechanism by which human flesh is converted into gold and circulates, within and outside the country, in the form of letters of exchange. Slavery distrusts commerce, as it distrusts any agency of progress, whether it is a businessman's office, a railroad station, or a primary school; yet slavery needs commerce — and so the latter tries to live with it on the best possible terms. But so long as slavery endures, commerce must always be the servant of a class, and not an independent national agent; it cannot thrive under a régime that will not permit it to enter into direct relations with consumers, and will not allow the population of the interior to rise into that category.

Of the classes whose growth slavery artificially stimulates, none is more numerous than that of government employees. The close relation between slavery and the mania for officeholding is as indisputable as the relation between slavery and the superstition of the All-Providing State. . . . Take at random any twenty or thirty Brazilians in any place where our most cultured society is to be found; all were, or are, or will be government employees — if not they, then their sons.

Officeholding is . . . the asylum of the descendants of formerly rich and noble families that have squandered the fortunes made from slavery, of which it can be said, as a rule, as of fortunes made by gambling, that they neither last nor bring happiness. But officeholding is also our political olive tree, that shelters all those young men of brains and ambition but no money who form the great majority of our talented people. Draw up a list of distinguished Brazilian statesmen who solved their personal problem of poverty by marrying wealth (which meant, in the great majority of cases, becoming humble clients of the slaveowners); make up another list of those who solved that problem by acquiring government jobs; in those two lists you will find the names of virtually all our outstanding politicians. But what this means is that the national horizons are closed in all directions — that fields that might offer a livelihood to men of other than commercial talents, such as literature, science, journalism, and teaching, are severely restricted, while others that might attract men of business ability are so many closed doors, thanks to lack of credit, to the narrow scope of commerce, to the rudimentary structure of our economic life. . . .

But can we have this consolation, that having degraded the various professions and reduced the nation to a proletariat, slavery at least succeeded in making the landowners a superior class, prosperous, educated, patriotic, worthy of representing the country intellectually and morally?

As concerns wealth, we have already seen that slavery ruined a generation of farmers whose place was taken by slave labor. From 1853 to 1857, when the obligations formed during the period of the slave traffic should have been in the process of liquidation, the mortgage debt of the city and province of Rio de Janeiro rose to sixty-seven thousand *contos.* The present generation has been no more fortunate. A large part of its profits was converted into human flesh, at a high price, and if an epidemic were to devastate the coffee plantations today, the amount of capital that the agriculture of the whole Empire could raise for new plantings would horrify those who believe it to be in a flourishing state. On top of this, for the past fifteen years there has been talk of nothing but "aid to agriculture." In 1868 appeared a little work by Sr. Quintino Bocayuva, *The Crisis of*

Agriculture, in which that notable journalist wrote: "Agriculture can only he revived by the simultaneous application of two types of aid that cannot be longer delayed: the establishment of agricultural credit and the procurement of labor." The first measure was to be "a vast emission" based on the landed property of the Empire, which would thus be converted into ready money; the second should be Chinese colonization.

For fifteen years we have heard on all sides the cry that agriculture is in *crisis,* in need of aid, in agony, facing imminent bankruptcy. The government is daily denounced for not making loans and increasing the imposts in order to enable the fazendeiros to buy still more slaves. A law of November 6, 1875, authorized the government to give its guarantee to the foreign bank — no other could make its notes circulate in Europe — which would lend money to the planters at a rate lower than that of the domestic money market. In order to have sugar centrals and improve their product, the landowners must have the nation build them at its expense. The same favor has been asked for coffee. On top of sugar centrals and money at low interest rates, the great planters demand railroad freight rates set to their liking, official expositions of coffee, Asiatic immigration, exemption from any direct tax, and an employment law that would make the German, English, or Italian colonist a white slave. Even the native population must be subjected to a new agricultural recruitment in order to satisfy certain Chambers of Commerce; and, above all, the rate of exchange, by an economic fallacy, must be kept as low as possible so that coffee, which is paid for in gold, may be worth more in paper money. . . .

As concerns its social functions, a landed aristocracy can serve its country in different ways: by working to improve the condition of the surrounding population and of the countryside in which its estates are situated; by taking the direction of the progress of the nation into its own hands; by cultivating or protecting art and literature; by serving in the army and the navy or distinguishing itself in a variety of careers; by becoming the embodiment of all that is good in the national character, of the superior qualities of the people — of all that merits being preserved as tradition. We have already seen what our landed aristocracy achieved in each of these respects, when we noted what the slave system over which it presides has done to the land and the people, to the masters and the slaves. Since the class for whose profit it was created and exists is not an aristocracy of money, birth, intelligence, patriotism, or race, what is the permanent role in Brazil of a heterogeneous aristocracy that cannot even maintain its identity for two generations?

When we turn from the different classes to social institutions, we see that slavery has either turned them to its own interests, when of compromising tendency, or created a vacuum about them, when hostile, or hampered their formation, when incompatible with the slavery system.

Among the institutions that have identified themselves with slavery from the start, becoming instruments of its pretensions, is the Church. Under the system of domestic slavery, Christianity became mixed with fetichism, just as the two races mixed with each other. Through the influence of the wet-nurse and the house slaves on the training of the children, the mumbo-jumbo terrors of the converted fetichist exert . . . the most depressing influence on the minds of the young. The faith, the religious system that results from this fusion of African traditions with the antisocial ideal of the fanatical missionary is a jumble of contradictions that only a total lack of principle can seek to reconcile. What is true of religion is true of the Church.

Our bishops, vicars, and confessors do not find the sale of human beings repugnant; the Bulls that condemn it have become obsolete. Two of our prelates were sentenced to imprisonment at hard labor for declaring war on Freemasonry; none, however, was willing to incur the displeasure of the slavocracy. . . .

Take another social force that slavery has appropriated in the same way — patriotism. The slavocracy has always exerted itself to identify Brazil with slavery. Whoever attacks it immediately falls under suspicion of connivance with foreigners, of hostility toward the institutions of his own country. Antonio Carlos de Andrada was accused by the slave power of being un-Brazilian. To attack monarchy in a monarchical country, to attack Catholicism in a Catholic country, is perfectly proper, but to attack slavery is national treason and felony. . . .

But as with all the moral forces that it subjugated, slavery degraded patriotism even as it bent it to its will. The Paraguayan War offers the best illustration of what it did to the patriotism of the slaveowning class, to the patriotism of the masters. Very few of them left their slaves to serve their country; many freed a few blacks in order to win titles of nobility. It was among the humblest strata of our population, descendants of slaves for the most part — the very people that slavery condemns to dependence and misery — among the illiterate proletarians whose political emancipation slavery indefinitely postponed — that one felt beating the heart of a new *patria*. It was they who produced the soldiers of the Volunteer Battalions. With slavery, said José Bonifacio de Andrada in 1825, "Brazil will never form, as she must form, a spirited army and a flourishing navy" — because with slavery there can be no true patriotism, but only a patriotism of caste or race; that is, a sentiment that should unite all the members of society is used to divide them. . . .

Among the forces of progress and change around which slavery has created a vacuum as hostile to its interests, the press is notable — and not only the newspaper but the book, and everything that concerns education. To the credit of our journalism, the press has been the great weapon of struggle against slavery, the instrument for the propagation of new ideas; efforts to found a "black organ" have always collapsed. Whether insinuated timidly or affirmed with energy, the dominant sentiment in all our journalism, from North to South, is emancipation. But in order to create a vacuum around the newspaper and the book, and around all that could foster abolitionist sentiment, slavery has instinctively repelled the school and public education, maintaining the country in ignorance and darkness — the milieu in which it can prosper. The slave hut and the school are poles that repel each other.

The state of public education under a slave system interested in universal ignorance is well illustrated by the following excerpt from a notable report by Sr. Ruy Barbosa, reporter for the Commission on Public Instruction of the Chamber of Deputies:

"The truth — and your Commission wants to be very explicit on this point, displease whom it may — is that our public instruction is as backward as is possible in a country that regards itself as free and civilized; that decadence and not progress prevails; that we are a people of illiterates, and that the rate of illiteracy is declining at an intolerably slow rate if it is declining at all; that our academic instruction is infinitely below the scientific level of the age;

that our youth leave the secondary schools more and more poorly prepared for advanced study; and that popular education, in the capital as in the provinces, is merely a desideratum. . . . "

Among the forces whose emergence slavery has impeded is public opinion, the consciousness of a common destiny. Under slavery there cannot exist that powerful force called public opinion, that simultaneously balances and offers a point of support to the individuals who represent the most advanced thought of the country. Just as slavery is incompatible with spontaneous immigration, so will it prevent the influx of new ideas. Itself incapable of invention, it will have nothing to do with progress. . . .

And because we lack this force of social change, Brazilian politics are the sad and degrading struggle for spoils that we behold; no man in public life means anything, for none has the support of the country. The president of the council lives at the mercy of the Crown, from which he derives his power; even the appearance of power is his only when he is regarded as the Emperor's lieutenant and is believed to have in his pocket the decree of dissolution — that is, the right to elect a chamber made up of his own henchmen. Below him are the ministers, who live by the favor of the president of the council; farther down still, on the third plane, are found the deputies, at the mercy of the ministers. The representative system, then, is a graft of parliamentary forms on a patriarchal government, and senators and deputies only take their roles seriously in this parody of democracy because of the personal advantages they derive therefrom. Suppress the subsidies, force them to stop using their positions for personal and family ends, and no one who had anything else to do would waste his time in such *skimaxai,* such shadow boxing, to borrow a comparison from Cicero.

Ministers without support from public opinion, who when dismissed fall into the limbo of forgotten things; presidents of the council who spend their days and nights seeking to fathom the esoteric thinking of the Emperor; a chamber of Deputies conscious of its nullity and wanting only to be left alone; a Senate reduced to being a *prytaneum;* political parties that are nothing more than employment agencies and mutual benefit societies for their members. All these ostensible evidences of a free government are preserved by national pride like the consular dignity in the Roman Empire, but what we really have is a government of primitive simplicity in which responsibilities are infinitely divided while power is concentrated in the hands of one man. He is the chief of State. When some leader seems to have effective authority and power, individual prestige, it is because at that particular moment he happens to be standing in the light cast by the throne. Let him take one step to the right or left away from that sphere of light, and he vanishes for ever into the darkness. . . .

There is only one autonomous, irresponsible power among us; only that power is sure of the morrow; it alone represents a permanent national tradition. The ministers are nothing more than secondary and sometimes grotesque incarnations of that superior entity. Casting his eyes about him, the Emperor finds not a single will, individual or collective, that limits his own. In that sense he is as absolute as the Czar or the Sultan, although he is at the center of a modern government provided with all the superior organs, such as parliament, which neither Russia nor Turkey possesses; parliamentary supremacy, which Germany does not have; freedom of the press, which very few countries have. What this means is that instead of being called an absolute ruler the Emperor should rather be called the permanent prime minister of Brazil. He does not appear before the chambers; he allows great latitude, especially in matters of finance and legislation, to the cabinet; but not for a single day does he lose sight of the march of affairs or fail to be the arbiter among his ministers.

This so-called *personal government* has been explained by the absurd theory that the Emperor corrupted an entire people; that he demoralized our politicians by means of supreme temptations after the manner of Satan; that he stole the virtue of parties which never had ideas or principles, save as a field of exploitation. The truth is that this government is the direct result of the practice of slavery in our country. A people accustomed to slavery does not prize liberty or learn to practice self-government. Hence the general abdication of civic functions, the distaste for the obscure and anonymous exercise of personal responsibility, without which no people can be free, since a free people is only an aggregate of free individuals. These are the causes that have resulted in the supremacy of the only permanent and perpetual element — the monarchy.

5. THE NEW FAZENDA

The abolition of slavery in 1888, so ruinous to the interests of the sugar planters of the North, coincided with the start of a coffee boom in São Paulo, whose landowners had been gradually shifting to the use of free labor. A fertile "red soil," the increase in European and North American demand for coffee, and the rapid immigration of millions of European laborers, made possible the vast expansion of the coffee industry. To the old type of plantation, worked by slave labor and frequently embodying a feudal-patriarchal way of life, succeeded a new fazenda, operated by tenant sharecroppers whose only ties to the landowner were economic ones. Pierre Denis describes life and labor on a coffee fazenda of the new type.[7]

I VISITED a great many [*fazendas*] during my stay in San Paolo; and the same observations would be true of nearly all. There is scarcely any difference: a more or less perfect equipment in the way of plant, a more or less expensive installation of drying machines and store-houses; but the same picturesque aspect, the same terraces, like great stairs, in the hard-beaten red earth; the same labouring population in clothes smeared with red (the livery of the red soil); the same methods of work, the same gestures, the same cares, the same enjoyments.

The houses of the colonists are not as a rule scattered among the coffee-shrubs; they form, according to the importance of the fazenda, a hamlet or village of regular construction, having nothing of the disorder of a European village. To be precise, it is really only a small city of labourers, just as the colonist is only a rural proletariat. The house is of bricks or mud, often white-washed, and only moderately comfortable, but the climate of San Paolo is extremely mild, and life is passed almost entirely in the open air. As for diet, it is sufficient. Bread is rare, for neither wheat nor rye is a usual crop, but they are replaced by meal prepared from boiled maize, polenta, manioc, and black beans.

Each fazenda constitutes a little isolated world, which is all but self-sufficient and from which the colonists rarely issue; the life is laborious. The coffee is planted in long regular lines in the red soil, abundantly watered by the rains, on which a constant struggle must be maintained against the invasion of noxious weeds. The weeding of the plantation is really

[7] Pierre Denis, *Brazil*, translated by Bernard Miall, London, 1911, pp. 199–207.

the chief labour of the colonist. It is repeated six times a year. Directly after the harvest, if you ride on horseback along the lines of shrubs, which begin, as early as September, to show signs of their brilliant flowering season, you will find the colonists, men and women, leaning on their hoes, while the sun, already hot, is drying behind them the heaps of weeds they have uprooted.

Each family is given as many trees as it can look after; the number varies with the size of the family. Large families will tend as many as eight or ten thousand trees; while a single worker cannot manage much more than two thousand.

Like the vine, coffee requires a large number of labourers in proportion to the area under cultivation; it supports a relatively dense population. The two thousand trees which one colonist will receive will not cover, as a matter of fact, more than five to seven acres; yet the coffee supports other labourers who work on the fazenda, in addition to the labourers proper, or colonists. Pruning, for instance, which so far is not universally practised, is never done by the colonists, but by gangs of practised workmen, who travel about the State and hire themselves for the task. The colonist is only a labourer; if he were allowed to prune the shrubs he would kill them. Heaven knows, the pruners to whom the task is confided ill-treat the trees sufficiently already! They use pruning-hook and axe with a brutality that makes one shudder.

When the coffee ripens, towards the end of June, the picking of the crop commences. Sometimes, in a good year, the crop is not all picked until November. The great advantage enjoyed by San Paolo, to which it owes its rank as a coffee-producing country, is that the whole crop arrives at maturity almost at the same moment. The crop may thus be harvested in its entirety at one picking; the harvester may pick all the berries upon each tree at once, instead of selecting the ripe berries, and making two or three harvests as is necessary in Costa Rica or Guatemala. This entails a great reduction in the cost of production and of labour. San Paolo owes this advantage to the climate, which is not quite tropical, and to the sequence of well-defined seasons and their effect upon the vegetation.

At the time of picking the colonists are gathered into gangs. They confine themselves to loading the berries on carts, which other labourers drive to the fazenda; there the coffee is soaked, husked, dried, and selected, and then dispatched to Santos, the great export market. All these operations the colonists perform under the supervision of the manager of the fazenda. A bell announces the hour for going to work; another the hour of rest; another the end of the day; the labourers have no illusions of independence. In the morning the gangs scatter through the plantation; in the evening they gradually collect on the paths of the fazenda, and go home in family groups, tired after the day's work, saving of words, saluting one another by gestures. On Sunday work is interrupted; games are arranged; parties are made up to play *mora,* or Italian card games, with *denari* and *bastoni.* Women hold interminable palavers. Sometimes, on an indifferent nag, borrowed at second or third hand from a neighbour, the colonist will ride as far as the nearest town, to see his relations, exercise his tongue, and pit himself against such hazards of fortune as the world outside the fazenda may offer.

What are the annual earnings of the agricultural worker? The conditions vary in different localities, but we may estimate that the colonist receives about 60 or 80 milreis — £4 to £5 7s. at the present rate of exchange — per 1,000 stems of coffee. This is a certain resource; a sort of fixed minimum wage. To this we must add the price of several days' labour at about 2 milreis, or 2s.8d. A still more irregular element in the profits of a colonist's family is the amount it receives for the harvest. By consulting the books of several fazendas I was able to realize the extent of this irregularity. Sometimes the wage paid for the harvest is insignificant, while sometimes it is greater by itself than all the other sources of income put together. It is calculated at so much per measure of berries given in by the colonist. When the branches are heavily laden, not only is the total quantity greater, but the labour is performed more rapidly, and each day is more productive. Years of good harvest are for the colonist, as for the planter, years of plenty. With this important element essentially variable, how can we estimate the annual earnings of the colonist?

His expenses, again, cannot be estimated with any exactitude. An economic family will reduce them to practically nothing, if it has the good fortune to escape all sickness, and so dispense with the doctor, the chemist, and the priest. What really enables the colonists to make both ends meet is the crops they have the right to raise on their own account, sometimes on allotments reserved for the purpose set apart from the coffee, and sometimes between the rows of the coffee-trees. They often think more of the clauses in their contract which relate to these crops than to those which determine their wages in currency. A planter told me that he had learned that a party of colonists intended to leave him after the harvest. We met some of them on the road, and I questioned them. "Is it true that you are engaged to work on Senhor B——'s fazenda for the coming year?" — "Yes." — "What reason have you for changing your fazenda? Will you be better paid there? Don't you get over £6 a thousand trees here?" — "Yes." — "How much do they offer you over there?" — "Only £4." — "Then why do you go?" — "Because there we can plant our maize among the coffee."

The culture of coffee is thus combined with that of alimentary crops. Almost all the world over the important industrial crops have to make room in the neighbourhood for food crops. Every agricultural country is forced to produce, at any rate to some extent, its own food, and to live upon itself if it wishes to live at all. In Brazil the dispersion of food crops is extreme, on account of the difficulties of transport; it is hardly less in San Paolo, in spite of the development of the railway system. Each fazenda is a little food-producing centre, the chief crops being maize, manioc, and black beans, of which the national dish, the *feijoada,* is made.

It even happens at times that the colonists produce more maize than they consume. They can then sell a few sacks at the nearest market, and add the price to their other resources. In this way crops which are in theory destined solely for their nourishment take on a different aspect from their point of view, yielding them a revenue which is not always to be despised.

The colonists make their purchases in the nearest town, or, more often, if the fazenda is of any importance, there is a shop or store — what the Brazilians call a *negocio* — in the neighbourhood of the colonists' houses. Its inventory would defy enumeration; it sells at the same time cotton prints and cooking-salt, agricultural implements and petroleum. An examination of the stock will show one just what the little economic unit called a fazenda really is. Although the colonists are to-day almost always free to make their purchases where they please, the trade of shopkeeper on a fazenda is still extremely profitable. He enjoys a virtual monopoly; the fazendeiro sees that no competitor sets up shop in the neighbourhood. The shop is the planter's property; he lets it, and usually at a high rent, which represents not only the value of the premises, but also the commercial privilege which goes with it. It is a sort of indirect commercial tariff levied by the planter on the colonists; a sign of the ever so slightly feudal quality of the organization of property in San Paolo. The custom that used to obtain, of the planter himself keeping shop for the profit, or rather at the expense of his colonists, has generally disappeared.

One of the most serious of the planter's anxieties is the maintenance of the internal discipline of the fazenda. This is a task demanding ability and energy. One must not be too ready to accuse the planters of governing as absolute sovereigns. I myself have never observed any abuse of power on their part, nor have I seen unjustifiable fines imposed. The fazendeiro has a double task to perform. He employs his authority not only to ensure regularity in the work accomplished, but also to maintain peace and order among the heterogeneous population over which he rules. He plays the part of a policeman. The public police service cannot ensure the respect of civil law, of the person, or of property. How could the police intervene on the plantation, which is neither village nor commune, but a private estate? It falls to the planter to see that the rights of all are protected. Many colonists have a preference for plantations on which the discipline is severe; they are sure of finding justice then. The severity of the planter is not always to the detriment of the colonist.

Individually the colonists are often turbulent and sometimes violent; collectively they have hitherto shown a remarkable docility. On some fazendas, however, there have been labour troubles, and actual strikes; but they have always been abortive. The strikes have not lasted, and have never spread. One of the means by which the planters maintain their authority and prevent the colonists from becoming conscious of their strength is the prohibition of all societies or associations. They have had little trouble in making this prohibition respected. Among an uneducated group of labourers, of various tongues and nationalities, the spirit of combination does not exist. We have seen the development of working-men's societies, of socialistic tendencies, in the cities of San Paolo, but no-

where in the country. An incoherent immigrant population, but lightly attached to the land, is not a favourable soil for the growth of a party with a socialistic platform. One must not look for agricultural trades-unions in San Paolo. The contract between the planter and his labourers is never a collective but always an individual contract.

Accounts are settled every two months. It often happens, even to-day, that the colonist is in the planter's debt. The planter has kept up the custom of making advances, and every family newly established in the country is, as a general rule, in debt. But the advances are always small, the colonist possessing so little in the way of securities; he has few animals and next to nothing in the way of furniture. His indebtedness towards the planter is not enough, as it used to be, to tie him down to the plantation; that many of them continue to leave by stealth is due to their desire to save their few personal possessions, which the planter might seize to cover his advances. At the last payment of the year all the colonists are free; their contract comes to an end after the harvest. Proletarians, whom nothing binds to the soil on which they have dwelt for a year, they do not resume their contracts if they have heard of more advantageous conditions elsewhere, or if their adventurous temperament urges them to try their luck further on.

The end of the harvest sees a general migration of the agricultural labourers. The colonists are true nomads. All the planters live in constant dread of seeing their hands leave them in September. Even the most generous fazendeiros experience the same difficulty. According to the Director of Colonisation, 40 per cent to 60 per cent of the colonists leave their fazendas *annually*. It is difficult to confirm this statement; but at least it is no exaggeration to say that a third of the families employed on the plantations leave their places from year to year. Towards September one meets them on the roads, most often travelling afoot; the man carrying a few household goods and the woman a newly-born child, like the city labourers at the end of the season. One can imagine what a serious annoyance this instability of labour must be to the coffee-planter. Long before the harvest the planter is planning to fill up the gaps that will appear in the colony directly after the harvest. He secretly sends out hired recruiting agents to the neighbouring fazendas or to the nearest town; he employs for this purpose some of the shrewder colonists, to whom he pays a commission for every family engaged. Finally, at the end of his resources, if he no longer has any hope of finding workmen in the neighbourhood who are experienced in plantation work, he decides to apply to a colonisation agent in San Paolo, and resigns himself to the employment of an untrained staff, whom he will have to spend several months in training.

The instability of agricultural labour is the most striking characteristic of rural life in the State of San Paolo. It is a result of the unusual and even artificial nature of the hasty development of coffee-planting.

The agricultural workers of San Paolo are for the most part of Italian nationality. It is Italy that has furnished the greatest proportion of immigrants. Many fazendas are peopled entirely by Italians, and in some municipalities they surpass in number the Brazilians and the immigrants of all other nationalities together. From 1891 to 1897 the Italians formed three-fourths or four-fifths of the total immigration, according to the year.

Part Eight

Latin America in the Twentieth Century

IN THE TWENTIETH CENTURY the Latin-American republics struggled to achieve the political stability and economic maturity enjoyed by the advanced countries of Europe and North America. Spurred by difficulties arising from two world wars and a great depression, they strove with some success to diversify their economies. Less successfully, they sought to eliminate from their political life the dreary cycle of dictatorship and revolution.

The Mexican Revolution that began in 1910 had profound repercussions at home and abroad. The Cárdenas land reform — the first serious attack on the hacienda system in Latin-American history — offered object lessons to other lands with grave agrarian problems, such as Guatemala and Bolivia. The intense nationalism of the Mexican Revolution — reflected above all in the expropriation of foreign oil properties in 1938 — influenced the policies of other republics that wished to achieve economic sovereignty. At mid-century the Revolution had not attained all its goals, but few denied that it had resulted in solid economic, moral, and political advantages.

Masses of European immigrants poured into Argentina and Brazil in the first decades of the twentieth century, giving a great impetus to the advance of agriculture and cattle raising. The Great Depression, exposing the narrowness of the economic base in both countries, drove them to adopt State-directed economies biased in favor of industrialization. In both countries the course of World War II inspired hopes for a greater measure of democracy — hopes that were partially fulfilled in Brazil, frustrated in Argentina.

The machine and new social doctrines entered Latin America together. Labor parties and trade unions grew in number and influence. The movement for women's rights registered important gains in many lands. But the Church, linked by strong ties to the past, lost some of its influence in this time of change.

Latin-American esteem for the United States, strong during the greater part of the nineteenth century, suffered as a result of numerous American interventions in Latin-American affairs and territories in the decades after 1900. Between 1933 and 1945 the operation of the Good Neighbor Policy recovered the good will that had been lost, but after World War II vexing problems of trade, investments, and economic aid arose, and it seemed to some Latin Americans that the United States had abandoned the spirit if not the letter of the Good Neighbor Policy.

348

XXIX

The Mexican Revolution

THE MEXICAN REVOLUTION OF 1910 developed into the first major effort in Latin-American history to uproot the system of great estates and peonage, to curb foreign control over the national resources, and to raise the living standards of the masses of small farmers and workers. The famous Constitution of 1917 spelled out this social content of the revolution.

The revolution did not begin as a clear-cut social movement. Its first leader, the martyred Madero, emphasized narrow political objectives: "effective suffrage and no re-election." Under popular pressure his constitutional successor, Carranza, adopted a program of reform for which he felt no real sympathy. Reconstruction began with the return of peace in 1920, but the tempo of reform was slow, its aims uncertain. By 1928 a conservative reaction had set in as many revolutionary leaders, grown wealthy and corrupt, abandoned their early ideals.

Popular discontent with the rule of "millionaire socialists" produced an upsurge of change in the administration of President Cárdenas (1934-1940). Cárdenas distributed a vast amount of land to the villages, strengthened labor's hand, and weakened foreign economic influence by the expropriation of the oil industry. His middle-of-the-road successors, Presidents Ávila Camacho (1940–1946), Alemán (1946–1952), and Ruiz Cortines (1952–1958), virtually abandoned land reform but promoted irrigation and electrification projects and supported industry, which made notable progress as a result of wartime needs and government protection.

As the Mexican Revolution entered its fifth decade, native and foreign observers debated the measure of its achievement. The land monopoly had been broken, food production had kept pace with the growing population, new industries had arisen, and Mexicans enjoyed a freedom to write, speak, and organize unknown in the days of Don Porfirio. But the standard of living of the mass of the population had risen only slightly; more than half of the nation remained outside a money economy; and the growth of industry threatened to outstrip the extremely low purchasing power of the people. At mid-century it appeared that the Revolution had only partly achieved its great ideals.

1. PORFIRIO DÍAZ, VICEROY OF MEXICO

The Age of Díaz (1876–1911) enriched a favored few at the expense of Mexico's millions. Shortly after the dictator's fall from power a cultured Mexican exile wrote the following appraisal of his régime.[1]

"MEXICO," said a popular maxim, "is the mother of foreigners and the stepmother of Mexicans." This saying, which passed from mouth to mouth and even appeared in books by foreigners,[2] summed up in a few words the financial, administrative, domestic, and foreign policies of General Díaz. And nothing explains better why,

while foreign countries showered decorations on Díaz and his sons, nephews, kinsmen, and lackeys and exalted him as the greatest statesman of Latin America, the Mexican people, outside the circle of his adoring favorites, heaped curses on him and waited impatiently for death to snatch him from the Presidency of the Republic or for some man to arise and topple him from his pinnacle of power. . . .

The object of every national government is to improve the social and political condition of its people. A good government does not reject foreign aid, for that would be absurd and even impossible in the present state of civilization, but it insists that this cooperation always be subordinated to the national interest. Immigration is only desirable when the immigrant represents a civilizing force and joins his interests to those

[1] Luis Para y Pardo, *De Porfirio Díaz a Francisco Madero*, New York, 1912, pp. 81–97. (Excerpt translated by the editor.)

[2] See Terry's *Mexico*.

349

of the country in which he makes his residence.

Only colonial governments of the worst type have for their sole object the unrestrained, senseless, and disorderly exploitation of the national resources for the benefit of foreigners and the enslavement or extermination of the natives. The government of General Díaz belongs in this unhappy category. . . .

The dazzling prosperity of the Díaz era was due in very large part to the exploitation of certain resources — of minerals, above all — on a greater scale than ever before. The export of these commodities, as well as that of certain tropical products in great demand abroad, increased in an astounding way. In only twenty years of Díaz' rule the export of minerals rose from a value of 36 million pesos (in 1890) to more than 111 millions (in 1910). In the same period the export of henequen increased from a value of less than 6 million to more than 20 million pesos, and the export of other tropical products, such as fine woods, tobacco, coffee, etc., also rose sharply.

But aside from henequen, coffee, and some other products of particular regions, this prosperity was based on the exploitation of exhaustible resources owed by foreigners who did not even reside in Mexico. The lion's share of the 120 million pesos of exported minerals went into dividends for foreign stockholders; only the extremely low wages paid to the workers remained in the country. As in colonial times, ships sailed from Mexico with treasure drawn from the bowels of the earth by enslaved Indians, for the benefit of foreign masters who never set eyes on the places where those riches were produced.

As in colonial times, around these mines arose populous and hastily built centers. But again as in colonial times, the day had to come when the veins would be exhausted and the people would depart with empty purses, leaving only skeleton cities, vast cities of the dead like Zacatecas, Guanajuato, Taxco, that retain only the vestiges of their ancient splendor.

The same happened with our agricultural exports, except for henequen and coffee. . . . As concerns the exploitation of the fine woods, it is well known that it was carried on in such a destructive way that whole forests were ravaged without seeding a single useful plant in the looted soil.

Meanwhile agricultural production for the internal market, the cultivation of the grains on which our people live, remained stationary or even declined in relation to the population;

year after year it was necessary to import North American corn and wheat to fill the needs of the internal market.

Equally dismal are the statistics for industry: There were 123 textile factories in 1893; eighteen years later the number was 146. And only the fact that the textile industry, almost entirely monopolized by Spaniards and Frenchmen, enjoyed privileges that closed the door to similar foreign articles and compelled the people to buy high-priced articles of inferior quality, made this achievement possible. The tobacco and liquor industries, on the other hand, advanced by leaps and bounds. There were 41 factories manufacturing cigarettes and cigars in 1893; in 1909 their number had increased to 437 — that is, ten times. The production of rum reached 43 million liters in 1909.

The panegyrists of General Díaz proclaim his greatness as an administrator. They base their claim above all on the construction of more than 20,000 kilometers of railroads. I have already explained the open-handed generosity of Díaz in granting concessions to American capitalists for the construction of railroads.[3] Each of these concessions was a gift, made directly to the capitalist involved or through the mediation of some favorite that he had bribed. All Mexico knows that many families owe their present wealth to concessions secured from General Díaz and sold to foreign capitalists. In the ministry of communications there were employees who defrauded the state of millions of pesos, taking bribes from individuals who obtained concessions and subventions for the construction of railways. It is no mystery that many of those roads were not constructed with the aim of favoring commerce or of meeting the needs of particular regions. . . .

The official statistics maintain a profound silence concerning the nationality of the directors of the mining companies, the great agricultural enterprises, and of the manufacturing industries of Mexico. But everyone knows that more than 75 per cent of them are foreign; as for the railroads, their foreign character is so marked that English has been the official language of the majority of lines.

In order to explain and justify this situation, which became so acute during the rule of General Díaz that it caused almost a crisis of "antiforeignism," some say that our lack of enter-

---

[3] In an earlier chapter Pardo explained Díaz' rise to power by American assistance, allegedly given in exchange for future economic concessions. B.K.

prise, our apathy, and our ignorance render us unfit to exploit our own resources, and that these must inevitably pass into the hands of foreigners.

I do not deny that from lack of education and on account of the social conditions in our country the Mexican people suffers from such defects. Nor do I make the mistake of attributing this state of affairs to General Díaz, or of demanding that he explain why the national character did not experience a radical change under his rule.

But this is not the only reason that Mexico is absolutely dominated by foreigners at present; furthermore, the government of General Díaz made not the slightest effort to keep the foreign invasion within the limits of fair dealing and the national interest. The monopolization of business by foreigners would have been legitimate and beneficial for the country if it had been the result of free competition between the natives and the immigrants — if the latter, through their capital and their spirit of enterprise, employed within just and legal limits, had emerged victorious. . . .

But for every property legitimately acquired, for every dollar, or franc, or mark, or pound sterling invested in enterprises that yielded benefits to the country, how many monopolies, servitudes, ruinous and truly iniquitous contracts did the government of General Díaz not leave behind it!

Not apathy and ignorance but tyranny deprived the Mexicans of the possession and exploitation of their own resources. If a Mexican sought the grant of a waterfall, a forest, a piece of land, a mine, or a deposit of coal or oil, his petition had to be supported and endorsed by some minion of the President who secured at an exorbitant price the favor of having the matter attended to with fair dispatch. Frequently the Mexican, having purchased in this manner the services of public officials, would receive a round "No" for an answer; and in a little while he would see in the Official Daily the announcement that the favor he was applying for had been graciously granted — to none other than the person whose intercession he had sought!

And if this happened to Mexicans on a social level close to that of the privileged class, what must have been the condition of laborers, small farmers, and artisans! Pity the unhappy peasant who, loving the soil he had inherited from his forefathers and seized with a sudden passion for progress, undertook to irrigate his inheritance,

to buy machines and use fertilizers, and who by means of patient and painful effort succeeded in obtaining the best yields and in attracting the attention of the neighborhood to his land! From that moment was awakened the rapacity of the *jefe político,* of the military commander, of the secretary of the state government, or of the curate, canon, or archbishop, who would not rest until they had despoiled him of his property; and if he defended it with the admirable tenacity with which the Indian defends his land, he would land in the barracks, condemned to the slavery of the soldier-convict, or a group of soldiers would take him out of jail and shoot him in the back while on the march.

In the court archives of Mexico there are thousands of episodes of this kind. I have seen many of them; I know in detail histories that would fill books — stories of people dragged from their farms by soldiers in order to satisfy the greed of the governor, or the local commander, or the foreigner, supported by General Díaz.

In 1863 President Juarez, wishing to promote agriculture, issued the law of vacant lands *(terrenos baldíos),* by which public lands were ceded to whoever would locate, survey, and exploit them, paying for them at a fixed price and receiving a part gratis in return for his engineering services. Basing itself on this law, the government of General Díaz committed the greatest iniquities. Documents published in Mexico show that time and time again certain magnates, seized by the fever of speculation in lands called "vacant," despoiled not only individuals but entire towns that had worked and made their living from those lands for centuries.

Among the many notions that certain sociological theories proclaim, and that serve to justify robbery by conquest, there is a fine-sounding doctrine that dazzles even educated and thoughtful persons. It affirms that if the owner of a source of wealth does not exploit it he may rightly be despoiled whenever there appears a claimant capable of making better use of it.

It would not have been so bad if this doctrine had really inspired and justified all these iniquities. One would have less cause for complaint if the natives had changed from the class of owners to that of tenants, or even to that of employees, peons, day laborers of the new owner, and if land once barely cultivated had begun to produce in abundance with the aid of irrigation, the plow, fertilizer. If all the square kilometers of land seized from their legitimate owners during the reign of Don Porfirio were now in production, even at the extremely low level of production typical of Mexican agriculture, all the granaries of the Republic would now be filled, and from our ports would depart ships loaded with wheat, flour, corn, and the many other products that the benign climate of Mexico yields.

But that is not what happened; in the great majority of cases the inhabitants were simply expelled and the lands closed to exploitation, awaiting the coming of some Yankee prospector in search of vast tracts — to be used in bamboozling his countrymen through the organization of one of many fraudulent agricultural companies. In official newspapers of the States I have seen the orders given by the authorities to inhabitants of villages and towns to abandon their homes and give up their lands to avaricious claimants. And those unhappy Indians, whose only crime was that they lacked a written title to the lands on which their forefathers had peacefully lived since long before the birth of Columbus, frequently preferred to die hunted down like wild beasts, or to rot in jail, to leaving voluntarily what for them was their only *patria*. . . .

Governmental expenditures during the thirty-five years' reign of Don Porfirio amounted to more, much more, than 2 billion pesos. This vast sum was entirely at his disposal; it was tribute paid by the country that General Díaz could have invested in bettering the social condition of Mexico. But of this immense sum of money not a cent was ever invested in irrigating or fertilizing the land on which 12,000,000 Indians passed their lives in struggle for a handful of grain with which to sate their hunger. Nor was any part of it used to bring to these people — the largest social class, the only class devoted to the cultivation of the soil — some notion of justice or some education that would enable them to take a step toward civilization. Not the least effort was made to liberate the rural population from the slavery that made its life almost intolerable. Calling itself paternal, his government made not the slightest effort to rescue this enormous mass of people from the clutches of alcoholism, which a rapacious master-class injected into the veins of the people the better to ensure its domination.

That is why at the end of those thirty-five years the rural population of Mexico continues under a régime of true slavery, receiving a daily wage of a few cents, sunk in ignorance, without

hope of redemption. And since the monopolies have greatly raised the cost of living, the situation of the people in general is much worse than when General Díaz rose to power. Above that great oppressed mass arose a wealthy, brutal, splendid caste — but when has the wealth of a master-class served any other purpose than to oppress and degrade the serfs? Has it ever served to liberate them?

The influence of General Díaz was as disastrous and corrupting on the political as on the social life of Mexico. Arrived at the pinnacle of power, he could and should have modified his system without danger to himself in such a way that the people could gradually have been educated in the exercise of their rights. . . .

But instead his policy of extermination, degradation, and prostitution was directed toward the concentration of power, and all the important changes that he made in the Mexican constitution were highly lethal to liberty and rendered the people increasingly incapable of governing itself. Thus, his most important reforms were designed to restrict the sphere of action of the town councils. Not even in the capital of the Republic — the center of culture, where the district action of the federal government was greatest — did he permit the existence of an elected council that would have charge of municipal taxation. On the contrary, he stripped the council of all its powers, converting it into an ornamental body, and put the municipal administration in the hands of the ministries. Another of his important reforms was to restrict trial by jury, and later he reformed the *ley de amparo* to the point where it was made inapplicable in civil cases. . . .

These were the salient features of the political system of General Díaz, and they justify my affirmation that his government was a viceroyalty, bringing a peace of extermination and oppression; pompous, brilliant, and profitable to foreigners, but productive of ills to the *patria* that future generations may be unable to cure.

2. THE WAYS OF TREASON

The Revolution proclaimed on November 20, 1910, by Francisco I. Madero toppled the Díaz dictatorship with astounding ease. But Madero, elected to the Presidency in the following year, did not hold office long. Kind and well-intentioned, but vacillating and excessively trustful, he fell victim to a conspiracy organized by reactionary military elements with the support of the American Ambassador, Henry Lane

Wilson. José Vasconcelos (1881–   ), a leading Mexican educator, historian, and philosopher, relates one of the darkest chapters in the history of the Revolution.[4]

I WAS INTRODUCED to His Excellency, Henry Lane Wilson, at the University Club, after he arrived in Mexico in the last days of *Porfirismo.* After Madero's victory I was assigned to establish friendly but unofficial contacts between Don Francisco and the American Ambassador. I arranged for them to meet at a dinner given by Rafael Hernández, a minister who had represented Madero in De la Barra's cabinet. Wilson, a man of literary tastes, was much pleased with the change that had taken place in the country. He preferred the cultured statesman to the uncouth ex-dictator. It flattered his vanity to be counted among the precursors of the new order as a result of his speech on "the Rock of the Constitution." The relations between the two men, then, began in a most promising way. Wilson even appeared enthusiastic about Madero. With the frankness natural to intelligent men and to the Yankees of that day, he approached me after the meal and said: "My congratulations; you have a great man; I am charmed with him. . . . Have you noted," he added, "what beautiful eyes he has — the eyes of an apostle, of a mystic? Wonderful!"

Mutual friends in the American colony in Mexico City kept me informed of the state of the barometer in the Embassy. I never stepped into the Foreign Office, but whenever it seemed necessary I called on Madero and reported to him. It was now more than a year after the dinner at the Club, and in the meantime the situation had changed. Wilson at first maintained a suave air, but little by little he grew demanding, later impertinent; now, it was said, he openly encouraged the disaffected, receiving them in his house. The North American newspaper, the *Mexican Herald,* obedient to the wishes of the Ambassador, developed a violent campaign of truly insolent opposition to Madero. The hatred of this newspaper had a cause. Its principal owner had made a fortune, thanks to the protection of Limantour, by selling furnishings to all the public offices at prices that were privately fixed. Now Madero purchased through public bidding; he had no favorites; and the new ministers not only had no friends — they did not even engage in business. But

[4] José Vasconcelos, *Ulises criollo,* México, 1937, pp. 500–535. (Excerpt translated by the editor.)

this does not explain, nor does anything else explain, the change of front of the Ambassador, who was irreproachable in his business dealings. My own opinion is that Wilson's injured pride was the cause. He had assumed that a little flattery and some words of advice would make Madero recognize his experience and consult him on the most delicate affairs of state. Instead he found in Madero a man of character. Where Porfirio Díaz and his ministers would say "yes" to everything that the Great Man might ask, Madero rose in all his pride as the President of a sovereign people. The sporadic excesses against American citizens that occurred in the wake of the Revolution provided Wilson with excuses for demands that steadily grew more irritating. From Washington came peremptory notes, suggesting that if the Mexican Government was incapable of defending the lives and properties of Americans, the United States would be forced to take measures on its own account. The moderate but firm tone of Madero's replies astounded a public accustomed to Díaz' ready compliance.

"The Embassy regards this as very serious," a friend who daily visited Wilson said to me. "You should intervene; all the Ambassador wants is to be treated with more consideration." Accordingly I sought the best occasion for a long talk with Madero: his morning walk in the park. I tried to make him see the necessity of a reconciliation; I even urged him to placate Wilson beforehand in order to gain it. But for the first time I saw Madero become excited. "You can't imagine," he said to me, "the impertinence that we have tolerated from him. Finally, the other day, he began to shout at me — but I would not permit it. He must learn that the days of Don Porfirio are gone forever. The American Ambassador is no longer master in this country. . . ." "Anyway," said Madero, confident and smiling, "he has little time left. . . . In a few months my friend Woodrow Wilson becomes President of the United States, and the first favor that I shall ask of him is to replace his Ambassador here. This Henry Lane Wilson is an alcoholic; he drinks himself to sleep every night with champagne."

Fortune had so often justified Madero's optimism that it infected us all. I forgot about the Ambassador, and my respect grew for a President who honored his office. His aides, educated in the Military College, admired his physical stamina, displayed on the horseback rides that they took on Sunday mornings. All who surrounded Madero admired him, and each for a different reason. . . . His was a great and serene destiny, but this was not a propitious time. When the excitement of the struggle had passed the people returned to their apathy. Small errors, such as those of certain appointments, magnified by lack of understanding, provoked wrathful reproaches. Foreign capitalists, angered by the suppression of the system of concessions, subsidized the anti-government press. The Johnny-come-lately revolutionaries, wishing to bury in oblivion their passivity in the days of trial, now took refuge in the "House of the People," where they thundered against Madero, proclaiming him a reactionary. Among them was Díaz Soto, disinterested in matters of money but wounded in his pride; also Luis Morones, of subsequent unhappy fame. . . . The late followers of Reyes in the Chamber of Deputies, for their part, calling themselves "Renovators," under the direction of Luis Cabrera, presented demands, obstructed the work of administration, and sowed the germs of the Carranza plague. Carranza himself, in the North, murmured and refused to give account of some regiments that he maintained in defiance of the law.

Yet the government appeared stable. It had crushed three rebellions with dazzling speed. The mass of the people were content and free for the first time in history. There was real prosperity. The railway workers were organized, the workers of Orizaba gained social and political power, the miners had greater security of employment and higher wages from their employers. Madero would never have fallen if treason had not conquered him. Against treason even the strongest is helpless. We do not call Lincoln incompetent because a madman fired a shot at him. It would be as unjust to say that Madero fell because he was *weak*. Much stronger than others who outlasted him, Madero humbled his enemies on the field of battle and in the greater struggle between Good and Evil. He was struck down by a barrack-room revolt that represented a return to barbarism. The Aztec manes took revenge upon the white Quetzalcoatl who had abolished human sacrifices. That was all. . . .

In a few more weeks a change of government in Washington would free us from the provoking Ambassador. A few more rounds of diplomatic fencing and then, with Taft's retirement, the notes would cease, the international climate would change. The Ambassador and the traitors who frequented the Embassy were probably making the same calculations. With incredible shamelessness they not only drew up but

signed a document which they made public after their triumph — the Pact of the Ciudadela, a treaty among swine, an agreement of matricides. By this pact the conspirators connived with the agent of Washington to overthrow the only legitimate government in all Mexican history.

The principal leaders of the conspiracy were prisoners, yet the rumors that circulated cited dates and names, spoke of regiments involved in the conspiracy. For myself, I had seen the malcontents fail so often, and the government had reacted so vigorously in the past, that I did not take the danger seriously. My frequent contact with different zones of various States confirmed my optimism. Everywhere men thought only of honest labor under the protection of a government whose honesty they recognized. And the people enjoyed their new-found liberty. So it was without concern that I left for Tampico to carry out a professional assignment, the authorization for a new refinery. . . .

The telephone rang some hours after daybreak. Only my colleague in Tampico knew where I was staying. He told me the stupendous news: General Reyes had been killed in combat shortly after being freed. Madero was a prisoner in Chapultepec. Tampico was calm, as was the rest of the country.

We speedily prepared to return by the first train. . . . As we drew near the center of the country more details began to come in. The Cavalry School and two regiments had freed the leaders of the two previous rebellions; Reyes and Díaz. The former was slain in the attack on the Palace. The second escaped, taking refuge in the Ciudadela, the military prison, where he was defending himself with three or four hundred men. There was no great cause for alarm. It was unthinkable that four hundred disloyal soldiers could overthrow a regime that enjoyed the support of the nation.

There was one dark cloud, however. General Lauro Villar, commanding the Mexico City garrison, had been wounded in the first encounter and had been replaced by General Victoriano Huerta, who offered Madero his sword. In that moment he became the military chief of the capital of the country.

It was almost midnight when our train arrived at Colonia Station. There were no taxis, so, followed by porters, we went on foot to Adriana's house in Colonia Juárez. Traffic had been prohibited in the center of the city, but there was movement in the residential zones. Suddenly we heard the distant firing of a machine gun. We talked for a long while, then slept for a few hours. It had barely dawned when I set out for my house, going through the suburb of the Hippodrome as far as Tacubaya. At home there was nothing new; my family confirmed the accounts I had already had. Going to the roof, they showed me the havoc wrought by cannon fire on the besieged ward. There was no telephone service; trolleys and taxis had stopped running. Removing the dust from a bicycle long stored away, I set out for Chapultepec by back streets. . . .

I entered the Castle by a private elevator. The serene rosebushes on the terrace gave no hint of alarm. In one of the observatories I found Sarita Madero. She was surrounded by military men, among them the Director of the Military College, situated in the Annex. Presenting me to the officers, she informed me that they were members of General Huerta's staff. There was no love lost between Madero's people and the officer class; we greeted each other without shaking hands. Then Madame Madero said: "Pancho is in the Palace and wants very much to see you. It's not easy to cross the city, but these gentlemen happen to be going there right now and I shall ask them to take you. What news do you bring?" "The country is at peace," I replied, "but there is great anxiety over the rumor that President Madero is a prisoner; I am glad to learn that it is not true." Taking me apart, she said, "Tell Pancho that. . . . He is not a prisoner, but who knows. . . . No one trusts General Huerta; go quickly to see Pancho, I beg you. . . ."

As we were going down the slope to where the car was waiting, one of the officers said to me: "Listen, Doctor, we'll take you; but I must warn you that you're running a risk, especially in a military car; the other day we got some bullets through the top. . . . If you'd rather go by yourself. . . . " He was a polished officer, gold sash, wristwatch, cocky like his colleagues. I immediately replied, looking directly at them, making no effort to conceal my hostility: "Don't be afraid, you're safe with me. . . . I'm a lucky fellow."

They didn't hit me then and there, because their hands were tied. The hour of treason had not yet arrived. They swallowed my sarcasm and even let me take the seat of honor in the powerful car. Without incident we crossed the deserted streets and entered the Palace. The only serious danger I ran was that they might get the idea of handing me over to the rebels. On the way they spoke of the bloodcurdling perils of the past days. They had all managed to keep their persons out of harm's way. I found Madero in the Blue Room. After an affectionate embrace I repeated my watchword: "The country is at peace; but it is said that Huerta has taken power into his own hands and has made you his prisoner." At that instant Victoriano Huerta himself came up with the slinking walk of a wary beast. Madero laughed at my remark. . . . "Listen to this, General, hear what Vasconcelos is saying. . . . " Without looking me in the face, the crafty devil listened and remained silent. Not a muscle trembled in his dark face. His eyes were shifty, his lips closed. . . . Madero spoke: "See for yourself. . . . Here is the general, the soul of loyalty." And as Madero put his arm over his shoulder, the traitor managed to slip away.

As we walked about, Madero explained the situation to me. The attack on the Ciudadela had not been carried out, for fear of causing destruction to neighboring houses. The American ambassador threatened a naval landing in Vera Cruz if a single American in the menaced zone suffered injury. On the previous day the whole diplomatic corps, at the instance of the Ambassador, had called on him to request that he resign. Madero had dismissed them, denying their right to express opinions on questions of Mexican politics. "Go to my private office," he concluded, "and come back in time to lunch with us. And don't worry, we shall conquer, for right is on our side."

In his office I found less optimism. Grouped about Sánchez Ancona were Madero's old lieutenants. Many of us had not set foot in the Palace for months, partly because of small slights suffered from Madero's closest collaborators. The present danger united us again. I remember, among others, Bordés Mangel and Urueta. Urueta loudly commented on the passivity of the ministers, especially the notorious incapacity of the Minister of War. "What Madero should do," exclaimed Chucho Urueta, "is send his whole Cabinet packing and form another Cabinet composed of young men of proven loyalty."

I returned to the Presidential rooms a few minutes before lunch, and Madero resumed our conversation. "As soon as this is over," he affirmed, "I shall change the Cabinet. My ministers are all very honorable men, but I need more active people. The responsibility must fall

on you younger men. You are not going to refuse me. You'll see; this business will be over in
a few days, and then we shall reorganize the
government. We must triumph, because we represent the force of good. Unhappy Mexico, if
these swine were to come to power! But it cannot be. Good must triumph. . . . " In the dining
room of the Palace we sat down to a light but
tastefully prepared meal. A Barsac wine, drawn
from the old stocks, gave the glasses a golden-
greenish glow. The President's conversation was
animated, but his ministers wore a gloomy air.

From time to time a shell exploded on the
roof, shattering some tile and making the glass-
ware tremble slightly. "Why," I asked, turning
to the Minister of War after one of these explo-
sions, "why is the aim of the rebels so good, and
why do our guns never make a hit on the Ciudadela?"

The view that the rebels and the beseigers
were in collusion had just been confirmed for me
in Madero's office. But the Minister of War had
the face not of a traitor but of a fool. "Why
don't you attack and finish off that nest of rats
in two hours?" I insisted. "It is a disgrace that
four hundred men should hold in check a whole
nation that is at peace and firmly behind the
government." Only then the minister replied:
"That is not my business; General Huerta has
responsibility for the situation."

I had also been urged to influence Madero to
strip Huerta of his command and give it to
General Ángeles, of unquestioned loyalty. The
day before, Huerta had committed an act of infamy that justified not only removal but a court-
martial. He had placed a force of Maderista
irregulars in a narrow street that opened on the
Ciudadela. The besieged, doubtless warned beforehand, had only to open up with their machine guns. The whole city saw the slaughter
and the treason. "But Madero doesn't see!" everyone exclaimed.

Either he did not see in time or he believed
it more opportune to temporize, submitting to
necessity, pretending confidence in Huerta in
order to disarm him, and also because he already felt himself in his power. This hypothesis,
however, seems inconsistent with Madero's character. His fundamental bravery would have rebelled at dissembling with a swine. It is more
probable that destiny, in achieving its tortuous
ends, blinds the most clear-sighted at the instant
of approaching destruction. The curse that
weighs upon our country darkened the mind of
the wisest of its sons. It made sluggish the ac-

tions of its most agile hero. Shadows enveloped
Madero. What great spirit has not known such
eclipses? From the darkness he would emerge
clean and glorious, a scintillating comet in the
sky of our history. But the nation would fall
into an abyss from which it has not yet emerged.

The popular versions of what happened were
strictly in accord with the facts. Victoriano
Huerta was visiting the American Embassy at
night to meet with the rebellious chiefs; if he
had not yet consummated the act of treason it
was only because they were not agreed as to who
should hold power. For his part, the Ambassador was in a hurry. On March 4 he must quit
his post, and it was now the middle of February.
The success of the rebellion depended on recognition of the *coup d'état* by the American Government.

More days of anguish and boredom. Intermittent cannon fire reminded the city that the
bloody struggle was continuing. In Adriana's
ward, among the gardens and luxurious chalets,
pyres of corpses were made in order to burn the
fallen of the neighborhood. In the mornings,
when I had the means of transportation, I
would go to the Palace. Afternoons I passed
with Adriana, the evenings at home. A rumor
circulated that an attack might be undertaken
with reinforcements arrived from the states. In
reality the reinforcements consisted of Blanquet's
battalion, the same one that months before had
machine-gunned the Maderistas in Puebla. This
Blanquet, a crony of Huerta's, claimed the distinction of having been the soldier who gave
Maximilian the *tiro de gracia*. It seems that this
sort of executioner's feat assures permanent consideration in some armies. The declarations that
the newspapers obtained from Blanquet were
not reassuring. He asserted that his mission was
to contribute to the pacification of the country,
but he said not a word about his loyalty, which
was already being questioned.

Finally, one noonday, Victoriano Huerta
proved himself capable of giving lessons to more
recent homicides: Amaro, Calles, or Eulogio Ortiz. In the history of Mexican crime the murder
of Gustavo Madero compares with the ambush
that Carranza set for Zapata, or that which
Obregón and Calles set for Villa. . . .

Gustavo had established himself in the Palace
at the side of his brother. He had shown himself to be a dangerous man, having personally
compelled the surrender of a whole group of
officers when the Reyistas assaulted the Palace.
They no longer joked about him; they feared

him. So Victoriano Huerta invited him to dinner. "This very afternoon," he told him, "I
shall take the Ciudadela, but first I am going to
lunch in the Gambrinus Restaurant [in the center of the city] and I want you to accompany us.
Some of my aides and intimate friends will be
along. Two officers will call for you at noon."
Gustavo was a daring man. He had no respect
for Huerta, but he would have thought it unworthy to show indecision at a time when it was
dangerous to enter or leave the Palace. He accepted.

Félix Díaz distrusted Huerta and demanded
proof of his good faith. "Hand Gustavo over to
me," he told him, "then I shall know that you
are not setting a trap for me in proposing that
I surrender." The pact, meanwhile, had already
been signed. The followers of Félix Díaz were
to recognize Huerta as President if he overthrew
Madero; in return they would receive some posts
in his Cabinet. They demanded their sacrifice
of human flesh. Huitzilopochtli was about to
resume his reign, interrupted by Madero's triumph.

Two future "generals" called for Gustavo and
took him to the private dining room at the Gambrinus. All the business establishments in the
vicinity were closed, but the restaurant had been
ordered to open for the sole purpose of consum-
mating the villainy. There Gustavo found other
officers, who asked him to wait a short while.
Huerta soon arrived; he embraced Madero, and
the meal began. Huerta continually looked at
the clock and talked half-drunkenly. Finally,
interrupting himself, he exclaimed: "I'll be back
in a moment, pay no attention to me." He left,
and Madero's table companions immediately
fell upon their guest, gagged him, and forced
him into a car previously made ready. On the
way they struck him on the head with their pistols to prevent him from struggling and to stop
his cries for help.

In the Ciudadela the caudillo Félix Díaz
awaited his prey. He personally tormented Gustavo, who was already badly wounded. Others
jabbed bayonets into his stomach. They tore off
his clothes. . . . Then they trampled on his body.
Perhaps they fired a last merciful shot. What is
certain is that the corpse was not turned over to
his family. There was no autopsy; the shattered
remains were secretly buried. And Gustavo's
glass eye passed from hand to hand as a trophy.

When he had concluded this Aztec rite, the
caudillo of the Ciudadela (as the nephew of the
dictator now officially styled himself) retired to
his private apartments. He received his concu-
bine, took a bath, perfumed himself. Then he
mounted a fine horse and set off with his host for
the Palace to congratulate the new President.
Not a few ladies of the old Porfirista aristocracy
wet their handkerchiefs with patriotic tears and
cast them before the conqueror, who, "pale and
smiling," said the newspapers the next day, displayed a nosegay in his buttonhole.

As soon as Huerta learned that Gustavo had
been handed over, he tossed off his habitual
glass of rum, shut himself up in the guardroom,
and from there directed the assault. A strong
squad under the command of two officers of his
staff entered the Council Room. Approaching
Madero, they declared him a prisoner. At that
moment the Presidential aide, Gustavo Gar-
mendia, killed one traitorous officer with a shot
in the head, wounded the other, and put the
squad to flight — but not before it had fired,
killing one of Madero's friends who had been
talking with him.

As soon as the corpses had been removed,
Madero gathered his few followers and strode to
the balcony of the Palace, intending to call on the
people to aid him. Outside the streets were totally deserted, showing the care that Huerta had
taken to isolate his prisoner. In any case, the
people would not move. A few days earlier, after
printing a proclamation calling on them to defend the government, we had driven in a car
through all the humble wards where once we
had strong support. Everywhere the people received us with distrust. And they were right, for
we did not give them arms; the city was no
longer ours. . . .

Retiring from the balcony, Madero understood
that his only hope was to get out of the Palace
alive. Outside he hoped to find armed elements
that would protect him. He would rush the
guard, attempt one of those audacious strokes
that at other times had brought him victory
when apparently all was lost. Descending in the
private elevator, he entered the antechamber below without opposition. But as he came out into
the corridor his advance was blocked by none
other than General Blanquet, at the head of his
battalion of illiterates. Madero faced these men,
who pointed their rifles at him; he signaled them
to stop and exclaimed: "I am the President of
the Republic, down with those arms!" The
troop vacillated for a moment; then Blanquet,
trembling, advanced, pistol in hand. "Surrender," he stammered. His officers threw themselves upon Madero, held him fast, searched him

for arms. Without a pistol, he had overawed a hundred gunmen!

The Ministers who had descended with Madero were also imprisoned. Madero was placed in an interior room, within sight of a sentry; later they shut him up together with his Cabinet, placing a guard at the door.

Now it was Victoriano Huerta who strode out on the balcony. The bells of the Cathedral, which was in the power of his henchmen, launched peals of triumph. A few curious people timidly approached. Huerta, who was drunk, "discoursed" to the people. He had assumed power. He would save the country. He would lower the price of bread and onions (sic). He would make the people happy. Then he went to interview his prisoners. He began by offering his hand to Madero, who refused it, calling him a traitor. He also offered his hand to the ministers. All, with a single exception, refused to clasp it. Soon afterwards he decreed the freedom of the ministers, but the President and Vice-President remained prisoners. . . .

The whole world knows what happened later. The Chamber of Deputies could have saved Mexico if it had resisted armed pressure. But most of the leaders of the government groups failed to meet the test. The most outstanding figure among them, Luis Cabrera, had absented himself from Mexico City weeks before the events, perhaps warned by old friends in the Reyes circle. Gustavo, the chief of the majority, had just been killed. No more than half a dozen deputies voted against accepting Madero's resignation.

Some were surprised, knowing Madero's character, that he agreed to resign. He did it because he felt unsupported by the people, and because he was told that thereby he could save the lives of all his imprisoned friends.

Later there occurred another, most reprehensible resignation: that of the Secretary of Foreign Relations, who, according to law, now became president and who instantly resigned in order to allow the Chamber to designate Victoriano Huerta as Provisional President. Some excused their acts of cowardice on the grounds that by yielding completely to the traitor they would at least save the lives of President Madero and his Vice-President, Pino Suárez. Momentarily paralyzed, the nation contemplated the debacle, fascinated by the final fate of the imprisoned Heads of State.

The next morning my office was informed that Sarita, with the rest of the Madero family, had taken refuge in the Japanese Embassy. I telephoned there to offer my services and they asked me to use my influence with Henry Lane Wilson. He alone could save Francisco Madero from the fate of Gustavo. I had not had any dealings with Wilson for a considerable time. Nevertheless, at the risk of suffering some slight, I telephoned the embassy. With the invariable courtesy of the Yankee official, the Ambassador spoke to me in person. "Don't worry, my friend." A special train would take Madero to Vera Cruz and he would be sent into exile; that had been agreed upon; he was in no danger whatever. "I've told those fellows that there has been enough vengeance and that they must stop killing people. . . . But be very careful. Stay out of it." The assurances of the ambassador who had compounded the infamous plot reassured Madero's friends, just the same. For me there began a curious agony. I was appalled by the fate of Madero, expelled from the country and consequently almost pardoned. In the end, it seemed, Huerta would emerge as the hero who had freed the country from a bad, a weak government. And the same criminals who had just assassinated Gustavo, the vile traitors who were already beginning to loot the nation, would not only go unpunished but receive praise. The Ambassador had doubtless given them sound advice. To pardon Madero was to save them from history, to consolidate their power. . . .

One morning the train that was to conduct Madero into exile was held ready in the station, but before the prisoner had arrived the order was countermanded and the journey canceled. The reason was not made public, but it has been linked to the unexpected action of a military man who had a moment of courage. General Velasco, military commander of Veracruz and the future scourge of Pancho Villa, said that if Madero came to Veracruz he would accord him Presidential honors. His resignation had been obtained under pressure; the course of events dishonored the Army. . . . It is a pity that Velasco could not maintain his position to the end; he soon put himself at the service of Huerta. But for the moment his attitude prevented Madero's departure.

At the same time the new government received news of which the public was ignorant. In different parts of the country uprisings occurred under the banner of Madero. In the United States meetings were held in certain cities to protest the manner in which the Ambassador was liquidating democracy in Mexico. The villains became increasingly uneasy, and they finally decided to get rid of their prey. The rooms of the National Palace, now transformed into a den of criminals, heard altercations which reached the public in more or less altered form. It was reported that when the crime was proposed the pious De la Barra said: "God's will be done," and that Félix Díaz demanded that the prisoners be turned over to him as had been done with Gustavo. The fact is that the moral responsibility attaches to all who then and later served the seedy soldier who styled himself President. The mode of the execution was left to the skill of the generals. That relic of the Juárez army, he who gave Maximilian the *tiro de gracia,* the heroic Blanquet, took charge of the affair. He made use of a certain Cárdenas, one of the colonels who applied the *ley de fuga* in the times of Porfirio Díaz; Cárdenas had the orders repeated by Huerta himself and by Mondragón and Blanquet, now Ministers of State. Then, in the darkness of the night of February 22, 1913, one week after the *coup d'état,* he prepared and carried out the sacred festival of Aztec militarism — the sacrifice of the prisoners.

3. FOR LAND AND LIBERTY

In his call for revolution, the Plan of San Luis Potosí, Madero had emphasized political objectives, only lightly touching on the subject of land reform. But in the mountainous southern state of Morelos, where the Indian communities had long waged a losing struggle against the encroaching sugar haciendas, the revolution, led by Emiliano Zapata, began under the slogan Tierra y Libertad ("Land and Liberty"). When Zapata became convinced that Madero did not intend to carry out his promise to restore land to the villages, he revolted and issued his own program, the Plan of Ayala, for which he continued to battle until the great guerrilla fighter was slain by treachery in 1919. Zapata's principled and tenacious struggle and the popularity of his ideas, among the landless peasantry contributed to the adoption of a bold program of agrarian reform in the Constitution of 1917. Important provisions of the Plan of Ayala follow.[5]

THE LIBERATING PLAN of the sons of the State of Morelos, members of the insurgent army that

[5] Gildardo Magaña, *Emiliano Zapata y el agrarismo en México,* México, 1934–1937, 2 vols., I, 126–130. (Excerpt translated by the editor.)

demands the fulfillment of the Plan of San Luis Potosí, as well as other reforms that it judges convenient and necessary for the welfare of the Mexican Nation.

We, the undersigned, constituted as a Revolutionary Junta, in order to maintain and obtain the fulfillment of the promises made by the revolution of November 20, 1910, solemnly proclaim in the face of the civilized world . . . , so that it may judge us, the principles that we have formulated in order to destroy the tyranny that oppresses us. . . .

1. . . . Considering that the President of the Republic, Señor Don Francisco I. Madero, has made a bloody mockery of Effective Suffrage by . . . entering into an infamous alliance with the *científicos,* the *hacendados,* the feudalists, and oppressive *caciques,* enemies of the Revolution that he proclaimed, in order to forge the chains of a new dictatorship more hateful and terrible than that of Porfirio Díaz. . . : For these reasons we declare the said Francisco I. Madero unfit to carry out the promises of the Revolution of which he was the author. . . .

4. The Revolutionary Junta of the State of Morelos formally proclaims to the Mexican people:

That it endorses the Plan of San Luis Potosí with the additions stated below for the benefit of the oppressed peoples, and that it will defend its principles until victory or death. . . .

6. As an additional part of the plan we proclaim, be it known: that the lands, woods, and waters usurped by the *hacendados, científicos,* or *caciques* through tyranny and venal justice henceforth belong to the towns or citizens who have corresponding titles to these properties, of which they were despoiled by the bad faith of our oppressors. They shall retain possession of the said properties at all costs, arms in hand. The usurpers who think they have a right to the said lands may state their claims before special tribunals to be established upon the triumph of the Revolution.

7. Since the immense majority of Mexican towns and citizens own nothing but the ground on which they stand and endure a miserable existence, denied the opportunity to improve their social condition or to devote themselves to industry or agriculture because a few individuals monopolize the lands, woods, and waters — for these reasons the great estates shall be expropriated, with indemnification to the owners of one third of such monopolies, in order that the

towns and citizens of Mexico may obtain *ejidos,* colonies, town sites, and arable lands. Thus the welfare of the Mexican people shall be promoted in all respects.

8. The properties of those *hacendados, cientificos,* or *caciques* who directly or indirectly oppose the present Plan shall be seized by the nation, and two thirds of their value shall be used for war indemnities and pensions for the widows and orphans of the soldiers who may perish in the struggle for this Plan.

9. In proceeding against the above properties there shall be applied the laws of disentail and nationalization, as may be convenient, using as our precept and example the laws enforced by the immortal Juárez against Church property — laws that taught a painful lesson to the despots and conservatives who at all times have sought to fasten upon the people the yoke of oppression and backwardness.

4. The Mexican Land Reform

Peace returned to Mexico in 1920. Under Presidents Obregón (1920–1924) and Calles (1924–1928) the work of reconstruction was begun. Some land was distributed to the villages; a young, dynamic Minister of Education, José Vasconcelos, organized a program of popular education that attracted much interest abroad; and a magnificent new art that expressed and served the ideals of the Revolution took form at the hands of great painters like José Clemente Orozco, Diego Rivera, and David Alfaro Siqueiros. But the affluent twenties corroded the moral fiber of many of the revolutionary leaders, and the pace of reform finally slowed down to a standstill. It required the Great Depression and rumblings of revolt among the people to produce a sweeping new advance under the leadership of President Cárdenas (1934–1940). Perhaps the most important and controversial achievement of his régime was its land redistribution program. Nathan Whetten, author of a monumental study of rural Mexico, summarizes the main results of the Cárdenas land reform.[6]

The great land monopoly which has plagued Mexico since colonial times and which reached its height under the régime of Porfirio Díaz has now been broken. There still remain many large private holdings in various parts of the country, particularly in the semiarid regions, where with-

out water the land is not suitable for cultivation; but the intolerable situation wherein about 90 per cent of the rural population had no land whatsoever, while a small minority owned or controlled almost all the land resources of the nation, has now been rather thoroughly liquidated. The ejidatarios have possession of about half the crop land and 22 per cent of all the land that was censused in 1940. In addition to the ejido program, small farms have been created out of lands made available through national irrigation and colonization projects. The Mexican government is pledged to continue to bring new lands into production through irrigation and colonization.

In 1940 there were 1,601,392 ejidatarios, and the total population living on ejidos amounted to 4,992,058 inhabitants, or one-fourth the total inhabitants of Mexico. In addition, there were 928,593 small private landholders having plots of 5 hectares, or less, in size. If we assume that the population on these small private holdings is distributed in about the same way as on the ejidos, it would mean that approximately 2,894,-424 inhabitants live in families having access to these plots and that 40 per cent of the total population of Mexico live either on the ejidos or on small privately owned holdings of 5 hectares or less. This indicates a high degree of land diffusion among the population in contrast to the land monopoly that existed previously. Nevertheless, there are still many rural families who have no land, and there are many sons and daughters of the ejidatarios becoming of age each year with little or no land available for them. Some land will be made available in the future through continuation of federal construction of irrigation projects and through drainage and malarial control in the sparsely populated coastal areas, but it is unlikely that these lands will be developed fast enough to take care of the needs of a rapidly increasing population. The cry of *tierra y libertad* is likely to continue until industrialization develops to the point at which it can absorb the surplus rural population and until efficient techniques of farming have become widespread enough to increase the present low yield of crops far beyond those realized by the present inefficient techniques that are generally practiced.

Mexico has not yet solved the problem of efficient agricultural production on the ejidos. Some ejidos are operating efficiently, but the vast majority are operated on a subsistence basis, with the crop land providing a little corn for

6 Nathan Whetten, *Rural Mexico,* Chicago, The University of Chicago Press, 1948, pp. 565–568. Copyright, 1948, by the University of Chicago Press, and reprinted by permission of the University of Chicago Press.

household use and the pasture land maintaining a few head of livestock, usually of poor quality. Very few products are realized for sale. In most cases the peasants were given land without any equipment for working it, and they have had no training or experience in preparation for the transition from peon to proprietor. Ancient and inefficient techniques of production are widely used, and in many instances the parcels of land given to ejidatarios are either too small or too poor in quality to produce a living for the family with the existing techniques of production. On some of the collective ejidos, where the land is of good quality, efficient production sometimes is handicapped by lack of efficient management and by lack of discipline among the workers. The devising of effective methods of stimulating efficient agricultural production on the ejidos is one of Mexico's most serious and urgent problems.

The government has attempted to provide agricultural credit for the ejidos through a national Ejido Bank. The needs have been far greater, however, than could be supplied up to the present. The Ejido Bank is therefore working with only about 15 per cent of the ejidatarios, while, with a few exceptions, the rest have no way of getting credit except at an appalling rate of interest. High interest rates for credit to the ejidos are due partly to the fact that the land cannot be mortgaged or transferred and production is often insufficient to provide the necessary surplus with which to pay off a loan. The Ejido Bank is concentrating its loans largely in restricted areas, where a good deal of supervision can be given, in the hope that, little by little, areas may be developed into efficient producing units so that production will be sufficient to warrant the investment of capital. In a few areas this policy seems to be meeting with success. In these areas ejidatarios are meeting payments on their loans promptly and are receiving credit each year in increasing amounts. In some of these areas the most modern of farm machinery and agricultural techniques are used. Extension of these practices to ejidatarios in general, however, is a matter to be hoped for but one which may take generations to accomplish.

One of Mexico's most serious problems is the rapid depletion of her soil. This began many generations before the agrarian program came into existence, but the author is convinced that its seriousness has been aggravated by the agrarian program. The Mexican peasant is generally unaware of efficient land-use practices. He cuts down the timber on the steep slopes and replaces it with row crops. Overgrazing is conspicuous in many areas, and much of the land is furrowed by deep gullies. Competent soil specialists report that in some of the more densely populated areas much of the topsoil has already been washed away. The federal government has recently organized a soil-conservation service which is carrying on demonstration projects in various parts of the country. A good beginning has been made, and modern methods are being used; but the program is on a small scale, while the needs are tremendous. It will take a long time, even with a broad educational program financed by adequate resources, to correct the wasteful land-use practices that have been in effect for centuries.

The net effect of the revolutionary programs on the agricultural productivity of the nation is very complex and difficult to measure. Production seems to have declined for a few of the basic commodities such as corn, wheat, and beans, but many other products have come into production which more than counterbalance these. Production has greatly increased for such products as pineapples, bananas, tomatoes, rice, sugar cane, cotton, chickpeas, and cattle. Mexico has imported corn and wheat in recent years; she also did so very often during the Díaz régime. Her total exports of agricultural products, however, are greater than during the Díaz régime, even though by 1945 the population had increased 46 per cent over 1910. Thus there appears to be ample evidence that total agricultural production has increased since the Revolution. This does not mean that production is more efficient on the ejido than on the hacienda. The increase may be due in part to the bringing of new land into production through irrigation projects, to the more intensive use of lands that formerly lay idle on the hacienda, to more efficient farming on small private holdings resulting from the breakup of the hacienda, and the shift in certain cases to products better adapted to the soil. At the present time, production appears to be less efficient on the ejidos than on the private holdings. Data in Chapter X indicate that the total production of cotton per hectare in the Laguna region has never been so high since expropriation as it was before and that production per hectare is lower on the ejidos of the region than on the private holdings. The total production in the area has increased, however, and all admit that business activity is much greater in the Laguna region now than ever before. This suggests that the profits from agriculture are being distributed more widely among the local inhabitants instead of being spent in European capitals by the former landlords.

5. CÁRDENAS SPEAKS

Mexico's struggle for economic sovereignty reached a high point under Cárdenas. In 1937 a dispute between American and British oil companies and the unions erupted into a strike, followed by legal battles between the contending parties. When the oil companies refused to accept a Supreme Court verdict in favor of the unions, Cárdenas intervened. On March 18, 1938 — celebrated by Mexicans as marking their declaration of economic independence — the President announced in a radio speech that the properties of the oil companies had been expropriated in the public interest. An excerpt from his message to the nation follows.[7]

THE HISTORY OF THIS LABOR DISPUTE, which culminates in this act of economic emancipation, is the following:

In connection with the strike called in 1934 by the various workers' unions in the employ of the Compañía Mexicana de Petróleo "El Águila," the Federal Executive agreed to intervene as arbitrator to secure a conciliatory agreement between both parties.

In June, 1934, the resultant Award was handed down and, in October of the same year, this was followed by an explanatory decision establishing adequate procedure for revising those resolutions which had not already been agreed to.

At the end of 1934 and early in 1936, the Chief of the Labor Department, delegated by me for that purpose, handed down several decisions with respect to wage levels, contractual cases, and uniformity of wages, on the basis of the Constitutional principle of equal pay for equal work.

The same Department, for the purpose of eliminating certain anomalous conditions, called the representatives of the various trade-union groups into a conference at which an agreement was reached on numerous pending cases, others being reserved for subsequent investigation and analysis by commissions composed of labor and employer representatives.

The Union of Oil Workers then issued a call for a special assembly in which they laid down the terms of a collective contract which was re-

jected by the oil companies on its presentation.

Out of consideration for the wishes of the companies and in order to avert a strike, the Chief of the Labor Department was instructed to secure the acquiescence of both parties to the holding of a worker-employer convention to be entrusted with the task of establishing, by mutual agreement, the terms of the collective contract. The agreement to hold the convention was signed November 27, 1936, and in the meetings the companies presented their counter-proposals. Because of the slow progress being made, it was then decided to divide the clauses of the contract into economic, social, and administrative categories, so that an immediate examination of the first-named group might be undertaken.

The difficulties preventing an agreement between the workers and the companies were clearly revealed by the discussions; their respective points of view were found to be very far apart, the companies maintaining that the workers' demands were exaggerated and the workers, for their part, pointing to the companies' intransigence in refusing to understand their social necessities. As a result of the breakdown of the negotiations, the strike began in May, 1937. In response to my appeals, the companies then offered an increase in wages and a betterment of certain other conditions, and the Union of Oil Workers decided to resume work on June 9th, at the same time bringing an economic action against the companies before the Board of Conciliation and Arbitration.

As a result of these events, the Board of Conciliation and Arbitration took jurisdiction in the case and, in accordance with the provisions of the law, a commission of experts, composed of persons of high moral standing and adequate preparation, was designated by the President of the Board.

The commission's report found that the companies could afford to meet the disbursements recommended in it, namely, an annual increase of 26,332,756 pesos, as against the offer made by the seventeen oil companies at the time of the strike in May, 1937. The experts specifically stated that the conditions recommended in the report would be totally satisfied with the expenditure of the sum stipulated, but the companies argued that the amount recommended was excessive and might signify an even greater expenditure, which they estimated at a total of 41,000,000 pesos.

[7] *Mexico's Oil*, México, 1940, pp. 878–879.

In view of these developments, the Executive then suggested the possibility of an agreement between representatives of the Union of Oil Workers and the companies, duly authorized to deal with the dispute, but this solution proved impossible because of the refusal of the companies.

Notwithstanding the failure of this effort, the Public Power, still desirous of securing an extrajudicial agreement between the parties at issue, instructed the Labor Authorities to inform the companies of its willingness to intervene with the purpose of persuading the Labor Unions to accept the interpretations necessary to clarify certain obscure points of the Award which might later lend themselves to misunderstandings, and to assure the companies that in no case would the disbursements ordered by the Award be allowed to exceed the above-mentioned sum of 26,332,756 pesos; but in spite of this direct intervention of the Executive, it was impossible to obtain the results sought.

In each and every one of the various attempts of the Executive to arrive at a final solution of the conflict within conciliatory limits, and which include the periods prior to and following the *amparo* action which has produced the present situation, the intransigence of the companies was clearly demonstrated.

Their attitude was therefore premeditated and their position deliberately taken, so that the Government, in defense of its own dignity, had to resort to application of the Expropriation Act, as there were no means less drastic or decision less severe that might bring about a solution of the problem.

For additional justification of the measure herein announced, let us trace briefly the history of the oil companies' growth in Mexico and of the resources with which they have developed their activities.

It has been repeated *ad nauseam* that the oil industry has brought additional capital for the development and progress of the country. This assertion is an exaggeration. For many years, throughout the major period of their existence, the oil companies have enjoyed great privileges for development and expansion, including customs and tax exemptions and innumerable prerogatives; it is these factors of special privilege, together with the prodigious productivity of the oil deposits granted them by the Nation often against public will and law, that represent almost the total amount of this so-called capital.

Potential wealth of the Nation; miserably underpaid native labor; tax exemptions; economic privileges; governmental tolerance — these are the factors of the boom of the Mexican oil industry.

Let us now examine the social contributions of the companies. In how many of the villages bordering on the oil fields is there a hospital, or school or social center, or a sanitary water supply, or an athletic field, or even an electric plant fed by the millions of cubic meters of natural gas allowed to go to waste?

What center of oil production, on the other hand, does not have its company police force for the protection of private, selfish, and often illegal interests? These organizations, whether authorized by the Government or not, are charged with innumerable outrages, abuses, and murders, always on behalf of the companies that employ them.

Who is not aware of the irritating discrimination governing construction of the company camps? Comfort for the foreign personnel; misery, drabness, and insalubrity for the Mexicans. Refrigeration and protection against tropical insects for the former; indifference and neglect, medical service and supplies always grudgingly provided, for the latter; lower wages and harder, more exhausting labor for our people.

The tolerance which the companies have abused was born, it is true, in the shadow of the ignorance, betrayals, and weakness of the country's rulers; but the mechanism was set in motion by investors lacking in the necessary moral resources to give something in exchange for the wealth they have been exploiting.

Another inevitable consequence of the presence of the oil companies, strongly characterized by their anti-social tendencies, and even more harmful than all those already mentioned, has been their persistent and improper intervention in national affairs.

The oil companies' support to strong rebel factions against the constituted government in the Huasteca region of Veracruz and in the Isthmus of Tehuantepec during the years 1917 to 1920 is no longer a matter for discussion by anyone. Nor is anyone ignorant of the fact that in later periods and even at the present time, the oil companies have almost openly encouraged the ambitions of elements discontented with the country's government, every time their interests were affected either by taxation or by the modification of their privileges or the withdrawal of the customary tolerance. They have had money, arms, and munitions for rebellion, money for the anti-patriotic press which defends them, money with which to enrich their unconditional defenders. But for the progress of the country, for establishing an economic equilibrium with their workers through a just compensation of labor, for maintaining hygenic conditions in the districts where they themselves operate, or for conserving the vast riches of the natural petroleum gases from destruction, they have neither money, nor financial possibilities, nor the desire to subtract the necessary funds from the volume of their profits.

Nor is there money with which to meet a responsibility imposed upon them by judicial verdict, for they rely on their pride and their economic power to shield them from the dignity and sovereignty of a Nation which has generously placed in their hands its vast natural resources and now finds itself unable to obtain the satisfaction of the most elementary obligations by ordinary legal means.

As a logical consequence of this brief analysis, it was therefore necessary to adopt a definite and legal measure to end this permanent state of affairs in which the country sees its industrial progress held back by those who hold in their hands the power to erect obstacles as well as the motive power of all activity and who, instead of using it to high and worthy purposes, abuse their economic strength to the point of jeopardizing the very life of a Nation endeavoring to bring about the elevation of its people through its own laws, its own resources, and the free management of its own destinies.

With the only solution to this problem thus placed before it, I ask the entire Nation for moral and material support sufficient to carry out so justified, important, and indispensable a decision.

The Government has already taken suitable steps to maintain the constructive activities now going forward throughout the Republic, and for that purpose it asks the people only for its full confidence and backing in whatever dispositions the Government may be obliged to adopt.

Nevertheless, we shall, if necessary, sacrifice all the constructive projects on which the Nation has embarked during the term of this Administration in order to cope with the financial obligations imposed upon us by the application of the Expropriation Act to such vast interests; and although the subsoil of the country will give us considerable economic resources with which to meet the obligation of indemnification

which we have contracted, we must be prepared for the possibility of our individual economy also suffering the indispensable readjustments, even to the point, should the Bank of Mexico deem it necessary, of modifying the present exchange rate of our currency, so that the whole country may be able to count on sufficient currency and resources with which to consolidate this act of profound and essential economic liberation of Mexico.

It is necessary that all groups of the population be imbued with a full optimism and that each citizen, whether in agricultural, industrial, commercial, transportation, or other pursuits, develop a greater activity from this moment on, in order to create new resources which will reveal that the spirit of our people is capable of saving the nation's economy by the efforts of its own citizens.

And, finally, as the fear may arise among the interests now in bitter conflict in the field of international affairs that a deviation of raw materials fundamentally necessary to the struggle in which the most powerful nations are engaged might result from the consummation of this act of national sovereignty and dignity, we wish to state that our petroleum operations will not depart a single inch from the moral solidarity maintained by Mexico with the democratic nations, whom we wish to assure that the expropriation now decreed has as its only purpose the elimination of obstacles erected by groups who do not understand the evolutionary needs of all peoples and who would themselves have no compunction in selling Mexican oil to the highest bidder, without taking into account the consequences of such action to the popular masses and the nations in conflict.

6. THE BALANCE SHEET OF THE REVOLUTION

In 1945, a quarter-century after the constructive phase of the Mexican Revolution began, a noted Mexican economist, editor, and government official, Jesús Silva Herzog (1893–   ), attempted to appraise the achievements and failures of the movement to date. His major conclusions follow.[8]

LAND HUNGER was a fundamental cause of the Mexican Revolution. Because it was a necessary

[8] Jesús Silva Herzog, *Un ensayo sobre la revolución mejicana,* México, Cuadernos Americanos, 1946, pp. 62–114. (Excerpt translated by the editor.) Reprinted by courtesy of *Cuadernos Americanos.*

task that could not be deferred, the revolutionary governments were compelled to distribute the land of the hacendados without previously drawing up a complete and perfected technical plan.

To those who criticize the agrarian program, saying that land has been distributed hastily, the answer must be that if a man on the point of death from hunger presents himself at your door, you do not go in search of a doctor to tell you what would be the most suitable diet; you give the man a piece of bread or any other food at hand in order to save his life. That is what happened in Mexico with regard to the agrarian question. It was necessary to give land to those who had a right to it, for the simple reason that they had a right to eat. The revolutionary governments did well in what they did, despite the inevitable imperfections of the procedures followed. It was a matter of solving with speed a grave, age-old problem.

Later, a few years after the transformation of the agrarian system had begun, the revolutionary governments began to concern themselves with improving agricultural techniques, with giving credits to the *ejidatario* and the small independent farmer, and with raising the cultural level of the farmers and their children. . . .

During the six years of the Cárdenas regime more land was distributed to the people than in all the previous administrations put together.

One criticism that can be leveled at the agrarian reform from a revolutionary point of view, with which the author of this essay associates himself, is that the peasant families have received very small parcels of land or land of very poor quality, with the result that in the majority of cases there has been only a very slight advance in the standard of living — and in other cases there has been no improvement at all. Frequently land of a quantity or quality inadequate to satisfy the most elementary needs has been distributed, just to solve the political problems of the moment. It is true that one could point to numerous instances in which it was impossible to make larger grants of land in a given region; but it is equally true that in other cases larger allotments could have been made. We know, of course, that the maximum amount of land that can be given to an individual family by way of *dotación* or *restitución* is fixed by law; but it is precisely with this legal criterion that we disagree. We hold that land distribution is not a gift but a right, that the agrarian reform should not simply consist in keeping the millions of Mexican peasants who still constitute the majority of our population from dying from hunger or from being vilely exploited, but in transforming their conditions of life, in raising their economic and cultural level until they become a consumer class, having at least a modest purchasing power, and actually and definitively incorporated into civilization. . . .

Not enough care has been taken to orient the peasant in political and social questions, or to create in him a firm and clear revolutionary ideology. That is why there are cases of *ejidatarios* who hire laborers, people even poorer and less fortunate than themselves. We recall a recent and impressive instance. A group of *ejidatarios* from the State of Morelos were discussing with a public official the price that the Government should set on their rice harvest. One of the group, speaking of the rise in the cost of production, said to the official: "The trouble is, Señor, the peons demand such high wages nowadays."

It cannot and should not be denied that errors have been committed in carrying out the agrarian reform. Yet we firmly believe that the advantages obtained have been enormous, that the result shows a favorable balance. Most important of all is the fact that hundreds of thousands of serfs have been transformed into men, into citizens who know how to defend their rights. Now we must neither retreat nor halt; we must march forward, continuing and perfecting the reform by correcting the mistakes of yesterday and making necessary adjustments. . . .

Much has been said of the decline in the country's agricultural production as a result of the agrarian reform, and there are those — generally incurable reactionaries — who assure us with pontifical emphasis that in 1944 less was produced than in the good old days of General Porfirio Díaz.

It seems obvious that such a profound transformation in the system of land tenure as was accomplished in Mexico must inevitably affect certain branches of agricultural production until the factors of production had made the necessary adjustments. But to say that we are producing less now than in the first decade of the century is, at best, incredible nonsense. For how will those gentlemen explain the fact that as a result of a population increase of more than five million people and the decline (according to them) of food production, devastating famines have not taken place in Mexican territory? And let them not reply that the famines were averted by the importation of wheat and corn, for if this is partly true it is also true that wheat and corn were imported more than once during the Díaz regime. They need to be reminded that from 1903–1904 to 1911–1912 we imported corn to the value of twenty-six million pesos and other grains to the value of ninety-four million pesos. At that time the value of the pesos was at least five or six times greater than at present. . . .

In 1926 there were organized four Agricultural Ejido Banks and the National Bank of Agricultural Credit. The four Agricultural Ejido Banks were established in the cities of Tula (Hidalgo), Celaya (Guanajuato), Morelia (Michoacán), and Durango (Durango), with a capital of 200,000 pesos each and an organization similar to that of cooperative credit societies. The experiment was unsuccessful, for these four small banks, as well as two or three more of the same type that were later established in other towns, were closed a few years after their formation. The National Bank of Agricultural Credit, on the other hand, has continued to operate down to the present, granting credit to *ejidatarios* and independent small farmers until 1935, and from 1936 to 1944 only to the latter, as a result of the founding of the National Bank of Ejidal Credit. During its nineteen years of operation the Agricultural Bank has lent 173 million pesos in round figures, of which it has recovered 125. As for the National Bank of Ejidal Credit, its loans to ejidatarios from 1936 to December 31, 1943, amounted to 536 million pesos, of which 366 millions were recovered.

The reader will probably think, with reason, that the percentage of recovery is very low; but it must be remembered that these banks are not operated, nor should or can they be operated, on a commercial basis; they are institutions for the benefit of society, and consequently their losses are at least understandable. When the primary objective is the satisfaction of collective necessities by financial organs of social progress, it is logical that the profit motive should occupy a secondary place in the minds of the directors, and that significant losses should occur. Clearly this is not the best solution, for in such cases the ideal would be to realize the social objective without detriment to the public Treasury.

In 1926 there were also established in different parts of the country various agricultural schools of a special type, intended to teach modern agricultural techniques to the sons of *ejida-*

tarios and the owners of small agricultural properties.

The use of agricultural machinery, which was hardly known in our country at the opening of the present century, is slowly becoming general. The value of the imports of implements and machinery rose in 1910 to 986,708,000 pesos and in 1926 to more than seven million pesos; in 1944 it exceeded 20 million pesos. At present the production of agricultural implements in the country is sufficient to meet all domestic requirements, and in the city of Saltillo a large factory is under construction — a subsidiary of International Harvester — for the production of agricultural machinery. This last fact demonstrates the growth of the national market and the consequent strong tendency toward modernization of agriculture.

Under General Díaz there was no plan for large-scale construction of irrigation works for increasing the cultivated area. The few small dams that were constructed at that time were built in the great majority of cases through the initiative and financial contributions of a few progressive hacendados.

In 1926 the National Irrigation Commission was founded, with the object of undertaking the construction of irrigation works at government expense, on the assumption that this was one of the most urgent of tasks, one that could not be put off. During the sixteen years that this Commission has functioned, 615,379 hectares have been placed under cultivation, at an approximate cost of 494 million pesos.

The construction of dams should be a source of pride to our revolutionary governments. To be sure, some irrigation systems have proven too costly, and errors were made in calculating the irrigable areas; but it is also true, on the one hand, that such errors may be excused by the lack of data and technical experience, and, on the other, by the fact that in the matter of costs per hectare the prevailing point of view was not a commercial but an economic-social one; the object was to increase agricultural production and bring former desert zones to permanent life.

Mining has traditionally been the chief source of Mexican wealth. Today it still has great importance, though not so much as in the past — not because production has diminished, but because of the development of other branches of the national economy. Unfortunately, the mines, like the metal-processing plants, are in the hands of foreign enterprises, North American and English, many of them connected with great economic organizations of immense financial power. In this respect the Republic is a semi-colonial country, and it can be said that the mineral wealth of Mexico belongs not to the Mexicans but to a few millionaires or multi-millionaires, "sleeping partners" who were born outside our borders and who live in London or some great North American city. In any case (this does not imply, however, that we are content with the situation) we benefit by the wages, the imports, and part of the raw materials obtained from the exploitation of the mines. . . .

Before the Revolution, Mexico's mineral production consisted of precious metals. Since 1920 the industrial metals have acquired a well-known importance and today constitute a significant source of wealth. The production of copper, lead, and zinc increased very significantly after 1914 and remained high, despite various fluctuations, between 1920 and 1944.

The mining companies in our country have enjoyed a privileged status. For example, one could cite the exceptionally low railroad freight rates that they have enjoyed for a long time. The National Railroads have tried to raise them on different occasions, but they have always been defeated by the influence of these great enterprises. Mexico cannot sell the minerals extracted from its subsoil directly to any country that it chooses; it cannot do so because the mining companies will not permit it. The sales contracts must be signed in New York or in London. . . .

As for petroleum, in 1910 about four million barrels were produced; in 1920, 157 millions; in 1930, 40 millions; and in 1944, 38 millions. In recent years production has been maintained at about 40 million barrels. . . .

With respect to industry, a few facts may be presented. The Monterey Steel and Iron Company produced 45 thousand tons of iron ingots in 1910, 133 thousand in 1944.

In 1910 there were 127 factories spinning and weaving cotton; there were 193 in 1940. The number of looms was 26,184 in the former year and 37,000 in 1945; the number of spindles was 723,963 and 900,000 respectively. The consumption of cotton rose from 35,169 tons in 1910 to 69,000 in 1944. . . .

One of the greatest concerns of the Revolution has been to raise the cultural level of the Mexican people. Since 1921 an important work has been accomplished in the cities and in the countryside — a difficult and complicated task, because in Mexico there is not an educational problem but "educational problems," owing, among other factors, to the differing levels of development of the population. It was impossible to solve the problems of cultural advance in the cities and in the countryside or, for example, among the peasants of Nayarit and those of Tabasco or Yucatan, with a single formula. The lack of resources and of teachers, moreover, has hindered the solution of a question so vital for the future of Mexico. It was necessary to reduce the number of illiterates, who in 1910 composed 70 per cent of the population; it was necessary to teach agricultural technique to the peasants; it was necessary to establish technical schools to prepare the youth for the tasks connected with modern economic development; for these purposes cultural missions were organized which went to different parts of the country to impart useful knowledge to the people. Teachers and rural schools have been established within the limits of the budgets; secondary and technical schools have been organized that are open to all social classes without distinction; in fine, efforts have been made that could be called titanic, and that have been well oriented as concerns their direction. Yet it must be confessed that we are far from achieving our goal. The number of illiterates had fallen to 65 per cent in 1921 and to 59.26 per cent in 1930; by now — September, 1945 — the proportion of persons who cannot read or write must be a little under 50 per cent. Something has been done; but much more remains to be done. The total number of elementary and secondary schools, meanwhile, rose from 9,541 in 1907 to 19,538 in 1930, and to 23,434 in 1940.

That the Revolutionary Governments have labored constructively in the field of education cannot be denied. But worthy, very worthy, as this work has been, it is still far from approaching even relative perfection. True, illiteracy has fallen considerably, and this in itself is an achievement of first-rate significance; but it must be noted that what has been gained in quantity in the large cities, especially in Mexico City, has been lost in quality. The level of primary education — I refer now solely to the Capital of the Republic, because that is a matter known to me at first hand — has declined in recent years.

In the field of higher education, the Revolution has notable accomplishments to its credit as concerns technical instruction, but the same cannot be said of university culture, of science and philosophy. The revolutionary governments have treated the universities of the country with unjustified neglect. The National University of Mexico has existed and does exist in shameful poverty, and the universities organized in various cities of the Republic are in even worse condition. The professors receive salaries lower than those paid to janitors in government offices, with the result that the profession of university teacher hardly exists in Mexico. The professors must earn a living by some other activity, and their teaching is a supplementary chore, and hence they frequently come to the lecture-room unprepared. Some teachers offer admirable examples of sacrifice and heroism, but their heroism and sacrifices, praiseworthy as they may be, do not guarantee that their instruction will be particularly profitable. For how can a teacher, self-sacrificing and capable as he may be, perform really fruitful intellectual labor when he must teach five and six hours a day — an exhausting labor — when he has no money to buy books and is sometimes oppressed by urgent financial worries?

Mexican universities lack modern laboratories and modern libraries; their enrolments, on the other hand, are so large as to make the work of teaching difficult and sometimes impossible. An example: In the National School of Medicine of the University of Mexico groups of two hundred, three hundred, and even four hundred students assemble in a hall with seats for one hundred and twenty to listen (but not very attentively) to the sage words of a professor who hurriedly arrives from a consultation or from some office job that has kept him busy for six or eight hours. . . .

Public health is one of the most serious questions confronting the nation. The lack of hygiene is shocking. Infant mortality reaches frightful figures. Hundreds of millions of pesos are needed for sanitation work in all parts of the Republic, for construction of, among other things, drainage and public water systems in the towns. Some efforts have been made in this direction, it is true; new hospitals have been constructed; the Social Security System is successfully beginning its vast and complex labor; and in recent years, between 1933 and 1944, the National Mortgage Bank has invested twenty-one million pesos to provide public water and drainage systems to 138 towns, with resulting benefits to more than one million seven hundred thousand inhabitants. The Federal Government, for its part, has directly invested considerable sums in such works.

The standard of living of the population has unquestionably risen a little, only a little, and more in the towns than in the countryside. But we are still a vast distance from our goal. There are many population groups in different parts of the Republic which do not enjoy the benefits of the Revolution — whose members live as their forefathers lived two or three centuries ago.

The Revolutionary Governments have favored the formation of trade unions, and for many years we have had a labor law that is certainly one of the most advanced codes in the world. It can be said that the immense, the overwhelming majority of Mexican industrial workers have their trade union organizations, which enable them to struggle in defense of their interests, frequently with unquestioned success.

The author of this essay approves without qualifications the organization of the working class. We regard as perfectly proper and fitting the organization of trade unions and the use of strikes as a weapon of struggle, for we know that only in this way can the proletariat compel the bourgeoisie to improve its living conditions. But we disapprove the lack of political education of the workers, their unclear class consciousness that on occasion causes them to speak out against their own interests; and we energetically censure certain lying leaders, traitors to their class, who have no moral backbone and whose sole object is getting rich in a hurry. We must criticize even more energetically, with deep concern and sadness, the workers who tolerate their betrayers, for this is an alarming symptom of the internal decay that has overtaken certain workers' groups.

Mexican trade-unionism was organized, at least in part and in its beginnings, from above, in official spheres. Here, perhaps, are the roots of some of its principal defects, among other reasons, because its leaders were not developed in the hard day-to-day struggle for existence but obtained their positions through the intrigues of political cliques, in the antechambers of ministers and by means of official favoritism. It is obvious that the above remark does not apply to all cases, but it applies to not a few.

Our foreign policy was exemplary from Carranza to the time of Cárdenas, and basically it has been so during the administration of General Ávila Camacho. Our attitude in Geneva, always in defense of weaker peoples and in support of the Spanish Republic, has given great moral stature to Mexico. For the rest, Mexico has been the asylum of all the victims of persecution, without distinction of creed or race; Spanish republicans, German or Polish Jews, Central Americans, and the sons of some South-American republics have all found refuge and friendly reception here. We have shared with them the little or the much that we had.

Notwithstanding the above, some find small blemishes here and there. Some criticize the Bucareli Treaties; others find fault with the settlement of the oil question between President Calles and Ambassador Morrow [9]; there are many, finally, who question the wisdom of certain aspects of the foreign policy of Doctor Ezequiel Padilla during his tenure as Secretary of Foreign Relations.

We are glad and even proud that we joined the Allied Powers in good time in their struggle against the totalitarian régimes; we agree that Mexico should cultivate sincerely friendly relations with the United States. But we dislike an attitude of excessive politeness; it hurts to see us placed psychologically in the attitude of a servant who stands on the sidewalk and speaks in humble tones to his master as he looks out of a third-story window. . . .

Concerning the public administration, we are compelled to say unpleasant things. And not from a desire to criticize, but from a sense of civic duty and with the hope that the indicated evils, which are not at all peculiar to Mexico or the Mexican Government, may some day be corrected. Certainly there have been and there are honest officials and employees in the Revolutionary governments; otherwise there could not have been and could not be effective government. But it has not been possible to have model governments because there have been and there are unscrupulous employees and officials, corrupted by a growing immorality. A few weeks ago Doctor Eduardo Suárez, Secretary of the Treasury, said in a speech before the Confederation of the Chambers of Commerce: "I must call atention to the frail morality of a large number of government agents — especially those employed by the treasury. Confronted with this sad state of affairs, the public limits itself to the composition of ingenious lampoons, to leveling sharp criticisms against the government, and to viewing the reprehensible practices with apathy and indifference, falling at last into an immoral collusion with the dishonest agent. There is a need, I am sure you will agree, for a vigorous reaction of the social organism against the wave of corruption and immorality which threatens to destroy the very basis of authority and to poison the very founts of social life."

The explanation of this phenomenon is complex. It is to be found in the crisis of values through which the world is going; in the decomposition of an economic structure very near its end; in the complicity of hundreds of individuals, especially among those who make up the so-called "living forces": merchants, industrialists, professional men, etc. It is to be found, finally — why not admit it? — in the case of the lower public officials, in the low salaries which sometimes do not cover their most elementary needs. There are doubtless other causes which it would take too long to analyze here. The problem is serious; it is a purulent wound that threatens to infect the whole organism and calls for the surgeon's knife. It is necessary to cut off the infected members if we want Mexico to be a nation respected by its own sons and by the citizens and subjects of other countries.

Another criticism that can and should be leveled at the Revolution in the sphere of government consists in noting that it has neglected in a most lamentable way, or at least has not given sufficient care to, the formation of a collective revolutionary spirit. The ideas of the revolutionary movement have not penetrated clearly and precisely the minds of all our people. The fact is that the majority of the organs of publicity have been in the power of enemies of the revolution. The radio stations and the newspapers of wide circulation are commercial enterprises, and logically and inevitably must serve those who pay for the advertisements and broadcasts — and those who pay for the advertisements and broadcasts do not, as a rule, sympathize with principles of social progress. They are the only ones who feel at home in this world that has lost its bearings. . . .

In fine, we have neglected a fundamental task, the propagation of the new principles; and it must be confessed that it was an error, an omission that showed a lack of vision, not to have concerned ourselves with a matter of such transcendent importance, an omission whose negative effects can be incalculable.

For the rest . . . , the Revolution has not proved capable of creating a revolutionary *mystique*. I do not use the word in a religious

[9] By the Bucareli agreements of 1923 the Mexican Government gave assurances to the United States concerning the future security of American property, especially petroleum holdings. Ambassador Morrow's diplomacy obtained the annulment of petroleum laws that violated the Bucareli agreements. B. K.

sense, as meaning a drawing of the soul nearer to Divinity, but in the sense of a fervent passion and ardent desire to serve with love and disinterestedness a cause that is considered useful and beneficial to the country or the social group of which one forms part.

In the matter of domestic policy there are two completely positive factors to be noted, particularly since 1935; respect for human life and freedom of thought. At this moment, we can say with satisfaction, there are no political prisoners in any part of the national territory; everyone can express his ideas, whatever they may be, without danger; one can attack the government, one can even attack the President anywhere; one can write against the authorities; nothing will happen to the writer, the orator, the agitator.

The fact that Mexico has been and is a refuge for the victims of political persecution; the fact that the Federal Government has consecrated the principle of respect for human life; and, finally, the fact that it has converted into reality the aspiration to freedom of action and thought — these are permanent values, results of the ascending process of the Mexican Revolution, that are enough to justify it fully before the conscience of the man of today and tomorrow.

It is true that the Revolution faces a crisis. I said it two years ago and I repeat it now with equal conviction. The crisis springs from the confusion in ideas and the corruption of principles — it is an ideological and a moral crisis. Yet we are certain, and want to be certain, that the honest and sincere revolutionaries, who have not enriched themselves in public office, will find ways to master the crisis by purifying their ranks, by imbuing the revolutionary movement with lofty ideals, with the new sap of the younger generation, that always embodies noble aspirations and the promise of victory.

XXX

Storm Over the Andes

IN THE TWENTIETH CENTURY a broad movement on behalf of the Indian, counterpart of a similar tendency in the Mexican Revolution, acquired special importance in the preeminently Indian republics of Peru, Bolivia, and Ecuador. An elastic concept, *Indianismo* came to include a variety of ideas and approaches, ranging from the vision of a new social order based on Indian communal traditions to more modest efforts to raise the material and cultural level of the Indian by providing him with land, technical assistance, and schools. Common to all varieties of Indianism is their ultimate goal: to incorporate the Indian into the economic, political, and cultural life of the nation.

A giant of Peruvian literature, Manuel González Prada, ushered in the Indianist movement in his country with spirited protests against oppression of the Indians. Two of his disciples, José Carlos Mariátegui and Victor Raúl Haya de la Torre, attempted to give Indianism a body of doctrine and an organized political expression. In his famous *Seven Essays on Peruvian Reality*, Mariátegui approached the Indian problem from an explicitly socialist viewpoint. Haya de la Torre made Indianism a major plank in the platform of his Aprista party. Now in political eclipse, for a time this liberal middle-class movement enjoyed considerable influence throughout Latin America.

Notwithstanding its wide popular appeal and notable cultural achievements, at midcentury Indianism and allied movements could record little progress toward solution of the Indian problem, which was closely linked to the problem of land tenure. A copious body of protective legislation had proven largely ineffective. The need and pressure for reform were dramatically illustrated in 1952, when the Bolivian National Revolutionary Movement swiftly overthrew a conservative régime with the aid of armed Indian miners and peasants. The new government promptly announced a program for nationalization of the tin mines and agrarian reform.

1. THE GREAT ICONOCLAST

Manuel González Prada (1848–1918), one of Latin America's most distinguished literary figures, initiated a new era of social unrest and intellectual ferment in Peru. He launched his "prose thunderbolts" against all that was sacrosanct in Peruvian society: the Army, the church, the State, the creole aristocracy. "Écrasez l'infâme!" could have been his motto, as it was of Voltaire. His honesty, unflinching courage, and social passion won him the respect and even the veneration of younger men who followed the trail that he had blazed. In the following selection González Prada states his views on the Indian question with characteristic vigor.[1]

DOES THE INDIAN suffer less under the Republic than under Spanish rule? The *corregimientos* and *encomiendas* are gone, it is true, but forced labor and conscription remain. Humanity may well curse us for our treatment of the Indian. We keep him in ignorance and serfdom; we debase him in our barracks; we brutalize him with alcohol; we hurl him to his destruction in our civil wars; and from time to time we organize Indian hunts and massacres like those of Amantani, Ilave, and Huanta.

There is an unwritten axiom that the Indian has no rights — only obligations. In his case an individual complaint becomes an act of insubordination; a collective petition, an effort at rebellion. The Spanish royalists slew the Indian when he sought to throw off the yoke of the conquistadores; we republicans exterminate him when he protests against heavy taxes or when he will no longer endure in silence the injustices of some provincial despot.

In the last analysis our form of government is but a great lie, for a state in which two or three million people live outside the protection of the law does not deserve to be called a democratic republic. If on the coast there appears some glimmer of legal guarantees under a semblance of republican government, in the interior the violation of all rights under a true feudal regime appears in all its nakedness. There neither law codes nor law courts prevail, because the landowners and *gamonales* decide everything, arrogating to themselves the roles of judges and executors of their verdicts. The political authorities, far from aiding the weak and the poor, nearly always aid the powerful and the rich. There are regions where the justices of the peace

and the governors form part of the labor force of the hacienda. What governor, prefect, or subprefect dares to defy an hacendado?

An hacienda is formed by the accumulation of small parcels of land seized from their rightful owners. The master exercises over his peons the authority of a Norman baron. Not only does he influence the appointment of governors, alcaldes, and justices of the peace; he arranges marriages, designates heirs, divides inheritances. In order that sons may satisfy the debts of their fathers, he fastens upon them a servitude that commonly lasts for a lifetime. He inflicts severe punishments like the stocks, floggings, the *cepo de campaña*,[2] and death; or "funny" penalties like shaving off their hair or administering enemas of cold water. It would be a miracle if one who respects neither life nor property had any respect for the honor of women; every Indian woman, single or married, is fair game for the brutal desires of the master. A rape or violation means nothing to one who thinks that Indian women must be had by force. Yet the Indian never speaks to the *patrón* without going on his knees and kissing his master's hand.

Don't think that the lords of the land act in this way from ignorance or lack of culture. The sons of some hacendados go to Europe as children, are educated in France or England, and return to Peru having all the appearance of civilized people. But as soon as they shut themselves up in their haciendas they lose their European varnish and act with greater inhumanity and violence than their fathers; along with the high, wide-brimmed hat, the poncho, and the spurs reappears the beast. In fine, the haciendas constitute so many kingdoms in the heart of the republic, and the hacendados are so many autocrats in the midst of Peruvian democracy.

In order to justify the neglect of the government and the inhumanity of the exploiters, some pessimists of the school of Le Bon brand the Indian's brow with a defamatory stigma: they accuse him of obstinately resisting civilization. One might think that all our towns maintain splendid schools filled with brilliant, well-paid teachers, and that the classrooms remain empty because the children, obeying their parents' orders, refuse to attend. One might think also that the natives refuse to follow the edifying exam-

---

[1] Manuel González Prada, *Horas de lucha*, Callao, 1924, pp. 326–338. (Excerpt translated by the editor.)

[2] "An old form of military punishment in which the thumbs were tied together, the knees put between the arms, and one or two rifles placed on the arms between these and the legs." *Appleton's New Spanish Dictionary*, 3rd. ed., 1942.

ples of the governing classes or crucify without the least compunction all exponents of advanced and generous ideas. The Indian receives what we give him: fanaticism and rum.

Come, what do we mean by "civilization"? Above industry and art, above erudition and science, morality shines like a luminous point at the vertex of a great pyramid. Not a theological morality founded on a theological sanction, but human morality, which seeks no sanction and would not dream of seeking it far from the earth. The sum of morality for societies and individuals alike consists in having transformed life from a struggle of man against man into an accord for mutual aid. Where there is no justice, mercy, or benevolence, there is no civilization; where the "struggle for existence" is proclaimed a social law, barbarism reigns. What good is it for a man to acquire the knowledge of an Aristotle, if he keeps the heart of a tiger? Or to possess the artistic gift of a Michelangelo, if he has the soul of a hog? It is better to go through life distilling the honey of goodness than to shed the light of art or science. Only those societies deserve to be called highly civilized in which doing good has ceased to be an obligation and become a custom, in which the generous act has been transformed into an instinctive impulse. Have the rulers of Peru acquired that level of morality? Have they the right to consider the Indian a being incapable of being civilized? . . .

The facts give the lie to the pessimists. The Indian trained in a *colegio* or educated by simple contact with civilized persons acquires the same level of morality and culture as the descendant of the Spaniard. Daily we meet yellow-skinned individuals who dress, eat, live, and think like the "honey-mouthed gentlemen" of Lima. We see Indians in the Congress, in the town councils, the magistracy, the universities, our literary societies, where they appear no more venal or ignorant than individuals of other races. It is impossible to apportion responsibilities in the *totum revolutis* of national politics so that one could say which evil was caused by the mestizos, which by the mulattoes, and which by the whites. There is such a promiscuity of blood and colors, each individual represents so many licit or illicit mixtures, that in the presence of a great many Peruvians one is at a loss to determine the proportion of black and yellow in their skins; no one merits the description of "pure white," even though his eyes be blue and his hair blond. I need only add that Santa Cruz, the

Peruvian ruler who had the broadest outlook of all, was of the Indian race. There were a hundred more, valiant to the point of heroism, like Cahuide, and faithful to the death, like Olaya. . . .

Is ignorance the sole cause of the degradation of the Indian? To be sure, the national ignorance seems incredible when one considers that in many towns of the interior not a single person knows how to read or write; that during the War of the Pacific the natives viewed the struggle of the two nations as a civil war between General Chile and General Peru; that not long ago the emissaries of Chucuito set out for Tacna, believing that they would find there the President of the Republic.

Some pedagogues (rivaling the peddlers of panaceas) believe that once a man knows the tributaries of the Amazon and the median temperature of Berlin he has gone halfway toward solving all social problems. If by some miracle all our illiterates were to wake up tomorrow not only knowing how to read and write but possessing university degrees, the problem of the Indian would not have been solved; the proletariat of the ignorant would be replaced by that of bachelors-of-arts and doctors. Doctors without patients, lawyers without clients, engineers without work, writers without readers, artists without commissions, teachers without students abound in the most civilized nations, forming an innumerable multitude of empty stomachs and brains filled with light. Where the coastal haciendas extend for four or five thousand *fanegadas,* where the estates of the sierra measure from thirty to fifty leagues, the nation must be divided into masters and slaves.

True, instruction can usually convert an impulsive brute into a reasonable and magnanimous being; education can light the way that a man must follow if he is not to go astray at the crossroads of life. But to see the way does not mean that one will follow it to the end; that requires a firm will and strong feet. One must also possess a proud and rebellious spirit, not the submissive and respectful spirit of the soldier and the monk. Education can reduce a man to a low and servile state: the eunuchs and grammarians of Byzantium were educated men. . . .

Nothing changes a man's psychology more swiftly and radically than the possession of property; by throwing off the "slavery of the belly" he grows a hundred feet. The mere acquisition of some property enables an individual to ascend a few steps on the social ladder, because in the last analysis classes are groups classified according to the amount of their wealth. Unlike the balloon, the man who weighs more rises higher. To him who preaches *the school*, let the answer be *school* and *bread*.

The Indian question, then, is an economic and social question, rather than one of pedagogy. How shall it be solved? Not long ago a German conceived the idea of restoring the Inca Empire; he learned Quechua, introduced himself to the Indians of Cuzco, began to win partisans, and might have attempted an uprising if death had not surprised him while he was returning from a voyage to Europe. But would such a restoration have any meaning today? Even if tried and accomplished, it would only yield a Lilliputian mockery of a vanished grandeur.

The condition of the Indian can be improved in one of two ways; either the oppressor's heart will be softened to the point of recognizing the rights of the oppressed, or the spirit of the oppressed will acquire sufficient strength to give a terrible lesson to the oppressor. If the Indian spent on rifles and cartridges the money he wastes on alcohol and fiestas, or if he hid a weapon in a corner of his hut or in the crevice of a cliff, he would compel respect for his life and property. He would reply to violence with violence, chastising the *patrón* who takes his wool, the soldier who conscripts him in the name of the government, the outlaw who steals his sheep and work animals.

Do not preach humility and resignation to the Indian; rather teach him pride and rebellion. What have three or four hundred years of conformity and patience gotten him? The more authorities he has over him, the greater are the evils from which he suffers. Here is a telling fact: Greater well-being prevails in the districts farthest removed from the haciendas; greater order and tranquillity prevail in the towns less frequented by the authorities.

In fine, the Indian must achieve his redemption through his own efforts, not through the humanity of his oppressors. To a greater or lesser degree, every white is a Pizarro, a Valverde, or an Areche.

2. THUNDER ON THE LEFT

Some of González Prada's young disciples went beyond Don Manuel's unsystematic radicalism in their search for solutions to Peru's problems. Basing his thinking on the revolutionary experience of other lands, on Indian communal practices and traditions, and on his study of history and economics, José Carlos Mariátegui (1895–1930) concluded that socialism offered the only certain cure for his country's ills. By contrast with the lava-like flow of González Prada's prose, Mariátegui's style, in the words of Jorge Basadre, is "as precise as an engineer's, aseptic as a physician's." In the following essay Mariátegui discusses the Indian problem.[3]

ALL APPROACHES to the Indian problem that ignore or evade its socio-economic essence are so many sterile theoretical exercises — sometimes on a purely verbal level — that are doomed to absolute discredit. The sincerity of some of these approaches does not save them. In practice, they serve only to conceal or distort the reality of the problem. A socialist critique discloses and illuminates that reality, because it seeks its causes in the country's economy, not in its administrative, juridical, or ecclesiastical mechanism or in the duality or plurality of its races or in its cultural and moral conditions. The Indian question derives from our economy. It has its roots in the system of land tenure. Every effort to solve it with administrative or protective measures, with educational methods or road-building projects, represents a superficial labor as long as the feudalism of the great landowners exists.

Gamonalismo inevitably invalidates every law or ordinance for the protection of the Indian. The landowner, the *latifundista,* is a feudal lord. Against his authority, supported by the milieu and by custom, the written law is impotent. The law forbids unpaid labor, yet unpaid labor and even forced labor survive on the latifundio. The judge, the subprefect, the commissary, the teacher, the tax-collector, are vassals of the great landowners. The law cannot prevail against the gamonales. The official who should obstinately strive to impose it would be abandoned and sacrificed by the central government, over which the influence of gamonalismo, acting directly or through Parliament, ever with the same efficacy, is always omnipotent.

The new approach to the Indian problem, therefore, is much less concerned with devising Indian protective legislation than with the consequences of the system of land tenure. . . .

This critique rejects as invalid the various approaches that evaluate the question according

[3] José Carlos Mariátegui, *Siete ensayos de interpretación de la realidad peruana,* Lima, 1928, pp. 25–32. (Excerpt translated by the editor.)

to one or another of the following unilateral and exclusive criteria: administrative, juridical, ethnic, moral, educational, ecclesiastical.

The first and most evident rout has been suffered by those who would reduce the protection of the Indian to a problem of ordinary administration. Since the days of Spanish colonial legislation, wise and comprehensive ordinances, framed after conscientious inquiries, have proven totally fruitless. The Republican era has been particularly fecund in the production of decrees, laws, and provisions directed toward the protection of the Indians against extortion and abuse. But the gamonal of today, like the encomendero of yesterday, has very little to fear from administrative theory. He knows that the practice is different.

The individualistic character of the Republican legislation unquestionably favored the absorption of Indian property by the latifundio. In this respect Spanish legislation viewed the situation of the Indian with greater realism. But juridical reform has no more value than administrative reform, given the existence of a feudalism intact in its economic structure. The expropriation of the greater part of Indian individual and communal property has already been completed. For the rest, the experience of all countries that have emerged from their feudal age shows that without the dissolution of the feudal estate a liberal legal system cannot function anywhere.

The view that the Indian problem is an ethnic problem draws on the most ancient repertory of imperialist ideas. The concept of inferior races served the white West in its work of expansion and conquest. To expect Indian emancipation to result from an active crossing of the aboriginal race with white immigrants is an example of sociological naiveté that could only arise in the rudimentary brain of an importer of merino sheep. The Asiatic peoples, to whom the Indian people is not at all inferior, have admirably assimilated the most dynamic and creative elements in Western culture without transfusions of European blood. The degeneracy of the Peruvian Indian is a cheap invention of legal lickspittles at the feudal table.

The tendency to consider the Indian problem as a moral problem embodies a liberal, humanitarian, eighteenth-century enlightened conception that in Europe finds expression in the organization of "Leagues of the Rights of Man." This view, which has always placed excessive faith in its appeal to the moral sense of civilization, inspired the European anti-slavery conferences and societies that more or less fruitlessly denounced the crimes of the colonizers. González Prada showed that he shared this hope when he wrote that the "condition of the Indian can be improved in one of two ways: either the hearts of the oppressors will be softened to the point of recognizing the rights of the oppressed, or the spirit of the oppressed will acquire sufficient strength to give a terrible lesson to the oppressors." . . . The experiment has been carried out far enough, in Peru and throughout the world. Humanitarian preachments have not restrained or abashed European imperialism, or improved its methods. The struggle against imperialism now relies solely on the solidarity and strength of the emancipation movements of the colonial masses. . . .

In the field of reason and morality, the religious approach was applied centuries ago, with greater energy, or at least with greater authority, than today. This crusade, however, only yielded laws and provisions of very sage inspiration. The lot of the Indians was not substantially altered. González Prada, who, as we know, did not view these matters from what one might call a properly sectarian or socialist point of view, found the explanation for this fiasco in the economic bowels of the question: "There could be no other result; exploitation was officially ordered; it was proposed to commit iniquities humanely, and to consummate injustices equitably. In order to eradicate abuses, it would have been necessary to abolish the repartimientos and the mita — in a word, to change the whole colonial system. Without the toil of the American Indian, the coffers of the Spanish treasury would have been emptied." Yet the religious preachment had greater possibilities of success than the liberal preachment. The former appealed to the exalted and operative Spanish Catholicism, whereas the latter addressed its pleas to the thin and formal creole liberalism.

But today the hope of an ecclesiastical solution is indisputably the most obsolete and unhistoric of all. The individuals who represent it do not even concern themselves, like their distant — ever so distant! — teachers, with obtaining a declaration of Indian rights, or with the appointment of qualified officials and the adoption of just laws, but instead propose to entrust to the missionary the function of mediating between the Indian and the gamonal. If the

Church could not accomplish its task in a medieval social order — in which its intellectual and spiritual capacity could be measured by friars of the stature of Father Las Casas — what chance of success does it have now? . . .

The concept that the Indian problem is an educational problem appears to lack support even from a strictly pedagogical point of view. Modern pedagogy more than ever takes socio-economic factors into account. The modern educator knows perfectly well that education is not a mere question of school and teaching methods. The socio-economic milieu inexorably conditions the work of the teacher. Gamonalismo is fundamentally hostile to the education of the Indian; it has the same interest in maintaining the Indian in ignorance as it has in cultivating his alcoholism. The modern school — even supposing that under existing conditions it were possible to multiply the number of schools in proportion to the school-age population of the countryside — is incompatible with the feudal latifundio. The mechanics of serfdom would totally annul the action of the school if the latter, by some miracle inconceivable within the existing social framework, could preserve its pure educational mission in a feudal atmosphere. The school and the teacher are inevitably condemned to deformation under the pressure of the feudal milieu, incompatible with the most elementary progressive or evolutionary conception of things. When this truth is half understood, the redeeming formula is found in boarding schools for native students. But the egregious inadequacy of this formula appears in all its nakedness, when one reflects on the insignificant percentage of the school population that could be lodged in these schools.

The pedagogical solution, advanced by many persons with perfect sincerity, is now discarded even in official quarters. The educators, I repeat, are the last people to think of asserting their independence of the socio-economic reality. There remains, then, in effect, nothing but a vague and formless suggestion for which no group or body of doctrine assumes responsibility.

The new approach consists in identifying the Indian problem with the problem of land.

We who study and define the Indian problem from a socialist point of view begin by declaring that the old humanitarian and philanthropic points of view are absolutely superseded. Our first concern is to establish its character as an essentially economic problem. We revolt, in the first place, against the instinctive — and defensive — tendency of the creole or *misti* to reduce it to an exclusively administrative, pedagogic, ethnic, or moral problem, in order to escape at all costs from the economic plane. The most absurd of the charges leveled against us, therefore, is that of assuming lyrical or literary attitudes. By placing the socio-economic problem on the first plane, we assume the least lyrical or literary attitude possible. We are not content with championing the right of the Indian to education, culture, progress, love, and heaven too. We begin with a categorical affirmation of his right to own land. This perfectly materialist position should suffice to distinguish us from the heirs and disciples of Father Las Casas. For the rest, our materialism does not hinder us from feeling the most fervent admiration and regard for the great Spanish friar.

And this problem of land — whose connection with the Indian problem is only too evident — we do not attenuate or minimize in an opportunistic manner. Quite the contrary. For myself, I propose to state the problem in absolutely unequivocal and plain terms.

The agrarian problem appears, above all, as the problem of liquidating feudalism in Peru. This liquidation should have been accomplished by the democratic-bourgeois regime formally established by the revolution of independence. But in Peru, in a century of the Republic, we have not had a true bourgeois or capitalist class. The ancient feudal class — camouflaged or masked as a republican bourgeoisie — has preserved its positions. The policy of disentail of agrarian property, initiated by the revolution of independence as a logical consequence of its ideology, did not lead to the development of small landed property. The old landholding class had not lost its domination. The survival of a latifundiary regime produced, in practice, the maintenance of the latifundio. It is well known that the policy of disentail attacked above all the Indian community. And the fact is that in the course of a century of the republic, the great agrarian property has been strengthened and increased despite the theoretical liberalism of our Constitution and the practical needs of the development of our capitalist economy.

The expressions of our surviving feudalism are two: latifundio and serfdom. These are related and consubstantial expressions, whose analysis leads to the conclusion that the serfdom that weighs down the Indian race cannot be liquidated without liquidating the latifundio.

The agrarian problem in Peru, posed in this way, does not lend itself to equivocal distortions. It appears in all its magnitude as a socio-economic — and therefore political — problem, in the domain of men who concern themselves with social and economic facts and ideas. And it is vain, for example, to try to convert it into a technical-agricultural problem in the domain of agronomists.

Everyone knows that the liberal solution for this problem, in conformity with individualist ideology, would be to break up the latifundio in order to create small landed properties. So great is the ignorance of the elementary principles of socialism among us that it is not stating the obvious or unnecessary to emphasize that this formula — the break-up of the latifundio in favor of small landed property — is neither utopian, heretical, nor revolutionary, neither Bolshevik nor advanced, but orthodox, constitutional, democratic, capitalist, and bourgeois. And that it has its origin in the liberal ideology which underlies the constitutions of all the bourgeois-democratic states. And that in the countries of Central and Eastern Europe — where the war crisis brought down with a crash the last ramparts of feudalism with the consent of the capitalist West (which henceforth opposed to Russia this bloc of anti-Bolshevik lands) — in Czechoslovakia, Rumania, Poland, Bulgaria, etc., agrarian laws have been passed that in principle limit the ownership of land to a maximum of 500 hectares.

In conformity with my ideological position, I think that in Peru the hour for trying the liberal method, the individualist formula, has already passed. Leaving doctrinal reasons aside, I regard as fundamental an indisputable and concrete factor that gives a peculiar stamp to our agrarian problem: the survival of the Indian community and of elements of practical socialism in Indian life and agriculture.

But those who cling to the democratic-liberal formula — if they really seek a solution for the Indian problem that will redeem the Indian from serfdom, above all — can direct their gaze toward the Czech or Rumanian experience, since the Mexican experiment, given its inspiration and course, may appear to set a dangerous example. There is still time for them to champion the liberal formula. If they should do so, they would at least ensure that the liberal thinking that, according to written history, has dominated the life of the Republic since the founda-tion of the Republic will not be completely missing from the debate on the agrarian problem that the new generation has provoked.

3. THE INDIAN PROBLEM TODAY

In recent decades the Indian problem has become the focal point of a large and important body of social science research, centered since 1941 in the Inter-American Indian Institute. The Mexican scholar Moisés Sáenz (1888–1941) was a major pioneer and promoter of this activity. In his basic study of the modern Peruvian Indian he demonstrates with an impressive array of data that the Indian problem in Peru is "not a theory, but a condition." [4]

FEUDALISM STILL EXISTS in modern Peru. Even in regions as unfavorable for large-scale agriculture as Huanta and Ayacucho, latifundismo or its dynamic expression, gamonalismo, is to be found on all sides. Anco is a little town situated on the road between Mejorada and Ayacucho, inhabited by serfs belonging to two haciendas which meet in this town, divided only by a street. Nothing ever reminded me so much of the Middle Ages as this place. It is completely steeped in a monastic and archaic atmosphere; all the people seemed to belong to a lay brotherhood. It actually is a brotherhood of serfs. We came across a strapping youth . . . [and] asked him what he did; he could hardly speak to us, but a woman told us that he was a servant of the master's. "What does he earn?," we asked. "He doesn't earn anything," she replied. "His parents also were in the master's service." On the road we met an aged Indian who was traveling with his daughter, a girl of about twenty. Her hat was covered with flowers that she had cut on the way; she looked like a shepherdess out of the Middle Ages. We asked them in what town they lived and they replied: "We belong to Don Guillermo Pacheco. . . ." This gentleman, master of men, is the hacendado of Llaccria; it seems that his serfs know to whom they belong, but not where they live.

THE LATIFUNDIO ON THE COAST

Feudalism has two aspects: the latifundio and gamonalismo. The latifundio exists in Peru; on the coast it has taken possession of all the oases formed by the waters that descend from the

[4] Moisés Sáenz, *Sobre el indio peruano y su incorpora-ción al medio nacional*, México, 1933, pp. 171–190. (Excerpt translated by the editor.)

mountains, and of the surrounding desert as far as was desired. It is said that the coastal latifundio results from the system of irrigation made necessary by the scarcity of water, which must be captured and distributed by costly processes that by their very nature are beyond the means of small landowners. Properties have also been consolidated by the efforts of foreign capital, which has acquired estates and expanded them in order to establish capitalist agricultural-industrial enterprises producing for export. The exploitation of labor on the coastal estates has been modernized; the sugar and cotton plantations are businesses that employ machinery for cultivation and processing and use all the processes of modern technique. The system of labor in these enterprises is largely based on the use of contract laborers (braceros), generally brought from the sierra. In colonial times Negro slaves were imported; in the middle of the last century coolies were transported from the East; neither system took root on the coast. At present the estates largely depend for their labor on men from the sierra.

THE LATIFUNDIO IN THE SIERRA

The latifundio in the sierra is entirely different from the one just described. It exists throughout the zone, but its presence is most marked in the southern part. The haciendas of the sierra sometimes constitute estates of enormous extent, but the lands suitable for cultivation are relatively small, irregular, and broken up by the rugged terrain. The haciendas possess infinite quantities of puna and mountain, the former suitable for pasture, the second entirely useless, for the cordilleras that rise above the sierra are generally bare, and consequently do not even represent a source of forest wealth. The labor of the Highland hacienda is as rudimentary as that of the Indian; the hacendado is not an agricultural entrepreneur; he leaves cultivation in the hands of Indians, yanaconas and colonos. The nature of the terrain and the general lack of enterprise impede the use of machinery; the cultivated fields are scattered about according to the configuration of the soil. Cattle raising is the principal branch of economic activity. The hacendado has his animals and the Indian laborer attached to the estate has his flock. The Indian families are responsible for pasturing the master's animals as well as their own. Each family has charge of a certain number of animals; each lives on a farm separated from the others. The hacienda, consequently, presents the picture of a fragmented enterprise. In reality, the hacienda is a latifundio in which small agricultural-pastoral units operate with primitive methods under the control of the owner or his representative. The labor system of the hacienda uses resident serfs, yanaconas, persons who are allotted a piece of land on the master's property and who have the right to pasture their animals, performing in return services that are more or less specified and more or less gratuitous.

The yanacona and his family are settled on the hacienda. This arrangement may have had its origin in a debt that the laborer contracted with the landowner, in the sale of his own land to the hacendado, in a spoliation suffered by the Indian at the hands of the gamonal (in which case his situation changes from that of a free owner to that of a renting tenant), or, finally, in the continuation of an arrangement begun in former times by the parents or grandparents of the worker. The yanaconas are obliged to tend the flocks of the master. At fixed times the agents of the hacendado come to count the animals, to demand an accounting from the Indian. There are many cases in which the Indian must make good from his own flocks losses caused by death or any other accident. These workers must also transport loads when ordered by the hacendado or his employees, at their own expense; they must also serve as pongos — that is, render personal service in the house of the master, sometimes at the hacienda, sometimes in the city. This service corresponds exactly to that called huasicamia in Ecuador. The yanacona must work in the master's fields a certain number of days. As a rule he receives no wages for this labor; in case some wage is provided, it is always less than the prevailing wage in the region. The yanaconas are allotted small parcels of land which they may cultivate as they please for themselves. The size of these tracts varies considerably. Frequently it does not exceed the typical small plot of the Indian comunero. In general, the land is of poor quality. These peons also have the right to pasture their animals and live in humble dwellings which as a rule they themselves have built. The hacendados also employ paid laborers at a fixed wage which varies according to the region and the time. Last year (1931) the wage paid in Ayacucho, Puno, and Cuzco was from 40 to 50 centavos daily.

The haciendas of the Department of Cuzco also employ, though on a small scale, the system of rental, by which the haciendas rent land to comuneros. Francisco Ponce de León has made a study of the system of rental of arable lands in the Department of Cuzco and lists the following forms: rental for money, rental for labor, rental for produce, sharecropping (*aparcería* or *compañía*), and mixed rental. . . . I quote from Ponce de León: "In the province of Paucartambo the landowner grants the use of land to a group of Indians on condition that they do all the work required to cultivate the hacienda fields which the patrón has reserved for himself. The renters or yanaconas, as they are called in this province, must also carry the hacendado's crops to Cuzco on the backs of their own animals without remuneration; they must also serve as pongos on the hacienda, or more commonly in Cuzco, where the landowners prefer to reside. They render pongo service by turns, for several weeks or months at a time, with or without compensation: that depends on the extent of the land they cultivate, on the number of renters, and on the kindness of the patrónes. There are estates so vast and extensive that they contain within their limits as many as a dozen *ayllus* or little Indian towns, which may possess some communal lands but whose members in large part live as renters of the hacienda that surrounds or adjoins them. One such property contains within its boundaries seven ayllus, each composed of 20 to 70 families. This hacienda constantly provides fourteen pongos for the service of various families of Cuzco's high society.

"The lands are not divided equally among the renters; instead each cultivates as much as he can (this is called his *mañay*); and the conditions of rental are the same whether one cultivates more or less. My informants assure me that they never manage to cultivate all the land that is allotted them because of its great extent, so that each renter possesses five or six sections or lots (*suertes*), as they call them, of which he cultivates only one each year, leaving the rest uncultivated until their turn comes again after a rest of three or four years. This circumstance gives some idea of the nature of the rented lands, which are usable only once every three or four years and whose cultivation involves breaking the ground anew each time.

"The widows or aged women who are renters, being unable to pay their rent in the hard labor of the fields, substitute for it by providing a laborer or rendering services in the master's house (under the name of *mittanes*), taking turns with each other. . . ."

As concerns the service of *pongueaje,* it represents one of the most humiliating forms of human bondage. Service in the master's house is sufficiently oppressive, but on top of this the pongo can be given or sold to friends during his term of service. When the Indian goes to perform his service he even loses his name; he is simply called pongo, and he is regarded as if he were a small, inoffensive, and useful domestic animal. In Puno and in La Paz the pongo must wear a cap different from that worn by other Indians; with that distinctive headgear the unhappy Indian servant is subject to abuse by all in the streets and markets.

The cases in which payment of rent is made with labor, on the basis of a fixed daily wage, are very frequent; the general rule in such cases is that the daily wage is less than the prevailing wage in the region. The free renters, if one can give that name to those who pay their rent with a stipulated number of work days, are free to dispose of the produce of the rented lands, selling or using it as they please; but very frequently special circumstances compel them to sell all their production to the landowner; in that case the price of sale is almost always lower than the prevailing market price. This phenomenon is particularly noticeable in the *montaña* lands, where coca is grown.

GAMONALISMO

Gamonalismo is the second aspect of Peruvian agrarian feudalism today. The term signifies the spoliation and abuse suffered by the Indian at the hands of monopolistic landowners and the constant extortion to which the landowners and even the authorities subject him. Gamonalismo is an order of things, a social condition, an attitude; it refers to the unequal status of the Indian in relation to the other social classes of the country—his "extra-social" condition, as Mariátegui called it; it is the colonialism and clericalism that have cast their shadow over a century of Peru's independent life; it signifies spoliation, neo-feudalism; it means the connivance of the social classes, the authorities, the clergy, the landowners, in exploiting the Indian without scruple and without conscience.

Alarmed by the risings of the Indians, the landowners undertook a campaign of defense and explanation. Pedro Irigoyen, speaking for the hacendados, wrote some articles in *El Comercio* of Lima, which he later reprinted in a pamphlet under the title of *The Indian Conflict and Problem.* No one can charge Señor

Irigoyen with bias against the latifundista and the hacendado; for this reason what he has to say about the gamonales carries particular weight.

"It is notorious, of course," he writes, "and no one will seek to deny it, that the so-called gamonales exist, that they have established great latifundios through the gradual and progressive seizure of lands belonging to the ayllus or Indian communities — lands that they have usurped by violence or fraud, frequently availing themselves of the complacency of the political authorities or the venality of certain judicial officers. They are the great enemies of the Indian race and the Peruvian nation. They not only constitute an affront to our country and a constant threat to the existing social order; they are the most effective contributors to the mistaken views held concerning the Indian problem, and to its transformation into a national conflict."

How the Indian is Despoiled of His Land

A favorite and systematic activity of the *gamonales* is the spoliation of the Indian lands. I take the following account of a typical case from the book *Indian Questions,* by Luis F. Aguílar. "The landowner establishes friendly relations with some villager and then sets a legal trap for the Indian, inducing him to grant him a written power of attorney for his defense, since it is a rare Indian property that is not either involved in a lawsuit or in imminent danger of such involvement. . . . Some time passes, and the pretended defender appears before the judge to demand possession of the Indian's land, since the supposed power of attorney was no such thing, but an instrument of sale, drawn up in connivance with the notary public, witnesses, and pettifogging lawyers. The formalities of possession are carried out and the buyer is legally accredited with full rights. Having surmounted all legal barriers, published the necessary notices in the newspapers, and proved his rights, he demands the expulsion of the usurper from his land. . . . Since the Indian's devotion to his hut and land is beyond the power of words to express, in the majority of cases he will not leave them, preferring to submit to slavery and remain in the capacity of a tenant on his own land, while the pretended attorney becomes its owner."

The incredible proceeding described by Aguílar actually occurred and is all too typical. Alberto A. Salas, secretary of the *Junta del Patronato Indigena* of the Department of Cuzco, asserts in an official report sent to Lima that about two thirds of the complaints of the Indians before the Junta have to do with fraudulent purchases of their age-old properties, made by gamonales in the way described above. . . .

The Hacienda vs. the Comunidad

"Peruvian latifundismo is a historic creation of the Spanish domination and has its original and authentic title in usurpation. . . ." "The latifundio was created through spoliation of Indian lands, sometimes by dissolution of the ayllus, sometimes by their ejection, and in the majority of cases by swallowing them up and subjecting them to servitude."

These concise words of Abelardo Solís give the key to the historic conflict between the latifundio, the hacienda, on the one side, and the Indian community on the other. It is a struggle in which material values are at stake but in which moral factors, above all, have played their part. The conflict, in effect, confronts the enslaving drive of the latifundista, who wants to preserve colonial feudal traditions, with the still older tendency of the Indian to maintain his condition of a freeman living on his own land. An effort was made in Peru to establish individual property at the expense of communal lands, but this — as we have seen — far from producing individual property as the dominant form, gave rise to the formation of latifundios on a large scale, and to the engulfment of many comuneros by a regime of servitude and virtual slavery. The Indian, dispossessed of his land, prefers to accept the servitude of the hacienda rather than leave his ancestral hearth. Entire communities have been swallowed up by the hacienda. The estates of today were the communal lands of yesterday. The Indian yanacona or colono pays with unremunerated labor for the privilege of continuing to live on the land which has been the home of his people since time immemorial. In the majority of cases the attack of the hacienda destroys, dislocates, or disintegrates the community. The phenomenon is a familiar one in Peru. The members of the dissolved communities either enter the hacienda as resident peons or become laborers who hire themselves out here and there as opportunity offers, or go to the mines or to the populous centers, where they form the lowest stratum of the proletariat, or, in the case of the most rebellious elements, take to the roads and become bandits. The coastal hacienda also destroys the Indian after a fashion, but at the same time it absorbs him and transforms him into a valuable element, as a rule; the hacienda of the sierra destroys the community and transforms the free comunero into a slave beyond redemption, or hurls him into the trackless desert of social maladjustment. Unfortunately, neither in Peru nor in other countries — the phenomenon is general in Latin America — are there statistics that reveal numerically the results of this tragic struggle between the hacienda and the community; the engulfment of the small property, lost by the Indian, gained by the hacienda; the slow and brutal destruction of men until they surrender from hunger; their transformation into pariahs and slaves; and the rebellion and departure of the strongest, or their angry uprising, leaving them in either case in a more maladjusted condition than that from which they escaped. But the lack of statistics does not conceal the reality of the phenomenon. In Peru, as elsewhere, the hacienda has grown at the expense of the community; freemen have been made slaves. "In Peru," says Carlos Váldez de la Torre, "the number of haciendas has grown astonishingly. In Puno, for example, it increased a hundredfold between 1860 and 1915."

In his study of native criminality, José Antonio Encinas shows that criminality is greater in the sierra than on the coast and that nearly all the crimes are motivated by hatred, vengeance, and repression. In his opinion the criminality of the Indian is intimately connected with his misery and, in general, with his economic condition. The presence of the latifundio determines the ascending curve of criminality, according to the eminent ex-rector of the University of San Marcos; there is more criminality in the sierra, where the latifundio and gamonalismo are more widespread than on the coast. In those regions, in particular, where gamonalismo is most in evidence, criminality is also greater.

COMUNEROS AND COLONOS

The difference between the members of the Indian communities and the peons (colonos) of the haciendas is enormous. The comunero retains his property and his condition of a free human being. In discussing the Indian communities, I noted that they fall into different classes, according to the land system that prevails among them; but all of them, typically, have preserved their integrity in the degree that they have been able to keep their land and their tie with the earth. The comunero is a member of a group, retains many of the traditions and customs of his group. The colono is a defeated man; his economic and cultural condition is inferior to that of a comunero. Where the difference is most evident is in the spiritual totality of the one and the other; the Indian colono is duller, more conservative, more sullen, less adaptable, than the freeman. It is well known that the colonos are less rebellious than the comuneros — not because the former lack causes for complaint, of which they have plenty, but because they are so crushed that they do not even know how to protest. After all, even to struggle for freedom one must enjoy a certain amount of liberty.

From the economic point of view, the hacienda of the sierra has little advantage over the small native proprietor; the methods of cultivation are equally backward, the harvests equally meager. We do not know the extent of the communal lands, and I might say that the extent of hacienda land is equally obscure. Consequently we cannot make a quantitative comparison of yields. . . .

INDIAN UPRISINGS

Native uprisings in Peru have been a frequent phenomenon throughout the history of the Republic, but after 1920 they increased to the point of inspiring a genuine alarm in the landowners. "All the Indian risings or riots," says Aguílar, "have no other cause than seizures, injuries, theft of their property, but only when the sufferers are comunitarios; when they are individual farmers the offense is consummated tranquilly. . . ."

Pedro Irigoyen, an apologist for the hacendados, explains the native uprisings in his own way. "Let it be well understood that the colono is not dissatisfied, nor is he the promoter of the late tumults. They have not resulted from his protests, much less from his action. They have been exclusively the work of the Indians of the ayllus, communities, or *parcialidades,* which enjoy less favorable economic conditions and unfortunately are within easier reach of their exploiters. It is these Indians who, incited and agitated by anarchist elements, as they may be called, have attacked estates and have spread among their race the ideal of reconstituting the Empire of Tahuantisuyo, of which they can really neither know nor remember anything. They have become enemies of the hacendados, whom they charge with being intruders on their properties, and to whom they attribute the decadence and degeneracy of their race. They have been persuaded that by suppressing the haciendas they could restore their sway over this entire territory. . . . "

The Indian risings have, as a rule, been violent acts of protest, not motivated initially by the desire for robbery and vandalism. It is important to emphasize that the majority of the tumults do in fact originate among the communities, as Irigoyen says, not because the colonos would not wish to protest but because they no longer have the spirit to do it.

Instead of looking for anarchist and communist agitators created by the tormented imaginations of the gamonales and conservatives, these gentlemen would do better to reflect on this statement of the *Junta Central del Patronato de la Raza Indigena,* presided over by the Archbishop of Lima — a statement that could help them to understand the real cause of the Indian risings: "The memorials presented by the Indians during the past year and more have been of such a nature that to read their contents produces a feeling of horror. They may be exaggerated, but experience teaches that that is not the case. Because of lack of education they may not express themselves with complete clarity and may even say something other than they mean, but the substance of their complaints makes all too clear the cruelty of their oppressors and the unhappy condition of the natives. . . . We must all join in the effort to improve in the shortest possible time the condition of the Indian. Let us not forget that oppression always produces disastrous reactions."

4. REPORT FROM BOLIVIA

In the desolate mining camps of Bolivia, 12,000 to 15,000 feet above the sea, the Indian problem and the labor problem merge into one. Unsatisfactory living and working conditions have caused frequent clashes between the Indian miners and the companies. In 1943, in response to an official Bolivian request, the United States Government dispatched a joint commission to survey conditions in the tin mines and to make recommendations to the authorities. The commission arrived in the country just after the "Catavi Massacre," in which an undetermined number of strikers were killed by troops. In the selection below, an American labor member of the commission reports to his organization on his visit to Bolivia. (In 1952 the tin mines were nationalized by a new revolution-ary government, and the miners' trade union was given a share in their management.) [5]

BOLIVIA has an area of 416,040 square miles. Its geography has three main divisions; the Andean plateau — bleak, desolate, treeless, dominated by the majestic snowcapped peaks like Illimani; the Yungas — picturesque mountain valleys that lead like gigantic steps down from the cordillera; the Llanos of the east — thousands of square miles of fertile plains and forbidding jungle. In the highlands is Lake Titicaca with an area of over 3,000 square miles, the highest navigable lake in the world.

Geography and the long indifference of man have isolated Bolivia from the rest of the world and from itself. In the rainy season the eastern lowlands lose contact with the midlands and the west. It sometimes takes forty days to make the journey overland, from Santa Cruz to Cochabamba, in the wet season. The lowlands look to the east; the highlands look to the west; the midlands look to themselves.

Bolivia's enormous size, her sparse population, her lack of roads, have caused it to lose territory to her neighbors in a series of tragic wars. Defeated by Chile in the War of the Pacific (1879–1883) Bolivia lost access to the sea. This is an important fact in the geography of Bolivia and in the psychology of the Bolivians.

Of Bolivia's 3,457,000 inhabitants, more than one-half are pure Indian. The cholos or mestizos of mixed blood number less than a million; there are less than half a million whites. The Indians are divided into the two main groups, viz: the Aymaras and the Quechuas — descendants of proud civilizations of centuries past. It is the Indian population which provides the man-power for the mines, the factories, the haciendas, or farms, and the army.

For centuries, the Indian has been set apart almost as a necessary evil. Individual members of his race have shown ability, skill and talent. But, as a group, they have been "kept in their place." Today, the Indian of Bolivia lives in dire poverty; as a worker, his normal span of life is thirty years; he carries his poverty with dignity, silent contempt and a hatred which occasionally boils over in overt acts of resistance to exploitation and repression.

The deliberate lack of educational opportunities has kept the Indian ignorant. In 1940 there

[5] Martin Kyne, *Report to the Congress of Industrial Organizations on Labor Conditions in Bolivia,* Washington, D.C., 1943, pp. 7–24.

were only about 120,000 children in the primary schools. There were only about 6,000 in secondary schools. The farm child is lucky if he can finish three years of elementary schooling. Boys and girls leave school at the age of seven, eight and nine years to learn a trade, to tend the sheep in the pastures or to sort rocks in the mines. In recent years, there was a movement to create a system of Indian schools which might teach the practical, useful things the people most need: agriculture, handcrafts, personal hygiene, cooperation, reading, writing and arithmetic. Powerful landlords have done away with those schools, undermining them by stealth or destroying them by force. As a result, 75 per cent of the people of Bolivia are illiterate.

Bolivia has lived mostly by selling tin to the world. The tin mines are located in the Andean highlands to the south of La Paz and Oruro. The mines also produce tungsten and antimony. Bolivian tin has traditionally been shipped to England; part of it is now coming to the United States.

The Yungas and the eastern lowlands are agricultural. Sugar, cotton, coffee, wheat and maize could be grown in abundance, more than enough to feed the whole country. But the roads are few. Transportation costs are high, so the workers of the highlands depend mainly on supplies of imported foods. In the south, toward the Argentine frontier, there are rich oil fields. Bolivia consumes little of its own petroleum products because the long haul up the valleys and mountains to the more populous west is slow and very expensive.

To the northeast in the province of El Beni are the rubber lands, lying in the heart of the Amazon basin. Cattle raising is important in this area, but the beef rarely gets to La Paz, Oruro or Potosí. It is cheaper to send it to Argentina. . . .

The Bolivian workers are organized in the Confederación Sindical de Trabajadores de Bolivia, referred to by its initials, CSTB. The confederation is formed by departmental and industrial federations which, in turn, are made up of single labor unions or *sindicatos*. The executive authority of the CSTB is its Central Committee, composed of the representatives of the departmental and industrial federations.

The chief elective officer is the Secretary General, corresponding to the president of a national union in the United States. The most important federations are those of La Paz, Oruro, Sucre, Tarija, El Beni, Cochabamba and Santa Cruz. The National Federation of Teachers, the Confederation of Railway and Transport Workers, the Union of Miners of the Patiño Enterprises, the University Federation of Bolivia, the Union of Industrial Workers and the National Federation of Chauffeurs are allowed one delegate each to the Central Committee.

The constitution of CSTB provides that manual and intellectual workers shall be admitted to the organization. Its principal aims are to improve the economic, cultural, social and political conditions of the Bolivian workers; to affirm the solidarity of the working classes; to organize labor throughout the republic; and to establish national and international relations with labor groups that pursue similar aims.

The constitution also declares in favor of the principle of industrial unionism and proclaims trade union democracy operating through a general assembly or congress and councils in each plant and industry. A minimum of fifteen workers is required to set up a union. The national congress is required to meet regularly. Members of the central executive committee may not hold office simultaneously in any member federation. There are standing committees on press, education, finances, statistics, farm labor, cooperatives, organization and negotiation of contracts.

The strongest unions in Bolivia are the miners' of Potosí; the Union of Industrial Workers of La Paz; the miners' of Oruro; the miners' of Patiño Enterprises, and the railway and transport union, are the only ones that can be considered as labor organizations in the European or North American sense of the word. Many small unions of petty craftsmen join the CSTB, but these represent very little organized strength.

Some miners work only about half of the year; they spend the rest of the time on their patches of land in the *yungas* or in the highlands. Moreover, the miners are obliged to return periodically to lower altitudes from the mines, which are at 12,000 to 15,000 feet above sea level.

In spite of its limited numbers, and in spite of difficulties, such as the illiteracy of the majority of the workers, the Bolivian trade union movement has been a militant one. It has fighting traditions. Organizational work began around 1921 in the mines and factories, in the agricultural areas around 1930. In 1936 the CSTB was founded in La Paz, and this organization is now a member of the Confederation of Latin American Workers.

June 4, 1923, is a memorable date in the his-

tory of Bolivian labor. On that day the miners'
of Unica, which belongs to the Patiño Enterprises, struck for a working day of eight hours.
The government, following the traditional pattern, suppressed the strike in which a large number of workers were shot down in cold blood.

In 1926 the railway workers of the entire country called a strike for a salary of 50 cents a day
U.S. currency. In 1928 and 1929 important
strikes took place in the tin mines. In 1930 and
1931 the government again resorted to martial
law to suppress the legitimate aspiration of the
workers for higher wages. The general strike of
1936 resulted in the downfall of the government. In 1938 strikes again broke out in the
mines of Oruro and Potosí. In 1941, the entire
working class supported the railway and transport workers in their demands for a 30 per cent
increase in wages. In this they were successful. . . .

Before describing the present state of the
workers in the Republic of Bolivia, it is necessary to understand the attitude of the employers
toward labor, especially in the mining industry.

First of all, it should be noted that the man
who directs Bolivia's largest tin mining enterprise, is an absentee owner. Enormously wealthy,
Simón Patiño has not lived in his country since
1924. He has spent his later life in the fine spots
of Europe, living in luxury as a diplomatic representative of Bolivia. He holds 30 per cent of
the stock of a Delaware corporation which has
an authorized capitalization of 50 million dollars and owns more than 150 mining concessions
and in 1942 his mines produced 47 per cent of
the tin exported by Bolivia.

The next largest tin operator is Mauricio
Hochschild, whose mines produced 25 per cent
of tin exports in 1942. The third of the Big
Three of Bolivian tin is Carlos Victor Aramayo,
who produced about seven per cent of the 1942
tin exports. Below these three there is a large
number of small producers, who represent about
21 per cent of tin production. The Big Three
— Patiño, Hochschild and Aramayo — are the
ones who took the lead in organizing the united
front of mining operators which refused to negotiate with the workers in December, 1942,
thus leading the way directly to the Catavi
strike.

The big mine operators have fostered the
legend of the incapacity of the Bolivian to progress. A spokesman for Hochschild, Dr. A.
Blum, wrote a few months ago: "It seems to be
a fact . . . that the Bolivian Indian has only a
very limited interest in better living conditions.

. . . Things in Bolivia are somewhat different,
and as stated already, there is only a limited
tendency in higher and lower classes for such
improvement and development."

The mine operators in the tin industry appear
to have rights which the workers do not enjoy.
They interpret labor laws and declare them unconstitutional when it suits their interest. This
is a prerogative of the Bolivian Government,
but in practice the employers often pre-empt this
function. In accordance with this practice, one
large tin operator on a certain occasion refused
to abide by the minimum hour law on the
ground that it was unconstitutional.

In the days preceding the Catavi strike, the
Big Three advised the Minister of Labor that
the strike was illegal and bluntly told the Minister what his duties and obligations were in
the matter.

I also found that the big operators in the tin
industry show as little consideration for the government as they do for the workers, even though
they interpret the laws of the land to suit their
own interests. From September to December,
1942, the operators dictated policy to the Ministry of Labor with regard to the Catavi workers' demands. This policy was subsequently carried out almost step by step as outlined by the
Patiño interests and their fellow employers. Yet,
this is what Dr. Blum, a representative of Hochschild, had to say: "The government has neglected very much its obligations in the past,
though at least during the last years the government revenues were such that it would have
been possible to do something; instead the
money was spent for the army, for unnecessary
luxurious buildings, for the increase of the number of public officials, for public works which
responded to the interests of small regions and
did not contribute to the general development
of the country."

An important fact to keep in mind is that the
mining operators act as a unit, as a united front,
working in full concert with one another against
labor. A few months before the Catavi incident,
mine owners held a national convention in
which they laid the foundation for this unity. In
contrast, leaders of labor could not move from
one part of Bolivia to another without special
permits which enabled the police to keep them
under constant surveillance. Later the state of
siege prevented the holding of regional or national meetings.

The united front of the Big Three operators
extended even to Washington. When they found
that the Catavi affair had been brought to the

attention of public opinion in the United States, Patiño, Hochschild and Aramayo convened in New York and planned their joint strategy. So far as I know not a single authorized spokesman of the Bolivian miners has been heard either in New York or Washington.

It should not be gathered from what has been said that standards and practices are the same in all the mines. Some mines have gone farther than others in recognizing that the intolerable conditions which have existed cannot continue forever without creating resentment and rebellion among the workers. But we American workers should be careful lest we accept a Cook's tour of the works of benevolent paternalism as proof that the basic ills of the Bolivian miners are being attacked in a sound, just and humane fashion. . . .

We may now consider the conditions under which the Bolivian workers actually live.

The pay of workers in industry and mining fluctuates considerably from one region to another. Full and reliable statistics on wages are not to be had, but the examples which are set forth below are typical of the wage situation in mining and industry. At the time to which these figures apply the monetary unit, the boliviano, was worth slightly more than two cents United States currency.

In 1940, in the Department of La Paz the annual earnings of industrial workers were about 4,304 bolivianos (approximately $90.00). The average daily wage, taking the prices of food prevailing at that time, would have enabled him to buy one quart of milk a day, a pound of meat or two pounds of potatoes, for a day's pay. In 1942 average wages in the mines of Colquiri were 44.79 bolivianos, average wages in the mill 24.22 bolivianos, average surface wages 32.85 bolivianos, and average of all wages 34.57 bolivianos (about 70 cents U.S.). The average wage in the Potosí mines at that time was 36.72 bolivianos.

In December, 1942, women were paid from 9.00 to 15.00 bolivianos a day for surface work. Unskilled adult males on surface work were paid the following minimum wages at different mines: San José, 13.20 bolivianos; Arca, 23.50; Pulacayo, 10.00; Corocoro, 10.45; Huanuni, 20.00; Llallagua, 21.70; Colquiri, 12.00; Unificada, 10.75. The lowest reported daily average wage of which I was able to obtain a record was 5.00 bolivianos in some of the mills.

Another report showed that one mine, the Compañía Minera Unificada of Potosí (Hochs-

child) was paying a few months ago the following rates: 884 workers, 5 to 10 bolivianos a day; 1,183 workers, 10 to 15 bolivianos; 1,169 workers, 15 to 20 bolivianos; 2,251 workers, 20 to 30 bolivianos; 152 workers, 30 to 40 bolivianos. The distribution of wages is shown also in the following table of earnings of mine workers compiled by the Workers' Insurance and Savings Fund:

1,998 Workers earning 5 to 10 bolivianos a day.
2,595 Workers earning 10 to 15 bolivianos a day.
2,555 Workers earning 15 to 20 bolivianos a day.
3,631 Workers earning 20 to 30 bolivianos a day.
6,314 Workers earning 30 to 40 bolivianos a day.
  225 Workers earning 40 to 50 bolivianos a day.
  192 Workers earning 50 to 60 bolivianos a day.

In other words, according to this table, 10 out of 17 miners were earning $.60 U.S. a day or less; only 225 out of 17,348 were earning 80 cents a day or more.

Putting it in terms of the pay envelope, a case was reported, which could not be taken as unusual, of a miner who worked 156 hours in 19.5 working days. He was paid at the rate of 19 bolivianos a day. His total pay was 370.50 bolivianos. After a deduction of 233.80 bolivianos was made for groceries, and payments for insurance, his total cash in hand was 118 bolivianos or about $2.35 U.S. currency.

Some mining firms have increased wages more than others in the last decade. Some mines provide better housing and lower prices in the *pulperías* (company stores) than others. It is the consensus of expert opinion, that wages have increased only about half as fast as retail prices since 1930.

One argument that is advanced by employers in favor of low wages is that if the Indian miners are paid more they will only squander it on drink. Another is that the workers are compensated by the low prices they pay in the company stores. Still another is that the stock of consumer's goods is limited and higher wages would only send prices still higher. It should be said also that much of the data on wages given by the employers are in averages rather than in breakdowns by groups or types of employment.

With regard to the value of the services provided by the employers, such as housing, medical aid and education, it has been stated that these services practically double the real wages of the miners. If this is taken without argument, the real wages of hundreds of miners with families would still be no more than 10 to 20 bolivianos a day, or 20 to 40 cents U.S. currency; 66 per cent would still receive $1.20 or less a day.

It has also been said that the miners are as a group better paid than the other classes of Bolivian workers. This is undoubtedly true, especially if they are compared with the agricultural workers of the eastern lowlands, many of whom do not get any wages at all. Even so, it must be emphasized that the work in the mines is dangerous, and exhausting. The incidence of silicosis and tuberculosis is high. Work is done at an altitude of 12,000 to 15,000 feet. In brief, wages are higher in the mines than in some of the other industries, but working conditions are worse.

Prices and pulperías. The many references which have been made to the company store indicate the important role that this well-known institution plays in the life of the Bolivian miner. The workers don't like the company store, have asked that it be abolished, but they have never been able to shake it off. The employers claim they don't like it, that they are kept on the verge of bankruptcy by it, but they have never been able to free themselves from its grip. The truth is that the company store, in Bolivia plays a multiple role — economic, social and even political. The proof of the latter is that when miners go on strike the company stores are closed, because the workers often have no other source of food and they will return to work much sooner. The operation of the company store system has been aptly described as chaotic; further, it provides a stranglehold on the economic life of the worker.

The *pulperías*, aside from their own inherent evils, have been subject to the steady inflationary trend of the last ten years that has affected all of Bolivia. This inflation has been caused partly by the increase in paper money, the steady advance of freight rates, handling charges and insurance since 1930. Prices of fifteen basic commodities, like rice, coffee, sugar, maize, potatoes, cheap cotton and beef increased more than eleven times between 1931 and 1942. The price of homespun cotton increased nearly 20 times during that period. Taking the year 1930 as a basis, the cost of living in La Paz increased from 196 points in May, 1936, to 856 in January, 1941. The index rose steadily to 1,252 points in March, 1942. It is reported to have reached 1,497 by the end of last year.

Internal revenue taxes, collected by the municipalities or by the departments are another cause of high living costs in Bolivia. A pair of imported overalls sold in Oruro will include in the price paid by the worker a customs duty, a surcharge of one per cent; warehouse, handling and consular fees; a statistical and transportation tax; a cathedral, university and paving tax; a municipal tax; and freight charges.

An argument advanced by employers in proof of their deep interest in the welfare of the miners is the fact that they have to stand heavy losses in the operation of company stores, which are often the only stores to be found in a mining camp. A statement made by the Aramayo Company in January, 1943, indicates that its stores were buying dried beans at 1.56 bolivianos a pound and selling them at .60 bolivianos. Coffee cost the company 5.22 bolivianos a pound and sold for 2.00 bolivianos. The loss on lard was 2.46 bolivianos a pound; on milk, 2.01 bolivianos a can; and on sugar, .87 bolivianos a pound. A boliviano is now worth .0238 U.S. currency.

There is no doubt that the company stores have to bear losses. The law gives them the option of selling certain articles of prime necessity at 30 per cent below cost or at cost plus 10 per cent. If the companies prefer the latter, they are obliged to make wage adjustments. However, several other facts about the operation of this system should be noted. The companies regard these losses as part of their labor costs, and fix wages accordingly. Low wages paid in some mines are justified on this ground. Also, the stores are not restricted as to prices on articles other than those included in the official list. There is a tendency, therefore, to sell other articles at prices which help cover the losses. It is not a small advantage, either, to tie wages and prices into a confused knot, which no miracle of accounting could undo, and which makes it impossible to settle wage questions on their merits. It is also an advantage to the employers to have taxes for compensation and industrial accidents tied to money wages.

The price control measures which the national government has tried have been effective only in regard to a few of the basic imported commodities. Retail price ceilings are not applied to the company stores, which operate on the principle of optional sales at 30 per cent below cost already referred to.

The high price of food is also the result of Bolivia's dependence on imported agricultural products that it could supply for itself with better utilization of its native resources. Up until four years ago Bolivia was importing potatoes, wheat, sugar, rice, meat and cheese. The largest imports were those of wheat and sugar. The southern mining towns of the republic are more removed, because of lack of roads, from the cattle country of the Bolivian lowlands than from the Argentine stockyards.

Taking imports with national production of foodstuffs in 1938 and dividing by the population of the republic, the consumption per capita of potatoes were slightly over 60 lbs. a year; of corn, 52 lbs.; of wheat, 57 lbs.; of sugar, 6.5 lbs.; of rice, 13 lbs.; of meat, 15 lbs.; of cheese, 6.5 lbs.

The Bolivian Indians supplement their meager diet by chewing the coca leaf, which presumably has a narcotic effect and dulls the pangs of hunger. Coca is sold in all the company stores, and indeed it is said that no mining camp could keep its workers if they are not provided with this drug. Coca production is an important industry in the *yungas*.

Housing is provided by the large mining companies in row houses, usually of one room, with an outside kitchen. Often a single room provides shelter for more than one family. Sanitary installations are at a premium, although in some camps efforts are being made to improve these conditions. Electric light is available to a practically negligible percentage of the workers.

There is a perpetual housing shortage, even of the one-room mud houses commonly found in the highlands. Employers state that construction labor is costly; that materials have become scarcer than ever on account of the war; that the miners do not know how to take care of improved houses; and that narrow profit margins do not allow for better housing standards.

Sanitation leaves a great deal to be desired in the mining areas. In one camp there were several hundred row houses without a single toilet. On the outskirts of Oruro at the edge of the city, miners' families have no sanitary facilities other than the open hillside close to the mines.

Labor turnover is one of the serious problems of Bolivian mining, and one which the war has aggravated. Traditionally the miners have gone back to their small farms after a period of time working in the mines. They thus retain in part their status as agricultural workers and do not become thoroughly specialized in mining. It is obvious that other conditions in the mining camps are not favorable to stability of employment. Better wages in the Argentine mines, for example, have attracted thousands of Bolivian miners. Others have migrated to the farms of northern Argentina. The attachment for the soil, plus the hard and lonely life of the highlands, makes for a constant shifting of the working population.

Another factor that plays an important role in Bolivian mining is the hiring of workers by the *enganchador* or labor contractor. The *enganchador* travels through the agricultural districts, making attractive offers to the peasants, who live in conditions bordering on medieval serfdom on the haciendas. Usually the contractor makes an advance of one or two hundred bolivianos, payable out of wages to be earned later. The contractor receives so much per head, and is responsible for returning the worker to his home if he is turned down by the mining company. One of the serious evils of this system is that in such cases the *enganchador* is as apt as not to leave the worker stranded with no means for returning home.

The Busch Code provides that only the government shall conduct free labor recruitment services. When this provision is actually carried out, one essential step toward the improvement of working conditions in Bolivia will have been accomplished.

Collective bargaining is guaranteed by the Constitution but in practice it can hardly be said to exist. Insofar as I could determine, there was not a single genuine written collective contract in effect in the entire republic. In this connection I can do no better than quote the statement of the joint commission on this subject:

"The Political Constitution of 1938 explicitly guarantees the right of free association for occupational and trade union purposes and recognizes the right of the workers to strike in defense of their interests. . . . After explicitly legalizing the formation of unions for the defense of collective interests, and authorizing strikes and lockouts, the Busch Code provides that 'the labor inspectors shall attend the meetings of the Committee (of every industrial association) and supervise its activities,' that 'an industrial association shall not be constituted by less than . . . 50 per cent of the employes of an undertaking . . .' and that employes shall be entitled to declare a strike only provided 'that the decision to strike is adopted by not less than three-fourths of the total number of the workers actually employed.' The Busch Code does not contain provisions which would protect or enforce the rights conceded to the workers.

"The evidence collected by the commission is sufficient to show that trade union activities do not pursue a free and normal course in Bolivia. There is an almost total absence of the kind of straightforward collective bargaining that is an accepted feature of modern democratic communities.

"The unsatisfactory situation in Bolivia with respect to the freedom of association and collective bargaining must, in the opinion of the commission, be attributed mainly to three causes: the reserved and suspicious attitude that is often adopted by the authorities; the economic control that is exercised by many enterprises over their employes; and the fundamental hostility of many of the employers.

"The commission recommended the deletion or the amendment of the three restrictive provisions referred to, and suggested that the efforts of the workers to organize in defense of their legitimate interests 'be met with respect and objectivity by the employers instead of being viewed with suspicion or hostility.'"

It was the absence of respect and objectivity by employers with respect to the efforts of the workers to defend their legitimate interests that led to the strike of Catavi and its aftermath of armed repression, exile and intimidation of trade union leaders.

XXXI

The New Argentina

A FLOOD OF EUROPEAN IMMIGRANTS and capital transformed the face of Argentina in the last decades of the nineteenth century. Cattle raising and agriculture made great advances, and a flourishing middle class, largely of immigrant origin, arose in Buenos Aires and other urban centers. But agrarian interests continued to dominate Argentine life; they were virtually unchallenged until 1930, when the Great Depression sharply reduced exports and imports and promoted a rapid growth of domestic industry.

The outbreak of World War II caused serious tension between pro-Allied and pro-Axis elements in Argentina. On the eve of the election of 1943 an army revolt, engineered by the powerful Group of United Officers, brought to power a government dominated by militarists and ultra-nationalists.

A young army colonel, Juan Domingo Perón (elected President of Argentina in 1946, reëlected in 1952), soon rose to leadership of the Nationalist movement. Perón imposed curbs on opposition parties and newspapers and purged university staffs of his political opponents. Labor was kept in line by official interventions, demagogic promises, and limited concessions. The Nationalist régime made some progress toward its goals of industrialization and economic independence. But a spiraling inflation kept discontent alive among the workers, while declining demand and prices for Argentine exports created difficulties for Perón's expensive program.

1. THE BIRTH OF THE NEW ARGENTINA

Between 1880 and 1900 the immigrant, the railroad, the refrigerator ship, and other agencies of progress rapidly transformed the primitive Argentina pictured in Sarmiento's Facundo. *Of all the factors making for change, none exceeded immigration in importance. An Argentine historian, José Luis Romero, surveys the economic and social consequences of this great movement.*[1]

[1] José Luis Romero, *Las ideas políticas en Argentina,* México, Fondo de Cultura Económica, 1946, pp. 169–183. (Excerpt translated by the editor.) Reprinted by courtesy of the Fondo de Cultura Económica.

THE ECONOMIC TRANSFORMATION

IN THE HALF-CENTURY between 1810 and 1859 — the period which may be called "creole" in the strict sense — the population of the country rose from 405,000 to 1,300,000 inhabitants. This growth, due almost entirely to natural increase, amounted to less than 900,000 in half a century — that is, to an average of 18,000 a year. For a territory of almost 3,000,000 square kilometers this rate of natural increase was insignificant. Clearly, the conquest of the desert could not be achieved by this means alone. A vigorous policy of stimulating immigration was needed, and that was the policy adopted by the Argentine government from the very beginning of the organized Republic.

The results were impressive. Thanks to active propaganda and generous official aid, a tidal wave of immigrants inundated the country. During the first administration of President Roca (1880–1886), 483,000 immigrants entered the country, and the average of 80,000 a year was exceeded several times, rising to 261,000 in 1889 and even more in 1906. Italians and Spaniards predominated, but there were smaller contingents of different national origins. This stream of immigration also stimulated natural increase. As a result of these developments, a rapid transformation of the Argentine population took place.

The first national census, taken in 1869, revealed a population of 1,830,214 inhabitants. Twenty-six years later, in 1895, the number had risen to 3,956,060 — an increase of more than two millions, or an average gain of 81,500 inhabitants a year. Of that total, more than a million were foreigners and belonged almost entirely to the immigrant element. This will suffice to give an idea of the rapid transformation of Argentine society, especially if one considers that in 1869 the number of foreigners barely exceeded 300,000; their share in the population had thus risen from 16.6 per cent to 25.4 per cent. The passage of time strengthened this trend. The census of 1914 disclosed a population of 7,885,-237; the increase of almost four millions in a space of nineteen years gave an average growth of 207,000 inhabitants a year, and the proportion of foreigners rose to more than 30 per cent of the population. And in the sixteen years between 1914 and 1930 the population continued to increase at an annual rate of 223,000, until it reached the figure of 11,452,374.

This growing population tended to concentrate in the zone of the littoral, in the urban centers above all. Meanwhile the rural population, whose growth a sound policy would have encouraged, suffered a sharp decline. In 1869 the rural sector comprised 65.8 per cent of the total population; in 1895, only 57.2 per cent; in 1914, a bare 42.6 per cent. And this process of decline has continued right down to the present, when the corresponding figure is 31.8 per cent. The tendency toward urban concentration was most marked in Buenos Aires, which had only 85,400 inhabitants in 1852. After 1870 the city experienced an extremely rapid growth. By 1889 its population had passed the half-million

mark, and the number doubled in less than twenty years, reaching 1,244,000 in 1909. In the next twenty years it doubled again, and, although it did not maintain that pace, it continued to grow at a rate that was always disproportionate to that of the rest of the country. Buenos Aires had the largest concentration of foreigners; it also had the greatest concentration of economic activity. Meanwhile the population of the interior regions — particularly of the Northwest — remained static as a result of their economic decay. Few immigrants settled in these zones, whose inhabitants retained the traditional creole traits. A marked contrast arose between the interior and the littoral, and this contrast soon became a distinctive characteristic of Argentine social life.

Population growth, added to other factors, gave an extraordinary stimulus to economic advance. Stock raising continued for some time to be the principal activity, but the crossing of breeds and other improvements changed its character. The new cattle industry opened wide vistas to our commerce, especially with the coming of refrigerator ships. But agriculture was the activity that benefited most from the new immigrant type of population. After the establishment of the colony of Esperanza in 1856, in the province of Sante Fe, important agricultural centers began to arise in the littoral. Fencing of the fields to protect them from the herds was begun, not without opposition, and cultivation was expanded and improved. The cultivated area increased from two million hectares in 1880 to five million in 1895, twelve million in 1905, twenty-six million in 1923, and thirty million hectares at present. This advance of agriculture, which contributed materially to the growth of wealth, was accompanied by a certain amount of division of the land. But over vast regions there existed — and still exist — extensive latifundia kept intact not so much by the needs of the cattle industry as by the stubborn monopolistic policy of the landowning classes. The development of mineral resources (especially of petroleum, after 1907) also made progress, but this expansion did not match the mighty advance of the agricultural industries, particularly in respect to exportable surpluses. Manufacturing and processing industry also grew after 1880. In 1895 there were 24,114 industrial establishments in the country, employing 175,000 workers. By 1913 the number of establishments had doubled, and the number of workers employed had risen to 410,000, with a five-fold increase in the capital invested. But industrial growth lagged far behind the expansion of foreign trade. From the time when the export of grain began — in the presidency of Avellaneda — exports and imports made equally rapid gains. The foreign-trade figures reveal a massive economic activity, and in particular show the increasing volume of the capital involved. From 104 millions in 1880, the value of trade rose to 254 millions in 1889, and after a difficult period of political and financial crisis it reached 241 in 1898 and 724 in 1910. Aside from money in circulation, there was a sharp expansion of bank credits for both productive and speculative purposes, and large loans were contracted abroad, especially for public works.

In this field, extension of the railway network was the principal concern. "Whoever has attentively followed the progress of this country," said General Roca to the Congress on assuming the presidency in 1880, "must have noted the profound economic, social, and political revolution brought about by the railroad and the telegraph as they penetrate the interior. These powerful agents of civilization have made possible the achievement of national unity, the conquest and extermination of banditry, and the solution of problems that appear insoluble, at least at the present time. Rich and fertile provinces only await the coming of the railroad to increase their productive forces a hundredfold, thanks to the ease with which it brings to the markets and ports of the littoral all their varied and excellent productions. . . . " This conviction guided Roca's economic policy. The 2,313 kilometers of track in existence when he came to power had increased to 5,964 when he left office in 1886. Four years later, on the outbreak of the revolution of 1890 during the administration of Juárez Celman, there were 9,254 kilometers of track; at the end of Roca's second administration, in 1904, the corresponding figure was 19,430. At the same time large sums were expended on other types of public works: the construction of bridges, dikes, and public buildings, and, above all, of the port of Buenos Aires, cost immense sums, which the State obtained by the use of its foreign and domestic credit, supported by the certainty that prosperity was a law of Argentine economic development. . . .

Even a superficial consideration of the economic transformation that took place reveals its immense significance for Argentine social life. The rapid irruption of foreign elements, difficult to assimilate, changed the face of our population; the revolution in economic life produced an equally profound disturbance in the system of social relations. Of the old creole Argentina, ethnically and socially homogeneous, with its elementary economic system, there soon remained but a vague recollection, nostalgically preserved by certain groups that had lost their influence on the direction of our collective life. After 1880, approximately, the alluvial Argentina, the Argentina that arose from that upheaval, grew, evolved, and struggled to achieve a balance that only the slow processes of time could bring about. Meanwhile the social and political history of Argentina developed to the rhythm of that process of stabilization, and the forms it assumed revealed their essential instability.

THE PSYCHOLOGICAL MAKE-UP OF THE NEW SOCIETY

The society formed by the incorporation of the immigrant mass in the creole element acquired the characteristics of a conglomerate, that is, of a formless mass, without definite relations between its parts or definite characteristics as a whole. The immigrant mass, considered by itself, had certain peculiar traits, but it soon entered into contact with the creole mass, and from this relation there arose reciprocal influences that modified the one as much as the other.

The psychology of the immigrant was determined by the impulse that had moved him to abandon his native land and seek his fortune in America. That impulse was fundamentally economic, and stemmed from the certainty that American life offered unlimited opportunities in return for intensive effort — effort that yielded only meager returns in zones of more advanced economy. Wealth, then, was the decisive motive, and everything that stood in its way appeared dispensable.

The conditions under which the immigrant mass began its search for wealth could not have been more favorable. In the atmosphere of our expanding economy a man of enterprising spirit, aided by the habits of hard work natural to the lands from which the immigrants came, had to triumph. And the immigrant triumphed in the majority of cases — which led to the rapid rise of a moneyed class psychologically characterized by an overvaluation of economic success. That, however, was not its only characteristic. The immigrant had broken his ties to his native land, and with them he abandoned the system of norms and principles that had regulated his conduct. As a citizen and as an ethical person the immigrant was an uprooted being to whom his adopted country could not offer — given its scanty population and the peculiar stage of development in which it found itself — a categorical, inevitable social and moral imperative in place of that which he had abandoned. The immigrant began to move between two worlds, and out of this situation arose a peculiar attitude which Sarmiento observed and defined as the early fruit of the policy of encouraging immigration. "The emigrant to South America," he wrote, "constantly dreams of returning to the homeland which he idealizes in his fantasy. His adopted land is a vale of tears that prepares him for a better life. The years go by, his business gradually attaches him to the soil, his family creates indissoluble bonds, gray hairs appear, and he continues to believe that some day he will return to that homeland of his golden dreams. Yet if one out of a thousand does finally return there, he discovers that it is no longer his homeland, that he is a stranger in it, and that he has left behind position, satisfactions, affections, whose place nothing can take. Thus, living two existences, he has not enjoyed the one and cannot enjoy the other; citizen of neither country, he is unfaithful to both, since he fails to perform the duties that both countries impose on those who are born and reside in them."

This attitude had no other basis than satisfaction with economic success; the immigrant preferred to feel that he was a foreigner, because in that status he could affirm his economic efficiency, his triumph, in contrast with the creole mass that lived in its own fashion, poor though not miserable, and enjoying its scanty spiritual pleasures. "In Buenos Aires," observed Sarmiento, "there takes place the transformation of the obscure immigrant who arrives with a stoop to his back, dressed as a peasant or worse, and dazed by the great city — first into a man conscious of his worth, next into a Frenchman, Italian, or Spaniard, according to his origin, then into a foreigner, with a title and dignity, and finally into a being superior to all about him."

This feeling of satisfaction was understandable. The immigrant was creating an economy which he dominated; with that economy he smashed the economic system that enabled the creole mass to preserve its humble dignity and the humble enjoyment of its spontaneous spiritual life. In the conflict between the two forms of economic life the rout of the traditional and the victory of the new were inevitable. As a result there arose a certain mutual hostility, expressed in the covert contempt with which the creole called the immigrant "gringo." In effect, the immigrant was displacing the creole and creating a standard of economic efficiency which made the latter his inferior economically, and, before long, socially as well.

Yet there soon began a rapid crossing between the immigrant mass and the creole mass. Frequent in the lower classes, it was no less so in the middle class that made its appearance at this time and was largely created by the upward movement of the successful immigrant. José S. Álvarez, in his *Tales of Fray Mocho*, documents with deft irony the social significance of this phenomenon, from which gradually emerged the typical Argentine middle class of the alluvial era, whose characteristics, not yet fixed, reveal the coexistence of creole ideals and the ideals of the immigrant mass, sometimes in struggle with each other, sometimes in process of fusion, and yet again juxtaposed without having made their definite adaptation.

The creole elite could hardly escape contact with the ascending immigrant wave, and within a few generations the descendants of immigrants began to merge with it; but the elite made an evident effort to preserve at least the institution of the creole landed estate, by means of a deliberate overvaluation of its characteristic mode of life. A leisurely manner, indifference to economic problems, country ways, and many other characteristics derived from the old rural and patriarchal view of life, now acquired a seal of elegance and became indispensable for whoever aspired to conquer the highest social positions. In the middle classes, on the other hand, immigrant social and economic ideals took firmer root, while among the humblest classes, even though immigrants and their descendants predominated, the creole spirit preserved a certain force that perhaps had its rhetorical aspects but nevertheless was the force of an elemental tradition, simple and rooted in the natural conditions of life. As concerns the folklore of the cities, at the opening of the century the popular song and dance began to assume hybrid forms that revealed the opposition between the new way of daily life and a design for living that seemed rooted in the earth; thus there arose the Argentine tango, saturated with creole spirit in its rhythmic, melodic, and literary elements, but also reminiscent of the more energetic attitude of the creole-immigrant conglomerate.

The principal stage for the activity of this conglomerate was Buenos Aires. "Who," asked Sarmiento shortly before his death, "are the citizens of this *El Dorado* foreseen by the ancient conquistadores, since of the four hundred thousand persons who inhabit it, the most industrious and modern part proclaims itself to be foreign, or at most acknowledges that it is the maker and builder of this transformation that is no transubstantiation, since each remains what he was: instrument, maker, builder . . . ? And so there rises a great American city, all to let, with few householders, to be peopled by that world on the march which drops away from Europe like ripe fruit and is borne by the trade winds to our shores. Thus, growing by leaps and bounds, we shall have — if we do not already have — an American Tower of Babel, built by artisans of all tongues, who persist in retaining their separate languages and thus cannot understand each other. And so the great hope of the world of the future against a new cataclysm and deluge will be dissipated at the breath of any untoward event: a prolonged drouth, a foreign or civil war. For it is impossible to build a *patria* without patriotism, or a city without citizens, the soul and glory of nations." Thus did Sarmiento, a champion of immigration and unlimited economic progress, complain of the outcome of his program, of this serious impediment to the development of Argentine nationality. Another architect of progress, Roca, roundly affirmed that Buenos Aires was not a part of the nation, "because it is a foreign province." But neither Roca nor the other members of the oligarchy which dominated the country for so long a time could or would do anything to channel a larger volume of immigration toward the countryside. To do that it would have been necessary to modify the system of land use, create new centers of economic interest in the interior, assist new arrivals (who under existing conditions had no choice but to work as peons for low wages on the immense estates of the rich) to obtain homesteads. But nothing of this kind was done, and the immigrant took his revenge by remaining in Buenos Aires, where he sought his fortune not in productive tasks but in the business of distribution, thus augmenting the number of those who would enrich themselves by engaging in the secondary forms of economic life. "The city grew up in rivalry with the republic," Ezequiel Martínez Estrada points out — and that rivalry grows day by day, aggravated by the nature of the social content of the one

and the other; because Buenos Aires is an amorphous conglomerate, still striving to take form; and the country is only in part that same conglomerate, in constant struggle with the forces of *criollismo,* tense and hostile in the zones beyond immigrant influence. And this duel obscures — and in large part explains — the indefiniteness of our social existence and the vicissitudes of our political life.

2. THE RADICAL TRIUMPH

In the period after 1880 the landed aristocracy — the principal beneficiary of the great economic movement created by the enterprise of the immigrant — grew increasingly indifferent to the popular interests and wishes. Middle-class resentment of oligarchical control of political life resulted in the formation of the Radical Party. From 1890 to 1912 the Radical Party fought the oligarchy with agitation for electoral reform, revolts, and boycottes of elections. In 1916 the first truly free election in Argentine history raised the Radical leader Hipólito Irigoyen (1852–1933) to the presidency. Irigoyen's biographer and ardent admirer, Manuel Gálvez (1882–), interprets the meaning of the Radical triumph.[2]

BEFORE THE ADVENT of the Radicals, government was monopolized by the people of quality: the lawyers, the physicians, the *estancieros,* the intellectuals, the "well-born." The middle class, like the common people, was kept away from power, save for an occasional youth who had distinguished himself by his merits and gained entrance into society by means of an advantageous marriage. The lads of "good family," especially in the provinces, were members by birth of the National Party, whether they knew it or not. But the party only existed in name. There were no registers or members. On the eve of elections a handful of politicians formed committees financed by rich people — in exchange for future posts and other advantages — and sometimes by the unwilling contributions of officeholders. The local caudillos dragged their people to the committee meetings. At these affairs they did not discuss politics or enlighten the citizens concerning their civic duties. The meetings were Homeric feasts, built around barbecues in which whole steers were roasted and the people drank beer and rum and played at jackstones.

2 Manuel Gálvez, *Vida de Hipólito Irigoyen,* Buenos Aires, n.d., pp. 190–193. (Excerpt translated by the editor.)

That was the extent of popular participation in political life. The estancieros forced their peons to vote for aristocrats whose ideas were opposed to the interests of the poor. The industrialists and all other employers of labor did the same. The government gave no thought to the oppressed classes. The lawyers who held the high government posts and received fancy salaries from great foreign firms let these enterprises exploit the Argentine worker without mercy.

With the triumph of Radicalism the middle class and the people entered on the scene. The colonial names went into eclipse. Henceforth government jobs would go to the sons of Spanish or Italian immigrants. In order not to scare the upper classes and create too many enmities at the start, Irigoyen cleverly appointed persons of high social position to occupy certain important posts. But for each such appointment he made hundreds of the other kind. High society, the Old Guard, the opposition newspapers, waxed indignant or jeered at certain appointments. Even the neutrals joined in the laughter. There was a prevailing belief, of colonial origin, that only men of ancient lineage were qualified to govern or hold administrative positions. A minister without an illustrious name, or a fortune, or intellectual prestige, was unthinkable. The Radicals, never having governed, could not have held posts; and not only political power, but university education, and all activities in general, had been monopolized by the oligarchy.

The discharged dandies ridiculed the names of the new rulers — and their dress. They reported that the impossible cutaway of the Minister of the Interior — a provincial — had been presented to him by a certain large store on condition that he say that it was the product of a rival establishment. For the *porteño,* ill-fitting dress is proof of inferiority. A certain citizen of the Capital, seeing the celebrated writer Barrès at an affair in Paris, affirmed that a man who wore such "funny little pants" could not have talent. The Minister of Public Instruction, a primary-school teacher but also a lawyer, provoked a burst of hilarity. A detestably written "reflection" of his, in which he made malaprop use of a Latin sentence, won him an outpouring of burlesque Latin verses. The opposition exercised its wit — sometimes cruel — on the new government officials.

Only since the passage of the Sáenz Pena Law had the common people taken part in political life, not as a decorative element or as a gang grouped around its caudillo, but in its own name. Now the people ruled. The Radicals elected their candidates in direct primaries, and their opponents found it necessary to do the same; they too must organize themselves in committees, create a new political life. The picture of provincial politics drawn by Pellegrini, in which the governors were satraps, was no longer possible. A new day had come. It was the hour of democracy.

The Government House had changed its aspect. It was no longer the cold, almost abandoned place of yesterday. Formerly not a soul could be seen in the corridors, aside from employees. Now it was like a Moroccan mosque, smelling of the multitude, full of rumors, passions, hopes. The government of Irigoyen, like the Radical Party, was very much alive. Its spirit, its coloration, was that of the people.

The Radical Party was idealistic and romantic. Leandro Alem, the John the Baptist of the new credo, infused it with his ideals: free elections, administrative honesty, the equality of men before the ballot box. The Radical party was romantic because it was governed by sentiments, not by ideas. It believed that with its coming to power that program had been realized or was about to be realized. The Radical government had only to put into effect the perfect election law and carry out vigorously the promise of administrative honesty.

As a political party — that, and no more — the Radicals had no ideas. But all parties, sometimes without knowing or desiring it, follow some system of ideas. One of these ideas was the romantic spirit, which logically led the Radical Party to anti-intellectualism. Another was its democratic character. Irigoyen gathered all authority to himself and in certain cases imposed his will, but he treated his adherents with simplicity and dominated in suave and indirect ways. For him there were no rich or poor; all were equal. The Radical committees led their own independent and sometimes excessively tumultuous life. They freely elected their own officers, and even their candidates for deputies, senators, and governors. As President, Irigoyen only intervened to veto or recommend some nomination, but this by way of exception and always through his satellites, who would portentously affirm that they knew his preference.

The Radical Party, then, had come to power without a definite program. There was something utopian in Irigoyen's dreams. Perfect governments do not exist anywhere. Caudillos and party chiefs promise what they cannot fulfill, and they promise because they know that they cannot fulfill. That was not the case with Irigoyen. Introverted and fanatical, a man of very few ideas, he was convinced that the country only needed free elections to be absolutely transformed. . . .

But if the Radical Party had no program of ideas, Irigoyen did, although it was more a matter of intuition than of will and, naturally, not yet defined. That program had its origin in certain principles — half derived from the German philosopher Kraus and half Christian — in which he believed. We already know what they were: the equality of men and nations, human fraternity, peace, an austere life. His sense of human equality and fraternity was the source of his labor policy, which, in our milieu and in relation to the social policy of previous governments, was revolutionary. His love of peace and his concept of the "Nation" dictated his policy of neutrality during World War I. His belief in the equality of nations — a Krausian principle — guided his attitude in the League of Nations. But Irigoyen did not formulate his program beforehand or have it clear in his mind. He was to formulate it and apply it according to the rhythm of events.

3. PERÓN'S BLUEPRINT FOR ARGENTINA

Popular hopes for a flowering of democracy under Radical leadership were not fulfilled. The Radicals proved incapable of giving a new direction to Argentine economic and social life. In 1930, at the first impact of the Great Depression, an army revolt ousted them from power without a fight. Their successors of the Conservative Restoration (1930–1943) proved equally lacking in solutions for Argentina's urgent problems. The Nationalist Revolution of June, 1943, followed by the speedy rise to power of Army Colonel Juan Domingo Perón, marked a turning point in Argentine history. A North American student of rural Argentina summarizes the ambitious economic and social program of the Perón régime.[3]

FOUR YEARS AGO when he was leaving Argentina the writer recorded in his diary the following five broad conclusions about that country's economy and culture: "(1) The economy of Argentina is very much a slave of foreign markets. (2) There is a great geographic disequilibrium in the coun-

---

[3] Carl C. Taylor, *Rural Life in Argentina*, Baton Rouge, Louisiana State University Press, 1948, pp. 445–452. Reprinted by permission of the Louisiana State University Press.

try's economic development. (3) There is a marked unevenness in the distribution of wealth and income and an equal unevenness in the social and cultural status of various segments of the population. (4) Argentina's educational system does not develop technicians who are capable of guiding the physical and economic development of her resources and economy. (5) The country desires to increase its population but will be unable to do so to any considerable extent unless its total economy is changed."

Before the war, Argentina stood first among the nations of the world in the export of beef, corn, linseed, oats, and rye, and second in the export of wheat, mutton, wool, and barley. Its chief imports are petroleum, cotton fabrics, and coal. Most of its farm products are grown primarily for export. Agriculture in Argentina is an extensive, low-production-cost type of agriculture. Its exports are raw, not processed, products. More than 87 per cent of its people live in the east central part of the country, one fourth of these in the metropolitan area of Greater Buenos Aires City. The concentration of population, industry, wealth, income, and even agricultural production within a radius of 250 miles of Buenos Aires is astounding. One who knows Argentina cannot therefore escape the conclusion that the Five Year Plan, to whatever extent it may work out in practice, is focused on the major economic and social problems of the country. Its provisions for industrialization bulk large because it is by means of industrialization that the greater development of natural resources is expected.

Power is recognized as basic to industry and hydroelectric energy is known to be the one outstanding power resource. Because of this fact and because the building of great dams is a dramatic undertaking many people think of hydroelectric development as the heart of the Five Year Plan. Others believe that the plans for controlling international trade are of first importance because, they say, such control will accumulate within the country the capital essential to industrial development. Still others believe that the provisions for improved education and increased immigration are even more important than control of international trade and equally as important as, in fact a concomitant of, industrialization.

The proposals for regularizing and controlling international trade are already largely in effect in terms of government purchases and sales of principal farm products and the manipulation of exchange rates on imports. The Argentine Institute for the Promotion of Trade is responsible for both of these activities. It purchases and sells farm products and it is the government purchasing agent abroad. Vast powers are contained in the charter of this organization and in addition the Congress has empowered the president to raise or lower duties 50 per cent and to impose duties as high as 25 per cent on products that are now free. The exchange rates are varied so as to invite imports that are desired and to restrict those which are not desired.

President Perón in his presentation of the plan stated four reasons why new industries are needed: (1) to increase the economic independence of the country, (2) to avoid postwar unemployment, (3) to increase the nation's income, and (4) to increase the financial stability of the country. He stated that toward these ends the country must guard against dumping from other countries and provide a program of protection especially for new industries to be developed in the interior.

The plan states that the first task is to consolidate and expand those existent industries which manufacture prime materials, especially derivatives of agricultural products, and the second is the development of new industries which will provide additional products for domestic consumption, foreign exports, and national defense. The industries listed for outstanding development may be enumerated in four groups, in the following order of magnitude, (1) *textiles:* cotton, wool, rayon, and the washing of wool; (2) *paper* of all kinds; (3) *minerals* in the following order: (a) tin plate, (b) iron or steel ingots, (c) zinc, and (d) tin; (4) *chemicals:* (a) soda, (b) oxide of zinc, (c) red ocher, (d) citric acid, and (e) other minor ones.

Hydroelectric power development is already under way but the big expansion is planned for the immediate future. Three projects are scheduled for completion and three for initiation in 1947, fifteen for initiation in 1948, seven in 1950, and eight in 1951. It is estimated that these will increase hydroelectric power from 45,000 kws, to 1,400,000 kws. Many dams will be dual or multiple purpose and they together with special irrigation works will supply water to more than two million acres of farm land.

In addition to the expansion of tillable lands, by way of irrigation, there are a number of other agricultural planks of the Five Year Plan. All the lands to be irrigated are to be purchased by the government, at raw-land values, before water is made available to them and are then to be colonized. Argentina already has on the statute books an outstanding colonization or land-settlement law. . . . That law, with slight modifications, is to be used in the colonization program. It provides for a long amortization period, low rates, promotion of co-operatives, technical education and guidance for colonists, and improved housing. Foreign immigrants may be interviewed and selected in their home countries, and the colonization agency may actually promote such selective immigration.

In addition to lands to be brought under cultivation by irrigation from large dams, it is also planned to promote vigorously settlement of "fiscal lands," i.e., federally owned lands, some of which are to be irrigated, some now occupied by squatters, and hundreds of thousands of acres which are being used by large operators who have never proved title to them. The colonization program will give special attention to the development and settlement of these lands as a means of partially correcting the disequilibrium of population distribution.

The plan definitely provides for an attack on the latifundia by means of an additional tax on lands which are "not worked" and progressive taxes on large holdings, "including those whose owners are corporations." The proposal is that all holdings of over 7,000 hectares (approximately 17,000 acres) shall be forced to subdivide or be expropriated. Although it is not provided for in the Five Year Plan, the Director of the Institute for Promotion of Trade recently threatened to expropriate all croplands for which more than 30 per cent share rent was being charged and to turn these lands over to the occupying tenants, they to amortize the purchase price of the land by paying 25 per cent of the crop.

It is also proposed to amend and improve "the law of rural rents". . . . This is one of the oldest and most frequently amended rural reform laws in Argentina. The plan proposed to revise the scale of rents, forbid subrenting, prescribe what landlords must furnish by way of living accommodations, guarantee tenants against crop losses due to bad seasons and plagues, and permit tenants to purchase land when it is offered for sale. The proposed law is not greatly different from the one now on the statute books. . . .

The plan for immigration is co-ordinated with the plans for both industrial and agricultural expansion and it is specified that the types of immigrants desired are those who will be assimilated into the "spiritual and social unity" of the Argentine people and who possess "moral and physical health"; especially desired are "agriculturists, fishermen, technical and specialized industrial workers." It is the plan to co-ordinate immigration with the construction of great works of irrigation, land conservation, building communication lines, and colonization. It is assumed that immigrants will find ready employment in the immense public works incident to the Five Year Plan, that they will find positions in the new industries to be established, and that later a number of them will locate on lands to be irrigated by water impounded behind these dams. Argentina has had practically no unemployment since World War II began. Industry and commerce were booming during the war and have continued to boom since. There has been a great exodus of agricultural workers into industrial and commercial jobs and newly arriving immigrants, of which there have been a good many thousands, have had no difficulty in finding either industrial or agricultural employment. An official commission spent a number of months in the early part of 1947 recruiting immigrants in Italy. An immigration treaty was negotiated between Italy and Argentina which provides that Argentina will advance money and even provide boats for the passage of immigrants and guarantee them equal treatment with Argentine citizens. This treaty implies that Argentina expects many, if not most, of them to become colonists.

The plan provides for practically a whole new system of education from the secondary schools to the universities, for universal education of all children from six to fourteen years of age in the common schools and for free secondary schools. It provides for a great many trade or technical schools to help farm and urban youth to become skilled workmen and technicians and for an elaborate system of scholarships for the sons and daughters of farmers and workingmen. Some of these are to be "traveling schools" which will penetrate isolated areas where the population is too sparse to justify school buildings. A number of these trade and technical schools have been in operation now for six months. The university plan is already enacted into law. It provides for hundreds of scholarships for sons and daughters of industrial workers and farmers and a great increase in engineering and agricultural education by the universities. The plan states that the whole educational system is to "educate

all citizens for a democracy" and to provide technicians for developing industry and agriculture.

Education is to be compulsory for all children from six to fourteen years of age and divides common school education into three parts, two years of kindergarten, five years of primary, and two years of office, manual-arts, and artisan training. It also provides for secondary education for those children whose parents cannot afford to pay for it and for free scholarships for such children in both secondary and technical schools. Secondary education is to be for five years, the last two years to be in the theory and practice of arts and trades. It is stated that secondary education shall qualify students for entrance to universities. At the present time this is not universally true. Free transportation, free school meals, and free textbooks are to be provided.

Technical education is to be free for "all workers who live by their work and for all those who depend on them," and technical education is to range all the way from workers' schools through secondary schools to institutions of higher learning. All industrial or commercial firms operating with a capital of as much as $125,000 must provide scholarships for a minimum of three grades of technical training. In areas where it is not feasible to establish these technical schools itinerant schools are to be provided. In provinces and territories there are to be installed technical schools "oriented to the economies of the areas." A number of workers' schools were opened in March and a plan for the establishment of the first technological college, a school of mines in the Province of Jujuy, is now under way.

President Perón proposed a detailed plan for university education and prefaced his plan with a statement to the effect that the present university regime is not democratic, that the universities have "demonstrated their absolute separation from the people," and that this has kept the humble classes "from studying in them." He asserted that university professors have not dedicated their lives to university teaching but instead have made their academic careers side lines and have often used them as platforms from which to promote political and social doctrines. The remedies he proposed are (1) that graduates from secondary schools shall be permitted to enter the universities, (2) that scholarships shall be provided for poor students, and that (3) professors shall give full time to university teaching and research. The scholarships are to cover all or part of the cost of living of the students' dependents if such is deemed necessary.

Perón proposed that all professors must secure appointment by competition but once having been appointed shall have absolute liberty to exercise their functions. He stated, however, that it is not intended that said liberty shall include the right to go beyond these functions, and that university teachers should have the right and obligation of exposition and criticism of all political and social doctrines but not the right to manifest political partisanship. The universities are to be financially supported by direct appropriations from the federal government by an income tax which all employed persons must pay, by matriculation and other fees, and from donations, or other bequests. These proposals, with some slight modifications, have already been enacted into law.

A law has already been passed and appropriations made for a National Agricultural Experiment Station, patterned to a considerable extent on the Beltsville Station in the United States. The plan calls for the establishment of regional experiment stations in each of the major-type farming areas, cereal, cotton, sugar cane, vines, fruits, and livestock. It also provides for strengthening the agricultural colleges at each of the national universities. The "Superior Technical Schools" are not attached to the university system but instead are the capstone of three levels of technical education. In the United States the three levels would be called trade schools, vocational schools, and colleges. A great expansion in both industrial and agricultural education is contemplated, the schools to be distributed throughout the country.

The plan recommends elaborate programs for the conservation and development of timber resources and the creation of a national institute of forestry to carry out this program. The space given to forestry in the published plan is an indication of the great value that is placed on this hitherto neglected natural resource of Argentina.

Because the territories have always been neglected and their development is essential to the correction of the disequilibrium of the national economy, and also because they are primarily agricultural areas, the plan provides for raising them one after the other to provincial status.

The plan as presented by President Perón was very broad, for the most part merely a statement of things that should be done. Congress is now enacting one piece of legislation after the other

to put the plan in force. More laws have been passed to implement the industrial and labor sections than have been enacted to augment the agricultural parts of the plan. Some of the laws already passed provide for minimum wages for industry and farm laborers, for retirement or pension systems, for reorganization of the university system, for the establishment of trade or technical schools, for the public ownership of electric power, for the building of dams, for the construction of a pipe line from the oil fields in eastern Chubut to Buenos Aires, for the construction of roads, and for the colonization of immigrants.

No one knows how successful the Five Year Plan may be but it is clear that it is a heroic attempt to develop the natural resources of Argentina, to decentralize its industry and population, and to distribute its wealth and income more widely among all the people. Whether it succeeds in all its details or in its stated purposes, it is intended to deal with the problems which the writer believed after a year's study in Argentina to be central to the economic and social development of that country. He was privileged to spend the months of January, February, and March of 1947 in Argentina, during which time he witnessed the extreme enthusiasm of the working people for the Five Year Plan. He also witnessed the hectic play of forces operating there under the impact of the proposed reforms of the Five Year Plan. What he has said here should not be taken as a prediction of the degree of success which the plan may ultimately have but only as a brief account of the things which it proposes.

4. THE PERÓN ERA:
AN INTERPRETATION

Controversy surrounds the origins, aims, and fundamental character of the movement called Peronismo. Whereas some observers stress its avowed objectives of social reform and economic independence, others lay a heavier emphasis on the "totalitarian implications" of the Perón régime. The following selection from a recent study of the Perón era illustrates this second point of view.[4]

THE PERÓN ERA promises to alter the whole course of Argentine history. The government of General Domingo Perón is something more than

[4] Robert J. Alexander, *The Perón Era*, New York, Columbia University Press, 1951, pp. 218–223. Reprinted by permission of the Columbia University Press.

the run-of-the-mill Latin-American strong-arm regime. It is a totalitarian administration which not only demands that the citizen must submit to its high-handed conduct of public affairs, but must give active demonstration of support.

Slowly but surely all phases of Argentine life are being made to conform to the Peronista model. The trade unions have been converted into little more than a tool of the government. The worker is being taught that he cannot reach out and try to make economic and social gains on his own account, but must accept only what "El Líder," "Evita," and the rest of the gang see fit to give him. An independent trade union movement is anathema in the Argentina of President-General Juan Domingo Perón.

All phases of economic life are being brought within a single strait-jacket. The export of basic crops is converted into a tool for the ambitions and the policies of the ruling clique. The nation's wheat and corn growers, cattle raisers and shepherds are thus put completely under the power of the ruling group in the "just" regime of "El Líder."

The industrialists, too, are meeting the same fate. Industrialization is being carried out under completely political control and much of it under actual military control. All independent organizations of Argentine industrialists have been either "intervened" or otherwise forced to conform. Individual anti-Perón industrialists, such as the chemical magnate Massone, have been forced to take refuge in Montevideo.

All means of communication and discussion are being made mere mouthpieces for the regime. The great radio stations of Buenos Aires and the provinces have been forced by subordination, purchase, or intimidation to become cogs in the wheel of the Peronista propaganda machine. All newspapers, with but one exception, have been forced either to become part of the propaganda apparatus or to go underground. The great motion picture industry — which was one of the prides of Argentina — has become but one more weapon in the armory of the Peronista politicos.

Nor have the great social and political institutions of the country escaped this all-encompassing totalitarian trend. The Catholic Church was first inveigled into a compromising position of political support of the regime, and then found itself helpless to withdraw from this alliance.

The Army seems to have been purged of all those who might question or be jealous of the authority of the Dictator and his friends. Militarism is entering into every phase of the country's public life. Military men hold civilian positions — elected and appointive — in great profusion. A large segment of the nation's economy has been placed under the direct control of the Ministry of Defense. By means of large appropriations, munificent salaries, and greatly heightened prestige within the nation, the Armed Forces have been bribed into acquiescence and cooperation with the Peronista rulers.

Education is confounded with propaganda. From infancy, Argentine children are now being taught that their nation's history virtually began with Juan Domingo Perón, and that anyone who does not agree completely with the policies, ideas, and institutions of the Peronista state is a traitor to the nation and to humanity itself. "Loyalty checks" by political Federal Police are demanded of teachers and students alike. All faculty members, whether in primary, secondary, or higher schools, whose allegiance to Peronismo is in the least open to question, have been ousted.

The checks and balances of a political democracy are being steadily eliminated. Not only does the Peronista group refuse to seat some of the elected opposition members, but it cavalierly ousts from their posts as the people's representatives those leaders of the opposition whom it considers too dangerous. The Supreme Court has been converted into a Peronista tool, by means of a wholesale purge; lesser judicial bodies have received similar treatment.

Thus, though the average visitor to Buenos Aires probably is not all aware of the spreading pall of the totalitarianism which is slowly but nonetheless completely blacking out the cultural diversity, the vigorous market of ideas, and the democratic spirit which have made Argentina one of the great nations of the hemisphere, the process is nonetheless moving relentlessly on.

The nature of Argentine totalitarianism leads to much confusion among outside observers. On the one hand, there are those Liberals who, because they have labeled the Argentine regime as "Fascist," cannot see that the basis of Perón's support among the people of Argentina is the program of social and economic reform he pursued in the middle years of the 1940's. These Liberals pronounce his social legislation as nothing more than "demagoguery," and refuse to admit that he really received the backing of the great mass of the leadership and the membership of the country's trade union movement. The Liberals are willing enough to believe that Perón is converting the trade union movement into a species of Labor Front — which is true —

but they are not willing to admit that he was in a position to do so only because that same labor movement was responsible for keeping him in power, once the Army had put him there — which is also true.

It was this same lack of appreciation of Perón's program which led the opposition to underestimate the influence he had gained in the ranks of the workers. The Radicals and Socialists, who make up the bulk of the opposition to Perón, did not understand until it was too late that Perón really had done things which the workers felt were in their interest and which therefore won him their gratitude and loyalty. The opposition has now awakened to this fact, but it may be too late, despite the gallantry and heroism of the anti-Peronista forces.

On the other hand there are those — and many of them are found in high places — who refuse to recognize the totalitarian nature of the Peronista regime. Because it has until recently allowed the two papers *La Nación* and *La Prensa* to continue publication, because there *is* still a Congress with a number of opposition deputies sitting in Buenos Aires, because Perón *has* carried out a program of economic development and social reform which is commendable, this group fails to recognize, or at least to admit, that the Peronista regime is nonetheless dangerous.

This group, many of whose members seem to be in the State Department, the halls of the United States Congress, and in other positions of trust, therefore continues to treat the Argentine regime as if it were one more Good Neighbor. It carries "appeasement" to the extreme of advocating — and then granting — loans to Perón's Argentina. It seems to overlook the extensive work of propaganda and subversion which Perón and his friends are conducting in other Latin American countries. It seems to refuse to believe in the possibility that Perón may succeed in his cherished aim of forming a Latin-American bloc independent of and defiant of the United States.

Not all the people in this second group are to be found in the United States. The British, for instance, for long overlooked the totalitarian implications of the Peronista regime. All too many Latin-American politicians and labor leaders notice only the labor legislation Perón has put on the books, or his success in defying the United States, and do not see the dangers which the Peronista movement and administration augur for themselves and their countries.

It is high time that people in both these camps took another look at the Peronista administration as it really is. If the Liberals want to call Perón "fascist," that is well and good. However, they should recognize the nature of the appeal which he has made. They should realize the implications of the fact that the people of once-proud Argentina were willing to sell their liberty for supposed economic and social benefits. This is the real lesson of Argentina's experience for the Liberals.

On the other hand, the statesmen of Latin America should come to realize without equivocation that although Perón may be successful in defying the United States, he has also been eminently successful in wiping out civil liberty and economic, social, and political freedom within the borders of Argentina. They should remember that Perón was the leader of the brutally imperialist-minded Grupo de Oficiales Unidos, which made little secret of its desire to dominate the South American continent and impose upon it a concentration camp regime patterned on those of Hitler's Europe. Nor should they forget the economic treaties which Perón offered his neighbors in the first flush of exuberance in 1946 and 1947: treaties which would have gone far toward destroying what economic independence those nations now enjoy and, in the long run, subverting their political independence as well.

North Americans, too, should be wide-awake to the dangers of Perón and his regime. Perón's Argentina is the spearhead of the reactionary dictatorial bloc among American nations. This bloc has no regard for the political democracy and freedom for which the United States stands in the world. Under Argentine leadership this bloc seeks to destroy the still-remaining democracies in the Western Hemisphere. Unless the United States is careful, she will one day wake up to find a united front of totalitarian military dictatorships among the nations to the South, proudly headed and dominated by El Líder — Su Excelencia Señor Presidente de la República Argentina, General Juan Domingo Perón.

XXXII

Republican Brazil

THE BRAZILIAN REVOLUTION OF 1889 moved the center of political gravity from the North to the South. The new republican constitution of 1891 granted the States a large measure of autonomy, but in practice the coffee planters and cattle raisers of São Paulo and Minas Gerais held the levers of power. A new economic and mental climate arose in the cities, where banks, stock exchanges, and corporations enjoyed a rapid growth, but the life of the countryside remained largely unchanged. The single-crop plantation system, under altered forms, continued to dominate economic activity, preventing balanced development and keeping the great majority of the people in poverty and ignorance.

Coffee was king under the Republic, while sugar, which had been seriously affected by the abolition of slavery, declined in importance. Cotton, cacao, and rubber were other leading export products in the twentieth century. The problem of overproduction and falling prices for coffee inspired schemes of "valorization" — official efforts to maintain prices at a high level by artificial means. After 1920 the chronic coffee crisis diverted some workers and capital to manufacturing industry, which had a considerable growth in São Paulo, Rio de Janeiro, and other centers. But at mid-century Brazil remained a predominantly agrarian country.

The collapse of the coffee industry in 1929, combined with bitter interprovincial rivalries, enabled Getúlio Vargas, a shrewd *caudilho* from Rio Grande do Sul, to seize power through a *coup d'état*. The years of the Vargas dictatorship (1930–1945) saw sweeping centralization of power in the central government, assistance to the new industrialists as well as to agriculture, and drastic curbs on labor and all opposition elements. Friendly to the United States, largest market for Brazil's coffee, Vargas took his country into the war against the Axis in 1942. Ousted by an army revolt in October, 1945, Vargas continued active in politics under the new constitution of 1945, and in 1950 won election as President of Brazil. A mounting inflation, an unfavorable balance of trade, and the disasters of drought and famine in certain northern provinces were among the problems faced by his Administration. The gravity of Brazil's economic and political crisis found dramatic expression when President Vargas took his own life on August 24, 1954, leaving a suicide note in which he laid the blame for Brazil's difficulties on predatory "international economic and financial groups."

1. "THE OLD ORDER CHANGETH ..."

The abolition of slavery in 1888, followed the next year by the establishment of the Republic, consummated a long evolution in Brazil's economic and social life. An eminent Brazilian historian, Pedro Calmon (1902–   ), interprets these important developments.[1]

IN BRAZIL, the historical and chronological epochs do not coincide.

Our sixteenth century began in 1532, with

[1] Pedro Calmon, *História Social do Brasil*, vol. 3, *A Época Republicana*, São Paulo, 1939, pp. 1–6. (Excerpt translated by the editor.)

the founding of S. Vicente; the seventeenth, in 1625, with the restoration of Bahia; the eighteenth, in 1694, with the discovery of the mines; the nineteenth, in 1808, with the arrival of the Portuguese Court. Our twentieth century began in 1888–89, with the abolition of slavery, which transformed the economy, and the foundation of the Republic, which changed the political face of the country.

The Revolution of 1888–89 was profound and general in its consequences.

More than a government fell before the advance of the new conditions of national life, before Federalism and revolutionary, Americanist liberalism. To the hierarchical and respectable society of the Empire succeeded a different society. The skilful, conciliatory formulas of Dom Pedro's parliamentary regime had long put off or concealed the collapse of the equilibrium between the old antagonisms of Brazilian society — the capital and the provinces, agriculture and industry, French and American models, order and idealism, the barons of the monarchy and the lawyers, traditional stability and rapid progress. But the machine went off its course amid the tumults of the eighties; there was the abolitionist campaign, the military question, the skepticism of the disgruntled parties (the Liberal Party, whose idealism had lost it the elections of 1881 and 1884, and the Conservative Party, which won empty victories in its exhausting struggle against erupting reforms), and the weight of years and illness pressing upon the Emperor.

A new generation demanded new laws.

The provinces of the South wanted tariff protection for industry; the North demanded protection for its decaying agriculture, credits, and free trade.

The sudden emancipation of the slaves inaugurated the epoch of immigration. High prices for coffee enabled São Paulo to bear the blow of abolition without disruption of its aristocratic plantation system. The *fazendeiros* could pay for labor and thus retain the workers they had acquired in recent years from the slave traders. Foreign colonists (beginning in 1888, 100,000 entered each year through the port of Santos!) swelled the ranks of the labor force.

But in the province of Rio de Janeiro and in the Recôncavo, agriculture languished and withered because of unfavorable conditions: an exhausted soil, ancient and divided estates of scanty yield, the patriarchal character of the economy, kept alive only by class spirit and the historic ties of the great families to the land on which they had lived for three centuries. The *usina,* the great sugar factory, destroyed the sugar mill of colonial type and swallowed up the properties of the old nobility. . . . The axis of wealth, and with it the axis of power, shifted from the Recôncavo to the South. In 1887 the political poles were Cotegipe and Antonio Prado, or Paulino and Silveira Martins. The cycle of sugar against that of coffee and cattle. The binomial of the nineteenth century (sugar and coffee), perhaps the agricultural formula of the unity of the Empire in the epoch of the aristocratic latifundio and the baron-colonels, was shattered. Coffee could survive without the slave, and withstood the blow of abolition. But

sugar, blockaded in Brazil by the terrific development of other sugar-producing centers, could not endure that shock. Sugar gave Brazil its independence in 1822. Coffee made the Republic in 1889.

Not that the conservative coffee planters were anti-monarchical by conviction and temperament. On the contrary, until 1888 they regarded the monarchy as their chief point of support. But they were tied to the mentality of a swift-moving civilization. They belonged to a time of audacious enterprises.

The divergence between the two economic zones was essentially a contrast in rhythms. Sugar moved slowly, coffee at a dizzy pace; one was a fixed, static culture, the other was extensive and expansive. The vertical line (sugar) combined with the horizontal (coffee) to define the "dynamism" of Brazil: solid and unstable, paralyzed in a conquest, the structural Brazil of the North, the polymorphic Brazil of the South. . . .

The coffee planters and a climate of liberalism, well suited to the pursuit of individual and unlimited prosperity, arose together. They had no use for the maturity and serenity of that other agriculture, the slow-moving culture of the cane, which crystallized its social types in the shadow of the colonial sugar-mill, gaining in deep, sentiment-steeped roots what the coffee-planter gained in new horizons. . . .

If one word can sum up the political confusion of that phase of transition from one regime to another, that word is — impatience.

The effect of abolition was as great in the minds of men as in the material realm.

Three days had sufficed to bring crashing down the infamous system that had lasted three centuries. If total reforms were so easy, why hesitate to illuminate the land with the ardent new lights of the time? Federation in American style; a republic *à la française;* a strong government as taught by Auguste Comte; industries, factories, companies, banks, inflation, business, as in the United States — and away with senile caution!

The movement of ideas that brought the *coup d'état* of November 15 was freighted with that formless impatience as the summer wind is freighted with the tepidity of the earth, the fire of space. . . . There arose a vague crusade against dogmas. A spiritual insurrection against the past, against consecrated values. A change of symbols, of principles, of ends. Instead of political continuity, the revolution; instead of monarchical ruralism, republican citizenship; no more national *unity,* but *union* of autonomous States; strong government, and not weak cabinet governments; speeches in the streets, not in Parliament; a "Jacobin" and lyrical nationalism, as in 1831, but with different models — democratic equality, a clamor of popular demands, and, in place of the ancient Emperor, a President-marshal. Let the giant learn to walk . . . , urged the liberal propagandists. Let a democracy of labor replace patriarchal customs; let the States place no impediment in the way of prosperity; let the citizen not feel the restraining hand of government upon his new-found liberty, cut to the patterns of Gambetta and Castellar.

The army removed the barrier of the Empire from that road. . . . The army precipitated the transformation; most important of all, it insured external peace, the appearance of transition without disorder. In the paralysis of the constitutional parties, of the old governing class, with its sense of organization it gave discipline and order to the nascent federation. An officer assumed the government of the province; supported by its garrison, he kept the officials at their posts, protected the magistrates in the performance of their duties. Anarchy was thus avoided.

Indeed, the least dramatic revolution was the political: the overthrow of the throne by the second brigade of Rio de Janeiro, commanded by Marshal Manoel Deodoro da Fonseca. It was Brazilian society that experienced change from top to bottom. No superficial tempest, this; all social strata were affected by the upheaval. It was not so much a new régime as a new century that arose. Republic? Say, rather, the twentieth century.

Aristides Lobo, correspondent of the *Diario Popular* of São Paulo, wrote for his readers a letter that has the revealing quality of a portrait, on November 15, 1889:

"For the time being the aspect of the government is purely military, and so it should be. Theirs was the work, only theirs, because the action of civilian elements was practically nil. The people looked on, stupefied, astonished, dumbfounded, without an inkling of what it all meant. Many honestly believed that they were watching a parade."

2. " . . . YIELDING PLACE TO NEW"

In the wake of the revolution came a flurry of modernization, of changes in manners, in values, and even in the physical appearance of some of Brazil's great urban centers. These changes were most marked in the Federal Capital, made into a beautiful and healthful city through the initiative and efforts of Prefect Pereira Passos and the distinguished scientist Oswaldo Cruz.[2]

1890 WAS A YEAR of rash gaiety, of a revolution in manners more intense and profound than the political revolution.

Gone were the restraints of the hierarchy, of the polished and sober *bon ton* of the Empire. Rio de Janeiro was transformed from top to bottom. The new "republican equality" cut off its peaks; the new police force of Sampaio Ferraz cleansed its roots. The Great Boom, the *Encilhamento,* subverting economic values and making wealth a common and dominant ideal, suddenly destroyed the moderate and elegant conception of life that had long prevailed and that had been inherent and implicit in the monarchical system, with its lifetime Senate, the honors of the Court, the tradition that statesmen should grow poor in the public service instead of enriching themselves, the radiant, fastidious honesty of the Palace of São Cristovão. Barons with recently acquired titles jostled each other in the corridors of the Stock Exchange or in the Rua da Alfândega, buying and selling stocks; the tilburies that filled the length of São Francisco Street were taken by a multitude of millionaires of recent vintage — commercial agents, bustling lawyers, promoters of all kinds, politicians of the new generation, the men of the day. They were shunned with dignity by the nonconformists, members of the old nobility, politicians of the Empire who held aloof; another year, and their number would be swollen by the disillusioned. But the Republic was not simply a movement against "Your Excellencies" in the name of plain "you." It took strong measures against hooliganism, against the disorders of the popular wards. In the very first days of the regime, Sampaio Ferraz cleaned out the vagabonds who had infested the city for a hundred years. . . . The gangs and the "young gentlemen of quality" went out together. The symbol of the new governing class was the horse car — leaving from the corner of Gonçalves Dias Street — whose "bourgeois benches" united all the citizens in perfect equality.

Pleasure — easy, commercial, exotic — held sway. The coffee-houses were full, the Rua do Ouvidor thronged, the horse cars crowded. Roulette-wheels were installed in private houses; the

2 Pedro Calmon, *História Social do Brasil,* Vol. 3, *A Época Republicana,* São Paulo, 1939, pp. 143–145, 164–169. (Excerpt translated by the editor.)

club became a business center; the vicissitudes of the Great Boom were discussed at the tables of the confectionery-shops where literati, financiers, gamblers, and courtesans congregated and astounded, dazzled provincials looked on. "City of vice and pleasure" was how the annoyed Anselmo Coelho Neto described "the Federal Capital." . . .

THE EPIDEMIC

That Federal Capital, refulgent in spirit and quivering with civic excitement, had its fashionable season and its season of gloom. The *carioca* unquestionably grew accustomed to yellow fever. He came to regard it as a cyclical scourge, his summer ailment, recurring each year between December and April and terrible at the start, especially for foreigners; but that soon ceased to disturb the routine life of the great city, which solved the problem as best it could. The people went to the mountains. They fled to the high spots of the surrounding countryside. They returned to nature, abandoning the city — and with it those who could not get away — to its periodic tragedy. There remained only the poor, the merchants, the officials. Petropolis offered its charms of a European city to the invaders of the upper class. It was even more imperial under the Republic, more opulent, more desired, but now without the examples of sobriety, the lessons in modesty, of Dom Pedro II.

In connection with the commemoration of the fiftieth anniversary of the arrival of the Sisters of Notre Dame de Sion in Brazil (they landed at Rio on October 9, 1888), their "diary" was published, with its disillusioned impressions of the plague-ridden Rio summer, of the horror inspired by the fever. . . . One of the nuns, Mother Felix, soon died, and the others left for Petropolis. They were ordered to remain there, together with their school for girls, which, between 1889 and 1892, functioned part of the year in Rio and the rest of the time in the mountains. A teacher who kept his pupils in the city during the period of the epidemic, that is, during the summer, would have committed a crime. The capital became uninhabitable, particularly for foreigners. The obituary lists caused terror. Hundreds died each month.

THE RENOVATION OF RIO DE JANEIRO

Oswaldo Cruz and Prefect Passos were the powerful arms that awoke the sleeping city. It awoke with a start at the sight of the gangs of workmen that began to demolish the old Rio. . . .

The monarchy fell in effigy in 1889.

The past really fell in 1904, with the passing of the narrow streets in the center of the city, with the widening of the city's heart, with the construction of modern avenues that would permit the free movement of a people fascinated by the civilization which thus made its triumphant entrance.

If the duel between sanitation and popular distrust had its trying aspects, from cold incredulity to armed resistance, the struggle of the city planner with the spirit of routine was no less dramatic and difficult. Both men could count on the absolute solidarity of the Federal Government; Cruz and Passos would not accept their dangerous and decisive missions on any other terms. The law of December 29, 1902, placed in the authoritarian hands of the Prefect almost dictatorial powers. Article 25, for example, authorized him to remove the occupants of condemned dwellings with the aid of the police and without judicial appeal. He got everything he asked for. Recalcitrants who beat at the doors of justice found themselves escorted away by armed soldiers. Passos was arbitrariness itself. It was a terribly lawless situation, in which a single man, absorbed in the mysteries of his plans, decided the fate of a city. But it was effective and necessary. A loan of six million pounds sterling that the Prefecture was empowered to float failed in Europe: Rio's business community covered it to the amount of four million pounds. Force and money — Passos' iron will would do the rest. That will did not weaken.

Cruz and Passos, working in concert, cultivated an ungrateful soil.

Hygiene depended on remodeling the city, on doing away with the cesspools and dissolving the ancient filth; and the old Rio could be made over only by conquering yellow fever. Each in his own field, the two dictators of public improvement encountered the same hostility. Oswaldo Cruz fought the battle of convictions — his struggle was the more abstract. Pereira Passos confronted a league of vested interests — his fight was more concrete. He faced the hostility of business, the property owners, the stubbornly, solidly conservative classes. The passivity of tenants, the force of habit, the new liberalism that taught the inviolability of the home, the old customs. . . .

Had he attempted to realize partial reforms, like those carried out at the end of the Empire, like the opening of Gonçalves Dias (1854) and

Senador Dantas streets or the ward of Vila Isabel, he would have met with universal applause. But his program, just like the hygienist's, was total and brusque.

Since 1871, as a member of the commission named by Minister João Alfredo, Passos had meditated on his grand project. He kept it to himself until 1902. In 1882, together with Teixeira Soares, he had obtained the franchise for the construction of the Corcovado Railroad. . . . Now his plan consisted in tearing down the old buildings, in rectifying with rectilinear and tree-covered designs the tortuous colonial plan. No more unlighted hovels and big old houses falling into ruins, no more dirty streets and discolored façades, no more repellent odors of pestilent alleys, no more oppressive atmosphere of the colonial city. He used his engineering equipment like a broom. He had to sweep away the filth of a commercial city that had grown too fast within the small area that housed its asphyxiated prosperity and its slums, its plenty and its poverty, its warehouses and its congested society that gasped for breath within the narrow bounds of its historic walls. Passos attacked the problem as a whole. He dislodged without pity the merchants affected by the condemnations, and took for their basis the low declarations of value made for tax purposes. He gave the construction of the new arteries the appearance of a catastrophe. . . . He worked with great haste. He knew that without drive and energy, without closing his eyes to cases of individual hardship, he could not carry his plan through. And the worst of all would be to leave the job half done, the houses torn down, the avenues still unopened, all buried in the rubble of the demolitions, with nothing to show for the destruction he had wrought. He had to be adamant in order to be efficient. On all sides he met with resistance. The newspapers hurled insults at him; the merchants whose interests were affected opposed him. He would be handed a court summons by day and by that night begin levelling the walls. The controversy increased as endless points of law were invoked — but meanwhile the pickaxes did not stop. Without that useful and massive violence he would have failed at the very start — he and Oswaldo Cruz. His heroism consisted in making himself insensible to all protests. President Rodrigues Alves armed himself with the same stoicism. The tactic was a skillful one: first tear down, then be free to rebuild at will. . . .

The first section of the new port at Rio de Janeiro was inaugurated November 8, 1906.

That year electric lights bathed the city in their luminous glow.

The Prefect wanted Rio to be the best illuminated city in the world.

It was the touch of magic needed to make the prodigy visible; from the deep ruins of the year of devastations emerged the modern outlines of the rejuvenated city.

"Rio is becoming civilized," sang the minstrels of the people. The patriarchal city that on other nights, dimly lit by gas lamps, had resounded with their languid serenades, was fleeing before their eyes. The hills of Rio, the Santo Antonio, the Castelo, the Conceição, the Favela, now ceased to be the refuges of poverty. Down below, swarms of workers advanced over the clouds of dust raised by the demolitions. And from the rubble emerged the shining tracks of the tilbury and the newly-arrived automobile.

3. THE COFFEE CYCLE, 1889–1930

The republican revolution left intact the traditional structure of the Brazilian economy. As before, and even more so, Brazil's fortunes were linked to those of a single export product. Coffee, which had shared economic leadership with sugar in the late Empire, now achieved a commanding position. But like its predecessors, the coffee cycle soon began to wane as a result of external factors over which Brazil had little or no control. A Brazilian historian relates the rise and fall of King Coffee.[3]

COFFEE HOLDS THE FIRST and sovereign place among all modern Brazilian products. In an earlier phase, under the Empire, we observed its ascendant progress, bringing under its sway the best and most important activities of the country. Now, under the Republic, we see it attaining the zenith of its grandiose course and establishing itself on a level that definitely put in the shade all other Brazilian products. Even in absolute and world terms, coffee acquired an outstanding position. In the twentieth century it was, if not the first, at least among the first food products of international trade; and Brazil, with 70 per cent of the world's coffee production, enjoyed an undisputed supremacy.

The natural conditions of the country, or rather of some of its regions (climate, quality of the soil), contributed in large part to this

[3] Caio Prado Junior, *História econômica do Brasil*, São Paulo, Editora Brasilense Ltda., 1945, pp. 237–248. (Excerpt translated by the editor.) Reprinted by permission of Editora Brasilense Ltda.

result. But undoubtedly the decisive factor in the enormous upsurge of Brazilian coffee production was the European imigration that provided the necessary supply of labor. This close connection between immigration and the progress of coffee was always known and very well understood. The Administration of the State of São Paulo (the principal producer, autonomous under the new republican federative regime) made assistance to immigration its central activity, and solved the problem by means of a system that may be regarded as perfected and complete. The immigrant, generally an Italian, was brought with official aid and protection from his home in the most remote village of the Apennines, or any other region, to the coffee plantation, by an organization whose responsibilities ranged from propaganda concerning Brazil in Europe to the perfectly regulated distribution of the laborers among the different properties in the State. To this complex and expensive service, the foundation stone of Paulist prosperity, the Government of São Paulo always assigned its best efforts and revenues. Its success was notable, for between 1889 and 1930 the State received more than two million immigrants (of whom more than half received financial aid), the majority of whom were destined to labor on the coffee plantations. This was the result, not of chance or fortuitous circumstances, but of a long and persistent effort carried on with intelligence and notable organizational activity.

The advance of coffee agriculture in Brazil since the last decade of the nineteenth century, remarkable when regarded as a whole, was nevertheless very irregular if we consider the different regions of the country. There was no uniform and harmonious development; expansion in some sectors coincided with decline and even complete annihilation in others. We noted this cyclical evolution of coffee under the Empire — an evolution in which the space of a few decades saw an ascending phase followed by another of decadence in each producing zone. The great area of progress in the period under discussion was the western portion of São Paulo, an almost desert region that was rapidly conquered and brought under cultivation.

A very different development occurred in other sectors of older occupation. The decay of coffee agriculture, already begun under the Empire, became complete over a large part of these regions. Only the ruins of old seignorial mansions, the former homes of wealthy planters, here

and there recalled the rapid transit of coffee's prosperity; the plantations had disappeared, and their place was taken by poor pastures that supported a few miserable cattle. Of coffee agriculture there remained only scanty patches of cultivated land, in full process of decay and extinction. Only in Minas Gerais was some modest progress made, and this was limited to certain sectors, where use was made of the remaining arable land.

Outside São Paulo (and the adjoining zone of Northern Paraná, reached by the Paulist march to the west), only Espiritu Santo witnessed an appreciable advance of coffee agriculture. Here use was made of reserves of virgin land which the incipient colonization of the region had left untouched to that moment. As in São Paulo, but on a much smaller scale, the planters relied on a regular stream of immigrants to satisfy their labor needs. But Espiritu Santo could not progress very far, for, unlike São Paulo, it lacked an abundance of suitable land; for this reason its agriculture would always be relatively mediocre. As for the coffee-producing regions of the North (Bahia, Pernambuco, and a small part of Ceará), they were doomed to remain on the same third-rate level as before. The soil factor — that is, the lack of lands suitable for coffee cultivation — was the principal cause of their stagnation. The climate, more markedly tropical and therefore less attractive for European colonists, was also partly responsible.

To sum up, the presence of virgin lands in western São Paulo, with its magnificent soils, its regular terrain that simplified the problem of transportation, and a climate to which the European laborer easily adjusted himself, diverted to it the best efforts and resources of the country; here was concentrated more than half the total number of coffee trees, producing more than 60 per cent of the total national production. It was São Paulo's massive contribution that enabled Brazil to achieve such a brilliant position in the world coffee trade.

But the quantitative advance of coffee cultivation in Brazil was not accompanied by an equal qualitative progress. By and large, the rudimentary agricultural processes of the past continued to be employed. A certain improvement was evident in the preparation and processing of the product: the cleaning and stripping of the "berries." For this purpose better machinery and installations were introduced. But as concerned cultivation proper (the care of the soil and the plant, selection of varieties, etc.), on the whole matters stood as before. And this was the principal reason for the invariable decline in the productivity of plantations, even though they were located in regions of superior soils and highly favorable natural conditions.

The only notable, large-scale innovation in agriculture in the period under discussion was the general introduction of free labor, and particularly of the European immigrant — which led to a considerable improvement in the conditions of agricultural exploitation by comparison with those prevailing under slavery. On the coffee plantations in general, and particularly in São Paulo, a labor system was adopted which combined wages (a fixed annual wage, plus a quota for the harvest that varied according to the size of the latter), with the right granted to the laborer to cultivate certain pieces of land for himself. Side by side with this type of worker (called *colono*), but generally in much smaller numbers, was found the pure wage-worker or day-laborer. The fazenda supplied its workers with homes, but not with the instruments of labor. These were very simple — a hoe and nothing more; the cultivation of coffee, a permanent plant harvested by hand, does not employ machinery.

Another aspect of coffee production, much more important in its history, as well as in the evolution of the Brazilian economy in general, was its financial vicissitudes in the period that opened with the establishment of the Republic. If the large expansion of production brought the country wealth and progress, it also brought a problem of overproduction that began to plague Brazil's coffee economy only a few years after the start of its great cycle of growth and that has continued to the present day, with profound and varied repercussions on the general evolution of the Brazilian economy. I have already noted that the first signs of disequilibrium appeared in 1896. It was the result of the extensive plantings made during the first years of the Republic, and which now began to bear fruit (let us recall again that the coffee tree is a plant that begins production at the age of four or five years). At that time appeared the classic symptoms of overproduction: decline in prices, the formation of unsalable stocks.

In the first years of the fall of prices, the devaluation of Brazilian currency still partly concealed the situation; in paper money, the price of coffee did not fluctuate greatly. It was as a result of the stabilization and revaluation of the currency after the financial restoration of 1898 that the full effect of the fall in prices was felt. Toward 1905, in gold, this amounted to more than 50 per cent. At the same time ever greater stocks of unsalable merchandise were accumulated. In 1905 they amounted to 11 million bags of 60 ks., representing 70 per cent of the world consumption for one year.

Undoubtedly the chief cause of the crisis was the increase in plantings. In the period from 1890 to 1900 the plantings of São Paulo doubled (220 and 520 million coffee trees, respectively). A remedy for the evil was sought by restricting cultivation, and in São Paulo (1902) a tax was placed on new plantings.

The fall in price and the difficult market situation considerably reduced the rate of growth. In the following decade (1901–1910) the number of coffee trees in São Paulo barely rose by 150 millions. The same phenomenon was observed among Brazil's competitors, whose production actually declined. But all this did not prevent a chronic disequilibrium between world consumption and production. The saturation of consumers' markets had clearly placed a ceiling on coffee production.

To be sure, production was always very variable, with great oscillations that resulted from the alternation of years or periods of favorable and unfavorable climatic conditions. The care given to the plantings, which varied according to market prospects and the financial situation of the producers, also influenced these oscillations. Thus, as a rule, the surpluses of one moment were compensated for by the shortages of the next. Taking more or less extensive periods as a whole, production proceeded about on a par with consumption. Only after 1925 did permanent surpluses arise that forced the destruction of great quantities of coffee. But this long-range equilibrium did not prevent momentary overproductions that sometimes were prolonged for several years in succession. Hence the successive crises that became almost permanent, and that have characterized the history of coffee to the present.

Commercial speculation intervened in this situation for its own benefit, and this was of great importance, not only in the particular sector of coffee production and commerce but in the economic and financial life of Brazil in general. Dependent as it was on its principal product, the Brazilian economy suffered all the vicissitudes through which coffee passed. I have already indicated how commercial speculation first intervened in the coffee industry in 1896.

From then on, its maneuvers largely conditioned the evolution of the coffee economy. Good harvests were utilized for the formation of reserves that dragged prices down or were doled out later, in years of poor harvests, at advantageous prices. The planters, compelled to dispose of their products without delay in order to pay the costs of production, lost the difference in price to the middlemen, who in the last analysis were large financial houses and international banks operating under cover. Maneuvers of this type were carried out even within the space of a single agricultural year. The coffee harvest in Brazil occupies the relatively short space of four months (May to August), when production flows to the ports, forcing a fall in prices. This is followed by a period of shortages of the product, when prices rise. The commercial middlemen would be buyers in the first phase, sellers in the second. In this way they monopolized the major part of the profits of the business, to the detriment of the producers.

It was the necessity of defending themselves against this state of things that caused the producers to resort to measures designed to maintain and stabilize the price of coffee. This took place for the first time in 1906, when a truly grave situation arose. Prices, long in decline as a result of the revaluation of currency, fell to a level clearly below the costs of production, with serious consequences to the planters. Meanwhile the world position of coffee was not unfavorable. In previous years production had maintained itself below consumption; a sharp increase in the latter compensated for the expansion in production, and in the period 1901–1905 there was a deficit of almost 5,000,000 bags. One could confidently expect that the accumulated stocks would be rapidly absorbed. And it is worthy of note that despite the decline in market quotations, the price paid by the consumer remained unchanged. The crisis affected only the producer.

It was these circumstances that determined the first official intervention in the coffee market. The problem could have been solved by means of a system of credit that would have protected the producers and not left them in the necessity of selling their production precipitately. But this was not the solution selected. An opportunistic expedient was chosen which consisted in intervening in the market with massive purchases in order to force prices up. It is difficult to ascertain to what degree the maneuvers of concealed interests contributed to this solution, so highly precarious and speculative. The large profits drawn from it by financial groups who had nothing in common with the producers permit us to indulge in these conjectures. The producers themselves were benefited, to be sure, but only momentarily; the lion's share of the profits was not for them.

Be that as it may, the proposed plan found a warm reception in many important sectors of the country, and an imposing campaign in its favor was unleashed in the press and in the Congress. The opposition was no less strong, both in the country and abroad. The Federal Government itself long hesitated before accepting it, and the burden of its realization fell on the principal producing States (São Paulo, Rio de Janeiro, and Minas Gerais). And it was São Paulo, the most interested State, and the only one that possessed adequate financial resources, that effectively assumed the responsibility.

The first difficulty was that of obtaining the necessary resources. Brazil's weak national finances were inadequate for such a large-scale operation; an appeal for foreign credit was rejected by Brazil's bankers in Europe (the Rothschild House and group). Directly or indirectly, they were too closely tied to established interests to accept any modification of the existing order in the coffee business. Now there entered upon the scene other financial groups, who took advantage of the opportunity (it may even be that they had prepared that opportunity) to change in their favor the control of the coffee trade. First entered a great German exporting firm, Theodor Wille & Co. This marked the simultaneous entrance of German imperialism, which until that time had played only a modest role in Brazilian affairs. Behind Theodor Wille were aligned the principal financial groups of that country: the Discount Gesellschaft and the Dresden Bank. They were joined by English and French bankers who formed an opposition in their countries to the groups that had held Brazilian finances in their hands. They were J. Henry Schroder and Co. of London, and the Société Générale of Paris. The National City Bank of New York also joined this aggregation. It furnished São Paulo with the necessary means to implement the valorization plan, making credits available to the amount of 4,000,000 pounds.

In the face of this development, Rothschild, seeing that his previous refusal had been without effect and unwilling to remain on the outside and compromise his position, hastened to join the group. Through him São Paulo received 3,000,000 pounds more. The Bank of France, representing the established financial and commercial interests in the coffee business, refused to accept coffee warrants calculated on a basis higher than 40 francs a bag (the price reached by coffee at that time fluctuated around 50 francs); in this way it hoped to neutralize the maneuvers of valorization. At the same time the importing firms of Havre, the great French center of the coffee trade, unleashed a powerful campaign to discredit the loans being floated by Brazil in Europe.

But the battle was finally won by the "bulls." In order to consolidate the previous loans and carry the operation to a conclusion, fifteen more millions were obtained; intervention in the market continued until 1910, when, tension having eased and prices stabilized, the purchases were finally suspended. During the period 1906–1910 nearly 8,500,000 bags had been withdrawn from the free market.

The financial interests involved in the operation thus won the contest. And it was they, much more than the producers in whose name the operation had been conducted, who reaped its best fruits. The merchandise acquired during the earlier phase of operations could now be sold at a large margin of profit, and the official stocks retired from the market remained in their hands for speculative purposes. In order to direct these maneuvers and proceed with the liquidation of the unsold stocks, a special body was established — the Coffee Commission of the State of São Paulo — in which the bankers had almost complete control (five members against one named by the Government of São Paulo). Thus they remained effectively, and for a long time, in control of the coffee market. The importance of this control can be gauged by the protests raised by those who were left on the outside of the scheme, by the competing financial groups who saw themselves denied opportunities now reserved to the fortunate agents of the valorization plan. The question even had repercussions in the German and French Parliaments, in which drastic measures were proposed to force the Commission to part with its stocks. The pretext was the interest of consumers (an entirely baseless pretext, since the consumer price never changed, either during the previous price decline or during the subsequent rise), and the socialist parties, in particular, from demagogic motives made an issue of the matter without suspecting that they were serving as mere instruments of despised financial interests. In the United States the question assumed another aspect, and on the grounds that the retention of stocks infringed the Sherman Anti-Trust Act, the Commission was judicially compelled to dispose of its holdings in that country. Elsewhere, the Commission continued in control of the market until World War I, by which time the remaining stocks had been exhausted, with the exception of the part held in Germany, which was confiscated by the government of that country when Brazil declared war on it.

While the financial agents of the valorization reaped large profits from the operation, the producers, though enjoying better and more stable prices for some years, later had to bear its entire burden. It was they who assumed the responsibility for the large debts contracted in order to execute the plan. For this purpose there was established a new tax of five gold francs per bag of coffee exported. This tax was used to pay the principal and interest of the debt, which even today, more than thirty years later, and when the valorization of 1906–1910 has passed entirely into the realm of history, has not been entirely liquidated. The momentary profits of valorization cost the producers and the Brazilian economy in general very dear.

Such, in brief, is the history of the first valorization, of such fundamental importance in the economic evolution of Brazil. It was repeated, though on a much smaller scale, in the course of the War of 1914–1918, when the disorganization of international trade and the contraction of consumers' markets caused a new fall of prices and a reduction of Brazilian exports. This time the final solution came in the form of the great frost of 1918, which devastated São Paulo's coffee plantations, reducing the production of several consecutive years and thus restoring equilibrium.

After the War, coffee enjoyed a new period of prosperity as a result of the return of normalcy to Europe and the great upsurge of economic activity that accompanied it. World consumption expanded, prices rose. Only a small crisis, a reflection of the financial storm which swept over Europe in 1921, interrupted this trend. But the upward movement of prices was soon resumed. Production was stimulated, above all, by the postwar financial boom, reflected in Brazil in the general intensification of business activity, the expansion of credit, and, after 1923, large issues of paper money designed to meet the needs of the upsurge of business and the activization of

economic life that was taking place. All this provoked a large increase in coffee plantings. Between 1918 and 1924 the number of coffee trees
in São Paulo rose from 828 to 949 millions. And
the old story of overproduction was repeated.

But this time (1924) much more ample measures were taken. Instead of simple expedients
and momentary operations (as in 1906), an ambitious scheme of permanent valorization was
adopted. The fact was that conditions had
changed. The Great War profoundly modified
the conditions of the coffee trade, and it ceased
to be, as in the past, the agitated scene of struggle between the financial interests of numerous
competing groups. From the great conflict of
1914–1918 resulted — in this as in the other
great sectors of the world economy — the formation of new and much greater financial trusts
which now ruled alone, each in its own field and
without any competitors of note. It was under
the auspices of one of these great international
groups that the new operation of valorization
took place in Brazil. Without opposition, it established a new financial sway, much greater
and more absolute than that of its predecessors
of 1906 in the field of the Brazilian coffee economy. This was the group of Lazard Brothers &
Co., Ltd., of London.

In São Paulo was created a special organization, the Institute of Coffee, designed to control
entirely the export trade in the product, regulating the market offerings and maintaining an
equilibrium between supply and demand. For
this purpose the Institute had the right to withdraw coffee production in unlimited quantity,
storing it in warehouses and releasing it only according to the needs of export trade. Thus, in
contrast with the plan of 1906 and later plans,
the agency of valorization did not intervene directly in the market to buy and sell the product; it only regulated the supply to the market,
seeking to establish an equilibrium with the
rhythm of exportation.

From this arose the necessity of financing the
producers, whose harvests were withheld from
the market. An official bank of the State of São
Paulo provided the producers with loans of up
to 50 per cent of the value of the merchandise
withheld.

The same bank also dealt in mortgages on
agricultural properties. The Institute and the
whole plan were of Paulista initiation, and
were only concerned with the coffee and commerce of São Paulo. By agreement, the other
producing States adopted similar and parallel
measures with regard to their product. For all
these operations Lazard Bros. advanced the
necessary resources; and there was imposed a
new coffee tax of a thousand gold milreis per
bag (that is, 2 s. 3 d. in English money), designed
to cover the costs of the plan and the service of
the contracted debts.

This whole scheme, designed initially and
ostensibly only to regulate the disposal of Brazil's
coffee production and maintain price stability,
soon was transformed into an immense corner
on coffee. With sixty per cent of the total world
production, Brazil was in a position to launch
a large-scale speculative manipulation designed
to force prices up. That is what was done, particularly after 1926. All that had to be done
was to reduce the market offerings to a suitable
figure, which the establishment of the Institute
of Coffee made possible. The bankers and other
international interests who manipulated the Institute behind the scenes reaped considerable
profits from the maneuver.

But the result was an accumulation of stocks
that constantly increased. The situation grew
worse from year to year because the high prices
greatly stimulated production. In São Paulo
alone, the number of coffee trees rose from 949
millions in 1924 to 1,155,000,000 in 1930. This
increase was made possible almost entirely
through large-scale extension of credit, and the
planters found themselves heavily in debt. A
factor that aggravated the situation still further
was the expansion of production by Brazil's
competitors, by Colombia above all. For this
reason the maintenance of prices required considerable withdrawals of coffee production.

The condition of agriculture was seemingly
prosperous: the high prices of coffee promised a
large margin of profit — but only promised, for
in reality only a part of production was sold and
exported. The rest remained withdrawn, in anticipation of an opportunity which never came.
The worst was that after some years of operation
of the plan, there was no way out of the artificial
and precarious situation that had been created.
The planters' debts had been contracted on the
basis of high prices; it was necessary, therefore,
to maintain prices at that level. And this became increasingly more difficult, requiring withdrawals that increased from year to year and
hence new loans to finance an output that was
not sold.

The climax came with the stock-market crash
in New York in October, 1929. Coffee quotations could not resist the tremor that ran

throughout the financial world, and fell abruptly by 30 per cent. Their subsequent decline was even sharper. At the same time foreign credit dried up and the financing of withdrawn coffee was suspended; this was followed by the liquidation of the contracted debts. Lazard Bros. threw in an additional 20 million pounds in an effort to salvage something from the disaster. But this had little effect; the new prices of coffee did not permit the planters to cover the debts they had contracted. Their ruin was complete.

The rest of the story has to do with the liquidation of the mountain of debt left by the adventure of valorization. But this episode forms part of a larger story — that of the general crisis of Brazil's economic system.

4. Getúlio Vargas and the "Estado Novo"

The collapse of Brazil's coffee industry in 1929–1930 had serious political and economic consequences. Widespread distress and discontent with Paulista domination of the national government brought to power a "liberal" caudilho from the cattle-raising state of Rio Grande do Sul — Getúlio Vargas. In the protective shadow of the Great Depression, and with lavish assistance from the strongly nationalistic Vargas government, Brazil's infant industries made notable strides. Meanwhile Getúlio governed Brazil with an authoritarian régime that borrowed many of its trappings from the fascist states of Europe. The following selection describes Vargas' rise to power and some salient features of his so-called "New State" (Estado Novo).[1]

EMPEROR TO PRESIDENT

THE GOVERNMENT to which poverty-stricken Brazilians now look for some improvement of their lot came into being as the result of the intolerable jealousies of the various states. Under the high-minded liberalism of Brazil's last Emperor, Dom Pedro II, some progress was being made toward unity. The Emperor's policy encouraged immigration and the development of the country as a whole, fostered representative government, and allowed such freedom of the press that a newsboy loudly peddling a paper called *A República* could follow the Emperor as he walked down the street and not be molested by the

police. And when the bloodless coup d'état of 1889 drove the benevolent and bewhiskered old monarch into exile a knowing observer, the President of Venezuela, remarked: "That is the end of the only republic that ever existed in America."

The dominant influence of the states was apparent in the legislative assembly of the new republic. The delegates did not seat themselves according to party lines — there were no parties as we know them — but sat in groups by states. The natural result of this grouping was to put the central government into the power of a coalition of the biggest states. It became established practice that the presidency and the better Cabinet posts were to alternate between candidates from São Paulo and Minas Gerais, two states that alone hold nearly a third of Brazil's people.

The gap between the states was further widened by export taxes levied even on products for other Brazilian states. At late as 1937 Pernambuco got 36 per cent of its income from export taxes and little Rio Grande do Norte got 60 per cent. Often the state laws were in conflict with the federal laws, and federal laws were put into effect only as the states saw fit. States maintained their own military establishments and in some cases had fair-sized standing armies. School children might know the name of their state Governor, but might not be able to tell who the President was. Rio seldom knew or cared what went on in the states so long as they did not plot revolution and so long as their delegations to the Assembly did not get too far out of hand. But the stresses created by the system were great enough so that in all but two of the twelve administrations between 1889 and 1930 the President felt it necessary at some time to declare a "state of siege" and to rule by decree for a period lasting anywhere from three weeks to two years.

As time passed, the strains between the states became greater rather than less. Following the brilliant conquest of yellow fever by Oswaldo Cruz around the turn of the century, the South gained in population, and coffee production expanded. At the same time the wealth of the North was on the wane. Cuba and the East Indies crowded Pernambuco from the world's sugar market, the rise of plantation rubber in the Dutch and British colonies almost wiped out the trade in Amazonian wild rubber, and the rising production of the African Gold Coast began to limit the market for Baía's cacao. So the South of Brazil pulled ahead of the North, and the

4 "South America VI: Brazil," *Fortune*, XIX, No. 6 (June, 1939), pp. 137–142. Reprinted from the June 1939 issue of *Fortune* Magazine by special permission of the editors; copyright 1939 by Time, Inc.

state of São Paulo pulled ahead of the rest of the South, to such an extent that Washington Luis, onetime Governor of São Paulo and President of Brazil for the 1926–30 term, felt strong enough to try to keep himself and his fellow Paulistas in power.

Accordingly, he caused his own "official" candidate to be nominated for the elections of 1930 and the "official" candidate, as was to be expected, won easily over the "popular" candidate, Getúlio Vargas, Governor of Rio Grande do Sul. But Vargas would not accept his defeat quietly. Aided by his fellow gaúcho, Oswaldo Aranha, he organized a coalition of army officers and malcontents from the states of Paraíba and Minas Gerais and raised the standard of revolution. After much maneuvering and little fighting Washington Luis was sent "to promenade" in Europe, and Vargas was installed as provisional President.

The new government rode into office on promises of a square deal for the northern states and better conditions for the laboring classes. But as no move was made to return to a constitutional form of government, various parts of the country began to grow restive under the rule of the new Federal Interventors who had been sent out to each of the states to enforce the wishes of Rio. In 1931 a brief revolt broke out in Pernambuco. There was discontent even in Getúlio's home state of Rio Grande do Sul. By 1932 the Paulistas, feeling that the demand for a constitution was sufficient excuse and wanting to recapture their former power, started a full-dress revolution, which lasted three months but caused the deaths of less than 1,000 combatants.

The Paulista revolt failed. The fiat money issued by the revolutionaries was redeemed by the government but set up as a debt against the state to bear 6 per cent interest. And Getúlio — he is almost always referred to by his first name in Brazil — called a Constitutional Convention and was later duly elected President for a term of four years from 1934.

THE GREEN SHIRTS

Even then there was no end to trouble. In 1935 came a brief and unsuccessful "communist" revolt, led by Luis Carlos Prestes, involving many army officers and other noncommunist elements. Next came the fascist movement led by Plinio Salgado. He and his green-shirted Integralistas got a real start toward political importance from the anxiety aroused by the "communist" outbreak. Many was the frightened rich man that Plinio shook down for a contribution in 1935 and 1936, and many were the shoeless fellows who were only too delighted to get fine green shirts free of charge. Few people took their parades and posturing very seriously, but Plinio Salgado was one of the three candidates in the presidential campaign of 1937.

In the field against him were Armando Salles, an engineer and administrator respected in São Paulo, and José Americo, a liberal from Paraíba in the Northeast, and the "official" candidate of the governors of the other states. As the campaign grew hot, Getúlio was at first expected to declare his preference, but he only pointed to the constitution, which bade him keep his hands off. He did go so far as to consent to review an Integralista parade in which Salgado had promised there would be at least 100,000 marchers. There were, he discovered, only 27,000 Integralistas in line.

The elections were scheduled for January, but they never took place. Late in September, on the pretext that civil war was being fomented by the ardor of the three parties in the field, Getúlio declared a state of martial law, called off campaigning, and waited for an overt act. Four months before, he had quietly prepared a constitution fit for just such an emergency. It came on November 9 when a member of the Assembly read out a declaration that the government should be overthrown by force. That night Getúlio sent fifty mounted policemen to take over the Chamber, and proclaimed the new constitution, which gave him emergency powers that could be indefinitely prolonged. The morning of the tenth the President of the Assembly, not having read the papers, turned up as usual, only to be told to his great embarrassment that the Assembly no longer existed.

It was immediately concluded in most foreign countries and by many Brazilians that Brazil had finally gone fascist. The new constitution gave extraordinary powers to the President, allowed very little discretion to the states, and set up on paper, where it still remains, a National Economic Council representing the various occupations and smacking familiarly of the corporative state. But Italy and Germany rejoiced too soon. In March, 1938, came a decree abolishing all "shirt" organizations and political clubs. It had become apparent that German agents were actively backing the Integralista movement and doing their best to stir up German settlers throughout Brazil. The decree abolishing the local organizations they had sponsored was met by some scattered rioting, but there was nothing serious until the abortive putsch of May 11, 1938. On that night when the guard outside Guanabara Palace was relieved, it joined with the fresh detail and attacked. Getúlio and his daughter Alzira were defended by two plainclothes men and a couple of the guardsmen who had refused to join in the plot, and a spirited exchange of shots took place. The attackers had done a poor job of wire cutting and one telephone in the palace remained connected. Troops were called, but their officers apparently waited to see whether the attack would succeed and did not turn up for three hours. When they did, the attackers meekly surrendered their arms.

Whether the Germans had any part of this plot was never proved, but the plotters were known to have strong Integralista leanings. Some time after this episode the German Ambassador attempted to dictate to Getúlio against interference with Nazi agents; he was rebuffed, and went home to consult. His government was asked by Brazil to keep him there. Since that time Brazil has had no trouble to speak of. But neither has there been the plebiscite, as called for in the new constitution, nor have the legislative provisions of the constitution been put into effect. Getúlio just goes on running the country, and it is quite probable that the majority of the people would vote to keep him at it if he ever gave them a chance.

Estado Novo

At this point the main elements of the current political situation may be set in order. The Brazilian Government is a dictatorship, under a constitution that takes effect only as it is implemented by the dictator's decrees. Although there are liberal tendencies in the regime — labor laws, public works, and certain cooperative economic controls — the usual forms of democracy have been abandoned and probably will remain in the discard for some time to come. The reason is quite simple. Brazilian politics are dominated, as are politics in nearly all Latin-American countries, by the influence of the leading army officers, whose hold over their troops is based on personal loyalty. In Brazil this group felt a natural affinity for the Integralista movement and its fascist doctrine. They were thoroughly tired of the squabbles and the oratorical displays of the sectional politicians. Getúlio saw early in 1937 that if the choice lay between the

Integralistas and a democratic President supported by a popular assembly, then the preponderant weight of the army would be thrown to the Integralistas and Brazil would indeed be delivered over to fascism. Moved by this perception, and perhaps even more by a politician's desire to hold on to a job, Getúlio took over the government himself. It was the only way to keep the army in line, and how narrowly it succeeded was shown by the Integralista and army plot just described. While putting down fascism with one hand, Getúlio now spares no pains to keep the army happy and to play off its leaders against one another. The new barracks just completed at Recife include a purple swimming pool and a movie auditorium. Integralistas could scarcely do more. The army is kept busy with its own internal feuds and does not have to worry about politics. And so, as long as the threat of fascism remains, Brazil, by ironic circumstance, is being made safe for democracy by dictatorial means.

The man who is preserving this delicate balance came to prominence up the customary political ladder: military academy, law school, small state jobs, deputy in Rio, Cabinet Minister, and Governor of his native state. Now fifty-six years old, Getúlio is physically a little man, with fine eyes, a strong profile, and a corporeal outline that would at once win him the nickname of "Tubby" in an American university. He laughs often and heartily, and the laughter is not forced. An enthusiastic beginner at golf — he sometimes breaks 110 — he gets in a round at least every Sunday. Getúlio has three sons and two daughters, most prominent of whom is the younger daughter, Alzira, who collects a salary for her titular job as lawyer to the Bank of Brazil, works closely with her father, and calls him "boss," for, unlike Getúlio, she speaks English well. Getúlio is genuinely popular, and although there are many in São Paulo who refer to him as "that man" or call him by his full name, Getúlio Vargas, rather than the usual Getúlio, the President is widely liked because of his engaging personality and admired for his uncanny political shrewdness. He is careful never to take too much responsibility. If, for instance, the military ask for an appropriation of 10,000 contos for ammunition, he turns the request over to the Finance Minister. The appropriation is cut in half. Then Getúlio intercedes and gets it raised to, say, 7,000 contos.

Naturally enough, the present regime in Brazil is presented to the people as something a good deal more philosophical than a mere political expedient. Indeed the regime arrogates to itself the best features of all popular systems and proudly labels them the New State, *Estado Novo*. The name came into use just after the *golpe* (coup d'état) of November 10, 1937, when Getúlio seized power and closed both federal and state legislatures; but subsequently the designation *Estado Novo* has been used retroactively on the theory that the *golpe* was a logical, planned step in an evolution that started in 1930. And that evolution presents certain alarming traits: extreme nationalism, Red-baiting, censorship, army control, and the turgid rhetoric of men straining to justify themselves. Let us take up these traits one by one.

The *Estado Novo* is decidedly nationalistic. Two-thirds of all employees in each job category in a foreign company must be Brazilians. Pilots of planes flying on national lines (as contrasted with international through routes) must be Brazilians. Brazilians must be paid the same salary as foreigners if they hold the same jobs. Waterpower and mineral resources can be exploited today only by companies controlled by Brazilians, and oil can be exploited only by the government. The constitution provides that all banks and insurance companies are to be nationalized (but so far foreign banks and insurance companies still operate as before). Twenty per cent of the coal bought by a factory must be national coal, although the quality is so poor that some factories simply buy it and pile it up in a dump heap. Alcohol made from Brazilian sugar must be mixed with all gasoline, the percentage varying in different states. Manioc flour must be mixed with wheat flour. A bachelor's tax is contemplated.

Getúlio has said: "The *Estado Novo* does not recognize individual rights against the collective state. Individuals have no rights, they have duties. The rights belong to the collective state." The worst sin a Brazilian can commit is to be a Communist; or to be what is known in this country as a "fellow traveler." Or even to possess volumes of Karl Marx. A man who is not a Communist may still get a couple of months in jail if someone complains that he is a Communist. Today, the upraised hand of the Fascist is nearly as evil as the clenched fist. In fact the Brazilian cannot belong to any political group whatever. Obviously he cannot get up on a box on the Avenida Rio Branco in Rio and make a political speech, nor can he hold political meetings within four walls, whether he is one of those comical Rio monarchists aching for the return from France of the young imperial pretender, or an ardent believer in liberal democracy.

A censor from the police is assigned to every newspaper office and his pencil deletes whatever is construed as prejudicial to the *Estado Novo*. Often his chore includes international news: he will demand soft pedaling of a renewed Nazi drive against Jews, as last winter, or the final absorption of Czechoslovakia by Germany. Part of this is policy, to avoid the appearance of taking sides on international questions; part of it is laziness, the reluctance of the censor to stand up under the accusations of prejudice leveled at him by local German officials. The censor also has a special interest to see that the military are treated with the utmost respect. Mail is censored to an unknown extent, but most letters from Europe are strictly inspected for communism.

Getúlio has said: "That negligible minority made up of the spiteful, the malcontents, of those who circulate rumors, of those who have been defeated, and of the saboteurs waste their time, and those who dare to disturb the order, under whatever pretext, will be punished." Keeping an eye on malcontents is the job of the police, and there are four different kinds of police in Rio, totaling about 10,000 in all. Besides the police, the army, numbering 65,000 effectives, and on the increase, is always available for real trouble. State police, which in the *Estado Novo* are under federal authority, add at least 30,000 more. The army is trained by a French mission, and the navy, with 12,500 men, has U. S. instruction. Appropriations for the army and navy departments for the current year are officially set at about one-quarter of the total budget, but the amount will probably prove to be an under-statement of actual expenditures. The new armament program, projected for ten years, amounts to some $10,000,000 a year, with large orders in England now for six cruisers and other orders totaling $40,000,000 placed with Krupp for the eventual delivery of arms, which, incidentally, will use up a lot of the bloated compensation-mark balance. Over a period of years Brazil's expenditures on the armed forces have taken as much as 50 per cent of the tax revenue remaining after payments on the debt.

5. BRAZIL — LAND OF THE FUTURE?

The Vargas dictatorship fell in 1945 amid public rejoicing over the defeat of the Axis. But Getúlio

*continued to be an influential name in Brazilian poli-
tics, and in the election of 1950 he was returned to
the presidency by a large popular majority. The
Vargas Era saw a considerable industrial advance,
paced by the rapidly-growing textile and steel industries. Yet Brazil at mid-century remained a predominantly agricultural country, and the majority of her
rural population continued to live under conditions
of extreme economic dependence and poverty. To
many observers it appeared that the existence of the
latifundium — the great landed property — constituted the major obstacle to the rise of a strong and
prosperous Brazil. A sympathetic North American
observer appraises the future prospects of this vast and
richly endowed land.*[5]

BRAZIL, LAND OF THE FUTURE? Many have answered this question with an unqualified "yes";
others are not so sure; and some have been impelled to damn all Brazil and everything Brazilian. That Brazil has secured the frontiers to a
large share of the world's unsettled and sparsely
settled territory, there can be no doubt. Fortunately, for South America and the world, the
Portuguese colonies were held together. Innumerable separatist movements were suppressed, so
that there has emerged one great nation and not
a host of small bickering states. Also beyond
question is the fact that there are vast undevel-
oped resources within the borders of South
America's giant. Just what they are is still to
be determined. However, even though failure
to distinguish between lush vegetation and rich
soil has been widespread, one may be sure that
there is a basis for the support of millions of
more people in Brazil. But resources and space
of themselves do not guarantee that Brazil is on
the verge of assuming world or even hemispheric
leadership. The cultural heritage, particularly
the economic organization, and the efforts made
to develop to the fullest the human potentialities are the important points to consider.

Land of the future? Yes, providing Brazilians
learn and apply even more of the medical and
sanitary techniques which alone can make life
healthful in the tropics; providing they make
the fullest use of modern technology so that they
may cease their fierce destruction of natural resources; and providing they borrow or devise a
more equitable system for distributing the results of the productive process among capital,

management, and labor. Only a cultural equipment primarily designed to safeguard health,
comparable to that employed in the Canal Zone,
will make possible the presence of a great population in the Amazon Valley, that is, in the
greater portion of unsettled Brazil. If the hand
of man is not strengthened for its struggle with
nature by the employment of power and labor-
saving equipment, the population of Brazil
might some day approach that of China or India
and without any happier results. If the vicious
destruction of the forests is paralleled for other
natural resources, much of Brazil's potentialities
can be dissipated before there is a chance to use
them for human welfare. If the millions of
Brazilians who make up the nation's labor force
do not receive more of the total national production, preferably in the form of education,
sanitation, medical care, and the other services
which valorize men, Brazil may continue to be
for generation after generation merely a land of
the future.

Viewing the immediate future from the vantage point of recent trends, certain observations
and predictions, with a few recommendations,
may be made. It seems fairly certain that fire
agriculture, the primitive system which wastes
Brazil's human, timber, and soil resources, will
gradually be eliminated. Slowly but surely it
will give way to the more rational, efficient, and
less destructive agricultural methods which had
their origin in Europe. Brazil will be fortunate
if the models followed are those from northern
Europe where animal traction, the plow, and the
four-wheeled farm wagon are integral parts of
the cultural heritage. Except for coffee and a
few other crops this heritage need never place
a dead weight upon the possible level of living
by relying upon the hoe culture of southern
Europe. The Brazilians of Polish and German
descent can help greatly to diffuse better farming methods throughout the length and breadth
of the republic, to spread the knowledge that
will sound the death knell of primitive fire agriculture.

Cultural lag is such a heavy drag, however,
that sudden changes should not be expected.
Although Saint-Hilaire would never recognize
the São Paulo of today as the decadent, poverty-
stricken area he encountered a little over a century ago, that state is an exception. The change
for the better probably will not be so rapid in
most other sections. Nevertheless, the adoption
of better agricultural methods will do much to
improve the situation throughout the entire na-

[5] T. Lynn Smith, *Brazil: People and Institutions,* Baton
Rouge, Louisiana State University Press, 1946, pp. 787–794.
Reprinted by permission of the Louisiana State University
Press.

tion. Coupled with this, the use of animal traction and the farm wagon can help man and woman to rise above their present beast-of-burden status.

Brazil would do well to give considerable attention to its population policy. The cry of *falta de braços* is sure to continue, and with it a strong pressure from the landed proprietors for the importation of cheap labor. Immigration per se should not be considered an unmixed blessing. Any immigrants who would be content for long with the status of farm laborers should be shunned as the plague. The large landowners are not likely to be enthusiastic about any others. On the other hand, there will not be many special-interest groups seeking to encourage the immigration of independent farm families, nor the provision of a liberal homestead policy that would enable them quickly to develop farms and become owners of land. However, Brazil probably never again will allow foreign nationality groups to establish their own miniature societies, to seal themselves off hermetically and form little worlds of their own. This will avoid the one serious disadvantage which has arisen from the importation of German, Italian, and Polish settlers into south Brazil. After the war the recent Japanese immigrants also probably will be disseminated much more widely. At least officials of the Japanese government will no longer be allowed to herd the immigrants and their children about.

The birth rate in Brazil seems likely to remain at a high level for some time to come. Therefore, even a slight reduction in mortality will be sharply reflected in the greater natural increase of the population. The control of the infectious diseases, and improved infant, child, and maternal care can bring about a tremendous saving of life. Fortunately, these are the aspects of the mortality problem that are most susceptible to human control. The amount of $1,000,000 spent on a campaign to reduce infant mortality, mainly on educating mothers about the care and feeding of children, probably would increase Brazil's population far more than a similar amount expended for the subsidization of immigration.

Only an increase in longevity, a fall in the birth rate, or both, can greatly reduce the ratio of Brazilians in the dependent ages to those in the productive ages. Therefore, for some time to come the average Brazilian producer will have more mouths to feed than his fellows in North America or Europe. Unless his efforts are correspondingly more productive, this means that the quality of the population will suffer to some extent.

The future of Brazil is dependent upon the land system it adopts or fails to adopt more than upon any other factor. That settlement will continue to advance, to project long fingers into the interior, is surely to be expected. But it will make a difference whether it is merely the haphazard occupation that has gone forward in north and central Brazil, the better-planned colonization such as has been carried on in the south, or a still more rational plan for establishing people on the land. There is no logical reason why Brazil should not make use of the best experience that has been gained in the settlement of North America. It still is not too late for Brazil to establish a national land system.

Brazil's land surveys, titles, and records could be made fully as simple as those in the United States and Canada. Simplification would be highly advantageous and could be done without the necessity of incurring any of the disadvantages inherent in the system of squares, which is characteristic of the two North American countries. . . .

In addition to systematic surveys, Brazil needs to adopt a homestead law. A wise land policy would encourage actual settlers to occupy and develop unused public lands. By so doing they should become entitled to deeds to the land they settle. There should be no thought of having them pay another price for parts of the public domain. All official efforts should be directed to guiding the settlement in a systematic manner. A considerable amount of public land, as much as one or two sections in every 25, should be reserved as a patrimony for educational purposes. The sections to be reserved should have the same number in every square, and the oncoming generations should never be betrayed by allowing the school lands to be juggled. The amount of land to which one man is entitled should be liberal from the standpoint of the family farm, but small enough to discourage the large landed proprietor. The upper limit might well be around 200 hectares in areas suitable for agriculture, 750 in those adapted only to stock raising. Above all, Brazil should seek to get large acreages of public lands into the hands of those who themselves will till them adequately.

On the lands that have already passed into private ownership it will be more difficult to make the desirable changes. Improvements will be easiest in parts of south Brazil, where the pooling of resources through the property tax, and the investment of the funds in education, roads, and sanitation, would add greatly to the worth of the average man. Elsewhere the problem of the latifundium is widespread. For dealing with this there is nothing so effective as the property tax, especially the graduated property tax. Regardless of the means used, the objective should be to get these large, unused tracts into the hands of people who themselves will till the earth. In all of this, Brazil would be wise to utilize the small farmers from the colonial areas of the south to instruct its other millions in European methods of agriculture, in the use of the wheel, the plow, draft animals, and all the other parts of modern agriculture which do so much to increase the production per man.

The renting of lands probably will increase in relative importance. Farm tenancy has already made great headway in São Paulo, and it is likely to come about by farm laborers improving their social status and not because owners slip back into tenancy. However, in Rio Grande do Sul, Santa Catarina, and Paraná, there probably will be an increased tendency for owners to drop down one rung on the agricultural ladder, for renting to become more prevalent.

Over most of Brazil, holdings will probably be reduced in size. In many places the subdivision of estates by inheritance may bring acute problems such as those already present in parts of São Paulo and Minas Gerais. The subdivision of *fazendas* brought about by taking them for the establishment of colonies of small farmers offers greater promise. But this division of land will not be universal. In the sugar areas the concentration of landownership and control may be expected to continue unabated. Some coffee estates will be split up among several heirs but it will be some time before they are likely to be greatly subdivided. Cocoa and rubber plantations will continue to be of enormous size. However, many of the huge cattle ranches of Rio Grande do Sul, Mato Grosso, and Goiaz are likely to be subdivided into farms.

The standards and levels of living in Brazil are sure to improve. This can hardly be done rapidly, but more education, the growth of cities, the improvement of communication and transportation, and the diffusion of new systems of merchandising and display will increase the wants of millions of Brazilians. The nation-wide diffusion of knowledge concerning life in south Brazil and in other countries will have the same effect. By degrees the increased wants will lead to more regular work activities, to greater production, and to a higher level of living. The social legislation now being placed on the books will cause some landed proprietors to improve the living and working conditions of the families on their places. Many others may be shamed into doing the same.

The small *municipio* found in São Paulo and Minas Gerais is well on the way of becoming a genuine urban community. This tendency will be promoted if certain of its functions are strengthened. Most important of all is the establishment of a high school for each little city that forms the seat of a municipio. Increased local taxation with the proceeds used for the more adequate provision of essential governmental services also would contribute to this end. Brazil's leaders should not try to do everything from Rio de Janeiro. The municipio is the logical unit of organization for use in the provision of more adequate protection for life and property, health and welfare services, education, and roads.

Brazil would be wise to double, double again, and then redouble, the number of students it is sending to study in foreign universities. The utmost encouragement and support should be given to those who go in search of scientific training at the graduate level. The need to send people abroad for training in the humanities is much less. With personnel trained abroad, plus those prepared in the national institutions of higher learning, Brazil soon would be able to staff more universities and technical schools. Then it would be equipped to train the teachers for the secondary schools which it is opening throughout the length and breadth of the land. Along with this the program of establishing more public elementary schools and of increasing the length of the elementary course, could be pushed ahead even more rapidly than in the last decade. As the teachers receive better training and become more experienced, professional standards will regulate many of the details of school activity which it is now thought necessary to handle through legislation.

All of this will cost money. Many will ask, some of them with scorn, "Can Brazil afford such improvements?" From the purely economical point of view it is difficult to see how it can afford not to make them. After all, the money necessary is *cruzeiros,*[6] not dollars or other foreign exchange. One need not be a narrow ex-

[6] The *cruzeiro* is the new unit of exchange. At present rates it is worth about 5 cents.

ponent of the labor theory of value to hold that this means merely putting a larger share of the nation's effort into educational line. Except for the small amounts necessary to send people abroad for training, money spent on education remains in the country. Resources are not de-pleted or exported. Brazil can build a great educational system, valorize its people, merely by directing a greater portion of the productive efforts of its population into educational activities. This is exactly what it has been necessary for other countries to do.

XXXIII

Latin-American Society in Transition

IN THE TWENTIETH CENTURY — particularly after 1920 — the pace of social change in Latin America quickened. The advance of industry, the growth of the cities, the rise of the middle and working classes, steadily weakened the foundations of the old aristocratic order. New doctrines infiltrated the continent, creating discontent with existing political and economic arrangements. The widespread and growing demand for reform was reflected in the elaborate social content of many modern Latin-American constitutions.

The rate of change was naturally swifter in the cities than in the countryside. An ambitious industrialist class wrested social as well as economic leadership from the landed aristocracy in the larger metropolitan centers. In the factories that arose in and about the cities thousands of former peons learned new work skills and habits, exchanged clan and village loyalties for the larger loyalties of their class and nation, and struggled to assimilate a world of new political and social ideas. For some members of this group, at least, the shift to the city meant a higher standard of living.

The status of women gradually improved; women obtained the vote in a growing number of countries, rose to high official positions in some, and in increasing numbers entered the factories, offices, and professions. But the tradition of the patriarchal family, of closely supervised courtship and marriage, remained strong, especially among the upper and middle classes.

The Church, shorn of much of its former political and economic power, continued to dominate the religious life of Latin America, although skepticism and indifferentism were widespread among upper and middle-class males. Outside Brazil, Protestant missionary activity made relatively slight headway in the area.

Latin America, with Brazil in the van, made progress toward amalgamation of its diverse ethnic strains. Notions of Indian and Negro racial inferiority were everywhere officially disapproved, but race prejudice and discrimination had not been completely overcome, particularly on the part of aristocratic white elites.

1. THE UPROOTED

Change — economic, political, social — was in the air of Latin America at mid-century. Large numbers of country folk, drawn from their isolation to the new factories, mines, and plantations, cast off the traditional attitude of submission to their betters and acceptance of inherited social status, and demanded a better life for themselves and their children. A North American social scientist describes the results of cultural displacement in present-day Guatemala.[1]

ESTEBAN PAZUJ was an Indian carpenter in Guatemala. He made chairs and tables from a poor

[1] Richard F. Behrendt, "The Uprooted: A Guatemala Sketch," *New Mexico Quarterly Review*, XIX, No. 1 (Spring, 1949), pp. 25–31. Reprinted by permission of the *New Mexico Quarterly Review*.

type of pine, fitted together without nails. In order to find customers, he had to take them from Totonicapán to Guatemala City, one hundred and twenty miles of mountain road at altitudes ranging down from eight thousand to four thousand feet. He carried on his shoulders and back the table and six chairs suspended from a tump-strap pressed against his forehead. He had to take his food along and would spend the nights in caves or under trees near the road. It took him eight days to reach the capital, several days to sell his goods on a special market, and another week to return home. He used to get three dollars for the table and the chairs or forty cents for each chair if sold separately. He charged for the lumber and his work only, not for the time spent en route. When he returned home, he had usually just enough left to buy more lumber and sustain himself and his family until his next sale.

During a few weeks every year, Esteban and his family used to go down to the western slopes of the volcanic mountain range, at about 3000 feet altitude, to pick coffee beans on a large plantation owned by Germans. He received twenty cents a day and his children, who were working with him in the field, ten cents a day. They lived in a large shack together with dozens of other families of seasonal workers. Each family prepared its meals, consisting mostly of corn and beans, over open fires inside the building. They slept on homemade woolen blankets spread on the dirt floor. There was no furniture of any kind. The women got their water from a brook half a mile away. Nature served as an open-air toilet. The Indian workers greeted the German administrators or their families, when these happened to cross their path, with bare heads and folded arms. If the workers broke any of the rules they were denied payment or put in the stocks for a night or longer.

Four years ago, an agent of the United Fruit Company came to Esteban's home town near Totonicapán to hire workers for the banana plantations around Tiquisate, in the lowlands of the west coast. He offered seventy cents a day, free housing, food at lower prices than it could be had in the stores, and the use of a plot of land for any worker who wanted to grow food of his own. It sounded fantastic to Esteban, but he accepted.

Now he loads banana stems on railway lorries from six o'clock in the morning to two o'clock in the afternoon. Sometimes he works overtime and is paid fifty per cent extra. In the afternoon he works for a few hours on his lot, if he feels like it. He and his family occupy a medium-sized room in a low, long wooden building housing several families. They have a kitchen of their own and share a toilet with their neighbors. They have electric light. They can buy rations of staple foods in the company commissary, at prices lower than those in regular stores. Their children go to a near-by school provided by the company, as required by the law of the country. The company fights the malaria-carrying mosquitoes and provides safe water supply. The company hospital, the second largest in the country, gives free service to the workers and their families.

But Esteban is not happy. For one thing, he and his family have never liked the hot, humid climate of the lowlands. He knows that he, his wife, and his children have more things to eat and a better place to live than before. However, to get these things he had to leave his village where generations of his family had spent their lives. His neighbors are comparative strangers, not related to him by blood, custom or even language. Esteban does not speak Spanish very well and his neighbors, having come from other parts of the country, do not speak his language, which is Quiché. He had to discard his aboriginal dress, with its patterns and colors distinctive of his native village. He now lives on an outlying *finca*, very different from his old, tight little home town whose people had been organized for centuries in kinships, *cofradías* (civic hereditary fraternities), and parishes. There everybody knew — although not necessarily spoke to — everybody else, and there everyone's position in the community was strictly defined by tradition.

Tiquisate is very different indeed from those parts of Guatemala where Esteban spent his earlier life. There are no old buildings; everything seems to him too new. In fact, the entire town and the outlying plantations were established only fifteen years ago when the fruit company shifted part of its operations from the Atlantic to the Pacific coast, because of plant diseases and soil exhaustion. There was then very little population and very little of anything — except climate and soil. Workers like Esteban had to be hired in the highlands where too many people try to eke out a living from thin soil on steep hillsides. Housing, transportation, communications, sanitation, irrigation, schools, hospital, entertainment had to be provided by the company. People from various countries, speaking different languages, professing even different religions, having different traditions and customs — and very different living standards — came to live here.

Esteban, and some ten thousand workers like him, with their families, changed from a form of life which had remained essentially fixed for centuries, almost unaffected by outside influences, in which people had obeyed traditional institutions and leaders, to a new, planned form of life which was organized by a foreign corporation for the one purpose of producing and marketing a profitable commodity. The company is an anonymous entity of which they know nothing except that it is controlled by an indefinite number of foreigners, somewhere in the United States, nobody knows exactly how. They have never seen those people and never will. Some foreigners they do see: the North Americans who manage and supervise local operations. The Guatemalan workers do not bow with folded arms to them. Nor are they put in the stocks for infractions. Still they are not closer to them than they were to their German bosses. The *americanos* live in a small town of their own, divided from the "native" town by a barbed wire fence. They have their own school, commissary, club house, swimming pool, and pleasant one-family bungalows on well-kept grounds. Esteban and most of his fellow workers do not see much of the *americanos,* because the time keepers and foremen are Guatemalans; but they know that those *americanos* are the bosses. Or, rather, that they represent the real bosses who live in a faraway country where everything seems to be plentiful, and whence they send orders which may mean great changes for every one of the thirty thousand or more people of Tiquisate, even the loss of their jobs. Formerly, Esteban had lived in his own house, poor as it was, and most of the time he had been his own boss, engaged in a fairly steady trade, even if it paid him only a barest living.

Thus, Esteban is torn between gratification and dissatisfaction. He is bewildered. He is not sure that the advantages of his new life outweigh its disadvantages. In spite of the fact that he earns more than he ever did before, he sometimes feels that he is not paid enough. He knows of neighbors who earn as much as one quetzal (equal to a dollar) or one quetzal and forty cents a day. They were skilled workers: sprayers, or banana pickers, or mechanics, or drivers. They have mastered certain techniques and know how to handle some of the innumerable tools and machines which were unknown to them and most of their fellows until they came to work for the

North Americans. These better paid skilled workers have gone to school and can read, write, and use elementary arithmetic. Their number is increasing steadily, as more efficient, more highly mechanized methods of production and transportation are being introduced and elementary school instruction is becoming more common. Esteban's children will probably belong to them.

Strangely enough, the skilled workers are more dissatisfied than Esteban. It is they who are most active in the labor unions which were founded during the last few years, taking advantage of the liberal laws adopted after the overthrow of the dictatorship in 1944. It is they who demand higher wages, better working conditions, free transportation on vacation trips, more school facilities, and many other things of which Esteban would never have dreamed a few years ago in his highland village. Some of these people have even learned English so that they can read the company's reports on its earnings. They now claim that the foreign owners of the company are taking too much money out of the country and they should be forced to leave greater benefits to the nationals, by paying higher wages and offering more social services of all kinds. They are not impressed with the arguments that the company already pays the best wages in the country, and that Esteban and his fellows would still be living the miserable, unhealthy, undernourished, and illiterate life of the past if it had not been for the many millions of dollars of North American capital invested by the company's stockholders. Some of the leaders of the union of which Esteban is a member, though not a very active one, even say that they, the Guatemalans, can take over the banana industry if the North Americans want to pull out of the country — just as the Guatemalans have taken charge of the German coffee and sugar plantations since the last war.

Esteban and his fellow workers have moved from a stationary way of life to a way of life where change — technological, economic, social, geographic — is the rule. They are not yet adjusted to it, but they are becoming accustomed to change. In fact, they may want to operate changes of their own, against the powerful corporation which has exposed them to this new way of life. Up to now, change has been planned and administered by the businessmen and engineers from the United States. New techniques, machinery, and skills were taught by these people to the natives of an economically backward country. Material inducements were offered to them for working in new places and unaccustomed enterprises. Now the principle of change is going farther than its original sponsors had intended. Social status and income are no longer determined by tradition and the accident of birth and, therefore, no longer accepted without criticism or ambition for improvement, as they were for centuries. On the other hand, the new factors on which one's place in life now depends are uncertain and not clearly understood.

If ambition and change are good and should take the place of conformity and tradition, for the sake of progress and a better life, why not push change until Esteban and *all* Guatemalans will enjoy the good things which are now reserved to the gringos and a few Guatemalans? If children of illiterate Guatemalan peasants can learn how to operate a railway engine, repair a truck, service an airplane, and do double-entry bookkeeping, things which only foreigners did thirty years ago, why can't they also learn to run *all* of Tiquisate — for their own benefit? And if the ability to operate machines and to plan and administer the work of many men is not limited to the members of certain master races or superior nations or ruling classes — why not change the traditional division of property under which a few families have owned most of the good lands and exploited the majority of the landless people who have had to work for them? Why put up any longer with the rule of privileged cliques in politics and public administration? If Esteban's children can learn things he never learned, as they do right now in school and shops, things which until recently were considered the prerogative of the overlords, what will stop them, or their children, from taking the place of those overlords?

Esteban Pazuj is representative not only of some thousands of fellow workers on the banana plantations of Guatemala but of millions of people working in many parts of the world. They are all going through essentially the same experience. Soon there will be even more Estebans.

Someone in a discussion of the evils of cultural displacement uttered this baroque epigram which sums up aptly the risks of the situation: "The uprooted and the roots of the uprooted are roots of revolution."

2. THE URGE TO INDUSTRIALIZE

Two World Wars and a great depression exposed the narrowness of Latin America's monocultural economy and stimulated demands for basic changes in the economic structure. Governments and peoples alike have come to regard industrialization as the key to economic independence and higher standards of living. In a number of countries — notably in Brazil, Argentina, Mexico, Chile, and Colombia — industrialization has made significant gains. A North American economist describes the background of this incipient industrial revolution and the measure of its achievement.[2]

THE DEPENDENCE of Latin America upon foreign markets and foreign investment did not become generally recognized as a serious problem until the 1930's when the great depression set in. If we go back to the years before the First World War, few Latin Americans were aware of such a problem, or even of the basic problem inherent in the failure of standards of living to rise in Latin America as the world's economic productivity went up by leaps and bounds. Undoubtedly the tendency to ignore this basic question of standards of living is explained by the fact that the educated people, who were but a handful in numbers, were not themselves faring badly. The large numbers of Latin Americans who lived in poverty and in permanent poor health were inarticulate.

Aside from this basic and important problem of low living standards, it may be said that the results of the close tie between Latin America and the industrialized economies of the world were favorable before 1914. The patterns of economic specialization in Latin America which directed commercially productive activity in the main toward industrial raw materials and foodstuffs, were fashioned in the fifty years or so before the First World War. On the whole they were satisfactory during that period because the world enjoyed a workable international economy in which products, capital, and people moved across international boundaries with relative freedom.

To illustrate this, we may appeal to the economic experience of Argentina. . . . From about 1880 to 1915 Argentina made great strides in economic development on the basis of producing meat and grains for export. The markets were found in the industrialized countries of western Europe. Technical developments, such as the introduction of barbed wire and refrigerated shipping, played a large part in making it possible for Argentina to supply these markets. But other forces also made important contributions.

2 Sanford Mosk, *Industrial Revolution in Mexico*, Berkeley, Calif., University of California Press, 1950, pp. 10–20. Reprinted by permission of the University of California Press.

Notable among these was the inflow of European capital (for example, for railroad construction) and immigration derived from European peoples. In short, the rapid economic advance of Argentina before 1915 was the product of a smoothly functioning international economic order.

This international economy was shaken loose from its foundations by the First World War, and it is well known that the strenuous efforts made subsequently to reconstruct it were without success. The atmosphere in which economic relations were conducted among nations in the 1920's was distinctly unhealthy. In addition, the prices of raw materials and foodstuffs declined, relatively, that is, to the prices of manufactured goods. Thus the Latin-American countries, together with the other colonial economies around the world, suffered an added disadvantage in the international economic setting of the postwar period.

The full consequences of their dependence upon export markets and foreign capital were brought home to the Latin-American republics during the economic depression of the 1930's. As world trade shrank to a fraction of its former volume after 1929 the Latin-American countries suffered great losses in export markets. In some countries the drop in exports reached almost fantastic proportions. In Chile the recession from 1929 to 1932 amounted to 88 per cent. Her foreign trade suffered more in those years than that of any other country in the world. Bolivia experienced an 80 per cent fall in exports between 1929 and 1932, while Cuba also had the doubtful honor of sharing the lead in this respect with a decline of 70 per cent. For the twenty Latin-American republics as a group, the aggregate value of exports fell by approximately 65 per cent in the short span of three years.

At the same time the flow of capital to Latin America slowed down and in some cases it came entirely to a halt. In the absence of aggregate figures, this may be illustrated from the experience of Argentina and Chile. In Argentina there was a net inflow of capital amounting to 500 million pesos in the period 1926–28. In 1929, however, capital imports stopped entirely. For 1930 there was again a net movement of capital into the country, amounting to 500 million pesos, only to be followed by a net outflow in the years 1931–1932. Chile underwent a similar experience about the same time. Loans from abroad reached a total of 1,100 million gold pesos in the years 1929–1930. In the following two years, however, the total was only 75 million, and in 1933 no new foreign investments at all were made.

Thus in the depression period of the 1930's a decline in exports with a parallel decline in new foreign investment combined to exert a strong depressive influence on economic conditions in Latin America. However, many foreigners acquainted with Latin America are inclined to believe that, since widespread unemployment was not apparent, the depression was not severely felt there. Large numbers of farmers engaged in self-sufficient agriculture were, they point out, unaffected by what happened in foreign trade. Such farmers were not integrated into the market structure enough to react to demand and price changes.

It is true that there is a dichotomy in the economies of virtually all the Latin-American countries, and that one of the two parts is subsistence farming. In many of the countries, especially where Indian populations or Indian mores prevail, this sector of the economy includes most of the population. In every one of the twenty republics, with the possible exceptions of Argentina and Uruguay, it embraces a substantial fraction of the inhabitants. In Mexico about 70 per cent of the population has lived wholly or largely outside the commercial framework, although Mexico actually has had a more diversified economy than most of the Latin-American countries. Subsistence farmers in Latin America have produced mostly for their own consumption; they have had only minor contacts with commercial markets and their purchases have been limited to essentially local barter transactions. Since they practice primitive farming methods, their crop yields have been meager. Their standards of living have also been very low.

The other part of the typical Latin-American economy may be called, for want of a better term, "modern." It includes the producers of export commodities, and all the commercial, financial, and transport organizations that deal with exports and imports. Commercial production for domestic markets also fits into this sector of the economy. Finally, the governments of the Latin-American republics obtain almost all their revenues from the "modern" parts of their economies.

The economic processes analyzed in the preceding pages have been related only to the "modern" sector. It is there that we find the institutions that are directly and readily influenced by international trade and international capital movements. But this does not mean that the subsistence sector is untouched by these influences. It, too, has a stake in the prosperity of the "modern" sector.

The two parts of the economy are connected by the movement of persons from one to the other. In times of prosperity, some people leave the rural communities and shift into the "modern" sector, where employment yields as a rule higher standards of living. In times of depression, the movement of people is reversed. This shift, which is both regional and occupational, explains why unemployment never reaches large proportions in a Latin-American country. Instead of suffering absolute unemployment in time of depression, workers transfer themselves to much less productive occupations.

The subsistence economy thus serves as a shock absorber, because strong family ties make it possible for persons to return to their former places in rural life. Given the low productivity of the agricultural organization to which they return, they add very little if anything to farm output. And yet they consume. Thus the cost of depression adjustment is borne by the rural families and communities as a whole, in the form of reduced consumption and lowered standards of living. The impact of a depression may be less forceful and less striking in the subsistence sector than in the "modern" part of the economy, but it is nonetheless real.

The depression of the 1930's in Latin America, therefore, penetrated the whole economic and social structure. Hardly anyone was sheltered from its impact. Unemployment figures were not large and bread lines were unknown, but these facts should not be allowed to obscure the reality of the depression experience.

From the Latin-American point of view the great depression of the 1930's appeared as an import — an import received from the industrialized nations which had failed to keep up their purchases of Latin-American export products and their flow of capital to Latin America. The validity of this viewpoint can hardly be doubted. The industrialized areas have been the centers of cyclical disturbances which have spread from them to the nonindustrialized parts of the world. The economically colonial areas have played a passive role. Depressions have originated in the industrialized countries as a group out of forces peculiar to a highly industrialized society, and they have been transmitted to the remainder of the world principally through a fall in demand for raw materials and foodstuffs and through a slackening in foreign investment. Decline in demand for imported manufactured goods in the economically colonial areas has been of a secondary and cumulative nature, and not a primary force in generating a depression.

The impact of the depression of the 1930's in Latin America reacted strongly on the thinking of statesmen and others who were concerned with national problems. The Latin American countries, it was agreed, were far too vulnerable to external economic factors. Their economies were too specialized. Even a minor change in market conditions in the industrialized countries, such as a change in consuming habits or in a manufacturing process, could have serious effects on a country that depended upon exports of only one or two products as the mainstay of its economic life, and a general depression in the industrialized nations was sure to create havoc. Even the kinds of measures which in the industrialized countries proved partly effective to combat deflationary pressures from abroad were difficult to adopt in Latin America because of extreme economic specialization.

Thus in Latin America in the 1930's the costs of specialization came to be regarded as excessive. Obviously, the solution for this problem was to diversify their economies, to establish a broader foundation for economic activity, to develop along new lines so that they would no longer be economically "one-sided," and, of the various means by which economic diversification could be achieved, industrialization was considered the most promising.

This whole trend of thinking in favor of economic diversification was reinforced by the experience of the Latin-American countries in trade negotiations in the 'thirties. The international economy, which had broken down badly in the 'twenties, collapsed utterly during the depression of the early 'thirties. Nation after nation adopted measures to promote recovery by expanding exports and by curtailing imports. In effect, countries were trying to pass the burden of the depression along to their neighbors, and to stage their own recovery at the expense of other nations. Tariffs were raised, import quotas and other restrictions were introduced, currencies were depreciated, and exchange controls were put into effect. Economic nationalism was dominant.

Although no basic change in international economic relations occurred following revival of business from the low point of the depression, new trading alignments were worked out by negotiation among countries. Some of these new arrangements were strictly of a bilateral nature whereas others followed a multilateral pattern, and they lasted for varying periods of time. In all cases, however, they involved bargaining between one country and another. It was in this connection that the Latin-American republics felt keenly their lack of economic weight and their dependence upon the industrialized economies. In bargaining with the highly industrialized nations they were at a great disadvantage. This disadvantage, inherent in their economically colonial position, was magnified by the degree to which exports were concentrated in a few products, or in even a single product.

It is not surprising that a number of Latin American countries, like countries in southeastern Europe, fell victims to the bold and ruthless trade methods of the Nazis in the 1930's. A well-known illustration of how they fared is found in the Brazilian-German clearing agreements. But even the reciprocal trade agreements which they made with the United States, in which this country refrained from making the most of its economic weight (because of the very nature of the reciprocal trade agreements program), found them at a considerable disadvantage. In many cases the United States was the largest market for their products, whereas they were only minor markets for American exports.

There is some significance in the fact that United States exports to Latin America increased more in the years 1938 to 1940 than United States imports from that area. The trade agreements cannot be held solely responsible for this outcome, since there were many other forces also playing across the lines of international commerce during the same period, but they must bear some responsibility. And in any event, Latin Americans came to think of the United States trade agreements program as a device for increasing United States exports, and they have doubted that Latin-American nations could ever benefit from the program until they have achieved a greater degree of economic independence.

International commercial negotiations as well as the depression, therefore, directed the Latin-American countries toward economic diversification during the 1930's. The main expression of this diversification was found in the development of manufacturing, and government after government adopted policies to stimulate industrial expansion. Some of these policies actually operated through negative measures, especially exchange control; foreign companies, unable to send all their profits abroad, were induced to invest in local manufacturing enterprises. On the whole, however, the positive measures, such as subsidies and protection from foreign competition, were more important.

The gains in industrial development were naturally distributed among the twenty republics of Latin America in a very uneven manner. The greatest strides were made in Argentina, Brazil, Mexico, Chile, and Colombia. To illustrate the significance of the manufacturing development achieved by Argentina, we need only point out that the proportion of imports in its annual consumption dropped from 38 per cent in 1914–1918 to 26 per cent in 1936–1938. The advances made by Mexico, where policies specifically designed to promote manufacturing development in the 'thirties were less actively pushed than in the other four countries named, are described in Chapter IV of this volume.

Some time toward the end of the 'thirties decade two other explanations of the need to industrialize in Latin America came into prominence. Neither was new, but neither had been featured in the earlier part of the decade. One was the now familiar proposition that industrialization was the best means, of attaining higher standards of living. The other was the thesis that the nation which is dependent economically upon other countries has a weak foundation for its political independence.

In view of all that has been heard about the first of these propositions in more recent years, it is curious that it did not emerge earlier as a major slogan with which to justify the promotion of industrialism. Nor is it clear why it came to the fore so strongly in the last years of the 'thirties. Possibly this development was associated with the growing strength of the labor movement in Latin America, and in particular with the formation in 1938 of the Confederación de Trabajadores de América Latina (CTAL), an international labor federation for Latin America.

The emergence of the second proposition may be ascribed to the wave of nationalism which has been sweeping through Latin America with growing force since the First World War. To build stronger national states has become a recognized objective in all the countries of Latin America, with full public support behind it. The Second World War has quite naturally strengthened the nationalistic point of view in Latin America, already on the upswing in 1939.

During the Second World War manufacturing development took a pronounced spurt in Latin America. This was especially true in the five countries which were already leading the field, but it was experienced everywhere. Many of the manufactured goods formerly imported could not be obtained abroad at all during the war, or could be secured only in limited quantities. In the face of a reduced supply, the demand for such commodities was actually increased through the operation of strong inflationary forces. These conditions were ideal for the establishment of new manufacturing plants and for the expansion of those already in existence, whenever the necessary equipment could be obtained.

Given the background circumstances which we have sketched above, the industrial expansion of the war period in Latin America is far from being regarded as a temporary development, to be written off now that more normal conditions are being restored. The industrial gains achieved since 1939 are looked upon as a base from which to score further and more important advances, and in almost every one of the twenty countries ambitious undertakings of an industrial nature have been started or planned since the end of the war.

Thus, prospects of industrialization are giving new vitality to economic life in Latin America, and the attitudes of businessmen and statesmen are being shaped accordingly. These attitudes are more sharply defined in some countries than in others, but they are sufficiently common to all alike to produce a uniform outlook on questions of international economic policy. The homogeneity and the tenacity of their viewpoint has shown itself especially in their opposition to the international economic program sponsored by the United States. This has been abundantly clear since early 1945, when the Inter-American Conference on Problems of War and Peace (Chapultepec Conference) was held in Mexico City.

The economic issues taken up at the Chapultepec Conference gave rise to lively and vigorous debate — much more so than the military, political, and social questions on the agenda. The spirited discussion which took place on economic problems was centered on a group of proposed resolutions which the United States delegation submitted under the rather grandiose title of the "Economic Charter of the Americas."

This document set forth basic objectives and guiding principles for economic development and economic policy in the Western Hemisphere. Although the United States delegates expected to have their proposal undergo a certain amount of modification in the conference, they were obviously surprised at the strength of the Latin-American reaction to it, and they were clearly disappointed over the result. The Latin-American delegates as a whole were opposed to important items in the proposal, they expressed their opposition strongly and with a frankness seldom manifested in international gatherings, and they put through significant changes in substance.

One of the questions most vigorously debated at the conference related to the reduction of trade barriers. The United States asked for an unqualified commitment on lowering barriers to international trade, with discussions on ways and means to be scheduled for an early date. A number of pertinent general questions were raised by Latin-American delegates. Should not the larger trading nations, those which weighted heavily in world economy such as the United States and Great Britain, take the first steps? How far was the United States itself prepared to go in lowering tariffs? (At the time of the Mexico City conference, it should be recalled, the U. S. Congress had not yet taken even the modest step of extending the Reciprocal Trade Agreements Act). In so far as past experience could be relied upon as a guide, there was little to warrant the belief that the United States would actually welcome imports on any very large scale.

In addition, the Latin Americans wondered about the real meaning of Assistant Secretary of State Will Clayton's plea for reducing tariffs and other barriers to trade in order to bring about a substantial expansion in world economy. "Most of the *latinos*," reports one observer, "understood 'expanding economy' to mean increased exports to Latin America." Clearly what they were most afraid of was the industrial power of the United States.

In harmony with their broad viewpoint, the Latin Americans at Chapultepec presented a united front on three other questions. (1) Protection for their new industries was justified on "infant industry" grounds. (2) Any program to reduce tariffs needed to take account of relative states of economic development — that is, the standards appropriate for economically advanced countries cannot be applied to nonindustrialized nations. (3) Endorsement of the

Bretton Woods monetary plan made it necessary to institute a certain measure of control over imports. As one of the Colombian delegates express it: "We want to pay fully for all that we buy, and to guarantee complete freedom for transfers. But precisely for this reason we must reserve the right of refraining from buying unless we believe that we can pay without causing grave disturbances in our monetary economy."

Thus the Latin Americans at Chapultepec held firmly to the position that import regulations, in one form or another, were necessary for two purposes, (1) to prevent economic dislocations in the postwar transition period, and (2) to attain suitable long-run national objectives in economic development, especially in industrialization. As a consequence, the resolution finally adopted on the question of trade barriers was softened and qualified so as to be free of any definite commitment whatever.

A further indication of the desire of Latin-American countries for greater economic independence came out in the discussion of foreign capital. The United States had proposed freedom of investment for foreign capital. This was accepted, but it was hedged in with one very important qualification sponsored by Latin American delegates, namely, "except when the investment of . . . foreign capital would be contrary to the fundamental principles of public interest." In this way the governments of Latin America reserved the right to influence investment decisions which might vitally affect their economies. The requirements of national interest were definitely placed above those of freedom of action for foreign investors.

As a final illustration from the experience of the Mexico City conference, we may cite the proposed United States resolution entitled "Elimination of Economic Nationalism." The original text — which dealt with this point briefly and bluntly — would have committed the signatory nations to the following policy:

In order that international economic collaboration may be realistic and effective, to work for the elimination of economic nationalism in all its forms.

Thanks to the Latin Americans, the tone of the final version was very different. Entitled "Elimination of Excesses of Economic Nationalism," it read:

To cooperate for the general adoption of a policy of international economic collaboration to eliminate the excesses which may result from economic nationalism, including the excessive restriction of imports and the dumping of surpluses of national production in world markets.

The effect of using the words "excesses" and "excessive" is obvious. But attention should also be called to the fact that dumping was specifically named as an undesirable practice. This was aimed at the United States. Again it reflected the fear of Latin Americans that their new industries would be stifled by competition from this country.

Even this brief survey of the results of the Chapultepec conference shows that the Latin Americans, in effect, transformed the "Economic Charter of the Americas" into a "Declaration of Economic Independence for Latin America." In doing so, they expressed their deep-seated conviction that the Latin-American nations must diversify themselves economically, and that this must be achieved mainly by means of industrial development.

This conviction is just as firmly entrenched in the minds of Latin Americans today as it was at the time of the Chapultepec meeting — perhaps more so. Certainly the issues upon which the clash of viewpoints occurred at Chapultepec are now more immediate and more practical issues than they were at that time. Postwar readjustments have helped to make them so. But even more important is the attempt, sponsored chiefly by the government of the United States, to get an effective international agreement for reducing the barriers to trade in all parts of the world.

Shortly after V–J Day, the United States government advanced a plan for freer international trade in the form of a State Department publication entitled *"Proposals for Expansion of World Trade and Employment."* This document became the nucleus of a draft charter for an International Trade Organization (ITO), drawn up at Geneva in 1947 by a special committee of the Economic and Social Council of the United Nations. In November of the same year, the Council staged at Havana a World Conference on Trade and Employment for the purpose of putting the ITO charter in final form. It was expected that the conference would concern itself with finishing touches, and that it would do its work quickly and adjourn. The results, however, were quite different. The conference dragged on for about four months, major differences of viewpoint were expressed vigorously, and the tone of the ITO charter was much modified prior to approval.

What occurred at Havana was a clash between

the industrialized nations and the countries with colonial economies. The latter, with Latin American nations taking the leadership, contended that the Geneva version of the ITO charter did not allow them the latitude they needed in commercial policy if they were to develop economically via the industrialization route. The arguments of the Latin Americans at Chapultepec were stated again, more fully and more vigorously if anything, because more was now at stake. They fought hard to strike out a clause requiring countries to eliminate quantitative restrictions on imports. They were not successful in their effort to have the offending clause removed. Nevertheless, in a combined effort with other underdeveloped countries, they did succeed in introducing escape clauses which give ample scope for taking steps of a protective nature. Even the right to establish quantitative trade controls was recognized under certain conditions. As a general proposition, it was agreed that underdeveloped nations have the right to protect, not only those industries which got a start during the war years, but also industries which might be established in the future to achieve a fuller use of their primary resources. By such action the republics of Latin America made it clear at Havana that they will not easily put aside their ambitions to industrialize.

3. THE MOVEMENT FOR SOCIAL REFORM

The progress of industrialization and the rise of organized labor have stimulated the adoption of elaborate social legislation by many Latin-American countries. The fact that until recently almost all large industrial enterprises were foreign-owned gave the sanction of a growing nationalism to the clamor for labor and social legislation. Although very unevenly enforced, this body of law points to the better future which Latin Americans are seeking to achieve. The little republic of Uruguay has been the undisputed leader in the adoption of an advanced program of social reform. Under the leadership of a remarkable President, José Batlle y Ordóñez (1856–1929), it became "the chief laboratory for social experimentation in the Americas and a focal point of world interest." The following excerpt describes Batlle's economic creed.[3]

WHEN JOSÉ BATLLE Y ORDÓÑEZ became president on 1 March 1903, the salient features of his

[3] Simon G. Hanson, *Utopia in Uruguay, Chapters in the Economic History of Uruguay*, New York, Oxford University Press, 1938, pp. 19–25. Reprinted by permission of the Oxford University Press and of the author.

philosophy had not yet been disclosed. In those days candidates for office in Uruguay did not win election by convincing the voters of the merits of their party platform. Politics were fiercely personal; membership in the two major parties was traditional and disassociated from belief in their principles; voters were regarded not as participants in the political scene of a democracy but as mere spectators whose periodic approval by vote was commanded rather than sought. Batlle's prestige was greater than that of his party. He was the son of a former president, had led the fight for honest government for a quarter of a century, and had demonstrated ability as the head of a department and in the legislature. He was the most influential journalist in the country. He had resurrected his party and given it his ideals, chief of which was that Uruguay should become a true democracy. "I am convinced," he said shortly before his election, "that the remedy for all our ills lies in electoral freedom, in honest elections." Factious opposition for a time interfered with the execution of the politics he believed essential. A fortnight after taking office he encountered resistance from the rival party, which feared encroachment on its dominance of a number of states won earlier as the price of peace. Rebellion was temporarily averted by a compromise but the tension continued and finally civil war broke out. Opinions differ as to responsibility for the outbreak. Since Batlle was not inclined to compromise, many have reasoned that he could not have been expected to tolerate a division of the nation into two sections, in one of which the legally constituted authority had to accept the mandates of a political group as an alternative to revolution. Whatever his share of the obloquy of the proceedings, the civil war was the last great use of force in Uruguay and ended in unification of the country.

His first term occupied largely with internal strife and the problems of reconstruction, Batlle left office in 1907 without having formulated or offered a well-articulated progressive program. From his writings and recommendations to the legislature, however, the public had gained an inkling of his pattern of thought and it was with dire forebodings that many witnessed his announcement of candidacy for a second term after spending the years since 1907 abroad. Safely in office in 1911, he launched the most progressive administration in Uruguayan history and one that has few parallels in any South American country. Within a year he recommended legislation providing State monopolies of insurance and electric light and power, reorganization of the State bank, the eight-hour day, a compulsory full day of rest for every five working days, regulation of the conditions of work, university education for women, secondary education for the rural districts, creation of institutes and experiment stations to aid the basic industries. These measures were followed by advocacy of a State mortgage bank, a scheme for construction of State railways, establishment of a chemical institute, increased protection for domestic industry, laws to protect animals against the abuses of such sports as bull fighting, old-age pensions, workmen's compensation, indemnification of discharged employees, protection of natural children and the right to investigate illegitimate paternity, proposals for monopoly of the manufacture of alcohol and tobacco, universal free education from the kindergarten through the university. Divorce at the will of the wife and the abolition of capital punishment were earlier accomplishments. Meanwhile Batlle maintained a consistently aggressive attitude toward the Church which finally brought in 1919 the separation of Church and State.

We are not concerned here with the political reforms instituted by Batlle. For our purposes it is enough to note that elections became more orderly and reasonably fair, that the constitutional guarantees of free speech and free press were restored, that efforts to perpetuate regimes by electoral frauds ceased, that the disillusioning experience with democratic institutions was replaced by a new faith in the vote as the expression of a true democracy. Batlle's advocacy of such innovations as proportional representation, universal suffrage, the secret ballot, model electoral laws, and especially the plural executive, was aimed at achievement of governments truly representative of the people. Once they had attained the new freedom in political life, Batlle believed that the same power of an effective ballot would bring them a new economic freedom.

"There is great injustice," he declared, "in the enormous gap between the rich and the poor." "Our population may be divided into those who have received more than they deserve and those who have received less. . . . But this does not mean that a man is either exploited or an exploiter. The inequality is not deliberate on the part of the more fortunate." "Nor is there reason for class hatred, for we all covet riches." "The real source of equality is in the difficulty of arriving at a just distribution." "The gap must be narrowed — and it is the duty of the State to attempt that task." The extreme concern of twentieth-century Uruguay for the rights of one group in the community — labour — derived from this belief in the necessity for state intervention to lessen economic inequality.

Batlle had defended labour's right to organize and to strike long before he reached the presidency. In *El Día,* which he had founded and used to propagate his ideas, at a time when the official policy was to discourage organization, Batlle wrote: "We sympathize with the strikers. A strike means that the weak have made themselves strong and having first implored justice now demand it." When a strike among the railway employees failed in 1908, the same paper published a strong leader: "Every strike is justified and it would be ideal if all could be successful. Since the all-important matter is that the time be opportune, let the State help by keeping the workers informed on conditions in various industries, markets, availability of strike-breakers, and the technique of labour organizations abroad." "After all," observed Batlle, "the workers merely seek a greater share of the wealth they create, and they use no weapon other than that of abstaining from work when they have lost hope of improvement otherwise. If their absence causes great difficulties, it is merely proof of the importance of their labour." However, since the power of capital and labour was so unequal, Batlle preferred not to depend on the strike alone: "Modern industry must not be allowed to destroy human beings. The State must regulate it to make more happy the life of the masses."

But the ideal was more clearly defined than the means of attaining it. Obviously one method of levelling out the inequalities would be to take from the rich and give to the poor. But the rich of Uruguay were the large landowners and whether out of respect for wealth derived from the land or unwillingness to alienate further a class already largely enrolled in the opposition party, Batlle did not seek a redistribution of their wealth by such methods as confiscatory taxation. "There is no pressing agrarian problem requiring the attention of the government," he emphasized in the campaign of 1910. "The division of the landed estates will take place in response to natural forces operating in our rural industries."

Toward foreign capital he displayed no such tenderness. From Paris in 1907 he had written: "We can make great progress during the next twenty years if we have honest government and especially if we are less generous in handing out money to foreign corporations." Concessions won by labour in its strikes in the foreign-owned enterprises were hailed as master achievements. "Without this strike," gloated the administration newspaper on the occasion of a victory of the tramway workers, "this wage increase amounting to $167,000 per annum would have continued to go, together with the rest of the abundant profits, to London and Berlin to swell the pockets of British and German shareholders. Now it remains here to be distributed among our own people." This hostility to foreign capital was one of Batlle's reasons for advocating state industry. "From the point of view of the national economy," ran one remarkable exposition of Batlle's theory, "a wasteful administration by the State is always preferable to the efficient management of an industry by foreign enterprise." The argument followed that efficiency of the foreigner merely increased the amount of dividends sent abroad without aiding domestic industry, while the State, when guilty of overstaffing or of paying excessively high wages, added to domestic purchasing power.

"The sphere of state intervention is expanding in every civilized country," noted Batlle in 1911 as he urged the legislature to create government monopolies. "Modern conditions have increased the number of industries that fall under the heading of public service. . . . Competition has ceased to mean something invariably beneficial, monopoly is not necessarily condemnable. . . . The modern state unhesitatingly accepts its status as an economic organization. It will enter industry when competition is not practicable, when control by private interests vests in them authority inconsistent with the welfare of the State, when a fiscal monopoly may serve as a great source of income to meet urgent tax problems, when the continued export of national wealth is considered undesirable." "State socialism makes it possible to use for the general good that portion of the results of labour which is not paid to labour."

Here, then, was the creed which guided the course of Uruguayan development. Steadfast faith in the ballot — with a consequent solicitude for such major voting elements as labour and the bureaucracy. Unrestrained nationalism — involving among other things unconcealed antagonism to foreign capital and willingness to aid domestic enterprise except when its interests conflicted with that of labour. Confidence in the ability of the State to participate directly and successfully in industry and trade. Inflexible belief that the primary obligation of the State is to secure for labour a larger share of the national wealth and income — with the stipulation, however, that it shall not involve a redistribution of the landowners' property.

4. Of Man, Woman, and Time

In the first half of the twentieth century Latin-American women made large strides toward emancipation from political, economic, and legal disabilities. But Latin-American society remained strongly man-centered, and the barriers of prejudice crumbled more slowly than those of law. Writing in the mid-thirties, a distinguished Chilean feminist and educational reformer, Amanda Labarca Hubertson (1886–   ), surveyed the status of women in Latin America.[4]

PROGRESS is as tortuous as the advance of the tide. An inviting beach beckons it inland; a rocky shore detains it. So it has been with the wave of feminism. Great Britain, Scandinavia, the Soviet Republics, North America, have incorporated its theses — once regarded as so daring — in their daily life. France and many of the Latin countries only tolerate it in their mental diet, without having fully digested it; and doubtless in more than one secluded valley of the Cauca or the Amur one can still live pleasantly under the omnipotent rod of the patriarchal master. What is true of the horizontal of geography is also true of the vertical of social classes. Conduct that the aristocracy regards as scandalously emancipated is an imperative not even discussed in the classes that live under the lash of poverty. And for the Latin girl of the middle class it is often a tragicomedy.

The first theorists of feminism paid dearly for their apostolate. They consoled themselves, in part, by reflecting that the sorrows they endured would help to fill the cup of happiness of the future. Has their hope been realized? Or, after the solution of certain problems, have not other, unforeseen problems arisen, perhaps more difficult than the old ones? Has not that cup of happiness been dearly paid for? Has feminism brought gains or losses to the Latin-American middle-class girl of today?

Gains. First of all, the consciousness of her own worth in the totality of human progress.

4 Amanda Labarca Hubertson, *¿A dónde va la mujer?*, Santiago de Chile, 1934, pp. 241–247. (Excerpt translated by the editor.)

Today's girl knows that there are no insurmountable obstacles to the flight of her intelligence; that the question of whether her entire sex is intelligent will not be raised before she is permitted to engage in any intellectual activity; that in the eyes of the majority her womanhood does not mark her with the stigma of irremediable inferiority, and that if she has talent she will be allowed to display it.

The law codes have returned to her, in large part, control over her life and property. She has well-founded hopes of seeing abolished within her lifetime the laws that still relegate her, in certain aspects, to the position of a second-class citizen, and that accord her unequal legal treatment.

She has made progress in economic liberty, basis of all independence, whether it be a question of a simple individual or one of nations. Today she is gaining admission into fields of labor forbidden to her mother.

Before her extends an unbounded horizon of opportunities. Hopes! She can live her years of illusions imagining — like every adolescent male — that the whole world awaits her, and that only her own limitations can prevent her from ascending the highest peaks of this world.

She has won liberty, including — it may seem ridiculous to mention it — the liberty of going about without papa or the classic brother at her side. To be sure, I do not speak of a nineteen-year-old Amy Johnson, who cleaves the air in a fantastic flight, without other pilot or mechanic than her youth, her skill, and valor, from England to remote Australia, in a secondhand plane that any established ace would have scorned as useless.

She has lost, in the first place, the respect of the male majority. One might say that formerly consideration for women formed part of good breeding, and it was denied only to one who by her conduct showed that she did not merit it. Today it is the other way around. In general, woman receives no tribute, and she must prove convincingly that she is a distinguished personage before receiving the homage that once was common.

Which has diminished — the respect or the quality of respectability?

It is worth one's while to analyze the point.

Men used to expect of women a stainless virtue, perfect submission — after God, thy husband, orders the epistle of St. Paul — and a lifelong devotion to the orbit in which her man revolved. A saint in the vaulted niche of her home, saint to the world, mistress of her four walls, and slave to her man. In exchange for this — respect and devotion. True, the father or husband sometimes played the role of sacristan to the saint. They allowed no one to fail to reverence her, but they themselves took liberties and even mistreated her — conduct that the saint had to bear with resignation . . . she had no recourse. It is also true that there are personalities that break all shackles, and that, with or without laws, ever since the world began there have been women who with the rosy point of a little finger, or armed with a gossamer web, have governed husband, children, home, and estate as they willed. But we are not concerned with male or female exceptions.

It is unnecessary to refer again to the upheavals that the invention of machinery brought to the world, the sharp rise in the cost of living, and the pauperization of the household, which from producer was reduced to being a simple consumer. It became impossible for a man of average means to satisfy the needs of all his womenfolk, and women had to enter offices, the professions, and other remunerative employment that had been men's traditional source of income. Woman has gone out into the world, and although this fact in itself is an economic imperative and does not essentially imply the abandonment of any virtue, the ordinary man has denied her his respect. As if it were not much more difficult, and consequently more meritorious, to preserve one's purity, sweetness, and delicacy amid the turmoil of the world than in the secluded garden of the old-time home!

On entering the economic struggle she rubs shoulders with misery. Yesterday she only knew of it by hearsay. Today it bespatters her. The rawness of life surrounds her. Often she must solve the problem of staying in the path of rectitude without the help of, or even defending herself from, the man who is ready to exploit any of her weaknesses. For the ordinary man, woman's freedom is license; her equality, the right to treat her without courtesy.

She has lost in opportunities for marriage, for establishing a household, and for satisfying that yearning for maternity that is her fundamental instinct. The more cultured a woman, the more difficult for her to find a husband, because it is normal for her to seek refuge, understanding, and guidance in a person superior to herself. And the latter do not always prefer cultured women. They imagine that knowledge makes them unfeeling — an absurd notion — that it makes them domineering — which concerns not acquired knowledge but character — or that it makes them insufferably pedantic. I regret to say that here they have a little justice on their side. Knowledge is such a recent attainment of women that the majority make an excessive show of it. We play the role of the *nouveaux-riches* of the world of culture. For their wives men prefer the "old-fashioned" girl.

That is the pathos of the tragedy of middle-class women in the Latin countries. Evolution has taken place in opposition to the fundamental convictions of men, who only tolerate it — in the case of their daughters, for example — because imperious necessity dictates it, and only with profound chagrin. Men — I repeat that I speak of the majority — continue to judge women from the viewpoint of fifty years ago, and if they retain some respect and esteem in their inner beings, they tender it to the woman who remained faithful to the classic type — the woman who has progressed they place very close to those for whom they have no respect.

Men cannot understand that external conditions — culture, profession, liberty — have not radically transformed the classic femininity, the maternal instincts, the impulses of the sweet Samaritan, the yearnings of a noble spirituality. The cases of this kind that he knows about do not convince him; he imagines that they constitute exceptions.

Nor are men of more advanced ideas free from this attitude. And it would be amusing — if it did not have tragic implications — to observe what a socialist, a radical, a communist, proclaims on the public platform and what he praises in the intimacy of his home.

Man and woman. Feared and beloved master; slave, sweetly or tyrannically subjugated; wall and ivy. Today divergent and almost hostile, but not comrades. Woman and man cannot yet be comrades, save in an infinitely small number of cases. The relationship of comrades implies equality, confidence, and the same criteria for judging each other.

"But if she acknowledges her bitter lot, why not turn back?" more than one naive soul asks. Impossible. Time does not turn back. The sharp point of its whirling lance moves on, heedless of shattered lives. New social theories will solve these problems and create new ones on the way to an inscrutable future that human faith — a flame that wavers but that only death can extinguish — imagines must be a better one.

Meanwhile, sisters, let us not preach feminism to women; let us win over the men, in the hope that our daughters may pay less dearly for their cup of happiness.

5. TEACHERS TO THE SOUTH

In recent decades some Latin-American republics — Mexico is a conspicuous example — have made marked progress in extending the benefits of public education to the rural masses that form the overwhelming majority of the population of the continent. But the handicaps of limited resources, and in some cases of ruling classes and governments indifferent to the popular needs, are enormous; as a result, in most countries the illiteracy rate is still well above 50 per cent. As in other lands, the social and economic status of the teaching profession has an important relation to the effectiveness of the educational effort. The selection given below, written by the Peruvian educator Carlos Cueto, describes the position of the teacher in his country.[5]

IN PERU, as in all Latin-American countries, the teaching profession is relatively young. If a profession is constituted by a group of persons who have received technical training in a specialised school, who exercise certain social functions within their community, who, in return for their services, have attained a certain economic level, and lastly, who present a fairly high degree of cohesion among themselves — then the teaching profession in the Latin-American countries has made its appearance in social life only in the course of the twentieth century. The first normal schools were set up many years after the beginning of this century. The idea that teaching implies a social function is being accepted very slowly. In societies which, in many ways, still maintain a feudal structure, the teacher's remuneration is painfully low. It is not easy to find professional solidarity in associations whose functioning is restricted by a number of factors.

In Peru, teaching continues to be a socially inferior profession. Only small groups of non-professional teachers, especially university professors, have been able to escape this connotation of inferiority. The factors which have determined this state of affairs in Peru are manifold and varied. We shall mention only two; both deeply rooted in the traditions of the country. In the first place, education was organised for the promotion of an *elite*. The idea of education for a minority group has prevailed for centuries. The civilisation of the Incas reserved the instruction given by the *amautas* to the members of the nobility. Even when, in 1551, a uni-

---

[5] *The Year Book of Education, 1953*, edited by R. K. Hall, N. Hans, and J. A. Lauwerys, Yonkers-on-Hudson, N.Y., World Book Company, 1953, pp. 572–579. Reprinted by permission of the World Book Company.

versity was founded in Peru with the purpose of spreading the culture of the West in the New World, social and economic conditions were such that a university education remained inaccessible to those who did not belong to the upper classes. The colonial period ended in the third decade of the nineteenth century; but to this day colonial practices and the system created by the aristocracy have persisted in the organisation of education. In a society ruled by groups of persons enjoying the twofold privilege of "blood" and wealth, teaching is not a liberal profession, i.e., a profession of free men. There is a profound separation between the great mass of the people and the ruling class. Consequently, the idea of a single nation hardly exists, and the teacher is not considered to have a social function.

In addition to the *elite*-oriented character of education, another no less important factor must be mentioned as a cause for the low regard accorded to the teaching profession: the centralisation of political power, a feature stemming from the earliest days of the country's history. The administration of education is bureaucratically controlled from the capital of the republic, and the teachers are but obedient servants carrying out orders which include even insignificant details. By means of decrees, regulations, and resolutions, the Ministry of Public Education prescribes the duties and obligations of teachers. This legislation, casuistic and microscopic in its attention to detail, crushes the teacher's initiative. Article 109 of the Regulations for Secondary Education states fourteen prohibitions for teachers, one of which reads as follows: "Teachers are forbidden to criticise the orders of higher authorities or of superiors."

The teaching profession in Peru falls into three distinct classes. Even where such stratification corresponds to differences that exist all over the world, the social and economic distances between these groups, the intellectual standing and, consequently, the personal prestige accorded to their members, are so great that it seems necessary to study them separately. These classes are university, secondary, and primary teachers respectively.

UNIVERSITY LEVEL: THE "CATEDRÁTICO"

The first university teachers in Peru were members of the clergy, and this is the reason why here, as in most Latin-American countries, they are called *catedráticos*. The root of this term is the same as that of "cathedral," the church where the bishop has his seat. *Catedrático* always denotes a high official of the church, a person who enjoys considerable prestige and power, a member of the intelligentsia. However, it was not long before the clergy had to share their functions with the lay dignitaries of the colony. In a society where personal significance could not be achieved through work, skills, or political power, university teaching and university degrees were considered solely as a means for the attainment of personal prestige. The occupation of a university professor was in no way a profession: it was simply a decorative activity carried on side by side with other occupations; it might also be described as a means used for the achievement of more important ends. This same tradition has prevailed since the establishment of the republic in 1821: the university professors are the heirs of the old colonial nobility. Besides their teaching, they have other occupations which definitely rank more highly in their esteem: they are lawyers, physicians, engineers, owners of large landed estates, and, frequently, prominent politicians with the greatest of influence on the public affairs of the country. Their true professional sphere is not in the university but outside it. The university is an episode, a secondary activity, a non-professional occupation taking up not more than a few hours per week. These conditions still prevail to a large extent in 1953. There are very few persons in the universities of Peru who devote themselves exclusively and professionally to the service of the institution. There have been two fundamental consequences of this system: the university has failed to fulfil its research function, and the students have had no tutors, guides, or masters.

The incipient industrialisation that developed in Peru during the years following World War I favoured the growth of a middle class. The members of the upper classes became attracted by economic activities; and middle-class individuals were channelled towards the university. This change must be considered as important. However, it still holds true that the title of university professor constitutes a mark of personal prestige, a means for consolidating the careers of doctors, lawyers, engineers, politicians, businessmen.

Owing to its position as a stronghold of the socially and economically powerful classes, the university used to constitute one of the politicians' major preoccupations. The invasion of the university by professors and students of middle-class origin, which has been taking place during the last years, has produced effects of the greatest importance: these middle classes, which have risen quickly towards "enlightenment" (the use of this term is intended to evoke historical associations), are agents of protest against the traditional social order. For this reason the university continues to be a focus of preoccupation to politicians. Peruvian universities frequently become the scene of tumultuous political agitation. All this brings discredit to the status and position of the university professor. Very few persons are willing to stake their future on one single card, that of the university, when it is known that the position of the *catedrático* may at any moment be revoked by a reform, a reorganisation, or by the closing of an institution. It is felt among teachers that one may have a position to-day, but that nobody can predict what will be happening to it to-morrow.

The lower grades of the university career in Peru comprise the instructors, who serve as assistants in courses requiring some form of supervision of the students' practical work (e.g. laboratory practice, clinical practice in medicine, archaeological exploration, teaching practice, etc.). Interim professors are required to lecture; they may be either assistant or full professors. In either case they are appointed for one academic year (which begins on April 1st and ends on March 31st), at the end of which their appointment may be renewed. Senior professors (*catedráticos*) are appointed for a five-year period at first; for ten years the second time; and for an unlimited term the third time. The direction of the faculties and of the university is restricted to senior professors. Only persons holding a doctoral degree are eligible for a professorship. The top rank of the career is reached by the professor who, having devoted himself fully to the university to the exclusion of any other occupation, is entitled to certain extra allowances and to indefinite tenure. The salaries of professors in the lower ranks go up to 300 *soles* per month; those of porters, gardeners, guards, carpenters, electricians, etc., employed in the university are never less than 500 *soles* per month. The income of top-ranking professors in the University of Lima, which is the wealthiest in the country, may in exceptional cases be as much as 4,000 *soles* per month, i.e. equivalent to the salary earned by third-class employees in insurance companies, banks, or industrial firms, and there-

fore below the income of a middling member of the liberal professions.

There are no associations of university professors in Peru. On the other hand, all the liberal professions are organised in professional and cultural associations. It should, perhaps, be mentioned here that another factor preventing the final professionalisation of university teaching lies in the frequent demands made on professors to serve in government posts, owing to the small number of qualified persons available. Such demands lead to their temporary or permanent estrangement from the university.

SECONDARY LEVEL: THE "PROFESSOR"

The present Law of Public Education (Law No. 9,359 of April 1st, 1941) requires secondary school teachers to hold a professional diploma awarded either by the pedagogical institutes which are directly subordinated to the Ministry of Public Education, or by the education schools of the universities. The same law stipulates, however, that if no candidates with teacher's diplomas are available, persons holding other professional diplomas or academic degrees may be appointed. The great majority of individuals who are, at present, teaching in the secondary schools or *colegios* of Peru hold no professional diploma whatsoever. According to statistics published in the so-called "Plan of National Education" (1950), only 20 per cent of active secondary teachers have a teacher's diploma proper; 12 per cent have other diplomas (lawyers, doctors, engineers, bachelors of science or literature, etc.); and 57 per cent of all secondary teachers are persons without any university education whatever.

The fact that the great majority (practically 80 per cent) of secondary school teachers in Peru lack a teacher's diploma shows that the profession is, in reality, still very weak. It is weak, not only as a social force, but even in its own sphere, in the secondary school, and in the field of educational activities. The professional secondary teachers constitute a minority in comparison with those persons who do the same type of work but whose interest is merely accessory and circumstantial. Like the university professors, these latter have occupations outside the school which are economically more rewarding and to which, therefore, they pay more attention.

The causes for this situation are analogous to those mentioned with reference to university professors. Until recent times, secondary education has been the privilege of the upper social classes. The majority of those engaged in teaching at the secondary level were members either of these classes or of the clergy, without any interest in the development of the teaching profession as such. Education has lacked social significance and failed to fulfil its function of social integration; thus, the social conditions necessary to the formation of a strong teaching profession have been absent.

The statistical figures mentioned above are subject to an important qualification. In the secondary schools of Lima, and a few large cities, professional teachers do not constitute such a striking minority as in the schools of the more remote towns. They are reluctant to go to places where there are no other prospects but teaching, with its implication of a low economic level and, above all, of life in an environment lacking in cultural stimulation. Moreover, in these towns the stability of the teacher's position is constantly threatened by powerful influences exercised from the capital. Senators and representatives intervene frequently and decisively in the Ministry of Education in matters concerning the appointment and dismissal of teachers. The dismissed teacher has to undertake a long journey to the capital, where the administrative apparatus that determines his fate is concentrated. The outcome of his appeal is never certain. Under such conditions, one can easily understand his reluctance to move to small towns or remote regions.

The relatively insignificant number of qualified teachers, the instability of their posts, the centralisation of administration, the casuistic regulations that control every aspect of the teacher's activity, the absorbing demands of a rigid curriculum and of inflexible study plans — all these are detrimental to the teacher's initiative. Hampered by these factors, he is forced to fall back on routine.

There are, in Peru, associations of secondary teachers, but they have no significance whatsoever from either the professional or the cultural point of view. Their existence is a passive one, and very often their activities are controlled by the authorities of the Ministry of Public Education.

The system of remuneration of secondary teachers reflects the conditions described above. As only part of their time is devoted to teaching, they do not receive a fixed salary corresponding to their professional training. Their remuneration is determined by the number of hours taught per week; and it varies according to the category of their schools. Schools are classified according to two criteria: location and number of students. The highest salaries are paid to teachers in military colleges; the next highest are those paid to teachers employed in the capital; remuneration is somewhat lower in some other large cities; it is lowest in the provincial towns.

The maximum earnings of a secondary teacher devoting practically all his time to teaching are below those of a young sub-lieutenant in the army. Even in Lima, the maximum salary of a secondary school teacher is below that of an army major.

The new Regulations for Secondary Education issued by the Military Government of Peru establish various hierarchies for the career of the secondary school teacher. It has been the aim of these Regulations to increase the number of full-time teachers. The hierarchy of the teaching career has to a large extent been modelled on the military hierarchy. The highest posts are those of the so-called "directive personnel"; and those who do not hold such directive posts merely carry out orders received from their superiors.

ELEMENTARY LEVEL: THE "MAESTRO"

The position of the primary school teacher in Peru is in many ways an inferior one. In addition to his extremely low economic status and his quite insignificant social influence, he is a subaltern in the ranks of his own profession. The educational level of secondary teachers is generally considered to be of university standing. The primary teacher, on the other hand, does not reach this level, his training being shorter than that of the former. Thus there exist, within the framework of the teaching profession in Peru, notable differences between secondary and primary school teachers, which are reflected by the lack of professional and cultural connections between the two groups as well as by the feelings of superiority of the former in relation to the latter.

Owing to the low level of the requirements for entry into the primary teaching profession, candidates tend to come from the lowest social classes; and their choice is determined not by vocational reasons but solely by the desire for security, although the career is a modest one and offers no possibilities for personal advancement.

The number of women teachers is increasing steadily, while the number of men is on the decrease.

Primary school teachers are divided into four categories. The first consists of the holders of the urban normal school diploma (awarded after five years of secondary education and four years in the urban normal school). The second group comprises the graduates of rural normal schools (three years of secondary education and three years in the rural normal school). The third category includes those who have concluded their secondary education but have not taken a normal school course; and the fourth consists of persons whose qualifications are lower still. According to official statistics published by the Ministry of Education ("Plan of National Education," 1950), more than 50 per cent of all primary teachers in Peru fall into the third and fourth categories.

A teacher classified in the first category earns a monthly salary of 710 soles; the salary of an army sub-lieutenant (a rank which is reached at about 22 years of age) is 1,121 soles. Teachers in the second, third, and fourth categories receive 570 soles, 410 soles, and 328 soles per month, respectively. Whereas the salary of sub-lieutenant constitutes an initial step in a career which offers constant opportunities for advancement, the teacher's remuneration remains relatively unchanged throughout his life. Possible increments are the following: for each child, an allowance of 30 soles per month; for every five years of service, an increase of 5 per cent; a special allowance for teachers serving in schools in outlying regions amounting to between 5 and 20 per cent of their salary. These economic conditions account for the very low prestige of the primary teaching career. It should be added that primary school teachers, unlike their colleagues in secondary schools and universities, have no possibility of supplementing their income by means of additional activities.

During recent years, a few primary school teachers working in towns that have universities (Lima, Arequipa, Cuzco, and Trujillo) have been taking courses in the Faculties of Education, which has enabled them to go on to secondary teaching. This trend is undoubtedly desirable from the teacher's personal point of view; but it tends to create what may eventually become a grave problem for the elementary school: the loss of its best elements.

The Ministry of Public Education has on repeated occasions organised holiday courses for teachers in the lower categories with the aim of making it possible for them to rise to the next higher rank. Time and again, however, these courses had to be abandoned: their excessively short duration, the high costs involved, and the difficulty of gathering the participants in appropriate places, rendered them ineffectual.

Primary teachers are appointed and dismissed by the Director of Primary Education in the Ministry of Education in Lima. Appointments are usually proposed by the provincial inspector. The influence of some political figure is very rarely absent in these matters.

Both primary and secondary teachers are required to follow faithfully the instructions issued by the Ministry. They are under the constant pressure of the weight of decrees, regulations, and circulars, as well as the severe authority of the school director and the inspector. The primary teachers are in a position of complete subordination in relation to the legal apparatus and the officials controlling it.

The fundamental disadvantage is perhaps the lack of social influence on the part of the primary teacher. The social action of teachers and schools is practically non-existent in a country where it is needed with tragic urgency. The primary teachers are not prepared professionally for such a task; but even if they were, the conditions under which they are forced to work — vertical control, inflexible authorities, lack of textbooks and materials, extensive curricula — all these would prevent any action reaching beyond the daily routine. In any case, a teacher is considered progressive if he is interested in pedagogical problems, i.e. in the technical aspect of his profession. It may be considered a symptom that there is much talk about "pedagogy," and that the meaning of the term has been distorted so as to reduce it to the methodology for the transmission of knowledge. Very seldom, on the other hand, do teachers refer to "education" as a social activity. This attitude is characteristic of the whole of Latin America, with very few exceptions.

6. THE NEGRO IN BRAZIL

Special historic circumstances have given the "race problem" in Latin America a milder character than in some other parts of the world. The experience of Brazil, with its large Negro population, is particularly enlightening in this respect. Donald Pierson, a North American sociologist and teacher at the Escola Livre de Sociologia e Política of São Paulo, offers some con-

clusions based on careful study of race relations in the city of Salvador (Bahia).[6]

IN BAHIA there is probably little or no race prejudice in the sense in which that term is used in the United States. There are no castes based on race; there are only classes. This does not mean that there is nothing which might be properly called prejudice but that such prejudice as does exist is *class* rather than *caste* prejudice. It is the kind of prejudice which exists *inside* the ranks of the Negro in the United States, the amount and intensity of which is actually very great.

That race prejudice has not arisen in Brazil is perhaps due to the fact that the Brazilian white has never at any time felt that the black or the mixed-blood offered any serious threat to his status. The past and present experiences of the ethnic groups have not been such as would call out in the whites feelings of fear, distrust, apprehension, dread, resentment, or envy, all of which probably enter into the attitude of race prejudice. Besides, there has not been in Brazil that obscure sense of guilt which men sometimes feel toward those they have wronged or toward those by whom they themselves have been wronged. There have been few or no incidents which the Europeans resent and tend to construe as affronts or unwarranted aggressions and attacks; no events, like those attendant on our Civil War and its aftermath, which would stir the Europeans, arouse their feelings, and give to their conception of the Negro a new meaning and content. . . .

Brazilian society nowhere passed through a comparable period of social upheaval in which a threatened reversal of the status structure elicited such deep-seated fear and apprehension that generations later it is so vividly recalled by the descendants of those who lived through it. The rape of white women by colored men, either real or fancied, has been unknown in Brazil. There has not been anything remotely comparable to the conquest of our South by northern armies, the imposition, for years, of onerous political control from without, and the consequent development of feelings of resentment and bitterness which, lacking normal expression (by reason of the North's formidable power), in the form of effective aggression toward the actual offending object, became displaced upon the more or less helpless Negro when northern force was withdrawn. On the contrary, the relations between the races in Brazil have always been, to a considerable extent, intimate and cordial. The moral order of the Bahian *engenhos*, which, as we have seen, was organized largely on a familial and personal basis, has persisted relatively undisturbed down to the present day, and the members of the different races have, by way of personal feelings and sentiments, long identified themselves with each other, entered into each other's personal experiences, and come to appreciate their common human character. Instead of conceiving the Negro as an abstract object, the Bahian white tends to think of him as João or Maria and as being wholly human like himself.

It is true that the Europeans at Bahia, like all groups, are ethnocentric, and individual whites share a general feeling of the superiority of their group. Many of them are adverse to the (to them) strange and bizarre behavior represented by the *candomblé* ritual and other African cultural survivals. In some minds at least these acts have taken on a disgusting and even offensive character and many have evoked deeply rooted antipathies. However, these antagonisms are directed at *cultural* rather than at *racial* variations, and they tend to disappear when the Negro, as he is now rapidly doing, gives up his identification with African cultural forms and becomes assimilated into the European world. The antipathy does not extend, therefore, to the Negro as such but rather to the *Africano,* the foreigner, he who constitutes an alien cyst in the social organism. This attitude is not greatly different from that characteristic of descendants of the first English settlers in the United States toward recent immigrants from southern and eastern Europe who for a time continue to live much to themselves and to cling tenaciously to Old World customs and traditions.

One might note that the Brazilian case of racial contact definitely supports Faris' challenge of a popular assumption which, confusing the customary with the natural, maintains that race prejudice is instinctive and hereditary. If race prejudice were organic, it obviously would appear in all cases of racial contact. If, then, we discover cases in which it does not appear, the hypothesis that race prejudice is instinctive is no longer valid.

What we find, then, in Bahia is a multiracial class society. There is no caste based upon race; there are only classes; these classes are still largely identified with color, it is true, but they are classes nonetheless and not castes. The most characteristic tendency of the Bahian social order is the gradual but persistent reduction of all distinguishing racial and cultural marks and the fusing, biologically and culturally, of the African and the European into one race and one common culture.

The actual situation in any case of race contact can perhaps be precisely defined by a diagram which distinguishes between caste and class relations. In a caste system the racial lines may run thus:

White
Race lines	Mixed-blood
Black

In case the structure of society is organized on the basis of class, as in Brazil or Hawaii, the color lines run vertically, cutting across class lines:

Class lines	White	Mixed-blood	Black

Each race, including the mixed-bloods, is likely to be represented in all the occupational classes. The hierarchy of occupations will inevitably take the form of a pyramid, but the percentage of each racial stock in each occupational class will indicate the occupational status of the different racial elements. And since the group with superior status will have proportionately larger numbers in the upper brackets, and the groups with inferior status will have larger numbers in the lower brackets, one may describe a racial situation statistically. Thus, on the basis of a sample census recently taken, the relation to the class structure of the respective ethnic elements in the population at Bahia may be described as shown in Table 16.

TABLE 16

Racial Distribution in the Classes at Bahia, 1936

Ethnic Groups	Intelligentsia		Marginal		Lower Class	
	No.	Per Cent	No.	Per Cent	No.	Per Cent
Blacks	5	0.4	23	5.1	1,245	75.2
Mixed-Bloods	222	15.7	255	56.3	386	23.3
Whites	1,183	83.9	175	38.6	25	1.5
Totals	1,410	100.0	453	100.0	1,656	100.0

... If now one were able to obtain statistics showing the extent of intermarriage between, on the one hand, members of the different racial stocks in the same occupational class and, on the other hand, between the different classes in the same racial stock, those facts should provide an accurate statistical description of what the racial situation actually is. If one finds that, as in the United States, marriages between different occupational classes within each racial group are more frequent than intermarriage between members of the different racial groups in the same class, we should expect to find solidarity

and co-operation for common ends organized along racial lines. The racial group would then assume more or less the character of a nationality or of a racial minority. On the other hand, if solidarity and co-operation were organized along class lines, then the struggle for status would take more or less the form of a class struggle.

Statistical data to resolve this problem are unfortunately not available in any depository in Bahia. Such information as it was possible to secure in the course of this study indicated that marriages cross race lines more often than class lines and that solidarity and co-operation tend to be organized along class lines.

Since, then, the blacks, mixed-bloods, and whites in Bahia do not constitute endogamous occupational groupings, the social structure is not that of caste. Although the hierarchy of occupations still takes a decidedly pyramidal form, and the white race, occupying superior status, has predominantly larger numbers in the upper brackets, and the black race, representing inferior status, is overwhelmingly dominant in the lower brackets, each race and the mixed-bloods are represented in all the occupational classes.

To the extent that the blacks-mixed-bloods, and whites fall into endogamous but not necessarily occupational groupings, one might say that the structure here takes the form of a racial minority, or a nationality, in free association with, but not accepted on a basis of social equality by, a dominant racial majority. Such is the relation of the Jew in Europe and, increasingly now, of the Negro in the United States. Of the latter, Park has said:

Although caste still persists and serves in a way to regulate race relations, many things — education, the rise within the Negro community of a professional class (teachers, ministers, and physicians) and of an intelligentsia, seeking to organize and direct the Negro's rising race consciousness — have conspired not merely to undermine the traditional caste system but to render it obsolete.

Meanwhile, the slow but steady advance of the Negro, as a result of a competition within and without the group, and the gradual rise of a Negro society within the limits of the white man's world have changed the whole structure of race relations in the United States, both in the North and in the South.

The restrictions on intermarriage still persist and continue to make of the Negro an endogamous social group, in much the same sense that the Jews, the Mennonites, and any of the more primitive religious sects are endogamous. On the other hand, in view of the fact that he has developed a society in which all the professions and many, if not most, occupations are represented, the Negro has an opportunity now, which he did not have earlier, to rise within the limits of the Negro world. Under those circumstances the Negro group has gradually ceased to exhibit the characteristics of a caste and has assumed rather the character of a racial or national minority.

With the Negro in Brazil endogamy is far from absolute, breaking down particularly along the biological borders of the race, probably increasingly, with the passage of time and the continued rise of individuals from the inferior status group. The scale of race distinctions, including the Negro at the bottom and the white at the top, seems to correspond in a general way to the scale of color distinctions *within the Negro minority* in the United States.

Although color and negroid features are still indicative of slave origin and still tend to be closely identified with low status and hence to constitute a considerable handicap to marriage into the upper classes, these characteristics lose their limiting and restrictive character in proportion as the degree of European intermixture increases or their symbolic reference is called into question by evidence of status-enhancing qualities in a given individual. Similarly, personal competence or individual achievement admit persons possessing considerable color into such status-symbolizing institutions as exclusive clubs. Race consciousness is at a minimum, "passing" has no point, and the circumstances are not ordinarily conducive to the appearance of the "marginal man." The organization of society tends to take the form of a competitive order in which the individual finds his place on the basis of personal competence rather than of racial descent.

The racial situation at Bahia probably is, in a general way, typical of all Brazil. At the same time a considerable immigration of Europeans during the past century into the southern Brazilian states, especially São Paulo, Santa Catharina, and Rio Grande do Sul, and the gradual development of an industrial society in São Paulo, may have modified somewhat the attitudes formerly prevailing in these areas. A Bahian mixed-blood recently returned from Rio Grande do Sul with the statement that he had there been referred to as a "Negro" and had otherwise felt uncomfortable distinctions to which in Bahia he had been unaccustomed. That there is some prejudice in the cosmopolitan city of Rio de Janeiro is attested by the organization in 1935 of O Movimento Brasileiro Contra o Preconceito Racial ("The Brazilian Movement against Race Prejudice"), sponsored by the prominent intellectuals, Arthur Ramos and Roquette Pinto. In São Paulo, the organization in 1924 of a Negro journal, *O Clarim d'Alvorada,* and later of others like *A Chibata, Cultura, O Clarim,* and *A Voz da Raça* ("The Voice of the Race"); of several Negro clubs for recreational and literary purposes like the Club 15 de Novembro, Club 13 de Maio, Gremio Dramatus e Recreativo Kosmos, and the Gremio União da Mocidade; of the Negro women's organization, Centro Civico Palmares; and, in 1931, of the Frente Negra Brasileira ("Brazilian Negro Front") with the aim of "bringing together the Negroes of all Brazil," clearly indicates at least some race consciousness on the part of the Negroes of São Paulo and consequently reflects feelings of exclusion and discrimination; as also do the subsequently organized Associação dos Brasileiros de Côr in Santos and the Frente Negra Pelotense in Pelotas, Rio Grande do Sul.

However, these indications of a measure of race consciousness are probably exceptions to the general Brazilian cultural pattern and not typical of it. Organizers for the Frente Negra do Brasil, after several weeks of fruitless effort, gave up an attempt to organize a chapter at Bahia. The fact that noted intellectuals band together to resist attitudes prejudicial to racial minorities is in itself an evidence of the racial ideology which we have noted. That these intellectuals are not atypical persons is attested by the general tenor of the spontaneous utterances, as well as formal remarks, of numerous Brazilians. It may be that Bahia, by reason of long being a passive cultural area in comparison to the more active cultural areas of the South, is more characteristically representative of the original Brazilian mores than São Paulo and certain other southern zones. But even in São Paulo the journals referred to above have one by one suspended publication, a fact which would seem to indicate no great amount of race consciousness. The study of intermarriage made in São Paulo by Dr. Lowrie would appear merely to confirm the fact that in Brazil still today the Negro in most cases lacks class. At least it is true that several individuals with some colored blood occupy important positions in the Paulista community or have married into white families.

The race problem in Brazil, in so far as there is a race problem, tends rather to be a consequence of the resistance which an ethnic group offers, or is thought to offer, to absorption. Recent opposition to Japanese immigration into São Paulo apparently has been largely motivated by apprehension that the Japanese would constitute a group difficult to assimilate. In an attempt to refute this imputation, the Japanese embassy in Rio published a pamphlet entitled *Intermixture among the Japanese: The Myth That They Do not Interbreed with Other Races,* to which were appended several photographs of mixed Japanese-Brazilian families.

Of the Negroes, Brazilians ordinarily say there is no Negro problem, because the Negroes are in process of absorption and eventually will be completely incorporated. To individuals from all classes of the population this eventual amalgamation and assimilation of diverse ethnic units is a matter of pride and self-commendation.

In summary, one might set down in the form of hypotheses for further testing what appear to be the more significant facts about the racial situation in Brazil, especially as it is related to the career of the African and his descendants.

1. Although probably more Africans were imported into Brazil than into the United States, or into any other region of the New World, the Brazilian Negro, as a racial unit, like the Brazilian Indian before him, is gradually but to all appearances inevitably disappearing, being biologically absorbed into the predominantly European population. Race mixture has gone on in an unobtrusive way over a long period of time. In few places in the world, perhaps, has the interpenetration of diverse races proceeded so continuously and on so extensive a scale.

2. There is not growing up a relatively permanent mixed racial stock, like the "Cape Coloured" of South Africa, the Macanese in China, or the Goanese in India. The Brazilian mixed-bloods are absorbing the blacks and are themselves in turn being absorbed by the predominantly European population.

3. In answer to the normal needs of a racial and cultural frontier a tradition of intermarriage arose and became firmly fixed in the colonial mores. This appears to be the natural response in all cases of racial contact where the sex ratio is out of balance.

4. Miscegenation, particularly when linked with intermarriage, resulted in bonds of sentiment between parents and offspring which hindered the arising of attitudes of prejudice and at the same time placed the mixed-bloods in a favorable position for social advancement.

5. With rise in class, intermarriage between mixed-bloods (especially those of the lighter shades) and whites became increasingly common. Thus, endogamy has for some time been breaking down, particularly along the biological borders of the races, and, with the continued rise of individuals from the inferior status group, this tendency is evidently increasing. Although color and negroid features are still symbolic of slave origin, still tend to be closely identified with low status and hence to constitute an undeniable handicap to marriage into the upper

classes, these physical marks lose their restraining character in proportion to the degree white intermixture increases or — what is even more important — in proportion to the degree their symbolic reference is called into question by evidence of other qualities of a status-enhancing character in a given individual.

6. In general, slavery in Brazil, as also in the United States, was characterized by the continuous growth of intimate, personal relations between master and slave which tended gradually to humanize the institution and undermine its formal character. The Brazilian moral order became organized, to a considerable extent, on a familial and personal basis.

7. The custom of manumission became firmly intrenched in the Brazilian mores, constituting, under certain circumstances, universally expected behavior. Brazilian Negroes were thus released from a servile status gradually and under circumstances which favored the continuance of those intimate personal ties already built up.

8. Emancipation sentiment in Brazil never suffered from a wave of fear like that which swept our South after the Negro uprising in Haiti and the disorders attendant on the subsequent annihilation of the Haitian whites.

9. Abolition sentiment and agitation were not limited to any one section of Brazil but, on the contrary, penetrated every community, even that of Bahia, where the institution of slavery was apparently very firmly intrenched. Thus, the "struggle for consistency" in the Brazilian mores went on *inside* each local community, where it had in its favor the intimate and personal relations of individuals who not only lived in close proximity to each other but were also bound together by ties of family, religion, and friendship.

10. Final emancipation came about as the culmination of a widespread liberation movement which for years had dominated the public mind. The release of the last slaves in bondage did not, as in the United States, occur as an incident of civil strife, nor were the race relations which have normally grown up under slavery ever exacerbated by a program of "reconstruction" imposed by armed conquest from without.

11. The Brazilian white has never at any time felt that the black or the mixed-blood offered any serious threat to his own status. No feelings of fear, distrust, apprehension, dread, resentment, or envy have been stirred up, as in our South during and following the Civil War,

no sense of unwarranted aggressions or attacks.

12. Today, the blacks and the mixed-bloods are represented throughout the entire occupational scale, although, as is to be expected, considering the original slave status of the Negro, his relatively disadvantaged position upon receiving his liberty, and the comparatively brief time he has enjoyed a freely competitive status, the darker portion of the population is still concentrated in the low-pay low-status employments. However, the blacks, ordinarily but not always paced by the mixed-bloods, are gradually rising in the occupational scale.

13. This rise in class of the blacks and the mixed-bloods is recognized not merely in a Negro world, as is largely true of similar advancement in the United States, but by all members of the Brazilian community.

14. Since, then, the blacks, the mixed-bloods, and the whites do not constitute endogamous occupational groupings, the social structure is not that of caste.

15. Nor does the Negro in Brazil appear to be, as he is in the United States, developing into a self-conscious racial minority in free association with, but not accepted by, a dominant racial majority.

16. Instead, the entire organization of society tends to take the form of a competitive order in which the individual finds his place on the basis of personal competence and individual achievement more than upon the basis of racial descent. This fact is perhaps best reflected in the common saying: "A rich Negro is a white man, and a poor white man is a Negro."

17. The Brazilian racial situation is, then, sufficiently distinct from that in India, for example, where the social order is organized on the principle of caste, and from those in many parts of the world where a national or racial minority (or minorities) is in free association with, but not accepted by, a dominant national or racial majority, to constitute, along with the Hawaiian racial situation and certain others, a distinct type: a *multiracial class society*.

18. There is not deliberate segregation as one finds where races have been embittered for a long time; spatial distribution is largely the consequence of economic sifting. Such isolation as exists is largely due to varying educational levels or to identification with elements of African culture, particularly the fetish cult.

19. For the assimilation of the *Africanos* at Bahia, while now far advanced, is not yet complete. African survivals still persist, setting apart

to some extent a (comparatively small) portion of the black population.

20. Lynching and the rape of white women by colored men are both unknown, "passing" has no point, and circumstances are not ordinarily conducive to the appearance of the "marginal man."

21. One drop of African blood does not, as in the United States (if known), class a mixed-blood as a Negro. Instead, many individuals are listed in the official statistics as whites, and are similarly known in the community, who not only have African ancestors but actually give some evidence of this descent in their color and features.

22. Prejudice exists in Brazil; but it is *class* rather than *race* prejudice. It is the kind of prejudice which one finds inside the ranks of the Negro in the United States.

23. It is possible that the Brazilian blacks and mixed-bloods, lacking as they do in most cases the sense of inferiority long characteristic of the Negro in the United States, particularly of the mixed-blood, have been less activated by personal ambition. Feeling themselves less under the necessity of demonstrating to a hostile white world their individual talents and abilities, they have not had the same incentive for social advancement and, consequently, have not, perhaps, as a group, risen in class as rapidly as has the Negro in the United States.

24. Although Brazil seems never to have had a formal racial policy, the traditional behavior which originally grew up and took shape under the influence of the immediate and unreflecting responses to the circumstances and conditions of colonial life gave rise to an *informal* racial policy, or racial ideology, which underlies and gives consistency to the mores, appearing only when they are challenged from without and individuals seek to rationalize and to defend their customary conduct. This ideology is perhaps best summarized in the commonly heard phrase, "We Brazilians are becoming one people."

Thus, the race problem in Brazil, in so far as there is a race problem, tends to be identified with the resistance which an ethnic group offers, or is thought to offer, to absorption and assimilation.

This is not to say that there are no social distinctions in Brazil; for such are obviously common to all societies, one thing or another serving as a basis. Neither does it mean that there is no discrimination or that the blacks and mixed-bloods are completely satisfied with their lot. But it does mean (a) that a man of color may, by reason of individual merit or favorable circumstance, improve his status and even achieve position in the upper levels of society and (b) that this position will then be with reference not merely to the darker group whose color he shares but to the total community.

XXXIV

The Flowering of Latin-American Culture

BY THE MIDDLE OF THE TWENTIETH CENTURY Latin-Amerian culture had attained maturity in a number of fields. Art and scholarship drew closer to the people and its problems, and at the same time displayed a growing mastery of the refinements of technique.

Literature first raised the standard of revolt against an aristocratic conception of culture. Before his death Darío himself had shown a new concern with political and social themes. Enrique González Martínez formally challenged the aristocratic tradition with his celebrated sonnet "Wring the Neck of the Swan" (1910). The ideals of literary Americanism and realism gradually triumphed over the cult of Art for Art's sake.

The portrayal of man's struggle against an untamed nature or an unsatisfactory environment came to occupy a central place in the literature of the novel. Typical of this new trend were such masterpieces as *Los de abajo* (1916), by Mariano Azuela, *La vorágine* (1924), by José Eustasio Rivera, and *Doña Bárbara* (1929), by Rómulo Gallegos.

Latin-American music — like the literature — made more use of folk materials and displayed increasing mastery of all modern technical resources. But it was in the field of painting that Latin-American culture burned with the most brilliant flame. The Mexican school, led by Diego Rivera, José Clemente Orozco, and David Alfaro Siqueiros, won world acclaim with its bold, socially-conscious art. Modern Brazilian architecture also impressed foreign observers with its audacity and its skilful solutions of problems of light and air.

Meanwhile the social scientists turned away from antiquarian concerns to explore the cultural contributions of the Negro and the Indian, to document the case for social reform, and to attack racial myths. Gilberto Freyre and Arturo Ramos in Brazil and Fernando Ortiz in Cuba rendered notable services to sociology. Archaeology and ethnology made large strides in Peru and Mexico. Extremely significant was the rise of centers for advanced study, staffed by scholars of the highest qualifications, such as the Colegio de México and the Instituto de Filología of the University of Buenos Aires.

1. "Wring the Neck of the Swan"

In a famous sonnet the Mexican poet Enrique González Martínez (1871–1952) attacked Darío's proud swan, symbol of beauty as an end in itself, and praised the sober owl, symbol of the quest for wisdom. In a general way, the poem foreshadowed the rise of a new spirit of sincerity, realism, and social consciousness in Latin-American literature. Miss Muna Lee has skillfully turned González Martínez' lines into English verse.[1]

WRING THE NECK OF THE SWAN

Wring the neck of the lying feathered swan
That gives a white note to the azure fountain!
It glides in grace, but never thinks upon
The soul of things, the voice from out the mountain.

Flee from every form and every fashion
Through which life's latent rhythm does not roll;
Only life itself adore with passion,
And let life know this homage of your soul.

Observe that sober owl which takes his flight
From Olympus and the refuge Pallas made
To rest himself in silence on his tree.
Although he has no swan's grace, you can see
His sober profile sharp against the shade
Interpreting the mystery of night.

2. In Search of a New Expression

The 'twenties were a period of intense literary activity in Latin America. Latin-American poets and novelists strove, with considerable success, to express the essence of their lands in an original and truly native way. In their search for a new expression they received guidance from one of Latin America's most eminent men of letters, the Dominican literary critic and historian Pedro Henríquez Ureña (1884–1946).[2]

THE PROBLEM OF EXPRESSION presents itself in all the Latin-American arts. But in literature it is doubly complex. The musician could renounce the tonal language of Europe if he found in such rejection the guarantee of originality; the dweller in lands where the Indian survives — as in Peru and Bolivia — can utilize the archaic but enduring native system, which is different from the European, to begin with, in its pentatonic scale. And one who lives in countries where the creole spirit dominates is heir to materials that are precious though not strictly native — music brought from Europe or Africa but impregnated with the flavor of new lands and a new life — a flavor that insinuates itself into the rhythm and the melodic design.

In the plastic arts, too, it is possible to turn one's back on Europe, as in the Mexican system of Adolfo Best, constructed on the basis of the seven lineal elements of Aztec drawing, with a frank acceptance of its limitations. Or, if we consider such rejection excessive, there are at least suggestions of various kinds in the art work of the Indian, in that of colonial creole artists who made European technique their own and achieved such splendid mastery in architecture, in the popular art of our time, even in the stone and wood, the fibre and dye, that our native lands provide.

In any case, in music and in the plastic arts the parting of the ways is clear: either the European or the Indian way, or at any rate the creole way, still unclear and difficult. The Indian way

---

[1] Quoted from Arturo Torres-Ríoseco, *The Epic of Latin-American Literature*, New York, Oxford University Press, 1942, pp. 111–112. Reprinted by permission of Miss Muna Lee.

[2] Pedro Henríquez Ureña, *Siete ensayos en busca de nuestra expresión*, Buenos Aires, 1928, pp. 18–35. (Excerpt translated by the editor.)

may represent impoverishment and limitation, and for those whose cities do not know the tread of the ancient lords of the land it seems an exotic road; a typical Latin-American paradox. But, strange or familiar, distant or near, the tonal language and the plastic language of native stock are intelligible.

In literature the problem is complex, is double; the poet, the writer, expresses himself in a language received from Spain. The Catalan or the Gallego has only to write in his vernacular tongue, and he has the illusion of feeling himself different from the Spaniard. For us that illusion is a forbidden or inaccessible fruit. Return to the Indian languages? The educated person generally does not know them, and the difficult task of studying them and writing in them would finally lead to his being understood by a very few, and to the immediate reduction of his reading public. Verse and prose in the Indian language were composed after the Conquest and are still being composed today, because there yet exist enormous and widely diffused native populations that speak a hundred — if not more — native tongues; but that literature is rarely inspired by clear objectives of survival and opposition to the dominant language. Should we create our own languages, offspring and successors to Castilian? A hundred years ago — a source of grave fear to some, of insane hope for others — there existed the idea that we were all unknowingly embarked on an effort to create native tongues. That mist has been dispelled by the unifying pressure of constant relations between the Hispanic peoples. The effort, supposing it were possible, would have required centuries of digging moat after moat between the language of Castile and the emergent languages of America, would have meant resigning ourselves with Franciscan heroism to an abject, impoverished dialectal expression until there appeared the Dante that could give it wings and talons. Let us note, in passing, that the gaucho language of the Rio de la Plata, the principal substance of that dissipated mist, does not possess sufficient diversity to attain even the stature of a dialect like that of León or Aragón; its light special tint does not materially distinguish it from Castilian, and *Martín Fierro* and *Fausto* are no more offshoots from the linguistic trunk than are the *coplas* of Andalucía or Murcia.

We have not renounced writing in Spanish, and our problem of achieving an original and native expression begins there. Every language is a crystallization of ways of thought and feeling, and all that is written in it is bathed in the colors of that crystal. Our expression will require a double vigor to superimpose its tonality on the red-and-gold.[3]

THE FORMULAS OF AMERICANISM

Let us examine the principal solutions proposed and tested for the problem of our expression in literature. And do not charge me prematurely with being a naive optimist because I give provisional approval to all of them; my reason will become clear in the end.

In the first place — nature. Descriptive literature, I think, must for a long time be the voice of the New World. At present the idea does not find favor; it has been abused in its application; there are as many landscapes in our romantic poetry as in our Impressionist painting. The task of description, born of enthusiasm, degenerated into a mechanical habit. But it has educated our eyes; the conventional picture of the first colonial writers, in whose works the genuine aspect of the land appears only by way of a very rare exception, as in the Peruvian mountains of the Inca Garcilaso, was gradually left behind, and at last, with the aid of Alexander von Humboldt and Chateaubriand, we attained the direct vision of nature. It would be a labor of justice and delight to make a collection of the vividly drawn landscapes and miniatures of fauna and flora that appear in many forgotten works of the nineteenth century. We need only think back in order to understand — perhaps with surprise — how we have mastered, one after another, the pictorial elements of our continents and even the spiritual bouquet they exhale — the colossal mountains; the vast plateaus of thin air and tranquil light where every profile is sharply outlined; the warm lands of the tropics, with their tangled forests, their deafening sea and their intoxicating light; the broad pampa; the "inexorable and sullen" desert. Our interest in the landscape engenders preferences that we defend with vehement words; we have partisans of the plains and partisans of the mountain. And while the former, whose eyes are accustomed to no other bounds than the horizon, feel oppressed by the proximity of heights, like Miguel Cané in Venezuela and Colombia, the latter complain of an "excessively flat" landscape, like the character in *Xaimaca* by Güiraldes, or, wishing to love it, conquer the initial impression of monotony and desolation and tell

3 The Spanish national colors. B.K.

how, after journeying across the pampa for some time, one no longer sees it: one sees a new pampa that has taken form in the soul (Gabriela Mistral). Or turn to the spectacle of the torrid zone: for the native it is rich in light, heat, and color, but languid and soft; for him all dissolves into long contemplations, pleasurable discussions, slow dances:

> And in the ardent summer nights
> the mandolin and the lengthy song
> that joins its music to the murmur of the river . . .

But the man of temperate climes sees the tropics under an aspect of oppressive glare. That is how Mármol saw them in Brazil, in those celebrated verses, half verbiage, half revelation of reality; that is how Sarmiento saw them in that brief yet comprehensive note on Rio de Janeiro:

"The insects are carbuncles or rubies, the butterflies plumes of gold, the birds painted and adorned with tufts of feathers and fantastic decorations, the vegetation green emerald, the flowers perfumed and purple, the light of heaven is palpable, the air blue cobalt, the clouds gilded and touched with fire, red the earth, and the sands intermixed with diamonds and topazes."

To nature add the primitive American. Go to the Indian! Each generation has seen that program born and reborn under a multitude of forms, in all the arts. In literature our interpretation of the Indian has been irregular and capricious. We have added little to that strong vision of conquistadores like Hernán Cortés, Ercilla, and Cieza de León and of missionaries like Fray Bartolomé de las Casas. They succeeded in defining two exemplary types, which Europe received and incorporated in its repertory of human figures: the "clever and discreet Indian," educated in his own complex and exquisite civilizations, singularly well endowed for art and industry; and the "virtuous savage," who lacks mechanical skills but lives in order, justice, and goodness — the figure that was so useful to European thinkers in creating the image of the hypothetical man of the "state of nature" before the social contract. Throughout our hundred years of independence our romantic idleness has prevented us from devoting much attention to those magnificent empires whose literary interpretation would require previous archaeological studies; until recent years our lack of human sympathy has kept us from drawing near to the surviving Indians of today, save in such cases as that memorable one of the *Ranqueles* Indians; and, finally, apart from Mansilla's incomparable

and delicious book, the best works on the Indian have been written in countries like Santo Domingo and Uruguay where the pure-blooded native barely survives in some remote corner and has dissolved into a sentimental memory. "The spirit of men floats above the land in which they lived, and we breathe it in," said Martí.

After the Indian, the creole literary movement has intermittently existed in all of Spanish America, and has sought to depict the manifestations of popular life, urban and rural, with a natural preference for the countryside. Its limits are vague; in the Argentine pampa the creole stands in opposition to the Indian, his traditional enemy, while in Mexico, in Central America, throughout the Andean region and its Pacific watershed, there does not always exist a perceptible frontier between creole and Indian customs. Mexican literature reflects this mixture in the *romances* of Guillermo Prieto and the *Periquillo* of Lizardi, dawn of the novel in our America as well as the swan song of the Spanish picaresque novel. There is not a single country in which creole life has not inspired pictures of distinctive coloration. Argentine literature, above all others, has shown its ability — in literary language as well as in that of the countryside — to capture gaucho life with a vision as vast as the pampa. Facundo Quiroga, Martín Fierro, Santos Vega, are figures that will stand for all time on the ideal horizon of our peoples. And I do not believe in the reality of the quarrel of Fierro and Quiroga. Sarmiento, as a civilizer, driven to action, tormented by haste, chose the European and North American short cut as the way that his country should travel, instead of the creole road, as yet formless, long, slow, perhaps interminable or leading into a blind alley; but none felt better than he the proud impetus, the acrid originality of the barbarism that he sought to destroy. In such oppositions, in such decisions, the aquiline Sarmiento stands revealed; his inflexible hand chooses, but the broad spirit opens to all the winds. Who understood Spain better than he — that Spain whose evil heritage he would cast into the fire, that land which he visited "with the saintly object of taking testimony against it," but which sometimes moved him to storms of sympathy? Who recognized better than he the limitations of the United States, those United States whose constructive perseverance he exalted as an exemplary model?

There exists another Americanism, which shuns Indianism and picturesque *criollismo* and the halfway bridge of the colonial era, place of rendezvous for many before and after Ricardo Palma; its only precept is to stick to the New World in the matter of thematics, in poetry as in the novel and the drama, in criticism as in history. And it seems to me that with that formula, as with the others, we have achieved in felicitous moments the living expression that we seek. In felicitous moments, let us remember...

THE CULT OF EUROPE

Now let us turn our gaze to the admirers of Europe, to those who, dissatisfied with any Americanism that aspires to achieve a native flavor and discontented even with our nature, promise us spiritual health if we but maintain firm the bond that links us to European culture. They believe that our function is not to create, beginning anew, going to the roots of things, but to continue, proceed, develop, without breaking traditions or ties.

And we know the examples that they would invoke, the very examples that served us in tracing the origins of our nationalist rebellion: Rome, the Middle Ages, the Renaissance, the French hegemony of the eighteenth century.... Let us pause again before them. May it not be that the classic archetypes are preferable to the romantic liberty that we use and abuse? May not the only secret of perfection be in holding to the ideal line that Western culture has pursued since its remote origins? To the criollista who defends himself — perhaps for the only time in his life — with the example of Greece, it would be easy to show that the Greek miracle, even though more unique, more original than the creations of their successors, incorporated venerable heritages. Not even miracles spring from the void; Greece, mother of so many stupendous inventions, utilized the work of others, retouching and perfecting but, in her opinion, seeking to approach the canons, the paradigms that other nations, her predecessors or contemporaries, sought with confused intuition.

All isolation is illusory. The history of the spiritual organization of our America, from the time of our political emancipation, tells us that our guides were "Europeanizers" at the appropriate moment: Andrés Bello, who launched from London the declaration of our literary independence, was dubbed a "Europeanizer" by the Argentine exiles a quarter-century later, when Bello was organizing Chilean culture; and the most violent censors of Bello, on returning to their homeland, in their turn had to undertake the task of "Europeanization," only to be condemned by the devotees of pure criollismo.

Let us hasten to give the admirers of Europe their due, but nothing more, and at the same time let us set the mind of the criollista at rest. Not only would isolation be an illusion — the network of communications prevents it — but we have a right to all the benefits of Western culture. And in literature — confining ourselves to our problem — let us recall that Europe will be present, at least, in the historical trump card of language.

Let us frankly accept as inevitable the complex situation: our expression will have to include, side by side with that portion that is our own (child of our own life, sometimes of Indian heritage), another substantial portion — though it be only the impress — that we received from Spain. I go further: Not only do we write the language of Castile, but we belong to Romania, to that Romanic family that still constitutes a community, a unity of culture, descendant of the one that Rome organized under its sway; we belong — in the phrase frequently repeated by Sarmiento — to the Roman Empire. From the viewpoint of literature, ever since the Romance languages acquired a fulness of life, Romania has never lacked a center, a successor to the Eternal City; from the eleventh to the fourteenth century it was France, with initial oscillations between North and South; with the Renaissance it shifted to Italy; then, for a short time, it tended to situate in Spain; since the time of Louis XIV it has again been France. Romania has often extended its influence to foreign zones, and we know how Paris governed Europe and, in passing, the two Americas, in the eighteenth century; but from the beginning of the nineteenth century there appeared, in open and enduring opposition, rival zones: the Germanic zone, instigator of rebellion; the English, which embraces England with its empire, now in dissolution, and the United States; the Slav... Even politically we were born and raised in Romania. Antonio Caso has listed with forceful precision the three European events whose influence on our own peoples has been decisive: the Discovery, a Spanish event; the Renaissance, Italian; the Revolution, French. The Renaissance gave form — in Spain only partially — to the culture that would be transplanted to our world; the Revolution was the antecedent of our Wars of Independence. The three events were the work of Romanic peoples. We have no direct relationship with the Reformation or with English constitutional evolution, and even the independence and the Constitution of the United States owe their prestige among us to the use that French propaganda made of those events.

THE NATIVE ENERGY

Granted all this, which is all that the admirers of Europe can rightfully claim, let us set the mind of the loyal creole at rest by reminding him that the existence of Romania as a unity, as a collective unity of culture, and the existence of an orienting center only affect the forms of culture, while the original character of peoples comes from their spiritual depths, from their native energy.

Aside from fleeting moments, when there has been adopted with excessive rigor a narrow formula, through excessive faith in rhetorical doctrine, or during periods in which a national decay of all the energies has caused it to fall silent, each people has expressed itself with a fulness of individual character within the imperial community. And in Spain, within the central language, not to mention its rivals, the regions sometimes display their own unique profiles in literary expression. Thus, among the poets, there is the secular opposition between Castile and Andalucia, the contrast between Fray Luis de León and Fernando de Herrera, between Quevedo and Góngora, between Espronceda and Becquer.

The fact of a shared language does not oblige us to lose ourselves in the mass of a chorus whose direction is out of our hands; it only obliges us to refine our expressive note, to seek an unmistakable accent. All the perplexities of the past hundred years have arisen from the desire to achieve and maintain that accent: hence the formulas of Americanism, the promises made by each generation, only to have the next forget or reject them, and hence the pro-European reaction, daughter of an unacknowledged discouragement.

THE YEARNING FOR PERFECTION

We come to the end of our journey through the labyrinthine palace, through that wearisome maze of our literary aspirations, in search of our original and genuine expression. And in emerging, I believe that I return with the hidden thread that served to guide me.

My guiding thread has been the thought that there is only one secret of expression: to work for it profoundly, to seek to purify it, going to the roots of the things we wish to say, to polish, to refine, with a desire for perfection.

The desire for perfection is the only norm. If we are content to use the discovery made by another, whether he be a foreigner or a countryman, we shall never communicate our own intimate revelation; if we are content with the weak and confused enunciation of our intuitions, they will lose their virtue for the reader and he will find them commonplace. But when we have achieved the firm expression of an artistic intuition, it goes freighted not only with universal meaning but with the essence of the spirit that possessed it and the flavor of the land that nourished it.

Every formula of Americanism can be useful (that is why I gave them all a provisional approval); those that we have surveyed form an aggregate of useful approaches that render flexible and malleable the material of American origin. But any formula when repeated degenerates into a mechanism and loses its pristine effectiveness; it becomes a prescription and engenders rhetoric.

Every great work of art creates its own appropriate and distinctive means of expression; it utilizes previous experiences, but it refashions them, because it is not a sum total but a synthesis, an invention. The enemies we face in searching for the expression of our world are the lack of effort and the absence of discipline — offspring of indolence and the lack of culture or of a life of perpetual disturbance and change, full of preoccupations alien to the purity of artistic work. Our poets, our writers, were and still are in the majority of cases men driven to action, active in political affairs and even in war, and among them there have been the guides and enlighteners of nations.

THE FUTURE

Now, at least in the Rio de la Plata, there has begun to arise the literary profession. With it should come the discipline, the repose required for serious undertakings. And the lively and understanding collaboration of the public is also required; too long has it oscillated between lack of attention and excessive indulgence. The public must be demanding, but it should display interest in American works. For great poets, said Walt Whitman, you must have great audiences.

Only one fear gives me pause, and I dislike darkening with a pessimistic note the song of hope. Now that we appear to be sailing toward a sure port — shall we not arrive too late? Will the man of the future continue to interest himself in artistic and literary creation, in the perfect expression of the highest aspirations of the spirit? The Westerner of today is less interested in them than the man of yesterday, and much less so than one of remote times. A hundred, or fifty years ago, when the disappearance of art was foretold, the augury was shrugged off with easy gestures: "There will always be poetry." But since then — a new phenomenon in the history of the world, unsuspected and surprising — we have seen the rise of prosperous, active, and seemingly happy societies, of Western culture, that are not concerned with artistic creation — societies for which industry is enough, or that are content with art reduced to industrial processes: Australia, New Zealand, Canada. And may not the United States represent the intermediate stage? Even in Europe, although artistic and literary production is abundant, the interest of contemporary man is not what it once was. Up to now art has served two human aims: one, the expression of profound aspirations, of the yearning for eternity, of the utopian and ever renewed dream of perfect life: the other, the aim of play, the imaginative solace that rests the spirit. The art and literature of our time have almost forgotten their ancient transcendent function; there is only left to us the aim of play. And art reduced to diversion — even though it be intelligent diversion, pyrotechnics of wit — ends in producing tedium.

I do not want to end on a pessimistic note. If the light of the arts and letters does not go out, we have the right to consider our future secure. We shall exchange the modest box in which we now keep our few jewels for a treasure chest, and we shall not have to fear the alien stamp of the language in which we write, for by that time the spiritual axis of the Hispanic world shall have passed to these Atlantic shores.

3. IN DUBIOUS BATTLE

Seeking to achieve an original and authentically American expression in literature, Latin-American writers discovered the beauty and terror of their landscape. In La vorágine, by José Eustasio Rivera (1889–1928), a violent tale of rubber collectors in the Amazon jungle, the implacable wilderness joins the "rubber lords" in debasing men, in shattering their hopes and bodies. *The following excerpt from Rivera's book illustrates the power of his description of the world of the jungle.*[4]

"WE ARE LOST!" Simple and common words — yet uttered in the jungles they strike terror in the heart. To the mind of the person who hears them comes the vision of a man-consuming hell, a gaping mouth swallowing men whom hunger and disappointment place in the jaws.

Neither vows, nor warnings, nor the tears of the guide, who promised to find his way again, could serve to calm the men's panic.

"This old fellow is to blame! He lost his way because he wanted to go to the Vaupés!"

"Wretch! Bandit! You were deceiving us. You were taking us to sell us, God knows where!"

"Yes, you criminal! But God blasted your schemes!"

Seeing that his crazed companions might kill him, old man Silva started to run, but the treacherous lianas of a tree caught his legs and tripped him. There they tied him up, while Peggi urged that they rip him to shreds. Then it was that Don Clemente spoke the words that saved him.

"You want to kill me?" he said. "How can you do anything without me? I'm your only hope!"

The men stopped mechanically.

"Yes, yes, it's necessary that he live in order to save us."

"But without letting him loose, or he'll escape!"

And although they would not unfasten him, they knelt before him to beg him to save them.

"Don't desert us!"

"Let's return to the hut!"

"If you abandon us, we'll starve!"

Don Clemente's explanations gradually made them amenable to reason. What had happened, he told them, was nothing unusual in the lives of guides and hunters. It was foolish to give up hope at the very first mishap, especially as there were so many ways of getting out of the difficulty. Why had they scared him? Why had they thought of the possibility of getting lost? Had he not told them again and again to resist all such thoughts, so easily aroused by the accursed jungles that seem eager to bewilder and confuse men? Had he not warned them not to look at the trees, because they beckon to one; not to listen to murmurings because they whisper things; not to speak, because the heavy foli-

4 José Eustasio Rivera, *The Vortex*, translated by Earle James, New York, G. P. Putnam, 1927, pp. 242–249.

age echoes back the voice? Far from following these instructions, they jested with the forest, and its witchery fell upon them, spreading from one to another as if by contagion; and he, too, although walking on ahead, had started feeling the influence of the evil spirits; the jungle began to move, the trees to dance before his eyes, the undergrowth to resist his efforts to blaze a trail; the branches hid from his knife, or sometimes sought to wrest it from him with a mighty grip. Who was to blame?

And now why the devil start yelling? And what good would shooting do? Who but the jaguar would run to find them? Would they like a visit from him? If so, they could wait until nightfall. He'd come then!

This terrified them and they were silent. Yet had they wished it, they could not have made their voices heard more than a couple of yards — their outcries had parched their throats. They spoke hoarsely, with the guttural pantings of geese.

Long before the sun was pluming with crimson those upper reaches they could not see, the smudge fire had to be lighted, for darkness falls upon the forest early. They cut branches on which to rest, scattering them on the mud, there to await the anguish of the inky shadows. Oh, the torture of a long night of hunger, of thoughts that terrify; yawning, always yawning, knowing that the next day the yawning will be worse! Oh, the depressing effect of the incessant sobbing in the shadows, of comforting words that are in vain, for they only hide death! Lost, lost! Sleeplessness brought its train of phantoms — and the agony of the helpless who feel unseen eyes spying on them from the darkness. The sounds came — the nocturnal voices, the creeping steps — silences as appalling as gaps in eternity.

Don Clemente, his head in his hands, searched his memory for some clarifying hint. Only the sky could help him. Let it only tell him where the light of dawn came. There would be enough to plan another route.

Through a clear space in the lofty ceiling of foliage, a skylight in the forest, he saw a fragment of blue, fractured by the riblike branches of a withered bough. He recalled his map again. To see the sun, to see the sun! That was the key. If those tall cones of green, which every day saw it pass over them, could only speak! Why should the silent trees refuse to tell a man what to do that he might not die? And, thinking again on God, he began to pray to the

jungle, a prayer that begged forgiveness for the injury done the forests through bantering talk.

To climb one of those giants was next to impossible: the enormous trunks, the remote branches, dizziness lurking in the foliage to overtake the one who dared. If Lauro Coutinho, dozing nervously, were to try. . . .

Silva was about to call him when a noise, as of rats gnawing on fine wood, scratched across the stillness. It was the teeth of his companions, chewing on the hard seeds of the vegetable ivory tree.

Don Clemente felt a surge of compassion. He would console them, even though by lying.

"What is it?" they whispered, bringing their shadowed faces near.

And anxious hands felt the knots of the cords that bound him.

"We are saved!"

Dulled with joy, they repeated the words: "Saved! Saved!" They knelt down and pressed the mud with their knees, for suffering had left them contrite. Without even asking what it was that offered them salvation, they gave vent to a hoarse prayer of thanks. It was enough that another promised it.

Don Clemente received embraces, entreaties of forgiveness, apologies to amend the wrong they had done him. Some took all the credit for the miracle:

"The prayers of my little mother!"

"The Masses that I offered!"

"The blessed amulet I carry!"

And meanwhile, in the shadows, death must have laughed!

Dawn broke.

The hope that sustained them accentuated the tragedy on their faces. Emaciated, feverish, with bloodshot eyes and fluttering pulses, they waited for the sun to rise. Their actions inspired fear. They had forgotten how to smile, or if they thought of smiling, only a frightful grimace moved their lips.

Vainly they searched for a place where they might see the sun. Then softly it began to rain. No one said a word. They understood. The sun was not to be theirs.

They decided to return, traveling over the trails traversed the previous day, skirting a swamp where footprints left tiny pools into which waters gurgled — and wiped away the traces. Yet the guide stuck to the route. Silently they kept on until about nine in the morning, when they entered a heavy growth of coarse and matted bamboo. There they encountered flocks of rabbits and trogons, which, stupefied, ran between their legs seeking refuge. A few moments later and a sound of swirling rapids was heard reverberating through the wilderness.

"Good God! The tambochas!"

Flight was the only thought then. Turning, they stumbled back and then plunged into the swamp until the stagnant waters swept over their shoulders. Better the leeches than the ants.

From there they watched the first swarm pass by. Like ashes thrown from a distant conflagration, clouds of fugitive roaches and coleoptera swept down on the waters, while the edges of the marsh grew dense with arachnids and reptiles, forcing the men to splash the foul waters so that the insects would not come toward them. A continual tremor agitated the ground, as if the vegetation of the jungles were boiling. From under trunks and roots came the tumultuous invaders; over the trees spread a dark stain, sheathing the trunks like a flowering shell that crept upward implacably to torture the branches, plunder the nests, swarm the apertures and cracks. A blind weasel, a tardy lizard, a newborn rat — these were coveted prey for the avaricious army which, grating shrilly, stripped the bones of flesh like some fast-dissolving acid.

How long did the martyrdom of those men last? Buried to the chin in the slimy liquid, with terror-stricken eyes, they watched the swarms of the enemy passing, passing, and again passing. Nerve-racking hours, during which they sipped and sipped the bitter depths of slow torture. When at length the last swarm was sweeping into the distance, they tried to emerge; but their limbs were numb, too weak to wrench themselves from the hungry mud that gripped them.

Yet they must not die there. They must struggle out. The Indian Venancio managed to grasp some plants and began to pull. Then he caught hold of a clump of reeds. Several stray tambochas gnawed the flesh of his hands, eating deeply. Little by little he felt the clammy mold that gripped him loosening its hold. His legs, as they tore from the bottom, cracked loudly. *"Upa!* Once more, and don't faint! Courage! Courage!"

He's out. The waters gurgled and bubbled in the hole he left.

Panting, on his back, he heard his despairing comrades calling on him for help. "Let me rest! Let me rest!"

An hour later, by means of branches and lianas, he had managed to get them all out.

This was the last time they suffered together. Which way had they been going? They felt their heads in flames, their bodies stiff. Pedro Fajardo began to cough convulsively. Of a sudden he fell bathed in frothy blood that he vomited in an attack of hemoptysis.

But they could feel no pity for the dying man. Coutinho the elder advised them to lose no time. "Take his knife from his belt and leave him there. Why did he come if he was ill? He mustn't hamper us!" So saying, he forced his brother to climb a copaiba to seek the sun.

The unfortunate youth bound his ankles with strips of shirt. Vainly he tried to grip the tree-trunk. They raised him on their shoulders so that he might catch hold higher up. He continued his efforts, but the bark peeled off. He would slide down, to start anew. They held him up, propping him with long, forked branches and feeling their height tripled in their effort to help him. Finally he grasped the first branch. Stomach, arms, chest, and knees shed blood. "Do you see anything? Do you see anything?" they asked. And with his head he answered: "No!"

They no longer remembered to be silent in order not to provoke the jungle. An absurd violence filled them, and the fury of drowning people surged through them, the fury that knows neither friend nor relative, fighting off those who would clamber into a boat that can hold no more. With their hands they gesticulated heavenwards as they called to Lauro Coutinho.

"You see nothing? Climb higher — and look well."

Lauro, on a branch, clutching the trunk, panted without replying. At such a height he seemed a wounded monkey, trying to squirm into frantic hiding from the hunter. "Coward! You must climb higher! And those below, mad with rage, threatened him.

Suddenly, however, the youth started to descend. A roar of hate rose from the ground. Lauro, terrified, tried to explain. "More tambochas — coming — com . . . "

The last syllable died in his throat. The elder Coutinho, with a shot from his rifle, had pierced his chest. The youth fell like a plummet.

The fratricide stood still, his eyes on the crumpled, bleeding body.

"My God!" he broke out suddenly. "I've killed my brother — killed my brother!" Then, throwing away his gun, he fled. The others ran too, not knowing where. And they scattered never to meet again.

Many nights later Don Clemente heard them shouting, but he was afraid they would kill him. He, too, had lost all pity. The jungle possessed him. Then remorse set him weeping, although the need for saving his own life justified his act before his conscience. Eventually he went back to look for them. He found the skulls and a few femurs.

Without fire or gun, he wandered two months, reduced almost to imbecility, deprived of his senses, animalized by the jungle, despised even by death, chewing roots, husks, mushrooms like an herbivorous animal, with the sole difference that he had to watch what kind of fruit or berries the monkeys ate in order to avoid the poisonous ones.

But one morning he had a sudden revelation. He stopped before a cananguche palm, and to his mind came the tradition that tells how this species follows the sun, like a sunflower. Never had he given the matter any thought before. He spent anxious moments watching, and he thought he saw the lofty foliage slowly bending, with the rhythm of a head that took exactly twelve hours to move from the right shoulder over to the left. The secret voice filled his soul. Was it possible that this palm, planted in the wilderness like an index pointing to the blue, was showing him his route? True or false, he heard it speak. And he believed! That was all he needed — belief. And from the course the palm tree followed he plotted his own.

So it was that he reached the banks of the Tiquié. That river, narrow and curving, seemed more like a stagnant pond in the marshes than a stream. He began throwing leaves into the water to see if they moved. The Albuquerque brothers found him thus occupied and, almost dragging him, took him to the shelter.

"Who's that scarecrow you've found?" the rubber-gatherers asked.

"A fugitive who can only say: 'Coutinho! . . . . Peggi! . . . Souza Machado! . . . .'"

Then after working there a year, he escaped in a dugout to the Vaupés.

Now he's sitting here in my company, waiting for dawn to break before going down to the shacks of Guaracu. Perhaps he's thinking of Yaguanarí, of Yavaraté, of his lost companions. "Don't go to Yaguanarí!" he's always telling me. But I, remembering Alicia and my enemy, cry angrily:

"I'll go! I'll go! I'll go!"

4. The Corn and the Wheat

In 1926 (see page 442), the critic Pedro Henríquez Ureña complained of the "lack of human sympathy" that prevented Latin-American writers from going to the Indian for their material. Since that time Latin-American novelists have made full amends for past shortcomings in this respect. The Indianist novel today dominates the field in Bolivia, Peru, and Ecuador and enjoys a strong vogue in Mexico and Central America. Its main theme is the struggle — generally unsuccessful — of Indian groups against enslavement by native or foreign landlords and mine owners. The prize-winning book Ancho y ajeno es el mundo *of the Peruvian Ciro Alegría (1909–) represents, according to Professor Torres-Rioseco, the "culminating work of the modern* novela indianista." *The following excerpt from this work depicts the peaceful life of an Indian mountain community before its destruction by an ambitious white landlord who wishes to extend his properties.[5]*

The sun had become wheat, and the wheat, sheaves. It was the harvest. An easy, sweet harvest over the dark blanket of the earth. The sickles were taken down from the eaves where they hung and carried to the wheat field. As they cut they made a swishing noise, and the stiff stalks yielded and the ears swayed and trembled as they were carried to the threshing pile. The men disappeared from sight beneath their huge loads of sheaves, which looked as though they were moving by themselves. But talk and laughter went on under them. On the threshing floor the pile was growing higher, and, after they left their load the threshers took a swallow of chicha and returned where the others were chopping away at a wall that, instead of falling, kept retreating. Now all the wheat was on the threshing pile. A high, round, golden pile was the testimonial of faith of these peasants, who had bent over the earth all year with a gesture that man has forgotten to attribute to God.

The next day came the threshing. The grain was piled up at the entrance to the village. Many Indians climbed up on the pile and threw the first layer of wheat down on the hard clay floor with their wooden pitchforks. The mares that were grazing in the stubble were brought in, and in a circle around the threshing floor

[5] Ciro Alegría, *Broad and Alien Is the World*, translated by Harriet de Onís, New York, 1941, pp. 138–143. Copyright, 1941, by Rinehart & Company, Inc., and reprinted by permission of Rinehart & Company, Inc., Publishers.

stood all the villagers, men, women, children, holding on to a cord made of a number of lariats joined together. They made a living, multicolored fence. And the threshers, riding the best horses, drank the ration of chicha to warm them up and then leaped over the cord with their horses. The threshing had begun. The shouts, the galloping, the breaking up of the straw, and the beating out of the grain had begun. The harvest sun was there too. The sun solidified in the heap of grain, fell, and broke into fragments at the feet of those who were holding the cord. The chicha went from hand to hand in shiny gourds, for the refreshment of all. The riders shouted, the mares ran, the sun, the heart, the hills all took part in the threshing. The chicha, the colors, the shouting and the grain rejoiced the soul.

One of the threshers, the one with the clearest voice, gave a high, full shout, almost musical, "Uuuaaaay," and the others, "Uooy" . . . "Uaay" . . . "Uooy" . . . "Uaay" . . . "Uoooy," forming a chorus that rang through the hills. From time to time some of the riders came out and others went in to replace them with new energy and voices.

One of them, drunk with happiness and liquor, got off his horse and stood by, watching the threshing. One of his children, a little fellow, came over to ask him:

"Father, why do they shout like that, as though they were calling to one another, and answering?"

"That's our way of singing."

Yes, to those whom Nature has not blessed with a voice to sing huainos or with the gift to play instruments, once a year comes a chance to raise their voices in a hymn, a powerful, happy hymn. It was the hymn to the sun which had become ears of wheat and which now helped with the threshing. It was the hymn to the fruit which is the beginning and the end, the promise become grain, and the annunciation in the simple miracle of the seed. The hymn to the creative force of the land and the rain and the tireless arms and the faith of the sower, beneath the majestic aegis of the sun. The hymn to the dynamic force that strips away straw and chaff to leave, full and generous, the bounty of life. A hymn to the true food, the sacred food of man, that is like the blood in his veins.

The pile had disappeared and the last round had been made on the threshing floor. The mares were led out and the Indians with their pitchforks threw the straw into the center of the

ring, and the women, with large switch brooms swept even the last grain toward the center too. A low curving hill, on whose summit the twilight was melting away, announced that the task was finished. Already the cord had been dropped, the many-colored circle had broken up, the shouts had died away. And just as it seemed that the growing shadows of the night were about to throw a veil of sadness over everything, the pulsations of the harp and the humming of the rustic violins were heard, as were the melodies of the flutes and the reedy *antaras*. The snare drums rattled and the bass drums boomed deeply. People were eating and drinking. And later, in the darkness lighted by the stars and then by the gleam of the moon, the instruments played on and voices were raised in a dance. Men and women moved in joyous rhythm in the bodily dialogue of surrender and refusal which each couple carried on in the measures of the huaino.

The corn had been shelled and the wheat had been winnowed. The winnowing was long and slow, as was to be expected from the lazy wind that had to be called on for help.

"Wind, wind, wind . . ." pleaded the women with a sweet cry. The men called to it with a peculiar whistle, with many inflections at the start and ending up on a sharp, humming note like that of a bullet.

Every now and then the languid wind moved its big wings and the forks threw the grain toward the top of the fragile hill: the wind carried away the straw as the grain fell. When the heavier straw had been winnowed out, the pitchforks were changed for wooden shovels. The heap of grain grew higher as a rain of wheat fell on it from the air. The wind heaped up a pile of straw a little further off.

During the nights groups of villagers built bonfires of winnowed straw and roasted squashes in them. They talked gaily as they ate the sweet slices, and then they contentedly chewed their coca while somebody told a story. Once Amadeo Illas was asked to tell one and he told the story called *"The Rivals and the Judge."* On a certain occasion he had told it in town and a gentleman who heard it said it contained a great deal of wisdom. Amadeo never thought of it in this light, because he did not know what wisdom was, and he told it only because he liked it. He had heard it from his mother, who was now dead, and she had learned it from a famous storyteller known as the Story Man.

Amadeo Illas was a handsome lad, with a smooth face, who always wore dark-red ponchos with blue stripes, which were woven by his wife, who was young, too. He had already made a name for himself as a storyteller, and some of the villagers, carried away by their enthusiasm, no doubt, said he was better than the oldest storytellers of Rumi. At any rate, he had many listeners. Here is the story he told this time:

There was once a toad who was very proud of his voice and he spent the night singing: toc, toc, toc . . . And there was a katydid that was even prouder of her voice and she spent the whole night, and the whole day, too, singing: chirr, chirr, chirr.

One day they met and the toad said to the katydid:

"My voice is better than yours."

"Mine is better," the katydid answered.

They got into an argument which seemed as though it would never end. The toad said he sang all night. The katydid said she sang day and night. The toad said his voice carried further and the katydid said her voice could always be heard. They began to sing in turn: toc, toc, toc . . . chirr, chirr, chirr. Neither one could convince the other.

So the toad said:

"Not far from here on the shore of a lake, lives a heron. Let's ask her to be the judge."

And the katydid said:

"Let's."

They hopped along and hopped along till they came to the heron. She was gray and stood there on one leg, looking into the water.

"Heron, can you sing?" called out the katydid.

"Yes, I can," answered the heron, looking at them out of the corner of her eye.

"Let's hear you sing. We want to hear you so we can name you judge," said the toad.

The heron had her own plans, and answered:

"And who are you to ask me for proofs? My singing is very delicate, you contemptible screamers. If you want my opinion, you have it; if not, you can go on your way." And with a bored expression she stretched out her other leg.

"That's right," said the toad, "we have no reason to pass judgment on our judge."

"Heron, all we want you to do is to say which of us sings better," the katydid cried out.

"Then come over closer," the heron answered, "so I can hear you well."

The toad said to the katydid:

"Maybe it would be best for us not to get any closer and to let the whole thing go."

But the katydid was sure she would win and, carried away by vanity, she said:

"Oh, you know your voice isn't as good as mine and now you're afraid you're going to lose."

The toad became angry and said:

"All right, now you're going to hear some real singing." And he hopped away as fast as he could to the heron followed by the katydid. The heron turned around and said to the toad:

"Now sing."

The toad began to sing, paying no attention to anything, so sure was he of victory. In the meantime the heron ate up the katydid. When the toad had finished the heron said:

"Now you two can go on with your argument in my crop," and she ate him too. And the heron, satisfied with herself, drew up one leg, and went on looking calmly at the water.

The group returned to the village and only Fabian Caipo and his wife remained out by the pile of wheat to see that it was not trampled down. The wheat field had been opened up, too, and day and night the stock wandered freely about the fields and village. Men and animals were living on terms of complete intimacy.

One night Marguicha and Augusto discovered that it was very nice on the big straw pile and they delayed their return. The night hour was beautiful. The large full moon, slow and round, lighted up the calm slopes, the sleeping village, the high hills, the far-off, solitary, snow-covered heights. A bird sang in the top of an elder tree. Beside the straw stack, a mare and a horse stood with their necks crossed over each other's. The tender love of the night had surely united Fabian and his wife under their improvised yellow shelter. And Augusto, without saying a word, drew Marguicha close and she gave herself to him, joyously yielding up her beautiful young body drenched with the moonlight.

The crop was divided up among the villagers, according to their needs, and the remainder was to be kept for sale.

Somebody had spilled a little wheat in the square, and Rosendo Maqui began to shout:

"Gather that wheat up, gather it up right away. I would rather see money thrown away than God's grain, our food, man's blessed nourishment."

Thus, once more, the corn and the wheat were garnered from the earth. They were the life of the community. They were the history of Rumi. Rosendo Maqui considered different events the history of his people, because to him the earth was life itself and not its memories. This history seemed very full. But these events had been spread over fifty, a hundred, two hundred years or more — many of the things he knew only by hearsay — and the life of the community had taken on a character of peace and uniformity and had acquired its real meaning in the cultivation of the earth. Sowing, plowing, reaping were the true pivotal point of its existence. The wheat and the corn — "blessed nourishment" — had become symbols. Just as other men build their structures upon positions, honors, arts or finances, it was upon the earth and its products that the villagers of Rumi built their homes. And for them the earth and its products were, first of all, a creed of brotherly love.

5. FAREWELL TO THE GAUCHO

Creole life in all its manifestations, urban and rural, attracted the attention of Latin-American writers of the twentieth century. The gaucho theme, rapidly nearing exhaustion as prosaic hired hands replaced the picturesque wanderers of the plains in the cattle industry, was exploited once more with incomparable artistry and a nostalgic spirit by the Argentine novelist Ricardo Güiraldes (1886–1927). The following description of gaucho merrymaking is taken from his masterpiece, Don Segundo Sombra.[6]

IN THE PATH OF LIGHT thrusting from the door toward the night, the men stood thick as maggots in a cheese. Pedro stepped ahead of me and we went in; but my poor herder's clothes made me feel stiff, and we stayed near the door. The girls, wrapped in their modesty, were tempting as mellow fruit, brightly waiting for someone to pick them and enjoy them. I ran over the assortment; not one held me. All of a sudden I spied my girl. She wore a red dress with a sky blue bandanna round her neck; and it seemed to me that all her gay glamour was for me alone. An accordion and a couple of guitars struck up the polka. Nobody budged.

I had the illusion that these country folk were alive only in their hands. And they were heavy lumps in the laps of the women, dead weights hanging from the arms of the men: idle, they were senseless. Suddenly, all faces turned toward the door, like a field of wheat swayed by a new wind. The squire, a brawny fellow, with pepper and salt whiskers, greeted us with a mischievous laugh:

"Now, boys, why aren't you dancing and having the good time God wants you to have? Come along, Remigio, and you, Pancho, and you, Don Primitivo, sir, and the rest of you. Felisario, Sofanor, Ramón, Telmo . . . let's get our partners."

We two were shoved aside by the men named. But the squire's brisk voice had joined the rest together, as if they were going to a charge. And at that, it's no small deed for men, who live most of their days miles from all human contact except their families, suddenly to step out and take a strange woman by the waist! A troop had formed in the middle of the room and was milling around restlessly, like thirsty cattle at a water hole, before they could make up their minds to move on the chairs of the women. But once they'd done it, each man's self-importance was doubled by his partner. The leader, with his accordion, struck up a fast waltz.

"Everybody to the right, and no bumping!" shouted the master of ceremonies. And the couples, with their feet close and their chests drawn back in order not to touch, began to whirl around, defying dizziness and fatigue. The dance was on. After the waltz came a mazurka. Young men, old men, boys, danced solemnly, and no face betrayed the slightest pleasure. Their enjoyment was mingled with amaze: to be touching the body of a woman, to feel beneath the hand the archaic rigor of a corset or the soft, pliant flesh, to be joined in motion with a blushing girl, was nothing to laugh at. There were a few shallow ones, however, to give the voice that must rise from every human feeling.

I was getting nervous at Pedro's side, and feeling out of place as if in a church. Shyness and the need to dance with my red-dressed girl were battling in me. The accordion's motions stopped. The master of ceremonies clapped his hands:

"Now the chair polka!"

One of the onlookers lugged a chair awkwardly to the middle of the floor. The squire opened the dance with a girl in green who after two giddy whirls around the room was plunked back in her chair where she sat all puffed up as if she were sitting for her portrait.

"There's a parrot for my cage!" said Pedro. But like everybody else, I was waiting to see what would come next.

"Feliciano Gómez!"

A great country bumpkin tried to run away, but they caught him and shoved him into the

---

6 Ricardo Güiraldes, *Don Segundo Sombra*, translated by Harriet de Onís, New York, 1935, pp. 87–98. Copyright, 1935, by Rinehart & Company, Inc., and reprinted by permission of Rinehart & Company, Inc., Publishers.

open space where he stood like a lost sheep.

"Let him get a look at the decoy!" shouted Pedro.

The poor chap did what he could to play up to the fun but his face was full of the confusion of the simple man who suddenly finds himself conspicuous. At last he plucked up courage and took six long strides to the little girl in green. She gave him an insolent eye from head to foot and then turned her chair round, her back to him. The man turned helplessly to the squire:

"You shouldn't try to hitch an old nag like me, sir, to a neat little mare like that."

"Don Fabián Luna!"

An old man with a long beard and arched legs came boldly forward, and got the same treatment.

"One's too ugly," he said, "and one's too old." And let out a guffaw that would have scared the ducks off a lagoon.

The squire pretended he was discouraged.

"What you want," Don Fabián advised him, "is a smarter younger chap."

"That's it. You pick him."

"Mebbe that young herder . . ."

That was all I could hear, but it made me feel like a pony with a tight hobble. I was against the wall, too far from the door: there was no chance of slipping out. Everyone was looking. And that brought me back to the old days when I had been the town kid and knew my crowd. So I stepped squarely over to the girl, pushed back my hat, folded my arms, and waited. The girl tried to outstare me, as she had done the others.

"The longer you look at me," said I, "the surer you are to buy me."

The next moment we were whirling our two regulation turns around the room, within the circle of stares.

"I wonder what the boys from the North like," said the girl as if talking to herself, when I had set her back in her chair.

"We tilt our hats to the right," I hinted.

She took three steps to the right, and then stopped, uncertain.

"We get off our ponies on the side of the lasso."

But my hints were not sharp enough; so I recited this verse:

"My girl is white as the cloud above
But she blushes red when I tell her my love."

This time she understood, and I got my reward for my nerve later when I danced the little brunette out of the room — though I doubt if we were in step.

At midnight they brought in trays of food for the womenfolk. Wines and liquors were served: cakes, pies, cookies. And the dames who were really hungry went out to the tent for roast meat. The men made a crowd around the booths where Pedro and I had looked longingly and vainly at the bottles earlier in the evening, and drank their gin, anisette, peach and cherry brandies. From that time on, a current of life, ever more highly charged, flowed between the ballroom and the tent. The accordion player was replaced by a much livelier one: polkas, mazurkas, with cadenzas and arpeggios and trills, leapt from his fingers. Jokes grew loud; girls laughed heartily, their careful dignity forgotten.

I grabbed off four dances with my girl in red and to the lilt of the guitar poured out flowery nothings which she sipped with the proper blushes. Betweentimes, I went back to Pedro Barrales whose delicious comments on the dance I could not do without.

"You're a booby," I said. "Why don't you dance? You're as glum as a shoat that's left the teat."

"You think I'm crazy like you to go jumping all over the floor?"

"Crazy?"

"So crazy the water's boiling in your head."

I made believe I was hurt, and he took me affectionately by the arm.

"Never mind, buddy. You're like the canebrake at Cruz: got your good side and your bad."

"Then here goes for the good!" And I went back to my fandango.

The excitement kept on rising and we had to dance faster and faster. Then the leader again clapped his hand:

"Now then, folks, let's have a gato sung like it should be danced by them that know their steps!"

The accordion player made room for the guitarist who was going to sing. Two couples took their place near the musicians. The women kept their eyes on the ground and the men turned up the hat brims from their faces. The guitars began to strum. Flexible wrists swayed and balanced above the strings; sharp twangs gave the accent, cutting the rhythmic murmur of the strum like a knife. The intermittent lash of the measure, like a drum roll, began to irradiate daring in the air. The dancers stood, until the vibrant fires of the music became the very soul of their long-fibered muscles, of their lithe, slow backs, of their eager shoulders.

Gradually, the room was drenched in the song. The white walls shutting in the tumult were steeped in the song.

The door cut four rigid lines into a night made of infinitude and stars above fields that cared only to sleep. The candles trembled like old grandmothers. The floor tiles rang with the feet of the dancers. Everything had succumbed to the proud male strum of the music!

The singer bespoke his tenderness in tense tones:

"All I need is a ladder of love
All I need is a ladder of love
To reach the heaven of your throat, my life."

The two women and the two men began to dance. The men moved agile and insistent, like amorous cocks flapping their wings. The women kept inside the prescribed circle and sent discreet glances over their shoulders. The four made a turn; and the singer continued:

"Fly, unhappy one, fly, I'm going to sea
In a little boat, my life, in a little boat."

The women picked up their skirts with careful fingers and opened them fanwise, as to receive a gift or defend something. Shadows flickered on the walls, touched the roof, and fell like rags to be trod on by gallant steps. Haste suddenly roused the two male bodies. Their boots rustled and shuffled a prelude; heels and soles clicked a multiplying rhythm that caught the guitars' accent to mark it and make it hurry. The moving folds of the chiripás sounded like faint waters. But the dance steps grew vigorous as a broncho's leaps, complementing in resonant counterpoint the melodious strings.

Turn and tapping were repeated. A guitar strummed four measures alone. Then the dance fell back into long tuneful measures. But the heels and spurs rose again, grew agitated. The skirts spread more sumptuously than ever, the percale gleamed like little fields of clover blooming in rustic pomp.

The dance died on a hard, emphatic note. Several of the women pursed their lips in disdain at these country dances, trying to ignore them. But a wild gladness mastered us all, for we felt that here was the pantomime of our true loves and delights.

I took part in one dance with Don Segundo and my girl.

It was a gato with words. When silence had made a ring around us, I spoke out my verses sharply:

"To come to this dance a star was my guide,
For I knew that here I should find my bride."

We gave a turn to the right and tapped out a figure. I waited quietly for the answer, that came without delay:

"I know naught of this love you're talking about;
But if you're a good teacher, I'll soon find out."

Next was Don Segundo's turn, and he advanced menacingly to his partner:

"One, two, three, four,
If you don't love me, everything's o'er."

Doña Encarnación, his voluminous partner, made her turn and with a great indifferent shrug of her shoulders replied:

"One, two, three,
A lot it matters to me!"

The verse play went on, alternating jest and gallantry.

We danced a triunfo and a *prado*: my little brown one and I got so warmed up that we sent signals to each other which we thought were hidden by the rhymes from the crowd.

One of the girls sang. A man had to improvise an answer in rhymed couplets, for that is the custom. But who would dare pace the silent room from one end to another, declaiming original, versed jokes as he went? Don Segundo stood at once in the middle of the ring.

We were all hushed with excitement. My godfather took off his hat and passed his forearm over his brow, a sign of hard mental work. At last he seemed to find his inspiration. He gave a circular glance round the room, and his strong voice spoke:

"I'm an old ram from the San Blas pack . . ."

He turned slowly on his heels:

"You've all seen me from the front . . ."

He moved, slow and sly, toward the door; and as he disappeared, in a bored tone:

"Now have a look at my back."

My brown girl was the liveliest little piece at the party; and as the coming dawn hinted tender release I, too, lost myself in her sparkling eyes and in the fleshly laughter of her mouth made for amorous answers. My tricks and her consent to them had warmed me up and I tried to get her alone by inviting her to have a feed in the tent. It took some maneuvering and a lot of energy; but at last I got her out of sight behind the improvised canvas. I took her hand and at once tried to kiss her. We struggled a moment and she repulsed me with her anger. I did not know how to soothe her, so I took her back to the ballroom. Three times I asked her for a dance and she turned me down each time with a trivial excuse.

By now I was mad, and I remembered the girl in green. It looked like quick sweet work with her, and I began calling myself a fool for all the time I had wasted on the other. Tenderly, we concluded a polka and I squeezed her hand. But I had sure got in wrong that night! For the little one squared off in front of me, and asked scornfully:

"So you think I'm a broom to sweep up other people's leavings?"

That was good-by to my fun for the night. The crowd rubbing elbows with me got on my nerves. I was sore, as if a horse had rolled on me at a round-up.

I fell back on Pedro.

"Look!" He pointed at a couple of gringos who were bobbing along in the dance. "Aren't they the grand gauchos, the way they are pulling out nails with their heels?"

Then he saw my glumness and turned his jokes on me:

"Didn't I tell you no good comes of hopping like a monkey on a stick? Did they do you dirt, buddy? Poor kid! You look like someone's taken away your bottle."

I fled into the breaking day to spread my saddle blanket and get a few hours' sleep.

XXXV

The Two Americas

A FEELING OF GREAT ADMIRATION dominated the attitude of Latin-American leaders toward the United States from the era of independence to the closing years of the nineteeth century. That feeling, explains the Mexican philosopher Leopoldo Zea, "derived from the negative attitude of the Latin American toward his own historical and cultural heritage." But in the case of some, notably among the Mexicans, the sentiment of admiration was tempered by resentment and misgivings over past and prospective territorial losses to the young colossus of the North. And others, like the Chilean Francisco Bilbao, already questioned the North American scale of values, and opposed Latin love of beauty and the spiritual values to alleged Yankee materialism and egotism.

After 1890 the increasingly aggressive foreign policy of the United States toward some of its southern neighbors rapidly depleted the Latin-American reservoir of good will toward the Republic of the North. The "Yankeemania" of Sarmiento turned into the "Yankeephobia" of Manuel Ugarte, Eduardo Prado, and Rufino Blanco Fombona. The transition in attitude was strikingly revealed in the writings of José Martí, epic chronicler of the United States from 1880 to 1895, whose reportage, long favorable to the United States, grew increasingly hostile toward the end of his journalistic career.

In the 1920's, impressed by the undesirable economic and political consequences of Latin-American ill will, Republican Administrations began a gradual liquidation of the old-style imperialism. But the flowering of the Good Neighbor Policy came under the second Roosevelt. Between 1933 and 1945 the old one-sided treaties were abrogated, the right of intervention was completely abandoned, and economic and cultural relations were greatly expanded. The Good Neighbor Policy proved its value during the critical years of World War II.

After 1945 a certain deterioration took place in inter-American relations. Despite formal pledges of mutual loyalty made by governments at conferences and in treaties, many observers agreed that the rising wave of economic nationalism and social unrest in Latin America was creating serious differences between the two Americas that were not always reflected on the official level.

1. THE UNITED STATES AS MODEL

Latin-American leaders in the nineteenth century, seeking to orient their countries in new and progressive directions, regarded the United States and England as their models. None expressed such passionate attachment for the United States and its institutions as did the Argentine Sarmiento, who visited this country in 1847 and again (as Argentine minister) in 1865–1868. The following selection is from his Travels in Europe, Africa, and America.[1]

EUROPEANS and even South Americans find fault with the Yankees for many defects of character. For my part, I respect these very defects, which I attribute to the whole human race, to our times, to hereditary preoccupations, and to the imperfection of our minds. A people composed of every nationality on earth, as free as the air, and with no tutors, armies, or bastilles, is the product of all their human predecessors, European and Christian. Their defects, therefore, must be those of the human race at any given period of its development. But as a nation, the United States is the final result of human logic. They have no kings, nobles, privileged classes, men born to command, or human machines born to obey. Is not this result consonant with the ideas of justice and equality which Christianity accepts in theory? Well-being is more widely distributed among them than among any other people. Their population is increasing at an unparalleled rate. Production is making astounding progress. Do freedom of action and lack of government enter into this, as Europeans assert? They say that this prosperity is all due to the case of taking up new land. But why, in South America, where it is even easier to take up new land, are neither population nor wealth on the increase, and cities and even capitals so static that not a hundred new houses have been built in them during the past ten years? No census has yet been taken on the mental capacity of the people of any nation. Population is counted by noses, and, from such figures, the strength and position of a nation are computed. Perhaps for war — looking at man as an engine of destruction — such statistical data may be significant, but one peculiarity of the American invalidates even this calculation. One Yankee is worth many of other nationalities for killing men, and therefore the destructive capacity of the United States might be estimated at two hundred mil-

lion people. The rifle is the national weapon, target shooting is the sport of children in the forest states, and the practice of knocking squirrels out of trees by shooting their feet off, in order not to injure the pelt, produces an astonishing skill which is universally acquired.

United States statistics show that the number of adult males corresponds to a population of twenty million inhabitants — all educated, able to read and write, and enjoying political rights, with exceptions which do not vitiate the essential correctness of the deduction. The American male is a man with a home or with the certainty of owning one, beyond the reach of hunger and despair, able to hope for any future that his imagination is capable of conjuring up, and endowed with political feelings and needs. In short, he is a man who is his own master, and possessed of a mind elevated by education and a sense of his own dignity. . . .

Railroads, as an instrument of wealth and civilization, are common both to Europe and to the United States, and since in both regions they date only from yesterday, the spirit that prevails in the two societies can be studied from them. In France, the work of leveling the roadbed, and every operation connected with railroading, is carefully examined by engineers before the trains are permitted to move. Wooden fences guard both sides of the right of way; double tracks of cast-iron rails facilitate traffic in either direction; and if a local road crosses the track, strong gates guard the crossing, which is carefully closed a quarter of an hour before the train is due, in order to avoid accidents. At intervals along the entire length of the road, guards are stationed to keep the tracks clear and to give warning with different colored flags of any dangers or obstructions. The train does not leave the platform until four minutes after an army of guards has ascertained that every traveler is in his seat, all doors are closed, the road is free, and no one is within a yard of where the train will pass. Everything has been foreseen, calculated, and checked so that the passengers may sleep soundly in their hermetically sealed jail.

Let us now examine what happens in the United States. The railroad crosses miles of primeval forest with no human habitation. As the company has little capital, the rails are wooden, with iron plates on top of them, which frequently work loose. Consequently, the engineer's eye is ever on the alert to avert a disaster. A single track suffices for traffic in both directions, as sidings are constructed at intervals, on which the

[1] Allison Williams Bunkley, ed., *A Sarmiento Anthology,* Princeton, N.J., Princeton University Press, 1948, pp. 220–226.

up train halts to let the down train pass on the main track. There is not a soul to give warning of such accidents as may occur. The tracks run through villages, and children stand at their front doors or in the middle of the roadbed itself, to wait for the train to pass — a favorite diversion. The railroad is not only a thoroughfare but also a local street and the passengers can see the people moving aside enough to let it pass before immediately continuing on their way. Instead of gates across the country crossings, there is simply a sign saying, "Listen for the bell before crossing," a warning to the teamster that he will be cut in two if he is imprudent enough to cross the track at the moment the train is passing. The train starts slowly from its platform, and when it is already in motion and has gathered speed passengers jump aboard, fruit and newspaper vendors hop off or walk back and forth, passing from one coach to another, for amusement or the feeling of their own freedom, even after the train is traveling fast. Since cows like to rest on the tracks, American locomotives carry a cowcatcher, whose charitable purpose it is to push imprudent animals to one side in order to prevent their being run over, and it is not unusual for a boy, asleep on the tracks, to be thrown four yards to one side by the cowcatcher, thereby saving his life even though a limb may have been broken or dislocated.

The physical and moral results of the two systems are only too perceptible. . . . The European is a minor, under the protection of the state. . . . The Yankee stands on his own two feet, and if he wishes to commit suicide no one will say him nay. If he runs after a train and dares to jump and catch hold of a bar to pull himself out of the way of the wheels, he is at liberty to do so. If a newsboy, in his eagerness to sell one more paper, has allowed the train to pick up speed before he jumps off, everybody will applaud his skill as he lands on his feet and saunters away. This is the way that nations' characters are formed and that liberty is used. There may be a few more victims of accidents, but on the other hand there are free men, not disciplined prisoners whose whole life is regulated. The word "passport" is unknown in the United States and the Yankee who comes across one of the European documents on which every movement of the traveler is inscribed, displays it to his compatriots with every indication of horror and loathing. The child who wishes to take a train, steamship, or canal boat, or the unmarried girl who goes on a six-hundred-mile visit, will find nobody to question why they are making the trip, or whose permission they have obtained before leaving home. They are simply availing themselves of their freedom and right to move about. That is why the Yankee child of ten astounds the European by his assurance, prudence, and knowledge of life. . . .

The Yankee ship is the best, cheapest, and largest in the world. If, on a stormy day, you should spy a ship running swiftly before the storm, its sails, topgallants, royals, and lower studs bellied out by the wind, the French, Spanish, or English captain of your ship who has reefed in even his mainsail, will instantly tell you its nationality. He will inform you, grating his teeth angrily, that it is a Yankee clipper. He recognizes it by its size and daring and even more by the way that it fairly grazes his own vessel without hoisting its flag to salute him.

In European ports and docks your eyes will be greeted by a special section where are moored colossal clippers that seem to belong to another world and to other men. They are Yankee ships that began to increase in size, at first in order to carry more bales of cotton, and have ended by becoming a special type of naval construction. Fifteen of the Hudson River steamboats, placed stem to stern, would make a wooden street a mile long. If, on a stormy day, you see a ship insisting on standing out to sea from Le Havre to Liverpool, it is sure to be a Yankee vessel whose departure had been posted for that day. The honor of its pennant and the glory of the stars and stripes would preclude it from postponing its departure until the wind abated, as ships of any other nationality would do. What are the ships that hunt the whale in the polar seas? Almost invariably they are American, and within the solitary hull of those squatters of the seas you will find a small crew that drinks nothing alcoholic, because every one of its members belongs to the Temperance Society. They are men inured to hardship, who snatch a tidy fortune from the jaws of death to set themselves up upon their return to the United States by purchase of a piece of land. This they clear, build a house on it, and around the cast-iron stove tell their sea adventures to their children. Last year, Queen Victoria was aboard her sumptuous yacht in Falmouth Bay accompanied by Prince Albert. Every ship was fully dressed in honor of the royal visitors. At the masthead atop the mainmast of an American frigate, a Yankee sailor was to be seen standing, swaying with the ship as it rolled at anchor, and holding his hat aloft in one hand as a salute. This was the symbolical expression of the Yankee navy. The queen turned queasy at the sight of him. National pride made one of the English sailors wish to imitate him, but the queen forbade it with every indication of horror. . . .

I lay especial emphasis upon this matter of the United States marine, because the nation which has the swiftest ships — those of cheapest construction and therefore of lowest freight rates — is king of the universe. . . . God has at last permitted the concentration in a single nation of enough virgin territory to permit society to expand indefinitely without fear of poverty. He has given it iron to supplement human strength, coal to turn its machines, forests to provide material for naval construction, popular education to develop the productive capacity of every one of its citizens, religious freedom to attract hundreds of thousands of foreigners to its shores, and political liberty which views despotism and special privilege with abhorrence. It is the republic, in short — strong and ascendant like a new star in the firmament. All of these factors are interdependent: freedom and abundant land; iron and industrial genius; democracy and the superiority of American ships. Try as you will to disjoin them in theory, assert that liberty and popular education have nothing to do with this unexampled prosperity which is leading inexorably to undisputed supremacy, the fact will still remain that European monarchies are an amalgam of decrepitude, revolution, poverty, ignorance, barbarism, and the degradation of the majority. Spit at heaven if you like and extol the advantages of monarchy. Its soil will still turn barren under your feet, and the republic will export its grain to feed you. The ignorance of the populace serves to prop up your thrones, and the crown that ornaments your temples shines like a flower growing out of a ruin. Half a million soldiers are required to keep in equilibrium the jealousy and envy of one sovereign for another, while the republic, placed in a fair land by Providence, like a beehive, saves immense sums of money which it turns into steppingstones to prosperity, yielding interest in increments of power and strength. Your science and vigils serve merely to increase that republic's splendor. *Sic vos non vobis*, you may invent telegraphy to bind your communications closer; *sic vos non vobis*. You may manufacture rails, but they will carry American products and commerce. Franklin had the temerity to appear at the most ostentatious court in the world, dressed in coarse clothes and hobnailed laborer's shoes. Someday

you will have to hide your scepters, crowns, and gilded baubles ere you may present yourself before the republic, for fear it may show you the door, like comedians or buffoons at carnival time.

2. THE TWO AMERICAS

The Chilean writer Francisco Bilbao, though not unmindful of the achievements of American democracy, called attention to certain defects in the American character and sounded the alarm against the expansionist designs of the United States against Latin America. It should be noted that he wrote the following lines at a time (1856) of aggressive North American diplomacy and filibustering expeditions designed to secure Cuba, Central America, and portions of Mexico for the United States.[2]

TODAY WE BEHOLD empires reviving the ancient idea of world domination. The Russian Empire and the United States, two powers situated at the geographical as well as political extremes, aspire, the one to extend Russian slavery under the mask of Pan-Slavism, the other to secure the sway of Yankee individualism. Russia is very far away, the United States is near. Russia sheathes its claws, trusting in its crafty snares; but the United States daily extends *its* claws in the hunting expedition that it has begun against the South. Already we see fragments of America falling into the jaws of the Saxon boa that hypnotizes its foes as it unfolds its tortuous coils. First it was Texas, then it was Northern Mexico and the Pacific that hailed a new master.

Today the skirmishers of the North are awakening the Isthmus with their shots,[3] and we see Panama, that future Constantinople of America, doubtfully suspended over the abyss and asking itself: Shall I belong to the South or to the North?

There is the danger. Whoever fails to see it, renounces the future. Is there so little self-awareness among us, so little confidence in the intelligence of the Latin-American race, that we must wait for an alien will and an alien intellect to organize us and decide our fate? Are we so poorly endowed with the gifts of personality

2 Francisco Bilbao, *América en peligro*, Santiago de Chile, 1941, pp. 144–154. (Excerpt translated by the editor.)
3 The reference is to the filibustering expedition of the American adventurer William Walker, who established a short-lived dictatorship in Nicaragua. He was executed by the Hondurans in 1860. B.K.

that we must surrender our own initiative and believe only in the foreign, hostile, and even overbearing initiative of individualism?

I do not believe it, but the hour for action has arrived.

This is the historic moment of South American unity; the second campaign, that will add the association of our peoples to the winning of independence, has begun. Its motive is the danger to our independence and the threat of the disappearance of the initiative of our race. . . .

The United States of South America has sighted the smoke of the campfires of the United States. Already we hear the tread of the young colossus that with its diplomacy, with that swarm of adventurers that it casts about like seed, with its growing power and influence that hypnotize its neighbors, with its intrigues among our peoples, with its treaties, mediations, and protectorates, with its industry, its merchant marine, its enterprises — quick to note our weaknesses and our weariness, quick to take advantage of the divisions among our republics, ever more impetuous and audacious, having the same faith in its imperial destiny as did Rome, infatuated with its unbroken string of successes — that youthful colossus advances like a rising tide that rears up its waters to fall like a cataract upon the South.

The name of the United States — our contemporary, but one that has left us so far behind — already resounds throughout the world. The sons of Penn and Washington opened a new historical epoch when, assembled in Congress, they proclaimed the greatest and most beautiful of all existing Constitutions, even before the French Revolution.

Then they caused rejoicing on the part of sorrowing humanity, which from its torture-bed hailed the Atlantic Republic as an augury of Europe's regeneration. Free thought, self-government, moral freedom, and land open to the immigrant, were the causes of its growth and its glory. It was the refuge of those who sought an end to their misery, of all who fled the theocratic and feudal slavery of Europe; it provided a field for utopias, for all experiments; in short, it was a temple for all who sought free lands for free souls.

That was the heroic moment of its annals. All grew: wealth, population, power, and liberty. They leveled the forests, peopled the deserts, sailed all the seas. Scorning tradition and systems, and creating a spirit that devours space and time, they formed a nation, a particular genius. And turning upon themselves and beholding themselves so great, they fell into the temptation of the Titans. They believed they were the arbiters of the earth, and even rivals of Olympus.

Personality infatuated with itself degenerates into individualism; exaggeration of personality turns into egotism; and from there to injustice and callousness is but a step. They would concentrate the universe in themselves. The Yankee replaces the American; Roman patriotism, philosophy; industry, charity; wealth, morality; and self-interest, justice. They have not abolished slavery in their States; they have not preserved the heroic Indian races — nor have they made themselves champions of the universal cause, but only of the American interest, of Saxon individualism. They hurl themselves upon the South, and the nation that should have been our star, our model, our strength, daily becomes a greater threat to the independence of South America.

Here is a providential fact that spurs us to enter upon the stage of history, and this we cannot do if we are not united.

What shall be our arms, our tactics? We who seek unity shall incorporate in our education the vital elements contained in the civilization of the North. Let us strive to form as complete a human entity as possible, developing all the qualities that constitute the beauty or strength of other peoples. They are different but not antagonistic manifestations of human activity. To unite them, associate them, to give them unity, is our obligation.

Science and industry, art and politics, philosophy and Nature should march in a common front, just as all the elements that compose sovereignty should live inseparable and indivisible in a people: labor, association, obedience, and sovereignty.

For that reason let us not scorn, let us rather incorporate in ourselves all that shines in the genius and life of North America. Let us not despise under the pretext of individualism all that forms the strength of the race.

When the Romans wished to form a navy, they took a Carthaginian ship for their model; they replaced their sword with that of Spain; they made their own the science, the philosophy, and the art of the Greeks without surrendering their own genius; they raised a temple to the gods of the very peoples that they fought, as if in order to assimilate the genius of all races and the power of all ideas. In the same way should we grasp the Yankee axe in order to clear the earth; we should curb our anarchy with liberty, the only Hercules capable of overcoming that hydra; we should destroy despotism with liberty, the only Brutus capable of extinguishing all tyrants. And the North possesses all this because it is free, because it governs itself, because above all sects and religions there is a single common and dominant principle: freedom of thought and the government of the people.

Among them there is no State religion because the religion of the State is the State: the sovereignty of the people. That spirit, those elements, we should add to our own characteristics. . . .

Let us not fear movement. Let us breathe in the powerful aura that emanates from the resplendent star-spangled banner, let us feel our blood seething with the germination of new enterprises; let us hear our silent regions resounding with the din of rising cities, of immigrants attracted by liberty; and in the squares and woods, the schools and congresses, let the cry be repeated with all the force of hope: forward, forward! . . .

We know the glories and even the superiority of the North, but we too have something to place in the scales of justice.

We can say to the North:

Everything has favored you. You are the sons of the first men of modern Europe, of those heroes of the Reformation who crossed the great waters, bringing the Old Testament, to raise an altar to the God of conscience. A knightly though savage race received you with primitive hospitality. A fruitful nature and an infinite expanse of virgin lands multiplied your efforts. You were born and reared in the wooded fields, fired with the enthusiasm of a new faith, enlightened through the press, through freedom of speech — and your efforts were rewarded with abundance.

You received a matchless education in the theory and practice of sovereignty, far from kings, being yourselves all kings, far from the sickly castes of Europe, from their habits of servility and their domesticated manners; you grew with all the vigor of a new creation. You were free; you wished to be independent and you made yourselves independent. Albion fell back before the Plutarchian heroes that made of you the greatest federation in history. It was not so with us.

Isolated from the universe, without other light than that which the cemetery of the Escorial

permitted, without other human voice than that of blind obedience, pronounced by the militia of the Pope, the friars, and by the militia of the kings, the soldiers — thus were we educated. We grew in silence, and regarded each other with terror.

A gravestone was placed over the continent, and upon it they laid the weight of eighteen centuries of slavery and decadence. And withal there was word, there was light in those gloomy depths; and we shattered the sepulchral stone, and cast those centuries into the grave that had been destined for us. Such was the power of the impulse, the inspiration or revelation, of the Republic.

With such antecedents, this result merits being placed in the balance with North America.

We immediately had to organize everything. We have had to consecrate the sovereignty of the people in the bosom of theocratic education.

We have had to struggle against the sterile sword that, infatuated with its triumphs, believed that its tangent of steel gave it a claim to the title of legislator. We have had to awaken the masses, at the risk of being suffocated by their blind weight, in order to initiate them in a new life by giving them the sovereignty of the suffrage.

We who are poor have abolished slavery in all the republics of the South, while you who are rich and fortunate have not done so; we have incorporated and are incorporating the primitive races, which in Peru form almost the totality of the nation, because we regard them as our flesh and blood, while you hypocritically exterminate them.

In our lands there survives something of that ancient and divine hospitality, in our breasts there is room for the love of mankind. We have not lost the tradition of the spiritual destiny of man. We believe and love all that unites; we prefer the social to the individual, beauty to wealth, justice to power, art to commerce, poetry to industry, philosophy to textbooks, pure spirit to calculation, duty to self-interest. We side with those who see in art, in enthusiasm for the beautiful (independently of its results), and in philosophy, the splendors of the highest good. We do not see in the earth, or in the pleasures of the earth, the definitive end of man; the Negro, the Indian, the disinherited, the unhappy, the weak, find among us the respect that is due to the name and dignity of man!

That is what the republicans of South America dare to place in the balance opposite the pride, the wealth, and the power of North America.

But our superiority is latent. We must develop it. That of the North is present and is growing.

Just as Cato the Censor ended all his speeches with the destructive phrase *Delenda est Carthago,* thus at the end of all argument only one creative idea presents itself: the necessity of an American Union.

What nation shone more brilliantly in history than Greece? Possessing in the highest degree all the elements and qualities that man can display in the plenitude of his powers, united for the full development of personality, she succumbed through internal division, and division quenched the light that her heroism had maintained. We are barely born, and in our cradle serpents assault us. Like Hercules, we must strangle them. Those serpents are anarchy, division, national pettiness. The battle summons us to perform the twelve symbolic labors of the hero. In the forest of our prejudices monsters lurk, spying upon the hour and the duration of our lethargy. Today the columns of Hercules are in Panama. And Panama symbolizes the frontier, the citadel, and the destiny of both Americas.

United, Panama shall be the symbol of our strength, the sentinel of our future. Disunited, it will be the Gordian knot cut by the Yankee axe, and will give the possession of empire, the dominion of the second focus of the ellipses described by Russia and the United States in the geography of the globe.

3. ARIEL AND CALIBAN

In the closing years of the nineteenth century Latin-American "Yankeemania" began to give way to "Yankeephobia." José Marti, perhaps the keenest Latin-American student of North American affairs of that time, expressed growing alarm over what he regarded as the imperialist direction of United States foreign policy, and viewed with increasing gloom the political and social scene in the United States. A chorus of Latin-American voices echoed his criticism. In a book published in 1900 the Uruguayan philosopher José Enrique Rodó (1871–1917) made his famous comparison between the materialistic "Caliban," the United States, and "Ariel," the embodiment of man's higher aspirations, represented by Latin America. Frequently overlooked was his call for a fruitful fusion of North American vigor and material progress with Latin spirituality. Rodó's book, written

in a style of classic grace and beauty, once enjoyed great influence in Latin-American cultured circles, but today its aristocratic tone and premises find little acceptance.[4]

THE UTILITARIAN CONCEPTION as the idea of human destiny, and equality at the mediocre as the norm of social proportion, make up the formula which in Europe they call the spirit of Americanism. It is impossible to think on either of these as inspirations for human conduct or society, while contrasting them with those which are opposed to them, without at once conjuring up by association a vision of that formidable and fruitful democracy there in the North, with its manifestations of prosperity and power, as a dazzling example in favour of the efficacy of democratic institutions and the correct aim of its ideas. If one could say of utilitarianism that it is the word of the English spirit, the United States may be considered the incarnation of that word. Its Evangel is spread on every side to teach the material miracles of its triumph. And Spanish America is not wholly to be entitled, in its relation to the United States, as a nation of Gentiles. The mighty confederation is realizing over us a sort of moral conquest. Admiration for its greatness, its strength, is a sentiment that is growing rapidly in the minds of our governing classes, and even more, perhaps, among the multitude, easily impressed with victory or success. And from admiring it is easy to pass to imitating. Admiration and belief are already for the psychologist but the passive mood of imitation. "The imitative tendency of our moral nature," says Bagehot, "has its seat in that part of the soul where lives belief." Common sense and experience would suffice of themselves to show this natural relation. We imitate him in whose superiority and prestige we believe. So it happens that the vision of a voluntarily delatinized America, without compulsion or conquest, and regenerate in the manner of its Northern archetype, floats already through the dreams of many who are sincerely interested in our future, satisfies them with suggestive parallels they find at every step, and appears in constant movements for reform or innovation. We have our *mania for the North.* It is necessary to oppose to it those bounds which both sentiment and reason indicate.

Not that I would make of those limits an

[4] José Enrique Rodó, *Ariel*, Boston, Houghton Mifflin Company, 1922, pp. 89–129. Reprinted by permission of Houghton Mifflin Company.

absolute negation. I well understand that enlightenment, inspiration, great lessons lie in the example of the strong; nor do I fail to realize that intelligent attention to the claims of the material and the study of the useful, directed abroad, is of especially useful result in the case of people in the formative stage, whose nationality is still in the mould. I understand how one must try by persevering education to rectify such traits of a society as need to be made to fit in with new demands of civilization and new opportunities in life, thus by wise innovation counteracting the forces of heredity or custom. But I see no good in denaturalizing the character of a people — its personal genius — to impose on it identity with a foreign model to which they will sacrifice the originality of their genius, that, once lost, can never be replaced; nor in the ingenuous fancy that this result may ever be obtained artificially or by process of imitation. That thoughtless attempt to transplant what is natural and spontaneous in one society into the soil of another where it has no roots, historically or naturally, seemed to Michelet like the attempt to incorporate by mere transference a dead organism in a living body.

In societies, as in art or literature, blind imitation gives but an inferior copy of the model. And in the vain attempt there is also something ignoble; a kind of political snobbery, carefully to copy the ways and acts of the great; as, in Thackeray's satire, those without rank or fortune ineffectually imitate only the foibles of the mighty. Care for one's own independence, personality, judgment, is a chief form of self-respect. A much-commented passage of Cicero teaches how it is our duty sedulously to preserve our original character; that which differentiates and determines, so far as may wisely be, the primal natural impulses, as they derive from a various distribution of natural gifts and so make up the concert and the order of the world. And even more would this seem to be true as applied to human collectivities. But perhaps you will say that there is no seal, no peculiar and definite thing to mark the quality for whose permanence and integrity we should do battle in the actual organization of our people. Perhaps there lacks in our South American character the definite contour of a personality. But even so, we Latin-Americans have an inheritance of Race, a great ethnic tradition to maintain, a sacred bond which unites us to immortal pages of history and puts us on our honour to preserve this for the future. That cosmopolitanism which we

have to respect as the irresistible tendency of our development need not exclude that sentiment of fidelity to the past, nor that moulding and directing force of which the genius of our race must avail itself in the fusing of the elements that shall constitute the American of the future.

It has more than once been pointed out that the great epochs of history, its most fertile periods, are always the result of distinct but coexisting forces which by their very agreement to oppose maintain the interest and stimulus of life, which in the quietism of a universal accord might tend to disappear. So the two extremes of Athens and Sparta revolve on an axle around which circles the race of greatest genius man has known. So America needs at this time to maintain its original duality, which has converted from classic myth to actual history the story of the two eagles, loosed at the same moment from either pole, to arrive at the same moment at each one's limit of dominion. This difference in genius does not exclude honourable emulation, nor discourage in very many relations agreement or even solidarity. And if one can dimly foresee even a higher concord in the future, that will be due not to a one-sided imitation of one race by the other, but to a reciprocity of influences and a skilful harmonizing of those attributes which make the peculiar glory of either race.

Still, the dispassionate study of that civilization which some would offer to us as a model, affords a reason no less potent than those which are based only on the indignity and unworthiness of mere imitation to temper the enthusiasm of those who propose it as our model. . . . And now I come to the very theme of my discourse, and the relation to it of this spirit of imitation. Any severe judgment formed upon our neighbours of the North should begin, like the courteous fencer, by lowering a rapier in salute to them. Easy is this for me. Failure to recognize their faults does not seem to me so insensate as to deny their qualities. Born — to employ Beaudelaire's paradox — with the innate experience of liberty, they have kept themselves faithful to the law of their birth; and have developed, with the precision and certainty of a mathematical progression, the fundamental principles of their organization. This gives to their history a unity which, even if it has excluded the acquirement of different aptitudes or merits, has at least the intellectual beauty of being logical. The traces of its progress will never be expunged from the annals of human right, because they have been the first to evoke our modern ideal of liberty and to convert it from the uncertainty of experiment and the visions of Utopia into imperishable bronze and living reality. For they have shown by their example the possibility of extending the immovable authority of a republic over an immense national commonwealth, and, with their federal organization, have revealed — as de Tocqueville felicitously put it — the manner in which the brilliancy and power of great states may be combined with the felicity and peace of little ones. . . .

Theirs are many of the most daring deeds for which the perspective of time shall distinguish this century; theirs is the glory of having revealed completely the greatness and dignity of labour, thereby accentuating the firmest note of moral beauty in all our civilization; that blest force which antiquity abandoned to the abjection of slavery, and which to-day we identify with the highest expression of human dignity, based on the consciousness and the exertion of its own merit. Strong, tenacious of purpose, holding inaction as opprobrious, they have placed in the hands of the mechanic of their shops and the farmer of their fields the mystic key of Hercules, and have given to human genius a new and unwonted beauty, girding it with the leathern apron of the hand-worker. Each one of these presses on to conquer life as his Puritan ancestors did the wilderness. Persistent followers of that creed of individual energy which makes of every man the artificer of his destiny, they have modelled their commonwealth on a kind of imaginary population of Crusoes, who, as soon as they have roughly attended to their training in the art of taking care of themselves, will turn to the making of themselves into a stable State. And, never sacrificing to this their conception of the sovereign individual, they yet have known how at the same time to make of their association the most admirable instrument of their grandeur and empire; they have got from the sum of their energies, as devoted to research, industry, philanthropy, results that are the more marvellous in that they were secured with the most absolute integrity of their personal liberty.

They have a sleepless and insatiable instinct of curiosity, an impatient eagerness for the light; and, carrying a fondness for public education almost to the point of monomania, have made the common school the surest prop of their prosperity, believing that the mind of the child should be the most cherished of their

precious things. Their culture, while far from being spiritual or refined, has an admirable efficiency so far as it is directed to practical ends and their immediate realization. And, while they have not added to the acquisitions of science a single general law, one new principle, they have done wonders in its application to new inventions and made giant strides in its service to utilities; in the steam boiler, the electric dynamo, are now billions of invisible slaves who centuple for their Aladdin the power of the magic lamp. The growth of their greatness and power will astonish future generations. By their marvellous gift for improvisation they have found a spur to time, so that in a few years they conjure, as it were from a desert, the fruitage hitherto the work of centuries.

And that Puritan liberty which gave them light in the past unites with that light a piety which still endures. Beside the factory and the school it has erected churches whence ascend the prayers of millions of free consciences. They have been able to save from the shipwreck of all the idealities that which is the highest of all, and kept alive the tradition of a religious sentiment which, if it does not uplift on wings of the highest idealism, spirituality, at least maintains over the utilitarian stampede some rein of the moral sense. Also, they have known how to maintain a certain primitive robustness even amidst the refinements of a highly civilized life; they hold to the pagan cult of health, sanity, and strength; they preserve in strong muscles the instrument of a strong will; obliged by their insatiable ambition to employ all human energies, they fit the torso of the athlete over the heart of the free man. And from all this springs a dominant note of optimism, confidence, faith, which makes them face the future with a proud and stubborn assurance; the note of "Excelsior" and the "Psalm of Life," which their poets have opposed as a balsam to melancholy or bitterness of spirit.

Thus it is that their Titanic greatness impresses even those made most distrustful by their exaggerations of character and the recent violences of their history; and I, who do not love them, as you see, admire them still. I admire them, first, for their formidable power of *desire*; I bow before that *"school of will and work"* — which Philarete Chasles tells us they have inherited from their forbears.

In the beginning was Action. With these famous words of Faust the future historian of the great Republic may begin; the Genesis, not yet concluded, of their national existence. Their genius may be defined as the universe of the *Dynamists:* force in movement. Above all, it has the capacity, the enthusiasm, the fortunate vocation, for doing things; volition is the chisel which has shapen this people from hard rock. Their characteristic points are manifestations of the will-power, originality, and audacity. Their history is above all a very paroxysm of virile activity. Their typical figure should be entitled, not Superman, but He who wants. And if anything saves them collectively from vulgarity, it is that extraordinary *verve* of energy which they always show and which lends a certain epic character to even the struggles of self-interest and the material life. So Bourget could say, of the speculators of Minneapolis and Chicago that they are of the mould of gladiators, that their fighting power of attack or of defence is as of Napoleon's soldiers of the Guard. Yet that supreme energy with which the North American seems to cast, as if by hypnotizing, a spell and suggestion over the Fates, is found only in just those things which are presented to us as exceptional, divergent, in their civilization. No one will say that Edgar Poe was not an anomalous individual, rebellious to the influences around him: his chosen spirit represented a particle inassimilable by the national soul, which vainly struggled to express itself to others as from an infinite solitude; yet the fundamental note — Baudelaire has pointed it out — in the character of Poe's heroes is still the inner shrine, the unconquerable resistance of the will. When he imagined Ligeia, most mysterious and adorable of his creatures, he symbolized in the inextinguishable light of her eyes the hymn of the triumph of man's will over death.

If now by a sincere recognition of what is great and brilliant in the genius of that mighty country I have acquired the right to complete the picture by meting even-handed justice, one question, full of interest, still presents itself: Does that society realize, or at least tend to realize, the ideal of such rational conduct as satisfies, to the heart's desire, the intellectual and moral dignity of our civilization? Is it there that we shall find the most approximate image of our perfect State? That feverish unrest which seems to centuple in its bosom the movement, the intensity of life — has it an end that is worth while and a motive sufficient for its justification?

Herbert Spencer, when with a noble sincerity he framed his parting address to the democracy of America at a New York banquet, marked as the chief feature of North American life that same overflowing unrest which shows itself both in the infinite passion for work and in vainglory in all forms of material expansion. Later he said that so exclusive a preoccupation with those activities which make for immediate utility revealed a notion of life, tolerable indeed in a young country as a provisional stage of civilization, but which already needed rectifying as it tended to make "useful" labor the end and object of all living; whereas in no case can it mean more than the accumulation of those things which are only the necessary elements to a full and harmonious development of our being. And he added that it behooved them now to teach their people the gospel of rest or recreation; and we, identifying these words with the *otium* of the ancients, will include in this gospel to be taught those restless toilers *any* ideal concern, *any* disinterested employment of one's time, *any* object of meditation or study divorced from all relation to immediate utilitarian interest.

North American life, indeed, describes that vicious circle which Pascal remarked in the ceaseless seeking for well-being when it has no object outside of oneself. Its prosperity is as immense as its incapability of satisfying even a mediocre view of human destiny. Titanic in its enormous concentration of human will-power, in its unprecedented triumph in all spheres of material aggrandizement, its civilization yet produces as a whole a singular impression of insufficiency, of emptiness. And if man's spirit demands, with all the reason that thirty centuries of growth under classic and under Christian influence have conferred upon it, *what* are in this new world the dirigent principles — the ideal substratum, the ulterior end of all this concernment with the positive interests that so informs that mighty multitude — he will only be met, as a definite formula, by that same exclusive interest in material triumphs. Orphaned of the profound tradition that attended his birth, the North American has not yet replaced the inspiring ideality of his past with any high unselfish conception of the future. He lives for the immediate reality of the present, and for this subordinates all his activities in the egoism of material well-being, albeit both individual and collective. Of all his aggregation of the elements of wealth and power, one might say, what Bourget said of the intelligence of his character the Marquis Norbert, "a mountain of wood to which they have not yet known how to set fire."

The vital spark is lacking to throw up that flame of the ideal, restless, life-giving, from that mountain of dead wood. Not even the selfishness of patriotism, for want of higher impulses, nor the pride of race, both of which transfigured and exalted in ancient days even the prosaic hardness of the life of Rome, can light a glimmer of ideality or beauty in a people where a cosmopolite confusion and the atomism of a badly understood democracy impede the formation of a veritable national conscience.

One might think that the positivist genius of England has suffered a sea change in crossing the Atlantic so as to fill its sons there with a spirit deprived of those elements of ideality which tempered it at home, and thus really reducing it to the crudeness which only the exaggeration of passion or satire has ascribed to its English form. For the English spirit, under its rough utilitarian exterior, its mercantile cynicism, its Puritanic severity, always concealed a rare poetic genius and a deep respect for the finer sensibility, which caused Taine to hold that at the bottom of the Teutonic nature, which is the base of the English race, must exist, however modified by the pressure of conquest or the habit of trade, an extraordinary exaltation of the emotional qualities. But the American spirit has not inherited this ancestral poetic instinct, which gushes like a clear fountain from the British rock when it is a Moses of high art who touches it. The English people possess in their institution of aristocracy (however unequal and out of date it may appear in the political aspect) a lofty and solid bulwark to oppose to the shop-keeping spirit and the encroachment of a prosaic world; so solid and lofty that Taine could say that since Grecian times history has presented no example of a society more fit to breed noble men and a noble spirit. But in the ambient of America's democracy there are no heights so lofty as to escape the climbing of the flood of vulgarity, and it spreads and extends itself freely as over a level plain.

Sensibility, intelligence, manners — each is marked in that enormous people by a radical unaptness for selection; and this, with the mechanical ordering of their material activities, makes a chaos of all that pertains to the realm of the ideal. It were easy to follow this unaptness from its most obvious manifestations to the more intimate and essential one. Prodigal of riches — for meanness is not his fault — the North American has learned only to acquire by them the satisfaction of his vanity and material luxury, but not the chosen note of good taste.

In such a surrounding true art can only exist as the rebellion of an individual. Emerson, Poe, are as estrays of a fauna expelled from their true habitat by some geological catastrophe. In "Outre Mer" Bourget speaks of the solemn tone in which the North American utters the word Art, when he, a self-made man, has achieved riches which he now desires to crown with all the human refinements; but he never has felt the divine frenzy of poem or picture; he would buy but to add to his collection a new toy, to satisfy at once his vanity and his acquisitive instinct. That in it which is disinterested, chosen, rare, he ignores, despite the munificence with which he scatters his individual fortune to found schools of art, form popular taste, build splendid museums, patronize huge expositions, and deck his cities with monuments and his streets with bronze and marble. And if one had to characterize his taste, in a word, it would be that which in itself involves the negation of great art; strained brutality of effect, insensibility to soft tones or an exquisite style, the cult of bigness, and that sensationalism which excludes all noble serenity as incompatible with the hurry of his hectic life.

The ideal of beauty does not appeal to the descendants of the austere Puritan, nor even a passionate worship of the truth; they care little for any thinking that has no immediate practical object — it seems to them idle and fruitless; even to science they bring no selfless interest for discovery, nor do they seem capable of loving its truth only because they are true; investigation is merely the necessary antecedent of practical application. Their praiseworthy efforts to extend the benefits of popular education are inspired with the noble motive of communicating the rudiments of knowledge to the masses; but it does not appear that they also concern themselves over-much with that higher education which shall rise above the general mediocrity. And so the outcome is that of all their struggle with ignorance the only gain has been a sort of universal semiculture and a profound indifference to the higher. . . . As fast as the general ignorance decreases, so, in the air of that giant democracy, decreases the higher learning and vanishes genius itself. This is why the story of their intellectual activity is of a retrogression in brilliance and originality. For while at the era of their Independence and Constitution many famous names illustrate their history in thought as well as in action, a half-century later de Tocqueville could say of them, the Gods are disappearing. And, when he wrote his master work, there still radiated from Boston, the Puritan home, the city of learning and tradition, a glorious pleiad which holds in the intellectual story of our century a universal fame. Who since has picked up the heritage of Emerson, Channing, Poe? The levelling by the middle classes tends ever, pressing with its desolating task, to plane down what little remains of *intelligentsia:* the flowers are mown by the machine when weeds remain.

Long since their books have ceased to soar on wings beyond the common vision. To-day the most actual example of what Americans like best in literature must be sought in the gray pages of magazines or periodicals which seldom remind one that that mode of publication was employed in the immortal "Federalist."

In the domain of moral sentiment, the mechanical impulse for the utilitarian has, indeed, encountered a certain balance-wheel in a strong religious tradition; but one may not conclude that even this has given to the direction of conduct a real, disinterested principle. . . . American religiosity, derived from the English and exaggerated, is merely an auxiliary force for the penal law, and would disappear on the day it was found possible without it to give to utilitarian morality that religious sanction which Mill desired for it. The very culmination of that morality is only that of Franklin; a philosophy of conduct which has for its goal a commonplace sagacity, a prudent usefulness, in whose bosom will never rise the emotions of holiness or heroism; and which, fit only to give to one's conscience in the common affairs of life a certain moral support — like the appletree cane with which Franklin ever walked — is but a fragile staff with which to surmount great heights. And yet his was its supreme height: it is in the valleys where one must seek for its actuality. Even if the moral critique were not to descend below the probity and moderation of Franklin's standard, its necessary termination, as de Tocqueville wisely said of a society educated narrowly with similar notions of duty, would surely not be in that superb and noble decadence which give us to measure a Satanic beauty of tragedy in the downfall of empires, but rather a kind of pallid materialism, drab culture, and finally the sleep of an enervation without brilliancy in the silent decay of all the mainsprings of the moral life. In that society whose precept tends to put outside of what is obligatory the higher manifestations of abnegations and of virtue, practical considerations will always make the limits of obligation recede indefinitely. And the school

of material prosperity, always a rude teacher of republican austerity, has carried even further that simplicity of the conception of a rational conduct which now obsesses the mind. To Franklin's code have succeeded others franker still in their expression of the national wisdom. A book by one Swett Marden was recently published in Boston, "Pushing to the Front," which announced, apparently with much popular approval, as a new moral law, that success is the final end of life; this book was praised even in church circles, and compared to the "Imitation" of à Kempis! . . .

And public life does not escape the consequences of the growth of this germ of disorganization in society generally. Any casual observer of their political customs will tell you how the obsession of material interest tends steadily to enervate and eradicate the sentiment of law or right; the civic virtue of a Hamilton is an old and rusty sword, every day the more forgotten, lost in the cobwebs of tradition; venality, beginning at the polls, spreads through the working of all their institutions; the government by a mediocrity renders vain that emulation which exalts the character and the intelligence, and imposes itself even on the imagination as an unavoidable future. A democracy not subject to a superior instruction, not trained in liberal schools to the understanding of true human excellence, tends always to that abominable brutality of the majority which despises the greater moral benefits of liberty and annuls in public opinion all respect for the dignity of the individual. And to-day a new and formidable power arises to accentuate this absolutism of numbers: the political influence of a plutocracy represented only by the agents of the trusts, monopolies of production, and lords of the economic life, one of the most noteworthy and significant features of the United States of to-day. Their advent has caused almost everybody to recall the coming of that proud and over-rich class which at the end of the Roman Republic preceded the tyranny of the Caesars and the ruin of liberty. And the exclusive preoccupation with material aggrandizement, the deity of such a civilization, has its logical result on the State as on the individual, putting the *struggle-for-life* principle also at the head of national policy, and making its representative the supreme personification of the national energy — the *postulant* of Emerson, the ruling *personage* of Taine.

To the impulse which drives the spiritual life toward that deorientation of the ideal to the selfishly useful corresponds physically that other principle which in the astounding increase of that people impels both the multitude and the initiative ever in the direction of that boundless West which in the times of their first independence was all mystery, veiled behind the forests of the Mississippi. In fact that improvised West — which grows so formidable to the older Atlantic States and already claims hegemony in the near future — is where the most faithful representation of American life is to be found at this moment of its evolution. It is there where the definite results, the logical and natural fruits of the spirit that has guided the great democracy from its origin, are brought into relief for the observer so that he can picture to himself the aspect of its immediate future. To the Virginian, the Yankee, has succeeded the master of the yesterday empty prairies, of whom Michel Chevalier predicted, half a century since, "The last shall one day be the first." Utilitarianism, empty of all ideal content, a certain cosmopolitan levity of spirit, and the levelling of a falsely conceived democracy, will in him reach their ultimate victory. Every noble element of that civilization, all which binds it to the generous traditions and lofty origin of its historic dignity — the arrival of the men of the Mayflower, the memory of the Patricians of Virginia and the warriors of New England, the spirit of the people and lawmakers of the Emancipation — will remain only in the older States, where a Boston or a Philadelphia still maintain "the palladium of the Washington tradition." Chicago will arise to reign. And its overweening superiority over the original States of the Atlantic shore is based on its belief that they are reactionary, too European, too subject to tradition. History confers no claims on any, where popular election confers the purple.

As fast as the utilitarian genius of that nation takes on a more defined character, franker, narrower yet, with the intoxication of material prosperity, so increases the impatience of its sons to spread it abroad by propaganda, and think it predestined for all humanity. To-day they openly aspire to the primacy of the world's civilization, the direction of its ideas, and think themselves the forerunners of all culture that is to prevail. The colloquial phrase, ironically quoted by Laboulaye, "America can beat the world," is taken seriously by almost any virile Westerner. At the bottom of their open rivalry with Europe lies a contempt for it that is almost naive, and the profound conviction that within a brief period they are destined to eclipse its

glory and do away with its spiritual superiority; thus once more fulfilling, in the progress of civilization, the hard law of the ancient mysteries, whereby the initiated shall put to death the initiator. It were useless to seek to convince them that, although their services to inventions and material advance have been doubtless great, even rising to the measure of a universal human obligation, they do not of themselves suffice to alter the axis of the earth. It were useless to seek to convince them that the fires lit upon European altars, the work done by peoples living these three thousand years gone by about the shores of the Mediterranean, though rising to glorious genius when bound with the olive and the palm of Athens, a work still being carried on and in whose traditions and teachings we South Americans live, makes a sum which cannot be equalled by any equation of Washington plus Edison. Would they even revise the Book of Genesis, to put themselves upon the front page?

But, aside from the insufficiency of the part that is given them to play in the education of humanity, their own character itself precludes all possibility of their hegemony. Nature has not granted them the genius for propaganda, the vocation of the apostle. They lack that great gift of *amiability* — likeableness, in a loftly sense; that extraordinary power of sympathy with which those races endowed by Providence for the task of education know how to make of their culture a beauty, as did Greece, loveable, eternal, and yet always with something of their own.

North American civilization may abound — it does abound — in fertile suggestions, profitable examples; it may inspire admiration, astonishment, respect; but it is rare for the foreigner to feel his heart come to his mouth with strong emotion when first he sees that Bartholdi statue holding high its torch of Liberty over New York Harbour; that thrill profound with which the ancient traveller saw the rosy light of the marble and the sheen of Athena's spear over the early dawn on the Acropolis.

But please remember that when I, in the name of their soul's rights, deny to their utilitarianism the right to impose itself as typical of the future on the world as mould or model, I do not in the least assert that its labours are wasted even in relation to those things which we may call soul-interests. . . . Without the arm which clears and constructs, there might now be no shelter for the brain that thinks; without some certain conquest of the materialities, the rule of the spiritualities in human societies becomes impossible. Renan's aristocratic idealism recognized, even from the point of view of the moral interest of the race and its future spiritual development, the import of the utilitarian labour of this century; "To get away from need is to redeem oneself." In the remote past even the prosaic and selfish activities of the merchant resulted in putting for the first time a people in relation with others, and thus had a far-reaching effect on men's ideas; since this had much to do with multiplying the means of intelligence, refining and softening manners, perhaps even showing the way to a more advanced morality; and the same positive force appears later, favoring the higher ideals of civilization. It was the gold accumulated by the merchants of the Italian republics that paid, says Saint-Victor, for the works of the Renaissance. The ships that came back from the countries of the Thousand and One Nights, laden with ivory and spices, made it possible for Lorenzo di Medici to renew in Florentine merchants' houses the feast of Plato. All history shows a definite relation of growth between the progress of utilitarian activity and the ideal. And just as the former can be turned into a shelter and protection for the latter, so the ideas of the mind often give rise to utilitarian results, above all when these latter are not sought directly. For instance, Bagehot remarks that the immense positive benefits of navigation might never have been attained for humanity if in earliest times there had not been dreamers, apparently idle — and certainly misunderstood by their contemporaries — who were interested solely in the contemplation of the movements of the stars.

This law of harmony bids us also respect the arm that labours arduously in what seems a barren and prosaic soil. The work of North American positivism will also at the end serve the cause of Ariel. That which this people of Cyclops have achieved for the direct purpose of material advantage, with all their sense for what is useful and their admirable faculty of mechanical invention, will be converted by other peoples, or later, even by themselves, to a wealth of material for the higher selection. Thus that most precious and fundamental invention of the alphabet, which gives the wings of immortality to the spoken word, originated in Phoenician shops, the discovery of merchants who only desired to keep their accounts. Using it for purposes merely mercenary, they never dreamed that the genius of a superior race would transfigure and transform it to a means of perpetuating the light and the learning of their being. The relation between material good and good that is intellectual or moral is thus only a new aspect of that modern doctrine which we call the transformation of energy; material well-being may be transformed into spiritual superiority.

But North American life does not as yet offer us any new example of this indisputable relation, nor even dimly suggest it as the triumph of the generation to come.

Our wish and our belief, indeed, incline us to hope that a superior destiny may be reserved for that civilization in a time not too remote for prophecy; the more that, under the spur of their energy, even the brief time that separates them from their dawn has sufficed to satisfy the expenditure of the vitality required for such immense achievement. Their past, their present, must be but the entry-way to a great future. Yet all shows that this is still far away from its definitive. The assimilative energy which has so far enabled them to maintain a certain uniformity as well as some touch of genius, despite the enormous inrush of ethnic elements opposed to those which have so far made the basis of their character, will have to do battle every day more strenuous, and in their utilitarianism, which proscribes all ideality, will find no inspiration sufficiently strong to maintain their solidarity with the older ideal. The illustrious thinker, who compared the slave of olden times to an atom outside the attraction of the social orbit, might well use the same comparison to characterize that numerous colony of German origin now peopling the Middle and Northern West, which preserves intact in their nature, their society, and their customs, the impression of that German spirit which in many of its profoundest and strongest characteristics must be considered as the actual antithesis of the American. . . . And also, a civilization which is destined to survive and spread throughout the world; which has not mummified itself in the manner of the Chinese by losing all capability of change; cannot indefinitely prolong the direction of its energies to one order of things alone. Let us hope, then, that the spirit of that Titanic organism, which has so far been utility and will-power only, may some day also be intelligence, sentiment, ideality; that from that mighty forge may arise, in last result, the noble human figure, harmonious, select, that Spencer foreshadowed in the discourse I have adverted to. But we may not look for him in the present reality of that people, nor in their immediate future; and we must give up hoping to find the perfect type of an exemplary civilization in what is now but a rough sketch, huge and misshapen, having to pass through many correcting hands before it assumes the serene, the perfect shape of a people that have fully developed their genius and contemplate their work, *finis coronat,* gloriously crowned.

4. THE GOOD NEIGHBOR POLICY

Latin-American ill will toward the United States, stimulated by numerous acts of American intervention in Caribbean lands, reached a climax in the 1920's. Official awareness of the adverse economic and political results of this hostility, and pressure from an aroused public opinion in the United States, brought a gradual reorientation of United States policy toward Latin America. Begun under Presidents Coolidge and Hoover, the Good Neighbor Policy attained its full development in the Roosevelt era. A State Department official describes the genesis and the substance of that policy.[5]

IN EXTERNAL AFFAIRS, the first century and a quarter of our independent existence was characterized primarily by "expansionism." From 13 States along the Atlantic seaboard, our country grew to 48, touching upon two oceans and including many territorial and island possessions. This growth in the national domain was justified by a curious philosophy which may be termed "manifest destiny." In his *Farewell Address,* George Washington laid down certain precepts for the guidance of our foreign relations. He said: "Observe good faith and justice toward all nations. Cultivate peace and harmony with all." Nevertheless, within a very short time, in extenuation of the growth in territory and power of the United States, the other American republics heard such statements as these:

In explaining the argument of natural law, Representative Wilde of Georgia declared with respect to the lands held by the Cherokee Nation:

And if it were possible to perpetuate the race of Indians, what would be the consequence? Why, that a

hundred or a thousand fold the number of white men would not be born, because the Indians would roam over and possess, without enjoying, the land which must afford the future whites subsistence.

Or Representative Duncan, in extolling the extension-of-freedom doctrine, which was employed to cover the annexation of Texas, Oregon, and California:

If ours is to be the home of the oppressed, we must extend our territory in latitude and longitude to the demand of the millions who are to follow us, as well of our own posterity as those who are invited to our peaceful shores to partake in our republican institutions.

It was only natural that generations of territorial expansion should give rise to deep distrust and fear on the part of our immediate neighbors. Only as recently as a generation ago, the United States purchased the Virgin Islands 1 year after President Wilson had stated "America does not want any additional territory."

As the era of territorial aggrandizement drew toward an end, the United States assumed a new role equally objectionable to our southern neighbors, that of international police power. In this connection Dr. Ricardo Alfaro, former President of Panama, recently placed in juxtaposition two statements of President Theodore Roosevelt. Dr. Alfaro said:

In 1906 President Theodore Roosevelt in a message to Congress stated:

"In many parts of South America there has been much misunderstanding of the attitude of the United States toward the other American republics. An idea has become prevalent that our assertion of the Monroe Doctrine implied or carried with it the assumption of superiority and of a right to exercise some kind of protectorate over the countries to whose territory that doctrine applies. Nothing could be farther from the truth."

Yet, Colonel Roosevelt throughout his two terms of office maintained and enforced the famous Corollary to the Monroe Doctrine which he formulated as follows:

"Chronic wrongdoing, or an impotence which results in a general loosening of the ties of civilized society, may in America, as elsewhere, ultimately require intervention by some civilized nation, and in the Western Hemisphere the adherence of the United States to the Monroe Doctrine may force the United States, however reluctantly, in flagrant cases of such wrongdoing or impotence, to the exercise of an international police power."

[5] Address by Laurence Duggan, Chief of the Division of the American Republics, at Philadelphia, April 2, 1938, before the American Academy of Political and Social Science. Department of State, *Press Releases,* April 2, 1938. Quoted in: James W. Gantenbein (ed.), *The Evolution of Our Latin American Policy: A Documentary Record,* New York, Columbia University Press, 1950, pp. 188–193.

The exercise of this assumed police power, which resulted in the infringement of sovereignty of many nearby nations, met with a growing hue and cry throughout the other republics of this hemisphere. The wave of nationalism which swept the world after the war brought them fortitude and determination. Their opposition to the philanthropies of intervention on the part of the United States became open, direct, and acrid. At the Inter-American Conference in 1928, the Argentine delegation withdrew from the Conference because of the opposition of the United States delegation to discussion of the question of intervention, then very alive because of the presence of United States marines in Nicaragua. In the United States people began to ask themselves in what way the national welfare which cost the lives of many marines and the expenditure of considerable money was advanced by a policy of intimidation and intervention.

Although the first indications that the United States Government likewise entertained doubts occurred under the tenure of Secretary Stimson, it was left to the present administration to give tangible proofs by a series of definite visible steps of a determination to conduct its relations with the other American republics. The principles of understanding, confidence, friendship, and respect have been proclaimed by every President. What is new is a new and more far-reaching application of these principles. As the references earlier given show, in the past there has been no lack of willingness to employ specious moral principles to justify actions contrary to the basic principles enunciated in the first days of our independent existence as the bases of our foreign relations, or to pervert or distort those basic principles to explain deeds of a totally irreconcilable nature. However, it is my belief that a careful examination will disclose no period in our relations with the other American republics when there has been as close a correlation between declared purpose and fulfillment, between theory and fact, as during the past 5 years.

It might be interesting to consider the reasons for the change in popular attitude which was given form by the present administration.

First of all it had become apparent that the antagonisms fired by our past activities had resulted in the erection of a barrier of distrust more efficacious in its insulating quality than any physical barrier of distance or topography. At international gatherings the United States delegations instead of being welcomed as friends and associates were eyed askance and with misgivings. This suspicion extended beyond the confines of the Government to include our citizens, regardless of walk of life. They were distinctly handicapped because they discovered that outside the confines of the United States they were considered to possess to a greater or lesser degree the same qualities that their country was considered to have exhibited in its international dealings. They found that the influence of the United States was related directly to that flowing from the might of material strength. They came to realize that the United States had few real friends on this hemisphere, friends who shared a similar outlook, friends whose sympathy and aid could be counted upon in case of need. And as storm clouds arose in other parts of the world, and the depression deepened, our people wondered whether this was a healthy situation.

Moreover, the antagonisms were adversely affecting our commerical interests. During the periods of the second intervention in Nicaragua (1926–1933) and of the acute period of our intervention in Haiti (1920–1930), groups in many countries boycotted United States goods. While for a variety of reasons the trade statistics are poor indices of the force of those boycotts, our businessmen were well aware of the business actually lost because of the ill feeling toward the United States. Their concern was not alleviated by the passage of the Smoot-Hawley tariff of 1930, which, because of its very substantial increases on many important export products of other American countries, caused deep resentment. Retaliatory tariffs were erected, and the new far-reaching trade controls instituted during the depression were sometimes availed of to our disadvantage. Some of the more enlightened and far-sighted American businessmen even took steps of their own to endeavor to correct some of the misconceptions regarding the United States — for there were many of these. For instance the Inter-American Committee, composed of several of the important business interests, took several useful steps in the early thirties along this line.

Finally, considering that the other American countries have known us by our interventions and dollars, it was not surprising that the United States should have been regarded as a great culture desert, void of art, music, literature — in short, of a soul. Oases here and there were admitted, but they were not considered typical and were generally believed to be nourished by subterranean foreign springs. Of course there were persons in every one of the American countries who knew that the United States was not a cultural vacuum. They have stood out like lighthouses. To them, this country owes a deep debt of gratitude for their efforts to interest their countrymen in the cultural activity of the United States. If they have not been successful, the fault is not theirs. It lies with the antagonisms created by our past policies, and with the indifference of our scholars and scientists and foundations to the almost uncharted sea of cultural cooperation in the Americas. With a steadfastness reminiscent of the captain's daughter lashed to the mast of the *Hesperus,* they have kept their attentions and activities riveted on the Old World.

These then are the principal, if not all, of the motives that led directly to a reorientation of policy. This picture may omit the overtones and shadings that give perspective and body to the central theme. But in its essentials it is my belief that it is accurate.

Let us now briefly consider the bases upon which the "good neighbor" policy rests.

First of all, the President declared in December 1933 that "the definite policy of the United States from now on is one opposed to armed intervention." The Government has ratified two inter-American treaties, one adopted at Montevideo, the other Buenos Aires, that contain the provision that no country has the right to intervene directly or indirectly in the internal or external affairs of another. Thus the peril of intervention by the United States which has hung over some countries like a sword of Damocles has been removed.

The question may be raised as to what attitude this country would take if confronted with a break-down of law and order in any country of this hemisphere. Contemplating that contingency, the President has said: "It is only if and when the failure of orderly processes affects the other nations of the continent that it becomes their joint concern; and the point to stress is that in such an event it becomes the joint concern of a whole continent in which we are all neighbors."

Secondly, the Government is endeavoring to improve and extend the trade relations, principally through the medium of the trade-agreements program, which has been fully discussed by others at this conference. The United States has negotiated agreements with 9 of the 20 countries.

Thirdly, the United States has ratified every one of the 10 inter-American peace treaties. This

machinery has been constructed little by little as experience and need have shown desirable. The prestige and influence which this body of international law is acquiring is revealed by the rapidity with which a direct settlement was arrived at between the Dominican Republic and Haiti after the latter had invoked one of the important peace instruments. While doubtlessly there are imperfections in this machinery, it would seem advisable to give prolonged and careful consideration before scrapping it for a completely new mechanism. For instance if it is generally believed desirable to provide for regular meetings of foreign ministers during the intervals between the formal conferences, the objectives might be attained by amendment to the existing treaties that provide for consultation.

Fourthly, the United States has ratified the convention for the maintenance, preservation, and reestablishment of peace adopted at the Buenos Aires Conference which provides for consultation "in the event that the peace of the American Republics is menaced." Moreover, in the declaration of principles of inter-American solidarity and cooperation the American republics stated: "That every act susceptible of disturbing the peace of America affected each and every one of them, and justifies the initiation of the procedure of consultation" provided for in the convention just mentioned. This Government stands ready to consult at the moment that any country on this hemisphere requests consultation in the belief that there exists a threat to the peace of the Americas. The convention and the declaration of necessity could not precisely define what constitutes a threat to the peace of the Americas. A threat probably would include the attempt at the use of armed force against any country of this hemisphere by any foreign power. However, a threat might also be considered to include many other actions, however veiled they may be, and in this connection there comes to mind another pertinent quotation from Washington's *Farewell Address:* "Against the insidious wiles of foreign influence . . . the jealousy of a free people ought to be *constantly* awake, since history and experience prove that foreign influence is one of the most harmful foes of republican government."

Fifthly, if there is to be real understanding between this country and the other American countries, it is essential that our people through education come to an appreciation of the many aspects of life and culture in the other American republics, and in turn that these countries develop an appreciation of the nonmaterial aspects of the civilization that is in process of dynamic development in the United States. The Department of State is now giving careful study to the way in which it can interest and cooperate with private organizations in this important work.

In the "good neighbor" policy this Government believes that it is contributing its share toward the improvement of international relationships on this hemisphere. The general acceptance and support of this policy by the nations of the New World is the most convincing testimony of the soundness and broad applicability of its principles that could be adduced. Indeed no higher plane of international relationships can be conceived than one of fair play, equity, mutual accommodation, and mutual trust. It is superfluous to mention that departures from this plane by any country at any time presents large difficulties for the other countries who recognize not only that their own particular advantage but the welfare of all is advanced by conducting their relations on that plane. There may have existed a day when a country could go its own way without greatly affecting the destinies of other countries, but, if that day ever existed, it has now passed. Our present civilization is characterized by the interdependence of peoples and nations, and it is therefore more than ever desirable that some common and satisfactory basis for the conduct of international relationships be found. It is my belief that the "good neighbor" policy provides that basis.

5. THE AMERICAS AT MID-CENTURY

The Good Neighbor Policy was unquestionably successful in winning the good will and cooperation of Latin America with the United States. During World War II all of the Latin-American republics except Argentina supported in varying degrees the war effort of the United States. However, in the years that followed the war, rifts began to appear in the New World alliance. Dissatisfaction with United States foreign economic policy, and a rising wave of nationalism that resented all foreign-owned enterprises in the area were among the sources of friction between the erstwhile "good neighbors." A recent volume of the important annual publication The United States in World Affairs *discusses the state of inter-American relations at the mid-century.*[6]

[6] *The United States in World Affairs, 1952*, by Richard P. Stebbins, New York, Harper and Brothers (for the Council on Foreign Relations), pp. 263–267.

WHILE THEIR CLOSE ECONOMIC TIES with this country ensured a measure of continuing collaboration independent of the surface tides of politics, opinion in the Latin-American republics tended to concentrate more on the shortcomings than on the mutual benefits of this relationship. Those Latin Americans who found satisfaction or advantage in repeating outmoded slogans about the "North American colossus" and "*Yanqui*" imperialism complained in one breath that this country was discriminating against its closest neighbors by channeling the bulk of its economic aid to Europe and Asia; in the next they asserted that Latin America was being "exploited" or even "strangled" by United States capital. A steady growth in "anti-imperialist" agitation, in this case directed almost exclusively against the United States and against enterprises owned or controlled by United States citizens, was the most noteworthy development on the Latin-American scene in 1952 and formed the chief link with related trends in other parts of the free world. Developments in Latin America offered more than one parallel to the agitation against the British oil company in Iran and the Arab revulsion against defense cooperation with the West.

Among the sharpest indications of anti-United States feeling, both as a popular force and as an influence upon the policies of Latin-American governments, was the widespread resistance stirred up by this country's plans for closer military cooperation with individual Latin-American countries in the defense of the Western Hemisphere. Although the importance of Hemisphere defense had been emphasized in numerous inter-American declarations, it had not hitherto figured very prominently in the postwar military policy of the United States. The Pentagon, however, was anxious not to have to assume major defense responsibilities in Latin America in case of war, and for that reason was desirous of helping selected Latin-American countries toward a position in which they would be better able to protect their own territory and maintain "common lines of communication and base installations." Thus it was proposed to furnish certain Latin-American nations with a limited amount of military assistance on a grant basis, over and above the more substantial assistance in equipment and training which Latin-American governments were receiving from this country for payment. Appropriations of $38.2 million for 1951–52 and $62.4 million (later cut to $51.7 million) for 1952–53 were expected to suffice for the rehabilitation of obsolescent material and complete the "capital equipment" of the most important Latin-American forces designated for the defense of the Hemisphere.

Eight Latin-American countries had been tentatively selected by the Joint Chiefs of Staff as the most suitable participants in this program; but action could not begin until they had fulfilled certain special requirements laid down by Congress. Under the terms of the Mutual Security Act of 1951, military aid to Latin American countries could be furnished on a grant basis only in accordance with approved defense plans which required the recipient country "to participate in missions important to the defense of the Western Hemisphere"; further, each recipient of aid was required to sign an agreement "designed to assure that the assistance will be used to promote the defense of the Western Hemisphere." This requirement was interpreted by the executive branch as covering various forms of cooperation with the United States in which Congress was particularly interested and which, moreover, had been emphasized in resolutions adopted by the consultative meeting of American Foreign Ministers in 1951. Thus the draft agreements prepared for discussion with potential beneficiaries provided that each recipient government should facilitate United States access to strategic materials, cooperate in limiting trade with the Communist bloc, fulfill its military obligations under existing treaties, and "make, consistent with its own political and economic stability, the full contribution permitted by its manpower, resources, facilities, and general economic conditions to the development and maintenance of its own defensive strength and the defensive strength of the free world."

Logical though such stipulations might be from the standpoint of the United States, in Latin America they were widely interpreted as encroachments on the "sovereignty" of the prospective recipient countries. In some instances they occasioned a response hardly less violent than that of Indonesia and Iran when confronted with similar requests. No great difficulty was encountered in negotiating satisfactory agreements with Ecuador (February 20), Peru (February 22), Cuba (March 27), and Colombia (April 17). Opposition centered primarily in Mexico, Brazil, Chile, and Uruguay — countries that happened to be among the most democratically governed in Latin America and which might therefore have been expected to respond most readily to suggestions from the United

States. Moreover, although the Communists in each of these countries were among the most vigorous opponents of the agreements, the reaction against them was obviously much wider in character. Apparently they formed a convenient target for the discharge of negative feelings toward the United States which had been building up for some time past.

Initially the most serious difficulty developed in Mexico, where both Communists and conservatives raised such a hue and cry that the government felt constrained to discontinue negotiations with this country before any agreement could be concluded. Considerably greater success attended the United States negotiators in Brazil (March 15), Chile (April 9), and Uruguay (June 30); but here, too, there had been such signs of opposition from non-Communist as well as Communist quarters that ratification by the respective legislatures threatened to be extremely difficult. In Chile, ratification was not completed until July 3, after stormy scenes which necessitated the protection of the legislators by a police cordon. In Brazil and Uruguay the agreements were strenuously debated during the autumn but the chambers adjourned for the year without taking any final action.

The most striking feature of this development was not the fact that Latin-American Communists saw fit to oppose the agreements just as violently as their European counterparts had opposed the Atlantic Pact and the European military aid program. More significant was the fact that here the Communists were able, in certain instances, to paralyze governmental action as they had seldom if ever been able to do in Western Europe. The reason, obviously, was not that the Communists were stronger in Latin America than in France or Italy, but that their agitation against the United States policies exactly coincided with tendencies that were also dominant in important non-Communist quarters. It was the combined attack from Left and Right that had blocked three of the eight military assistance agreements and seriously threatened a fourth. This convergence of Communist agitation with other tendencies which may properly be called Rightist or even neo-Fascist in character — and which, moreover, were not less strenuously opposed to the United States than Communism itself — was the phenomenon that gave Latin-American politics in the early 1950's their peculiar quality and justified the particular concern of many United States observers.

It is true that opinion in this country, in so

far as it was alerted to possible political dangers within the hemisphere, still reserved its chief misgivings for the various evidences of direct Communist penetration in Latin America. Thus attention in the United States tended to focus primarily on countries like Guatemala, where Communists had undoubtedly gained a remarkable ascendency over the government of President Jacobo Arbenz Guzmán, and Brazil, where they appeared to exercise a wholly undesirable influence in the armed forces as well as in parliamentary circles. What sometimes escaped United States observers was the degree to which a handful of genuine Communists were magnifying their normal influence by associating themselves with a much broader movement of Latin-American opinion. In fact, the Communists in Latin America were riding a wave of nationalism which they had not produced but were finding it just as profitable to encourage as did the Tudeh party amid the not wholly dissimilar conditions of Dr. Mosaddeq's Iran. Communist agitation in Latin America, dangerous as it undoubtedly was, was only one manifestation of deeply rooted social and political maladjustments which seemed to be producing a gradual but profound transformation in Latin-American political relationships.

Closely linked with the popular reaction against the United States, and possibly even more fundamental in character, was a reaction against the democratic processes of government which had been considered normal in the inter-American family even when neglected in practice. In parts of Latin America, democracy had never been strong; yet seldom had it seemed so widely in retreat as in the period since World War II. Within the preceding four or five years, a whole series of Latin-American countries had succumbed to military dictatorships or embraced authoritarian regimes of one kind or another. In 1952 the pace was accelerated, with revolutionary *coups d'état* in Cuba and Bolivia, perpetuation of the military dictatorship in Venezuela, and the installation of a potentially authoritarian government by popular vote in Chile.

It would be incorrect to suggest that all anti-democratic movements in Latin America were necessarily hostile toward the United States. Military dictatorships established with little or no semblance of popular consent, such as those in Peru and Venezuela, sometimes looked more benevolently on this country than did the authoritarian or semiauthoritarian regimes installed by popular majority like that of President Perón in Argentina. This fact in itself was an indication that anti-United States feeling in Latin America was a widespread psychological tendency, not the monopoly of any political movement.

Glossary

of

Spanish, Portuguese, and Indian Terms

adelantado — Governor of a frontier district in colonial times.

alcabala — Tax on sales.

alcalde — Head of municipal government; mayor.

alcalde mayor — Governor of a municipal district in colonial times.

alfaquí — Moslem spiritual leader and teacher of the Koran.

alguacil — Constable.

aliama or **aljama** — Name applied to a Moslem or Jewish community or quarter in a medieval Spanish city.

amauta — An Inca sage.

amin — A kind of Jewish broth.

andén — Agricultural terrace, widely used in Inca agriculture.

añus — A Peruvian grain.

apoderado — Attorney.

Aprista — Follower of APRA (**Alianza Popular Revolucionaria Americana**), a Peruvian political movement.

arroba — Measure of weight (about 25 pounds).

asesor — Assessor, adviser.

audiencia — High administrative and judicial court in the Spanish colonies.

ayllu — Indian village community in the Andean highlands.

azumbre — A liquid measure, containing about two liters.

balanghai (balangay) — A kind of large swift native canoe or boat.

Bandeirantes — Portuguese gold- and slave-hunters in the interior of Brazil.

barrio — Ward or precinct.

caatinga — Semi-arid part of northeastern Brazil.

cabildo — Municipal council.

caboclo — Indian, also applied to mixture of white and Indian (Brazil).

cacique — Indian chieftain.

capataz — Overseer or foreman.

capitão-do-campo — "Bush-captain," official charged with recapture of fugitive slaves in colonial Brazil.

capitão-môr — Commander-in-chief of the military forces of a Brazilian province in colonial times.

carga — A measure of six and one-half bushels.

carioca — Citizen of Rio de Janeiro.

cascalhão — Alluvium containing gold or diamonds.

catedrático — University professor.

caudilho — Military or political leader.

caudillo — *See* **caudilho.**

chapetón — Name applied to European-born Spaniards in the South American colonies.

chinampas — Small garden tracts artificially formed in the lakes of the Valley of Mexico.

chiripá — A long fringed shawl, held at the waist by a belt, that was worn by the gaucho (Argentina).

cielito — Gaucho song and dance (Argentina).

científico — Name given to group of Porfirio Diaz' close advisers who made a fetish of scientific efficiency in government administration.

colegio — College, secondary school.

colono — Andean highland farmer, enjoying use of land in return for labor.

común — Community, committee.

comunero — In Andean highlands, member of settlement of Indians who hold their land communally.

consulado — Colonial guild merchant and tribunal of commerce.

conto — Brazilian monetary unit, 1000 **milreis.**

copla — Song or ballad.

coroza — A peaked headdress.

corregidor — Governor of a municipal district.

corregimiento — Territory governed by a **corregidor.**

cortes — Spanish parliament.

criollismo — Nativism.

criollista — Nativist.

cruzado — Ancient Portuguese gold coin.

cruzeiro — Brazilian monetary unit.

curiboca — Mixture of white and Indian (Brazil).

donatário — Proprietor of an original land grant in early Brazil.

dotación — Grant of land to an individual in accordance with Mexican agrarian laws.

ejidatario — Member of an **ejido.**

ejido — An agricultural community which has received land in accordance with Mexican agrarian laws.

Encilhamento — Great movement of financial speculation in first years of the Brazilian republic.

encomendero — Holder of an **encomienda**.

encomienda — Assignment of Indian tribute to individuals or institutions.

estado — Measure of length (1.85 yards).

estancia — Ranch (Argentina and Uruguay).

fanega — A measure of grain (about 1.60 bushels).

fanegada — A measure of land equal to one and one-tenth acres.

fazenda — Large estate (Brazil).

fazendeiro — Owner of a **fazenda**.

festa — Holiday.

finca — Farm or ranch.

fiscal — Crown attorney.

fuero — Privilege or exemption.

gachupín — Name applied to European-born Spaniards in New Spain.

gamonal — Large landowner (Peru).

gamonalismo — The system of large landholdings (Peru).

gaucho — Cowboy of the Plate region.

grajas — A kind of crow.

guaca — *See* **huaca.**

guaipil (**huipil**) — Square, sleeveless blouse worn by Indian women in some parts of Mexico and Central America.

hacendado — Owner of an **hacienda.**

hacienda — Landed estate.

hidalgo — Nobleman.

huaca (**guaca**) — Inca shrine or sacred object.

ingenuo — Child of a slave mother, born free after passage of the emancipation law of 1871 (Brazil).

jagunço — Inhabitant of Brazilian backlands.

jefe político — Governor of a district.

juicio de amparo — Protective writ; writ of injunction (Mexico).

junta — Council.

latifundio — Large landed estate.

latifundista — Holder of a **latifundio.**

lépero — Vagabond, disorderly element (Mexico).

llanero — Plainsman.

maestro — Teacher.

mameluco (**mamaluco**) — Mixture of white and Indian (Brazil).

maravedí — An old Spanish coin.

mayordomo — Administrator of a landed estate.

mestizo — Mixture of white and Indian.

milpa — Plot of Indian maize land in Mexico.

milreis — Brazilian monetary unit (replaced in 1942 by the *cruzeiro*).

mita — Periodic conscription of Indian labor in the Spanish colonies.

mitimaes — Colonists sent by the Incas to consolidate control of newly-won territory.

mocambo (**mucambo**) — Fugitive-slave settlement in Brazil.

obraje — Textile factory in the Spanish colonies.

oidor — Spanish colonial judge, member of **audiencia.**

orejón — Member of the Inca aristocracy.

ouvidor — Portuguese colonial judge and administrative officer.

pai — Father.

palmo — A measure of length (eight inches).

papa — Potato.

páramo — High and cold region.

pardelas — A bird about the size of a pigeon.

pardo — Mulatto or Negro.

patria — Fatherland.

patrón — Master, landlord.

patronato real — Right of the Spanish kings to dispose of all ecclesiastical benefices.

peso — Spanish coin and monetary unit.

pongo — The domestic servant of a landowner, selected by draft from among his Indian tenants (Peru).

porteño — Citizen of Buenos Aires.

principales — Leading men.

puna — Bleak, arid table-land.

quintal — Quintal, a hundred pounds.

quinua — A Peruvian grain.

quipu — Inca counting device and memory aid.

rancho — Farm or cattle ranch.

real — A Spanish coin.

regidor — Councilman.

reis — Plural of **real.**

repartimiento — (*a*) The distribution of Indians or land among Spanish settlers during the first years of the Conquest, (*b*) the periodic conscription of Indians for labor useful to the Spanish community, (*c*) the mandatory purchase of merchandise by Indians from colonial officials.

residencia — Judicial review of an official's conduct at the end of his term of office.

restitución — Restoration of lands that had been illegally taken from Mexican villagers.

roda dos engeitados — Foundling home.

romance — Ballad.

roto — Chilean common laborer.

sertanejo — Inhabitant of the **sertão.**

sertão — The semi-arid, isolated interior of the Brazilian Northeast.

sol — Peruvian silver coin.

tercio — Bundle or bale.

tiro de gracia — Literally, a "merciful shot," that ends the sufferings of a dying man.

vara — Variable unit of length, about 2.8 ft.

visitador general — Official charged with the inspection or investigation of an entire viceroyalty or captaincy-general.

yanacona — Inca and colonial servant or serf class; tenant farmer holding land in retur[n] for labor (Peru).

yungas — Temperate zone on eastern side of the Bolivian Andes.

zambahigo — Mixture of Indian and Chinese.

zambo — Mixture of Indian and Negro.